Criminal Procedure

EIGHTH EDITION

Joel Samaha

Horace T. Morse Distinguished Teaching Professor

University of Minnesota

WADSWORTH
CENGAGE Learning

Australia • Brazil • Japan • Korea • Mexico • Singapore • Spain • United Kingdom • United States

WADSWORTH
CENGAGE Learning™

Criminal Procedure, **Eighth Edition**
Joel Samaha

Senior Publisher: Linda Schreiber-Ganster

Senior Acquisitions Editor: Carolyn Henderson Meier

Senior Assistant Editor: Erin Abney

Editorial Assistant: Virginette Acacio

Media Editor: Ting Jian Yap

Senior Marketing Manager: Michelle Williams

Marketing Assistant: Sean Foy

Marketing Communications Manager: Heather Baxley

Senior Content Project Manager: Christy Frame

Creative Director: Rob Hugel

Senior Art Director: Maria Epes

Senior Print Buyer: Karen Hunt

Rights Acquisitions Account Manager: Dean Dauphinais

Production Service: Ruth Cottrell

Text Designer: Lisa Devenish

Copy Editor: Lura Harrison

Proofreader: Martha Ghent

Indexer: Kathy Garcia

Cover Designer: Riezebos Holzbaur Design Group

Cover Image: Top: Dennie Cody/Getty Bottom: Fat Chance Productions/Corbis

Compositor: PreMediaGlobal

For product information and technology assistance, contact us at **Cengage Learning Customer & Sales Support, 1-800-354-9706**

For permission to use material from this text or product, submit all requests online at **www.cengage.com/permissions** Further permissions questions can be e-mailed to **permissionrequest@cengage.com**

Library of Congress Control Number: 2010936203

Student Edition ISBN-10: 0-495-91335-9

Student Edition ISBN-13: 978-0-495-91335-1

Wadsworth
20 Davis Drive
Belmont, CA 94002-3098
USA

Cengage Learning is a leading provider of customized learning solutions with office locations around the globe, including Singapore, the United Kingdom, Australia, Mexico, Brazil, and Japan. Locate your local office at **www.cengage.com/global**

Cengage Learning products are represented in Canada by Nelson Education, Ltd.

To learn more about Wadsworth, visit **www.cengage.com/wadsworth**

Purchase any of our products at your local college store or at our preferred online store **www.cengagebrain.com**

Printed in the United States of America
1 2 3 4 5 6 7 14 13 12 11 10

*For my students, my sons Adam and Luke,
and my dear friends Steve and Doug*

ABOUT THE AUTHOR ‖‖

Professor Joel Samaha teaches Criminal Law, Criminal Procedure, and Introduction to Criminal Justice at the University of Minnesota. He is both a lawyer and an historian whose primary interest is crime control in a constitutional democracy. He received his B.A., J.D., and Ph.D. from Northwestern University. Professor Samaha also studied under the late Sir Geoffrey Elton at Clare Cambridge University, England. He was named the College of Liberal Arts Distinguished Teacher in 1974. In 2007 he was awarded the title of University of Minnesota Morse Alumni Distinguished Teaching Professor and inducted into the Academy of Distinguished Teachers.

Professor Samaha was admitted to the Illinois Bar in 1962 and practiced law briefly in Chicago. He taught at UCLA before going to the University of Minnesota in 1971. At the University of Minnesota, he served as Chair of the Department of Criminal Justice Studies from 1974 to 1978. He now teaches and writes full time. He has taught both television and radio courses in criminal justice and has co-taught a National Endowment for the Humanities seminar in legal and constitutional history.

In addition to *Law and Order in Historical Perspective* (1974), an analysis of law enforcement in pre-industrial Essex County, England, Professor Samaha has transcribed and written a scholarly introduction to a set of local criminal justice records from the borough of Colchester during the reign of Elizabeth I. He has also written several articles on the history of criminal justice, published in the *Historical Journal, The American Journal of Legal History, Minnesota Law Review, William Mitchell Law Review*, and *Journal of Social History*. He has also written two other textbooks, *Criminal Law* in its tenth edition, and *Criminal Justice* in its seventh edition.

Balancing the power of government to enforce the criminal law against the rights of individuals to come and go as they please without government interference is the central problem in the law of criminal procedure in a constitutional democracy. It's also the heart of *Criminal Procedure, 8th Edition*. It's a problem that always fascinates my students, stimulates them to think, and provokes them to discuss it not only in class but also with their friends and family outside class. I'm not surprised.

The balance between government power and individual rights has fascinated me since I studied criminal procedure at Northwestern University Law School decades ago under the sparkling Claude R. Sowle and the legendary Fred E. Inbau. Professor Sowle, a brilliant advocate and a distinguished teacher, emphasized the philosophical underpinnings of the law of criminal procedure. Professor Inbau, a famous interrogator and a highly respected student of the law of interrogation, spoke from the 1930s right up to his death in the late 1990s with the authority of one who has actually applied abstract principles to everyday police practices.

In 1971, I taught criminal procedure for the first time. I've done so ever since. My students have included undergraduates, graduate students, and law students. That many of these students are now police officers and administrators; corrections officers and administrators; criminal defense attorneys, prosecutors, and judges; and legislators testifies to their enduring interest in the law of criminal procedure and to their commitment to the application of formal law to informal real-life decision making.

Criminal Procedure, Eighth Edition, like its predecessors, reflects my conviction that the best way to learn the law of criminal procedure is both to understand general principles *and* critically examine the application of these principles to real problems. By "critically," I don't mean "negatively"; *Criminal Procedure* doesn't trash the system. Rather, it examines and weighs the principles that govern the balance between government power and individual life, liberty, privacy, and property. It tests the weight of strong, honest feelings about this balance in the bright light of reason, logic, and facts. *Criminal Procedure* proceeds on the assumptions that the general principles governing the balance between government power and individual rights have real meaning only in the context of a specific reality, and that reality makes sense only when seen in the light of general principles applied to specific facts in particular circumstances.

|||||||||||||||||||||||||||||||||||||||||||||||||||||||||||||||||||||||||||||||||||||||||||||||||||||||||||||||||||||||||||||||||

TEXT AND CASES

Criminal Procedure, Eighth Edition, is a text-case book, meaning that it contains both text and excerpts of actual court opinions that apply the general principles discussed in the text to concrete cases. The text and case excerpts complement each other. The text enriches the understanding of the cases, while the cases enhance the understanding of the constitutional principles in the text. The cases aren't just examples, illustrations, or attention grabbers; they explain, clarify, elaborate, and apply the general principles and constitutional provisions to real-life situations. Moreover, the cases are excellent tools for developing the critical thinking skills of students at all levels of formal learning and beyond to everyday life.

The cases and the text are independent enough of each other, and they can each stand alone. Design differences clearly mark one from the other. This separation of text from cases allows instructors who favor the case analysis approach to emphasize cases over text, leaving the text for students to read if they need to in order to understand the cases. Instructors who favor the text approach can focus on the text, allowing students to read the cases as enrichment or as examples of the principles, constitutional provisions, and rules discussed in the text.

The case excerpts are edited for nonlawyers to supply students with a full statement of the facts of the case; the court's application of the law to the facts of the case; key portions of the reasoning of the court; and the court's decision. Excerpts also contain portions of the dissenting opinions and, when appropriate, parts of the concurring opinions.

The question that opens each case focuses students on the main principle of the case. The case history gives a brief procedural history of the case. And the questions at the end of the case excerpts test whether students know the facts of the case, understand the law of the case, and comprehend the application of the law to the facts of the case. The questions also supply the basis for developing critical thinking skills, not to mention provoking class discussions on the legal, ethical, and policy issues raised by the case.

|||||||||||||||||||||||||||||||||||||||||||||||||||||||||||||||||||||||||||||||||||||||||||||||||||||||||||||||||||||||||||||||||

KEY CHANGES TO THE EIGHTH EDITION

New Cases A number of new cases and many re-edited existing cases appear in the eighth edition. I added, replaced, and re-edited cases for three reasons. First, I wanted to reflect new developments in the law since the last edition. Second, I included cases I've found since the last edition that explain the law better and apply the law to the facts in clearer and more interesting ways for students. Third, experiences through actual use in the classroom led me to re-edit some cases and sometimes cut excerpts from previous editions.

Streamlining I worked especially hard to streamline the case excerpts and the text throughout. The result is a shift from excerpts making up the largest proportion of the book to more text. I expanded descriptions, explanations, and analyses of the law.

Empirical Research *Criminal Procedure*, Eighth Edition, continues the practice of recent editions to include more of the growing, rich social science research that explains and evaluates criminal procedures.

Criminal Procedure in Crises Times Chapter 15 stresses the need during national emergencies to recalibrate the balance between government power and individual liberty and privacy. *Criminal Procedure,* Eighth Edition, retains the historical overview of the recalibration. Then, we home in on the period since September 11, 2001, and the major recalibrations that continue in 2010—adoption and revisions to the USA Patriot Act, other legislation, military tribunals, and the latest U.S. Supreme Court cases applying these laws. In this edition, we've added a new section on another national emergency—immigration laws and their enforcement in our constitutional democracy.

PEDAGOGY

However it's organized and presented, the law of criminal procedure is a complicated subject that embraces a lot of technical concepts. I've tried to help students work through these complexities, primarily by writing clear, direct prose. But there are special features as well. Each chapter begins with a Chapter Outline, a list of the Learning Objectives, and an introductory discussion. I also boldfaced key terms in the text, which appear in a list at the end of each chapter as well as in the Glossary at the end of the book. There's also a Summary at the end of each chapter, which is made up of a bulleted list of the chapter's main points. Review Questions follow and provide a good test of whether students have identified and understood the main points in the chapter.

Additionally, to reflect emerging trends and issues in criminal procedure, I added two new boxed features to the eighth edition:

- New "Ethical Issues" boxes in every chapter put students in the role of the decision maker, challenging them to apply the legal concepts presented in the chapter to real-world situations. Working through ethical dilemmas now helps students build a solid foundation that will serve them well wherever their career paths may lead.
- New "White Collar Crime: The 'Other' World of Criminal Procedure" boxes in some chapters keep students on the cutting edge, presenting real-world criminal law issues from this increasingly high-profile area. These crimes are overlooked in most other criminal procedure texts (which focus exclusively on traditional "street" crime).

CHAPTER-BY-CHAPTER REVISIONS

Chapter 1, Crime Control in a Constitutional Democracy

New

- Ethical Issues: "Is Torture Ever Ethical?"
- White Collar Crime: "FDA Law Enforcers Crack Down on Illegal Botox Scammers"

Revised

- Sections: Streamlined "The Text-Case Method"; combined "The Parts of Case Excerpts" and "Briefing the Cases" subsections

Chapter 2, Criminal Procedure and the Constitution

New

- Ethical Issues: "Should Prosecutors Help Claimants Prove Their Discrimination Case against the Government?"
- White Collar Crime: "Federalism and White Collar Crime Investigation"

Revised

- Sections: Substantially rewrote "*Hurtado* and Charging by Information," "The 'Scottsboro Boys' and Due Process," and "*Brown v. Mississippi* and Coerced Confessions"; expanded "Equal Protection of the Law"
- Case: Streamlined *U.S. v. Armstrong* excerpt

Chapter 3, The Definition of Searches and Seizures

New

- Ethical Issues: "Should the Government Use Snitches?"

Revised

- Section: Expanded and rewrote "Electronic Surveillance"

Chapter 4, Stop and Frisk

New

- Ethical Issues: "Is It Ethical to Stop and Frisk More Innocent Black and Hispanic Men than White Men?"
- Sections: "Questioning Stopped Suspects," "Traffic Stops and Frisks," and "Frisking People in Stopped Vehicles"
- Cases: *Hiibel v. Sixth Judicial District Court* excerpt, on questioning stopped suspects; *Arizona v. Johnson* excerpt, on frisking passengers in stopped vehicles
- Graphics: Table 4.4, "Stops and Arrests, NYPD," and Table 4.5, "Facts Supporting Stops and Arrest" (empirical findings)

Revised

- Chapter: Streamlined by 25 percent and revised entire chapter content
- Sections: Rewrote and expanded "High Crime Area"; expanded *Illinois v. Wardlow* Questions (to emphasize empirical research)
- Cases: Removed case excerpts from earlier editions and incorporated their main points into text:
    a. *U.S. v. Cortez* (1979)
    b. *Florida v. J. L.* (2000)
    c. *U.S. v. Sharpe and Savage* (1985)
    d. *U.S. v. Sokolow* (1989)
    e. *U.S. v. McCargo* (2006)

Chapter 5, Seizure of Persons: Arrest

New

- Ethical Issues: "Issue a Citation or Make a Full Custodial Arrest?"

- Case: *Brigham City, Utah v. Charles Stuart and others* (2006) excerpt, on police entering a home without a warrant or exigent circumstances
- Graphics: Table 5.5, "Lower Courts' Applications of 'Objective Standard of Reasonable Force' Test"; Figure 5.1, "Number of K9 Dog-Bite Patients in Police Custody"; Figure 5.2, "Some Characteristics of Dog-Bite Patients by Percent"

Revised

- Section: Added empirical research on dog bite-and-hold policies to "Nondeadly Force"
- Cases: Removed *U.S. v. Watson* (1976) and *Payton v. New York* (1980) excerpts from earlier editions and incorporated their main points into text

Chapter 6, Searches for Evidence

New

- Ethical Issues: "Is It Ethical for the Courts to Find Consent Voluntary Because Law Enforcement Officers Believe They're in Danger?"
- Section: "Occupants' Failure to Respond to Officers' Announcement"
- Case: *Arizona v. Gant* (2009)
- Graphics: Table 6.1, "*New York v. Belton* (1981) Majority's Argument"; Table 6.2, "Circumstances That May Form Part of Voluntary Consent"; Table 6.3, "'Unequivocal' Withdrawal of Consent"
- Exploring Further: "Did He Consent to the Search of His Crotch?" *U.S. v. Blake* (1988)

Revised

- Chapter: Streamlined by 14 percent and revised entire chapter content
- Sections: Expanded and rewrote "Third-Party Consent Searches"; rewrote "Vehicle Searches" for clarity, adding historical perspective
- Cases: Removed *U.S. v. Banks* and *U.S. v. Gray* excerpts from earlier editions and incorporated their main points into text

Chapter 7, "Special Needs" Searches

New

- Ethical Issues: "Should Hospitals Test Maternity Patients Suspected of Using Cocaine?"
- Sections: "Testing and Storing Prisoners' DNA" and "Prenatal Drug Testing in Hospitals"
- Cases: *Bull v. City of San Francisco* (2010) excerpt, found strip search of jail inmates reasonable; *State v. Ellis* (2006) excerpt, on college dorm room inspections; and *Ferguson v. City of Charleston* (2001) excerpt, on hospital urine testing of prenatal patients suspected of drug use

Revised

- Section: Expanded "College Dormitory Room Checks," adding Table 7.1, "Justifications for Reduced Privacy in College and University Dorm Rooms"
- Cases: Removed excerpts from earlier editions and incorporated their main points into text:
  a. *Mary Beth G. v. City of Chicago* (1983)
  b. *Board of Education of Independent School District No. 92 of Pottawatomie County v. Earls* (2002)

Chapter 8, Self-Incrimination

New

- Ethical Issues: "Do the Police Have an "Ethical" Responsibility to Video Record Interrogations?"
- Section: "False Confessions: Popular Belief and Empirical Evidence"; includes five new subsections
- Case: *Berghuis v. Thompkins* (2010) excerpt, found suspects have to assert their right to remain silent unambiguously; silence can denote implicit waiver

Revised

- Cases: Removed excerpts from earlier editions and incorporated their main points into text:
  a. *Schmerber v. California* (1966)
  b. *Brewer v. Williams* (1977)
  c. *Moran v. Burbine* (1986)

Chapter 9, Identification Procedures

New

- Ethical Issues: "Do Police Departments Have an Ethical Responsibility to Adopt Lineup Procedure Reforms? Hennepin County Pilot Project"
- Sections: "Psychological Research and Eyewitness Identification" (includes new subsections "Identification Research Methods" and "Eyewitness Retrospective Self-Reports"); "Recommendations for Reforming Identification Procedures"
- Cases: *State v. Clopten* (2009) excerpt, allowing expert witness to testify about the social psychological research on eyewitness reliability; *District Attorney's Office for the Third Judicial District v. Osborne* (2009) excerpt, convicted prisoner's right to DNA evidence collected by the state

Revised

- Sections: Expanded and rewrote "Social Science and Mistaken Eyewitness Identification," increasing the social science research content by 45 percent; streamlined and rewrote "DNA Profile Identification"

Chapter 10, Remedies for Constitutional Violations I: The Exclusionary Rule and Entrapment

New

- Ethical Issues: "Is It Ethical Public Policy to Let Criminals Go Free Because Police Officers Violated the Fourth Amendment to Obtain Evidence?"
- Case: *Herring v. U.S.* (2009) excerpt, on expanding the "good faith" exception to the exclusionary rule

Revised

- Chapter: Streamlined by 15 percent
- Sections: Rewrote "The Good Faith Exception," exception to the exclusionary rule, and "Social Costs and Deterrence: The Empirical Findings"
- Cases: Removed *U.S. v. Leon* (1984) and *Arizona v. Evans* (1995) excerpts from earlier editions and incorporated their main points into text

Chapter 11, Constitutional Violations II: Other Remedies against Official Misconduct

New

- Ethical Issues: "Does Ethical Policy Demand That It's Time to End Absolute Immunity for Prosecutors?"

Revised

- Chapter: Rewrote the chapter introduction; streamlined and updated chapter text

Chapter 12, Court Proceedings I: Before Trial

New

- Ethical Issues: "Is It Ethical to Allow Prosecutors to Appoint Their Opposing Defense Lawyers?"
- White Collar Crime: "The Grand Jury and White Collar Crime"
- Section: "The Right to the Counsel of Your Choice"
- Cases: *Rompilla v. Beard* (2005), right to effective counsel, and *Renico v. Lett* (2010), hung jury

Revised

- Case: Removed *Gideon v. Wainwright* (1963) excerpt from earlier editions and incorporated its main points into text

Chapter 13, Court Proceedings II: Trial and Conviction

New

- Ethical Issues: "Should It Be Ethical to Take Race, Ethnicity, and Gender into Account When Selecting Jurors?"
- White Collar Crime: "Refusing to Plea Bargain Extracts a Heavy Price"
- Case: *Snyder v. Louisiana* (2008), race-based peremptory prospective juror challenges
- Graphic: "Types of Felony Convictions in State Courts," illustrates magnitude of guilty plea cases over trial

Revised

- Chapter: Expanded by 22 percent; expanded introductory text, emphasizing that most cases are pleaded out rather than allowed to go to trial
- Sections: Expanded "Jury Selection" to include new material on race and jury selection and the new *Snyder v. Louisiana* (2008) excerpt; expanded "Conviction by Guilty Plea" to include:
  a. History of plea bargaining
  b. Description of the complexity of the plea-bargaining system
  c. More detailed discussion of important Supreme Court cases dealing with the constitutionality of plea bargaining and guilty pleas
  d. Description and analysis of empirical research and plea bargaining, particularly from law and behavioral science scholarship, questioning whether decision making by parties to plea bargaining is made rationally
- Cases: Removed *Ballew v. Georgia* (1978) and *Lockhart v. McCree* (1986) excerpts from earlier editions and incorporated their main points into text

Chapter 14, After Conviction

New

- Ethical Issues: "Juveniles: A Life Sentence without the Chance of Parole?"
- White Collar Crime: "Sentencing White Collar Offenders after *U.S. v. Booker* (2005)"
- Cases: *Lockyer v. Andrade* (2003) excerpt, sentence of 50 years for stealing $150 worth of videos under California 3-strikes law isn't cruel and unusual punishment; *Gall v. U.S.* (2007) excerpt, judicial discretion reducing Brian Gall's conviction for distributing "ecstasy" under U.S. sentencing guidelines
- Graphics: Figure 14.1, "Minnesota Sentencing Guidelines Grid," and Figure 14.3, "Death Penalty: The Numbers," which depicts the odds of receiving a sentencing departure from the death sentence by race, ethnicity, sex, and age

Revised

- Chapter: Expanded by 21 percent
- Sections: Expanded "Sentencing Guidelines," "The Proportionality Principle and the Sentence of Death," and "The Proportionality Principle and Sentences of Imprisonment"; also expanded the discussion of how sentencing guidelines work in "Sentencing Guidelines and Mandatory Minimum Sentences," including the two new graphics and empirical research on the
    a. Influence of race, ethnicity, gender, and age on granting unwarranted departures from sentences recommended in the guidelines
    b. Influence of judge's political affiliation on unwarranted departures
        - Expanded "Habeas Corpus (Collateral Attack)" with
    a. More detailed description and explanation
    b. History of habeas corpus and its importance in understanding its present meaning
    c. Importance of the Antiterrorism and Effective Death Penalty Act (AEDPA) in habeas corpus proceedings

Chapter 15, Criminal Procedure in Crises Times

New

- Ethical Issues: "Is It Ethical to Refuse to Enforce Arizona's Immigration Law?"
- White Collar Crime: "The Christmas Day Bomb Suspect"
- Sections: "Trials in Federal Courts," "Debate: Military Commissions vs. Trial in U.S. Federal Courts," and "Illegal Immigrants and the Constitution"
- Cases: *Boumediene v. Bush* (2008) excerpt, the latest case on Guantanamo Bay detainees right to habeas corpus; *Demore v. Kim* (2003) excerpt, on detention of illegal immigrants pending deportation

Revised

- Chapter: Expanded by 33 percent
- Section: Rewrote "Detention" and its subsections; expanded and rewrote "Interrogation" and its subsection "*Miranda v. Arizona* and Terrorism Suspects"

‖‖

SUPPLEMENTS

To access additional course materials, please visit www.cengagebrain.com. At the CengageBrain.com home page, search for the ISBN of your title (from the back cover of your book) using the search box at the top of the page. This will take you to the product page where these resources can be found.

Wadsworth provides a number of supplements to help instructors use *Criminal Procedure*, Eighth Edition, in their courses and to aid students in preparing for exams. Supplements are available to qualified adopters. Please consult your local Wadsworth/ Cengage sales representative for details.

For the Instructor

Instructor's Resource Manual with Test Bank An improved and completely updated *Instructor's Resource Manual with Test Bank* has been developed by Barbara Belbot at the University of Houston, Downtown. The manual includes learning objectives, detailed chapter outlines, key terms, chapter summaries, and questions for review and discussion. Each chapter's test bank contains questions in multiple-choice, true–false, fill-in-the-blank, and essay formats, with a full answer key. The test bank is coded to the chapter objectives that appear in the main text and includes the page numbers in the main text where the answers can be found. Finally, each question in the test bank has been reviewed carefully by experienced criminal justice instructors for quality, accuracy, and content coverage. Our "Instructor Approved" seal, which appears on the front cover, is our assurance that you're working with an assessment and grading resource of the highest caliber.

PowerPoint® Slides Created by Mark Brown, University of South Carolina at Columbia, these handy Microsoft® PowerPoint slides, which outline the chapters of the main text in a classroom-ready presentation, will help you in making your lectures engaging and in reaching your visually oriented students. The presentations are available for download on the password-protected website and can also be obtained by e-mailing your local Cengage Learning representative.

ExamView® Computerized Testing The comprehensive Instructor's Manual described above is backed up by ExamView, a computerized test bank available for PC and Macintosh computers. With ExamView you can create, deliver, and customize tests and study guides (both print and online) in minutes. You can easily edit and import your own questions and graphics, change test layouts, and reorganize questions. And using ExamView's complete word-processing capabilities, you can enter an unlimited number of new questions or edit existing questions.

WebTutor™ on Blackboard® and WebCT® Jump-start your course with customizable, rich, text-specific content within your Course Management System. Whether you want to web-enable your class or put an entire course online, WebTutor delivers. WebTutor offers a wide array of resources, including media assets, a test bank, practice quizzes linked to chapter learning objectives, and additional study aids. Visit www .cengage.com/webtutor to learn more.

The Wadsworth Criminal Justice Video Library So many exciting new videos—so many great ways to enrich your lectures and spark discussion of the material in this text. Your Cengage Learning representative will be happy to provide details on our video policy by adoption size. The library includes these selections and many others:

- *ABC® Videos*. ABC videos feature short, high-interest clips from current news events as well as historic raw footage going back 40 years. Perfect for discussion starters or to enrich your lectures and spark interest in the material in the text, these brief videos provide students with a new lens through which to view the past and present. The videos will greatly enhance their knowledge and understanding of significant events and open up to them new dimensions in learning. Clips are drawn from such programs as *World News Tonight*, *Good Morning America*, *This Week*, *PrimeTime Live*, *20/20*, and *Nightline*, as well as numerous ABC News specials and material from the Associated Press Television News and British Movietone News collections.
- *Cengage Learning's "Introduction Criminal Justice Video Series."* This series features videos supplied by the BBC Motion Gallery. These short, high-interest clips from CBS and BBC news programs—everything from nightly news broadcasts and specials to *CBS News Special Reports*, *CBS Sunday Morning*, *60 Minutes*, and more—are perfect classroom discussion starters. Clips are drawn from the BBC Motion Gallery.
- *Films for the Humanities*. Choose from nearly two hundred videos on a variety of topics such as elder abuse, supermax prisons, suicide and the police officer, the making of an FBI agent, and domestic violence.

For the Student

Current Perspectives: Readings from InfoTrac® College Edition These readings, designed to give students a closer look at special topics in criminal justice, include free access to InfoTrac College Edition. The timely articles are selected by experts in each topic from within InfoTrac College Edition. They're available free when bundled with the text and include the following titles:

- Cyber Crime
- Victimology
- Juvenile Justice
- Racial Profiling
- White Collar Crime
- Terrorism and Homeland Security
- Public Policy and Criminal Justice
- Technology and Criminal Justice
- Ethics in Criminal Justice
- Forensics and Criminal Investigation
- Corrections
- Law and Courts
- Policy in Criminal Justice

CourseMate Cengage Learning's Criminal Justice CourseMate brings course concepts to life with interactive learning, study, and exam preparation tools that support the printed textbook. CourseMate includes an integrated eBook, quizzes mapped to chapter Learning Objectives, flashcards, videos, and Engagement Tracker, a first-of-its-kind tool that monitors student engagement in the course. The accompanying instructor website offers access to password-protected resources, such as an electronic version of the instructor's manual and PowerPoint® slides. The web quizzing was created by Cornel Plebani of Husson University.

Criminal Justice Media Library Cengage Learning's Criminal Justice Media Library includes nearly three hundred media assets on the topics you cover in your courses. Available to stream from any web-enabled computer, the Criminal Justice Media Library's assets include such valuable resources as

- Career Profile Videos, featuring interviews with criminal justice professionals from a range of roles and locations
- Simulations that allow students to step into various roles and practice their decision-making skills
- Video clips on current topics from ABC® and other sources
- Animations that illustrate key concepts
- Interactive learning modules that help students check their knowledge of important topics
- Reality Check exercises that compare expectations and preconceived notions against the real-life thoughts and experiences of criminal justice professionals

The Criminal Justice Media Library can be uploaded and used within many popular Learning Management Systems. The library allows you to customize it to meet your own course material needs. You can also purchase an institutional site license. Please contact your Cengage Learning representative for ordering and pricing information.

***Careers in Criminal Justice Website* (available bundled with this text at no additional charge)** Featuring plenty of self-exploration and profiling activities, the interactive Careers in Criminal Justice website helps students investigate and focus on the criminal justice career choices that are right for them. It includes interest assessment, video testimonials from career professionals, resume and interview tips, and links for reference.

CLeBook Cengage Learning's Criminal Justice ebooks allow students to access our textbooks in an easy-to-use online format. Highlight, take notes, bookmark, search your text, and, for most texts, link directly into multimedia. In short, CLeBooks combine the best features of paper books and ebooks in one package.

ACKNOWLEDGMENTS

Criminal Procedure, Eighth Edition, didn't get here by my efforts alone; I had a lot of help. I'm grateful for all those who have provided feedback over the years and as always, I'm particularly indebted to the reviewers of this edition:

Dana Cook Baer, Waynesburg University
Becky Kohler da Cruz, Armstrong Atlantic State University
Dr. Dorinda L. Dowis, Columbus State University
Jacinta M. Gau, California State University, San Bernardino

Criminal Justice Editor Carolyn Henderson Meier has helped me at every stage of the book. Christy Frame ironed out all kinds of rough spots along the way. The book also benefited yet one more time from Lura Harrison's painstaking copy editing. Ruth Cottrell's calm efficiency, warm kindnesses, careful editing, and extraordinary patience were as welcome and necessary as they have been in earlier editions. Luke Samaha did most of the preliminary work on the Chapter Outlines, Learning Objectives, Summaries, and Review Questions.

What would I do without Doug and Steve? Doug takes me there and gets me here and everywhere, day in and day out, days that now have stretched into years. And my old and dear friend Steve, who from the days when he watched over my kids to now decades later when he keeps the Irish Wolfhounds, the Siamese cat, the Standard Poodle, me, and a lot more around here in order. And they do it all while putting up with what my beloved mentor at Cambridge, Sir Geoffrey Elton, called "Joel's mercurial temperament." Only those who really know me can understand how I can try the patience of Job! Friends and associates like these have made *Criminal Procedure*, Eighth Edition, whatever success it enjoys. As for its faults, I claim total ownership.

JOEL SAMAHA
Minneapolis

Criminal Procedure

EIGHTH EDITION

1

LEARNING OBJECTIVES

1 Appreciate that at the heart of our constitutional democracy is the idea of balancing values—community safety versus individual autonomy and the means versus the ends in obtaining the correct result.

2 Appreciate that the balance between result and process never rests easily at a point that satisfies everyone and that the balance shifts, depending on the circumstances, especially during emergencies.

3 Appreciate that the deep commitment to the value of equality in U.S. society reflects our deep commitment to equal justice for all in the law and the practice of criminal procedure.

4 Know, understand, and appreciate the importance to criminal procedure of both formal decision making according to written rules and informal discretionary decision making according to judgments based on official training and experience.

5 Know, understand, and appreciate the importance of the objective basis requirement that the government has to back up with facts every officially triggered restraint on the rights of individuals to come and go as they please and to be let alone by the government.

6 Know and appreciate that the exclusionary rule requires courts to throw out "good" evidence if the government used "bad" methods to obtain it.

7 Understand the importance of empirical and social scientific research in balancing the core values of liberty and order.

8 Know the importance of prior case decisions (precedent) and the obligation to follow prior decisions (stare decisis) in judicial reasoning and decision making.

Crime Control in a Constitutional Democracy

If men were angels, no government would be necessary. If angels were to govern men, neither external nor internal controls on government would be necessary. In framing a government which is to be administered by men over men, the great difficulty lies in this: You must first enable the government to control the governed; and in the next place, oblige it to control itself. *James Madison ([1787], 1961, 349)*

If we lived in a police state, officials could break into our houses in the dead of night and shoot us in our beds based on nothing more than the whim of the current dictator. If we lived in a *pure* democracy, the majority who won the last election could authorize the police to shoot anyone who they had a hunch was a street gang member. But we live in a **constitutional democracy**, where neither a single dictator nor an overwhelming majority of the people has total power over us as individuals. Our constitutional democracy balances the need to provide for the public's safety and security against other equally important values—individual liberty, privacy, and dignity.

In the U.S. version of constitutional democracy, a majority of the people's elected representatives have wide latitude to *create* criminal laws that define criminal behavior and punishment. But in *enforcing* the criminal law, officials are much more restricted by the law of criminal procedure. *Criminal Procedure 8* takes you on a journey through the law of criminal procedure (Figure 1.1) and its day-to-day operations: from police investigation of suspicious behavior on the streets and other public places; then, to detention and further investigation at not-so-public police stations; next, to trials and sentencing in trial courts; and finally, to review of convictions in courts of appeals.

In our *federal* form of constitutional democracy, local and state officials have a monopoly on these day-to-day operations. The law of criminal procedure that controls their monopoly is mostly *constitutional* law. Most constitutional law in the United States is made by judges and published in the reports of their decisions. Specifically, we're referring here to U.S. Supreme Court cases, which you're going to be reading a lot of in this book.

According to respected experts, Supreme Court justices are the "primary generators of rules for regulating the behavior of police, prosecutors, and the other actors who administer the criminal process" (Allen, Hoffman, Livingston, and Stuntz 2005, 77). One distinguished federal judge called the Supreme Court's opinions interpreting the Bill of Rights—the part of the Constitution where most of these rules originate—a national "code of criminal procedure" (Friendly 1965, 929).

This code of criminal procedure gives government officials the power to protect public safety by enforcing the criminal law. But, at the same time, it also limits that power by guaranteeing the fair and equal administration of criminal justice to everybody, including criminal suspects, defendants, and convicted offenders. All the specific rules made by the Supreme Court spring from two clauses in the Fourteenth Amendment to the U.S. Constitution: "Due process of law" guarantees fairness, and "equal protection of the laws" guarantees equality.

U.S. Supreme Court justices don't make all criminal procedure law. States are free to rely on their own state constitutions to raise minimum operating procedures established by the U.S. Supreme Court. (You'll learn about some other sources later in this chapter and scattered throughout the remaining chapters.)

Finally, and this is very important, judge-made law leaves plenty of "play in the joints" for criminal justice professionals to exercise discretionary decision making. This, too, we'll discuss later in this chapter, and throughout the remainder of the book, where you'll discover just how important discretion is in the day-to-day operation of the criminal process.

In Chapter 1, we begin with a central issue in criminal procedure in a constitutional democracy: the need to balance values that protect both public safety and individual freedoms. In that light, we examine what equality for all means before the law. Next, we see how discretionary decision making can affect balance and equality at every level of criminal procedure. That discretion still has to satisfy the standards set by objective basis requirements for criminal prosecution. And you'll see how "good" evidence gathered by "bad" methods is handled under the law.

FIGURE 1.1 A General View of the Criminal Justice System

This chart seeks to present a simple yet comprehensive view of the movement of cases through the criminal justice system. Procedures in individual jurisdictions may vary from the pattern shown here. The differing weights of the line indicate the relative volumes of cases disposed of at various points in the system, but this is only suggestive since no nationwide data of this sort exists.

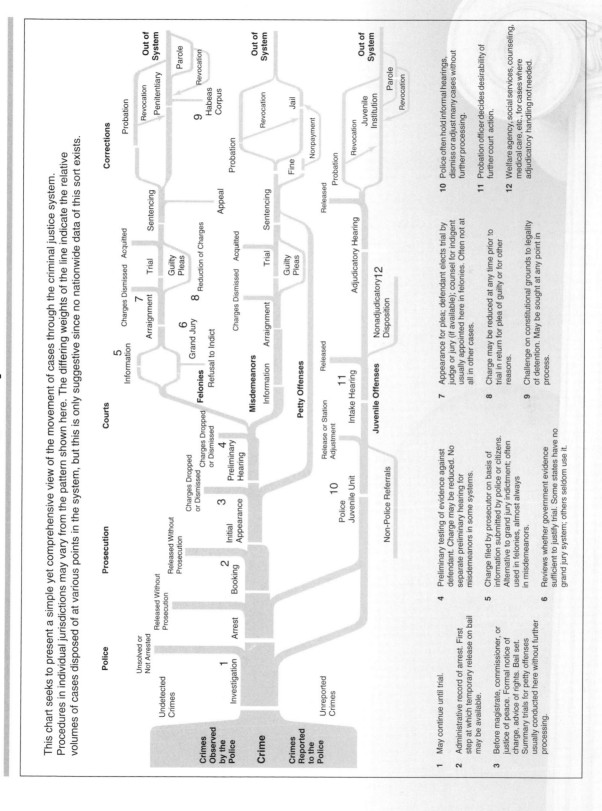

1　May continue until trial.

2　Administrative record of arrest. First step at which temporary release on bail may be available.

3　Before magistrate, commissioner, or justice of peace. Formal notice of charge, advice of rights. Bail set. Summary trials for petty offenses usually conducted here without further processing.

4　Preliminary testing of evidence against defendant. Charge may be reduced. No separate preliminary hearing for misdemeanors in some systems.

5　Charge filed by prosecutor on basis of information submitted by police or citizens. Alternative to grand jury indictment; often used in felonies, almost always in misdemeanors.

6　Reviews whether government evidence sufficient to justify trial. Some states have no grand jury system; others seldom use it.

7　Appearance for plea; defendant elects trial by judge or jury (if available); counsel for indigent usually appointed in felonies. Often not at all in other cases.

8　Charge may be reduced at any time prior to trial in return for plea of guilty or for other reasons.

9　Challenge on constitutional grounds to legality of detention. May be sought at any point in process.

10　Police often hold informal hearings, dismiss or adjust many cases without further processing.

11　Probation officer decides desirability of further court action.

12　Welfare agency, social services, counseling, medical care, etc. for cases where adjudicatory handling not needed.

5

Your understanding of how the courts try to effect balance in the law would not be complete without a look at the role empirical and social scientific research play in creating normative criminal procedure. Last, you'll learn the basics of the text-case method, which you'll use to enhance your understanding of the criminal procedure used in cases included throughout the text.

Balancing Values in Criminal Procedure

LO 1

At the heart of our constitutional democracy is the idea of balancing values, balances between values we believe essential to the quality of life. Let's look at two sets of these values: first, balances between community security and individual autonomy and, then, between ends and means. Next, we'll look at the history of balancing values in our society and at what happens to that balance during national emergencies.

Community Security and Individual Autonomy

LO 1

The objective of community security is a community where we're safe, or at least where we *feel* safe. Our lives are safe from murder; our bodies are safe from rape and other assaults; our homes are safe from burglars, arsonists, and trespassers; our secrets are safe from exposure; and our "stuff" is safe from thieves and vandals.

Individual autonomy means individuals control their own lives. They can come and go as they please; develop their body and mind as they wish to do; believe whatever or whomever they want to believe; worship any god they like; associate with anybody they choose to be with; and do whatever else they wish to do in the privacy of their own homes (assuming that they're competent adults and what they want to do doesn't include committing crimes that violate the community's or other persons' safety against their will). In other words, they can't tip the balance between community security and individual autonomy in their favor whenever and however they want.

Weighed on one side of the balance is the amount of government power needed to control crime for everybody's safety and security. Weighed on the other side is the amount of control individuals have over their own lives. James Madison (see the passage quoted in the chapter opener) and others who wrote and adopted the U.S. Constitution in the 1700s were realists. They accepted human nature for what it is: People aren't angels. Left to do as they please, ordinary individuals will break the law. And, because they're people, too, government officials left to do as they please will abuse their power. So the Founders expected excesses from both ordinary people and government officials who live in a real world inhabited by imperfect people. Let me be clear right at the beginning of our journey through the criminal process: I subscribe to Madison's view of human nature and the world.

Because both community security, in the form of crime control, and individual autonomy are highly valued "goods," striking the balance between them is difficult, and where it's struck never satisfies anyone completely.

The late U.S. Supreme Court Chief Justice William Rehnquist (1974) expressed the challenge this way:

> Throughout the long history of political theory and the development of constitutional law in our country, the most difficult cases to decide have been those in which two competing values, each able to marshal respectable claims on its behalf, meet in a contest in which one must prevail over the other. (1)

The balance between crime control and individual rights is flexible. Where exactly the balance is struck shifts, depending on the circumstances. Put another way, the right balance falls within a zone; it's not a point on the spectrum between total control and total freedom (*Llaguno v. Mingey* 1985, 1565). The most extreme examples are emergencies, especially wartime. As one lawyer prosecuting suspected disloyalists during the Civil War put it (I'm paraphrasing here), "During wartime the Bill of Rights is put to sleep. We'll wake it up when the emergency passes" (Gayarré 1903, 601). But it's not just during emergencies such as wars that we'll see the balance struck in various places in the zone. We'll see many examples where courts move around in the zone between order and liberty.

Ends and Means

LO 1

The quality of life also depends on a second balance of values—between ends and means. Or, to be more precise, the balance between result and process. In criminal procedure, the "ends" side of the balance consists of the search for the truth to obtain the correct result in individual cases. The correct result has two dimensions: (1) catching, convicting, and punishing guilty people and (2) freeing, as soon as possible, innocent people caught up in government efforts to control crime. Keep in mind these words of the late Professor Jerome Hall (1942) as we make our journey through the law of criminal procedure:

> [Criminal law's] ultimate ends are dual and conflicting. It must be designed from inception to end to acquit the innocent as readily as to convict the guilty. This presents the inescapable dilemma of criminal procedure . . . that the easier it is made to prove guilt, the more difficult it becomes to establish innocence. (728)

At the "means" end of the end-means balance is the commitment to fairness in dealing with suspects, defendants, and offenders in all cases. In our constitutional democracy, we don't believe in catching, convicting, and punishing criminals *at any price*. According to one court, "Truth, like all other good things, may be loved unwisely, may be pursued too keenly, may cost too much" (*Pearce v. Pearce* 1846, 950). The U.S. Constitution and provisions in every state constitution limit public officials' power to control crime (Chapter 2, "Due Process of Law" and "Equal Protection of the Law").

Balancing ends and means creates an uncomfortable tension. The rules that protect everybody against government abuses of power also can get in the way of the search for truth in individual cases. This interference can, and probably does, reduce the security of all people. Some guilty individual will go free in one case today to make sure the government will play by the rules in all cases tomorrow!

It might help you to understand and accept the importance of this balance between ends and means if you frequently remind yourself that the rules we make to control crime apply to all government officials and all suspects, defendants, and offenders. In other words, the rules don't just apply to good cops and prosecutors who follow the rules for catching and convicting bad (guilty) people. They also apply to bad cops and prosecutors who abuse their power when they apprehend and prosecute innocent people.

The balance between result and process never rests easily at a point that satisfies everyone. Throughout our history, the particular balance struck has caused great frustration, even anger. Those who fear criminals more than they fear government abuses of power stress the importance of the value of the correct result in the case at hand. They complain of rules or "technicalities" that "handcuff the police" and allow criminals to go free. Those who fear government abuses of power more than they fear criminals complain that we haven't obliged the government to "control itself," as Madison warned us to do.

The great U.S. Court of Appeals Judge Learned Hand clearly took the side of government power in this debate. According to Judge Hand (1922), accused persons have all the advantages.

> Our dangers do not lie in too little tenderness to the accused. Our procedure has been always haunted by the ghost of the innocent man convicted. It is an unreal dream. What we need to fear is the archaic formalism and the watery sentiment that obstructs, delays, and defeats the prosecution of crime. (659)

Professor Joseph Goldstein (1960), weighing in on the side of controlling government, strongly disagrees with Judge Hand's position. Goldstein believes that modern criminal procedure "gives overwhelming advantage to the prosecution." The result is "rejection of the presumption of innocence in favor of a presumption of guilt" (1152).

ETHICAL ISSUES

Is Torture Ever Ethical?

Did saving a young girl justify torturing her kidnapper to find out where he had buried her alive? According to criminologist Carl Klockars (1980), that is the ethical issue posed by the 1971 movie classic *Dirty Harry*:

> Policing constantly places its practitioners in situations in which good ends can be achieved by dirty means. When the ends to be achieved are urgent and unquestionably good and only dirty means will work to achieve them, the policeman faces a genuine moral dilemma. A genuine moral dilemma is a situation from which one cannot emerge innocent no matter what one does—employ a dirty means, employ an insufficiently dirty means, or walk away. (33)

INSTRUCTIONS

1. Watch the 1971 film *Dirty Harry*. Then, answer the following questions about the film:
   a. Is psychopathic kidnapper Scorpio able to provide Detective "Dirty Harry" Callahan the information he wants?
   b. Do you think that Dirty Harry's nondirty means would have saved Scorpio's victim?
   c. Did Dirty Harry's dirty means save Scorpio's victim?
   d. Does the possibility or likelihood that the victim is already dead destroy or weaken the justification for Dirty Harry's use of dirty means?

2. Read Carl Klockars's "The Dirty Harry Problem." See the link under the Chapter 1 Ethical Issues section of the Companion Website—login at www.cengagebrain.com.

3. Write an essay in which you:

   a. Summarize the dirty means Dirty Harry used in the film.

   b. State the elements of the "Dirty Harry" problem, according to Klockars.

   c. Explain why you agree or disagree with Klockars's that the Dirty Harry problem creates a moral dilemma "from which one cannot emerge innocent no matter what one does."

   d. Explain why you agree or disagree with Klockars's conclusion that "the only means of assuring that dirty means will not be used too readily or too crudely is to punish those who use them and the agency which endorses their use."

The History of Balancing Values

LO 2

Some have argued that the history of criminal justice in the Western world, from the Roman Republic to today, has been like a pendulum swinging back and forth between periods of result and process alternately holding the upper hand. When there was an excess of one, then the pendulum swung back to the other, and so on throughout Western history (Pound 1921).

Let's enter the story in the 1960s, when evidence of excessive police power spawned a reaction called the **due process revolution**. Led by the U.S. Supreme Court (called the "Warren Court" after its chief justice, Earl Warren), this revolution tilted the balance of power toward process and individual rights. According to its critics, it tilted the balance too far—so far that it created a criminal procedure soft on criminals and hard on victims (Cronin, Cronin, and Milakovich 1981).

From the late 1960s to 2010, as I write this book, the pendulum has swung from process back to result. In 1968, presidential candidate Richard Nixon promised to appoint "law and order" judges. And President Nixon did what Candidate Nixon promised. He started in 1969 by nominating a "tough on crime" U.S. Court of Appeals judge, Warren Burger, to succeed the retiring Earl Warren as chief justice of the United States.

All the presidents since President Nixon have appointed justices who've voted to "curb" the process precedents created by the Warren Court. *Curbed* but not *obliterated*—most of the rest of this book is about how the Court has limited the Warren Court precedents. As you read the book and study the cases in your class, you decide for yourself how to characterize this now 40-year history. You'll be better equipped to answer these and other questions: How much has changed? Is the trend only rebalancing result and process to where it was before 1960? Is the post-1960 trend good or bad? Is it right or wrong?

One thing is not in question: With some significant exceptions, which we'll cover where appropriate, the trend is away from process, intended to protect defendants, toward result, intended to get at the truth to convict criminals and release innocent suspects and defendants.

Balancing Values during Emergencies

LO 2

Nothing in recent history has tested the balances between community security and individual autonomy, and between ends and means, more than two "wars": first on drugs and now on terror. Putting aside ordinary rules during extraordinary emergencies is a fact of life in every society under every form of government (Rossiter 1948).

Even during ordinary times, individuals demand extraordinary measures when they're victims or *feel* like victims. During the 1970s, a Minneapolis police chief told me the story of a woman who came into a Minneapolis Police Department precinct office and demanded the officer in charge go into her neighbor's house and get a television set she was sure the neighbor had taken. "We can't just go in there because you tell us to," said the officer. "Why not?" the woman asked. "Because you need a warrant," the officer explained. "And you can't get a warrant without probable cause, and you don't have probable cause. That's the law." Without pausing for a second, the woman asked, "How do we get this law changed?" (As you'll learn in Chapter 6, the "law" she was talking about is the Fourth Amendment right against "unreasonable searches and seizure," an essential part of the Bill of Rights.)

THE OTHER CRIMINAL PROCEDURE **White Collar Crime**

FDA Law Enforcers Crack Down on Illegal Botox Scammers

In November 2004, when four people became paralyzed after purportedly receiving Botox Cosmetic injections at a medical clinic in Oakland Park, Fla., the Food and Drug Administration's (FDA) Office of Criminal Investigations (OCI) was called to investigate. The four victims were hospitalized with severe botulism poisoning. The paralysis was temporary—a result of being injected with potent, unapproved botulinum toxin. The doctor who injected the toxin had passed it off as Botox Cosmetic, an FDA-approved drug to treat forehead wrinkles.

What began as one OCI investigation of a Florida medical clinic escalated into 210 investigations of health care professionals throughout the United States. As of July 2008, the work of OCI has led to 31 arrests and 29 convictions of individuals who purposely injected an unapproved, cheaper substitute toxin for FDA-approved Botox Cosmetic into nearly 1,000 unknowing patients.

Under federal law, no form of botulinum toxin may be commercially distributed for use on humans unless it has been approved by FDA. At this time, Botox Cosmetic, made by Allergan Inc. of Irvine, Calif., is the only type of botulinum toxin approved by FDA to temporarily soften the frown lines between the eyebrows. Botox Cosmetic is a sterile, purified version of the same toxin that causes botulism, a severe form of foodborne illness. In both cases, the toxin is produced by the bacterium *Clostridium botulinum*. The injectable form of sterile, purified botulinum toxin, when used in small doses, locally affects the muscles' ability to contract, smoothing out frown lines to make them nearly invisible.

Source of the Problem

OCI agents traced the fake Botox Cosmetic used in the Florida clinic to a California laboratory that sold botulinum toxin for research purposes. The agents found more of the laboratory's research product at Toxin Research International Inc. (TRI) in Tucson, Ariz. TRI was selling the unapproved toxin to health care professionals as a cheaper alternative to Botox Cosmetic. In December 2004, OCI agents seized vials of the botulinum toxin from TRI, along with numerous marketing materials targeted to physicians.

The vials were clearly labeled, "For Research Purposes Only, Not For Human Use." Invoices and product information sheets carried the same warning. Physicians who bought the cheaper, unapproved product from TRI increased their profits on each treatment by charging their patients the same fee as if they were using the FDA-approved Botox Cosmetic.

OCI agents arrested four individuals associated with TRI. Chad Livdahl, TRI's president, was convicted of fraud and misbranding a drug and sentenced to nine years in prison. His wife and co-owner, Zahra Karim, was sentenced to almost six years in prison. Other co-conspirators got lesser sentences.

OCI Special Agents examined TRI shipping records to track down more than 200 health care professionals who bought the unapproved drug from TRI. "The physicians were located throughout the country, from Manhattan to Las Vegas," says Philip Walsky, Assistant Special Agent in Charge in FDA's OCI Headquarters office. "They'd learn about the drug by going to a conference where TRI would give a spiel and demonstration to sell their product."

Many of the purchasers of the TRI product have been prosecuted. Some are serving time in federal prison and were ordered to pay restitution to their patients. "Someone who abuses a position of trust for financial gain and subjects patients to unknown safety risks from unapproved medications will be held accountable," says Kim A. Rice, FDA Special Agent in Charge of OCI's Metro Washington Field Office. "FDA will aggressively pursue those who willfully circumvent laws that are in place to protect the consuming public." OCI continues to investigate these cases, says Walsky.

How Patients Were Scammed

According to OCI agents, most of the health care professionals misrepresented the fake product to patients, leading them to believe they were receiving the real Botox Cosmetic. Some of the tactics they used were

- advertising in brochures, magazines, and on Websites that they specialized in treating facial wrinkles with Botox Cosmetic
- displaying a certificate indicating they received training by the Botox Cosmetic manufacturer, when they did not
- informing patients they would be receiving Botox Cosmetic
- failing to tell patients they were getting a drug not approved for human use
- asking patients to sign a consent form indicating they would be receiving injections of FDA-approved Botox Cosmetic

Sample Botox Cases Investigated by FDA's Office of Criminal Investigations

Defendant	Illegal Action	Result
Gayle Rothenberg, M.D., operator of Center for Image Enhancement, Houston	Injected more than 170 patients with unapproved drug, representing it as approved Botox Cosmetic	Indicted for mail fraud, misbranding a drug, making false statements to a federal agent; June 13, 2008, sentenced to 27 months in prison, restitution of $98,426, fine of $1,000
Mark E. Van Wormer, M.D., operator of GreatSkin Clinic, Albuquerque, N.M.	Injected patients with unapproved drug, representing it as approved Botox Cosmetic	Indicted for fraud, misbranding a drug, tampering with documents; Dec. 14, 2007, sentenced to 1 year and 1 day in prison, restitution of $65,265, fine of $3,000
Albert Poet, M.D., operator of offices in Stafford Township and Montclair, N.J.	Injected patients with unapproved drug without telling patients	Indicted for mail fraud, misbranding a drug; Sept. 28, 2007, sentenced to 14 months in prison

Defendant	Illegal Action	Result
Ivyl Wells, former M.D. and operator of Skinovative Laser Center, Boise, Idaho; surrendered medical license after charges were filed	Injected about 200 patients with unapproved drug, representing it as approved Botox Cosmetic	Indicted for mail fraud, misbranding a drug; Dec. 11, 2006, sentenced to 6 months in prison, 6 months home detention, restitution of $88,000, fine of $40,000, 300 hours community service
Jerome Lentini, M.D., operator of A Younger You clinics, Salem and Tigard, Ore., and his assistant, Cathryn Garcia, R.N.	Injected about 800 patients with unapproved drug, representing it as approved Botox Cosmetic	Indicted for misbranding a drug; Aug. 14, 2006, Garcia sentenced to 1 year in prison; Dec. 11, 2006, Lentini sentenced to 18 months in prison, restitution of $330,000
Chad Livdahl and Zarah Karim, owners of Toxin Research International, Tucson, Ariz.	Sold unapproved botulinum toxin, labeled "Not for Human Use," to more than 200 physicians throughout the U.S. to use on their patients	Indicted for mail and wire fraud, misbranding a drug; Jan. 26, 2006, Livdahl sentenced to 9 years in prison, restitution of $345,567, forfeiture of $882,565; Karim sentenced to 5.8 years in prison, restitution of $345,567

Tips for Consumers Considering Botox Injections

- Botox Cosmetic is an injectable drug and should be administered by a trained, qualified health care professional.

- Know what you are being injected with. Make sure your health care professional is using only an FDA-approved product purchased within the United States. If he or she refuses to give you this information, look for another health care professional.

- Make sure the benefits and risks are fully explained to you in a patient consultation.

- Fully disclose any medical conditions you might have and medications you are taking, including vitamins and over-the-counter drugs.

- Botox Cosmetic should be administered in an appropriate setting using sterile instruments. A non-physician who is appropriately licensed and trained may perform the injections under the supervision of a qualified physician. Malls and private homes are not medical environments and may be unsanitary. (Adapted from the American Society for Aesthetic Plastic Surgery)

Source: U.S. Food and Drug Administration. http://www.fda.gov/ForConsumers/ConsumerUpdates/ucm048377.htm (updated February 20, 2009; visited July 5, 2010).

WHAT DO *YOU* THINK?

1. Should there be a separate law enforcement agency within the FDA?

2. In times of budget crises, should white-collar law enforcement be confined within the FBI?

|||||||||||||||||||||||||||||||||||||||||||||||||||||||||||||||||||||||||||||||||||||||||||||||||||||

Equality

LO 3

Most of the history of criminal procedure, especially state criminal procedure since the Civil War, developed in response to racial discrimination (Chapter 2). You can't understand the law of criminal procedure unless you put it into this sociohistorical context. Racial discrimination has definitely lessened, but it hasn't disappeared. At all stages in the criminal process, race can infect decision making, especially at the early stages of the process, such as street stops and frisks (Chapter 4).

Racial discrimination is only one dimension of a threat to our deep commitment to the ideal of equal justice for all. This ideal includes class, gender, ethnic, religious, and sexual orientation discrimination. Gender can affect who's excused from jury duty or excluded from jury service (Chapter 13). Ethnicity affects the same types of decisions as race (noted earlier; see also Chapter 4, "Race and Ethnicity"). Religion combined with ethnicity affects decisions involving terrorist crimes (Chapter 15).

Further, money can determine who gets the best lawyer, how early in the criminal process she gets one, and who can pay for expensive appeals. Despite the U.S. Supreme Court's command that the Sixth Amendment's right to counsel guarantees the right to "effective" counsel, even when you're too poor to afford a lawyer, the reality falls far short of the constitutional command (Chapter 12, "Right to Counsel").

Discretion

You can't really understand how the ideal of equality and the balancing of values work in practice—or, for that matter, most of what else is happening in your journey through the law of criminal procedure—unless you understand the importance of discretionary decision making. And you can't understand the importance of discretion until you understand the difference between decisions made according to the formal law of criminal procedure and the leeway within the formal law given to informal official discretionary decision making. So let's look briefly at these differences.

Formal decision making consists of decisions made according to the law of criminal procedure—namely, the rules spelled out in the Constitution, judicial opinions, laws, other written sources you'll learn about throughout the text, and cases. **Discretionary decision making**—informal decision making, or judgments by professionals based on their training and experience and unwritten rules—is how the process works on a day-to-day basis.

Think of each step in the criminal process, from investigation to appeals from convictions, as a decision point. Each step presents a criminal justice professional with the opportunity to decide whether to start, continue, or end the criminal process. Both formal rules and discretionary judgment inform these decisions.

The police can investigate suspects, or not, and arrest them, or not—initiating the formal criminal process, or stopping it. Prosecutors can charge suspects and continue the criminal process, divert suspects to some social service agency, or take no further action—effectively terminating the criminal process.

Defendants can plead guilty (usually on their lawyers' advice) and avoid trial. Judges can suspend sentences or sentence convicted offenders to the maximum allowable penalty—hence, either minimizing or maximizing the punishment the criminal law prescribes.

Justice, fairness, and predictability all require the certainty and the protection against abuses that written rules assure. These same goals also require discretion to soften the rigidity of written rules. The tension between formal law and informal discretion—a recurring theme in criminal procedure—is as old as law. Arguments raged over it in Western civilization as early as the Middle Ages.

In the end, the criminal process in practice is a blend of the formal law of criminal procedure and informal influences that enter the process by way of discretion. Discretion and law complement each other in promoting and balancing the interests in criminal procedure.

The Objective Basis Requirement

LO 5

However much "play in the joints" discretion creates in the formal rules of law, one thing is certain: The agents of crime control aren't free to do whatever they please. That's because of another principle of criminal procedure you need to carry with you in your journey through the law of criminal procedure, the **objective basis requirement**. The requirement is that the government has to back up with facts every officially triggered restraint on the rights of individuals to come and go as they please and be let alone by the government. Hunches are never enough.

There's also a related requirement (there's no official name for it; we'll call it the **graduated objective basis requirement**) that goes like this: The greater the limit, the more facts required to back it up. So to arrest a person, police have to have enough facts to add up to probable cause (Chapter 5), but to convict a defendant, the government has to marshal enough evidence to prove guilt beyond a reasonable doubt (Chapter 13).

"Good" Evidence and "Bad" Methods

LO 6

Most of the cases you're going to read in this book are in court because defendants want to take advantage of the trump card of fair procedures—the **exclusionary rule** (Chapter 10). This rule requires courts to throw out "good" evidence (evidence that proves defendants are guilty) if the government got it by "bad" methods (methods that violate the U.S. or state constitutions).

These methods most often include violations of suspects' and defendants' rights guaranteed by the U.S. Constitution's ban on unreasonable search and seizures (Chapters 3–7) and the Fifth Amendment's ban on self-incrimination (Chapter 8). Referring to the exclusionary rule, the great judge Benjamin Cardozo once asked, "Should the culprit go free because the constable has blundered?" (*People v. Defore* 1926). The answer by supporters of the rule: "Well, if the culprit goes free, it's the Constitution that set him free."

Social Scientific Research and Criminal Procedure

LO 7

In 2009, two law professors with different backgrounds and perspectives joined forces to advocate "a new generation of criminal procedure." Together, the conservative—whose background was in engineering—and the liberal—who holds a Ph.D. in Political Science—penned an article calling for a new criminal procedure "that places empirical and social scientific evidence at the very heart of" judicial decision making.

The goal is to make criminal procedure decisions and decision making more transparent. Transparency results when judges identify the social science research and empirical research that support their assertions of facts. At the core of criminal procedure normative judgments is the intent to balance the interests of public safety with individual liberty and privacy.

Modern constitutional criminal procedure started with real-world experiences—namely, practical concerns about police investigative practices, their encounters with individuals on the streets and other public places, police interrogations and identification procedures, and the effect of these practices on individual civil liberties. These concerns later extended to the entire criminal process, from investigation, to pretrial, trial, sentencing, and postconviction review of lower court decisions. And, it's now a widespread practice to describe and think about criminal procedure constitutional rights as "guaranteeing a reasonable balance between liberty and order" (737).

It was a natural consequence of these practical concerns that judicial decision making and academic writing in criminal procedure focused on two empirical questions: (1) How effective are these practices in controlling crime? (2) What is their effect on individual liberty and privacy (736–37)? To judge the proper balance between the interest in public safety and the liberty and privacy interests of individuals calls for accurate, reliable, *neutral* empirical and social scientific evidence. This won't "guarantee the *right* answers in criminal procedure. But use of empirical evidence will produce a *clearer* picture of the existing constitutional landscape and spotlight the normative judgments at the heart of criminal procedure" (735).

You'll encounter empirical evidence throughout the book, whenever it's available to elaborate on, correct, and modify the courts' rulings. This evidence will enable you to see judgments balancing order and liberty more clearly and completely in the light of the real-world decision making of criminal justice officials and the suspects, defendants, and convicted offenders their decisions affect.

This evidence happily exists for several important topics in the book, especially for searches and seizures (Chapters 4–7); the right against self-incrimination and confessions (Chapter 8); witness identification procedures (Chapter 9); the exclusionary rule (Chapter 10); pretrial proceedings (Chapter 12); guilty pleas (Chapter 13); and sentencing (Chapter 14). So even though courts are unaware of it, or consciously ignore it, or take pains to reject it outright, we'll include it.

||||||||||||||||||||||||||||||||||||||||||||||||||||||||||||||||||||||||||||||||||||||||||||||||||||||||||||||||||||||||||||||||||||||

The Text-Case Method

LO 8

You won't be ready to begin your journey through the criminal process until you understand the method of *Criminal Procedure 8*. Your book is what I call a *text-case book*; it's part text and part excerpts from real criminal procedure cases, edited for nonlawyers. The text part of the book explains the general principles, practices, and issues related to the law of criminal procedure.

The case excerpts provide you with encounters that actually took place between real criminal suspects, defendants, and offenders on one side and law enforcement officers, prosecutors, defense lawyers, and judges on the other. The excerpts let you see how the general principles apply to the specifics of real situations, allowing you to think critically about the principles and the issues they raise. I believe the best way to test whether you understand the principles and issues is to apply them to concrete situations. So although you can learn a lot from the text alone, you won't get the full benefit of what you've learned without applying and thinking about it by reading the case excerpts.

FIGURE 1.2 The Structure of the U.S. Federal Court System

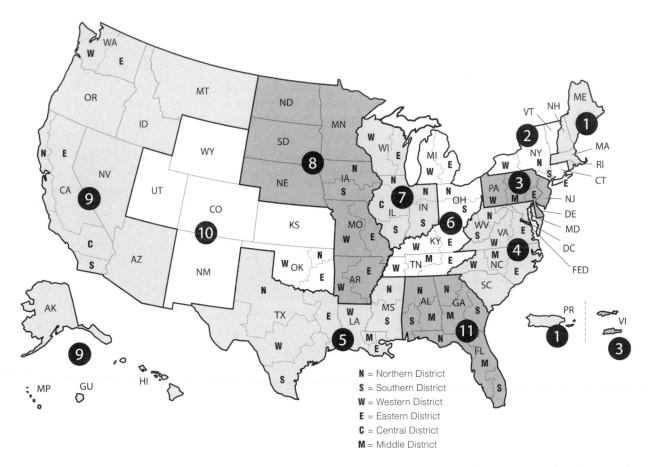

N = Northern District
S = Southern District
W = Western District
E = Eastern District
C = Central District
M = Middle District

Most of the case excerpts are U.S. Supreme Court cases because, as pointed out earlier, Supreme Court justices are the "primary generators of rules for regulating the behavior of police, prosecutors, and the other actors who administer the criminal process" (page 4).

Sometimes, you'll also read U.S. Courts of Appeals (see Figure 1.2) cases. These cases are included when they deal with issues not yet decided by the U.S. Supreme Court or when they interpret rules already established by the Supreme Court. Occasionally, you'll also read cases from state courts. State cases are important for at least two reasons. First, every state has a bill of rights that contains provisions similar or identical to those in the U.S. Bill of Rights. State courts decide for themselves how to interpret and apply their own state constitutional provisions.

Let's take a closer look at what you'll be reading in excerpts from these cases throughout the book. We'll begin with a look at the parts of the case excerpts, which will help you to write out your own case summary. Then, we'll examine the importance of precedent, stare decisis, and appellate cases.

The Eight Parts of a Case Summary

Don't worry if reading cases intimidates you at first. Like so many students before you, you'll get the hang of it before long. To help you get the most out of the case excerpts, in this section, I've included a set of detailed instructions for reading and analyzing the excerpts. (Because they're excerpts, I've also included instructions for finding cases. This way you can read the whole case if your instructor assigns it or if you'd like to read it unedited.)

Next, I've outlined the main parts of each case, the (1) title, (2) citation, (3) procedural history, (4) judge, (5) facts, (6) constitutional question, (7) decision, and (8) opinion. Learn and become familiar with them right at the beginning, and I'm sure you'll catch on to how to read cases sooner. You should also write out summaries of these parts in what lawyers call **briefing a case**. I recommend using a separate card or sheet of paper for each case. At the top of each card or sheet, put the name and the citation of the case. Then, summarize briefly and accurately the parts of the case.

1. *Title.* The **title of the case** in criminal cases consists of two names, one on either side of "v." (the abbreviation for "versus" or "against"). The government (U.S. or the state, called variously "State," "People," or "Commonwealth," depending on what the state calls itself) is always the first party in the trial court because the government starts all criminal cases. The name on the right in the trial court is always the defendant's.

There are no trial court cases in this book because, unfortunately, trial records aren't published. We enter the case after the trial court has decided an issue in the case, a higher court has reviewed the trial court's decision, and it has decided to publish its opinion. (Reviewing courts don't have to publish their opinions; the decision to publish is discretionary.)

The placement of names to the left or right of the "v." in cases of appeal varies. In federal cases, the party appealing the decision of the court below is placed to the left of the "v." Some states follow the federal practice. The others keep the order of the original case; that is, the name of the state is always to the left, and the defendant's is always to its right.

Keep in mind that the government can't appeal a verdict of "not guilty." Why? Because the double jeopardy clause of the U.S. Constitution forbids it (Chapter 12). The government can appeal some trial court decisions (which, occasionally, we'll encounter) but never an acquittal.

2. *Citation.* After the title of the case, you'll see a string of letters and numbers. These are called the **case citation**. The case citation (like a footnote, endnote, or other reference in articles and books) tells you the source of the material quoted or relied upon. So the citation tells you where you can find the published report of the case. The information in the citation tells you: (a) the court that's reporting the case, (b) the date the court decided the case, and (c) the book, volume, and page where the case report begins.

For example, in *Rochin v. California* (excerpted in Chapter 2), the citation reads "342 U.S. 165 (1952)." This means that you'll find the case reported in Volume 342 of the *United States Reports* (abbreviated "U.S."), beginning on page 165; the volume includes cases decided by the Court in the year 1952. *United States Reports* is the official U.S. government publication of U.S. Supreme Court cases. Two other widely used nongovernment publications, *Supreme Court Reporter* (S.Ct.) and the *Lawyer's Edition* (L.Ed.), also report U.S. Supreme Court cases. The U.S. Court of Appeals decisions are reported in *The Federal Reporter* (F., F.2d, and F.3d).

3. *History.* The **procedural history of the case** refers to the formal procedural steps the case has taken and the decisions at each of these steps, beginning usually with the indictment and moving through the trial court and appellate courts to the court whose excerpt you're briefing. This part of your brief puts the excerpt in its correct procedural place so that you'll know where the case has been, what decisions were made before it got to the appellate court, and the decision of the appellate court in the case whose excerpted facts and opinion you're about to read.

4. *Judge.* Judge refers to the name of the judge who wrote the opinion and issued the court's judgment in the case. Supreme Court judges and most state supreme court judges have the title "Justice"; intermediate appeals court judges have the title "Judge."

5. *Facts.* The facts of the case are the critical starting point in reading and analyzing cases. If you don't know the facts, you can't understand the principle the case is teaching. One of my favorite law professors used to tell us again and again: "Remember cases are stories with a point. You can't get the point if you don't know the story." He also told us something else I think will help you: "Forget you're lawyers. Tell me the story as if you were telling it to your grandmother who doesn't know anything about the law." Take Professor Hill's advice. I do, because it's still good advice.

There are two types of relevant facts in criminal procedure cases: acts by government officials and the objective basis for the actions.

a. *Acts by government officials.* These are the actions that defendants claim violated the Constitution. List each act by the government accurately and in chronological order. Also, include circumstances surrounding the acts. I recommend that you put each act and circumstance on a separate line of your brief. Think of these facts as notes for a story you're going to tell someone who isn't familiar at all with what government officials did and the circumstances surrounding the acts.

b. *Objective basis (quantum of proof).* Objective basis (also called the **quantum of proof**) means the facts and circumstances that back up the act by government officials. As you'll learn over and over in your study of criminal procedure, government officials can't restrict your freedom of movement or your privacy on a *hunch* (also known as "mere suspicion"); they have to justify their actions by facts and circumstances that backed up their actions. For example, a law enforcement officer can't back up patting you down by claiming she had a "hunch" you were carrying a gun. But she can back it up by saying there was a bulge at your waist inside your shirt that resembled the shape of a gun.

6. *Constitutional (legal) question.* The point of the case stories is the **constitutional question** they raise. For example, "Was ordering the passenger Jimmy Lee Wilson out of the car stopped for speeding a 'reasonable' Fourth Amendment seizure?" (*Maryland v. Wilson,* Chapter 4).

7. *Judgment (disposition) of the case.* The court's **judgment (disposition) of the case** is the most important legal action of the court, because it decides what happens to the defendant and the government. The judgment refers to the court's decision in the case. In the trial court, the judgments are almost always guilty or not guilty. In appeals courts, the judgments are affirmed, reversed, or reversed and remanded.

8. *Court opinion.* **Court opinions** explain why courts decided and disposed of the case the way they did. The opinion contains two essential ingredients:

a. *Holding of the court.* The **holding of the court** refers to the legal rule the court applied to the facts of the case.

b. *Reasoning of the court.* The **reasoning of the court** refers to the reasons and arguments the court gives to support its holding.

Appellate courts, whether federal or state, can issue four types of opinions:

a. *Majority opinion.* The U.S. Supreme Court consists of nine justices, each of whom has a vote and the right to submit an opinion. The **majority opinion** is the law. In most cases, five justices make up the majority. Sometimes, less than nine justices participate; in these cases, the majority can be less than five.

b. *Concurring opinion.* **Concurring opinions** occur when judges agree with the conclusions of other judges in the case but rely on different reasons to reach the same conclusion.

c. *Plurality opinions.* If a majority of the justices agree with the decision in a case but they can't agree on the reasons, the opinion with the reasoning agreed to by the largest number of justices is called the **plurality opinion.** For example, suppose that seven justices agree with the result and four give one set of reasons, three give another set of reasons, and two dissent. The opinion to which the four subscribe is the plurality opinion. A plurality opinion is a weak precedent.

d. *Dissenting opinion.* If justices don't agree with the court's decision and/or its reasoning, they can write their own **dissenting opinions** explaining why they don't agree with the majority's or plurality's reasoning, their decision, or both.

Often, the dissenting opinions point to the future; many majority opinions of today are based on dissents from the past. The late Chief Justice Charles Evans Hughes once said a dissent should be "an appeal to the brooding spirit of the law, to the intelligence of a future day" (Lewis 1994, A13).

Courts don't have to write opinions. Many times (and in trial courts in almost every case) they don't, which as students is our loss (or maybe to you it's a blessing). The judgment of the case is the only binding action of the court. It states what's going to happen to the judgment of the court below and, ultimately, to the defendant or convicted offender. Common judgments in criminal cases include affirmed, reversed, or reversed and remanded.

a. *Affirmed.* **Affirmed** means the appellate court upheld a lower court's judgment.

b. *Reversed and/or remanded.* **Reversed** means the appellate court set aside, or nullified, the lower court's judgment. **Remanded** means that the appellate court sent the case back to the lower court for further action.

Notice that neither reversed nor remanded means that the defendant automatically goes free. Fewer than half the defendants who win their cases in the Supreme Court ultimately triumph when their cases are reversed and/or remanded to lower courts, particularly to state courts. For example, in the famous *Miranda v. Arizona* case (Chapter 8), the prison gates didn't open for Ernesto Miranda. He was detained in jail while he was retried without the confession he made, promptly convicted, and sent from jail to prison.

The conflicting arguments and reasoning in the majority, plurality, concurring, and dissenting opinions challenge you to think about the issues in the cases, because, most of the time, all the justices argue their views of the case convincingly. First, the majority opinion, then the concurring opinion(s), and finally the dissenting opinion(s) present arguments that will sway your opinion one way and then another. This is good. It teaches you that there's more than one reasonable position on all the important issues in the law of criminal procedure. Reasonable people do disagree!

Precedent and Stare Decisis

You'll notice that court opinions refer to past cases to back up their reasons and their decision in the present case. These prior decisions are called **precedent**. They're part of the way lawyers think. The ancient and firmly entrenched doctrine called **stare decisis** binds judges to follow precedent.

But stare decisis only binds judges to the prior decisions of either their own court or of courts superior to theirs in their own jurisdiction. **Jurisdiction** refers to the power to hear and decide cases in a specific geographical area (such as a county, a state, or a federal district) or the subject matter (for example, criminal appeals) that the court controls.

Supreme Court Justice and respected judicial philosopher Benjamin Cardozo (1921) once said this about precedent and the doctrine of stare decisis:

> "It is easier to follow the beaten track than it is to clear another. In doing this, I shall be treading in the footsteps of my predecessors, and illustrating the process that I am seeking to describe, since the power of precedent, when analyzed, is the power of the beaten path." (62)

The idea of precedent isn't special to the law of criminal procedure, nor is it the basis only of legal reasoning (Schauer 1987, 571). We're accustomed to the basic notion of precedent in ordinary life. We like to do things the way we've done them in the past. For example, if a professor asks multiple-choice questions covering only material in the text on three exams, you expect multiple-choice questions on the fourth exam. If you get an essay exam instead, you won't like it. Not only won't you like it; you'll probably think it's "unfair." Why? Because precedent—the way we've done things before—makes life stable and predictable.

Knowing what to expect, and counting on it, guides our actions in the future so we can plan for and meet challenges and solve problems. Changing this without warning is unfair. In ordinary life, then, as in criminal procedure, following past practice gives stability, predictability, and a sense of fairness and justice to decisions.

Of course, doing things the way we've always done them isn't always right or good. When we need to, we change (admittedly often reluctantly) and do things differently. These changes themselves become guides to future action—so, too, with legal precedent. Courts occasionally change precedent but not often, and then only reluctantly.

Courts, like individuals in ordinary life, don't like to change, particularly when they have to admit they were wrong. That's why, as you read the case excerpts, you'll rarely find a court that comes right out and says, "We were wrong, so we overrule our prior decision." Instead, when courts decide to get off the beaten path, they do it by **distinguishing cases**, meaning that a court decides that a prior decision doesn't apply to the current case because the facts are different. For example, the rule that controls the right to a lawyer in death penalty cases doesn't have to apply to a case punishable by a fine. As the Court has noted, "Death is different" (Schauer 1987, 571).

Appellate Court Cases

Most of the cases in this textbook are **appellate court cases**. In appellate cases, a lower court has already taken some action in the case and one of the parties has asked a higher court to review the lower court's action. Parties seek appellate review of what they claim were errors by the trial court or unlawful actions by police, judges, prosecutors, or defense lawyers.

Only defendants can appeal convictions, but the government can never appeal acquittals. However, many appellate reviews arise out of proceedings before trial and convictions. Both the government and the defendant can appeal pretrial proceedings. Most appellate cases in this book arise out of defendants' motions to throw out evidence obtained by law enforcement officers during searches and seizures, interrogation, and identification procedures, such as lineups. These motions are heard in a proceeding called a **suppression hearing**.

Courts call parties in appellate courts by different names. The most common parties in the appellate courts are the **appellant** (the party appealing) and the **appellee** (the party appealed against). Both of these terms originate from the word *appeal*. In the excerpts of older cases, you'll find other names for the parties. The older cases refer to the "plaintiff in error," the party that claims the lower courts erred in their rulings, and to the "defendant in error," the party who won in the lower court. These names stem from an old and no longer used writ called the "writ of error."

A **petitioner** is a defendant in a noncriminal case. The petitioner asks the higher court to review a decision made by either a lower court or some other official. The two main petitions you'll encounter in case excerpts are habeas corpus, Latin for "you have the body," and certiorari, Latin for "to be certified":

1. *Habeas corpus.* Called a **collateral attack** because it's a separate proceeding from the criminal case, **habeas corpus** is a **civil action** (a noncriminal proceeding) that reviews the constitutionality of the petitioner's detention or imprisonment. You can recognize these proceedings by their title. Instead of the name of a state or the United States, you'll see two individuals' names, such as in *Adams v. Williams* (excerpted in Chapter 4). Williams, a state prisoner, sued Adams, the warden of the prison where Williams was held. Williams petitioned the court to order Adams to prove that Williams was being imprisoned lawfully.

2. *Certiorari.* Most appeals to the U.S. Supreme Court are based on writs of certiorari. **Certiorari** is a proceeding in the U.S. Supreme Court to review decisions of lower courts. These proceedings begin when petitioners ask for reviews of court decisions.

The Court doesn't grant certiorari to prevent the punishment of innocent defendants. Petitioners would get nowhere if their petitions read, "I'm innocent; they convicted the wrong person." As a legal matter, the Court isn't interested in whether individual defendants are innocent or guilty; that's the job of the lower courts. The Supreme Court grants certiorari because a case raises an important constitutional issue that affects large numbers of individuals; in a sense, the defendant in the case reviewed represents these other individuals.

Granting certiorari is wholly discretionary, and the Court grants it—that is, it issues a **writ of certiorari** (an order to the court that decided the case to send up the record of its proceedings to the U.S. Supreme Court for review)—in only a tiny percentage of petitions. Four of the nine Supreme Court justices have to vote to review a case, a requirement known as the **rule of four**, before the Court will hear an appeal by issuing a writ of certiorari.

Summary

LO 1

- At the heart of our constitutional democracy is the idea of balancing values essential to the quality of life. One balance is between the value of the safety and security of the whole community and the value of individual autonomy, consisting of life, liberty, property, privacy, and dignity.

LO 1, LO 3, LO 6

- The quality of life in our constitutional democracy also depends on another balance—between ends and means, more precisely between result and process. The ends consist of the use of government power to search for truth and obtain the "right" result in each case—namely, convicting the guilty and freeing the innocent. At the "means" end of the end-means balance is the commitment to fairness in dealing with suspects, defendants, and offenders in all cases. The rules that control crime don't just apply to good cops and prosecutors who follow the rules for catching and convicting bad (guilty) people. They also apply to bad cops and prosecutors who abuse their power when they apprehend and prosecute innocent people.

LO 2
- Because both crime control and individual autonomy are highly valued "goods," striking the optimum balance is difficult and never satisfies anyone completely. The balance between crime control and individual autonomy is also flexible; it shifts, depending on the circumstances, particularly during emergencies.

LO 3
- Throughout U.S. history, the ideals of equality and equal justice have ranked high. Most of the history of criminal procedure, especially state criminal procedure since the Civil War, developed in response to racial discrimination. The ideal of equal justice reaches beyond the need to root out racial discrimination; it includes class, gender, ethnic, religious, and sexual orientation discrimination.

LO 4
- In criminal procedure, both formal decision making, according to written rules, and informal discretionary decision making, according to judgments based on official training and experience, play a crucial rule. Each step in the criminal process from investigation to appeals from convictions is a decision point. Each step presents a criminal justice professional with the opportunity to decide whether to start, continue, or end the criminal process. Discretion and law complement each other in promoting and balancing the interests in criminal procedure.

LO 5
- In U.S. criminal procedure, government officials have to back up with facts every officially triggered restraint on the rights of individuals to come and go as they please and to be let alone by the government. So, despite a lot of "play in the joints" that discretion creates in the formal rules of law, one thing is certain: The agents of crime control aren't free to do whatever they please.

LO 6
- Most of the cases excerpted are in court because "guilty" defendants wanted to take advantage of the trump card of fair procedures, the exclusionary rule. The rule requires courts to throw out "good" evidence if the government used "bad" methods to obtain it. "Good" evidence refers to evidence that would prove the defendant's guilt if admitted. "Bad" methods refer most of the time to violations of criminal suspects' and defendants' rights guaranteed by the criminal procedure provisions in the U.S. Constitution's Bill of Rights.

LO 7
- Social scientific research adds to our knowledge about how to balance the core values of liberty and order. To judge the proper balance between the interest in public safety and the liberty and privacy interests of individuals calls for accurate, reliable, neutral empirical and social scientific evidence.

LO 8
- Throughout the book, you'll notice that court opinions refer to past cases to support their reasoning and their decisions. This reliance on prior cases (precedent) is part of how lawyers think. Related to reliance on precedent is the doctrine of stare decisis, which requires courts to follow precedent in their decisions.

Review Questions

1. Identify and describe the difference between crime control for a police state, a pure democracy, and a constitutional democracy.
2. Identify the stages of the day-to-day operations of criminal procedure, which crime control agencies and officials control these operations, and the kind of law that controls their monopoly.

3. What does it mean to say the Bill of Rights is "a code of criminal procedure"? Identify and define the two clauses in the Fourteenth Amendment from which all criminal procedure stems.

4. What does it mean to say that judge-made law leaves plenty of "play in the joints"?

5. Who makes most constitutional law in the United States?

6. Describe the two elements of balancing community security and individual autonomy in a constitutional democracy. Give an example of each element.

7. Explain the significance of the quote, "During wartime the Bill of Rights is put to sleep."

8. Describe the two elements of balancing ends and means in criminal procedure. Give an example of each.

9. Why is it said that "Criminal law's ultimate ends are dual and conflicting"?

10. To whom do the rules we make to control crime apply? Why is it important to remind yourself of the answer to this question?

11. How does balancing ends and means create an uncomfortable tension for those trying to enforce the law? Summarize the positions of Judge Learned Hand and Professor Joseph Goldstein to illustrate this tension.

12. Describe the pendulum swings in the U.S. history of criminal procedure from the 1960s to the present.

13. Identify and describe two emergencies that have tested the balance between community security and individual autonomy.

14. Explain the significance of racial discrimination in the history of U.S. criminal procedure since the Civil War.

15. Identify and describe two types of decision making in criminal procedure.

16. What is meant by the phrase, "Hunches are never enough"?

17. Describe "good" evidence and "bad" methods in the law of criminal procedure.

18. Explain the importance of empirical and social scientific research in balancing the values at the core of criminal procedure.

Key Terms

2

CASES COVERED

Rochin v. California, 342 U.S. 165 (1952)

U.S. v. Armstrong, 517 U.S. 456 (1996)

LEARNING OBJECTIVES

1 Appreciate that the final authority of criminal procedure lies in the U.S. Constitution, especially in the Bill of Rights.

2 Appreciate that the U.S. Supreme Court has the final word in defining what constitutional law and rights mean.

3 Know that every state constitution guarantees its citizens parallel criminal procedure rights. Also, understand that states might guarantee broader criminal procedure rights than federal rights but can't reduce state rights below the federal minimum standard defined by the U.S. Supreme Court.

4 Know that, in the 1960s "due process revolution," the U.S. Supreme Court expanded the meaning of criminal procedure rights within the federal system and, at the same time, ruled that most of these expanded rights applied to state and local criminal justice, too.

5 Know, understand, and appreciate that after a decades-long struggle within the Court, a majority came to agree that "due process" requires the incorporation of the specific criminal procedure provisions in the U.S. Bill of Rights and that the Constitution commands equal protection of the laws.

Criminal Procedure and the Constitution

The state is free to regulate the procedure of its courts in accordance with its own conceptions of policy, unless in so doing it offends some principle of justice so rooted in the traditions and conscience of our people as to be ranked as fundamental. . . . The rack and torture chamber may not be substituted for the witness stand. The state may not permit an accused to be hurried to conviction under mob domination—where the whole proceeding is but a mask—without supplying corrective process. *Chief Justice Charles Evans Hughes*

(Brown v. Mississippi *1936)*

"**W**e must never forget that it is a constitution we are expounding," Chief Justice John Marshall wrote in the great case of *McCulloch v. Maryland* (1819). The chief justice was referring to a deeply embedded idea in our constitutional democracy—the idea of **constitutionalism**. The core of the idea is that constitutions adopted by the whole people are a higher form of law than ordinary laws passed by legislatures. Constitutions are forever; ordinary laws are for now. Laws are detailed, constantly changing rules passed by legislatures; constitutions are a set of permanent (or at least very hard to change), general principles. We can boil down the difference between laws and constitutions into six contrasting characteristics (Gardner 1991, 814):

1. Constitutions are a higher form of law that speak with a political authority that no ordinary law or other government action can ever match.

2. Constitutions express the will of the whole people.

3. Constitutions always bind the government.

4. Constitutions can't be changed by the government.

5. Only the direct action of the whole people can change constitutions.

6. Constitutions embody the fundamental values of the people.

The **law of criminal procedure** consists of the rules that government has to follow to detect and investigate crimes, apprehend suspects, prosecute and convict defendants, and punish criminals. The dominant source, and the one you'll learn the most about, is the U.S. Constitution, particularly the criminal procedure clauses in the Bill of Rights. Equally important are the rules generated by the U.S. Supreme Court cases based on the Bill of Rights. From time to time, you'll also learn about criminal procedure law included in the lower federal court cases—namely, those of the U.S. Courts of Appeals and the U.S. District Courts; state and federal statutes; state constitutions and state cases; the rules of courts and law enforcement agencies; and the American Law Institute's (hereafter ALI) remarkable ***Model Code of Pre-Arraignment Procedure*** (1975). ALI is a group of distinguished judges, lawyers, criminal justice professionals, law enforcement professionals, and scholars. The *Model Code* is a model of criminal procedure law for law enforcement and courts.

The U.S. Constitution is the highest authority in criminal procedure; it trumps all other sources. There are two criminal procedure provisions in the body of the Constitution: Article I, § 9, recognizes habeas corpus (the right of individuals to challenge any government detention) (Chapter 14), and Article III, § 2, guarantees trial by jury in the community where the crimes were committed (Chapter 13).

Most criminal procedure provisions are in the Fourth, Fifth, Sixth, Eighth, and Fourteenth Amendments to the Constitution, the part known as the Bill of Rights. These amendments contain 18 guarantees to persons suspected of, charged with, and convicted of crimes (Table 2.1). At first, the guarantees listed in Table 2.1 applied only to the federal government, but in a series of U.S. Supreme Court cases in the 1960s, the Court decided that most of the criminal procedure rights apply to state and local governments, too.

In this chapter, we look at the U.S. Constitution and the principle of judicial review by courts, state constitutions and the authority of state courts, the meaning of due process before the law, and how the courts have judged equal protection before the law.

TABLE 2.1

Criminal Procedure Protections in the Bill of Rights

(See the Appendix for the full text of these amendments.)

Fourth Amendment

1. The right to be free from unreasonable searches
2. The right to be free from unreasonable seizures
3. The right to probable cause to back up searches and seizures

Fifth Amendment

4. The right to grand jury indictment in federal cases
5. The right against double jeopardy
6. The right to due process in federal cases
7. The right against self-incrimination

Sixth Amendment

8. The right to a speedy trial
9. The right to a public trial
10. The right to an impartial jury
11. The right to have a jury made up of persons from the state and district where the crime was committed
12. The right to be informed of the charges against the accused
13. The right to confront witnesses against the accused
14. The right to a compulsory process to obtain witnesses in favor of the accused
15. The right of the accused to defense counsel

Eighth Amendment

16. The right against excessive bail
17. The right against excessive fines
18. The right against cruel and unusual punishment

Fourteenth Amendment

19. The right to due process of law in state criminal proceedings
20. The right to equal protection of the law in state criminal proceedings

LO 1, LO 2

The U.S. Constitution and the Courts

According to the U.S. Constitution, Article VI (the **supremacy clause**), the U.S. Constitution is the last word in criminal procedure. True as this may be, the Constitution doesn't come with an instruction manual. It requires—and gets—a lot of interpretation. Who tells officials (and us) what the Constitution means?

Chief Justice John Marshall answered the question in the great case of *Marbury v. Madison* (1803). Writing for the Court, Marshall established what later courts would call the principle of **judicial review**. According to that principle, courts and, ultimately, the U.S. Supreme Court, not the Congress and not the president, have the final word in saying what the Constitution's provisions mean.

The supremacy clause and judicial review together establish that criminal procedure has to answer to the U.S. Constitution, and courts determine which procedures are in line with the Constitution. All courts can interpret the Constitution, but the U.S. Supreme Court has the last word. Its decisions bind all other courts, legislatures, executives, and criminal justice officials.

Despite this enormous power, you should remember two important limits on the Court's power. First, the U.S. Constitution and Supreme Court are at the top of a pyramid with a very wide state and local base of criminal justice administration. So the Supreme Court has to depend on local courts, prosecutors, and police officers to apply its decisions to day-to-day operations. Second, and just as important, U.S. Courts of Appeals, U.S. District Courts, and state courts answer constitutional questions the Supreme Court hasn't answered yet—and often never will (Amsterdam 1970, 785).

One final point: The U.S. Supreme Court has more power over criminal procedure in lower federal courts than it does over state courts. Why? Because it has **supervisory power** over them—that is, the power to make rules to manage how lower federal courts conduct their business. The Court can only control the law of criminal procedure in state courts if the states' rules violate the U.S. Constitution. Many procedures (some of them very important for defendants and the state) don't violate the Constitution.

||||||||||||||||||||||||||||||||||||||||||||||||||||||||||||||||||||||||||||||||||||||||||||||||||||||||||||||

State Constitutions and State Courts

Every state constitution guarantees its citizens **parallel rights**—rights similar to those in the U.S. Constitution and the Bill of Rights. For example, every state constitution guarantees rights against self-incrimination and unreasonable searches and seizures, as well as the right to counsel and to jury trial. In addition to parallel rights, some state constitutions provide rights not specifically mentioned in the U.S. Constitution, such as the right to privacy.

State courts are a source of criminal procedure law in two types of cases: (1) those involving the U.S. Constitution that the U.S. Supreme Court hasn't decided yet and (2) those involving their own state constitutions. In cases involving the U.S. Constitution, state court decisions aren't final. They can always be appealed to federal courts. Many cases excerpted in this book started in state courts and ended in the U.S. Supreme Court. But, in practice, most criminal cases never get past state courts.

State courts are the final authority in cases based on their own state constitutions and statutes. The federal courts—even the U.S. Supreme Court—can't interpret state constitutions and statutes unless the state provisions and state courts interpreting them fail to meet the minimum standards set by the U.S. Constitution. In referring to this **federal rights floor**, a Supreme Court justice once said, "It doesn't pay a law much of a compliment to declare it constitutional." States are free to raise the minimum, and, sometimes they do, but they can never lower the floor.

||||||||||||||||||||||||||||||||||||||||||||||||||||||||||||||||||||||||||||||||||||||||||||||||||||||||||||||

Due Process of Law

The application of the Bill of Rights to state proceedings in the 1960s "due process revolution" expanded the rights of individuals. How was this expansion accomplished? First, more classes of people (the vulnerable as well as the powerful, including criminal suspects, defendants, and offenders) were included within the scope of constitutional protection. Second, states as well as the federal government were compelled to guarantee those rights to these vulnerable classes.

The bases for this two-pronged expansion were two guarantees states have to provide according to the Fourteenth Amendment: due process and equal protection of the law. The Fourteenth Amendment commands that

> No state shall . . . deprive any citizen of life, liberty, or property without due process of law; nor deny to any person within its jurisdiction the equal protection of the laws.

From colonial times until the Civil War, criminal justice was a local affair. In view of this history, it's not surprising that the Bill of Rights wasn't applied to the states. As early as 1833, Chief Justice John Marshall noted that the question of whether the Bill of Rights extended to the states was "of great importance, but not of much difficulty" (*Barron v. Baltimore* 1833, 247). If the Congress that created the Bill of Rights had meant to take the highly unusual step of applying them to the states, it would have said so, "in plain and intelligible language" (250).

The Fourteenth Amendment, adopted in the aftermath of the Civil War, changed all that (Nelson 1988, Chapter 2). A main goal of the war was to establish federal supremacy over states' rights (vindicated by the crushing defeat of the Confederacy). A second principle, that everyone was entitled to equal rights, triumphed at least on paper in the abolition of slavery.

The drafters of the amendment left the definitions of due process and equal protection general (and not by accident, vague). You should already know one reason why they did: They were constitutional provisions, not ordinary laws. The other reason is rooted in the history of the time: States' rights and equality were enormously controversial issues. No matter how decisive in military terms the victory of the Union and the defeat of the secessionists were, the outcome couldn't guarantee the triumph of the great principles for which millions had fought and died. Don't forget this history. It will help you to appreciate the struggle to define the due process and equal protection guarantees.

Let's look next at the meaning of due process, some famous cases that led to U.S. Supreme Court rulings on due process, and two contrasting views on how the Fourteenth Amendment should be applied to state criminal proceedings: the fundamental fairness doctrine and the incorporation doctrine.

THE OTHER CRIMINAL PROCEDURE ## White Collar Crime

Federalism and White Collar Crime Investigation

The characteristics of many white collar crimes mandate that they be addressed at the federal level rather than by state or local law enforcement agencies. One very common characteristic of white collar crime is that it tends to be interstate in nature; that is, an offender who is located in one government agency/geographic area causes victimization in other jurisdictions and geographic areas. Statutory authority possessed by state and local agencies is generally limited to the state in which they are located. Thus, success in interstate white collar crime investigations by state/local agencies would be largely dependent upon cooperation between jurisdictions (and no doubt, there has been excellent cooperation in many instances), and not because of reciprocal law enforcement powers between the jurisdictions. One good example of an important limitation would be obtaining business records in one state using the legal powers of process (e.g., subpoena) from another state. To be sure, under these circumstances many legitimate business entities may honor the out-of-state process out of a willingness to cooperate with an official investigation being conducted by a bona fide authority. However, note the conditions of "legitimate business entities" and "willingness to cooperate." When these conditions are not present, obtaining basic records necessary to pursue an investigation of an out-of-state offender could become very difficult.

Conversely, federal agencies possess nationwide authority to investigate offenses, and the legal process available to them must be honored throughout the United States. Federal investigators in one part of the country can travel to another part of the country to conduct an investigation, although in practice they usually will coordinate with their agency's local office when doing so, as a matter of courtesy and/or policy. This highlights another important asset federal agencies possess incident to investigating multijurisdictional offending: These agencies typically have investigative personnel assigned to various parts of the country. State/local agencies might undertake an investigation of an out-of-state offender because of many victims within their jurisdiction. In federal investigations, the same offender would most likely be targeted by the appropriate federal agency office in closest proximity to the offender, thus eliminating the travel time and expense that would have to be incurred at the state/local level. Moreover, in federal cases that require investigative work to be completed in a distant location, these investigators can often be assisted by their agency counterparts in this area, unlike their state/local counterparts who might have to travel to this jurisdiction even to complete the simplest investigative pass.

Another distinction between the state/local and federal level lies in the traditional areas of enforcement responsibility. Under our federal system of government, state and local governments have responsibility for investigating conventional parts, for example, homicide, rape, robbery, assault, burglary, larceny, and drug enforcement. Unfortunately, these crimes are all too abundant in our society and there tends to be a very clear public mandate that they be addressed. This burden falls on our state and local agencies and a good deal of investigative resources is directed in these areas.

In addition to being better able to address crimes committed on an interstate basis, many white collar crimes have an inherent federal connection. For instance, federal law plays a large role in regulating the banking and securities industries. Moreover, the federal government underwrites the lawful operation of these industries by providing the public insurance against bank failures and malfeasance in the securities industry. These are complex industries and have spawned bodies of specialized knowledge, both for those who work in these areas and for those who oversee the operations. Thus, the federal government has established highly specialized and trained enforcement agencies to investigate both criminal and civil violations in these industries. This same scenario plays out when one considers the oversight required for the Medicare program and the proper administration of many other government spending programs.

Thus, the federal government not only has the investigative authority and powers necessary to address white collar crimes, but in many instances it has an inherent mandate to do so. Accordingly, the federal government has established many specialized agencies to address a vast array of white collar offending, the majority of which fall outside the purview and resource limitations of state and local agencies.

Again, however, it must be *emphasized* that state and local agencies play an important role in white collar crime enforcement. Not only do they address the white collar crimes that are captured in the UCR (FBI Uniform Crime Reports) and NIBRS (National Incident-Based Reporting System), but also most states do take on regulatory functions that mirror federal activities, although again their focus is usually limited to within state borders. For instance, many states have very active consumer protection agencies that have enforcement powers. In addition, most states have environmental protection agencies that aggressively take on polluters. The banking and insurance industries in most states come under the oversight of state regular regulatory agencies, and the healthcare program for the poor is monitored by Medicare fraud units. The position being taken here is to encourage even greater involvement by state and local agencies in white collar crime enforcement through increased funding and authority as a means to better address the enormity of this national problem.

Nevertheless, the comprehensive investigative approach presented here will have a federal orientation for two reasons. First, a myriad of statutory and procedural variations across the 50 states prevents a common state-level approach to white collar crime investigations. Second, white collar crime enforcement responsibility in this country lies predominantly within the federal domain. Again, however, just as there are common steps in both criminal and noncriminal investigations, there are more similarities than differences between investigations conducted at the federal and state/local levels.

Source: Bazley, Tom D., "Investigating White Collar Crime," 1st edition, © 2008. Printed and electronically reproduced by permission of Pearson Education, Inc., Upper Saddle River, New Jersey.

WHAT DO *YOU* THINK?

1. Why isn't white collar crime investigation more integrated?

2. Should it be?

The Meaning of Due Process

How do the courts, particularly the U.S. Supreme Court, define **due process**, this broad and vague idea that lends itself to many interpretations? Some emphasize the "process" part, contending that due process guarantees fair procedures for deciding cases. (A piece of advice: Whenever you see "due process" think "fair process.") We call this **procedural due process**. This is the meaning we'll discuss in this book. (We leave aside substantive due process, the other meaning of due process, which is a topic for courses in constitutional and criminal law, not criminal procedure.)

What fair procedures does due process guarantee? The Bill of Rights lists several. Are these the specific ones due process guarantees? Yes, say some experts. According to these experts, the authors of the Bill of Rights were codifying a specific list of hard-fought and proudly won procedures to protect private persons against government excesses.

Other experts disagree. They maintain that if due process is just shorthand for the Bill of Rights, then the Fourteenth Amendment due process clause is wasted language, because the Fifth Amendment already includes a due process clause, "No person shall be denied life, liberty, or property without due process of law" (*Adamson v. California* 1947).

Besides, they say, the framers wouldn't have frozen criminal procedure at a particular 18th-century moment. The authors of the Constitution looked forward; they hoped the meaning of due process would evolve and expand to meet the needs and wants of an ever-advancing society. Until the 1930s, the U.S. Supreme Court time and again—sometimes exasperated that lawyers didn't get the message—stubbornly refused to apply the Fourteenth Amendment due process clause to state criminal proceedings.

Hurtado v. California and Due Process

LO 5

Hurtado v. California, decided in 1884, began a line of cases that rejected the idea that due process was shorthand for the application of the specific provisions in the Bill of Rights to state criminal proceedings. The case involved Joseph Hurtado and José Estuardo, who'd been close friends for several years. Then, Hurtado discovered Estuardo was having an affair with his wife. When confronted, Estuardo admitted it and said, "I'm the meat and you're the knife; kill me if you like." Instead, Hurtado demanded that Estuardo leave Sacramento. Estuardo promised to leave but then reneged and renewed his pursuit of Hurtado's wife.

The case began with a brawl in a Sacramento tavern. Hurtado assaulted Estuardo. A few days later, Hurtado shot Estuardo in the chest. When Estuardo turned to flee, Hurtado shot him in the back. Estuardo fell to the ground; Hurtado shot him again and then bludgeoned him with the pistol (Cortner 1981, 18–19).

In the federal courts, and in most state courts of the time, a grand jury would have decided whether to indict Hurtado. But California didn't follow the practice of indictment by grand jury review. California was one of a number of states that during the 1800s replaced the grand jury with a procedure known as **charging by information**.

In proceeding by information, prosecutors charged criminal defendants directly; they didn't have to rely on grand juries. But there was a problem: The Fifth Amendment requires indictment by a grand jury in capital, or otherwise "infamous," crimes. Following Hurtado's conviction, the judge sentenced him to "be hung by the neck until he is dead." After losing an appeal based on trial errors, Hurtado appealed to the U.S. Supreme Court. The basis of his appeal was that failure to indict him by grand jury review violated his Fifth Amendment right to grand jury indictment in a capital case. Hurtado's lawyer made the then novel argument that Fourteenth Amendment due process commanded states to provide Fifth Amendment grand jury indictment in capital cases.

Hurtado's lawyer relied on an earlier U.S. Supreme Court case that decided due process required "a fair trial in a court of justice, according to the modes of proceeding applicable to such case." Hurtado's lawyer argued that due process meant more than that; namely, it included all the ancient common-law rights inherited from England and recognized as fundamental to free people. Grand jury indictment, he maintained, was one of these fundamental rights.

The Court rejected this argument, affirming Hurtado's conviction. According to Justice Stanley Matthews, adhering only to provisions in the Bill of Rights would freeze the law in 1789 when it was written. But the authors of the Constitution and due process made them for an unknown and growing future, full of "new and various experiences" that will mold it into new and "useful forms" (530).

Justice John Marshall Harlan, the lone dissenter, argued that the Fourteenth Amendment due process clause "imposed upon the states the same restrictions, in respect of proceedings involving life, liberty, and property, which had been imposed upon the general government" (541).

Lawyers tried more than once to get the Court to see things the way Justice Harlan did. In the 1960s, the Court adopted Justice Harlan's position when it subscribed to the incorporation doctrine (discussed later). But for the time being, the Court stuck steadfastly to its position that state criminal procedure was a local matter and none of the federal government's business.

The "Scottsboro Boys," Due Process, and the Right to Counsel

LO 5

Then came the German war machine of the First World War and the rise of fascism and other totalitarian governments of the 1920s and 1930s. These developments revived old American suspicions of arbitrary government. It was probably no coincidence that the U.S. Supreme Court first applied the Fourteenth Amendment due process clause to state criminal procedures in a case it decided just as Hitler was rising to power in Nazi Germany (Allen 1978, 157–58).

That first case began in northern Alabama one morning in March 1931 when seven scruffy White boys came into a railway station in northern Alabama and told the stationmaster that a "bunch of Negroes" had picked a fight with them and thrown them off a freight train. The stationmaster phoned ahead to Scottsboro, where a deputy sheriff deputized every man who owned a gun. When the train got to Scottsboro, the posse rounded up nine Black boys and two White girls. The girls were dressed in men's caps and overalls. Five of the boys were from Georgia and four from Tennessee. They ranged in age from 12 to 20. One was blind in one eye and had only 10 percent vision in the other; one walked with a cane; all were poor and illiterate.

After the deputy sheriff had tied the boys together and was loading them into his truck, Ruby Bates told the sheriff that the boys had raped her and her friend, Victoria Price. By nightfall, a mob of several hundred people had surrounded the little Scottsboro jail, vowing to avenge the rape by lynching the boys.

When the trial began on Monday morning, April 6, 1931, 102 National Guardsmen struggled to keep several thousand people at least one hundred feet away from the courthouse. Inside the courtroom, Judge Alfred E. Hawkins offered the job of defense attorney to anyone who would take it. Only Chattanooga lawyer Stephen Roddy—an alcoholic already drunk at 9:00 A.M.—who admitted he didn't know anything about Alabama law, accepted. Judge Hawkins then appointed as defense counsel "all members" of the local bar present in the courtroom.

By Thursday, eight of the boys had been tried, convicted, and sentenced to death. Only 12-year-old Roy Wright remained because the jury hung, with seven demanding death and five holding out for life imprisonment. Judge Hawkins declared a mistrial in Roy Wright's trial and sentenced the others to death by electrocution.

Liberals, radicals, and Communists around the country rallied to the defense of the "Scottsboro boys," as the defendants became popularly known. In March 1932, the Alabama Supreme Court upheld all of the convictions except for Eugene Williams, who was granted a new trial as a juvenile. In November, the U.S. Supreme Court ruled in *Powell v. Alabama* (1932) that Alabama had denied the boys due process of law.

According to Justice Sutherland, there are exceptions to the sweeping rule in *Hurtado* that the criminal procedure amendments in the Bill of Rights don't apply to states. If under "compelling considerations," denying a right in the Bill of Rights violates "fundamental principles of liberty and justice which lie at the base of all our civil and political institutions," then it's "embraced within the due process clause of the Fourteenth Amendment." Under the facts of this case, the right to a lawyer is "of this fundamental character."

What facts? The Court focused on these six:

1. The ignorance and illiteracy of the defendants
2. Their youth
3. The circumstances of public hostility
4. The imprisonment and the close surveillance of the defendants by the military forces
5. The fact that the defendants' friends and families were all in other states and communication with them was necessarily difficult
6. Above all, that they stood in deadly peril of their lives (64–71)

Two members of the Court dissented. Justices James McReynolds and Pierce Butler argued that the record in the case failed to show that the proceedings denied the "Scottsboro boys" any federal constitutional right (76–77).

Brown v. Mississippi, Due Process, and Coerced Confessions

LO 5

With monsters like Hitler, Stalin, Mussolini, and Franco in the background providing hideous examples of what governments can do to individuals not protected by rights, the Court soon revisited the problem of state criminal justice. In 1936, the Court inched ahead the process of applying the due process clause to state criminal proceedings in *Brown v. Mississippi.*

On the night of March 30, 1934, a deputy sheriff named Dial and other White men came to Yank Ellington's house and took him to a dead White man's house. There, they accused Ellington, a Black man, of murdering Raymond Stewart, the dead White man. When he denied it, they grabbed him, and with the deputy's help, they hanged him by a rope to the limb of a tree, let him down, hung him again, and let him down a second time. When he still protested his innocence, they tied him to a tree and whipped him. When he continued to refuse demands that he confess, they finally released him. With difficulty, he got home, "suffering intense pain and agony" (281).

A day or two later, the deputy and another man returned to Ellington's house and arrested him. While on the way to jail, the deputy stopped along the way, and severely whipped him, telling Ellington that "he would continue the whipping until he confessed." Ellington agreed to whatever statement "the deputy would dictate." After he signed the statement, they put him in jail (281–82).

Two other "ignorant negroes," Ed Brown and Henry Shields, were also arrested and locked up in the same jail. On Sunday night, April 1, 1934, Deputy Dial, another officer, the jailer, and a number of other White men forced Brown and Shields to strip, laid them over chairs, and "their backs were cut to pieces with a leather strap with buckles on it." Deputy Dial made clear to them that the whipping would continue "unless and until they confessed in every matter of detail" that those present demanded. The defendants confessed the crime, and, as the whipping continued, they "changed or adjusted their confession in all particulars of detail so as to conform to the demands of their torturers" (281–82).

When the "mob" got the confessions in "the exact form and contents" they wanted, they left with the warning that if the defendants changed their story they'd be back to "administer the same or equally effective treatment" (281–82).

On the next day, eight men, including the sheriff and other deputies, came to the jail to "hear the free and voluntary confession of these miserable and abject defendants" (282).

On April 5, the so-called trial began and ended the next day, April 6, 1934, resulting in a "pretended conviction with death sentences." The Mississippi Supreme Court affirmed the convictions.

In later reversing the convictions, U.S. Supreme Court Chief Justice Charles Evans Hughes wrote that the trial "transcript reads more like pages torn from some medieval account than a record made within the confines of a modern civilization which aspires to an enlightened constitutional government."

Deputy Dial admitted the whippings. When asked how severely Ellington was whipped, Dial replied, "Not too much for a negro; not as much as I would have done if it were left to me" (284–85).

During the trial, the sheriff admitted that one of the defendants was limping as he came to confess, didn't sit down, and said that "he had been strapped so severely that he could not sit down." The sheriff also admitted that the "signs of the rope on the neck of another of the defendants were plainly visible to all" (282).

According to the Chief Justice, the trial court had enough evidence before it to prove that the confessions "were not, beyond all reasonable doubt, free and voluntary; and the failure of the court to exclude the confessions is sufficient to reverse the judgment, under every rule of procedure that has heretofore been prescribed, and hence it was not necessary subsequently to renew the objections by motion or otherwise" (282–83).

In the opinion reversing the convictions, Chief Justice Hughes wrote:

> The state is free to regulate the procedure of its courts in accordance with its own conceptions of policy, unless in so doing it "offends some principle of justice so rooted in the traditions and conscience of our people as to be ranked as fundamental." . . . The rack and torture chamber may not be substituted for the witness stand. The state may not permit an accused to be hurried to conviction under mob domination—where the whole proceeding is but a mask—without supplying corrective process.
>
> It would be difficult to conceive of methods more revolting to the sense of justice than those taken to procure the confessions of these petitioners, and the use of the confessions thus obtained as the basis for conviction and sentence was a clear denial of due process. (285–86)

The Fundamental Fairness Doctrine and Due Process

LO 2, LO 4, LO 5

The two great cases *Powell v. Alabama* and *Brown v. Mississippi* established what came to be called the fundamental fairness doctrine of due process. According to the **fundamental fairness doctrine**, due process is a command to the states to provide two basics of a fair trial:

1. Notice to defendants of the charges against them
2. A hearing on the facts before convicting and punishing defendants

The doctrine leaves it up to the individual states to determine the specifics of notice and hearing, and to develop notions of **natural law** (a body of unchanging moral principles regarded as a basis for all human conduct).

From the 1930s through the 1950s, except for cases of extreme physical brutality like *Brown* and *Powell*, where Mississippi and Alabama provided no real hearing at all, a majority of the Court continued to reject the claim that the specific rights guaranteed by the Bill of Rights applied to state criminal justice.

In *Palko v. Connecticut* (1937), "one of the most influential [opinions] in the history of the court," Justice Cardozo conceded that the Bill of Rights might include some of these fundamental rights. In *Palko*, the question was whether double jeopardy was one of them. Justice Cardozo put it this way: Did exposing Frank Palko to double jeopardy subject him to a hardship so shocking that our polity will not endure it? Does it violate those "fundamental principles of liberty and justice which lie at the base of all our civil and political institutions"? No, the Justice answered to both of his own questions (328).

Justice Felix Frankfurter, the greatest defender of fundamental fairness, tried to capture its essence in two phrases: procedures that "offend the community's sense of fair play and decency" (*Rochin v. California* 1952, 173; excerpted starting on p. 37) and "conduct that shocks the conscience" (172).

The Incorporation Doctrine and Due Process

LO 1, LO 2, LO 4, LO 5

During the 1940s and 1950s, all the justices came to accept the idea that the Bill of Rights does impose limits on state criminal procedure. But they disagreed hotly over exactly why and what those limits are. The fundamental fairness doctrine, the idea that some higher law than the Bill of Rights defined due process, fueled a great debate on and off the Court.

A growing minority on the Court came to reject the fundamental fairness doctrine. In its place, they argued for the **incorporation doctrine**, which defined Fourteenth Amendment due process as applying the specific provisions of the Bill of Rights to state criminal procedure. By the 1960s, incorporation had claimed a majority of the Court as advocates. Part of the explanation was that the Court's membership changed. The leaders of fundamental fairness, Justices Felix Frankfurter and Charles Whittaker, an ally of Justice Frankfurter, retired in 1962. President John F. Kennedy replaced them with two incorporationists, Justices Byron R. White and Arthur J. Goldberg.

The fundamental fairness doctrine and the incorporation doctrine differed significantly. First, the fundamental fairness doctrine focused on general fairness, whereas the incorporation doctrine focused on specific procedures. The proponents of fundamental fairness relied on commentators who traced its origins to the Magna Carta, which they believed had established a flexible standard of justice "less rigid and more fluid" than the rights named in the Bill of Rights (Israel 1982, 274). According to proponents of the fundamental fairness doctrine, due process might include some of the specific procedural rights in the Bill of Rights, but, if it does, it's purely by chance.

On the other hand, the incorporation doctrine says that due process is shorthand for the specific procedural guarantees in the Bill of Rights. Justice Hugo L. Black, the incorporation doctrine's strongest advocate, maintained that due process grants only a "right to be tried by an independent and unprejudiced court using established procedures and applying valid pre-existing laws" (*Duncan v. Louisiana* 1968, 145). According to Justice Black, due process absorbs every specific right listed in the Bill of Rights (169).

Second, fundamental fairness and incorporation differ over the degree of uniformity of procedures required in state and local systems of criminal justice. According to the fundamental fairness doctrine, states could define most of their own criminal procedure law. The incorporation doctrine says that the states have to apply the procedures outlined in the Bill of Rights.

TABLE 2.2

Fundamental Fairness and Total and Selective Incorporation

Fundamental Fairness	Total Incorporation	Selective Incorporation
General fairness	Entire Bill of Rights incorporated	Some of Bill of Rights incorporated
States define their own provisions	States have to follow procedures exactly as defined by U.S. Supreme Court	States have to follow those procedures defined by U.S. Supreme Court

When the Court finally adopted the incorporation doctrine, justices continued to disagree strongly over which provisions the Fourteenth Amendment incorporated. A few justices, such as Justice Black, called for **total incorporation,** meaning that all the provisions were incorporated under the due process clause. Most supported the more moderate **selective incorporation doctrine**, meaning that some rights were incorporated and others weren't (Table 2.2).

The conflict over the fundamental fairness and incorporation doctrines is clear in our first case excerpt, *Rochin v. California* (1952). Although the case was decided before the Court's shift to selective incorporation, it's an excellent example of the two doctrines and how they apply to police actions. Writing for the Court majority, Justice Frankfurter applied the fundamental fairness doctrine but not without spirited dissenting opinions from Justices Black and Douglas, who favored the incorporation doctrine. Before you read the excerpt, study "The Eight Parts of a Case Summary" (Chapter 1, page 16).

The conflict over the fundamental fairness and incorporation doctrines is clear in our first case excerpt, Rochin v. California (1952).

CASE Did the Police Actions "Shock the Conscience"?

Rochin v. California
342 U.S. 165 (1952)

HISTORY

Antonin Rochin was brought to trial before a California Superior Court, sitting without a jury, on the charge of possessing "a preparation of morphine" in violation of the California Health and Safety Code. Rochin was convicted and sentenced to sixty days' imprisonment. The chief evidence against him were the two capsules. They were admitted over petitioner's objection.

On appeal, the District Court of Appeal affirmed the conviction, despite the finding that the officers "were guilty of unlawfully breaking into and entering defendant's room and were guilty of unlawfully assaulting and battering defendant while in the room," and "were guilty of unlawfully assaulting, battering, torturing and falsely imprisoning the defendant at the alleged hospital."

One of the three judges, while finding that "the record in this case reveals a shocking series of violations of constitutional rights," concurred only because he felt bound by decisions of his Supreme Court. These, he asserted, "have been looked upon by law enforcement officers as an encouragement, if not an invitation, to the commission of such lawless acts."

The Supreme Court of California denied without opinion Rochin's petition for a hearing. This Court granted certiorari, because a serious question is raised as to the limitations which the Due Process Clause of the Fourteenth Amendment imposes on the conduct of criminal proceedings by the States.

FRANKFURTER, J.

FACTS

Having "some information that Rochin was selling narcotics," three deputy sheriffs of the County of Los Angeles, on the morning of July 1, 1949, made for the two-story dwelling house in which Rochin lived with his mother, common-law wife, brothers and sisters. Finding the outside door open, they entered and then forced open the door to Rochin's room on the second floor. Inside they found petitioner sitting partly dressed on the side of his bed, upon which his wife was lying. On a "night stand" beside the bed the deputies spied two capsules. When asked, "Whose stuff is this?" Rochin seized the capsules and put them in his mouth. A struggle ensued, in the course of which the three officers "jumped upon him" and attempted to extract the capsules. The force they applied proved unavailing against Rochin's resistance.

He was handcuffed and taken to a hospital. At the direction of one of the officers a doctor forced an emetic solution through a tube into Rochin's stomach against his will. This "stomach pumping" produced vomiting. In the vomited matter were found two capsules which proved to contain morphine.

OPINION

In our federal system the administration of criminal justice is predominantly committed to the care of the States. . . . Broadly speaking, crimes in the United States are what the laws of the individual States make them. . . . Accordingly, in reviewing a State criminal conviction under a claim of right guaranteed by the Due Process Clause of the Fourteenth Amendment . . . we must be deeply mindful of the responsibilities of the States for the enforcement of criminal laws, and exercise with due humility our merely negative function in subjecting convictions from state courts to the very narrow scrutiny which the Due Process Clause of the Fourteenth Amendment authorizes. Due process of law, itself a historical product, is not to be turned into a destructive dogma against the States in the administration of their systems of criminal justice.

However, this Court too has its responsibility. Regard for the requirements of the Due Process Clause inescapably imposes upon this court an exercise of judgment upon the whole course of the proceedings . . . in order to ascertain whether they offend those canons of decency and fairness which express the notions of justice of English speaking peoples even toward those charged with the most heinous offenses. These standards of justice are not authoritatively formulated anywhere as though they were

specifics. Due process of law is a summarized constitutional guarantee of respect for those personal immunities which are "so rooted in the traditions and conscience of our people as to be ranked as fundamental," or are "implicit in the concept of ordered liberty."

The vague contours of the Due Process Clause do not leave judges at large. We may not draw on our merely personal and private notions and disregard the limits that bind judges in their judicial function. Even though the concept of due process of law is not final and fixed, these limits are derived from considerations that are fused in the whole nature of our judicial process. These are considerations deeply rooted in reason and in the compelling traditions of the legal profession.

The Due Process Clause places upon this Court the duty of exercising a judgment upon interests of society pushing in opposite directions. In each case "due process of law" requires an evaluation based on a detached consideration of conflicting claims, on a judgment duly mindful of reconciling the needs both of continuity and of change in a progressive society.

Applying these general considerations to the circumstances of the present case, we are compelled to conclude that the proceedings by which this conviction was obtained do more than offend some fastidious squeamishness or private sentimentalism about combating crime too energetically. This is conduct that shocks the conscience. Illegally breaking into the privacy of Rochin, the struggle to open his mouth and remove what was there, the forcible extraction of his stomach's contents—this course of proceeding by agents of government to obtain evidence is bound to offend even hardened sensibilities. They are methods too close to the rack and the screw to permit of constitutional differentiation.

On the facts of this case the conviction of Rochin has been obtained by methods that offend the Due Process Clause. The judgment below must be REVERSED.

CONCURRING OPINION

BLACK, J.

. . . I believe that faithful adherence to the specific guarantees in the Bill of Rights insures a more permanent protection of individual liberty than that which can be afforded by the nebulous standards stated by the majority. What the majority hold is that the Due Process Clause empowers this Court to nullify any state law if its application "shocks the conscience," offends "a sense of justice" or runs counter to the "decencies of civilized conduct."

Of even graver concern, however, is the use of philosophy [of natural law] to nullify the Bill of Rights. I long ago concluded that the accordion-like qualities of this philosophy must inevitably imperil all the individual liberty safeguards specifically enumerated in the Bill of Rights.

QUESTIONS

1. Why did the police actions violate Rochin's due process?
2. Does the police conduct in this case "shock your conscience"? Why or why not?
3. Are "shocks the conscience," offending the "community's sense of fair play and decency," "traditions and conscience of our people," and "those canons of decency and fairness which express the notions of justice of English speaking peoples" purely a matter of personal opinion, or are they objective tests? Explain.
4. Summarize how Justice Frankfurter defines and defends the fundamental fairness doctrine.
5. Summarize how Justice Black defines and defends the incorporation doctrine.
6. In your opinion, which doctrine is better? Back up your answer with the facts of the case and the arguments of the majority and concurring opinions.

During the 1960s, the majority of the Supreme Court opted for the selective incorporation doctrine. By 1970, Justice William Brennan (1977) wrote, the incorporation doctrine had changed the "face of the law" (493). Cases decided in the 1960s specifically incorporated all but four of the Bill of Rights guarantees relating to criminal justice: public trial, notice of charges, prohibition of excessive bail, and prosecution by indictment (Table 2.3). In cases decided since the 1960s, the Court has implied that the Fourteenth Amendment due process absorbs all but indictment by grand jury.

Incorporated rights apply to the states exactly as the U.S. Supreme Court mandates the federal courts to practice them. States have to apply the rights "jot-for-jot and case for case," as one of the doctrine's severest critics, Justice John Harlan, put it. Justice Brennan defended the jot-for-jot standard: "Only impermissible subjective judgments can explain stopping short of the incorporation of the full sweep of the specific being absorbed" (Friendly 1965, 936).

The Court didn't just shift its reason for intervening in state criminal procedure, it did something far more consequential and controversial for day-to-day criminal procedure. It expanded its intervention from the courtroom to the police station in interrogation and right to counsel (Chapter 8); search and seizure (Chapters 3–7); identification procedures (Chapter 9); and even onto the street and other public places (stop and frisk, Chapter 4).

The labels used to describe this expansion of federal intervention in local law enforcement ("handcuffing the police," "constitutionalizing criminal procedure," "policing the police," "judicial lawmaking") only hint at the firestorm of controversy the highest court in the land (and the least democratic branch of the government) set off when the U.S. Supreme Court got involved in reviewing the day-to-day activities of police officers in every city, town, and village in the country (Graham 1970).

The critics of incorporation—it had and still has many—charged that incorporation destroys federalism, interferes with local criminal justice, and guts the need for both local variety and experiments with different solutions to problems in criminal justice administration. They maintain that the great differences among the states and among federal, state, and local systems of criminal justice demand local control and variation.

Critics rightly observe that federal criminal justice consists mainly of cases involving fraud, tax evasion, and other complex crimes. Investigation takes place largely in offices, not in the field. Local law enforcement deals mainly with the hurly-burly street crimes that bring local police into contact with violent individuals and strangers who are difficult to identify, apprehend, and bring to trial. As a result, the critics say, the Bill of Rights works well for federal but not state and local criminal justice. Furthermore,

TABLE 2.3

Bill of Rights Provisions Incorporated (as of 2010)

Bill of Rights Provision	Case
Unreasonable searches and seizures	*Wolf v. Colorado* (1949)
Exclusionary rule applied to state searches and seizures	*Mapp v. Ohio* (1961)
Self-incrimination	*Malloy v. Hogan* (1964)
Assistance of counsel	*Gideon v. Wainwright* (1963)
Confront witnesses against the accused	*Pointer v. Texas* (1965)
Compulsory process to obtain witnesses	*Washington v. Texas* (1967)
Speedy trial	*Klopfer v. North Carolina* (1967)
Cruel and unusual punishment	*Robinson v. California* (1962)

most local police aren't highly trained college graduates, as are the federal police agents. So, according to the critics, the incorporation doctrine works effectively for the 0.6 percent of federal criminal cases but not for the remaining 99.4 percent of state cases (Graham 1970).

The criticisms target all criminal justice agencies, but perhaps nothing generates more controversy than whether uniform standards ought to apply to local police departments. Cries that the U.S. Supreme Court was "running local police departments" from Washington and "handcuffing" local police by doing so were common during the late 1960s, following the decision in the *Miranda* case (Chapter 8). So damaging to the Court's prestige was *Miranda v. Arizona* (1966) that the decision was labeled one of three times in its history that the Court struck a "self-inflicted wound" (Graham 1970).

The Court may have wounded itself, but, by most accounts, contrary to its opponents' fears, the incorporation doctrine hasn't wounded criminal justice. The Supreme Court's flexible interpretations of the constitutional protections permit plenty of local diversity and experimentation. A good example is *Chandler v. Florida* (1981).

Noel Chandler argued that Florida's practice of televising trials violated his right to a fair trial. The Court rejected Chandler's claim. Chief Justice Warren Burger, no fan of television in the courts, supported the right of local jurisdictions to follow their own practices. He wrote that the Constitution didn't give the Court power to "oversee or harness" the states' efforts to experiment with procedures. The Court has to trust state courts to look out for procedures that "impair the fundamental rights of the accused." Unless the procedures are shown to establish a "prejudice of constitutional dimensions to these defendants, there is no reason for this Court either to endorse or to invalidate Florida's experiment" (582).

Equal Protection of the Law

LO 5

Constitutional democracy couldn't survive without protecting our right to fair procedures guaranteed by due process of law. But neither could it survive without the equal protection of those procedures for everybody. Equality is embedded deeply in the concept of U.S. constitutionalism. In the years just prior to the Revolution, one commentator wrote, "The least considerable man among us has an interest equal to the proudest nobleman, in the laws and constitution of his country" (Inbau and others 1984, 209). I remember a blunter expression of the value of equality from the 1960s: "If the rich can beat the rap, then everyone should get to beat the rap."

Equality before the law is more than a slogan in criminal justice; since 1868, it's been a constitutional command. According to the Fourteenth Amendment to the U.S. Constitution:

> No state shall . . . deny to any person within its jurisdiction the equal protection of the laws.

Equal protection claims can arise out of actions throughout the criminal process. Examples include during the police investigation, pretrial bail, appointment of counsel, charging by the prosecutor, jury selection, and in right-to-trial transcripts.

Be aware that **equal protection** of the law doesn't mean state officials have to treat everybody exactly alike. It means they can't investigate, apprehend, convict, and punish people *unreasonably*. So courts look suspiciously at the reasonableness of certain classifications, particularly those based on race or ethnicity.

In practice, it's difficult to prove claims that officials denied equal protection because of two facts claimants have to prove. First, they have to prove that the official action had a **discriminatory effect**—that race or some other illegal group characteristic (not a legitimate criterion, such as seriousness of the offense or criminal record) accounts for the official decision.

Second, and far more difficult, claimants have to prove **discriminatory purpose**—that, in the case at hand, the specific officer intended to discriminate against the complainant because of her race or other illegal criteria. For example, proving an official said (and meant) "I hate Hispanics" isn't good enough to win an equal protection case. The claimant has to prove, for example, that a police officer decided to arrest a specific Hispanic because of her Hispanic ethnicity. So proving the officer said (and meant), "I arrested her because she was Hispanic" would be good enough. Of course, in this day and age of political correctness, it's unlikely any officer would say that. And without such an admission, the claimant probably couldn't prove discriminatory intent.

In addition to the difficulty of proving discriminatory effect and discriminatory purpose, there's another hurdle: the **presumption of regularity.** Government actions are presumed lawful unless there's "clear evidence to the contrary." Equal protection claimants have the heavy burden of proving that they were denied equal protection. Many equal protection claims have reached federal and state courts, but few claimants have overcome the heavy burden of overcoming the presumption of regularity (LaFave and others 2009, 720).

Many, if not most, of the equal protection cases that reach the courts aren't about whether there actually was discrimination. They're about getting information from the government that can help claimants carry their heavy burden to overcome the presumption of regularity. This is called **discovery**, a legal action asking a court order to compel one side in a case to turn over information that might help the other side.

Our next case excerpt, the leading U.S. Supreme Court discovery case, *U.S. v. Armstrong* (1996), included a claim of discriminatory prosecution. The U.S. Supreme Court ruled that Christopher Lee Armstrong and four other Black men hadn't overcome the presumption of regularity in their claim for information to prove they were prosecuted for drug crimes because they're Black.

*Our next case excerpt is U.S. v. Armstrong
(1996), the leading U.S. Supreme Court
discovery case, in which the Court found that
the presumption of regularity hadn't been
overcome in a claim of race-based prosecution.*

CASE Was the Race-Based Drug Prosecution Provable?

U.S. v. Armstrong

517 U.S. 456 (1996)

HISTORY

Christopher Lee Armstrong, Aaron Hampton, Freddie Mack, Shelton Martin, and Robert Rozelle (respondents) were indicted on charges of conspiring to possess with intent to distribute more than 50 grams of cocaine base (crack) and conspiring to distribute the same, in violation of 21 U.S.C. §§ 841 and 846, and federal firearms offenses. They entered a motion for discovery on a claim of selective prosecution. (*Discovery* is a legal action asking for a court order to compel one side—the U.S. Attorney's office in this case—to turn over information that might help the other side—in this case, the respondents.)

The U.S. District Court for the Central District of California granted the motion. A three-judge panel of the U.S. Ninth Circuit Court of Appeals reversed. Rehearing **en banc** (hearing by all the judges on the Court) was granted. The full Court of Appeals affirmed the District Court. The U.S. Supreme Court granted certiorari, reversed the en banc decision, and remanded the case.

REHNQUIST, C.J., joined by O'CONNOR, SCALIA, KENNEDY, SOUTER, THOMAS, and GINSBURG, JJ.

In this case, we consider the showing necessary for a defendant to be entitled to discovery on a claim that the prosecuting attorney singled him out for prosecution on the basis of his race. We conclude that respondents failed to satisfy the threshold showing: They failed to show that the Government declined to prosecute similarly situated suspects of other races.

FACTS

For three months prior to the indictment, agents of the Federal Bureau of Alcohol, Tobacco, and Firearms and the Narcotics Division of the Inglewood, California, Police Department had infiltrated a suspected crack distribution ring by using three confidential informants. On seven separate occasions during this period, the informants had bought a total of 124.3 grams of crack from

respondents and witnessed respondents carrying firearms during the sales.

The agents searched the hotel room in which the sales were transacted, arrested respondents Armstrong and Hampton in the room, and found more crack and a loaded gun. The agents later arrested the other respondents as part of the ring.

In response to the indictment, respondents filed a motion for discovery or for dismissal of the indictment, alleging they were selected for federal prosecution because they are black. In support of their motion, they offered only an affidavit by a "Paralegal Specialist," employed by the Office of the Federal Public Defender representing one of the respondents.

The only allegation in the affidavit was that, in every one of the 24 § 841 or § 846 cases closed by the office during 1991, the defendant was black. Accompanying the affidavit was a "study" listing the 24 defendants, their race, whether they were prosecuted for dealing cocaine as well as crack, and the status of each case.

The Government opposed the discovery motion, arguing . . . that there was no evidence or allegation "that the Government has acted unfairly or has prosecuted non-black defendants or failed to prosecute them."

The District Court granted the motion. It ordered the Government

1. to provide a list of all cases from the last three years in which the Government charged both cocaine and firearms offenses,

2. to identify the race of the defendants in those cases,

3. to identify what levels of law enforcement were involved in the investigations of those cases, and

4. to explain its criteria for deciding to prosecute those defendants for federal cocaine offenses.

The Government moved for reconsideration of the District Court's discovery order. With this motion it submitted affidavits and other evidence to explain why it had chosen to prosecute respondents and why respondents' study did not support the inference that the Government was singling out blacks for cocaine prosecution.

The federal and local agents participating in the case alleged in affidavits that race played no role in their investigation. An Assistant United States Attorney explained in an affidavit that the decision to prosecute met the general criteria for prosecution, because

> there was over 100 grams of cocaine base involved, over twice the threshold necessary for a ten year mandatory minimum sentence; there were multiple sales involving multiple defendants, thereby indicating a fairly substantial crack cocaine ring; . . . there were multiple federal firearms violations intertwined with the narcotics trafficking; the overall evidence in the case was extremely strong, including audio and videotapes of defendants; . . . and several of the defendants had criminal histories including narcotics and firearms violations.

The Government also submitted sections of a published 1989 Drug Enforcement Administration report which concluded that "large-scale, interstate trafficking networks controlled by Jamaicans, Haitians and Black street gangs dominate the manufacture and distribution of crack."

In response, one of respondents' attorneys submitted an affidavit alleging that an intake coordinator at a drug treatment center had told her that there are "an equal number of Caucasian users and dealers to minority users and dealers."

Respondents also submitted an affidavit from a criminal defense attorney alleging that in his experience many nonblacks are prosecuted in state court for crack offenses, and a newspaper article reporting that federal "crack criminals . . . are being punished far more severely than if they had been caught with powder cocaine, and almost every single one of them is black."

The District Court denied the motion for reconsideration. When the Government indicated it would not comply with the court's discovery order, the court dismissed the case.

A divided three-judge panel of the Court of Appeals for the Ninth Circuit reversed, holding that, because of the proof requirements for a selective-prosecution claim, defendants must "provide a colorable basis for believing that 'others similarly situated have not been prosecuted'" to obtain discovery.

The Court of Appeals voted to rehear the case en banc, and the en banc panel affirmed the District Court's order of dismissal, holding that "a defendant is not required to demonstrate that the government has failed to prosecute others who are similarly situated." We granted certiorari to determine the appropriate standard for discovery for a selective-prosecution claim.

OPINION

The *presumption of regularity* supports prosecutorial decisions and, in the absence of clear evidence to the contrary, courts presume that they have properly discharged their official duties. In the ordinary case, so long as the prosecutor has probable cause to believe that the accused committed an offense defined by statute, the decision whether or not to prosecute, and what charge to file or bring before a grand jury, generally rests entirely in his discretion.

Of course, a prosecutor's discretion is "subject to constitutional constraints." The decision whether to prosecute may not be based on "an unjustifiable standard such as race, religion, or other arbitrary classification." A defendant may demonstrate that the administration of a criminal law is "directed so exclusively against a particular class of persons with a mind so unequal and oppressive" that the system of prosecution amounts to "a practical denial" of equal protection of the law.

In order to dispel the presumption that a prosecutor has not violated equal protection, a criminal defendant must present "clear evidence to the contrary." Judicial deference to the decisions of these executive officers rests in part on an assessment of the relative competence of prosecutors and courts. "Such factors as the strength of the case, the prosecution's general deterrence value, the Government's enforcement priorities, and the case's relationship to the Government's overall enforcement plan are not readily susceptible to the kind of analysis the courts are competent to undertake."

It also stems from a concern not to unnecessarily impair the performance of a core executive constitutional function. "Examining the basis of a prosecution delays the criminal proceeding, threatens to chill law enforcement by subjecting the prosecutor's motives and decision making to outside inquiry, and may undermine prosecutorial effectiveness by revealing the Government's enforcement policy."

The requirements for a selective-prosecution claim draw on "ordinary equal protection standards." The claimant must demonstrate that the federal prosecutorial policy "had a discriminatory effect and that it was motivated by a discriminatory purpose." To establish a discriminatory effect in a race case, the claimant must show that similarly situated individuals of a different race were not prosecuted. . . .

Having reviewed the requirements to prove a selective prosecution claim [itself], we turn to the showing necessary to obtain discovery in support of such a claim. If discovery is ordered, the Government must assemble from its own files documents which might corroborate or refute the defendant's claim. Discovery . . . will divert prosecutors' resources and may disclose the Government's prosecutorial strategy. The justifications for a rigorous standard for the elements of a selective-prosecution claim thus require a correspondingly rigorous standard for discovery in aid of such a claim. . . .

In this case we consider what evidence constitutes "some evidence tending to show the existence" of the discriminatory effect element. The Court of Appeals held that a defendant may establish a colorable basis for discriminatory effect without evidence that the Government has failed to prosecute others who are similarly situated to the defendant. We think it was mistaken in this view. . . .

In the case before us, respondents' "study" did not constitute "some evidence tending to show the existence of the essential elements of" a selective-prosecution claim. The study failed to identify individuals who were not black and could have been prosecuted for the offenses for which respondents were charged, but were not so prosecuted. This omission was not remedied by respondents' evidence in opposition to the Government's motion for reconsideration.

The newspaper article, which discussed the discriminatory effect of federal drug sentencing laws, was not relevant to an allegation of discrimination in decisions to prosecute. Respondents' affidavits, which recounted one attorney's conversation with a drug treatment center employee and the experience of another attorney defending drug prosecutions in state court, recounted hearsay and reported personal conclusions based on anecdotal evidence.

The judgment of the Court of Appeals is therefore REVERSED, and the case is REMANDED for proceedings consistent with this opinion.

DISSENT

STEVENS, J.

. . . The Court correctly concludes that in this case the facts presented to the District Court in support of respondents' claim that they had been singled out for prosecution because of their race were not sufficient to prove that defense. Moreover, I agree with the Court that their showing was not strong enough to give them a right to discovery. . . .

Like Chief Judge Wallace of the Court of Appeals, however, I am persuaded that the District Judge did not abuse her discretion when she concluded that the factual showing was sufficiently disturbing to require some response from the United States Attorney's Office. Perhaps the discovery order was broader than necessary, but I cannot agree with the Court's apparent conclusion that no inquiry was permissible.

The District Judge's order should be evaluated in light of three circumstances that underscore the need for judicial vigilance over certain types of drug prosecutions. First, the Anti-Drug Abuse Act of 1986 and subsequent legislation established a regime of extremely high penalties for the possession and distribution of so-called "crack" cocaine. Those provisions treat one gram of crack as the equivalent of 100 grams of powder cocaine. The distribution of 50 grams of crack is thus punishable by the same mandatory minimum sentence of 10 years in prison that applies to the distribution of 5,000 grams of powder cocaine.

The Sentencing Guidelines extend this ratio to penalty levels above the mandatory minimums: For any given quantity of crack, the guideline range is the same as if the offense had involved 100 times that amount in powder cocaine. These penalties result in sentences for crack offenders that average three to eight times longer than sentences for comparable powder offenders.

Second, terms of imprisonment for drug offenses tend to be substantially lower in state systems than in the federal system. Under California law at the time of the offenses, possession for sale of cocaine base involving 50 grams carried a penalty of imprisonment for either three, four, or five years. If the defendant had no prior convictions, he could be granted probation. § 11370. For each prior felony drug conviction, the defendant received an additional 3-year sentence. § 11370.2. Thus, with three priors and the possibility of work time reductions, Hampton could have served as little as six years under California law.

Finally, it is undisputed that the brunt of the elevated federal penalties falls heavily on blacks. While 65% of the persons who have used crack are white, in 1993 they represented only 4% of the federal offenders convicted of trafficking in crack. Eighty-eight percent of such defendants were black. During the first 18 months of full guideline implementation, the sentencing disparity between black and white defendants grew from preguideline levels: Blacks on average received sentences over 40% longer than whites.

The extraordinary severity of the imposed penalties and the troubling racial patterns of enforcement give rise to a special concern about the fairness of charging practices for crack offenses. Evidence tending to prove that black defendants charged with distribution of crack in the Central District of California are prosecuted in federal court, whereas members of other races charged with similar offenses are prosecuted in state court, warrants close scrutiny by the federal judges in that district.

In my view, the District Judge, who has sat on both the federal and the state benches in Los Angeles, acted well within her discretion to call for the development of facts that would demonstrate what standards, if any, governed the choice of forum where similarly situated offenders are prosecuted.

Respondents submitted a study showing that of all cases involving crack offenses that were closed by the Federal Public Defender's Office in 1991, 24 out of 24 involved black defendants. To supplement this evidence, they submitted affidavits from two of the attorneys in the defense team. The first reported a statement from an intake coordinator at a local drug treatment center that, in his experience, an equal number of crack users and dealers were Caucasian as belonged to minorities.

The second was from David R. Reed, counsel for respondent Armstrong. Reed was both an active court-appointed attorney in the Central District of California and one of the directors of the leading association of criminal defense lawyers who practice before the Los Angeles County courts. Reed stated that he did not recall "ever handling a [crack] cocaine case involving non-black defendants" in federal court, nor had he even heard of one. He further stated that "there are many crack cocaine sales cases prosecuted in state court that do involve racial groups other than blacks."

The majority discounts the probative value of the affidavits, claiming they recounted "hearsay" and reported "personal conclusions based on anecdotal evidence." But the Reed affidavit plainly contained more than mere hearsay; Reed offered information based on his own extensive experience in both federal and state courts. Given the breadth of his background, he was well qualified to compare the practices of federal and state prosecutors.

In any event, the Government never objected to the admission of either affidavit on hearsay or any other grounds. It was certainly within the District Court's discretion to credit the affidavits of two members of the bar of that Court, at least one of whom had presumably acquired a reputation by his frequent appearances there, and both of whose statements were made on pains of perjury.

The criticism that the affidavits were based on "anecdotal evidence" is also unpersuasive. I thought it was agreed that defendants do not need to prepare sophisticated statistical studies in order to receive mere discovery in cases like this one. Certainly evidence based on a drug counselor's personal observations or on an attorney's practice in two sets of courts, state and federal, can "'tend to show the existence'" of a selective prosecution.

Even if respondents failed to carry their burden of showing that there were individuals who were not black but who could have been prosecuted in federal court for the same offenses, it does not follow that the District Court abused its discretion in ordering discovery. There can be no doubt that such individuals exist, and indeed the Government has never denied the same. In those circumstances, I fail to see why the District Court was unable to take judicial notice of this obvious fact and demand information from the Government's files to support or refute respondents' evidence.

Also telling was the Government's response to respondents' evidentiary showing. It submitted a list of more than 3,500 defendants who had been charged with federal narcotics violations over the previous three years. It also offered the names of 11 nonblack defendants whom it had prosecuted for crack offenses. All 11, however, were members of other racial or ethnic minorities. The District Court was authorized to draw adverse inferences from the Government's inability to produce a single example of a white defendant, especially when the very purpose of its exercise was to allay the court's concerns about the evidence of racially selective prosecutions. As another court has said: "Statistics are not, of course, the whole answer, but nothing is as emphatic as zero. . . ."

In sum, . . . "while the exercise of discretion by prosecutors and investigators has an impact on sentences in almost all cases to some extent, because of the 100-to-1 quantity ratio and federal mandatory minimum penalties, discretionary decisions in cocaine cases often have dramatic effects."

The severity of the penalty heightens both the danger of arbitrary enforcement and the need for careful scrutiny of any colorable claim of discriminatory enforcement. In this case, the evidence was sufficiently disturbing to persuade the District Judge to order discovery that might help explain the conspicuous racial pattern of cases before her court. I cannot accept the majority's conclusion that the District Judge either exceeded her power or abused her discretion when she did so. I therefore respectfully dissent.

QUESTIONS

1. **Summarize the facts presented by the defendants in favor of the discovery of information to support a claim of selective enforcement of the drug laws.**
2. **Summarize the facts presented by the government against the discovery of information to support a claim of selective enforcement of the drug laws.**
3. **Assume that you're the defendants' lawyer. Argue the case in favor of discovery.**
4. **Assume that you're the prosecutor. Argue the case against discovery.**
5. **Now, assume that you're the judge. Rule on the motion to discover. State your reasons for your ruling on the motion.**

ETHICAL ISSUES

Should Prosecutors Help Claimants Prove Their Discrimination Case against the Government?

Should prosecutors help claimants prove their case of race-based criminal drug offense charges, even if the equal protection clause doesn't compel them to?

You learned from *U.S. v. Armstrong* that it's difficult to prove an equal protection claim. It's even difficult to get information from the government to help prove the claim. The Court's decision resolved the constitutional question, but did it leave an ethical dilemma unresolved—namely, whether the prosecutor should provide the information, even if the Constitution doesn't command her to provide it?

INSTRUCTIONS

1. Go to the Companion Website and read *U.S. v. Armstrong*. See the link under the Chapter 2 Ethical Issues section of the Companion Website—login at www.cengagebrain.com.

   a. From each brief, list the arguments that would support an ethical—not legal—obligation to provide information to defendants.

   b. From each brief, list the arguments that would support an ethical—not legal—obligation *not* to provide information to defendants.

2. Relying on the information you've acquired, do you favor an ethical obligation to provide or not to provide the information?

3. If you can't decide, what more would you need to help you answer?

Summary

LO 1, LO 2

- The final authority on criminal procedure lies in the U.S. Constitution, especially in the Bill of Rights. The Constitution and these rights are a higher law than ordinary statutes, court decisions, and crime control agency rules. But applying the Court's decisions in day-to-day operations depends on both the lower federal courts, federal prosecutors, and law enforcement and the state and local courts, prosecutors, and law enforcement officers.

LO 2, LO 3

- Every state constitution guarantees its citizens parallel criminal procedure rights, such as the rights against self-incrimination and unreasonable searches and seizures. State courts are a source of criminal procedure law in two types of cases: (1) those involving the U.S. Constitution that the U.S. Supreme Court hasn't decided yet and (2) those involving their own state constitutions. State courts are the final authority in cases based on their own state constitutions and statutes. State criminal procedure rights might be broader than federal rights, but they can't fall below the federal minimum standard defined by the U.S. Supreme Court.

LO 1, LO 2 LO 4

- From the adoption of the Bill of Rights until the 1960s, criminal procedure rights applied only to federal criminal justice. Then, the U.S. Supreme Court, in a series of decisions in the 1960s called the "due process revolution," expanded the meaning of these rights within the federal system. At the same time, the Court ruled that most of these expanded rights applied to state and local criminal justice, too.

LO 1, LO 5

- The Supreme Court relied on two Civil War amendment guarantees to accomplish its revolution: the due process and equal protection clauses of the Fourteenth Amendment. After a decades-long struggle within the Court, a majority came to agree that "due process" requires the incorporation of the specific criminal procedure provisions in the U.S. Bill of Rights. The Court also came to agree that the idea of equality is embedded deeply within our history and that, since the Civil War, the Constitution commands equal protection of the laws.

  Be aware that equal protection of the law doesn't mean state officials have to treat everybody exactly alike. It means they can't investigate, apprehend, convict, and punish people *unreasonably*. So courts look suspiciously at the reasonableness of certain classifications, particularly those based on race or ethnicity. In practice, it's difficult to prove claims that officials have denied equal protection of the laws.

Review Questions

1. Describe the differences between constitutions and laws.

2. Identify six characteristics of constitutionalism.

3. Identify the five amendments to the U.S. Constitution that contain the criminal procedure amendments, and list the specific rights guaranteed in each amendment.

4. Identify and describe two limits imposed on the U.S. Supreme Court's powers.

5. Explain the significance of the phrase, "It doesn't pay a law much of a compliment to declare it constitutional."

6. Describe how the expansion of the Bill of Rights to state proceedings changed the due process and equal protection of law clauses.

7. Trace the development of the application of the Bill of Rights to criminal procedure from colonial times to the present.

8. Identify the major aspects of the 1960s "due process revolution."

9. Identify the significance of *Hurtado v. California* to the Fourteenth Amendment.

10. Summarize the ruling in *Powell v. Alabama*. Explain how political movements in Europe and the social reality in the United States probably affected the decision.

11. Describe the significance of *Brown v. Mississippi* for the Fourteenth Amendment. Explain how political movements in Europe and the social reality at home probably affected the decision.

12. Explain the differences between the fundamental fairness doctrine and the incorporation doctrine.

13. List the arguments for and against the fundamental fairness doctrine and the incorporation doctrine.

14. Identify and describe the two elements claimants have to prove violated their right to equal protection of the law.

15. Explain why it's difficult to win claims that the government denied a person equal protection of the law.

Key Terms

constitutionalism, p. 26
law of criminal procedure, p. 26
Model Code of Pre-Arraignment Procedure, p. 26
supremacy clause, p. 27
judicial review, p. 27
supervisory power, p. 28
parallel rights, p. 28
federal rights floor, p. 28
due process, p. 31
procedural due process, p. 31
charging by information, p. 32

fundamental fairness doctrine, p. 35
natural law, p. 35
incorporation doctrine, p. 36
total incorporation, p. 37
selective incorporation doctrine, p. 37
equal protection, p. 41
discriminatory effect, p. 41
discriminatory purpose, p. 41
presumption of regularity, p. 41
discovery, p. 41
en banc, p. 42

CASES COVERED

LEARNING OBJECTIVES

1 Understand that crime control depends on information but that information usually comes from reluctant sources.

2 Know that Fourth Amendment analysis follows a three-step process based on answering three questions in the following order: (1) Was the law enforcement action a "search" or a "seizure"? (2) If the action was a search or a seizure, was it reasonable? (3) If the action was an unreasonable search, does the Fourth Amendment ban its use as evidence?

3 Know that, originally, search and seizure were government operations used to enforce sedition and customs laws, not ordinary crimes.

4 Appreciate that the Fourth Amendment balances government power to control crime and the right of people to be let alone by the government.

5 Know that the Fourth Amendment doesn't ban all searches and seizures, only "unreasonable" ones.

6 Understand that the Fourth Amendment applies only to government actions, not actions of private individuals.

7 Know that if government actions don't invade a reasonable expectation of privacy, the Fourth Amendment doesn't apply; these actions are left to individual officers' discretion.

8 Understand that government actions aren't searches unless they invade a person's reasonable expectation of privacy.

9 Know that discoveries of evidence in plain view, in public places, in open fields, or on abandoned property aren't searches, and so the Fourth Amendment doesn't apply to them.

10 Appreciate that people aren't "seized" whenever officers approach them and ask questions; they're seized only when they're either physically detained or submit to an officer's display of authority.

The Definition of Searches and Seizures

> The right of the people to be secure in their houses, persons, papers, and effects against unreasonable searches and seizure, shall not be violated; and no warrants shall be issued but upon probable cause, supported by oath or affirmation, and particularly describing the place to be searched, and the persons or things to be seized.

Fourth Amendment, U.S. Constitution

For clarity and consistency, the law of the fourth amendment is not the Supreme Court's most successful product. In Mr. Justice Frankfurter's graceful phrase, "the course of the true law pertaining to searches and seizures has not run smooth." Professor LaFave, who borrowed that phrase to title an article, observed that no "area of the law has more bedeviled the judiciary, from the Justices of the Supreme Court down to the magistrate." In a badly fractured recent decision, one of the few passages that commanded a majority of the Court, conceded that "it would be nonsense to pretend that our decision reduces Fourth Amendment law to complete order and harmony." A subsequent article concluded that "the fourth amendment cases are a mess."

Anthony Amsterdam (1974, 349)

LO 1

Crime control in a constitutional democracy depends on information. Almost all information the police need comes from what they see and hear. As long as what they see and hear by watching and listening is available to the general public, they're "free to use that tactic [surveillance] when and on whom they wish, free of legal constraint" (Stuntz 2002, 1387).

Unfortunately, information isn't always accessible to the naked eye and ear (or nose or fingers) in public. It comes from reluctant, sometimes stubborn, fearful, and even hostile, sources—criminals, suspects, victims, and witnesses. Criminals don't want to incriminate themselves. Potential criminals don't want to give away their criminal schemes. Victims and other witnesses often are afraid to talk, or they don't want to give up their friends and family. So law enforcement officers, sometimes, have to rely on four involuntary methods to get information—searches and seizures (Chapters 3–7), interrogation (Chapter 8), and identification procedures (Chapter 9).

All four of these methods of obtaining evidence, which aren't available to the general public, are limited by the Fourth Amendment ban on "unreasonable searches and seizure" (discussed in this and the next four chapters); the Fifth Amendment ban on self-incrimination; and the right to due process (discussed in Chapters 8 and 9). In practice, when law enforcement officers use these methods, they have to follow rules generated by the U.S. Supreme Court in cases, many of which you'll read in excerpts in this chapter and in Chapters 4 through 9. Incidentally, all the federal and state courts, the U.S. Congress and state legislatures, and city councils and all other governing and administrative bodies are also bound by the Supreme Court's rules.

Getting information to control crime is the main purpose of searches and seizures, but there are searches and seizures that go beyond law enforcement purposes to satisfy special needs. These special-needs searches include searches and seizures to:

- Protect officers from armed suspects (Chapters 4, 6)
- Prevent drunk driving (Chapter 4)
- Protect the property of detained suspects from loss or damage (Chapter 7)
- Protect officials from lawsuits (Chapter 7)
- Detect drug use among students and public employees (Chapter 7)

In this chapter, we'll first examine the history and purposes of the Fourth Amendment. Then, we'll turn to the three main steps in Fourth Amendment analyses, phrased here in the form of three questions:

LO 2

1. *Was the law enforcement action a "search" or a "seizure"?* (the subject of this chapter). If it wasn't, the Fourth Amendment isn't involved at all, and the analysis ends.

2. *If the action was a search or a seizure, was it reasonable?* (Chapters 4–7). If it was, the inquiry ends because the Fourth Amendment bans only *unreasonable* searches and seizures.

3. *If the action was an unreasonable search, does the Fourth Amendment ban its use as evidence?* (Chapter 10). If it does, the case isn't necessarily over because there may be enough other evidence to convict the defendant, either now or sometime in the future.

The first question may be the most important of the three. Why? Because if a law enforcement action isn't a search or a seizure, then it's beyond the reach of the limits mandated by the Fourth Amendment. Taking the action outside the Fourth Amendment means that appropriate law enforcement action depends on the good judgment (discretion) of individual officers. In Judge Charles E. Moylan's blunt language, if there's no search, "the law does not give a constitutional damn about noncompliance" (1977, 76).

Be careful that you don't carry the "constitutional damn" idea too far. Judge Moylan is referring specifically to the Fourth Amendment. Other constitutional provisions, such as the due process and equal protection clauses (Chapter 2), may apply. Also, officers' actions might be federal and/or state crimes (Chapter 11). Furthermore, the actions might give rise to private lawsuits in which plaintiffs can recover money awards for wrongdoing by law enforcement officials (Chapter 11). Finally, the actions might violate law enforcement agency rules that can result in agency disciplinary actions, such as demotions or termination (Chapter 11).

The History and Purposes of the Fourth Amendment

LO 3

The Fourth Amendment was created to make sure the government doesn't use illegal methods to get evidence. To understand why, let's look at a little history. Search and seizure law began long before the adoption of the Fourth Amendment. It started with the invention of the printing press and had nothing to do with the crimes law enforcement is concerned with today—murder, rape, robbery, burglary, theft, and crimes against public order and morals, such as prostitution, pornography, and especially illegal drug crimes.

Let's enter the story in the 1700s, when English monarchs had for two centuries been sending out their agents to conduct search and destroy missions against *seditious libels* (printed criticism of the government) and libelers. The practice reached a high point in the 1700s. The low respect the English had for their imported German kings (the four Georges of the House of Hanover) raised the number of seditious libels to epidemic proportions.

To fight this epidemic, the Crown relied on **writs of assistance**, granting royal agents two enormous powers. The first part, called the "**general warrant**," empowered royal agents to search anyone, anywhere, anytime. The second part, the writ of assistance, empowered the agents to order anyone who happened to be nearby to help execute the warrant. Writs of assistance were issued at the beginning of a new monarch's reign and were good for the life of the monarch. Like the holder of a blank check who can fill in the amount, the writ permitted the officer to fill in names of persons, homes, shops, offices, private papers, and other items the officer wanted to search. So for the life of the monarch, officers of the Crown had total discretion as to whom, where, and what to search and seize. In the case of George III, that meant the authority was good for 60 years! (George III was king from 1760 to 1820.)

CHAPTER 3 • The Definition of Searches and Seizures

Writs of assistance weren't used just to search for and destroy seditious libels. They were also used to collect taxes on a long list of the most widely used commodities, including cider, beer, and paper. The British hated paying these taxes, and the American colonists hated paying customs duties on them; both were notorious for not paying any of them.

Smuggling goods into and out of the American colonies was rampant. The writs of assistance became the main weapon used to collect the hated customs in the American colonies. Notice what these original searches and seizures were *not* directed at: looking for and gathering evidence of felonies against individuals and their property or arresting suspects involved in these activities. So their purposes were very different from what they're used for today (Taylor 1969, Part I).

It was the use of the hated writs of assistance in these political and tax collection cases that prompted William Pitt to speak in the House of Commons the most famous words ever uttered against the power of government to search:

> The poorest man may in his cottage bid defiance to all the forces of the Crown. It may be frail—its roof may shake—the wind may blow through it—the storm may enter—but the King of England cannot enter—all his force dares not cross the threshold of the ruined tenement. (Quoted in Hall 1993, 2:4)

In the United States, it was in a customs case that the young lawyer and future president John Adams watched the great colonial trial lawyer James Otis attack the writs of assistance in a Boston courtroom. Otis argued that writs of assistance were illegal because they were general warrants.

According to Otis, only searches with specific dates, naming the places or persons to be searched and seized were lawful where free people lived. Otis's argument moved John Adams to write years later: "There was the Child Independence born" (Smith 1962, 56). But the powerful oratory hurled against the writs of assistance didn't stop either the English Crown or American governors from using them.

LO 4

The authors of the Bill of Rights didn't forget their hatred for the general warrant, and they wrote their opposition to it into the Fourth Amendment to the U.S. Constitution. But the Fourth Amendment wasn't aimed at *crippling* law enforcement's power to protect the value of property and personal security. It was aimed only at limiting that power enough so as not to infringe "unreasonably" on two other values at the heart of a free society: (1) **liberty**, the right to come and go as we please, sometimes called the "right of locomotion," and (2) **privacy**, the right to be let alone by the government.

LO 5

The Fourth Amendment is supposed to make sure the government has enough power to make us safe and secure by looking for, getting, and using the evidence it needs to control crime, protect officers, seize suspects, and meet special needs beyond criminal law enforcement. It just can't do any of these by *unreasonable* searches and seizures.

LO 6

In all of what follows in this chapter, and in Chapters 4 through 7, keep in mind that the Fourth Amendment protects us only from invasions by *law enforcement officers*; it doesn't protect us from invasions by *private persons*. Protections against invasions of our liberty and privacy—for example, false imprisonment, trespass, and invasions of privacy (Chapter 11)—by private persons depend on federal and state laws.

Now, let's turn to the topics in the rest of the chapter: When are law enforcement actions searches and seizures?

Searches

LO 5

Until 1967, the U.S. Supreme Court defined searches according to the **trespass doctrine**. According to the Court's definition of the trespass doctrine, to amount to a "search," officers had to invade physically a "constitutionally protected area." Constitutionally protected areas were the places named in the Fourth Amendment—persons, houses, papers, and effects (personal stuff).

According to the Supreme Court, searching of persons that amounted to trespassing included touching their bodies, rummaging through their pockets, taking blood tests, and performing surgery to remove bullets. On the other hand, the Court ruled that ordering suspects to give handwriting samples, voice samples, or hair specimens aren't searches of their person because they're less invasive. Houses include apartments, hotel rooms, garages, business offices, stores, and even warehouses. Papers include a broad range of personal writings, including diaries and letters. Effects include many items of personal property: cars, purses, briefcases, and packages.

In our study of searches, we'll look at the privacy doctrine, the impact of electronic surveillance on privacy, the differences between the plain view and the open fields doctrines and how they affect our privacy rights, and the issue of whether we have any right to privacy with regard to property we abandon.

The Privacy Doctrine

LO 4, LO 5, LO 7, LO 8

The privacy doctrine was first suggested in a famous dissent in a Prohibition Era case, *Olmstead v. U.S.* (1928). In *Olmstead*, the defendants' telephones were tapped without a warrant to find evidence of violations of alcohol laws. The government collected more than 775 pages of notes from the wiretaps and, based on this information, indicted more than seventy people. The Supreme Court applied the trespass doctrine to the case, holding that the government wiretaps were not Fourth Amendment searches of the defendants' houses, papers, or effects, because no officers physically entered the defendants' buildings. Disagreeing with the majority, Justice Louis Brandeis wrote one of the most famous dissents in the history of the Court. He conceded that wiretaps were not physical trespasses. He argued that, nevertheless,

> The makers of the Constitution recognized the significance of man's spiritual nature of his feelings and of his intellect. They knew that only a part of the pain, pleasure and satisfactions of life are to be found in material things. They sought to protect Americans in their beliefs, their thoughts, their emotions and their sensations. They conferred, as against the Government, the right to be let alone—the most comprehensive of rights and the right most valued by civilized men. (478)

In 1983, the late senator and constitutional scholar Sam Ervin (1983) reaffirmed Brandeis's notion of the right to privacy:

> The oldest and deepest hunger in the human heart is for a place where one may dwell in peace and security and keep inviolate from public scrutiny one's innermost aspirations and thoughts, one's most intimate associations and communications, and one's most private activities. This truth was documented by Micah, the prophet, 2,700 years ago when he described the Mountain of the Lord as a place where "they shall sit every man under his own vine and fig tree and none shall make them afraid." (283)

TABLE 3.1

The Expectation of Privacy and Places Where We Expect It

Search	No Search
Eavesdropping on telephone conversations	Overhearing a conversation on the street
Climbing over a backyard fence	Observing a backyard from the window of an airplane
Hiding in the bushes outside a house looking inside	Standing on the street and looking into the living room through open curtains
Opening a briefcase and looking inside	Observing someone carrying a briefcase

Source: Based on Stuntz 2002, 1387.

LO 7, LO 8

In 1967, Justice Brandeis's dissent became the law of the land when, in the landmark case *Katz v. U.S.*, the Supreme Court replaced the trespass doctrine with the **privacy doctrine**. Justice Potter Stewart, a leading expert on Fourth Amendment law, wrote the majority opinion in the case. Justice Stewart was not only an expert on the law, he was one of the Court's masters at turning phrases. One of his most memorable was the one he wrote about the privacy doctrine—"The Fourth Amendment protects people, not places" (351).

Before we go on, let's clarify a point about Justice Stewart's wonderful phrase. In applying the privacy doctrine, the expectation of privacy depends almost always on *where* people expect privacy. So places are still important. (See examples in Table 3.1.) Justice John Marshall Harlan's concurring opinion in *Katz* established the two-pronged expectation-of-privacy test that the Supreme Court has followed ever since. The two prongs are:

1. *Subjective privacy.* Whether the "person exhibited an actual [personal] expectation of privacy"

2. *Objective privacy.* Whether the subjective expectation of privacy is reasonable—that is, an expectation "that society is prepared to recognize as 'reasonable'"

Before you read *Katz*, you should be aware of an important point. Courts consider the expectation of privacy at the moment law enforcement officers observe an action. "The duration and intensity" of the observation don't matter. For example, it's not a search if police officers stake out a private home, move into a house across the street, and watch who and what's coming and going for weeks. Similarly, it's not a search if officers follow someone down the street and into a restaurant, watch her while she eats, follow her when she leaves, enter several stores to watch her shop, and then follow her into any other public place. Why aren't they searches? Because any member of the public could've done the same thing. Of course, the actions might be something else—for example, stalking, which is a crime in many states today (Stuntz 2002, 1387).

In *theory*, the privacy doctrine is a fine example of balancing the government's power to control crime and the individual's right to be let alone by the government. In *practice*, as you learned in the last paragraph, it allows the police a lot of leeway. A **reasonable expectation of privacy** is the kind of expectation any citizen might have with respect to any other citizen.

A fair translation of that standard might go as follows:

Police can see and hear the things that any member of the public might see and hear, without fear of Fourth Amendment regulation. Only when they see and hear things that members of the public would not be allowed to see and hear, has a 'search' taken place. (Stuntz 2002, 1387)

In our next excerpted case, *Katz v. U.S.* (1967), the U.S. Supreme Court created and applied the privacy doctrine. Charles Katz went into a public telephone booth, closed the door, put his money in the slot, and took bets on the upcoming week's college basketball games. Katz was a bookie and his customers were from around the country. It was from these very unremarkable facts that the privacy test was created and that the majority of the Court decided that Katz had a reasonable expectation of privacy in his end of the betting conversations. Justice Harlan's concurring opinion coined the exact statement of the privacy test currently used by the Court. Justice Black flatly rejected the new test because it created law based on the justices' personal opinions instead of on the original intent of those who wrote the Fourth Amendment.

This narrow conception of the privacy doctrine led Professor William Heffernan (2001–2002) to conclude that we have a reasonable expectation of privacy only when we can demonstrate "eternal vigilance." In Professor Heffernan's words, "Even the slightest exposure of an item to the public can defeat a privacy claim" (38). As you read the *Katz v. U.S*, and the "Exploring Further" excerpts, think about what Professor Heffernan says.

*Our next excerpted case, **Katz v. U.S.**, is the one from which the privacy test was created when the majority of the Court decided that Katz, a bookie, had a reasonable expectation of privacy for his phone calls.*

CASE   Did He Have a Right to Privacy That Society Recognizes?

Katz v. U.S.
389 U.S. 347 (1967)

HISTORY

Charles Katz was convicted under a federal statute of transmitting wagering information by telephone across state lines. The court of appeals affirmed the conviction. The Supreme Court granted certiorari and reversed.

STEWART, J.

FACTS

[The facts are taken from Katz v. U.S., *369 F.2d 130 (9th Cir. 1966).]*

In February of 1965 Charles Katz was seen placing calls from a bank of three public telephone booths during certain hours and on an almost daily basis. He was never observed in any other telephone booth. In the period of February 19 to February 25, 1965, at set hours, Special

Agents of the Federal Bureau of Investigation placed microphones on the tops of two of the public telephone booths normally used by Katz. The other phone was placed out of order by the telephone company.

The microphones were attached to the outside of the telephone booths with tape. There was no physical penetration inside of the booths. The microphones were activated only while Katz was approaching and actually in the booth. Wires led from microphones to a wire recorder on top of one of the booths. Thus the F.B.I. obtained a record of Katz's end of a series of telephone calls. A study of the transcripts of the recordings made of Katz's end of the conversations revealed that the conversations had to do with the placing of bets and the obtaining of gambling information by Katz.

At the trial evidence was introduced to show that from February 19 to February 25, 1965, inclusive, the appellant placed calls from two telephone booths located in the 8200 block of Sunset Boulevard in Los Angeles. The conversations were overheard and recorded every day except February 22. The transcripts of the recordings and the normal business records of the telephone company were used to determine that the calls went to Boston, Massachusetts, and Miami, Florida.

The testimony of Joseph Gunn of the Administrative Vice Division of the Los Angeles Police Department, who was the expert called by the government in the area of bookmaking, was that the transcripts of the conversations showed that bets were made and information assisting in the placing of bets was transmitted on the dates and at the times alleged in the indictment. Bets were recorded like "Give me Duquesne minus 7 for a nickel." Information relating to the line and the acquiring of credit was also transmitted.

From all of the evidence in the case the court found the volume of business being done by Katz indicated that it was not a casual incidental occupation of Katz. The court found that he was engaged in the business of betting or wagering at the time of the telephone conversations, which were transmitted and recorded. Katz was convicted of transmitting wagering information by telephone from Los Angeles to Miami and Boston, in violation of a federal statute.

OPINION

The Fourth Amendment cannot be translated into a general constitutional "right to privacy." That Amendment protects individual privacy against certain kinds of governmental intrusion, but its protections go further, and often have nothing to do with privacy at all. The protection of a person's general right to privacy—his right to be let alone by other people—is, like the protection of his property and of his very life, left largely to the law of the individual States.

The parties have attached great significance to the characterization of the telephone booth from which the petitioner placed his calls. The petitioner has strenuously argued that the booth was a "constitutionally protected area." The Government has maintained with equal vigor that it was not. But this effort to decide whether or not a given "area," viewed in the abstract, is "constitutionally protected" deflects attention from the problem presented by this case. For the Fourth Amendment protects people, not places. What a person knowingly exposes to the public, even in his own home or office, is not a subject of Fourth Amendment protection. But what he seeks to preserve as private, even in an area accessible to the public, may be constitutionally protected.

The Government stresses the fact that the telephone booth from which the petitioner made his calls was constructed partly of glass, so that he was as visible after he entered it as he would have been if he had remained outside. But what he sought to exclude when he entered the booth was not the intruding eye—it was the uninvited ear. He did not shed his right to do so simply because he made his calls from a place where he might be seen. No less than an individual in a business office, in a friend's apartment, or in a taxicab, a person in a telephone booth may rely upon the protection of the Fourth Amendment. One who occupies it, shuts the door behind him, and pays the toll that permits him to place a call is surely entitled to assume that the words he utters into the mouthpiece will not be broadcast to the world. To read the Constitution more narrowly is to ignore the vital role that the public telephone has come to play in private communication.

We conclude that the "trespass" doctrine can no longer be regarded as controlling. The Government's activities in electronically listening to and recording the petitioner's words violated the privacy upon which he justifiably relied while using the telephone booth and thus constituted a "search and seizure" within the meaning of the Fourth Amendment. The fact that the electronic device employed to achieve that end did not happen to penetrate the wall of the booth can have no constitutional significance.

JUDGMENT REVERSED.

CONCURRING OPINION

HARLAN, J.

As the Court's opinion states, "the Fourth Amendment protects people, not places." The question, however, is what protection it affords to those people. Generally, as here, the answer to that question requires reference to a "place." My understanding of the rule that has emerged from prior decisions is that there is a twofold requirement, first that a person have exhibited an actual (subjective) expectation of privacy and, second, that the expectation be one that society is prepared to recognize as "reasonable."

Thus a man's home is, for most purposes, a place where he expects privacy, but objects, activities, or statements that he exposes to the "plain view" of outsiders are not "protected" because no intention to keep them to himself has been exhibited. On the other hand, conversations in the open would not be protected against being overheard, for the expectation of privacy under the circumstances would be unreasonable.

The critical fact in this case is that "one who occupies it (a telephone booth) shuts the door behind him, and pays the toll that permits him to place a call is surely entitled to assume" that his conversation is not being intercepted. The point is not that the booth is "accessible to the public" at other times, but that it is a temporarily private place whose momentary occupants' expectations of freedom from intrusion are recognized as reasonable.

DISSENT

BLACK, J.

If I could agree with the Court that eavesdropping carried on by electronic means (equivalent to wiretapping) constitutes a "search" or "seizure," I would be happy to join the Court's opinion. My basic objection is twofold: (1) I do not believe that the words of the Amendment will bear the meaning given them by today's decision, and (2) I do not believe that it is the proper role of this Court to rewrite the Amendment in order "to bring it into harmony with the times" and thus reach a result that many people believe to be desirable.

While I realize that an argument based on the meaning of words lacks the scope, and no doubt the appeal, of broad policy discussions and philosophical discourses on such nebulous subjects as privacy, for me the language of the Amendment is the crucial place to look in construing a written document such as our Constitution.

The first clause protects "persons, houses, papers, and effects, against unreasonable searches and seizures." These words connote the idea of tangible things with size, form, and weight, things capable of being searched, seized, or both. The second clause of the Amendment still further establishes its Framers' purpose to limit its protection to tangible things by providing that no warrants shall issue but those "particularly describing the place to be searched, and the persons or things to be seized."

Tapping telephone wires, of course, was an unknown possibility at the time the Fourth Amendment was adopted. But eavesdropping (and wiretapping is nothing more than eavesdropping by telephone) was an ancient practice which at common law was condemned as a nuisance. In those days the eavesdropper listened by naked ear under the eaves of houses or their windows, or beyond their walls seeking out private discourse. There can be no doubt that the Framers were aware of this practice, and if they had desired to outlaw or restrict the use of evidence obtained by eavesdropping, I believe that they would have used the appropriate language to do so in the Fourth Amendment. They certainly would not have left such a task to the ingenuity of language-stretching judges. No one, it seems to me, can read the debates on the Bill of Rights without reaching the conclusion that its Framers and critics well knew the meaning of the words they used, what they would be understood to mean by others, their scope and their limitations.

I do not deny that common sense requires and that this Court often has said that the Bill of Rights' safeguards should be given a liberal construction. This principle, however, does not justify construing the search and seizure amendment as applying to eavesdropping or the "seizure" of conversations. The Fourth Amendment was aimed directly at the abhorred practice of breaking in, ransacking and searching homes and other buildings and seizing people's personal belongings without warrants issued by magistrates.

Since I see no way in which the words of the Fourth Amendment can be construed to apply to eavesdropping, that closes the matter for me. In interpreting the Bill of Rights, I willingly go as far as a liberal construction of the language takes me, but I simply cannot in good conscience give a meaning to words which they have never before been thought to have and which they certainly do not have in common ordinary usage. I will not distort the words of the Amendment in order to "keep the Constitution up to date" or "to bring it into harmony with the times." It was never meant that this Court have such power, which in effect would make us a continuously functioning constitutional convention.

With this decision the Court has completed, I hope, its rewriting of the Fourth Amendment, which started only recently when the Court began referring incessantly to the Fourth Amendment not so much as a law against unreasonable searches and seizures as one to protect an individual's privacy.

By clever word juggling the Court finds it plausible to argue that language aimed specifically at searches and seizures of things that can be searched and seized may, to protect privacy, be applied to eavesdropped evidence of conversations that can neither be searched nor seized. Few things happen to an individual that do not affect his privacy in one way or another. Thus, by arbitrarily substituting the Court's language, designed to protect privacy, for the Constitution's language, designed to protect against unreasonable searches and seizures, the Court has made the Fourth Amendment its vehicle for holding all laws violative of the Constitution which offend the Court's broadest concept of privacy.

The Court talks about a constitutional "right of privacy" as though there is some constitutional provision or provisions forbidding any law ever to be passed which might abridge the "privacy" of individuals. But there is not. The Fourth Amendment protects privacy only to the extent that it prohibits unreasonable searches and seizures of "persons, houses, papers, and effects." No general right is created by the Amendment so as to give this Court the unlimited power to hold unconstitutional everything which affects privacy. Certainly the Framers, well acquainted as they were with the excesses of governmental power, did not intend to grant this Court such omnipotent lawmaking authority as that. The history of governments proves that it is dangerous to freedom to repose such powers in courts.

For these reasons I respectfully dissent.

QUESTIONS

1. List the specific government invasions in the case.
2. State the privacy and trespass doctrines.
3. Why did the majority of the Court reject the trespass doctrine?
4. State Justice Harlan's formulation of the privacy test.
5. Using Justice Harlan's formulation of the test, in your opinion, did Katz have a subjective and objective expectation of privacy in his conversations?
6. On the basis of the facts, is Justice Stewart correct that the Fourth Amendment protects people, not places?
7. Is Justice Black right in his dissent that there is no right to privacy in the Fourth Amendment? Explain your answer.
8. What if it's true that the framers of the Fourth Amendment didn't intend to protect us from government eavesdropping? Should something written over two hundred years ago bind the Court (and us) today? Explain your answer.
9. Do you agree that the Supreme Court doesn't have the authority to keep the Constitution "up to date"? Explain your answer.

EXPLORING FURTHER

··

The Expectation of Privacy

1. *Did He Have a Reasonable Expectation of Privacy in His Bank Records?*

U.S. v. Miller, 425 U.S. 435 (1976)

FACTS In response to an informant's tip, a deputy sheriff from Houston County, Georgia, stopped a van-type truck occupied by two of Mitch Miller's alleged co-conspirators. The truck contained distillery apparatus and raw material. A few weeks later, a fire broke out in a Kathleen, Georgia, warehouse rented to Miller. During the blaze, firefighters and sheriff's department officials discovered a 7,500-gallon-capacity distillery, 175 gallons of non-tax-paid whiskey, and related paraphernalia.

Two weeks later agents from the Treasury Department's Alcohol, Tobacco, and Firearms Bureau presented grand jury subpoenas to the presidents of the Citizens & Southern National Bank of Warner Robins and the Bank of Byron, where Miller maintained accounts. The subpoenas required the two presidents to appear in court and to produce all records of accounts—savings, checking, loan or otherwise, in the name of Mr. Mitch Miller. The banks didn't tell Miller about the subpoena but ordered their employees to make the records available and to provide copies of any documents the agents desired.

At the Bank of Byron, an agent was shown microfilm records of the relevant account and provided with copies of one deposit slip and one or two checks. At the Citizens & Southern National Bank, microfilm records also were shown to the agent, and he was given copies of the records of the respondent's account during the applicable period. These included all checks, deposit slips, two financial statements, and three monthly statements. The bank presidents were then told that it wouldn't be necessary to appear in person before the grand jury.

In a motion to suppress the bank records, Miller contended that the bank records were seized illegally. Did Miller have a reasonable expectation of privacy in his bank records?

DECISION The trial court overruled the motion, and the U.S. Supreme Court agreed. According to the Court:

> Miller urges that he has a Fourth Amendment interest in the records kept by the banks because he has a reasonable expectation of privacy [in the records]. We perceive no legitimate "expectation of privacy" in their contents. The checks are not confidential communications but negotiable instruments to be used in commercial transactions. All of the documents obtained, including financial statements and deposit slips, contain only information voluntarily conveyed to the banks and exposed to their employees in the ordinary course of business.

> The depositor takes the risk, in revealing his affairs to another, that the information will be conveyed by that person to the Government. This Court has held repeatedly that the Fourth Amendment does not prohibit the obtaining of information revealed to a third party and conveyed by him to Government authorities, even if the information is revealed on the assumption that it will be used only for a limited purpose and the confidence placed in the third party will not be betrayed.

Justice Brennan dissented. According to Justice Brennan:

> The customer of a bank expects that the documents, such as checks, which he transmits to the bank in the course of his business operations, will remain private, and that such an expectation is reasonable. The prosecution concedes as much, although it asserts that this expectation is not constitutionally cognizable. Representatives of several banks testified at the suppression hearing that information in their possession regarding a customer's account is deemed by them to be confidential.

2. *Did He Have a Reasonable Expectation of Privacy in Numbers Dialed from His Home Telephone?*

Smith v. Maryland, 442 U.S. 745 (1979)

FACTS In Baltimore, Maryland, Patricia McDonough was robbed. She gave the police a description of the robber and of a 1975 Monte Carlo automobile she had observed near the scene of the crime. After the robbery, McDonough began receiving threatening and obscene phone calls from a man identifying himself as the robber. On one occasion, the caller asked that she step out on her front porch; she did so, and saw the 1975 Monte Carlo she had earlier described to police moving slowly past her home. On March 16, police spotted a man who met McDonough's description driving a 1975 Monte Carlo in her neighborhood. By tracing the license plate number, police learned that the car was registered in the name of Michael Lee Smith.

The next day, the telephone company, at police request, installed a pen register at its central offices to record the numbers dialed from the telephone at Smith's home. The police didn't get a warrant or court order before having the pen register installed. The register revealed that on March 17 a call was placed from Smith's [the defendant's] home to McDonough's phone.

On the basis of this and other evidence, the police obtained a warrant to search the petitioner's residence. The search revealed that a page in Smith's phone book was turned down to the name and number of Patricia McDonough; the phone book was seized. Smith was arrested, and a six-man lineup was held on March 19. McDonough identified the petitioner as the man who had robbed her.

Smith was indicted in the Criminal Court of Baltimore for robbery. He moved to suppress "all fruits derived from the pen register" on the ground that the police had failed to secure a warrant prior to its installation. Did he have a reasonable expectation of privacy in the numbers he dialed from his home telephone?

DECISION No, said the U.S. Supreme Court. According to the majority:

> We doubt that people in general entertain any actual expectation of privacy in the numbers they dial. Smith can claim no legitimate expectation of privacy here. When he used his phone, Smith voluntarily conveyed numerical information to the telephone company and "exposed" that information to its equipment in the ordinary course of business. In so doing, he assumed the risk that the company would reveal to police the numbers he dialed. The switching equipment that processed those numbers is merely the modern counterpart of the operator who, in an earlier day, personally completed calls for the subscriber.

DISSENT Justice Stewart disagreed. (Recall that Justice Stewart wrote the opinion in *Katz v. U.S.*) According to his dissent:

> I think that the numbers dialed from a private telephone—like the conversations that occur during a call—are within the constitutional protection recognized in *Katz*. It seems clear to me that information obtained by pen register surveillance of a private telephone is information in which the telephone subscriber has a legitimate expectation of privacy. The information captured by such surveillance emanates from private conduct within a person's home or office—locations that without question are entitled to Fourth and Fourteenth Amendment protection.
>
> The numbers dialed from a private telephone—although certainly more prosaic than the conversation itself—are not without "content." Most private telephone subscribers may have their own numbers listed in a publicly distributed directory, but I doubt there are any who would be happy to have broadcast to the world a list of the local or long distance numbers they have called. This is not because such a list might in some sense be incriminating, but because it easily could reveal the identities of the persons and the places called, and thus reveal the most intimate details of a person's life.

Justice Marshall also dissented:

> Just as one who enters a public telephone booth is "entitled to assume that the words he utters into the mouthpiece will not be broadcast to the world," so too, he should be entitled to assume that the numbers he dials in the privacy of his home will be recorded, if at all, solely for the phone company's business purposes. Accordingly, I would require law enforcement officials to obtain a warrant before they enlist telephone companies to secure information otherwise beyond the government's reach.

3. Did They Have a Reasonable Expectation of Privacy in Their Trash?

California v. Greenwood, 486 U.S. 35 (1988)

FACTS Investigator Jenny Stracner of the Laguna Beach Police Department received information indicating that Billy Greenwood might be engaged in narcotics trafficking. Stracner asked the neighborhood's regular trash collector to pick up the plastic garbage bags that Greenwood had left on the curb in front of his house and to turn the bags over to her without mixing their contents with garbage from other houses. The trash collector cleaned his truck bin of other refuse, collected the garbage bags from the street in front of Greenwood's house, and turned the bags over to Stracner. The officer searched through the rubbish and found items indicative of narcotics use.

Stracner recited the information that she had gleaned from the trash search in an affidavit in support of a warrant to search Greenwood's home. Police officers encountered both Greenwood and Dyanne Van Houten at the house later that day when they arrived to execute the warrant. The police discovered quantities of cocaine and hashish during their search of the house. Did Greenwood and Van Houten have a reasonable expectation of privacy in the trash?

DECISION No, said the U.S. Supreme Court. According to Justice White, writing for the majority:

> It may well be that respondents did not expect that the contents of their garbage bags would become known to the police or other members of the public. An expectation of privacy does not give rise to Fourth Amendment protection, however, unless society is prepared to accept that expectation as objectively reasonable. Here, we conclude that respondents exposed their garbage to the public sufficiently to defeat their claim to Fourth Amendment protection.
>
> It is common knowledge that plastic garbage bags left on or at the side of a public street are readily accessible to animals, children, scavengers, snoops, and other members of the public. Moreover, respondents placed their refuse at the curb for the express purpose of conveying it to a third party, the trash collector, who might himself have sorted through respondents' trash or permitted others, such as the police, to do so. Accordingly, having deposited their garbage "in an area particularly suited for public inspection and, in a manner of speaking, public consumption, for the express purpose of having strangers take it," respondents could have had no reasonable expectation of privacy in the inculpatory items that they discarded.
>
> Furthermore, as we have held, the police cannot reasonably be expected to avert their eyes from evidence of criminal activity that could have been observed by any member of the public. Hence, "what a person knowingly exposes to the public, even in his own home or office, is not a subject of Fourth Amendment protection."

DISSENT Justices Brennan and Marshall disagreed. Justice Brennan wrote in his dissent:

> Every week for two months, and at least once more a month later, the Laguna Beach police clawed through the trash that Greenwood left in opaque, sealed bags on the curb outside his home. Complete strangers minutely scrutinized their bounty, undoubtedly dredging up intimate details of Greenwood's private life and habits.
>
> A trash bag is a common repository for one's personal effects and is therefore inevitably associated with the expectation of privacy. Almost every human activity ultimately manifests itself in waste products. If you want to know what is really going on in a community, look at its garbage. A single bag of trash testifies eloquently to the eating, reading, and recreational habits of the person who produced it. A search of trash, like a search of the bedroom, can relate intimate details about sexual practices, health, and personal hygiene.
>
> Beyond a generalized expectation of privacy, many municipalities, whether for reasons of privacy, sanitation, or both, reinforce confidence in the integrity of sealed trash containers by prohibiting anyone, except authorized employees of the Town to rummage into, pick up, collect, move or otherwise interfere with articles or materials placed on any public street for collection.
>
> Had Greenwood flaunted his intimate activity by strewing his trash all over the curb for all to see, or had some nongovernmental intruder invaded his privacy and done the same, I could accept the Court's conclusion that an expectation of privacy would have been unreasonable. But all that Greenwood "exposed to the public" were the exteriors of several opaque, sealed containers. Until the bags were opened by police, they hid their contents from the public's view.
>
> In holding that the warrantless search of Greenwood's trash was consistent with the Fourth Amendment, the Court paints a grim picture of our society. It depicts a society in which local authorities may command their citizens to dispose of their personal effects in the manner least protective of the sanctity of the home and the privacies of life, and then monitor them arbitrarily and without judicial oversight—a society that is not prepared to recognize as reasonable an individual's expectation of privacy in the most private of personal effects sealed in an opaque container and disposed of in a manner designed to commingle it imminently and inextricably with the trash of others.
>
> The American society with which I am familiar chooses to dwell in reasonable security and freedom from surveillance, and is more dedicated to individuals' liberty and more sensitive to intrusions on the sanctity of the home than the Court is willing to acknowledge.

Electronic Surveillance

LO 2, LO 4,
LO 5, LO 7,
LO 8

The subject of undercover agents and informants is sensitive and controversial. Before *Katz v. U.S.*, the Supreme Court dealt with several cases involving undercover agents and informants who talked with suspects. The story that led to the U.S. Supreme Court decision in *Hoffa v. U.S.* (1966) began in late autumn 1964, when labor union boss James Hoffa was charged with violating the Taft-Harley labor law. He was tried by a jury in a trial that lasted several weeks in a Nashville, Tennessee, federal court. The trial ended in a hung jury.

In 1964, Hoffa and others were convicted of trying to bribe members of the 1962 hung trial jury. The government's proof that led to the convictions consisted largely of a witness named Edward Partin, who testified to several incriminating statements which he said Hoffa had made in his presence during the course of the 1962 trial. The Supreme Court upheld the convictions. It held that the informant Edward Partin's success in gaining Hoffa's confidence to get an incriminating statement from him didn't invoke Fourth Amendment issues because it involved only "a wrongdoer's misplaced belief that a person to whom he voluntarily confided his wrongdoing would not reveal it" (302).

In the same year as *Hoffa*, the U.S. Supreme Court decided *Lewis v. U.S.* On December 3, 1964, Edward Cass, an undercover federal narcotics agent, telephoned Duke Lewis's home to inquire about buying marijuana. Cass, who previously had not met or dealt with Lewis, falsely identified himself as "Jimmy the Polack." He said that a mutual friend had told him Lewis might be able to get him marijuana. Lewis replied, "Yes, I believe, Jimmy, I can take care of you," and directed Cass to his home, where Lewis indicated a sale of marijuana would occur.

Cass drove to Lewis's home, knocked on the door, identified himself as "Jim," and Cass let him in. After discussing the possibility of regular future dealings at a discounted price, Lewis led Cass to a package located on the front porch of his home. Cass gave Lewis $50, took the package, and left. The package contained five bags of marijuana. A second sale took place on December 17, 1964. Once again, Cass paid the petitioner $50, but this time he received a package containing six bags of marijuana.

Lewis was charged with selling marijuana. The U.S. District Court for the District of Massachusetts convicted him; the U.S. Court of Appeals affirmed. Lewis contended that "any official intrusion upon the privacy of a home" without a warrant violated the Fourth Amendment, and that the fact the suspect invited the intrusion cannot be held a waiver when the invitation was induced by fraud and deception" (208).

In affirming the Court of Appeals, Chief Justice Warren noted that Lewis had invited undercover agent Cass to his home for the specific purpose of selling the marijuana to Cass—a federal felony. Lewis's only concern was whether Cass was a "willing purchaser who could pay the agreed price. Indeed, to convince the agent that his patronage at Lewis's home was desired, Lewis told him that, if he became a regular customer there, he would in the future receive an extra bag of marijuana at no additional cost; and in fact petitioner did hand over an extra bag at a second sale which was consummated at the same place and in precisely the same manner" (208).

Chief Justice Warren concluded:

> Were we to hold the deceptions of the agent in this case constitutionally prohibited, we would come near to a rule that the use of undercover agents in any manner is virtually unconstitutional per se. Such a rule would, for example, severely hamper the Government in ferreting out those organized criminal activities that are characterized by covert dealings with victims who either cannot or do not protest. A prime example is provided by the narcotics traffic. (208)

ETHICAL ISSUES

Should the Government Use Snitches?

Yes, say supporters like Bill McCollum:

> I have no problems with informants because while they may not always be reliable, they give us leads and you go on and find other proof and when you go to try somebody in court, you have to prove they're guilty to a jury beyond a reasonable doubt, and if you can gain information from informants or snitches, that's fine. That's not what necessarily convicts somebody. That would be just one piece of evidence. But it does give you a lead. And you need that lead. How else are we going to find the bad guy? If you don't have informants and you can't eavesdrop, law enforcement would never be able to protect society from these major criminal enterprises.
>
> *Bill McCollum, former U.S. Congressman*

No, says defense attorney Bob Clark:

> Snitches are used by the government because it makes their life a lot easier. You put everybody in prison, and then you cut deals with those that are willing to rat on everybody else. And people generally tell the government what they want to hear. In fact, when they try people here in the southern district of Alabama, they put all the rats and

the snitches together in one cell. And after they testify, they go back to the snitch cell and compare stories and compare notes. Do I feel that snitches lie? Only when their mouth is moving. You know, if they're asleep, most of the time they don't—oh, they'll say anything. They're prostitutes. I mean it is—I don't know how you could run a criminal justice system without the use of informants, but at the same time, it allows itself for such abuse. I mean absolutely unbelievable abuse.

Bob Clark, Defense Attorney

INSTRUCTIONS

1. Visit the Companion Website and read the two selections linked there. See the links under the Chapter 3 Ethical Issues section of the Companion Website—login at www .cengagebrain.com.

2. List all the arguments made for and against the use of "snitches" in prosecuting crime.

3. Write an essay addressing the question: "Is the use of 'snitches' ethical in prosecuting crime?" Back up your answers with the information you listed in 2.

Source: Frontline, "Snitch" transcript. 1999. http://www.pbs.org/wgbh/pages/frontline/ shows/snitch/etc/script.html.

Both *Hoffa* and *Lewis* involved information given to a "false friend" (undercover informant) who didn't record or electronically transmit the information to government backup agents. What if the informant is wired for sound to backup agents? Does the target of the conversation, who doesn't know the "false friend" is wired to the police, have a reasonable expectation of privacy in the transmitted and/or recorded conversations? No, said the U.S. Supreme Court in our next case excerpt, *U.S. v. White.*

In **U.S. v. White,** *the U.S. Supreme Court decided when recording a suspect undercover is a Fourth Amendment search.*

CASE Were Statements Made to an Informant Wired for Sound to the Police Searches?

U.S. v. White
401 U.S. 745 (1971)

HISTORY

James A. White, Defendant, was convicted in the U.S. District Court for the Northern District of Illinois, Eastern Division, of two narcotics violations. He was fined, and sentenced as a second offender to 25-year concurrent sentences. He appealed. The U.S. Court of Appeals for the Seventh Circuit reversed and remanded. The U.S. Supreme

Court granted certiorari and reversed the judgment of the Court of Appeals.

WHITE, J. (Plurality of 4)

FACTS

The issue before us is whether the Fourth Amendment bars from evidence the testimony of governmental agents who related certain conversations which had occurred between defendant White and a government informant,

Harvey Jackson, and which the agents overheard by monitoring the frequency of a radio transmitter carried by Jackson and concealed on his person.

On four occasions the conversations took place in Jackson's home; each of these conversations was overheard by an agent concealed in a kitchen closet with Jackson's consent and by a second agent outside the house using a radio receiver. Four other conversations—one in White's home, one in a restaurant, and two in Jackson's car—were overheard by the use of radio equipment. The prosecution was unable to locate and produce Jackson at the trial and the trial court overruled objections to the testimony of the agents who conducted the electronic surveillance. The jury returned a guilty verdict and defendant appealed.

OPINION

The Fourth Amendment affords no protection to a wrongdoer's misplaced belief that a person to whom he voluntarily confides his wrongdoing will not reveal it. A police agent who conceals his police connections may write down for official use his conversations with a defendant and testify concerning them, without a warrant authorizing his encounters with the defendant and without otherwise violating the latter's Fourth Amendment rights.

For constitutional purposes, no different result is required if the agent instead of immediately reporting and transcribing his conversations with defendant, either simultaneously records them with electronic equipment which he is carrying on his person or carries radio equipment which simultaneously transmits the conversations either to recording equipment located elsewhere or to other agents monitoring the transmitting frequency. If the conduct and revelations of an agent operating without electronic equipment do not invade the defendant's constitutionally justifiable expectations of privacy, neither does a simultaneous recording of the same conversations made by the agent or by others from transmissions received from the agent to whom the defendant is talking and whose trustworthiness the defendant necessarily risks.

Our problem is not what the privacy expectations of particular defendants in particular situations may be or the extent to which they may in fact have relied on the discretion of their companions. Very probably, individual defendants neither know nor suspect that their colleagues have gone or will go to the police or are carrying recorders or transmitters. Otherwise, conversation would cease and our problem with these encounters would be nonexistent or far different from those now before us.

Our problem, in terms of the principles announced in *Katz*, is what expectations of privacy are constitutionally "justifiable"—what expectations the Fourth Amendment will protect in the absence of a warrant. So far, the law permits the frustration of actual expectations of privacy by permitting authorities to use the testimony of those associates who for one reason or another have determined to turn to the police, as well as by authorizing the use of informants. If the law gives no protection to the wrongdoer whose trusted accomplice is or becomes a police agent, neither should it protect him when that same agent has recorded or transmitted the conversations which are later offered in evidence to prove the State's case.

Inescapably, one contemplating illegal activities must realize and risk that his companions may be reporting to the police. If he sufficiently doubts their trustworthiness, the association will very probably end or never materialize. But if he has no doubts, or allays them, or risks what doubt he has, the risk is his. In terms of what his course will be, what he will or will not do or say, we are unpersuaded that he would distinguish between probable informers on the one hand and probable informers with transmitters on the other.

Given the possibility or probability that one of his colleagues is cooperating with the police, it is only speculation to assert that the defendant's utterances would be substantially different or his sense of security any less if he also thought it possible that the suspected colleague is wired for sound. At least there is no persuasive evidence that the difference in this respect between the electronically equipped and the unequipped agent is substantial enough to require discrete constitutional recognition, particularly under the Fourth Amendment which is ruled by fluid concepts of "reasonableness."

Nor should we be too ready to erect constitutional barriers to relevant and probative evidence which is also accurate and reliable. An electronic recording will many times produce a more reliable rendition of what a defendant has said than will the unaided memory of a police agent. It may also be that with the recording in existence it is less likely that the informant will change his mind, less chance that threat or injury will suppress unfavorable evidence and less chance that cross-examination will confound the testimony. Considerations like these obviously do not favor the defendant, but we are not prepared to hold that a defendant who has no constitutional right to exclude the informer's unaided testimony nevertheless has a Fourth Amendment privilege against a more accurate version of the events in question.

The judgment of the Court of Appeals is REVERSED. It is so ordered.

DISSENT

DOUGLAS, J.

The issue in this case is clouded and concealed by the very discussion of it in legalistic terms. What the ancients knew as "eavesdropping," we now call "electronic surveillance"; but to equate the two is to treat man's first gunpowder on the same level as the nuclear bomb. Electronic surveillance is the greatest leveler of human privacy ever known. How most forms of it can be held "reasonable" within the meaning of the Fourth Amendment is a mystery.

To be sure, the Constitution and Bill of Rights are not to be read as covering only the technology known in the

18th century. At the same time the concepts of privacy which the Founders enshrined in the Fourth Amendment vanish completely when we slavishly allow an all-powerful government, proclaiming law and order, efficiency, and other benign purposes, to penetrate all the walls and doors which men need to shield them from the pressures of a turbulent life around them and give them the health and strength to carry on.

We have become a fearful people. There was a time when we feared only our enemies abroad. Now we seem to be as fearful of our enemies at home, and depending on whom you talk to, those enemies can include people under thirty, people with foreign names, people of different races, people in the big cities. We have become a suspicious nation, as afraid of being destroyed from within as from without. Unfortunately, the manifestations of that kind of fear and suspicion are police state measures.

Must everyone live in fear that every word he speaks may be transmitted or recorded and later repeated to the entire world? I can imagine nothing that has a more chilling effect on people speaking their minds and expressing their views on important matters. The advocates of that regime should spend some time in totalitarian countries and learn firsthand the kind of regime they are creating here.

A technological breakthrough in techniques of physical surveillance now makes it possible for government agents and private persons to penetrate the privacy of homes, offices, and vehicles; to survey individuals moving about in public places; and to monitor the basic channels of communication by telephone, telegraph, radio, television, and data line. Most of the "hardware" for this physical surveillance is cheap, readily available to the general public, relatively easy to install, and not presently illegal to own.

As of the 1960s, the new surveillance technology is being used widely by government agencies of all types and at every level of government, as well as by private agents for a rapidly growing number of businesses, unions, private organizations, and individuals in every section of the United States. The scientific prospects for the next decade indicate a continuing increase in the range and versatility of the listening and watching devices, as well as the possibility of computer processing of recordings to identify automatically the speakers or topics under surveillance. These advances will come just at the time when personal contacts, business affairs, and government operations are being channeled more and more into electronic systems such as data-phone lines and computer communications.

DISSENT

HARLAN, J.

We deal here with the constitutional validity of instantaneous third-party electronic eavesdropping, conducted by federal law enforcement officers, without any prior judicial approval of the technique utilized. The critical question is whether under our system of government, as reflected in the Constitution, we should impose on our citizens the risks of the electronic listener or observer without at least the protection of a warrant requirement. This question must, in my view, be answered by assessing the nature of a particular practice and the likely extent of its impact on the individual's sense of security balanced against the utility of the conduct as a technique of law enforcement. For those more extensive intrusions that significantly jeopardize the sense of security which is the paramount concern of Fourth Amendment liberties, I am of the view that more than self-restraint by law enforcement officials is required and at the least warrants should be necessary.

The impact of the practice of third-party bugging, must, I think, be considered such as to undermine that confidence and sense of security in dealing with one another that is characteristic of individual relationships between citizens in a free society. It goes beyond the impact on privacy occasioned by the ordinary type of "informer" investigation. The argument of the plurality opinion, to the effect that it is irrelevant whether secrets are revealed by the mere tattletale or the transistor, ignores the differences occasioned by third-party monitoring and recording which insures full and accurate disclosure of all that is said, free of the possibility of error and oversight that inheres in human reporting.

Authority is hardly required to support the proposition that words would be measured a good deal more carefully and communication inhibited if one suspected his conversations were being transmitted and transcribed. Were third-party bugging a prevalent practice, it might well smother that spontaneity—reflected in frivolous, impetuous, sacrilegious, and defiant discourse—that liberates daily life. Much offhand exchange is easily forgotten and one may count on the obscurity of his remarks, protected by the very fact of a limited audience, and the likelihood that the listener will either overlook or forget what is said, as well as the listener's inability to reformulate a conversation without having to contend with a documented record. All these values are sacrificed by a rule of law that permits official monitoring of private discourse limited only by the need to locate a willing assistant.

Finally, it is too easy to forget—and, hence, too often forgotten—that the issue here is whether to interpose a search warrant procedure between law enforcement agencies engaging in electronic eavesdropping and the public generally. By casting its "risk analysis" solely in terms of the expectations and risks that "wrongdoers" or "one contemplating illegal activities" ought to bear, the plurality opinion, I think, misses the mark entirely. *On Lee* [omitted here] does not simply mandate that criminals must daily run the risk of unknown eavesdroppers prying into their private affairs; it subjects each and every law-abiding member of society to that risk. The very purpose of interposing the Fourth Amendment warrant requirement is to redistribute the privacy risks throughout society.

The interest that *On Lee* fails to protect is the expectation of the ordinary citizen, who has never engaged in illegal conduct in his life, that he may carry on his private discourse freely, openly, and spontaneously without measuring his every word against the connotations it might carry when instantaneously heard by others unknown to him and unfamiliar with his situation or analyzed in a cold, formal record played days, months, or years after the conversation.

Interposition of a warrant requirement is designed not to shield "wrongdoers," but to secure a measure of privacy and a sense of personal security throughout our society. The Fourth Amendment does, of course, leave room for the employment of modern technology in criminal law enforcement, but in the stream of current developments in Fourth Amendment law I think it must be held that third-party electronic monitoring, subject only to the self-restraint of law enforcement officials, has no place in our society.

QUESTIONS

1. Is the plurality saying it's reasonable to expect people we confide in might be wired for sound to the police? Do you expect this?
2. Which is most intrusive: listening to James White in his home, in Harvey Jackson's home, in a restaurant, on the street, or in a car? Or are they all about the same? Why? Why not?
3. Does Justice Douglas in his dissent have a point when he says that everyone will live in fear that what she or he says will be reported, or transmitted by radio, to the police? Explain.
4. Should the police have been required to get a warrant here? Explain your answer.

Technology that allows officers to get information about possible suspects has advanced significantly since 1971 when the Court decided *U.S. v. White*. One of those advances is the development of **thermal imagers**, devices that detect, measure, and record infrared radiation invisible to the naked eye. The imagers convert radiation into images based on the amount of heat (black is cool, white is hot, shades of gray are in between).

What if unknown to you, police officers parked on the street outside your house, aimed a thermal imager at your house and measured and recorded the amount of heat coming out of various parts of your house? Do you have an expectation of privacy in these heat waves? If you do, is it an expectation society is prepared to recognize? The U.S. Supreme Court held that the discovery and measurement of heat—something invisible to the naked eye—escaping from your home is a Fourth Amendment search in *Kyllo v. U.S.* (2001).

In Kyllo v. U.S. (2001), the U.S. Supreme Court ruled that the discovery and measurement of heat from a home by law enforcement is a Fourth Amendment search.

CASE Was Measuring the "Heat" from Outside the House a Search?

Kyllo v. U.S.
533 U.S. 27 (2001)

HISTORY

After unsuccessfully moving to suppress evidence, Danny Kyllo entered a conditional guilty plea to manufacturing marijuana, and then appealed. Following remand, the U.S. District Court for the District of Oregon again denied Kyllo's suppression motion; Kyllo appealed again. The Ninth Circuit Court of Appeals affirmed. Certiorari was granted. The U.S. Supreme Court (5 to 4) reversed and remanded.

SCALIA, J.

FACTS

In 1991 Agent William Elliott of the United States Department of the Interior came to suspect that marijuana was being grown in the home belonging to petitioner Danny Kyllo, part of a triplex on Rhododendron Drive in Florence, Oregon. Indoor marijuana growth typically requires high-intensity lamps. In order to determine whether an amount of heat was emanating from Kyllo's home consistent with the use of such lamps, at 3:20 A.M. on January 16, 1992, Agent Elliott and Dan Haas used an Agema Thermovision 210 thermal imager to scan the triplex. Thermal imagers detect infrared radiation, which virtually all objects emit but which is not visible to the naked eye. The imager converts radiation into images based on relative warmth—black is cool, white is hot, shades of gray connote relative differences; in that respect, it operates somewhat like a video camera showing heat images.

The scan of Kyllo's home took only a few minutes and was performed from the passenger seat of Agent Elliott's vehicle across the street from the front of the house and also from the street in back of the house. The scan showed that the roof over the garage and a side wall of Kyllo's home were relatively hot compared to the rest of the home and substantially warmer than neighboring homes in the triplex. Agent Elliott concluded that Kyllo was using halide lights to grow marijuana in his house, which indeed he was.

Based on tips from informants, utility bills, and the thermal imaging, a Federal Magistrate Judge issued a warrant authorizing a search of Kyllo's home, and the agents found an indoor growing operation involving more than 100 plants. Kyllo was indicted on one count of manufacturing marijuana, in violation of 21 U.S.C. § 841(a)(1). He unsuccessfully moved to suppress the evidence seized from his home and then entered a conditional guilty plea. The Court of Appeals for the Ninth Circuit remanded the case for an evidentiary hearing regarding the intrusiveness of thermal imaging. On remand the District Court found that the Agema 210 "is a non-intrusive device which emits no rays or beams and shows a crude visual image of the heat being radiated from the outside of the house"; it "did not show any people or activity within the walls of the structure"; "the device used cannot penetrate walls or windows to reveal conversations or human activities"; and "no intimate details of the home were observed."

Based on these findings, the District Court upheld the validity of the warrant that relied in part upon the thermal imaging, and reaffirmed its denial of the motion to suppress. A divided Court of Appeals initially reversed, but that opinion was withdrawn and the panel (after a change in composition) affirmed, with Judge Noonan dissenting. The court held that Kyllo had shown no subjective expectation of privacy because he had made no attempt to conceal the heat escaping from his home, and even if he had, there was no objectively reasonable expectation of privacy because the imager "did not expose any intimate details of Kyllo's life," only "amorphous 'hot spots' on the roof and exterior wall." We granted certiorari.

OPINION

At the very core of the Fourth Amendment stands the right of a man to retreat into his own home and there be free from unreasonable governmental intrusion. With few exceptions, the question whether a warrantless search of a home is reasonable and hence constitutional must be answered no. On the other hand, the antecedent question whether or not a Fourth Amendment "search" has occurred is not so simple. As Justice Harlan's oft-quoted concurrence [in *Katz v. U.S.*, p. 56] described it, a Fourth Amendment search occurs when the government violates a subjective expectation of privacy that society recognizes as reasonable.

The present case involves officers on a public street engaged in more than naked-eye surveillance of a home. We have previously reserved judgment as to how much technological enhancement of ordinary perception from such a vantage point, if any, is too much. It would be foolish to contend that the degree of privacy secured to citizens by the Fourth Amendment has been entirely unaffected by the advance of technology. The question we confront today is what limits there are upon this power of technology to shrink the realm of guaranteed privacy. While it may be difficult to refine *Katz* when the search of areas such as telephone booths, automobiles, or even the curtilage and uncovered portions of residences is at issue, in the case of the search of the interior of homes there is a ready criterion, with roots deep in the common law, of the minimal expectation of privacy that exists, and that is acknowledged to be reasonable.

To withdraw protection of this minimum expectation would be to permit police technology to erode the privacy guaranteed by the Fourth Amendment. We think that obtaining by sense-enhancing technology any information regarding the interior of the home that could not otherwise have been obtained without physical "intrusion into a constitutionally protected area," constitutes a search—at least where (as here) the technology in question is not in general public use. This assures preservation of that degree of privacy against government that existed when the Fourth Amendment was adopted. On the basis of this criterion, the information obtained by the thermal imager in this case was the product of a search.

The Government maintains, however, that the thermal imaging must be upheld because it detected "only heat radiating from the external surface of the house." While the technology used in the present case was relatively crude, the rule we adopt must take account of more sophisticated systems that are already in use or in development.

The Government also contends that the thermal imaging was constitutional because it did not "detect private activities occurring in private areas." The Fourth

Amendment's protection of the home has never been tied to measurement of the quality or quantity of information obtained. In *Silverman*, for example, we made clear that any physical invasion of the structure of the home, "by even a fraction of an inch," was too much, and there is certainly no exception to the warrant requirement for the officer who barely cracks open the front door and sees nothing but the nonintimate rug on the vestibule floor. In the home, our cases show, all details are intimate details, because the entire area is held safe from prying government eyes.

We have said that the Fourth Amendment draws "a firm line at the entrance to the house." That line, we think, must be not only firm but also bright—which requires clear specification of those methods of surveillance that require a warrant. While it is certainly possible to conclude from the videotape of the thermal imaging that occurred in this case that no "significant" compromise of the homeowner's privacy has occurred, we must take the long view, from the original meaning of the Fourth Amendment forward.

Where, as here, the Government uses a device that is not in general public use, to explore details of the home that would previously have been unknowable without physical intrusion, the surveillance is a "search" and is presumptively unreasonable without a warrant.

Since we hold the Thermovision imaging to have been an unlawful search, it will remain for the District Court to determine whether, without the evidence it provided, the search warrant issued in this case was supported by probable cause—and if not, whether there is any other basis for supporting admission of the evidence that the search pursuant to the warrant produced.

The judgment of the Court of Appeals is REVERSED; the case is REMANDED for further proceedings consistent with this opinion.

DISSENT

STEVENS, J.

There is, in my judgment, a distinction of constitutional magnitude between "through-the-wall surveillance" that gives the observer or listener direct access to information in a private area, on the one hand, and the thought processes used to draw inferences from information in the public domain, on the other hand. The Court has crafted a rule that purports to deal with direct observations of the inside of the home, but the case before us merely involves indirect deductions from "off-the-wall" surveillance, that is, observations of the exterior of the home. Those observations were made with a fairly primitive thermal imager that gathered data exposed on the outside of Kyllo's home but did not invade any constitutionally protected interest in privacy.

The notion that heat emissions from the outside of a dwelling are a private matter implicating the protections of the Fourth Amendment is quite difficult to take seriously. Heat waves, like aromas that are generated in a kitchen, or in a laboratory or opium den, enter the public domain if and when they leave a building. A subjective expectation that they would remain private is not only implausible but also surely not "one that society is prepared to recognize as 'reasonable.'"

There is a strong public interest in avoiding constitutional litigation over the monitoring of emissions from homes, and over the inferences drawn from such monitoring. Just as "the police cannot reasonably be expected to avert their eyes from evidence of criminal activity that could have been observed by any member of the public," so too public officials should not have to avert their senses or their equipment from detecting emissions in the public domain such as excessive heat, traces of smoke, suspicious odors, odorless gases, air-borne particulates, or radioactive emissions, any of which could identify hazards to the community. In my judgment, monitoring such emissions with "sense-enhancing technology," and drawing useful conclusions from such monitoring, is an entirely reasonable public service.

On the other hand, the countervailing privacy interest is at best trivial. After all, homes generally are insulated to keep heat in, rather than to prevent the detection of heat going out, and it does not seem to me that society will suffer from a rule requiring the rare homeowner who both intends to engage in uncommon activities that produce extraordinary amounts of heat, and wishes to conceal that production from outsiders, to make sure that the surrounding area is well insulated. The interest in concealing the heat escaping from one's house pales in significance to "the chief evil against which the wording of the Fourth Amendment is directed," the "physical entry of the home," and it is hard to believe that it is an interest the Framers sought to protect in our Constitution.

Since what was involved in this case was nothing more than drawing inferences from off-the-wall surveillance, rather than any "through-the-wall" surveillance, the officers' conduct did not amount to a search and was perfectly reasonable.

I respectfully DISSENT.

QUESTIONS

1. **Describe specifically the information agents Elliott and Haas got from Kyllo's house.**
2. **Describe exactly how the officers got the information.**
3. **Summarize the arguments the majority makes to support its conclusion that getting and recording thermal images are searches and seizures.**
4. **Summarize the arguments the dissent makes to support its conclusions that they aren't searches and seizures.**

The Plain View Doctrine

LO 9

According to the **plain view doctrine**, individuals have no reasonable expectation of privacy in what officers discover by their ordinary senses. Although the doctrine takes its name from the sense of sight, it applies to discovery by the other senses, too—namely, hearing, smell, and sometimes even touch. (Unless otherwise noted, we'll use "plain view" to include all the ordinary senses.)

There are two kinds of plain view. In both kinds, the issue is rarely whether there's a *search*; it's whether officers can *seize* the items in plain view. The first type is **search-related plain view**. It refers to items in plain view that officers discover while they're searching for items for which they're specifically authorized to search. For example, in one leading Supreme Court case, an officer had a warrant to search for jewelry taken during a robbery. During the search, he saw an Uzi machine gun and other weapons in plain view (*Horton v. California* 1990). This kind of plain view we'll discuss in relation to seizures during frisks in Chapter 4; during arrests in Chapter 5; during searches for evidence in Chapter 6; and during inventory searches in Chapter 7.

The second type, **nonsearch-related plain view**, refers to plain view that doesn't involve a Fourth Amendment intrusion at all. This can occur in several settings. Here are a few examples: An officer sees a diner in a restaurant take a "joint" out of her pocket; an officer sees a passenger in a car stopped at a stoplight hand a joint to the driver; or an officer walking down the street sees a resident smoking pot in her living room in front of her ground-level apartment window that is clearly visible from the public sidewalk.

All three of our examples satisfy the two conditions of the plain view doctrine, which says that discoveries made under two conditions aren't searches:

1. Officers are where they have a legal right to be—namely, any place where you or I could lawfully be.

2. Officers haven't beefed up their ordinary senses with advanced technology that's not readily available to you or me.

Condition 2 requires that courts distinguish between technological enhancements that many people use and anyone can get easily—flashlights, bifocals, and magnifying glasses—and high-powered devices that only a few people have or can get easily. So eyesight enhanced by a flashlight is treated like ordinary eyesight; eyesight enhanced by X-ray isn't.

In *U.S. v. Kim* (1976), for example, FBI agents used an 800-millimeter telescope with a 60-millimeter opening to observe activities in Earl "The Old Man" Kim's apartment. The surveillance took place nearly a quarter mile from the apartment. The telescope was so powerful the agents could even see what Kim was reading. According to the U.S. District Court for the District of Hawaii, "It is inconceivable that the government can intrude so far into an individual's home that it can detect the material he is reading and still not have engaged in a search" (1255).

The U.S. Supreme Court came to a different result when it applied the plain view doctrine in *California v. Ciraolo* (1986). The police saw marijuana growing in Dante Ciraolo's yard from a plane 1,000 feet in the air. The police had hired the plane because two privacy fences blocked their view from the ground. According to the Court, the use of the plane didn't enhance the officers' naked eye such that it turned the observation into a Fourth Amendment search.

In a similar case, *Dow Chemical Corporation v. U.S.* (1986), Dow maintained elaborate security around a 2,000-acre chemical plant that bars ground-level observation.

When Dow refused the Environmental Protection Agency's (EPA's) request for an on-site inspection, the EPA employed a commercial air photographer to fly over the plant and take photographs to determine whether Dow was complying with EPA standards. The U.S. Supreme Court ruled that such aerial observation and photography weren't Fourth Amendment searches.

We've discussed so far only the application of the doctrine to what officers *see* (1) when they're where they have a legal right to be and (2) without the aid of technology not available to the general public. But, as we mentioned earlier, the doctrine also applies to what officers hear, smell, and even, sometimes, what they feel.

In Illinois v. Caballes (2005), the U.S. Supreme Court held that the Fourth Amendment didn't apply to a drug-sniffing dog that alerted officers at the trunk of Roy Caballes's car to what turned out to be marijuana inside.

CASE   Was the Dog Sniff a Search?

Illinois v. Caballes
543 U.S. 405 (2005)

HISTORY

Roy I. Caballes, Defendant, was convicted of cannabis trafficking, following a bench trial in the Circuit Court, La Salle County, and sentenced to 12 years' imprisonment and a $256,136 fine. He appealed. The Illinois Appellate Court affirmed. Granting petition for leave to appeal, the Illinois Supreme Court, reversed. The U.S. Supreme Court granted certiorari, vacated the judgment and remanded the case.

STEVENS, J.

FACTS

Illinois State Trooper Daniel Gillette stopped Roy Caballes for speeding on an interstate highway. When Gillette radioed the police dispatcher to report the stop, a second trooper, Craig Graham, a member of the Illinois State Police Drug Interdiction Team, overheard the transmission and immediately headed for the scene with his narcotics-detection dog. When they arrived, Caballes's car was on the shoulder of the road and Caballes was in Gillette's vehicle. While Gillette was in the process of writing a warning ticket, Graham walked his dog around Caballes's car. The dog alerted at the trunk. Based on that alert, the

officers searched the trunk, found marijuana, and arrested Caballes. The entire incident lasted less than 10 minutes.

OPINION

Official conduct that does not "compromise any legitimate interest in privacy" is not a search subject to the Fourth Amendment. Any interest in possessing contraband cannot be deemed "legitimate," and thus, governmental conduct that only reveals the possession of contraband compromises no legitimate privacy interest. This is because the expectation "that certain facts will not come to the attention of the authorities" is not the same as an interest in "privacy that society is prepared to consider reasonable."

In *U.S. v. Place* (1983), we treated a canine sniff by a well-trained narcotics-detection dog as unique because it discloses only the presence or absence of narcotics, a contraband item. Caballes likewise concedes that drug sniffs are designed, and if properly conducted are generally likely, to reveal only the presence of contraband. Although Caballes argues that the error rates, particularly the existence of false positives, call into question the premise that drug-detection dogs alert only to contraband, the record contains no evidence or findings that support his argument. Moreover, Caballes does not suggest that an erroneous alert, in and of itself, reveals any legitimate private information, and, in this case, the trial judge found that the dog sniff was sufficiently reliable to establish probable cause to conduct a full-blown search of the trunk.

Accordingly, the use of a well-trained narcotics-detection dog—one that does not expose noncontraband items that otherwise would remain hidden from public view during a lawful traffic stop, generally does not implicate legitimate privacy interests. In this case, the dog sniff was performed on the exterior of Caballes's car while he was lawfully seized for a traffic violation. Any intrusion on Caballes's privacy expectations does not rise to the level of a constitutionally cognizable infringement.

This conclusion is entirely consistent with our recent decision that the use of a thermal-imaging device to detect the growth of marijuana in a home constituted an unlawful search, *Kyllo v. U.S.* (2001) [excerpted on p. 65]. Critical to that decision was the fact that the device was capable of detecting lawful activity—in that case, intimate details in a home, such as "at what hour each night the lady of the house takes her daily sauna and bath."

The legitimate expectation that information about perfectly lawful activity will remain private is categorically distinguishable from Caballes's hopes or expectations concerning the nondetection of contraband in the trunk of his car. A dog sniff conducted during a concededly lawful traffic stop that reveals no information other than the location of a substance that no individual has any right to possess does not violate the Fourth Amendment.

The judgment of the Illinois Supreme Court is vacated, and the case is REMANDED for further proceedings not inconsistent with this opinion.

It is so ordered.

DISSENT

SOUTER, J.

The infallible dog is a creature of legal fiction. Although the Supreme Court of Illinois did not get into the sniffing averages of drug dogs, their supposed infallibility is belied by judicial opinions describing well-trained animals sniffing and alerting with less than perfect accuracy, whether owing to errors by their handlers, the limitations of the dogs themselves, or even the pervasive contamination of currency by cocaine. See, *e.g.*, *U.S. v. Kennedy* (C.A.10 1997) (describing a dog that had a 71% accuracy rate); *U.S. v. Scarborough* (C.A.10 1997) (describing a dog that erroneously alerted 4 times out of 19 while working for the postal service and 8% of the time over its entire career); *U.S. v. Limares* (C.A.7 2001) (accepting as reliable a dog that gave false positives between 7% and 38% of the time); *Laime v. State* (Ark 2001) (speaking of a dog that made between 10 and 50 errors); *U.S. v. $242, 484.00* (C.A.11 2003) (noting that because as much as 80% of all currency in circulation contains drug residue, a dog alert "is of little value"); *U.S. v. Carr* (C.A.3 1994) ("[A] substantial portion of United States currency . . . is tainted with sufficient traces of controlled substances to cause a trained canine to alert to their

presence"). Indeed, a study cited by Illinois in this case for the proposition that dog sniffs are "generally reliable" shows that dogs in artificial testing situations return false positives anywhere from 12.5% to 60% of the time, depending on the length of the search. K. Garner et al., Duty Cycle of the Detector Dog: A Baseline Study 12 (Apr. 2001) (prepared by Auburn U. Inst. for Biological Detection Systems). In practical terms, the evidence is clear that the dog that alerts hundreds of times will be wrong dozens of times.

Once the dog's fallibility is recognized, however, that ends the justification for treating the sniff as *sui generis* under the Fourth Amendment: the sniff alert does not necessarily signal hidden contraband, and opening the container or enclosed space whose emanations the dog has sensed will not necessarily reveal contraband or any other evidence of crime.

The sniff and alert cannot claim the certainty that *Place* assumed, both in treating the deliberate use of sniffing dogs as *sui generis* and then taking that characterization as a reason to say they are not searches subject to Fourth Amendment scrutiny. And when that aura of uniqueness disappears, there is no good reason to ignore the actual function that dog sniffs perform. They are conducted to obtain information about the contents of private spaces beyond anything that human senses could perceive, even when conventionally enhanced.

Thus in practice the government's use of a trained narcotics dog functions as a limited search to reveal undisclosed facts about private enclosures, to be used to justify a further and complete search of the enclosed area. And given the fallibility of the dog, the sniff is the first step in a process that may disclose "intimate details" without revealing contraband, just as a thermal-imaging device might do, as described in *Kyllo v. U.S.* (2001).

GINSBURG, J., joined by SOUTER J.

In my view, the Court diminishes the Fourth Amendment's force. A drug-detection dog is an intimidating animal. Injecting such an animal into a routine traffic stop changes the character of the encounter between the police and the motorist. The stop becomes broader, more adversarial, and (in at least some cases) longer. Caballes—who, as far as Troopers Gillette and Graham knew, was guilty solely of driving six miles per hour over the speed limit—was exposed to the embarrassment and intimidation of being investigated, on a public thoroughfare, for drugs. Even if the drug sniff is not characterized as a Fourth Amendment "search," the sniff surely broadened the scope of the traffic-violation-related seizure.

The Court has never removed police action from Fourth Amendment control on the ground that the action is well calculated to apprehend the guilty. Under today's decision, every traffic stop could become an occasion to call in the dogs, to the distress and embarrassment of the law-abiding population. . . .

QUESTIONS

1. List all the officers' acts that might qualify as ones in which there's a reasonable expectation of privacy.
2. Summarize the arguments in the majority and dissenting opinions regarding whether the dog sniff was (or wasn't) a search.
3. In your opinion, was the drug-sniffing dog circling Roy Caballes's car an enhancement of Officer Graham's sense of smell? Explain your answer.
4. In your opinion, what's the significance of the numbers Justice Souter cites in support of his argument?

Public Places

LO 2, LO 4, LO 5, LO 7, LO 8

The Fourth Amendment doesn't protect what officers can discover through their ordinary senses in public places, including streets, parks, and other publicly owned areas. Public places also include privately owned businesses that are open to the public. But "employees only" areas, such as offices, restrooms, basements, and other places not open to the public, aren't public places. Public restrooms are public places, too, even enclosed stalls—at least as much as officers can see over and under partitions or through cracks or other gaps in partitions (Hall 1993, 543–48).

The Open Fields Doctrine

LO 2, LO 4, LO 5, LO 7, LO 8

The Fourth Amendment protects our right to be secure in our persons, houses, papers, and effects, but through its decisions, the Supreme Court has made it clear that this protection doesn't extend to all places—namely, to open fields, public places, and abandoned property.

According to the **open fields doctrine**, "the special protection accorded by the Fourth Amendment to the people in their 'persons, houses, papers, and effects' is not extended to the open fields" (*Hester v. U.S.* 1924, 28). In *Oliver v. U.S.* (1984), the U.S. Supreme Court concluded that society isn't prepared to recognize any reasonable expectation of privacy in open fields because, open fields don't "provide the setting for those intimate activities that the Amendment is intended to shelter from government interference or surveillance. There is no societal interest in protecting the privacy of those activities, such as the cultivation of crops, that occur in open fields" (178).

What if owners give notice they expect privacy—for example, by building fences or putting up "No Trespassing" signs? Does the doctrine still apply? Yes, says the Supreme Court. Why? Because of the practical difficulties police officers would face in administering the policy with those kinds of exceptions. They'd have to "guess before every search" whether owners had erected fences high enough, or posted enough warning signs, or put contraband in an area secluded enough to "establish a right of privacy" (181).

On the other hand, the ground and buildings immediately surrounding a home (the **curtilage**), such as garages, patios, and pools, aren't open fields. Why? Because this is where family and other private activities take place. The Supreme Court has identified the following criteria to determine whether an area falls within the curtilage:

- The distance from the house
- The presence or absence of a fence around the area
- The use or purpose of the area
- The measures taken to prevent public view

In applying these criteria in *U.S. v. Dunn* (1987), the Court concluded that Ronald Dunn's barn wasn't part of the curtilage because it was 60 yards from the house; it was 50 yards beyond a fence surrounding the house; it wasn't used for family purposes; and Dunn took no measures to hide it from public view. So the crystal meth lab the officers discovered by shining a flashlight through a window in the barn wasn't a search.

Abandoned Property

LO 2, LO 4, LO 5, LO 7, LO 8

According to the U.S. Supreme Court, there's no "reasonable expectation of privacy" in abandoned property. But what does "abandoned" mean? There's a physical and a mental element to abandonment:

1. Physically giving up possession of something

2. Intending to give up the expectation of privacy

So I legally abandon an apple core when I throw it away after I've eaten what I want of the apple. But I don't abandon my car when I park it in the University of Minnesota parking ramp while I teach my "Criminal Procedure in U.S. Society" class. I've given it up only for the purpose of safekeeping until I'm ready to go home.

How does this relate to the law of searches? An officer's actions don't amount to a search if there's proof that the person gave up physical possession of something and that person also intended to give up a reasonable expectation of privacy in that something.

The U.S. Supreme Court has adopted a **totality-of-circumstances test** (a test you'll encounter frequently in the text and case excerpts) to determine whether throwing away property proves the intent to give up the reasonable expectation of privacy protected by the Fourth Amendment. The Court looks at all the facts in each case to determine the intent to abandon, the actions indicating abandonment, and therefore the termination of a reasonable expectation of privacy in the items seized by the government.

In the leading abandonment case decided during the Prohibition era, *Hester v. U.S.* (1924), revenue agents chased Hester through open fields. When the agents fired a shot, Hester dropped the illegal liquor he was carrying. The Supreme Court held that the facts indicated that Hester intended to abandon the alcohol. Later, in a famous Cold War case, immigration officials arrested suspected Communist spy Rudolf Abel. After Abel checked out of the hotel where FBI agents had arrested him, the agents searched his hotel room. They seized several items Abel had left behind in a wastepaper basket. The U.S. Supreme Court held that Abel had abandoned the room and, therefore, intended to give up his reasonable expectation of privacy in what he left behind in the wastepaper basket (*Abel v. U.S.* 1960).

Seizures

LO 10

When are individuals "seized" in the Fourth Amendment sense? According to the U.S. Supreme Court in the landmark "stop and frisk" case, *Terry v. Ohio* (1968), which we'll discuss in Chapter 4: "Only when the officer, by means of physical force or show of

TABLE 3.2

Show-of-Authority Seizures

Show of Authority	No Show of Authority
Setting up a roadblock	Approaching an individual on the sidewalk
Flashing an emergency light	Identifying oneself as a law enforcement officer
Ordering a person to leave a vehicle	Asking questions
Surrounding a car	Requesting to search
Drawing a weapon	Following a pedestrian in a police car
Several officers present	
Using a commanding tone of voice	

authority, has in some way restrained the liberty of a citizen may we conclude that a 'seizure' has occurred" (21).

Terry was the first case in which the Court took up the question of when contacts between individuals and law enforcement officers trigger the Fourth Amendment's protection against an officer's interference with our right to come and go as we please. We learned very little about when a contact becomes a seizure, because the case focused mainly on the officer's frisk of the defendant.

Unfortunately, what we didn't learn until later cases fleshed it out is that there are two kinds of Fourth Amendment seizures (also known as "stops")—actual seizures and show-of-authority seizures. **Actual seizures** occur when officers physically grab individuals with the intent to keep them from leaving. **Show-of-authority seizures** take place when officers display their authority by ordering suspects to stop, drawing their weapons, or otherwise acting such that a reasonable person wouldn't feel free to leave or "otherwise terminate the encounter, and individuals submit to the authority." (See Table 3.2 for examples.)

The Court revisited the problem of defining seizure 12 years later in *U.S. v. Mendenhall* (1980). Federal DEA agents approached Sylvia Mendenhall as she was walking through a concourse in the Detroit airport, identified themselves, and asked to see her ID and ticket, which she handed to them. Justice Potter Stewart, in a part of his opinion joined only by Justice William Rehnquist, concluded the agents hadn't seized Mendenhall.

Here's how Justice Stewart defined a Fourth Amendment seizure: "A person has been 'seized' within the meaning of the Fourth Amendment only if, in view of all of the circumstances surrounding the incident, a reasonable person would have believed that he was not free to leave" (555). Justice Stewart explained why:

> On the facts of this case, no "seizure" of the respondent occurred. The events took place in the public concourse. The agents wore no uniforms and displayed no weapons. They did not summon the respondent to their presence, but instead approached her and identified themselves as federal agents. They requested, but did not demand to see the respondent's identification and ticket. Such conduct without more, did not amount to an intrusion upon any constitutionally protected interest. The respondent was not seized simply by reason of the fact that the agents approached her, asked her if she would show them her ticket and identification,

and posed to her a few questions. Nor was it enough to establish a seizure that the person asking the questions was a law enforcement official. In short, nothing in the record suggests that the respondent had any objective reason to believe that she was not free to end the conversation in the concourse and proceed on her way, and for that reason we conclude that the agents' initial approach to her was not a seizure. (555)

A majority of the Court adopted Justice Stewart's **"reasonable person would not feel free to leave" definition of seizure** in *Florida v. Royer* (1983). Justice Byron White added this important passage to his opinion regarding officers who approach individuals and ask them questions:

Law enforcement officers do not violate the Fourth Amendment by merely approaching an individual on the street or in another public place, by asking him if he is willing to answer some questions, [or] by putting questions to him if the person is willing to listen. Nor would the fact that the officer identifies himself as a police officer without more, convert the encounter into a seizure. (*Florida v. Royer* 1983, 497)

LO 10

Because they're not "seized," individuals approached can walk away and ignore the officer's request. And walking away doesn't *by itself* provide the objective basis required to "seize" persons. Again, in Justice White's words:

The person approached, however, need not answer any question put to him; indeed, he may decline to listen to the questions at all and may go on his way. He may not be detained, even momentarily without reasonable, objective grounds for doing so; and his refusal to listen or answer does not, without more, furnish such grounds. (497–98)

The U.S. Supreme Court modified the "free to leave" definition when officers approach passengers in a bus who are physically able to leave, distinguishing it from when officers approach individuals in airports. *Florida v. Bostick* (1991) involved the boarding of a Greyhound bus by officers during a brief stop at Fort Lauderdale on its 19-hour trip from Miami to Atlanta. Most of the passengers couldn't afford to fly. One of the passengers, Terrence Bostick, a 28-year-old Black man, was asleep on the back seat (Cole 1999, 16) when two officers woke him up. They were wearing their bright green "raid" jackets with the Broward County Sheriff's Office insignia and displaying their badges; one carried a gun in a plastic gun pouch. They were "working the bus," looking for passengers who might be carrying illegal drugs.

The officers asked for Bostick's identification; he gave it to them. Then, they asked him if they could search his bag; he said yes. They found a pound of cocaine. The officers admitted that until they found the cocaine they had no basis for suspecting Bostick was guilty of any crime. "Working" buses is a common tactic in drug law investigation. And it works. One officer testified that he had searched 3,000 bags without once being refused consent (Cole 1999, 16); one 13-month period produced 300 pounds of cocaine, 800 pounds of marijuana, 24 handguns, and 75 suspected drug "mules" (16).

The Court in *Bostick* acknowledged that a reasonable person wouldn't feel free to leave the bus. Nonetheless, the Court concluded that no Fourth Amendment seizure took place. According to the Court:

Bostick's freedom of movement was restricted by a factor independent of police conduct, i.e., by his being a passenger on a bus. Accordingly, the "free to leave" analysis on which Bostick relies is inapplicable. In such a situation, the appropriate inquiry is whether a reasonable person would feel free to decline the officers' requests or otherwise terminate the encounter. (436)

The Court applied the *Bostick* standard in *U.S. v. Drayton* (2002). During a bus stop, the driver left the bus, leaving three police officers in charge of the bus. One stood guard at the front of the bus, another at the rear, while the third questioned every passenger without telling them their right not to cooperate. The Court held that there was no seizure because reasonable people would have felt free to get up and leave the bus. But, would they? Let's look at the answer provided by the empirical evidence.

Empirical Findings

It's clear from the discussion of *Mendenhall, Royer, Bostick,* and *Drayton* that the Supreme Court has firmly, and repeatedly, taken the position that police encounters with citizens are not usually coercive. Scientific findings, as you'll also learn in consent searches (Chapter 6), police interrogation (Chapter 8), and identification procedures (Chapter 9), don't support the Court's position.

Professor Janice Nadler (2002), in her survey of Fourth Amendment empirical research on encounters with law enforcement, has demonstrated an "ever-widening gap" between Fourth Amendment court decisions and scientific findings regarding the psychology of compliance. Whether an individual "feels free to terminate a police encounter" can't "reliably be answered solely from the comforts of one's armchair, while reflecting only on one's own experience."

> An examination of the existing empirical evidence on the psychology of coercion suggests that in many situations where citizens find themselves in an encounter with the police, the encounter is not consensual because a reasonable person would not feel free to terminate the encounter. Even worse, the existing empirical evidence also suggests that observers outside of the situation systematically overestimate the extent to which citizens in police encounters feel free to refuse. Members of the Court are themselves such outside observers, and this partly explains why the Court has repeatedly held that citizen encounters are consensual. (155–56)

Fleeing Suspects

When are you seized when you run away from the police? According to the U.S. Supreme Court in our next excerpt, *California v. Hodari D.* (1991), you're seized when you're either grabbed by the chasing officer or when you submit to a display of police authority.

Officers Brian McColgin and Jerry Pertoso were on patrol in a high-crime area of Oakland, California. When Hodari J., a juvenile, saw the officers, he ran. Just as Officer Pertoso was about to catch up to him, Hodari tossed a "rock" of crack cocaine away, and was later charged with possession of cocaine. The juvenile court denied his motion to suppress and found that he was in possession of cocaine. The California Court of Appeal reversed; the California Supreme Court denied the state's application for review; the U.S. Supreme Court reversed and remanded.

According to the U.S. Supreme Court in California v. Hodari D. (1991), you're seized when you're either grabbed by the chasing officer or when you submit to a display of police authority.

CASE   When Did the Police Seize Him?

California v. Hodari D.
499 U.S. 621 (1991)

HISTORY

Hodari D., a juvenile, appealed from an order of the Superior Court, Alameda County, denying his motion to suppress and finding that he was in possession of cocaine. The California Court of Appeal reversed. The California Supreme Court denied the state's application for review. Certiorari was granted. The Supreme Court reversed and remanded.

SCALIA, J., joined by REHNQUIST, C.J., and BLACKMUN, O'CONNOR, KENNEDY, and SOUTER, JJ.

FACTS

Late one evening in April 1988, Officers Brian McColgin and Jerry Pertoso were on patrol in a high-crime area of Oakland, California. They were dressed in street clothes but wearing jackets with "Police" embossed on both front and back. Their unmarked car proceeded west on Foothill Boulevard, and turned south onto 63rd Avenue. As they rounded the corner, they saw four or five youths huddled around a small red car parked at the curb. When the youths saw the officers' car approaching they apparently panicked, and took flight. The respondent here, Hodari D., and one companion ran west through an alley; the others fled south. The red car also headed south, at a high rate of speed.

The officers were suspicious and gave chase. McColgin remained in the car and continued south on 63rd Avenue. Pertoso left the car, ran back north along 63rd, then west on Foothill Boulevard, and turned south on 62nd Avenue. Hodari, meanwhile, emerged from the alley onto 62nd and ran north. Looking behind as he ran, he did not turn and see Pertoso until the officer was almost upon him, whereupon he tossed away what appeared to be a small rock. A moment later, Pertoso tackled Hodari, handcuffed him, and radioed for assistance. Hodari was found to be carrying $130 in cash and a pager; and the rock he had discarded was found to be crack cocaine.

In the juvenile proceeding brought against him, Hodari moved to suppress the evidence relating to the cocaine. The court denied the motion without opinion. The California Court of Appeal reversed, holding that Hodari had been "seized" when he saw Officer Pertoso running toward him, that this seizure was unreasonable under the Fourth Amendment, and that the evidence of cocaine had to be suppressed as the fruit of that illegal seizure. The California Supreme Court denied the state's application for review.

We granted certiorari.

OPINION

We have long understood that the Fourth Amendment's protection against "unreasonable seizures" includes seizure of the person. From the time of the founding to the present, the word "seizure" has meant a "taking possession." Hodari contends (and we accept as true for purposes of this decision) that Pertoso's pursuit qualified as a "show of authority" calling upon Hodari to halt. The narrow question before us is whether, with respect to a show of authority as with respect to application of physical force, a seizure occurs even though the subject does not yield. We hold that it does not.

Respondent contends that his position is sustained by the so-called *Mendenhall* test, formulated by Justice Stewart's opinion in *U.S. v. Mendenhall* (1980): A person has been "seized" within the meaning of the Fourth Amendment only if, in view of all the circumstances surrounding the incident, a reasonable person would have believed that he was not free to leave. In seeking to rely upon that test here, Hodari fails to read it carefully. It says that a person has been seized "only if," not that he has been seized "whenever"; it states a necessary, but not a sufficient, condition for seizure—or, more precisely, for seizure effected through a "show of authority."

Mendenhall establishes that the test for existence of a "show of authority" is an objective one: not whether the citizen perceived that he was being ordered to restrict his movement, but whether the officer's words and actions would have conveyed that to a reasonable person. Application of this objective test was the basis for our decision in the other case (*Michigan v. Chesternut*) principally relied upon by respondent, where we concluded that the police cruiser's slow following of the defendant did not convey the message that he was not free to disregard the police and go about his business. We did not address in *Michigan v. Chesternut*, however, the question whether, if the *Mendenhall* test was met—if the message that the defendant was not free to leave had been conveyed—a Fourth Amendment seizure would have occurred.

Quite relevant to the present case, however, was our decision in *Brower v. Inyo County* (1989). In that case, police cars with flashing lights had chased the decedent for 20 miles—surely an adequate "show of authority"—but he did not stop until his fatal crash into a police-erected blockade. The issue was whether his death could be held to be the consequence of an unreasonable seizure in violation of the Fourth Amendment. We did not even consider the possibility that a seizure could have occurred during the course of the chase because, as we explained, that "show of authority" did not produce his stop.

In sum, assuming that Pertoso's pursuit in the present case constituted a "show of authority" enjoining Hodari to halt, since Hodari did not comply with that injunction he was not seized until he was tackled. The cocaine abandoned while he was running was in this case not the fruit of a seizure, and his motion to exclude evidence of it was properly denied.

We REVERSE the decision of the California Court of Appeal, and REMAND for further proceedings not inconsistent with his opinion.

It is so ordered.

DISSENT

STEVENS, J., joined by MARSHALL, J.

The court's narrow construction of the word "seizure" represents a significant, and in my view, unfortunate, departure from prior case law construing the Fourth Amendment. Almost a quarter of a century ago, in two landmark cases—one broadening the protection of individual privacy [*Katz v. U.S.*] and the other broadening the powers of law enforcement officers [*Terry v. Ohio*]—we rejected the method of Fourth Amendment analysis that today's majority endorses. In particular, the Court now adopts a definition of "seizure" that is unfaithful to a long line of Fourth Amendment cases.

Even if the Court were defining seizure for the first time, which it is not, the definition that it chooses today is profoundly unwise. In its decision, the Court assumes, without acknowledging, that a police officer may now fire his weapon at an innocent citizen and not implicate the Fourth Amendment—as long as he misses his target.

Whatever else one may think of today's decision, it unquestionably represents a departure from earlier Fourth Amendment case law. The notion that our prior cases contemplated a distinction between seizures effected by a touching on the one hand, and those effected by a show of force on the other hand, and that all of our repeated descriptions of the *Mendenhall* test stated only a necessary, but not a sufficient, condition for finding seizures in the latter category, is nothing if not creative lawmaking. Moreover, by narrowing the definition of the term seizure, instead of enlarging the scope of reasonable justifications for seizures, the Court has significantly limited the protection provided to the ordinary citizen by the Fourth Amendment.

In this case the officer's show of force—taking the form of a head-on chase—adequately conveyed the message that respondent was not free to leave. There was an interval of time between the moment that respondent saw the officer fast approaching and the moment when he was tackled, and thus brought under the control of the officer.

The question is whether the Fourth Amendment was implicated at the earlier or the later moment. Because the facts of this case are somewhat unusual, it is appropriate to note that the same issue would arise if the show of force took the form of a command to "freeze," a warning shot, or the sound of sirens accompanied by a patrol car's flashing lights. In any of these situations, there may be a significant time interval between the initiation of the officer's show of force and the complete submission by the citizen.

At least on the facts of this case, the Court concludes that the timing of the seizure is governed by the citizen's reaction, rather than by the officer's conduct. One consequence of this conclusion is that the point at which the interaction between citizen and police officer becomes a seizure occurs, not when a reasonable citizen believes he or she is no longer free to go, but rather, only after the officer exercises control over the citizen.

It is too early to know the consequences of the Court's holding. If carried to its logical conclusion, it will encourage unlawful displays of force that will frighten countless innocent citizens into surrendering whatever privacy rights they may still have. The Court today defines a seizure as commencing, not with egregious police conduct, but rather, with submission by the citizen. Thus, it both delays the point at which "the Fourth Amendment becomes relevant" to an encounter and limits the range of encounters that will come under the heading of "seizure." Today's qualification of the Fourth Amendment means that innocent citizens may remain "secure in their persons against unreasonable searches and seizures" only at the discretion of the police.

Some sacrifice of freedom always accompanies an expansion in the executive's unreviewable law enforcement powers. A court more sensitive to the purposes of the Fourth Amendment would insist on greater rewards to society before decreeing the sacrifice it makes today. Alexander Bickel presciently wrote that "many actions of government have two aspects: their immediate, necessarily intended, practical effects, and their perhaps unintended or unappreciated bearing on values we hold to have more general and permanent interest." The Court's immediate concern with containing criminal activity poses a substantial, though unintended, threat to values that are fundamental and enduring.

I respectfully DISSENT.

QUESTIONS

1. What are the relevant facts in determining when the officer seized Hodari D.?
2. What criteria does the Court use in determining when seizures occur?
3. Why does the dissent see a danger in distinguishing between show-of-authority stops and actual-seizure stops? Do you agree that this poses a danger?
4. When do you think the officer stopped Hodari D.? Why is it important in this case?
5. Why is it important generally?
6. Consider the following remarks of Professor Richard Uviller, who observed the police in New York City for a period of a year:

    [T]he manifest confidence [exuded by the police] begets submission. And the cops learn the firm tone and hand that informs even the normally aggressive customer of the futility of resistance. It's effective. In virtually every encounter I have witnessed, the response of the person approached was docile, compliant, and respectful.

    Do you think Professor Uviller's observations support the argument that no reasonable person feels free to leave the presence of a police officer? Do you believe that it supports the argument that a request by a police officer is really a command that citizens aren't free to deny? Defend your answer.

Restraints on Movement That Are Not "Seizures"

It's important to note two kinds of restraints on freedom of movement that have no Fourth Amendment significance: psychological pressure and a sense of moral duty. You may feel a psychological pressure—and, as responsible members of your community, you *should* also feel a *moral* duty—to cooperate with police officers. But neither psychological pressure nor your sense of moral duty, by themselves, can turn a police encounter into a Fourth Amendment seizure (*INS v. Delgado* 1984). Why? Because these are self-imposed restraints; law enforcement officers didn't impose them on you.

The American Law Institute (ALI) (1975) also takes the position that simple questioning by law enforcement officers isn't a seizure. According to its respected *Model Code of Pre-Arraignment Procedure:*

§110.1 Requests for Cooperation by Law Enforcement Officers

(1) Authority to Request Cooperation.

A law enforcement officer may request any person to furnish information or otherwise cooperate in the investigation or prevention of crime. The officer may request the person to respond to questions, to appear at a police station, or to comply with any other reasonable request. In making requests no officer shall indicate that a person is legally obliged to furnish information or otherwise to cooperate if no such legal obligation exists.

Compliance with a request for information or other cooperation shall not be regarded as involuntary or coerced solely on the ground that such request was made by one known to be a law enforcement officer. (3)

Summary

LO 1, LO 9
- Crime control depends on information, but that information usually comes from reluctant sources. As long as the information that officers can see or hear is also available to the general public, they may use it without running afoul of the Fourth Amendment.

LO 2
- Fourth Amendment analysis follows a three-step process based on answering three questions in the following order: (1) *Was the law enforcement action a "search" or a "seizure"?* If it wasn't, the Fourth Amendment isn't involved at all, and the analysis ends. (2) *If the action was a search or a seizure, was it reasonable?* If it was, the inquiry ends because the Fourth Amendment bans only *unreasonable* searches and seizures. (3) *If the action was an unreasonable search, does the Fourth Amendment ban its use as evidence?* If it does, the case isn't necessarily over because there may be enough other evidence to convict the defendant, either now or sometime in the future.

LO 3
- The Fourth Amendment was created to make sure the government doesn't use illegal methods to get evidence in two kinds of cases prominent in British and American colonial history: government operations of the British Crown and colonial governors to enforce sedition and customs laws, not ordinary crimes. The Fourth Amendment was aimed at the same ideological and economic offenses.

LO 4, LO 5, LO 6
- The Fourth Amendment balances government power to control crime and the right of people to be let alone by the government. To accomplish this balance, the Fourth Amendment doesn't ban all searches and seizures, only "unreasonable" ones. And, it applies only to government actions, not actions of private individuals.

LO 7, LO 8, LO 9
- If government actions don't invade a reasonable expectation of privacy, the Fourth Amendment doesn't apply to the actions. They're left largely to individual officers' discretionary judgments based on their training and experience in the field. The Fourth Amendment doesn't apply to discoveries of evidence in plain view, in public places, in open fields, or on abandoned property.

LO 10
- People aren't "seized" any time officers approach them and ask questions. According to the U.S Supreme Court, they're seized only when they're either physically detained or submit to an officer's display of authority.

Review Questions

1. In a constitutional democracy, what does crime control depend on?
2. Identify four sources law enforcement officers depend on to obtain information. Why is each one reluctant to divulge information?
3. Identify four involuntary methods law enforcement officials use to obtain information.

4. Crime control is the main purpose of searches and seizures. Identify five special needs for searches and seizures that go beyond law enforcement purposes.

5. Identify and describe each element of the three main steps in Fourth Amendment analyses. Why is the first step the most important?

6. Explain the significance of the statement "the law does not give a constitutional damn about noncompliance" with the Fourth Amendment. Why should you not carry the "constitutional damn" idea too far?

7. Describe the origins and original purposes of searches and seizures.

8. Identify and describe the two values at the heart of a free society that the Fourth Amendment protects.

9. Identify and describe the balance of interests the Fourth Amendment is supposed to protect.

10. State the elements of the trespass and privacy doctrines. Compare the privacy doctrine in theory and in practice.

11. Identify the two-pronged expectation-of-privacy test the U.S. Supreme Court adopted in *Katz v. U.S.* List four examples that fall within reasonable expectation of privacy and four examples that don't. According to Professor William Heffernan, when can we claim a "reasonable expectation of privacy"?

12. What reason did Chief Justice Warren give for rejecting Duke Lewis's claim that the Fourth Amendment protected his conversations with the undercover informant Edward Cass?

13. Identify and give an example of the two types of plain view. Why can plain view searches be called *non*searches? State the two conditions that satisfy the plain view doctrine. Explain how courts distinguish between technologies that qualify under condition 2 and those that don't.

14. Why doesn't the Fourth Amendment protect "open fields"? Summarize the facts and the holding of *Hester v. U.S.* (1924). What is the significance of the case in Fourth Amendment law?

15. List the four criteria courts use to determine if property qualifies as curtilage.

16. Identify the mental and physical elements of abandonment.

17. Identify and describe two types of seizure "stops." Give examples of each.

18. Summarize the empirical findings regarding the coerciveness of police-citizen encounters.

19. Identify the two restraints on your freedom of movement that have no Fourth Amendment significance.

Key Terms

writs of assistance, p. 51
general warrant, p. 51
liberty, p. 52
privacy, p. 52

trespass doctrine, p. 53
privacy doctrine, p. 54
subjective privacy, p. 54
objective privacy, p. 54

4

CASES COVERED

LEARNING OBJECTIVES

1 Understand that Fourth Amendment stops are brief detentions that allow officers to freeze suspicious people and situations briefly to investigate possible criminal activity. Fourth Amendment frisks are pat downs of outer clothing to protect officers from use of concealed weapons during stops.

2 Know that reasonable stops require an objective basis to back them up; hunches that crime may be afoot aren't enough. Reasonable frisks require an independent objective basis to back them up; hunches about possible concealed weapons aren't enough.

3 Know that stops and frisks can be reasonable in the investigation of all kinds of crimes. Individualized and categorical suspicion, random procedures, and even race and actuarial tables can qualify as building blocks in reasonable suspicion.

4 Understand that the balancing test of the reasonableness of stops and frisks requires that the government interest in crime control and officer protection outweighs the invasions of individual liberty and privacy.

5 Appreciate that many innocent people will be stopped and frisked. Stops and frisks aren't supposed to be pleasant; they're supposed to be reasonable.

6 Understand that empirical and other social scientific research doesn't always support the factual assertions made in the balancing decision.

7 Know and appreciate that law enforcement officers have the power to freeze special situations (traffic stops and frisks, international borders, and checkpoints and roadblocks) briefly without individualized suspicion that a crime "may be afoot."

Stop and Frisk

Record Number of Innocent New Yorkers Stopped, Interrogated by NYPD

In just three months, the NYPD stopped enough totally innocent New Yorkers to fill the new Yankee Stadium three times over. Police made more than 151,000 stops of completely innocent New Yorkers—the overwhelming majority of whom were black and Latino. These innocent people did nothing wrong, but their names and addresses are now stored in a police database. The NYPD stopped and interrogated more innocent people during the first three months of 2009 than during any three-month period since the Department began collecting data on its troubling stop-and-frisk program. Over the past five years, New Yorkers have been subjected to the practice more than 2 million times—a rate of nearly 1,250 every day. *New York Civil Liberties Union, May 12, 2009*

The power to stop and question suspicious persons is ancient. From at least the Middle Ages, English constables were bound by their office to detain suspicious people, especially the dreaded "nightwalkers." (Anyone walking around between dusk and dawn was automatically suspected of being up to no good [Stern 1967, 532].) The English brought "stop and frisk" to their American colonies, and nobody challenged it until the 1960s.

Then, during the due process revolution of that decade (Chapter 2), civil libertarians did challenge the power of police to detain suspicious people on a hunch that they were up to no good. On what basis? Private individuals, they argued, especially "outsiders," need the courts to protect their rights whenever they're out on the streets and other public places.

Not surprisingly, law enforcement officers didn't see it that way. They argued that until they made an **arrest** (Chapter 5)—took suspects to the police station and kept them there against their will—their good judgment, based on their professional expertise gained from training and experience, was enough. Formal rules written by judges who had no knowledge and experience of the "street" and "street people" would only interfere with crime control (Remington 1960, 390).

Fourth Amendment stops are brief detentions that allow law enforcement officers to freeze suspicious people and situations briefly, so they can investigate them. Fourth Amendment seizures of persons include everything from these brief street stops to lengthy jail detentions (Figure 4.1). **Fourth Amendment frisks** are once-over-lightly pat downs of outer clothing by officers to protect themselves by taking away suspects' weapons. (We don't expect officers to risk their lives when they approach a person to check out possible danger.)

Fourth Amendment searches of persons include everything from these protective pat downs for weapons to strip and body-cavity searches. Chapters 5 and 6 analyze the greater invasions of arrests and full-blown searches in the unfamiliar and isolated surroundings of police stations and jails. This chapter examines stops and frisks, the least invasive seizures and searches of persons in familiar and more comfortable public places, such as streets, parks, and malls.

We've already touched on how the U.S. Constitution requires government officers to have an objective basis (suspicious facts and circumstances), not just hunches, to back up official unwanted interferences with individuals' rights (Chapters 2–3). We further noted that the greater the invasion, the greater the objective basis required by the Constitution to back it up. With specific reference to Fourth Amendment searches and seizures, this means officers need to prove fewer suspicious facts and circumstances to back up stops and frisks than they do for arrests (Chapter 5) and full-blown searches (Chapter 6).

Stops and frisks are the beginning of a chronological path through the investigative process, beginning with the more frequent and more-visible (but less-intrusive) searches and seizures in public to the more-intrusive (but less-visible) searches and seizures out of sight in police stations.

Stops and frisks aren't just fine points for constitutional lawyers and courts to debate. They also reflect broad public policies aimed at balancing the values of crime control and individual liberty and privacy. As we've just seen, although they may take place in the less-intimidating atmosphere of public places, and invade liberty and privacy less than arrests and searches, stops and frisks affect a lot more people. The ratio of stops to arrests is about one arrest to every nine stops (Spitzer 1999, Table I.B.1). In fact, for most people, stops and frisks are the only uninvited (and unwanted) contact with the police they'll ever have.

Just as important, because stops and frisks take place in public, the display of police power is there for everybody to see. This visibility of stops and frisks probably shapes public opinion of police power more than the greater invasions of arrest and searches that we never see. Deciding which is more important—crime control by means of less-intrusive public stops and frisks affecting more people or often invisible arrests and searches affecting fewer people—is both a constitutional and public policy question of great importance.

FIGURE 4.1 Seizures

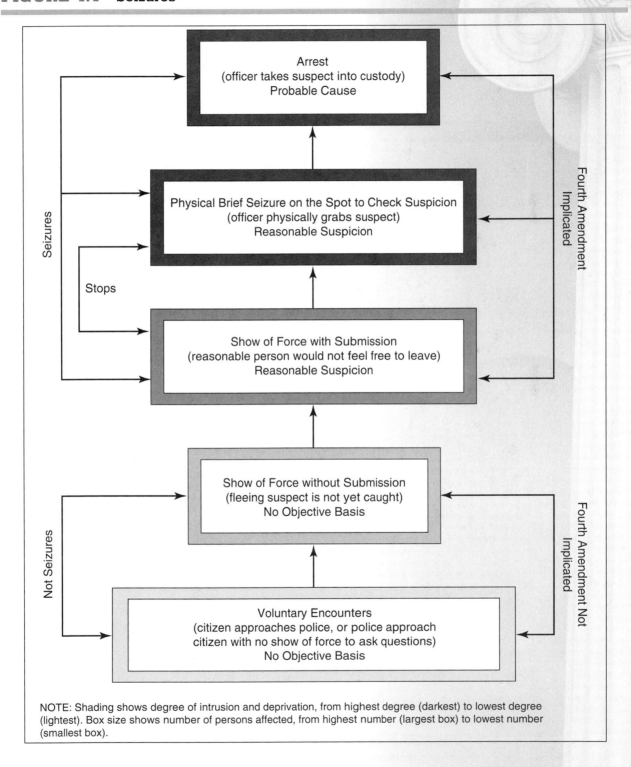

NOTE: Shading shows degree of intrusion and deprivation, from highest degree (darkest) to lowest degree (lightest). Box size shows number of persons affected, from highest number (largest box) to lowest number (smallest box).

The importance of the constitutional and policy dimensions of stops and frisks isn't due solely to their numbers but also to their geographic and demographic distribution. Black and Latino young men living in poor urban neighborhoods, or who happen to be in White neighborhoods, experience stops and frisks far more frequently than Whites. Even poor Whites living in the same poor neighborhoods as Blacks and Latinos experience fewer stops and frisks. (Spitzer 1999).

As we examine the realities of stop and frisk, keep in mind these four facts:

- Officers are going to stop many people who haven't done anything wrong, and they'll frisk lots of people who aren't armed.

- Most of these same people want police protection and (at least in high-crime neighborhoods) need it more than people who live in safe neighborhoods.

- Both lawbreakers and law abiders in high-street-crime neighborhoods form lasting opinions about the police from street encounters they've either watched or experienced.

- Stops and frisks aren't distributed evenly; they fall most heavily on Black and Latino young men in poor urban neighborhoods.

Stop-and-Frisk Law

Stop-and-frisk law follows the three-step analysis we used to decide whether an officer's action was a search or a seizure at all in Chapter 3:

1. Was the officer's action a stop or a frisk?

2. If the officer's action was a stop or a frisk, was it unreasonable?

3. If the stop or frisk was unreasonable, should evidence obtained during the stop and/or frisk be excluded from legal proceedings against the defendants (Chapter 10)?

If the action *wasn't* a stop or a frisk (step 1, Chapter 3), then the Fourth Amendment doesn't apply at all, and the analysis stops. This means the courts don't have the authority to review what officers do in such situations; it's left to officers' discretion. If the action was a stop or a frisk, then the analysis proceeds to the next step—namely, whether it was reasonable (step 2, this chapter). If it was reasonable, the analysis is over. If it was unreasonable, the analysis proceeds to decide whether the evidence has to be excluded (step 3, Chapter 10).

Two Approaches to Fourth Amendment Analysis

Before we analyze stops and frisks, we need to break down the two parts of the Fourth Amendment:

1. *Reasonableness clause.* "The right of the people to be secure in their persons, houses, papers, and effects against unreasonable searches and seizures shall not be violated."

2. *Warrant clause.* ". . . and no warrants shall issue but upon probable cause, supported by oath or affirmation, and particularly describing the place to be searched, and the persons or things to be seized."

Until the 1960s, the U.S. Supreme Court followed the **conventional Fourth Amendment approach**, which says the warrant and reasonableness clauses are firmly connected. Specifically, the reasonableness clause is just a stirring introduction to the heart of the people's right against unreasonable searches and seizures—the warrant clause. The warrant clause guarantees that only searches and seizures based on warrants and probable cause are reasonable.

In the 1960s, the Supreme Court shifted from this conventional approach to the **reasonableness Fourth Amendment approach**. It says the two clauses are separate, and they address separate problems. The warrant clause tells us what the Fourth Amendment requires only when law enforcement officers obtain warrants (Chapter 6). But only a tiny fraction of searches and seizures are made with warrants, and some searches and seizures don't require probable cause either. That means the warrant clause doesn't come into play very often.

So, according to the Court, the Fourth Amendment can't mean that searches and seizures without warrants and probable cause are *always* unreasonable. Since the 1960s, the Court has spent a lot of its time reviewing, case by case, the circumstances that make a search or seizure unreasonable. By now it should be clear to you that the Court's decisions aren't always clear. But don't blame the Court; after all, "unreasonable" is probably the vaguest, and therefore also one of the toughest to define, words in the Constitution.

The Fourth Amendment has generated more cases, and takes up more pages in criminal procedure books (including this one), than any other subject in the law of criminal procedure. Why? All lower courts have to follow these decisions. State legislatures also consult them when they write criminal procedure rules. And, most important, local police departments and police officers know their stop-and-frisk rules and actions might be reviewed by at least some court and could go all the way to the Supreme Court.

Reasonableness is a broad—and some say too subjective—standard. According to Professor John M. Copacino (1994), in balancing the interest of the government in crime control and special needs against the invasions of individual liberty and privacy, the Court has adopted a broad definition of the government's interest, usually without "any hard evidence" to justify it. At the same time, the Court has "proclaimed its subjective judgment" of the harm the government's intrusions cause to individuals without citing "any empirical evidence, expert testimony, or individual testimony from those who have been affected by the search or seizure" (236).

When the U.S. Supreme Court decided there were more reasonable searches and seizures without than with warrants, it created two major challenges:

1. When does the Fourth Amendment require warrants?

2. What does "unreasonable" mean?

LO 4

The Court has formulated a method for meeting these challenges. One type of reasonable search and seizure is based on warrants and probable cause. The other type—which, in practice, includes the vast majority of searches and seizures—has to pass the **reasonableness test**. The reasonableness test consists of two elements that it's the government's burden to prove:

1. *Balancing element.* The need to search and/or seize outweighs the invasion of liberty and privacy rights of the individuals.

2. *Objective basis.* There are enough facts and circumstances to back up the search and/or seizure.

According to the U.S. Supreme Court, courts have to decide whether searches and seizures are reasonable on a **case-by-case basis**. How do they do it? The Court has repeatedly *said* the lower courts have to look at the totality of circumstances surrounding the specific searches and seizures in individual cases. Officers make a preliminary (usually on the spur of the moment under pressure) reasonableness decision on the street and in police stations.

In making their decision, officers are allowed to view the totality of circumstances through the lens of their professional training and experience. But officers' decisions aren't final. That's left to judges. Judges review the totality of the circumstances the officers acted on and decide whether they meet the constitutional standard of reasonableness. But, as you'll learn later in this chapter (*Maryland v. Wilson*), and most of the others in the book, the Court has increasingly created (some critics say "legislated") "**bright-line**" [unambiguous] **rules** to tell officers, courts, and the rest of us what's reasonable.

The test of reasonableness also requires a case-by-case evaluation of whether there was enough objective basis to back up the searches and seizures. The objective basis ranges from the probable cause required to back up full-blown searches (Chapter 6) and seizures (arrests, Chapter 5) to the lesser reasonable suspicion required to back up stops and frisks. Both probable cause (always) and reasonable suspicion (usually) require *individualized suspicion*, meaning suspicion that points to specific individuals. However, DWI roadblocks (discussed later in this chapter) and some noncriminal law enforcement searches (Chapter 7) don't require individualized suspicion. In these cases, the objective basis consists of standard procedures such as random stops.

Today's stop-and-frisk law grew out of the Supreme Court's ruling in one case. Let's look at the Fourth Amendment issues surrounding that case, *Terry v. Ohio*, and at stop-and-frisk law after *Terry*.

Terry v. Ohio and Stop and Frisk

Today's stop-and-frisk law grew out of the practical problems police officers face in preventing and investigating crime on the streets and other public places in our largest cities. In these investigations, officers are usually dealing with people they don't know and probably won't ever see again. Usually, these strangers' suspicious behavior doesn't add up to the probable cause needed to arrest them (Chapter 5).

For example, suppose an officer doesn't have enough facts and circumstances viewed through the lens of her professional experience and training to arrest two men who peer into a store window, look around as if to see if anyone is watching them, and pace up and down repeating this pattern for several minutes. What should the officer do? Nothing? Keep watching them? Briefly detain them and pat them down for weapons? Take them to the police station? These were the issues raised in the famous *Terry v. Ohio* case.

The answer depends on three possible interpretations of the Fourth Amendment (Dix 1985, 853–55):

1. The Fourth Amendment applies only to full searches and arrests; so short of full arrests and searches, officers' discretion controls their contacts with individuals in public places.

2. Even brief street detentions are arrests, and pat downs are searches, so the police can't do anything unless they've got probable cause.

3. Stops and frisks are searches and seizures, but they're "minor" ones, so officers have to back them up with facts. But they need fewer facts than they'd need to arrest and search.

If officers can't take any action until they've got probable cause (alternative 2), crime control suffers because they'll probably never see the suspects again. But if the Fourth Amendment doesn't apply at all to these street encounters (alternative 1), then people on the street are subject to the whims of every officer. So both alternatives 1 and 2 are unacceptable; the U.S. Supreme Court chose alternative 3.

According to the Court, the Fourth Amendment gives the police enough power to "freeze" suspicious events and people briefly to find out if criminal activity "may be afoot." The Fourth Amendment also gives officers the power to protect themselves by frisking the people they stop. But officers can't freeze all the events and lay hands on all the people they've got a hunch may be up to no good; their stops and frisks have to be "reasonable." Courts can later review their stops and frisks to make sure they were reasonable.

What's "reasonable"? First, in the balance between crime control and individual freedom and privacy, in each case, the need to control crime has to outweigh the invasions against the individuals' rights. Second, officers can't stop and frisk people on a hunch, whim, or "mere suspicion." They need facts—not as many as would add up to probable cause (Chapters 5–6) but enough so that a neutral judge can decide later if there was enough objective basis to back up both the stop and the frisk.

*In the landmark case **Terry v. Ohio** (1968), our next case excerpt, the U.S. Supreme Court applied alternative 3, holding that the stop and frisk of John Terry satisfied the reasonableness requirement of the Fourth Amendment.*

CASE   Was He Seized and Searched?

Terry v. Ohio
392 U.S. 1 (1968)

HISTORY

John W. Terry was prosecuted for carrying a concealed weapon. The Court of Common Pleas of Cuyahoga County, Ohio, overruled a pretrial motion to suppress. Terry was convicted and sentenced to one to three years in the Ohio Penitentiary. Terry appealed. The Court of Appeals for the Eighth Judicial District of Ohio affirmed. The Ohio Supreme Court dismissed an appeal on the ground that no substantial constitutional question was involved. The U.S. Supreme Court granted certiorari, and affirmed.

WARREN, J.

This case presents serious questions concerning the role of the Fourth Amendment in the confrontation on the street between the citizen and the policeman investigating suspicious circumstances.

FACTS

Officer Martin McFadden testified that while he was patrolling in plain clothes in downtown Cleveland at approximately 2:30 in the afternoon of October 31, 1963, his attention was attracted by two men, Chilton and Terry, standing on the corner of Huron Road and Euclid Avenue. He had never seen the two men before, and he was unable to say precisely what first drew his eye to them. However, he testified that he had been a policeman for 39 years and a detective for 35 and that he had been assigned to patrol this vicinity of downtown Cleveland for shoplifters and pickpockets for 30 years. He explained that he had developed routine habits of observation over the years and that he would "stand and watch people or walk and watch people at many intervals of the day." He added: "Now, in this case when I looked over they didn't look right to me at the time."

His interest aroused, Officer McFadden took up a post of observation in the entrance to a store 300 to 400 feet away from the two men. "I get more purpose to watch them when I seen their movements," he testified.

He saw one of the men leave the other one and walk southwest on Huron Road, past some stores. The man paused for a moment and looked in a store window, then walked on a short distance, turned around and walked back toward the corner, pausing once again to look in the same store window. He rejoined his companion at the corner, and the two conferred briefly.

Then the second man went through the same series of motions, strolling down Huron Road, looking in the same window, walking on a short distance, turning back, peering in the store window again, and returning to confer with the first man at the corner.

The two men repeated this ritual alternately between five and six times apiece—in all, roughly a dozen trips. At one point, while the two were standing together on the corner, a third man approached them and engaged them briefly in conversation. This man then left the two others and walked west on Euclid Avenue.

Chilton and Terry resumed their measured pacing, peering and conferring. After this had gone on for 10 to 12 minutes, the two men walked off together, heading west on Euclid Avenue, following the path taken earlier by the third man.

By this time Officer McFadden had become thoroughly suspicious. He testified that after observing their elaborately casual and oft-repeated reconnaissance of the store window on Huron Road, he suspected the two men of "casing a job, a stick-up," and that he considered it his duty as a police officer to investigate further. He added that he feared "they may have a gun."

Thus, Officer McFadden followed Chilton and Terry and saw them stop in front of Zucker's store to talk to the same man who had conferred with them earlier on the street corner. Deciding that the situation was ripe for direct action, Officer McFadden approached the three men, identified himself as a police officer and asked for their names. At this point his knowledge was confined to what he had observed. He was not acquainted with any of the three men by name or by sight, and he had received no information concerning them from any other source.

When the men "mumbled something" in response to his inquiries, Officer McFadden grabbed petitioner Terry, spun him around so that they were facing the other two, with Terry between McFadden and the others, and patted down the outside of his clothing. In the left breast pocket of Terry's overcoat Officer McFadden felt a pistol. He reached inside the overcoat pocket, but was unable to remove the gun.

At this point, keeping Terry between himself and the others, the officer ordered all three men to enter Zucker's store. As they went in, he removed Terry's overcoat completely, removed a .38-caliber revolver from the pocket and ordered all three men to face the wall with their hands raised. Officer McFadden proceeded to pat down the outer clothing of Chilton and the third man, Katz. He discovered another revolver in the outer pocket of Chilton's overcoat, but no weapons were found on Katz.

The officer testified that he only patted the men down to see whether they had weapons, and that he did not put his hands beneath the outer garments of either Terry or Chilton until he felt their guns. So far as appears from the record, he never placed his hands beneath Katz' outer garments. Officer McFadden seized Chilton's gun, asked the proprietor of the store to call a police wagon, and took all three men to the station, where Chilton and Terry were formally charged with carrying concealed weapons.

OPINION

The Fourth Amendment right against unreasonable searches and seizures belongs as much to the citizen on the streets of our cities as to the homeowner closeted in his study to dispose of his secret affairs. Unquestionably Terry was entitled to the protection of the Fourth Amendment as he walked down the street in Cleveland. The question is whether in all the circumstances of this on-the-street encounter, his right to personal security was violated by an unreasonable search and seizure.

We would be less than candid if we did not acknowledge that this question thrusts to the fore difficult and troublesome issues regarding a sensitive area of police activity. In this context we approach the issues in this case mindful of the limitations of the judicial function in controlling the myriad daily situations in which policemen and citizens confront each other on the street.

The rule excluding evidence seized in violation of the Fourth Amendment has been recognized as a principal mode of discouraging lawless police conduct. But a stern refusal by this Court to condone such activity does not necessarily render it responsive to the exclusionary rule. Regardless of how effective the rule may be where obtaining convictions is an important objective of the police, it is powerless to deter invasions of constitutionally guaranteed rights where the police either have no interest in prosecuting or are willing to forgo successful prosecution in the interest of serving some other goal.

Proper adjudication of cases in which the exclusionary rule is invoked demands a constant awareness of these limitations. The wholesale harassment by certain elements of the police community, of which minority groups, particularly Negroes, frequently complain, will not be stopped by the exclusion of any evidence from any criminal trial. Yet a rigid and unthinking application of the exclusionary rule, in futile protest against practices which it can never be used effectively to control, may exact a high toll in human injury and frustration of efforts to prevent crime.

We turn our attention to the quite narrow question posed by the facts before us: whether it is always unreasonable for a policeman to seize a person and subject him to a limited search for weapons unless there is probable cause for an arrest.

Our first task is to establish at what point in this encounter Officer McFadden "seized" Terry and whether and when he conducted a "search." There is some suggestion in the use of such terms as "stop" and "frisk" that such police conduct is outside the purview of the Fourth Amendment because neither action rises to the level of a "search" or "seizure" within the meaning of the Constitution.

We emphatically reject this notion. Whenever a police officer accosts an individual and restrains his freedom to walk away, he has "seized" that person. And it is nothing less than sheer torture of the English language to suggest that a careful exploration of the outer surfaces of a person's clothing all over his or her body in an attempt to find weapons is not a "search." Moreover, it is simply fantastic to urge that such a procedure performed in public by a policeman while the citizen stands helpless, perhaps facing a wall with his hands raised, is a "petty indignity." It is a serious intrusion upon the sanctity of the person, which may inflict great indignity and arouse strong resentment, and it is not to be undertaken lightly.

The central inquiry under the Fourth Amendment is the reasonableness in all the circumstances of the particular governmental invasion of a citizen's personal security. In this case there can be no question that Officer McFadden "seized" Terry and subjected him to a "search" when he took hold of him and patted down the outer surfaces of his clothing. We must decide whether at that point it was reasonable for Officer McFadden to have interfered with petitioner's personal security as he did.

In determining whether the seizure and search were "unreasonable" our inquiry is a dual one—whether the officer's action was justified at its inception, and whether it was reasonably related in scope to the circumstances which justified the interference in the first place.

In justifying the particular intrusion the police officer must be able to point to specific and articulable facts which, taken together with rational inferences from those facts, reasonably warrant that intrusion. The Fourth Amendment is meaningful only if at some point the conduct of those charged with enforcing the laws can be subjected to the more detached, neutral scrutiny of a judge who must evaluate the reasonableness of a particular search or seizure. In making that assessment it is imperative that the facts be judged against an objective standard: would the facts available to the officer at the moment of the seizure or the search "warrant a man of reasonable caution in the belief" that the action taken was appropriate?

Anything less would invite intrusions upon constitutionally guaranteed rights based on nothing more substantial than inarticulate hunches. And simple "good faith on the part of the arresting officer is not enough." If subjective good faith alone were the test, the protections of the Fourth Amendment would evaporate, and the people would be "secure in their persons, houses, papers, and effects" only in the discretion of the police.

Applying these principles to this case, we consider first the nature and extent of the government interests involved. One general interest is of course that of effective crime prevention and detection; it is this interest which underlies the recognition that a police officer may in appropriate circumstances and in an appropriate manner approach a person for purposes of investigating possibly criminal behavior even though there is no probable cause to make an arrest. It was this legitimate investigative function Officer McFadden was discharging when he decided to approach Terry and his companions. He had observed Terry, Chilton, and Katz go through a series of acts, each of them perhaps innocent in itself, but which taken together warranted further investigation.

There is nothing unusual in two men standing together on a street corner, perhaps waiting for someone. Nor is there anything suspicious about people in such circumstances strolling up and down the street, singly or in pairs. Store windows, moreover, are made to be looked in.

But the story is quite different where, as here, two men hover about a street corner for an extended period of time, at the end of which it becomes apparent that they are not waiting for anyone or anything; where these men pace alternately along an identical route, pausing to stare in the same store window roughly 24 times; where each completion of this route is followed immediately by a conference between the two men on the corner; where they are joined in one of these conferences by a third man who leaves swiftly; and where the two men finally follow the third and rejoin him a couple of blocks away. It would have been poor police work indeed for an officer of 30 years' experience in the detection of thievery from stores in this same neighborhood to have failed to investigate this behavior further.

The crux of this case, however, is not the propriety of Officer McFadden's taking steps to investigate Terry's suspicious behavior, but rather, whether there was justification for McFadden's invasion of Terry's personal security by searching him for weapons in the course of that investigation. We are now concerned with more than the governmental interest in investigating crime; in addition, there is the more immediate interest of the police officer in taking steps to assure himself that the person with whom he is dealing is not armed with a weapon that could unexpectedly and fatally be used against him. Certainly it would be unreasonable to require that police officers take unnecessary risks in the performance of their duties.

We must still consider, however, the nature and quality of the intrusion on individual rights which must be accepted if police officers are to be conceded the right to search for weapons in situations where probable cause to arrest for crime is lacking. Even a limited search of the outer clothing for weapons constitutes a severe, though brief, intrusion upon cherished personal security, and it must surely be an annoying, frightening, and perhaps humiliating experience.

Our evaluation of the proper balance that has to be struck leads us to conclude that there must be a narrowly drawn authority to permit a reasonable search for weapons for the protection of the police officer, where he has reason to believe that he is dealing with an armed and dangerous individual. In determining whether the officer acted reasonably in such circumstances, due weight must be given, not to his inchoate and unparticularized suspicion or "hunch," but to the specific reasonable inferences which he is entitled to draw from the facts in light of his experience.

We must now examine the conduct of Officer McFadden in this case to determine whether his search and seizure of petitioner were reasonable, both at their inception and as conducted. He had observed Terry, together with Chilton and another man, acting in a manner he took to be preface to a "stick-up." We think on the facts and circumstances Officer McFadden detailed before the trial judge a reasonably prudent man would have been warranted in believing petitioner was armed and thus presented a threat to the officer's safety while he was investigating his suspicious behavior.

The actions of Terry and Chilton were consistent with McFadden's hypothesis that these men were contemplating a daylight robbery—which, it is reasonable to assume, would be likely to involve the use of weapons—and nothing in their conduct from the time he first noticed them until the time he confronted them and identified himself as a police officer gave him sufficient reason to negate that hypothesis. Although the trio had departed the original scene, there was nothing to indicate abandonment of an intent to commit a robbery at some point.

The manner in which the seizure and search were conducted is, of course, as vital a part of the inquiry as whether they were warranted at all. The Fourth Amendment proceeds as much by limitations upon the scope of governmental action as by imposing preconditions upon its initiation. Such a search is not justified by any need to prevent the disappearance or destruction of evidence of crime. The sole justification of the search in the present situation is the protection of the police officer and others nearby, and it must therefore be confined in scope to an intrusion reasonably designed to discover guns, knives, clubs, or other hidden instruments for the assault of the police officer.

The scope of the search in this case presents no serious problem in light of these standards. Officer McFadden patted down the outer clothing of petitioner and his two companions. He did not place his hands in their pockets or under the outer surface of their garments until he had felt weapons, and then he merely reached for and removed the guns. Officer McFadden confined his search strictly to what was minimally necessary to learn whether the men were armed and to disarm them once he discovered the weapons. He did not conduct a general exploratory search for whatever evidence of criminal activity he might find.

We conclude that the revolver seized from Terry was properly admitted in evidence against him. Each case of this sort will, of course, have to be decided on its own facts.

We merely hold today that where a police officer observes unusual conduct which leads him reasonably to conclude in light of his experience that criminal activity may be afoot and that the persons with whom he is dealing may be armed and presently dangerous, where in the course of investigating this behavior he identifies himself as a policeman and makes reasonable inquiries, and where nothing in the initial stages of the encounter serves to dispel his reasonable fear for his own or others' safety, he is entitled for the protection of himself and others in the area to conduct a carefully limited search of the outer clothing of such persons in an attempt to discover weapons which might be used to assault him. Such a search is a reasonable search under the Fourth Amendment, and any weapons seized may properly be introduced in evidence against the person from whom they were taken.

AFFIRMED.

CONCURRING OPINIONS

HARLAN, J.

I would make it perfectly clear that the right to frisk in this case depends upon the reasonableness of a forcible stop to investigate a suspected crime. Where such a stop is reasonable, however, the right to frisk must be immediate and automatic if the reason for the stop is, as here, an articulable suspicion of a crime of violence. A limited frisk incident to a lawful stop must often be rapid and routine. There is no reason why an officer, rightfully but forcibly confronting a person suspected of a serious crime, should have to ask one question and take the risk that the answer might be a bullet.

I would affirm this conviction for what I believe to be the same reasons the Court relies on. I would, however, make explicit what I think is implicit in affirmance on the present facts. Officer McFadden's right to interrupt Terry's freedom of movement and invade his privacy arose only because circumstances warranted forcing an encounter with Terry in an effort to prevent or investigate a crime. Once that forced encounter was justified, however, the officer's right to take suitable measures for his own safely followed automatically. Upon the foregoing premises, I join the opinion of the Court.

WHITE, J.

I think an additional word is in order concerning the matter of interrogation during an investigative stop. There is nothing in the Constitution which prevents a policeman from addressing questions to anyone on the streets. Absent special circumstances, the person approached may not be detained or frisked but may refuse to cooperate and go on his way.

However, given the proper circumstances, such as those in this case, it seems to me the person may be briefly detained against his will while pertinent questions are directed to him. Of course, the person stopped is not obliged to answer, answers may not be compelled, and refusal to answer furnishes no basis for an arrest, although it may alert the officer to the need for continued observation.

In my view, it is temporary detention, warranted by the circumstances, which chiefly justifies the protective frisk for weapons. Perhaps the frisk itself, where proper, will have beneficial results whether questions are asked or not. If weapons are found, an arrest will follow. If none are found, the frisk may nevertheless serve preventive ends because of its unmistakable message that suspicion has been aroused. But if the investigative stop is sustainable at all, constitutional rights are not necessarily violated if pertinent questions are asked and the person is restrained briefly in the process.

DISSENT

DOUGLAS, J.

The requirement of probable cause has roots that are deep in our history. The general warrant, in which the name of the person to be arrested was left blank, and the writs of assistance, against which James Otis inveighed, both perpetuated the oppressive practice of allowing the police to arrest and search on suspicion. Police control took the place of judicial control, since no showing of "probable cause" before a magistrate was required.

The infringement on personal liberty of any "seizure" of a person can only be "reasonable" under the Fourth Amendment if we require the police to possess "probable cause" before they seize him. Only that line draws a meaningful distinction between an officer's mere inkling and the presence of facts within the officer's personal knowledge which would convince a reasonable man that the person seized has committed, is committing, or is about to commit a particular crime.

To give the police greater power than a magistrate is to take a long step down the totalitarian path. Perhaps such a step is desirable to cope with modern forms of lawlessness. But if it is taken, it should be the deliberate choice of the people through a constitutional amendment. Until the Fourth Amendment is rewritten, the person and the effects of the individual are beyond the reach of all government agencies until there are reasonable grounds to believe (probable cause) that a criminal venture has been launched or is about to be launched.

There have been powerful hydraulic pressures throughout our history that bear heavily on the Court to water down constitutional guarantees and give the police the upper hand. That hydraulic pressure has probably never been greater than it is today. Yet if the individual is no longer to be sovereign, if the police can pick him up whenever they do not like the cut of his jib, if they can "seize" and "search" him in their discretion, we enter a new regime. The decision to enter it should be made only after a full debate by the people of this country.

QUESTIONS

1. **List in chronological order all of McFadden's actions from the time he started watching Terry until he arrested him.**
2. **According to Professor Lewis Katz (2004), who worked on one of the briefs in the case:**

    The Court played fast and loose with the most important fact in the case: the number of trips Terry and Chilton made up the street and how many times they looked into the store window. [Chief Justice] Warren reported that the two men looked into the window twenty-four times. That figure is reported with a certainty that the evidence does not support. McFadden was confused about how many times this occurred; a fair reading of the many times he stated what happened leads to the conclusion that they looked into the window between four and twenty-four times. His police report written immediately after the arrests stated that each man made three trips. This fact is critical because it is unclear as to whether the seizure would have been reasonable based on fewer observations of the store window. (454)

    Do you agree that Chief Justice Warren "played fast and loose with the most important fact in the case"? Does this added information affect your opinion? Does it bother you that the chief justice isn't clear on the facts? Explain your answers.
3. **According to the Court, at what point did McFadden seize Terry? Summarize the Court's reasons for picking that point.**
4. **According to the Court, at what point did McFadden search Terry? Summarize the Court's reasons for picking that point.**
5. **What was the objective basis (facts and circumstances) for McFadden's "stop" of Terry?**
6. **What was the objective basis (facts and circumstances) for McFadden's "frisk" of Terry?**
7. **Summarize the main points of Justice Harlan's concurring opinion. What do they add to your understanding of Chief Justice Warren's opinion?**
8. **During the oral argument before the Supreme Court, it came out that in all of Officer McFadden's experience, he'd never investigated a robbery; his experience was limited to spotting and investigating**

shoplifters and pickpockets. Does this matter? Explain your answer.

9. It was also learned during the oral argument that Terry, Chilton, and Katz were a lot bigger than Officer McFadden. Does this matter? Why? Why not?

10. Consider the following excerpt from an amicus curiae brief filed in *Terry v. Ohio:*

> In the litigation now before the Court—as is usual in cases where police practices are challenged—two parties essentially are represented. Law enforcement officers, legal representatives of their respective States, ask the Court to broaden police powers, and thereby to sustain what has proved to be a "good pinch."
>
> Criminal defendants caught with the goods through what in retrospect appears to be at least shrewd and successful (albeit constitutionally questionable) police work ask the Court to declare that work illegal and to reverse their convictions.
>
> Other parties intimately affected by the issues before the Court are not represented. The many thousands of our citizens who have been or may be stopped and frisked yearly, only to be released when the police find them innocent of any crime, are not represented. The records of their cases are not before the Court and cannot be brought here. Yet it is they, far more than those charged with crime, who will bear the consequences of the rules of constitutional law which this Court establishes.
>
> The determination of the quantum of "belief" or "suspicion" required to justify the exercise of intrusive police authority is precisely the determination of how far afield from instances of obvious guilt the authority stretches. To lower that quantum is to broaden the police net and, concomitantly, to increase the number (and probably the proportion) of innocent people caught up in it.
>
> The innocent are those this Court will never see. (Kurland and Casper 1975)

What's the point the brief makes? What's the importance of the point?

11. During oral arguments of the case before the Supreme Court, Louis Stokes, Terry's lawyer, revealed some of what happened at the suppression hearing. Stokes said, among other things, that Officer McFadden testified that he didn't know the men, that they walked normally, that they were standing in front of a store talking normally, and that they were facing away from the store windows. When asked why he approached Terry, Chilton, and Katz, Officer McFadden replied, "Because I didn't like them." Is this testimony important? Also, McFadden was White and Terry and Chilton were Black. Is this important?

Stop and Frisk after *Terry v. Ohio*

Judge Michael R. Juviler (1998) was a prosecutor in 1968. On the same day that *Terry v. Ohio* was argued, he argued in favor of the power to stop and frisk in a New York case before the U.S. Supreme Court. On the 30th anniversary of the decision, he recalled:

> After the *Terry* opinions were filed, we felt perhaps like the makers of the hydrogen bomb. What had we created? What had we contributed to? Would this lead to further racial divisions, police abuse, police "testilying [police perjury]"? (743–44)

At the time *Terry* was decided, many commentators, and some judges, interpreted the decision as a *grudging* watering down of the protections of the right against unreasonable search and seizure. This watering down seemed necessary in the climate of the times. The case was decided at a time when race riots, mass antiwar protests that sometimes turned violent, and skyrocketing crime rates (including murder) plagued our largest cities. Law enforcement had to have tools to respond to this violence, crime, and disorder. The decision was praised for balancing the need for safety and the rights of individuals.

As you read the remaining sections in the chapter, think about Judge Juviler's comment, and ask yourself whether his worries have come to pass. Certainly, it's true that the cases that followed *Terry* (some of which you'll read in the sections that follow) expanded the power of the police in several ways. First, they expanded the scope of the power beyond violent crimes against the person, such as armed robbery, to possessory crimes, especially illegal drug possession. Second, the cases expanded the time and location where the powers can be exercised. Third, the decisions expanded the objective basis for stops and frisks from firsthand observation by officers to include informants, anonymous tips, and even to profiles.

Four years after the Court decided *Terry v. Ohio*, it began to flesh out what the balancing element and objective basis of the reasonableness approach to Fourth Amendment stops meant. That fleshing out signaled a trend (broken only rarely) that the Court has followed up to 2010—tipping reasonableness in favor of law enforcement. The case in which the Court fleshed out the reasonableness approach elements was our next excerpt, *Adams v. Williams* (1971).

Adams v. Williams **decided that** *Terry v. Ohio* **wasn't limited to violent crimes against persons backed up by reasonable suspicion based on the direct observation of officers who stopped and frisked a suspect. It also applied to drug possession backed up by the secondhand hearsay of an informant.**

 **CASE** Was the Stop and Frisk Reasonable?

Adams v. Williams
407 U.S. 143 (1972)

HISTORY

Robert Williams (Respondent) was convicted in a Connecticut state court of illegal possession of a handgun found during a "stop and frisk," as well as of possession of heroin that was found during a full search incident to his weapons arrest. After respondent's conviction was affirmed by the Supreme Court of Connecticut, the U.S. Supreme Court denied certiorari. Williams' petition for federal habeas corpus relief was denied by the District Court and by a divided panel of the Second Circuit, but on rehearing en banc the Court of Appeals granted relief. That court held that evidence introduced at Williams' trial had been obtained by an unlawful search of his person and car, and thus the state court judgments of conviction should be set aside. Since we conclude that the policeman's actions here conformed to the standards this Court laid down in *Terry v. Ohio*, we reverse.

REHNQUIST, J.

FACTS

Police Sgt. John Connolly was alone early in the morning on car patrol duty in a high-crime area of Bridgeport, Connecticut. At approximately 2:15 A.M. a person known to Sgt. Connolly approached his cruiser and informed him that an individual seated in a nearby vehicle was carrying narcotics and had a gun at his waist.

After calling for assistance on his car radio, Sgt. Connolly approached the vehicle to investigate the informant's report. Connolly tapped on the car window and asked the occupant, Robert Williams, to open the door. When Williams rolled down the window instead, the sergeant reached into the car and removed a fully loaded revolver from Williams' waistband. The gun had not been visible to Connolly from outside the car, but it was in precisely the place indicated by the informant.

Williams was then arrested by Connolly for unlawful possession of the pistol. A search incident to that arrest was conducted after other officers arrived. They found substantial quantities of heroin on Williams' person and in the car, and they found a machete and a second revolver hidden in the automobile.

OPINION

Respondent contends that the initial seizure of his pistol, upon which rested the later search and seizure of other weapons and narcotics, was not justified by the informant's tip to Sgt. Connolly. He claims that absent a more reliable informant, or some corroboration of the tip, the policeman's actions were unreasonable under the standards set forth in *Terry v. Ohio.*

In *Terry* this Court recognized that "a police officer may in appropriate circumstances and in an appropriate manner approach a person for purposes of investigating possibly criminal behavior even though there is no probable cause to make an arrest." The Fourth Amendment does not require a policeman who lacks the precise level of information necessary for probable cause to arrest to simply shrug his shoulders and allow a crime to occur or a criminal to escape.

On the contrary, *Terry* recognizes that it may be the essence of good police work to adopt an intermediate response. A brief stop of a suspicious individual, in order to determine his identity or to maintain the status quo momentarily while obtaining more information, may be most reasonable in light of the facts known to the officer at the time.

The Court recognized in *Terry* that the policeman making a reasonable investigatory stop should not be denied the opportunity to protect himself from attack by a hostile suspect. "When an officer is justified in believing that the individual whose suspicious behavior he is investigating at close range is armed and presently dangerous to the officer or to others," he may conduct a limited protective search for concealed weapons. The purpose of this limited search is not to discover evidence of crime, but to allow the officer to pursue his investigation without fear of violence, and thus the frisk for weapons might be equally necessary and reasonable, whether or not carrying a concealed weapon violated any applicable state law. So long as the officer is entitled to make a forcible stop, and has reason to believe that the suspect is armed and dangerous, he may conduct a weapons search limited in scope to this protective purpose.

Applying these principles to the present case, we believe that Sgt. Connolly acted justifiably in responding to his informant's tip. The informant was known to him personally and had provided him with information in the past. This is a stronger case than obtains in the case of an anonymous telephone tip. The informant here came forward personally to give information that was immediately verifiable at the scene. Indeed, under Connecticut law, the informant might have been subject to immediate arrest for making a false complaint had Sgt. Connolly's investigation proved the tip incorrect.

Thus, while the Court's decisions indicate that this informant's unverified tip may have been insufficient for a narcotics arrest or search warrant, the information carried enough indicia of reliability to justify the officer's forcible stop of Williams.

In reaching this conclusion, we reject respondent's argument that reasonable cause for a stop and frisk can only be based on the officer's personal observation, rather than on information supplied by another person.

Informants' tips, like all other clues and evidence coming to a policeman on the scene, may vary greatly in their value and reliability. One simple rule will not cover every situation. Some tips, completely lacking in indicia of reliability, would either warrant no police response or require further investigation before a forcible stop of a suspect would be authorized. But in some situations—for example, when the victim of a street crime seeks immediate police aid and gives a description of his assailant, or when a credible informant warns of a specific impending crime—the subtleties of the hearsay rule should not thwart an appropriate police response.

While properly investigating the activity of a person who was reported to be carrying narcotics and a concealed weapon and who was sitting alone in a car in a high-crime area at 2:15 in the morning, Sgt. Connolly had ample reason to fear for his safety. When Williams rolled down his window, rather than complying with the policeman's request to step out of the car so that his movements could more easily be seen, the revolver allegedly at Williams' waist became an even greater threat. Under these circumstances the policeman's action in reaching to the spot where the gun was thought to be hidden constituted a limited intrusion designed to insure his safety, and we conclude that it was reasonable. The loaded gun seized as a result of this intrusion was therefore admissible at Williams' trial.

Under the circumstances surrounding Williams' possession of the gun seized by Sgt. Connolly, the arrest on the weapons charge was supported by probable cause, and the search of his person and of the car incident to that arrest was lawful [Chapter 5]. The fruits of the search were therefore properly admitted at Williams' trial, and the Court of Appeals erred in reaching a contrary conclusion.

REVERSED.

DISSENT

DOUGLAS, J., joined by MARSHALL, J.

The easy extension of *Terry v. Ohio*, to "possessory offenses" is a serious intrusion on Fourth Amendment safeguards. If it is to be extended to the latter at all, this should be only where observation by the officer himself or well authenticated information shows that criminal activity may be afoot.

BRENNAN, J.

The crucial question, as the Court concedes, is whether, there being no contention that Williams acted voluntarily in rolling down the window of his car, the State had shown sufficient cause to justify Sgt. Connolly's "forcible" stop. I would affirm, for the following reasons stated by Judge, now Chief Judge, Friendly, dissenting, that the State did not make that showing:

To begin, I have the gravest hesitancy in extending *Terry v. Ohio*, to crimes like the possession of narcotics. There is too much danger that, instead of the stop being the object and the protective frisk an incident thereto, the reverse will be true. Against that we have here the added fact of the report that Williams had a gun on his person. But Connecticut allows its citizens to carry weapons, concealed or otherwise, at will, provided only they have a permit, and gives its police officers no special authority to stop for the purpose of determining whether the citizen has one.

If I am wrong in thinking that *Terry* should not be applied at all to mere possessory offenses, I would not find the combination of Officer Connolly's almost meaningless observation and the tip in this case to be sufficient justification for the intrusion. The tip suffered from a threefold defect, with each fold compounding the others. The informer was unnamed, he was not shown to have been reliable with respect to guns or narcotics, and he gave no information which demonstrated personal knowledge or—what is worse—could not readily have been manufactured by the officer after the event.

Terry v. Ohio was intended to free a police officer from the rigidity of a rule that would prevent his doing anything to a man reasonably suspected of being about to commit or having just committed a crime of violence, no matter how grave the problem or impelling the need for swift action, unless the officer had what a court would later determine to be probable cause for arrest. It was meant for the serious cases of imminent danger or of harm recently perpetrated to persons or property, not the conventional ones of possessory offenses.

If it is to be extended to the latter at all, this should be only where observation by the officer himself or well authenticated information shows that criminal activity may be afoot. I greatly fear that if the (contrary view) should be followed, *Terry* will have opened the sluicegates for serious and unintended erosion of the protection of the Fourth Amendment."

MARSHALL, J., joined by DOUGLAS, J.

Four years have passed since we decided *Terry v. Ohio*, and its companion cases, *Sibron v. New York* and *Peters v. New York*. This case marks our first opportunity to give some flesh to the bones of *Terry*. Unfortunately, the flesh provided by today's decision cannot possibly be made to fit on *Terry*'s skeletal framework.

We upheld the stop and frisk in *Terry* because we recognized that the realities of on-the-street law enforcement require an officer to act at times on the basis of strong evidence, short of probable cause, that criminal activity is taking place and that the criminal is armed and dangerous. Hence, *Terry* stands only for the proposition that police officers have a "narrowly drawn authority to search for weapons" without a warrant.

In today's decision the Court ignores the fact that *Terry* begrudgingly accepted the necessity for creating an exception from the warrant requirement of the Fourth Amendment and treats this case as if warrantless searches were the rule rather than the "narrowly drawn" exception. This decision betrays the careful balance that *Terry* sought to strike between a citizen's right to privacy and his government's responsibility for effective law enforcement and expands the concept of warrantless searches far beyond anything heretofore recognized as legitimate. I dissent.

Mr. Justice Douglas was the sole dissenter in *Terry*. He warned of the "powerful hydraulic pressures throughout our history that bear heavily on the Court to water down constitutional guarantees." While I took the position then that we were not watering down rights, but were hesitantly and cautiously striking a necessary balance between the rights of American citizens to be free from government intrusion into their privacy and their government's urgent need for a narrow exception to the warrant requirement of the Fourth Amendment, today's decision demonstrates just how prescient Mr. Justice Douglas was.

It seems that the delicate balance that *Terry* struck was simply too delicate, too susceptible to the "hydraulic pressures" of the day. As a result of today's decision, the balance struck in *Terry* is now heavily weighted in favor of the government. And the Fourth Amendment, which was included in the Bill of Rights to prevent the kind of arbitrary and oppressive police action involved herein, is dealt a serious blow. Today's decision invokes the specter of a society in which innocent citizens may be stopped, searched, and arrested at the whim of police officers who have only the slightest suspicion of improper conduct.

QUESTIONS

1. List all of Officer Connolly's actions that infringed on Robert Williams's privacy and/or liberty.
2. List the facts that Connolly relied on to back up his actions.
3. Compare the facts in *Williams* with those in *Terry* in three respects: the crimes involved, the degree of the intrusions involved, and the objective basis for the officers' actions.
4. Summarize the majority opinion's reasons for ruling that the stop and frisk of Williams were reasonable.
5. Summarize the dissent's arguments for disagreeing with the majority opinion.
6. Do you agree more with the majority or the dissent? Explain your answer.

TABLE 4.1

Three Kinds of Police-Individual Contacts

Voluntary Encounters	Willing contacts without physical force or intimidation	Fourth Amendment doesn't apply
Stops	Brief (usually minutes), on-the-spot detentions that require reasonable suspicion to back them up	Fourth Amendment applies
Arrests	Longer detentions (hours or a few days) in police stations that require probable cause to back them up (Chapter 5)	Fourth Amendment applies

Now that you've got an overview of stops and frisks in the early cases, let's turn to a closer examination of each of these law enforcement actions. First, we'll look at stops, then at frisks, and finally at some special situations involving one or both—namely, vehicles, borders, and roadblocks.

Stops and the Fourth Amendment

LO 2

Beginning with *Terry v. Ohio*, we can divide the framework for analyzing police encounters with individuals into the three categories shown in Table 4.1. We've already examined the difference between voluntary encounters with the police (which are left to police discretion) and the two kinds of stops to investigate suspicious persons and circumstances that qualify as Fourth Amendment seizures (see Chapter 3, actual-seizure and show-of-authority stops).

Remember, the first question in the three-step analysis of Fourth Amendment seizures is, "Was the police action a stop?" If it wasn't, then the Fourth Amendment doesn't apply at all, and the analysis stops. But if the action was a stop, then the analysis proceeds to answering the question in step 2, "Was the stop reasonable?" What's a "reasonable" stop? Reasonableness depends on two elements:

1. Does the objective basis for the stop add up to reasonable suspicion? Reasonable suspicion (discussed later) consists of something more than a hunch but less than probable cause, the objective basis required to arrest a suspect (Chapter 5).

2. Are the requirements of the "scope of the stop" met?

    a. The *duration* is short.

    b. The *location* of the investigation is at or near the scene of the stop.

According to *Terry*, as long as officers can point to facts and circumstances amounting to reasonable suspicion, officers can "freeze" suspicious people and situations in time and space. But the freeze can last only long enough (duration) to let officers get enough information to arrest suspects; if they don't, they have to let them go. And the freeze has to take place (location) on the spot or very near the place where the stop took place.

How many facts are enough to add up to reasonable suspicion? How long is "only long enough," or, in Fourth Amendment terms, how long is reasonable? And exactly what is "on the spot"? How far, if any distance at all, is it reasonable for officers to move suspects from the spot? Let's try to answer these questions. First, we'll look at the objective basis for reasonable suspicion and then examine the scope of the stop allowed under the reasonableness test.

Reasonable Suspicion to Back Up Stops

LO 3

According to the U.S. Supreme Court in *Terry v. Ohio*, hunches aren't enough to back up even brief stops on the street or other public places. Officers have to point to **articulable facts** that show "criminal activity may be afoot." Simply put, articulable facts are facts that officers can name to back up their stops of private persons, and, by definition, "hunches" aren't enough. In *Terry*, the nameable facts included Officer McFadden's direct observation of Terry and Chilton pacing up and down and peering into a store window in downtown Cleveland. Seeing this aroused his suspicion that the three men were "casing" the store and were about to rob it.

Chief Justice Warren never used the words "reasonable suspicion," but Justice Harlan did. In his concurring opinion, Justice Harlan defined the standard the Court has followed right up to 2010:

> Officer McFadden had no probable cause to arrest Terry for anything, but he had observed circumstances that would reasonably lead an experienced, prudent policeman to suspect that Terry was about to engage in burglary or robbery. His justifiable suspicion afforded a proper constitutional basis for accosting Terry, restraining his liberty of movement briefly, and addressing questions to him, and Officer McFadden did so. (*Terry v. Ohio* 1968, 32)

In this book, we'll refer to **reasonable suspicion** as the totality of articulable facts and circumstances that would lead an officer, in the light of her training and experience, to *suspect* that crime *may* be afoot. (Notice the emphasis on "suspect" and "may" in contrast to the definition of arrest, which requires enough facts and circumstances to justify officers' *belief* that crime is afoot [Chapter 5].) The **totality-of-facts-and-circumstances test**—usually called just the "totality-of-circumstances test"—is a favorite standard the Court applies to decide whether official actions are constitutional. (You'll notice this as we work our way through the rest of the book.)

It might help you to call the test the **whole picture test**, an idea of Chief Justice Warren Burger. He wrote that the "essence" of reasonable suspicion is "that the totality of circumstances—the whole picture—must be taken into account." Based upon that whole picture, "the detaining officers must have a particularized and objective basis for suspecting the particular person stopped of criminal activity" (*U.S. v. Cortez* 1981, 417–18).

According to the chief justice:

> When used by trained law enforcement officers, objective facts, meaningless to the untrained, can be combined with permissible deductions from such facts to form a legitimate basis for suspicion of a particular person and for action on that suspicion. (419)

Information that officers can rely on to build reasonable suspicion comprises two types:

1. *Direct information.* Facts and circumstances officers learn firsthand from what they themselves see, hear, smell, and touch

2. *Hearsay information.* Facts and circumstances officers learn secondhand from victims, witnesses, other police officers, and anonymous, professional, or paid informants

Table 4.2 elaborates on direct and hearsay bases for reasonable suspicion.

TABLE 4.2

Direct and Hearsay Bases for Reasonable Suspicion

Direct Information	Hearsay Information
• Flight	• Victim statement
• Furtive movement	• Eyewitness statement
• Hiding	• Statements by fellow officers
• Resisting an officer	• Statements by informants
• Attempting to destroy evidence	• Anonymous tip
• Evasive answers	
• Contradictory answers	
• Weapons or contraband in plain view	

Recall that in 1968, when *Terry v. Ohio* was decided, reasonable suspicion was based on Officer McFadden's firsthand observations. Recall also, that four years later, in *Adams v. Williams*, the Court decided that an informant's tip plus the time (2:00 A.M.) and the location (a high-crime neighborhood) added up to reasonable suspicion to stop Williams. So officers can rely on secondhand information, or hearsay, either partly or completely.

LO 5

Officers usually get information secondhand through victims, witnesses, other police officers, and professional informants. In *Williams*, Officer Connolly knew the informant (even though he never named him). But what about anonymous tips? Are they enough to add up to reasonable suspicion? In *Alabama v. White* (1990), the police received an anonymous telephone tip

> stating that Vanessa White would be leaving 235-C Lynwood Terrace Apartments at a particular time in a brown Plymouth station wagon with the right taillight lens broken, that she would be going to Dobey's Motel, and that she would be in possession of about an ounce of cocaine inside a brown attaché case. (327)

By itself, the Court ruled, the tip wouldn't have justified a *Terry* stop. But when the officer's later direct observation confirmed the informant's prediction about White's movements, it was reasonable to suspect that the tipster had inside knowledge about the suspect and to credit his assertion about the cocaine. The Court called *White* a "close case." Then, in *Florida v. J. L.* (2000), the Court held unanimously that an anonymous tip that a "young Black male standing at a particular bus stop and wearing a plaid shirt was carrying a gun" did *not* amount to reasonable suspicion (268).

In addition to anonymous tips, Table 4.3 lists other reasons that, according to the courts, are insufficient to cross the reasonable suspicion threshold unless they're backed up by other evidence. The examples in Table 4.3 point to two other kinds of information officers use to back up reasonable stops: individualized suspicion and categorical suspicion (Harris 1998).

Individualized suspicion consists of "facts that would tell both the officer on the street and a court ruling on a suppression motion whether or not there was reasonable suspicion" (987). Terry and Chilton's casing Zucker's clothing store before Officer McFadden approached them is an excellent example of individualized suspicion. Individualized suspicion is necessary in all cases, but it may not be enough to amount to reasonable suspicion.

Categorical suspicion can also help to cross that threshold. Categorical suspicion refers to suspicion that falls on suspects because they fit into a broad category of

TABLE 4.3

Reasons Insufficient by Themselves for Reasonable Suspicion

1. General suspicion that drug dealing went on in a tavern (*Ybarra v. Illinois*, 444 U.S. 85 [1979])

2. Driver double-parked within 10 feet of a pedestrian in a drug-trafficking location (*Rivera v. Murphy*, 979 F.2d 259 [1st Cir. 1992])

3. Other bar patrons, not the one detained, possessed weapons and contraband (*U.S. v. Jaramillo*, 25 F.3d 1146 [2nd Cir. 1994])

4. Passenger leaving airplane appeared nervous in the presence of officers (*U.S. v. Caicedo*, 85 F.3d 1184 [6th Cir. 1996])

5. Driver of a car with out-of-state license plates and no noticeable luggage avoided eye contact with a police car (*U.S. v. Halls*, 40 F.3d 275 [8th Cir. 1995])

6. "Hispanic looking" males in a heavy truck near the border looked nervous, did not acknowledge police presence, and drove faster than the flow of traffic (*U.S. v. Garcia-Camacho*, 53 F.3d 244 [9th Cir. 1995])

7. Generalized suspicion of criminal activity in a high-crime neighborhood (*Brown v. Texas*, 443 U.S. 47 [1979])

8. Nervous man traveling alone who left an airline terminal quickly after picking up one suitcase and had a one-way ticket that he had bought with cash from a drug-source city (*U.S. v. Lambert*, 46 F.3d 1064 [10th Cir. 1995])

9. Driver failed to look at patrol car late at night (*U.S. v. Smith*, 799 F.2d 704 [11th Cir. 1986])

10. "Mexican appearing" person, driving a car with out-of-state license plates and no suitcases, appeared nervous in talking with officers during discussion of a speeding ticket (*U.S. v. Tapia*, 912 F.2d 1367 [11th Cir. 1990])

people, such as being in a particular location, being members of a particular race or ethnicity, or fitting a profile. Categorical suspicion is never enough by itself to amount to reasonable suspicion. But taken together with individualized suspicion, it can be one of the building blocks in the whole picture of reasonable suspicion.

The next three sections examine how the categories of location (with an in-depth look at flight from police officers in "high crime areas"), race and ethnicity, and profiles can support individualized suspicion when it's not enough by itself to amount to reasonable suspicion.

"High Crime Area"

LO 5

Whether you're stopped can depend on *where* you're stopped. The character of a neighborhood is a frequently used building block for establishing reasonable suspicion. Whether a neighborhood is considered a **"high crime area"** (or a variation of the phrase, such as "known for drug trafficking") is often the basis for successfully arguing that highly ambiguous conduct amounts to reasonable suspicion that justified a Fourth Amendment stop (Raymond 1999, 100).

However courts *define* "high crime area," the overwhelming majority of courts rely on law enforcement officers' testimony to *prove* that it's a "high crime area." Also, most have taken the officers at their word, allowing officer reports of their arrests—even statements as weak as "several arrests"—to qualify as proof of a high-crime area. But some courts demand something more than officers' unsupported testimony, such as police department findings, citizen complaints, or the number of prior arrests the testifying officer has made. As a result, "high crime area" differs from case to case, and from court to court, "because no court has required a threshold level of arrests, or complaints" (Ferguson and Bernache 2008, 1608–9).

A few courts have recognized the need for improved methods of proof. The U.S. Court of Appeals for the Ninth Circuit did so in *U.S. v. Montero-Camargo* (2000). The majority expressed concern that use of the term "high crime area" . . . "may well be an 'invitation to trouble'" (1139, note 32) and "can serve as a proxy for race or ethnicity" (1138). It held that it takes more than "mere war stories" to prove a location is a high-crime area (1139).

But, according to the distinguished Judge Alex Kozinski, who concurred in the court's opinion, the majority accepted "nothing more than the personal experiences of two arresting agents" to prove the location was a high-crime area:

> Both agents testified only that they had detected criminal violations after stopping people in the area. How often? One agent said he'd been involved in 15–20 stops over eight and a half years, and "couldn't recall anywhere we didn't have a violation of some sort." The other agent testified to "about a dozen" stops in the same period, all but one of which led to an arrest.
>
> Does an arrest every four months or so make for a high crime area? Can we rely on the vague and undocumented recollections of the officers here? Do the two officers' figures of "15–20" and "about a dozen" reflect separate pools of incidents, or do they include some where, as here, both officers were involved? Are such estimates sufficiently precise to tell us anything useful about the area? I wouldn't have thought so, although I could be persuaded otherwise. But my colleagues don't even pause to ask the questions. To them, it's a high crime area, because the officers say it's a high crime area.
>
> Just as a man with a hammer sees every problem as a nail, so a man with a badge may see every corner of his beat as a high crime area. Police are trained to detect criminal activity and they look at the world with suspicious eyes. This is a good thing, because we rely on this suspicion to keep us safe from those who would harm us. But to rely on every cop's repertoire of war stories to determine what is a "high crime area"—and on that basis to treat otherwise innocuous behavior as grounds for reasonable suspicion—strikes me as an invitation to trouble.
>
> If the testimony of two officers that they made, at most, 32 arrests during the course of a decade is sufficient to turn the road here into a high crime area, then what area under police surveillance wouldn't qualify as one? There are street corners in our inner cities that see as much crime within a month—even a week. I would be most reluctant to give police the power to turn any area into a high crime area based on their unadorned personal experiences. I certainly would not reach out to decide the issue. (1143)

Andrew Guthrie Ferguson, a staff attorney for the Washington, D.C., Public Defender's Office, and Damien Bernache, a staff attorney for the Nassau/Suffolk Law Services Committee (2008), have proposed an "objective, quantifiable approach" to the "high crime area" designation. It consists of three elements that the government has the burden of proving "to the appropriate standard":

1. *Crime and criminal activity.* The area has a high incidence of specific criminal activity compared to neighboring areas with objective and verifiable data. As a practical matter, government lawyers would have to introduce objective and verifiable evidence to support the claim. It could include certified arrest or conviction statistics from such areas as official crime "hot spots" or "drug free zones." It might also include crime mapping data, expert testimony, police logs, and citizen complaints. The key is "empirical data or documentation that could be verified and compared by the trial court" (1629–30). It might be difficult to draw the line as to how much

higher than the neighboring areas would qualify as high. Ten to twenty percent higher? Probably. Five to ten percent? Probably not.

2. *Geography and timing.* The area is defined narrowly to a certain location (for example, including specific blocks, parks, housing complexes, and intersections) and limited to recent criminal activity. Here, statistics have to relate to an area within specific boundaries, and they have to be recent.

   In practice, this will depend on how crime statistics are collected. It could be police districts, as it is in Chicago (see *Wardlow*, below), or it could be smaller. In Washington, D.C., the D.C. Police Department has a crime-mapping website where anyone can find out the number of crimes in the past two years for any block or intersection in the city (1631–32).

3. *Criminal activity/officer observation link.* There is a demonstrated connection between the specific criminal activity and the officer's observation. Why is this important? Because the only reason the criminal activity is relevant is because it makes the suspicion more reasonable. For example, if an area is verifiably high in burglaries, it's more reasonable to suspect that a person loitering with a bag over his or her shoulder might have just committed a burglary than it would be to suspect a person seen transferring money to someone might be dealing drugs. The crime/officer observation link prevents including too much within the "high crime area" designation (1635).

   Of course, the officer has to know that it's a "high crime area" *before* she observed the criminal activity; otherwise, the location is not a basis for suspicion.

The objective of these empirical elements is to guide litigants and courts in Fourth Amendment suppression hearings whenever the government raises the "high crime area" issue (1628).

In Illinois v. Wardlow *(5–4), the U.S. Supreme Court found that Sam Wardlow's unprovoked flight from Chicago police officers in "an area known for heavy narcotics trafficking" added up to reasonable suspicion to stop him.*

CASE   Does Sudden Unprovoked Flight in a "Heavy Narcotics Trafficking" Area Amount to Reasonable Suspicion?

Illinois v. Wardlow
528 U.S. 119 (2000)

HISTORY

William "Sam" Wardlow (respondent) was arrested and charged with unlawful use of a weapon by a felon. The Illinois trial court denied his motion to suppress and convicted Wardlow of unlawful use of a weapon by a felon. The Illinois Appellate Court reversed Wardlow's conviction.

The Illinois Supreme Court affirmed the Appellate Court's decision. Illinois petitioned for certiorari. The U.S. Supreme Court granted the petition and reversed (5–4).

REHNQUIST, C.J.

FACTS

On September 9, 1995, Officers Nolan and Harvey and six others were working as uniformed officers in the special operations section of the Chicago Police Department. The officers were driving the last car of a four-car caravan converging on an area known for heavy narcotics trafficking in order to investigate drug transactions. The officers were traveling together because they expected to find a crowd of people in the area, including lookouts and customers.

As the caravan passed 4035 West Van Buren, Officer Nolan observed Wardlow standing next to the building holding an opaque bag. Wardlow looked in the direction of the officers and fled. Nolan and Harvey turned their car southbound, watched him as he ran through the gangway and an alley, and eventually cornered him on the street. Nolan then exited his car and stopped Wardlow. He immediately conducted a protective pat-down search for weapons because in his experience it was common for there to be weapons in the near vicinity of narcotics transactions.

During the frisk, Officer Nolan squeezed the bag Wardlow was carrying and felt a heavy, hard object similar to the shape of a gun. The officer then opened the bag and discovered a .38-caliber handgun with five live rounds of ammunition. The officers arrested Wardlow.

OPINION

An individual's presence in an area of expected criminal activity, standing alone, is not enough to support a reasonable, particularized suspicion that the person is committing a crime. But officers are not required to ignore the relevant characteristics of a location in determining whether the circumstances are sufficiently suspicious to warrant further investigation. Accordingly, we have previously noted that a stop in a "high crime area" can be among the relevant contextual considerations in a *Terry* analysis [see *Adams v. Williams* (1972), excerpted on p. 95].

In this case, it was not merely Wardlow's presence in an area of heavy narcotics trafficking that aroused the officers' suspicion but his unprovoked flight upon noticing the police. Our cases have also recognized that nervous, evasive behavior is a pertinent factor in determining reasonable suspicion. Headlong flight—wherever it occurs—is the consummate act of evasion: it is not necessarily indicative of wrongdoing, but it is certainly suggestive of such.

In reviewing the propriety of an officer's conduct, courts do not have available empirical studies dealing with inferences drawn from suspicious behavior, and we cannot reasonably demand scientific certainty from judges or law enforcement officers where none exists. Thus, the determination of reasonable suspicion must be based on commonsense judgments and inferences about human behavior. We conclude Officer Nolan was justified in suspecting that Wardlow was involved in criminal activity, and, therefore, in investigating further.

When an officer, without reasonable suspicion or probable cause, approaches an individual, the individual has a right to ignore the police and go about his business. And any "refusal to cooperate, without more, does not furnish the minimal level of objective justification needed for a detention or seizure." But unprovoked flight is simply not a mere refusal to cooperate. Flight, by its very nature, is not "going about one's business"; in fact, it is just the opposite. Allowing officers confronted with such flight to stop the fugitive and investigate further is quite consistent with the individual's right to go about his business or to stay put and remain silent in the face of police questioning.

Wardlow also argues that there are innocent reasons for flight from police and that, therefore, flight is not necessarily indicative of ongoing criminal activity. This fact is undoubtedly true, but does not establish a violation of the Fourth Amendment. *Terry* recognized that the officers could detain the individuals to resolve the ambiguity. In allowing such detentions, *Terry* accepts the risk that officers may stop innocent people. If the officer does not learn facts rising to the level of probable cause, the individual must be allowed to go on his way. But in this case the officers found Wardlow in possession of a handgun, and arrested him for violation of an Illinois firearms statute.

The judgment of the Supreme Court of Illinois is REVERSED, and the case is REMANDED for further proceedings not inconsistent with this opinion. It is so ordered.

CONCURRING AND DISSENTING OPINIONS

STEVENS, J., joined by SOUTER, GINSBURG, and BREYER, JJ., concurring in part and dissenting in part.

The State of Illinois asks this Court to announce a "bright-line rule" authorizing the temporary detention of anyone who flees at the mere sight of a police officer. Wardlow counters by asking us to adopt the opposite *per se* rule—that the fact that a person flees upon seeing the police can never, by itself, be sufficient to justify a temporary investigative stop. The Court today wisely endorses neither *per se* rule. Instead, it adheres to the view that the concept of reasonable suspicion is not readily reduced to a neat set of legal rules, but must be determined by looking to the totality of the circumstances—the whole picture.

The question in this case concerns "the degree of suspicion that attaches to" a person's flight—or, more precisely, what "commonsense conclusions" can be drawn respecting the motives behind that flight.*

Given the diversity and frequency of possible motivations for flight, it would be profoundly unwise to endorse

---

*"Compare, Proverbs 28:1: 'The wicked flee when no man pursueth: but the righteous are as bold as a lion' with Proverbs 22:3: 'A shrewd man sees trouble coming and lies low; the simple walk into it and pay the penalty.' I have rejected reliance on the former proverb in the past, because its 'ivory-towered analysis of the real world' fails to account for the experiences of many citizens in this country, particularly those who are minorities. That this pithy expression fails to capture the total reality of our world, however, does not mean it is inaccurate in all instances."

either per se rule. The inference we can reasonably draw about the motivation for a person's flight, rather, will depend on a number of different circumstances. Factors such as the time of day, the number of people in the area, the character of the neighborhood, whether the officer was in uniform, the way the runner was dressed, the direction and speed of the flight, and whether the person's behavior was otherwise unusual might be relevant in specific cases.

This number of variables is surely sufficient to preclude either a bright-line rule that always justifies, or that never justifies, an investigative stop based on the sole fact that flight began after a police officer appeared nearby. Still, Illinois presses for a *per se* rule regarding "unprovoked flight upon seeing a clearly identifiable police officer." The phrase "upon seeing," as used by Illinois, apparently assumes that the flight is motivated by the presence of the police officer.*

Even assuming we know that a person runs because he sees the police, the inference to be drawn may still vary from case to case. Flight to escape police detection may have an entirely innocent motivation:

> It is a matter of common knowledge that men who are entirely innocent do sometimes fly from the scene of a crime through fear of being apprehended as the guilty parties, or from an unwillingness to appear as witnesses. Nor is it true as an accepted axiom of criminal law that "the wicked flee when no man pursueth, but the righteous are as bold as a lion." Innocent men sometimes hesitate to confront a jury—not necessarily because they fear that the jury will not protect them, but because they do not wish their names to appear in connection with criminal acts, are humiliated at being obliged to incur the popular odium of an arrest and trial, or because they do not wish to be put to the annoyance or expense of defending themselves. *Alberty v. U.S.*, 162 U.S. 499, 511 (1896).

In addition to these concerns, a reasonable person may conclude that an officer's sudden appearance indicates nearby criminal activity. And where there is criminal activity there is also a substantial element of danger—either from the criminal or from a confrontation between the criminal and the police. These considerations can lead

to an innocent and understandable desire to quit the vicinity with all speed.

Among some citizens, particularly minorities and those residing in high crime areas, there is also the possibility that the fleeing person is entirely innocent, but, with or without justification, believes that contact with the police can itself be dangerous, apart from any criminal activity associated with the officer's sudden presence.**

For such a person, unprovoked flight is neither "aberrant" nor "abnormal." . . .†

Many stops never lead to an arrest, which further exacerbates the perceptions of discrimination felt by racial minorities and people living in high crime areas. . . .‡

Even if these data were race neutral, they would still indicate that society as a whole is paying a significant cost in infringement on liberty by these virtually random stops. Moreover, these concerns and fears are known to the police officers themselves, and are validated by law enforcement investigations into their own practices. The Massachusetts Attorney General investigated allegations of egregious police conduct toward minorities. The report stated:

> Perhaps the most disturbing evidence was that the scope of a number of *Terry* searches went far beyond anything authorized by that case and indeed, beyond anything that we believe would be acceptable under the federal and state constitutions even where probable cause existed to conduct a full search incident to an arrest.
>
> Forcing young men to lower their trousers, or otherwise searching inside their underwear, on public streets or in public hallways, is so demeaning and invasive of fundamental precepts of privacy that it can

---

Note: Nowhere in Illinois' briefs does it specify what it means by "unprovoked." At oral argument, Illinois explained that if officers precipitate a flight by threats of violence, that flight is "provoked." But if police officers in a patrol car—with lights flashing and siren sounding—descend upon an individual for the sole purpose of seeing if he or she will run, the ensuing flight is "unprovoked." Illinois contends that unprovoked flight is "an extreme reaction," because innocent people simply do not "flee at the mere sight of the police." To be sure, Illinois concedes, an innocent person—even one distrustful of the police—might "avoid eye contact or even sneer at the sight of an officer," and that would not justify a *Terry* stop or any sort of per se inference. But, Illinois insists, unprovoked flight is altogether different. Such behavior is so "aberrant" and "abnormal" that a per se inference is justified.

**See Casimir, "Minority Men: We Are Frisk Targets," *N.Y. Daily News*, Mar. 26, 1999, p. 34 (informal survey of 100 young black and Hispanic men living in New York City; 81 reported having been stopped and frisked by police at least once; none of the 81 stops resulted in arrests); Brief for NAACP Legal Defense & Educational Fund as Amicus Curiae 17–19 (reporting figures on disproportionate street stops of minority residents in Pittsburgh and Philadelphia, Pennsylvania, and St. Petersburg, Florida); U.S. Dept. of Justice, Bureau of Justice Statistics, S. Smith, "Criminal Victimization and Perceptions of Community Safety in 12 Cities" (25 June 1998) (African-American residents in 12 cities are more than twice as likely to be dissatisfied with police practices than white residents in same community.)

†See e.g., Kotlowitz, "Hidden Casualties: Drug War's Emphasis on Law Enforcement Takes a Toll on Police," *Wall Street Journal*, Jan. 11, 1991 ("Black leaders complained that innocent people were picked up in the drug sweeps. . . . Some teenagers were so scared of the task force they ran even if they weren't selling drugs.")

‡See Goldberg, "The Color of Suspicion," *N.Y. Times Magazine*, June 20, 1999 (reporting that in a 2-year period, New York City Police Department Street Crimes Unit made 45,000 stops, only 9,500, or 20%, of which resulted in arrest); Casimir (reporting that in 1997, New York City's Street Crimes Unit conducted 27,061 stop-and-frisks, only 4,647 of which, 17%, resulted in arrest).

only be condemned in the strongest terms. The fact that not only the young men themselves, but independent witnesses complained of strip searches, should be deeply alarming to all members of this community.

Accordingly, the evidence supporting the reasonableness of these beliefs is too pervasive to be dismissed as random or rare, and too persuasive to be disparaged as inconclusive or insufficient. In any event, just as we do not require "scientific certainty" for our commonsense conclusion that unprovoked flight can sometimes indicate suspicious motives, neither do we require scientific certainty to conclude that unprovoked flight can occur for other, innocent reasons.

"Unprovoked flight," in short, describes a category of activity too broad and varied to permit a per se reasonable inference regarding the motivation for the activity. While the innocent explanations surely do not establish that the Fourth Amendment is always violated whenever someone is stopped solely on the basis of an unprovoked flight, neither do the suspicious motivations establish that the Fourth Amendment is never violated when a *Terry* stop is predicated on that fact alone.

Guided by that totality-of-the-circumstances test, the Court concludes that Officer Nolan had reasonable suspicion to stop respondent. In this respect, my view differs from the Court's. The entire justification for the stop is articulated in the brief testimony of Officer Nolan. Some facts are perfectly clear; others are not. This factual insufficiency leads me to conclude that the Court's judgment is mistaken.

Wardlow was arrested a few minutes after noon on September 9, 1995. Nolan was part of an eight-officer, four-car caravan patrol team. The officers were headed for "one of the areas in the 11th District [of Chicago] that's high [in] narcotics traffic." The reason why four cars were in the caravan was that "normally in these different areas there's an enormous amount of people, sometimes lookouts, customers." Officer Nolan testified that he was in uniform on that day, but he did not recall whether he was driving a marked or an unmarked car.

Officer Nolan and his partner were in the last of the four patrol cars that "were all caravaning eastbound down Van Buren." Nolan first observed respondent "in front of 4035 West Van Buren." Wardlow "looked in our direction and began fleeing." Nolan then "began driving southbound down the street observing [respondent] running through the gangway and the alley southbound," and observed that Wardlow was carrying a white, opaque bag under his arm.

After the car turned south and intercepted respondent as he "ran right towards us," Officer Nolan stopped him and conducted a "protective search," which revealed that the bag under respondent's arm contained a loaded handgun.

This terse testimony is most noticeable for what it fails to reveal. Though asked whether he was in a marked or unmarked car, Officer Nolan could not recall the answer. He was not asked whether any of the other three cars in the caravan were marked, or whether any of the other seven officers were in uniform. Though he explained that the size of the caravan was because "normally in these different areas there's an enormous amount of people, sometimes lookouts, customers," Officer Nolan did not testify as to whether anyone besides Wardlow was nearby 4035 West Van Buren. Nor is it clear that that address was the intended destination of the caravan.

As the Appellate Court of Illinois interpreted the record, "it appears that the officers were simply driving by, on their way to some unidentified location, when they noticed defendant standing at 4035 West Van Buren." Officer Nolan's testimony also does not reveal how fast the officers were driving. It does not indicate whether he saw respondent notice the other patrol cars. And it does not say whether the caravan, or any part of it, had already passed Wardlow by before he began to run. Indeed, the Appellate Court thought the record was even "too vague to support the inference that . . . defendant's flight was related to his expectation of police focus on him."

Presumably, respondent did not react to the first three cars, and we cannot even be sure that he recognized the occupants of the fourth as police officers. The adverse inference is based entirely on the officer's statement: "He looked in our direction and began fleeing." No other factors sufficiently support a finding of reasonable suspicion.

Though respondent was carrying a white, opaque bag under his arm, there is nothing at all suspicious about that. Certainly the time of day—shortly after noon—does not support Illinois' argument. Nor were the officers "responding to any call or report of suspicious activity in the area."

Officer Nolan did testify that he expected to find "an enormous amount of people," including drug customers or lookouts, and the Court points out that "it was in this context that Officer Nolan decided to investigate Wardlow after observing him flee." This observation, in my view, lends insufficient weight to the reasonable suspicion analysis; indeed, in light of the absence of testimony that anyone else was nearby when respondent began to run, this observation points in the opposite direction.

The State, along with the majority of the Court, relies as well on the assumption that this flight occurred in a high crime area. Even if that assumption is accurate, it is insufficient because even in a high crime neighborhood unprovoked flight does not invariably lead to reasonable suspicion.

On the contrary, because many factors providing innocent motivations for unprovoked flight are concentrated in high crime areas, the character of the neighborhood arguably makes an inference of guilt less appropriate, rather than more so. Like unprovoked flight itself, presence in a high crime neighborhood is a fact too generic and susceptible to innocent explanation to satisfy the reasonable suspicion inquiry.

It is the State's burden to articulate facts sufficient to support reasonable suspicion. In my judgment, Illinois has failed to discharge that burden. I am not persuaded that the mere fact that someone standing on a sidewalk looked in the direction of a passing car before starting to run is sufficient to justify a forcible stop and frisk.

I therefore respectfully DISSENT from the Court's judgment to reverse the court below.

QUESTIONS

1. Identify the "articulable" facts Officer Nolan relied on to stop Wardlow.
2. List the Court's reasons for concluding these facts added up to reasonable suspicion.
3. Compare the facts Nolan possessed with those possessed by Officer McFadden in *Terry v. Ohio*. In your opinion, which officer had more articulable facts?
4. Even if one had more than the other, did they both have reasonable suspicion? Defend your answer.
5. Is reasonable suspicion enough of a safeguard to the right of all people, innocent and guilty, to come and go as they please? Defend your answer.
6. List and summarize the empirical evidence Justice Stevens includes in his dissenting opinion. Is the evidence reliable? Assuming the evidence is reliable, does it have anything to do with whether Nolan's stop and frisk of Wardlow was reasonable? Defend your answer.
7. Neither the majority nor the dissent referred to data available regarding the "high crime area" part of the reasonable suspicion the officers had to stop Wardlow. According to its amicus brief, the National Association of Police Organizations, Policemen's Benevolent and Protective Association of Illinois, and Illinois Police Association (*Illinois v. Wardlow*, "Amicus Brief 1999, 11–12):

The reputation of an area for having substantial criminal activity can be based, not only on the objective knowledge and experience of police officers, but on verifiable and quantifiable data. Sophisticated data collection, geographical computer and other mapping, and detailed geographical analysis systems have all become an essential part of crime prevention. Determining which locales or neighborhoods are high crime areas, and knowing what types of crimes are prevalent in those areas, results in a more efficient allocation of resources and thus more effective law enforcement, as was occurring in this case.

Chicago Police District 11, where the Respondent fled from the police, is such a high crime area. In 1997, District 11 had a higher overall total crime rate than 13 of the 25 police districts, roughly an equal crime rate to two of the districts, and a lower crime rate than 9 of the districts. When broken down further, this data reveals that in 1997, District 11 had the highest number of murders and robberies, and the second highest

number of criminal sexual assaults and aggravated assaults, of all the police districts in Chicago. This data clearly indicates that District 11 is a high crime area, and contradicts the Respondent's assertion, as stated in his brief in opposition to the petition for a writ of certiorari, of lack of evidence on that issue.

The ability to quantify reports of crime refutes any claim that the police disproportionately or discriminatorily target areas that have large ethnic or racial minority populations, thus causing those areas to have higher than average arrest statistics, an argument which we anticipate may be posited by an *amicus curiae* on behalf of the Respondent. Any such assertion is erroneous for all the following reasons: first, victim reports and calls for service are factored into the data; and, second, research demonstrates that not all minority neighborhoods suffer from high crime and victimization, and that high crime also exists in other neighborhoods.

This is certainly the case in Chicago. The Chicago data set forth in this brief demonstrates that neighborhoods in Chicago, as elsewhere, do not have to be predominately populated by racial or ethnic minorities in order to be labeled as high crime areas. Thus, when patrolling any of these locales, a Chicago police officer would take into account that he or she is, in fact, in a high crime area, when considering the totality of the circumstances applying to a particularly suspicious individual or situation.

This rebuts insinuations that using area as a factor in determining reasonable belief has a discriminatory effect on racial or ethnic minorities. If anything, the opposite is true. While objective statistics do show that many high crime areas are found in urban neighborhoods with large racial or ethnic minority populations, data also show that the minority residents of these neighborhoods are much more concerned about crime and have higher victimization rates than any other demographic group. In fact, crime prevention efforts targeting specific neighborhoods have served as an invaluable tool in providing the residents of these communities with the protection that they not only desire, but so rightly deserve. To reduce law enforcement efforts in these neighborhoods would disproportionately subject their law-abiding residents to increasing victimization and would be a clear denial of the Equal Protection Clause of the Fourteenth Amendment.

Should the Court have referred to this information and argument? How does it change and/or enrich your understanding of the case? Explain.

8. **Consider Table 4.4 and Table 4.5, "Stops and Arrests, NYPD" and "Facts Supporting Reasonable Suspicion (NYPD)," respectively. What, if any, policies would you recommend on the basis of these numbers? Is there anything else you'd want to know before you recommended anything? Explain your answers.**

TABLE 4.4

Stops and Arrests, New York City Police Department (NYPD)

	Total Stops	Stops Resulting in Arrest	Ratio of Stops to Arrest
Facts articulate reasonable suspicion (stop meets constitutional standard of reasonable suspicion)	2,678	368	7.3
Facts do not articulate reasonable suspicion (stop does not meet constitutional standard of reasonable suspicion)	673	23	29.3
Insufficient information (evidence insufficient to determine whether constitutional standard of reasonable suspicion was met	1,032	76	13.6
Flight Alone[a,b]			
Fleeing crime scene	104	4	26.0
Attempted flight	79	5	15.8
Flight in High Crime Area			
Fleeing crime scene	61	3	20.3
Attempted flight	45	1	45.0
Total	4,383	467	9.4

Source: New York Office of the Attorney General. 1999 (December 1). *The New York City Police Department's "Stop and Frisk" Practices: A Report to the People of the State of New York from the Office of the Attorney General*; Meares and Harcourt 2000.

[a]We are grateful to Jeffrey Fagan, Center for Violence Research and Prevention, Columbia University, for the analysis of stops and arrests based on the flight codes.
[b]The data on flight were categorized in two ways: (1) attempting to elude police, which includes eluding police plus other factors/suspicious activity, and (2) fleeing the crime scene. Information relevant to the first category is evidence of an unconstitutional stop; evidence relevant to the second category is insufficient to make a determination.

Race and Ethnicity

LO 5

Should officers be allowed to view race and ethnicity through the lens of their training and experience as part of the totality of circumstances adding up to reasonable suspicion? Or must reasonable suspicion be color and ethnicity blind? Even asking this question generates explosive controversy (Kennedy 1997, Chapter 4).

The U.S. Supreme Court has made it clear that race and ethnicity by themselves can never amount to reasonable suspicion. But the Supreme Court and almost all lower courts have made it equally clear that when it comes to reasonable suspicion, color and ethnicity are *part* of reality, however uncomfortable that reality may be. "Facts are not to be ignored simply because they may be unpleasant," wrote U.S. Eighth Circuit Court of Appeals Judge Wollman in *U.S. v. Weaver* (1992, 394).

We need to distinguish between two uses of race and ethnicity as building blocks in reasonable suspicion. First, and usually not problematic, race or ethnicity is a building block when it's part of individualized suspicion, as when a witness identifies her attacker as White, or Black, or Hispanic. Second, race and ethnicity can be a building block when it's a categorical circumstance, such as it was in *U.S. v. Weaver*. The U.S. Eighth Circuit Court of Appeals held that law enforcement officers could use Weaver's race as *part* of reasonable suspicion.

Arthur Weaver caught the attention of Drug Enforcement Administration (DEA) agents and Kansas City detectives when he got off an early morning direct flight from

TABLE 4.5

Facts Supporting Reasonable Suspicion, NYPD

Reasonable Suspicion Standard	Types of Information Reported by Officers as Basis for Their Reasonable Suspicion
Facts articulate reasonable suspicion	Crime observed: drug sale, jumping turnstile/metrocard fraud, theft of service, buy & bust, graffiti; carrying theft equipment or other paraphernalia, placing or retrieving object (drugs), suspected break-in/burglary/on fire escape
	Fit description: fit the description, identified by or information from third party at scene, bail jumping, known and wanted by police, active warrant
	Weapon observed: waistband activity, bulge in waistband, observed object that could be (appeared to be) gun or weapon, laser light activity, toy guns
	Suspicious plus: eluding the police plus other factors; extended observation of suspicious activity: trying multiple car doors, extended observation activity, walking back and forth on same street for period of time, etc.
	Location prone to robbery plus suspicious behavior: pacing, talking to known dealers, loitering; location known for drug activity plus "suspicious behavior": pacing, standing around talking with passersby or known drug dealers; location known for prostitution plus suspicious behavior
Facts do not articulate reasonable suspicion; the stop is unconstitutional	Activity deemed suspicious: pocket or clothing activity, bulge in clothing, attempting to elude police, suspicious behavior (nervousness, pacing), suspicious clothing, looking into parked cars/trying one door, black or silver object/ exchange of object
	Wrong place: out of place; location known for drug activity; location prone to robbery/burglary/grand larceny; location known for prostitution
	Association with "wrong" people: a suspect or person arrested/known dealer, gang affiliation (known member or clothing), loitering, known to police, loitering on subway platform
Insufficient information	Person was in area that crime or suspicious activity was reported, fleeing crime scene, suspected drug sale, observed drug use, suspected or observed alcohol consumption or open bottle, moving furniture, carrying out of place objects (computers), panhandling, knife in pocket, questioned individual previously in an ongoing investigation
Flight[a] (Fleeing crime scene and attempted flight)	The data on flight were categorized in two ways: (1) attempting to elude police, which includes eluding police plus other factors/suspicious activity, and (2) fleeing the crime scene. The researchers considered information relevant to the first category evidence of an unconstitutional stop, and they considered evidence relevant to the second category insufficient to make a determination.

Source: New York Office of the Attorney General. 1999 (December 1). *The New York City Police Department's 'Stop and Frisk' Practices: A Report to the People of the State of New York from the Office of the Attorney General*; Meares and Harcourt 2009.

[a]We are grateful to Jeffrey Fagan, Center for Violence Research and Prevention, Columbia University, for the analysis of stops and arrests based on the flight codes.

Los Angeles. The DEA agent testified that several factors caused him to suspect that Weaver might be carrying drugs:

> Number one, we have intelligence information and also past arrest history on two black—all black street gangs from Los Angeles called the Crips and the Bloods. They are notorious for transporting cocaine into the Kansas City area from Los Angeles for sale. Most of them are young, roughly dressed male blacks. (394, n. 2)

According to Judge Wollman:

> We agree with the dissent that large groups of our citizens should not be regarded by law enforcement officers as presumptively criminal based upon their race. We would not hesitate to hold that a solely race-based suspicion of drug courier status would not pass constitutional muster. As it is, however, facts are not to be ignored simply because they may be unpleasant—and the unpleasant fact in this case is that Hicks had knowledge, based upon his own experience and upon the intelligence reports he had received from the Los Angeles authorities, that young male members of black Los Angeles gangs were flooding the Kansas City area with cocaine. To that extent, then, race, when coupled with the other factors Hicks relied upon, was a factor in the decision to approach and ultimately detain Weaver. We wish it were otherwise, but we take the facts as they are presented to us, not as we would like them to be. (394)

Chief Judge Arnold dissented:

> When public officials begin to regard large groups of citizens as presumptively criminal, this country is in a perilous situation indeed. Airports are on the verge of becoming war zones, where anyone is liable to be stopped, questioned, and even searched merely on the basis of the on-the-spot exercise of discretion by police officers.
>
> It's hard to work up much sympathy for Weaver. He's getting what he deserves, in a sense. What is missing here, though, is an awareness that law enforcement is a broad concept. It includes enforcement of the Bill of Rights, as well as enforcement of criminal statutes. Cases in which innocent travelers are stopped and impeded in their lawful activities don't come to court. They go on their way, too busy to bring a lawsuit against the officious agents who have detained them. (397)

ETHICAL ISSUES

Is It Ethical to Stop and Frisk More Innocent Black and Hispanic Men than White Men?

Just Take Away Their Guns?

The most effective way to reduce illegal gun carrying is to encourage the police to take guns away from people who carry them without a permit. This means encouraging the police to make street frisks. . . . Innocent people will be stopped. Young Black and Hispanic men will probably be stopped more often than older White Anglo males of any race. But we must get illegal guns off the street.

Wilson 1994, 46

You've learned that "stops and frisks" are reasonable under the Fourth Amendment. And we can all agree that guns can be dangerous when not owned and operated properly. But what about the ethics of what the distinguished political scientist James Q. Wilson proposes?

INSTRUCTIONS

1. Visit the Companion Website and read James Q. Wilson's full article, "Just Take Away Their Guns." Then, answer the questions that follow. (The links for all three articles referred to

here appear under the Chapter 4 Ethical Issues section of the Companion Website—login at www.cengagebrain.com.)

   a.   List Wilson's recommendations.

   b.   List his arguments to support them.

2.   Read "Racial Disparity in NYPD Stops-and-Frisks" (Center for Constitutional Rights 2009). List the major findings and recommendations of the center.

3.   For a modified assessment of the data and findings of the New York Center for Constitutional Rights, read the RAND Corporation's "Do NYPD's Pedestrian Stop Data Indicate Racial Bias?" List the major findings and recommendations of the RAND Research Brief.

4.   Explain your conclusions about race and stop and frisk based on these readings.

Profiles

LO 5

Profiles consist of lists of circumstances that might, or might not, be linked to particular kinds of behavior. Profiles have been popular law enforcement tools since the 1970s when the government introduced an airline hijacker profile.

In this section, we'll focus on **drug courier profiles**, lists of characteristics that drug traffickers are supposed to possess. Drug Enforcement Administration (DEA) Agent Paul Markonni developed the drug courier profile in 1974 while he was assigned to the Detroit DEA office and trained other agents in its use. Since then, it's become a "nationwide law enforcement tool." Officers stationed at airports observe travelers, looking for seven primary and four secondary characteristics (Table 4.6; *U.S. v. Elmore* 1979, 1039, n. 3).

If their suspicions are aroused, agents approach travelers, identify themselves, seek their consent to be questioned, and ask to see their identification and ticket. If this doesn't remove their suspicion, the agents ask travelers to come with them to another location, usually a room used by law enforcement officers. Once inside the room, agents ask travelers to consent to searches of their persons and luggage. If travelers refuse, agents either have to let them go or "seize" them (Cloud 1985, 848–49).

Since the introduction of the airport drug courier profile, law enforcement has introduced a number of other profiles: for illegal aliens entering the United States, international drug smugglers, customers of suspected domestic drug dealers, and highway drug couriers.

The Supreme Court, in *Reid v. Georgia* (1980), ruled that the drug courier profile *by itself* can't amount to reasonable suspicion. In *Reid*, a DEA agent suspected that Tommy Reid, Jr., possessed cocaine based on the DEA drug courier profile, "a somewhat informal compilation of characteristics typical of persons unlawfully carrying narcotics" (440).

The Georgia Court of Appeals held that the following elements of the profile were enough to satisfy the reasonable suspicion requirement.

1.   Reid had arrived from Fort Lauderdale, a principal place of origin of cocaine sold elsewhere in the country;

2.   Reid arrived in the early morning, when law enforcement activity is diminished;

TABLE 4.6

Primary and Secondary Characteristics of Drug Couriers

Primary Characteristics	Secondary Characteristics
• Arriving or departing from "source" cities	• Using public transportation when leaving airports
• Carrying little or no luggage, or empty suitcases	• Making telephone calls immediately after getting off the plane
• Traveling by an unusual itinerary	
• Using an alias	• Leaving false or fictitious callback numbers when leaving the plane
• Carrying unusually large amounts of cash	
• Purchasing tickets with large numbers of small bills	• Making excessively frequent trips to source or distribution cities
• Appearing unusually nervous	

3. Reid and his companion appeared to the agent to be trying to conceal the fact that they were traveling together, and

4. Reid and his companion apparently had no luggage other than their shoulder bags. (441–42)

The U.S. Supreme Court disagreed. The Court conceded that the agent's observing Reid looking back occasionally at his companion as they walked through the concourse "relates to their particular conduct." Nevertheless, the four elements in this profile listed "describe a very large category of presumably innocent travelers, who would be subject to virtually random seizures were the Court to conclude that as little foundation as there was in this case could justify a seizure." Therefore, the Court held, the profile by itself didn't add up to reasonable suspicion, and the possibility that Reid and his companion were trying to conceal that they were traveling together "is simply too slender a reed to support" Reid's stop (442).

What about the *characteristics* in the profiles that fit the individual defendant? Can officers use them as part of the totality-of-circumstances test amounting to reasonable suspicion? Yes, ruled the Supreme Court in the frequently cited *U.S. v. Sokolow* (1989).

DEA agents stopped Andrew Sokolow in Honolulu International Airport after his behavior indicated he might be a drug trafficker:

1. He'd paid $2,100 in cash for airline tickets..

2. He wasn't traveling under his own name.

3. His original destination was Miami.

4. He appeared nervous during the trip.

5. He checked none of his luggage. (3)

DEA agents arrested Sokolow and searched his luggage without a warrant. Later, at the DEA office, agents obtained warrants allowing more extensive searches, and they discovered 1,063 grams of cocaine. According to the Court, the agents had a reasonable suspicion that Sokolow "was engaged in wrongdoing." Just because some of that information is also part of a profile (probabilistic evidence) doesn't bar its use to build reasonable suspicion, as long as the "totality of the circumstances" adds up to reasonable suspicion (7–9).

The Scope of Reasonable Stops

LO 1

A brief freeze in time and in space—the scope of a reasonable stop has to include these two things. So there are two elements to the scope of a reasonable stop: short duration and on-the-spot location of the investigation. Let's look at each.

Short Duration

LO 1

According to the American Law Institute's (a group of distinguished prosecutors, defense lawyers, law enforcement officers, and academics) *Model Code of Pre-Arraignment Procedure* (1975), there ought to be a bright-line rule controlling the length of stops. Section 110.2 provides that law enforcement officers can stop a person "for such period as is reasonably necessary, but in no case for more than twenty minutes" to "obtain or verify" the stopped person's identification; to "obtain or verify an account of such person's presence or conduct"; or to determine whether to arrest the person.

The U.S. Supreme Court has so far declined to adopt this rule (*U.S. v. Sharpe and Savage* 1985). Why? Because the Court prefers to keep its options open and to give officers plenty of room for discretionary decision making. That way neither the Court nor officers are confined to a bright-line rule that may hamper crime control.

"On the Spot" Investigation

LO 1

Before *Terry v. Ohio* (1968), whenever a law enforcement officer moved a suspect to another place, it was an "arrest," requiring probable cause to back it up. For example, a court in one case ruled that taking the suspect to a police call box less than a block away was an arrest (*U.S. v. Mitchell* 1959). But today officers are allowed some leeway. According to search and seizure expert, Professor Wayne R. LaFave (2004), often quoted in criminal procedure cases, "*some* movement of the suspect in the *vicinity* of the stop is permissible without converting what would otherwise be a . . . [stop] into an arrest" (4:348). Recall that Officer McFadden moved Terry, Chilton, and Katz into the nearest store, and the Court didn't question this move.

Questioning Stopped Suspects

LO 7

During the brief, on-the-spot freeze, what can officers do to find further information that will lead either to arrest or release? Most often, officers ask the suspect questions. Lies, or statements "that are incriminating, implausible, conflicting, evasive or unresponsive," can lead to a longer, more invasive arrest (LaFave and others 2009, 179). Knowing a suspect's identity can clear suspects and allow both officers and suspects to get back to their business by leading to their quick release. This is the purpose of the **"stop-and-identify" statutes** in 21 states that allow officers to ask for suspects' names and identification.

Refusal to answer can lead to arrest and prosecution for failure to produce identification when a law enforcement asks for it. That's what happened to Larry Hiibel when he refused to identify himself to Humboldt County, Nevada, Deputy Sheriff Lee Dove in our next case excerpt, *Hiibel v. Sixth Judicial District Court of Nevada, Humboldt County et al.* (2004).

In Hiibel v. Sixth Judicial District Court of Nevada, Humboldt County et al. *(2004), the U.S. Supreme Court affirmed the Nevada Supreme Court's decision, supporting that state's "stop and identify" statute.*

 **CASE** Is the "Stop and Identify" Law Reasonable?

Hiibel v. Sixth Judicial Court of Nevada, Humboldt County et al.

542 U.S. 177 (2004)

KENNEDY, J., delivered the opinion of the Court, in which REHNQUIST, C.J., and O'CONNOR, SCALIA, and THOMAS, JJ., joined. STEVENS, J., filed a dissenting opinion. BREYER, J., filed a dissenting opinion, in which SOUTER and GINSBURG, JJ., joined.

FACTS

The sheriff's department in Humboldt County, Nevada, received an afternoon telephone call reporting an assault. The caller reported seeing a man assault a woman in a red and silver GMC truck on Grass Valley Road. Deputy Sheriff Lee Dove was dispatched to investigate. When the officer arrived at the scene, he found the truck parked on the side of the road. A man was standing by the truck, and a young woman was sitting inside it. The officer observed skid marks in the gravel behind the vehicle, leading him to believe it had come to a sudden stop.

The officer approached the man and explained that he was investigating a report of a fight. The man appeared to be intoxicated. The officer asked him if he had "any identification on him," which we understand as a request to produce a driver's license or some other form of written identification. The man refused and asked why the officer wanted to see identification. The officer responded that he was conducting an investigation and needed to see some identification. The unidentified man became agitated and insisted he had done nothing wrong. The officer explained that he wanted to find out who the man was and what he was doing there.

After continued refusals to comply with the officer's request for identification, the man began to taunt the officer by placing his hands behind his back and telling the officer to arrest him and take him to jail. This routine kept up for several minutes: The officer asked for identification 11 times and was refused each time. After warning the man that he would be arrested if he continued to refuse to comply, the officer placed him under arrest.

We now know that the man arrested on Grass Valley Road is Larry Dudley Hiibel. Hiibel was charged with "willfully resisting, delaying or obstructing a public officer in discharging or attempting to discharge any legal duty of his office" in violation of Nev.Rev.Stat. (NRS) § 199.280 (2003). The government reasoned that Hiibel had obstructed the officer in carrying out his duties under § 171.123, a Nevada statute that defines the legal rights and duties of a police officer in the context of an investigative stop. Section 171.123 provides in relevant part:

"1. Any peace officer may detain any person whom the officer encounters under circumstances which reasonably indicate that the person has committed, is committing or is about to commit a crime. . . .
3. The officer may detain the person pursuant to this section only to ascertain his identity and the suspicious circumstances surrounding his presence abroad. Any person so detained shall identify himself, but may not be compelled to answer any other inquiry of any peace officer."

Hiibel was tried in the Justice Court of Union Township. Hiibel was convicted and fined $250.

OPINION

NRS § 171.123(3) is an enactment sometimes referred to as a "stop and identify" statute. The statutes vary from State to State, but all permit an officer to ask or require a suspect to disclose his identity. Stop and identify statutes have their roots in early English vagrancy laws that required suspected vagrants to face arrest unless they gave "a good Account of themselves," a power that itself reflected common-law rights of private persons to "arrest any suspicious night-walker, and detain him till he give a good account of himself." In recent decades, the Court has found constitutional infirmity in traditional vagrancy laws.

The Court has recognized similar constitutional limitations on the scope and operation of stop and identify statutes. In *Brown v. Texas* (1979), the Court invalidated a conviction for violating a Texas stop and identify statute on Fourth Amendment grounds. The Court ruled that the initial stop was not based on specific, objective facts establishing reasonable suspicion to believe the suspect was involved in criminal activity. Absent that factual basis for detaining the defendant, the Court held, the risk of "arbitrary and abusive police practices" was too great and the stop was impermissible.

Here there is no question that the initial stop was based on reasonable suspicion, satisfying the Fourth Amendment requirements noted in *Brown*. Furthermore, the Nevada Supreme Court has interpreted NRS § 171.123(3) to require only that a suspect disclose his name. "The suspect is not required to provide private details about his background, but merely to state his name to an officer when reasonable suspicion exists." As we understand it, the statute does not require a suspect to give the officer a driver's license or any other document. Provided that the suspect either states his name or communicates it to the officer by other means—a choice, we assume, that the suspect may make—the statute is satisfied and no violation occurs.

Hiibel argues that his conviction cannot stand because the officer's conduct violated his Fourth Amendment rights. We disagree. Our decisions make clear that questions concerning a suspect's identity are a routine and accepted part of many *Terry* stops. Obtaining a suspect's name in the course of a *Terry* stop serves important government interests. Knowledge of identity may inform an officer that a suspect is wanted for another offense, or has a record of violence or mental disorder. On the other hand, knowing identity may help clear a suspect and allow the police to concentrate their efforts elsewhere. Identity may prove particularly important in cases such as this, where the police are investigating what appears to be a domestic assault. Officers called to investigate domestic disputes need to know whom they are dealing with in order to assess the situation, the threat to their own safety, and possible danger to the potential victim.

Although it is well established that an officer may ask a suspect to identify himself in the course of a *Terry* stop, it has been an open question whether the suspect can be arrested and prosecuted for refusal to answer. The principles of *Terry* permit a State to require a suspect to disclose his name in the course of a *Terry* stop. The reasonableness of a seizure under the Fourth Amendment is determined "by balancing its intrusion on the individual's Fourth Amendment interests against its promotion of legitimate government interests." The Nevada statute satisfies that standard. The request for identity has an immediate relation to the purpose, rationale, and practical demands of a *Terry* stop.

The threat of criminal sanction helps ensure that the request for identity does not become a legal nullity. On the other hand, the Nevada statute does not alter the nature of the stop itself: it does not change its duration, or its location. A state law requiring a suspect to disclose his name in the course of a valid *Terry* stop is consistent with Fourth Amendment prohibitions against unreasonable searches and seizures.

The judgment of the Nevada Supreme Court is AFFIRMED.

DISSENT

Justice BREYER, with whom Justice SOUTER and Justice GINSBURG join, dissenting.

This Court's Fourth Amendment precedents make clear that police may conduct a *Terry* stop only within circumscribed limits. And one of those limits invalidates laws that compel responses to police questioning. In *Terry v. Ohio* (1968), Justice White, in a concurring opinion, wrote: "Of course, the person stopped is not obliged to answer, answers may not be compelled, and refusal to answer furnishes no basis for an arrest, although it may alert the officer to the need for continued observation."

There is no good reason now to reject this generation-old statement of the law. There are sound reasons rooted in Fifth Amendment considerations for adhering to this Fourth Amendment legal condition circumscribing police authority to stop an individual against his will. Administrative considerations also militate against change. Can a State, in addition to requiring a stopped individual to answer "What's your name?" also require an answer to "What's your license number?" or "Where do you live?" Can a police officer, who must know how to make a *Terry* stop, keep track of the constitutional answers? After all, answers to any of these questions may, or may not, incriminate, depending upon the circumstances.

Indeed, as the Court points out, a name itself—even if it is not "Killer Bill" or "Rough 'em up Harry"—will sometimes provide the police with "a link in the chain of evidence needed to convict the individual of a separate offense." The majority reserves judgment about whether compulsion is permissible in such instances. How then is a police officer in the midst of a *Terry* stop to distinguish between the majority's ordinary case and this special case where the majority reserves judgment?

The majority presents no evidence that the rule enunciated by Justice White, which for nearly a generation has set forth a settled *Terry* stop condition, has significantly interfered with law enforcement. Nor has the majority presented any other convincing justification for change. I would not begin to erode a clear rule with special exceptions.

I consequently dissent.

QUESTIONS

1. State the elements of the Nevada "stop and identify" statute.
2. List all the facts relevant to deciding whether the stop-and-identify law is "reasonable."
3. Summarize the majority opinion's argument supporting its holding that the statute meets the constitutional requirement of reasonableness.
4. Summarize the dissent's arguments that the statute doesn't meet the constitutional requirement of reasonableness.

||||||||||||||||||||||||||||||||||||||||||||||||||||||||||||||||||||||||||||||||||||||||||||||||||||||||||||||

Frisks and the Fourth Amendment

LO 4

You learned in *Terry v. Ohio* (1968, p. 89) that there are two elements that make a frisk a reasonable Fourth Amendment search:

1.   The officer has made a lawful Fourth Amendment stop *before* she frisks a suspect).

2.   The officer reasonably suspects that the stopped suspect is armed and dangerous.

3.   The search is limited to a once-over-lightly pat down to detect weapons only (not contraband or evidence).

Frisks are the least invasive searches; body-cavity searches stand at the other extreme (Chapter 7). However, to say that frisks are the least invasive doesn't mean they're not invasions of privacy at all. After all, even a slight touch, when it's not wanted, can be highly offensive, not to mention the crime of battery. So it's not surprising that, since *Terry*, the U.S. Supreme Court has never wavered from calling frisks Fourth Amendment searches.

Whether a frisk is reasonable depends on balancing the government's interest in protecting law enforcement officers against the individual's privacy right not to be touched by an officer. The basic idea is that we shouldn't expect police officers to risk their lives unnecessarily to investigate suspicious persons and circumstances. At the same time, we have to obey the Fourth Amendment command to keep people "secure in their persons" against unreasonable searches.

Let's turn from the important question of balancing to the answers to two other critical questions regarding frisks: (1) What's reasonable suspicion to frisk? and (2) What's the scope of lawful frisks? (See Table 4.7 for the elements of lawful frisks.)

Reasonable Suspicion to Back Up Frisks

LO 2

Terry v. Ohio established that facts that back up a stop don't *automatically* also back up a frisk—with one major exception, when suspects are stopped for crimes of violence. The facts of *Terry* are an excellent example of the **violent crime–automatic-frisk exception**. Officer McFadden reasonably suspected that Terry and Chilton might be about to commit armed robbery. If it was reasonable to suspect that they might be about to commit armed robbery, it was also reasonable to suspect they might use weapons to commit it. So it was reasonable to frisk Terry and his companions for weapons.

In nonviolent crimes, the rule is that the circumstances must add up to a reasonable suspicion that stopped suspects may be armed. In practice, however, police frequently are told to assume that "every person encountered may be armed" (LaFave 2004, 624). Lower courts take the position that the power to frisk in a wide variety of situations and circumstances is automatic, including robbery, burglary, rape, assault with weapons, and dealing in large quantities of illegal drugs (625–26). Other offenses require specific facts suggesting suspects are armed. Table 4.7 lists some of the offenses courts have held don't justify automatic frisks.

Table 4.8 lists some of the many circumstances that courts have ruled justify frisks in crimes that don't qualify for automatic frisks.

Some critics claim that the lower courts have weakened the reasonable suspicion requirement so much that, in practice, the power to frisk is left almost entirely to law enforcement officers' discretion. In other words, the power to frisk, in practice, requires

TABLE 4.7

Examples of Circumstances That Don't Justify Automatic Frisks

• Trafficking in small amounts of illegal drugs	• Passing bad checks
• Possession of marijuana	• Underage drinking
• Illegal possession of alcohol	• Driving under the influence
• Prostitution	• Minor assault without a weapon
• Bookmaking	• Curfew violation
• Shoplifting	• Vagrancy

Source: LaFave 2004, 626–27.

TABLE 4.8

Circumstances That Justify Frisks

• Sudden inexplicable movement toward a pocket	• Awareness of suspect's previous serious criminal conduct
• Inexplicable failure to remove a hand from a pocket	• Awareness suspect had been armed previously
• Awkward movement in an apparent effort to conceal something	• Awareness of suspect's recent aggressive behavior
• Backing away from an officer	• Discovery suspect possessed another weapon
• Bulge in clothing	• Discovery suspect is wearing a bulletproof vest

Source: LaFave 2004, 628–30.

no separate reasonable suspicion that suspects may be armed and dangerous. Instead, it follows automatically from the lawful stop.

According to Professor David Harris (1998), one of the leading critics of the automatic power to frisk, the lower courts have "consistently expanded" the number of "dangerous" offenses that justify a frisk.

> When confronted with these offenses, police may *automatically* frisk, whether or not any individualized circumstances point to danger. Soon, *anyone* stopped by police may have to undergo a physical search at the officer's discretion, however benign the circumstances of the encounter or the conduct of the "suspect." (5)

The Scope of Reasonable Frisks

The same day the Supreme Court decided *Terry v. Ohio*, it decided *Sibron v. New York* (1968), another important but less-publicized case. In *Sibron*, the Court emphatically rejected New York's argument that after a lawful stop an automatic frisk for evidence and contraband was lawful. Why? Because, according to the Court, frisks are so intrusive that only the enormous interest in saving officers from "armed and dangerous" suspects who might wound or kill them justifies the invasion of a frisk during the brief "freeze" of a stop to investigate suspicious people and circumstances.

No matter how compelling the government's interest in protecting officers from armed and dangerous suspects is, they're allowed to use only the amount of bodily contact necessary to detect weapons. In most cases, this means officers may lightly

TABLE 4.9
Examples That Justify a Frisk beyond an Outer-Clothing Pat Down

- Feeling a hard object inside a coat pocket that could be a weapon authorizes reaching inside the coat.
- Encountering unusually bulky winter clothing may require feeling underneath the outer clothing.
- Suspecting the contents of a closed handbag might be illegal can justify opening the handbag.

touch suspects' outer clothing to locate and seize concealed weapons. Courts are vague about how much further police officers may lawfully go. Table 4.9 cites examples of when it may be permissible for officers to go further than pat downs of outer clothing.

In *Minnesota v. Dickerson*, our next case excerpt, the U.S. Supreme Court held that a Minneapolis police officer went too far when during a lawful frisk for weapons he rolled around a lump between his fingers to determine whether it was a rock of crack cocaine. But the Court made it clear that it's not *always* unreasonable to seize evidence and contraband during a frisk. Suppose an officer is patting down a suspect who was stopped lawfully and is reasonably suspected of being armed. She pats down the suspect and comes upon marijuana. Can she seize it? Yes, as long as the frisk for weapons isn't a pretext for looking for marijuana.

In Minnesota v. Dickerson, *the U.S. Supreme Court held that the discovery of crack cocaine on Timothy Dickerson took place within the lawful scope of a frisk.*

CASE   Was the Discovery of Crack Cocaine within the Lawful Scope of the Frisk?

Minnesota v. Dickerson
508 U.S. 366 (1993)

HISTORY

After the Hennepin County District Court in Minnesota denied his motion to suppress the seizure of crack cocaine, Timothy Dickerson, Respondent, was convicted of possession of crack cocaine and sentenced to two years probation. He appealed. The Minnesota Court of Appeals reversed. The State appealed. The Minnesota Supreme Court affirmed. The U.S. Supreme Court granted the State's petition for certiorari, and affirmed the Minnesota Supreme Court.

WHITE, J.

FACTS

On the evening of November 9, 1989, two Minneapolis police officers were patrolling an area on the city's north side in a marked squad car. At about 8:15 P.M., one of the officers observed Timothy Dickerson (respondent) leaving a 12-unit apartment building on Morgan Avenue North. The officer, having previously responded to complaints of drug sales in the building's hallways and having executed several search warrants on the premises, considered the building to be a notorious "crack house."

According to testimony credited by the trial court, respondent began walking toward the police but, upon spotting the squad car and making eye contact with one of the officers, abruptly halted and began walking in the opposite direction. His suspicion aroused, this officer watched as respondent turned and entered an alley on the other side of the apartment building. Based upon respondent's seemingly evasive actions and the fact that he had just left a building known for cocaine traffic, the officers decided to stop respondent and investigate further.

The officers pulled their squad car into the alley and ordered respondent to stop and submit to a patdown search. The search revealed no weapons, but the officer conducting the search did take an interest in a small lump in respondent's nylon jacket. The officer later testified:

> As I pat-searched the front of his body, I felt a lump, a small lump, in the front pocket. I examined it with my fingers and it slid and it felt to be a lump of crack cocaine in cellophane.

The officer then reached into respondent's pocket and retrieved a small plastic bag containing one fifth of one gram of crack cocaine. Respondent was arrested and charged in Hennepin County District Court with possession of a controlled substance.

Before trial, respondent moved to suppress the cocaine. The trial court first concluded that the officers were justified under *Terry v. Ohio* (1968), in stopping respondent to investigate whether he might be engaged in criminal activity. The court further found that the officers were justified in frisking respondent to ensure that he was not carrying a weapon. His suppression motion having failed, respondent proceeded to trial and was found guilty. On appeal, the Minnesota Court of Appeals reversed [CAC] [because] the officers had overstepped the bounds allowed by *Terry* in seizing the cocaine. In doing so, the Court of Appeals "declined to adopt the plain feel exception" to the warrant requirement.

The Minnesota Supreme Court affirmed. The court expressly refused "to extend the plain view doctrine to the sense of touch" on the grounds that "the sense of touch is inherently less immediate and less reliable than the sense of sight" and that "the sense of touch is far more intrusive into the personal privacy that is at the core of the Fourth Amendment." The court further noted that "even if we recognized a 'plain feel' exception, the search in this case would not qualify" because "the pat search of the defendant went far beyond what is permissible under *Terry*." As the State Supreme Court read the record, the officer conducting the search ascertained that the lump in respondent's jacket was contraband only after probing and investigating what he certainly knew was not a weapon.

We granted certiorari to resolve a conflict among the state and federal courts over whether contraband detected through the sense of touch during a patdown search may be admitted into evidence. We now AFFIRM.

OPINION

The Minnesota Supreme Court, after "a close examination of the record," held that the officer's own testimony "belies any notion that he 'immediately'" recognized the lump as crack cocaine. Rather, the court concluded, the officer determined that the lump was contraband only after "squeezing, sliding and otherwise manipulating the contents of the defendant's pocket"—a pocket which the officer already knew contained no weapon.

Under the State Supreme Court's interpretation of the record before it, it is clear that the court was correct in holding that the police officer in this case overstepped the bounds of the "strictly circumscribed" search for weapons allowed under *Terry*. Here, the officer's continued exploration of respondent's pocket after having concluded that it contained no weapon was unrelated to "the sole justification of the search under *Terry*: the protection of the police officer and others nearby." It therefore amounted to the sort of evidentiary search that *Terry* expressly refused to authorize, and that we have condemned in subsequent cases.

In *Arizona v. Hicks*, this Court held invalid the seizure of stolen stereo equipment found by police while executing a valid search for other evidence. Although the police were lawfully on the premises, they obtained probable cause to believe that the stereo equipment was contraband only after moving the equipment to permit officers to read its serial numbers. The subsequent seizure of the equipment could not be justified by the plain-view doctrine, this Court explained, because the incriminating character of the stereo equipment was not immediately apparent; rather, probable cause to believe that the equipment was stolen arose only as a result of a further search—the moving of the equipment—that was not authorized by a search warrant or by any exception to the warrant requirement.

The facts of this case are very similar. Although the officer was lawfully in a position to feel the lump in respondent's pocket, because *Terry* entitled him to place his hands upon respondent's jacket, the court below determined that the incriminating character of the object was not immediately apparent to him. Rather, the officer determined that the item was contraband only after conducting a further search, one not authorized by *Terry* or by any other exception to the warrant requirement. Because this further search of respondent's pocket was constitutionally invalid, the seizure of the cocaine that followed is likewise unconstitutional.

For these reasons, the judgment of the Minnesota Supreme Court is AFFIRMED.

CONCURRING OPINION

SCALIA, J.

I take it to be a fundamental principle of constitutional adjudication that the terms in the Constitution must be given the meaning ascribed to them at the time of their ratification. Thus, when the Fourth Amendment provides that "the right of the people to be secure in their persons, houses, papers, and effects, against *unreasonable searches and seizures,* shall not be violated" [emphasis added by Justice Scalia], it is to be construed in the light of what was deemed an unreasonable search and seizure when it was adopted. The purpose of the provision, in other words, is to preserve that degree of respect for the privacy of persons and the inviolability of their property that existed when the provision was adopted—even if a later, less virtuous age should become accustomed to considering all sorts of intrusion "reasonable."

My problem with the present case is that I am not entirely sure that the physical search—the "frisk"—that produced the evidence at issue here complied with that constitutional standard. I am unaware of any precedent for a physical search of a person temporarily detained for questioning. I frankly doubt, moreover, whether the fiercely proud men who adopted our Fourth Amendment would have allowed themselves to be subjected, on mere *suspicion* of being armed and dangerous, to such indignity—which is described as follows in a police manual:

> Check the subject's neck and collar. A check should be made under the subject's arm. Next a check should be made of the upper back. The lower back should also be checked.

A check should be made of the upper part of the man's chest and the lower region around the stomach. The belt, a favorite concealment spot, should be checked. The inside thigh and crotch area also should be searched. The legs should be checked for possible weapons. The last items to be checked are the shoes and cuffs of the subject.

QUESTIONS

1. Describe exactly the frisk of Dickerson conducted by the Minneapolis police officer.
2. State the test the U.S. Supreme Court applied to determine whether the frisk was within the scope of a lawful frisk.
3. Summarize Justice White's reasons for deciding the frisk exceeded its lawful scope.
4. Summarize Justice Scalia's reasons for agreeing with the Court's conclusion that the scope of the frisk was unreasonable.
5. In your opinion, should the frisk be considered reasonable?
6. Even if the frisk exceeded the permissible scope, should it be legal to seize the crack?

||||||||||||||||||||||||||||||||||||||||||||||||||||||||||||||||||||||||||||||||||||||||||||||||||||||||||||||||||||||||||||||||||||||||||

Special Situation Stops and Frisks

LO 7

In this last section, we'll look at the power of officers to freeze special situations briefly to check out their suspicions that a crime "may be afoot." These special situations include (1) traffic stops and frisks, (2) international borders, and (3) checkpoints and roadblocks.

Traffic Stops and Frisks

LO 6, LO 7

A multi-volume legal tome could be written on the topic, "The Constitution at Roadside." Few Terms of the Supreme Court pass without at least one case testing how the Constitution—usually, the Fourth Amendment—applies when police officers pull over a car or truck for a traffic stop. Among the multitude of factors that may influence the outcome is whether the constitutional complaint is by the driver or the passengers, whether the situation involves people inside the vehicle or outside of it, whether the stop was brief or lengthy, whether the stopped individuals did or did not feel free to leave, whether they cooperated or seemed to resist police inquiry, whether any suspicious items turn up in the officer's plain sight or after some kind of search, whether the suspicious items were located in the passenger compartment in the trunk, whether officers did or did not fear for their safety, or the safety of passersby, whether the occupants consent to a search, or not.

The Court, in analyzing such variables, usually focuses on the specific array of factual circumstances, but sometimes it tries to craft what it calls "bright-line rules" that are easy for police to follow and for the public to understand. That goal is quite elusive, because peculiar factual details often make all the difference, suggesting new exceptions or qualifications of previously written rules. (*Arizona v. Johnson* 2009)

If there's one theme that runs through the power to stop and frisk during police encounters with people in vehicles, it's officer safety. The idea runs deep in American culture that policing is dangerous work, and that idea clearly extends to traffic stops (Lichtenberg and Smith 2001, 419). This is true, even though empirical research suggests that *routine* traffic stops aren't as dangerous as many, including courts, believe.

Illya Lichtenberg and Alisa Smith set out to find out just how dangerous routine traffic stops are. They estimated the ratio of officers assaulted and killed over a 10-year period and the number of traffic stops over the same period. They found the ratio could be as "high" as one officer killed for every 10 million stops or as "low" as one officer killed for every 30 million. They also found that the stop-to-assault ratio ranged from a "high" of one police officer for every 8,274 stops to a low of one for every 13,847 stops (424–25). Furthermore, they found that "no data exist to support the proposition that greater intrusions of citizen privacy rights will ensure greater safety to police officers" (420).

Whatever the "real" danger, courts are extremely reluctant to limit or second-guess officers' decisions during vehicle stops. This extends even to "judicially legislating" that power by means of creating "bright-line" rules that attempt to limit or remove second-guessing. So what happens if an officer lawfully stops a vehicle but lacks reason to suspect the people in the stopped vehicle are armed? Is she banned from taking any action to protect herself? No.

We'll look at two situations where the U.S. Supreme Court has created bright-line rules to protect officers during vehicle stops: (1) ordering people in stopped vehicles to get out of the vehicles and (2) frisking people in stopped vehicles.

Ordering Drivers and Passengers to Get Out of Stopped Vehicles

LO 7

In *Pennsylvania v. Mimms* (1977), the Supreme Court created the bright-line rule that when an officer lawfully stops a vehicle, without any reason to suspect the driver is armed, the officer can *always* demand that the driver get out of the car to reduce "the possibility, otherwise substantial that the driver can make unobserved movements" (111). The Court concluded that removing the driver from the car is a "trivial invasion" because the driver is stopped already. Balancing the possible danger to the officer clearly outweighs the trivial invasion of removing the driver from the car.

But is it a trivial invasion to order *passengers* (who officers don't suspect of any wrongdoing) out of the car while officers sort out their suspicions of the driver? And is it lawful to frisk *passengers* in lawfully stopped vehicles? Yes, the U.S. Supreme Court answered to both questions, and both decisions were influenced heavily by the concern for officer safety.

This isn't surprising when we consider that in the cases the Court reviews, guns and/or drugs were found and seized, especially when frisks follow the stops (Allen and others 2005, 577). The Court doesn't hear, and we don't often read about, innocent people stopped in vehicles. Still, both the majority and dissents rely on numbers to support, or challenge, the true level of danger vehicle stops present to officers. This was true in our next case excerpt, *Maryland v. Wilson* (1997).

In Maryland v. Wilson, *the U.S. Supreme
Court held that* Pennsylvania v. Mimms
*applies to passengers in stopped vehicles, too.
Therefore, officers making a traffic stop may
order passengers to get out of the car pending
completion of the stop.*

CASE Was the Order to Get Out of the Car Reasonable?

Maryland v. Wilson
519 U.S. 408 (1997)

HISTORY

Jerry Lee Wilson, Respondent, moved to suppress crack cocaine seized by a police officer during a traffic stop. The trial court granted the motion. The State appealed. The Maryland Court of Special Appeals affirmed, ruling that *Pennsylvania v. Mimms* does not apply to passengers. The Maryland Court of Appeals denied certiorari. The U.S. Supreme Court granted certiorari and reversed and remanded the case.

REHNQUIST, C.J., joined by O'CONNOR, SCALIA, SOUTER, THOMAS, GINSBURG, and BREYER, JJ.

FACTS

At about 7:30 P.M. on a June evening, Maryland state trooper David Hughes observed a passenger car driving southbound on I-95 in Baltimore County at a speed of 64 miles per hour. The posted speed limit was 55 miles per hour, and the car had no regular license tag; there was a torn piece of paper reading "Enterprise Rent-A-Car" dangling from its rear. Hughes activated his lights and sirens, signaling the car to pull over, but it continued driving for another mile and a half until it finally did so.

During the pursuit, Hughes noticed there were three occupants in the car and that the two passengers turned to look at him several times, repeatedly ducking below sight level and then reappearing. As Hughes approached the car on foot, the driver alighted and met him halfway. The driver was trembling and appeared extremely nervous, but nonetheless produced a valid Connecticut driver's license.

Hughes instructed him to return to the car and retrieve the rental documents, and he complied. During this encounter, Hughes noticed that the front-seat passenger, Jerry Lee Wilson (the respondent), was sweating and also appeared extremely nervous. While the driver was sitting in the driver's seat looking for the rental papers, Hughes ordered Wilson out of the car. When Wilson exited the car, a quantity of crack cocaine fell to the ground.

OPINION

In *Mimms*, we considered a traffic stop much like the one before us today. There, Mimms had been stopped for driving with an expired license plate, and the officer asked him to step out of his car. When Mimms did so, the officer noticed a bulge in his jacket that proved to be a .38-caliber revolver, whereupon Mimms was arrested for carrying a concealed deadly weapon.

Mimms, like Wilson, urged the suppression of the evidence on the ground that the officer's ordering him out of the car was an unreasonable seizure, and the Pennsylvania Supreme Court, like the Court of Special Appeals of Maryland, agreed. We reversed, explaining that the touchstone of our analysis under the Fourth Amendment is always the reasonableness in all the circumstances of the particular governmental invasion of a citizen's personal security, and that reasonableness depends on a balance between the public interest and the individual's right to personal security free from arbitrary interference by law officers.

On the public interest side of the balance, we noted that the State "freely conceded" that there had been nothing unusual or suspicious to justify ordering Mimms out of the car, but that it was the officer's practice to order all drivers [CAC][stopped in traffic stops] out of their vehicles as a matter of course as a precautionary measure to protect the officer's safety. We thought it too plain for argument that this justification—officer safety—was both legitimate and weighty. In addition, we observed that the danger to the officer of standing by the driver's door and in the path of oncoming traffic might also be "appreciable."

On the other side of the balance, we considered the intrusion into the driver's liberty occasioned by the officer's ordering him out of the car. Noting that the driver's car was already validly stopped for a traffic infraction, we deemed the additional intrusion of asking him to step outside his car "de minimis" [trivial]. Accordingly, we concluded that once a motor vehicle has been lawfully detained for a traffic violation, the police officers may order the driver to get out of the vehicle without violating the Fourth Amendment's proscription of unreasonable seizures.

Wilson urges, and the lower courts agreed, that this *per se* rule does not apply to Wilson because he was a passenger, not the driver. We must therefore now decide whether the rule of *Mimms* applies to passengers as well as to drivers. On the public interest side of the balance, the same weighty interest in officer safety is present regardless of whether the occupant of the stopped car is a driver or passenger. Regrettably, traffic stops may be dangerous encounters. In 1994 alone, there were 5,762 officer assaults and 11 officers killed during traffic pursuits and stops. *Federal Bureau of Investigation, Uniform Crime Reports: Law Enforcement Officers Killed and Assaulted* 71, 33 (1994).

In the case of passengers, the danger of the officer's standing in the path of oncoming traffic would not be present except in the case of a passenger in the left rear seat, but the fact that there is more than one occupant of the vehicle increases the possible sources of harm to the officer.

On the personal liberty side of the balance, the case for the passengers is in one sense stronger than that for the driver. There is probable cause to believe that the driver has committed a minor vehicular offense, but there is no such reason to stop or detain the passengers. But as a practical matter, the passengers are already stopped by virtue of the stop of the vehicle. The only change in their circumstances which will result from ordering them out of the car is that they will be outside of, rather than inside of, the stopped car.

Outside the car, the passengers will be denied access to any possible weapon that might be concealed in the interior of the passenger compartment. It would seem that the possibility of a violent encounter stems not from the ordinary reaction of a motorist stopped for a speeding violation, but from the fact that evidence of a more serious crime might be uncovered during the stop. And the motivation of a passenger to employ violence to prevent apprehension of such a crime is every bit as great as that of the driver.

In summary, danger to an officer from a traffic stop is likely to be greater when there are passengers in addition to the driver in the stopped car. While there is not the same basis for ordering the passengers out of the car as there is for ordering the driver out, the additional intrusion on the passenger is minimal. We therefore hold that an officer making a traffic stop may order passengers to get out of the car pending completion of the stop.

The judgment of the Court of Special Appeals of Maryland is REVERSED, and the case is REMANDED for proceedings not inconsistent with this opinion. It is so ordered.

DISSENT

STEVENS, J., joined by KENNEDY, J.

My concern is not with the ultimate disposition of this particular case, but rather with the literally millions of other cases that will be affected by the rule the Court announces. Though the question is not before us, I am satisfied that—under the rationale of *Terry v. Ohio*—if a police officer conducting a traffic stop has an articulable suspicion of possible danger, the officer may order passengers to exit the vehicle as a defensive tactic without running afoul of the Fourth Amendment.

Accordingly, I assume that the facts recited in the majority's opinion provided a valid justification for this officer's order commanding the passengers to get out of this vehicle. But the Court's ruling goes much farther. It applies equally to traffic stops in which there is not even a scintilla of evidence of any potential risk to the police officer. In those cases, I firmly believe that the Fourth Amendment prohibits routine and arbitrary seizures of obviously innocent citizens.

The majority suggests that the personal liberty interest at stake here is outweighed by the need to ensure officer safety. The Court correctly observes that "traffic stops may be dangerous encounters." The magnitude of the danger to police officers is reflected in the statistic that, in 1994 alone, "there were 5,762 officer assaults and 11 officers killed during traffic pursuits and stops." There is, unquestionably, a strong public interest in minimizing the number of such assaults and fatalities. The Court's statistics, however, provide no support for the conclusion that its ruling will have any such effect.

Those statistics do not tell us how many of the incidents involved passengers. Assuming that many of the assaults were committed by passengers, we do not know how many occurred after the passenger got out of the vehicle, how many took place while the passenger remained in the vehicle, or indeed, whether any of them could have been prevented by an order commanding the passengers to exit.

There is no indication that the number of assaults was smaller in jurisdictions where officers may order passengers to exit the vehicle without any suspicion than in jurisdictions where they were then prohibited from doing so.

Indeed, there is no indication that any of the assaults occurred when there was a complete absence of any articulable basis for concern about the officer's safety—the only condition under which I would hold that the Fourth Amendment prohibits an order commanding passengers to exit a vehicle. In short, the statistics are as consistent with the hypothesis that ordering passengers to get out of a vehicle increases the danger of assault as with the hypothesis that it reduces that risk.

Furthermore, any limited additional risk to police officers must be weighed against the unnecessary invasion that will be imposed on innocent citizens under the majority's rule in the tremendous number of routine stops that occur each day. We have long recognized that because of the extensive regulation of motor vehicles and traffic the extent of police–citizen contact involving automobiles will be substantially greater than police–citizen contact in a home or office.

Most traffic stops involve otherwise law abiding citizens who have committed minor traffic offenses. A strong interest in arriving at a destination—to deliver a patient to a hospital, to witness a kick-off, or to get to work on time—will often explain a traffic violation without justifying it. In the aggregate, these stops amount to significant law enforcement activity.

Indeed, the number of stops in which an officer is actually at risk is dwarfed by the far greater number of routine stops. If Maryland's share of the national total is about average, the State probably experiences about 100 officer assaults each year during traffic stops and pursuits. Making the unlikely assumption that passengers are responsible for one-fourth of the total assaults, it appears that the Court's new rule would provide a potential benefit to Maryland officers in only roughly 25 stops a year. These stops represent a minuscule portion of the total. In Maryland alone, there are something on the order of one million traffic stops each year. Assuming that there are passengers in about half of the cars stopped, the majority's rule is of some possible advantage to police in only about one out of every twenty thousand traffic stops in which there is a passenger in the car. And, any benefit is extremely marginal. In the overwhelming majority of cases posing a real threat, the officer would almost certainly have some ground to suspect danger that would justify ordering passengers out of the car.

In contrast, the potential daily burden on thousands of innocent citizens is obvious. That burden may well be "minimal" in individual cases. But countless citizens who cherish individual liberty and are offended, embarrassed, and sometimes provoked by arbitrary official commands may well consider the burden to be significant. In all events, the aggregation of thousands upon thousands of petty indignities has an impact on freedom that I would characterize as substantial, and which in my view clearly outweighs the evanescent safety concerns pressed by the majority.

To order passengers about during the course of a traffic stop, insisting that they exit and remain outside the car, can hardly be classified as a trivial intrusion. The traffic violation sufficiently justifies subjecting the driver to detention and some police control for the time necessary to conclude the business of the stop. The restraint on the liberty of blameless passengers that the majority permits is, in contrast, entirely arbitrary.

In my view, wholly innocent passengers in a taxi, bus, or private car have a constitutionally protected right to decide whether to remain comfortably seated within the vehicle rather than exposing themselves to the elements and the observation of curious bystanders. The Constitution should not be read to permit law enforcement officers to order innocent passengers about simply because they have the misfortune to be seated in a car whose driver has committed a minor traffic offense.

Unfortunately, the effect of the Court's new rule on the law may turn out to be far more significant than its immediate impact on individual liberty. Throughout most of our history the Fourth Amendment embodied a general rule requiring that official searches and seizures be authorized by a warrant, issued "upon probable cause, supported by Oath or affirmation, and particularly describing the place to be searched, and the persons or things to be seized." During the prohibition era, the exceptions for warrantless searches supported by probable cause started to replace the general rule.

In 1968, in the landmark "stop and frisk" case *Terry v. Ohio*, the Court placed its stamp of approval on seizures supported by specific and articulable facts that did not establish probable cause. The Court crafted *Terry* as a narrow exception to the general rule that the police must, whenever practicable, obtain advance judicial approval of searches and seizures through the warrant procedure. The intended scope of the Court's major departure from prior practice was reflected in its statement that the "demand for specificity in the information upon which police action is predicated is the central teaching of this Court's Fourth Amendment jurisprudence."

In the 1970s, the Court twice rejected attempts to justify suspicionless seizures that caused only "modest" intrusions on the liberty of passengers in automobiles. Today, however, the Court takes the unprecedented step of authorizing seizures that are unsupported by any individualized suspicion whatsoever.

The Court's conclusion seems to rest on the assumption that the constitutional protection against "unreasonable" seizures requires nothing more than a hypothetically rational basis for intrusions on individual liberty. How far this ground-breaking decision will take us, I do not venture to predict. I fear, however, that it may pose a more serious threat to individual liberty than the Court realizes.

I respectfully DISSENT.

KENNEDY, J.

Traffic stops, even for minor violations, can take upwards of 30 minutes. When an officer commands passengers innocent of any violation to leave the vehicle and stand by the side of the road in full view of the public, the seizure is serious, not trivial. As Justice Stevens concludes, the command to exit ought not to be given unless there are objective circumstances making it reasonable for the officer to issue the order. (We do not have before us the separate question whether passengers, who, after all are in the car by choice, can be ordered to remain there for a reasonable time while the police conduct their business.)

Coupled with *Whren v. U.S.* [excerpted in Chapter 6] the Court puts tens of millions of passengers at risk of arbitrary control by the police. If the command to exit were to become commonplace, the Constitution would be diminished in a most public way. As the standards suggested in dissent are adequate to protect the safety of the police, we ought not to suffer so great a loss.

Most officers, it might be said, will exercise their new power with discretion and restraint; and no doubt this often will be the case. It might also be said that if some jurisdictions use today's ruling to require passengers to exit as a matter of routine in every stop, citizen complaints and political intervention will call for an end to the practice.

These arguments, however, would miss the point. Liberty comes not from officials by grace but from the Constitution by right. For these reasons, and with all respect for the opinion of the Court, I DISSENT.

QUESTIONS

1. List the specific invasions Jerry Lee Wilson experienced after the vehicle he was a passenger in was stopped.
2. Identify the government's interest that was furthered by ordering Wilson out of the car.
3. In your opinion, did the government's interest outweigh the degree of invasion against Wilson? In your answer, consider both the majority and dissenting opinions.
4. State specifically the objective basis for ordering Wilson out of the car.
5. State the Court's bright-line rule governing officers' power to order passengers out of cars they've stopped.
6. Summarize the arguments the majority gave to back up its bright-line rule.
7. Describe the empirical evidence the majority's opinion was based on. In view of the dissenting justices' criticism of the statistics, how much weight do they carry in your opinion?
8. How do the dissenting justices answer the majority's arguments in (7)? Which side has the better arguments? Defend your answer.
9. During oral arguments before the U.S. Supreme Court, Justice Scalia asked the Maryland attorney general:

   Can you tell me why we—I resent being put in the position of deciding this case on speculation. . . . You're telling us that it will increase police safety if we adopt this automatic rule. None of the briefs—and there's a brief here by 20 States or so—make any attempt to compare the assaults on police in the States that have the rule you're urging us to adopt and the States that don't have that rule, and that's the crucial question. We know we're going to inconvenience citizens to some extent. We don't know whether we're going to increase police safety. Why—aren't those statistics available? Why doesn't somebody come and say, this is the proof of what we're saying?

   If that's so, why do you think Justice Scalia voted with the majority? Should he have? How important do you believe this lack of empirical research should be?

Frisking People in Stopped Vehicles

LO 1, LO 4, LO 5, LO 7

What can officers do to protect themselves once they've got the drivers and/or passengers outside vehicles stopped for traffic violations? Can they order them to raise their hands above their heads until the summons is completed? Question them about possible weapons possession? Can they frisk them?

The Court demonstrated its continued deference to officers in our next case excerpt, *Arizona v. Johnson* (2009). The Court struck the balance in favor of officers' safety when it ruled that Officer Maria Trevizo and two detectives lawfully frisked Lemon Montrea Johnson, a passenger in a lawfully stopped vehicle. This was even though the officers didn't suspect Johnson of any crime, but they did suspect that he might be armed and dangerous.

In Arizona v. Johnson, our next case excerpt, the U.S. Supreme Court found that it was lawful to frisk a passenger in a lawfully stopped vehicle, even if he was not suspected of committing a crime.

Case Was the Frisk of a Passenger after He Received a Traffic Citation "Reasonable"?

Arizona v. Johnson
129 S.Ct. 781 (2009)

HISTORY

Lemon Montrea Johnson was charged in state court with possession of a weapon by a prohibited possessor. He moved to suppress the evidence as the fruit of an unlawful search. The trial court denied the motion, concluding that the stop was lawful and that Trevizo had cause to suspect Johnson was armed and dangerous. A jury convicted Johnson of the gun-possession charge, and sentenced him to 8 years in prison. A divided panel of the Arizona Court of Appeals reversed Johnson's conviction. The Arizona Supreme Court denied review. We granted certiorari, and now reverse the judgment of the Arizona Court of Appeals.

GINSBURG, J., delivered the opinion for a unanimous Court.

FACTS

On April 19, 2002, Officer Maria Trevizo and Detectives Machado and Gittings, all members of Arizona's gang task force, were on patrol in Tucson near a neighborhood associated with the Crips gang. At approximately 9 P.M., the officers pulled over an automobile after a license plate check revealed that the vehicle's registration had been suspended for an insurance-related violation. Under Arizona law, the violation for which the vehicle was stopped constituted a civil infraction warranting a citation. At the time of the stop, the vehicle had three occupants—the driver, a front-seat passenger, and a passenger in the back seat, Lemon Montrea Johnson, the respondent here. In making the stop the officers had no reason to suspect anyone in the vehicle of criminal activity.

The three officers left their patrol car and approached the stopped vehicle. Machado instructed all of the occupants to keep their hands visible. He asked whether there were any weapons in the vehicle; all responded no. Machado then directed the driver to get out of the car. Gittings dealt with the front-seat passenger, who stayed in the vehicle throughout the stop. While Machado was getting the driver's license and information about the vehicle's registration and insurance, Trevizo attended to Johnson.

Trevizo noticed that, as the police approached, Johnson looked back and kept his eyes on the officers. When she drew near, she observed that Johnson was wearing clothing, including a blue bandana, that she considered consistent with Crips membership. She also noticed a scanner in Johnson's jacket pocket, which "struck [her] as highly unusual and cause [for] concern," because "most people" would not carry around a scanner that way "unless they're going to be involved in some kind of criminal activity or [are] going to try to evade the police by listening to the scanner." In response to Trevizo's questions, Johnson provided his name and date of birth but said he had no identification with him. He volunteered that he was from Eloy, Arizona, a place Trevizo knew was home to a Crips gang. Johnson further told Trevizo that he had served time in prison for burglary and had been out for about a year.

Trevizo wanted to question Johnson away from the front-seat passenger to gain "intelligence about the gang [Johnson] might be in." For that reason, she asked him to get out of the car. Johnson complied. Based on Trevizo's observations and Johnson's answers to her questions while he was still seated in the car, Trevizo suspected that "he might have a weapon on him." When he exited the vehicle, she therefore "patted him down for officer safety." During the patdown, Trevizo felt the butt of a gun near Johnson's waist. At that point Johnson began to struggle, and Trevizo placed him in handcuffs.

OPINION

Terry v. Ohio established that when a stop is justified by suspicion that criminal activity is afoot, the police officer must be positioned to act instantly on reasonable suspicion that the persons temporarily detained are armed and dangerous. Recognizing that a limited search of outer clothing for weapons serves to protect both the officer and the public, the Court held the patdown reasonable under the Fourth Amendment. This Court has recognized that traffic stops are especially fraught with danger to police officers.

The risk of harm to both the police and the occupants of a stopped vehicle is minimized, we have stressed, if the officers routinely exercise unquestioned command of the situation. (*Maryland v. Wilson*, 1997) *Wilson* held that an officer making a traffic stop may order passengers to get out of the car pending completion of the stop.

The same weighty interest in officer safety, the Court observed, is present regardless of whether the occupant of the stopped car is a driver or passenger. The Court emphasized, the risk of a violent encounter in a traffic-stop setting stems not from the ordinary reaction of a motorist stopped for a speeding violation, but from the fact that evidence of a more serious crime might be uncovered during the stop. The motivation of a passenger to employ violence to prevent apprehension of such a crime, the Court stated, is every bit as great as that of the driver. Moreover, the Court noted, as a practical matter, the passengers are already stopped by virtue of the stop of the vehicle, so the additional intrusion on the passenger is minimal.

Completing the picture, officers who conduct routine traffic stops may perform a patdown of a driver and any passengers upon reasonable suspicion that they may be armed and dangerous.

A lawful roadside stop begins when a vehicle is pulled over for investigation of a traffic violation. The temporary seizure of driver and passengers ordinarily continues, and remains reasonable, for the duration of the stop. Normally, the stop ends when the police have no further need to control the scene, and inform the driver and passengers they are free to leave. An officer's inquiries into matters unrelated to the justification for the traffic stop, this Court has made plain, do not convert the encounter into something other than a lawful seizure, so long as those inquiries do not measurably extend the duration of the stop.

In sum, a traffic stop of a car communicates to a reasonable passenger that he or she is not free to terminate the encounter with the police and move about at will. Nothing occurred in this case that would have conveyed to Johnson that, prior to the frisk, the traffic stop had ended or that he was otherwise free "to depart without police permission." Officer Trevizo surely was not constitutionally required to give Johnson an opportunity to depart the scene after he exited the vehicle without first ensuring that, in so doing, she was not permitting a dangerous person to get behind her.

For the reasons stated, the judgment of the Arizona Court of Appeals is REVERSED, and the case is REMANDED for further proceedings not inconsistent with this opinion.

It is so ordered.

QUESTIONS

1. **List all the facts and circumstances relevant to deciding whether the frisk was reasonable.**
2. **Summarize the Court's arguments for deciding that Officer Maria Trevizo's frisk of Lemon Johnson was reasonable.**
3. **The Arizona Court of Appeals recognized that, initially, Johnson was lawfully detained incident to the legitimate stop of the vehicle in which he was a passenger. But, that court concluded, once Officer Trevizo undertook to question Johnson on a matter unrelated to the traffic stop (i.e., Johnson's gang affiliation), pat-down authority ceased to exist, absent reasonable suspicion that Johnson had engaged, or was about to engage, in criminal activity. Why would all justices disagree with the Arizona court's ruling? Does the Arizona court have a point?**

Detentions at International Borders

LO 7

The strong government interest in controlling who and what comes into the United States substantially reduces the liberty and privacy rights of individuals at the Mexican and Canadian land boundaries, at the seaports along the East and West Coasts, and at all airports on flights coming from foreign countries. Routine detentions don't require reasonable suspicion to back up lengthy detentions or frisks. This includes examining purses, wallets, and pockets (*Henderson v. U.S.* 1967) and up-close dog sniffs (*U.S. v. Kelly* 2002).

The strong government interest extends to many kinds of people and to many things that demand preventive measures, but here we'll use as our example preventing illegal drug smuggling. Specifically, we'll look at the difficulty that balloon swallowers create for law enforcement. (We'll take up preventing terrorist attacks and apprehending terrorist suspects in Chapter 15.) These are smugglers who bring illegal drugs into the country hidden in their alimentary canal or vaginas.

The U.S. Supreme Court upheld a 16-hour detention of Rosa Elvira Montoya de Hernandez, a suspected "balloon swallower," in close confinement under constant surveillance and a strip search at Los Angeles International Airport in *U.S. v. Montoya de Hernandez* (1985).

In U.S. vs. Montoya de Hernandez (1985), our next case excerpt, the U.S. Supreme Court found that an extended detention of Colombian national Rosa Elvira Montoya de Hernandez to determine whether she was a balloon swallower was a reasonable stop.

CASE   Is the 16-Hour Detention of a Suspected "Balloon-Swallower" a Reasonable Stop?

U.S. v. Montoya de Hernandez
473 U.S. 531 (1985)

HISTORY

Rosa Elvira Montoya de Hernandez was charged with narcotics violations. She moved to suppress the narcotics. The U.S. District Court denied the motion and admitted the cocaine in evidence. Montoya de Hernandez was convicted of possessing cocaine with intent to distribute and unlawful importation of cocaine. A divided U.S. Court of Appeals for the 9th Circuit reversed the conviction. The government appealed to the U.S. Supreme Court. The Supreme Court reversed.

REHNQUIST, J., joined by BURGER, C.J., and WHITE, BLACKMUN, POWELL, and O'CONNOR, JJ.

FACTS

Montoya de Hernandez arrived at Los Angeles International Airport shortly after midnight, March 5, 1983, on Avianca Flight 080, a direct 10-hour flight from Bogotá, Colombia. Her visa was in order so she was passed through Immigration and proceeded to the customs desk. At the customs desk she encountered Customs Inspector Talamantes, who reviewed her documents and noticed from her passport that she had made at least eight recent trips to either Miami or Los Angeles.

Talamantes referred respondent to a secondary customs desk for further questioning. At this desk Talamantes and another inspector asked Montoya de Hernandez general questions concerning herself and the purpose of her trip. Montoya de Hernandez revealed that she spoke no English and had no family or friends in the United States. She explained in Spanish that she had come to the United States to purchase goods for her husband's store in Bogotá.

The customs inspectors recognized Bogotá as a "source city" for narcotics. Montoya de Hernandez possessed $5,000 in cash, mostly $50 bills, but had no billfold. She indicated to the inspectors that she had no appointments with merchandise vendors, but planned to ride around Los Angeles in taxicabs visiting retail stores such as J.C. Penney and K-Mart in order to buy goods for her husband's store with the $5,000.

Montoya de Hernandez admitted she had no hotel reservations, but said she planned to stay at a Holiday Inn. Montoya de Hernandez could not recall how her airline ticket was purchased. When the inspectors opened Montoya de Hernandez's one small valise they found about four changes of "cold weather" clothing. Montoya de Hernandez had no shoes other than the high-heeled pair she was wearing. Although Montoya de Hernandez possessed no checks, waybills, credit cards, or letters of credit, she did produce a Colombian business card and a number of old receipts, waybills, and fabric swatches displayed in a photo album. At this point Talamantes and the other inspector suspected that Montoya de Hernandez was a "balloon swallower," one who attempts to smuggle narcotics into this country hidden in her alimentary canal. Over the years Inspector Talamantes had apprehended dozens of alimentary canal smugglers arriving on Avianca Flight 080.

The inspectors requested a female customs inspector to take Montoya de Hernandez to a private area and conduct a pat down and strip search. During the search the female inspector felt Montoya de Hernandez's abdomen area and noticed a firm fullness, as if Montoya de Hernandez were wearing a girdle. The search revealed no contraband, but the inspector noticed that Montoya de Hernandez was wearing two pairs of elastic underpants with a paper towel lining the crotch area.

When Montoya de Hernandez returned to the customs area and the female inspector reported her discoveries, the inspector in charge told Montoya de Hernandez that he suspected she was smuggling drugs in her alimentary canal. . . . The inspector then gave Montoya de Hernandez the option of returning to Colombia on the next available flight, agreeing to an x-ray, or remaining in detention until she produced a monitored bowel movement that would confirm or rebut the inspectors' suspicions.

Montoya de Hernandez chose the first option and was placed in a customs office under observation. She was told that if she went to the toilet she would have to use a wastebasket in the women's restroom, in order that female inspectors could inspect her stool for balloons or capsules carrying narcotics. The inspectors refused Montoya de Hernandez's request to place a telephone call.

Montoya de Hernandez sat in the customs office, under observation, for the remainder of the night. She remained detained in the customs office under observation, for most of the time curled up in a chair leaning to one side. She refused all offers of food and drink, and refused to use the toilet facilities. The Court of Appeals noted that she exhibited symptoms of discomfort with "heroic efforts to resist the usual calls of nature."

At the shift change at 4:00 the next afternoon, almost 16 hours after her flight had landed, Montoya de Hernandez still had not defecated or urinated or partaken of food or drink. At that time customs officials sought a court order authorizing an x-ray, and a rectal examination. The Federal Magistrate issued an order just before midnight that evening, which authorized a rectal examination and involuntary x-ray. A physician conducted a rectal examination and removed from Montoya de Hernandez's rectum a balloon containing a foreign substance. Montoya de Hernandez was then placed formally under arrest. By 4:10 A.M. Montoya de Hernandez had passed 6 similar balloons; over the next four days she passed 88 balloons containing a total of 528 grams of 80% pure cocaine hydrochloride.

After a suppression hearing, the District Court admitted the cocaine in evidence against Montoya de Hernandez. She was convicted of possession of cocaine with intent to distribute and unlawful importation of cocaine. A divided panel of the United States Court of Appeals for the Ninth Circuit reversed Montoya de Hernandez's convictions.

OPINION

The Fourth Amendment commands that searches and seizures be reasonable. What is reasonable depends upon all of the circumstances surrounding the search or seizure itself. The permissibility of a particular law enforcement practice is judged by "balancing its intrusion on the individual's Fourth Amendment interest against its promotion of legitimate governmental interests."

Here the seizure of Montoya de Hernandez took place at the international border. Since the founding of our Republic, Congress has granted the Executive plenary authority to conduct routine searches and seizures at the border, without probable cause or a warrant, in order to regulate the collection of duties and to prevent the introduction of contraband into this country. The Fourth Amendment's balance of reasonableness is qualitatively different at the international border than in the interior. Routine searches of the persons and effects of entrants are not subject to any requirement of reasonable suspicion, probable cause, or warrant, and first-class mail may be opened without a warrant on less than probable cause.

These cases reflect long-standing concern for the protection of the integrity of the border. This concern is, if anything, heightened by the veritable national crisis in law enforcement caused by smuggling of illicit narcotics and in particular by the increasing utilization of alimentary canal smuggling. This desperate practice appears to be a relatively recent addition to the smugglers' repertoire of deceptive practices, and it also appears to be exceedingly difficult to detect.

Balanced against the sovereign's interests at the border are the Fourth Amendment rights of Montoya de Hernandez. Having presented herself at the border for admission, and having subjected herself to the criminal enforcement powers of the Federal Government she was entitled to be free from unreasonable search and seizure.

But not only is this expectation of privacy less at the border than in the interior the Fourth Amendment balance between the interests of the Government and the privacy right of the individual is also struck much more favorably to the Government at the border.

We have not previously decided what level of suspicion would justify a seizure of an incoming traveler for purposes other than a routine border search. The Court of Appeals viewed "clear indication" as an intermediate standard between "reasonable suspicion" and "probable cause." No other court, including this one, has ever adopted "clear indication" language as a Fourth Amendment standard. We do not think that the Fourth Amendment's emphasis upon reasonableness is consistent with the creation of a third verbal standard in addition to "reasonable suspicion" and "probable cause."

We hold that detention of a traveler at the border, beyond the scope of a routine customs search and inspection, is justified at its inception if customs agents, considering all the facts surrounding the traveler and her trip, reasonably suspect that the traveler is smuggling contraband in her alimentary canal. The facts, and their rational inferences, known to customs inspectors in this case clearly supported a reasonable suspicion that Montoya de Hernandez was an alimentary canal smuggler.

The trained customs inspectors had encountered many alimentary canal smugglers and certainly had more than an inchoate and unparticularized suspicion or hunch, that Montoya de Hernandez was smuggling narcotics in her alimentary canal. The inspectors' suspicion was a common-sense conclusion about human behavior upon which practical people, including government officials, are entitled to rely.

The final issue in this case is whether the detention of Montoya de Hernandez was reasonably related in scope to the circumstances which justified it initially. In this regard we have cautioned that courts should not indulge in unrealistic second-guessing, and we have noted that creative judges, engaged in after the fact evaluations of police conduct can almost always imagine some alternative means by which the objectives of the police might have been accomplished.

The rudimentary knowledge of the human body which judges possess in common with the rest of humankind tells us that alimentary canal smuggling cannot be detected in the amount of time in which other illegal activity may be investigated through brief *Terry*-type stops. It presents few, if any external signs; a quick frisk will not do, nor will even a strip search.

In the case of Montoya de Hernandez, the inspectors had available, as an alternative to simply awaiting her bowel movement, an x-ray. They offered her the alternative of submitting herself to that procedure. But when she refused that alternative, the customs inspectors were left with only two practical alternatives: detain her for such a time as necessary to confirm their suspicions, a detention which would last much longer than the typical *Terry* stop, or turn her loose into the interior carrying the reasonably suspected contraband drugs.

The inspectors in this case followed this former procedure. They no doubt expected that Montoya de Hernandez, having recently disembarked from a 10-hour direct flight with a full and stiff abdomen, would produce a bowel movement without extended delay. But her visible efforts to resist the call of nature, which the court below labeled "heroic," disappointed this expectation and in turn caused her humiliation and discomfort.

Our prior cases have refused to charge police with delays in investigatory detention attributable to the suspect's evasive actions. Montoya de Hernandez alone was responsible for much of the duration and discomfort of the seizure. Under these circumstances, we conclude that the detention was not unreasonably long. It occurred at the international border, where the Fourth Amendment balance of interests leans heavily to the Government. Montoya de Hernandez's detention was long, uncomfortable indeed, humiliating; but both its length and its discomfort resulted solely from the method by which she chose to smuggle illicit drugs into this country.

REVERSED

CONCURRING OPINION

STEVENS, J.

If a seizure and search of the person of the kind disclosed by this record may be made on the basis of reasonable suspicion, we must assume that a significant number of innocent persons will be required to undergo similar procedures. The rule announced in this case cannot, therefore, be supported on the ground that Montoya de Hernandez's

prolonged and humiliating detention "resulted solely from the method by which she chose to smuggle illicit drugs into this country."

The prolonged detention of Montoya de Hernandez was, however, justified by a different choice that Montoya de Hernandez made; she withdrew her consent to an x-ray examination that would have easily determined whether the reasonable suspicion that she was concealing contraband was justified.

DISSENT

BRENNAN, J., joined by MARSHALL, J.

We confront a "disgusting and saddening episode" at our Nation's border. "That Montoya de Hernandez so degraded herself as to offend the sensibilities of any decent citizen is not questioned." That is not what we face. For "it is a fair summary of history to say that the safeguards of liberty have frequently been forged in controversies involving not very nice people." . . .

The standards we fashion to govern the ferreting out of the guilty apply equally to the detention of the innocent, and "may be exercised by the most unfit and ruthless officers as well as by the fit and reasonable." Nor is the issue whether there is a "veritable national crisis in law enforcement caused by smuggling illicit narcotics." In our democracy such enforcement presupposes a moral atmosphere and a reliance upon intelligence whereby the effective administration of justice can be achieved with due regard for those civilized standards in the use of the criminal law which are formulated in our Bill of Rights.

The issue, instead, is simply this: Does the Fourth Amendment permit an international traveler, citizen or alien, to be subjected to the sort of treatment that occurred in this case without the sanction of a judicial officer and based on nothing more than the "reasonable suspicion" of low ranking investigative officers that something might be amiss? The Court today concludes that the Fourth Amendment grants such sweeping and unmonitored authority to customs officials. I dissent.

Indefinite involuntary incommunicado detentions "for investigation" are the hallmark of a police state, not a free society. In my opinion, Government officials may no more confine a person at the border under such circumstances for purposes of criminal investigation than they may within the interior of the country. The nature and duration of the detention here may well have been tolerable for spoiled meat or diseased animals, but not for human beings held on simple suspicion of criminal activity.

Finally, I believe that the warrant and probable cause safeguards equally govern Justice STEVENS' proffered alternative of exposure to x-irradiation for criminal investigative purposes. The available evidence suggests that the number of highly intrusive border searches of suspicious-looking but ultimately innocent travelers may be very high. One physician who at the request of customs officials conducted many "internal searches"—rectal and vaginal examinations and stomach pumping—estimated that he had found contraband in 15 to 20 percent of the persons he had examined. It has similarly been estimated that only 16 percent of women subjected to body cavity searches at the border were in fact found to be carrying contraband. It is precisely to minimize the risk of harassing so many innocent people that the Fourth Amendment requires the intervention of a judicial officer.

The Court argues, however, that the length and "discomfort" of de Hernandez' detention "resulted solely from the method by which she chose to smuggle illicit drugs into this country," and it speculates that only her "heroic" efforts prevented the detention from being brief and to the point. Although we now know that de Hernandez was indeed guilty of smuggling drugs internally, such after the fact rationalizations have no place in our Fourth Amendment jurisprudence, which demands that we prevent hindsight from coloring the evaluation of the reasonableness of a search or seizure. At the time the authorities simply had, at most, a reasonable suspicion that de Hernandez might be engaged in such smuggling.

Neither the law of the land nor the law of nature supports the notion that petty government officials can require people to excrete on command; indeed, the Court relies elsewhere on "the rudimentary knowledge of the human body" in sanctioning the "much longer than typical" duration of detentions such as this. And, with all respect to the Court, it is not "unrealistic second-guessing," to predict that an innocent traveler, locked away in incommunicado detention in unfamiliar surroundings in a foreign land, might well be frightened and exhausted as to be unable so to "cooperate" with the authorities.

It is tempting, of course, to look the other way in a case that so graphically illustrates the "veritable national crisis" caused by narcotics trafficking. But if there is one enduring lesson to be learned in the long struggle to balance individual rights against society's need to defend itself against lawlessness, it is that it is easy to make light of insistence on scrupulous regard for the safeguards of civil liberties when invoked on behalf of the unworthy. It is too easy. History bears testimony that by such disregard are the rights of liberty extinguished, heedlessly at first, then stealthily, and brazenly in the end.

QUESTIONS

1. Identify the government interests the invasions of Montoya de Hernandez's liberty and privacy were intended to protect.

2. Compare the duration, location, and subjective invasiveness of Montoya de Hernandez's detention with that of John Terry in *Terry v. Ohio*.

3. Assume, first, you're a prosecutor and, then, a defense lawyer. Relying on the facts and opinion in *Terry v. Ohio*, argue, first, that the detention and searches of Montoya de Hernandez pass the reasonableness test and, then, that they fail the reasonableness test. Make sure you include all of the elements of reasonableness we've discussed in this chapter.

4. Now, assume you're a judge. Based on your view of the law, write an opinion supporting your decision whether the government actions in this case were reasonable under the Fourth Amendment.

Roadblocks and Checkpoints

LO 7

Roadblocks—stopping everyone who passes a point on a road during a specific time period—create a special Fourth Amendment problem: Can law enforcement officers stop groups of drivers and passengers without individualized suspicion that any one of them might be up to criminal activity? A few years after *Terry v. Ohio*, the U.S. Supreme Court upheld a permanent roadblock in southern California to check for illegal Mexican immigrants. Why? They cited balancing interests—namely, the "the need to make routine checkpoint stops is great and the consequent intrusion on Fourth Amendment rights is quite limited (*U.S. v. Martinez-Fuerte* 1976; excerpted in Chapter 15).

Amid a lot of controversy, a number of states have created roadblocks to prevent drunk driving and apprehend and prosecute drunk drivers (Hickey and Axline 1992; Weiner and Royster 1991). Are DWI roadblocks unreasonable stops? As you might expect by this point in reading the book, in *Michigan v. Sitz* (1990), our next case excerpt, the U.S. Supreme Court answered, "It all depends. . . ."

In **Michigan v. Sitz** *(1990), the U.S. Supreme Court found that highway sobriety checkpoint programs are reasonable stops of citizens even when there's no individualized suspicion.*

CASE Was the DWI Roadblock an Unreasonable Seizure?

Michigan v. Sitz
496 U.S. 444 (1990)

HISTORY

Rick Sitz and other drivers (respondents) brought an action to challenge the constitutionality of a highway sobriety checkpoint program. The Circuit Court of Wayne County, Michigan, invalidated the program, and the Michigan Department of State Police (petitioners) appealed. The Court of Appeals of Michigan affirmed. The U.S. Supreme Court granted certiorari. The Supreme Court reversed and remanded the case.

REHNQUIST, C.J., joined by WHITE, O'CONNOR, SCALIA, and KENNEDY, JJ.

FACTS

The Michigan Department of State Police and its Director (petitioners) established a sobriety checkpoint pilot program in early 1986. Under the plan, checkpoints would be set up at selected sites along state roads. All vehicles passing through a checkpoint would be stopped and their drivers briefly examined for signs of intoxication. In cases where a checkpoint officer detected signs of intoxication, the motorist would be directed to a location out of the traffic flow where an officer would check the motorist's driver's license and car registration and, if warranted, conduct further sobriety tests. Should the field tests and the officer's observations suggest that the driver was intoxicated, an arrest would be made. All other drivers would be permitted to resume their journey immediately.

The first—and to date the only—sobriety checkpoint operated under the program was conducted in Saginaw County with the assistance of the Saginaw County Sheriff's Department. During the hour-and-fifteen-minute duration of the checkpoint's operation, 126 vehicles passed through the checkpoint. The average delay for each vehicle was approximately 25 seconds. Two drivers were detained for field sobriety testing, and one of the two was arrested for driving under the influence of alcohol. A third driver who drove through without stopping was pulled over by an officer in an observation vehicle and arrested for driving under the influence.

On the day before the operation of the Saginaw County checkpoint, Sitz and the other drivers (respondents) filed a complaint in the Circuit Court of Wayne County seeking declaratory and injunctive relief from potential subjection to the checkpoints. Sitz and each of the other drivers "is a licensed driver in the State of Michigan who regularly travels throughout the State in his automobile." During pretrial proceedings, the Michigan Department of State Police (petitioners) agreed to delay further implementation of the checkpoint program pending the outcome of this litigation.

After the trial, at which the court heard extensive testimony concerning the "effectiveness" of highway sobriety checkpoint programs, the court ruled that the Michigan program violated the Fourth Amendment and Art. 1, § 11, of the Michigan Constitution. On appeal, the Michigan Court of Appeals affirmed the holding that the program violated the Fourth Amendment and, for that reason, did not consider whether the program violated the Michigan Constitution. After the Michigan Supreme Court denied Department of State Police's application for leave to appeal, we granted certiorari.

To decide this case the trial court performed a balancing test derived from our opinion in *Brown v. Texas* (1979). As described by the Court of Appeals, the test involved "balancing the state's interest in preventing accidents caused by drunk drivers, the effectiveness of sobriety checkpoints in achieving that goal, and the level of intrusion on an individual's privacy caused by the checkpoints."

The Court of Appeals agreed that the Brown three-prong balancing test was the correct test to be used to determine the constitutionality of the sobriety checkpoint plan. As characterized by the Court of Appeals, the trial court's findings with respect to the balancing factors were that the State has a "grave and legitimate" interest in curbing drunken driving; that sobriety checkpoint programs are generally "ineffective" and, therefore, do not significantly further that interest; and that the checkpoints' "subjective intrusion" on individual liberties is substantial. According to the court, the record disclosed no basis for disturbing the trial court's findings, which were made within the context of an analytical framework prescribed by this Court for determining the constitutionality of seizures less intrusive than traditional arrests.

OPINION

The Department of State police (petitioners) concede, correctly in our view, that a Fourth Amendment "seizure" occurs when a vehicle is stopped at a checkpoint. The question thus becomes whether such seizures are "reasonable" under the Fourth Amendment. We address only the initial stop of each motorist passing through a checkpoint and the associated preliminary questioning and observation by checkpoint officers.

Detention of particular motorists for more extensive field sobriety testing may require satisfaction of an individualized suspicion standard. No one can seriously dispute the magnitude of the drunken driving problem or the States' interest in eradicating it. Drunk drivers cause an annual death toll of over 25,000 and in the same time span cause nearly one million personal injuries and more than five billion dollars in property damage. For decades, this Court has repeatedly lamented the tragedy. Conversely, the weight bearing on the other scale—the measure of the intrusion on motorists stopped briefly at sobriety checkpoints—is slight. The trial court and the Court of Appeals, thus, accurately gauged the "objective" intrusion, measured by the duration of the seizure and the intensity of the investigation, as minimal.

With respect to what it perceived to be the "subjective" intrusion on motorists, however, the Court of Appeals found such intrusion substantial. The court first affirmed the trial court's finding that the guidelines governing checkpoint operation minimize the discretion of the officers on the scene. But the court also agreed with the trial court's conclusion that the checkpoints have the potential to generate fear and surprise in motorists. This was so because the record failed to demonstrate that approaching motorists would be aware of their option to make U-turns or turnoffs to avoid the checkpoints. On that basis, the court deemed the subjective intrusion from the checkpoints unreasonable.

We believe the Michigan courts misread our cases concerning the degree of "subjective intrusion" and the potential for generating fear and surprise. The "fear and surprise" to be considered are not the natural fear of one who has been drinking over the prospect of being stopped at a sobriety checkpoint but, rather, the fear and surprise engendered in law-abiding motorists by the nature of the stop.

The Court of Appeals went on to consider as part of the balancing analysis of the "effectiveness" of the proposed checkpoint program. Based on extensive testimony in the trial record, the court concluded that the checkpoint program failed the "effectiveness" part of the test, and that this failure materially discounted petitioners' strong interest in implementing the program.

We think the Court of Appeals was wrong on this point as well. Experts in police science might disagree over which of several methods of apprehending drunken drivers is preferable as an ideal. But for purposes of Fourth Amendment analysis, the choice among such reasonable alternatives remains with the governmental officials who have a unique understanding of, and a responsibility for, limited public resources, including a finite number of police officers.

This case involves neither a complete absence of empirical data nor a challenge of random highway stops. During the operation of the Saginaw County checkpoint, the detention of each of the 126 vehicles that entered the checkpoint resulted in the arrest of two drunken drivers. Stated as a percentage, approximately 1.5 percent of the drivers passing through the checkpoint were arrested for alcohol impairment.

In addition, an expert witness testified at the trial that experience in other states demonstrated that, on the whole, sobriety checkpoints resulted in drunken driving arrests of around 1 percent of all motorists stopped.

In sum, the balance of the state's interest in preventing drunken driving, the extent to which this system can reasonably be said to advance that interest, and the degree of intrusion upon individual motorists who are briefly stopped, weighs in favor of the state program. We therefore hold that it is consistent with the Fourth Amendment. The judgment of the Michigan Court of Appeals is accordingly reversed, and the case is remanded for further proceedings not inconsistent with this opinion.

REVERSED.

DISSENT

BRENNAN, J., joined by MARSHALL, J.

Some level of individualized suspicion is a core component of the protection the Fourth Amendment provides against arbitrary government action. By holding that no level of suspicion is necessary before the police may stop a car for the purpose of preventing drunken driving, the Court potentially subjects the general public to arbitrary or harassing conduct by the police.

I do not dispute the immense social cost caused by drunken drivers, nor do I slight the government's efforts to prevent such tragic losses. Indeed, I would hazard a guess that today's opinion will be received favorably by a majority of our society, who would willingly suffer the minimal intrusion of a sobriety checkpoint stop in order to prevent drunken driving. But consensus that a particular law enforcement technique serves a laudable purpose has never been the touchstone of constitutional analysis.

The Fourth Amendment was designed not merely to protect against official intrusions whose social utility was less as measured by some "balancing test" than its intrusion on individual privacy; it was designed in addition to grant the individual a zone of privacy whose protections could be breached only where the "reasonable" requirements of the probable cause standard were met. Moved by whatever momentary evil has aroused their fears, officials—perhaps even supported by a majority of citizens—may be tempted to conduct searches that sacrifice the liberty of each citizen to assuage the perceived evil. But the Fourth Amendment rests on the principle that a true balance between the individual and society depends on the recognition of "the right to be let alone"—the most comprehensive of rights and the right most valued by civilized men.

In the face of the "momentary evil" of drunken driving, the Court today abdicates its role as the protector of that fundamental right. I respectfully DISSENT.

STEVENS, J., joined by BRENNAN and MARSHALL, JJ.

The record in this case makes clear that a decision holding these suspicionless seizures unconstitutional would not impede the law enforcement community's remarkable progress in reducing the death toll on our highways. Because the Michigan program was patterned after an older program in Maryland, the trial judge gave special attention to that state's experience. Over a period of several years, Maryland operated 125 checkpoints; of the 41,000 motorists passing through those checkpoints, only 143 persons (0.3%) were arrested. The number of man-hours devoted to these operations is not in the record, but it seems inconceivable that a higher arrest rate could not have been achieved by more conventional means.

Any relationship between sobriety checkpoints and an actual reduction in highway fatalities is even less substantial than the minimal impact on arrest rates. As the Michigan Court of Appeals pointed out, Maryland had conducted a study comparing traffic statistics between a county using checkpoints and a control county. The results of the study showed that alcohol-related accidents in the checkpoint county decreased by ten percent, whereas the control county saw an eleven percent decrease; and while fatal accidents in the control county fell from sixteen to three, fatal accidents in the checkpoint county actually doubled from the prior year.

In light of these considerations, it seems evident that the Court today . . . overvalues the law enforcement interest in using sobriety checkpoints [and] undervalues the citizen's interest in freedom from random, unannounced investigatory seizures.

A Michigan officer who questions a motorist at a sobriety checkpoint has virtually unlimited discretion to detain the driver on the basis of the slightest suspicion. A ruddy complexion, an unbuttoned shirt, bloodshot eyes or a speech impediment may suffice to prolong the detention.

Any driver who had just consumed a glass of beer, or even a sip of wine, would almost certainly have the burden of demonstrating to the officer that her driving ability was not impaired.

These fears are not, as the Court would have it, solely the lot of the guilty. To be law abiding is not necessarily to be spotless, and even the most virtuous can be unlucky. Unwanted attention from the local police need not be less discomforting simply because one's secrets are not the stuff of criminal prosecutions. Moreover, those who have found—by reason of prejudice or misfortune—that encounters with the police may become adversarial or unpleasant without good cause will have grounds for worrying at any stop designed to elicit signs of suspicious behavior. Being stopped by the police is distressing even when it should not be terrifying, and what begins mildly may by happenstance turn severe.

In my opinion, unannounced investigatory seizures are, particularly when they take place at night, the hallmark of regimes far different from ours; the surprise intrusion upon individual liberty is not minimal. On that issue, my difference with the Court may amount to nothing less than a difference in our respective evaluations of the importance of individual liberty, a serious albeit inevitable source of constitutional disagreement. On the degree to which the sobriety checkpoint seizures advance the public interest, however, the Court's position is wholly indefensible.

The evidence in this case indicates that sobriety checkpoints result in the arrest of a fraction of one percent of the drivers who are stopped, but there is absolutely no evidence that this figure represents an increase over the number of arrests that would have been made by using the same law enforcement resources in conventional patrols. Thus, although the gross number of arrests is more than zero, there is a complete failure of proof on the question whether the wholesale seizures have produced any net advance in the public interest in arresting intoxicated drivers.

The most disturbing aspect of the Court's decision today is that it appears to give no weight to the citizen's interest in freedom from suspicionless unannounced investigatory seizures. On the other hand, the Court places a heavy thumb on the law enforcement. Perhaps this tampering with the scales of justice can be explained by the Court's obvious concern about the slaughter on our highways, and a resultant tolerance for policies designed to alleviate the problem by "setting an example" of a few motorists. . . .

This is a case that is driven by nothing more than symbolic state action—an insufficient justification for an otherwise unreasonable program of random seizures. Unfortunately, the Court is transfixed by the wrong symbol—the illusory prospect of punishing countless intoxicated motorists—when it should keep its eyes on the road plainly marked by the Constitution.

I respectfully DISSENT.

QUESTIONS

1. According to the Court, why are DWI checkpoints Fourth Amendment seizures?
2. Why, according to the Court, are they reasonable seizures?
3. What interests does the Court balance in reaching its result?
4. What does Justice Stevens mean when he says that he and the majority disagree over the meaning of freedom?
5. What does he have to say about the need for and effectiveness of DWI checkpoints?
6. What does Justice Brennan mean when he says that the degree of the intrusion begins, not ends, the inquiry about whether DWI checkpoints are reasonable seizures?
7. How would you identify and balance the interests at stake in the DWI checkpoints? Are the checkpoints effective? Explain.
8. According to the American Civil Liberties Union (ACLU), "highly publicized local law enforcement efforts such as random roadblocks" are "Orwellian intrusions into individual privacy." What does the ACLU mean? Do you agree? Explain.

Summary

LO 1
- Fourth Amendment stops are brief detentions that allow officers to freeze suspicious people and situations briefly to investigate possible criminal activity. Fourth Amendment frisks are pat downs of outer clothing to protect officers from use of concealed weapons during stops.

LO 1, LO 2
- The Fourth Amendment consists of two parts: (1) the reasonableness clause that applies to all searches and (2) the warrant clause that applies only to searches and arrest warrants based on warrants.

LO 2
- Reasonableness consists of two elements, a balancing element and an objective basis requirement. Both are determined on a case-by-case evaluation of the totality of circumstances.

LO 4
- *Terry v. Ohio* established the framework for stop-and-frisk analysis that continues to the present: In the balance between crime control and individual freedom and privacy, in each case, the need to control crime has to outweigh the invasions against the individuals' rights. Second, officers can only stop and frisk suspects if they have reasonable suspicion.

LO 2, LO 3, LO 5
- Fourth Amendment stops are reasonable if the totality of circumstances (whole picture) leads officers to suspect recent or present criminal activity in the case at hand. The whole picture can include direct and/or hearsay information, individualized and/or categorical suspicion, and actuarial information. Race, ethnicity, fleeing from the police, and drug courier profiles can be part of, but not by themselves, the "whole picture" in establishing reasonable suspicion.

LO 5, LO 6
- Empirical social scientific research has clarified and challenged the accuracy and weight of some categorical suspicion types, such as "high crime area," and the danger to police officers making traffic stops.

LO 2
- Fourth Amendment stops are reasonable in scope if they're brief, on-the-spot detentions, during which officers may question stopped individuals to help them decide quickly whether to arrest or free them.

LO 2, LO 4
- Fourth Amendment frisks are reasonable if the government interest in protecting law enforcement officers outweighs the individual's privacy right not to be touched by an officer. The elements of a reasonable frisk include: (1) the officer lawfully

stops an individual *before* she frisks him; (2) the officer reasonably suspects that the person stopped is armed; *and* (3) the officer limits her action to a once-over-lightly pat down of the outer clothing to detect weapons only.

LO 4, LO 5, LO 7

- Special situation stops and frisks require reasonably balancing special interests. The hundreds of millions of traffic stops every year have to balance officer safety against driver and passenger liberty and privacy. International border detentions balance the interest in controlling who and what enters and leaves the country against the privacy and liberty interests of U.S. citizens and noncitizens. Roadblocks balance the interest in apprehending specific fleeing suspects against the privacy and liberty interests of innocent people stopped. Checkpoints balance the interest in preventing drunk driving against apprehending drunk drivers.

Review Questions

1. Trace the history behind the modern power of police to stop and question suspicious persons.

2. Explain the difference between Fourth Amendment stops and arrests.

3. Explain the difference between Fourth Amendment frisks and other searches.

4. Why do stops and frisks have a greater impact on opinions of police power than arrests and full searches?

5. What's the ratio of stops to arrests?

6. Identify four facts about the realities of stop and frisk.

7. Identify the three steps in the analysis used to decide whether stops and frisks are reasonable Fourth Amendment searches and seizures.

8. Identify the two parts of the Fourth Amendment that play a role (and the role they play) in the conventional and reasonableness approaches to determining whether searches and seizures are constitutional.

9. Identify the two elements of the Fourth Amendment reasonableness test.

10. Explain how the "totality of circumstances" test works in practice.

11. Describe the background and significance of *Terry v. Ohio*.

12. Identify three possible interpretations of the Fourth Amendment and which interpretation the Supreme Court has settled on.

13. Explain why Judge Juviler said that since the Supreme Court decided *Terry v. Ohio*, he and other lawyers feel "like the makers of the hydrogen bomb."

14. Identify three kinds of police-individual encounters.

15. Reasonable stops depend on two elements. Identify and describe each.

16. Identify four sources of hearsay information officers can rely on to build reasonable suspicion. Give an example of each.

17. Describe the findings of empirical research regarding the designation of a location as a "high crime area." Compare the findings with the decision in *Illinois v. Wardlow*.

18. Summarize the findings reported in Table 4.4, "Stops and Arrests, New York City Police Department (NYPD)" and Table 4.5, "Facts Supporting Reasonable Suspicion (NYPD)."

19. Can race be used in building reasonable suspicion? Explain.

20. What's the difference between individualized suspicion and a profile?

21. Identify seven primary characteristics and four secondary characteristics of drug couriers.

22. Identify the two necessary elements that define the scope of a reasonable stop.

23. Describe the extent to which officers may question suspects they stop. What are the constitutional consequences for those who refuse to answer officers' questions during a lawful stop?

24. Identify three elements of a lawful frisk.

25. What's reasonable suspicion to frisk?

26. What's the scope of a lawful frisk?

27. Why is it reasonable to remove passengers from a stopped vehicle even when there's no suspicion that they might be involved in a crime?

28. Why are individuals' liberty and privacy severely restricted at international borders?

29. Identify the legitimate purposes for roadblocks, and explain the objective basis that makes roadblocks reasonable Fourth Amendment seizures.

Key Terms

arrest, p. 84
Fourth Amendment stops, p. 84
Fourth Amendment frisks, p. 84
reasonableness clause, p. 86
warrant clause, p. 86
conventional Fourth Amendment approach, p. 87
reasonableness Fourth Amendment approach, p. 87
reasonableness test, p. 87
balancing element, p. 87
objective basis, p. 87
case-by-case basis, p. 88
"bright-line" rules, p. 88
articulable facts, p. 99

reasonable suspicion, p. 99
totality-of-facts-and-circumstances test, p. 99
whole picture test, p. 99
direct information, p. 99
hearsay information, p. 99
individualized suspicion, p. 100
categorical suspicion, p. 100
"high crime area," p. 101
profiles, p. 111
drug courier profile, p. 111
"stop-and-identify" statutes, p. 113
violent crime–automatic-frisk exception, p. 116
roadblocks, p. 131

5

CASES COVERED

Draper v. U.S., 358 U.S. 307 (1959)

Brigham City, Utah v. Charles Stuart, Shayne Taylor, and Sandra Taylor, 547 U.S. 398 (2006)

Tennessee v. Garner, 471 U.S. 1 (1985)

Graham v. Connor, 490 U.S. 386 (1989)

Kuha v. City of Minnetonka, 365 F.3d 590 (CA8 Minn., 2003)

Atwater v. City of Lago Vista, 532 U.S. 318 (2001)

LEARNING OBJECTIVES

1 Understand that arrests are a vital tool that can help law enforcement officers catch the guilty and free the innocent.

2 Appreciate that the noble end of crime control doesn't justify unreasonable arrests to attain that end.

3 Know that arrests are Fourth Amendment seizures but are more invasive than stops.

4 Know that the Fourth Amendment's reasonableness requirement requires both probable cause before and a reasonable execution during and after arrest.

5 Appreciate that the probable cause requirement balances the societal interest in crime control and the individual right to free movement.

6 Know that officers can use both direct information and hearsay to build probable cause.

7 Know that arrest warrants are required to enter homes to arrest except where the need to act immediately exists at the time of the arrest.

8 Know that officers can use only the amount of force that is necessary to get and maintain control of suspects they have probable cause to arrest.

9 Know that after an arrest, felony suspects usually are taken to the police station for booking, photographing, and possible interrogation and identification procedures; misdemeanor suspects usually are released.

10 Understand that it's constitutionally reasonable, but not necessarily wise, for officers to make full custodial arrests for fine-only offenses.

Seizure of Persons: Arrest

At about 10:45 P.M. Memphis Police Officers Elton Hymon and Leslie Wright were dispatched to answer a "prowler inside call." Upon arriving at the scene they saw a woman standing on her porch gesturing toward the adjacent house. She told them she had heard glass breaking and that "they" or "someone" was breaking in next door. While Wright radioed the dispatcher to say that they were on the scene, Hymon went behind the house. He heard a door slam and saw someone run across the backyard. The fleeing suspect, 15-year-old Edward Garner, stopped at a 6-feet-high chain link fence at the edge of the yard. With the aid of a flashlight, Hymon was able to see Garner's face and hands. He saw no sign of a weapon, and though not certain, was "reasonably sure" and "figured" that Garner was unarmed. He thought Garner was 17 or 18 years old and about 5'5" or 5'7" tall.

> **While Garner was crouched at the base of the fence, Hymon called out "police, halt" and took a few steps toward him. Garner began to climb over the fence. Convinced that if Garner made it over the fence he would elude capture, Hymon shot him. The bullet hit Garner in the back of the head. Garner was taken by ambulance to a hospital, where he died on the operating table. Ten dollars and a purse taken from the house were found on his body.**
>
> *Tennessee v. Garner (1985), U.S. Supreme Court*

LO 1, LO 2, LO 3, LO 4

Arrests are a vital tool that can help law enforcement officers catch the guilty and free the innocent, but they also have to meet the requirements of the U.S. Constitution. The noble end of crime control doesn't justify unreasonable arrests to attain that end. Arrests, like the *stops* you learned about in Chapter 4, are Fourth Amendment seizures. But they're more invasive than stops, and they require a higher objective basis to make them reasonable.

Arrests are more invasive than stops in several ways. First, the duration is longer. Stops are measured in minutes; arrests can last hours, sometimes even days. Second, the location differs. Stops begin and end on streets and in other public places with other people around; arrested people are taken to the isolated and intimidating surroundings of the local police department and jail where they're held against their will for hours, sometimes even days.

Third, most stops don't get "written up"; arrests produce written documents that become part of a person's record, or "rap sheet." Fourth, stops (unless accompanied by frisks) don't involve body searches. Full-body searches (usually) and strip and body-cavity searches (sometimes) accompany arrests (Chapter 6). Interrogations (Chapter 8) and lineups (Chapter 9) can also accompany arrests (Table 5.1).

Last, arrests can produce fear, anxiety, and loss of liberty. They can also cause loss of income and even the loss of a job. Furthermore, these losses don't just affect arrested suspects who turn out to be guilty; they also affect millions of innocent arrested people. And arrests embarrass and cause economic hardship to the families of both the innocent *and* the guilty people arrested. These embarrassments and hardships rarely accompany a Fourth Amendment stop.

These are the characteristics of **custodial arrests**, defined as an officer taking a person into custody and holding her to answer criminal charges. But considerably less invasive seizures can also be arrests. Think of arrest as a zone, not a point, within a spectrum of invasions between investigatory stops at one end and imprisonment at the other end (see Table 5.2). That zone begins with detentions after stops end and continues through full custodial arrests that involve all the invasions listed in Table 5.1.

Within that zone, arrests may contain only some of the characteristics in Table 5.1. The duration and location also may vary significantly from the characteristics in the tables. How long does a seizure have to last to turn a stop into an arrest? How far do officers have to move an individual to turn a stop into an arrest? No "bright line" separates stops from arrests. But it

TABLE 5.1

Characteristics of a Custodial Arrest

- The police officer says to the suspect, "You're under arrest."
- The suspect is put into a squad car.
- The suspect is taken to the police station.
- The suspect is photographed, booked, and fingerprinted.
- The suspect is searched.
- The suspect is locked up either at the police station or in a jail cell.
- The suspect is interrogated.
- The suspect may be put into a lineup.

TABLE 5.2

Deprivations of Liberty from Stops to Imprisonment

Deprivation	Objective Basis	Duration	Location	Degree of Invasion
Voluntary contact	None	Brief	On the spot	Moral and psychological pressure
Stop	Reasonable suspicion	Minutes	At or near the stop on the street or in another public place	Reveal identification and explain whereabouts
Arrest	Probable cause	Hours to a few days	Usually removal to a police station	Fingerprints, booking, photograph, interrogation, identification procedures
Detention	Probable cause	Days to months	Jail	Inventory, full-body, strip, and body-cavity searches; restricted contact with the outside
Imprisonment	Proof beyond a reasonable doubt	Years to life	Prison	Same as detention with heightened invasions of privacy, liberty, and property

does matter where we draw the line because of one element common to all arrests within the zone: The Fourth Amendment requires probable cause to make them reasonable.

The remainder of this chapter describes and analyzes the reasonableness requirement in a lawful arrest. Reasonable arrests consist of two elements:

1. *Objective basis*. The arrest was backed up by probable cause.

2. *Manner of arrest*. The way the arrest was made was reasonable.

First, we'll look at what the law requires for probable cause to arrest. Then, you'll also learn how courts decide whether three kinds of actions taken by officers before, during, and after arrests are reasonable:

1. When it's reasonable to enter homes to make arrests

2. The kinds and degree of force that are reasonable to get and maintain control of suspects

3. The criteria for determining whether actions officers took *after* the arrests were reasonable

||||||||||||||||||||||||||||||||||||||||||||||||||||||||||||||||||||||||||||||||||||||||||||||||||||||||||||||||||||||||||||||||||

Probable Cause

LO 4, LO 5

Probable cause to arrest requires that an officer, in the light of her training and experience, knows enough facts and circumstances to reasonably believe that:

1. A crime has been, is being, or is about to be committed, *and*

2. The person arrested has committed, is committing, or is about to commit the crime

(Contrast this definition with the reasonable-grounds-to-suspect standard for stops discussed in Chapter 4.) Probable cause lies on a continuum between reasonable suspicion on one end and proof beyond a reasonable doubt on the other. Table 5.2 shows how the requirement for an objective basis increases as the level of invasiveness increases in criminal procedure.

The probable cause requirement balances the societal interest in crime control and the individual **right of locomotion**—the freedom to come and go as we please. According to the classic probable cause case *Brinegar v. U.S.* (1949), probable cause balances the interest in safeguarding individuals from "from rash and unreasonable interferences with privacy and from unfounded charges of crime," while giving law enforcement officers "fair leeway for enforcing the law in the community's protection." Because officers have to confront many ambiguous situations, we have to leave room for officers to make "some mistakes." But they have to be the mistakes of "reasonable men, acting on facts leading sensibly to their conclusions of probability" (176).

The day-to-day application of finding probable cause rests mainly with officers on the street who have to make quick decisions. They don't have the luxury that professors in their studies, judges in their chambers, and you wherever you're reading this chapter have to think deeply about technical matters. According to the Court in *Brinegar* (1949), "In dealing with probable cause, as the very name implies, we deal with probabilities. These are not technical; they are the factual and practical considerations of everyday life on which reasonable and prudent men, not legal technicians, act" (176).

So, although officers can't arrest on a hunch, a whim, or mere suspicion, and judges have the final say on whether the officers had probable cause, courts tend to accept the facts as police see them. According to one judge: Police officers don't "prearrange the setting" they work in and can't

> schedule their steps in the calm reflective atmosphere of some remote law library. Events occur without warning and policemen are required as a matter of duty to act as a reasonably prudent policeman would under the circumstances as those circumstances unfold before him. (*People v. Brown* 1969, 869)

The basis for reasonable belief can be either direct information or hearsay. Let's look at these two kinds of information.

Direct Information

LO 6

Direct information in probable cause to arrest is firsthand information known to arresting officers through what they see, hear, feel, taste, and smell. Direct information doesn't automatically make the case for probable cause. The courts look for patterns, or a totality of circumstances, that build the case for probable cause. Table 5.3 lists some of the facts and circumstances that officers usually know firsthand and which, either alone or in combination, form a pattern that a judge could find amounts to probable cause.

TABLE 5.3
Probable Cause Information Officers Know Firsthand

• Fleeing ("flight")	• Attempting to destroy evidence
• Resisting officers	• Matching fingerprints
• Making furtive movements	• Matching hair samples
• Hiding	• Matching blood samples
• Giving evasive answers	• Matching
• Giving contradictory explanations	• DNA profile

Hearsay

LO 6

Officers don't have to rely only on direct information to make their case for probable cause. They can (and often do) rely on hearsay in probable cause to arrest, information they get secondhand from victims, witnesses, other police officers, and professional informants. According to the **hearsay rule in arrests**, courts don't admit secondhand evidence to prove guilt, but, if it's reliable and truthful, they'll accept it to show probable cause to arrest. Why? Because arrests aren't trials.

Of course, arrests can still cost suspects their liberty—but only long enough to decide whether there's enough evidence to charge them with a crime (Chapter 12) and put them on trial (Chapter 13). At trial, there are legal experts in the courtroom to testify and plenty of time to weigh the evidence. However, police officers on the street—and at the precinct station—aren't lawyers, and they aren't supposed to be. They don't have the leisure to sort out the evidence they've acquired. As you learned earlier, officers either have to act immediately or forever lose their chance to arrest suspects. So allowing hearsay to show probable cause reflects the deference that courts concede to the realities of police work.

Not all hearsay carries equal weight; some informants are more trustworthy than others. In determining probable cause, magistrates weigh both the trustworthiness and the source of the information. So, according to the court in *Allison v. State* (1974), "If the citizen or victim informant is an eyewitness this will be enough to support probable cause even without specific corroboration of reliability." But this isn't true if victims or other witnesses refuse to identify themselves. So anonymous tips alone never are enough to establish probable cause to arrest (see *Draper v. U.S.* [1959], p. 144).

There's another problem. Bystander eyewitnesses aren't the source of most hearsay information; professional informants (almost always) are. And snitches create greater problems with credibility than victims and nonprofessional eyewitnesses. In *Jones v. U.S.* (1959), the U.S. Court of Appeals for the District of Columbia noted that drug informants are themselves often involved in drug trafficking, and paid for their information in cash, narcotics, immunity from prosecution, or lenient punishment.

> The present informer practice amounts to condoning felonies on condition that the confessed or suspected felon brings about the conviction of others. Under such stimulation it is to be expected that the informer will not infrequently reach for shadowy leads, or even seek to incriminate the innocent. The practice of paying fees to the informer for the cases he makes may also be expected from time to time, to induce him to lure no-users into the drug habit and then entrap them into law violations. (928)

(We'll discuss informants further and the test for evaluating their information in Chapter 6 when we get to probable cause to search.)

One of the best discussions of probable cause, and one of the clearest explanations of its application to the facts of an arrest based on a combination of direct and hearsay information (hearsay corroborated by an officer's direct observations), appears in our first case excerpt, *Draper v. U.S.* (1959).

In Draper v. U.S. (1959), the U.S. Supreme Court upheld the conviction of James Draper on a narcotics violation, even though hearsay evidence was used to establish probable cause.

CASE Does an Informant's Corroborated Tip Amount to Probable Cause to Arrest?

Draper v. U.S.
358 U.S. 307 (1959)

HISTORY

James Alonzo Draper was prosecuted for knowingly concealing and transporting heroin in violation of federal narcotics laws. The U.S. District Court for the District of Colorado denied Draper's motion to suppress the heroin, and Draper was convicted. Draper appealed. The U.S. Court of Appeals affirmed the conviction. The U.S. Supreme Court granted certiorari and affirmed.

WHITTAKER, J.

FACTS

Marsh, a federal narcotic agent with 29 years' experience, was stationed at Denver. Hereford had been engaged as a "special employee" of the Bureau of Narcotics at Denver for about six months, and from time to time gave information to Marsh regarding violations of the narcotics laws, for which Hereford was paid small sums of money, and that Marsh had always found the information given by Hereford to be accurate and reliable.

On September 3, 1956, Hereford told Marsh that James Draper recently had taken up abode at a stated address in Denver and "was peddling narcotics to several addicts" in that city. Four days later, on September 7, Hereford told Marsh "that Draper had gone to Chicago the day before (September 6) by train and that he was going to bring back three ounces of heroin and that he would return to Denver either on the morning of the 8th of September or the morning of the 9th of September also by train."

Hereford also gave Marsh a detailed physical description of Draper and of the clothing he was wearing. Hereford told Marsh that Draper was a Negro of light brown complexion, 27 years of age, 5 feet 8 inches tall, weighed about 160 pounds, and that he was wearing a light colored raincoat, brown slacks, and black shoes. He said that he would be carrying "a tan zipper bag," and that he habitually "walked real fast."

On the morning of September 8, Marsh and a Denver police officer went to the Denver Union Station and kept watch over all incoming trains from Chicago, but they did not see anyone fitting the description that Hereford had given. Repeating the process on the morning of September 9, they saw a person, having the exact physical attributes and wearing the precise clothing described by Hereford, alight from an incoming Chicago train and start walking "fast" toward the exit. He was carrying a tan zipper bag in his right hand and the left was thrust in his raincoat pocket.

Marsh, accompanied by the police officer, overtook, stopped and arrested him. They then searched him and found the two "envelopes containing heroin" clutched in his left hand in his raincoat pocket, and found the syringe in the tan zipper bag. Marsh then took Draper into custody. Hereford died four days after the arrest and therefore did not testify at the hearing on the motion.

OPINION

The Narcotic Control Act of 1956, provides: The Commissioner and agents, of the Bureau of Narcotics may— (2) make arrests without warrant for violations of any law of the United States relating to narcotic drugs where the violation is committed in the presence of the person making the arrest or where such person has reasonable grounds to believe that the person to be arrested has committed or is committing such violation.

The crucial question for us then is whether knowledge of the related facts and circumstances gave Marsh "probable cause" within the meaning of the Fourth Amendment, and "reasonable grounds" within the meaning of § 104(a) to believe that petitioner had committed or was committing a violation of the narcotics laws. The terms probable cause as used in the Fourth Amendment and reasonable grounds as used in § 104 (a) of the Narcotic Control Act, 70 Stat. 570, are substantial equivalents of the same meaning.

If it did, the arrest, though without a warrant, was lawful and the subsequent search of petitioner's person and the seizure of the found heroin were validly made incident to a lawful arrest, and therefore the motion to suppress was properly overruled and the heroin was competently received in evidence at the trial.

Petitioner (Draper) contends

(1) that the information given by Hereford to Marsh was "hearsay" and, because hearsay is not legally competent evidence in a criminal trial, could not legally have been considered, but should have been put out of mind, by Marsh in assessing whether he had "probable cause" and "reasonable grounds" to arrest petitioner without a warrant, and

(2) that, even if hearsay could lawfully have been considered, Marsh's information should be held insufficient to show "probable cause" and "reasonable grounds" to believe that petitioner had violated or was violating the narcotic laws and to justify his arrest without a warrant.

Considering the first contention, we find petitioner entirely in error. The criterion of admissibility in evidence, to prove the accused's guilt, of the facts relied upon to show probable cause goes much too far in confusing and disregarding the difference between what is required to prove guilt in a criminal case and what is required to show probable cause for arrest or search. It approaches requiring (if it does not in practical effect require) proof sufficient to establish guilt in order to substantiate the existence of probable cause. There is a large difference between the two things to be proved (guilt and probable cause), as well as between the tribunals which determine them, and therefore a like difference in the quanta and modes of proof required to establish them.

Nor can we agree with petitioner's second contention that Marsh's information was insufficient to show probable cause and reasonable grounds to believe that petitioner had violated or was violating the narcotic laws and to justify his arrest without a warrant. The information given to narcotic agent Marsh by "special employee" Hereford may have been hearsay to Marsh, but coming from one employed for that purpose and whose information had always been found accurate and reliable, it is clear that Marsh would have been derelict in his duties had he not pursued it.

And when, in pursuing that information, he saw a man, having the exact physical attributes and wearing the precise clothing and carrying the tan zipper bag that Hereford had described, alight from one of the very trains from the very place stated by Hereford and start to walk at a "fast" pace toward the station exit, Marsh had personally verified every facet of the information given him by Hereford except whether petitioner had accomplished his mission and had the three ounces of heroin on his person or in his bag. And surely, with every other bit of Hereford's information being thus personally verified, Marsh had "reasonable grounds" to believe that the remaining unverified bit of Hereford's information—that Draper would have the heroin with him—was likewise true.

In dealing with probable cause, as the very name implies, we deal with probabilities. These are not technical; they are the factual and practical considerations of everyday life on which reasonable and prudent men, not legal technicians, act. Probable cause exists where the facts and circumstances within their (the arresting officers') knowledge and of which they had reasonably trustworthy information are sufficient in themselves to warrant a man of reasonable caution in the belief that an offense has been or is being committed.

We believe that, under the facts and circumstances here, Marsh had probable cause and reasonable grounds to believe that petitioner (Draper) was committing a violation of the laws of the United States relating to narcotic drugs at the time he arrested him. The arrest was therefore lawful, and the subsequent search and seizure, having been made incident to that lawful arrest, were likewise valid. It follows that petitioner's motion to suppress was properly denied and that the seized heroin was competent evidence lawfully received at the trial.

AFFIRMED.

DISSENT

DOUGLAS, J.

Decisions under the Fourth Amendment, taken in the long view, have not given the protection to the citizen which the letter and spirit of the Amendment would seem to require. One reason, I think, is that wherever a culprit is caught redhanded, as in leading Fourth Amendment cases, it is difficult to adopt and enforce a rule that would turn him loose. A rule protective of law-abiding citizens is not apt to flourish where its advocates are usually criminals. Yet the rule we fashion is for the innocent and guilty alike. If the word of the informer on which the present arrest was made is sufficient to make the arrest legal, his word would also protect the police who, acting on it, hauled the innocent citizen off to jail.

Of course, the education we receive from mystery stories and television shows teaches that what happened in this case is efficient police work. The police are tipped off that a man carrying narcotics will step off the morning train. A man meeting the precise description does alight from the train. No warrant for his arrest has been—or, as I see it, could then be—obtained. Yet he is arrested; and narcotics are found in his pocket and a syringe in the bag he carried. This is the familiar pattern of crime detection which has been dinned into public consciousness as the correct and efficient one. It is, however, a distorted reflection of the constitutional system under which we are supposed to live.

The Court is quite correct in saying that proof of "reasonable grounds" for believing a crime was being committed need not be proof admissible at the trial. It could be inferences from suspicious acts, e.g., consort with known peddlers, the surreptitious passing of a package, an intercepted message suggesting criminal activities, or any number of such events coming to the knowledge of the officer. But, if he takes the law into his own hands and does not seek the protection of a warrant, he must act on some evidence known to him.

The law goes far to protect the citizen. Even suspicious acts observed by the officers may be as consistent with innocence as with guilt. That is not enough, for even the guilty may not be implicated on suspicion alone. The reason is, as I have said, that the standard set by the Constitution and by the statute is one that will protect both the officer and the citizen. For if the officer acts with "probable cause" or on "reasonable grounds," he is protected even though the citizen is innocent.

This important requirement should be strictly enforced, lest the whole process of arrest revert once more to whispered accusations by people. When we lower the guards as we do today, we risk making the role of the informer—odious in our history—once more supreme. Here the officers had no evidence—apart from the mere word of an informer—that petitioner was committing a crime. The fact that petitioner walked fast and carried a tan zipper bag was not evidence of any crime. The officers knew nothing except what they had been told by the informer.

If they went to a magistrate to get a warrant of arrest and relied solely on the report of the informer, it is not conceivable to me that one would be granted. For they could not present to the magistrate any of the facts which the informer may have had. They could swear only to the fact that the informer had made the accusation. They could swear to no evidence that lay in their own knowledge. They could present, on information and belief, no facts which the informer disclosed. No magistrate could issue a warrant on the mere word of an officer, without more. We are not justified in lowering the standard when an arrest is made without a warrant and allowing the officers more leeway than we grant the magistrate.

With all deference I think we break with tradition when we sustain this arrest. A search is not to be made legal by what it turns up. In law it is good or bad when it starts and does not change character from its success. In this case it was only after the arrest and search were made that there was a shred of evidence known to the officers that a crime was in the process of being committed.

QUESTIONS

1. List all the facts and circumstances supporting the conclusion there was probable cause to arrest Draper.
2. Identify which were firsthand, hearsay, or a combination of the two.
3. Do you think Justice Douglas is overreacting to the decision in this case? Or does he have a point that the hearsay provided by the informant amounts to nothing of substance that would lead a reasonable person to conclude that a crime was committed or in progress and that James Draper committed it?
4. Does the majority ruling favor crime control at the expense of procedural regularity and controlling government?
5. Does the Court give clear guidelines in regard to what constitutes probable cause to arrest? Explain.

EXPLORING FURTHER

....

Probable Cause

1. Did They Have Probable Cause?

State v. Bumpus, 459 N.W.2d 619 (Iowa 1990)

FACTS Des Moines police officers Gary Bryan and Michael Stueckrath were patrolling the vicinity of the Another World Lounge at about 11:00 P.M. They noticed Claude Bumpus, Marvin Taylor, and another man they didn't recognize in the parking lot of the lounge crouching behind a car. The officers observed that the men were exchanging something, but they couldn't see what it was. The Another World Lounge was a notorious site for drug transactions.

Based on their past experience with the location, the nature and furtiveness of the three men's actions, the notoriety of the location, and the lateness of the hour, the officers pulled their patrol car into the parking lot. Bumpus ran away from them into the bar. Once inside, Bumpus tried to conceal a black pouch from the officer who pursued him. Officer Bryan grabbed Bumpus's arm and asked him to step outside. Once outside, Bumpus threw the pouch over a fence and tried to flee. After a brief struggle, Bryan seized and arrested Bumpus.

The trial court decided that Officer Bryan arrested Bumpus not when he said, "You're under arrest," but when he grabbed his arm inside the bar and escorted him outside.

Did Bryan have probable cause at the moment of the arrest?

DECISION Yes, said the Iowa Supreme Court.

OPINION "While flight alone does not give rise to probable cause . . . in this case not only did Bumpus flee from officers but he also attempted to conceal the pouch." Therefore, when he grabbed Bumpus's arm, Officer Bryan had probable cause to arrest him.

2. Was There Probable Cause to Believe a Drug Deal Had Taken Place?

People v. Brown, 248 N.E.2d 867 (N.Y. 1969)

FACTS Detective Odesto, the arresting officer, testified at a suppression hearing that at 11:45 P.M., in a high-crime area in Manhattan, he observed Nathaniel Brown in the "company of someone he suspected of being a narcotics addict." The suspected addict walked away from Brown and entered a building, returning shortly to Brown. The two came "close together," Detective Odesto said, adding: "I observed what appeared to be a movement of hand. At that time I started to go across the street and intercepted the two persons when Mr. Brown walked in my direction with 'a fast shuffling gait' and the other person walked in the opposite direction."

Detective Odesto arrested Brown for possession of a narcotic drug. At the suppression hearing, Detective Odesto explained that this was typical behavior for drug transactions in that neighborhood:

> Most of its persons engaged in the selling of narcotics do not carry narcotics on them. They usually have a place where it is stored in or carried by someone else. Usually the person would have a conversation with the potential seller, give him his money and then the potential seller will go to his place where he stores the narcotics and bring it back, give it to that person, and they'll go in opposite directions.

Did Detective Odesto have probable cause to arrest Brown?

DECISION Yes, said the trial judge. The appellate court REVERSED.

OPINION Although the observed acts of the defendant and the suspected narcotic addict were not inconsistent with a culpable narcotics transaction, they were also susceptible to many innocent interpretations, even between persons with a narcotics background. The behavior, at most "equivocal and suspicious," was not supplemented by any additional behavior raising "the level of inference from suspicion to probable cause." Thus, for example, there was no recurring pattern of conduct sufficient to negate inferences of innocent activity, no overheard conversation between the suspects that might clarify the acts observed, no flight at the approach of the officer, and no misstatements when questioned about observed activity.

The logical and practical problem is that even accepting ungrudgingly, as one should, the police officer's expertness in detecting a pattern of conduct characteristic of a particular criminal activity, the detected pattern, being only the superficial part of a sequence, does not provide probable cause for arrest if some sketchy pattern occurs just as frequently or even more frequently in innocent transactions. The point is that the pattern is equivocal and is neither uniquely nor generally associated with criminal conduct, and unless it is there is no probable cause. Thus, for example, the observation of a known or obvious prostitute talking to a man she meets (or accosts) on the street does not establish probable cause. More of a pattern must be shown, either by proof of the conversation or ensuing culpable conduct.

3. Was "Flight" Enough to Amount to Probable Cause?

People v. Washington, 236 Cal.Rptr. 840 (Cal.App. 1987)

FACTS Officers Lewis and Griffin were in the vicinity of 1232 Buchanan Street. They observed Michael Washington, the defendant, along with four other individuals in a courtyard area between 1133 Laguna and 1232 Buchanan. Washington and the others were observed talking in a "huddle" formation with "a lot of hand movement" inside the huddle, but the officers could not see what was in the hands of any member of the group. The officers then walked toward the group, at which point everyone looked in the officers' direction, whispered, and quickly dispersed. When Washington saw the officers, he immediately turned around and started walking at a fast pace through the lobby of 1232 Buchanan.

The officers followed him for a quarter of a block when Officer Griffin called out to Washington. He replied, "Who, me?" Officer Griffin answered, "Yes," and Washington immediately ran away. The officers chased him. Two minutes later, while still chasing Washington, Officer Lewis saw him discard a plastic bag containing five white bundles. Officer Lewis scooped up the bag as he continued to give chase. Shortly thereafter, the officers apprehended Washington. Officer Lewis testified that during the four years he had been a patrolman he had made at least one hundred arrests concerning cocaine in the area frequented by the defendant that night. On cross-examination, Officer Lewis answered yes when asked if most of the black men he saw in the area usually had something to hide if they ran from police. The officer stated that prior to the chase he saw no contraband, nor was anything about the group's dispersal significant. Nor did the officer explain why they singled out the defendant to follow. The trial court denied the defendant's motion to suppress.

Did Officers Lewis and Griffin have probable cause to arrest Washington?

DECISION No, said the court.

OPINION Prior to defendant's abandonment of the cocaine, the police lacked the "articulable suspicion that a person has committed or is about to commit a crime." The officers spotted the group of men in an open courtyard at 6:15 P.M.; the men made no attempt to conceal them-selves and did not exhibit any furtive behavior. The hand gestures were, on the police officer's own testimony, in-conclusive and unrevealing. Furthermore, the time at which the detention occurred is not the "late or unusual hour from which any inference of criminality may be drawn." The fact that defendant was seen in what was a high crime area also does not elevate the facts into a reasonable suspicion of criminality. Courts have been re-luctant to conclude that a location's crime rate transforms otherwise innocent-appearing circumstances into circum-stances justifying the seizure of an individual.

Once the officers made their approach visible, they gave no justification for their decision to follow defendant apart from the others in the group. Neither officer knew defendant or knew of defendant's past criminal record, nor did Officer Lewis testify that defendant appeared to be a principal or a leader in the group. Further, the defendant had the right to walk away from the officers. He had no legal duty to submit to the attention of the officers; he had the freedom to "go on his way," free of stopping even mo-mentarily for the officers. By walking at a brisk rate away from the officers, defendant could have been exercising his right to avoid the officers or avoid any other person, or could have simply walked rapidly through sheer nervous-ness at the sight of a police officer.

We see no change in the analysis when defendant decided to run from the officers. Flight alone does not trigger an investigative detention; rather, it must be com-bined with other objective factors that give rise to an ar-ticulable suspicion of criminal activity. No such factors existed, nor does Officer Lewis's assertion that the "black men [they] see in the project usually have something to hide when they run" justify a detention. Mere subjective speculation as to the [person's] purported motives car-ries no weight. Thus, prior to defendant's abandonment of the contraband, the circumstances of defendant's ac-tions were not reasonably consistent with criminal activity.

Here, the officers conceded they had no objective fac-tors upon which to base any suspicions that the group was involved in illegal activity, and the officers offered no ex-planation why they singled out defendant to follow. In-deed, the only justification for engaging in pursuit was that defendant was a Black male, and that it was the offi-cer's subjective belief that Black men run from police when they have something to hide. Thus, a single factor—the defendant's race—triggered the detention. . . .

The Arrest Warrant Requirement

LO 7

In most situations, probable cause without an arrest warrant is enough to make an arrest a reasonable Fourth Amendment seizure. But, if officers want to arrest some-one in her home, they have to get an arrest warrant. For centuries, under the English and American common law, before the Fourth Amendment was adopted, warrants weren't required to make arrests outside the home for *felonies* lawful; probable cause was enough. However, in *misdemeanors*, warrants were required unless the offense took place in the officer's presence.

As the previous sections have shown, the vast majority of arrests don't require officers to get arrest warrants to make the arrest reasonable. Even though the Fourth Amendment doesn't demand that officers get arrest warrants to arrest felony suspects outside their homes, it may still be a good idea to do so. Why? Because a judge's ap-proval before making an arrest means officers don't have to worry about the lawfulness of arrests.

If officers need a warrant to make an arrest in a home, or if they want to get a war-rant to ensure an arrest is reasonable, the Fourth Amendment requires that arrest war-rants include three elements:

1. *A neutral magistrate.* A disinterested judge has to decide whether there is probable cause before officers arrest suspects.

2. *An affidavit (sworn statement).* This is made by someone (nearly always a law en-forcement officer) who swears under oath to the facts and circumstances amount-ing to probable cause.

3. *The name of the person to be arrested.* The warrant has to identify specifically the person(s) the officers are going to arrest.

Let's look more closely at each of these requirements.

A Neutral Magistrate

The requirement that officers get approval from a **neutral magistrate** (one who will fairly and adequately review the warrant) before they arrest assumes that magistrates carefully review the information that law enforcement officers supply them. However, both the outcomes of cases and social science research suggest otherwise:

> There is little reason to be reassured by what we know about magistrates in operation. The magistrate can know there are factual issues to be explored only if he looks behind the particulars presented. Yet it is rare for such initiatives to be taken. Most magistrates devote very little time to appraising the affidavit's sufficiency. They assume that the affiant is being honest.
>
> They tend to ask no questions and to issue warrants in routine fashion. Over the years the police have adapted their practice not only to the law's requirements but also to the opportunities presented by the manner in which the law is administered. They have often relied on the magistrate's passivity to insulate from review affidavits that are only apparently sufficient—sometimes purposely presenting them through officers who are "ignorant of the circumstances" and, therefore, less likely to provide awkward details in the unlikely event that questions are asked. . . . (Goldstein 1987, 1182)

Summarizing the results of a study of probable cause determination, Professor Abraham S. Goldstein (1987) found:

> Proceedings before magistrates generally lasted only two to three minutes and the magistrate rarely asked any questions to penetrate the boilerplate language or the hearsay in the warrant. Witnesses other than the police applicant were never called. And the police often engaged in "magistrate shopping" for judges who would give only minimal scrutiny to the application. (1183)

Whether a judge is, in fact, neutral can become an issue, when the validity of a warrant is challenged because it's charged that the magistrate failed to properly determine whether the requirements for showing probable cause had been met before issuing the warrant. This happened in *Barnes v. State* (1975):

> At the hearing held by the trial court (challenging the issuance of a warrant) in the absence of the jury, Justice of the Peace Matthews testified that, although he did not read all of the three-page, single-spaced affidavit presented him by Officers Blaisdale and Bridges, but only "touched the high parts," he did question the officers in detail about its contents and about the necessity of issuing the warrant. Further, he was acquainted with the requirements for showing probable cause, and it was only after satisfying himself that probable cause existed for the search of the premises described that he issued the warrant. (401)

According to the court, the charge that J. P. Matthews wasn't a "neutral and detached magistrate" had no merit (401).

An Affidavit

The Fourth Amendment requires that magistrates base their probable cause determination on written information sworn to under oath (**affidavit**). The pain of *perjury* (the crime of lying under oath) charges encourages truthfulness. If the affidavit establishes probable cause, the magistrate issues the warrant.

The written statement isn't always enough to establish probable cause; sometimes it's purposely vague. For example, police officers who want to preserve the anonymity of undercover agents may make only vague references to the circumstances surrounding the information (*Fraizer v. Roberts* 1971). In these cases, supplemental oral information can satisfy the requirement in some jurisdictions. However, other courts require that all information be in writing (*Orr v. State* 1980).

Officers usually appear before magistrates with the written affidavit, but not all jurisdictions require officers to appear in person. For example, the *Federal Rules of Criminal Procedure* (2002, 41[d][3]) authorize officers to phone or radio their information to a federal magistrate. The magistrate records the information verbatim. If the information satisfies the probable cause requirement, the magistrate authorizes the officer to sign the magistrate's name to a warrant.

Some argue that modern electronic advances should eliminate the need for most warrantless arrests. According to this argument, officers can always obtain advance judicial approval for arrests, except in emergencies, without hindering effective law enforcement. According to Professor Craig Bradley (1985), a former clerk to Chief Justice Rehnquist, if courts adopted this practice:

> The Supreme Court could actually enforce the warrant doctrine to which it has paid lip service for so many years. That is, a warrant is always required for every search and seizure when it is practicable to obtain one. However, in order that this requirement be workable and not be swallowed by its exception, the warrant need not be in writing but rather may be phoned or radioed into a magistrate (where it will be tape recorded and the recording preserved) who will authorize or forbid the search orally. By making the procedure for obtaining a warrant less difficult (while only marginally reducing the safeguards it provides), the number of cases where "emergencies" justify an exception to the warrant requirement should be very small. (1471)

The Name of the Person to Be Arrested

The Fourth Amendment requires specific identification of the person to be arrested. To satisfy this particularity requirement, the *Federal Rules of Criminal Procedure* provide that an arrest warrant "must contain the defendant's name or, if it is unknown, a name or description by which the defendant can be identified with reasonable certainty" (4[b][1][A]).

Arrests in Homes

LO 7

Probable cause without a warrant is enough to satisfy the Fourth Amendment reasonableness requirement when officers want to make felony arrests outside the home.

But they have to get a warrant to enter a home to make an arrest, except in emergencies. Let's look first at entering a home to make an arrest and then at the effect of exigent circumstances (emergencies) on the reasonableness of entering homes to make arrests without warrants.

Entering Homes to Arrest

LO 7

Why does the Fourth Amendment require an arrest warrant? Because officials entering homes "is the chief evil" the Fourth Amendment was intended to protect against (*U.S. v. U.S. District Court* 1972, 313). According to the U.S. Supreme Court, the Fourth Amendment has "drawn a firm line at the entrance to a home." To be arrested in your own home involves not just the invasion that accompanies all arrests; it also invades the sanctity of the home. According to the Court, "This is simply too substantial an invasion to allow without a warrant" (*Payton v. New York* 1980, 589; *Kirk v. Louisiana* 2002, 637). The U.S. Supreme Court in *Payton v. New York* found that "routine arrests in which there was ample time to obtain a warrant," require arrest warrants to enter homes.

In *Payton*, police officers had probable cause to believe that Theodore Payton had committed a robbery and a murder. At about 7:30 in the morning, six officers went to Payton's apartment without an arrest warrant, intending to arrest him. They heard music inside, and the lights were on. They knocked, but no one answered the door. After waiting for about a half hour, they broke open the metal door with crowbars, and entered. No one was there, but they seized an empty shell in plain view, which was later used as evidence in Payton's murder trial. The U.S. Supreme Court held that this was a routine arrest case, which required an arrest warrant. Accordingly, Justice Stevens wrote, "we have no occasion to consider the sort of emergency or dangerous situation, described in our cases as 'exigent circumstances,' that would justify a warrantless entry into a home for the purpose of either arrest or search" (583).

Exigent Circumstances

LO 7

In **exigent circumstances**, situations where officers have to take immediate action to make an arrest, officers don't need to get an arrest warrant before they enter a home to make an arrest. The most common exigency is "hot pursuit," first recognized by the U.S. Supreme Court in *Warden v. Hayden* (1967).

In that case, police were informed that an armed robbery had taken place, and that Bennie Joe Hayden had entered 2111 Cocoa Lane less than five minutes before the officers had arrived. According to the Court, the officers acted "reasonably when they entered the house and began to search for a man of the description they had been given and for weapons which he had used in the robbery or might use against them." The Fourth Amendment doesn't mandate that officers put off their investigation if the delay would "gravely endanger their lives or the lives of others. Speed here was essential, and only a thorough search of the house for persons and weapons could have insured that Hayden was the only man present and that the police had control of all weapons which could be used against them or to effect an escape (298–99)."

Table 5.4 lists the major exigent circumstances that allow officers to enter homes to arrest without a warrant.

TABLE 5.4

Exigent Circumstances That May Make Entering Homes to Arrest without Arrest Warrants Reasonable

"Hot pursuit." *Warden v. Hayden*, 387 U.S. 294 (1967)	Police were informed that an armed robbery had taken place and that Bennie Joe Hayden had entered 2111 Cocoa Lane less than five minutes before the officers had arrived.
Imminent destruction of evidence. *Colorado v. Mendez*, 986 P.2d 285 (Colo. 1999)	Two officers smelled the strong odor of burning marijuana coming from a hotel room. They instructed the manager to open the door with the master key, entered, and found Edgar Mendez flushing the marijuana down the toilet.
Imminent escape of suspect. *Warden v. Hayden*, 387 U.S. 294 (1967)	The police were informed that an armed robbery had taken place, and that the suspect had entered 2111 Cocoa Lane less than five minutes before they reached it. They acted reasonably when they entered the house and began to search for a man of the description they had been given and for weapons which he had used in the robbery or might use against them. Speed here was essential, and only a thorough search of the house for persons and weapons could have insured that Hayden was the only man present and that the police had control of all weapons which could be used against them or to effect an escape.

In **Brigham City, Utah v. Charles Stuart, Shayne Taylor, and Sandra Taylor** *(2006), our next case excerpt, the U.S. Supreme Court defined imminent danger as an exigent circumstance that can eliminate the need for an arrest warrant to enter homes.*

CASE Why Were the Circumstances Exigent?

Brigham City, Utah v. Charles Stuart, Shayne Taylor, and Sandra Taylor
547 U.S. 398 (2006)

HISTORY

Defendants, who were charged in state court with contributing to the delinquency of a minor, disorderly conduct, and intoxication, filed a motion to suppress. The First District Court, Brigham City Department, granted the motion. The City appealed. The Utah Court of Appeals affirmed. The City again appealed. The Utah Supreme Court affirmed. The U.S. Supreme Court reversed.

ROBERTS, C.J., delivered the opinion for a unanimous Court. STEVENS, J., filed a concurring opinion.

ROBERTS, J. for a unanimous Court.

In this case we consider whether police may enter a home without a warrant when they have an objectively reasonable basis for believing that an occupant is seriously injured or imminently threatened with such injury. We conclude that they may.

FACTS

This case arises out of a melee that occurred in a Brigham City, Utah, home in the early morning hours of July 23, 2000. At about 3 A.M., four police officers responded to a call regarding a loud party at a residence. Upon arriving at the house, they heard shouting from inside, and proceeded down the driveway to investigate. There, they observed two juveniles drinking beer in the backyard. They entered the backyard, and saw—through a screen door and windows—an altercation taking place in the kitchen of the home. According to the testimony of one of the officers, four adults were attempting, with some difficulty, to restrain a juvenile. The juvenile eventually "broke free, swung a fist and struck one of the adults in the face." The officer testified that he observed the victim of the blow spitting blood into a nearby sink. The other adults continued to try to restrain the juvenile, pressing him up against a refrigerator with such force that the refrigerator began moving across the floor. At this point, an officer opened the screen door and announced the officers' presence. Amid the tumult, nobody noticed. The officer entered the kitchen and again cried out, and as the occupants slowly became aware that the police were on the scene, the altercation ceased.

The officers subsequently arrested respondents and charged them with contributing to the delinquency of a minor, disorderly conduct, and intoxication. In the trial court, respondents filed a motion to suppress all evidence obtained after the officers entered the home, arguing that the warrantless entry violated the Fourth Amendment. The court granted the motion, and the Utah Court of Appeals affirmed.

Before the Supreme Court of Utah, Brigham City argued that although the officers lacked a warrant, their entry was nevertheless reasonable on either of two grounds. The court rejected both contentions and, over two dissenters, affirmed. First, the court held that the injury caused by the juvenile's punch was insufficient to trigger the so-called "emergency aid doctrine" because it did not give rise to an "objectively reasonable belief that an unconscious, semiconscious, or missing person feared injured or dead [was] in the home." Furthermore, the court suggested that the doctrine was inapplicable because the officers had not sought to assist the injured adult, but instead had acted "exclusively in their law enforcement capacity."

The court also held that the entry did not fall within the exigent circumstances exception to the warrant requirement. This exception applies, the court explained, where police have probable cause and where "a reasonable person [would] believe that the entry was necessary to prevent physical harm to the officers or other persons." Under this standard, the court stated, the potential harm need not be as serious as that required to invoke the emergency aid exception. Although it found the case "a close and difficult call," the court nevertheless concluded that the officers' entry was not justified by exigent circumstances.

We granted certiorari, in light of differences among state courts and the Courts of Appeals concerning the appropriate Fourth Amendment standard governing warrantless entry by law enforcement in an emergency situation.

OPINION

It is a basic principle of Fourth Amendment law that searches and seizures inside a home without a warrant are presumptively unreasonable. Nevertheless, because the ultimate touchstone of the Fourth Amendment is "reasonableness," the warrant requirement is subject to certain exceptions. We have held, for example, that law enforcement officers may make a warrantless entry onto private property to fight a fire and investigate its cause, to prevent the imminent destruction of evidence, or to engage in "hot pursuit" of a fleeing suspect. Warrants are generally required to search a person's home or his person unless the exigencies of the situation make the needs of law enforcement so compelling that the warrantless search is objectively reasonable under the Fourth Amendment.

One exigency obviating the requirement of a warrant is the need to assist persons who are seriously injured or threatened with such injury. The need to protect or preserve life or avoid serious injury is justification for what would be otherwise illegal absent an exigency or emergency. Accordingly, law enforcement officers may enter a home without a warrant to render emergency assistance to an injured occupant or to protect an occupant from imminent injury.

We think the officers' entry here was plainly reasonable under the circumstances. The officers were responding, at 3 o'clock in the morning, to complaints about a loud party. As they approached the house, they could hear from within "an altercation occurring, some kind of a fight." "It was loud and it was tumultuous." The officers heard "thumping and crashing" and people yelling "stop, stop" and "get off me." As the trial court found, "it was obvious that knocking on the front door" would have been futile. The noise seemed to be coming from the back of the house; after looking in the front window and seeing nothing, the officers proceeded around back to investigate further. They found two juveniles drinking beer in the backyard. From there, they could see that a fracas was taking place inside the kitchen. A juvenile, fists clenched, was being held back by several adults. As the officers watch, he breaks free and strikes one of the adults in the face, sending the adult to the sink spitting blood.

In these circumstances, the officers had an objectively reasonable basis for believing both that the injured adult might need help and that the violence in the kitchen was just beginning. Nothing in the Fourth Amendment required them to wait until another blow rendered someone "unconscious" or "semi-conscious" or worse before entering. The role of a peace officer includes preventing violence and restoring order, not simply rendering first aid to casualties; an officer is not like a boxing (or hockey) referee, poised to stop a bout only if it becomes too one-sided.

The manner of the officers' entry was also reasonable. After witnessing the punch, one of the officers opened the screen door and yelled in "police." When nobody heard him, he stepped into the kitchen and announced himself again. Only then did the tumult subside. The officer's announcement of his presence was at least equivalent to a knock on the screen door. Indeed, it was probably the only option that had even a chance of rising above the din. Under these circumstances, there was no violation of the Fourth Amendment's knock-and-announce rule.

Furthermore, once the announcement was made, the officers were free to enter; it would serve no purpose to require them to stand dumbly at the door awaiting a response while those within brawled on, oblivious to their presence.

Accordingly, we REVERSE the judgment of the Supreme Court of Utah, and REMAND the case for further proceedings not inconsistent with this opinion.

It is so ordered.

CONCURRENCE

STEVENS, J.

This is an odd flyspeck of a case. The charges that have been pending against respondents for the past six years are minor offenses—intoxication, contributing to the delinquency of a minor, and disorderly conduct—two of which could have been proved by evidence that was gathered by the responding officers before they entered the home. The maximum punishment for these crimes ranges between 90 days and 6 months in jail. And the Court's unanimous opinion restating well-settled rules of federal law is so clearly persuasive that it is hard to imagine the outcome was ever in doubt.

Under these circumstances, the only difficult question is which of the following is the most peculiar: (1) that the Utah trial judge, the intermediate state appellate court, and the Utah Supreme Court all found a Fourth Amendment violation on these facts; (2) that the prosecution chose to pursue this matter all the way to the United States Supreme Court; or (3) that this Court voted to grant the petition for a writ of certiorari.

A possible explanation for the first is that the suppression ruling was correct as a matter of Utah law, and neither trial counsel nor the trial judge bothered to identify the Utah Constitution as an independent basis for the decision because they did not expect the prosecution to appeal. The most plausible explanation for the latter two decisions is that they were made so police officers in Utah may enter a home without a warrant when they see ongoing violence—we are, of course, reversing the Utah Supreme Court's conclusion to the contrary. But that purpose, laudable though it may be, cannot be achieved in this case. Our holding today addresses only the limitations placed by the Federal Constitution on the search at issue; we have no authority to decide whether the police in this case violated the Utah Constitution.

The Utah Supreme Court, however, has made clear that the Utah Constitution provides greater protection to the privacy of the home than does the Fourth Amendment. And it complained in this case of respondents' failure to raise or adequately brief a state constitutional challenge, thus preventing the state courts from deciding the case on anything other than Fourth Amendment grounds. "Surprised" by "the reluctance of litigants to take up and develop a state constitutional analysis," the court expressly invited future litigants to bring challenges under the Utah Constitution to enable it to fulfill its "responsibility as guardians of the individual liberty of our citizens" and "undertake a principled exploration of the interplay between federal and state protections of individual rights." The fact that this admonishment and request came from the Utah Supreme Court in this very case not only demonstrates that the prosecution selected the wrong case for establishing the rule it wants, but also indicates that the Utah Supreme Court would probably adopt the same rule as a matter of state constitutional law that we reject today under the Federal Constitution.

Whether or not that forecast is accurate, I can see no reason for this Court to cause the Utah courts to redecide the question as a matter of state law. Federal interests are not offended when a single State elects to provide greater protection for its citizens than the Federal Constitution requires. Indeed, I continue to believe that a policy of judicial restraint—one that allows other decisional bodies to have the last word in legal interpretation until it is truly necessary for this Court to intervene—enables this Court to make its most effective contribution to our federal system of government. Thus, while I join the Court's opinion, I remain persuaded that my vote to deny the State's petition for certiorari was correct.

QUESTIONS

1. Summarize the details of the arrest of Charles Stuart, Shayne Taylor, and Sandra Taylor.
2. List the "exigent circumstances" that the U.S. Supreme Court found were present in the case.
3. Summarize the Court's arguments for finding that exigent circumstances were present.
4. List the reasons why Justice Stevens wrote a concurring opinion. Should the U.S. Supreme Court not have taken the case?
5. Why should anyone object to the officers' entering the house? Why did the officers enter the house? To arrest the adults or to help people in trouble?

EXPLORING FURTHER

. . . .

Entering Homes to Arrest

1. *Was the Arrest Made in His Home?*

State v. Holeman, 693 P.2d 89 (Wash. 1985)

FACTS Two uniformed police officers went to David Holeman's home to question him about the theft of a bicycle. David's father, Clarence Holeman, met the officers at the door and called David to the doorway. The officers, while remaining outside, questioned David as he was standing in the doorway. David denied any involvement in the theft. During the discussion, Clarence Holeman became angry and told the police they had no right to arrest David without a warrant. At this point, the officers read David his

Miranda rights and decided to question him at the police station despite the fact that they did not have a warrant. Both parties agree that at this point David was under arrest.

Was the arrest without a warrant reasonable?

DECISION No, according to the court.

OPINION This arrest of David was unlawful because, without a warrant and absent exigent circumstances, the police are prohibited from arresting a suspect while the suspect is standing in the doorway of his house. The Fourth Amendment has drawn a firm line at the entrance to the house. It is no argument to say that the police never crossed the threshold of David's house. A person does not forfeit his Fourth Amendment privacy interests by opening his door to police officers. A person's home can be invaded to the same extent when the police remain outside the house and call a person to the door as when the police physically enter the household itself. . . . Here the police did not have the proper authority of law; *i.e.*, a warrant. Consequently, this . . . arrest of David was unlawful.

2. *Did He Voluntarily Expose Himself to the Police?*

U.S. v. Vaneaton, 49 F.3d 1423 (CA9 Ore., 1995)

FACTS Armed with ample probable cause to arrest Jack Vaneaton for receiving stolen property officers went to his motel room to see if he was there and to arrest him if he was. Wearing their uniforms and with their guns in their holsters, Portland police officers knocked on the door to Vaneaton's motel room. They made no demands; in fact, they said nothing. Vaneaton opened the curtains of a window, saw the officers, and opened the door. Detective Carpenter asked him if he was Jack Vaneaton, and when he said he was, he was arrested.

At the moment of his arrest, Vaneaton was standing at the doorway but just inside the threshold. The arresting officer was immediately outside the threshold of the room and did not enter before advising Vaneaton he was under arrest. Vaneaton was then handcuffed.

Did the arrest require a warrant?

DECISION No. According to the court.

OPINION The question presented in this case is not decided only on the basis of whether Vaneaton was standing inside or outside the threshold of his room, but whether he "voluntarily exposed himself to warrantless arrest" by freely opening the door of his motel room to the police. If he so exposed himself, the presumption created by *Payton* is overcome. By opening the door as he did, Vaneaton exposed himself in a public place. His warrantless arrest, therefore, does not offend the Fourth Amendment.

DISSENT The majority's opinion is bad policy. It will have the effect of discouraging private citizens from answering knocks on the door by uniformed police officers, by subjecting citizens to warrantless arrests inside their own homes, stemming from nothing more than the exercise of common courtesy in answering a police officer's knock on the door. Indeed, it provides a justification for refusing to answer a police officer's knock. The result is bound to make routine police investigation more difficult and further to strain relations between the citizenry and police.

While making police work more difficult, the majority's decision simultaneously erodes the privacy interests protected by the Fourth Amendment. The majority has, quite literally, opened the door to warrantless invasions of the home, ignoring the Supreme Court's warning that the physical entry of the home is the chief evil against which the wording of the Fourth Amendment is directed.

Arrest by Force

LO 8

Whether the manner of an arrest was reasonable is affected by whether the amount of force, if any, was reasonably necessary. Usually, when we hear about the use of force to make an arrest, it's when the officers have killed a suspect. This distorts the public's view of the frequency of the use of **deadly force**—restraint capable of producing death. In reality, there are far more forcible arrests using nondeadly force than deadly force. And the vast majority of all arrests are made without the use of any force at all. Keeping these facts in mind, let's look at the use of deadly and nondeadly force to arrest suspects.

Deadly Force

LO 8

Throughout most of our history, states have followed the ancient common-law rule that allowed officers to use deadly force when it was necessary to apprehend fleeing felons. By the 1960s, many police departments had adopted rules that restricted this common-law rule. The gist of these rules is that officers can use deadly force only under two conditions: (1) it's necessary to apprehend "dangerous" suspects, *and* (2) it doesn't put innocent people in danger. In *Tennessee v. Garner* (1985), the U.S. Supreme Court adopted these two rules as Fourth Amendment requirements in using deadly force to make arrests. Read the excerpt to see how the Court applied the rules to the facts of the case.

In Tennessee v. Garner (1985), our next excerpt, the U.S. Supreme Court adopted two Fourth Amendment requirements for the test of whether deadly force by an officer is reasonable. The case involved the fatal shooting of 15-year-old Edward Garner by a Memphis police officer.

CASE Is Shooting a Fleeing Suspected Felon an Unreasonable Seizure?

Tennessee v. Garner
471 U.S. 1 (1985)

HISTORY

Fifteen-year-old Edward Garner was killed by Memphis Police Department Officer Elton Hymon when Garner fled the scene of a suspected burglary. His father, Cleamtree Garner, sued the Department under U.S.C.A. § 1983 [discussed in Chapter 11] for violating his son's Fourth Amendment right against unreasonable seizures. The U.S. District Court ruled that the shooting was not an unreasonable seizure. The U.S. Court of Appeals reversed. The U.S. Supreme Court affirmed.

WHITE, J., joined by BRENNAN, MARSHALL, BLACKMUN, POWELL, and STEVENS, JJ.

FACTS

At about 10:45 P.M. on October 3, 1974, Memphis Police Officers Elton Hymon and Leslie Wright were dispatched to answer a "prowler inside call." Upon arriving at the scene they saw a woman standing on her porch gesturing toward the adjacent house. She told them she had heard glass breaking and that "they" or "someone" was breaking in next door. While Wright radioed the dispatcher to say that they were on the scene, Hymon went behind the house. He heard a door slam and saw someone run across the backyard.

The fleeing suspect, Edward Garner, stopped at a 6-feet-high chain link fence at the edge of the yard. With the aid of a flashlight, Hymon was able to see Garner's face and hands. He saw no sign of a weapon, and though not certain, was "reasonably sure" and "figured" that Garner was unarmed. He thought Garner was 17 or 18 years old and about 5'5" or 5'7" tall. While Garner was crouched at the base of the fence, Hymon called out "police, halt" and took a few steps toward him.

Garner began to climb over the fence. Convinced that if Garner made it over the fence he would elude capture, Hymon shot him. The bullet hit Garner in the back of the head. Garner was taken by ambulance to a hospital, where he died on the operating table. Ten dollars and a purse taken from the house were found on his body.

In using deadly force to prevent escape, Hymon was acting under the authority of a Tennessee statute, *and* pursuant to Police Department policy. The statute provides that "if, after notice of the intention to arrest the defendant, he either flee or forcibly resist, the officer may use all the necessary means to effect the arrest." Tenn. Code Ann. § 40–7-108 (1982). The Department policy was slightly more restrictive than the statute, but still allowed the use of deadly force in cases of burglary. The incident was reviewed by the Memphis Police Firearm's Review Board and presented to a grand jury. Neither took any action.

Cleamtree Garner, Edward's father, then brought this action in the Federal District Court for the Western District of Tennessee, seeking damages under 42 U.S.C. § 1983 for asserted violations of Garner's constitutional rights. The complaint alleged that the shooting violated the Fourth, Fifth, Sixth, Eighth, and Fourteenth Amendments of the United States Constitution. It named as defendants Officer Hymon, the Police Department, its Director, and the Mayor and City of Memphis.

After a 3-day bench trial, the District Court entered judgment for all defendants. It dismissed the claims against the Mayor and the Director for lack of evidence. It then concluded that Hymon's actions were authorized by the Tennessee statute. Hymon had employed the only reasonable and practicable means of preventing Garner's escape. Garner had "recklessly and heedlessly attempted to vault over the fence to escape, thereby assuming the risk of being fired upon." The District Court found that the statute, and Hymon's actions, were constitutional. The Court of Appeals reversed and remanded.

OPINION

Whenever an officer restrains the freedom of a person to walk away, he has seized that person. There can be no question that apprehension by the use of deadly force is a seizure subject to the reasonableness requirement of the Fourth Amendment. A police officer may arrest a person if he has probable cause to believe that person committed a crime. Tennessee and the City of Memphis argue that if this requirement is satisfied the Fourth Amendment has nothing to say about how that seizure is made. The submission ignores the many cases in which this Court, by balancing the extent of the intrusion against the need for it, has examined the reasonableness of the manner in which a search or seizure is conducted.

The use of deadly force to prevent the escape of all felony suspects, whatever the circumstances, is constitutionally unreasonable. It is not better that all felony suspects die than that they escape. [Emphasis added] Where the suspect poses no immediate threat to the officer and no threat to others, the harm resulting from failing to apprehend him does not justify the use of deadly force to do so. It is no doubt unfortunate when a suspect who is in sight escapes, but the fact the police arrive a little late or are a little slower afoot does not always justify killing the suspect. A police officer may not seize an unarmed, nondangerous suspect by shooting him dead. The Tennessee statute is unconstitutional insofar as it authorizes the use of deadly force against such fleeing suspects.

Officer Hymon could not reasonably have believed that Garner—young, slight, and unarmed—posed any threat. Indeed, Hymon never attempted to justify his actions on any basis other than the need to prevent escape. The fact that Garner was a suspected burglar could not, without regard to the other circumstances, automatically justify the use of deadly force. Hymon did not have probable cause to believe that Garner, whom he correctly believed to be unarmed, posed any physical danger to himself or to others.

AFFIRMED.

DISSENT

O'CONNOR, J., joined by BURGER, C.J., and REHNQUIST, J.

The public interest involved in the use of deadly force as a last resort to apprehend a fleeing burglary suspect relates primarily to the serious nature of the crime. Household burglaries represent not only the illegal entry into a person's home, but also "pose a real risk of serious harm to others." According to recent Department of Justice statistics, "Three-fifths of all rapes in the home, three-fifths of all home robberies, and about a third of home aggravated and simple assaults are committed by burglars."

Against the strong public interests justifying the conduct at issue here must be weighed the individual interests implicated in the use of deadly force by police officers. The majority declares that "the suspect's fundamental interest in his own life need not be elaborated upon." This blithe assertion hardly provides an adequate substitute for the majority's failure to acknowledge the distinctive manner in which the suspect's interest in his life is even exposed to risk. For purposes of this case, we must recall that the police officer, in the course of investigating a nighttime burglary, had reasonable cause to arrest the suspect and ordered him to halt. The officer's use of force resulted because the suspected burglar refused to heed this command and the officer reasonably believed that there was no means short of firing his weapon to apprehend the suspect.

The policeman's hands should not be tied merely because of the possibility that the suspect will fail to cooperate with legitimate actions by law enforcement personnel.

QUESTIONS

1. **Should the Fourth Amendment apply to the manner of arrest? Defend your answer.**
2. **Professor H. Richard Uviller (1986), a longtime student of police power and the Constitution, commented on the decision in *Tennessee v. Garner*:**

   It is embarrassing for a law professor to be blindsided in his own territory. But the truth is, I didn't see it coming. It had never occurred to me that a police officer shooting to kill a fleeing felon might be engaging in an unconstitutional search and seizure. Of course, I can see the connection now that it has been explained to me, but I did not spontaneously equate a deadly shot with an arrest. And I have had some prior acquaintance not only with the fourth amendment, but specifically with the issue of the bullet aimed at the back of a retreating felon. (706)

   Should shooting a suspect be considered a Fourth Amendment "seizure"?
3. **Professor Uviller asks the following questions: Would the rule in this case permit an officer to shoot a drunk driver swerving erratically down the road headed toward a town? A person wanted for a series of violent crimes but not presently armed who flees from the police? How would you answer Professor Uviller's questions? Defend your answers.**
4. **Will this rule embolden criminals? Did the Court tilt the balance too far toward process and societal interests and too far away from the interest in results? Defend your answer.**

Nondeadly Force

Shooting is the most dramatic and publicized use of force to arrest suspects, but, in practice, officers are far more likely to use nondeadly force. In *Graham v. Connor* (1989), our next case excerpt, the Supreme Court applied the **objective standard of reasonable force** that it adopted in *Tennessee v. Garner*. According to the standard, the Fourth Amendment permits officers to use the amount of force necessary to apprehend and bring suspects under control. The standard is objective because it doesn't depend on the officer's intent or motives. So in law enforcement officers' use of nondeadly force, an arrest is reasonable when two elements are present:

1. Probable cause to arrest

2. The amount of force an officer uses is objectively reasonable

Under the objective standard of reasonableness, the Court points out: "An officer's evil intentions will not make a Fourth Amendment violation out of an objectively reasonable use of force; nor will an officer's good intentions make an objectively unreasonable use of force constitutional" (398).

In Graham v. Connor (1989), our next case excerpt, the U.S. Supreme Court established the criteria that lower courts have to use to decide the question of whether police use of force is "objectively reasonable."

CASE   Was the Police Use of Force Excessive?

Graham v. Connor
490 U.S. 386 (1989)

HISTORY

Dethorne Graham, a diabetic, sued several police officers to recover damages for injuries he suffered when the officers used physical force against him during an investigatory stop. The U.S. District Court directed a verdict for the defendant police officers. The court of appeals affirmed. The U.S. Supreme Court granted certiorari and reversed.

REHNQUIST, C.J., joined by WHITE, STEVENS, O'CONNOR, SCALIA, and KENNEDY, JJ.

FACTS

On November 12, 1984, Dethorne Graham, a diabetic, felt the onset of an insulin reaction. He asked a friend,

William Berry, to drive him to a nearby convenience store so he could purchase some orange juice to counteract the reaction. Berry agreed, but when Graham entered the store, he saw a number of people ahead of him in the checkout line. Concerned about the delay, he hurried out of the store and asked Berry to drive him to a friend's house instead.

Respondent Connor, an officer of the Charlotte, North Carolina, Police Department, saw Graham hastily enter and leave the store. The officer became suspicious that something was amiss and followed Berry's car. About one-half mile from the store, he made an investigative stop. Although Berry told Connor that Graham was simply suffering from a "sugar reaction," the officer ordered Berry and Graham to wait while he found out what, if anything, had happened at the convenience store. When Officer Connor returned to his patrol car to call for backup assistance, Graham got out of the car, ran around it twice, and finally sat down on the curb, where he passed out briefly.

In the ensuing confusion, a number of other Charlotte police officers arrived on the scene in response to Officer Connor's request for backup. One of the officers rolled Graham over on the sidewalk and cuffed his hands tightly behind his back, ignoring Berry's pleas to get him some sugar. Another officer said: "I've seen a lot of people with sugar diabetes that never acted like this. Ain't nothing wrong with the M. F. but drunk. Lock the S. B. up." Several officers then lifted Graham up from behind, carried him over to Berry's car, and placed him face down on its hood.

Regaining consciousness, Graham asked the officers to check in his wallet for a diabetic decal that he carried. In response, one of the officers told him to "shut up" and shoved his face down against the hood of the car. Four officers grabbed Graham and threw him headfirst into the police car. A friend of Graham's brought some orange juice to the car, but the officers refused to let him have it. Finally, Officer Connor received a report that Graham had done nothing wrong at the convenience store, and the officers drove him home and released him.

At some point during his encounter with the police, Graham sustained a broken foot, cuts on his wrists, a bruised forehead, and an injured shoulder; he also claims to have developed a loud ringing in his right ear that continues to this day. He commenced this action under 42 U.S.C. § 1983 against the individual officers involved in the incident, all of whom are respondents here, alleging that they had used excessive force in making the investigatory stop, in violation of "rights secured to him under the Fourteenth Amendment to the United States Constitution and 42 U.S.C. § 1983."

[Civil Rights Act actions (called § 1983 actions because they're brought under Title 42, Section 1983, of the Civil Rights Act of 1871, passed just after the Civil War) allow plaintiffs to go into federal courts to sue state police officers and their agency heads; county sheriffs and their deputies; and municipal police officers and their chiefs for violating plaintiffs' federal constitutional rights.]

The case was tried before a jury. At the close of petitioner's evidence, respondents moved for a directed verdict. In ruling on that motion, the District Court considered the following four factors, which it identified as "the factors to be considered in determining when the excessive use of force gives rise to a cause of action under § 1983":

1. the need for the application of force;
2. the relationship between that need and the amount of force that was used;
3. the extent of the injury inflicted; and
4. whether the force was applied in a good faith effort to maintain and restore discipline or maliciously and sadistically for the very purpose of causing harm.

Finding that the amount of force used by the officers was "appropriate under the circumstances," that "there was no discernable injury inflicted," and that the force used "was not applied maliciously or sadistically for the very purpose of causing harm," but in "a good faith effort to maintain or restore order in the face of a potentially explosive situation," the District Court granted respondents' motion for a directed verdict. A divided panel of the Court of Appeals for the Fourth Circuit affirmed. We granted certiorari, and now REVERSE.

OPINION

Many courts have seemed to assume, as did the courts in this case, that there is a generic "right" to be free from excessive force, grounded not in any particular constitutional provision but rather in basic principles of § 1983 jurisprudence. We reject this notion that all excessive force claims brought under § 1983 are governed by a single generic standard.

As we have said many times, § 1983 is not itself a source of substantive rights, but merely provides a method for vindicating federal rights elsewhere conferred. In addressing an excessive force claim brought under § 1983, analysis begins by identifying the specific constitutional right allegedly infringed by the challenged application of force. In most instances, that will be either the Fourth Amendment's prohibition against unreasonable seizures of the person, or the Eighth Amendment's ban on cruel and unusual punishments, which are the two primary sources of constitutional protection against physically abusive governmental conduct. The validity of the claim must then be judged by reference to the specific constitutional standard, which governs that right, rather than to some generalized "excessive force" standard.

Where, as here, the excessive force claim arises in the context of an arrest or investigatory stop of a free citizen, it is most properly characterized as one invoking the protections of the Fourth Amendment, which guarantees citizens the right "to be secure in their persons . . . against unreasonable . . . seizures" of the person.

Today we hold that all claims that law enforcement officers have used excessive force—deadly or not—in the course of an arrest, investigatory stop, or other "seizure" of a free citizen should be analyzed under the Fourth Amendment and its "reasonableness" standard, rather than under a "substantive due process" [general right against excessive force] approach. Because the Fourth Amendment provides an explicit textual source of constitutional protection against this sort of physically intrusive governmental conduct, that Amendment, not the more generalized notion of "substantive due process," must be the guide for analyzing these claims.

Determining whether the force used to effect a particular seizure is "reasonable" under the Fourth Amendment requires a careful balancing of "the nature and quality of the intrusion on the individual's Fourth Amendment interests" against the countervailing governmental interests at stake. Our Fourth Amendment jurisprudence has long recognized that the right to make an arrest or investigatory stop necessarily carries with it the right to use some degree of physical coercion or threat thereof to effect it.

With respect to a claim of excessive force, the standard of reasonableness at the moment applies: Not every push or shove, even if it may later seem unnecessary in the peace of a judge's chambers, violates the Fourth Amendment. The calculus of reasonableness must embody allowance for the fact that police officers are often forced to make split-second judgments—in circumstances that are tense, uncertain, and rapidly evolving—about the amount of force that is necessary in a particular situation.

As in other Fourth Amendment contexts, however, the "reasonableness" inquiry in an excessive force case is an objective one: the question is whether the officers' actions are "objectively reasonable" in light of the facts and circumstances confronting them, without regard to their underlying intent or motivation. An officer's evil intentions will not make a Fourth Amendment violation out of an objectively reasonable use of force; nor will an officer's good intentions make an objectively unreasonable use of force constitutional.

Because petitioner's excessive force claim is one arising under the Fourth Amendment, the Court of Appeals erred in analyzing it under the four-part *Johnson v. Glick* test. That test, which requires consideration of whether the individual officers acted in "good faith" or "maliciously and sadistically for the very purpose of causing harm," is incompatible with a proper Fourth Amendment analysis. We do not agree with the Court of Appeals' suggestion, that the "malicious and sadistic" inquiry is merely another way of describing conduct that is objectively unreasonable under the circumstances. Whatever the empirical correlations between "malicious and sadistic" behavior and objective unreasonableness may be, the fact remains that the "malicious and sadistic" factor puts in issue the subjective motivations of the individual officers, which our prior cases make clear has no bearing on whether a particular seizure is "unreasonable" under the Fourth Amendment.

Nor do we agree with the Court of Appeals' conclusion, that because the subjective motivations of the individual officers are of central importance in deciding whether force used against a convicted prisoner violates the Eighth Amendment, it cannot be reversible error to inquire into them in deciding whether force used against a suspect or arrestee violates the Fourth Amendment. Differing standards under the Fourth and Eighth Amendments are hardly surprising: the terms "cruel" and "punishment" clearly suggest some inquiry into subjective state of mind, whereas the term "unreasonable" does not. Moreover, the less protective Eighth Amendment standard applies only after the State has complied with the constitutional guarantees traditionally associated with criminal prosecutions.

The Fourth Amendment inquiry is one of "objective reasonableness" under the circumstances, and subjective concepts like "malice" and "sadism" have no proper place in that inquiry.

Because the Court of Appeals reviewed the District Court's ruling on the motion for directed verdict under an erroneous view of the governing substantive law, its judgment must be vacated and the case REMANDED to that court for reconsideration of that issue under the proper Fourth Amendment standard.

QUESTIONS

1. List all the specific uses of force by the officers.
2. State the standard that the Court adopted for determining whether the use of force violated the Fourth Amendment.
3. How does the Court's standard differ from the test that the Court of Appeals applied in the case?
4. Why did the Court change the standard? Which test do you favor? Explain your answer.
5. If you were applying the tests to the facts of this case, what decision would you reach? Defend your answer.

As noted in the text introducing *Graham v. Connor*, the Supreme Court left it to lower courts to apply the criteria of the objective-standard-of-reasonable-force test to a variety of types of force officers use to take and maintain control over arrested suspects. The major ones are listed in Table 5.5.

Our next excerpt, *Kuha v. Minnetonka* (2003), shows how one court applied the test, holding that the use of a dog trained in the **bite-and-hold technique** met the requirements of the test. According to the technique used in the excerpt, "if given a 'find' command, Arco [the dog] will find, 'bite' and 'hold' a suspect until commanded to release." This technique was used instead of the **find-and-bark technique**, in which dogs are trained to find suspects and then bark until officers can get control of the suspect.

TABLE 5.5

Lower Courts' Applications of "Objective Standard of Reasonable Force" Test

Type of Force	Case
Directing police dog to bite and hold	1. *Kuha v. City of Minnetonka* (see excerpt on p. 162)
	2. *Miller v. Clark County*, 340 F.3d 959 (CA9 2003). A deputy's use of a police dog to bite and hold a plaintiff's arm until backup arrived a minute later was objectively reasonable.
Pepper spraying	1. *Isom v. Town of Warren*, 360 F.3d 7 (CA1 2004). An officer's use of pepper spray to disarm a suspect armed with an axe was objectively reasonable.
	2. *McCormick v. City of Fort Lauderdale*, 333 F.3d 1234 (CA11 2003). It was objectively reasonable to use pepper spray against a suspect who had recently assaulted another person; "pepper spray ordinarily causes only temporary discomfort."
	3. *Vinyard v. Wilson*, 311 F.3d 1340 (CA11 2002). Using pepper spray in a minor crime when the suspect is secured, is not acting violently, and "there is no threat to officers or anyone else," is objectively unreasonable. But it is objectively reasonable when the "plaintiff was either resisting arrest or refusing police requests, such as requests to enter a patrol car or go to the hospital."
Firing lead-filled bean bag rounds from shotgun	1. *Bell v. Irwin*, 321 F.3d 637 (CA7 2003). Firing a bean from shotgun bag rounds when a suspect threatened to blow up a home with propane and kerosene and then "leaned toward a tank with what appeared to be a cigarette lighter" was objectively reasonable.
	2. *Deorle v. Rutherford*, 272 F.3d 1272 (CA9 2001). Use of lead-filled bean bag rounds is objectively reasonable only when a strong government interest compels its use, because it can cause serious injury.
Hog tying	*Cruz v. City of Laramie*, 239 F.3d 1183 (CA10 2001). Binding the ankles to the wrists behind a suspect's back is "forbidden when an individual's diminished capacity is apparent" because of the high risk of suffocation. When permissible "such restraint should be used with great care and continual observation of the well-being of the subject."
Tight handcuffing	1. *Payne v. Pauley*, 337 F.3d 767 (CA7 2003). Handcuffing a suspect tightly was objectively reasonable when the suspect "resisted arrest, failed to obey orders, [and] was accused of a more serious or violent crime."
	2. *Kopec v. Tate*, 361 F.3d 772 (CA3 2004). Placing excessively tight handcuffs on a suspect and needlessly failing to respond for 10 minutes to pleas to loosen them, causing permanent damage, was objectively unreasonable.
Tasering (stun gun)	*Draper v. Reynolds*, 369 F.3d 1270 (CA11 2004). A deputy's use of a Taser to bring a motorist under control in a difficult, tense situation where a "single use of the taser gun may well have prevented a physical struggle and serious harm to either" the driver or the officer was objectively reasonable.

In Kuha v. Minnetonka *(2003), our next case excerpt, a federal appeals court found that the city's dog bite-and-hold policy was objectively reasonable when officers used it to apprehend Jeff Kuha after he ran away during a traffic stop.*

CASE   Was Bite and Hold Excessive Force?

Kuha v. City of Minnetonka
365 F.3d 590 (CA8 Minn., 2003)

HISTORY

Jeff Kuha, who was bitten by a police dog, brought an action against the city of Minnetonka, Minnesota, and police officers William Roth, Dennis Warosh, and K-9 team member Kevin Anderson in charge of "Arco," alleging the use of excessive force in violation of his civil rights under § 1983, and asserting state law claims of assault and battery and negligence. The U.S. District Court for the District of Minnesota, granted summary judgment in favor of the defendants. Kuha appealed. The Court of Appeals affirmed in part and reversed in part, and rehearing was granted.

MELLOY, J.

FACTS

On the evening of September 22, 1999, Jeff Kuha went to a bar with friends. He had four or five beers at the bar and then drove to a friend's house. Kuha claims he left his friend's home at approximately 1:00 A.M., intending to drive home. Shortly after leaving, he drove his car into a roadside curb, damaging the car and flattening the tire. Kuha walked back to his friend's house to get help. He and his friend changed the tire and placed the damaged tire on the front seat of the car. Kuha then continued on his way home.

At approximately 5:30 A.M., Kuha encountered Officer Roth, a Minnetonka police officer, who was driving in the opposite direction. Kuha failed to dim his lights when he approached the oncoming police car. Officer Roth made a U-turn and pulled Kuha over. Officer Roth called in the vehicle's license plate information and started to get out of the car for what appeared to be a routine traffic stop.

At this point, Kuha opened his door, got out, looked at the officer, and ran from his car, heading for a ditch and swamp abutting the road. Officer Roth attempted to follow Kuha but Kuha disappeared into the swamp. Beyond the swamp was a hilly area with high grass and dense brush and foliage. Beyond that were apartment and office buildings. Officer Roth returned to his police car and called for back-up. While waiting for back-up, Officer Roth inspected Kuha's car, noting its damage and the flat tire on the front seat. He also found Kuha's wallet and concluded that the picture on the license matched that of the person who had fled from the scene.

Within minutes, Officers Warosh and Anderson arrived. They were accompanied by Officer Anderson's K-9 partner, "Arco." Arco is trained under a "bite and hold" method; thus, if given a "find" command, Arco will find, "bite" and "hold" a suspect until commanded to release. While tracking Kuha, Officer Anderson held Arco's leash in one hand and a flashlight in the other. Officer Warosh provided cover for the K-9 team. Arco remained on his leash as they tracked plaintiff up a steep, woody hill and toward a grassy field.

Approximately thirty minutes after the initial stop, and as the K-9 team reached the top of a hill, Arco alerted, indicating that Kuha was relatively nearby. At this point, Arco was around ten feet out on his lead. Arco bounded into the three-foot-high grass and "seized" Kuha. Arco is trained to bite and hold the first body part that he reaches. In this instance, Arco bit Kuha's upper leg. Kuha was naked except for his boxer shorts. He claims that he took off his clothes after swimming through the swamp because they were wet and cold.

Kuha states that he held his hands up to surrender as the officers approached and before Arco bit him, but concedes that the officers may not have seen him because of the high grass. The officers aver that they did not see the seizure but instead heard Kuha scream and arrived on the scene immediately thereafter. Prior to calling off Arco, Officers Anderson and Warosh inspected the area around and under Kuha to ensure he was unarmed. During this time, Kuha gripped Arco's head trying to free his hold. Officer Anderson repeatedly told Kuha he would not call off the dog until Kuha let go of the dog and put his hands up. Kuha eventually complied and Officer Anderson called off the dog. It is undisputed that the entire apprehension, from bite to release, took no more than ten to fifteen seconds.

The officers then handcuffed Kuha and noticed that Kuha was bleeding from the site where Arco bit him. They applied pressure to the wound and called for an ambulance. A subsequent medical examination revealed that Arco's bite had pierced plaintiff's femoral artery, causing substantial blood loss.

On May 25, 2000, Kuha pled guilty to the charge of disobeying a police officer. According to Kuha, he ran from Officer Roth because he feared he may have been over the legal alcohol consumption limit. Kuha claims he was afraid of being convicted for driving under the influence which would have severely hindered his prospects for a career as a commercial pilot. A sample of Kuha's blood was taken at the hospital when he was treated for the dog bite. The sample placed Kuha's blood alcohol level above the legal limit. He was not charged with driving under the influence, however, because of concerns that his blood loss may have altered the results of the test.

OPINION

Kuha asserts that Officers Anderson and Warosh used excessive force in violation of the Fourth and Fourteenth Amendments in:

(1) using a dog trained in the "bite and hold" method under the circumstances of the case—where Kuha had fled from a minor traffic violation and there was no legitimate concern that he was armed or dangerous;

(2) allowing the dog to attack Kuha without warning; and

(3) refusing to call off the dog when it was clear that Kuha was unarmed and not dangerous.

Kuha alleges municipal liability based on the City's failure to properly formulate a police dog policy that contemplates less dangerous methods—e.g., the "find and bark" method.

Kuha's excessive force claim is analyzed under the Fourth Amendment's "objective reasonableness" standard. The test of reasonableness under the Fourth Amendment is not capable of precise definition or mechanical application. However, its proper application requires careful attention to the facts and circumstances of each particular case, including the severity of the crime at issue, whether the suspect poses an immediate threat to the safety of the officers or others, and whether he is actively resisting arrest or attempting to evade arrest by flight. In sum, the nature and quality of the intrusion on the individual's Fourth Amendment interests must be balanced against the importance of the governmental interests alleged to justify the intrusion.

The reasonableness of a particular use of force must be judged from the perspective of a reasonable officer on the scene, rather than with the 20/20 vision of hindsight.

The calculus of reasonableness must embody allowance for the fact that police officers are often forced to make split-second judgments—in circumstances that are tense, uncertain, and rapidly evolving—about the amount of force that is necessary in a particular situation. The question is whether the officers' actions are "objectively reasonable" in light of the facts and circumstances confronting them, without regard to their underlying intent or motivation. An officer's evil intentions will not make a Fourth Amendment violation out of an objectively reasonable use of force; nor will an officer's good intentions make an objectively unreasonable use of force constitutional.

In reviewing Kuha's claims, the relevant inquiry is whether Kuha presented enough proof in support of his claim that a jury could properly find that the degree of force used against him was not objectively reasonable. We conclude that he did. We conclude that a jury could properly find it objectively unreasonable to use a police dog trained in the bite and hold method without first giving the suspect a warning and opportunity for peaceful surrender.

The presence or absence of a warning is a critical fact in virtually every excessive force case involving a police dog. The district court held that the officers were not required to put themselves in danger by giving away their location to a hiding suspect whom they did not know for certain was unarmed. We agree that officer safety is paramount but disagree that the district court properly decided as a matter of law that requiring a verbal warning will put officers at increased risk. To the contrary, such a practice would likely diminish the risk of confrontation by increasing the likelihood that a suspect will surrender.

While there may be exceptional cases where a warning is not feasible, we see no reason why, in this case, a rational jury would be precluded from finding that the officers could have placed themselves out of harm's way—e.g., at the top of the hill where they had a good vantage point, or behind one of the nearby apartment buildings—and given a loud verbal warning that a police dog was present and trained to seize by force. Although a verbal warning will not always result in a peaceful surrender, it may be, as argued by plaintiff, that, without such a warning, seizure by force is a nearly foregone conclusion.

Kuha contends that the use of a police dog trained only in the bite and hold method was objectively unreasonable. In essence, Kuha argues that the governmental interest in apprehending a fleeing misdemeanant will never outweigh the potential harm inherent in canine assisted apprehensions. We disagree. Police dogs serve important law enforcement functions, and their use is not inherently dangerous.

There are innumerable situations where the use of a properly trained and utilized police dog, even one trained only in the bite and hold technique, will not result in physical interaction with the suspect, most obviously because the dog remains on a leash until his handler releases him. Police are trained, and constitutionally obligated, to use only that amount of force reasonably necessary to effect a seizure. We will not presume that officers will abuse their discretion in this respect. And, as discussed above, we believe it will be the rare case where a verbal warning prior to releasing the dog would not facilitate a peaceful resolution of the situation.

In sum, the mere use of a police dog trained to bite and hold does not rise to the level of a constitutional violation. And in this particular case, we agree that, given the odd turn of events initiated by Kuha, the initial decision to use Arco to assist in Kuha's apprehension was objectively reasonable as a matter of law.

Kuha's claim of excessive force by the officers in the moments following his apprehension by Arco is a closer question. We must decide whether, construing the facts in the light most favorable to Kuha, a jury could properly conclude that it was objectively unreasonable for the officers to require Kuha to release Arco prior to calling off the dog. As Arco was biting Kuha's upper leg, Kuha's hands gripped the dog's head in an attempt to minimize the damage and pain. Officer Anderson repeatedly told Kuha that he would not call off the dog until Kuha raised his hands in the air. Kuha states that he tried to comply but his hands would instinctively return to the dog's head. Eventually Kuha did comply with Officer Anderson's order and the dog was called off. Kuha emphasizes that he was nearly naked during the attack, that he was clearly unarmed, and that the officers had no indication that he was dangerous.

Kuha's argument is compelling. It does not, however, end our analysis. *Graham* [*Graham v. Connor* excerpted p. 158] requires "careful attention to the facts and circumstances of each particular case," and cautions against hindsight. Here, the officers were confronted with an inexplicable flight from a minor traffic stop in the early hours of the morning. They knew the suspect had chosen to swim through a swamp rather than encounter a police officer. The area they were searching was difficult to traverse. The officers knew there were inhabited apartment buildings nearby and that residents would soon be leaving for work. They knew that Officer Roth had not seen a gun in the brief moments before Kuha fled, but, given the totality of the circumstances, they were reasonably wary of what they might encounter when they found Kuha, and reasonably concerned for their safety.

Turning to the actual seizure, it is undisputed that the entire incident lasted only ten to fifteen seconds. Moreover, we note that this is not a case where the officers are accused of siccing a police dog on a manifestly unarmed and compliant suspect. It appears uncontested that the officers did not see the initial seizure since Arco was ten feet ahead on his lead. They heard the scream and arrived immediately thereafter. On arrival, the officers were confronted with Arco "holding" a nearly naked suspect who had been hiding in three-feet-high grass. During the ten seconds or so that ensued, the officers were searching the area under and around Kuha to ensure that he was not hiding a weapon which could be used against the officers or the dog. At the same time, Officer Anderson was ordering Kuha to release the dog's head.

In light of the short time frame at issue and the conditions under which Kuha fled and was found, we conclude that as a matter of law the officers' actions after Kuha was bitten were not objectively unreasonable. We are mindful that we must construe the facts in the light most favorable to Kuha, and we do so. But we cannot ignore the undisputed facts that are equally relevant to our analysis. To do otherwise would vitiate *Graham*'s explicit recognition of, and allowance for, a measure of deference to officer judgment given the "tense, uncertain, and rapidly evolving" circumstances that officers often confront. . . .

With respect to Kuha's § 1983 claim, we REVERSE the district court's judgment in favor of the City and REMAND for further proceedings consistent with this opinion.

QUESTIONS

1. **List in chronological order all the actions taken by Officers William Roth, Dennis Warosh, and K-9 team member Kevin Anderson in charge of "Arco."**
2. **List the objective basis for each of the actions.**
3. **Summarize the court's arguments to support its decision.**
4. **Label each of the actions as either "objectively reasonable" or "objectively unreasonable." Defend your answer.**
5. **The Los Angeles Police Department changed from a "bite and hold" to "find and bark" policy in 1992. Researchers (Hutson and others 1997) reported the effects of the change of policy by collecting information about dog-bite patients in police custody from 1988 to 1995. Consider the results of their study in Figures 5.1 and 5.2. In view of these findings, is "bite and hold" instead of "find and bark" a reasonable use of force?**

FIGURE 5.1 Number of K-9 Dog-bite Patients in Police Custody

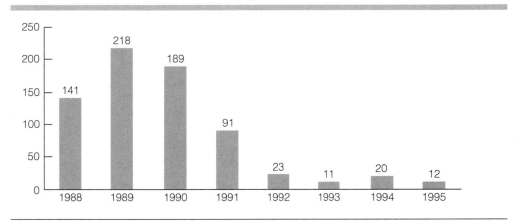

Hutson and others. 1997. p. 639.

FIGURE 5.2 Some Characteristics of Dog-bite Patients by Percent

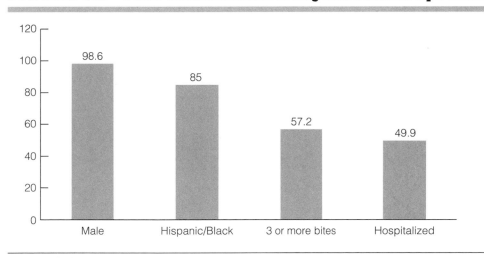

Hutson and others. 1997. p. 637.

After Arrest

LO 9

Immediately after an arrest, police officers may use force to subdue unruly suspects; to prevent escape; and to protect suspects, officers, other people, or property. When they arrest suspects for *felonies*, officers almost always take the following actions:

1. Search suspects (see Chapter 6)

2. Take suspects to the police station and then "book" them, by putting their name and address, the time the crime was committed, and other information into the police blotter

3. Photograph and fingerprint them

4. Interrogate them (Chapter 8)

5. Put them into lineups (Chapter 9)

6. Turn the results of the initial investigations over to prosecutors (Chapter 12)

7. Present prisoners to a magistrate (Chapter 12)

Misdemeanor suspects are not usually arrested; they're issued a **citation** (an order to appear before a judge on a certain date to defend against a charge, often a traffic violation). But not always. Sometimes, officers make a custodial arrest and take some or all of the seven actions in the preceding list. Are these full custodial arrests reasonable Fourth Amendment seizures? A sharply divided U.S. Supreme Court (5–4) answered yes in the next excerpted case, *Atwater v. City of Lago Vista*.

In Atwater v. City of Lago Vista (2001), the U.S. Supreme Court held that the Fourth Amendment authorized a police officer to make a full custodial arrest of Gail Atwater for committing a fine-only criminal offense in his presence.

CASE   Was the Custodial Arrest for Violating the Fine-Only Seat Belt Law Reasonable?

Atwater v. City of Lago Vista

532 U.S. 318 (2001)

HISTORY

Gail Atwater was charged with driving without her seat belt fastened, failing to secure her children in seat belts, driving without a license, and failing to provide proof of insurance. She pleaded no contest to the misdemeanor seat belt offenses and paid a $50 fine; the other charges were dismissed. Atwater and her husband, Michael Haas, sued Officer Bart Turek, the City of Lago Vista, and the Lago Vista Chief of Police Frank Miller. The City removed the suit to the U.S. District Court for the Western District of Texas. The District Court granted the City's summary judgment motion. A panel of the U.S. Court of Appeals for the Fifth Circuit reversed. Sitting en banc, the Court of Appeals vacated the panel's decision and affirmed the District Court's summary judgment for the City. The U.S. Supreme Court affirmed.

SOUTER, J., joined by REHNQUIST, C.J., and SCALIA, KENNEDY, THOMAS, JJ.

FACTS

[The facts are taken from 165 F.3d 380, 382–383 (1999).]

Gail Atwater and her family are long-term residents of Lago Vista, Texas, a suburb of Austin. She is a full-time mother and her husband is an emergency room physician at a local hospital. On the pleasant spring afternoon of March 26, 1997, as Gail Atwater was driving her children home after their soccer practice at 15 miles per hour through her residential neighborhood, she violated Section 545.413 of the Texas Transportation Code. Neither Gail Atwater, her four-year-old son Mac nor her six-year-old daughter Anya were wearing their seat belts.

Detecting this breach of the peace and dignity of the state, Lago Vista police officer, Bart Turek, set about to protect the community from the perpetration of such a crime. In doing so, he brought to bear the full panoply of means available to accomplish his goal—verbal abuse, handcuffs, placing Gail Atwater under custodial arrest, and hauling her to the local police station. It was not a proud moment for the City of Lago Vista.

When Officer Turek pulled over Atwater's pickup, she and her children remained in the vehicle. Officer Turek approached the driver's side window and aggressively jabbed his finger toward her face. Turek screamed either that they had met before or had this conversation before. Turek's conduct frightened her children, so Atwater calmly and in a normal tone requested that Turek lower his voice. According to Atwater, the request that Turek lower his voice further triggered his wrath. Turek responded immediately by telling Atwater that she was going to jail. Atwater remained calm. Atwater was not acting suspiciously, she did not pose any threat to Turek, and she was not engaged in any illegal conduct other than failing to wear a seat belt when Turek told her she was going to jail.

Turek continued to speak to Atwater in a verbally abusive manner, accusing her of not caring for her children. Atwater's children and bystanders including friends and other Lago Vista residents who drove or walked by witnessed Turek's tirade. Turek stated that he recently stopped Atwater for not having her children in seat belts, but such was not the case. Turek had in fact stopped her several months before for allowing her son to ride on the front seat arm rest, but the seat belt was securely fastened. No citation was issued.

After telling Atwater that she would be taken to jail, Turek demanded her driver's license and proof of insurance. When Atwater informed Turek that her license and insurance card were in her purse that had been stolen a couple of days before, Turek ridiculed her and implied she was a liar, even though, assuming he followed standard procedures during the previous stop, he knew she had a valid driver's license and was an insured driver. Atwater eventually provided her driver's license number and address from her check book. Atwater then asked Turek to allow her to take her children to a friend's home just two houses down before taking her to jail, but he refused her request. Turek stated that her children could accompany her to the police station. Fortunately, a friend of Atwater's who came to the scene took the children into her care.

Although under Texas law Turek could have issued Atwater a traffic citation if she signed a promise to appear, (1) he instead chose to handcuff Atwater with her hands behind her back, load her into his squad car, and take her to the police station. Once at the police station, Atwater was required to remove her shoes and glasses, empty her pockets and have her picture taken. She was then placed in a jail cell for approximately one hour before being taken before a magistrate.

Atwater pleaded no contest to not wearing a seat belt and allowing her children to not wear seat belts. Charges of driving without a license or proof of insurance were dismissed. This incident caused Atwater and her children extreme emotional distress and anxiety. Her youngest child has required counseling, and Atwater has been prescribed medication for nightmares, insomnia, and depression resulting from this incident.

Frank Miller, the chief of police for Lago Vista, was the ultimate authority in the police department in the areas of management of department personnel. Lago Vista's policy for enforcement of traffic violations allows for the use of custodial arrests to promote its goals of increased traffic ordinance compliance. The policy specifically leaves to the officer's judgment whether to take a motorist into custody for violations of a traffic ordinance, and according to Appellants, encourages the very conduct engaged in by Officer Turek.

OPINION

The question is whether the Fourth Amendment forbids a warrantless arrest for a minor criminal offense, such as a misdemeanor seat belt violation punishable only by a fine. We hold that it does not.

If we were to derive a rule exclusively to address the uncontested facts of this case, Atwater might well prevail. She was a known and established resident of Lago Vista with no place to hide and no incentive to flee, and common sense says she would almost certainly have buckled up as a condition of driving off with a citation. In her case, the physical incidents of arrest were merely gratuitous humiliations imposed by a police officer who was (at best) exercising extremely poor judgment. Atwater's claim to live free of pointless indignity and confinement clearly outweighs anything the City can raise against it specific to her case.

[Atwater argues for a new] arrest rule forbidding custodial arrest, even upon probable cause, when conviction could not ultimately carry any jail time and when the government shows no compelling need for immediate detention. But we have traditionally recognized that a responsible Fourth Amendment balance is not well served by standards requiring sensitive, case-by-case determinations of government need, lest every discretionary judgment in the field be converted into an occasion for constitutional review. Often enough, the Fourth Amendment has to be applied on the spur (and in the heat) of the moment, and the object in implementing its command of reasonableness is to draw standards sufficiently clear and simple to be applied with a fair prospect of surviving judicial second-guessing months and years after an arrest or search is made.

Courts attempting to strike a reasonable Fourth Amendment balance thus credit the government's side with an essential interest in readily administrable rules. See *New York v. Belton* [excerpted in Chapter 6] (Fourth Amendment rules "ought to be expressed in terms that are readily applicable by the police in the context of the law enforcement activities in which they are necessarily engaged" and not "qualified by all sorts of ifs, ands, and buts").

Atwater's rule promises very little in the way of administrability. It is no answer that the police routinely make judgments on grounds like risk of immediate repetition; they surely do and should. But there is a world of difference between making that judgment in choosing between the discretionary leniency of a summons in place of a clearly lawful arrest, and making the same judgment when the question is the lawfulness of the warrantless arrest itself. It is the difference between no basis for legal action challenging the discretionary judgment, on the one hand, and the prospect of evidentiary exclusion or (as here) personal § 1983 liability for the misapplication of a constitutional standard, on the other.

Atwater's rule therefore would not only place police in an almost impossible spot but would guarantee increased litigation over many of the arrests that would occur. For all these reasons, Atwater's various distinctions between permissible and impermissible arrests for minor crimes strike us as "very unsatisfactory lines" to require police officers to draw on a moment's notice.

One may ask, of course, why these difficulties may not be answered by a simple tie breaker for the police to follow in the field: if in doubt, do not arrest. Whatever help the tie breaker might give would come at the price of a systematic disincentive to arrest in situations where arresting would serve an important societal interest. [For example,] an officer not quite sure that drugs weighed enough to warrant jail time or not quite certain about a suspect's risk of flight would not arrest, even though it could perfectly well turn out that, in fact, the offense called for incarceration and the defendant was long gone on the day of trial. Multiplied many times over, the costs to society of such under enforcement could easily outweigh the costs to defendants of being needlessly arrested and booked, as Atwater herself acknowledges.

Just how easily the costs could outweigh the benefits may be shown by asking, as one Member of this Court did at oral argument, "how bad the problem is out there." The very fact that the law has never jelled the way Atwater would have it leads one to wonder whether warrantless misdemeanor arrests need constitutional attention, and there is cause to think the answer is no. So far as such arrests might be thought to pose a threat to the probable cause requirement, anyone arrested for a crime without formal process, whether for felony or misdemeanor, is entitled to a magistrate's review of probable cause within 48 hours, and there is no reason to think the procedure in this case atypical in giving the suspect a prompt opportunity to request release, see Tex. Tran. Code Ann. §543.002 (1999) (persons arrested for traffic offenses to be taken "immediately" before a magistrate).

Many jurisdictions, moreover, have chosen to impose more restrictive safeguards through statutes limiting warrantless arrests for minor offenses. It is, in fact, only natural that States should resort to this sort of legislative regulation, for it is in the interest of the police to limit petty-offense arrests, which carry costs that are simply too great to incur without good reason.

Finally, the preference for categorical treatment of Fourth Amendment claims gives way to individualized review when a defendant makes a colorable argument that an arrest, with or without a warrant, was "conducted in an extraordinary manner, unusually harmful to [her] privacy or even physical interests."

The upshot of all these influences, combined with the good sense (and, failing that, the political accountability) of most local lawmakers and law-enforcement officials, is a dearth of horribles demanding redress. Indeed, when Atwater's counsel was asked at oral argument for any indications of comparably foolish, warrantless misdemeanor arrests, he could offer only one. We are sure that there are others, but just as surely the country is not confronting anything like an epidemic of unnecessary minor-offense arrests. That fact caps the reasons for rejecting Atwater's request for the development of a new and distinct body of constitutional law.

Accordingly, we confirm today what our prior cases have intimated: the standard of probable cause "applies to all arrests, without the need to 'balance' the interests and circumstances involved in particular situations." If an officer has probable cause to believe that an individual has committed even a very minor criminal offense in his presence, he may, without violating the Fourth Amendment, arrest the offender.

Atwater's arrest satisfied constitutional requirements. There is no dispute that Officer Turek had probable cause to believe that Atwater had committed a crime in his presence. She admits that neither she nor her children were wearing seat belts, as required by Tex. Tran. Code Ann. §545.413 (1999). Turek was accordingly *authorized* (not *required*, but authorized) to make a *custodial* [italics added] arrest without balancing costs and benefits or determining whether or not Atwater's arrest was in some sense necessary. Nor was the arrest made in an "extraordinary manner, unusually harmful to her privacy or physical interests."

The question whether a search or seizure is "extraordinary" turns, above all else, on the manner in which the search or seizure is executed: *Tennessee v. Garner* (1985) ("seizure by means of deadly force") [excerpted earlier on p. 156], *Wilson v. Arkansas* (1995) ("unannounced entry into a home") [excerpted in Chapter 6], *Welsh v. Wisconsin* (1984) ("entry into a home without a warrant"), and *Winston v. Lee* (1985) ("physical penetration of the body").

Atwater's arrest was surely "humiliating," as she says in her brief, but it was no more "harmful to privacy or physical interests" than the normal custodial arrest. She was handcuffed, placed in a squad car, and taken to the local police station, where officers asked her to remove her shoes, jewelry, and glasses, and to empty her pockets. They then took her photograph and placed her in a cell, alone, for about an hour, after which she was taken before a magistrate, and released on $310 bond. The arrest and booking were inconvenient and embarrassing to Atwater, but not so extraordinary as to violate the Fourth Amendment.

The Court of Appeals' en banc judgment is AFFIRMED.

DISSENT

O'CONNOR, J., joined by STEVENS, GINSBURG, and BREYER, JJ.

The Court recognizes that the arrest of Gail Atwater was a "pointless indignity" that served no discernible state interest, and yet holds that her arrest was constitutionally permissible. Because the Court's position is inconsistent with the explicit guarantee of the Fourth Amendment, I dissent. A full custodial arrest, such as the one to which Ms. Atwater was subjected, is the quintessential seizure.

When a full custodial arrest is effected without a warrant, the plain language of the Fourth Amendment requires that the arrest be reasonable. "The touchstone of our analysis under the Fourth Amendment is always the reasonableness in all the circumstances of the particular governmental invasion of a citizen's personal security." We evaluate the search or seizure under traditional standards of reasonableness by assessing, on the one hand, the degree to which it intrudes upon an individual's privacy and, on the other, the degree to which it is needed for the promotion of legitimate governmental interests." In other words, in determining reasonableness, each case is to be decided on its own facts and circumstances.

A custodial arrest exacts an obvious toll on an individual's liberty and privacy, even when the period of custody is relatively brief. The arrestee is subject to a full search of her person and confiscation of her possessions. If the arrestee is the occupant of a car, the entire passenger compartment of the car, including packages therein, is subject to search as well. The arrestee may be detained for up to 48 hours without having a magistrate determine whether there in fact was probable cause for the arrest. Because people arrested for all types of violent and nonviolent offenses may be housed together awaiting such review, this detention period is potentially dangerous. And once the period of custody is over, the fact of the arrest is a permanent part of the public record.

If the State has decided that a fine, and not imprisonment, is the appropriate punishment for an offense, the State's interest in taking a person suspected of committing that offense into custody is surely limited, at best. This is not to say that the State will never have such an interest. A full custodial arrest may on occasion vindicate legitimate state interests, even if the crime is punishable only by fine. Arrest is the surest way to abate criminal conduct. It may also allow the police to verify the offender's identity and, if the offender poses a flight risk, to ensure her appearance at trial. But when such considerations are not present, a citation or summons may serve the State's remaining law enforcement interests every bit as effectively as an arrest.

Because a full custodial arrest is such a severe intrusion on an individual's liberty, its reasonableness hinges on the degree to which it is needed for the promotion of legitimate governmental interests. In light of the availability of citations to promote a State's interests when a fine-only offense has been committed, I cannot concur in a rule which deems a full custodial arrest to be reasonable in every circumstance. Giving police officers constitutional carte blanche to effect an arrest whenever there is probable cause to believe a fine-only misdemeanor has been committed is irreconcilable with the Fourth Amendment's command that seizures be reasonable.

Instead, I would require that when there is probable cause to believe that a fine-only offense has been committed, the police officer should issue a citation unless the officer is able to point to specific and articulable facts which, taken together with rational inferences from those facts, reasonably warrant the additional intrusion of a full custodial arrest.

The majority insists that a bright-line rule focused on probable cause is necessary to vindicate the State's interest in easily administrable law enforcement rules. While clarity is certainly a value worthy of consideration in our Fourth Amendment jurisprudence, it by no means trumps the values of liberty and privacy at the heart of the Amendment's protections.

The record in this case makes it abundantly clear that Ms. Atwater's arrest was constitutionally unreasonable. Atwater readily admits—as she did when Officer Turek pulled her over—that she violated Texas' seat belt law. While Turek was justified in stopping Atwater, neither law nor reason supports his decision to arrest her instead of simply giving her a citation. The officer's actions cannot sensibly be viewed as a permissible means of balancing Atwater's Fourth Amendment interests with the State's own legitimate interests.

There is no question that Officer Turek's actions severely infringed Atwater's liberty and privacy. Turek was loud and accusatory from the moment he approached Atwater's car. Atwater's young children were terrified and hysterical. Yet when Atwater asked Turek to lower his voice because he was scaring the children, he responded by jabbing his finger in Atwater's face and saying, "You're going to jail." Having made the decision to arrest, Turek did not inform Atwater of her right to remain silent. He instead asked for her license and insurance information.

Atwater asked if she could at least take her children to a friend's house down the street before going to the police station. But Turek—who had just castigated Atwater for not caring for her children—refused and said he would take the children into custody as well. Only the intervention of neighborhood children who had witnessed the scene and summoned one of Atwater's friends saved the children from being hauled to jail with their mother.

With the children gone, Officer Turek handcuffed Ms. Atwater with her hands behind her back, placed her in the police car, and drove her to the police station. Ironically, Turek did not secure Atwater in a seat belt for the drive. At the station, Atwater was forced to remove her shoes, relinquish her possessions, and wait in a holding cell for about an hour. A judge finally informed Atwater of her rights and the charges against her, and released her when she posted bond. Atwater returned to the scene of the arrest, only to find that her car had been towed.

Ms. Atwater ultimately pleaded no contest to violating the seat belt law and was fined $50. Even though that fine was the maximum penalty for her crime, and even though Officer Turek has never articulated any justification for his actions, the city contends that arresting Atwater was constitutionally reasonable because it advanced two legitimate interests: "the enforcement of child safety laws and encouraging [Atwater] to appear for trial." It is difficult to see how arresting Atwater served either of these goals any more effectively than the issuance of a citation. With respect to the goal of law enforcement generally, Atwater did not pose a great danger to the community.

She had been driving very slowly—approximately 15 miles per hour—in broad daylight on a residential street that had no other traffic. Nor was she a repeat offender; until that day, she had received one traffic citation in her life—a ticket, more than 10 years earlier, for failure to signal a lane change. Although Officer Turek had stopped Atwater approximately three months earlier because he thought that Atwater's son was not wearing a seat belt, Turek had been mistaken. Moreover, Atwater immediately accepted responsibility and apologized for her conduct. Thus, there was every indication that Atwater would have buckled herself and her children in had she been cited and allowed to leave. With respect to the related goal of child welfare, the decision to arrest Atwater was nothing short of counterproductive.

Atwater's children witnessed Officer Turek yell at their mother and threaten to take them all into custody. Ultimately, they were forced to leave her behind with Turek, knowing that she was being taken to jail. Understandably, the 3-year-old boy was "very, very, very traumatized." After the incident, he had to see a child psychologist regularly, who reported that the boy "felt very guilty that he couldn't stop this horrible thing . . . he was powerless to help his mother or sister." Both of Atwater's children are now terrified at the sight of any police car. According to Atwater, the arrest "just never leaves us. It's a conversation we have every other day, once a week, and it's—it raises its head constantly in our lives."

Citing Atwater surely would have served the children's interests well. It would have taught Atwater to ensure that her children were buckled up in the future. It also would have taught the children an important lesson in accepting responsibility and obeying the law. Arresting Atwater, though, taught the children an entirely different lesson: that "the bad person could just as easily be the policeman as it could be the most horrible person they could imagine."

The City also contends that the arrest was necessary to ensure Atwater's appearance in court. Atwater, however, was far from a flight risk. A 16-year resident of Lago Vista, population 2,486, Atwater was not likely to abscond. Although she was unable to produce her driver's license because it had been stolen, she gave Officer Turek her license number and address. In addition, Officer Turek knew from their previous encounter that Atwater was a local resident.

The city's justifications fall far short of rationalizing the extraordinary intrusion on Gail Atwater and her children. Measuring "the degree to which [Atwater's custodial arrest was] needed for the promotion of legitimate governmental interests," against "the degree to which it intruded upon her privacy," it can hardly be doubted that Turek's actions were disproportionate to Atwater's crime.

The majority's assessment that "Atwater's claim to live free of pointless indignity and confinement clearly outweighs anything the City can raise against it specific to her case," is quite correct. In my view, the Fourth Amendment inquiry ends there.

The Court's error, however, does not merely affect the disposition of this case. The per se rule that the Court creates has potentially serious consequences for the everyday lives of Americans. A broad range of conduct falls into the category of fine-only misdemeanors. In Texas alone, for example, disobeying any sort of traffic warning sign is a misdemeanor punishable only by fine, as is failing to pay a highway toll, and driving with expired license plates. Nor are fine-only crimes limited to the traffic context. In several States, for example, littering is a criminal offense punishable only by fine.

To be sure, such laws are valid and wise exercises of the States' power to protect the public health and welfare. My concern lies not with the decision to enact or enforce these laws, but rather with the manner in which they may be enforced. Under today's holding, when a police officer has probable cause to believe that a fine-only misdemeanor offense has occurred, that officer may stop the suspect, issue a citation, and let the person continue on her way. Or, if a traffic violation, the officer may stop the car, arrest the driver, search the driver, search the entire passenger compartment of the car including any purse or package inside, and impound the car and inventory all of its contents. Although the Fourth Amendment expressly requires that the latter course be a reasonable and proportional response to the circumstances of the offense, the majority gives officers unfettered discretion to choose that course without articulating a single reason why such action is appropriate.

Such unbounded discretion carries with it grave potential for abuse. The majority takes comfort in the lack of evidence of "an epidemic of unnecessary minor-offense arrests." But the relatively small number of published cases dealing with such arrests proves little and should provide little solace. Indeed, as the recent debate over racial profiling demonstrates all too clearly, a relatively minor traffic infraction may often serve as an excuse for stopping and harassing an individual. After today, the arsenal available to any officer extends to a full arrest and the searches permissible concomitant to that arrest. An officer's subjective motivations for making a traffic stop are not relevant considerations in determining the reasonableness of the stop. But it is precisely because these motivations are beyond our purview that we must vigilantly ensure that officers' poststop actions—which are properly within our reach—comport with the Fourth Amendment's guarantee of reasonableness.

The Court neglects the Fourth Amendment's express command in the name of administrative ease. In so doing, it cloaks the pointless indignity that Gail Atwater suffered with the mantle of reasonableness. I respectfully dissent.

QUESTIONS

1. List all of Officer Turek's actions leading up to, during, and following Gail Atwater's arrest.
2. List all the actions taken by booking officers after Officer Turek turned her over to them.
3. According to the majority opinion, what is the bright-line rule regarding arrests for fine-only offenses?
4. Summarize the majority's arguments supporting the bright-line rule.
5. According to the majority, what are the exceptions to the bright-line rule?
6. Summarize the dissent's arguments against the bright-line rule.
7. State the rule the dissent recommends for fine-only offenses.
8. Summarize the dissent's arguments in favor of the rule it recommends.
9. List the exceptions the dissent recommends should apply to its rule.

EXPLORING FURTHER
....

After Arrest

Was the Custodial Arrest Reasonable?

Hedgepeth v. Washington Metro Area Transit and others, 284 F.Supp.2d 145 (D.D.C. 2003)

FACTS It was the start of another school year and the Washington Metropolitan Area Transit Authority (WMATA) was once again getting complaints about bad behavior by students using the Tenleytown/American University Metro rail station. In response WMATA embarked on a week-long undercover operation to enforce a "zero-tolerance" policy with respect to violations of certain ordinances, including one that makes it unlawful for any person to eat or drink in a Metro rail station.

"Zero tolerance" had more fateful consequences for children than for adults. Adults who violate § 35–251(b) typically receive a citation subjecting them to a fine of $10 to $50. *Id.* § 35–253. District of Columbia law, however, does not provide for the issuance of citations for non-traffic offenses to those under eighteen years of age. Instead, a minor who has committed what an officer has reasonable grounds to believe is a "delinquent act" "may be taken into custody."

Committing an offense under District of Columbia law, such as eating in a Metro rail station, constitutes a "delinquent act." The upshot of all this is that zero-tolerance enforcement of § 35–251(b) entailed the arrest of every offending minor but not every offending adult.

The undercover operation was in effect on October 23, 2000, when twelve-year-old Ansche Hedgepeth and a classmate entered the Tenleytown/AU station on their way home from school. Ansche had stopped at a fast-food restaurant on the way and ordered a bag of french fries—to go. While waiting for her companion to purchase a fare-card, Ansche removed and ate a french fry from the take-out bag she was holding.

After proceeding through the fare-gate, Ansche was stopped by a plain-clothed Metro Transit Police officer, who identified himself and informed her that he was arresting her for eating in the Metro rail station. The officer then handcuffed Ansche behind her back while another officer searched her and her backpack. Pursuant to established procedure, her shoelaces were removed.

Upset and crying, Ansche was transported to the District of Columbia's Juvenile Processing Center some distance away, where she was fingerprinted and processed before being released into the custody of her mother three hours later.

The no-citation policy was not, it turned out, carved in stone. The negative publicity surrounding Ansche's arrest prompted WMATA to adopt a new policy effective January 31, 2001, allowing WMATA officers to issue citations to juveniles violating § 35–251(b). Zero tolerance was also not a policy for the ages. Effective May 8, 2001, WMATA adopted a new Written Warning Notice Program, under which juveniles eating in the Metro are neither arrested nor issued citations, but instead given written warnings, with a letter notifying their parents and school. Only after the third infraction over the course of a year may a juvenile be formally prosecuted.

On April 9, 2001, Ansche's mother Tracey Hedgepeth brought this action as Ansche's next friend in the United States District Court for the District of Columbia. The complaint was filed under 42 U.S.C. § 1983 and named WMATA, its General Manager, the arresting officer, and the District of Columbia as defendants. It alleged that Ansche's arrest was an unreasonable seizure under the Fourth Amendment. The complaint sought declaratory and injunctive relief against the enforcement policies leading to Ansche's arrest, and expungement of Ansche's arrest record.

Was the custodial arrest a reasonable Fourth Amendment seizure?

DECISION Yes, said the U.S. District of Columbia Court of Appeals.

OPINION Ansche Hedgepeth challenges her arrest on the ground that it was an unreasonable seizure in violation of the Fourth Amendment. This claim quickly runs into the Supreme Court's recent holding in *Atwater v. City of Lago Vista*. The Court in *Atwater* undertook a two-step inquiry in addressing the plaintiff's argument that a warrantless arrest for a fine-only offense was unreasonable under the Fourth Amendment. It first concluded that Atwater's argument that such arrests were not supported by the common law at the Founding, "while by no means insubstantial," ultimately failed.

The Court then declined the plaintiff's invitation "to mint a new rule of constitutional law" based on a balancing of competing interests and an assessment according to "traditional standards of reasonableness." Reasoning that "the standard of probable cause 'applies to all arrests, without the need to balance the interests and circumstances involved in particular situations,'" the Court concluded that "if an officer has probable cause to believe that an individual has committed even a very minor criminal offense in his presence, he may, without violating the Fourth Amendment, arrest the offender."

On the basis of this passage, the defendants argue that Ansche's arrest does not violate the Fourth Amendment, for it is undisputed that the arresting officer had probable cause to believe Ansche had committed a criminal offense, however minor. No balancing or inquiry into whether Ansche's probable cause arrest was otherwise reasonable is permitted. The Court acknowledged that "if we were to derive a rule exclusively to address the uncontested facts of this case, Atwater might well prevail." But because a rule allowing ad hoc reasonableness review of an arrest decision, even when there is probable cause, would hobble the officer's discretion, the Court declined to engage in any inquiry beyond probable cause.

In addition, the "very fact that [Fourth Amendment] law has never jelled the way Atwater would have it" led the Court to doubt "whether warrantless misdemeanor arrests need constitutional attention." The Court enumerated a number of protections, both constitutional and practical, that it thought obviated the need for reasonableness scrutiny above and beyond probable cause. The Court concluded that "the upshot of all these influences, combined with the good sense (and, failing that, political accountability) of most *local lawmakers* and law-enforcement officials, is a dearth of horribles demanding redress." The *Atwater* Court even cited WMATA's decision in this case to change its policy, and to provide for citations in lieu of arrest for "subway snackers," as an example of the efficacy of the "practical and political considerations" supporting the absence of a need for a reasonableness balancing beyond probable cause.

While we can inquire into the reasonableness of the manner in which an arrest is conducted, the only cases in which we have found it necessary actually to perform the balancing analysis involved searches and seizures conducted in an extraordinary manner, unusually harmful to an individual's privacy or even physical interests: *Graham v. Connor* [excerpted earlier on p. 158]; *Tennessee v. Garner* [excerpted earlier on p. 156]. The most natural reading of *Atwater* is that we cannot inquire further into the reasonableness of a decision to arrest when it is supported by probable cause. That is true whether the decision to arrest upon probable cause is made by the officer on the beat or at a more removed policy level.

ETHICAL ISSUES

Issue a Citation or Make a Full Custodial Arrest?

According to the U.S. Supreme Court five-member majority opinion in *Atwater v. City of Lago Vista* (2001), Lago Vista Police Department Officer Bart "Turek was *authorized* (not *required*, but authorized) to make a *custodial* arrest without balancing costs and benefits or determining whether or not Atwater's arrest was in some sense necessary." And the Court formulated this rule: "If an officer has probable cause to believe that an individual has committed even a very minor criminal offense in his presence, he may, without violating the Fourth Amendment, arrest the offender."

So, under the Fourth Amendment, making a full custodial arrest of Gail Atwater for the violation of the fine-only misdemeanor of allowing her children to ride in her car without their seat belts was a reasonable seizure. But was it ethical? Neither the five-member majority nor the four dissenters thought it was. What do you think?

INSTRUCTIONS

1. Read the excerpt from the brief of the National League of Cities, U.S. Conference of Mayors, National Association of Counties, National Conference of State Legislatures, National Governors Association, International City/County Management Association,

Council of State Governments, and International Municipal Lawyers Association as Amici Curiae supporting the City of Lago Vista, Officer Turek, and Lago Vista Police Chief Frank Miller. See the link under the Chapter 5 Ethical Issues section of the Companion Website—login at www.cengagebrain.com.

2. Write an essay that includes:

   a. A list of all actions Officer Turek took before and during the arrest

   b. Presentation of the arguments made by the amici that would support the conclusion that not only were Turek's actions constitutional, they were also ethical. (Of course, amici aren't arguing ethics, but the story they tell certainly lends itself to an ethics argument.)

   c. An explanation of why you believe Officer Turek's actions were ethical or unethical.

Summary

LO 1, LO 2

- Arrests are a vital tool that can help law enforcement officers catch the guilty and free the innocent. But arrests have to satisfy the reasonableness requirement of the Fourth Amendment.

LO 3

- Arrests are Fourth Amendment seizures but are more invasive than stops. Arrests can last longer, result in being taken to the police station, and are recorded.

LO 4

- To satisfy the Fourth Amendment's reasonableness requirement, arrests require both probable cause before and a reasonable execution during and after arrest.

LO 5, LO 6

- The probable cause requirement balances the societal interest in crime control and the individual right to free movement. Officers can use both direct information and hearsay to build probable cause.

LO 7

- Most arrests based on probable cause are reasonable without warrants. However, arrest warrants are required to enter homes to arrest unless exigent circumstances exist. The most common exigent circumstances include hot pursuit, need to protect officers, preventing the destruction of evidence, and preventing the escape of suspects.

LO 8

- During and after arrests, officers can use only the amount of force that is objectively reasonable to get and maintain control of suspects they have probable cause to arrest. Under this standard, "An officer's evil intentions will not make a Fourth Amendment violation out of an objectively reasonable use of force; nor will an officer's good intentions make an objectively unreasonable use of force constitutional." Furthermore, reasonableness is determined at the moment of the use of force. "Not every push or shove, even if it may later seem unnecessary in the peace of a judge's chambers, violates the Fourth Amendment."

LO 9

- After an arrest, felony suspects usually are taken to the police station for booking, photographing, and possible interrogation and identification procedures; misdemeanor suspects usually are released.

LO 10

- It's constitutionally reasonable, but not necessarily wise, for officers to make full custodial arrests for fine-only offenses.

Review Questions

1. Compare and contrast Fourth Amendment stops with full custodial arrests.
2. List the negative consequences of arrests.
3. Identify the characteristics of a full custodial arrest.
4. Identify the two elements of a reasonable arrest.
5. What two societal interests does the probable cause requirement balance?
6. Identify and define the two kinds of information officers can rely on to satisfy the probable cause to arrest requirement.
7. Identify and describe the two elements that satisfy the Fourth Amendment reasonableness of arrest requirement.
8. Why do officers need to obtain warrants to arrest a suspect in a home?
9. Identify and give an example of the exceptions to the arrest warrant requirement to enter homes.
10. Define and give an example of an exigent circumstance.
11. Identify and describe the three elements of an arrest warrant.
12. Identify a positive and a negative aspect to the neutral magistrate requirement.
13. Why are some arrest warrant affidavits purposely vague?
14. According to Professor Craig Bradley, what should the U.S. Supreme Court do regarding arrest warrants?
15. Contrast deadly force with nondeadly force. Which one is used more to subdue suspects?
16. What two conditions have to be satisfied to use deadly force?
17. Why is the standard of reasonable force to arrest an objective standard?
18. Identify the actions taken after an arrest for a felony.
19. Why is it reasonable for officers to arrest suspects for a misdemeanor?

Key Terms

custodial arrests, p. 140

probable cause to arrest, p. 142

right of locomotion, p. 142

direct information in probable cause to
  arrest, p. 142

hearsay rule in arrests, p. 143

neutral magistrate, p. 149

affidavit, p. 150

exigent circumstances, p. 151

deadly force, p. 155

objective standard of reasonable
  force, p. 158

bite-and-hold technique, p. 160

find-and-bark technique, p. 160

citation, p. 166

6

CASES COVERED

Wilson v. Arkansas, 514 U.S. 927 (1995)

Chimel v. California, 395 U.S. 752 (1969)

Arizona v. Gant, 129 S.Ct. 1710 (2009)

Knowles v. Iowa, 525 U.S. 113 (1998)

Whren v. U.S., 517 U.S. 806 (1996)

Schneckloth v. Bustamonte, 412 U.S. 218 (1973)

U.S. v. Rodney, 956 F.2d 295 (CADC 1992)

Illinois v. Rodriguez, 497 U.S. 177 (1990)

Wyoming v. Houghton, 526 U.S. 295 (1999)

LEARNING OBJECTIVES

1 Appreciate that crime control couldn't survive without searches, but the power to search comes at a price: It tempts those who hold it to abuse it.

2 Understand that searches hardly ever require warrants except when officers want to search homes. Know how officers can execute warrants to search homes "reasonably."

3 Know that search warrants require both particularity and probable cause. Appreciate that, with some exceptions, officers

have to knock, announce their presence, and give occupants an opportunity to open the door, before they enter.

4 Know and appreciate that the millions of searches incident to arrest are reasonable without warrants, because they protect officers, prevent escape, and preserve evidence.

5 Know that the millions of consent searches allow officers to search without warrants or probable cause. Appreciate that without consent, officers couldn't conduct the search.

6 Know how to determine the scope of consent; when consent can be withdrawn; and when one person can consent for another. Appreciate the significance of empirical research regarding consent searches.

7 Understand that the searches of vehicles without warrants are reasonable, constitutionally, because of their mobility and the reduced expectation of privacy in vehicles.

8 Know that searches of containers and persons within the vehicles without warrants are "reasonable" as long as they're based on probable cause.

9 Understand that emergency searches are based on the idea that it's sometimes impractical to require officers to obtain warrants before they search.

Searches for Evidence

Dylan Rodney stepped off a bus in Washington, D.C., arriving from New York City. As Rodney left the bus station, Detective Vance Beard, dressed in plainclothes and carrying a concealed weapon, approached him from behind. A second officer waited nearby. Beard displayed identification and asked if Rodney would talk to him. Rodney agreed. Beard asked Rodney whether he was carrying drugs in his travel bag. After Rodney said no, Beard obtained permission to search the bag. As he did so, the other officer advanced to within about five feet of Rodney. The search failed to turn up any contraband.

Beard then asked Rodney whether he was carrying drugs on his person. After Rodney again said no, Beard requested permission to conduct a body search. Rodney said "Sure" and raised his arms above his head. Beard placed his hands on Rodney's ankles and, in one sweeping motion, ran them up the inside of Rodney's legs. As he passed over the crotch area, Beard felt small, rock-like objects.

Rodney exclaimed: "That's me!" Detecting otherwise, Beard placed Rodney under arrest. *U.S. v. Rodney*, 956 F.2d 295 (CADC 1992)

LO 1

Crime control couldn't survive without searches, but, like all good things, the power to search comes at a price. Searches invade the privacy of individuals, their homes, their private papers, and their property. Like all power, the power to search tempts those who hold it to abuse it.

No one appreciated the price and the temptation to abuse the power to search more than U.S. Supreme Court Justice Robert H. Jackson. At the end of World War II, President Truman appointed Justice Jackson chief prosecutor at the Nazi war crimes trials in Nuremberg, Germany. There, Justice Jackson learned details of the Nazis' atrocities against the German people's "persons, houses, papers and effects" (Hockett 1991, 257–99).

These discoveries were a defining moment for Justice Jackson, and when he returned to the Supreme Court, he spoke eloquently of the right against unreasonable searches and seizures. Worried that Americans didn't fully appreciate the importance of the Fourth Amendment, Justice Jackson disapproved of what he believed was the Supreme Court's tendency to treat the rights against unreasonable searches and seizures as "second-class rights."

He wrote that the rights against unreasonable searches and seizures

> are not mere second-class rights but belong in the catalog of indispensable freedoms. Among deprivations of rights, none is so effective in cowing a population, crushing the spirit of the individual and putting terror in every heart. Uncontrolled search and seizure is one of the first and most effective weapons in the arsenal of every arbitrary government. And one need only briefly to have dwelt and worked among a people possessed of many admirable qualities but deprived of these rights to know that the human personality deteriorates and dignity and self-reliance disappear where homes, persons and possessions are subject at any hour to unheralded search and seizure by the police. But the right against searches and seizures is one of the most difficult to protect. Since the officers are themselves the chief invaders, there is no enforcement outside of court. (*Brinegar v. U.S.* 1949, 180–81)

Notice that Justice Jackson didn't condemn all searches, only "unreasonable" searches. That's because he knew how important searches are in controlling crime. (Jackson had been an aggressive prosecutor.) But he also knew that the Fourth Amendment doesn't just confer the power on *good* officers searching *bad* people, their homes, and stuff; it bestows the same power on bad officers searching good people. So, Jackson urged, courts had to balance the need for searches against the privacies they invade.

The three-step analysis we used to examine the government actions in Chapter 3, the stops and frisks in Chapter 4, and the arrests in Chapter 5 also applies to the searches we'll examine in this chapter:

1.   Was the government action a search? (Chapter 3)

2.   If it was a search, was it reasonable?

3.   If it was unreasonable, then should the evidence be excluded? (Chapter 10)

We won't repeat the first step in the analysis (the definition of search) because we already examined it in Chapter 3. We'll begin with the issues affecting the reasonableness of searches. We'll divide our discussion into searches for evidence of crime (this chapter) and special-needs searches that go beyond crime control (Chapter 7). In this chapter, we'll examine searches with and without warrants and then look at consent, vehicle-exception, and emergency searches.

Search Warrants

LO 2, LO 3

The Fourth Amendment commands that "no warrants shall issue, but upon probable cause, supported by oath or affirmation, and particularly describing the place to be searched, and the persons or things to be seized." According to the distinguished U.S. Supreme Court Justice Felix Frankfurter: "With minor and severely confined exceptions every search is unreasonable when made without a magistrate's authority expressed through a validly issued warrant" (*Harris v. U.S.* 1947, 162; see "Neutral Magistrates" in Chapter 5).

Despite Justice Frankfurter's often repeated words, there are so many exceptions to the warrant requirement (up to thirty, depending on how you count them) that the searches without warrants far outnumber searches with warrants. With that in mind, let's look at each of the three elements required to satisfy the Fourth Amendment's warrant requirement:

1.   Particularity

2.   An affidavit supporting probable cause

3.   The "knock and announce" rule

Particularity Requirement

LO 2, LO 3

To comply with the Fourth Amendment, search warrants have to "particularly describe the place to be searched"; this is known as the **particularity requirement**. The address of a single-dwelling house, "404 Blake Road," particularly describes the place to be searched; a warrant to search "1135 Stone Street," a 16-floor apartment complex, doesn't.

Warrants also have to "particularly describe the things to be seized." A warrant to search for and seize "one book entitled *Criminal Procedure*, 8th edition, by Joel Samaha" is good enough. So are warrants naming whole classes of items, such as "address books, diaries, business records, documents, receipts, warranty books, guns, stereo equipment, and a color television" in a list of stolen property. Catchall categories might also meet the requirement. For example, a search warrant that named "records, notes, and documents indicating involvement in and control of prostitution activity" was particular enough in one case, because the officers were directed to seize only items related to prostitution.

Probable Cause Affidavit

This is the same as the requirement for arrest warrants (Chapter 5), so we won't repeat the details here. One notable difference: The probable cause in search warrant affidavits has to include evidence to support the claim that the items or classes of items named in the warrant will be found in the place to be searched.

Knock-and-Announce Rule

LO 3

Most states and the U.S. government have many specific requirements for how search warrants are supposed to be executed. One of these rules, the **knock-and-announce rule**, has 700 years of English and U.S. history behind it; it also has centuries of controversy surrounding it. According to the rule, officers have to knock *and* announce that they're officers with a search warrant before they enter the places they're about to search.

Does the Fourth Amendment demand this knock-and-announce rule, or is a no-knock entry reasonable, too? Oddly enough, for all the history behind the rule, and the controversy surrounding it, the U.S. Supreme Court didn't answer this important question until 1995, when it decided that the Fourth Amendment commanded officers to knock and announce before they entered. It did so in *Wilson v. Arkansas*, our first case excerpt.

In Wilson v. Arkansas (1995), *the U.S. Supreme Court found that Sharlene Wilson's conviction for possession of illegal drugs, seized during a no-knock entry into her home, didn't meet Fourth Amendment "reasonable search" requirements.*

CASE Was the "No-Knock" Entry an Unreasonable Search?

Wilson v. Arkansas
514 U.S. 927 (1995)

HISTORY

Sharlene Wilson was charged with illegal possession of marijuana and methamphetamine. The Circuit Court, Hot Springs County, Arkansas, denied Wilson's motion to suppress marijuana, amphetamines, and other evidence seized during a "no knock" search of her house. She was convicted and sentenced to 32 years in prison. She appealed and the Arkansas Supreme Court affirmed. The U.S. Supreme Court granted certiorari and reversed and remanded.

THOMAS, J. for a unanimous court.

FACTS

During November and December 1992, Sharlene Wilson made a series of narcotics sales to a Joann Potts, an informant acting at the direction of the Arkansas State Police. In late November, Potts purchased marijuana and methamphetamine at the home that Wilson shared with Bryson Jacobs. On December 30, Potts telephoned Wilson at her home and arranged to meet her at a local store to buy some marijuana. According to testimony presented below, Wilson produced a semiautomatic pistol at this meeting and waved it in Potts's face, threatening to kill her if she turned out to be working for the police. Wilson then sold Potts a bag of marijuana.

The next day, police officers applied for and obtained warrants to search Wilson's home and to arrest both Wilson and Jacobs. Affidavits filed in support of the warrants set forth the details of the narcotics transactions and stated that Jacobs had previously been convicted of arson and firebombing. The search was conducted later that afternoon.

Police officers found the main door to Wilson's home open. While opening an unlocked screen door and entering the residence, they identified themselves as police officers and stated that they had a warrant. Once inside the home, the officers seized marijuana, methamphetamine, valium, narcotics paraphernalia, a gun, and ammunition. They also found Wilson in the bathroom, flushing marijuana down the toilet.

Wilson and Jacobs were arrested and charged with delivery of marijuana, delivery of methamphetamine, possession of drug paraphernalia, and possession of marijuana. Before trial, Wilson filed a motion to suppress the evidence seized during the search. Wilson asserted that the search was invalid on various grounds, including that the officers had failed to "knock and announce" before entering her home. The trial court summarily denied the suppression motion. After a jury trial, Wilson was convicted of all charges and sentenced to 32 years in prison.

The Arkansas Supreme Court affirmed Wilson's conviction on appeal. The court noted that "the officers entered the home while they were identifying themselves," but it rejected Wilson's argument that "the Fourth Amendment requires officers to knock and announce prior to entering the residence." Finding "no authority for Wilson's theory that the knock and announce principle is required by the Fourth Amendment," the court concluded that neither Arkansas law nor the Fourth Amendment required suppression of the evidence. We granted certiorari to resolve the conflict among the lower courts as to whether the common-law knock-and-announce principle forms a part of the Fourth Amendment reasonableness inquiry. We hold that it does, and accordingly reverse and remand.

OPINION

Although the common law generally protected a man's house as his "castle of defense and asylum," common-law courts long have held that "when the King is party, the sheriff (if the doors be not open) may break the party's house, either to arrest him, or to do other execution of the King's process, if otherwise he cannot enter." *Semayne's Case*, (K.B., 1603). To this rule, however, common-law courts appended an important qualification:

> But before he breaks it, he ought to signify the cause of his coming, and to make request to open doors, for the law without a default in the owner abhors the destruction or breaking of any house (which is for the habitation and safety of man) by which great damage and inconvenience might ensue to the party, when no default is in him; for perhaps he did not know of the process, of which, if he had notice, it is to be presumed that he would obey it. . . . (*Ibid.*, 77 Eng. Rep., at 195–196)

The common-law knock-and-announce principle was woven quickly into the fabric of early American law. Most of the States that ratified the Fourth Amendment had enacted constitutional provisions or statutes generally incorporating English common law. Our own cases have acknowledged that the common law principle of announcement is "embedded in Anglo-American law," but we have never squarely held that this principle is an element of the reasonableness inquiry under the Fourth Amendment.

We now so hold. Given the long-standing common-law endorsement of the practice of announcement, we have little doubt that the Framers of the Fourth Amendment thought that the method of an officer's entry into a dwelling was among the factors to be considered in assessing the reasonableness of a search or seizure. Contrary to the decision below, we hold that in some circumstances an officer's unannounced entry into a home might be unreasonable under the Fourth Amendment.

This is not to say, of course, that every entry must be preceded by an announcement. The Fourth Amendment's flexible requirement of reasonableness should not be read to mandate a rigid rule of announcement that ignores countervailing law enforcement interests. As even Wilson concedes, the common-law principle of announcement was never stated as an inflexible rule requiring announcement under all circumstances.

Thus, because the common-law rule was justified in part by the belief that announcement generally would avoid "the destruction or breaking of any house by which great damage and inconvenience might ensue," courts acknowledged that the presumption in favor of announcement would yield under circumstances presenting a threat of physical violence. See for example, *Mahomed v. The Queen* (1843): "While he was firing pistols at them, were they to knock at the door, and to ask him to be pleased to open it for them? The law in its wisdom only requires this ceremony to be observed when it possibly may be attended with some advantage, and may render the breaking open of the outer door unnecessary."

Similarly, courts held that an officer may dispense with announcement in cases where a prisoner escapes from him and retreats to his dwelling. Proof of "demand and refusal" was deemed unnecessary in such cases because it would be a "senseless ceremony" to require an officer in pursuit of a recently escaped arrestee to make an announcement prior to breaking the door to retake him.

Finally, courts have indicated that unannounced entry may be justified where police officers have reason to believe that evidence would likely be destroyed if advance notice were given.

We need not attempt a comprehensive catalog of the relevant countervailing factors here. For now, we leave to the lower courts the task of determining the circumstances under which an unannounced entry is reasonable under the Fourth Amendment. We simply hold that although a search or seizure of a dwelling might be constitutionally defective if police officers enter without prior announcement, law enforcement interests may also establish the reasonableness of an unannounced entry.

Arkansas contends that the judgment below should be affirmed because the unannounced entry in this case was justified for two reasons. First, Arkansas argues that police officers reasonably believed that a prior announcement would have placed them in peril, given their knowledge that Wilson had threatened a government informant with a semiautomatic weapon and that Mr. Jacobs had previously been convicted of arson and firebombing. Second, Arkansas suggests that prior announcement would have produced an unreasonable risk that Wilson would destroy easily disposable narcotics evidence.

These considerations may well provide the necessary justification for the unannounced entry in this case. Because the Arkansas Supreme Court did not address their sufficiency, however, we remand to allow the state courts to make any necessary findings of fact and to make the determination of reasonableness in the first instance.

The judgment of the Arkansas Supreme Court is REVERSED, and the case is REMANDED for further proceedings not inconsistent with this opinion. It is so ordered.

QUESTIONS

1. What does the history Justice Thomas relates have to do with whether the Fourth Amendment requires officers to "knock and announce"?
2. Did the officers satisfy the knock-and-announce rule? List the facts that might indicate that the officers satisfied the requirement.
3. Identify the three exceptions to the knock-and-announce rule Justice Thomas referred to in the excerpt from the Court's opinion. What do they all have in common? Do you agree that they should be exceptions? Explain.
4. Assume you're the prosecutor when the case is remanded. Argue that the facts of the case fit into one or more of the exceptions. Or think of other exceptions the court might accept.
5. Assume you're the judge on remand. Decide the case and give your reasons.

Let's look more closely at exceptions to the knock-and-announce rule and at what happens when occupants fail to respond to officers' announcement before entering.

Exceptions to the Knock-and-Announce Rule

LO 3

After *Wilson v. Arkansas*, we now know the "knock and announce rule" is part of the Fourth Amendment. We also know there are three major exceptions to the rule: to prevent violence, the destruction of evidence, and the escape of suspects. And there may be more to come. In the following excerpt from *Wilson v. Arkansas*, Justice Thomas sent a not-too-subtle invitation to lower courts to come up with more exceptions to the knock-and-announce rule:

> We need not attempt a comprehensive catalog of the relevant countervailing factors here. For now, we leave to the lower courts the task of determining the circumstances under which an unannounced entry is reasonable under the Fourth Amendment. We simply hold that although a search or seizure of a dwelling might be constitutionally defective if police officers enter without prior announcement, law enforcement interests may also establish the reasonableness of an unannounced entry. (936)

The Wisconsin Supreme Court wasted no time in accepting Justice Thomas's invitation in *State v. Richards* (1996) when it approved a blanket "drug house" exception to the knock-and-announce rule. Steiney Richards, the defendant, argued "The blanket 'drug house' exception to the 'knock and announce' rule violates the Fourth Amendment's reasonableness requirement" (219).

The Wisconsin Supreme Court disagreed, holding that "police are not required to adhere to the rule of announcement when executing a search warrant involving felonious drug delivery." According to the court:

> Exigent circumstances are always present in the execution of search warrants involving felonious drug delivery: an extremely high risk of serious if not deadly injury to the police as well as the potential for the disposal of drugs by the occupants prior to entry by the police. The public interests inherent in these circumstances far outweigh the minimal privacy interests of the occupants of the dwelling for which a search warrant has already been issued. (219)

Richards appealed to the U.S. Supreme Court (*Richards v. Wisconsin* 1997). Justice Stevens, writing for a unanimous Court, acknowledged that "flexible requirement of reasonableness should not be read to mandate a rigid rule of announcement that ignores countervailing law enforcement interests," and left "to the lower courts the task of determining the circumstances under which an unannounced entry is reasonable under the Fourth Amendment." But, he continued, "We disagree with the court's conclusion that the Fourth Amendment permits a blanket exception to the knock-and-announce requirement for this entire category of criminal activity" (387–88).

Nevertheless, the Court upheld the Wisconsin Supreme Court's decision "because the evidence presented to support the officers' actions in this case establishes that the decision not to knock and announce was a reasonable one under the circumstances" (388).

Occupants' Failure to Respond to Officers' Announcement

Announcing their presence doesn't automatically authorize officers to break and enter. They have to "wait a reasonable amount of time" before they break and enter, unless occupants refuse to allow them to come in (LaFave 2004, 2:672–73; *U.S. v. Spikes* 1998, 925). How long do they have to wait? There's no bright-line rule—that is, no rule that applies to all cases. The test is reasonableness, which depends on the totality of the circumstances in each individual case. The Sixth Circuit U.S. Court of Appeals put it this way: "The Fourth Amendment's 'knock and announce' cannot be distilled into a constitutional stop-watch where a fraction of a second assumes controlling significance" (*U.S. v. Spikes* 1998, 926). The totality of circumstances hardly ever makes very brief waits, say 2 to 4 seconds, reasonable; 10 to 20 seconds usually are (LaFave 2004, 673–74).

The U.S. Supreme Court ruled unanimously in *U.S. v. Banks* (2003) that the totality of circumstances made it reasonable for officers to use the "ultimate 'master key,' a battering ram," to break down Lashawn Banks's front door after calling out "police search warrant" and waiting 10 seconds (33). North Las Vegas Police Department officers had a warrant to search Banks's two-bedroom apartment, based on information that Lashawn Banks was selling cocaine at home. As soon as they got to the apartment at 2 o'clock in the afternoon, the officers called out "police search warrant" and rapped hard enough on the door to be heard by officers at the back door. After waiting for 15 to 20 seconds with no answer, the officers broke open the front door with the battering ram. They searched and found weapons, crack cocaine, and other evidence of drug dealing.

Banks was charged with drug and firearms offenses. Banks moved to suppress the evidence, arguing that the officers executing the search warrant waited an unreasonably short time before forcing entry and so violated the Fourth Amendment. The U.S. District Court for the District of Nevada denied the motion. Banks pleaded guilty, reserving his right to challenge the search on appeal. A divided panel of the U.S. Court of Appeals for the Ninth Circuit reversed the conviction. The U.S. Supreme Court reversed the Court of Appeals.

Writing for the unanimous Court, Justice Souter noted that the details of reasonable execution of search warrants have to be "fleshed out case by case," according to the totality of "facts of cases so various that no template is likely to produce sounder results than examining the totality of circumstances in a given case" (35–36). Although the Court found this case "a close one," it held that it was reasonable to "suspect imminent loss" of the cocaine after the 15 to 20 seconds the officers waited before they battered the door down:

> One point in making an officer knock and announce is to give a person inside the chance to save his door. That is why, in the case with no reason to suspect an immediate risk, the reasonable wait time may well be longer. The need to damage property in the course of getting in is a good reason to require more patience than it would be reasonable to expect if the door were open. Police seeking a stolen piano may be able to spend more time to make sure they really need the battering ram. (41)
>
> Attention to cocaine rocks and pianos tells a lot about the chances of their respective disposal and its bearing on reasonable time. Instructions couched in terms like "significant amount of time," and "an even more substantial amount of time," tell very little. (42)

Searches without Warrants

LO 2

The U.S. Supreme Court has repeatedly said that the Fourth Amendment expresses a strong preference for search warrants with only a few well-defined exceptions. That's the *law*, but what's the *practice*? The vast majority of searches are made without warrants, because the exceptions are interpreted broadly to satisfy the strong preference of law enforcement officers and the clear practical need for searches without warrants (Haddad 1977, 198–225; Sutton 1986, 411).

One former Washington, D.C., assistant U.S. attorney said of this practical element in searches without warrants: "As anyone who has worked in the criminal justice system knows, searches conducted pursuant to these exceptions, particularly searches incident to arrest, automobile and 'stop and frisk' searches, far exceed searches performed pursuant to warrants" (Bradley 1985, 1475). Why is this so? According to this same attorney, the reason "is simple: the clear rule that warrants are required is unworkable and to enforce it would lead to exclusion of evidence in many cases where the police activity was essentially reasonable" (1475).

Law enforcement officers frequently express frustration with the delay in getting search warrants. One police officer said it takes four hours from the time he decides he wants a warrant until the time he has one in his hand:

> And that's if everything goes right. You find people and get 'em typed and you can find the judges when they are sitting at the bench—because a lot of judges won't see people in their offices. If you miss them there, they leave and go to lunch and you have to wait until they come back for the afternoon dockets, and if they are already into the afternoon dockets, they are not going to interrupt the procedures

for a warrant. So you sit and wait through three or four docket sessions. It can take all day. (Sutton 1986, 411)

Frustration tempts officers to "get around" the Fourth Amendment. One way around is by "shamming" consent. One detective put it this way:

> You tell the guy, "Let me come in and take a look at your house." And he says, "No, I don't want to." And then you tell him, "Then I'm going to leave Sam here, and he's going to live with you until we come back. Now we can do it either way." And very rarely do the people say, "Go get your search warrant, then." (Sutton 1986, 415)

Let's look at the five major exceptions to the warrant requirement approved by the U.S. Supreme Court:

1. Searches incident to (at the time of) arrest
2. Consent searches
3. Vehicle searches
4. Container searches
5. Emergency searches (also called "exigent circumstances searches")

Searches Incident to Arrest

The brilliant constitutional lawyer and historian Telford Taylor (1969) concluded from his research into the history of search and seizure "that search of an arrested person and premises without warrants or probable cause is as old as the institution of arrest itself" (28). **Searches incident to arrest**—searches made of lawfully arrested suspects without probable cause or a warrant—are old. But are they reasonable Fourth Amendment searches? Yes, says the U.S. Supreme Court. Why? Three reasons:

1. They protect officers from suspects who might injure or kill them.
2. They prevent arrested suspects from escaping.
3. They preserve evidence that suspects might destroy or damage.

There's some debate about Professor Taylor's history (Davies 1999), but as for searches of arrested *persons* without warrants, there's no doubt about their constitutionality. The same certainty doesn't extend to searching the *place* where arrests take place. In fact, an analysis of decisions by the U.S. Supreme Court, the lower federal courts, and the state courts and commentators on this issue reveal zigging and zagging, creating enormous confusion.

As early as 1969, the U.S. Supreme Court tried to clear up the confusion over how far beyond the arrested person an officer can search. In *Chimel v. California* (1969), our next case excerpt, the Court decided that officers who arrested Ted Chimel in his home could search only as far as Chimel could reach either to grab a weapon or to destroy evidence.

Before we get to the case, you should be aware of one critical fact the cases hardly ever mention about what officers do in practice when they arrest suspects. According to available evidence, after officers arrest suspects, they immediately handcuff them. That's what department rules prescribe; it's what police cadets are trained to do; it's what most officers do (Moskovitz 2002). Keep this in mind as you read *Chimel* and all the materials in this section on searches incident to arrest.

In Chimel v. California (1965), *our next case excerpt, the U.S. Supreme Court reversed Ted Chimel's conviction for the burglary of a coin shop, because his home was searched without a warrant or his permission.*

CASE   Was the Search Incident to the Arrest?

Chimel v. California

395 U.S. 752 (1969)

HISTORY

Ted Chimel was prosecuted for the burglary of a coin shop. He was convicted in the Superior Court, Orange County, California, and appealed. The California Supreme Court affirmed, and Chimel petitioned the U.S. Supreme Court for a writ of certiorari. The Supreme Court granted the writ and reversed the California Supreme Court's judgment.

STEWART, J.

FACTS

Late in the afternoon of September 13, 1965, three police officers arrived at the Santa Ana, California, home of Ted Chimel with a warrant authorizing his arrest for the burglary of a coin shop. The officers knocked on the door, identified themselves to Chimel's wife, and asked if they might come inside. She ushered them into the house, where they waited 10 or 15 minutes until Chimel returned home from work. When Chimel entered the house, one of the officers handed him the arrest warrant and asked for permission to "look around." Chimel objected, but was advised that "on the basis of the lawful arrest," the officers would nonetheless conduct a search. No search warrant had been issued.

Accompanied by Chimel's wife, the officers then looked through the entire three-bedroom house, including the attic, the garage, and a small workshop. In some rooms the search was relatively cursory. In the master bedroom and sewing room, however, the officers directed Mrs. Chimel to open drawers and "to physically move contents of the drawers from side to side so that (they) might view any items that would have come from (the) burglary." After completing the search, they seized numerous items—primarily coins, but also several medals, tokens, and a few other objects. The entire search took between 45 minutes and an hour.

At Chimel's subsequent state trial on two charges of burglary, the items taken from his house were admitted into evidence against him, over his objection that they had been unconstitutionally seized. He was convicted, and the judgments of conviction were affirmed by both the California Court of Appeal, and the California Supreme Court. We granted certiorari in order to consider Chimel's substantial constitutional claims.

OPINION

When an arrest is made, it is reasonable for the arresting officer to search the person arrested in order to remove any weapons that the latter might seek to use in order to resist arrest or effect his escape. Otherwise, the officer's safety might well be endangered, and the arrest itself frustrated. In addition, it is entirely reasonable for the arresting officer to search for and seize any evidence on the arrestee's person in order to prevent its concealment or destruction. And the area into which an arrestee might reach in order to grab a weapon or evidentiary items must, of course, be governed by a like rule. A gun on a table or in a drawer in front of one who is arrested can be as dangerous to the arresting officer as one concealed in the clothing of the person arrested.

There is ample justification, therefore, for a search of the arrestee's person and the area "within his immediate control"—construing that phrase to mean the area from within which he might gain possession of a weapon or destructible evidence. There is no comparable justification, however, for routinely searching any room other than that in which an arrest occurs—or, for that matter, for searching through all the desk drawers or other closed or concealed areas in that room itself. Such searches, in the absence of well-recognized exceptions, may be made only under the authority of a search warrant. The "adherence to judicial processes" mandated by the Fourth Amendment requires no less.

It is argued in the present case that it is "reasonable" to search a man's house when he is arrested in it. But that argument is founded on little more than a subjective view regarding the acceptability of certain sorts of police conduct, and not on consideration relevant to Fourth Amendment interests. Under such an unconfined analysis, Fourth Amendment protection in this area would approach the evaporation point. After arresting a man in his house, to rummage at will among his papers in search of whatever will convict him, appears to us to be indistinguishable from what might be done under a general warrant; indeed, the warrant would give more protection, for presumably it must be issued by a magistrate.

Application of sound Fourth Amendment principles to the facts of this case produces a clear result. The search here went far beyond the petitioner's person and the area from within which he might have obtained either a weapon or something that could have been used as evidence against him. There was no constitutional justification, in the absence of a search warrant, for extending the search beyond that area. The scope of the search was, therefore, "unreasonable" under the Fourth and Fourteenth Amendments and the petitioner's conviction cannot stand.

REVERSED.

DISSENT

WHITE, J., joined by BLACK, J.

The Fourth Amendment does not proscribe "warrantless searches" but instead it proscribes "unreasonable searches" and this Court has never held nor does the majority today assert that warrantless searches are necessarily unreasonable. This case provides a good illustration that it is unreasonable to require police to leave the scene of an arrest in order to obtain a search warrant when they already have probable cause to search and there is a clear danger that the items for which they may reasonably search will be removed before they return with a warrant.

Chimel was arrested in his home. There was doubtless probable cause not only to arrest Chimel, but also to search his house. He had obliquely admitted, both to a neighbor and to the owner of the burglarized store, that he had committed the burglary. In light of this, and the fact that the neighbor had seen other admittedly stolen property in petitioner's house, there was surely probable cause on which a warrant could have issued to search the house for the stolen coins.

Moreover, had the police simply arrested Chimel, taken him off to the station house, and later returned with a warrant, it seems very likely that Chimel's wife, who in view of Chimel's generally garrulous nature must have known of the burglary, would have removed the coins. For the police to search the house while the evidence they had probable cause to search out and seize was still there cannot be considered unreasonable.

QUESTIONS

1. Describe the search that followed Chimel's arrest.
2. How does the Court define the area "within [a suspect's] immediate control"?
3. If you were defining the phrase, would you have included the whole house within the scope of the rule? Explain your answer, including what interests you consider paramount in formulating your definition.
4. Does Justice White, in his dissent, have the better argument in the case? Summarize his argument and then evaluate it.

Now, let's look at other issues raised by searches incident to arrests, including how the courts define the "grabbable"—or searchable—area and whether it extends to vehicles; the time frame officers have to conduct a search before it is no longer considered incident to the arrest; and searches incident to misdemeanors and pretext arrests.

The "Grabbable" Area

LO 4

According to *Chimel v. California*, law enforcement officers can only search the "**grabbable**" **area**—namely, the arrested person and the area under her immediate physical control. The rule seems clear enough, but confusion arose when police were faced with applying the rule to arrests of suspects in vehicles. The courts were divided over whether the grabbable area rule even applied to searches of vehicles. Some courts quickly said it did; others were reluctant.

New York v. Belton (1981) is a good example of this division. The trial court said the grabbable-area rule applied even when the arrested person was outside the car and under the control of the police and so highly unlikely to escape, grab a weapon, or destroy evidence inside the vehicle. The intermediate appeals court agreed, but a divided Court of Appeals, New York's highest court, said the rule didn't include a search of the car when the arrested suspects were outside the car. The U.S. Supreme Court *supposedly* resolved the problem, not only for New York but for the country, when it upheld the car search incident to Roger Belton's arrest by a vote of 5–4 in *New York v. Belton* (1981). (Also, see Table 6.1.)

TABLE 6.1
New York v. Belton (1981) Majority's Argument

1. Fourth Amendment protections can only be realized if the police are acting under a set of rules which, in most instances, make it possible to reach a correct determination beforehand as to whether an invasion of privacy is justified in the interest of law enforcement.
2. No straightforward rule has emerged from the decided cases respecting the question involved here.
3. This has caused the trial courts difficulty and has put the appeals courts in disarray.
4. The cases suggest that articles inside the passenger compartment of cars are, generally, if not inevitably, in an area that suspects can reach and grab a weapon or evidence.
5. So the workable rule in this category of cases is best achieved by holding that when a policeman has made a lawful custodial arrest of the occupant of an automobile, he may, as a *contemporaneous incident of that arrest,* search the passenger compartment of that automobile.
6. And it follows that the police may also examine the contents of any containers found within the passenger compartment, for if the passenger compartment is within reach of the arrestee, so also will containers in it be within his reach.

In *Belton,* New York State Trooper Douglas Nicot chased and pulled over a speeding car occupied by four college students. Trooper Nicot smelled burned marijuana, ordered the four young men out of the car, and arrested them for unlawful possession of marijuana. Then, he returned to the car. During a search of the passenger compartment, he found Roger Belton's black leather jacket on the back seat. He unzipped the pocket and removed the cocaine he found in it. Belton was convicted of attempted criminal possession of a small amount of cocaine, and he appealed. The New York Supreme Court, Appellate Division, affirmed. The New York Court of Appeals reversed. The U.S. Supreme Court granted certiorari and reversed (Table 6.1).

After *Belton,* lower courts *and* police officers treated searches incident to traffic arrests as "a police entitlement rather than as an exception to the warrant requirement justified by the twin rationales" of officer protection and evidence preservation (*Thornton v. U.S.* 2004, 624). As interpreted by those courts, officers could *always* search the passenger compartment and all the containers in it, as long as they had probable cause to arrest an occupant.

Also since *Belton,* officers can use searches incident to minor traffic offenses as a "powerful investigative tool" (Amacost 2010, 276). In these **pretext arrests,** officers can stop and arrest motorists for minor traffic offenses not to enforce the traffic laws but so they can search for evidence of more serious crimes that they don't have probable cause to arrest them for (see Chapter 5, "Probable Cause"). According to Jeffrey Fisher, in an amicus brief (2008) supporting Rodney Gant's side in *Arizona v. Gant* (2009), our next case excerpt, "The upshot of all this is that the current search-incident-to-arrest doctrine encourages officers to arrest people whom they would not otherwise arrest, in order to conduct exploratory searches they would not otherwise be allowed to conduct" (10).

In addition to the broad reading given to *Belton,* and the pretext traffic arrest problem, there's empirical research that challenges at least two of the *Belton* Court's generalizations listed in Table 6.1. This research was cited in *Arizona v. Gant:*

1. "The cases suggest that articles inside the passenger compartment of cars are, generally, if not inevitably, in an area which suspects can reach and grab a weapon or evidence."
2. It follows from the generalization in 1, "that the police may also examine the contents of any containers found within the passenger compartment, for if the passenger compartment is within reach of the arrestee, so also will containers in it be within his reach."

Before we look at these challenges raised by Myron Moskovitz's (2002) research, you should be aware of his sources and methods. Moskovitz wrote to police departments in California's thirty largest cities and about fifty of California sheriff's departments; about a dozen federal law enforcement agencies; and about thirty state and municipal police agencies around the country (664). Although his hit rate was "small," he "received enough information to challenge both generalizations."

As for the first challenge, he found wide support for it. In his inquiries to various police departments, "Not a single respondent said or even suggested that a police officer should search a vehicle while the arrestee is in the vehicle or unsecured" (675–76). According to Moskovitz, "No sensible police officer will allow an arrestee to remain in reach of any such area—he'll get the arrestee out of the car immediately" (674).

What about the second claim? Moskovitz found this generalization was even further from officers' actual procedures in the field:

> Because they are instructed to remove and secure the arrestee before searching the vehicle, it is highly unlikely (if not impossible) that an arrestee would be able to remove his handcuffs, escape from a police car and/or surveillance by a cover officer, run to the vehicle, enter it or reach into it, open a container, and remove a weapon or item of evidence—all before an officer could intervene and stop him. And yet this strange scenario would have to be the norm for *Belton* to mesh with *Chimel*'s rationales for a search incident to arrest. (677)

With the empirical reality of police work, lower court approval of its broad reading of the *Belton* bright-line rule, and a growing "chorus" of criticism of *Belton* by academic lawyers in the background, the U.S. Supreme Court decided *Arizona v. Gant* (2009), our next excerpted case.

In Arizona v. Gant (2009), the U.S. Supreme Court upheld a Fourth Amendment challenge to car searches incident to a traffic offense conducted after officers arrested, handcuffed, and placed the driver, Rodney Gant, in the police car.

CASE Was the Car Search "Incident" to the Driver's Arrest?

Arizona v. Gant
129 S.Ct. 1710 (2009)

HISTORY

Rodney Joseph Gant (Defendant) was convicted in the Superior Court, Pima County, Arizona, Clark W. Munger, J., of possession of a narcotic drug for sale and possession of drug paraphernalia. Defendant appealed. The Court of Appeals of Arizona, Brammer, J., reversed. The Supreme

Court of Arizona, Berch, Vice Chief Justice, affirmed. The U.S. Supreme Court affirmed.

STEVENS, J., joined by SCALIA, SOUTER, THOMAS, and GINSBURG, JJ.

FACTS

On August 25, 1999, acting on an anonymous tip that the residence at 2524 North Walnut Avenue was being used to sell drugs, Tucson police officers Griffith and Reed knocked on the front door and asked to speak to the owner. Gant answered the door and, after identifying himself, stated that he expected the owner to return later. The officers left the residence and conducted a records check, which revealed that Gant's driver's license had been suspended and there was an outstanding warrant for his arrest for driving with a suspended license.

When the officers returned to the house that evening, they found a man near the back of the house and a woman in a car parked in front of it. After a third officer arrived, they arrested the man for providing a false name and the woman for possessing drug paraphernalia. Both arrestees were handcuffed and secured in separate patrol cars when Gant arrived. The officers recognized his car as it entered the driveway, and Officer Griffith confirmed that Gant was the driver by shining a flashlight into the car as it drove by him. Gant parked at the end of the driveway, got out of his car, and shut the door. Griffith, who was about 30 feet away, called to Gant, and they approached each other, meeting 10-to-12 feet from Gant's car. Griffith immediately arrested Gant and handcuffed him.

Because the other arrestees were secured in the only patrol cars at the scene, Griffith called for backup. When two more officers arrived, they locked Gant in the backseat of their vehicle. After Gant had been handcuffed and placed in the back of a patrol car, two officers searched his car: One of them found a gun, and the other discovered a bag of cocaine in the pocket of a jacket on the backseat.

Gant was charged with two offenses—possession of a narcotic drug for sale and possession of drug paraphernalia (i.e., the plastic bag in which the cocaine was found). He moved to suppress the evidence seized from his car on the ground that the warrantless search violated the Fourth Amendment. Among other things, Gant argued that *Belton* did not authorize the search of his vehicle because he posed no threat to the officers after he was handcuffed in the patrol car and because he was arrested for a traffic offense for which no evidence could be found in his vehicle. When asked at the suppression hearing why the search was conducted, Officer Griffith responded: "Because the law says we can do it."

The trial court rejected the State's contention that the officers had probable cause to search Gant's car for contraband when the search began, but it denied the motion to suppress. Relying on the fact that the police saw Gant commit the crime of driving without a license and apprehended him only shortly after he exited his car, the court held that the search was permissible as a search incident to arrest. A jury found Gant guilty on both drug counts, and he was sentenced to a 3-year term of imprisonment.

OPINION

In *Chimel v. California* (excerpted on p. 186), we held that a search incident to arrest may only include "the arrestee's person and the area 'within his immediate control'" ("the area from within which he might gain possession of a weapon or destructible evidence"). In *New York v. Belton* (1981), we considered *Chimel*'s application to the automobile context. A lone police officer in that case stopped a speeding car in which Belton was one of four occupants. While asking for the driver's license and registration, the officer smelled burnt marijuana and observed an envelope on the car floor marked "Supergold"—a name he associated with marijuana. Thus having probable cause to believe the occupants had committed a drug offense, the officer ordered them out of the vehicle, placed them under arrest, and patted them down. Without handcuffing the arrestees, the officer split them up into four separate areas of the Thruway so they would not be in physical touching area of each other, and searched the vehicle, including the pocket of a jacket on the backseat, in which he found cocaine.

We held that when an officer lawfully arrests "the occupant of an automobile, he may, as a contemporaneous incident of that arrest, search the passenger compartment of the automobile" and any containers therein. That holding was based in large part on our assumption that articles inside the relatively narrow compass of the passenger compartment of an automobile are in fact generally, even if not inevitably, "within 'the area into which an arrestee might reach.'"

The Arizona Supreme Court read our decision in *Belton* as merely delineating "the proper scope of a search of the interior of an automobile" incident to an arrest. That is, *when* the passenger compartment is within an arrestee's reaching distance, *Belton* supplies the generalization that the entire compartment and any containers therein may be reached. On that view of *Belton*, the state court concluded that the search of Gant's car was unreasonable because Gant clearly could not have accessed his car at the time of the search. It also found that no other exception to the warrant requirement applied in this case. Gant now urges us to adopt the reading of *Belton* followed by the Arizona Supreme Court.

Despite the support for the Arizona Supreme Court's reading of *Belton*, our opinion has been widely understood to allow a vehicle search incident to the arrest of a recent occupant even if there is no possibility the arrestee could gain access to the vehicle at the time of the search. Since we decided *Belton*, Courts of Appeals have given different answers to the question whether a vehicle must be within an arrestee's reach to justify a vehicle search incident to arrest. As Justice O'Connor observed, "lower court decisions seem now to treat the ability to search a vehicle incident to the arrest of a recent occupant as a police entitlement rather than as an exception justified by the twin rationales of *Chimel*." Justice SCALIA has similarly noted that, although it is improbable that an arrestee could gain access to weapons stored in his vehicle after he has been handcuffed and secured in the backseat of a patrol car, cases allowing a search in "this precise factual scenario are legion." Indeed, some courts have upheld searches under *Belton* even when the handcuffed arrestee has already left the scene.

Under this broad reading of *Belton*, a vehicle search would be authorized incident to every arrest of a recent occupant notwithstanding that in most cases the vehicle's passenger compartment will not be within the arrestee's reach at the time of the search. Accordingly, we reject this reading of *Belton* and hold that the *Chimel* rationale authorizes police to search a vehicle incident to a recent occupant's arrest only when the arrestee is unsecured and within reaching distance of the passenger compartment at the time of the search.* We also conclude that circumstances unique to the vehicle context justify a search incident to a lawful arrest when it is reasonable to believe evidence relevant to the crime of arrest might be found in the vehicle. In many cases, as when a recent occupant is arrested for a traffic violation, there will be no reasonable basis to believe the vehicle contains relevant evidence. But in others, including *Belton*, the offense of arrest will supply a basis for searching the passenger compartment of an arrestee's vehicle and any containers therein.

Neither the possibility of access nor the likelihood of discovering offense-related evidence authorized the search in this case. Unlike in *Belton*, which involved a single officer confronted with four unsecured arrestees, the five officers in this case outnumbered the three arrestees, all of whom had been handcuffed and secured in separate patrol cars before the officers searched Gant's car. Under those circumstances, Gant clearly was not within reaching distance of his car at the time of the search. An evidentiary basis for the search was also lacking in this case. Whereas Belton was arrested for drug offenses, Gant was arrested for driving with a suspended license—an offense for which police could not expect to find evidence in the passenger compartment of Gant's car. Because police could not reasonably have believed either that Gant could have accessed his car at the time of the search or that evidence of the offense for which he was arrested might have been found therein, the search in this case was unreasonable.

The State argues that *Belton* searches are reasonable regardless of the possibility of access in a given case because that expansive rule correctly balances law enforcement interests, including the interest in a bright-line rule, with an arrestee's limited privacy interest in his vehicle. For several reasons, we reject the State's argument. First, the State seriously undervalues the privacy interests at stake. It is particularly significant that *Belton* searches authorize police officers to search not just the passenger compartment but every purse, briefcase, or other container within that space. A rule that gives police the power to conduct such a search whenever an individual is caught committing a traffic offense, when there is no basis for believing evidence of the offense might be found in the vehicle, creates a serious and recurring threat to the privacy of countless individuals.

Contrary to the State's suggestion, a broad reading of *Belton* is also unnecessary to protect law enforcement safety and evidentiary interests. Under our view, *Belton* permits an officer to conduct a vehicle search when an arrestee is within reaching distance of the vehicle or it is reasonable to believe the vehicle contains evidence of the offense of arrest. Other established exceptions to the warrant requirement authorize a vehicle search under additional circumstances when safety or evidentiary concerns demand. For instance, *Michigan v. Long* (1983), permits an officer to search a vehicle's passenger compartment when he has reasonable suspicion that an individual, whether or not the arrestee, is "dangerous" and might access the vehicle to "gain immediate control of weapons." If there is probable cause to believe a vehicle contains evidence of criminal activity, *United States v. Ross* (1982), authorizes a search of any area of the vehicle in which the evidence might be found. *Ross* allows searches for evidence relevant to offenses other than the offense of arrest, and the scope of the search authorized is broader. Finally, there may be still other circumstances in which safety or evidentiary interests would justify a search. *Maryland v. Buie* (1990) held that, incident to arrest, an officer may conduct a limited protective sweep of those areas of a house in which he reasonably suspects a dangerous person may be hiding.

These exceptions together ensure that officers may search a vehicle when genuine safety or evidentiary concerns encountered during the arrest of a vehicle's recent occupant justify a search. Construing *Belton* broadly to allow vehicle searches incident to any arrest would serve no purpose except to provide a police entitlement, and it is anathema to the Fourth Amendment to permit a warrantless search on that basis. For these reasons, we are unpersuaded by the State's arguments that a broad reading of *Belton* would meaningfully further law enforcement interests and justify a substantial intrusion on individuals' privacy.

We do not agree with the contention in Justice ALITO's dissent (hereinafter dissent) that consideration of police reliance interests requires a different result. Although it appears that the State's reading of *Belton* has been widely taught in police academies and that law enforcement officers have relied on the rule in conducting vehicle searches during the past 28 years, many of these searches were not justified by the reasons underlying the *Chimel* exception. Countless individuals guilty of nothing more serious than a traffic violation have had their constitutional right to the security of their private effects violated as a result. The fact that the law enforcement community may view the State's version of the *Belton* rule as an entitlement does not establish the sort of reliance interest that could outweigh the countervailing interest that all individuals share in having their constitutional rights fully protected. If it is clear that a practice is unlawful, individuals' interest in its discontinuance clearly outweighs any law enforcement "entitlement" to its persistence.

The experience of the 28 years since we decided *Belton* has shown that the generalization underpinning the broad reading of that decision is unfounded. We now know that

---

*Because officers have many means of ensuring the safe arrest of vehicle occupants, it will be the rare case in which an officer is unable to fully effectuate an arrest so that a real possibility of access to the arrestee's vehicle remains.

articles inside the passenger compartment are rarely within the area into which an arrestee might reach, and blind adherence to *Belton*'s faulty assumption would authorize myriad unconstitutional searches.

Police may search a vehicle incident to a recent occupant's arrest only if the arrestee is within reaching distance of the passenger compartment at the time of the search or it is reasonable to believe the vehicle contains evidence of the offense of arrest. When these justifications are absent, a search of an arrestee's vehicle will be unreasonable unless police obtain a warrant or show that another exception to the warrant requirement applies. The Arizona Supreme Court correctly held that this case involved an unreasonable search.

Accordingly, the judgment of the State Supreme Court is AFFIRMED. *It is so ordered.*

CONCURRING OPINION

SCALIA, J.

It is abundantly clear that traditional standards of reasonableness do not justify what I take to be the rule set forth in *New York v. Belton* (1981): that arresting officers may always search an arrestee's vehicle in order to protect themselves from hidden weapons. When an arrest is made in connection with a roadside stop, police virtually always have a less intrusive and more effective means of ensuring their safety—and a means that is virtually always employed: ordering the arrestee away from the vehicle, patting him down in the open, handcuffing him, and placing him in the squad car.

Law enforcement officers face a risk of being shot whenever they pull a car over. But that risk is at its height at the time of the initial confrontation; and it is *not at all* reduced by allowing a search of the stopped vehicle after the driver has been arrested and placed in the squad car. I observed in *Thornton v. U.S.* (2004) that the government had failed to provide a single instance in which a formerly restrained arrestee escaped to retrieve a weapon from his own vehicle. Arizona and its *amici* have not remedied that significant deficiency in the present case.

Justice STEVENS would retain the application of *Chimel v. California* (1969), in the car-search context but would apply in the future what he believes our cases held in the past: that officers making a roadside stop may search the vehicle so long as the "arrestee is within reaching distance of the passenger compartment at the time of the search." I believe that this standard fails to provide the needed guidance to arresting officers and also leaves much room for manipulation, inviting officers to leave the scene unsecured (at least where dangerous suspects are not involved) in order to conduct a vehicle search.

In my view we should simply abandon the *Belton-Thornton* charade of officer safety and overrule those cases. I would hold that a vehicle search incident to arrest is *ipso facto* "reasonable" only when the object of the search is evidence of the crime for which the arrest was made, or of another crime that the officer has probable cause to believe occurred. Because respondent was arrested for driving without a license (a crime for which no evidence could be expected to be found in the vehicle), I would hold in the present case that the search was unlawful.

DISSENT

ALITO, J., joined by ROBERTS, CJ., and KENNEDY, BREYER, JJ.

The precise holding in *Belton* could not be clearer. The Court stated unequivocally: "We hold that when a policeman has made a lawful custodial arrest of the occupant of an automobile, he may, as a contemporaneous incident of that arrest, search the passenger compartment of that automobile."

The *Chimel* Court concluded that there are only two justifications for a warrantless search incident to arrest—officer safety and the preservation of evidence. The Court stated that such a search must be confined to "the arrestee's person" and "the area from within which he might gain possession of a weapon or destructible evidence." Unfortunately, *Chimel* did not say whether "the area from within which [an arrestee] might gain possession of a weapon or destructible evidence" is to be measured at the time of the arrest or at the time of the search, but unless the *Chimel* rule was meant to be a specialty rule, applicable to only a few unusual cases, the Court must have intended for this area to be measured at the time of arrest.

This is so because the Court can hardly have failed to appreciate the following two facts. First, in the great majority of cases, an officer making an arrest is able to handcuff the arrestee and remove him to a secure place before conducting a search incident to the arrest. Second, because it is safer for an arresting officer to secure an arrestee before searching, it is likely that this is what arresting officers do in the great majority of cases. (And it appears, not surprisingly, that this is in fact the prevailing practice.) Thus, if the area within an arrestee's reach were assessed, not at the time of arrest, but at the time of the search, the *Chimel* rule would rarely come into play.

Moreover, if the applicability of the *Chimel* rule turned on whether an arresting officer chooses to secure an arrestee prior to conducting a search, rather than searching first and securing the arrestee later, the rule would create a perverse incentive for an arresting officer to prolong the period during which the arrestee is kept in an area where he could pose a danger to the officer. If this is the law, the D.C. Circuit observed, "the law would truly be, as Mr. Bumble said, 'a ass.'"

I do not think that this is what the *Chimel* Court intended. Handcuffs were in use in 1969. The ability of arresting officers to secure arrestees before conducting a search—and their incentive to do so—are facts that can hardly have escaped the Court's attention. I therefore believe that the *Chimel* Court intended that its new rule apply in cases in which the arrestee is handcuffed before the search is conducted.

QUESTIONS

1. List the facts relevant to deciding whether the search of Rodney Gant's car was a lawful search "incident" to Gant's car.
2. Summarize what Justice Stevens says is a misunderstanding that lower courts and law enforcement officers have of the Court's decision in *New York v. Belton*.
3. According to Justice Stevens, when is search of a vehicle incident to a recent passenger's arrest reasonable?
4. According to Justice Stevens, why will the Court's decision in *Gant* not endanger officer safety?
5. What does Justice O'Connor mean when she writes that "lower court decisions seem now to treat the ability to search a vehicle incident to the arrest of a recent occupant as a police entitlement rather than as an exception justified by the twin rationales of *Chimel*."
6. Summarize Justice Scalia's "less intrusive and more effective means of ensuring" officer safety.
7. According to Justice Scalia, when is a vehicle search incident to arrest reasonable?
8. According to Justice Alito, what "two facts" could the Court in *Chimel* "hardly have failed to appreciate"?
9. According to Justice Alito, what interpretation of *Chimel* would make the law "a ass"?

The Reaction to Arizona v. Gant

LO 4

When *Arizona v. Gant* came before the Supreme Court, law enforcement thought it was a "big deal" (Armacost 2010, 277). A long list of prosecutors, police chiefs, police organizations, and attorneys representing 25 states filed an amicus brief (*Arizona v. Gant*, Amicus Brief 2008) supporting *Belton* and predicting dire consequences if the Court did not reaffirm the *Belton* rule:

> *Belton*'s allowance of searches incident to arrest has protected officers and the public in a wide array of fast-moving and hazardous arrest situations involving automobiles. There should be no need to analyze the particulars of every arrest that occurs in public, on the side of the road, and involving a mobile vehicle; instead, even if it is later determined that the arrestees were secured and posed no danger, the need to search vehicles contemporaneous with such inherently dangerous arrests remains a vital tool in protecting the public and fighting crime.
>
> The need for continuance of the *Belton* rule is borne out by statistics showing rising violent crime rates, deaths and assaults involving officers while making arrests involving vehicles, as well as the continued rise in gang activity and drug trafficking. These acutely dangerous criminal activities make warrantless searches of vehicles incident to arrests an immensely important part of law enforcement's arsenal to protect the public and preserve evidence. Without the bright-line *Belton* rule, the effectiveness of law enforcement efforts will be diminished and the potential for volatile arrest situations to end in tragedy will increase. This Court should therefore reaffirm the *Belton* rule and overrule the Arizona Supreme Court's reasoning that the rule did not apply to Gant's case. (2–3)

Defense attorney organizations, such as the National Association of Criminal Defense Lawyers (NACDL), and the civil rights bars also thought *Gant* was "a very important case" (Armacost 2010, 278). Long-time criminal defense lawyer and NACDL President John Wesley Hall (2009) wrote in his President's column:

> For years we old-timers still *pretended* the Fourth Amendment was alive, even while legal scholars and courtroom defenders lamented that it had kicked the bucket. We had to. It was our job. That is, until April 2, 2009, when the Supreme Court handed down *Arizona v. Gant*, and ruled 5–4 that the *Fourth Amendment isn't dead; it's just been in a 28-year coma.* (italics in original) (5)

Law enforcement's reaction to *Gant*—at least up to the summer of 2010—has been "remarkably muted." Professor Barbara Armacost (2010) explains: "While there is widespread agreement that officers will have to learn new, more nuanced rules for conducting traffic stop searches, most police experts are predicting that, in the end, *Gant* won't make much difference" (279). On one police blog, an officer pointed out that there's "more than one way to skin a suspect. Let's not forget consent search. Inventory works, but why not just ask? You never know. In my experience, 90 percent of people say yes anyway" (Wellentine 2009).

EXPLORING FURTHER

••

Search Incident to Arrest

Was the Search of the Suitcase on the Road Next to the Suspect Reasonable?

People v. Brooks, 257 Cal.Rptr. 840 (Cal.App. 1989)

FACTS A California police officer discovered a pistol and drugs on a hitchhiker during a lawful pat down, arrested and handcuffed him, and put him into a police vehicle. Only then did a second officer open an unlocked suitcase that had been sitting on the road next to the suspect at the time of the arrest; inside the suitcase were more drugs.

Was the search of the suitcase incident to the arrest?

DECISION Yes, said the California Court of Appeals, holding that if a container is close enough that the arrested suspect *could* have reached it at the moment of arrest, it's reasonable to search it:

> A search does not become unlawful because the police first separate the arrestee from the reach of the article, or handcuff or otherwise restrain the arrestee, so long as the search is made immediately thereafter, while the arrestee is still nearby at the scene of the arrest and before the arresting officers have turned their attention to tasks unrelated to securing the safety of persons and property involved in the arrest.

The Time Frame of "Incident To"

According to the U.S. Supreme Court, **"incident to arrest"** (or as it's sometimes called, **"contemporaneous with arrest"**) includes the time before, during, and after arrest. For example, in *Cupp v. Murphy* (1973), *immediately before* Portland, Oregon, police officers arrested Daniel Murphy, they scraped his fingernails for blood residue to see if it matched his strangled wife's. The U.S. Supreme Court held that because the officers *could* have arrested Murphy before they searched him (they had probable cause), the search was incident to the arrest.

In *U.S. v. Edwards* (1974), Eugene Edwards was arrested shortly after 11:00 P.M. and put in jail. The *next morning*, officers took his clothing and searched it for paint chips that would link Edwards to a burglary. Despite the 10-hour gap between the arrest and the search, and over a strong dissent arguing the officers had plenty of time to present their evidence to a neutral magistrate to get a search warrant, the Supreme Court ruled that the search was incident to the arrest.

Searches Incident to Misdemeanor Arrests

Until now, we've looked at the reasonableness of searches incident to *felony* arrests, but what about the reasonableness of searches incident to arrests for misdemeanors? The U.S. Supreme Court answered the question in *U.S. v. Robinson* (1973). Officer Richard Jenks, a 15-year veteran of the Washington, D.C., Police Department, arrested Willie Robinson for driving without a license (a misdemeanor). Jenks then searched Robinson. During the search, Jenks felt a lump in Robinson's coat pocket. Reaching inside, he found a crumpled-up cigarette package. Jenks took the package out of Robinson's pocket, opened it, and found heroin inside.

Robinson was charged with illegally possessing narcotics. He moved to suppress the evidence, but the court denied his motion and admitted the heroin. The heroin was the main evidence that convicted Robinson. The Supreme Court upheld the conviction and formulated a bright-line *Robinson* **rule:** Officers can always search anyone they're authorized to take into custody. (Be clear that officers don't *have to* search; many times they don't, but whether they do is a matter of individual officer discretion.)

According to Justice Rehnquist, writing for the majority:

> A police officer's determination as to how and where to search the person of a suspect whom he has arrested is necessarily a quick ad hoc judgment which the Fourth Amendment does not require to be broken down in each instance into an analysis of each step in the search. A custodial arrest of a suspect based on probable cause is a reasonable intrusion under the Fourth Amendment; that intrusion being lawful, a search incident to the arrest requires no additional justification. It is the fact of the lawful arrest which establishes the authority to search, and we hold that in the case of a lawful custodial arrest a full search of the person is not only an exception to the warrant requirement of the Fourth Amendment, but is also a "reasonable" search under that Amendment. (234–35)

What's the justification for the bright-line *Robinson* rule? Two reasons, according to the Court:

1. The possible danger to police officers taking suspects into custody
2. The logical impossibility of the Court's reviewing every police decision

The bright-line *Robinson* rule shows the Court's reluctance to second-guess law enforcement decisions. Nevertheless, six state courts—Alaska, California, Hawaii, New York, Oregon, and West Virginia—haven't been so reluctant; they've rejected the bright-line *Robinson* rule. Five—Illinois, Michigan, Montana, New Hampshire, and Texas—have specifically adopted it (Latzer 1991, 64).

Are *automatic* searches incident to traffic citations reasonable under the *Robinson* rule? (*Citations* are substitutes for arrests.) A unanimous U.S. Supreme Court said no in our next excerpted case, *Knowles v. Iowa* (1998). The case challenged an Iowa statute that created a search-incident-to-citation exception to the warrant requirement.

In Knowles v. Iowa (1998), our next case excerpt, the U.S. Supreme Court said that automatic searches incident to traffic citations aren't reasonable under the Robinson rule.

CASE Was the Automatic Search Incident to Citation Reasonable?

Knowles v. Iowa
525 U.S. 113 (1998)

HISTORY

Patrick Knowles was charged with possession of marijuana and keeping marijuana in a car. After the court denied his motion to suppress the marijuana as evidence, he was convicted of both offenses. The Iowa Supreme Court affirmed. The U.S. Supreme Court granted certiorari and reversed and remanded the case.

REHNQUIST, C.J.

FACTS

Patrick Knowles was stopped in Newton, Iowa, after having been clocked driving 43 miles per hour on a road where the speed limit was 25 miles per hour. The police officer issued a citation to Knowles, although under Iowa law he might have arrested him. The officer then conducted a full search of the car, and under the driver's seat he found a bag of marijuana and a "pot pipe." Knowles was then arrested and charged with violation of state laws dealing with controlled substances.

Before trial, Knowles moved to suppress the evidence so obtained. At the hearing on the motion to suppress, the police officer conceded that he had neither Knowles' consent nor probable cause to conduct the search. He relied on Iowa law dealing with such searches. Iowa Code Ann. § 321.485(1)(a) provides that Iowa peace officers having cause to believe that a person has violated any traffic or motor vehicle equipment law may arrest the person and immediately take the person before a magistrate. Iowa law also authorizes the far more usual practice of issuing a citation in lieu of arrest or in lieu of continued custody after an initial arrest. Section 805.1(4) provides that the issuance of a citation in lieu of an arrest "does not affect the officer's authority to conduct an otherwise lawful search." The Iowa Supreme Court has interpreted this provision as providing authority to officers to conduct a full-blown search of an automobile and driver in those cases where police elect not to make a custodial arrest and instead issue a citation—that is, a search incident to citation.

OPINION

In *U.S. v. Robinson*, we noted the two historical rationales for the "search incident to arrest" exception: (1) the need to disarm the suspect in order to take him into custody, and (2) the need to preserve evidence for later use at trial. But neither of these underlying rationales for the search incident to arrest exception is sufficient to justify the search in the present case.

We have recognized that the first rationale—officer safety—is "both legitimate and weighty," *Maryland v. Wilson* [excerpted in Chapter 4]. The threat to officer safety from issuing a traffic citation, however, is a good deal less than in the case of a custodial arrest. In *Robinson*, we stated that a custodial arrest involves "danger to an officer" because of "the extended exposure which follows the taking of a suspect into custody and transporting him to the police station."

We recognized that "the danger to the police officer flows from the fact of the arrest, and its attendant proximity, stress, and uncertainty, and not from the grounds for arrest."

A routine traffic stop, on the other hand, is a relatively brief encounter and is more analogous to a so-called *Terry* stop than to a formal arrest. Where there is no formal arrest a person might well be less hostile to the police and less likely to take conspicuous, immediate steps to destroy incriminating evidence. This is not to say that the concern for officer safety is absent in the case of a routine traffic stop. It plainly is not. But while the concern for officer safety in this context may justify the "minimal" additional intrusion of ordering a driver and passengers out of the car, it does not by itself justify the often considerably greater intrusion attending a full field-type search.

Nor has Iowa shown the second justification for the authority to search incident to arrest—the need to discover and preserve evidence. Once Knowles was stopped for speeding and issued a citation, all the evidence necessary to prosecute that offense had been obtained. No further evidence of excessive speed was going to be found either on the person of the offender or in the passenger compartment of the car.

Iowa nevertheless argues that a "search incident to citation" is justified because a suspect who is subject to a routine traffic stop may attempt to hide or destroy evidence related to his identity (e.g., a driver's license or vehicle registration), or destroy evidence of another, as yet undetected, crime. As for the destruction of evidence relating to identity, if a police officer is not satisfied with the identification furnished by the driver, this may be a basis for arresting him rather than merely issuing a citation. As for destroying evidence of other crimes, the possibility that an officer would stumble onto evidence wholly unrelated to the speeding offense seems remote.

In *Robinson*, we held that the authority to conduct a full field search as incident to an arrest was a "bright-line rule," which was based on the concern for officer safety and destruction or loss of evidence, but which did not depend in every case upon the existence of either concern. Here we are asked to extend that "bright-line rule" to a situation where the concern for officer safety is not present to the same extent and the concern for destruction or loss of evidence is not present at all. We decline to do so.

The judgment of the Supreme Court of Iowa is REVERSED, and the cause REMANDED for further proceedings not inconsistent with this opinion. It is so ordered.

QUESTIONS

1. **Summarize the reasons for Iowa's claim that the search incident to a citation is reasonable. Do you agree? Explain.**
2. **Summarize the reasons why the U.S. Supreme Court decided that the Iowa statute was unconstitutional. Do you agree? Explain.**
3. **Do you think the Supreme Court retreated from its sweeping decision in *U.S. v. Robinson*? If so, do you think it's a good idea that it did? Defend your answer.**

Searches Incident to Pretext Arrests

LO 4

Suppose an officer has only a hunch that a college student has marijuana in her car. The officer sees her make a left turn without signaling. "What luck," he thinks, "Now, I've got my chance." He stops her for turning without signaling so that he can search the car for marijuana—the arrest is simply a pretext for the search. *Pretext arrests* (arrests for one offense where probable cause exists, motivated by officers' desire to search for evidence of another unrelated offense where probable cause doesn't exist) are powerful investigative tools in the "drug war." Most people commit traffic offenses, so officers can use this fact of life to act on their hunches that drivers are committing drug crimes.

Critics argue that searches incident to pretext traffic arrests put a heavy thumb on the government side of the balance between government and individuals. According to Professor Daniel S. Jonas (1989):

> The conflict between liberty and law enforcement is particularly sharp in the area of pretextual police conduct. Police would have a powerful investigative tool if it were constitutional, for example, to arrest a felony suspect on the basis of a parking ticket that had not been paid, when the facts relating to the felony did not provide probable cause. Precisely because its investigative potential is so great, pretextual police conduct poses an alarming threat to individual freedom from government intrusion. (1792)

In our next case excerpt, *Whren v. U.S.* (1996), a unanimous U.S. Supreme Court decided that police officers' search of Michael Whren's Nissan Pathfinder incident to Whren's arrest for traffic violations was a reasonable Fourth Amendment search.

In **Whren v. U.S.** *(1999), our next case excerpt, the U.S. Supreme Court held that Michael Whren's conviction was based on a reasonable search incident to his arrest for a traffic violation.*

CASE Was the Search Incident to a Pretext Arrest Reasonable?

Whren v. U.S.
517 U.S. 806 (1996)

HISTORY

Michael A. Whren and James L. Brown were convicted in the U.S. District Court for the District of Columbia of drug offenses, and they appealed. The Court of Appeals affirmed. The U.S. Supreme Court granted certiorari. The U.S. Supreme Court affirmed.

SCALIA, J.

FACTS

On the evening of June 10, 1993, plainclothes vice-squad officers of the District of Columbia Metropolitan Police Department were patrolling a "high drug area" of the city in an unmarked car. Their suspicions were aroused when they passed a dark Nissan Pathfinder with temporary license plates and youthful occupants waiting at a stop sign, the driver looking down into the lap of the passenger at his right. The Pathfinder remained stopped at the intersection for what seemed an unusually long time—more than 20 seconds.

When the police car executed a U-turn in order to head back toward the truck, the Pathfinder turned suddenly to its right, without signaling, and sped off at an "unreasonable" speed. The policemen followed, and in a short while overtook the Pathfinder when it stopped behind other traffic at a red light. They pulled up alongside, and Officer Ephraim Soto stepped out and approached the driver's door, identifying himself as a police officer and directing the driver, James Brown, to put the vehicle in park. When Soto drew up to the driver's window, he immediately observed two large plastic bags of what appeared to be crack cocaine in Michael Whren's hands. Brown and Whren were arrested, and quantities of several types of illegal drugs were retrieved from the vehicle.

Brown and Whren were charged in a four-count indictment with violating various federal drug laws, including 21 U.S.C. §§ 844(a) and 860(a). At a pretrial suppression hearing, they challenged the legality of the stop and the resulting seizure of the drugs. They argued that the stop had not been justified by probable cause to believe, or even reasonable suspicion, that they were engaged in illegal drug-dealing activity; and that Officer Soto's asserted ground for approaching the vehicle—to give the driver a warning concerning traffic violations—was pretextual.

The District Court denied the suppression motion. Whren and Brown were convicted. The Court of Appeals affirmed the convictions. The U.S. Supreme Court affirmed.

OPINION

The decision to stop an automobile is reasonable where the police have probable cause to believe that a traffic violation has occurred. Brown and Whren accept that Officer Soto had probable cause to believe that various provisions of the District of Columbia traffic code had been violated:

1. 18 D.C. Mun. Regs. §§ 2213.4 (1995) An operator shall . . . give full time and attention to the operation of the vehicle;

2. 2204.3 No person shall turn any vehicle . . . without giving an appropriate signal;

3. 2200.3 No person shall drive a vehicle . . . at a speed greater than is reasonable and prudent under the conditions.

They argue, however, that "in the unique context of civil traffic regulations" probable cause is not enough. Since, they contend, the use of automobiles is so heavily and minutely regulated that total compliance with traffic and safety rules is nearly impossible, a police officer will almost invariably be able to catch any given motorist in a technical violation. This creates the temptation to use traffic stops as a means of investigating other law violations, as to which no probable cause or even articulable suspicion exists.

Whren and Brown, who are both Black, further contend that police officers might decide which motorists to stop based on decidedly impermissible factors, such as the race of the car's occupants. To avoid this danger, they say, the Fourth Amendment test for traffic stops should be, not the normal one (applied by the Court of Appeals) of whether probable cause existed to justify the stop; but rather, whether a police officer, acting reasonably, *would* [emphasis added] have made the stop for the reason given.

Whren and Brown contend that the standard they propose is consistent with our past cases' disapproval of police attempts to use valid bases of action against citizens as pretexts for pursuing other investigatory agendas. We are reminded that in *Florida v. Wells* (1990), we stated that an inventory search must not be used as a ruse for a general rummaging in order to discover incriminating evidence; that in *Colorado v. Bertine* (1987), in approving an inventory search, we apparently thought it significant that there had been no showing that the police, who were following standard procedures, acted in bad faith or for the sole purpose of investigation; and that in *New York v. Burger* (1987), we observed, in upholding the constitutionality of a warrantless administrative inspection, that the search did not appear to be a pretext for obtaining evidence of violation of penal laws.

Not only have we never held, outside the context of inventory search [discussed in Chapter 7] or administrative inspection, that an officer's motive invalidates objectively justifiable behavior under the Fourth Amendment, but we have repeatedly held and asserted the contrary. [*The Court discussed several cases omitted here.*] We think these cases foreclose any argument that the constitutional reasonableness of traffic stops depends on the actual motivations of the individual officers involved.

We of course agree with Whren and Brown that the Constitution prohibits selective enforcement of the law based on considerations such as race. But the constitutional basis for objecting to intentionally discriminatory application of laws is the Equal Protection Clause, not the Fourth Amendment. Subjective intentions play no role in ordinary, probable-cause Fourth Amendment analysis.

Whren and Brown's claim that a reasonable officer *would not* [emphasis added] have made this stop is based largely on District of Columbia police regulations which permit plainclothes officers in unmarked vehicles to enforce traffic laws "only in the case of a violation that is so grave as to pose an immediate threat to the safety of others." This basis of invalidation would not apply in jurisdictions that had a different practice. And it would not have applied even in the District of Columbia, if Officer Soto had been wearing a uniform or patrolling in a marked police cruiser.

Whren and Brown argue that the balancing inherent in any Fourth Amendment inquiry requires us to weigh the governmental and individual interests implicated in a traffic stop such as we have here. That balancing, they claim, does not support investigation of minor traffic infractions by plainclothes police in unmarked vehicles; such investigation only minimally advances the government's interest in traffic safety, and may indeed retard it by producing motorist confusion and alarm—a view said to be supported by the Metropolitan Police Department's own regulations generally prohibiting this practice.

It is of course true that in principle every Fourth Amendment case, since it turns upon a "reasonableness" determination, involves a balancing of all relevant factors. With rare exceptions not applicable here, however, the result of that balancing is not in doubt where the search or seizure is based upon probable cause. Where probable cause has existed, the only cases in which we have found it necessary actually to perform the "balancing" analysis involved searches or seizures conducted in an extraordinary manner, unusually harmful to an individual's privacy or even physical interests—such as, for example, seizure by means of deadly force, see *Tennessee v. Garner* (1985) [excerpted in Chapter 5], unannounced entry into a home, see *Wilson v. Arkansas* (1995) [excerpted earlier on p. 180], entry into a home without a warrant, see *Welsh v. Wisconsin* (1984), or physical penetration of the body, see *Winston v. Lee* (1985).

The making of a traffic stop out-of-uniform does not remotely qualify as such an extreme practice, and so is governed by the usual rule that probable cause to believe the law has been broken "outbalances" private interest in avoiding police contact.

Whren and Brown urge as an extraordinary factor in this case that the "multitude of applicable traffic and equipment regulations" is so large and so difficult to obey perfectly that virtually everyone is guilty of violation, permitting the police to single out almost whomever they wish for a stop. But we are aware of no principle that would allow us to decide at what point a code of law becomes so expansive and so commonly violated that infraction itself can no longer be the ordinary measure of the lawfulness of enforcement. And even if we could identify such exorbitant codes, we do not know by what standard (or what right) we would decide, as Whren and Brown would have us do, which particular provisions are sufficiently important to merit enforcement.

For the run of the mine case, which this surely is, we think there is no realistic alternative to the traditional common-law rule that probable cause justifies a search and seizure. Here the District Court found that the officers had probable cause to believe that petitioners had violated the traffic code. That rendered the stop reasonable under the Fourth Amendment, the evidence thereby discovered admissible, and the upholding of the convictions by the Court of Appeals for the District of Columbia Circuit correct.

Judgment AFFIRMED.

QUESTIONS

1. List all the actions Officer Soto and his partner took that affected Whren and Brown's liberty and privacy.
2. What's the evidence that Officer Soto and his partner conducted a pretext search?
3. Did Officer Soto and his partner have probable cause to arrest Whren and Brown? List the relevant facts and circumstances relevant to deciding whether they had probable cause.
4. For what "crimes" did the officers have probable cause to arrest Brown and Whren?
5. Explain the "could have" and "would have" tests to determine the reasonableness of the pretext search. What test did the Court adopt? Why?
6. Do you agree with Professor Jonas in the quotation at the opening of this section that pretext searches threaten individual rights too much? That they give the government too much power? Or do you believe that the government needs this power to fight the "war on drugs"?
7. Consider the following excerpt from the Petitioner's Brief (*Whren v. U.S.* 1996a) in *Whren v. U.S.*:

Justice Jackson's observation nearly a half-century ago is no less true today: "I am convinced that there are many unlawful searches of homes and automobiles of innocent people which turn up nothing incriminating, in which no arrest is made, about which courts do nothing, and about which we never hear." *Brinegar v. U.S.*, 338 U.S. 160 (1949) (JACKSON, J., dissenting).

Because police do not generally keep records of traffic stops that turn up nothing and in which no one is ticketed, it is no simple matter to substantiate Justice Jackson's suspicions. However, reporters from the *Orlando Sentinel* had the unique opportunity to document this phenomenon when they obtained 148 hours of videotaped "traffic" stops of 1,084 motorists along Interstate 95 in Florida (Brazil and Berry, "Color of Driver Is Key to Stops in I-95 Videos," *Orlando Sentinel*, Aug. 23, 1992).

Although all of the stops were purportedly based on traffic violations, only nine drivers (less than one percent) were issued citations. Searches were made in almost half the stops, but only 5 percent of all stops resulted in an arrest. Most shocking is how racially disproportionate the stops were. Although blacks and Hispanics made up only 5 percent of the drivers on that stretch of I-95 and only 15 percent of traffic convictions statewide, approximately 70 percent of those stopped were black or Hispanic.

On average, stops of minority drivers lasted more than twice as long as stops of white drivers. For some, the tapes showed it was not the first time they had been singled out: "There is the bewildered black man who stands on the roadside trying to explain to the deputies that it is the seventh time he has been stopped. And the black man who shakes his head in frustration as his car is searched; it is the second time in minutes he has been stopped." This kind of baseless "checking out" of racial minorities generally gets public attention only when someone well-known speaks out.

Materials in a class action involving pretextual traffic stops along Interstate 95 near Philadelphia show a similar pattern. The class representatives alleged that, while returning from a church celebration in 1991, they were stopped and subjected to a sniff by a police dog before being told, "in order to make this a legitimate stop, I'm going to give you a warning for obstruction of your car's rear-view mirror." The only object hanging from the mirror was a thin piece of string on which an air freshener had once been attached. When the driver pointed out that the officer could not have seen the string, the officer stated that they were stopped "because you are young, black and in a high drug-trafficking area, driving a nice car."

Materials and follow-up interviews in the Tinicum Township case showed: First, the interdiction program is based on the power to make a pretextual traffic stop. Numerous vehicles have been stopped, for example, for having small items tied to their rearview mirrors, for outdated inspection stickers, or for other minor violations, all supposedly observed as the car passed the police at sixty miles per hour. Second, the stops are racially disproportionate. Third, claims of consent are rebutted by numerous innocent individuals who give consistent accounts of being told that they would have to wait for a police dog, have their car towed, or suffer other types of roadside detention unless they consented to a search. (24–27)

How does this passage affect your opinion of the reasonableness of pretext searches? Is it more relevant to claims under the equal protection than the due process clause? (Refer to Chapter 2 on due process and equal protection.)

8. Consider the following remarks made by a police officer to researchers Lawrence Tiffany and his colleagues (1967):

You can always get a guy legitimately on a traffic violation if you tail him for a while, and then a search can be made. You don't have to follow a driver very long before he will move to the other side of the yellow line and then you can arrest and search him for driving on the wrong side of the highway. In the event that we see a suspicious automobile or occupant and wish to search the person or the car, or both, we will usually follow the vehicle until the driver makes a technical violation of a traffic law. Then we have a means of making a legitimate search. (131)

What's your reaction to this comment? Do you think things might have changed since the 1950s when the research for this quote was completed? Explain your answer.

9. Present arguments that both defense lawyers and prosecutors might make to support the reasonableness and the unreasonableness of searches incident to pretext traffic arrests. Then, assume the role of judge and decide the reasonableness of pretext traffic arrest searches in light of Fourth Amendment reasonableness.

Consent Searches

LO 5, LO 6

Consent searches are searches in which individuals give officers permission to search them and/or their houses and personal belongings without either warrants or probable cause. It's difficult to estimate the number of consent searches, but they may be the most common. We do know that "the vast majority of people" who do consent to searches or to allow officers to conduct a pat down are innocent (Nadler 2002, 209–10). We also know that most of the people who consent are young, poor, and not White (Cole 1999, 28).

Consent searches also definitely make law enforcement officers' job easier, because they don't have to go through the hassle of either getting warrants before they search or proving probable cause to a judge later. We also know that consent searches allow officers to search where they couldn't otherwise, because they couldn't get warrants or they lacked probable cause.

Lawrence P. Tiffany, Donald M. McIntyre, Jr., and Daniel L. Rotenberg, in their classic *The Detection of Crime* (1967), studied consent searches as part of the distinguished American Bar Foundation's massive ethnographic research into the day-to-day operations of criminal justice in America. They found that officers prefer to search by consent even when they have probable cause to obtain warrants because consent searches are convenient. "Search warrant procedure is overly technical and time-consuming, and has no corresponding advantages for them or meaningful protections for the individual" (157–61).

But convenience isn't the only reason for consent searches. Necessity also drives police officers to ask individuals to consent to searches. Officers need consent when they don't have probable cause or *can't* get a warrant. For example, it's well known that drug dealers travel by bus or plane, but officers don't have probable cause to search most passengers. So they approach travelers, ask if they can talk to them, explain the seriousness of the drug problem, and ask them if they mind having officers search them and their belongings. According to the anecdotal evidence supplied by officers, most travelers give their consent, especially when officers are polite and respectful.

In *U.S. v. Blake* (1988), Detective Perry Kendrick, who worked the Fort Lauderdale Airport, testified that people willingly consent even to searches of their crotches in the public part of airports (*U.S. v. Rodney*, excerpted later in this chapter). In just one day,

> [H]e talked with 16 to 20 people and most consented, but one or two did not. He testified further that initially some complain after the search, but that after the deputies explain their mission in interdicting narcotics moving from airport to airport within the United States, that the persons understand and many "thank us for the job we're doing." (927)

Several legal questions surround consent. We'll concentrate on the following four:

1. Did the suspect consent?
2. What's the scope of consent?
3. When can consent be withdrawn after it's given?
4. When can one person consent to search for someone else, their houses, and personal belongings?

The Test of Consent

When police officers ask for consent to search, constitutionally, they're asking individuals to give up their right against unreasonable searches. It's a serious matter to give up one of the fundamental rights our ancestors fought the Revolutionary War to protect. So the U.S. Supreme Court demands that as a minimum requirement, the government has to prove by a preponderance of the evidence that the consent was voluntary. The **voluntariness test of consent searches** looks at the totality of circumstances in each case to determine if the suspect consented voluntarily (Table 6.2).

A signed consent form is another example of how officers can demonstrate that a suspect voluntarily consented to a search. The New Jersey "Consent to Search" form, adopted by the New Jersey State Police, is an example. It authorizes a trooper to conduct a "complete search" of a motor vehicle or other premises as described by the officer on the face of the form. The form also states:

1. I also authorize the above member of the New Jersey State Police to remove and search any letters, documents, papers, materials, or other property which is considered pertinent to the investigation, provided that I am subsequently given a receipt for anything which is removed.
2. I have knowingly and voluntarily given my consent to the search described above.
3. I have been advised by [the investigating officer] and fully understand that I have the right to refuse giving my consent to search.
4. I have been further advised that I may withdraw my consent at any time during the search.

TABLE 6.2

Circumstances That May Form Part of Voluntary Consent

- Knowledge of constitutional rights in general
- Knowledge of the right to refuse consent
- Sufficient age and maturity to make an independent decision
- Intelligence to understand the significance of consent
- Education in or experience with the workings of the criminal justice system
- Cooperation with officers, such as saying, "Sure, go ahead and search"
- Attitude toward the likelihood that officers will discover contraband
- Length of detention and nature of questioning regarding consent
- Coercive police behavior surrounding the consent

The form is filled out by the officer and includes, among other things, the officer's name and a description of the vehicle to be searched. Then, it's presented to the consenting person for his or her signature (*State v. Carty* 2002, 907).

In our first consent case excerpt, the leading U.S. Supreme Court consent search case, *Schneckloth v. Bustamonte* (1973), the Court adopted a totality-of-circumstances test and then applied it, holding that the search of the car, in which Clyde Bustamonte was a passenger, passed the test.

In Schneckloth v. Bustamonte *(1973), the U.S. Supreme Court upheld the search of the car Clyde Bustamonte was a passenger in because it passed the totality of circumstances test for consent searches.*

CASE   Was the Consent Voluntary?

Schneckloth v. Bustamonte
412 U.S. 218 (1973)

HISTORY

Clyde Bustamonte was tried in a California state court for possessing a check with intent to defraud. The trial judge denied his motion to suppress and Bustamonte was convicted. The California Court of Appeals affirmed. The California Supreme Court denied review. Bustamonte brought a petition for habeas corpus in the U.S. District Court for the Northern District of California. The District Court denied the petition. The U.S. Court of Appeals for

the Ninth Circuit vacated the District Court's order, and remanded. The U.S. Supreme Court reversed.

STEWART, J.

FACTS

While on routine patrol in Sunnyvale, California, at approximately 2:40 in the morning, Police Officer James Rand stopped an automobile when he observed that one headlight and its license plate light were burned out. Six men were in the vehicle. Joe Alcala and Robert Clyde Bustamonte were in the front seat with Joe Gonzales, the driver. Three older men were seated in the rear. When, in response to the policeman's question, Gonzales could not produce a driver's license, Officer Rand asked if any of the other five had any evidence of identification. Only Alcala produced a license, and he explained that the car was his brother's.

After the six occupants had stepped out of the car at the officer's request and after two additional policemen had arrived, Officer Rand asked Alcala if he could search the car. Alcala replied, "Sure, go ahead." Prior to the search no one was threatened with arrest and, according to Officer Rand's uncontradicted testimony, it "was all very congenial at this time." Gonzales testified that Alcala actually helped in the search of the car, by opening the trunk and glove compartment. In Gonzales' words: "[T]he police officer asked Joe (Alcala), he goes, 'Does the trunk open?' And Joe said, 'Yes.' He went to the car and got the keys and opened up the trunk." Wadded up under the left rear seat, the police officers found three checks that had previously been stolen from a car wash.

OPINION

It is well settled under the Fourth Amendment that one of the exceptions to the requirements of both a warrant and probable cause is a search that is conducted pursuant to consent. The precise question in this case is what must the prosecution prove to demonstrate that a consent was "voluntarily" given. And upon that question there is a square conflict of views between the state and federal courts that have reviewed the search involved in the case before us.

The Court of Appeals for the Ninth Circuit concluded that it is an essential part of the State's initial burden to prove that a person knows he has a right to refuse consent. The California courts have followed the rule that voluntariness is a question of fact to be determined from the totality of all the circumstances, and that the state of a defendant's knowledge is only one factor to be taken into account in assessing the voluntariness of a consent.

The most extensive judicial exposition of the meaning of "voluntariness" has been developed in those cases in which the Court has had to determine the "voluntariness" of a defendant's confession [Chapter 8]. The ultimate test has remained the same in Anglo-American courts for two hundred years: the test of voluntariness. Is the confession the product of an essentially free and unconstrained choice by its maker? If it is, if he has willed to confess, it may be used against him. If it is not, if his will has been overborne and his capacity for self-determination critically impaired, the use of his confession offends due process.

The significant fact about all of these decisions is that none of them turned on the presence or absence of a single controlling criterion; each reflected a careful scrutiny of all the surrounding circumstances. In none of them did the Court rule that the Due Process Clause required the prosecution to prove as part of its initial burden that the defendant knew he had a right to refuse to answer the questions that were put. While the state of the accused's mind, and the failure of the police to advise the accused of his rights, were certainly factors to be evaluated in assessing the "voluntariness" of an accused's responses, they were not in and of themselves determinative.

The question whether a consent to a search was in fact "voluntary" or was the product of duress or coercion is a question of fact to be determined from the totality of all the circumstances. While knowledge of the right to refuse consent is one factor to be taken into account, the government need not establish such knowledge as indispensable to an effective consent. As with police questioning, two competing concerns must be accommodated in determining the meaning of a voluntary consent—the legitimate need for such searches and the equally important requirement of assuring the absence of coercion.

In situations where the police have some evidence of illicit activity, but lack probable cause to arrest or search, a search authorized by a valid consent may be the only means of obtaining important and reliable evidence. In the present case for example, while the police had reason to stop the car for traffic violations, the State does not contend that there was probable cause to search the vehicle or that the search was incident to a valid arrest of any of the occupants. Yet, the search yielded tangible evidence that served as a basis for a prosecution, and provided some assurance that others, wholly innocent of the crime, were not mistakenly brought to trial. In short, a search pursuant to consent may result in considerably less inconvenience for the subject of the search, and, properly conducted, is a constitutionally permissible and wholly legitimate aspect of effective police activity.

But the Fourth Amendment requires that a consent not be coerced. In examining all the surrounding circumstances to determine if in fact the consent to search was coerced, account must be taken of subtly coercive police questions, as well as the possibly vulnerable subjective state of the person who consents. Those searches that are the product of police coercion can thus be filtered out without undermining the continuing validity of consent searches.

The approach of the Court of Appeals for the Ninth Circuit that the State must affirmatively prove that the subject of the search knew that he had a right to refuse consent, would, in practice, create serious doubt whether consent searches could continue to be conducted. There might be rare cases where it could be proved from the record that a person in fact affirmatively knew of his right to refuse—such as a case where he announced to the police that if he didn't sign the consent form, "you (police) are going to get a search warrant." But more commonly where there was no evidence of any coercion, the prosecution would nevertheless be unable to demonstrate that the subject of the search in fact had known of his right to refuse consent.

[Bustamonte also argues] that the Court's decision in the *Miranda* case [*excerpted in Chapter 8*] requires the conclusion that knowledge of a right to refuse is an indispensable element of a valid consent. In *Miranda* the Court found that the techniques of police questioning and the nature of custodial surroundings produce an inherently coercive situation. The Court noted that "without proper safeguards the process of in-custody interrogation of persons suspected or accused of crime contains inherently compelling pressures which work to undermine the individual's will to resist and to compel him to speak where he would not otherwise do so freely."

In this case, there is no evidence of any inherently coercive tactics—either from the nature of the police questioning or the environment in which it took place. Indeed, since consent searches will normally occur on a person's own familiar territory, the specter of incommunicado police interrogation in some remote station house is simply inapposite. There is no reason to believe, under circumstances such as are present here, that the response to a policeman's question is presumptively coerced; and there is, therefore, no reason to reject the traditional test for determining the voluntariness of a person's response.

It is also argued that the failure to require the Government to establish knowledge as a prerequisite to a valid consent, will relegate the Fourth Amendment to the special province of "the sophisticated, the knowledgeable and the privileged." We cannot agree. The traditional definition of voluntariness we accept today has always taken into account evidence of minimal schooling, low intelligence, and the lack of any effective warnings to a person of his rights; and the voluntariness of any statement taken under those conditions has been carefully scrutinized to determine whether it was in fact voluntarily given.

Our decision today is a narrow one. We hold only that when the subject of a search is not in custody and the State attempts to justify a search on the basis of his consent, the Fourth Amendment requires that it demonstrate that the consent was in fact voluntarily given, and not the result of coercion. Voluntariness is a question of fact to be determined from all the circumstances, and while the subject's knowledge of a right to refuse is a factor to be taken into account, the prosecution is not required to demonstrate such knowledge as a prerequisite to establishing a voluntary consent.

Judgment of Court of Appeals REVERSED.

DISSENT

MARSHALL, J.

I would have thought that the capacity to choose necessarily depends upon knowledge that there is a choice to be made. But today the Court reaches the curious result that one can choose to relinquish a constitutional right—the right to be free of unreasonable searches—without knowing that he has the alternative of refusing to accede to a police request to search. I am at a loss to understand why consent cannot be taken literally to mean a "knowing choice." In fact, I have difficulty in comprehending how a decision made without knowledge of available alternatives can be treated as a choice at all. I can think of no other situation in which we

would say that a person agreed to some course of action if he convinced us that he did not know that there was some other course he might have pursued.

The Court contends that if an officer paused to inform the subject of his rights, the informality of the exchange would be destroyed. I doubt that a simple statement by an officer of an individual's right to refuse consent would do much to alter the informality of the exchange, except to alert the subject to a fact that he surely is entitled to know. It is not without significance that for many years the agents of the Federal Bureau of Investigation have routinely informed subjects of their right to refuse consent, when they request consent to search.

I must conclude with some reluctance that when the Court speaks of practicality, what it really is talking of is the continued ability of the police to capitalize on the ignorance of citizens so as to accomplish by subterfuge what they could not achieve by relying only on the knowing relinquishment of constitutional rights. Of course it would be "practical" for the police to ignore the commands of the Fourth Amendment, if by practicality we mean that more criminals will be apprehended, even though the constitutional rights of innocent people also go by the board. But such a practical advantage is achieved only at the cost of permitting the police to disregard the limitations that the Constitution places on their behavior, a cost that a constitutional democracy cannot long absorb.

I find nothing in the opinion of the Court to dispel my belief that under many circumstances a reasonable person might read an officer's "May I" as the courteous expression of a demand backed by force of law. In most cases, in my view consent is ordinarily given as acquiescence in an implicit claim of authority to search. Permitting searches in such circumstances, without any assurance at all that the subject of the search knew that, by his consent, he was relinquishing his constitutional rights, is something that I cannot believe is sanctioned by the Constitution.

The proper resolution of this case turns, I believe, on a realistic assessment of the nature of the interchange between citizens and the police. Although the Court says it "cannot agree," the holding today confines the protection of the Fourth Amendment against searches conducted without probable cause to the sophisticated, the knowledgeable, and, I might add, the few. The Court's half-hearted defense, that lack of knowledge is to be "taken into account," rings rather hollow, in light of the apparent import of the opinion that even a subject who proves his lack of knowledge may nonetheless have consented "voluntarily," under the Court's peculiar definition of voluntariness. In the final analysis, the Court now sanctions a game of blindman's buff, in which the police always have the upper hand, for the sake of nothing more than the convenience of the police.

But the guarantees of the Fourth Amendment were never intended to shrink before such an ephemeral and changeable interest. The Framers of the Fourth Amendment struck the balance against this sort of convenience and in favor of certain basic civil rights. It is not for this

Court to restrike that balance because of its own views of the needs of law enforcement officers. I fear that that is the effect of the Court's decision today.

QUESTIONS

1. State the elements of the voluntariness test created by the U.S. Supreme Court.
2. List all the facts and circumstances relevant to deciding whether Clyde Bustamonte consented to the search of the car.
3. Describe the Court's application of the voluntariness test to consent in the case.
4. Explain why the Court says there's a fundamental difference between rights guaranteeing a fair trial and the rights against searches and seizures.
5. According to Justice Marshall, do individuals ever voluntarily consent to police requests, or are all police requests polite orders? Do you agree with Justice Marshall? Defend your answer.
6. State the elements of the waiver test favored by Justice Marshall.
7. Apply the majority's voluntariness test and the dissent's waiver test to the facts of the consent in the case.
8. Consider the consent form used by the St. Paul, Minnesota, Police Department in Figure 6.1. If Bustamonte had signed this form, would his consent have been voluntary? Would it matter if the officer just handed the form to him without explaining its importance? Explain your answer.

EXPLORING FURTHER

....

Consent Searches

1. *Was the Consent Given While Handcuffed, After Promises and Threats, Voluntary?*

U.S. v. Ceballos, 812 F.2d 42 (2d Cir. 1987)

FACTS Secret Service agents had information that Abraham Ceballos and Efrian Adames were counterfeiting U.S. currency. After a number of agents entered the P & J Printing Company where Ceballos worked, they handcuffed and escorted him out. Later, they advised him of his right to remain silent. Ceballos was taken to the field office and questioned. The agents warned him of the seriousness of a counterfeiting offense and threatened to get a search warrant unless he consented to a search of his apartment. They offered to help Ceballos obtain low bail and retain his job if he cooperated.

After a couple of hours, Ceballos consented to a search of his apartment. At the apartment, Ceballos located counterfeit plates and surrendered them to the agents. He was taken back to the field office, whereupon he and Adames were indicted on counterfeiting and conspiracy charges.

Did Ceballos voluntarily consent to the search of his apartment?

FIGURE 6.1   St. Paul, Minnesota, Consent Search Form

WAIVER AND CONSENT TO SEARCH

The undersigned _____

residing at _____

_____ hereby authorizes

the following named St. Paul Police Officers _____

to search the _____

_____

(insert description of place or auto, lic. number, etc.)

owned by/or in possession of the undersigned.
I do hereby waive any and all objections that may be made by me to said search and declare that this waiver and consent is freely and voluntarily given of my own free will and accord.

Signed _____ day of _____ 20 __ at _____ PM   AM

Signed _____

Witnessed _____

DECISION Yes, according to the U.S. Second Circuit Court of Appeals.

OPINION Agents forcibly removed Ceballos from his place of work in handcuffs. There is also no question that the agents sought to persuade Ceballos to consent to a search and to confess. They warned him of the disruption to his household of execution of a court-ordered search warrant. They promised him aid in obtaining low bail and retaining his job if he cooperated.

Nonetheless, the totality of the circumstances suggests that Ceballos' consent to search was voluntarily given. The record indicates that the only use of force was in connection with the arrest. Thereafter the agents gave Ceballos a *Miranda* warning. They questioned him at their field office for a couple of hours before he consented to the search. We find that the warnings made and promises offered by the agents did not overbear Ceballos' free will.

2. Was Consent Voluntary When Given After the Trooper Asked to Search the Stopped Car?

Ohio v. Robinette, 117 S.Ct. 417 (1996)

FACTS This case arose on a stretch of Interstate 70 north of Dayton, Ohio, where the posted speed limit was 45 miles per hour because of construction. Robert D. Robinette was clocked at 69 miles per hour as he drove his car along this stretch of road, and he was stopped by Deputy Roger Newsome of the Montgomery County Sheriff's office. Newsome asked for and was handed Robinette's driver's license, and he ran a computer check, which indicated that Robinette had no previous violations. Newsome then asked Robinette to step out of his car, turned on his mounted video camera, issued a verbal warning to Robinette, and returned his license.

At this point, Newsome asked, "One question before you get gone: Are you carrying any illegal contraband in your car? Any weapons of any kind, drugs, anything like that?" Robinette answered "no" to these questions, after which Deputy Newsome asked if he could search the car. Robinette consented. In the car, Deputy Newsome discovered a small amount of marijuana and, in a film container, a pill that was later determined to be Ecstasy (MDMA). Robinette was then arrested and charged with knowing possession of a controlled substance (Ohio Rev.Code Ann. § 2925.11(A) (1993)).

Did Robinette voluntarily consent to the search?

DECISION Yes, said the U.S. Supreme Court.

OPINION We have long held that the "touchstone of the Fourth Amendment is reasonableness." Reasonableness, in turn, is measured in objective terms by examining the totality of the circumstances. In applying this test we have consistently eschewed bright-line rules, instead emphasizing the fact-specific nature of the reasonableness inquiry. In *Schneckloth v. Bustamonte,* 412 U.S. 218 (1973), it was argued that such a consent could not be valid unless the defendant knew that he had a right to refuse the request. We rejected this argument: "While knowledge of the right to refuse consent is one factor to be taken into account, the government need not establish such knowledge as the sine qua non of an effective consent." And just as it "would be thoroughly impractical to impose on the normal consent search the detailed requirements of an effective warning," so too would it be unrealistic to require police officers to always inform detainees that they are free to go before a consent to search may be deemed voluntary.

Next, we examine what empirical research tells us about how citizens really feel about consent searches, how far searches can extend once a citizen gives consent, what constitutes a legal withdrawal of consent, and the circumstances under which third parties can give consent to search.

Empirical Research and Consent Searches

LO 6

The U.S. Supreme Court expressed great confidence that lower courts would carefully scrutinize the "totality of circumstances" in each case to make sure consent searches were voluntary. In practice, available empirical evidence shows that the lower courts find consent was voluntary in all but the most extreme cases.

One unpublished study conducted by a Georgetown University Law Center student (cited in Cole 1999) examined all consent cases decided by the U.S. D.C. Court of Appeals from January 1989 to April 15, 1995. In every case, the court found the consent was voluntary. In most of the cases, the court didn't even discuss the circumstances the Supreme Court said in *Schneckloth* were important in determining voluntariness. "When they did mention them, the courts turned a blind eye to factors strongly suggesting a less than voluntary encounter." In one case, the court found the consent given by a 24-year-old defendant with a 10th-grade education, who previously had refused to consent four times and was searched anyway, was voluntary (Cole 1999, 32).

The majority of justices in *Schneckloth v. Bustamonte* (1973) also claimed that if suspects know they have a right to refuse consent, it "would, in practice, create serious doubt whether consent searches could continue to be conducted" (229–30). Available empirical evidence suggests otherwise.

Professor Illya Lichtenberg (2001) examined Ohio State Police data on all highway stops between 1995 and 1997. These years included the year before and after the Ohio Supreme Court ruled that Ohio officers had to warn drivers stopped for traffic violations that they had the right to refuse officers' requests to search (Exploring Further, p. 206). He found no decrease in consent rates after police were required to give the warning.

Lichtenberg interviewed a random sample of a group of drivers from the Ohio data. Of the 54 in the sample, 49 consented; 5 refused (251). Of the 49 who consented, 47 said they consented because they were afraid of what would happen to them if they refused. Here are a few answers:

#15373. I knew *legally* I didn't have to, but I kind of felt I had to. (264)

#3371. It would be very, very inconvenient to be locked up for the night. I didn't know if that was an option, and I didn't want to find out. (261)

#4337. At first I didn't think there was any reason to [consent] and then I realized that if I didn't they would do it anyway. (261)

#16633. To this day I do not know what would have happened if I had said, "No, absolutely not." (263)

Finally, the Supreme Court interprets a consent search as an act of good citizenship; it reinforces the rule of law and should, in the words of Justice Kennedy for the majority in *U.S. v. Drayton* (2002), be "given a weight and dignity of its own" (207). Most of Lichtenberg's sample drivers gave more mixed interpretations. Three were definitely positive:

#01568. I wish they would do it more. (283)

#14735. I'm just glad I had nothing to hide. (284)

#07267. I guess they were just doing their job. (284)

The rest were strongly negative:

#14735. It was embarrassing. It pissed me off. . . . They just treat you like you're nothing. . . . I think about it every time I see a cop. (283)

#15494. I feel really violated. I felt like my rights had been infringed upon. I feel really bitter about the whole thing. (285)

#12731. I don't trust the police anymore. I've lost all trust in them. (288)

Professor Janice Nadler (2002) summed up Lichtenberg's findings in her survey of empirical studies of Fourth Amendment consent searches this way:

Consent search encounters with police often have a substantial impact on people—they do not forget about the experience quickly, and most people, in this sample at least, had lasting negatives toward the incident (and sometimes toward the police) as a result. Finally, unlike people who are discovered carrying unlawful contraband, innocent citizens who are subjected to coercive consent searches have no practical recourse—it is difficult to prove a constitutional violation even when their privacy interests protected by the Fourth Amendment were violated, and in any event the amount of money damages recovered is likely to be quite small. (212–13; see Chapter 11)

The Scope of Consent

LO 6

How far can officers go in searching *after* they get permission to search? Only as far as the person who gave it consented to. But how far is that? As far as the person who gave it intended the search to be or as far as the officer believes the consent goes? According to the U.S. Supreme Court, the consent is as broad as the officers *reasonably* believe it to be.

In *Florida v. Jimeno* (1991), officers asked for permission to search Jimeno's "car." He agreed. The police searched not only the car itself but also a brown paper bag found in the trunk of the car. (The officer found drugs in the paper bag.) The U.S. Supreme Court upheld the reasonableness of the search. According to the Court, "The Fourth Amendment is satisfied when, under the circumstances, it is objectively reasonable for the officer to believe that the scope of the suspect's consent permitted him to open a particular container within the automobile" (248–49).

The scope of consent searches is a major issue in so-called crotch searches, a tactic used in drug law enforcement. Specially trained officers who patrol bus stations, airports, and railway stations approach persons with no reasonable suspicion. They get into some light conversation and then ask, "Do you mind if I search you?" If the persons agree, the officers immediately pat down their crotch area.

The U.S. Supreme Court hasn't decided whether consent to search "you" includes searching the genital area, especially if the consent to search occurs on a public street or in the public areas of busy airports, bus stations, and railway stations.

The U.S. Circuit Courts are divided. Some say consent to search "you" includes the groin area. Others say officers have to ask specifically, "Can I search your genital area?" In the next excerpt, *U.S. v. Rodney* (1992), the D.C. Circuit Court decided that Dylan Rodney's consent to search his person included his groin area.

*In **U.S. v. Rodney** (1992), our next case excerpt, the U.S. District Court for the District of Columbia upheld Dylan Rodney's conviction after finding that he had consented to a crotch search, which revealed hidden drugs.*

CASE Did Dylan Rodney Consent to a Search of His Crotch?

U.S. v. Rodney
956 F.2d 295 (CADC 1992)

HISTORY

Dylan Rodney (Defendant) was convicted upon his guilty plea to possession with intent to distribute crack cocaine before the United States District Court for the District of Columbia, after the court denied his motion to suppress. Rodney appealed. The Court of Appeals panel affirmed (2–1), and held that: (1) the district court committed no clear error in finding consent to the search voluntary; (2) defendant's general consent to a body search for drugs, without more, authorized a *Terry* frisk which included defendant's crotch area; and (3) the officer had probable cause to make warrantless arrest of defendant. Before WALD, GINSBURG, and THOMAS, JJ.

THOMAS, Circuit Justice

FACTS

Dylan Rodney stepped off a bus that had arrived in Washington, D.C., from New York City. As Rodney left the bus station, Detective Vance Beard, dressed in plain clothes and carrying a concealed weapon, approached him from behind. A second officer waited nearby. Beard displayed identification and asked if Rodney would talk to him. Rodney agreed. Beard asked Rodney whether he lived in either Washington or New York. Rodney replied that he lived in Florida, but had come to Washington to try to find his wife. She lived on Georgia Avenue, Rodney said, although he was unable to identify any more precise location. Beard asked Rodney whether he was carrying drugs in his travel bag. After Rodney said no, Beard obtained permission to search the bag. As he did so, the other officer advanced to within about five feet of Rodney. The search failed to turn up any contraband.

Beard then asked Rodney whether he was carrying drugs on his person. After Rodney again said no, Beard requested permission to conduct a body search. Rodney said "sure" and raised his arms above his head. Beard placed his hands on Rodney's ankles and, in one sweeping motion, ran them up the inside of Rodney's legs. As he passed over the crotch area, Beard felt small, rock-like objects. Rodney exclaimed: "That's me!" Detecting otherwise, Beard placed Rodney under arrest. At the police station, Beard unzipped Rodney's pants and retrieved a plastic bag containing a rock-like substance that was identified as cocaine base. Rodney was charged with possession and intent to distribute.

OPINION

Rodney contends that the district court erred in finding that his consent to the body search was voluntary, and therefore not prohibited by the Fourth Amendment. In determining the voluntariness of a consent, a district court must examine the totality of all the surrounding circumstances—both the characteristics of the accused and the details of the interrogation. *Schneckloth v. Bustamonte* (1973). Relevant factors include: the youth of the accused; his lack of education; or his low intelligence; the lack of any advice to the accused of his constitutional rights; the length of detention; the repeated and prolonged nature of the questioning; and the use of physical punishment such as the deprivation of food or sleep.

On this record, we find no clear error. On the one hand, some evidence suggests an involuntary consent. Rodney testified that he thought three, rather than two, officers were covering him; that the officers were much bigger than he; and that he was young (twenty-four) and relatively uneducated (to the tenth grade) at the time. He also testified that before the events leading to his arrest, he had had four unpleasant encounters with the police:

each time he had refused their request to search him, but each time they had searched him anyway.

On the other hand, Beard's testimony indicates that the police conduct here bore no resemblance to the sort of aggressive questioning, intimidating actions, or prolonged police presence, that might invalidate a consent. During the encounter, according to Beard, his gun was concealed; he wore plain clothes and spoke in a conversational tone; and no other officer came within five feet of Rodney. The district court could have weighed Beard's evidence more heavily than Rodney's. Thus, even assuming that the court credited Rodney's testimony in addition to Beard's, the court committed no clear error in finding the consent voluntary.

Rodney next argues that even if he consented voluntarily to the body search, he did not consent to the search of his crotch area. A consensual search cannot exceed the scope of the consent. The scope of the consent is measured by a test of "objective reasonableness": it depends on how broadly a reasonable observer would have interpreted the consent under the circumstances. Here, Rodney clearly consented to a search of his *body* for *drugs*. We conclude that a reasonable person would have understood that consent to encompass the search undertaken here. In this case, Rodney authorized a search for drugs. Dealers frequently hide drugs near their genitals. Indeed, Beard testified that his colleagues make up to 75 percent of their drug recoveries from around the crotch area. For these reasons, we conclude that a request to conduct a body search for drugs reasonably includes a request to conduct some search of that area.

Although the scope of a search is generally defined by its expressed object, we doubt that the Supreme Court would have us apply that test unflinchingly in the context of body searches. At some point, we suspect, a body search would become so intrusive that we would not infer consent to it from a generalized consent, regardless of the stated object of the search. For example, although drugs can be hidden virtually anywhere on or in one's person, a generalized consent to a body search for drugs surely does not validate everything up to and including a search of body cavities.

The search undertaken here, however, was not unusually intrusive, at least relative to body searches generally. It involved a continuous sweeping motion over Rodney's outer garments, including the trousers covering his crotch area. At the suppression hearing, Rodney mimicked the search. Without objection, the prosecutor asked for the record to reflect that Rodney "ran both his hands from the base of his feet or ankle area up through the interior of his legs and including the crotch area with one motion." In this respect, the search was no more invasive than the typical pat-down frisk for weapons described by the Supreme Court in *Terry v. Ohio*.

We conclude that Rodney voluntarily consented to a search of his body for drugs, which encompassed the frisk undertaken here. As a result of that frisk, we conclude further, Beard had probable cause to arrest Rodney. Accordingly, the judgment of conviction is

AFFIRMED.

DISSENT

WALD, J.

The issue before us is whether a person against whom there is no articulable suspicion of wrongdoing who is asked to submit to a body search on a public street expects that search to include manual touching of the genital area. I do not believe any such expectation exists at the time a cooperative citizen consents to an on-the-street search. Rather, that citizen anticipates only those kinds of searches that unfortunately have become a part of our urban living, searches ranging from airport security personnel passing a hand-held magnometer over a person's body, to having a person empty his pockets, and subject himself to a patting-down of sides, shoulders, and back. Any search that includes touching genital areas or breasts would not normally be expected to occur in public.

In all aspects of our society, different parts of the body are subject to very different levels of privacy and expectations about intrusions. We readily bare our heads, arms, legs, backs, even midriffs, in public, but, except in the most unusual circumstances, certainly not our breasts or genitals. On the streets, in elevators, and on public transportation, we often touch, inadvertently or even casually, each others' hands, arms, shoulders, and backs, but it is a serious affront, and sometimes even a crime, to intentionally touch another's intimate body parts without explicit permission; and while we feel free to discuss other people's hair, facial features, weight, height, noses or ears, similar discussions about genitals or breasts are not acceptable. Thus in any consensual encounter, it is not "objectively reasonable" for a citizen desiring to cooperate with the police in a public place to expect that permission to search her body includes feeling, even "fully clothed," the most private areas of her body. Under our social norms that requires "special permission," given with notice of the areas to be searched.

Nor can the mere fact that drug couriers often hide their stash in the crotch area justify the search of such area without some elementary form of notice to the citizen that such an offensive procedure is about to take place. The ordinary citizen's expectation of privacy in intimate parts of her body is certainly well enough established to merit a particularized request for consent to such an intimate search in public.

Minimally, in my view, fourth amendment protection of a nonsuspect citizen's reasonable expectations of privacy requires that the police indicate that the search will entail a touching of private areas. A general consent to a search of a citizen's "person" in a public place does not include consent to touch the genital or breast areas. The majority today upholds a practice that allows police under the rubric of a general consent to conduct intimate body searches, and in so doing defeats the legitimate expectations of privacy that ordinary citizens should retain during cooperative exchanges with the police on the street. I believe the search was impermissible under the fourth amendment, and the drugs seized should have been suppressed.

QUESTIONS

1. State the specific rule the majority adopted to cover the scope of consent searches of a person.
2. State exactly what the officers asked Rodney to consent to.
3. Assume you're Rodney's lawyer. Relying on the facts as they're outlined in the case, argue that Rodney didn't consent to a search of his crotch.
4. Now assume you're the prosecutor, and argue that Rodney voluntarily consented to the search of his crotch.
5. Now assume you are the judge. Rule on the consent and its scope.

EXPLORING FURTHER
....

The Scope of Consent

Did He Consent to the Search of His Crotch?

U.S. v. Blake 888 F.2d 795 (CA11, 1989)

FACTS On December 11, 1987, three Broward County Sheriff's Deputies were working at the South Terminal in the Fort Lauderdale/Hollywood International Airport. As defendants Blake and Eason were leaving the Piedmont Airlines ticket counter and entering into the middle of an airport corridor, they were approached by two of the deputies. One of the officers testified that he had no reason for choosing the defendants, but that his actions were simply part of a random, voluntary drug interdiction policy. He admitted that he saw nothing suspicious about the defendants and that he was not relying upon a "drug courier" profile. The officers, dressed in plain-clothes, identified themselves as deputy sheriffs to Blake and Eason by showing their badges and asked Blake and Eason if they would consent to speak with them. After Blake and Eason gave their consent, the officers asked them for their plane tickets and identification. Blake responded that he had a driver's license; Eason said that he had no identification. One of the officers, Detective Hendrick, renewed the request to see their tickets. When Blake responded that the tickets were in his carry-on bag, Hendrick suggested that they move over to a bench approximately five feet away.

At the bench, Blake opened his bag and gave Hendrick the airline tickets. The tickets were one-way tickets to Baltimore in the names of "Omar Blake" and "Williams." After examining the tickets, Hendrick immediately returned them to Blake and again asked to see their identification. Blake gave Hendrick his driver's license, and Eason again responded that he did not have any identification.

Hendrick noted that Blake's driver's license was in his name and returned the license to him immediately.

Detective Hendrick then asked defendants for permission to search their baggage and their persons for drugs. He explained to Blake and Eason that they had the right to refuse consent to the search. Both defendants agreed to a search of their luggage and their persons. Within seconds of Blake's having given his consent, Hendrick reached into Blake's groin region where he did a "frontal touching" of the "outside of [Blake's] trousers" in "the area between the legs where the penis would normally be positioned." Upon reaching into Blake's crotch, Hendrick felt an object and heard a crinkling sound.

Hendrick repeated this procedure upon receiving Eason's consent and, as with Blake, felt a foreign object in Eason's crotch and heard a crinkling sound. Hendrick and the other officers then handcuffed Blake and Eason and advised them of their *Miranda* rights. Blake and Eason were then taken to the airport's drug interdiction office outside the public concourse where Hendrick removed a package of suspected crack cocaine from each of their crotches. A narcotics-sniffing dog was employed to search the defendants' bags. A subsequent search of the bag revealed drug paraphernalia in the form of numerous glassine envelopes and little zip-lock bags typically used for packaging crack cocaine among the contents of the luggage.

Was the search consensual?

DECISION No, said both the U.S. District Court and the U.S. 11th (now 5th) Circuit Court of Appeals.

OPINION Although defendants did consent to a brief, non-coercive encounter with the officers, defendants could not have possibly foreseen the course that the arresting officers would choose to pursue in their search of defendants. Defendants clearly did not consent to the intimate search of their persons that was conducted in the public area of the Fort Lauderdale Airport. The request by the officers to search defendants' "person" was ambiguous at best and it is not clear whether Defendants understood exactly what was entailed by the phrase "body search."

The consent given by the defendants allowing the officers to search their "persons" could not, under the circumstances, be construed as authorization for the officers to touch their genitals in the middle of a public area in the Fort Lauderdale Airport. The search constituted such a serious intrusion into the defendants' privacy that, under the circumstances, it could not be said that the defendants had knowingly and voluntarily consented to the search in question.

It must be remembered that the request for the search took place in a public airport terminal—a setting in which particular care needs to be exercised to ensure that police officers do not intrude upon the privacy interests of individuals. Given this public location, it cannot be said that a reasonable individual would understand that a search of one's person would entail an officer touching his or her genitals.

CONCURRING

Schoob, J.

I concur with the majority opinion but wish to express my opinion concerning the outrageousness of the conduct of the law enforcement officers in this case. I would hold that intimate searches may not occur as part of random airport stops absent explicit and voluntary consent. A layperson approached in an airport concourse by law enforcement officers making random stops ordinarily would consent to a search of his or her luggage and even a search of his or her person. I do not believe, however, that a layperson who consents to such a search would anticipate the kind of intrusive and intimate contact that occurred in this case.

I share the district court's "amazement that there have apparently been no complaints lodged or fists thrown by indignant travelers" subjected to these searches. A layperson consenting to a search in the public area of an airport might expect a search of his or her pockets, sides and shoulders or use of a hand-held magnometer. It is a different matter entirely when the search begins with the law enforcement officer's reaching for and touching the individual's genital area.

Airport terminals are settings where particular care must be exercised to protect the privacy rights of individuals. I would prefer a holding establishing that crotch searches during random airport stops must be preceded by a specific request and voluntary consent. In all other respects, I concur in the majority opinion.

ETHICAL ISSUES

Is It Ethical for the Courts to Find Consent Voluntary Because Law Enforcement Officers Believe They're in Danger?

James Harvey and five other Albuquerque police officers and DEA special agents in four police cars turned on all the police vehicles' spotlights so Jose Perea couldn't see anything behind the bright lights. All the police officers had their guns drawn and trained on Perea's Cadillac Escalade. One of those officers—armed with an AR-15 rifle—was stationed outside a nearby building. At the time the officers pulled over the Escalade, they didn't know the driver's identity.

The officers ordered Jose Perea out of his vehicle at gunpoint, handcuffed him, and placed him in the back of a police car. After about twenty minutes in custody, the officers asked Perea for permission to search his vehicle. Perea gave permission; the officers discovered one pound of crack cocaine. Charged with federal narcotics crimes, Perea moved to suppress the evidence on the ground that he didn't consent voluntarily. The district court denied the motion, holding that "based on the totality of the circumstances, Perea's consent was voluntary in that it was free of duress or coercion, it was specific and unequivocal, and it was freely and intelligently given" (*U.S. v. Perea* 2006).

According to Brian Sutherland (2006, 2194), "[I]t seems extraordinary to conclude that Perea believed that he could prevent the search of his vehicle by refusing permission":

> Why did the court find otherwise? Although mistaken, officers at the scene had good reason to believe that Perea was wanted in connection with a homicide. In light of what the officers believed to be true about Perea, the court found that the amount of force used to detain and question him was reasonable in order to protect their safety. Whether Perea actually found the police conduct coercive is unclear from the opinion, but the message of the case is clear: Consent is voluntary in the absence of police misconduct. (2194)

Based on Sutherland's statistical analysis of trial courts' findings of voluntariness, he concluded that "the voluntariness factors enumerated by the Supreme Court and circuit courts do not constrain or predict district court decision making in close cases. I argue that the best explanation for this result is that courts find consent voluntary if the evidence does not show police misconduct" (2195).

INSTRUCTIONS

1. Read the full version of *U.S. v. Perea*. See the link under the Chapter 6 Ethical Issues section of the Companion Website—login at www.cengagebrain.com.

2. Write an essay, answering the following questions:

    a. On the basis of the full version of the facts, was the court's finding of voluntariness ethical?

    b. On the basis of Sutherland's empirical research, should consent searches be ethical because they're "constitutional"?

Withdrawing Consent

LO 6

The U.S. Supreme Court hasn't decided if someone who has voluntarily consented to a search may later withdraw the consent. Lower federal courts and state courts have ruled unanimously that people can withdraw their consent but with a major qualification: "any such withdrawal must be supported by unambiguous acts or unequivocal statements" (*U.S. v. Sanders* 2005, 774).

In *U.S. v. Miner* (1973), two airline employees at Los Angeles International Airport asked Gary Miner to walk through a magnetometer, a gadget designed to detect the presence of metal on boarding passengers. Miner complied, but the machine did not register. Miner was then asked to open a small suitcase that he was carrying but refused saying, "No, it's personal." According to the court, "No, it's personal" signaled withdrawal of his consent, fulfilling the **unequivocal acts or statements withdrawal of consent rule**:

> At that point, the airline employees would have been justified in refusing to permit him to fly, but they could not compel him to submit to further search. Asking Miner to open his suitcase could be justified only if he continued to manifest an intention to board the plane, or if he otherwise consented to the search. (1077)

The court in *U.S. v. Gray* (2004) reached the opposite conclusion. Arkansas State Trooper Kyle Drown stopped a car and issued the driver a warning citation for following a truck too closely and weaving in her lane. After Drown issued the warning citation, he secured permission from both Denise Lawrence, the driver, and her companion, Darnell Gray, to search the vehicle. Not finding any contraband, he turned to Rudy, his drug detection dog, who alerted to narcotics.

After obtaining consent at about 11:09 A.M., Drown searched the vehicle and its contents for some 20 minutes without incident. Shortly after 11:30 A.M., Gray and Lawrence got impatient with the length of the search. Gray testified that he said, "This is ridiculous" and asked how long the search was going to take. A few minutes later, Gray and Drown had a second conversation, which they recall differently. Drown testified that Gray merely asked him to speed up the search but didn't withdraw consent. Gray testified that he attempted to withdraw consent by again saying the length of the search was "ridiculous" and told Drown twice that he and Lawrence were "ready to go now."

According to the court, withdrawing consent doesn't require "magic words," but those who give consent have to communicate their intent to withdraw by an "unequivocal act or statement" (Table 6.3). At most, Gray's conversations with Drown were only "an expression of impatience, which is not sufficient to terminate consent."

Third-Party Consent Searches

LO 6

Can you give police officers consent to search your roommate's bedroom? It depends. Sometimes, one person can consent to a search for another person; this is called a **third-party consent search**. It took the U.S. Supreme Court some time to settle on just what it takes to give someone else the power to consent for you (LaFave and others 2009, 284).

In *Stoner v. California* (1964), the U.S. Supreme Court adopted an **agency source of third-party consent authority** (consent by someone authorized to consent for someone else). In *Stoner*, when police officers asked a hotel night clerk if they could search Joey Stoner's room, the clerk replied, "I will be more than happy to give you permission and I will take you directly to the room" (485). First, the Court pointed out that it was Joey Stoner's constitutional right, not the hotel's or the clerk's that was at stake. So only Stoner could give it up, either "directly or through an agent. It is true that the night clerk clearly and unambiguously consented to the search" (489).

Then, in *Bumper v. North Carolina* (1968), the Court adopted a **property source of third-party consent authority** (consent based on the property interest of the consenting party). The Court found that police officers had coerced Mrs. Hattie Leath to consent to a search of her house where her grandson Wayne Bumper lived with her. They found a rifle that was later introduced in court to prove that Bumper had committed rape and felonious assault. Bumper conceded that if the consent had been voluntary it would've been binding on him. The Court agreed. Why? Because, the Court made clear, Mrs. Leath "owned the house and the rifle" (548).

TABLE 6.3
"Unequivocal" Withdrawal of Consent

- Defendant exclaimed, "The search is over. I am calling off the search." (*U.S. v. Dichiarinte* 1971)

- Prospective airline passenger balked at search of luggage, saying, "No, it's personal." (*U.S. v. Miner* 1973)

- Defendant's statement: "That's enough. I want you to stop." (*U.S. v. Bily* 1975)

- Motorist's act of closing and locking trunk of his car after a police officer's consensual warrantless search of trunk. (*U.S. v. Ibarra* 1990; noting motorist's actions constituted withdrawal of that consent and barred further search)

- After freely given consent to search his airplane, the defendant locked the plane after he taxied it to a hangar area and before being driven by police to a nearby motel. (*Cooper v. State* 1985)

Then, in *Frazier v. Cupp* (1969), the Court introduced the **assumption of risk source of third-party consent authority** (the consenting party takes the chance that someone else might consent for her). During a search of Jerry Lee Rawls's house, police officers asked if they could search Rawls's duffle bag, which he shared with his cousin Martin Frazier, and which was in the house. Rawls agreed. They found items of Frazier's clothing that they later used in court against Frazier. Frazier argued that Rawls couldn't consent for him. The Supreme Court concluded that Frazier's claim "could be dismissed rather quickly. Frazier, in allowing Rawls to use the bag and in leaving it in his house, must be taken to have assumed the risk that Rawls would allow someone else to look inside" (740).

Then came *U.S. v. Matlock* (1974). The Court made it clear that the authority to justify third-party consent doesn't depend on property law. It rests on two bases:

1. That the consenting party could permit the search "in his own right"

2. That the defendant had "assumed the risk" a co-occupant might permit a search (LaFave and others 2009, 285)

In *Matlock*, William Earl Matlock was arrested in the yard in front of the house where he lived with William Marshall, his wife, several of his children, including their 21-year-old daughter, Gayle Graff, and her three-year-old son. Three of the arresting officers went to the door. Graff, dressed in a robe and holding her son in her arms, let the officers in. They told her they were looking for money and a gun and asked if they could search the house. She consented. They searched the house, including the east bedroom on the second floor, which Graff said she and Matlock shared. In a diaper bag in the only closet in the room, they found $4,995 in cash (179).

Authority to search for others usually comes up in common relationships: spouse-spouse, parent-child, roommate-roommate, employer-employee, landlord-tenant, and school administrator-student. But these relationships don't automatically give one person the authority to consent for the other person. For example, consent to search given out of spite can invalidate the consent. Also, employers can't consent to searches of their employees' desks, because employees have a reasonable expectation of privacy in these concealed parts of their desks even if they're in their workplace.

In one case, a principal couldn't consent to searching a guidance counselor's desk that was locked; located in the counselor's office; and contained psychological profiles and other confidential student records. But in another case, a factory manager could consent to searching items on the top of an employee's workbench. In another ruling, janitors, clerks, and drivers couldn't consent to searches of their employers' premises, but managers could. (Table 6.4 lists examples of valid third-party consent searches.)

TABLE 6.4
Example of Valid Third-Party Consent Searches

- One lover consents to a search of the room shared with the other lover.
- One roommate consents to a search of an entire apartment, including the other roommate's separate bedroom.
- A homeowner consents to a search of the room that a houseguest occupies.
- One joint user of a duffel bag consents to a search of the shared duffel bag.
- A high-school principal consents to a search of high-school students' lockers.
- A college dean permits a search of students' rooms for marijuana.

Two rules, one objective and the other subjective, are used to decide whether one person can consent to a search for someone else.

1. *Actual authority (subjective) third-party consent.* Only someone who, in fact, has the legal authority to consent for someone else can give law enforcement officers permission to search that other person's house or stuff.

2. *Apparent authority (objective) third-party consent.* Consent given by someone who law enforcement officers reasonably believe (but who, in fact, doesn't) have the authority to consent for another makes the search reasonable.

Federal and state courts were divided over which of these two tests to adopt. In *Illinois v. Rodriguez* (1990), our next excerpt, the U.S. Supreme Court settled the question in the federal system by adopting the apparent-authority objective test as the minimum required by the Fourth Amendment.

In Illinois v. Rodriquez (1990), the next case excerpt, the U.S. Supreme Court applied the apparent authority third-party consent test to uphold a search of Edward Rodriquez's apartment based on Gail Fischer's consent to enter and search.

CASE Did She Have the Authority to Consent?

Illinois v. Rodriguez
497 U.S. 177 (1990)

HISTORY

Edward Rodriguez, who was charged with possession of a controlled substance with intent to deliver, moved to suppress seized evidence. The Circuit Court, Cook County, Illinois, granted the motion, and the People appealed. The Appellate Court affirmed. The People petitioned for leave to appeal. The Supreme Court denied the petition without published opinion. The People petitioned for a writ of certiorari. The Supreme Court granted the writ and reversed and remanded.

SCALIA, J., joined by REHNQUIST, C.J., and WHITE, BLACKMUN, O'CONNOR, and KENNEDY, JJ.

FACTS

On July 26, 1985, police were summoned to the residence of Dorothy Jackson on South Wolcott in Chicago. They were met by Ms. Jackson's daughter, Gail Fischer, who showed signs of a severe beating. She told the officers that she had been assaulted by Edward Rodriguez earlier that day in an apartment on South California. Fischer stated that Rodriguez was then asleep in the apartment, and she consented to travel there with the police in order to unlock the door with her key so that the officers could enter and arrest him. During this conversation, Fischer several times referred to the apartment on South California as "our" apartment, and said that she had clothes and furniture there. It is unclear whether she indicated that she currently lived at the apartment, or only that she used to live there.

The police officers drove to the apartment on South California, accompanied by Fischer. They did not obtain an arrest warrant for Rodriguez, nor did they seek a search warrant for the apartment. At the apartment, Fischer unlocked the door with her key and gave the officers permission to enter. They moved through the door into the living room, where they observed in plain view drug paraphernalia and containers filled with white powder that they believed (correctly, as later analysis showed) to be cocaine. They proceeded to the bedroom, where they found Rodriguez asleep and discovered additional containers of white powder in two open attaché cases. The officers arrested Rodriguez and seized the drugs and related paraphernalia.

Rodriguez was charged with possession of a controlled substance with intent to deliver. He moved to suppress all evidence seized at the time of his arrest, claiming that Fischer had vacated the apartment several weeks earlier and had no authority to consent to the entry. The Cook County Circuit Court granted the motion, holding that at the time she consented to the entry Fischer did not have common authority over the apartment.

The Court concluded that Fischer was not a "usual resident" but rather an "infrequent visitor" at the apartment on South California, based upon its findings that Fischer's name was not on the lease, that she did not contribute to the rent, that she was not allowed to invite others to the apartment on her own, that she did not have access to the apartment when Rodriguez was away, and that she had moved some of her possessions from the apartment.

The Circuit Court also rejected the State's contention that, even if Fischer did not possess common authority over the premises, there was no Fourth Amendment violation if the police reasonably believed at the time of their entry that Fischer possessed the authority to consent. The Appellate Court of Illinois affirmed the Circuit Court in all respects. The Illinois Supreme Court denied the State's petition for leave to appeal, and we granted certiorari.

OPINION

The Fourth Amendment prohibits the warrantless entry of a person's home, whether to make an arrest or to search for specific objects. The prohibition does not apply, however, to situations in which voluntary consent has been obtained, either from the individual whose property is searched, *Schneckloth v. Bustamonte* (1973) [excerpt on p. 202], or from a third party who possesses common authority over the premises, *U.S. v. Matlock* (1974). The State of Illinois contends that that exception applies in the present case.

As we stated in *Matlock*, "common authority" rests "on mutual use of the property by persons having joint access or control." The burden of establishing that common authority rests upon the State. On the basis of this record, it is clear that burden was not sustained. The evidence showed that although Fischer, with her two small children, had lived with Rodriguez beginning in December 1984, she had moved out on July 1, 1985, almost a month before the search at issue here, and had gone to live with her mother. She took her and her children's clothing with her, though leaving behind some furniture and household effects. During the period after July 1 she sometimes spent the night at Rodriguez's apartment, but never invited her friends there, and never went there herself when he was not home. Her name was not on the lease nor did she contribute to the rent. She had a key to the apartment, which she said at trial she had taken without Rodriguez's knowledge (though she testified at the preliminary hearing that Rodriguez had given her the key). On these facts the State has not established that, with respect to the South California apartment, Fischer had "joint access or control for most purposes." To the contrary, the Appellate Court's determination of no common authority over the apartment was obviously correct.

The State contends that, even if Fischer did not in fact have authority to give consent, it suffices to validate the entry that the law enforcement officers reasonably believed she did. Rodriguez asserts that permitting a reasonable belief of common authority to validate an entry would cause a defendant's Fourth Amendment rights to be "vicariously waived." We disagree.

What Rodriguez is assured by the Fourth Amendment is not that no government search of his house will occur unless he consents; but that no such search will occur that is unreasonable. Reasonableness does not demand that the government be factually correct. What is demanded is not that officers always be correct, but that they always be reasonable. As we put it in *Brinegar v. U.S.* (1949):

> Because many situations which confront officers in the course of executing their duties are more or less ambiguous, room must be allowed for some mistakes on their part. But the mistakes must be those of reasonable men, acting on facts leading sensibly to their conclusions of probability.

We see no reason to depart from this general rule with respect to facts bearing upon the authority to consent to a search. Whether the basis for such authority exists is the sort of recurring factual question to which law enforcement officials must be expected to apply their judgment;

and all the Fourth Amendment requires is that they answer it reasonably.

The Constitution is no more violated when officers enter without a warrant because they reasonably (though erroneously) believe that the person who has consented to their entry is a resident of the premises, than it is violated when they enter without a warrant because they reasonably (though erroneously) believe they are in pursuit of a violent felon who is about to escape.

What we hold today does not suggest that law enforcement officers may always accept a person's invitation to enter premises. Even when the invitation is accompanied by an explicit assertion that the person lives there, the surrounding circumstances could conceivably be such that a reasonable person would doubt its truth and not act upon it without further inquiry. As with other factual determinations bearing upon search and seizure, determination of consent to enter must be judged against an objective standard: would the facts available to the officer at the moment, warrant a man of reasonable caution in the belief that the consenting party had authority over the premises? *Terry v. Ohio* (1968) [excerpted in Chapter 4]. If not, then warrantless entry without further inquiry is unlawful unless authority actually exists. But if so, the search is valid.

In the present case, the Appellate Court found it unnecessary to determine whether the officers reasonably believed that Fischer had the authority to consent, because it ruled as a matter of law that a reasonable belief could not validate the entry. Since we find that ruling to be in error, we remand for consideration of that question.

The judgment of the Illinois Appellate Court is REVERSED, and the case is REMANDED for further proceedings not inconsistent with this opinion.

DISSENT

MARSHALL, J., joined by BRENNAN and STEVENS, JJ.

Dorothy Jackson summoned police officers to her house to report that her daughter Gail Fischer had been beaten. Fischer told police that Ed Rodriguez, her boyfriend, was her assaulter. During an interview with Fischer, one of the officers asked if Rodriguez dealt in narcotics. Fischer did not respond. Fischer did agree, however, to the officers' request to let them into Rodriguez's apartment so that they could arrest him for battery. The police, without a warrant and despite the absence of an exigency, entered Rodriguez's home to arrest him. As a result of their entry, the police discovered narcotics that the State subsequently sought to introduce in a drug prosecution against Rodriguez.

The Court holds that the warrantless entry into Rodriguez's home was nonetheless valid if the officers reasonably believed that Fischer had authority to consent. The majority's defense of this position rests on a misconception of the basis for third-party consent searches. That such searches do not give rise to claims of constitutional violations rests not on the premise that they are "reasonable" under the Fourth Amendment, but on the premise that a person may voluntarily limit his expectation of privacy by allowing others to exercise authority over his possessions.

Thus, an individual's decision to permit another joint access to or control over the property for most purposes, limits that individual's reasonable expectation of privacy and to that extent limits his Fourth Amendment protections. If an individual has not so limited his expectation of privacy, the police may not dispense with the safeguards established by the Fourth Amendment.

We have recognized that the physical entry of the home is the chief evil against which the wording of the Fourth Amendment is directed. We have further held that a search or seizure carried out on a suspect's premises without a warrant is per se unreasonable, unless the police can show that it falls within one of a carefully defined set of exceptions. The Court has often heard, and steadfastly rejected, the invitation to carve out further exceptions to the warrant requirement for searches of the home because of the burdens on police investigation and prosecution of crime.

Our rejection of such claims is not due to a lack of appreciation of the difficulty and importance of effective law enforcement, but rather to our firm commitment to the view of those who wrote the Bill of Rights that the privacy of a person's home and property may not be totally sacrificed in the name of maximum simplicity in enforcement of the criminal law. The concerns of expediting police work and avoiding paperwork are never very convincing reasons and, in these circumstances, certainly are not enough to by-pass the constitutional requirement. In this case, no suspect was fleeing or likely to take flight. The search was of permanent premises, not of a movable vehicle. No evidence or contraband was threatened with removal or destruction.

Unlike searches conducted pursuant to these recognized exceptions to the warrant requirement, third-party consent searches are not based on an exigency and therefore serve no compelling social goal. Police officers, when faced with the choice of relying on consent by a third party or securing a warrant, should secure a warrant and must therefore accept the risk of error should they instead choose to rely on consent.

A search conducted pursuant to an officer's reasonable but mistaken belief that a third party had authority to consent is on an entirely different constitutional footing from one based on the consent of a third party who in fact has such authority. Even if the officers reasonably believed that Fischer had authority to consent, she did not, and Rodriguez's expectation of privacy was therefore undiminished.

Our cases demonstrate that third-party consent searches are free from constitutional challenge only to the extent that they rest on consent by a party empowered to do so. The majority's conclusion to the contrary ignores the legitimate expectations of privacy on which individuals are entitled to rely. That a person who allows another joint access to his property thereby limits his expectation of privacy does not justify trampling the rights of a person who has not similarly relinquished any of his privacy expectation.

QUESTIONS

1. List all the facts relevant to determining whether the search in this case was a lawful search.
2. How does the majority define third-party consent? How does the dissent define it?
3. Why did the Supreme Court hold that Fischer's consent made the search of Rodriguez's apartment a lawful search?
4. Do you agree that someone can consent for another even when the person giving consent doesn't have the authority to do so?
5. Do you agree that if you share your property with someone else you "assume the risk" that the other person may give the police permission to search the property?
6. What arguments does the dissent make to reject the validity of Fischer's consent to search Rodriguez's apartment?
7. How do the majority and the dissent balance differently Rodriguez's rights and law enforcement's needs for consent searches? How would you balance the interests in the case?

EXPLORING FURTHER
·······························

Third-Party Consent

Can He Overrule His Estranged Wife's Consent?

Georgia v. Randolph, 126 S.Ct. 1515 (2006)

SOUTER, J.

FACTS Scott Randolph and his wife, Janet, separated in late May 2001, when she left the marital residence in Americus, Georgia, and went to stay with her parents in Canada, taking their son and some belongings. In July, she returned to the Americus house with the child, though the record does not reveal whether her object was reconciliation or retrieval of remaining possessions.

On the morning of July 6, she complained to the police that after a domestic dispute her husband took their son away, and when officers reached the house she told them that her husband was a cocaine user whose habit had caused financial troubles. Shortly after the police arrived, Scott Randolph returned and explained that he had removed the child to a neighbor's house out of concern that his wife might take the boy out of the country again.

One of the officers, Sergeant Murray, went with Janet Randolph to reclaim the child, and when they returned she not only renewed her complaints about her husband's drug use, but also volunteered that there were "items of drug evidence" in the house. Sergeant Murray asked Scott Randolph for permission to search the house, which he unequivocally refused. The sergeant turned to Janet Randolph for consent to search, which she readily gave. She led the officer upstairs to a bedroom that she identified as Scott's, where the sergeant noticed a section of a drinking straw with a powdery residue he suspected was cocaine.

Could Janet Randolph overrule Scott Randolph's refusal to consent?

DECISION No, said the majority of the U.S. Supreme Court.

OPINION We have lived our whole national history with an understanding of the ancient adage that a man's home is his castle to the point that the "poorest man may in his cottage bid defiance to all the forces of the Crown." Disputed permission is thus no match for this central value of the Fourth Amendment, and the State's other countervailing claims do not add up to outweigh it. Yes, we recognize the consenting tenant's interest as a citizen in bringing criminal activity to light. And we understand a co-tenant's legitimate self-interest in siding with the police to deflect suspicion raised by sharing quarters with a criminal.

This case invites a straightforward application of the rule that a physically present inhabitant's express refusal of consent to a police search is dispositive as to him, regardless of the consent of a fellow occupant. Scott Randolph's refusal is clear, and nothing in the record justifies the search on grounds independent of Janet Randolph's consent.

The State does not argue that she gave any indication to the police of a need for protection inside the house that might have justified entry into the portion of the premises where the police found the powdery straw (which, if lawfully seized, could have been used when attempting to establish probable cause for the warrant issued later). Nor does the State claim that the entry and search should be upheld under the rubric of exigent circumstances, owing to some apprehension by the police officers that Scott Randolph would destroy evidence of drug use before any warrant could be obtained.

The judgment of the Supreme Court of Georgia is therefore AFFIRMED.

DISSENT The dissent concluded otherwise. Chief Justice Roberts, joined by Justice Scalia, wrote:

> The rule the majority fashions does not implement the high office of the Fourth Amendment to protect privacy, but instead provides protection on a random and happenstance basis, protecting, for example, a co-occupant who happens to be at the front door when the other occupant consents to a search, but not one napping or watching television in the next

room. And the cost of affording such random protection is great, as demonstrated by the recurring cases in which abused spouses seek to authorize police entry into a home they share with a nonconsenting abuser.

The correct approach is clearly mapped out in our precedents: The Fourth Amendment protects privacy. If an individual shares information, papers, *or places* with another, he assumes the risk that the other person will in turn share access to that information or those papers *or places* with the government. Just because the individual happens to be present at the time, so too someone who shares a place with another cannot interpose an objection when that person decides to grant access to the police, simply because the objecting individual happens to be present.

A warrantless search is reasonable if police obtain the voluntary consent of a person authorized to give it. Co-occupants have assumed the risk that one of their number might permit a common area to be searched. Just as Mrs. Randolph could walk upstairs, come down, and turn her husband's cocaine straw over to the police, she can consent to police entry and search of what is, after all, her home, too.

THOMAS, J.

The Court has long recognized that it is an act of responsible citizenship for individuals to give whatever information they may have to aid in law enforcement. No Fourth Amendment search occurs where, as here, the spouse of an accused voluntarily leads the police to potential evidence of wrongdoing by the accused.

Vehicle Searches

LO 7

Searching vehicles without warrants began with a 1789 act of Congress. This was the same Congress that had adopted the Fourth Amendment, so the hated British general warrants were fresh in Congress's mind. Despite these bitter memories, the 1789 statute authorized law enforcement officers without a warrant "to enter any ship or vessel, in which they shall have reason to suspect any goods, wares or merchandise subject to duty shall be concealed; and therein to search for, seize, and secure any such goods, wares or merchandise."

Ships were one thing; homes were quite another. Officers who suspected people were hiding taxable stuff in their houses had to get a warrant based on probable cause before they searched. Why the difference between boats and houses? Necessity: "Goods in course of transportation and concealed in a movable vessel readily could be put out of reach of a search warrant."

In 1815, Congress authorized officers "not only to board and search vessels within their own and adjoining districts, but also to stop, search, and examine any vehicle, beast, or person on which or whom they should suspect there was merchandise which was subject to duty." In the Indian Appropriation Act of 1917, Congress authorized officers without warrants to seize and forfeit "automobiles used in introducing or attempting to introduce intoxicants into the Indian territory." (*Carroll v. U.S.* 1925, 152–53)

Not a single U.S. Supreme Court case ever challenged this exception until 1925 during Prohibition when the modern history of the vehicle exception began. You saw the impact of technology on the Fourth Amendment in several cases in Chapter 3 (eavesdropping microphones in *Katz v. U.S.*, radio transmitters in *U.S. v. White*, and thermal imaging in *Kyllo v. U.S.*). Their impact, however, can't compare with the single greatest technological advance of the 20th century that affected the Fourth Amendment—the car, and now SUVS and trucks.

As car ownership spread throughout all classes in society, its use as a crime tool advanced and so did Fourth Amendment law. The U.S. Supreme Court added another rationale for the **vehicle exception**—a reduced expectation of privacy in vehicles. Prohibition, the fear of alcohol-related crimes, and the ubiquity of the car were behind the landmark vehicle exception case, *Carroll v. U.S.* (1925), in the 1920s. (The fear of illegal drugs still drives the interpretation of the Fourth Amendment that so many cases in Chapters 3 through 6 clearly demonstrate.)

In *Carroll*, federal Prohibition agents Cronenwett, Scully, and Thayer and Michigan state trooper Peterson had probable cause to believe bootleggers George Carroll and John Kiro were illegally carrying liquor from Detroit to Grand Rapids in their Oldsmobile convertible. While on regular duty patrolling the road looking for Prohibition law violations, they stopped the car and searched it without a warrant. They found 68 bottles of blended Scotch whiskey and Gordon gin stuffed in hollowed-out upholstery, which they had to rip open to find.

The U.S. Supreme Court upheld the search without a warrant based on the rationale that it was "not practicable to secure a warrant, because the vehicle can be quickly moved out of the locality or jurisdiction in which the warrant must be sought" (153).

The decision was immediately controversial. We were fighting an earlier war on drugs; alcohol was the drug. Cars were a new technological weapon used by the enemy and the government. As in our own drug wars, critics complained that we were sacrificing our rights to fight the war. The dissent joined the critics. Justice McReynolds wrote:

> The damnable character of the "bootlegger's" business should not close our eyes to the mischief which will surely follow any attempt to destroy it by unwarranted methods. To press forward to a great principle by breaking through every other great principle that stands in the way of its establishment; in short, to procure an eminent good by means that are unlawful, is as little consonant to private morality as to public justice. (163)

Following *Carroll*, the Court began a slow, although not steady, expansion of what was soon called the vehicle exception to the warrant requirement. One expansion was to add to the mobility of vehicles the rationale that there's a reduced expectation of privacy in vehicles. In a series of other decisions, the exception came to include all searches of vehicles without warrants, as long as they're based on probable cause to believe they contain contraband or evidence. The exception extended to the passenger compartment, the glove compartment, and the trunk. Then, the Court turned its attention to two other very important related searches: of containers inside vehicles and to occupants and their belongings. Let's look at each of these searches.

Searches of Containers in Vehicles

LO 8

Officers with probable cause but without warrants can search containers inside vehicles that aren't an essential part of the vehicle. Until 1991, officers could only search containers in vehicles if they had separate probable cause to search both the vehicle and the container. If they had probable cause to search the container but not the vehicle, they had to get a warrant.

The Court established the rule governing searches of containers in vehicles in *California v. Acevedo* (1991). Police officers observed Charles Acevedo leave an apartment where officers knew there was marijuana. Acevedo was carrying a brown paper bag the size of marijuana packages the officers had seen earlier. Acevedo put the bag into the trunk of his car. As he drove away, the police stopped his car, opened the trunk, opened the bag, and found marijuana in it. The Court held it was reasonable to search the container without a warrant because they had probable cause to believe the bag contained marijuana. The Court acknowledged Acevedo's expectation of privacy in the brown bag, but concluded that the risks the car might drive off and the marijuana might disappear trumped Acevedo's expectation of privacy.

Searches of Vehicle Passengers

LO 8

Before *Acevedo*, car searches focused on *containers* (luggage, purses, and paper bags) and a debate over if and when the Fourth Amendment allowed officers to open to see what was inside them. *Acevedo* seemed to settle the debate: As long as officers have probable cause to believe they contain contraband, they can search containers in the vehicle. But it didn't. Left unsettled was whether officers could search containers attached to people in the car, such as the wallet in the pocket of the jacket you're wearing, or in the purse hanging over your shoulder, or on the seat beside you.

Recall that one of the reasons for the vehicle exception to the warrant requirement is a reduced expectation of privacy in vehicles. Do passengers as well as drivers have a reduced expectation of privacy? And, if they do, can officers search a passenger's purse when they have no probable cause to suspect her of the crime they arrested the driver for? In our next excerpt, *Wyoming v. Houghton* (1999), a divided U.S. Supreme Court answered, yes.

In **Wyoming v. Houghton *(1999)***, our next case excerpt, the U.S. Supreme Court found that the search of passenger Sandra Houghton's purse met the vehicle-exception rule.*

CASE Was Her Purse Part of the Vehicle Exception?

Wyoming v. Houghton
526 U.S. 295 (1999)

HISTORY

Sandra Houghton was convicted in the District Court, Natrona County, Wyoming, of felony possession of methamphetamine, and she appealed. The Wyoming Supreme Court reversed and remanded. The U.S. Supreme Court granted certiorari and reversed.

SCALIA, J., joined by REHNQUIST, C.J., and O'CONNOR, KENNEDY, THOMAS, and BREYER, JJ.

FACTS

In the early morning hours of July 23, 1995, a Wyoming Highway Patrol officer (Officer Baldwin) stopped an automobile for speeding and driving with a faulty brake light. There were three passengers in the front seat of the car: David Young (the driver), his girlfriend, and Diane Houghton. While questioning Young, the officer noticed a hypodermic syringe in Young's shirt pocket. He left the occupants under the supervision of two backup officers as he went to get gloves from his patrol car. Upon his return, he instructed Young to step out of the car and place the syringe on the hood. The officer then asked Young why he had a syringe; with refreshing candor, Young replied that he used it to take drugs.

At this point, the backup officers ordered the two female passengers out of the car and asked them for identification. Houghton falsely identified herself as "Sandra James" and stated that she did not have any identification. Meanwhile, in light of Young's admission, the officer searched the passenger compartment of the car for contraband. On the back seat, he found a purse, which Houghton claimed as hers. He removed from the purse a wallet containing Houghton's driver's license, identifying her properly as Sandra K. Houghton. When the officer asked her why she had lied about her name, she replied: "In case things went bad."

Continuing his search of the purse, the officer found a brown pouch and a black wallet-type container.

Houghton denied that the former was hers, and claimed ignorance of how it came to be there; it was found to contain drug paraphernalia and a syringe with 60 cc's of methamphetamine.

Houghton admitted ownership of the black container, which was also found to contain drug paraphernalia, and a syringe (which Houghton acknowledged was hers) with 10 cc's of methamphetamine—an amount insufficient to support the felony conviction at issue in this case. The officer also found fresh needle-track marks on Houghton's arms. He placed her under arrest.

The State of Wyoming charged Houghton with felony possession of methamphetamine in a liquid amount greater than three-tenths of a gram. After a hearing, the trial court denied her motion to suppress all evidence obtained from the purse as the fruit of a violation of the Fourth and Fourteenth Amendments. The court held that the officer had probable cause to search the car for contraband, and, by extension, any containers therein that could hold such contraband. A jury convicted Houghton as charged.

The Wyoming Supreme Court, by divided vote, reversed the conviction and announced the following rule:

> Generally, once probable cause is established to search a vehicle, an officer is entitled to search all containers therein which may contain the object of the search.
>
> However, if the officer knows or should know that a container is the personal effect of a passenger who is not suspected of criminal activity, then the container is outside the scope of the search unless someone had the opportunity to conceal the contraband within the personal effect to avoid detection.

The court held that the search of Houghton's purse violated the Fourth and Fourteenth Amendments because the officer "knew or should have known that the purse did not belong to the driver, but to one of the passengers," and because "there was no probable cause to search the passengers' personal effects and no reason to believe that contraband had been placed within the purse."

OPINION

We have read the historical evidence to show that the Framers would have regarded as reasonable (if there was probable cause) the warrantless search of containers within an automobile. In *U.S. v. Ross* (1982), we upheld as reasonable the warrantless search of a paper bag and leather pouch found in the trunk of Ross's car by officers who had probable cause to believe that the trunk contained drugs.

To be sure, there was no passenger in *Ross*, and it was not claimed that the package in the trunk belonged to

anyone other than the driver. Even so, a passenger's personal belongings, just like the driver's belongings or containers attached to the car like a glove compartment, are "in" the car, and the officer has probable cause to search for contraband in the car. Passengers, no less than drivers, possess a reduced expectation of privacy with regard to the property that they transport in cars.

Whereas the passenger's privacy expectations are considerably diminished, the governmental interests at stake are substantial. Effective law enforcement would be appreciably impaired without the ability to search a passenger's personal belongings when there is reason to believe contraband or evidence of criminal wrongdoing is hidden in the car. As in all car-search cases, the "ready mobility" of an automobile creates a risk that the evidence or contraband will be permanently lost while a warrant is obtained. In addition, a car passenger will often be engaged in a common enterprise with the driver, and have the same interest in concealing the fruits or the evidence of their wrongdoing.

To be sure, these factors favoring a search will not always be present, but the balancing of interests must be conducted with an eye to the generality of cases. To require that the investigating officer have positive reason to believe that the passenger and driver were engaged in a common enterprise, or positive reason to believe that the driver had time and occasion to conceal the item in the passenger's belongings, surreptitiously or with friendly permission, is to impose requirements so seldom met that a "passenger's property" rule would dramatically reduce the ability to find and seize contraband and evidence of crime.

Of course these requirements would not attach (under the Wyoming Supreme Court's rule) until the police officer knows or has reason to know that the container belongs to a passenger. But once a "passenger's property" exception to car searches became widely known, one would expect passenger-confederates to claim everything as their own. And one would anticipate a bog of litigation—in the form of both civil lawsuits and motions to suppress in criminal trials—involving such questions as whether the officer should have believed a passenger's claim of ownership, whether he should have inferred ownership from various objective factors, whether he had probable cause to believe that the passenger was a confederate, or to believe that the driver might have introduced the contraband into the package with or without the passenger's knowledge.

When balancing the competing interests, our determinations of "reasonableness" under the Fourth Amendment must take account of these practical realities. We think they militate in favor of the needs of law enforcement, and against a personal-privacy interest that is ordinarily weak. . . .

We hold that police officers with probable cause to search a car may inspect passengers' belongings found in the car that are capable of concealing the object of the search.

The judgment of the Wyoming Supreme Court is REVERSED.

CONCURRING OPINION

BREYER, J.

I point out certain limitations upon the scope of the bright-line rule that the Court describes. Obviously, the rule applies only to automobile searches. Equally obviously, the rule applies only to containers found within automobiles. And it does not extend to the search of a person found in that automobile. As the Court notes, the search of a person, including even "a limited search of the outer clothing," is a very different matter in respect to which the law provides "significantly heightened protection."

Less obviously, but in my view also important, is the fact that the container here at issue, a woman's purse, was found at a considerable distance from its owner, who did not claim ownership until the officer discovered her identification while looking through it. Purses are special containers. They are repositories of especially personal items that people generally like to keep with them at all times. So I am tempted to say that a search of a purse involves an intrusion so similar to a search of one's person that the same rule should govern both. However, given this Court's prior cases, I cannot argue that the fact that the container was a purse automatically makes a legal difference, for the Court has warned against trying to make that kind of distinction.

But I can say that it would matter if a woman's purse, like a man's billfold, were attached to her person. It might then amount to a kind of "outer clothing." In this case, the purse was separate from the person, and no one has claimed that, under those circumstances, the type of container makes a difference. For that reason, I join the Court's opinion.

DISSENT

STEVENS, J., joined by SOUTER and GINSBURG, JJ.

In all of our prior cases applying the automobile exception to the Fourth Amendment's warrant requirement, either the defendant was the operator of the vehicle and in custody of the object of the search, or no question was raised as to the defendant's ownership or custody. In the only automobile case confronting the search of a passenger defendant—*U.S. v. Di Re* (addressing searches of the passenger's pockets and the space between his shirt and underwear, both of which uncovered counterfeit fuel rations)—the Court held that the exception to the warrant requirement did not apply.

In *Di Re*, as here, the information prompting the search directly implicated the driver, not the passenger.

Today, instead of adhering to the settled distinction between drivers and passengers, the Court fashions a new rule that is based on a distinction between property contained in clothing worn by a passenger and property contained in a passenger's briefcase or purse. In cases on both sides of the Court's newly minted test, the property is in a "container" (whether a pocket or a pouch) located in the vehicle.

Moreover, unlike the Court, I think it quite plain that the search of a passenger's purse or briefcase involves an intrusion on privacy that may be just as serious as was the intrusion in *Di Re*. I am not persuaded that the mere spatial association between a passenger and a driver provides an acceptable basis for presuming that they are partners in crime or for ignoring privacy interests in a purse. Whether or not the Fourth Amendment required a warrant to search Houghton's purse, at the very least the trooper in this case had to have probable cause to believe that her purse contained contraband. The Wyoming Supreme Court concluded that he did not.

Finally, in my view, the State's legitimate interest in effective law enforcement does not outweigh the privacy concerns at issue. I am as confident in a police officer's ability to apply a rule requiring a warrant or individualized probable cause to search belongings that are—as in this case—obviously owned by and in the custody of a passenger as is the Court in a "passenger-confederate's" ability to circumvent the rule. Certainly the ostensible clarity of the Court's rule is attractive. But that virtue is insufficient justification for its adoption. Moreover, a rule requiring a warrant or individualized probable cause to search passenger belongings is every bit as simple as the Court's rule; it simply protects more privacy.

Instead of applying ordinary Fourth Amendment principles to this case, the majority extends the automobile warrant exception to allow searches of passenger belongings based on the driver's misconduct. Thankfully, the Court's automobile-centered analysis limits the scope of its holding. But it does not justify the outcome in this case.

I respectfully dissent.

QUESTIONS

1. State the rule the majority of the Court adopted for searching passengers' "containers."
2. Explain how the majority applied the rule to the search of Sandra Houghton's purse.
3. Summarize the dissent's arguments for concluding the purse search was unreasonable.
4. Summarize Justice Breyer's hesitation about supporting the majority decision.
5. Consider your summaries. Which opinion do you think is the most convincing? Defend your answer.

Emergency Searches

LO 9

Emergency searches (also called *exigent circumstance searches*) are based on the idea that it's sometimes impractical (even dangerous) to require officers to obtain warrants before they search. The danger might be (1) to officers' safety, justifying frisks or pat downs for weapons (Chapter 4); (2) that suspects or others might destroy evidence during the time it takes to get a search warrant; (3) that fleeing felons might escape while officers are trying to obtain search warrants, or (4) that individuals in the community are in immediate danger. Because we've already examined frisks, in which officers' reasonable suspicion that a lawfully stopped suspect is armed justifies a pat down for weapons (Chapter 4), we won't repeat that discussion here. Let's look at the other three types of emergencies.

Destruction of Evidence

LO 9

If police officers have probable cause to search, *and* they reasonably believe evidence is about to be destroyed right now, they can search without a warrant. For example, in *Cupp v. Murphy* (1973), the U.S. Supreme Court held that police officers who had probable cause to believe Daniel Murphy had strangled his wife didn't need a warrant to take scrapings of what looked like blood under his fingernails. Why? Because Murphy knew the officers suspected he was the strangler, so he had a motive to destroy the short-lived bloodstain evidence.

In *Schmerber v. California* (1966; Chapter 8), the Supreme Court held that rapidly declining blood alcohol levels justified giving a blood alcohol test to Schmerber without a warrant. And in *Ker v. California* (1963), the Court held that a warrantless entry into a home was justified by the reasonable fear that Ker was about to destroy or hide marijuana.

Hot Pursuit

LO 9

Hot pursuit is another emergency created by the need to apprehend a fleeing suspect. If officers are chasing a suspect whom they have probable cause to arrest, they can follow the suspect into a house without getting a warrant (*U.S. v. Santana* 1976). So officers wouldn't need a warrant to enter a home to search for a fleeing armed robbery suspect and weapons.

But how extensive can the search be? Only as extensive as is necessary to prevent the suspect from escaping or resisting. So officers can't search every nook and cranny of a house just because they got in lawfully during a hot pursuit (*Warden v. Hayden* 1967). For example, they can't search dresser drawers for contraband. Nor can they search every room of a hotel because a robber entered the hotel (*U.S. v. Winsor* 1988).

Danger to the Community

LO 9

Police officers can sidestep the warrant requirement if they have probable cause to believe either that a suspect has committed a violent crime or that they or others in the community are in immediate danger. So officers could enter and search a house in a residential area because they reasonably believed guns and bombs were in the house (*U.S. v. Lindsey* 1989). It was also reasonable to enter a house without a warrant to search for a weapon when police found a dead body on the front porch (*U.S. v. Doe* 1985).

Other dangers to the public include fires and explosions. Police officers at the scene of a fire don't need a warrant to stay inside a burned building long enough to look for possible injured victims and to investigate the cause of the fire or explosion. But once they determine the cause of the fire, officers have to get a warrant if they want to search for evidence of a crime (*Michigan v. Clifford* 1984). Furthermore, they can't enter just because a fire or explosion might be in the offing. For example, a court ruled that it wasn't reasonable for officers to enter a house where they knew a man had kept dangerous chemicals in his house for two weeks and wasn't at home (*U.S. v. Warner* 1988).

Summary

LO 1
- Crime control couldn't survive without searches, but the power to search comes at a price. The Fourth Amendment doesn't condemn all searches, only "unreasonable" searches. But the Fourth Amendment doesn't just confer the power to search on "good" officers searching "bad" people, their homes, and stuff; it bestows the same power on bad officers searching good people.

LO 2, LO 3
- Searches of homes require warrants to be "reasonable." To comply with the Fourth Amendment, search warrants have to include a detailed description of the place to be searched, the things to be seized, and an affidavit supporting probable cause. With important exceptions, when executing warrants to search homes, officers have to "knock and announce" their presence before entering.

LO 4
- Most searches don't require warrants to be reasonable. Some require neither warrants nor probable cause. Millions of searches incident to lawful arrests based on probable cause are reasonable without warrants, because they protect officers, prevent escape, and preserve evidence. They include searches of arrested persons and the "grabbable area" around them and to the passenger compartment of vehicles they occupied when they were arrested. The motive of the arresting officer is irrelevant as long as probable cause supports the arrest.

LO 5, LO 6
- Millions of consent searches require neither warrants nor probable cause, allowing officers to search where they couldn't otherwise do so. The government has to prove consent was voluntary. Consenting persons can withdraw their consent at any time if they can demonstrate their clear intent to stop the search. The scope of the consent depends on what the officer reasonably believes the person has consented to. Third-party consents are lawful as long as an officer reasonably believes the third person has the authority to consent. Empirical research demonstrates that most people who consent to searches are innocent, and they're young, poor, and non-White.

LO 7
- Searches of vehicles without warrants are reasonable, constitutionally, because of vehicle mobility and the reduced expectation of privacy in vehicles.

LO 8
- Searches of containers and persons within the vehicles without warrants are "reasonable" as long as they're based on probable cause.

LO 9
- Emergency searches are based on the idea that it's sometimes impractical to require officers to obtain warrants before they search.

Review Questions

1. Describe Supreme Court Justice Jackson's experience in dealing with search and seizure law. What does he mean by "second class rights"?

2. Identify and describe each of the elements required to meet the Fourth Amendment's warrant requirement.

3. According to the "knock and announce" rule, what's a reasonable amount of time to wait before breaking and entering?

4. Identify and describe the main exceptions to the knock-and-announce rule.

5. Compare and contrast the preference and practice regarding searches with warrants and without.

6. Identify five major exceptions to the warrant requirement approved by the U.S. Supreme Court.

7. List three reasons why searches incident to arrest are reasonable.

8. Identify the scope and time frame of "incident" to arrest.

9. Describe the *Robinson* rule and the justification for it.

10. Describe why pretext arrests are a powerful investigative tool.

11. In a consent search, what's the person really consenting to?

12. Identify some characteristics the courts use to determine the voluntariness of consent.

13. Summarize the main empirical research findings regarding consent searches.

14. Describe the elements of scope of consent and the withdrawal of consent.

15. Give an example of a third-party consent search.

16. Identify the subjective and objective elements in determining whether one person can consent to a search for someone else.

17. Identify the two reasons why vehicle searches are reasonable without warrants.

18. According to *Wyoming v. Houghton,* what's the rule regarding searches of containers in passenger vehicles?

19. Identify three emergency searches, and tell why the Supreme Court finds them reasonable searches without warrants.

Key Terms

7

CASES COVERED

South Dakota v. Opperman, 428 U.S. 364 (1976)

Bull and others v. City and County of San Francisco, 595 F.3d 964 (CA9, Cal. 2010)

Samson v. California, 126 S.Ct. 2193 (2006)

State v. Ellis, 2006 WL 82736 (OhioApp. 2006)

Ferguson and others v. City of Charleston and others, 532 U.S. 67 (2001)

LEARNING OBJECTIVES

1 Understand that special-needs searches are directed at people generally, can result in criminal prosecution, and don't require warrants or probable cause.

2 Know that following routine, department-approved procedures allows law enforcement to conduct inventory searches without probable cause or warrants to protect the owners' belongings, to prevent lawsuits against law enforcement departments, and to protect law enforcement agents.

3 Know that the special need of the United States to control who and what comes into its borders makes international border searches reasonable without warrants or probable cause.

4 Understand that the special need to maintain airport security outweighs the minimal invasions of walking through metal detectors and allowing luggage to be observed by X-ray.

5 Appreciate that the special needs to maintain safety, security, and discipline over people locked up in jails and prisons, probationers, and parolees outweigh the significantly reduced expectation of privacy that society grants to people in the custody of the criminal justice system.

6 Appreciate that probationers and parolees have diminished Fourth Amendment rights, even though they're not locked up.

7 Understand that the reasonableness of a public college's or university's entry and inspection of dormitory rooms requires balancing the institution's responsibility to provide a suitable learning environment against the students' right not to have unreasonable searches of their "home."

8 Appreciate that searches for employee drug use through drug testing are directed at the special need to reduce danger to public safety, not to collect evidence of crime.

9 Understand that it's not reasonable for public hospital administrators to turn over to local law enforcement the results of urine tests performed without probable cause on pregnant mothers suspected of "crack" cocaine use.

10 Know that drug testing of students who participate in *any* school activity is a reasonable search.

"Special Needs" Searches

A Resident Assistant in the university dormitory where Sherman Ellis lived, entered Ellis's room to conduct an unannounced safety inspection. These inspections were done on a regular basis by Resident Assistants and were not performed for obtaining evidence for criminal prosecution. These searches were conducted consistent with the policies and procedures set forth by the University.

Upon entering the room, and joined shortly thereafter by another Resident Assistant, a beer can was discovered on a desk top. Possession of alcoholic beverages is a violation of the University policies and procedures. During the course of obtaining the beer, the Resident Assistant observed an open drawer in the desk and could smell, as well as see, bags of what he referred to as "weed," which he identified as marijuana.

University police officers were notified and watched while the Resident Assistants completed their safety search and inspection. The police officers did not participate in the search. The Resident Assistants turned over several items obtained from their search, which were later used to prosecute Sherman Ellis. *State v. Ellis* (2006)

Until now, we've only discussed searches and seizures conducted for the purpose of gathering evidence of crime, but crime control isn't the only reason for searches. The U.S. Supreme Court has applied the Fourth Amendment to a wide range of searches that go beyond criminal law enforcement to meet "special needs." In this chapter, we'll discuss the following **special-needs searches**:

- *Inventory searches.* Documenting inventory searches of persons and containers in government custody to protect the owners from theft and damage, government agencies from lawsuits, and jails from danger

- *International border searches.* Conducting international border checks to control who and what comes into and goes out of the country

- *Airport searches.* Examining airport passengers and their baggage to protect the safety of travelers

- *Custody-related searches.* Searching prisoners, probationers, parolees, and visitors and employees of prisons and jails to control contraband

- *Employee workplace drug testing.* Testing employees for drug use to increase workplace safety

- *Prenatal patient drug testing.* Testing pregnant public hospital clinic patients suspected of illegal drug use

- *Public high school student drug testing.* Testing students to maintain a thriving learning environment

- *Public college and university dormitory inspections.* Conducting health, safety, and drug and alcohol inspections to provide a healthy school environment

Other special-needs searches include "inspecting" businesses, such as restaurants and bars, to make sure they're complying with health and safety codes, and conducting vehicle safety checks to make the roads safer.

"Special needs" doesn't mean that these searches are totally unrelated to law enforcement. Take the best example, the frisks you learned about in Chapter 4. Their sole purpose is to protect officers, but if evidence of a crime turns up during the frisk, officers can seize it, prosecutors can use it to charge and prosecute defendants, and courts can introduce it to convict defendants in criminal cases. The same is true of all the special-needs searches that you'll learn about in this chapter; in fact, many of the cases discussed in the chapter involve evidence of crimes discovered during the special need beyond law enforcement that justified the search in the first place.

LO 1

Despite their variety, special-needs searches have four common characteristics:

- They're directed at people generally, not criminal suspects and defendants specifically.

- They can result in criminal prosecution and conviction.

- They don't require warrants or probable cause.

- Their reasonableness depends on balancing special government needs against invasions of individual privacy.

Let's look at several of these special-needs searches to gain a greater understanding of how they serve the aims of protecting the public.

Inventory Searches

LO 2

Inventory searches commonly occur when persons and/or their property is in police custody. **Inventory searches** consist of making a list of people's personal property and containers that the government holds in custody. Containers include vehicles, purses, clothing, or anything else where people in custody might put their belongings. After looking through ("searching") the containers, officials make a list of the items and put them away ("seize") for safekeeping.

The reasonableness of an inventory search depends on satisfying two elements (Chapter 4):

1. *Balancing interests.* Searches have to balance the government's special need to inspect against the invasion of individuals' privacy caused by the search. If the government's special need outweighs the individual's right to privacy (courts almost always find that it does), the search is reasonable.

2. *Objective basis.* Routine procedures, not probable cause or even reasonable suspicion, are required in special-needs searches.

Let's look at each element.

Law enforcement officers take inventories to satisfy three government interests that aren't directly connected to searching for evidence of a crime:

1. To protect owners' personal property while they, or their vehicles and other containers, are in police custody

2. To protect law enforcement agencies against lawsuits for the loss, destruction, or theft of owners' property

3. To protect law enforcement officers, detained suspects, and offenders from the danger of bombs, weapons, and illegal drugs that might be hidden in owners' property

According to the U.S. Supreme Court, inventories made by law enforcement officers are Fourth Amendment searches, but they're reasonable without either probable cause or warrants. Why? Because, they're not searches conducted for the purpose of gathering evidence to prosecute crime. This doesn't mean inventory special-needs searches are left entirely to officers' discretion. The objective basis that satisfies the reasonableness requirement is the use of **routine-procedure limits** that police departments adopt, and officers follow, for conducting inventory searches. Following routine, department-approved, written procedures can take the place of probable cause and reasonable suspicion in inventory searches.

Inventory searches of vehicles were firm and long-established practices, but they received no attention in their most common "special needs" form until the 1970s. In 1976, the U.S. Supreme Court agreed to hear *South Dakota v. Opperman,* our next case excerpt. The Court held that the Vermillion, South Dakota, police department's inventory search procedures were reasonable Fourth Amendment searches.

In South Dakota v. Opperman (1976), the U.S. Supreme Court held that the Vermillion, South Dakota, police department's inventory search procedures were reasonable Fourth Amendment searches.

CASE Was the Inventory a Reasonable Search?

South Dakota v. Opperman

428 U.S. 364 (1976)

Donald Opperman was convicted before the District County Court, Second Judicial District, Clay County, South Dakota, of possession of less than one ounce of marijuana, and he appealed. The South Dakota Supreme Court reversed, and certiorari was granted. The U.S. Supreme Court reversed the South Dakota Supreme Court and remanded.

BURGER, C.J.

FACTS

Local ordinances prohibit parking in certain areas of downtown Vermillion, S. D., between the hours of 2 A.M. and 6 A.M. During the early morning hours of December 10, 1973, a Vermillion police officer observed respondent's (Donald Opperman) unoccupied vehicle illegally parked in the restricted zone. At approximately 3 A.M., the officer issued an overtime parking ticket and placed it on the car's windshield. The citation warned: "Vehicles in violation of any parking ordinance may be towed from the area."

At approximately 10 o'clock on the same morning, another officer issued a second ticket for an overtime parking violation. These circumstances were routinely reported to police headquarters, and after the vehicle was inspected, the car was towed to the city impound lot. From outside the car at the impound lot, a police officer observed a

watch on the dashboard and other items of personal property located on the back seat and back floorboard. At the officer's direction, the car door was then unlocked and, using a standard inventory form pursuant to standard police procedures, the officer inventoried the contents of the car, including the contents of the glove compartment, which was unlocked. There he found marijuana contained in a plastic bag. All items, including the contraband, were removed to the police department for safekeeping.

During the late afternoon of December 10, Opperman appeared at the police department to claim his property. The marijuana was retained by police. At Opperman's trial, the officer who conducted the inventory testified as follows:

Q: And why did you inventory this car?

A: Mainly for safekeeping, because we have had a lot of trouble in the past of people getting into the impound lot and breaking into cars and stealing stuff out of them.

Q: Do you know whether the vehicles that were broken into . . . were locked or unlocked?

A: Both of them were locked, they would be locked.

In describing the impound lot, the officer stated:

A: It's the old county highway yard. It has a wooden fence partially around part of it, and kind of a dilapidated wire fence, a makeshift fence.

Opperman was subsequently arrested on charges of possession of marijuana. His motion to suppress the evidence yielded by the inventory search was denied; he was convicted after a jury trial and sentenced to a fine of $100 and 14 days' incarceration in the county jail. On appeal, the Supreme Court of South Dakota reversed the conviction. The court concluded that the evidence had been obtained in violation of the Fourth Amendment prohibition against unreasonable searches and seizures. We granted certiorari, and we reverse.

OPINION

In the interests of public safety and as part of community caretaking functions, automobiles are frequently taken into police custody. When vehicles are impounded, local police departments generally follow a routine practice of securing and inventorying the automobiles' contents. These procedures developed in response to three distinct needs: the protection of the owner's property while it remains in police custody; the protection of the police against claims or disputes over lost or stolen property; and the protection of the police from potential danger. The practice has been viewed as essential to respond to incidents of theft or vandalism. In addition, police frequently attempt to determine whether a vehicle has been stolen and thereafter abandoned.

The Vermillion police were indisputably engaged in a caretaking search of a lawfully impounded automobile. The inventory was conducted only after the car had been impounded for multiple parking violations. The owner, having left his car illegally parked for an extended period, and thus subject to impoundment, was not present to make other arrangements for the safekeeping of his belongings. The inventory itself was prompted by the presence in plain view of a number of valuables inside the car. There is no suggestion whatever that this standard procedure, essentially like that followed throughout the country, was a pretext concealing an investigatory police motive. The inventory was not unreasonable in scope. Opperman's motion to suppress in state court challenged the inventory only as to items inside the car not in plain view. But once the policeman was lawfully inside the car to secure the personal property in plain view, it was not unreasonable to open the unlocked glove compartment, to which vandals would have had ready and unobstructed access once inside the car.

On this record we conclude that in following standard police procedures, prevailing throughout the country and approved by the overwhelming majority of courts, the conduct of the police was not "unreasonable" under the Fourth Amendment. The judgment of the South Dakota Supreme Court is therefore reversed, and the case is remanded for further proceedings not inconsistent with this opinion.

REVERSED and REMANDED.

DISSENT

MARSHALL, J., joined by BRENNAN and STEWART, JJ.

The Court's opinion appears to suggest that its result may be justified because the inventory search procedure is a "reasonable" response to "three distinct needs: the protection of the owner's property while it remains in police custody; the protection of the police against claims or disputes over lost or stolen property; and the protection of the police from potential danger. It is my view that none of these "needs," separately or together, can suffice to justify the inventory search procedure approved by the Court.

First, this search cannot be justified in any way as a safety measure, for though the Court ignores it, the sole purpose given by the State for the Vermillion police's inventory procedure was to secure valuables. Nor is there any indication that the officer's search in this case was tailored in any way to safety concerns, or that ordinarily it is so circumscribed. I do not believe that any blanket safety argument could justify a program of routine searches of the scope permitted here. Ordinarily there is little danger associated with impounding unsearched automobiles. Thus, while the safety rationale may not be entirely discounted when it is actually relied upon, it surely cannot justify the search of every car upon the basis of undifferentiated possibility of harm; on the contrary, such an intrusion could ordinarily be justified only in those individual cases where the officer's inspection was prompted by specific circumstances indicating the possibility of a particular danger. The very premise of the State's chief argument, that the cars must be searched in order to protect valuables because no guard is posted around the vehicles, itself belies the argument that they must be searched at the city lot in order to protect the police there.

The Court suggests a further "crucial" justification for the search in this case: protection of the public from vandals who might find a firearm, or contraband drugs. There is simply no indication the police were looking for dangerous items. Indeed, even though the police found shotgun shells in the interior of the car, they never opened the trunk to determine whether it might contain a shotgun. Aside from this, the suggestion is simply untenable as a matter of law. If this asserted rationale justifies search of all impounded automobiles, it must logically also justify the search of all automobiles, whether impounded or not, located in a similar area, for the argument is not based upon the custodial role of the police. But this Court has never permitted the search of any car or home on the mere undifferentiated assumption that it might be vandalized and the vandals might find dangerous weapons or substances.

Second, the Court suggests that the search for valuables in the closed glove compartment might be justified as a measure to protect the police against lost property claims. Again, this suggestion is belied by the record, since although the Court declines to discuss it, the South Dakota

Supreme Court's interpretation of state law explicitly absolves the police from any obligation beyond inventorying objects in plain view and locking the car.

Moreover, it may well be doubted that an inventory procedure would in any event work significantly to minimize the frustrations of false claims. Even were the State to impose a higher standard of custodial responsibility upon the police, however, it is equally clear that such a requirement must be read in light of the Fourth Amendment's pre-eminence to require protective measures other than interior examination of closed areas. Indeed, if such claims can be deterred at all, they might more effectively be deterred by sealing the doors and trunk of the car so that an unbroken seal would certify that the car had not been opened during custody.

Finally, the Court suggests that the public interest in protecting valuables that may be found inside a closed compartment of an impounded car may justify the inventory procedure. I recognize the genuineness of this governmental interest in protecting property from pilferage. But even if I assume that the posting of a guard would be fiscally impossible as an alternative means to the same protective end, I cannot agree with the Court's conclusion.

In my view, if the owner of the vehicle is in police custody or otherwise in communication with the police, his consent to the inventory is prerequisite to an inventory search. The Constitution does not permit such searches as a matter of routine; absent specific consent, such a search is permissible only in exceptional circumstances of particular necessity.

The Court's result in this case elevates the conservation of property interests, indeed mere possibilities of property interests, above the privacy and security interests, protected by the Fourth Amendment. For this reason I dissent. On the remand it should be clear in any event that this Court's holding does not preclude a contrary resolution of this case or others involving the same issues under any applicable state law.

STATEMENT

WHITE, J.

Although I do not subscribe to all of my Brother MARSHALL's dissenting opinion, particularly some aspects of his discussion concerning the necessity for obtaining the consent of the car owner, I agree with most of his analysis and conclusions and consequently dissent from the judgment of the Court.

QUESTIONS

1. List all the actions taken by the Vermillion police department related to the inventory of Donald Opperman's impounded car.
2. List all of Opperman's personal belongings the police inventoried, and state where they were found.
3. Summarize the majority opinion's arguments for finding the inventory search was reasonable.
4. Summarize the dissent's arguments for concluding that the inventory search was unreasonable.
5. Do you agree with the dissent that, "The Constitution does not permit such searches as a matter of routine; absent specific consent, such a search is permissible only in exceptional circumstances of particular necessity"? Defend your answer.

Most courts have adopted the majority rule in *Opperman* that "following standard police procedures" is enough to satisfy the minimum standard of Fourth Amendment reasonableness. But some courts have adopted a narrower rule that officers conducting inventory searches of vehicles without warrants can't exceed what they can see in plain view (LaFave and others 2009, 235). And the U.S. Supreme Court has rejected the dissenters' call for "reasonable efforts under the circumstances to identify and reach the owner of the property to facilitate alternative means of security or to obtain his consent to the search." In *Colorado v. Bertine* (1987), the Court held that the Fourth Amendment doesn't require police officers to use the least intrusive means to secure property of seized vehicles. But they have to follow "standardized criteria" spelled out in police regulations.

||||||||||||||||||||||||||||||||||||||||||||||||||||||||||||||||||||||||||||||||||||||||||||||||||||||||||||||

International Border Searches

LO 3

According to the U.S. Supreme Court in *U.S. v. Ramsey* (1977), searches at international borders are reasonable even without warrants or probable cause. This is known as the **border search exception**. The special need of border searches is the right to control who and what comes into and goes out of the country.

In *Ramsey*, a batch of incoming, letter-sized airmail envelopes from Thailand (a known source of narcotics) was bulky and much heavier than normal airmail letters. So a customs inspector opened the envelopes for inspection at the General Post Office in New York City (considered a "border") and found heroin in them. The inspector seized the heroin and used it to convict the recipient. The customs inspector didn't obtain a warrant to search the envelopes, even though he had time to get one.

Still, according to the U.S. Supreme Court, it wasn't an illegal search and seizure. Border searches are reasonable simply because they're conducted at international borders. The Court turned to history to support this holding:

> The Congress which proposed the Bill of Rights, including the Fourth Amendment, to the state legislatures on September 25, 1789 had, some two months prior to that proposal, enacted the first customs statute. Section 24 of this statute granted customs officials "full power and authority" to enter and search "any ship or vessel, in which they shall have reason to suspect any goods, wares or merchandise subject to duty shall be concealed. . . ." This acknowledgement of plenary customs power was differentiated from the more limited power to enter and search "any particular dwelling-house, store, building, or other place where a warrant was required." The historical importance of the enactment of this customs statute by the same Congress which proposed the Fourth Amendment is, we think, manifest. (616)

Applying the balancing test to border searches, the U.S. Supreme Court found that the national interest in controlling our international borders outweighs the invasions of individual privacy caused by border searches. So border checks require neither warrants nor individualized suspicion. However, reasonable suspicion is required to back up strip searches for contraband and weapons, because people coming into the country are "forced to disrobe to a state which would be offensive to the average person." Body-cavity searches at the border are reasonable only if they're backed up by probable cause (LaFave and others 2009, 265).

||||||||||||||||||||||||||||||||||||||||||||||||||||||||||||||||||||||||||||||||||||||||||||||||||||||||||||||||||||||||||||||||||||||||||||||||||

Airport Searches

Ever since a series of airline hijackings and terrorist bombings in the 1970s, travelers have had to pass through detectors before they can board airplanes. Passengers also must pass their luggage through X-ray machines for examination. Additionally, inspectors sometimes open and look through baggage. If they discover suspicious items, they investigate further.

Applying the balancing test of Fourth Amendment reasonableness, the U.S. Supreme Court has held that airport searches are reasonable even without warrants or probable cause. According to the Court, airport searches serve two extremely important special needs—the security and the safety of air travelers. These special needs clearly outweigh the minimal invasion of privacy caused by having passengers pass through metal detectors and allowing their luggage to be observed by X-ray. Furthermore, these invasions apply equally to all passengers, who are notified in advance that they're subject to them. So passengers are free not to board the airplane if they don't want to subject their person and their luggage to these intrusions (LaFave and Israel 1984, 1:332–33).

Since September 11, 2001, the searches have become more frequent and more intrusive but so has the sense of urgency about security. To date, there have been no court challenges to these security changes. But if a court challenge arises, it's not likely that the balance will be struck against the current practice. Of course, if passengers are singled out for more-frequent and more-invasive measures because of their Middle Eastern background and/or their Muslim religion, that's a different matter.

|||||||||||||||||||||||||||||||||||||||||||||||||||||||||||||||||||||||||||||||||||||||||||||||||||||||||||||||||||||||||||||||||||||

Custody-Related Searches

LO 5

Prisoners and their cells; prison visitors and employees; prisoners released on parole; probationers who could be but aren't locked up; and even defendants detained *before* they're convicted all can be searched without warrants or probable cause—and sometimes without any individualized suspicion at all. Why? Because the special need to maintain safety, security, and discipline over people locked up in jails and prisons, and probationers and parolees under state supervision in the community, outweighs the significantly reduced expectation of privacy that society grants to people in the custody of the criminal justice system.

Let's examine this balance as it applies to prisoners, probationers, and parolees and prison visitors and employees.

Searches of Prisoners

LO 5

Historically, prisoners had no Fourth Amendment rights; the Constitution stopped at the prison gate. Referring to convicted prisoners, the Virginia court in *Ruffin v. Commonwealth* (1871) said, "The bill of rights is a declaration of general principles to govern a society of freemen." Prisoners "are the slaves of the State" (1025). As for people detained in jails before they're convicted, in *Lanza v. New York* (1962), the U.S. Supreme Court ruled that "a jail shares none of the attributes of privacy of a home, automobile, an office or hotel room, and official surveillance has traditionally been the order of the day in prisons" (139).

In the 1980s, the Court conceded that prisoners have an expectation of privacy that society recognizes. According to the Court, in *Hudson v. Palmer* (1984), "We have repeatedly held that prisons are not beyond the reach of the Constitution. No 'iron curtain' separates one from the other." *But*, the Court continued, "imprisonment carries with it the circumscription or loss of many significant rights" (523).

The reasonableness of prisoner searches depends on balancing the need to maintain prison and jail security, safety, and discipline against the invasion of prisoners' substantially reduced reasonable expectation of privacy. The Court applied the balancing approach in *Hudson v. Palmer* (1984). According to the prisoner, Russell Thomas Palmer,

> Officer Hudson shook down my locker and destroyed a lot of my property, i.e.: legal materials, letters, and other personal property only as a means of harassment. Officer Hudson has violated my Constitutional rights. The shakedown was no routine shakedown. It was planned and carried out only as harassment. Hudson stated the next time he would really mess my stuff up. I have plenty of witnesses to these facts. (541)

The Court accepted Palmer's version of the facts. Still, Chief Justice Burger, writing for the majority, held that the "shakedown routine"—unannounced searches of prisoners and their cells for weapons and contraband—was not a search at all. "Society is not prepared to recognize as legitimate any expectation of privacy that a prisoner might have in his prison cell," so "the Fourth Amendment proscription against unreasonable searches does not apply within the confines of the prison cell." Privacy for prisoners in their cells "cannot be reconciled with the concept of incarceration and the needs and objectives of penal institutions" (525–26).

The Court went further, holding that the Fourth Amendment doesn't apply even if the motive behind the shakedown was harassment. Four justices disagreed. According to Justice Stevens, writing for the dissenters:

> Measured by the conditions that prevail in a free society, neither the possessions nor the slight residuum of privacy that a prison inmate can retain in his cell, can have more than the most minimal value. From the standpoint of the prisoner, however, that trivial residuum may mark the difference between slavery and humanity.
>
> Personal letters, snapshots of family members, a souvenir, a deck of cards, a hobby kit, perhaps a diary or a training manual for an apprentice in a new trade, or even a Bible—a variety of inexpensive items may enable a prisoner to maintain contact with some part of his past and an eye to the possibility of a better future. Are all of these items subject to unrestrained perusal, confiscation, or mutilation at the hands of a possibly hostile guard? Is the Court correct in its perception that "society" is not prepared to recognize any privacy or possessory interest of the prison inmate—no matter how remote the threat to prison security may be? . . . (542–43)
>
> The restraints and the punishment which a criminal conviction entails do not place the citizen beyond the ethical tradition that accords respect to the dignity and intrinsic worth of every individual. By telling prisoners that no aspect of their individuality, from a photo of a child to a letter from a wife, is entitled to constitutional protection, the Court breaks with the ethical tradition that I had thought was enshrined forever in our jurisprudence. (557–58)

Now, let's look at two other Fourth Amendment issues that prisoners have raised: strip and body-cavity searches and testing their DNA and storing it.

Strip and Body-Cavity Searches of Prisoners

The U.S. Supreme Court concedes that full-body, strip, and body-cavity searches are Fourth Amendment searches, but they're reasonable without either warrants or probable cause *if*, in the particular situation, the need for security, safety, or discipline outweighs prisoners' reasonable expectation of privacy in the particular circumstances of the case. For example, in *Bell v. Wolfish* (1979; Chapter 12), the U.S. Supreme Court ruled that it was reasonable to require jail inmates awaiting trial to expose their body cavities for visual inspection after every visit with a person from outside the jail. The Court said these body-cavity searches were reasonable to maintain safety and order in the jail.

As broad as the government's power is, the Fourth Amendment doesn't leave prisoners' rights completely up to the discretion of government officials. Sometimes, the balance between the special need and individual privacy weighs in favor of prisoners. Highly intrusive custodial searches when security, safety, and discipline don't require them can violate the rights of prisoners. Mary Beth G. and Sharon N., for example, were arrested for traffic violations and taken to detention centers because of outstanding parking tickets against their cars. They were strip-searched according to the Chicago Police Department policies.

Female police personnel (1) lifted their blouses and sweaters, (2) unhooked their brassieres to visually inspect their breast area, (3) pulled up their skirts, (4) lowered their underwear, and (5) made them squat two or three times and bend over to permit visual inspection of their vaginal and anal areas. The Seventh Circuit U.S. Court of Appeals held that the strip searches were unreasonable Fourth Amendment searches (*Mary Beth G. and Sharon N. v. City of Chicago* 1983).

But in our next excerpted case, *Bull v. City and County of San Francisco* (2010), the U.S. Ninth Circuit Court of Appeals ruled, over a vigorous dissent, that San Francisco's policy of strip-searching all arrested persons confined in the general jail population of the San Francisco jails was reasonable.

In Bull v. City and County of San Francisco (2010), our next case excerpt, the U.S. Ninth Circuit Court of Appeals ruled that San Francisco's policy of strip-searching all arrested persons confined in the general jail population of the San Francisco jails was reasonable.

CASE Was the Strip-Search Policy Reasonable?

Bull and others v. City and County of San Francisco

595 F.3d 964 (CA9, Cal. 2010)

HISTORY

Mary Bull, Charli Johnson, Sister Bernie Galvin, Michael Marron, Laura Timbrook, Deborah Flick, Salome Mangosing, and Leigh Fleming, pre-arraignment arrestees, brought a § 1983 class action, challenging the sheriff's department's strip search policy. The U.S. District Court for the Northern District of California denied defendants' motion for summary judgment. The Sheriff appealed. A Court of Appeals panel affirmed. Rehearing en banc was granted. The Court of Appeals, Ikuta, Circuit Judge, held that policy was reasonable under Fourth Amendment.

IKUTA, Circuit Judge

FACTS

San Francisco's six county jails struggle with a serious, ongoing problem of drugs, weapons, and other contraband being smuggled into jail facilities. The record contains hundreds of pages of incident reports, indicating that between April 2000 and December 2003, searches of the San Francisco general jail population resulted in the discovery of 1,574 items of contraband, including 662 assorted controlled substance pills, 106 shanks and other weapons, 1 screwdriver, 17 jail-made handcuff keys, 42.88 grams of rock cocaine, 2.75 grams of powder cocaine, 6.70 grams of methamphetamine, 6.24 grams of tar heroine, 71.93 grams of marijuana, 4 ecstasy pills, 32 assorted pipes, 1 hypodermic needle, and 24 gallons of homemade alcohol known as "Pruno."

During this period, new arrestees entering the San Francisco County jail system were transported to County Jail No. 9, a temporary intake and release facility, where they were pat-searched, scanned with a metal detector, booked into the system, and fingerprinted. The arrestees were then placed in holding cells. Those eligible to post bail were given access to a telephone and afforded up to 12 hours to secure their release on bond. Individuals arrested because of intoxication were released when they became sober. Arrestees who were statutorily eligible were cited and released. None of these arrestees was strip searched under the challenged policy.

Because County Jail No. 9 is a temporary intake facility equipped with holding cells but no beds, those arrestees not eligible for release were transported to a jail with housing facilities. Arrestees were then transferred into the facility's general jail population, which included pretrial detainees and convicted inmates. Pursuant to the Booking Searches policy, these individuals were strip searched prior to admission into the general population in order to prevent the smuggling of contraband into the facilities.

Under the policy, a strip search was to be performed "in a professional manner in an area of privacy" by an officer of the same sex as the arrestee. The arrestee was required "to remove or arrange some or all of his or her clothing so as to permit a visual inspection of the underclothing, breasts, buttocks or genitalia of such person." The search included "a visual inspection of the mouth, ears, hair, hands, skin folds, [and] armpits as well as a thorough search of all clothing items." San Francisco Sheriff's Dep't Proc. No. E-03, E-03(III). The policy authorized a visual search only; officers were not allowed to physically touch inmates' body cavities. The written policy instructions for conducting strip searches stated:

1. Strip searches include a visual body cavity search. A strip search *does not* include a physical body cavity search.

2. The search will be conducted in a professional manner in an area of privacy so that the search cannot be observed by persons not participating in the search.

3. The searching officer will instruct the arrestee to:

    a. Remove his/her clothing.

    b. Raise his/her arms above their head and rotate 360 degrees.

    c. To bend forward and run his/her hands through his/her hair.

    d. To turn his/her head first to the left and then to the right so the searching officer can inspect the arrestee's ear orifices.

    e. To open his/her mouth and run his/her finger over the upper and lower gum areas; then raise his/her tongue so the officer can inspect the interior of the arrestee's mouth. Remove dentures if applicable.

    f. To turn around and raise first one foot, then the other so the officer can check the bottom of each foot.

4. The searching officer will visually inspect the arrestee's breasts, buttocks, and genitalia.

5. The searching officer will thoroughly search the arrestee's clothing, underclothing, shoes, and socks.

6. At the completion of the search, the searching officer will instruct the arrestee to dress.

Strip searches conducted under the Booking Searches policy uncovered significant amounts of contraband hidden in and on arrestees' bodies. For example, San Francisco "produced evidence that from April 2000 through April 2005 strip searches at County Jail No. 9 resulted in the discovery of 73 cases of illegal drugs or drug paraphernalia hidden in body cavities." Contraband discovered in arrestees' body cavities included handcuff keys, syringes, crack pipes, heroin, crack-cocaine, rock cocaine, and marijuana. In the same time period, strip searches uncovered various concealed weapons, including a seven-inch folding knife, a double-bladed folding knife, a pair of 8-inch scissors, a jackknife, a double-edged dagger, a nail, and glass shards. Jail officials found contraband on arrestees charged with a range of offenses, including non-violent offenses such as public drunkenness, public nuisance, and violation of a court order. For example, a man arrested on a warrant for public nuisance was found smuggling a plastic bag of suspected cocaine powder.

OPINION

Because San Francisco's policy applied to arrestees introduced into the general jail population for custodial housing, we are required to evaluate the plaintiffs' constitutional claims in the light of the central objective of prison administration—safeguarding institutional security. Even if we disagree with the judgment of corrections officials about the extent of the security interests affected and the means required to further those interests, we may not engage in an impermissible substitution of our view on the proper administration of a corrections facility for that of the experienced administrators of that facility.

The San Francisco strip search procedures governing the scope and manner of the searches limited the searches to visual inspection and expressly prohibited tactile strip searches. Moreover, the San Francisco procedures required officials to conduct strip searches in a professional manner and in a place that afforded privacy. Furthermore, the record reveals a pervasive and serious problem with contraband inside San Francisco's jails, as well as numerous instances in which contraband was found during a search, indicating that arrestees' use of body cavities as a method of smuggling drugs, weapons, and items used to escape custody is an immediate and troubling problem for San Francisco jail administrators.

In sum, the balance between the need for the San Francisco strip search policy and the invasion of personal rights that the search entails must be resolved in favor of the jail system's institutional concerns. While strip searches are invasive and embarrassing, and while this type of security measure instinctively gives us the most pause, we must conclude that San Francisco's strip search policy was reasonable and therefore did not violate the class members' Fourth Amendment rights.

We conclude that San Francisco's policy requiring strip searches of all arrestees classified for custodial housing in the general population was reasonable under the Fourth Amendment, notwithstanding the lack of individualized reasonable suspicion as to the individuals searched.

We reverse the district court's grant of plaintiffs' motion for partial summary judgment as to Fourth Amendment liability.

REVERSED.

DISSENT

THOMAS, J., joined by WARDLAW, BERZON, and RAWLINSON, JJ.

1. Mary Bull was arrested at a political protest for pouring red dye mixed with corn syrup on the ground. At the police station, according to her testimony, she was pushed to the floor and her clothes forcibly removed. Her face was smashed against the concrete cell floor while jailors performed a body cavity search. She was left naked in the cell for eleven hours, then subjected to a second body cavity search. After another twelve hours in the jail, she was released on her own recognizance. She was never charged with a crime.

2. Charli Johnson was arrested for operating a motor vehicle with a suspended license. She alleges she was forcibly strip searched by male officers in a hallway, and that she was kept in a cold room, naked for twelve hours with male officers regularly viewing her. No contraband was found. She was released the next day. No charges were ever filed.

3. Sister Bernie Galvin, a Catholic nun and a member of the Sisters of Divine Providence, was arrested at an anti-war demonstration for trespassing. She was strip searched at the jail. No contraband was found.

4. Michael Marron was arrested for alleged credit card fraud at the Hotel Nikko, strip searched, and allegedly beaten and left naked in a cell for over ten hours. No contraband was found. All charges were eventually dismissed.

5. Laura Timbrook, who was arrested for bouncing small checks, was body cavity searched twice. No contraband was found.

6. Deborah Flick alleges she was arrested for public intoxication, forcibly strip searched and left naked and bleeding in a cell overnight.

7. Salome Mangosing, arrested for public drunkenness, was strip searched and forced to remain naked for twelve hours. Again, no contraband was found.

8. Leigh Fleming was arrested for disturbing the peace. She was body cavity searched and confined naked in a cold room for five hours. No contraband was found, and she was never charged with a crime.

[These are allegations not yet proven.]

No officer testified that anyone suspected any of these individuals were hiding contraband in body orifices and, to no one's surprise, no contraband was found. Rather, they were forcibly stripped and searched under a policy that mandated routine body cavity searches of everyone arrested in San Francisco classified for the general jail population, regardless of how petty the offense.

In holding that such searches were unconstitutional, the district court faithfully applied a quarter century of Ninth Circuit law, which was consistent with the law of all but one of our sister circuits. Under that nearly uniform interpretation of constitutional law, a body cavity strip search of a detainee is only justified by individualized reasonable suspicion that the search will bear fruit. If jailors have no reasonable suspicion, the search must be categorically reasonable based on empirical evidence that the policy is necessary. Jailors are entitled to strip search those whose arrest charges, criminal history, probation status, or suspicious behavior create a reasonable justification for believing the person arrested might be concealing contraband in a body cavity. That interpretation was consistent with the leading Supreme Court case on the topic, *Bell v. Wolfish*, 441 U.S. 520, 559, 99 S.Ct. 1861, 60 L.Ed.2d 447 (1979), which required "balancing of the need for the particular search against the invasion of personal rights that the search entails."

The majority sweeps away twenty-five years of jurisprudence, giving jailors the unfettered right to conduct mandatory, routine, suspicionless body cavity searches on any citizen who may be arrested for minor offenses, such as violating a leash law or a traffic code, and who pose no credible risk for smuggling contraband into the jail. Under its reconfigured regime, the majority discards *Bell*'s requirement to balance the need for a search against individual privacy and instead blesses a uniform policy of performing body cavity searches on everyone arrested and designated for the general jail population, regardless of the triviality of the charge or the likelihood that the arrestee is hiding contraband.

The rationale for this abrupt precedential departure is founded on quicksand. Indeed, the government's entire argument is based on the logical fallacy that happenstance implies causation. The government argues that contraband has been found in the San Francisco jails. Thus, the government reasons, individuals who are arrested must be smuggling contraband into the jail. Therefore, the government concludes it must body cavity search everyone who is arrested, even those who pose no risk of concealing contraband, much less of trying to smuggle contraband into the jail.

Not all searches are created equal. The Fourth Amendment differentiates between more and less intrusive searches, and requires varying levels of need to justify different kinds of searches. The scope of the particular intrusion, in light of all the exigencies of the case, is a central element in the analysis of reasonableness. Because the Fourth Amendment requires a balancing of the need for the particular search against the invasion of personal rights that the search entails, the most invasive search is justified only by the most compelling need.

The strip searches in this case are the most serious of personal invasions. The intrusiveness of a body-cavity search cannot be overstated. Strip searches involving the visual exploration of body cavities are dehumanizing and humiliating. Only a truly compelling need justifies such an invasive search. Because there is absolutely no evidence that contraband was smuggled into the prison by eligible class members, San Francisco had no reason—categorical or otherwise—to suspect that arrestees falling into the class of plaintiffs certified in this case were smuggling contraband. Thus, San Francisco's strip search policy was unreasonable and violates the Fourth Amendment.

For decades, we have followed Supreme Court precedent and required that body cavity strip searches of arrestees be based on reasonable suspicion, created either by individual circumstances or reasonable objective factors. The reinstallation of a more constitutionally sound policy has, according to government filings, worked well and has struck the right balance between safety and the rights of inmates.

Our longstanding precedent also struck the right balance. It allowed strip searches of those whose arrest charges, criminal history, probation status, or suspicious behavior would create a reasonable justification for believing the person arrested might be concealing contraband in a body cavity. It precluded jailors from strip searching those who posed no credible risk of secreting contraband. Rather than bringing competing interests into equilibrium, today's decision removes the balancing scales altogether—to the detriment of constitutional rights and human dignity.

Nor should we take solace in the fact that every person is subject to a humiliating strip search, whether it be Sister Bernie Galvin, an honored long-time community advocate for the poor who was arrested at an anti-war rally, or a pusher armed with weapons and caught in a crack house. Our constitutional oath requires us to do justice—not injustice—without respect to persons. Invading the rights of everyone, regardless of whether we have reason to suspect them or not, should give no one illusory comfort that we are providing justice for all.

I respectfully dissent.

QUESTIONS

1. State the San Francisco policy for conducting strip searches in the county jails.
2. State the narrow class of arrested persons who are subject to the strip-search policy.
3. State the government and individual interests that the policy requires the court to balance.
4. Summarize the majority's reasons for concluding that the policy strikes the appropriate balance between the interests you identified in question 3.
5. Summarize the dissent's reasons for concluding that the policy comes down heavily on the government side of the balance.
6. On which side do you come down? Back up your answer with facts and arguments from the court opinions.

Testing and Storing Prisoners' DNA

Every state and the federal government now have statutes that mandate DNA testing of all incarcerated felons (*State v. Raines* 2004). Courts have defined the testing and storing of DNA as Fourth Amendment searches and seizures. The U.S. Supreme Court hasn't ruled on the reasonableness of the testing, but the U.S. Eleventh Circuit Court of Appeals upheld Georgia's statute (*Padgett v. Donald* 2005). The statute requires convicted, incarcerated felons to provide a sample of their DNA to the Georgia Department of Corrections for analysis and storage in a data bank maintained by the Georgia Bureau of Investigation (1275).

The DNA profiles can be released from the data bank "to federal, state, and local law enforcement officers upon a request made in furtherance of an official investigation of any criminal offense." The statute applies to all persons convicted of a felony and incarcerated on or after July 1, 2000, and all felons incarcerated as of that date (1275):

> In implementing the statute, the Georgia Department of Corrections (DOC) formulated policy dictating that members of the prison staff obtain the samples by swabbing the inside of felons' mouths for saliva. The GDOC then sends the swabs to the GBI for typing and placement in the DNA database. Inmates that refuse to submit to the procedure are subjected to disciplinary reports followed by hearings and possible disciplinary action. If any inmate still refuses to cooperate, the prison staff takes the sample by force. (1275–76)

Roy Padgett and several other imprisoned convicted felons brought a civil suit asking for an injunction against testing them on the ground that it was an illegal search and seizure of their saliva. The U.S. Court of Appeals affirmed the U.S. District Court's rejection of the prisoners' claim. The court found that the statute was "reasonable under a totality of the circumstances analysis":

> We employ a balancing test, weighing the degree to which the search intrudes on an individual's privacy against the degree to which it promotes a legitimate governmental interest. Because we believe that Georgia's legitimate interest in creating a permanent identification record of convicted felons for law enforcement purposes outweighs the minor intrusion involved in taking prisoners' saliva samples and storing their DNA profiles, given prisoners' reduced expectation of privacy in their identities, we . . . hold that the statute does not violate the Fourth Amendment. (1280)

Searching Probationers and Parolees

LO 5, LO 6

Probationers and parolees also have diminished Fourth Amendment rights, even though they're not locked up (LaFave and others 2009, 272–74). Their reduced expectation of privacy subjects probationers and parolees to arrest and searches of their persons, their vehicles, and their houses without warrants or probable cause. Why? Three theories:

1. *Custody.* Some courts say it's because they're still in state custody, and conditional release is a privilege, not a right. After all, they could still be locked up; it's only by the grace of the state they're conditionally released, and one of the conditions for release is to be searched at the discretion of the state.

2. *Consent.* Other courts say they're consent searches and seizures, signed and agreed to in their "contract" of release.

3. *Balancing.* Still other courts adopt a balancing approach to the searches of probationers and parolees. On the "special need" side of the balance is the government's interest in protecting society and reducing recidivism; on the other side is privacy and the right against unreasonable searches and seizures. Let's look more closely at each group.

Searching Probationers

The U.S. Supreme Court applied the balancing approach in *Griffin v. Wisconsin* (1987), the first and still the most frequently cited case involving the Fourth Amendment rights of probationers. Wisconsin law puts probationers in the custody of the Wisconsin Department of Health and Social Services. One of the department's regulations permits probation officers to search probationers' homes without a warrant as long as the searches are backed up by reasonable suspicion that contraband is in the house (870–71).

Michael Lew, Joseph Griffin's probation officer's supervisor, had reasonable suspicion that "there might be guns in Griffin's house." Lew went to the house without a warrant and searched the house. He found a handgun, a violation of Griffin's probation. Griffin was charged with possession of a firearm by a convicted felon, a felony in Wisconsin. The trial court denied Griffin's motion to suppress the gun, a jury convicted him, and the court sentenced him to two years in prison. The Wisconsin Court of Appeals and the Wisconsin Supreme Court affirmed his conviction (871–72).

The U.S. Supreme Court also affirmed. According to the Court, the Fourth Amendment protects probationers' homes from "unreasonable searches." Probationers and parolees don't enjoy "the absolute liberty to which every citizen is entitled, but only conditional liberty properly dependent on observance of special [probation] restrictions." The "special need" of supervision allows relaxing the probable cause and warrant requirements that apply to ordinary people's houses (873–74):

> These restrictions are meant to assure that the probation serves as a period of genuine rehabilitation and that the community is not harmed by the probationer's being at large. These same goals require and justify the exercise of supervision to assure that the restrictions are in fact observed. Supervision, then, is a "special need" of the State permitting a degree of impingement upon privacy that would not be constitutional if applied to the public at large. (875)

The matter of balancing seemed settled: *Probation officers* can search probationers' homes without warrants as long as they're backed up by reasonable suspicion. Then, 13 years later, *U.S. v. Knights* (2001) expanded the relaxed standard of reasonableness to searches by *law enforcement officers*.

Mark James Knights was convicted of a drug offense and was placed on probation, subject to the condition that he "submit his person, property, place of residence, vehicle, personal effects, to search at anytime, with or without a search warrant, warrant of arrest or reasonable cause by any probation officer or law enforcement officer." Knights signed the probation order, which stated immediately above his signature that "I HAVE RECEIVED A COPY, READ AND UNDERSTAND THE ABOVE TERMS AND CONDITIONS OF PROBATION AND AGREE TO ABIDE BY SAME" (114). Three days later, Todd Hancock, a sheriff's detective, without Knights' knowledge or participation, searched his apartment without a warrant but with enough information to suspect, reasonably, that there might be "incendiary materials" in the apartment (115–16).

A unanimous U.S. Supreme Court ruled that the search passed the balancing test. Conceding that the search condition "significantly diminished Knights' reasonable expectation of privacy" (120), the Court turned to the special-needs side of the balance:

> The State has a dual concern with a probationer. On the one hand is the hope that he will successfully complete probation and be integrated back into the community. On the other is the concern, quite justified, that he will be more likely to engage in criminal conduct than an ordinary member of the community. We hold that when an officer has reasonable suspicion that a probationer subject to a search condition is engaged in criminal activity, there is enough likelihood that criminal conduct is occurring that an intrusion on the probationer's significantly diminished privacy interests is reasonable. (120–21)

Searching Parolees

According to the U.S. Supreme Court, parolees have less Fourth Amendment expectation of privacy than probationers because

> parole is an established variation of imprisonment of convicted criminals. The essence of parole is release from prison, before the completion of the sentence, on the condition that the prisoner abides by certain rules during the balance of the sentence. (*Samson v. California* 2006, 2198)

Not all members of the Court subscribe to this view, and there's a lot of controversy over whether the empirical data support the majority view. You'll learn more about the majority's and the dissent's views of parole and the empirical data in our next case excerpt, *Samson v. California* (2006).

In Samson v. California (2006), the Court expanded the rule in Knights when it held that law enforcement officers can search parolees' homes without either warrants or individualized reasonable suspicion.

CASE Was the Suspicionless Search of the Parolee's Home Reasonable?

Samson v. California
126 S.Ct. 2193 (2006)

HISTORY

Donald Curtis Samson, Defendant, was convicted by a jury in the California Appellate Division of the Superior Court of possession of methamphetamine, and sentenced to seven years in prison. The California Court of Appeal affirmed. The U.S. Supreme Court granted certiorari and affirmed.

THOMAS, J., joined by ROBERTS, C.J., and SCALIA, KENNEDY, GINSBURG, and ALITO, JJ.

CASE

California law provides that every prisoner eligible for release on state parole "shall agree in writing to be subject to search or seizure by a parole officer or other peace officer at any time of the day or night, with or without a search warrant and with or without cause." Cal.Penal Code Ann. § 3067(a). We granted certiorari to decide whether a suspicionless search, conducted under the authority of this statute, violates the Constitution. We hold that it does not.

FACTS

In September 2002, petitioner Donald Curtis Samson was on state parole in California, following a conviction for being a felon in possession of a firearm. On September 6, 2002, Officer Alex Rohleder of the San Bruno Police Department observed petitioner walking down a street with a woman and a child. Based on a prior contact with petitioner, Officer Rohleder was aware that petitioner was on parole and believed that he was facing an at large warrant. Accordingly, Officer Rohleder stopped petitioner and asked him whether he had an outstanding parole warrant. Petitioner responded that there was no outstanding warrant and that he "was in good standing with his parole agent." Officer Rohleder confirmed, by radio dispatch, that petitioner was on parole and that he did not have an outstanding warrant.

Nevertheless, pursuant to Cal.Penal Code Ann. § 3067(a) and based solely on petitioner's status as a parolee, Officer Rohleder searched petitioner. During the search, Officer Rohleder found a cigarette box in petitioner's left breast pocket. Inside the box he found a plastic baggie containing methamphetamine.

We granted certiorari, to answer a variation of the question this Court left open in *U.S. v. Knights* (2001)—whether a condition of release can so diminish or eliminate a released prisoner's reasonable expectation of privacy that a suspicionless search by a law enforcement officer would not offend the Fourth Amendment. Answering that question in the affirmative today, we affirm the judgment of the California Court of Appeal.

OPINION

An inmate-turned-parolee remains in the legal custody of the California Department of Corrections through the remainder of his term, and must comply with all of the terms and conditions of parole, including mandatory drug tests, restrictions on association with felons or gang members, and mandatory meetings with parole officers. Parolees may also be subject to special conditions, including psychiatric treatment programs, mandatory abstinence from alcohol, residence approval, and "any other condition deemed necessary." The extent and reach of these conditions clearly demonstrate that parolees have severely diminished expectations of privacy by virtue of their status alone.

Additionally, the parole search condition under California law—requiring inmates who opt for parole to submit to suspicionless searches by a parole officer or other peace officer "at any time" was "clearly expressed" to petitioner. He signed an order submitting to the condition and thus was "unambiguously" aware of it. Examining the totality of the circumstances pertaining to petitioner's status as a parolee, an established variation on imprisonment, including the plain terms of the parole search condition, we conclude that petitioner did not have an expectation of privacy that society would recognize as legitimate.

The State's interests, by contrast, are substantial. This Court has repeatedly acknowledged that a State has an "overwhelming interest" in supervising parolees because "parolees are more likely to commit future criminal offenses." Similarly, this Court has repeatedly acknowledged that a State's interests in reducing recidivism and thereby promoting reintegration and positive citizenship among probationers and parolees warrant privacy intrusions that would not otherwise be tolerated under the Fourth Amendment.

The empirical evidence presented in this case clearly demonstrates the significance of these interests to the State of California. As of November 30, 2005, California had over 130,000 released parolees. California's parolee population has a 68-to-70 percent recidivism rate. This Court has acknowledged the grave safety concerns that attend recidivism. The Fourth Amendment does not render the States powerless to address these concerns *effectively*. California's ability to conduct suspicionless searches of parolees serves its interest in reducing recidivism, in a manner that aids, rather than hinders, the reintegration of parolees into productive society.

The California Legislature has concluded that, given the number of inmates the State paroles and its high recidivism rate, a requirement that searches be based on individualized suspicion would undermine the State's ability to effectively supervise parolees and protect the public from criminal acts by reoffenders. This conclusion makes eminent sense. Imposing a reasonable suspicion requirement, as urged by petitioner, would give parolees greater opportunity to anticipate searches and conceal criminality. This Court concluded that the incentive-to conceal concern justified an "intensive" system for supervising probationers in *Griffin*. That concern applies with even greater force to a system of supervising parolees.

Thus, we conclude that the Fourth Amendment does not prohibit a police officer from conducting a suspicionless search of a parolee. Accordingly, we AFFIRM the judgment of the California Court of Appeal. *It is so ordered.*

DISSENT

STEVENS, J., joined by SOUTER and BREYER, JJ.

Our Fourth Amendment jurisprudence does not permit the conclusion, reached by the Court here for the first time, that a search supported by neither individualized suspicion nor "special needs" is nonetheless "reasonable." The suspicionless search is the very evil the Fourth Amendment was intended to stamp out. While individualized suspicion is not an irreducible component of reasonableness under the Fourth Amendment, the requirement has been dispensed with only when programmatic searches were required to meet a "'special need' divorced from the State's general interest in law enforcement."

None of our special needs precedents has sanctioned the routine inclusion of law enforcement, both in the design of the policy and in using arrests, either threatened or real, to implement the system designed for the special needs objectives. Ignoring just how closely guarded is that category of constitutionally permissible suspicionless searches, the Court for the first time upholds an entirely suspicionless search unsupported by any special need. And it goes further: In special needs cases we have at least insisted upon programmatic safeguards designed to ensure evenhandedness in application; if individualized suspicion is to be jettisoned, it must be replaced with measures to protect against the state actor's unfettered discretion. Here, by contrast, there are no policies in place—no standards, guidelines, or procedures, to rein in officers and furnish a bulwark against the arbitrary exercise of discretion that is the height of unreasonableness.

The Court is able to make this unprecedented move only by making another. Prisoners have no legitimate expectation of privacy; parolees are like prisoners; therefore, parolees have no legitimate expectation of privacy. The conclusion is remarkable not least because we have long embraced its opposite.

Threaded through the Court's reasoning is the suggestion that deprivation of Fourth Amendment rights is part and parcel of any convict's punishment. If a person may be subject to random and suspicionless searches in prison, the Court seems to assume, then he cannot complain when he is subject to the same invasion outside of prison, so long as the State still *can* imprison him. Punishment, though, is not the basis *[for depriving prisoners of their Fourth Amendment rights]*.

Had the State imposed as a condition of parole a requirement that petitioner submit to random searches by his parole officer, who is supposed to have in mind the welfare of the parolee and guide the parolee's transition back into society, the condition might have been justified either under the special needs doctrine or because at least part of the requisite "reasonable suspicion" is supplied in this context by the individual-specific knowledge gained through the supervisory relationship. Likewise, this might have been a different case had a court or parole board imposed the condition at issue based on specific knowledge of the individual's criminal history and projected likelihood of reoffending, or if the State had had in place programmatic safeguards to ensure evenhandedness.

Under either of those scenarios, the State would at least have gone some way toward averting the greatest mischief wrought by officials' unfettered discretion. But the search condition here is imposed on *all* parolees—whatever the nature of their crimes, whatever their likelihood of recidivism, and whatever their supervisory needs—without any programmatic procedural protections.

The Court seems to acknowledge that unreasonable searches "inflict dignitary harms that arouse strong resentment in parolees and undermine their ability to reintegrate into productive society." It is satisfied, however, that the California courts' prohibition against "arbitrary, capricious or harassing" searches suffices to avert those harms—which are of course counterproductive to the State's purported aim of rehabilitating former prisoners and reintegrating them into society.

I am unpersuaded. The requirement of individualized suspicion, in all its iterations, is the shield the Framers selected to guard against the evils of arbitrary action, caprice, and harassment. To say that those evils may be averted without that shield is, I fear, to pay lip service to the end while withdrawing the means.

Respectfully, I dissent.

QUESTIONS

1. Identify the government's "special needs" and Donald Curtis Samson's diminished expectations of privacy. How would you balance the needs and this reduction of privacy? Explain your answer.

2. Summarize the arguments of the majority supporting its decision that searches of parolees' homes without either warrants or reasonable suspicion are reasonable.

3. Summarize the dissent's argument that searches of parolees' homes without either warrants or reasonable suspicion are unreasonable.

4. Which side has the better arguments? Explain your answer without just repeating the arguments.

||||||||||||||||||||||||||||||||||||||||||||||||||||||||||||||||||||||||||||||||||||||||||||||||||||||||||||||||||||||||||||||||||||||||||||||||||||

College Dormitory Room Checks

LO 7

The U.S. Supreme Court hasn't answered the question of how much protection the Fourth Amendment guarantees to college students in their dormitory rooms, and surprisingly few lower federal and state courts have done so either. As of 2006, there were only 29 reported appellate court cases involving college and university dormitory room searches (*People v. Superior Court of Santa Clara County* 2006, 844).

Before we go further into these few cases, it's important to recall that the Fourth Amendment's ban covers only *government* officers' or their agents' actions (Chapter 3). Why is this important? Because public college officials are state agents and, therefore, restricted by the Fourth Amendment; private school officials aren't. So

> the fourth amendment protections against unreasonable searches and seizures are wholly inapplicable to a search or seizure, even an unreasonable one, effected by a private individual not acting as an agent of the Government or with the participation or knowledge of any governmental official. (*Duarte v. Commonwealth* 1991, 42, quoting *U.S. v. Jacobsen* 1984, 113)

Public college dormitory room search cases fall into two subdivisions—searches conducted by college officials and those conducted by local government law enforcement officers. Although the Fourth Amendment binds public college officials, the cases suggest that they have more leeway to conduct nonconsensual searches than local law enforcement (Jones 2007, 603). According to an Alabama U.S. District Court, public colleges have an "obligation to promulgate and to enforce reasonable regulations designed to protect campus order and discipline and to promote an environment consistent with the educational process" (*Moore v. Student Affairs Committee of Troy State University* (1968, 729–30).

All the cases acknowledge the college's or university's claim to "preserve a healthy, structured, and safe learning environment." But courts vary as to the value they place on students' right against unreasonable searches. As a result, individual dormitory room searches boil down to "an undefined balancing test weighing the student's right to privacy against the college's or university's right to maintain a desired campus environment" (Jones 2007, 606).

The cases have variously adopted and blended three justifications to analyze and support their balancing responsibilities:

1. Emergency or exigent circumstances that require immediate action

2. The "special relationship" between the college or university and students

3. The college's or university's duty to provide the appropriate environment for learning. (Table 7.1)

TABLE 7.1

Justifications for Reduced Privacy in College and University Dorm Rooms

Justification	Example
Emergency	University administrator permitted police officers to enter and search the room of a student suspected of burglary, because the administrator might "reasonably have concluded that any delay in ascertaining facts regarding the use of the room would indicate condonation of wrongful acts and would reflect discredit on the school, and therefore the circumstances called for immediate action." *People v. Kelly*, 195 Cal. App. 2d 669 (1961)
Special relationship between student and college or university	The Dean of Men allowed local police officers to search a student's room, where they found a small matchbox containing marijuana. The search was reasonable because "College students who reside in dormitories have a special relationship with the college involved. The relationship grows out of the peculiar and sometimes the seemingly competing interests of college and student. A student naturally has the right to be free of unreasonable search and seizures, and a tax-supported public college may not compel a 'waiver' of that right as a condition precedent to admission. The college, on the other hand, has an 'affirmative obligation' to promulgate and to enforce reasonable regulations designed to protect campus order and discipline and to promote an environment consistent with the educational process." *Moore v. Student Affairs Committee of Troy State University*, 284 F.Supp. 725, D.C.Ala. (1968).
Duty to maintain a "clean, safe, and well-disciplined environment"	Officials discovered marijuana while searching dormitory rooms following multiple reports of vandalism to the Director of Housing and Food Services. The search was reasonable because students "require and are entitled to an atmosphere that is conducive to educational pursuits. In a dormitory situation, it is the university that accepts the responsibility of providing this atmosphere. Thus, it is incumbent upon the university to take whatever reasonable measures are necessary to provide a clean, safe, well-disciplined environment." *State v. Hunter*, 831 P.2d 1033 (Utah App. 1992)

The Ohio Court of Appeals reversed and remanded Sherman Ellis's conviction and five-year sentence for trafficking in marijuana, because the evidence was seized during an unreasonable search by the campus police.

CASE Was the Dormitory Room Search Reasonable?

State v. Ellis

2006 WL 82736 (OhioApp. 2006)

HISTORY

Sherman Ellis (Defendant) was indicted on one count of trafficking in marijuana, R.C. 2925.03(A)(2), and one count of possession of criminal tools, R.C. 2923.24(A), following a seizure by campus police of drugs that were found in Ellis's dormitory room at Central State University. Ellis filed a motion to suppress the evidence that was seized. The trial court overruled Ellis's motion to suppress following a hearing. Ellis then entered a plea of no contest to the trafficking in marijuana charge. In exchange, the State dismissed the criminal tools charge. The trial court found Ellis guilty of the marijuana charge and on his conviction sentenced Ellis to five years of community control sanctions and a two hundred fifty dollar fine. Ellis appealed to this court from his conviction and sentence, challenging the trial court's decision overruling his motion to suppress evidence. The Appeals court reversed and remanded.

Grady, J.

FACTS

Sherman Ellis (Defendant), on October 7, 2004, was a student attending Central State University. Ellis was residing on campus in a dormitory room located on the campus of Central State University, Wilberforce, Ohio. As a student at Central State University, Ellis was subject to the safety and security policies and procedures set forth by the University. Ellis had agreed to recognize and be subject to the safety and security policies and procedures while a resident on the campus at Central State University. Ellis is not contesting the applicability of the safety and security policies and procedures.

Pursuant to these safety policies and procedures, a Resident Assistant in the dormitory in which Ellis resided was acting in accordance with the Resident's Hall Health and Safety checks portion of the policy and procedure by entering the room of Ellis to conduct an unannounced safety inspection. These inspections were done on a regular basis by Resident Assistants and were not performed for the purpose of obtaining evidence solely for the purpose of criminal prosecution. These searches were conducted consistent with the policies and procedures set forth by the University.

Upon entering the room, and joined shortly thereafter by another Resident Assistant, a beer can was discovered on a desk top. Possession of alcoholic beverages is a violation of the University policies and procedures. During the course of obtaining the beer, the Resident Assistant observed an open drawer in the desk and could smell, as well as see, bags of what he referred to as "weed," which he identified as marijuana.

Central State University police officers were then notified, who upon their later arrival, observed while the Resident Assistants completed their safety search and inspection. As a result of the inspection and search, the Resident Assistants turned over several items obtained from the dormitory to the Central State Police Department. While the police officers were at the dormitory after being notified, they did not participate in the search, which was conducted by the Resident Assistants. The Resident Assistants conducted the administrative search pursuant to the Resident's Hall Health and Safety checks pursuant to the University residence policies and the code of student conduct.

OPINION

A college student's dormitory room is entitled to the same protection against unreasonable search and seizure that is afforded to a private home for purposes of the Fourth Amendment. The state cannot condition attendance at a state college on a waiver of constitutional rights, nor can it require students to waive their right to be free from unreasonable searches and seizures as a condition of occupancy of a college dormitory room.

The Fourth Amendment limits only official government behavior or state action: it does not regulate searches by private persons. The mere fact that evidence found and obtained during a search by a private person is ultimately turned over to the police does not destroy the private nature of the search and render it official government action subject to the exclusionary rule. If a private person acts as the agent of the police, however, the result is different. Official participation in the planning or implementation of a private person's efforts to secure evidence may taint the operation sufficiently as to require suppression of the evidence. The test of government participation is whether under all the circumstances the private individual must be regarded as an agent or instrument of the state.

The evidence presented in this case demonstrates that the University's Resident Assistants entered Ellis's dormitory room and the rooms of other students to determine whether students were bringing prohibited items such as alcohol or drugs to their rooms, a common occurrence during the school's homecoming celebrations. The search was conducted in accordance with Central State University's policies and procedures governing residence halls, which authorizes the Residence staff to inspect student rooms at any time to determine compliance with the University's safety and hygiene policies governing residence halls. Therefore, as the trial court found, the search the Resident Life staff performed, which yielded the marijuana that campus police seized, was an administrative search by private persons, and therefore not a search subject to the Fourth Amendment's warrant requirement.

Ellis argues that because campus police were in the room while the Resident Assistants conducted their search, and the police officers told the staff members to place the evidence they found on a desk or table in the room, that the Resident Assistants acted as agents of police in performing their search. While the question is a close one, we believe that more is required to show agency. There must be some evidence that police directed private persons where and how to search and what to look for. That's lacking here because the officers merely stood by in Ellis's room while the Resident Assistants searched it.

However, that does not resolve the Fourth Amendment issue that Ellis's motion to suppress presented. The problem arises in this case because, after the resident advisors initially discovered marijuana in Ellis's room and notified campus police, the campus police then came to the scene and *entered* Ellis's room. Police remained inside Ellis's room and observed while the Resident Assistants continued their search. After the Resident Assistants had completed their search and placed the contraband they discovered in a central location in the room, as the officers had directed, the police then seized and removed that contraband from Ellis's room.

By entering Ellis's dormitory room, campus police infringed upon the reasonable expectation of privacy that Ellis had in that place which, as we previously mentioned, is entitled to the same level of protection against unreasonable search and seizure as a private home. In order to lawfully enter Ellis's room, police needed either a warrant, which they did not have, or an established exception to the warrant requirement. None applies in this case, and the State argued none in opposition to Ellis's motion to suppress.

There was no consent given by Ellis for police to enter his room. He was not even present during the search. The plain view exception does not apply because police did not observe the contraband until after they had unlawfully entered Ellis's room, and any intrusion affording the plain view observation must otherwise be lawful. Neither does the exigent or emergency circumstances exception justify the entry, for instance to prevent the concealment or destruction of evidence. The Resident Assistants were in the room, Defendant was not, and Defendant could have easily been kept out of the room by police and the evidence preserved until police had secured a warrant.

We conclude that by entering Ellis's dormitory room without a warrant or an applicable recognized exception to the warrant requirement, and by further seizing and removing from that room contraband discovered by the Resident Assistants during their private search of that room, campus police violated Ellis's Fourth Amendment rights. Accordingly, the trial court erred when it denied Ellis's motion to suppress evidence.

The judgment of the trial court will be REVERSED and this case REMANDED for further proceedings consistent with this opinion.

QUESTIONS

1. List all the actions taken by the Resident Assistants and the Central State Police Department officers that invaded Ellis's reasonable expectation of privacy.
2. Explain why the court concluded that the Resident Assistants' actions were reasonable Fourth Amendment searches but the police officers' actions were unreasonable. Do you agree? Defend your answer.
3. Assume you're Ellis's lawyer. Argue that the search by Resident Assistants was unreasonable. Back up your answer with facts and arguments made by the state in the case.
4. Do you think that Ellis's privacy outweighs the college's special needs? Back up your answer.
5. Does it matter whether the Resident Assistants, campus police, or city police conducted the search? Defend your answer.

‖‖

Drug Testing

LO 8, LO 9, LO 10

Courts, willingly, have relaxed Fourth Amendment warrant and probable cause requirements when it comes to upholding government alcohol and other drug testing that aims at the special need to protect the public health and safety. The Fourth Amendment requires courts to balance the legitimate government need to protect public health and safety against the privacy of individuals subject to the testing. According to U.S. Supreme Court Justice Sandra Day O'Connor, dissenting in *Vernonia School District v. Acton* (1995, 672): "State-compelled, state-monitored collecting of urine, while perhaps not the most intrusive of searches (visual body cavity searches) is still particularly destructive of privacy and offensive to personal dignity."

We'll examine the application of the balancing test in the leading U.S. Supreme Court cases in three settings: (1) testing employees in the workplace; (2) testing pregnant patients in hospitals; and (3) testing students in high schools and colleges.

Employee Drug Testing in the Workplace

LO 8

The Court dealt with the problem of balancing the government's need and employees' privacy in the companion cases of *Skinner v. Railway Labor Executive Association* (1989) and *National Treasury Employees Union v. Von Raab* (1989). The Court ruled in both cases that testing the blood, breath, and urine of some public employees, in accordance with administrative regulations, without either warrants or individualized suspicion, is reasonable.

In *Skinner*, the Court upheld Federal Railroad Administration (FRA) regulations mandating alcohol and other drug testing of employees following their involvement in major accidents and breath and urine tests for employees who violated safety rules. The Court stressed the need to "prevent and deter that hazardous conduct" (633) by "those engaged in safety-sensitive tasks" (620). It also stressed "the limited discretion exercised" by the employers during the testing (633).

Von Raab approved Treasury regulations that required testing U.S. Customs Service employees whenever they were transferred or promoted to positions directly related to drug interdiction or to positions requiring them to carry firearms. According to the Court, the testing regulations passed the balancing test because although tests invade privacy, the "Government's compelling interest in preventing the promotion of drug users to positions where they might endanger the integrity of our Nation's borders or the life of the citizenry" outweighs the privacy interests of individual employees (672).

Justices Marshall and Brennan dissented in both cases, reiterating their opposition to any "special needs" exception to the probable cause requirement. They further protested the expansion of the exception to include body searches (breath, urine, and blood tests) without even reasonable suspicion and challenged the majority's tipping the balance in favor of the government.

Justices Stevens and Scalia dissented in *Von Raab*. They argued that whereas the result in *Skinner* was supported by "the demonstrated frequency of drug and alcohol use by the targeted class of employees, and the demonstrated connection between such use and grave harm," in *Von Raab*, the government didn't cite a single instance "in which the cause of bribe-taking, or of poor aim, or of unsympathetic law enforcement, or of compromise of classified information was drug use" (683).

According to Justice Scalia, who wrote the dissent:

> I do not believe for a minute that the driving force behind these drug-testing rules was any of the feeble justifications put forward by counsel here and accepted by the Court. The only plausible explanation, in my view, is what the Commissioner himself offered in the concluding sentence of his memorandum to Customs Service employees announcing the program: "Implementation of the drug screening program would set an important example in our country's struggle with this most serious threat to our national health and security." . . . (686)
>
> What better way to show that the Government is serious about its "war on drugs" than to subject its employees on the front line of that war to this invasion of their privacy and affront to their dignity? To be sure, there is only a slight chance that it will prevent some serious public harm resulting from Service employee drug use, but it will show to the world that the Service is "clean," and—most important of all—will demonstrate the determination of the Government to eliminate this scourge of our society! I think it obvious that this justification is unacceptable; that the impairment of individual liberties cannot be the means of making a point; that symbolism, even symbolism for so worthy a cause as the abolition of unlawful drugs, cannot validate an otherwise unreasonable search. (686–87)

Those who lose because of the lack of understanding that begot the present exercise in symbolism are not just the Customs Service employees, whose dignity is thus offended, but all of us—who suffer a coarsening of our national manners that ultimately give the Fourth Amendment its content, and who become subject to the administration of federal officials whose respect for our privacy can hardly be greater than the small respect they have been taught to have for their own. (687)

Prenatal Drug Testing in Hospitals

LO 9

"Cocaine: A Vicious Assault on a Child"
"Crack's Toll among Babies: A Joyless View"
"Studies: Future Bleak for Crack Babies"

These are sample headlines from the 1980s and 1990s when "crack cocaine" use drew national attention and generated widely publicized fears that pregnant "crack" users "would produce a generation of severely damaged children." Researchers systematically following "crack babies" are finding that—so far anyway—the long-term effects of cocaine exposure on children's brain development and behavior "appear relatively small." That doesn't mean there are *no* effects. "Cocaine is undoubtedly bad for the fetus." But not as bad as alcohol—and similar to tobacco. According to Dr. Deborah Frank, a pediatrician at Boston University, "The argument is not that it's O.K. to use cocaine in pregnancy, any more than it's O.K. to smoke cigarettes. Neither drug is good for anybody" (Okie 2009).

In April 1989, staff members at the Charleston, South Carolina, public hospital operated by the Medical University of South Carolina (MUSC) responded to the fear of crack babies by ordering drug screens on urine samples of maternity patients suspected of using cocaine. Patients who tested positive were referred to the county substance abuse commission for counseling and treatment, but cocaine use remained unchanged. So MUSC offered to cooperate with the city in prosecuting mothers whose children tested positive for drugs at birth. A task force made up of MUSC representatives, police, and local officials developed a policy that

1. Established procedures for identifying and testing pregnant patients suspected of drug use

2. Required that a chain of custody be followed when obtaining and testing patients' urine samples

3. Provided education and treatment referral for patients testing positive

4. Contained police procedures and criteria for arresting patients who tested positive

5. Prescribed prosecutions for drug offenses and/or child neglect, depending on the stage of the defendant's pregnancy (*Ferguson v. City of Charleston* 2001, 67)

Ten state hospital patients arrested under the policy sued the hospital, the city of Charleston, the state police, and medical personnel for damages suffered by violating their Fourth Amendment rights. The U.S. Supreme Court agreed (6–3) with the patients, over a strong dissent. The case, *Ferguson v. City of Charleston* (2001), is our next case excerpt.

In Ferguson v. City of Charleston (2001), the U.S. Supreme Court held that forced drug testing and arrests of pregnant patients who tested positive for drug use violated their Fourth Amendment rights.

CASE Were the Urine Tests Unreasonable Searches?

Ferguson and others v. City of Charleston and others

532 U.S. 67 (2001)

HISTORY

State hospital obstetrics patients who were arrested after testing positive for cocaine, in urine tests conducted by the Charleston, South Carolina public hospital, operated by the Medical University of South Carolina (MUSC), pursuant to a policy developed in conjunction with police, sued the hospital, state solicitor, city and state police, and individual medical personnel, alleging, that they had violated the Fourth Amendment. The United States District Court for the District of South Carolina, entered judgment for defendants, and the patients appealed. The United States Court of Appeals for the Fourth Circuit, affirmed. Certiorari was granted. The Supreme Court, Justice Stevens, held that: (1) urine tests were "searches" within meaning of Fourth Amendment, and (2) tests, and reporting of positive test results to police, were unreasonable searches absent patients' consent, in view of policy's law enforcement purpose. Reversed and remanded.

STEVENS, J., joined by O'CONNOR, SOUTER, GINSBURG, and BREYER, JJ.

In this case, the question is whether the interest in using the threat of criminal sanctions to deter pregnant women from using cocaine can justify a departure from the general rule that an official nonconsensual search is unconstitutional if not authorized by a valid warrant.

FACTS

In the fall of 1988, staff members at the public hospital operated in the city of Charleston by the Medical University of South Carolina (MUSC) became concerned about an apparent increase in the use of cocaine by patients who were receiving prenatal treatment. (As several witnesses testified at trial, the problem of "crack babies" was widely perceived in the late 1980s as a national epidemic, prompting considerable concern both in the medical community and among the general populace.) In response

to this perceived increase, as of April 1989, MUSC began to order drug screens to be performed on urine samples from maternity patients who were suspected of using cocaine. If a patient tested positive, she was then referred by MUSC staff to the county substance abuse commission for counseling and treatment.

However, despite the referrals, the incidence of cocaine use among the patients at MUSC did not appear to change. Some four months later, Nurse Shirley Brown, the case manager for the MUSC obstetrics department, heard a news broadcast reporting that the police in Greenville, South Carolina, were arresting pregnant users of cocaine on the theory that such use harmed the fetus and was therefore child abuse. Nurse Brown discussed the story with MUSC's general counsel, Joseph C. Good, Jr., who then contacted Charleston Solicitor Charles Condon in order to offer MUSC's cooperation in prosecuting mothers whose children tested positive for drugs at birth.

Petitioners are 10 women who received obstetrical care at MUSC and who were arrested after testing positive for cocaine. Four of them were arrested during the initial implementation of the policy; they were not offered the opportunity to receive drug treatment as an alternative to arrest. The others were arrested after the policy was modified in 1990; they either failed to comply with the terms of the drug treatment program or tested positive for a second time. Respondents include the city of Charleston, law enforcement officials who helped develop and enforce the policy, and representatives of MUSC.

Petitioners claimed that warrantless and nonconsensual drug tests conducted for criminal investigatory purposes were unconstitutional searches. The U.S. District Court jury found for the City of Charleston. The Court of Appeals affirmed, holding that the searches were reasonable as a matter of law under our line of cases recognizing that "special needs" may, in certain exceptional circumstances, justify a search policy designed to serve non-law-enforcement ends. On the understanding "that MUSC personnel conducted the urine drug screens for medical purposes wholly independent of an intent to aid law enforcement efforts," the majority applied the balancing test, and concluded that the interest in curtailing the pregnancy complications and medical costs associated with maternal cocaine use outweighed what the majority termed a minimal intrusion on the privacy of the patients. We conclude that the judgment should be reversed and the case remanded for a decision on the consent issue.

OPINION

Because the hospital seeks to justify its authority to conduct drug tests and to turn the results over to law enforcement agents without the knowledge or consent of the patients, this case differs from the four previous cases in which we have considered whether comparable drug tests "fit within the closely guarded category of constitutionally permissible suspicionless searches." In three of those cases, we sustained drug tests for railway employees involved in train accidents, *Skinner v. Railway Labor Executives' Assn.*, 489 U.S. 602, (1989), for United States Customs Service employees seeking promotion to certain sensitive positions, *Treasury Employees v. Von Raab*, 489 U.S. 656, (1989), and for high school students participating in interscholastic sports, *Vernonia School Dist. 47J v. Acton*, 515 U.S. 646, (1995). In the fourth case, we struck down such testing for candidates for designated state offices as unreasonable, *Chandler v. Miller*, 520 U.S. 305, (1997).

In each of those cases, we employed a balancing test that weighed the intrusion on the individual's interest in privacy against the "special needs" that supported the program. As an initial matter, we note that the invasion of privacy in this case is far more substantial than in those cases. In the previous four cases, there was no misunderstanding about the purpose of the test or the potential use of the test results, and there were protections against the dissemination of the results to third parties. The use of an adverse test result to disqualify one from eligibility for a particular benefit, such as a promotion or an opportunity to participate in an extracurricular activity, involves a less serious intrusion on privacy than the unauthorized dissemination of such results to third parties. The reasonable expectation of privacy enjoyed by the typical patient undergoing diagnostic tests in a hospital is that the results of those tests will not be shared with nonmedical personnel without her consent. In none of our prior cases was there any intrusion upon that kind of expectation.

The critical difference between those four drug-testing cases and this one, however, lies in the nature of the "special need" asserted as justification for the warrantless searches. In each of those earlier cases, the "special need" that was advanced as a justification for the absence of a warrant or individualized suspicion was one divorced from the State's general interest in law enforcement. In this case, however, the central and indispensable feature of the policy from its inception was the use of law enforcement to coerce the patients into substance abuse treatment. This fact distinguishes this case from circumstances in which physicians or psychologists, in the course of ordinary medical procedures aimed at helping the patient herself, come across information that under rules of law or ethics is subject to reporting requirements, which no one has challenged here.

Respondents argue in essence that their ultimate purpose—namely, protecting the health of both mother and child—is a beneficent one. In *Chandler*, however, we did not simply accept the State's invocation of a "special need." Instead, we carried out a "close review" of the scheme at issue before concluding that the need in question was not "special," as that term has been defined in our cases. In this case, a review of the M-7 policy plainly reveals that the purpose actually served by the MUSC searches "is ultimately indistinguishable from the general interest in crime control."

In looking to the programmatic purpose, we consider all the available evidence in order to determine the relevant primary purpose. In this case, it is clear from the record that an initial and continuing focus of the policy was on the arrest and prosecution of drug-abusing mothers. Tellingly, the document codifying the policy incorporates the police's operational guidelines. It devotes its attention to the chain of custody, the range of possible criminal charges, and the logistics of police notification and arrests. Nowhere, however, does the document discuss different courses of medical treatment for either mother or infant, aside from treatment for the mother's addiction.

Moreover, throughout the development and application of the policy, the Charleston prosecutors and police were extensively involved in the day-to-day administration of the policy. Police and prosecutors decided who would receive the reports of positive drug screens and what information would be included with those reports. Law enforcement officials also helped determine the procedures to be followed when performing the screens. In the course of the policy's administration, they had access to Nurse Brown's medical files on the women who tested positive, routinely attended the substance abuse team's meetings, and regularly received copies of team documents discussing the women's progress. Police took pains to coordinate the timing and circumstances of the arrests with MUSC staff, and, in particular, Nurse Brown.

While the ultimate goal of the program may well have been to get the women in question into substance abuse treatment and off of drugs, the immediate objective of the searches was to generate evidence *for law enforcement purposes* in order to reach that goal. The threat of law enforcement may ultimately have been intended as a means to an end, but the direct and primary purpose of MUSC's policy was to ensure the use of those means. In our opinion, this distinction is critical. Because law enforcement involvement always serves some broader social purpose or objective, under respondents' view, virtually any nonconsensual suspicionless search could be immunized under the special needs doctrine by defining the search solely in terms of its ultimate, rather than immediate, purpose. Such an approach is inconsistent with the Fourth Amendment. Given the primary purpose of the Charleston program, which was to use the threat of arrest and prosecution in order to force women into treatment, and given the extensive involvement of law enforcement officials at every stage of the policy, this case simply does not fit within the closely guarded category of "special needs."

Respondents have repeatedly insisted that their motive was benign rather than punitive. Such a motive, however, cannot justify a departure from Fourth Amendment protections, given the pervasive involvement of law enforcement with the development and application of the MUSC policy. The stark and unique fact that characterizes this case is that Policy M-7 was designed to obtain evidence of criminal conduct by the tested patients that would be turned over to the police and that could be admissible in subsequent criminal prosecutions. While respondents are correct that drug abuse both was and is a serious problem, the gravity of the threat alone cannot be dispositive of questions concerning what means law enforcement officers may employ to pursue a given purpose. The Fourth Amendment's general prohibition against nonconsensual, warrantless, and suspicionless searches necessarily applies to such a policy.

Accordingly, the judgment of the Court of Appeals is REVERSED, and the case is REMANDED for further proceedings consistent with this opinion.

It is so ordered.

DISSENT

SCALIA, J., joined by REHNQUIST, C.J., and THOMAS, J.

There is always an unappealing aspect to the use of doctors and nurses, ministers of mercy, to obtain incriminating evidence against the supposed objects of their ministration—although here, it is correctly pointed out, the doctors and nurses were ministering not just to the mothers but also to the children whom their cooperation with the police was meant to protect. But whatever may be the correct social judgment concerning the desirability of what occurred here, that is not the issue in the present case.

The Constitution does not resolve all difficult social questions, but leaves the vast majority of them to resolution by debate and the democratic process—which would produce a decision by the citizens of Charleston, through their elected representatives, to forbid or permit the police action at issue here. The question before us is a narrower one: whether, whatever the desirability of this police conduct, it violates the Fourth Amendment's prohibition of unreasonable searches and seizures. In my view, it plainly does not.

The first step in Fourth Amendment analysis is to identify the search or seizure at issue. There is only one act that could conceivably be regarded as a search of petitioners in the present case: the *taking* of the urine sample. I suppose the *testing* of that urine for traces of unlawful drugs could be considered a search of sorts, but the Fourth Amendment protects only against searches of citizens' "persons, houses, papers, and effects"; and it is entirely unrealistic to regard urine as one of the "effects" (*i.e.*, part of the property) of the person who has passed and abandoned it.

It is rudimentary Fourth Amendment law that a search which has been consented to is not unreasonable. There is no contention in the present case that the urine samples were extracted forcibly. The only conceivable bases for saying that they were obtained without consent are the contentions (1) that the consent was coerced by the patients' need for medical treatment, (2) that the consent was uninformed because the patients were not told that the tests would include testing for drugs, and (3) that the consent was uninformed because the patients were not told that the results of the tests would be provided to the police. Until today, we have *never* held—or even suggested—that material which a person voluntarily entrusts to someone else cannot be given by that person to the police, and used for whatever evidence it may contain.

There remains to be considered the first possible basis for invalidating this search, which is that the patients were coerced to produce their urine samples by their necessitous circumstances, to wit, their need for medical treatment of their pregnancy. If that was coercion, it was not coercion applied by the government—and if such nongovernmental coercion sufficed, the police would never be permitted to use the ballistic evidence obtained from treatment of a patient with a bullet wound. And the Fourth Amendment would invalidate those many state laws that require physicians to report gunshot wounds, evidence of spousal abuse, and (like the South Carolina law relevant here, see S.C.Code Ann. § 20–7-510 (2000)) evidence of child abuse.

As I indicated at the outset, it is not the function of this Court—at least not in Fourth Amendment cases—to weigh petitioners' privacy interest against the State's interest in meeting the crisis of "crack babies" that developed in the late 1980s. I cannot refrain from observing, however, that the outcome of a wise weighing of those interests is by no means clear. The initial goal of the doctors and nurses who conducted cocaine testing in this case was to refer pregnant drug addicts to treatment centers, and to prepare for necessary treatment of their possibly affected children. When the doctors and nurses agreed to the program providing test results to the police, they did so because (in addition to the fact that child abuse was required by law to be reported) they wanted to use the sanction of arrest as a strong incentive for their addicted patients to undertake drug-addiction treatment. And the police themselves used it for that benign purpose, as is shown by the fact that only 30 of 253 women testing positive for cocaine were ever arrested, and only 2 of those prosecuted. It would not be unreasonable to conclude that today's judgment, authorizing the assessment of damages against the county solicitor and individual doctors and nurses who participated in the program, proves once again that no good deed goes unpunished.

But as far as the Fourth Amendment is concerned: There was no unconsented search in this case. And if there was, it would have been validated by the special-needs doctrine. For these reasons, I respectfully dissent.

QUESTIONS

1. Identify the special needs that the hospital was addressing in its policy of drug testing suspected pregnant "crack" users.

2. List the facts relevant to deciding whether this case is about law enforcement, some other need beyond law enforcement, or a combination.

3. Summarize the majority's arguments supporting its holding that the policy was a law enforcement policy.

4. Summarize the dissent's arguments that this was enough of a non–law enforcement policy to make the testing a reasonable search and seizure.

5. Which do you agree with more—the majority or the dissent? Back up your answer with specifics from the case excerpt.

ETHICAL ISSUES

Should Hospitals Test Maternity Patients Suspected of Using Cocaine?

One sister is 14; the other is 9. They are a vibrant pair: The older girl is high-spirited but responsible, a solid student and a devoted helper at home; her sister loves to read and watch cooking shows, and she recently scored well above average on citywide standardized tests. There would be nothing remarkable about these two happy, normal girls if it were not for their mother's history. Yvette H., now 38, admits that she used cocaine (along with heroin and alcohol) while she was pregnant with each girl. "A drug addict," she now says ruefully, "isn't really concerned about the baby she's carrying."

When the use of crack cocaine became a nationwide epidemic in the 1980s and '90s, there were widespread fears that prenatal exposure to the drug would produce a generation of severely damaged children. Newspapers carried headlines like "Cocaine: A Vicious Assault on a Child," "Crack's Toll among Babies: A Joyless View," and "Studies: Future Bleak for Crack Babies."

But now researchers are systematically following children who were exposed to cocaine before birth, and their findings suggest that the encouraging stories of Ms. H.'s daughters are anything but unusual. So far, these scientists say, the long-term effects of such exposure on children's brain development and behavior appear relatively small.

INSTRUCTIONS

1. Read Susan Okie's, "The Epidemic That Wasn't." See the link under the Chapter 7 Ethical Issues section of the Companion Website—login at www.cengagebrain.com.

2. After reading the article and gathering information from this section of your text, write an essay, answering the following questions:

    a. Is it ethical to conduct urine tests of pregnant women suspected of using cocaine?

    b. Under what conditions?

Student Drug Testing in High Schools

LO 10

For centuries, minors have lacked some fundamental rights enjoyed by adults, including the right to be let alone by the government. This is especially true while they're in school. According to the legal doctrine *in loco parentis*, school administrators are substitute parents while students are in school. Inspections of students, their personal belongings, their lockers, and their cars during school hours and activities are searches. To determine whether they're reasonable searches, courts weigh the special need for schools to maintain an environment where learning can thrive against students' privacy.

The U.S. Supreme Court had to balance the special need of high schools against high-school students' privacy in *New Jersey v. T. L. O.* (1985). A teacher at a New Jersey high school caught T. L. O., a 14-year-old freshman, and a friend smoking cigarettes in the girls' bathroom. The teacher took them to the principal's office. T. L. O. denied she was smoking; in fact, she denied that she smoked at all.

The assistant vice-principal demanded to see her purse, opened it, and found a pack of cigarettes; he also noticed a pack of cigarette rolling papers commonly used to smoke marijuana. So he searched the purse more thoroughly and found marijuana, a pipe, plastic bags, a fairly substantial amount of money, and two letters that implicated T. L. O. in marijuana dealing.

The state brought delinquency charges, and the case eventually reached the U.S. Supreme Court, where the Court had to decide whether the Fourth Amendment applied to searches by school officials. Two questions confronted the Court: Does the Fourth Amendment apply to school searches? And was this search reasonable? According to the Court, the answer to both questions is yes. The Court held that the Fourth Amendment's ban on unreasonable searches and seizures applies to searches conducted by public school officials.

Furthermore, school officials can't escape the commands of the Fourth Amendment because of their authority over schoolchildren. When they search students, they aren't *in loco parentis* (acting as parents); so students have a reasonable expectation of privacy. But that expectation is limited. Striking a balance between students' reasonable expectations of privacy and the school's legitimate need to maintain a healthy learning environment calls for easing the restrictions on searches of students. Therefore, school officials don't have to get warrants, and they don't need probable cause before they search students. Reasonable suspicion is enough. Does the right to search high-school students extend to testing some for drugs?

High school student athlete drug testing to provide a healthy and safe learning environment is the special need that most courts have dealt with, and it was the subject of the first case to reach the U.S. Supreme Court. In *Vernonia School District v. Acton* (1995), the Court found that random (without individualized suspicion) drug testing of all students voluntarily participating in the school district's athletic programs was reasonable.

According to school policy, all students who wished to participate in school sports had to sign a form consenting to urinalysis for drugs. (Parental consent was also required.) Athletes were tested at the beginning of the season for their sport. Then, once a week, 10 percent of the teams were selected blindly for follow-up testing. A same-sex adult accompanied an athlete to a restroom for the test. Each fully clothed boy produced a sample at a urinal with his back to the monitor, standing 12 to 15 feet behind the boy. The monitor was allowed to (but didn't always) watch while the sample was produced and to listen for "normal sounds of urination" (650). Girls produced their samples in an enclosed bathroom stall, where monitors could hear, but not observe, them. If athletes tested positive, they had to take a second test. If they tested positive twice, they had the option of participating in a six-week assistance program, including weekly testing, or being suspended from athletics for a specific time period.

To determine reasonableness, the Court balanced the competing interests. On the privacy side, Justice Scalia pointed out that high-school students have a lesser expectation of privacy than adults. Student athletes can expect even less privacy than other students, because they have to suit up and shower in public locker rooms. Furthermore, the way the testing was done minimized the privacy reduction—boys were observed only from behind; girls were behind closed stall doors.

On the special-need side, the Court called the government's interest in deterring drug use by students "important—indeed, perhaps compelling," and concluded that the special need trumped the student athletes' privacy. Therefore, the Court held that the warrantless searches without individualized suspicion were reasonable. According to the Court, much of the student body, especially school athletes, "was in a state of rebellion; disciplinary actions had reached epidemic proportions; and the rebellion was being fueled by alcohol and drug abuse as well as by the student's misperceptions about the drug culture" (661–63).

Vernonia wasn't the Court's last word on school drug testing. In *Board of Education of Independent School District No. 92 of Pottawatomie County v. Earls* (2002), the Court decided the reasonableness of a drug-testing policy that applied to all students who participated in *any* extracurricular activity, including Academic Team, Future Farmers of America, Future Homemakers of America, band, choir, pom-pom, cheerleading, and athletics. All students who wanted to participate had to agree to urinalysis similar to that in *Earls*. Random tests followed, and positive results could lead to suspension from the activity, but the school didn't give the results to law enforcement. Unlike the athletes in *Earls*, these students weren't likely to engage in "communal undress" or other forms of reduced privacy. Also unlike the athletes in *Earls*, participants in these activities weren't engaging in increased drug use.

The U.S. Supreme Court majority held that the urinalysis policy was reasonable under the Fourth Amendment, discounting the differences with *Earls*. Justice Thomas wrote, for the 5-member majority, that the decision in *Earls* didn't depend on the reduced privacy of athletes; that evidence of increased drug use isn't necessary to justify drug testing; and that

> the safety interest furthered by drug testing is undoubtedly substantial for all children, athletes and nonathletes alike. Indeed, it would make little sense to require a school district to wait for a substantial portion of its students to begin using drugs before it was allowed to institute a drug testing program designed to deter drug use. (836–37)

Summary

LO 1, LO 2

- Special-needs searches are directed at people generally due to a public need such as public protection. Because special-needs searches aren't the result of suspicion about someone, they require an objective basis (e.g., routine procedure limit). But warrants and probable cause aren't required. Even though the procedure is routine, criminal prosecution still results if evidence of crime is discovered. Frisks are intended to protect officers but also turn up evidence and result in convictions.

LO 1–LO 10

- A special-needs search is reasonable when a court finds the government need is more important than the privacy loss that results.

LO 2

- Courts find inventory searches by law enforcement, when routine, often meet a variety of needed public protections, ranging from protection of private property from theft to protection of law enforcement from wrongful blame.

LO 3

- Nations regulate borders. This special need results in the routine and warrantless inspection of packages crossing the border. Criminal evidence is often found, and criminal prosecution results.

LO 4
- The special need of government to provide public safety at airports receives much weight due to recent events. Generally, it isn't necessary to establish probable cause or secure a warrant when public officials use metal detectors, X-ray, and other means to provide for public safety and security.

LO 5
- When an individual is in custody, the need for security and discipline increases while the expectation of privacy decreases. Courts maintain that prisoners retain few, but some, privacy rights. DNA databases demonstrate how public need outweighs a prisoner's reduced privacy rights.

LO 6
- When prisoners are released on parole, they regain a measure of privacy. Still, they're often subject to conditions for release that mitigate their expectation of privacy. Some courts consider parolees to be in custody; others say parolees consent to search as a condition of release. Some courts afford parolees limited privacy and seek to balance needs. On balance, the public need for safety means probationers and parolees might be subjected to routine procedures that give them less privacy.

LO 7
- Officials at public colleges and universities represent the public sector. This means they're restricted in their abilities to infringe on privacy rights. But their need to preserve a safe atmosphere conducive to learning affords them additional leeway.

LO 8
- Drug-testing policies for public employees are justifiable in court when a routine is established to retain public safety. Drug testing with the goal of finding criminals isn't justifiable.

LO 9
- Privacy concerns take on special considerations in a hospital. Still, it's possible for public needs to assert themselves. In the case of a prenatal crack epidemic, the standard of probable cause is justified.

LO 10
- Minors lack the rights of adults, especially in school. The privacy concerns that exist are outweighed by the special needs of schools when routine drug tests are applied as a condition for students who enroll in school activities.

Review Questions

1. Identify four characteristics that all special-needs searches have in common.
2. Identify the two elements that have to be satisfied for an inventory search to be reasonable.
3. Under the balancing element, identify the three government interests that make the taking of inventories by law enforcement officers reasonable.
4. Identify the objective basis for an inventory search.
5. Identify the border exception and the special need the government balances at international borders.
6. Identify two extremely important special needs airport searches serve.
7. Why does the court approve of such minimal invasions of privacy during airport searches?
8. Identify the balance in custody-related searches for prisoners, probationers, and parolees.

9. Identify the special need and the objective basis for searches of prisoners.

10. When are strip and body-cavity searches of prisoners reasonable? Explain.

11. Summarize the facts and explain the significance of the Supreme Court's holding in *Hudson v. Palmer*. Summarize the dissent's argument in the case.

12. What, if any significance, does harassment have on prison shakedowns?

13. Explain the significance of testing and storing the DNA of incarcerated felons.

14. Identify two reasons why courts say that probationers and parolees have diminished Fourth Amendment rights.

15. What is the significance of *U.S. v. Knights* in dealing with searches and seizures of probationers?

16. Why do parolees have even more diminished rights against searches and seizures than probationers?

17. Why are employee drug tests reasonable without warrants or probable cause?

18. Identify the special need and the expectation of privacy balanced in searches of high-school students as outlined by the U.S. Supreme Court in *New Jersey v. T. L. O.*

19. Identify the special need and privacy balanced in searches of high-school students.

20. Summarize the facts and the majority and dissenting opinions in *Vernonia School District v. Acton*.

21. Summarize the facts and the majority and dissenting opinions in *State v. Ellis*.

22. How does the setting of searches of college students differ from the setting of searches of high-school students?

23. According to *State v. Ellis*, why are searches of college students' dorm rooms reasonable only if backed up by warrants and probable cause?

24. When are drug-testing policies for public employees justifiable?

25. In the case of a prenatal crack epidemic, what objective basis is required to justify testing hospital patients, and why is it required?

Key Terms

special-needs searches, p. 230
inventory searches, p. 231
routine-procedure limit, p. 232

border search exception, p. 234
in loco parentis, p. 256

8

CASES COVERED

Miranda v. Arizona, 384 U.S. 436 (1966)

Berkemer, Sheriff of Franklin County v. McCarty, 468 U.S. 420 (1984)

Berghuis v. Thompkins, 130 S.Ct. 2250 (2010)

Colorado v. Connelly, 479 U.S. 157 (1986)

LEARNING OBJECTIVES

1 Understand confessions and incriminating statements.

2 Know the amendments that impact criminal confessions. Know which stages of the criminal process are relevant to each.

3 Understand the due process, right-to-counsel, and self-incrimination approaches to criminal confession and their history.

4 Understand the Fifth Amendment protection against being compelled to witness against oneself. Know what falls under that protection and what doesn't.

5 Understand the "bright line" established in *Miranda v. Arizona* and why it's important to custodial interrogation.

6 Understand the wide variety of police behavior that can be considered interrogation.

7 Know the factors considered when individuals waive the right to remain silent—implicitly or explicitly.

8 Understand the factors that affect innocent people when they confess to crimes they didn't commit.

Self-Incrimination

People intuitively feel that they would never confess to something they did not do. But people do confess. They confess to things they actually do (in confessionals, in psychotherapy, and in police interrogations). And they confess to things they did not do. One goal of our legal system must be to secure conviction of the guilty, but another must be to minimize wrongful convictions, including those involving false confessions. *Elizabeth Loftus (2004, i)*

"Miranda has become embedded in routine police practice to the point where the warnings have become part of our national culture." These are the words of Chief Justice William Rehnquist (2000). What was the occasion for his comment? He was reading the U.S. Supreme Court's decision in *Dickerson v. U.S.* (2000). In that case, the Court ruled that Congress doesn't have the power to overrule *Miranda v. Arizona* (1966), something it had tried to do in 1968. In that year, in a burst of "get tough on criminals" legislation, Congress passed a law saying officers don't have to warn suspects of their rights to a lawyer and against self-incrimination before they interrogate them.

Federal and state officials ignored the law until 1997 when a Virginia federal court relied on the 1968 statute to admit Charles Dickerson's confession obtained after FBI agents gave him defective *Miranda* warnings. The 1968 law, the 1997 case relying on it, and the Supreme Court's decision declaring the law unconstitutional reflect a long and emotional debate over the right against self-incrimination.

In this chapter, we'll look at (1) the role of confessions, (2) what the Constitution has to say about self-incrimination, (3) the landmark *Miranda v. Arizona* case and how it has changed the way confessions and interrogations are handled by the law, (4) what happens when suspects waive their right to remain silent and voluntarily incriminate themselves, and (5) the problem of false confessions.

The Nature and Role of Confessions

LO 1

Confessions (suspects' written or oral acknowledgement of guilt, often including details about the crime) play an ambivalent role in society and law, and that ambivalence is ancient. In many religions, confession is the first step to forgiveness and finally redemption; in the law, they're the proof that justifies blame and punishment. Because confessions create access to defendants' innermost beliefs, knowledge, and thinking, they're uniquely powerful evidence of guilt *and* contrition. But they can also be uniquely dangerous and misleading. "The upshot has been heavy reliance on confessions coupled with extensive regulation of their use" (Seidman 2002, 229).

Defendants confess their guilt, or make **incriminating statements**, in four different settings. (Incriminating statements refers to statements that fall short of full confessions.) First, some confess to their friends and associates, who report the statements to officials. These confessions can be used against those who make them, with a major exception you'll learn about when we look at the right to counsel. Second, anyone who pleads guilty confesses his or her guilt; these are far and away the most common confessions in the criminal justice system (Chapter 13). Third, convicted offenders make incriminating statements during the sentencing process, most often because they want to demonstrate they're sorry.

Fourth, and most important to us in this chapter, suspects confess, or at least make incriminating statements, during police interrogations after they're arrested. These confessions have generated controversy and a complicated set of rules regulating them.

We'll devote most of the chapter to confessions made during police interrogation. But we'll also examine broader questions related to confessions and self-incrimination, including the importance of the constitutional provisions that regulate them; the growing body of empirical social science research on interrogation and confessions; and recommendations to ensure that we obtain the confessions of the *guilty* and not accept the confessions of the guilty.

The Self-Incrimination Setting

LO 1

Chief Justice Rehnquist was certainly right in his chapter opening quote—*Miranda* is part of our culture. But what he left out is it's also part of our culture "wars." Perhaps no procedure has generated more hostility between social conservatives and social liberals. Every week (from 1993 to 2005, and now in reruns), audiences watched *NYPD Blue*'s "good cops," Andy Sipowicz and whoever his current partner was (it was a long list), wage a "war on *Miranda*." In almost every episode, a "scumbag" murderer—or his lawyer—made a "mockery of the system" by taunting the cops with his "rights." Then, Sipowicz and his partner threatened, shoved, and usually wound up beating a confession out of the "worthless animal" called a "suspect." We all knew he was guilty (it was always a man by the way), and we were invited to hate not only the murderer but also the system that provided such scumbags with rights.

But this popular portrayal of saintly cops and satanic criminals hid the complexity of self-incrimination in practice where it most frequently occurs, during police interrogations and resulting confessions. The atmosphere in police stations is (and it's supposed to be) strange, intimidating, and hostile to criminal suspects. It's not like being stopped, asked a few questions, and frisked in the familiar surroundings of public places (Chapter 4).

In police stations, suspects are searched thoroughly—sometimes strip-searched and, occasionally, subjected to body-cavity searches (Chapter 7); they have to stand in lineups (Chapter 9); and, they're interrogated incommunicado. (This isn't a criticism; it's a description.) Being taken to police stations isn't supposed to be pleasant for suspects. The atmosphere and the actions are supposed to flush out the truth about suspects' possible criminal behavior, or what they know about someone else's criminal behavior.

By the time officers bring arrested suspects to police stations, their investigation has focused on those particular suspects. This period when the police have shifted their attention from a general investigation of a crime to building a case against a named individual is called the **accusatory stage of the criminal process**. During this stage, balancing the needs of law enforcement against the interests of individual privacy and liberty carries higher stakes for both suspects and law enforcement. Defining the proper balance between these competing social interests during the period when the police hold suspects in custody, but before prosecutors have charged them with crimes, has always generated controversy over how much the U.S. Constitution protects criminal suspects in police custody.

These aren't black-and-white issues. Consider the following hypothetical situations. In which cases can the persons "be compelled to be witnesses" against themselves?

- A police officer asks a man he has stopped on the street, "What are you doing out at 1:30 A.M.?" The man replies, "I'm trying to buy some crystal meth, as if it's any of your business."

- An officer hears screams coming from an apartment. He enters without knocking and asks, "What's going on here?" A woman answers, "I just beat up my baby."

- An elderly woman is beaten when she won't give her purse to three muggers. She is left on the street and dies of exposure. Officers in relays question an 18-year-old suspect for six hours without a break. Some officers get tough, bullying the youth and telling him he's in "big trouble" if he doesn't talk. But they never touch him. One officer befriends him, telling him the officer knows whoever took the purse didn't mean to kill the woman and that, anyway, it was really her fault for resisting. The young man finally weakens and confesses.

- A police officer, while interrogating a suspect in the police station, promises, "If you'll just tell me the truth about raping the college student, I'll see to it that the prosecutor only charges you with misdemeanor assault." The suspect asks, "You can do that?" The officer replies, "Sure, I wouldn't tell you something I couldn't do." The suspect says, "O.K., I did it." He later puts the confession in writing.

- An officer tells a suspect brought to the police station for questioning, "You might as well admit you killed your husband, because your neighbor already told us he saw the whole thing." The officer is lying. The suspect replies, "My God, I knew I should've pulled the shades; that nosy bastard's always spying on me."

Reconsider your answers after you've read the rest of the chapter. In the meantime, to understand the law of self-incrimination, interrogation, and confessions better, we'll examine their importance and look at the potential for the abuse of interrogation.

The Importance of Confessions and Interrogation

LO 1

Almost a half century ago, U.S. Supreme Court Justice Felix Frankfurter (*Culombe v. Connecticut* 1961) explained why he believed police interrogation and confessions were important:

> Despite modern advances in the technology of crime detection, offenses frequently occur about which things cannot be made to speak. And where there cannot be found innocent human witnesses to such offenses, nothing remains—if police investigation is not to be balked before it has fairly begun—but to seek out possible guilty witnesses and ask them questions, witnesses, that is, who are suspected of knowing something about the offense precisely because they are suspected of implication in it. (571)

Fred Inbau (1961)—for 60 years a professor of law, author of the leading manual on police interrogation, and one of the best interrogators of his time—gave three reasons why he supported Justice Frankfurter's position:

1. Police can't solve many crimes unless guilty people confess or suspects give police information that can convict someone else who's guilty.

2. Criminals don't confess unless the police either catch them in the act or interrogate them in private.

3. Police have to use "less refined methods" when they interrogate suspects than are "appropriate for the transaction of ordinary, every-day affairs by and between law-abiding citizens." (19)

We don't know, empirically, how close to the truth Justice Frankfurter and Professor Inbau were about the importance of interrogations and confessions. U.S. Supreme Court Chief Justice Earl Warren—himself an experienced and effective former prosecutor—explained why: "Interrogation still takes place in privacy. Privacy results in secrecy and this in turn results in a gap in our knowledge as to what in fact goes on in the interrogation room" (*Miranda v. Arizona* 1966).

Later in the chapter, we'll delve more deeply into some important empirical questions and research regarding interrogations and confessions, particularly the problem of false confessions. We'll also look at some recommended reforms to improve the central purposes of interrogations and confessions—to make sure we secure the confessions of *guilty* people, and not believe and admit the false confessions of *innocent* people.

The Constitution and Self-Incrimination

LO 1, LO 2, LO 3

The right to remain silent in the face of an accusation has ancient religious and legal origins. The ancient Talmudic law, which put the teachings of Moses into writing, contained an absolute ban on self-incrimination. The ban couldn't ever be waived because self-incrimination violated the natural right of survival.

Jesus was probably exercising this right when he stood before the Roman governor Pontius Pilate, who demanded to know if Jesus was guilty of treason. When Pilate asked, "Art thou King of the Jews?" Jesus artfully replied, "Thou sayest." Then, the chief priests and elders accused Jesus of many crimes. Jesus stood and "answered them nothing."

Surprised at Jesus' obstinacy, Pilate demanded, "'Hearest thou not how many things they witness against thee?' And still Jesus answered him to never a word, insomuch that the governor marveled greatly" (Matt. 27:11–14 Authorized [King James] Version).

The origin of the right to remain silent also is tied to another ancient rule, the common-law rule that confessions had to be voluntary. By the time the right to remain silent appeared in the Fifth Amendment to the U.S. Constitution, it had followed a controversial and complicated history (Levy 1968).

The U.S. Supreme Court has relied on three provisions in the U.S. Constitution to develop rules to control police interrogation and confessions (Table 8.1):

1. *Fourteenth Amendment due process clause.* "No state shall . . . deprive any person of life, liberty, or property without due process of law."

2. *Sixth Amendment right-to-counsel clause.* "In all criminal prosecutions, the accused shall . . . have the assistance of counsel for his defense."

3. *Fifth Amendment self-incrimination clause.* "No person . . . shall be compelled in any criminal case to be a witness against himself."

Each of these constitutional provisions has led to a different approach to police interrogation and suspects' confessions. We'll look at all three: the due process approach, the right-to-counsel approach, and the self-incrimination approach.

The Due Process Approach

LO 1, LO 2, LO 3

The due process, right-to-counsel, and self-incrimination approaches overlap, but they follow a roughly chronological line. In *Brown v. Mississippi* (1936), the U.S. Supreme Court applied the Fourteenth Amendment due process clause to the confessions extracted by torture in that tragic case (Chapter 2).

TABLE 8.1
The U.S. Constitution and Self-Incrimination

Amendment	Stage of Criminal Process Where It's Applicable
Fourteenth Amendment due process clause	All stages
Sixth Amendment right-to-counsel clause	All stages after formal charges
Fifth Amendment self-incrimination clause	Custodial interrogation and all following stages

The basic idea behind the **due process approach to confessions** is that confessions must be voluntary. Involuntary confessions violate due process, not because they're "compelled," but because they're not reliable (meaning they might be false). The **reliability rationale for due process** is that admitting unreliable evidence to prove guilt denies defendants the right to their lives (Brown, Stewart, and Ellington were sentenced to death) without due process of law. In *Brown*, the confessions were the only evidence against the defendants.

Here's what Chief Justice Hughes wrote for the Court:

> The state is free to regulate the procedure of its courts in accordance with its own conceptions of policy. But the freedom of the state in establishing its policy is limited by the requirement of due process of law. The rack and torture chamber may not be substituted for the witness stand. And the trial is a mere pretense where the state authorities have contrived a conviction resting solely on the confessions obtained by violence. It would be difficult to conceive of methods more revolting to the sense of justice than those taken to procure the confessions of these petitioners, and the use of the confessions thus obtained as the basis for conviction and sentence was a clear denial of due process. (286)

The unreliability of coerced confessions provided the rationale for the reviews of most of the early state confessions cases decided by the U.S. Supreme Court after *Brown v. Mississippi*. After several cases intimated there was a second rationale for reviewing state confession cases, the Court made the accusatory system rationale explicit in *Rogers v. Richmond* (1961). According to the **accusatory system rationale**, forced confessions violate due process even if they're true, because under our system the government alone has the burden of proving guilt beyond a reasonable doubt. In applying the accusatory system rationale in *Rogers*, the Court threw out a confession that the police got after they threatened to bring Rogers's arthritic wife in for questioning.

According to Justice Felix Frankfurter:

> Our decisions under the Fourteenth Amendment due process clause have made clear that convictions following the admission into evidence of confessions which are involuntary, i.e., the product of coercion, either physical or psychological, cannot stand. This is so not because such confessions are unlikely to be true but because the methods used to extract them offend an underlying principle in the enforcement of our criminal law: that ours is an accusatorial and not an inquisitorial system—a system in which the State must establish guilt by evidence independently and freely secured and may not by coercion prove its charge against an accused out of his own mouth.

The Court relied on a third rationale for reviewing state confessions in *Townsend v. Sain* (1963). Ailing Frank Sain's confession was obtained by questioning him after he received "truth serum"; the interrogating police officers were unaware of the drug's effects. According to the **free will rationale**, involuntary confessions aren't just unreliable and contrary to the accusatory system of justice; they're also coerced if they're not "the product of a rational intellect and a free will" (307).

During the 30 years between *Brown v. Mississippi* (1936) and *Miranda v. Arizona* (1966), the Supreme Court threw out 40 state confessions because they violated due process. Most of the early cases involved southern White mobs who had rounded up poor, illiterate Blacks and tortured them until they confessed. The Court was much more reluctant to overturn the convictions of less "sympathetic criminals" from other parts of the country. In *Lisenba v. California* (1941), for example, Ray Lisenba (an educated White business executive from California) confessed he'd "tied his wife to a chair, subjected her to rattlesnake bites, and then drowned her in a pond." The police grilled Lisenba in several all-night sessions for two weeks, refusing to grant his repeated demands to see a lawyer and to remain silent until he did.

But even in the face of these tactics, the Court refused to overturn Lisenba's conviction by throwing out his confession. According to the Court, his incriminating statements, looked at in the light of his intelligence and business experience, were not caused by police "overbearing his will" but instead were "a calculated attempt to minimize his culpability after carefully considering statements by the accomplice."

In *Stein v. New York* (1953), another case of "unsympathetic criminals"—this time involving clever, experienced White robbers in rural New York State—Justice Jackson impatiently referred to the defendants as criminals who were "convinced their dance was over and the time had come to pay the fiddler." According to Justice Jackson, "The limits in any case depend upon a weighing of the circumstances of pressure against the power of resistance of the person confessing. What would be overpowering to the weak of will or mind might be utterly ineffective against an experienced criminal" (184).

The Right-to-Counsel Approach

LO 1, LO 2, LO 3

At the same time the U.S. Supreme Court was developing the due process approach to the review of state confessions cases, a growing minority of the Court was looking for tougher measures to control police interrogation. They found one of these tougher measures in the Sixth Amendment, which reads: "In all criminal prosecutions, the accused shall . . . have the assistance of counsel for his defense." The problem is the phrase "all criminal prosecutions"; it suggests proceedings in court, not in police stations.

But by 1958, four of nine justices, including Chief Justice Warren and Associate Justices Black, Douglas, and Brennan, were calling custodial interrogation a **critical stage in criminal prosecutions** (the point when suspects' right to a lawyer kicked in).

In *Crooker v. California* (1958), John Russell Crooker, Jr., was a former law student working as a houseboy for a woman with whom he was having an affair. She broke off the affair when she found another boyfriend. After 14 hours in police custody, Crooker confessed to stabbing and strangling her. Although the police wouldn't let Crooker call his lawyer, there was no evidence officers had forced him to confess. He was allowed to eat, drink, and smoke, and interrogation sessions lasted only about an hour at a time. The U.S. Supreme Court affirmed Crooker's conviction, but Chief Justice Warren and Justices Black, Douglas, and Brennan dissented. Justice Douglas explained, "The mischief and abuse of the third degree will continue as long as an accused can be denied the right to counsel at the most critical period of his ordeal. For what takes place in the secret confines of the police station may be more critical than what takes place at trial" (444–45).

A change in the Court's membership brought to a slim majority of 5–4 the number of justices who favored the **right-to-counsel approach** to police interrogation and confessions. In 1964, in *Escobedo v. Illinois* (1964), the Supreme Court by a 5–4 vote turned to the Sixth Amendment right-to-counsel clause as the basis for reviewing state confessions cases.

Danny Escobedo asked his Chicago police interrogators to let him see his lawyer. They refused. His lawyer came to the station at Escobedo's mother's behest, but the officers repeatedly refused his requests to see Danny. Finally, Escobedo confessed. The Supreme Court threw out the confession because Escobedo had given it without the advice of his lawyer. According to the Court, as soon as a police investigation focuses on a particular suspect (the accusatory stage), criminal prosecution begins and the right to counsel attaches. If defendants don't have a right to a lawyer until they go to trial and they confess before trial without a lawyer, then the trial is "no more than an appeal from the interrogation."

Four dissenting justices argued that allowing lawyers in interrogation rooms would kill the use of confessions. Why? Because, "Any lawyer worth his salt will tell the suspect in no uncertain terms to make no statement to the police under any circumstances" (*Watts v. Indiana* 1949, 59). According to Justice White, dissenting in *Escobedo*, "I do not suggest for a moment that law enforcement will be destroyed by the rule announced today. The need for peace and order is too insistent for that. But it will be crippled and its task made a great deal more difficult" (499).

The Self-Incrimination Approach

LO 1, LO 2, LO 3

In 1966, just two years after adopting the right-to-counsel approach to custodial interrogations, the Court abruptly dropped it. In a 5–4 decision in the landmark *Miranda v. Arizona* (1966) case, the Court majority relied on the Fifth Amendment self-incrimination clause to decide the constitutionality of custodial interrogation.

The due process, right-to-counsel, and self-incrimination doctrines are all still applied in combination to decide cases. To decide whether a police custodial interrogation before formal charges was inherently coercive, the Court relies on the Fifth Amendment self-incrimination clause. To decide whether coercion was used after formal charges, the Court relies on the Sixth Amendment right to counsel. To review whether suspects and defendants have knowingly and voluntarily made incriminating statements whenever they take place, the Court relies on the Fourteenth Amendment due process clause (Table 8.1).

To claim successfully that their Fifth Amendment right against self-incrimination was violated, defendants have to prove three elements:

1. *Compulsion.* "No person . . . shall be compelled . . ."
2. *Incrimination.* ". . . in any criminal case"
3. *Testimony.* "to be a witness against himself"

TABLE 8.2

Incriminating Evidence Not Protected by the Fifth Amendment

• Weapons	• Products of consent searches
• Photographs	• Hair samples
• Contraband	• Books, papers, documents
• Appearance in lineup	• Voice samples
• Stolen property	• Records required by law to be kept
• Bullets removed from the body	• Fingerprints
• Handwriting samples	

This is the order the elements appear in within the self-incrimination clause, but we'll begin with the preliminary requirement: testimony. Then, we'll discuss what it means to be "compelled" to be a witness against oneself.

The Meaning of "Witness against Himself"

The Fifth Amendment says you can't be compelled to be a "witness" against yourself, but what does this mean? According to the U.S. Supreme Court, it means the government can't force you to give **testimony** (the content of what you say and write) against yourself. But content doesn't include the voice that spoke the words. So the government can compel you to speak particular words that might help a witness identify your voice. Also, drivers involved in accidents don't incriminate themselves when they have to give their names and addresses to the police. And if some law says you have to turn over information in your personal books, papers, bank accounts, and other records, you aren't being compelled to incriminate yourself. Further, in *Schmerber v. California* (1966), the Supreme Court decided that taking blood alcohol samples from Armando Schmerber against his will didn't compel him to be a witness against himself. (See Table 8.2 for more examples.)

The Meaning of "Compelled"

The due process approach to self-incrimination relied on the voluntariness test to decide whether suspects were "compelled" to be witnesses against themselves. According to the voluntariness test of self-incrimination, confessions and other incriminating statements violate due process if the totality of circumstances surrounding the statements shows that suspects didn't confess voluntarily.

In 1966, a combination of three factors produced one of the most famous (and most controversial and hated) decisions in U.S. constitutional history—*Miranda v. Arizona:*

1. Uneasiness about tactics used against suspects in the intimidating atmosphere of police stations

2. Dissatisfaction with the vagueness of the totality-of-circumstances approach

3. Impatience with the case-by-case approach to deciding whether confessions were voluntarily given and gotten

Let's turn now to an analysis of this famous case, and it's importance in several key areas: self-incrimination, confessions, police interrogation, and the right to counsel.

|||||||||||||||||||||||||||||||||||||||||||||||||||||||||||||||||||||||||||||||||||||||||||||||||||||||||||||||||||||

Miranda v. Arizona

LO 4

In *Miranda v. Arizona* (1966), a bare 5–4 majority of the U.S. Supreme Court established a "bright-line" rule to govern **custodial interrogation**. (We define custodial interrogation as police questioning suspects while holding them against their will, usually in a police station, but sometimes in other places.) According to the Court majority, custodial interrogation is "**inherently coercive**." Why? First, because suspects are held in strange surroundings where they're not free to leave or even to call for emotional support from relatives and friends. Second, skilled police officers use tricks, lies, and psychological pressure to "crack" the will of suspects. These circumstances, according to the Court, require strong measures to prevent involuntary confessions.

Those measures (what we all know as the *Miranda* warnings) mandated by the Court majority in its decision and the reasons for them were hotly debated in our next case excerpt, *Miranda v. Arizona*.

In Miranda v. Arizona *(1966), the U.S. Supreme Court held that police officers violated Ernesto Miranda's Fifth Amendment right against self-incrimination during Miranda's custodial interrogation.*

CASE Does the Fifth Amendment Apply to Custodial Interrogation?

Miranda v. Arizona
384 U.S. 436 (1966)

HISTORY

Ernesto Miranda was convicted of rape and robbery in the Superior Court, Maricopa County, Arizona, and sentenced to twenty to thirty years in prison for each crime. He appealed. The Arizona Supreme Court affirmed. The U.S. Supreme Court granted certiorari and reversed.

WARREN, C.J.

FACTS

On March 13, 1963, Ernesto Miranda, was arrested at his home and taken into custody to a Phoenix police station. He was there identified by the complaining witness. The police then took him to "Interrogation Room No. 2" of the detective bureau, where two police officers questioned him. The officers admitted at trial Miranda was not advised he had a right to have an attorney present. Two hours later, the officers emerged from the interrogation room with a written confession signed by Miranda. At the top of the statement was a typed paragraph stating the confession was made voluntarily, without threats or promises of immunity and "with full knowledge of my legal rights, understanding any statement I make may be used against me." One of the officers testified he read this paragraph to Miranda. Apparently, however, he did not do so until after Miranda had confessed orally.

At his trial before a jury, the written confession was admitted into evidence over the objection of defense counsel, and the officers testified to the prior oral confession made by Miranda during the interrogation. Miranda was found guilty of kidnapping and rape. He was sentenced to 20 to 30 years' imprisonment on each count, the sentences to run concurrently. On appeal, the Supreme Court of Arizona held that Miranda's constitutional rights were not violated in obtaining the confession and affirmed the conviction. In reaching its decision, the court emphasized heavily the fact that Miranda did not specifically request counsel.

OPINION

The constitutional issue we decide is the admissibility of statements obtained from a defendant questioned while in custody or otherwise deprived of his freedom of action in any significant way. The modern practice of in-custody interrogation is psychologically rather than physically oriented. Interrogation takes place in privacy and privacy results in secrecy.

In *Miranda*, we concern ourselves primarily with this interrogation atmosphere and the evils it can bring. The police arrested Miranda and took him to a special interrogation room where they secured a confession. Miranda was thrust into an unfamiliar atmosphere and run through menacing police interrogation procedures. The potentiality for compulsion is forcefully apparent, for example, where the indigent Mexican defendant was a seriously disturbed individual with pronounced sexual fantasies. To be sure, the records do not evince overt physical coercion or patent psychological ploys.

We have concluded that without proper safeguards the process of in-custody interrogation contains inherently compelling pressures which work to undermine the individual's will to resist and to compel him to speak where he would not otherwise do so freely. In order to combat these pressures and to permit a full opportunity to exercise the privilege against self-incrimination, the accused must be adequately and effectively apprised of his rights and the exercise of those rights must be fully honored.

If a person in custody is to be subjected to interrogation, he must first be informed in clear and unequivocal terms that he has the right to remain silent. Such a warning is an absolute prerequisite in overcoming the inherent pressures of the interrogation atmosphere. The Fifth Amendment privilege is so fundamental to our system of constitutional rule and the expedient of giving an adequate warning as to the availability of the privilege so simple, we will not pause to inquire in individual cases whether the defendant was aware of his rights without a warning being given.

The warning of the right to remain silent must be accompanied by the explanation that anything said can and will be used against the individual in court. This warning is needed in order to make him aware not only of the privilege, but also of the consequences of forgoing it. This warning may serve to make the individual more acutely aware that he is faced with a phase of the adversary system—that he is not in the presence of persons acting solely in his interest.

We hold that an individual held for interrogation must be clearly informed that he has the right to consult with a lawyer and to have the lawyer with him during interrogation under the system for protecting the privilege we delineate today. As with the warnings of the right to remain silent and that anything stated can be used in evidence against him, this warning is an absolute prerequisite to interrogation. No amount of circumstantial evidence that the person may have been aware of this right will suffice to stand in its stead.

In order fully to apprise a person interrogated of the extent of his rights under this system, it is necessary to warn him not only that he has the right to consult with an attorney, but also that if he is indigent [poor] a lawyer will be appointed to represent him. Without this additional warning, the admonition of the right to consult with counsel would often be understood as meaning only that he can consult with a lawyer if he has one or has the funds to obtain one. The warning of a right to counsel would be hollow if not couched in terms that would convey to the indigent that he too has a right to have counsel present.

Once warnings have been given, the subsequent procedure is clear. If the individual indicates in any manner, at any time prior to or during questioning, that he wishes to remain silent, the interrogation must cease. If the individual states that he wants an attorney, the interrogation must cease until an attorney is present. If the individual cannot obtain an attorney and he indicates that he wants one before speaking to police, they must respect his decision to remain silent.

If the interrogation continues without the presence of an attorney and a statement is taken, a heavy burden rests on the government to demonstrate that the defendant knowingly and intelligently waived his privilege against self-incrimination and his right to retained or appointed counsel. Since the State is responsible for establishing the isolated circumstances under which the interrogation takes place and has the only means of making available corroborated evidence of warnings given during incommunicado interrogation, the burden is rightly on its shoulders.

In dealing with statements obtained through interrogation, we do not purport to find all confessions inadmissible. Confessions remain a proper element in law enforcement. Any statement given freely and voluntarily without any compelling influences is, of course, admissible in evidence.

A recurrent argument made in these cases is that society's need for interrogation outweighs the privilege. But if the individual desires to exercise his privilege, he has the right to do so. This is not for the authorities to decide.

An attorney may advise his client not to talk to police until he has had an opportunity to investigate the case, or he may wish to be present with his client during any police questioning. This is not cause for considering the attorney a menace to law enforcement. He is merely carrying out what he is sworn to do under his oath—to protect to the extent of his ability the rights of his client. In fulfilling this responsibility the attorney plays a vital role in the administration of criminal justice under our Constitution.

Over the years the Federal Bureau of Investigation has compiled an exemplary record of effective law enforcement while advising any suspect or arrested person, at the outset of an interview, that he is not required to make a statement, that any statement may be used against him in court, that the individual may obtain the services of an attorney of his own choice and, more recently, that he has a right to free counsel if he is unable to pay. A letter received from the Solicitor General in response to a question from the Bench makes it clear that the present pattern of warnings and respect for the rights of the individual followed as a practice by the FBI is consistent with the procedure which we delineate today. The practice of the FBI can readily be emulated by state and local enforcement agencies.

The argument that the FBI deals with different crimes than are dealt with by state authorities does not mitigate the significance of the FBI experience.

It is also urged upon us that we withhold decision on this issue until state legislative bodies and advisory groups have had an opportunity to deal with these problems by rule making. The Constitution does not require any specific code of procedures for protecting the privilege against self-incrimination during custodial interrogation. Congress and the States are free to develop their own safeguards for the privilege, so long as they are fully as effective as those described above in informing accused persons of their right of silence and in affording a continuous opportunity to exercise it.

But the issues presented are of constitutional dimensions and must be determined by the courts. The admissibility of a statement in the face of a claim that it was obtained in violation of the defendant's constitutional rights is an issue the resolution of which has long since been undertaken by this Court. Judicial solutions to problems of constitutional dimension have evolved decade by decade. As courts have been presented with the need to enforce constitutional rights, they have found means of doing so. Where rights secured by the Constitution are involved, there can be no rule making or legislation which would abrogate them.

From the testimony of the officers and by the admission of Arizona, it is clear that Miranda was not in any way apprised of his right to consult with an attorney and to have one present during the interrogation, nor was his right not to be compelled to incriminate himself effectively protected in any other manner. Without these warnings the statements were inadmissible. The mere fact that he signed a statement which contained a typed-in clause stating that he had "full knowledge" of his "legal rights" does not approach the knowing and intelligent waiver required to relinquish constitutional rights.

Judgment of the Supreme Court of Arizona REVERSED.

DISSENT

CLARK, J.

It is with regret that I find it necessary to write in this case. However, I am unable to join in the Court's criticism of the present practices of police and investigatory agencies as to custodial interrogation. The police agencies—all the way from municipal and state forces to the federal bureaus—are responsible for law enforcement and public safety in this country. I am proud of their efforts, which in

my view are not fairly characterized by the Court's opinion.

HARLAN, J., joined by STEWART and WHITE, JJ.

The new rules are not designed to guard against police brutality or other unmistakably banned forms of coercion. The thrust of the new rules is to negate all pressures, to reinforce the nervous or ignorant suspect, and ultimately to discourage any confession at all. The aim in short is toward "voluntariness" in a utopian sense, or to view it from a different angle, voluntariness with a vengeance.

Without at all subscribing to the generally black picture of police conduct painted by the Court, I think it must be frankly recognized at the outset that police questioning may inherently entail some pressure on the suspect and may seek advantage in his ignorance or weaknesses. The atmosphere and questioning techniques, proper and fair though they be, can in themselves exert a tug on the suspect to confess. Until today, the role of the Constitution has been only to sift out undue pressure, not to assure spontaneous confessions.

The Court largely ignores that its rules impair, if they will not eventually serve wholly to frustrate, an instrument of law enforcement that has long and quite reasonably been thought worth the price paid for it. There can be little doubt that the Court's new code would markedly decrease the number of confessions. To warn the suspect that he may remain silent and remind him that his confession may be used in court are minor obstructions. To require also an express waiver by the suspect and an end to questioning whenever he demurs must heavily handicap questioning. And to suggest or provide counsel for the suspect simply invites the end of the interrogation.

How much harm this decision will inflict on law enforcement cannot fairly be predicted with accuracy. Evidence on the role of confessions is notoriously incomplete. But we do know that some crimes cannot be solved without confessions, that ample expert testimony attests to their importance in crime control, and that the Court is taking a real risk with society's welfare in imposing its new regime on the country. The social costs of crime are too great to call the new rules anything but a hazardous experimentation. . . .

WHITE, J., joined by HARLAN and STEWART, JJ.

More than the human dignity of the accused is involved; the human personality of others in the society must also be preserved. Thus the values reflected by the privilege are not the sole desideratum; society's interest in the general security is of equal weight.

The obvious underpinning of the Court's decision is a deep-seated distrust of all confessions. This is the not so subtle overtone of the opinion—that it is inherently wrong for the police to gather evidence from the accused himself. And this is precisely the nub of this dissent. I see nothing wrong or immoral, and certainly nothing unconstitutional, in the police's asking a suspect whom they have reasonable cause to arrest whether or not he killed his wife or in confronting him with the evidence on which the arrest was based, at least where he has been plainly advised that he may remain completely silent. Moreover, it is by no means certain that the process of confessing is injurious to the accused. To the contrary it may provide psychological relief and enhance the prospects for rehabilitation.

There is, in my view, every reason to believe that a good many criminal defendants who otherwise would have been convicted on what this Court has previously thought to be the most satisfactory kind of evidence will now under this new version of the Fifth Amendment, either not be tried at all or will be acquitted if the State's evidence, minus the confession, is put to the test of litigation. I have no desire whatsoever to share the responsibility for any such impact on the present criminal process.

In some unknown number of cases the Court's rule will return a killer, a rapist or other criminal to the streets and to the environment which produced him, to repeat his crime whenever it pleases him. As a consequence, there will not be a gain, but a loss, in human dignity. The real concern is not the unfortunate consequences of this new decision on the criminal law as an abstract, disembodied series of authoritative proscriptions, but the impact on those who rely on the public authority for protection and who without it can only engage in violent self-help with guns, knives and the help of their neighbors similarly inclined. . . .

QUESTIONS

1. According to the Supreme Court, what do the words *custody* and *interrogation* mean?
2. Why is custodial interrogation "inherently coercive," according to the majority?
3. Identify and explain the criteria for waiving the right against self-incrimination in custodial interrogation.
4. On what grounds do the dissenters disagree with the majority's decision? What interests are in conflict, according to the Court?
5. How do the majority and the dissent explain the balance of interests established by the Constitution?
6. Which makes more sense regarding the law of police interrogation, the majority's bright-line rule, requiring warnings, or the dissent's due process test, weighing the totality of circumstances on a case-by-case basis? Defend your answer.

Just what impact do the *Miranda* warnings have on interrogation and confessions? To answer this, we'll examine the *Miranda* bright-line rules, the meaning of "custody," the public safety exception to the rules, and the Fifth and Sixth Amendment meanings of "interrogation."

The *Miranda* "Bright-Line" Rules

The Supreme Court intended the *Miranda* warnings to provide a *bright-line rule*— sometimes called a "per se rule"—to prevent police coercion while still allowing police pressure. The rule is that whenever police officers conduct a custodial interrogation, they have to give suspects the now famous four warnings:

1. You have a right to remain silent.
2. Anything you say can and will be used against you in court.
3. You have a right to a lawyer.
4. If you can't afford a lawyer, one will be appointed for you.

What's the reason for the bright-line rule? To avoid what the Court called the "inherently coercive nature of custodial interrogation."

The Court created five more bright-line rules for the interrogating officer, prosecutors, and judges. But police officers don't have to tell suspects about these rules:

1. Suspects can claim their right to remain silent at any time. If at any time they indicate in any way they don't want to talk, the interrogation has to stop immediately.

2. If, before interrogation begins, suspects indicate in any manner they want a lawyer, interrogation can't start; if it has started already, it has to stop immediately.

3. Any statement obtained without a lawyer present puts a "heavy burden" on the prosecution to prove defendants waived two constitutional rights: the right against

self-incrimination and the right to a lawyer. Neither silence nor later confessions count as a waiver. (See the case excerpt from *Berghuis v. Thompkins* 2010, p. 282.)

4. Statements obtained in violation of the rules can't be admitted into evidence.

5. Exercising the right against self-incrimination can't be penalized. So prosecutors can't suggest or even hint at trial that the defendant's refusal to talk is a sign of guilt.

One final point about the bright-line *Miranda* rule: On TV cop shows, whenever, wherever, and as soon as police officers arrest anyone, they "mirandize" her or him immediately or say something like, "Read her her rights." However, *Miranda v. Arizona* doesn't command officers to warn suspects "whenever" they arrest them. Officers have to give the famous warnings only if they intend both to (1) take the suspects into custody *and* (2) interrogate them. These limits still leave the police plenty of leeway for questioning individuals who aren't in custody, including:

1. Questioning people at crime scenes

2. Questioning people before they become suspects

3. Questioning people during Fourth Amendment stops (Chapter 4)

The Meaning of "Custody"

In *Miranda*, the U.S. Supreme Court defined **custody** as being held by the police in a police station or depriving an individual of "freedom of action in any significant way." According to the Court, deciding whether suspects are in "custody" boils down to "whether there was a formal arrest or restraint on freedom of movement of the degree associated with a formal arrest." The Court used this language to prevent police officers from getting around the *Miranda* requirements by questioning suspects away from a police station. The Court was sending the message that *Miranda* targets coercive atmospheres, not just coercive places.

Whether suspects are in custody depends on a case-by-case evaluation of the totality of circumstances surrounding the interrogation. These circumstances include:

1. Whether officers had probable cause to arrest

2. Whether officers intended to detain suspects

3. Whether suspects believed their freedom was significantly restricted

4. Whether the investigation had focused on the suspect

5. The language officers used to summon suspects

6. The physical surroundings

7. The amount of evidence of guilt officers presented to suspects

8. How long suspects were detained

9. The amounts and kinds of pressure officers used to detain suspects

Three types of detentions don't qualify as being in custody:

1. Detaining drivers and passengers during routine traffic stops (*Berkemer v. McCarty* 1984)

2. Requiring probationers to attend routine meetings with their probation officers (*Minnesota v. Murphy* 1984)

3. Detaining persons during the execution of search warrants (*Michigan v. Summers* 1981)

What about questioning suspects in their homes? It depends on the totality of the circumstances in each case. In *Orozco v. Texas*, four police officers entered Reyes Arias Orozco's bedroom at 4:00 A.M., woke him up, and immediately started questioning him about a shooting. The Court held that even though Orozco was at home in his own bed he was still in custody, because he was "deprived of his liberty in a significant way." The Court relied heavily on the officers' testimony that from the moment Orozco gave them his name, he wasn't free to go anywhere. On the other hand, the Court ruled that Carl Mathiason (*Oregon v. Mathiason* 1977) and Jerry Beheler (*California v. Beheler* 1983) were not in custody when they went voluntarily to their local police stations and confessed.

In our next case excerpt, *Berkemer v. McCarty* (1984), the U.S. Supreme Court applied the totality-of-circumstances test to Richard McCarty, a suspect questioned about his sobriety while he was stopped for a traffic violation.

In Berkemer v. McCarty (1984), the U.S. Supreme
Court held that brief questioning during a
traffic stop was not a "custodial interrogation."

CASE   Was He "in Custody"?

Berkemer, Sheriff of Franklin County v. McCarty
468 U.S. 420 (1984)

HISTORY

Richard McCarty was convicted of operating a motor vehicle while under the influence of alcohol and/or drugs. The U.S. District Court for the Southern District of Ohio denied his petition for habeas corpus. The U.S. Court of Appeals reversed. The U.S. Supreme Court granted certiorari and affirmed.

MARSHALL, J.

FACTS

On the evening of March 31, 1980, Trooper Williams of the Ohio State Highway Patrol observed Richard McCarty's car weaving in and out of a lane on Interstate Highway 270. After following the car for two miles, Williams forced McCarty to stop and asked him to get out of the vehicle. When McCarty complied, Williams noticed that he was having difficulty standing. At that point, "Williams concluded that McCarty would be charged with a traffic offense and, therefore, his freedom to leave

the scene was terminated." However, McCarty was not told he would be taken into custody. Williams then asked McCarty to perform a field sobriety test, commonly known as a "balancing test." McCarty could not do so without falling.

While still at the scene of the traffic stop, Williams asked McCarty whether he had been using intoxicants. McCarty replied "he had consumed two beers and had smoked several joints of marijuana a short time before." McCarty's speech was slurred, and Williams had difficulty understanding him. Williams thereupon formally placed McCarty under arrest and transported him in the patrol car to the Franklin County Jail.

At the jail, McCarty was given an intoxilyzer test to determine the concentration of alcohol in his blood. The test did not detect any alcohol whatsoever in his system. Williams then resumed questioning McCarty in order to obtain information for inclusion in the State Highway Patrol Alcohol Influence Report. McCarty answered affirmatively a question whether he had been drinking. When then asked if he was under the influence of alcohol, he said, "I guess, barely." Williams next asked McCarty to indicate on the form whether the marihuana he had smoked had been treated with any chemicals. In the section of the report headed "Remarks," McCarty wrote, "No angel dust or PCP in the pot."

At no point in this sequence of events did Williams or anyone else tell McCarty that he had a right to remain silent, to consult with an attorney, and to have an attorney appointed for him if he could not afford one.

McCarty was charged with operating a motor vehicle while under the influence of alcohol and/or drugs. Under Ohio law, that offense is a first-degree misdemeanor and is punishable by fine or imprisonment for up to six months. Incarceration for a minimum of three days is mandatory. McCarty moved to exclude the various incriminating statements he had made to Trooper Williams on the ground that introduction into evidence of those statements would violate the Fifth Amendment insofar as he had not been informed of his constitutional rights prior to his interrogation.

When the trial court denied the motion, McCarty pleaded "no contest" and was found guilty. He was sentenced to 90 days in jail, 80 of which were suspended, and was fined $300, $100 of which were suspended. According to Ohio law, "The plea of no contest does not preclude a defendant from asserting upon appeal that the trial court prejudicially erred in ruling on a pretrial motion, including a pretrial motion to suppress evidence." We granted certiorari to resolve confusion in the federal and state courts regarding the applicability of our ruling in *Miranda* to questioning of motorists detained pursuant to traffic stops.

OPINION

To assess the admissibility of the self-incriminating statements made by McCarty prior to his formal arrest, we are obliged to decide whether the roadside questioning of a motorist detained pursuant to a routine traffic stop should be considered "custodial interrogation." A traffic stop significantly curtails the "freedom of action" of the driver and the passengers of the detained vehicle. Certainly few motorists would feel free either to disobey a directive to pull over or to leave the scene of a traffic stop without being told they might do so. Thus, we must decide whether a traffic stop exerts upon a detained person pressures that sufficiently impair his free exercise of his privilege against self-incrimination to require that he be warned of his constitutional rights.

Two features of an ordinary traffic stop mitigate the danger that a person questioned will be induced "to speak where he would not otherwise do so freely." First, the vast majority of roadside detentions last only a few minutes. A motorist's expectations, when he sees a policeman's light flashing behind him, are that he will be obliged to spend a short period of time answering questions and waiting while the officer checks his license and registration, that he may then be given a citation, but that in the end he most likely will be allowed to continue on his way. In this respect, questioning incident to an ordinary traffic stop is quite different from stationhouse interrogation, which frequently is prolonged, and in which the detainee often is aware that questioning will continue until he provides his interrogators the answers they seek. Second, circumstances associated with the typical traffic stop are not such that the motorist feels completely at the mercy of the police. To be sure, the aura of authority surrounding an armed, uniformed officer and the knowledge that the officer has some discretion in deciding whether to issue a citation, in combination, exert some pressure on the detainee to respond to questions.

But other aspects of the situation substantially offset these forces. Perhaps most importantly, the typical traffic stop is public. Passersby, on foot or in other cars, witness the interaction of officer and motorist. This exposure to public view both reduces the ability of an unscrupulous policeman to use illegitimate means to elicit self-incriminating statements and diminishes the motorist's fear that, if he does not cooperate, he will be subjected to abuse. The fact that the detained motorist typically is confronted by only one or at most two policemen further mutes his sense of vulnerability. In short, the atmosphere surrounding an ordinary traffic stop is substantially less "police dominated" than that surrounding the kinds of interrogation at issue in *Miranda*.

The safeguards prescribed by *Miranda* become applicable as soon as a suspect's freedom of action is curtailed to a "degree associated with formal arrest." If a motorist who has been detained pursuant to a traffic stop thereafter is subjected to treatment that renders him "in custody" for practical purposes, he will be entitled to the full panoply of protections prescribed by *Miranda*.

Turning to the case before us, we find nothing in the record that indicates that McCarty should have been given *Miranda* warnings at any point prior to the time Trooper Williams placed him under arrest. We reject the contention that the initial stop of McCarty's car, by itself, rendered him "in custody." And McCarty has failed to demonstrate that, at any time between the initial stop and the arrest, he was subjected to restraints comparable to those associated with a formal arrest. Only a short period of time elapsed between the stop and the arrest. At no point during that interval was McCarty informed that his detention would not be temporary.

Nor do other aspects of the interaction of Williams and McCarty support the contention that McCarty was exposed to "custodial interrogation" at the scene of the stop. A single police officer asked McCarty a modest number of questions and requested him to perform a simple balancing test at a location visible to passing motorists. Treatment of this sort cannot fairly be characterized as the functional equivalent of formal arrest.

We conclude that McCarty was not taken into custody for the purposes of *Miranda* until Williams arrested him. Consequently, the statements McCarty made prior to that point were admissible against him.

AFFIRMED.

QUESTIONS

1. List all the facts relevant to deciding whether Richard McCarty's freedom was "limited in any significant way."
2. Summarize the arguments the Court gives for its rule that people stopped for traffic violations aren't typically in custody.
3. List the facts and circumstances in *Miranda* and *McCarty* that differ.
4. According to the Court, when can a noncustodial traffic stop turn into a custodial stop for purposes of *Miranda*?
5. Summarize how the Court applied its definition of "custody" to the stop of Richard McCarty.

The Public Safety Exception

What if "mirandizing" a suspect before questioning her would endanger an officer or someone nearby? Would officers have to give the warnings anyway? No, said the U.S. Supreme Court in *New York v. Quarles* (1984), a case that created a **public safety exception** to *Miranda*.

In *Quarles*, a woman came up to two NYPD officers and told them she had been raped by a man carrying a gun who had just gone into a supermarket across the street. Officer Kraft ran to the market and saw Benjamin Quarles, who fit the woman's description. Kraft briefly lost sight of Quarles, then saw him again, pulled his own gun, ordered Quarles to stop and put his hands over his head, frisked him, discovered an empty shoulder holster, and handcuffed him. Without "mirandizing" Quarles, Kraft asked him where the gun was. Nodding to some cartons, Quarles said, "The gun's over there." Among the cartons, Kraft found a loaded .38 caliber revolver.

By a 5–4 vote, the Court decided Officer Kraft didn't have to warn Quarles. According to the Court, the cost of *Miranda* is that some guilty people will go free, a cost worth paying in most cases because of the premium we put on the right against coerced self-incrimination. But the cost is too high if giving the warning would endanger public safety. According to the Court, "the need for answers to questions in a situation posing a threat to the public safety outweighs the need for the rule protecting the privilege against self-incrimination" (657). Writing for the majority, Justice Rehnquist wrote,

> We decline to place officers in the untenable position of having to consider, often in a matter of seconds, whether it best serves society for them to ask the necessary questions without the *Miranda* warnings and render whatever probative evidence they uncover inadmissible, or for them to give the warnings in order to preserve the admissibility of evidence they might uncover but possibly damage or destroy their ability to obtain that evidence and neutralize the volatile situation confronting them. (657–58)

Justice O'Connor, who agreed that the exception made sense, nonetheless, dissented because of the confusion she believed making exceptions to *Miranda's* bright-line rule would cause: "In my view, a 'public safety' exception unnecessarily blurs the edges of the clear line heretofore established and makes *Miranda*'s requirements more difficult to understand" (662–64).

The Meaning of "Interrogation"

LO 6

The word *interrogation* doesn't appear in the Fifth Amendment self-incrimination clause or the Sixth Amendment right-to-counsel clause. But, as you've already learned (p. 273), it appears in the *Miranda* bright-line rules that inform officers of what they don't have to tell suspects in custody whom they want to question.

The U.S. Supreme Court has adopted two tests to determine whether police questioning amounts to **interrogation**:

1. *The Fifth Amendment "Functional Equivalent of a Question" Test*
2. *The Sixth Amendment "Deliberately Eliciting a Response" Test*

Let's look more closely at each of the tests.

The Fifth Amendment "Functional Equivalent of a Question" Test

The Supreme Court adopted and applied the **"functional equivalent of a question" test** in *Rhode Island v. Innis* (1980). Thomas Innis, a cab driver, was arrested for robbing and murdering another cab driver, John Mulvaney, with a sawed-off shotgun. Officers immediately, and several times after that, gave Innis the *Miranda* warnings; Innis said he wanted to talk to a lawyer. Three officers put Innis in the squad car to take him to the station. On the way, the officers talked among themselves about finding the shotgun because there was a school for handicapped kids nearby. At that point, Innis said he'd show them where the gun was; he did.

The Rhode Island state court tried and convicted Innis of murder. The Rhode Island supreme court overturned the conviction because the officers got his confession by "subtle coercion" that was equivalent to *Miranda* interrogation (296). The U.S. Supreme Court was faced with choosing between a narrow view of interrogation—namely, that it includes only direct questions—and a broad view like that adopted by the Rhode Island court. According to the Court, "'Interrogation' under *Miranda* refers not only to express questioning, but also to any words or actions on the part of the police that the police should know are reasonably likely to elicit an incriminating response from the suspect" (300–3).

The Sixth Amendment "Deliberately Eliciting a Response" Test

The *Innis* "functional equivalent" definition is based on the Fifth Amendment right against self-incrimination. It differs from the Sixth Amendment right-to-counsel clause, which applies only to interrogation after formal charges are brought. (The Sixth Amendment commands that "in all criminal prosecutions, the accused shall . . . have the assistance of counsel.") The test for interrogation after formal charges, called the **"deliberately eliciting a response" test,** focuses squarely on police intent.

The "deliberately elicited" test provides broader protection to interrogated suspects and more restrictions on interrogating officers. Notice that the Sixth Amendment says nothing about coercion; it guarantees the right to counsel in *all* criminal prosecutions (italics added). "Prosecution" means when the government starts formal proceedings (formal charge, preliminary hearing, indictment, information, or arraignment). At that point, the Sixth Amendment kicks in and defendants can always have their lawyers present. Any incriminating statements suspects make when a lawyer isn't present, *even if they're voluntary*, violate the suspect's right to counsel.

For example, in *Massiah v. U.S.* (1964), Winston Massiah was indicted for cocaine dealing and released on bail. While he was on bail, the police arranged for Massiah's co-defendant to discuss with him the pair's pending trial in a car while the co-defendant was wired with a radio transmitter hooked up to police officers. The Court held that Massiah's right to counsel was violated even though officers never directly asked him anything. According to the Court, the incriminating words Massiah communicated to his co-defendant resulted from interrogation because they "were deliberately elicited from him" by federal agents.

Why has the Supreme Court interpreted interrogation broadly once the right to counsel kicks in? Two reasons: First, once formal proceedings begin, all the power of the government is aimed at convicting criminal defendants. Second, at this stage, technical knowledge of the law and its procedures becomes critical. Defendants need experts (defense lawyers) to guide them through the maze of highly technical rules and procedures just as the state relies on its own experts (prosecutors) to do the same for the government.

In *Brewer v. Williams* (1977), the Court applied the "deliberately elicited" test to Robert Williams's confession (although it was true) to the grisly murder of a 10-year-old girl on Christmas Eve in Des Moines, Iowa. Shortly after the murder, Williams drove to Davenport, 160 miles east of Des Moines. On the morning of December 26, on the advice of his lawyer, Williams turned himself in to the Davenport police.

In the presence of the Des Moines Chief of police and Detective Leaming, Henry McKnight, Williams's lawyer, told Williams that Des Moines police officers would be coming to pick him up and take him back to Des Moines. He assured Williams that the officers wouldn't interrogate him, or mistreat him, and told him that he shouldn't talk to the officers. In the meantime, Williams was arraigned before a Davenport judge on an outstanding arrest warrant. The judge gave Williams his *Miranda* warnings and ordered him locked up in jail.

Detective Leaming and a fellow officer picked up Williams at about noon. Detective Leaming repeated the *Miranda* warnings and told Williams that they knew he was represented by a local attorney and McKnight in Des Moines. He told Williams, "I want you to remember this, because we'll be visiting between here and Des Moines." On the trip, Williams told the officers several times, "When I get to Des Moines and see Mr. McKnight I'm going to tell you the whole story" (391). Leaming knew that Williams was a former mental patient and that he was deeply religious.

Not long after they left Davenport, Leaming delivered what came to be known as his "Christian burial" speech. Referring to Williams as "Reverend," the detective said,

> I want to give you something to think about while we're traveling down the road. Number one, I want you to observe the weather conditions, it's raining, it's sleeting, it's freezing, driving is very treacherous, visibility is poor, it's going to be dark early this evening. They are predicting several inches of snow for tonight, and I feel that you yourself are the only person that knows where this little girl's body is, that you yourself have only been there once, and if you get a snow on top of it you yourself may be unable to find it. And, since we will be going right past the area on the way into Des Moines, I feel that we could stop and locate the body, that the parents of this little girl should be entitled to a Christian burial for the little girl who was snatched away from them on Christmas Eve and murdered. And I feel we should stop and locate it on the way in rather than waiting until morning and trying to come back out after a snow storm and possibly not being able to find it at all. (392–93)

As the car approached Mitchellville, Iowa, Williams told the officers that he'd show the officers where the body was; he took them to the victim's body.

Williams was indicted for first-degree murder. Before trial, his counsel moved to suppress all evidence relating to or resulting from any statements Williams had made during the automobile ride from Davenport to Des Moines. The U.S. Supreme Court granted a writ of habeas corpus to Williams. According to the majority,

The crime of which Williams was convicted was senseless and brutal, calling for swift and energetic action by the police to apprehend the perpetrator and gather evidence with which he could be convicted. No mission of law enforcement officials is more important. Although we do not lightly affirm the issuance of a writ of habeas corpus in this case, so clear a violation of the Sixth and Fourteenth Amendments as here occurred cannot be condoned. The pressures on state executive and judicial officers charged with the administration of the criminal law are great, especially when the crime is murder and the victim a small child. But it is precisely the predictability of those pressures that makes imperative a resolute loyalty to the guarantees that the Constitution extends to us all. (406)

The majority decision provoked strong dissents from several justices, one of them extremely angry that this horrible crime was going to go unpunished:

The consequence of the majority's decision is extremely serious. A mentally disturbed killer whose guilt is not in question may be released. Why? The police did nothing wrong, let alone anything unconstitutional. To anyone not lost in the intricacies of the prophylactic rules of *Miranda v. Arizona*, the result in this case seems utterly senseless. (439)

Eventually, Williams was retried, convicted, and the Court upheld his conviction, in *Nix v. Williams* (1984).

‖‖‖

The Waiver of the Right to Remain Silent

LO 7

After *Miranda v. Arizona* was decided there was a lot of talk about "handcuffing the police." The talk was created by a fear that suspects wouldn't talk if officers told them they had a right not to talk to police and to have lawyers with them if they did talk. As it turned out, these fears were greatly exaggerated. Most defendants waived their rights and talked to the police anyway. They still do. Richard Leo (1996) estimates that about 75 percent of suspects routinely waive their *Miranda* rights and talk to the police (653). Based on this reality, the Supreme Court said, "Giving the warnings and getting a waiver has generally produced a virtual ticket of admissibility" (*Missouri v. Seibert* 2004, 601).

Because so many suspects waive their rights and talk to interrogators with no lawyer in sight, two questions are of great constitutional *and* practical importance:

1. What is a valid waiver of the right against self-incrimination?
2. What is a voluntary confession?

In *Miranda v. Arizona* (1966), the Court addressed the issue of what constitutes a valid waiver:

An express statement that the individual is willing to make a statement and does not want an attorney followed closely by a statement could constitute a waiver. But a valid waiver will not be presumed simply from the silence of the accused after warnings are given or simply from the fact that a confession was in fact eventually obtained. (475)

This statement strongly suggests that the Court was referring to an **express waiver test**, which means that suspects have to make clear statements that indicate they know their rights, know they're giving them up, and know the consequences of giving them

TABLE 8.3

Circumstances Relevant to Showing a Knowing Waiver

- Intelligence
- Physical condition
- Education
- Mental condition

- Age
- Ability to understand English
- Familiarity with the criminal justice system

TABLE 8.4

Cases in Which Courts Found a Knowing Waiver

- No evidence showed the suspect was threatened, tricked, or cajoled. (*Connecticut v. Barrett* 1987)

- The suspect invoked the right to counsel and then after a five-hour ride in the back of a squad car signed a waiver when police officers asked "if there was anything he would like to tell them." (*Henderson v. Florida* 1985)

- The suspect asked for a lawyer, didn't get one, and then signed a waiver after repeated warnings and "nagging" by police officers. (*Watkins v. Virginia* 1986)

- After refusing to sign an express waiver, the defendant talked to the police. (*U.S. v. Barahona* 1993)

- The defendant said "I don't got nothing to say" when he was presented with a waiver form but then answered questions during an interview that followed. (*U.S. v. Banks* 1995)

- The defendant remained silent throughout most of nearly three hours of questioning after being advised of his *Miranda* rights, but he responded "Yes" when asked if he prayed for forgiveness for killing the victim. (*Berghuis v. Thompkins* 2010)

up. But the Court doesn't require *express* waivers. Instead, it has adopted an **implied waiver test**, which says the totality of circumstances in each case has to prove that before suspects talked, they knew they had the rights *and* they knew they were giving them up.

In *North Carolina v. Butler* (1979), officers read Willie Butler his *Miranda* rights. Butler said he knew his rights, but he refused to sign a waiver form. ("I will talk to you but I am not signing any form" [371].) The North Carolina trial court threw out the confession because Butler didn't expressly waive his right to remain silent. The North Carolina supreme court affirmed. The U.S. Supreme Court reversed, adopting instead the **implied waiver test**.

According to Justice Stewart, writing for the majority, an express written or oral waiver of the right to remain silent and/or the right to counsel is "usually strong proof" that the waiver is valid, but it's not always

> either necessary or sufficient to establish waiver. The courts must presume that a defendant did not waive his rights; the prosecution's burden is great; but in at least some cases waiver can be clearly inferred from the actions and words of the person interrogated. [A valid waiver depends on] the particular facts and circumstances surrounding that case, including the background, experience, and conduct of the accused. (373–75)

Circumstances commonly considered in making the waiver determination are listed in Table 8.3, and examples of cases in which courts ruled there was a knowing waiver appear in Table 8.4.

In *Berghuis v. Thompkins* (2010), our next case excerpt, the U.S. Supreme Court revisited the waiver question in a contentious 5–4 decision.

In Berghuis v. Thompkins *(2010), the U.S. Supreme Court (5–4) held that criminal suspects who want to protect their right to remain silent have to speak up and unambiguously invoke it.*

CASE   Did He "Speak Up" and "Unambiguously" Invoke and Waive His Right to Remain Silent?

Berghuis v. Thompkins
130 S.Ct. 2250 (2010)

HISTORY

Van Chester Thompkins was charged with first-degree murder. The trial court denied his motion to suppress his confession. The jury convicted him and the judge sentenced him to life in prison without parole. Thompkins appealed. The Michigan Court of Appeals affirmed. The U.S. District Court denied his petition for habeas corpus. The U.S. Sixth Circuit Court of Appeals reversed. The U.S. Supreme Court granted certiorari. Mary Berghuis, the warden of a Michigan correctional facility is the petitioner here, and Van Chester Thompkins, who was convicted, is the respondent. The Supreme Court reversed the Sixth Circuit Court.

KENNEDY, J., joined by ROBERTS, C.J., and SCALIA, THOMAS, and ALITO, JJ.

FACTS

On January 10, 2000, a shooting occurred outside a mall in Southfield, Michigan. Among the victims was Samuel Morris, who died from multiple gunshot wounds. The other victim, Frederick France, recovered from his injuries and later testified. Thompkins, who was a suspect, fled. About one year later he was found in Ohio and arrested there. Two Southfield police officers traveled to Ohio to interrogate Thompkins, then awaiting transfer to Michigan. The interrogation began around 1:30 P.M. and lasted about three hours. The interrogation was conducted in a room that was 8 by 10 feet, and Thompkins sat in a chair that resembled a school desk (it had an arm on it that swings around to provide a surface to write on). At the beginning of the interrogation, one of the officers, Detective Helgert, presented Thompkins with a form derived from the *Miranda* rule. It stated:

Notification of constitutional rights and statement

1. You have the right to remain silent.
2. Anything you say can and will be used against you in a court of law.
3. You have a right to talk to a lawyer before answering any questions and you have the right to have a lawyer present with you while you are answering any questions.
4. If you cannot afford to hire a lawyer, one will be appointed to represent you before any questioning, if you wish one.
5. You have the right to decide at any time before or during questioning to use your right to remain silent and your right to talk with a lawyer while you are being questioned.

Helgert asked Thompkins to read the fifth warning out loud. Thompkins complied. Helgert later said this was to ensure that Thompkins could read, and Helgert concluded that Thompkins understood English. Helgert then read the other four *Miranda* warnings out loud and asked Thompkins to sign the form to demonstrate that he understood his rights. Thompkins declined to sign the form. The record contains conflicting evidence about whether Thompkins then verbally confirmed that he understood the rights listed on the form. At a suppression hearing, Helgert testified that Thompkins verbally confirmed that he understood his rights. At trial, Helgert stated, "I don't know that I orally asked him" whether Thompkins understood his rights.

Officers began an interrogation. At no point during the interrogation did Thompkins say that he wanted to remain silent, that he did not want to talk with the police, or that he wanted an attorney. Thompkins was "largely" silent during the interrogation, which lasted about three hours. He did give a few limited verbal responses, however, such as "yeah," "no," or "I don't know." And on occasion he communicated by nodding his head. Thompkins also said that he "didn't want a peppermint" that was offered to him by the police and that the chair he was "sitting in was hard."

About 2 hours and 45 minutes into the interrogation, Helgert asked Thompkins, "Do you believe in God?" Thompkins made eye contact with Helgert and said "Yes," as his eyes "welled up with tears." Helgert asked, "Do you pray to God?" Thompkins said "Yes." Helgert asked, "Do you pray to God to forgive you for shooting that boy down?" Thompkins answered "Yes" and looked away. Thompkins refused to make a written confession, and the interrogation ended about 15 minutes later.

OPINION

The *Miranda* Court formulated a warning that must be given to suspects before they can be subjected to custodial interrogation. All concede that the warning given in this case was in full compliance with these requirements. The dispute centers on the response—or nonresponse—from the suspect.

Thompkins contends that he invoked his privilege to remain silent by not saying anything for a sufficient period of time, so the interrogation should have ceased before he made his inculpatory statements. This argument is unpersuasive. In the context of invoking the *Miranda* right to counsel, the Court in *Davis v. United States* (1994) held that a suspect must do so "unambiguously." If an accused makes a statement concerning the right to counsel "that is ambiguous or equivocal" or makes no statement, the police are not required to end the interrogation, or ask questions to clarify whether the accused wants to invoke his or her *Miranda* rights.

There is good reason to require an accused who wants to invoke his or her right to remain silent to do so unambiguously. A requirement of an unambiguous invocation of *Miranda* rights results in an objective inquiry that avoids difficulties of proof and provides guidance to officers on how to proceed in the face of ambiguity. If an ambiguous act, omission, or statement could require police to end the interrogation, police would be required to make difficult decisions about an accused's unclear intent and face the consequence of suppression if they guess wrong. Suppression of a voluntary confession in these circumstances would place a significant burden on society's interest in prosecuting criminal activity. Thompkins did not say that he wanted to remain silent or that he did not want to talk with the police. Had he made either of these simple, unambiguous statements, he would have invoked his right to cut off questioning. Here he did neither, so he did not invoke his right to remain silent.

We next consider whether Thompkins waived his right to remain silent. Even absent the accused's invocation of the right to remain silent, the accused's statement during a custodial interrogation is inadmissible at trial unless the prosecution can establish that the accused in fact knowingly and voluntarily waived *Miranda* rights when making the statement. The waiver inquiry has two distinct dimensions: waiver must be voluntary in the sense that it was the product of a free and deliberate choice rather than intimidation, coercion, or deception, and made with a full awareness of both the nature of the right being abandoned and the consequences of the decision to abandon it.

The record in this case shows that Thompkins waived his right to remain silent. There is no basis in this case to conclude that he did not understand his rights; and on these facts it follows that he chose not to invoke or rely on those rights when he did speak. First, there is no contention that Thompkins did not understand his rights; and from this it follows that he knew what he gave up when he spoke. There was more than enough evidence in the record to conclude that Thompkins understood his *Miranda* rights. Thompkins received a written copy of the *Miranda* warnings; Detective Helgert determined that Thompkins could read and understand English; and Thompkins was given time to read the warnings. Thompkins, furthermore, read aloud the fifth warning, which stated that "you have the right to decide at any time before or during questioning to use your right to remain silent and your right to talk with a lawyer while you are being questioned." He was thus aware that his right to remain silent would not dissipate after a certain amount of time and that police would have to honor his right to be silent and his right to counsel during the whole course of interrogation. Those rights, the warning made clear, could be asserted at any time. Helgert, moreover, read the warnings aloud.

Second, Thompkins's answer to Detective Helgert's question about whether Thompkins prayed to God for forgiveness for shooting the victim is a "course of conduct indicating waiver" of the right to remain silent. If Thompkins wanted to remain silent, he could have said nothing in response to Helgert's questions, or he could have unambiguously invoked his *Miranda* rights and ended the interrogation. The fact that Thompkins made a statement about three hours after receiving a *Miranda* warning does not overcome the fact that he engaged in a course of conduct indicating waiver. Police are not required to rewarn suspects from time to time. Thompkins's answer to Helgert's question about praying to God for forgiveness for shooting the victim was sufficient to show a course of conduct indicating waiver. This is confirmed by the fact that before then Thompkins had given sporadic answers to questions throughout the interrogation.

Third, there is no evidence that Thompkins's statement was coerced. Thompkins does not claim that police threatened or injured him during the interrogation or that he was in any way fearful. The interrogation was conducted in a standard-sized room in the middle of the afternoon. It is true that apparently he was in a straight-backed chair for three hours, but there is no authority for the proposition that an interrogation of this length is inherently coercive. Indeed, even where interrogations of greater duration were held to be improper, they were accompanied, as this one was not, by other facts indicating coercion, such as an incapacitated and sedated suspect, sleep and food deprivation, and threats. The fact that Helgert's question referred to Thompkins's religious beliefs also did not render Thompkins's statement involuntary. The Fifth Amendment privilege is not concerned with moral and psychological pressures to confess emanating from sources other than official coercion. In these circumstances, Thompkins knowingly and voluntarily made a statement to police, so he waived his right to remain silent.

The judgment of the Court of Appeals is REVERSED, and the case is REMANDED with instructions to deny the petition.

It is so ordered.

DISSENT

SOTOMAYOR, J., joined by STEVENS, GINSBURG, and BREYER JJ.

The Court concludes today that a criminal suspect waives his right to remain silent if, after sitting tacit and uncommunicative through nearly three hours of police interrogation, he utters a few one-word responses. The Court also concludes that a suspect who wishes to guard his right to remain silent against such a finding of waiver must, counterintuitively, speak—and must do so with sufficient precision to satisfy a clear-statement rule that construes ambiguity in favor of the police. Both propositions mark a substantial retreat from the protection against compelled self-incrimination that *Miranda v. Arizona* (1966) has long provided during custodial interrogation. Because I believe that Thompkins' statements were admitted at trial without the prosecution having carried its burden to show that he waived his right to remain silent, I respectfully dissent.

The strength of Thompkins' *Miranda* claims depends in large part on the circumstances of the 3-hour interrogation, at the end of which he made inculpatory statements later introduced at trial. The Court's opinion downplays record evidence that Thompkins remained almost completely silent and unresponsive throughout that session. One of the interrogating officers, Detective Helgert, testified that although Thompkins was administered *Miranda* warnings, the last of which he read aloud, Thompkins expressly declined to sign a written acknowledgment that he had been advised of and understood his rights. There is conflicting evidence in the record about whether Thompkins ever verbally confirmed understanding his rights. The record contains no indication that the officers sought or obtained an express waiver.

As to the interrogation itself, Helgert candidly characterized it as "very, very one-sided" and "nearly a monologue." Thompkins was "peculiar," "sullen," and "generally quiet." Helgert and his partner "did most of the talking," as Thompkins was "not verbally communicative" and "largely" remained silent. To the extent Thompkins gave any response, his answers consisted of "a word or two. A 'yeah,' or a 'no,' or 'I don't know.' . . . And sometimes . . . he simply sat down . . . with his head in his hands looking down. Sometimes . . . he would look up and make eye-contact would be the only response." After proceeding in this fashion for approximately 2 hours and 45 minutes, Helgert asked Thompkins three questions relating to his faith in God. The prosecution relied at trial on Thompkins' one-word answers of "yes."

Even when warnings have been administered and a suspect has not affirmatively invoked his rights, statements made in custodial interrogation may not be admitted as part of the prosecution's case in chief unless and until the prosecution demonstrates that an individual knowingly and intelligently waived his rights. It is undisputed here that Thompkins never expressly waived his right to remain silent. His refusal to sign even an acknowledgment that he understood his *Miranda* rights evinces, if anything, an intent not to waive those rights. That Thompkins did not make the inculpatory statements at issue until after approximately 2 hours and 45 minutes of interrogation serves as strong evidence against waiver.

Today's decision ignores the important interests *Miranda* safeguards. The underlying constitutional guarantee against self-incrimination reflects many of our fundamental values and most noble aspirations, our society's preference for an accusatorial rather than an inquisitorial system of criminal justice; a fear that self-incriminating statements will be elicited by inhumane treatment and abuses and a resulting distrust of self-deprecatory statements; and a realization that while the privilege is sometimes a shelter to the guilty, it is often a protection to the innocent.

For these reasons, we have observed, a criminal law system which comes to depend on the confession will, in the long run, be less reliable and more subject to abuses than a system relying on independent investigation. By bracing against the possibility of unreliable statements in every instance of in-custody interrogation, *Miranda*'s prophylactic rules serve to protect the fairness of the trial itself. Today's decision bodes poorly for the fundamental principles that *Miranda* protects.

Today's decision turns *Miranda* upside down. Criminal suspects must now unambiguously invoke their right to remain silent—which, counterintuitively, requires them to speak. At the same time, suspects will be legally presumed to have waived their rights even if they have given no clear expression of their intent to do so. Those results, in my view, find no basis in *Miranda* or our subsequent cases and are inconsistent with the fair-trial principles on which those precedents are grounded. I respectfully dissent.

QUESTIONS

1. List all the facts relevant to deciding whether Van Chester Thompkins (a) invoked his right to remain silent, and, if he did (b) whether he at some point waived it.

2. Summarize the majority's arguments for holding that Thompkins (a) didn't invoke his right to remain silent, but, if he did, that (b) he later waived it.

3. Summarize the dissent's arguments that Detective Helgert and his partner violated Thompkins's right to remain silent.

4. Which side has the better arguments? Which side do you agree with more? Explain your answers.

5. After you've read the section "False Confessions" (p. 290), return to question 4. Would you now answer it differently? Explain why or why not.

|||||||||||||||||||||||||||||||||||||||||||||||||||||||||||||||||||||||||||||||||||||||||||||||||||||||||||||||||||||||

Voluntary Self-Incrimination

Great fears and equally great hopes—depending on whether those who voiced them were more afraid of street criminals or of government abuse of power—were expressed that *Miranda v. Arizona* (1966) would kill police interrogation as a tool to collect evidence. But it didn't happen. As we've already learned, Richard Leo found that only 25 percent of suspects invoke their right to remain silent and/or to speak to a lawyer (p. 280). One experienced interrogator, Sergeant James DeConcini (now retired), of the Minneapolis Police Department, suggests the reason is that knowledge is a two-way street. Not only do police officers want to find out what suspects know about crimes they're investigating, but suspects also want to know how much police officers know. Suspects believe that by cooperating with the police, they might find out if they "have something on them."

That most suspects waive their right to remain silent and agree to custodial interrogation brings us back to the due process requirement of voluntariness. Even if officers have warned suspects and gotten a knowing waiver, they still may not have gotten the incriminating statements that follow voluntarily. (See also "False Confessions" later in the chapter.)

To determine whether incriminating statements were made voluntarily, the U.S. Supreme Court adopted another of its totality-of-circumstances tests: Confessions are involuntary only if the totality of the circumstances proves two things:

1. Officers engaged in coercive conduct during the interrogation.

2. The coercive conduct caused the suspect to make incriminating statements.

The most common circumstances courts consider in determining whether coercive state action caused people to confess include the following:

- The location where the questioning took place

- Whether the suspect initiated the contact with law enforcement

- Whether the *Miranda* warnings were given

- The number of interrogators

- The length of the questioning

- Whether food, water, and toilet facilities were denied

- Whether the police used threats, promises, lies, or tricks

- Whether the suspect was denied access to a lawyer

- The suspect's characteristics, such as age, gender, race, physical and mental condition, education, drug problems, and experience with the criminal justice system

Courts have ruled that none of the following actions caused suspects to confess (*Twenty-Sixth Annual Review of Criminal Procedure* 1997, 967–68):

- Promises of leniency
- Promises of treatment
- Confronting the accused with other evidence of guilt
- The interrogator's appeal to the defendant's emotions
- False and misleading statements made by the interrogator

In our next case excerpt, *Colorado v. Connelly* (1986), the U.S. Supreme Court ruled that Francis Connelly's confession was voluntary even though his serious mental illness led him to believe God ordered him to "confess or commit suicide."

> *In our next case excerpt,* **Colorado v. Connelly**
> *(1986), the U.S. Supreme Court ruled that*
> *Francis Connelly's confession was voluntary*
> *even though his serious mental illness led*
> *him to believe God ordered him to "confess or*
> *commit suicide."*

CASE Did He Confess Voluntarily?

Colorado v. Connelly
479 U.S. 157 (1986)

HISTORY

The trial court suppressed statements made by Francis Barry Connelly. The state appealed. The Colorado Supreme Court affirmed. The U.S. Supreme Court granted certiorari, reversed, and remanded the case.

REHNQUIST, C.J., joined by WHITE, POWELL, O'CONNOR, and SCALIA, JJ., and, in all but Part III-A, BLACKMUN, J.

FACTS

On August 18, 1983, Officer Patrick Anderson of the Denver Police Department was in uniform, working in an off-duty capacity in downtown Denver. Francis Connelly approached Officer Anderson and, without any prompting, stated he had murdered someone and wanted to talk about it. Anderson immediately advised Connelly he had the right to remain silent, that anything he said could be used against him in court, and that he had the right to an attorney prior to any police questioning. Connelly stated that he understood these rights but he still wanted to talk about the murder. Understandably bewildered by this confession, Officer Anderson asked Connelly several questions.

Connelly denied he had been drinking, denied he had been taking any drugs, and stated that, in the past, he had been a patient in several mental hospitals. Officer Anderson again told Connelly he was under no obligation to say anything. Connelly replied it was "all right," and that he would talk to Officer Anderson because his conscience had been bothering him. To Officer Anderson, Connelly appeared to understand fully the nature of his acts.

Shortly thereafter, Homicide Detective Stephen Antuna arrived. Connelly was again advised of his rights, and Detective Antuna asked him "what he had on his mind." Connelly answered that he had come all the way from Boston to confess to the murder of Mary Ann Junta, a young girl whom he had killed in Denver sometime during November 1982. Connelly was taken to police headquarters, and a search of police records revealed that the body of an unidentified female had been found in April 1983. Connelly openly detailed his story to Detective Antuna and Sergeant Thomas Haney, and readily agreed to take the officers to the scene of the killing. Under Connelly's sole direction, the two officers and Connelly proceeded in a police vehicle to the location of the crime.

Connelly pointed out the exact location of the murder. Throughout this episode, Detective Antuna perceived no indication whatsoever that Connelly was suffering from any kind of mental illness. Connelly was held overnight.

During an interview with the public defender's office the following morning, he became visibly disoriented. He began giving confused answers to questions, and for the first time, stated "voices" had told him to come to Denver and he had followed the directions of these voices in confessing. Connelly was sent to a state hospital for evaluation. He was initially found incompetent to assist in his own defense. By March 1984, however, the doctors evaluating Connelly determined he was competent to proceed to trial.

At a preliminary hearing, Connelly moved to suppress all of his statements. Dr. Jeffrey Metzner, a psychiatrist employed by the state hospital, testified that Connelly was suffering from chronic schizophrenia and was in a psychotic state at least as of August 17, 1983, the day before he confessed. Metzner's interviews with Connelly revealed that he was following the "voice of God." This voice instructed him to withdraw money from the bank, to buy an airplane ticket, and to fly from Boston to Denver. When he arrived from Boston, God's voice became stronger and told him either to confess to the killing or to commit suicide. Reluctantly following the command of the voices, he approached Officer Anderson and confessed.

Dr. Metzner testified that, in his expert opinion, Connelly was experiencing "command hallucinations." This condition interfered with his "volitional abilities—that is, his ability to make free and rational choices." Dr. Metzner further testified that Connelly's illness did not significantly impair his cognitive abilities. Thus, he understood the rights he had when Officer Anderson and Detective Antuna advised him that he need not speak. Dr. Metzner admitted that the "voices" could in reality be Connelly's interpretation of his own guilt, but explained that in his opinion, Connelly's psychosis motivated his confession.

Although the Colorado trial court found that the police had done nothing wrong or coercive in securing Connelly's confession, his illness destroyed his volition and compelled him to confess. The trial court also found that Connelly's mental state vitiated his attempted waiver of the right to counsel and the privilege against compulsory self-incrimination. Accordingly, Connelly's initial statements and his custodial confession were suppressed. The Colorado Supreme Court affirmed the trial court's decision to suppress all of Connelly's statements.

OPINION

The cases considered by this Court over the 50 years since *Brown v. Mississippi* have focused upon the crucial element of police overreaching. While each confession case has turned on its own set of factors justifying the conclusion that police conduct was oppressive, all have contained a substantial element of coercive police conduct. Absent police conduct causally related to the confession, there is simply no basis for concluding that any state actor has deprived a criminal defendant of due process of law.

Connelly correctly notes that as interrogators have turned to more subtle forms of psychological persuasion, courts have found the mental condition of the defendant a more significant factor in the "voluntariness" calculus. But this fact does not justify a conclusion that a defendant's mental condition, by itself and apart from its relation to official coercion, should ever dispose of the inquiry into constitutional "voluntariness."

Our "involuntary confession" jurisprudence is entirely consistent with the settled law requiring some sort of "state action" to support a claim of violation of the Due Process Clause of the Fourteenth Amendment. The Colorado trial court found that the police committed no wrongful acts, and that finding has been neither challenged by Connelly nor disturbed by the Supreme Court of Colorado. The latter court, however, concluded that sufficient state action was present by virtue of the admission of the confession into evidence in a court of the State. The difficulty with the approach of the Supreme Court of Colorado is that it fails to recognize the essential link between coercive activity of the State, on the one hand, and a resulting confession by a defendant, on the other.

The flaw in Connelly's constitutional argument is that it would expand our previous line of "voluntariness" cases into a far-ranging requirement that courts must divine a defendant's motivation for speaking or acting as he did even though there be no claim that governmental conduct coerced his decision. We have previously cautioned against expanding currently applicable exclusionary rules by erecting additional barriers to placing truthful and probative evidence before state juries. We abide by that counsel now.

The central purpose of a criminal trial is to decide the factual question of the defendant's guilt or innocence, and while we have previously held that exclusion of evidence may be necessary to protect constitutional guarantees, both the necessity for the collateral inquiry and the exclusion of evidence deflect a criminal trial from its basic purpose. Connelly would now have us require sweeping inquiries into the state of mind of a criminal defendant who has confessed, inquiries quite divorced from any coercion brought to bear on the defendant by the State.

We think the Constitution rightly leaves this sort of inquiry to be resolved by state laws governing the admission of evidence and erects no standard of its own in this area. A statement rendered by one in the condition of Connelly might be proved to be quite unreliable, but this is a matter to be governed by the evidentiary laws of the forum, and not by the Due Process Clause of the Fourteenth Amendment.

We hold that coercive police activity is a necessary predicate to the finding that a confession is not "voluntary" within the meaning of the Due Process Clause of the Fourteenth Amendment. We also conclude that the taking of Connelly's statements, and their admission into evidence, constitute no violation of that Clause.

We think that the Supreme Court of Colorado erred in importing into this area of constitutional law notions of "free will" that have no place there. The sole concern of the Fifth Amendment, on which *Miranda* was based, is governmental coercion. Indeed, the Fifth Amendment privilege is not concerned with moral and psychological pressures to confess emanating from sources other than official coercion. The voluntariness of a waiver of this privilege has always depended on the absence of police overreaching, not on "free choice" in any broader sense of the word.

Connelly urges this Court to adopt his "free will" rationale, and to find an attempted waiver invalid whenever the defendant feels compelled to waive his rights by reason of any compulsion, even if the compulsion does not flow from the police. But such a treatment of the waiver issue would "cut this Court's holding in *Miranda* completely loose from its own explicitly stated rationale." *Miranda* protects defendants against government coercion leading them to surrender rights protected by the Fifth Amendment; it goes no further than that. Connelly's perception of coercion flowing from the "voice of God," however important or significant such a perception may be in other disciplines, is a matter to which the United States Constitution does not speak.

The judgment of the Supreme Court of Colorado is accordingly REVERSED, and the cause is REMANDED for further proceedings not inconsistent with this opinion. . . .

DISSENT

BRENNAN, J., joined by MARSHALL, J.

Today the Court denies Mr. Connelly his fundamental right to make a vital choice with a sane mind, involving a determination that could allow the State to deprive him of liberty or even life. This holding is unprecedented: Surely in the present stage of our civilization a most basic sense of justice is affronted by the spectacle of incarcerating a human being upon the basis of a statement he made while insane. Because I believe that the use of a mentally ill person's involuntary confession is antithetical to the notion of fundamental fairness embodied in the Due Process Clause, I dissent.

Connelly's seriously impaired mental condition is clear on the record of this case. At the time of his confession, Mr. Connelly suffered from a "longstanding severe mental disorder," diagnosed as chronic paranoid schizophrenia. He had been hospitalized for psychiatric reasons five times prior to his confession; his longest hospitalization lasted for seven months. Mr. Connelly heard imaginary voices and saw nonexistent objects. He believed that his father was God, and that he was a reincarnation of Jesus.

The state trial court found that the "overwhelming evidence presented by the Defense" indicated that the prosecution did not meet its burden of demonstrating by a preponderance of the evidence that the initial statement to Officer Anderson was voluntary. While the court found no police misconduct, it held: There's no question that the Defendant did not exercise free will in choosing to talk to the police. He exercised a choice both of which were mandated by auditory hallucination, had no basis in reality, and were the product of a psychotic break with reality. The Defendant at the time of the confession had absolutely in the Court's estimation no volition or choice to make.

The absence of police wrongdoing should not, by itself, determine the voluntariness of a confession by a mentally ill person. The requirement that a confession be voluntary reflects a recognition of the importance of free will and of reliability in determining the admissibility of a confession, and thus demands an inquiry into the totality of the circumstances surrounding the confession. Today's decision restricts the application of the term "involuntary" to those confessions obtained by police coercion.

Confessions by mentally ill individuals or by persons coerced by parties other than police officers are now considered "voluntary." The Court's failure to recognize all forms of involuntariness or coercion as antithetical to due process reflects a refusal to acknowledge free will as a value of constitutional consequence. But due process derives much of its meaning from a conception of fundamental fairness that emphasizes the right to make vital choices voluntarily: The Fourteenth Amendment secures against state invasion the right of a person to remain silent unless he chooses to speak in the unfettered exercise of his own will. This right requires vigilant protection if we are to safeguard the values of private conscience and human dignity.

A true commitment to fundamental fairness requires that the inquiry be not whether the conduct of state officers in obtaining the confession is shocking, but whether the confession was free and voluntary. Since the Court redefines voluntary confessions to include confessions by mentally ill individuals, the reliability of these confessions becomes a central concern. A concern for reliability is inherent in our criminal justice system, which relies upon accusatorial rather than inquisitorial practices. While an inquisitorial system prefers obtaining confessions from criminal defendants, an accusatorial system must place its faith in determinations of guilt by evidence independently and freely secured.

In *Escobedo v. Illinois* (1964), we justified our reliance upon accusatorial practices: We have learned the lesson of history, ancient and modern, that a system of criminal law enforcement which comes to depend on the "confession" will, in the long run, be less reliable and more subject to abuses than a system which depends on extrinsic evidence independently secured through skillful investigation.

I dissent.

QUESTIONS

1. List all the facts relevant to deciding whether Francis Connelly's confession was voluntary.
2. What are the two parts of the test that the U.S. Supreme Court announced for determining whether confessions are voluntary?
3. Do you agree with the majority that the confession was voluntary? If yes, what persuaded you? If no, do you agree with the dissent? Explain why.

EXPLORING FURTHER

··

Voluntary Self-Incrimination

Was He Coerced by a Private Person?

State v. Bowe, 881 P.2d 538 (1994)

FACTS On January 21, 1990, a brawl involving a number of individuals occurred at one of the dormitory buildings on the University of Hawai`i-Manoa (UH) campus. During the fight, Steven Oshiro (Victim) was beaten and sustained physical injuries.

On February 9, 1990, Sergeant John Pinero (Sergeant Pinero) of the Honolulu Police Department (HPD) contacted Wallace, head coach of the UH Men's Basketball Team. He requested Wallace's assistance in making arrangements for the police to interview certain members of the basketball team, who were suspected of being involved in the January 21, 1990, fight. Sergeant Pinero provided Wallace with a list of suspects that included Troy Bowe. Wallace later told Bowe that he needed to go to the police station and that he would go with him if he required assistance.

On February 12, 1990, Bowe went to the police station accompanied by Wallace. Bowe was given *Miranda* warnings and subsequently signed an HPD Form 81, waiving his constitutional rights to counsel and to remain silent. After waiving his constitutional rights, an interrogation commenced in which Bowe admitted assaulting the victim.

On September 17, 1991, an Oahu Grand Jury indicted Defendant and Vincent Smalls for Assault in the Second Degree. On November 21, 1991, Bowe filed a Motion to suppress evidence on the grounds that his February 12, 1990, statement to the police was involuntary because it was obtained through the use of official state coercion in violation of Bowe's constitutional right to due process. On May 8, 1992, the circuit court granted Bowe's motion to suppress.

In determining that Defendant's statement was coerced, the circuit court entered the following findings of fact:

1. On or about January or February of 1990, Sergeant John Pinero was an employee of the [HPD], who was at that time working on an investigation of an assault which allegedly involved TROY BOWE.

2. In his capacity as a police officer with the [HPD], Sergeant Pinero called Riley Wallace, at that time basketball coach of the University of Hawaii at Manoa Basketball Team (hereinafter "Basketball Team"), and gave Wallace a list of suspects who were on the Basketball Team that Sergeant Pinero wanted Wallace to bring down to the [HPD] (hereinafter "List").

3. Wallace, as head basketball coach, had the authority to suspend athletes or remove them from the Basketball Team and, in the case of scholarship-athletes, to initiate procedures to withdraw their athletic-scholarships.

4. TROY BOWE was a scholarship-athlete on the Basketball Team.

5. TROY BOWE was on said List.

6. Sergeant Pinero specifically asked Wallace to locate the individuals on the List and have them meet with Sergeant Pinero.

7. Sergeant Pinero, however, did not request that Wallace use force or coercion while attempting to have individuals on the List meet with Sergeant Pinero.

8. Wallace then contacted Defendant TROY BOWE and informed him that he had to go down to the [HPD] to meet with Sergeant Pinero.

9. Wallace informed TROY BOWE that Wallace would accompany him to the [HPD] in place of an attorney and instructed TROY BOWE to make a statement to Sergeant Pinero.

10. Wallace did not inform TROY BOWE that he could or should have an attorney present with him when he went to be interviewed by Sergeant Pinero.

11. TROY BOWE believed that he could not refuse to follow Wallace's directions because if he did so Wallace could suspend him from the Basketball Team or institute procedures to revoke Defendant TROY BOWE's athletic-scholarship.

Was the coercive conduct of Coach Wallace, a private person, sufficient to render Bowe's confession inadmissible?

DECISION Yes, said the Hawaii supreme court.

OPINION While the Supreme Court in *Connelly* stated that, "the sole concern of the Fifth Amendment is governmental coercion," we have recognized that one of the basic considerations underlying the exclusion of confessions obtained through coercion is the "inherent untrustworthiness of involuntary confessions." Accordingly, we reject the Supreme Court's narrow focus on police coercion in *Connelly*.

We recognize that an individual's capacity to make a rational and free choice between confessing and remaining silent may be overborne as much by the coercive conduct of a private individual as by the coercive conduct of the police. [Therefore,] we hold that the coercive conduct of a private person may be sufficient to render a confession inadmissible based on article 1, sections 5 and 10 of the Hawaii Constitution.

Nevertheless, we acknowledge that some sort of state action is required to support a defendant's claim that his due process rights were violated. Although no state action is involved where an accused is coerced into making a confession by a private individual, we find that the state participates in that violation by allowing the coerced statements to be used as evidence.

What happens when the self-incriminatory confession given is false? We turn next to the troubling and tragic issue of false confessions.

||||||||||||||||||||||||||||||||||||||||||||||||||||||||||||||||||||||||||||||||||||||||||||||||||||||||||||||||||||||||||||||||||||||||||||

False Confessions: Popular Belief and Empirical Evidence

LO 8

There are no scientific estimates of the numbers of false confessions, or of how many of them lead to convicting innocent people. Most police departments—and other organizations, for that matter—don't routinely collect, analyze, and report interrogation information. Furthermore, most police departments don't record interrogations and confessions. So it's difficult, if not impossible, to find out if confessions are true. This doesn't mean that the study of police interrogation and false confessions is useless. Social scientists can still understand and explain how and why false confessions occur, even if they can't estimate the number and rates that occur (Drizin and Leo 2003–4, 930–31).

Steven Drizin and Richard Leo (2003–4) examined 125 *proven* cases of individuals who confessed to crimes they didn't commit. Drizin and Leo "proved" the confessions were false in four ways:

1. *The crime didn't happen.* For example, an Alabama jury convicted three mentally retarded defendants of killing Victoria Banks's unborn child; Banks wasn't capable of getting pregnant.

2. *The defendant couldn't have committed the crime.* For example, jail records proved that Mario Hayes, Miguel Castillo, and Peter Williams were locked up when the crimes they confessed to were committed.

3. *The actual criminal is proven to have committed the crime.* For example, Christopher Ochoa, a former high school honor student confessed to raping and murdering Nancy DePriest in an Austin, Texas, Pizza Hut. He was freed when Achim Marino came forward and admitted that he killed DePriest. Marino led authorities to the weapon he used and the bag he put the money in.

4. *DNA evidence exonerated the defendant.* For example, Michael Crowe, Joshua Treadway, and Aaron Houser confessed to murdering Crowe's 12-year-old sister. DNA testing proved that blood found on mentally ill Richard Tuite's sweatshirt matched the victim's. (925–26)

What did Drizin and Leo learn about *proven* false confessions beyond the fact that people do confess to crimes they didn't commit? Here are some of their findings:

1. 101 out of 125 (81%) proven innocent defendants who decided to go to trial were convicted—wrongly—"beyond a reasonable doubt," even though their confessions were later proved false (995–96).

2. More than 80 percent of interrogations lasted more than 6 hours; half lasted more than 12 hours. The average length was 16.3 hours, the median was 12 hours. Drizin and Leo found these figures "especially striking" compared to Leo's earlier observation of 500 routine police interrogations, where the average interrogation lasted less than 2 hours (948).

3. "Virtually all false confessions result in some deprivation of the false confessor's liberty" (949). Of course, some of these are false confessions that lead to conviction. But even those who weren't convicted still lost significant time locked up before exoneration. And they suffered other losses as well, including the stigma of a criminal accusation; damage to their personal and professional reputation; loss of income and savings; loss of their job; separation and divorce; and emotional strain (949–50).

4. The most vulnerable populations (84 out of 125) are overrepresented in the sample, including:

   a. 44 juveniles under 18 (7 under 14)

   b. 28 mentally retarded

   c. 12 mentally ill (963–74)

5. "The 125 *proven* false confessions may be a more serious problem than previously imagined" (996).

In the remainder of this chapter, we look more closely at false confessions, including (1) why people confess to crimes they didn't commit, (2) the impact of those false confessions, and (3) reforms that aim to reduce false confessions.

Why Do Innocent People Confess to Crimes They Didn't Commit?

LO 8

Researchers divide proven false confessions into three categories:

1. Voluntary false confessions

2. Compliant false confessions

3. Internalized false confessions (Kassin and Gudjonsson 2004, 46)

1. *Voluntary False Confessions.* Some innocent people confess without police prompting or pressure. These confessions are called **voluntary false confessions**. Why do innocent people confess? Possible reasons include (1) a desire for notoriety; (2) a need for self-punishment to remove guilt feelings; (3) an inability to separate reality from fantasy; and (4) a desire to help and protect the real criminal. But there are many more. In one case, an innocent man confessed to murder to impress his girlfriend. Another innocent man, angry with the police for arresting him while he was drinking at a party, confessed to murder to get revenge by misleading the police (49).

2. *Compliant False Confessions.* Some innocent people confess because of police pressure during custodial interrogation. **Compliant confessions** are "mere acts of public compliance by a suspect who comes to believe that the short-term benefits of confession . . . outweigh the long-term costs." Suspects give in to demands for admissions and confessions for instrumental reasons: to escape an uncomfortable situation; to avoid a threat; or to receive a reward. Specific incentives for compliant false confessions include being allowed to sleep, eat, make a phone call, or go home (49–50).

3. *Internalized False Confessions.* Innocent, but vulnerable, suspects subjected to "highly suggestive interrogation tactics" come not just to give in to get the situation

over with but to believe that they actually committed the crime. One frequently cited tragic example of **internalized false confession** is the case of 18-year-old Peter Reilly. Although Reilly called the police immediately after he discovered his murdered mother, the police suspected that Reilly murdered her. After they gained his trust, his interrogators told Reilly that he failed his lie detector test (a lie), and that the test indicated that he was guilty even though he couldn't remember killing his mother.

After hours of "relentless interrogation, Reilly underwent a chilling transformation from adamant denial through confusion, self-doubt, conversion ('Well, it really looks like I did it'), and eventual full confession ('I remember slashing once at my mother's throat with a straight razor I used for model airplanes. . . . I also remember jumping on my mother's legs')." Two years later, evidence proved that Reilly couldn't have killed his mother (50).

Studies of wrongful convictions based on these *proven innocent* people's false confessions stem from two sources: (1) certain police interrogation techniques and (2) jurors' belief in the confessions. When innocent people confessed, went to trial, and pleaded guilty, jury conviction rates ranged from 73 percent, in one study, to 81 percent in a second (56).

These figures led Drizin and Leo (2004) to conclude that confession evidence is "inherently prejudicial and highly damaging to a defendant, even if it is the product of coercive interrogation, and even if it is ultimately proven false beyond any reasonable doubt" (959).

The Impact of False Confessions

LO 8

Do juries uncritically accept confessions, even if they're the product of coercive interrogation? And can ordinary people, in general, and law enforcement professionals, in particular, tell the difference between true and false confessions? Let's look at the psychological experts' answers to these questions.

According to Kassin and Gudjonsson (2004, 56), research in a wide variety of settings shows that jurors may credit confessions obtained during "high pressure" interrogation methods because of **fundamental attribution error**. They overestimate the role of defendants' "nature" (disposition) in evaluating their actions, while they underestimate the role of the interrogation situation. The explanation for this error is that people tend to "draw quick and automatic inferences, taking behavior at face value, but then because of a lack of motivation or cognitive capacity fail to adjust or correct for situational influences" (56–57).

The impact of false confessions doesn't stop with its influence on juries. False confessions tend to "overwhelm other information, such as alibis and other evidence of innocence, resulting in a chain of adverse legal consequences—from arrest through guilty pleas, prosecution, and conviction, and incarceration." For example, Bruce Godschalk spent 15 years in prison until DNA exonerated him from two rape convictions. Even so, the Montgomery County, Pennsylvania, district attorney, Bruce L. Castor Jr., whose office convicted Godschalk, refused to let him out of prison, saying that he believed Godschalk was guilty and that the DNA testing was flawed. Asked what scientific basis he had for concluding that the testing was flawed, Castor said, "I have no scientific basis. I know because I trust my detective and my tape-recorded confession. Therefore the results must be flawed until someone proves to me otherwise" (Rimer 2002, A18).

Do people know a false confession when they hear one? The research has "yielded sobering results." Experiments in the lab showed that student observers didn't do better than chance in picking out false from true confessions (Kassin and Gudjonsson 2004, 57–58). What about police professionals in actual crimes? Let's look closer at Kassin, Meissner, and Norwick's 2005 study.

They recruited male prisoners to take part in a pair of videotaped interviews. For one interview, the researchers instructed each inmate to give a full confession to the crime they were sent to prison for. In the second interview, prisoners were given a brief description of a crime committed by one of the other prisoners and told to make up a false confession to it. The prisoners were paired so that each inmate's true confession was paired with another prisoner's false confession to the same crime.

Then, researchers used five of the true confessions and their five false counterparts to create a videotape depicting ten different prisoners confessing to aggravated assault, armed robbery, burglary, breaking and entering, or car theft. They also made auditory tapes of the same confessions to correct for research finding that people are better lie detectors when they use auditory instead of visual cues, which are often misleading. College students and law enforcement officers judged both the video and audio taped confession interviews.

The result: Neither the students nor the officers produced "high rates of accuracy," although the officers were more confident in their performance than the students. Accuracy improved when the subjects listened to the audio tapes. Students, but not the police, exceeded chance in this performance, although once again the police officers were more confident. Officers didn't differ from students in their hit rate, but they exceeded the students in the number of false positives. Officers included those with extensive law enforcement experience and those with special training in interviewing and interrogation. This result doesn't show that police are predisposed to see deception but, instead, to infer guilt—an "inference that rested upon a tendency to believe false confessions" (Kassin and Gudjonsson 2004, 58)

Why did police officers not do better at distinguishing false from true confessions? And why did "naïve" college students exceed officers' accuracy? Kassin and Gudjonsson offer two possible reasons. First, law enforcement officers *may* introduce a bias that reduces accuracy. This possible explanation draws support from findings that police are trained to be suspicious and to see deception in other people. Second, the experiment's design (half the confessions were false) might have compromised the officers' judgment accuracy. Law enforcement work might lead to officers' reasonable belief that most confessions are true; hence, they import their bias from the station to the study.

In a second study, Kassin, Meissner, and Norwick (2005) told subjects that half the confessions were true and half were false. This manipulation reduced the total number of "true" confession judgments and also reduced the number of "false positives." But the police still maintained a pattern of low accuracy and high confidence compared to the students (58).

Reforms Aimed at Reducing the False Confession Problem

LO 8

DNA exonerations have proven that about 25 percent of the wrong convictions were due to innocent people confessing to crimes they didn't commit (Innocence Project 2010). In light of these cases, many of which were highly publicized, and advances in psychological research, calls for reform in interrogation and confession procedures have grown among social scientists. They want collaboration among law enforcement professionals, prosecutors, defense attorneys, judges, policy makers, and social scientists to evaluate current interrogation and confession practices. All these parties agree that the objective of interrogation is to obtain confessions from *guilty* suspects and not from *innocent* people (Kassin and Gudjonsson 2004, 59).

A few state legislatures, courts, and police departments have implemented some reforms.

We'll look at three of these proposed reforms: (1) reducing the length of time in custody and interrogation; (2) eliminating police use of false information during interrogations; and (3) videotaping interrogations and confessions.

Limit Time in Custody and Interrogation

Psychological research has documented that the "human needs for belonging, affiliation, and social support, especially in times of stress, are a fundamental human motive" (Kassin and Gudjonsson 2004, 60). Prolonged custody and interrogation can lead suspects to confess to escape these deprivations. Although most *documented* interrogations last for less than two hours, proven false confessions resulted from interrogations that lasted much longer (average 16.3 hours) (Drizin and Leo 2004). In the infamous Central Park Jogger false confession case, the five boys underwent interrogation from 14 to 30 hours before they confessed falsely to beating and raping the jogger. At this time, no rules regulate the length of time of interrogation and custody.

Restrict Police Use of False Information during Interrogations

Bluntly, we're talking here about police lies to suspects, such as telling suspects that nonexistent eyewitnesses identified them; officers found their fingerprints, hair, or blood when they didn't; or that they failed a lie detector test when they actually passed.

The U.S. Supreme Court has explicitly sanctioned police use of lies as part of the totality of circumstances in determining whether confessions are voluntary. In *Frazier v. Cupp* (1969), police officers falsely told Martin Frazier that his cousin Jerry Rawls, who had been with him on the night of the crime, had confessed. The Court considered that this "misrepresentation, while relevant, is insufficient in our view to make this otherwise voluntary confession inadmissible" (739).

Although it's had many opportunities to do so, and substantial research raises questions about this ruling, the Court has never changed its position (Magid 2001, 1176). Research shows that presenting suspects with "false evidence substantially increases false confessions" (Kassin and Gudjonsson 2004, 60). This research and the proven false confession cases led Kassin and Gudjonsson to recommend that "the Court should revisit the wisdom of its prior ruling and declare: 'Thou shalt not lie'" (60).

Video Record Interrogations and Confessions

"Calls to electronically record interrogations are almost as old as the technology itself. For more than seventy years, reformers from all ranks, including some from law enforcement, have seen recording requirements as a way to eliminate secrecy in the stationhouse" and to "recognize the value that neutral, contemporaneously made records could have in law enforcement" (Drizin and Reich 2004, 620, 621). In his 1932 classic *Convicting the Innocent*, Edwin Borchard recommended that the solution to protecting suspects' right against self-incrimination and to preventing unreliable confessions was to make "phonographic records, which shall alone be introducible as evidence of the prisoner's statements" (370–71). Beyond transparency and objectivity, videotaping interrogation confessions provides a means to improve the ability of police, judges, prosecutors, defense attorneys, and juries (and social scientists) to assess the procedure more objectively.

Many state courts have spoken warmly of recording the whole process of interrogation from *Miranda* warnings, through interrogation, to the confession (*State v. Cook* 2004). Despite this history, the DNA exonerations, the psychological research findings we've touched on, and the warm words of some courts, only four states at the time of this writing have mandatory video recording requirements—Alaska, Illinois, Maine, and Minnesota.

The arguments in favor of recording include:

1. It creates an objective, reviewable record.

2. It enhances jurors' and judges' assessment of credibility by providing a complete record.

3. It provides judges and juries with a more accurate picture of what was said; words can convey different meanings, depending on the tone of voice or nuance used.

4. It can improve the quality of police work by providing law enforcement officials with the ability to monitor the quality of the interrogation process, and recordings can be used in training courses to demonstrate effective versus ineffective, or legally impermissible, interrogation techniques.

5. It preserves judicial resources by discouraging defendants from raising "frivolous" pretrial challenges to confessions. (*State v. Cook* 2004, 556–57)

There are also drawbacks to videotaping. They include:

1. The cost, including purchasing the equipment, maintenance, storage, transcription, and remodeling interrogation rooms, can be high.

2. It can interfere with interrogation techniques and hamper officers' ability to obtain truthful confessions.

3. Suspects may be reluctant to speak candidly in front of cameras. (557–58)

ETHICAL ISSUES

Do the Police Have an "Ethical" Responsibility to Video Record Interrogations?

Fifteen-year-old Katrina Suhan was murdered sometime in the early morning hours of Saturday, February 14, 1998. Katrina's body was found on the afternoon of Sunday, February 15. She had been brutally beaten. Her body was positioned face downward and a jacket covered her head; her pants had been pulled below her waist. Large pieces of concrete lay atop her hands and head and an overturned red shopping cart was situated in front of, and partially on, her body. A trail of blood led to the body and to several rocks near her head. A forensic pathologist expressed the view that Katrina died of blunt trauma injury to the head. There was injury also to her left breast that was consistent with a bite mark; there were no other physical signs of sexual assault.

Tomahl Cook, Defendant, who was twenty-four years old at the time of the murder, was arrested and interrogated. Although a tape recorder was available during the interview, the officers did not tape any portion of the interrogation.

INSTRUCTIONS

1. Read the excerpt from *State v. Cook* (2004). See the link under the Chapter 8 Ethical Issues section of the Companion Website—login at www.cengagebrain.com.

2. Summarize the arguments for and against video recording police interrogations.

3. On the basis of the arguments, write an essay arguing one of the following positions.

    a. Police have an ethical obligation to start recording interrogations immediately to establish an objective record of what goes on behind the closed doors of the interrogation room.

    b. Police have an ethical obligation to conduct pilot projects to decide whether to adopt a recording requirement.

    c. Police have an ethical duty to conduct noncoercive interrogations but not to record them.

Summary

LO 1

- Confessions acknowledge guilt, and, as such, they're uniquely powerful evidence. Incriminating statements fall short of full confessions. Confessions are made to friends and family, during interrogation, in guilty pleas, and during sentencing in the form of apologies.

LO 2

- The Fifth Amendment prevents law enforcement from compelling people to make self-incriminating statements, the Sixth Amendment ensures the right to counsel, and the Fourteenth Amendment guarantees due process.

LO 2, LO 3

- Protections of the Fifth and Fourteenth Amendments apply to all stages of the criminal process, the Sixth Amendment after formal charges are brought, and the Fifth Amendment in custodial interrogation and thereafter.

LO 3

- Due process, right to counsel, and self-incrimination are approaches to criminal confession, and their influences overlap in history.

LO 3

- The due process approach emphasized the voluntary nature of confession, stating that involuntary confessions violate due process only because they're unreliable.

LO 3

- The right-to-counsel approach sought to toughen controls on police interrogation by applying the Sixth Amendment's right to counsel to the custodial period in the police station.

LO 3, LO 4

- The self-incrimination approach applied the Fifth Amendment to custodial interrogation. Compulsion, incrimination, and testimony are all required to prove violation of Fifth Amendment rights in a criminal case.

LO 4

- The Fifth Amendment protection against being compelled to "witness" against oneself applies to forced testimony but not personal paperwork, weapons, hair samples, blood samples used for alcohol testing, and more.

LO 4, LO 5

- Whether one is "compelled" is difficult to define. The voluntariness of the confession is critical. In *Miranda*, judges moved away from weighing "totality of circumstances" on a case-by-case basis and, instead, required that a specific police warning be given in every case at the time suspects were taken into custody.

LO 5

- The "bright line" of *Miranda v. Arizona* defines custodial interrogation. In custodial interrogation, suspects are held against their will.

LO 5, LO 6

- Interrogation refers not only to direct questioning but also to subtle coercion that acts as the functional equivalent of a question and to officers that "deliberately elicit a response" from suspects in custody.

LO 5, LO 6

- Interrogation in the accusatory phase is performed in an intentionally intimidating setting conducive to self-incrimination.

LO 5, LO 6, LO 8

- Interrogation is an essential tool without which many prosecutions would go nowhere. Still, courts warn that the same atmosphere that breaks a criminal's will to lie may break an innocent person's will to adhere to the truth.

LO 7

- A waiver of Fifth Amendment and some other rights can be implied, given a totality of circumstances (e.g., age, intelligence, mental condition, education) that indicate suspects knew their rights and gave them up voluntarily.

LO 8

- Voluntary false confessions aren't a theoretical risk but a proven fact. Reforms focus on making video recordings of interrogations and confessions, limiting time in custody, and restricting the use of false information intended to elicit confessions.

Review Questions

1. Describe the ambivalence surrounding confessions in social and legal history.
2. Identify four different settings where defendants confess their guilt or make incriminating statements.
3. Identify when the accusatory stage of the criminal process triggers the rights afforded to suspects.
4. Identify three reasons why Fred Inbau supported interrogations.
5. List four findings of Richard Leo's research on police interrogation, and describe what his findings are based on.
6. List arguments both in favor of and against videotaping interrogations.
7. What is the meaning and significance of the statement, "Pressure yes; coercion no"?
8. Identify and state the contents of the three provisions in the U.S. Constitution that limit police interrogation and confessions.
9. What is the basic idea behind the due process approach to confessions?
10. What is the significance of *Rogers v. Richmond*?
11. What is the significance of *Townsend v. Sain*?
12. When does the right to counsel kick in during interrogations?
13. What three elements have to be satisfied for defendants to claim that their Fifth Amendment rights were violated?
14. Can physical evidence serve as a witness against a suspect? Explain.

15. Describe the voluntariness test of self-incrimination.

16. Identify three factors behind the decision in *Miranda v. Arizona*.

17. *Miranda v. Arizona* established a "bright-line" rule regarding warnings to suspects. State and give the reasons for the rule.

18. State the two circumstances that exist before officers have to give the *Miranda* warnings.

19. Identify five circumstances to determine custody.

20. Identify three types of detentions that aren't custodial.

21. State and summarize the reason for the public safety exception to the *Miranda* warnings.

22. Identify and describe the Fifth Amendment test used to determine interrogation.

23. Identify and describe the Sixth Amendment test used to determine when the right to counsel kicks in.

24. Identify the two elements of a valid wavier of the rights to counsel and to remain silent.

25. List some circumstances relevant to showing a knowing wavier.

26. Identify the two elements of involuntary confessions.

27. List some circumstances courts consider in determining whether coercive action caused people to confess.

28. List some circumstances that courts have determined don't cause suspects to confess.

Key Terms

CHAPTER

9

CASES COVERED

Manson v. Brathwaite, 432 U.S. 98 (1977)

State v. Clopten, 223 P.3d 1103 (Utah 2009)

District Attorney's Office for the Third Judicial District and others v. William G. Osborne, 129 S.Ct. 2308 (2009)

LEARNING OBJECTIVES

1 Know that, in a lineup, witnesses try to pick the suspect out of a group of individuals who are present. In a show-up, witnesses match the suspect with one person, who is either present or pictured in a "mug shot."

2 Understand that courts recognize a violation of due process as a ground for rejecting identification testimony, but that due process challenges rarely succeed.

3 Understand the preponderance of evidence standard and how it affects defense efforts to challenge identification procedures.

4 Know that identification procedures are rejected by courts only when they're unnecessarily suggestive and create a very substantial likelihood of misidentification.

5 Understand and appreciate the impact of the proven incorrect assumptions that we make about how people acquire memories.

6 Know and appreciate the significant role that suggestion plays in witnesses' adding unobserved details to their stories.

7 Understand that social science research has demonstrated that factors such as lineup composition, neutrality of lineup administrators, pre-lineup instructions, and the way the lineup is presented can affect the accuracy of identification.

8 Know that psychological research shows that our perceived ability to identify a culprit varies from our actual ability. Understand that the amount of time a witness spent observing a culprit is often less important than what the witness paid attention to during that time.

9 Know that DNA technology has prompted the reevaluation of many past convictions. Appreciate that these reevaluations can and have led to not only exonerations of the innocent but also further proof against the guilty.

Identification Procedures

Several men entered a bank, tied up the only guard in the lobby, told the customers to lie down on the floor, and demanded that the tellers hand over all their money. The robbers then left. There were five tellers, two officers, one guard, and five customers in the bank at the time. When the police took their statements over the next hour, there was little consensus among the 13 witnesses as to the number of robbers, what they looked like, what they did, the presence of weapons, or how long the robbery lasted.

Video cameras in the bank recorded the robbery. Comparing these recordings to the descriptions provided by the witnesses, it was found that no single witness gave an accurate report of the sequence of events, nor did any single witness provide a consistently accurate description of any of the robbers. Further, in subsequent photo identification lineups, half of the witnesses made serious errors: Four of the 13 witnesses erroneously selected as a robber, either a teller or a customer who had been in the bank during the robbery; three of the 13 erroneously selected a photograph of someone who had not been in the bank at all. All seven of these witnesses said they were "sure" they'd correctly identified one of the robbers and that they were willing to testify to their identification. *Haber and Haber 2000, 1058*

Proving that a crime was committed is often a lot easier than identifying who committed it. Of course, some culprits are caught red-handed; others confess. Technological advances help to identify others; DNA (deoxyribonucleic acid) evidence may be the "single greatest advance in the search for truth since cross-examination" (Coleman and Swenson 1994, 11). And, most important, victims and others who know perpetrators can virtually always identify the culprit. But, in the cases that frighten most of us—violent personal crimes like rape and robbery committed by *strangers*, eyewitness identification remains the most widely used, and often the only, way to identify and prove guilt.

In this chapter, you'll learn how the U.S. Supreme Court relies on the U.S. Constitution to provide minimum safeguards to protect against convictions based on mistaken identifications. The dominant theme in the Court's decisions is balancing the need to protect defendants from wrongful convictions without encroaching on the jury's prerogative to decide guilt. According to the Court, identification evidence should be admitted unless identification procedures create a "very substantial likelihood of irreparable misidentification." Short of that, "We are content to rely upon the good sense and judgment of American juries. Juries are not so susceptible that they cannot measure intelligently the weight of identification testimony that has some questionable feature" (*Manson v. Brathwaite* 1977, 116, excerpted later on p. 306).

Then, we'll examine the highly risky business of eyewitnesses (usually victims) identifying strangers who committed the crimes. We'll rely heavily on the empirical psychological studies of perception, memory, and recall to demonstrate the substantial shortcomings of the rules the Supreme Court adopted to reduce the likelihood of eyewitness misidentification. Then, relying again on empirical research by psychologists, we'll examine and evaluate some leading recommendations for improving the reliability of eyewitness identification.

Finally, we'll look at the growing reliance on DNA testing, its reliability, and convicted defendants' right to access it to help prove they were convicted wrongly.

|||||||||||||||||||||||||||||||||||||||||||||||||||||||||||||||||||||||||||||||||||||||||||||||||||||||||||||||||||||||||||||||||||||

The Constitution and Identification Procedures

LO 1, LO 2

"That's him," says the witness, pointing to the defendant sitting in the courtroom. That's the image you've all seen in a dramatic moment in courtroom dramas. But what you probably don't know, or don't think much about, is that these witnesses have all made an earlier identification of the defendant—before trial and out of court. These out-of-court pretrial identifications consist of two procedures that we'll discuss in more detail later: lineups and show-ups.

1. *Lineups.* In live lineups, witnesses try to pick the suspect out of a group of individuals who are present. In photo lineups, witnesses look for the suspect in a group of photos, or a **photo array.** Although the lineups you see on TV might be live, most places in the United States use photo lineups. Even in places that still use live lineups, they're frequently preceded by photo lineups. (Wells, Memon, and Penrod 2006, 50)

2. *Show-ups.* Witnesses try to match the suspect with one person, either live or a "mug shot" photo.

The *Wade-Gilbert-Stovall* Trio

LO 1, LO 2

Until 1967, the courts, including the U.S. Supreme Court, adopted a "hands off" approach to admitting evidence of lineups and show-ups. Their reasoning was that it was up to juries to assess the reliability of this evidence, not courts. Then came a trio of eyewitness cases that the U.S. Supreme Court decided on the same day. The first two cases brought the Sixth Amendment right to counsel into the evaluation of eyewitness identification.

In *U.S. v. Wade* (1967), Billie Joe Wade participated in a lineup conducted *after* he was indicted, without his lawyer present. The Court held that the lineup after indictment without his lawyer there violated Wade's Sixth Amendment right to counsel. *Gilbert v. California* (1967) held that a "bright-line" *per se* exclusionary rule banned the introduction of an out-of-court lineup identification made in violation of Jesse James Gilbert's right to counsel.

The third case, *Stovall v. Denno* (1967), introduced due process rights into determining the admissibility of evidence derived from a pretrial show-up *before* indictment. In *Stovall*, Dr. Paul Behrendt was stabbed to death in his kitchen. His wife, also a doctor, followed her husband to the kitchen and jumped the assailant, who knocked her down and stabbed her 11 times. The police found a shirt on the floor with keys in the pocket, which they traced to Ted Stovall. Seven police officers brought Stovall to Dr. Behrendt's hospital room the day after she underwent surgery to save her life. Stovall, handcuffed to one of the seven officers, was the only Black in the room. Dr. Behrendt identified him. At trial, Dr. Behrendt testified to her out-of-court identification and identified Stovall again in the courtroom (295).

Although the Court upheld the admissibility of the show-up, it recognized, for the first time, that due process was a basis for challenging identification testimony on constitutional grounds. Whether the hospital room show-up was a violation of due process depended on whether the circumstances were "so unnecessarily suggestive and conducive to irreparable mistaken identification that he was denied due process of law." Under the totality of the circumstances, the Court ruled that showing Stovall to Mrs. Behrendt immediately was imperative. "Here was the only person in the world who could possibly exonerate Stovall. Her words, and only her words, 'He is not the man' could have resulted in freedom for Stovall. Under these circumstances, the usual police station line-up was out of the question" (302).

"Reliability Is the Linchpin"

LO 1, LO 2, LO 3

Some of the Court's language in *Stovall* suggested, and some lower courts adopted, a bright-line *per se* rule that focused on the susceptibility of identification procedures to suggestion. The rule is that identifications that result from "unnecessarily suggestive" identification procedures should be excluded from trial. But, in later decisions, the Court brought the Constitution only a small way into eyewitness identification procedures. Why? Because, to exclude identification evidence on due process grounds, defendants have to prove by a **preponderance of the evidence** (it's more likely than not) that the totality of the circumstances shows that:

1. The identification procedure was unnecessarily suggestive.
2. The unnecessarily suggestive procedure created a very substantial likelihood of misidentification.

Notice the effect of the two-pronged test: **Unnecessarily and impermissibly suggestive** identifications are admissible *unless* defendants can prove that they create a **"very substantial likelihood of misidentification."** The two-prong test demonstrates that, in *Manson's* majority opinion, "reliability is the linchpin" of due process in eyewitness identification. It shouldn't surprise you to learn that *courts* rarely, if ever, throw out eyewitness identification evidence (Table 9.1). Juries, of course, can choose to give it little or no weight, depending on the circumstances.

The Court has identified five factors in the "totality of circumstances" that should weigh heavily in determining whether the "unnecessarily and impermissibly suggestive" procedure created a "very substantial likelihood of misidentification" in lineups and show-ups:

1. Witnesses' opportunity to view defendants at the time of the crime
2. Witnesses' degree of attention at the time of the crime
3. Witnesses' accuracy of description of defendants prior to the identification
4. Witnesses' level of certainty when identifying defendants at the time of the identification procedure
5. The length of time between the crime and the identification (*Manson v. Brathwaite* 1977, p. 306)

In *Manson v. Brathwaite* (1977), our next case excerpt, the Court rejected Nowell Brathwaite's claim that State Trooper Jimmy Glover's single photo show-up identification violated due process.

TABLE 9.1
Application of Due Process Test of Eyewitness Identification Reliability

Lower Federal Court Cases	Court's Holding	Eyewitness Identification
U.S. v. Wong, 40 F.3d 1347 (CA2 1994)	Not impermissibly suggestive; if it was, it was still reliable and admissible	In restaurant shooting of a Green Dragon gang member: • Witness saw shooter for a "few seconds" as she ducked under a table • Viewed 3 photo lineups, couldn't be sure; during third: "It looked like" the shooter • Officers told her repeatedly they believed they had the right man
Clarke v. Caspari, 274 F.3d 507 (CA8 2002)	Reliable	Two liquor store clerks viewed two handcuffed Black suspects "surrounded by White officers, one of whom was holding a shotgun"
Howard v. Bouchard, 405 F.3d 459 (CA6 2008)	Reliable, only "minimally suggestive"	Witness saw defendant at defense table with his lawyer about one hour before lineup could have unnecessarily suggested he was the culprit

State Court Cases

State v. Thompson, 839 A.2d 622 (Conn.App. 2004)	Reliable and admissible	• Police officer drove witness to show-up at the place where suspect was apprehended • Officer told witness, "We believe we have the person. We need you to identify him." Asked witness to identify the person, who was "probably the shooter" • Shined spotlights and headlights on squad car, then removed suspect from back of the car for the show-up
State v. Johnson, 836 N.E. 2d 1243 (OhioApp. 2005)	Reliable	• Murder victim's wife failed to identify juvenile suspect from photo lineup a month after the murder • Seven months later, she identified juvenile dressed in Department of Youth Services clothing, maybe handcuffed, the only young Black sitting at the defense table, at a court hearing in juvenile court to transfer him for trial as an adult
Bynum v. State, 929 So.2d 324 (Miss.App. 2005)	Reliable	• One week after a robber attacked the victim, she selected, from a photo lineup, the suspect and one other person • Victim stated that Bynum "looked the most like the attacker" • Four days later, in second photo lineup containing Bynum but not the second person she selected in the first lineup, victim selected Bynum "positively and unequivocally" • Second individual witnessed the crime, wasn't able to pick out the attacker from the lineup, but later identified Bynum as the robber • Third witness identified Bynum in the lineup, later testified he was "100% certain" of his identification

In Manson v. Brathwaite *(1977), our next case excerpt, the Court rejected Nowell Brathwaite's claim that State Trooper Jimmy Glover's single photo show-up identification violated due process.*

CASE   Did the Photo Show-Up Create a "Very Substantial Likelihood of Misidentification"?

Manson v. Brathwaite
432 U.S. 98 (1977)

HISTORY

Nowell Brathwaite was charged with possession and sale of heroin. The jury found him guilty, and the judge sentenced him to not less than six nor more than nine years. The Supreme Court of Connecticut affirmed. Fourteen months later, Brathwaite filed a petition for habeas corpus in the U.S. District Court for the District of Connecticut. The District Court dismissed his petition. On appeal, the U.S. Court of Appeals for the Second Circuit reversed. The U.S. District Court for the District of Connecticut denied relief, and Brathwaite appealed. The Court of Appeals, Second Circuit, reversed. The U.S. Supreme Court granted certiorari and reversed.

BLACKMUN, J.

FACTS

Jimmy D. Glover, a trained Black undercover state police officer was assigned to the Narcotics Division in 1970. On May 5 of that year, at about 7:45 P.M., EDT, and while there was still daylight, Glover and Henry Alton Brown, an informant, went to an apartment building at 201 Westland, in Hartford, to buy narcotics from "Dickie Boy" Cicero, a known narcotics dealer.

Cicero, it was thought, lived on the third floor of that apartment building. Glover and Brown entered the building, observed by back-up Officers D'Onofrio and Gaffey, and proceeded by stairs to the third floor. Glover knocked at the door of one of the two apartments served by the stairway. It appears that the door on which Glover knocked may not have been that of the Cicero apartment. Petitioner [John Manson, Commissioner of Corrections] concedes that the transaction "was with some other person than had been intended." The area was illuminated by natural light from a window in the third floor hallway.

The door opened 12 to 18 inches. Glover observed a man standing at the door and, behind him, a woman. Brown identified himself. Glover then asked for "two

things" of narcotics. The man at the door held out his hand, and Glover gave him two $10 bills. The door closed. Soon the man returned and handed Glover two glassine bags. . . . This was Glover's testimony. Brown later was called as a witness for the prosecution. He testified on direct examination that, due to his then use of heroin, he had no clear recollection of the details of the incident. On cross-examination, as in an interview with defense counsel the preceding day, he said that it was a woman who opened the door, received the money, and thereafter produced the narcotics. On redirect, he acknowledged that he was using heroin daily at the time, that he had had some that day, and that there was "an inability to recall and remember events."

While the door was open, Glover stood within two feet of the person from whom he made the purchase and observed his face. Five to seven minutes elapsed from the time the door first opened until it closed the second time.

Glover and Brown then left the building. This was about eight minutes after their arrival. Glover drove to headquarters where he described the seller to D'Onofrio and Gaffey. Glover at that time did not know the identity of the seller. He described him as being "a colored man, approximately five feet eleven inches tall, dark complexion, black hair, short Afro style, and having high cheekbones, and of heavy build. He was wearing at the time blue pants and a plaid shirt."

D'Onofrio, suspecting from this description that Brathwaite might be the seller, obtained a photograph of him from the Records Division of the Hartford Police Department. He left it at Glover's office. D'Onofrio was not acquainted with Brathwaite personally but did know him by sight and had seen him "several times" prior to May 5. Glover, when alone, viewed the photograph for the first time upon his return to headquarters on May 7; he identified the person shown as the one from whom he had purchased the narcotics.

Brathwaite was arrested on July 27 while visiting at the apartment of a Mrs. Ramsey on the third floor of 201 Westland. This was the apartment where the narcotics sale took place on May 5. Brathwaite testified: "Lots of times I have been there before in that building." He also testified that Mrs. Ramsey was a friend of his wife, that her apartment was the only one in the building he ever visited, and that he and his family, consisting of his wife and five children, did not live there but at 453 Albany Avenue, Hartford.

Brathwaite was charged, in a two-count information, with possession and sale of heroin. At his trial in January 1971, the photograph from which Glover had identified Brathwaite was received in evidence without objection on the part of the defense. Glover also testified that, although he had not seen Brathwaite in the eight months that had elapsed since the sale, "there was no doubt whatsoever" in his mind that the person shown on the photograph was respondent. Glover also made a positive in-court identification without objection. No explanation was offered by the prosecution for the failure to utilize a photographic array or to conduct a lineup.

Brathwaite, who took the stand in his own defense, testified that on May 5, the day in question, he had been ill at his Albany Avenue apartment ("a lot of back pains, muscle spasms, a bad heart, high blood pressure, neuralgia in my face, and sinus") and that at no time on that particular day had he been at 201 Westland. His wife testified that she recalled, after her husband had refreshed her memory, that he was home all day on May 5.

Doctor Wesley M. Vietzke, an internist and assistant professor of medicine at the University of Connecticut, testified that Brathwaite had consulted him on April 15, 1970, and that he took a medical history from him, heard his complaints about his back and facial pain, and discovered that he had high blood pressure. The physician found Brathwaite, subjectively, "in great discomfort." Brathwaite in fact underwent surgery for a herniated disc at L5 and S1 on August 17.

The jury found Brathwaite guilty on both counts of the information. He received a sentence of not less than six nor more than nine years. His conviction was affirmed by the Supreme Court of Connecticut. That court noted the absence of an objection to Glover's in-court identification and concluded that Brathwaite "has not shown that substantial injustice resulted from the admission of this evidence." Under Connecticut law, substantial injustice must be shown before a claim of error not made or passed on by the trial court will be considered on appeal.

Fourteen months later, Brathwaite filed a petition for habeas corpus in the U.S. District Court for the District of Connecticut. On appeal, the United States Court of Appeals for the Second Circuit reversed. We granted certiorari.

OPINION

The petitioner, Connecticut Commissioner of Corrections, acknowledges that "the procedure in the instant case was suggestive (because only one photograph was used) and unnecessary" (because there was no emergency or exigent circumstance). Brathwaite, in agreement with the Court of Appeals, proposes a per se rule of exclusion that he claims is dictated by the demands of the Fourteenth Amendment's guarantee of due process. He rightly observes this is the first case in which this Court has had occasion to rule upon out-of-court identification evidence of the challenged kind.

Since the decision in *Neil v. Biggers*, the Courts of Appeals appear to have developed at least two approaches to such evidence. The first, or **per se approach** [looking at the totality of circumstances to determine whether an identification should be admitted into evidence], employed by the Second Circuit in the present case, focuses on the procedures employed and requires exclusion of the out-of-court identification evidence, without regard to reliability, whenever it has been obtained through unnecessarily suggestive confrontation procedures. The justifications advanced are the elimination of evidence of uncertain reliability, deterrence of the police and prosecutors, and the fair assurance against the awful risks of misidentification.

The second, or more lenient, approach is one that continues to rely on the **totality of the circumstances** [weighing all the facts surrounding the government's establishing identification of the suspect to determine if it's reliable enough to be admitted]. [This approach] permits the admission of the confrontation evidence if, despite the suggestive aspect, the out-of-court identification possesses certain features of reliability. Its adherents feel that the per se approach is not mandated by the Due Process Clause of the Fourteenth Amendment. This second approach, in contrast to the other, is ad hoc and serves to limit the societal costs imposed by a sanction that excludes relevant evidence from consideration and evaluation by the trier of fact.

Mr. Justice STEVENS, in writing for the Seventh Circuit in *Kirby v. Illinois*, observed: "There is surprising unanimity among scholars in regarding such a rule (the per se approach) as essential to avoid serious risk of miscarriage of justice." He pointed out that well-known federal judges have taken the position that "evidence of, or derived from, a showup identification should be inadmissible unless the prosecutor can justify his failure to use a more reliable identification procedure." Indeed, the ALI *Model Code of Pre-Arraignment Procedure* §§ 160.1 and 160.2 (1975), frowns upon the use of a showup or the display of only a single photograph.

Brathwaite stresses the same theme and the need for deterrence of improper identification practice, a factor he regards as pre-eminent. Photographic identification, it is said, continues to be needlessly employed. He notes that the legislative regulation "the Court had hoped would engender," has not been forthcoming. He argues that a totality rule cannot be expected to have a significant deterrent impact; only a strict rule of exclusion will have direct and immediate impact on law enforcement agents.

Identification evidence is so convincing to the jury that sweeping exclusionary rules are required. Fairness of the trial is threatened by suggestive confrontation evidence, and thus, it is said, an exclusionary rule has an established constitutional predicate.

There are, of course, several interests to be considered and taken into account. The driving force behind *United States v. Wade* (1967), *Gilbert v. California* (1967) (right to counsel at a post-indictment line-up), and *Stovall,* all decided on the same day, was the Court's concern with the problems of eyewitness identification. Usually the witness must testify about an encounter with a total stranger under circumstances of emergency or emotional stress. The witness' recollection of the stranger can be distorted easily by the circumstances or by later actions of the police.

Thus, *Wade* and its companion cases reflect the concern that the jury not hear eyewitness testimony unless that evidence has aspects of reliability. It must be observed that both approaches before us are responsive to this concern. The per se rule, however, goes too far since its application automatically and peremptorily, and without consideration of alleviating factors, keeps evidence from the jury that is reliable and relevant.

The second factor is deterrence. Although the per se approach has the more significant deterrent effect, the totality approach also has an influence on police behavior. The police will guard against unnecessarily suggestive procedures under the totality rule, as well as the per se one, for fear that their actions will lead to the exclusion of identifications as unreliable.

The third factor is the effect on the administration of justice. Here the per se approach suffers serious drawbacks. Since it denies the trier reliable evidence, it may result, on occasion, in the guilty going free. Also, because of its rigidity, the per se approach may make error by the trial judge more likely than the totality approach. And in those cases in which the admission of identification evidence is error under the per se approach but not under the totality approach—cases in which the identification is reliable despite an unnecessarily suggestive identification procedure—reversal is a Draconian sanction. Unlike a warrantless search, a suggestive preindictment identification procedure does not in itself intrude upon a constitutionally protected interest.

Thus, considerations urging the exclusion of evidence deriving from a constitutional violation do not bear on the instant problem. Certainly, inflexible rules of exclusion that may frustrate rather than promote justice have not been viewed recently by this Court with unlimited enthusiasm. The standard, after all, is that of fairness as required by the Due Process Clause of the Fourteenth Amendment.

We turn, then, to the facts of this case and apply the analysis:

1. *The opportunity to view.* Glover testified that for two to three minutes he stood at the apartment door, within two feet of the respondent. The door opened twice, and each time the man stood at the door. The moments passed, the conversation took place, and payment was made. Glover looked directly at his vendor. It was near sunset, to be sure, but the sun had not yet set, so it was not dark or even dusk or twilight. Natural light from outside entered the hallway through a window. There was natural light, as well, from inside the apartment.

2. *The degree of attention.* Glover was not a casual or passing observer, as is so often the case with eyewitness identification. Trooper Glover was a trained police officer on duty—and specialized and dangerous duty—when he called at the third floor of 201 Westland in Hartford on May 5, 1970. Glover himself was a Negro and unlikely to perceive only general features of "hundreds of Hartford black males," as the Court of Appeals stated. It is true that Glover's duty was that of ferreting out narcotics offenders and that he would be expected in his work to produce results. But it is also true that, as a specially trained, assigned, and experienced officer, he could be expected to pay scrupulous attention to detail, for he knew that subsequently he would have to find and arrest his vendor. In addition, he knew that his claimed observations would be subject later to close scrutiny and examination at any trial.

3. *The accuracy of the description.* Glover's description was given to D'Onofrio within minutes after the transaction. It included the vendor's race, his height, his build, the color and style of his hair, and the high cheekbone facial feature. It also included clothing the vendor wore.

    No claim has been made that Brathwaite did not possess the physical characteristics so described. D'Onofrio reacted positively at once. Two days later, when Glover was alone, he viewed the photograph D'Onofrio produced and identified its subject as the narcotics seller.

4. *The witness's level of certainty.* There is no dispute that the photograph in question was that of Brathwaite. Glover, in response to a question whether the photograph was that of the person from whom he made the purchase, testified: "There is no question whatsoever." This positive assurance was repeated.

5. *The time between the crime and the confrontation.* Glover's description of his vendor was given to D'Onofrio within minutes of the crime. The photographic identification took place only two days later. We do not have here the passage of weeks or months between the crime and the viewing of the photograph.

These indicators of Glover's ability to make an accurate identification are hardly outweighed by the corrupting effect of the challenged identification itself. Although identifications arising from single-photograph displays may be viewed in general with suspicion, we find in the instant case little pressure on the witness to acquiesce in the suggestion that such a display entails. D'Onofrio had left the photograph at Glover's office and was not present when Glover first viewed it two days after the event. There thus was little urgency and Glover could view the photograph at his leisure. And since Glover examined the photograph alone, there was no coercive pressure to make an identification arising from the presence of another. The identification was made in circumstances allowing care and reflection.

Although it plays no part in our analysis, all this assurance as to the reliability of the identification is hardly undermined by the facts that Brathwaite was arrested in the very apartment where the sale had taken place, and that he acknowledged his frequent visits to that apartment. Mrs. Ramsey was not a witness at the trial.

Surely, we cannot say that under all the circumstances of this case there is "a very substantial likelihood of irreparable misidentification." Short of that point, such evidence is for the jury to weigh. We are content to rely upon the good sense and judgment of American juries, for evidence with some element of untrustworthiness is customary grist for the jury mill. Juries are not so susceptible that they cannot measure intelligently the weight of identification testimony that has some questionable feature.

Of course, it would have been better had D'Onofrio presented Glover with a photographic array including "so far as practicable a reasonable number of persons similar to any person then suspected whose likeness is included in the array." *Model Code*, § 160.2(2). The use of that procedure would have enhanced the force of the identification at trial and would have avoided the risk that the evidence would be excluded as unreliable. But we are not disposed to view D'Onofrio's failure as one of constitutional dimension to be enforced by a rigorous and unbending exclusionary rule. The defect, if there be one, goes to weight and not to substance.

We conclude that the criteria laid down in *Biggers* are to be applied in determining the admissibility of evidence offered by the prosecution concerning a post-*Stovall* identification, and that those criteria are satisfactorily met and complied with here.

The judgment of the Court of Appeals is REVERSED.

CONCURRING OPINION

STEVENS, J.

The arguments in favor of fashioning new rules to minimize the danger of convicting the innocent on the basis of unreliable eyewitness testimony carry substantial force. Nevertheless, I am persuaded that this rulemaking function can be performed more effectively by the legislative process than by a somewhat clumsy judicial fiat and that the Federal Constitution does not foreclose experimentation by the States in the development of such rules.

DISSENT

MARSHALL, J., joined by BRENNAN, J.

It is distressing to see the Court virtually ignore the teaching of experience and blindly uphold the conviction of a defendant who may well be innocent. Relying on numerous studies made over many years by such scholars as Professor Wigmore and Mr. Justice Frankfurter, the Court in *U.S. v. Wade* (1967), concluded that "the vagaries of eyewitness identification are well-known; the annals of criminal law are rife with instances of mistaken identification."

It is, of course, impossible to control one source of such errors—the faulty perceptions and unreliable memories of witnesses—except through vigorously contested trials conducted by diligent counsel and judges. The Court acted, however, to minimize the more preventable threat posed to accurate identification by "the degree of suggestion inherent in the manner in which the prosecution presents the suspect to witnesses for pretrial identification."

Despite my strong disagreement with the Court over the proper standards [totality of circumstances] to be applied in this case, assuming applicability of the totality test, the facts of the present case require the exclusion of the identification in this case because it raises a very substantial likelihood of misidentification.

I consider first the opportunity that Officer Glover had to view the suspect. Careful review of the record shows he could see the heroin seller only for the time it took to speak three sentences of four or five short words, to hand over some money, and later after the door reopened, to receive the drugs in return. The entire face-to-face transaction could have taken as little as 15 or 20 seconds. But during this time, Glover's attention was not focused exclusively on the seller's face. He observed that the door was opened 12 to 18 inches, that there was a window in the room behind the door, and, most importantly, that there was a woman standing behind the man. Glover was, of course, also concentrating on the details of the transaction—he must have looked away from the seller's face to hand him the money and receive the drugs. The observation during the conversation thus may have been as brief as 5 or 10 seconds.

As the Court notes, Glover was a police officer trained in and attentive to the need for making accurate identifications. Nevertheless, both common sense and scholarly study indicate that while a trained observer such as a police officer is somewhat less likely to make an erroneous identification than the average untrained observer, the mere fact that he has been so trained is no guarantee that he is correct in a specific case. His identification testimony should be scrutinized just as carefully as that of the normal witness.

Another factor on which the Court relies, the witness' degree of certainty in making the identification, is worthless as an indicator that he is correct. Even if Glover had been unsure initially about his identification of Brathwaite's picture, by the time he was called at trial to present a key piece of evidence for the State that paid his salary, it is impossible to imagine his responding negatively to such questions as "is there any doubt in your mind whatsoever" that the identification was correct. As the Court noted in *Wade:* "It is a matter of common experience that, once a witness has picked out the accused at the (pretrial confrontation), he is not likely to go back on his word later on."

Next, the Court finds that because the identification procedure took place two days after the crime, its reliability is enhanced. While such nearness in time makes the identification more reliable than one occurring months later, the fact is that the greatest memory loss occurs within hours after an event. After that, the dropoff continues much more slowly. Thus, the reliability of an identification is increased only if it was made within several hours of the crime.

Finally, the Court makes much of the fact that Glover gave a description of the seller to D'Onofrio shortly after the incident. Despite the Court's assertion that because "Glover himself was a Negro and unlikely to perceive only general features of hundreds of Hartford black males," the description given by Glover was actually no more than a general summary of the seller's appearance. We may discount entirely the seller's clothing, for that was of no significance later in the proceeding. Indeed, to the extent that Glover noticed clothes, his attention was diverted from the seller's face.

Otherwise, Glover merely described vaguely the seller's height, skin color, hairstyle, and build. He did say that the seller had "high cheekbones," but there is no other mention of facial features, nor even an estimate of age. Conspicuously absent is any indication that the seller was a native of the West Indies, certainly something which a member of the black community could immediately recognize from both appearance and accent. Brathwaite had come to the United States from his native Barbados as an adult.

In contrast, the procedure used to identify Brathwaite was both extraordinarily suggestive and strongly conducive to error. By displaying a single photograph of Brathwaite to the witness Glover under the circumstances in this record almost everything that could have been done wrong was done wrong.

In the first place, there was no need to use a photograph at all. Because photos are static, two-dimensional, and often outdated, they are clearly inferior in reliability to live person lineups and showups. While the use of photographs is justifiable and often essential where the police have no knowledge of an offender's identity, the poor reliability of photos makes their use inexcusable where any other means of identification is available.

Here, since Detective D'Onofrio believed he knew the seller's identity, further investigation without resort to a photographic showup was easily possible. With little inconvenience, a live person lineup including Brathwaite might have been arranged. Indeed, the police carefully staged Brathwaite's arrest in the same apartment that was used for the sale, indicating that they were fully capable of keeping track of his whereabouts and using this information in their investigation.

Worse still than the failure to use an easily available live person identification was the display to Glover of only a single picture, rather than a photo array. With good reason, such single-suspect procedures have been widely condemned. They give no assurance the witness can identify the criminal from among a number of persons of similar appearance, surely the strongest evidence that there was no misidentification.

The danger of error is at its greatest when the police display to the witness only the picture of a single individual. The use of a single picture (or the display of a single live suspect, for that matter) is a grave error, of course, because it dramatically suggests to the witness that the person shown must be the culprit. Why else would the police choose the person? And it is deeply ingrained in human nature to agree with the expressed opinions of others—particularly others who should be more knowledgeable—when making a difficult decision.

In this case, moreover, the pressure was not limited to that inherent in the display of a single photograph. Glover, the identifying witness, was a state police officer on special assignment. He knew that D'Onofrio, an experienced Hartford narcotics detective, presumably familiar with local drug operations, believed respondent to be the seller. There was at work, then, both loyalty to another police officer and deference to a better-informed colleague.

While the Court is impressed by D'Onofrio's immediate response to Glover's description, the detective, who had not witnessed the transaction, acted on a wild guess that Brathwaite was the seller. D'Onofrio's hunch rested solely on Glover's vague description, yet D'Onofrio had seen Brathwaite only "several times, mostly in his vehicle." There was no evidence that Brathwaite was even a suspected narcotics dealer, and D'Onofrio thought that the drugs had been purchased at a different apartment from the one Glover actually went to. The identification of Brathwaite provides a perfect example of the investigator and the witness bolstering each other's inadequate knowledge to produce a seemingly accurate but actually worthless identification.

The Court discounts this overwhelming evidence of suggestiveness, however. It reasons that because D'Onofrio was not present when Glover viewed the photograph, there was "little pressure on the witness to acquiesce in the suggestion." That conclusion blinks psychological reality. There is no doubt in my mind that even in D'Onofrio's absence, a clear and powerful message was telegraphed to Glover as he looked at respondent's photograph. He was emphatically told that "this is the man," and he responded by identifying Brathwaite then and at trial whether or not he was in fact "the man."

I must conclude that this record presents compelling evidence that there was "a very substantial likelihood of misidentification" of respondent Brathwaite. The suggestive display of Brathwaite's photograph to the witness Glover likely erased any independent memory Glover had retained of the seller from his barely adequate opportunity to observe the criminal.

Accordingly, I dissent.

QUESTIONS

1. Describe the three approaches to dealing with misidentifications outlined by the majority opinion.
2. Which approach does the Court adopt? Why?
3. List the facts in each of the five factors and the majority opinion's assessment of them.
4. List the facts in the same way and the dissent's assessment of them.
5. Do you think the circumstances demonstrate "a very substantial likelihood of irreparable misidentification"?
6. Summarize the dissent's argument in favor of the per se test and against the totality test. Is the dissent correct in arguing that the Court wrongfully evaluated the impact of the exclusionary rule and the totality of circumstances? Evaluate those arguments.
7. Is the dissent's stress on Brathwaite's Barbados ancestry important? Explain.
8. Would you side with the dissent or the majority in this case? Defend your answer.

||||||||||||||||||||||||||||||||||||||||||||||||||||||||||||||||||||||||||||||||||||||||||||||||||||||||||||||||||||||||||

Social Science and Mistaken Eyewitness Identification

LO 5

Do you believe that you're aware of what you can and can't remember? To introduce you to the impressive empirical research findings on the psychology of human perception and memory and their effect on mistaken eyewitness identification, answer the questions that follow. Decide whether you agree strongly, agree, disagree, or disagree strongly with these 10 statements about memory, which researchers presented to "typical people":

1. Memory is like a video recording of your observations that can be played back at will to remind you of what you saw.

2. When you're very confident about your memory for an event you observed, you're much more likely to be correct.

3. Your memory is stable over time.

4. Your memory for what you originally saw can be kept separate from things you learned from observing the event.

5. People's faces stand out when you observe them, and it's easy to remember faces; so recognition of faces is rarely wrong.

6. An eyewitness report is accurate evidence as to who was present and what happened.

7. Having to tell the same story of what happened over and over reinforces it and makes it more resistant to change.

8. When a weapon is visible during a crime, witnesses are more accurate in remembering the details of a crime.

9. Personally experienced traumatic events are remembered more accurately than everyday ones.

10. Observed violent events are remembered more accurately than everyday events. (Haber and Haber 2000, 1057–58)

Most "typical people" agreed or strongly agreed with all 10 of the statements. In contrast, the majority of **memory experts** ("scientists whose profession is providing empirical demonstrations of how memory actually functions") disagree. So the descriptions of the robbery in the chapter don't surprise law enforcement professionals and lawyers; they "treat this example as a common occurrence." Why? Because they've learned through experience that multiple eyewitnesses frequently describe the same event differently; that no single witness accurately describes the entire event; and that eyewitnesses frequently misidentify, with great confidence, individuals connected with the event (1058).

Relying on eyewitness identification of *strangers* in criminal cases is a risky business. The risks of mistaken identification are high, even in ideal settings, and the most common identification procedures—live and photo lineups and show-ups—don't take place in ideal settings. According to most experts, mistaken identification of strangers "is the single greatest cause of the conviction of the innocent" (Scheck 1997). The best guess (there aren't any reliable exact figures) is that eyewitness misidentifications account for 75 percent of the wrongful convictions of those exonerated by DNA testing (Innocence Project, "Eyewitness," 2010).

Let's look at the three stages of natural human memory—acquisition, retention, and recall—and how they can lead to mistakenly identifying strangers as culprits in criminal cases.

Memory and the Identification of Strangers

LO 5, LO 6

When we experience an important event, it's a much more complex process than simply recording it in our memories as a video camera would do. The camera just stores the event for later recall. Human memory, on the other hand, is both subjective and malleable. Eyewitness evidence is a form of "trace evidence." Instead of leaving physical traces like blood or semen, eyewitness evidence leaves a "memory trace" in the witness's mind, which we try to extract without damaging (Loftus 1996, 21–22; Wells and Olson 2003, 279; Shay and O'Toole 2006, 118–19).

Psychologists separate memory into three phases:

1. *Acquisition of memory.* The *perception* of an event, when information is first entered into memory

2. *Retention of memory.* The process of storing information during the period of time between an event and the "eventual recollection of a particular piece of information" (Loftus 1996, 21)

3. *Retrieval of memory.* The time when a person recalls the stored information about an event for the purpose of identifying a person in an event

Let's look more closely at each of these stages of memory and their implications for identifying strangers in criminal cases.

The Acquisition Stage

Contrary to common belief, the brain isn't a digital video recorder (DVR) that records everything witnesses see. For well over a century, psychologists have proven repeatedly that the brain doesn't record exact images sent to it through our eyes. Unlike cameras, people have expectations, and our expectations and our highly developed thought processes heavily influence our acquisition of information. In short, our perceptions often trump reality. Like beauty, the physical characteristics of criminals are in the eye of the beholder, and our subjective perceptions influence heavily what happens during events, including crimes.

Attention also shapes our observations. Observers—even trained ones—don't take in everything that happens during a crime. We all pay only selective attention to what's going on around us, and this selective attention leaves wide gaps in the information we acquire during events.

The accuracy of witnesses' first observation of strangers during a crime depends on the interaction among five circumstances:

1. *Length of time* to observe the stranger

2. *Distractions* during the observation

3. *Focus* of the observation

4. *Stress* on the witness during the observation

5. *Race* of the witness and the stranger (Wells and Olson 2003, 279)

The longer a witness observes a stranger, the more reliable the observation. The problem is, most crimes last only seconds. Even when they last longer, other obstacles interfere with accurate observation. Descriptions witnesses give of obvious (but crucial) details, such as age, height, and weight, are often highly inaccurate. Time estimates are also unreliable, particularly during stressful situations like getting robbed or raped.

Witnesses also get distracted from focusing on the physical description to other "details" like the gun the robber waved or the knife a rapist held to his victim's face. Understandable as this "weapons focus" is, the weapon is obviously not as important as the description of the robber or rapist. Also, crimes aren't always committed under physical conditions ideal for accurately describing details; bad lighting is a good example. Equally important, stress distorts our observations.

It may *sound* convincing when a witness says, "I was so scared I could never forget that face," but research demonstrates convincingly that accuracy sharply declines during stressful events. According to C. Ronald Huff, an identification expert who conducted one study, many robbery and rape victims who were close enough to the offender to "get a look at him" were mistaken, because they were under conditions of "extreme stress. Such stress can significantly affect perception and memory and should give us cause to question the reliability of such eyewitness testimony" (reported in Yant 1991, 99).

Discouraging as the natural limits of observation, distracted focus, poor lighting, and stress are to accurate identification, race complicates matters further. Researchers have demonstrated that identifying strangers of another race substantially increases the risk of mistaken identification. In one famous experiment, researchers showed observers a photo of a White man waving a razor blade in an altercation with a Black man on a subway. When asked immediately afterward to describe what they saw, over half the subjects reported that the Black man was carrying the weapon. Furthermore, increased contact with persons of another race doesn't improve the ability to perceive their physical characteristics (Gross 1987, 398–99).

The Retention Stage

LO 5, LO 6

Information that's perceived has to be stored. Fading memory of stored information raises the already high risk of mistake caused by faulty observation. Memory fades most during the first few hours after an event (the time when it's most important to retain it). After these first hours, it fades more slowly for months and years. Curiously, at the same time witnesses' memory is fading, their confidence in their memory is rising. Unfortunately, courts and juries place enormous weight on witnesses' confidence, even in the face of clear proof that confidence isn't related to accuracy.

Memories don't just fade. Many things can happen to a witness during this critical retention period. Sometimes, new items are added to our memory bin. Witnesses talk about the event, overhear conversations about it, or read, hear, or watch news stories about it, all of which "bring about powerful and unexpected changes in the witness's memory" (Loftus 1996, 21–22).

Retrieval: Recall and Recognition

After a crime, someone may ask the witness questions about it. At this point, the witness has to retrieve from long-term memory the specific information she needs to answer the questions. This retrieval comes from information acquired from both the original experience and information added during the retention period (22).

Retrieval arises from two phenomena: recall and recognition. In **eyewitness recall**, eyewitnesses are given hints, such as a time frame, and then asked to report what they observed. In **eyewitness recognition**, eyewitnesses are shown persons or objects and then asked to indicate whether they were involved in the crime. Retrieval errors can be either **errors of omission** (for example, failure to recall some detail or to recognize a perpetrator) or **errors of commission** (picking an innocent person in a photo array) (Wells 2002, 665).

The Power of Suggestion

LO 6

As if faulty observation and fading and malleable memory aren't enough to shake our confidence in the accuracy of memory during the retrieval stage, the strong power of **suggestion** contributes further to mistaken identification. According to the widely accepted findings of psychologists, most mistaken identifications happen because of a combination of the natural imperfections of memory and the normal susceptibility to innocent and subtle suggestion (Wells and Olson 2003, 277).

Suggestion is particularly powerful (and most threatening to accuracy) during the retention and retrieval phases. Witnesses store details in one "memory storage bin," which contains information about the crime they acquired by faulty perception at the time of the crime *and* information that they added later during the retention stage. In her famous experiments, psychologist and eyewitness expert Elizabeth Loftus (1996) found that witnesses add to their stories of crimes. What they add depends on how *she* describes what happened. Loftus found that the power of her suggestions shapes what witnesses later take out of their memory bin and recall during the identification process.

Steven Penrod, Distinguished Professor of Psychology at John Jay College, says witnesses (like all of us) embellish their stories: "A witness tells his story to the police, to the family, then to friends, then to the prosecutor. As the story gets retold, it becomes more epic legend than a few facts." Witnesses "feel very confident about what they now think happened and that confidence is communicated to the jury" (quoted in Yant 1991, 100).

Let's now discuss specifically the influence of suggestion on procedures to identify strangers in criminal cases.

Psychological Research and Eyewitness Identification

LO 6

Every day, courts hear defense attorneys challenge the accuracy of eyewitness identification evidence because of suggestive eyewitness identification procedures. Here are some common arguments:

1. The police used a show-up when they could've used a lineup.

2. The police used a lineup in which the suspect stood out.

3. The police didn't tell the witness that the culprit might not be in the lineup.

4. The police showed the witness a photo of the suspect before they conducted the lineup.

5. The police told a witness who was potentially not confident that she picked the "right" person in the lineup.

6. The police conducted a second lineup in which the only person who appeared in both lineups was the suspect. (Wells and Quinlivan 2009, 1)

Defense counsel lose these arguments in almost every case because of the **reliability test of eyewitness evidence** established in *Manson v. Brathwaite* (1977, excerpt on p. 306). Recall that the test (1) allows the admission of identification evidence based on "unnecessarily suggestive" identification procedures, (2) *unless* defendants can prove that the suggestive procedure creates a "very substantial likelihood of misidentification." In the Court's words, "Reliability is the linchpin." The reliability test remains the law of the land, despite an enormous body of empirical research that casts doubt on the reliability it was designed to enhance.

The test has also remained in the face of the widely reported finding that an embarrassing 75 percent of defendants exonerated by DNA are cases of mistaken eyewitness identification—more than all other causes combined (Wells and Quinlivan 2009). These DNA exonerations represent only a tiny fraction of actual mistaken identity, because they're limited to cases where there's a likelihood of finding DNA. That eliminates most old cases where DNA has deteriorated, is lost, or been destroyed. It also excludes almost all crimes except sexual assault because that's where the DNA is. In addition, sexual assault victims are probably better witnesses, probably among the most reliable, because they usually get a longer and closer look at the culprit than witnesses to other crimes, such as robbery (Wells and Quinlivan 2009, 2).

One final note about the exoneration cases—they all had the "benefit" of the *Manson* reliability test when they were tried. Let's look at some of this rich body of research. It's probably coincidental that at the same time the Supreme Court decided *Manson v. Brathwaite* (1977), psychologists were conducting eyewitness identification experiments that examined the influence of suggestive identification procedures (Wells and Quinlivan 2009, 1).

Hundreds of published experiments later, Professor Penrod (2003) concluded that "research conducted by psychologists raises serious questions about the reliability of witness performance." Keep in mind that the Supreme Court justices who decided *Manson* didn't have the benefit of this more than thirty years of research. Nevertheless, Justice Marshall, in his dissent, relied heavily on research available at the time to bolster his support for a bright-line rule that would exclude eyewitness identification evidence based on "unnecessarily suggestive" identification procedures.

Before we look at the psychological empirical research findings, you should be aware of two preliminary matters: (1) the research methods of the eyewitness studies and some criticisms of it and (2) the problem of witness self-reporting in court with regard to three of the factors in the reliability part of the *Manson* reliability test.

Identification Research Methods

Psychologists rely on two principal methods to study eyewitness identification, both common in all scientific research: archival and experimental. **Archival research** consists of analyzing real procedures used in actual criminal cases. Only a small portion of the research is archival, so we'll concentrate on the much larger experimental research. In **experimental research**, researchers *create* crimes (live staged or videotaped) that unsuspecting people witness. Then, researchers question them about what they witnessed and show them a lineup. Typical experiments have from 100 to 300 witnesses to stabilize the data and test hypotheses.

Because researchers create the "crime," there's no ambiguity about the actors' actions or words and the culprit's identity. So researchers can score witnesses' errors accurately. They also can manipulate variables, such as witness characteristics, viewing conditions, and lineups, enabling them to study the effects of these manipulations on witnesses' errors (Wells and Quinlivan 2009, 5).

Those who criticize the experimental method do so on several grounds. First, experiments usually use college students as witnesses; obviously most actual eyewitnesses in criminal cases *aren't* college students. But researchers have also used young children, adolescents, middle-aged people, and the elderly. These studies show consistently that college students *outperform* the other groups. They're less influenced by suggestive procedures and more likely to make accurate identifications. "Therefore, if anything, college students as witnesses underestimate the magnitude of the problem" (Wells and Quinlivan 2009, 6).

Second, witnesses in experiments don't experience the stress and fear that real witnesses experience. But experiments that have "managed to induce significant stress have shown that stress interferes with, rather than helps, the formation of reliable memories" (6). Third, experiment witnesses know there are no serious consequences for mistaken identifications; actual witnesses are too cautious to make these mistakes. Archival research has demonstrated that real eyewitnesses who select someone from a lineup identify an innocent filler on average 30 percent of the time (6, reporting results from Behrman and Richards 2005). Obviously, these real witnesses weren't too cautious to select innocent persons.

Eyewitness Retrospective Self-Reports

LO 7

Courts rely heavily on **eyewitness retrospective self-reports** (witnesses' in-court recollections) when it comes to three of the five *Manson* reliability factors: their view, attention, and certainty. Psychologists are highly skeptical of retrospective self-reports, because they're highly malleable in response to even slight changes in context, such as:

1. The social desirability of the responses
2. The need to appear consistent
3. Reinterpretations of the past based on new events (Wells and Quinlivan 2009, 9)

Wells and Quinlivan (2009) point out that it's "somewhat odd" to ask eyewitnesses to report on their own credibility, when it's their credibility that's at stake. It would be like giving a student a grade based on the student's own report on how hard he or she studied (9).

Assessments of Lineups

LO 7

Now, let's look at some major empirical assessments of lineups, including their composition; pre-lineup instructions; suggestive behavior by the administrator during the procedure; and suggestive behavior by the administrator immediately after the procedure.

The Lineup Composition

LO 7

The choice of suspects and foils can infect the reliability of lineups by suggesting whom the eyewitness should select. To reduce the chance of infection by suggestion, psychologists recommend that a lineup *always* include one suspect but no more than one. (Be clear here: A suspect might *not* be the culprit.) *All* the rest should be **fillers** (persons known to be innocent).

The reason for fillers is to make sure the lineup doesn't suggest the target of the police investigation. Research has consistently found that fillers who don't fit the witness's previous description of the culprit "dramatically" increase the chances that the witness will identify the wrong person—an *innocent* suspect (7). So lineups should consist of a suspect and fillers who resemble one another: They're the same race, ethnicity, and skin color; they're similar in age, height, weight, hair color, and body build; and they're wearing similar clothing.

Unfortunately, live lineups often fall short of these recommendations. Understand that this gap is hardly ever intentional; it's almost always because the only people available to put in lineups are police officers and jail inmates. It's easier to put together a photo lineup because of the large numbers of mug shots. But no matter how wide the gap, most courts don't throw out lineup identifications. Why? Courts trust jurors' common sense and daily experience to detect wrong identifications (See "The Constitution and Identification Procedures," p. 303).

A substantial body of empirical research demonstrates that courts' trust in jurors' ability to discern witness lineup misidentifications is misplaced. When Jennifer Davenport and Steven Penrod (1997) surveyed the studies on this issue, they reported one study suggesting that jurors might believe as many as "three out of four mistaken identifications" (348).

Pre-Lineup Instructions

LO 7

Witnesses have a tendency to think of lineups as multiple-choice tests without a "none of the above" choice. They feel pressured by the possibility they might look foolish if they "don't know the answer." So they tell themselves the culprit *has to be* in the lineup. This leads witnesses to make a **relative judgment**; namely, they select the person in the lineup who looks most like the culprit. In other words, they're ripe for suggestion, particularly in uncomfortable or threatening situations, such as a police lineup. The very fact that police have arranged an identification procedure puts pressure on witnesses. They believe that the police must have found the culprit, or they wouldn't have gone to the trouble of arranging the lineup.

A major thrust of psychological research deals with the effect of the **might-or-might-not-be-present instruction**. The administrator tells witnesses *before* they view the lineup that the culprit "might or might not" be present. Specifically, the question researchers ask is whether this instruction reduces the pressure of the inherent suggestiveness of lineups. The science gives a clear answer: "Mistaken identifications from culprit-absent lineups are significantly higher when the witness is not given the pre-lineup instruction than when the witness is given the pre-lineup instruction." Administrators who don't give the instruction can infect the pre-lineup procedure even further in culprit-absent lineups by telling witnesses such things as, the police have found the culprit, they know who committed the crime, or they already have plenty of evidence against the culprit (6–7).

Suggestive Behavior by the Lineup Administrator

LO 7

Researchers have shown that the administrator's knowledge or expectations influence the witness. Wells and Quinlivan (2009, 8) give several simple examples of verbal and nonverbal cues to the administrator's knowledge and expectations:

1. A witness calls out the number of a filler photo. The administrator, knowing it's a filler, urges the witness to "Make sure you look at all the photos before you finally make up your mind."

2. The witness names the suspect. The administrator says, "Good, tell me what you remember about that guy."

3. The witness names a filler. The administrator says nothing but frowns and moves his head left to right.

4. The witness names a suspect. The administrator smiles and nods her head up and down.

These cues aren't intentional or even conscious. They're "natural behavior of all testers" in all scientific experiments when "they think they know the correct answer or have expectations about how the tested person will or should behave." In experiments, when lineup administrators are misled into believing that one member in the lineup is the culprit, it influences witnesses' identification decision (8).

Show-Ups

Although, until now, we've devoted the discussion mainly to empirical research on lineups, recall that it was a show-up that the U.S. Supreme Court affirmed in *Manson.* Before we move on to looking closer at the *Manson* reliability factors, let's make a few important points about show-ups. *Show-ups*—identifications of a single person—are substantially less reliable than lineups, because presenting only one person to identify is more suggestive than providing a group of people to choose from. Nevertheless, courts usually admit show-up identification evidence.

Here are three common situations in which courts are likely to admit show-up identifications:

1. Witnesses accidentally run into suspects, such as in courthouse corridors.

2. Witnesses identify suspects during emergencies, such as when witnesses are hospitalized. (*Stovall v. Denno* 1967, p. 303)

3. Witnesses identify suspects while they're loose and being pursued by police, such as when police cruise crime scenes with witnesses. (*McFadden v. Cabana* 1988)

Psychologists' experiments have found that show-ups suggest to witnesses the person to identify—the person in the show-up. The advantage of a lineup is that wrong choices will be distributed among known innocent *fillers*, a harmless choice because they obviously won't be charged with crimes. In a show-up, the error can do greater harm because the person in the show-up is a *suspect* who the police believe is the culprit. So a show-up is worse than a *good* lineup (a lineup consisting of one suspect plus five innocent fillers). But a show-up is better than a bad lineup—namely, one made up of less than two fillers (Wells and Quinlivan, 7).

Psychological Research and the *Manson* Reliability Variables

LO 6, LO 8

Psychologists have studied extensively three variables that *Manson* includes in its reliability-prong circumstances—(1) eyewitnesses' opportunity to view the culprit; (2) the amount of attention witnesses devoted to looking at the culprit; and (3) witnesses' confidence (also called certainty) in their identifications. Researchers have found that suggestion seriously infects all three.

The Witness's Opportunity to View the Culprit

Recall that opportunity to view is the first of the five circumstances in the reliability prong of the *Manson* test. A witness's opportunity to view the culprit at the time of the crime is obviously important. Distance is part of that opportunity. Distance played a significant role in a case that began on the day Alaskans received their 1997 annual $1500 oil dividend. Four youths took to the streets of Fairbanks, violently attacking random individuals. In a trial later, the prosecutor, who lacked convincing evidence of who killed a teen-age boy and an older man, introduced the eyewitness testimony of Arlo Olson. He testified that "while standing in the doorway of Eagles Hall in downtown Fairbanks, he had watched in horror as a group of men, whom he later identified as the defendants, accosted and savagely beat Mr. Dayton in a parking lot a couple of blocks away" (Loftus and Harley 2005, 43).

The distance between Olson and the "group of men" was 450 feet. An eyewitness expert for the defense testified that "seeing someone from 450 ft away is what one is doing when one is sitting high in the center field bleachers of Yankee Stadium, looking across the ballpark at another individual sitting in the stands behind home plate" (44). Most people can clearly view a human face up to about 25 feet; it gradually diminishes to zero at about 150 feet (Wells and Quinlivan 2009, 9–10).

In addition to distance, witnesses are also asked how long they saw the culprit's face and whether their view was blocked for any part of the time. Researchers have found only a weak link between the length of time the witness viewed the culprit and correct identification, especially when there was stress or anxiety during the viewing. Also, witnesses greatly overestimate the time they viewed the culprit, and they greatly underestimate how long their view was blocked (Wells and Quinlivan, 10).

In a series of published experiments from a variety of labs, witnesses to simulated crimes were shown lineups that didn't include the culprit, *and* they mistakenly identified one of the foils. After their mistaken identification, the lineup administrator said either, "Good, you identified the suspect," or said nothing.

Later, all witnesses were asked, "How good was the view that you had of the culprit?" and "How well could you make out the details of the culprit's face while witnessing the crime?" All witnesses had the same (poor) view. Of the witnesses who didn't receive the positive feedback, none reported that they had a "good" or "excellent" view, and none said they could easily make out the details of the face. Among those who got the positive feedback, 27 percent said their view was good or excellent, and 20 percent said they could easily make out the face (Wells and Quinlivan, 10).

The Witness's Attention

LO 8

The Supreme Court in *Manson* equated attention with the *amount* of time witnesses spent looking at the culprit's face. Eyewitness identification psychologists have concluded that it's not the amount of time spent but what witnesses do with the time. For example, devoting time to specific facial features (eyes, nose, mouth) takes a lot more time than judging what the whole face looks like. But researchers have found that the whole face view, which can happen rapidly, leads to recognizing that face in a lineup. On the other hand, in reconstructing a face (for a composite drawing), attention to specific facial features is better than a whole face view (Wells and Quinlivan, 10–11).

People naturally have a limited capacity to take in information, so paying attention to one part of an event takes away from concentrating on another. The "weapons effect" (see "weapons focus," discussed on p. 313) is a good example of this. Paying attention to the weapon reduces the capacity to recognize the face. Also, research demonstrates that the better witnesses can describe peripheral details ("I noticed the window was open"), the poorer their description of the culprit's face (Wells and Leippe 1981).

The Witness's Certainty

LO 8

"How certain are you that you identified the right person?" "How confident are you that you identified the right person?" Researchers ask these questions about the certainty (also called confidence) of a witness's identification in virtually all experiments. Certainty, another circumstance in the *Manson* liability prong, is "one of the most researched variables in the eyewitness literature" (Wells and Quinlivan 11).

Witness confidence was one of the totality of circumstance variables that the Supreme Court in *Manson v. Braithwaite* (1977) used to assess the reliability of the unnecessarily suggestive identification procedure in that case. But witness confidence affects not only jury decisions during trial but also whether prosecutors will charge suspects in the first place. It further affects whether they go to trial or negotiate a plea with charged defendants. So it's no surprise that researchers have devoted so much time to the link between eyewitness confidence in their identifications and the reliability of those identifications.

What have researchers found? Psychologists have concluded that "eyewitness certainty, although of limited utility, can have *some* diagnostic value." But that's only where there were no suggestive procedures. When there are, such as when a lineup administrator confirms a witness's choice ("You picked the right one"), the research has consistently shown that it inflates the confidence of witnesses who pick the wrong person (Wells and Quinlivan 2009, 11–12). For example, in one study, less than 15 percent of eyewitnesses who picked the wrong person said that, at the moment when they made the identification, they were "positive or nearly positive" about their selection. But after a group of mistaken witnesses were told by administrators, "Good, you identified the actual suspect," 50 percent said they were positive or nearly positive at the moment of identification (Bradfield, Wells, and Olson 2002).

You should know three further findings. First, witnesses soon forget that they were uncertain at the moment of identification; instead, they believe they were certain all along. Second, the boost in confidence is stronger in *mistaken* witnesses than it is in witnesses who are right (Wells and Quinlivan 2009, 12). Finally, administrators' confidence-boosting remarks infect witnesses in several ways, including affecting other *Manson* reliability variables. In one series of experiments, participants who received confirming feedback reported the following:

1. Recalling greater certainty in their identification

2. Having a better view

3. Being better able to make out details of the person's face from the video

4. Paying more attention to the video

5. Having a better basis for their identification

6. Making their identification more easily

7. Being better able to identify strangers

8. Having a better image in their mind of the person's face

9. Being more willing to testify about their identification (Douglass and McQuiston-Surrett 2006, 999)

Recommendations for Reforming Identification Procedures

It should be clear by now that an enormous body of psychology research, only a tiny bit of which we've surveyed here, has exposed serious shortcomings in the *Manson* reliability test's capacity to produce accurate (reliable) eyewitness identifications. So it's not surprising that the test's shortcomings have generated considerable criticism and a variety of calls for reform, even though it satisfies the due process rights guaranteed by the U.S. Constitution. Let's look at some of the criticism and some specific recommended reforms.

Recommendations by Psychologists and Lawyers

Psychologists have tried for decades to make the legal and criminal justice communities aware of their findings and to change police identification procedures based on the findings.

Defense lawyers have tried to get courts to accept expert eyewitness identification psychologists' testimony on human perception and memory and on the shortcomings of eyewitness identification evidence. Defense lawyers also have urged judges to instruct jurors that eyewitnesses can wrongly identify defendants.

Legal commentators argue that the *Manson* test is a poor way to decide the reliability of identifications at trial. To improve reliability, they have recommended several reforms that courts can implement, including:

1. A per se rule excluding all evidence based on suggestive procedures

2. Looser standards for admitting expert testimony on human perception and memory and on the shortcomings of eyewitness identification

3. Requiring corroboration of eyewitness identifications in some cases, such as cross-racial identifications (Nartarajan 2003, 1845–48)

4. Mandating certain police identification procedures recommended by psychologists, such as the sequential lineup (Sussman 2001–2)

Recommendations by Legislatures and Law Enforcement Agencies

A few state legislatures, such as New Jersey, Virginia, and Wisconsin, and a few police departments, including Minneapolis and several of its suburbs and Seattle, have adopted identification procedures based on the psychology research you learned about earlier. Wisconsin's recommendations include the following:

1. Utilize nonsuspect fillers chosen to minimize any suggestiveness that might point toward the suspect.

2. Utilize a "double blind" procedure, in which the administrator (called a **blind administrator**) doesn't know who the suspect is and, therefore, isn't in a position to influence the witness's selection unintentionally.

3. Instruct eyewitnesses that the real perpetrator might or might not be present and that the administrator doesn't know which person is the suspect.

4. Present the suspect and the fillers sequentially (one at a time, or **sequential presentation**) rather than simultaneously (all at once, or **simultaneous presentation**). In a sequential presentation, the witness is asked to answer "yes" or "no" as each person in the lineup is presented. This discourages relative judgment and encourages absolute judgments of each person presented, because eyewitnesses are unable to see the subjects all at once or to know when they've seen the last subject.

5. Assess eyewitness confidence immediately after identification.

6. Avoid multiple identification procedures in which the same witness views the same suspect more than once. (Wisconsin Attorney General 2010, 3)

State Court Opinions

Some state courts have responded to the legal and social science criticisms of the *Manson* reliability test by interpreting their state constitutions or state statutes, or by court rule making, to provide more protection than *Manson* (Shay and O'Toole 2006, 115; Table 9.1).

The Utah Supreme Court, in *State v. Long* (1986), as early as 1986 recognized that "research has convincingly demonstrated the weaknesses inherent in eyewitness identification" (490). The court also recognized that "jurors are, for the most part, unaware of these problems" (490). As a result, the court ruled that trial courts had to give jurors **"cautionary instruction,"** explaining the weaknesses of eyewitness identification evidence.

But the court also acknowledged that a cautionary instruction is "plainly not a panacea." In 2009, the Utah Supreme Court, in *State v. Clopten*, our next case excerpt, recognizing the limits of the cautionary instruction, added a second requirement—the use of expert witnesses to explain to the jury the limits of human perception and memory and how that affects eyewitness identification evidence.

In 2009, the Utah Supreme Court, in State v. Clopten, *our next case excerpt, required that expert witnesses be used to explain to juries the limits of human perception and memory and how that affects eyewitness identification evidence.*

CASE Did He Have a "Right" to an Expert Witness?

State v. Clopten
223 P.3d 1103 (Utah 2009)

HISTORY

Deon Lomax CLOPTEN (Defendant) was convicted by a jury in the Third District Court, Salt Lake Department, of murder, failing to respond to a police command, and possession of a dangerous weapon. Defendant appeals his conviction for murder on grounds that the trial court abused its discretion when it excluded expert testimony regarding the reliability of eyewitness identification. Following existing Utah precedent, the court of appeals affirmed Clopten's conviction while inviting this court to revisit our position on the admissibility of such expert testimony. We reverse the decision of the court of appeals, vacate the conviction, and remand for a new trial.

DURHAM, C.J.

FACTS

Tony Fuailemaa, the victim in this case, was shot and killed outside a nightclub following a rap concert. An undercover police officer responded and was told by the victim's girlfriend, Shannon Pantoja, that the shooter was "the guy in the red." The officer gave chase and saw several men jump into a Ford Explorer and drive away at high speed. A police pursuit ensued and resulted in the capture of Clopten and three other men. Clopten was in the driver's seat of the Explorer at the time of the arrest. Freddie White, the individual identified by Clopten as the shooter, was in the rear passenger seat. Both Clopten and White are African-American. Clopten was wearing both a red hooded sweatshirt and red pants at the time of arrest, while White was wearing a red T-shirt. Another red hooded sweatshirt was later found in the Explorer near where White had been sitting; the evidence suggested that White had been wearing it earlier in the evening. The handgun was found on the side of a road, having been thrown from the Explorer during the pursuit.

The State was unable to link Clopten to the handgun using fingerprints or other forensic evidence. Instead, the State relied heavily on eyewitness testimony of Shannon Pantoja and Melissa Valdez. Both Valdez and Pantoja witnessed a brutal crime committed by a stranger. They each saw the shooter for no more than a few seconds, from some distance away, at night, and while in extreme fear for their own lives. The shooter's facial features were likely disguised by a hood. The shooter was of a different race than either eyewitness, and the presence of a weapon may have served as a significant distractor. Pantoja's identification may have been biased by her expectations, since Fuailemaa had told her just before the murder that he and Clopten were enemies. Her identification may also have been affected by circumstances that occurred later, such as the fact that Clopten was the only individual wearing a red sweatshirt at the time of the initial "show up" identification. Pantoja's statement that she was urged by police to go identify a perpetrator for the sake of her murdered boyfriend, at a time when she was still extremely distraught, also creates doubts as to her accuracy. Finally, the fact that Pantoja insisted that she remembered the shooter's distinctive hairline, when others testified that the shooter's head was covered, raises a fair question as to whether Pantoja actually recalled the shooter's hairline, or if she later incorporated that feature into her memory after seeing pictures of Clopten.

In February 2006, Clopten was convicted of first-degree murder. As part of his defense, Clopten sought to introduce the testimony of Dr. David Dodd, an expert on eyewitness identification. Clopten intended to elicit testimony from Dr. Dodd regarding various factors that can affect the accuracy of eyewitness identifications, including cross-racial identification, the impact of violence and stress during an event, the tendency to focus on a weapon rather than an individual's facial features, and the suggestive nature of certain identification procedures used by police.

At trial, the district court initially allowed the expert testimony, but later reversed itself and ruled that Dr. Dodd could not testify. The trial court reasoned that the testimony was unnecessary since potential problems with eyewitness identification could be explained using a jury instruction, as has been the common practice in Utah since this court's decision in *State v. Long*, 721 P.2d 483 (Utah 1986). The trial court concluded that the jury instruction (hereinafter a "*Long* instruction") "does an adequate job" and that Dr. Dodd's testimony would be "superfluous" and "would only confuse the issue."

Clopten appealed the trial court's ruling. The court of appeals held that trial judges are afforded "significant deference to exclude expert testimony on this topic" and upheld the conviction. However, the court also cited numerous studies concluding "that jury instructions and cross-examinations do not adequately address the vagaries of eyewitness identification." Judge Thorne wrote a separate concurrence, in which he urged this court to "revisit the boundaries of trial court discretion in excluding expert testimony on the subject." We granted certiorari review.

OPINION

When we decided *State v. Long* in 1986, it was already apparent that although research has convincingly demonstrated the weaknesses inherent in eyewitness identification, jurors are, for the most part, unaware of these problems. In *Long*, we considered the appropriateness of jury instructions as a way of familiarizing the fact-finder with these issues. There, the defendant was convicted of aggravated assault based on an identification made by the victim, who had been wounded by a shotgun blast and acknowledged that his vision was "glossy" when he saw the shooter. Counsel for the defendant requested a cautionary instruction regarding the accuracy of the identification, which the trial court declined to give. We reversed Long's conviction, and remanded the case for a new trial. In addition, we directed trial courts to provide instructions "whenever eyewitness identification is a central issue in a case and such an instruction is requested by the defense."

We also acknowledged that, because of doubts regarding its effectiveness in educating the jury, a cautionary instruction plainly is not a panacea. It was never the intent of this court to establish cautionary instructions as the sole means for educating juries about eyewitness fallibility. Indeed, we carefully acknowledged that "full evaluation of the efficacy of cautionary instructions must await further experience." With the benefit of hindsight, however, it is clear that *Long* actually discouraged the inclusion of eyewitness expert testimony by failing to dispel earlier notions that such testimony would constitute a "lecture to the jury about how they should perform their duties." As a result, trial judges reached two logical conclusions: (1) when in doubt, issuing cautionary instructions was a safe option; and (2) allowing expert testimony was hazardous if the expert "lectured the jury" about the credibility of a witness.

Subsequent decisions reinforced this bias. In addition, we held that a *Long* instruction is enough to render an erroneous exclusion harmless, even if the instruction failed to mention significant portions of the proffered

expert testimony. Finally, neither this court nor the court of appeals has ever reversed a conviction for failure to admit eyewitness expert testimony. Given this history, it is not surprising that there is a de facto presumption against eyewitness expert testimony in Utah's trial courts.

This trend, acknowledged by both parties, is troubling in light of strong empirical research suggesting that cautionary instructions are a poor substitute for expert testimony. Decades of study, both before and particularly after *Long*, have established that eyewitnesses are prone to identifying the wrong person as the perpetrator of a crime, particularly when certain factors are present. For example, people identify members of their own race with greater accuracy than they do members of a different race. In addition, accuracy is significantly affected by factors such as the amount of time the culprit was in view, lighting conditions, use of a disguise, distinctiveness of the culprit's appearance, and the presence of a weapon or other distractions.

Moreover, there is little doubt that juries are generally unaware of these deficiencies in human perception and memory and thus give great weight to eyewitness identifications. Indeed, juries seemed to be swayed the most by the confidence of an eyewitness, even though such confidence correlates only weakly with accuracy. That the empirical data is conclusive on these matters is not disputed by either party in this case and has not been questioned by this court in the decisions that followed *Long*.

The remaining issue is whether expert testimony is generally necessary to adequately educate a jury regarding these inherent deficiencies. As discussed below, we are now convinced that it is. In the absence of expert testimony, a defendant is left with two tools—cross-examination and cautionary instructions—with which to convey the possibility of mistaken identification to the jury. Both of these tools suffer from serious shortcomings when it comes to addressing the merits of eyewitness identifications.

The most troubling dilemma regarding eyewitnesses stems from the possibility that an inaccurate identification may be just as convincing to a jury as an accurate one. The challenge arises in determining how best to provide that assistance in cases where mistaken identification is a possibility. It is apparent from the research that the inclusion of expert testimony carries significant advantages over the alternatives, namely cross-examination and jury instructions.

Typically, an expert is called by a criminal defendant to explain how certain factors relevant to the identification in question could have produced a mistake. Such testimony teaches jurors about certain factors—such as "weapon focus" and the weak correlation between confidence and accuracy—that have a strong but counterintuitive impact on the reliability of an eyewitness. In other words, the testimony enables jurors to avoid certain common pitfalls, such as believing that a witness's statement of certainty is a reliable indicator of accuracy. Second, it assists jurors by quantifying what most people already know. Expert testimony does not unfairly favor the defendant by making the jury skeptical of all eyewitnesses. In fact, when a witness sees the perpetrator under favorable conditions, expert testimony actually makes jurors more likely to convict. When expert testimony is used correctly, the end result is a jury that is better able to reach a just decision.

In the absence of expert testimony, the method most commonly used to challenge the veracity of eyewitnesses is cross-examination. But because eyewitnesses may express almost absolute certainty about identifications that are inaccurate, research shows the effectiveness of cross-examination is badly hampered. Cross-examination will often expose a lie or half-truth, but may be far less effective when witnesses, although mistaken, believe that what they say is true. In addition, eyewitnesses are likely to use their "expectations, personal experience, biases, and prejudices" to fill in the gaps created by imperfect memory. Because it is unlikely that witnesses will be aware that this process has occurred, they may express far more confidence in the identification than is warranted.

Trial courts in Utah and around the nation have often tried to remedy the possibility of mistaken identification by giving cautionary instructions to the jury. The standard instruction consists of general cautions about many factors known to contribute to mistaken identifications, such as brief exposure time, lack of light, presence of disguises and distractions, and effects of stress and cross-racial identification. At the time it was adopted, it seemed logical that this measure would substantially enhance a jury's ability to evaluate eyewitness accuracy.

Subsequent research, however, has shown that a cautionary instruction does little to help a jury spot a mistaken identification. While this result seems counterintuitive, commentators and social scientists advance a number of convincing explanations. First, instructions "given at the end of what might be a long and fatiguing trial, and buried in an overall charge by the court" are unlikely to have much effect on the minds of a jury. Second, instructions may come too late to alter the jury's opinion of a witness whose testimony might have been heard days before. Third, even the best cautionary instructions tend to touch only generally on the empirical evidence. The judge may explain that certain factors are known to influence perception and memory, but will not explain how this occurs or

to what extent. As a result, instructions have been shown to be less effective than expert testimony.

In conclusion, there is little reason to be confident that cross-examination and cautionary instructions alone provide a sufficient safeguard against mistaken identifications. In contrast, expert testimony has been shown to substantially enhance the ability of juries to recognize potential problems with eyewitness testimony.

We REVERSE the decision of the court of appeals, vacate Clopten's conviction and REMAND for a new trial in accordance with our decision today.

CONCURRING AND DISSENTING OPINION

DURRANT, A.C.J.

Our case law has consistently recognized that the decision to admit or exclude expert testimony is within the discretion of the district court. It is fundamentally a product of the structure of our judicial system, in which district court judges are placed in a superior position to evaluate the proffered testimony in light of the principles set out in the rules of evidence.

I would simply instruct the district courts that they are to treat eyewitness expert testimony like any other type of expert testimony and determine its admissibility based on the requirements of the rule. I would neither create a presumption in favor, nor one against, the admission of eyewitness expert testimony, and district court rulings on the admissibility of such expert testimony would be entitled to the same deference we have traditionally accorded rulings on the admissibility of other types of expert testimony.

QUESTIONS

1. Describe the details of the basis for the two eyewitnesses' identification of Deon Clopten.
2. Describe the police identification procedure during which the witnesses identified Clopten.
3. Summarize the court's reasons for holding that the trial court should've allowed expert witness testimony.
4. Summarize Judge Durrant's concurring/dissenting opinion disagreements with the majority.

ETHICAL ISSUES

Do Police Departments Have an Ethical Responsibility to Adopt Lineup Procedure Reforms? Hennepin County Pilot Project

There is a persuasive body of research concerning new methods to secure eyewitness identifications from photographic lineups. This research shows that relatively simple changes in lineup procedures can lead to stronger eyewitness identifications, making it more likely that the right person is held responsible for the crime. Accordingly, in the interests of justice, the Hennepin County Attorney's Office spearheaded an initiative to improve traditional lineup procedures. In the fall of 2003, the office worked with several police departments to adopt a new photographic lineup protocol consistent with recent scientific evidence on procedures designed to minimize the risk of misidentifications. The county attorney's office developed a year-long pilot program to examine recommended eyewitness procedures in real police field investigations. The results of this project, detailed below, represent the first available field data on blind sequential lineup performance.

Amy Klobuchar, Hennepin County Attorney

INSTRUCTIONS

1. Visit the Companion Website and read "Improving Eyewitness Identifications: Hennepin County's Blind Sequential Lineup Pilot Project" (Klobuchar, Steblay, and Caligiuri 2006). See the link under the Chapter 9 Ethical Issues section—login at www.cengagebrain.com.

2. Summarize the results of the research on the blind sequential lineup project.

3. Summarize the implementation results in Part VI of the article.

4. In light of the summaries in 2 and 3, do you believe *all* police departments have an ethical duty to implement one, or both, of these reforms? If not, what, if any, ethical duties do police departments in Hennepin County, or any other departments around the country, have regarding police lineup procedures?

DNA Profile Identification

LO 9

Because of scientific advances in the testing of deoxyribonucleic acid, particularly Short Tandem Repeat (STR) DNA testing, one of the most important criminal law issues of our day is whether there exists under the Constitution of the United States a right, post-conviction, to access previously produced forensic evidence for purposes of DNA testing in order to establish one's complete innocence of the crime for which he has been convicted and sentenced.

There is now widespread agreement within the scientific community that this technology can distinguish between any two individuals on the planet, other than identical twins, the statistical probabilities of STR DNA matches ranging in the hundreds of billions, if not trillions. In other words, STR DNA tests can, in certain circumstances, establish to a virtual certainty whether a given individual did or did not commit a particular crime. (Judge Michael Luttig, *Harvey v. Horan* 2002, 304–5)

U.S. Fourth Circuit Court Judge Luttig, who wrote these words, concluded that there is a "core liberty interest protected by the Due Process Clause of the Fourteenth Amendment which, in certain, very limited circumstances, gives rise to access previously produced forensic evidence for purposes of STR DNA testing" (308). Judge Luttig believes that judicial recognition of **DNA profiling**, this new science for determining innocence and guilt, should be "ungrudging." He recognizes that such a right will place burdens on the courts and lead to difficult questions concerning standards for access of the evidence for testing and for its use in court (306). Nevertheless, he wrote:

But no one, regardless of his political, philosophical, or jurisprudential disposition, should be otherwise troubled that a person who was convicted in accordance with law might thereafter be set free, either by the executive or by the courts, because of evidence that provides absolute proof that he did not in fact commit the crime for which he was convicted. Such is not an indictment of our system of justice, which, while insisting upon a very high degree of proof for conviction, does not, after all, require proof beyond *all* doubt, and therefore, *is* capable of producing erroneous determinations of both guilt and innocence. To the contrary, it would be a high credit to our system of justice that it recognizes the need for, and imperative of, a safety valve in those rare instances where objective proof that the convicted actually did not commit the offense later becomes available through the progress of science. (306)

Finally, Judge Luttig makes clear that this constitutional right of access should not be "constitutionally required or permitted as a matter of course or even frequently" (306).

In *District Attorney's Office for the Third Judicial District and others v. William G. Osborne* (2009), our next case excerpt, the U.S. Supreme Court (5–4) decided that there's no constitutional right of access to forensic evidence.

In **District Attorney's Office for the Third Judicial District and others v. William G. Osborne** *(2009), our next case excerpt, the U.S. Supreme Court (5–4) decided that there's no constitutional right of access to forensic evidence.*

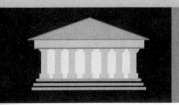

CASE Does a State's Refusal to Grant a Request for DNA Testing Deny the Prisoner's Due Process Right?

District Attorney's Office for the Third Judicial District and others v. William G. Osborne

129 S.Ct. 2308 (2009)

HISTORY

After the Court of Appeals of Alaska affirmed the denial of his request for further DNA testing of evidence used to convict him, State prisoner William Osborne brought a § 1983 action to compel release of certain biological evidence so that it could be subjected to DNA testing. The United States District Court for the District of Alaska dismissed the action. Osborne appealed. The United States Court of Appeals for the Ninth Circuit reversed. On remand, the District Court awarded summary judgment for Osborne, and the Court of Appeals affirmed. The U.S. Supreme Court reversed and remanded.

ROBERTS, C.J., joined by SCALIA, KENNEDY, THOMAS, and ALITO, JJ.

FACTS

On the evening of March 22, 1993, two men driving through Anchorage, Alaska, solicited sex from a female prostitute, K.G. She agreed to perform fellatio on both men for $100 and got in their car. The three spent some time looking for a place to stop and ended up in a deserted area near Earthquake Park. When K.G. demanded payment in advance, the two men pulled out a gun and forced her to perform fellatio on the driver while the passenger penetrated her vaginally, using a blue condom she had brought. The passenger then ordered K.G. out of the car and told her to lie face-down in the snow. Fearing for her life, she refused, and the two men choked her and beat her with the gun. When K.G. tried to flee, the passenger beat her with a wooden axe handle and shot her in the head while she lay on the ground. They kicked some snow on top of her and left her for dead.

K.G. did not die; the bullet had only grazed her head. Once the two men left, she found her way back to the road, and flagged down a passing car to take her home. Ultimately, she received medical care and spoke to the police. At the scene of the crime, the police recovered a spent shell casing, the axe handle, some of K.G.'s clothing stained with blood, and the blue condom.

Six days later, two military police officers at Fort Richardson pulled over Dexter Jackson for flashing his headlights at another vehicle. In his car they discovered a gun (which matched the shell casing), as well as several items K.G. had been carrying the night of the attack. The car also matched the description K.G. had given to the police. Jackson admitted that he had been the driver during the rape and assault, and told the police that William Osborne had been his passenger. Other evidence also implicated Osborne. K.G. picked out his photograph (with some uncertainty) and at trial she identified Osborne as her attacker. Other witnesses testified that shortly before the crime, Osborne had called Jackson from an arcade, and then driven off with him. An axe handle similar to the one at the scene of the crime was found in Osborne's room on the military base where he lived.

Osborne and Jackson were convicted by an Alaska jury of kidnapping, assault, and sexual assault. They were acquitted of an additional count of sexual assault and of attempted murder. Finding it "nearly miraculous" that K.G. had survived, the trial judge sentenced Osborne to 26 years in prison, with 5 suspended. His conviction and sentence were affirmed on appeal.

OPINION

Modern DNA testing can provide powerful new evidence unlike anything known before. Since its first use in criminal investigations in the mid-1980s, there have been several major advances in DNA technology, culminating in STR technology. It is now often possible to determine whether a biological tissue matches a suspect with near certainty. DNA testing has exonerated wrongly convicted people, and has confirmed the convictions of many others. The availability of technologies not available at trial cannot mean that every criminal conviction, or even every criminal conviction involving biological evidence, is suddenly in doubt. The dilemma is how to harness DNA's power to prove innocence without unnecessarily overthrowing the established system of criminal justice.

That task belongs primarily to the legislature. The States are currently engaged in serious, thoughtful examinations of how to ensure the fair and effective use of this testing within the existing criminal justice framework. Forty-six States have already enacted statutes dealing specifically with access to DNA evidence. The State of Alaska itself is considering joining them. The Federal Government has also passed the Innocence Protection Act of 2004, which allows federal prisoners to move for court-ordered DNA testing under certain specified conditions. That Act also grants money to States that enact comparable statutes, and as a consequence has served as a model for some state legislation. At oral argument, Osborne agreed that the federal statute is a model for how States ought to handle the issue.

These laws recognize the value of DNA evidence but also the need for certain conditions on access to the State's evidence. A requirement of demonstrating materiality is common, but it is not the only one. The federal statute, for example, requires a sworn statement that the applicant is innocent. States also impose a range of diligence requirements. Several require the requested testing to have been technologically impossible at trial. Others deny testing to those who declined testing at trial for tactical reasons.

Alaska is one of a handful of States yet to enact legislation specifically addressing the issue of evidence requested for DNA testing. But that does not mean that such evidence is unavailable for those seeking to prove their innocence. Instead, Alaska courts are addressing how to apply existing laws for discovery and postconviction relief to this novel technology. Both parties agree that under Alaska Stat. § 12.7, "a defendant is entitled to post-conviction relief if the defendant presents newly discovered evidence that establishes by clear and convincing evidence that the defendant is innocent." If such a claim is brought, state law permits general discovery. Alaska courts have explained that these procedures are available to request DNA evidence for newly available testing to establish actual innocence.

In addition to this statutory procedure, the Alaska Court of Appeals has invoked a widely accepted three-part test to govern additional rights to DNA access under the State Constitution. Drawing on the experience with DNA evidence of State Supreme Courts around the country, the Court of Appeals explained that it was "reluctant to hold that Alaska law offers no remedy to defendants who could prove their factual innocence." It was "prepared to hold, however, that a defendant who seeks post-conviction DNA testing must show (1) that the conviction rested primarily on eyewitness identification evidence, (2) that there was a demonstrable doubt concerning the defendant's identification as the perpetrator, and (3) that scientific testing would likely be conclusive on this issue." Thus, the Alaska courts have suggested that even those who do not get discovery under the State's criminal rules have available to them a safety valve under the State Constitution.

"No State shall . . . deprive any person of life, liberty, or property, without due process of law." U.S. Const., Amdt. 14, § 1; accord Amdt. 5. This Clause imposes procedural limitations on a State's power to take away protected entitlements. Osborne argues that access to the State's evidence is a "process" needed to vindicate his right to prove himself innocent and get out of jail. Process is not an end in itself, so a necessary premise of this argument is that he has an entitlement (what our precedents call a "liberty interest") to prove his innocence even after a fair trial has proved otherwise. We must first examine this asserted liberty interest to determine what process (if any) is due.

Osborne has a liberty interest in demonstrating his innocence with new evidence under state law. A criminal defendant proved guilty after a fair trial does not have the same liberty interests as a free man. At trial, the defendant is presumed innocent and may demand that the government prove its case beyond reasonable doubt. But once a defendant has been afforded a fair trial and convicted of the offense for which he was charged, the presumption of innocence disappears. Given a valid conviction, the criminal defendant has been constitutionally deprived of his liberty.

The State accordingly has more flexibility in deciding what procedures are needed in the context of postconviction relief. We see nothing inadequate about the procedures Alaska has provided to vindicate its state right to postconviction relief in general, and nothing inadequate about how those procedures apply to those who seek access to DNA evidence. Alaska provides a substantive right to be released on a sufficiently compelling showing of new evidence that establishes innocence. It exempts such claims from otherwise applicable time limits. The State provides for discovery in postconviction proceedings, and has—through judicial decision—specified that this discovery procedure is available to those seeking access to DNA evidence.

And there is more. While the Alaska courts have not had occasion to conclusively decide the question, the Alaska Court of Appeals has suggested that the State Constitution provides an additional right of access to DNA. In expressing its "reluctance to hold that Alaska law offers no remedy" to those who belatedly seek DNA testing, and in invoking the three-part test used by other state courts, the court indicated that in an appropriate case the State Constitution may provide a failsafe even for those who cannot satisfy the statutory requirements under general postconviction procedures.

To the degree there is some uncertainty in the details of Alaska's newly developing procedures for obtaining postconviction access to DNA, we can hardly fault the State for that. Osborne has brought this § 1983 action without ever using these procedures in filing a state or federal habeas claim relying on actual innocence. In other words, he has not tried to use the process provided to him by the State or attempted to vindicate the liberty interest that is now the centerpiece of his claim. When Osborne *did* request DNA testing in state court, he sought RFLP testing that had been available at trial, not the STR testing he now seeks, and the state court relied on that fact in denying him testing under Alaska law.

His attempt to sidestep state process through a new federal lawsuit puts Osborne in a very awkward position. If he simply seeks the DNA through the State's discovery procedures, he might well get it. If he does not, it may be for a perfectly adequate reason, just as the federal statute

and all state statutes impose conditions and limits on access to DNA evidence. It is difficult to criticize the State's procedures when Osborne has not invoked them. This is not to say that Osborne must exhaust state-law remedies. But it is Osborne's burden to demonstrate the inadequacy of the state-law procedures available to him in state postconviction relief. These procedures are adequate on their face, and without trying them, Osborne can hardly complain that they do not work in practice.

Osborne asks that we recognize a freestanding substantive due process right to DNA evidence untethered from the liberty interests he hopes to vindicate with it. We reject the invitation and conclude, in the circumstances of this case, that there is no such substantive due process right. Osborne seeks access to state evidence so that he can apply new DNA-testing technology that might prove him innocent. The elected governments of the States are actively confronting the challenges DNA technology poses to our criminal justice systems and our traditional notions of finality, as well as the opportunities it affords. To suddenly constitutionalize this area would short-circuit what looks to be a prompt and considered legislative response.

DNA evidence will undoubtedly lead to changes in the criminal justice system. It has done so already. The question is whether further change will primarily be made by legislative revision and judicial interpretation of the existing system, or whether the Federal Judiciary must leap ahead—revising (or even discarding) the system by creating a new constitutional right and taking over responsibility for refining it.

Federal courts should not presume that state criminal procedures will be inadequate to deal with technological change. The criminal justice system has historically accommodated new types of evidence, and is a time-tested means of carrying out society's interest in convicting the guilty while respecting individual rights. That system, like any human endeavor, cannot be perfect. DNA evidence shows that it has not been. But there is no basis for Osborne's approach of assuming that because DNA has shown that these procedures are not flawless, DNA evidence must be treated as categorically outside the process, rather than within it. That is precisely what his § 1983 suit seeks to do, and that is the contention we reject.

The judgment of the Court of Appeals is REVERSED, and the case is REMANDED for further proceedings consistent with this opinion.

It is so ordered.

CONCURRING OPINION

Justice ALITO, with whom Justice KENNEDY joins, and with whom Justice THOMAS joins as to Part II, concurring.

Respondent was convicted for a brutal sexual assault. At trial, the defense declined to have DNA testing done on a semen sample found at the scene of the crime. Defense counsel explained that this decision was made based on fear that the testing would provide further evidence of respondent's guilt. After conviction, in an unsuccessful attempt to obtain parole, respondent confessed in detail to the crime. Now, respondent claims that he has a federal constitutional right to test the sample and that he can go directly to federal court to obtain this relief without giving the Alaska courts a full opportunity to consider his claim. A defendant who declines the opportunity to perform DNA testing at trial for tactical reasons has no constitutional right to perform such testing after conviction.

DISSENT

Justice STEVENS, with whom Justice GINSBURG and Justice BREYER join, and with whom Justice SOUTER joins as to Part I, dissenting.

The State of Alaska possesses physical evidence that, if tested, will conclusively establish whether respondent William Osborne committed rape and attempted murder. If he did, justice has been served by his conviction and sentence. If not, Osborne has needlessly spent decades behind bars while the true culprit has not been brought to justice. The DNA test Osborne seeks is a simple one, its cost modest, and its results uniquely precise.

Throughout the course of state and federal litigation, the State has failed to provide any concrete reason for denying Osborne the DNA testing he seeks, and none is apparent. Because Osborne has offered to pay for the tests, cost is not a factor. And as the State now concedes, there is no reason to doubt that such testing would provide conclusive confirmation of Osborne's guilt or revelation of his innocence. In the courts below, the State refused to provide an explanation for its refusal to permit testing of the evidence, and in this Court, its explanation has been, at best, unclear. Insofar as the State has articulated any reason at all, it appears to be a generalized interest in protecting the finality of the judgment of conviction from any possible future attacks.

While we have long recognized that States have an interest in securing the finality of their judgments, finality is not a stand-alone value that trumps a State's overriding interest in ensuring that justice is done in its courts and secured to its citizens. Indeed, when absolute proof of innocence is readily at hand, a State should not shrink from the possibility that error may have occurred. Rather, our system of justice is strengthened by recognizing the need for, and imperative of, a safety valve in those rare instances where objective proof that the convicted actually did not commit the offense later becomes available through the progress of science. DNA evidence has led to an extraordinary series of exonerations, not only in cases where the trial evidence was weak, but also in cases where the convicted parties confessed their guilt and where the trial evidence against them appeared overwhelming.

The arbitrariness of the State's conduct is highlighted by comparison to the private interests it denies. It seems to me obvious that if a wrongly convicted person were to produce proof of his actual innocence, no state interest would be sufficient to justify his continued punitive detention. If such proof can be readily obtained without imposing a significant burden on the State, a refusal to provide access to such evidence is wholly unjustified.

SOUTER, J.

Alaska argues against finding any right to relief in a federal § 1983 action because the procedure the State provides is reasonable and adequate to vindicate the post-trial liberty interest in testing evidence that the State has chosen to recognize. When I first considered the State's position I thought Alaska's two strongest points were these: (1) that in Osborne's state litigation he failed to request access for the purpose of a variety of postconviction testing that could not have been done at time of trial (and thus sought no new evidence by his state-court petition); and (2) that he failed to aver actual innocence (and thus failed to place his oath behind the assertion that the evidence sought would be material to his postconviction claim). Denying him any relief under these circumstances, the argument ran, did not indicate any inadequacy in the state procedure that would justify resort to § 1983 for providing due process.

Yet the record shows that Osborne has been denied access to the evidence even though he satisfied each of these conditions. As for the requirement to claim testing by a method not available at trial, Osborne's state-court appellate brief specifically mentioned his intent to conduct short tandem repeat (STR) analysis, and the State points to no pleading, brief, or evidence that Osborne ever changed this request.

The State's reliance on Osborne's alleged failure to claim factual innocence is equally untenable. While there is no question that after conviction and imprisonment he admitted guilt under oath as a condition for becoming eligible for parole, the record before us makes it equally apparent that he claims innocence on oath now. His affidavit filed in support of his request for evidence under § 1983 contained the statement, "I have always maintained my innocence," followed by an explanation that his admission of guilt was a necessary gimmick to obtain parole. Since the State persists in maintaining that Osborne is not entitled to test its evidence, it is apparently mere makeweight for the State to claim that he is not entitled to § 1983 relief because he failed to claim innocence seriously and unequivocally.

This is not the first time the State has produced reasons for opposing Osborne's request that collapse upon inspection. Arguing before the Ninth Circuit, the State maintained that the DNA evidence Osborne sought was not material; that is, it argued that a test excluding

Osborne as the source of semen in the blue condom, found near the bloody snow and spent shell casing in the secluded area where the victim was raped by one man, would not "establish that he was factually innocent" or even "undermine confidence . . . in the verdict." Such an argument is patently untenable, and the State now concedes that a favorable test could "conclusively establish Osborne's innocence."

Standing alone, the inadequacy of each of the State's reasons for denying Osborne access to the DNA evidence he seeks would not make out a due process violation. But taken as a whole the record convinces me that, while Alaska has created an entitlement of access to DNA evidence under conditions that are facially reasonable, the State has demonstrated a combination of inattentiveness and intransigence in applying those conditions that add up to procedural unfairness that violates the Due Process Clause.

QUESTIONS

1. **Summarize the reasons the majority held that Osborne had no constitutional right to obtain the DNA evidence that the state of Alaska possesses.**
2. **Summarize the reasons the dissents argue that Osborne has a constitutional right to obtain the DNA evidence that the state of Alaska possesses.**
3. **In your opinion, should Osborne have a constitutional right to obtain the DNA evidence? Back up your answer with points made in the Court's opinion.**
4. **What do you make of the disagreement between the majority and the dissents about the facts in the case?**
5. **Summarize Justice Alito's point in his concurring opinion. Do you agree with him? Explain your answer.**

Summary

LO 1
- In a lineup, witnesses try to pick the suspect out of a group of individuals who are present. In a show-up, witnesses match the suspect with one person, who is either present or pictured in a "mug shot."

LO 2
- Courts took a "hands off" approach to identification evidence and its admissibility until 1967 when it first recognized due process challenges to identification testimony.

LO 3, LO 4
- Eyewitness identifications are almost never rejected by courts. To have them rejected, defendants must demonstrate by a preponderance of the evidence that the identification procedure was unnecessarily suggestive and created a very substantial likelihood of misidentification.

LO 5
- Scientists who study memory refute common assumptions about how memory functions and under what circumstances it's likely to be reliable.

LO 5, LO 7
- When memories are acquired, the brain doesn't act as a video recorder storing a stream of images. Observational accuracy is affected by duration, distraction, stress, race, and other factors.

LO 5
- Retrieval blends information from the original experience with information added during the retention period. Eyewitness identification is subject to errors of omission (failure to recall) and errors of commission (incorrect recall).

LO 5, LO 6
- Suggestion is particularly powerful during the retention and recollection phase. Research finds that witnesses add to a story based on what information researchers give them. People aren't good at keeping memories acquired during an incident separate from suggestions that occur thereafter.

LO 5, LO 6
- Identification research relies on both new experiments and archival data. Experimental research needs to make sure that volunteers resemble average real-world witnesses under stress.

LO 5, LO 6
- Eyewitness retrospective self-reports are the basis of identification testimony. The social desirability of the response, the need to appear consistent, and reinterpretation of past events due to new events all affect such reports.

LO 7
- The composition of the lineup and the instructions given prior to the lineup influence identifications. Instructions that seem reasonable are often more suggestive than we realize.

LO 7
- Show-ups are substantially less reliable than lineups. Courts admit show-up identifications even if a witness runs into a suspect in the courthouse, saw police pursuing the suspect, and under other potentially misleading situations.

LO 8
- Research shows that our reported opportunity to view a culprit varies widely from our actual opportunity to do so. The amount of time spent observing a culprit is less important than what the witness did with the time and where he or she focused attention.

LO 7, LO 8
- Reform of identification procedures and testimony includes recommendations allowing expert testimony on memory, mandating sequential lineups, conducting double-blind administration of lineups, warning the witness that the suspect might or might not be in the lineup, and obtaining a witness confidence statement immediately following the identification.

LO 9
- DNA is some of the most powerful evidence imaginable. One of the most important criminal law issues of our day is whether there's a postconviction constitutional right to access DNA evidence for the purpose of exonerating sentenced convicts.

Review Questions

1. Why is identification of strangers risky in criminal cases?
2. Identify and define three mental processes that account for mistakes in identifying strangers.
3. Identify five circumstances that affect the accuracy of identifying strangers.
4. Describe how memory affects the accuracy of eyewitness identification.
5. Describe how suggestion works based on Elizabeth Loftus's research.
6. Describe how witnesses' descriptions of criminal events change over time.
7. When is the effect of suggestion most powerful and threatening? Why?
8. Explain why the procedures used to identify strangers add to the problem of misidentification.
9. Identify and describe three ways to reduce the inaccuracy of eyewitness identification by police procedures and legal rules.
10. Identify three constitutional provisions identification procedures can violate and when in the criminal process they kick in.
11. Summarize what empirical research has shown about the reliability of lineups.
12. Describe and give an example of how the power of suggestion works in administering lineups.

13. Identify the two prongs in the totality-of-circumstances due process test of admissibility of eyewitness identification created by the U.S. Supreme Court.

14. Identify, describe, and give an example of the five circumstances in the totality-of-circumstances due process test you identified in question 15.

15. Why are photo identifications the most unreliable eyewitness identification procedure?

16. List four recommendations made by legal commentators to improve eyewitness identification reliability.

17. List the six recommendations made by the Wisconsin legislature and law enforcement to improve eyewitness identification.

18. Identify and compare the three legal tests for admitting DNA evidence in court.

19. Summarize the importance jurors, lawyers, and judges attach to scientific evidence as proof of guilt.

Key Terms

lineup, p. 303

photo array, p. 303

show-up, p. 303

preponderance of the evidence, p. 304

unnecessarily and impermissibly suggestive, p. 304

very substantial likelihood of misidentification, p. 304

per se approach, p. 307

totality of the circumstances, p. 307

memory experts, p. 311

acquisition of memory, p. 312

retention of memory, p. 312

retrieval of memory, p. 312

eyewitness recall, p. 314

eyewitness recognition, p. 314

errors of omission, p. 314

errors of commission, p. 314

suggestion, p. 314

reliability test of eyewitness evidence, p. 315

archival research, p. 316

experimental research, p. 316

eyewitness retrospective self-reports, p. 316

fillers, p. 317

relative judgment, p. 317

might-or-might-not-be-present instruction, p. 318

blind administrator, p. 322

sequential presentation, p. 322

simultaneous presentation, p. 322

cautionary instruction, p. 322

DNA profiling, p. 326

10

CASES COVERED

Mapp v. Ohio, 367 U.S. 643 (1961)

Herring v. U.S., 129 S.Ct. 695 (2009)

Jacobson v. U.S., 503 U.S. 540 (1992)

LEARNING OBJECTIVES

1 Know that there's no constitutional right to have evidence that was collected illegally excluded at trial. Courts exclude evidence to enforce other established rights.

2 Understand how Fourth, Fifth, Sixth, and Fourteenth Amendment rights can be violated by bad practices in law enforcement.

3 Understand how and why the "fruit of the poisonous tree" doctrine prevents the government from being better off after violating the Constitution.

4 Understand how courts exclude evidence to preserve judicial integrity and to deter officers from breaking the law.

5 Know the exceptions under which evidence excluded from the main prosecution can be used in other parts of the legal process.

6 Understand entrapment and that it occurs when agents get people to commit crimes they wouldn't have otherwise committed.

7 Understand that the entrapment defense isn't provided by constitutional right and how it has been defined by statutes and courts.

8 Know the difference between the subjective test for entrapment (predisposition of the suspect) and the objective test for entrapment (hypothetical person) and when each is used.

Remedies for Constitutional Violations I: The Exclusionary Rule and Entrapment

CHAPTER OUTLINE

The Exclusionary Rule
History
Justifications for the Exclusionary Rule
Exceptions to the Exclusionary Rule
Collateral Use
Cross-Examination

Attenuation, Independent Source, and
Inevitable Discovery
The Good-Faith Exception
Social Costs and Deterrence: The Empirical
Findings

The Defense of Entrapment
The Subjective Test
The Objective Test

On a July afternoon in 2004, Bennie Dean Herring came to the Coffee County Sheriff's Department to retrieve his belongings from a vehicle impounded in the Department's lot. Investigator Mark Anderson, who was at the Department that day, knew Herring from prior interactions: Herring had told the district attorney, among others, of his suspicion that Anderson had been involved in the killing of a local teenager, and Anderson had pursued Herring to get him to drop the accusations. Informed that Herring was in the impoundment lot, Anderson asked the Coffee County warrant clerk whether there was an outstanding warrant for Herring's arrest. Anderson arrested Herring when a law enforcement clerk told him that there was an outstanding warrant against Herring. It turned out later that the clerk was mistaken. *Herring v. U.S.* 1990, 705–6

When I was a very junior member of a Minneapolis mayor's committee to examine police misconduct, our committee held a neighborhood meeting to educate residents about our work. But I learned a lot more than the residents. One resident that night made a comment and then asked a great question. His comment: "We all know what happens when we break the law—we get arrested and prosecuted." His question: "What I want to know is what happens when the police break the law against us? What recourse do we have?"

The answer is, "We have lots of remedies" (at least, on paper).

We'll divide the discussion of the remedies into two types and between this chapter and the next. First, we'll look at remedies that can affect the outcome of the state's criminal case against defendants (the trial stage). They're part of the criminal case against defendants. Two of these remedies are the subject of this chapter:

1. ***Exclusionary rule***. The government throws out illegally obtained evidence in the case against the defendant (by far the most frequently used remedy).

2. ***Defense of entrapment***. The government dismisses cases against defendants who committed crimes they (or a hypothetical reasonable person) wouldn't have committed if law enforcement officers hadn't encouraged them to commit them.

"**Encouragement**" is a widely used undercover police tactic directed mainly at consensual crimes, such as official corruption, and crimes without complaining victims, such as illegal drugs, pornography, and prostitution.

LO 1

Citizens have no constitutional right to either the exclusionary rule or the defense of entrapment. The exclusionary rule is a device created by the U.S. Supreme Court to enforce constitutional rights, but it's not a right on its own. The defense of entrapment is a right created by either federal and state statutes or court decisions.

The remedies covered in Chapter 11 require proceedings separate from the criminal case against defendants. Some of these proceedings take place inside, and others outside, the judicial system. They include:

1. *Criminal prosecution* of police officers for their illegal actions

2. *Civil lawsuits* to seek and obtain remedies from individual officers, and/or the administrators of departments and government units responsible for their wrongdoing

3. *Administrative review* of police misconduct to discipline officers who break police rules

The Exclusionary Rule

LO 1, LO 2

The U.S. legal system, like all others, excludes the use of some irrelevant or untrustworthy evidence. But the *exclusionary rule,* mandating courts to ban the introduction of "good" evidence obtained by "bad" law enforcement, is more prevalent in the United States than in most other countries' legal systems. In Judge Cardozo's famous words, "Should the culprit go free because the constable has blundered?" (*People v. Defore* 1926, 587).

"**Good evidence**" refers to **probative evidence**—evidence that proves (or at least helps to prove) defendants committed the crimes they're charged with. "**Bad methods**" refers to police actions and procedures that violate any of five constitutional rights:

1. The Fourth Amendment ban on unreasonable searches and seizures (Chapters 3–7)
2. The Fifth Amendment ban on coerced incriminating statements (Chapter 8)
3. The Sixth Amendment right to counsel (Chapter 12)
4. The Fifth and Fourteenth Amendment guarantees of due process of law in administering identification procedures (Chapter 9)

In this section, we'll trace the history of the exclusionary rule. Then, we'll examine the rationales for and the scope of the rule; what happens when people are brought to court based on illegal arrests; the reasonable, good-faith exception to the exclusionary rule; whether bad methods employed by non–law enforcement government officials should result in the exclusion of evidence obtained based on their mistakes; and the social costs of the exclusionary rule.

History

LO 1, LO 3

The Bill of Rights to the U.S. Constitution doesn't mention the exclusionary rule (or for that matter any other remedies we'll be discussing in this chapter and Chapter 11). James Madison, in an address to Congress in 1789 (*Annals of Congress* 1789), explains this silence:

> If these rights are incorporated into the Constitution, independent tribunals of justice will consider themselves in a peculiar manner the guardians of those rights; they will be an impenetrable bulwark against every assumption of power in the Legislative or Executive; they will naturally be led to resist every encroachment upon rights expressly stipulated for in the Constitution by the declaration of rights. (457)

In other words, the Constitution didn't have to spell out the remedies because judges would create appropriate ones to fit the circumstances of each case.

Until the 20th century, the only remedies for constitutional violations were private lawsuits against officials. All this changed dramatically in 1914, when the U.S. Supreme Court created the exclusionary rule in *Weeks v. U.S.* (1914). In that case, while Fremont Weeks was at work in Union Station, Kansas City, Kansas, local police officers broke into his house without a warrant. They searched the house and seized "all of his books, letters, money, papers, notes, evidences of indebtedness, stock certificates, insurance policies, deeds, abstracts of title, bonds, candies, clothes, and other property." After taking the evidence to the U.S. Marshal's office, local officers and a marshal arrested Weeks while he was at work. Soon, Weeks was charged with illegal gambling.

The trial court refused Weeks's motion to return the seized evidence, and he was convicted and sentenced to a fine and imprisonment. On appeal, the U.S. Supreme Court reversed the conviction and ordered the return of his documents because to allow the government to seize his private papers and use them to convict him violated his Fourth Amendment right against unreasonable searches and seizures.

Notice two points here. First, the rule established in *Weeks* applied only to *federal* law enforcement; the *states* could choose any remedy they saw fit to enforce their own citizens' constitutional rights under their state constitutions. Second, the rule applied only to Weeks's private papers and other belongings he legally possessed. The Court said nothing about what it would have decided if Weeks had demanded the return of contraband. *Weeks* began a trend toward the use of the exclusionary rule to enforce law enforcement violations of constitutional rights.

The Court broadened the *Weeks* rule in *Silverthorne Lumber Co. v. U.S.* (1920). After arresting Fred Silverthorne and his father, Justice Department officers and a U.S. marshal "without a shadow of authority" went to the Silverthornes' Lumber Company office and "made a clean sweep of all the books, papers and documents found there." The officers immediately took all the stuff they seized to the office of the U.S. District Attorney's office.

The Silverthornes demanded and got back their illegally seized books and papers, but, by that time, the government had already copied and photographed them. They used the copies and photographs to get a subpoena from the trial court, ordering the Silverthornes to turn over the originals. When the Silverthornes refused to obey the subpoena, the trial court fined and jailed them for contempt.

According to Justice Oliver Wendell Holmes, the government's search and seizure "was an outrage." And as for the government's claims that "it may study the papers before it returns them, copy them, and then use the knowledge" to order the owners to turn over the papers: That's "not the law." The government's claimed power "reduces the Fourth Amendment to a form of words." The purpose of the rule that forbids acquiring evidence in a certain way is not only that the government can't use the evidence in court, but also that it can't use the evidence "at all" (392).

This expansion of the exclusionary rule to ban the use of evidence indirectly based on an illegal government action is called the **fruit-of-the-poisonous-tree doctrine**. The idea behind the doctrine is that the government should never be in a *better* position after violating the Constitution than it was before it broke the law. We'll discuss later the opposite idea: The government shouldn't be in a *worse* position after violating the Constitution than it was before.

Weeks and *Silverthorne* restricted the exclusionary rule to private papers. But in *Agnello v. U.S.* (1925), the Court created "a full-blown rule of exclusion at federal trials." The government had seized cocaine from Frank Agnello's house illegally, and Agnello argued that the court should have suppressed the cocaine at his trial. The Supreme Court agreed, expanding the rule beyond papers to include the contraband cocaine. Years later, Justice Potter Stewart (1983) contended that after the decision in *Agnello* in 1925, "the annexation of the exclusionary rule to the Fourth Amendment was complete" (1376–77).

As we've already noted, *Weeks*, *Silverthorne*, and *Agnello* applied only to *federal* cases. States still were free to apply the exclusionary rule or not. (Remember, it wasn't until the 1930s that the Court began to apply the Bill of Rights to state criminal proceedings [discussed in Chapter 2].) So the Court would have to decide in future cases whether the Fourteenth Amendment due process clause ("no state shall deny any person of life, liberty, or property without due process of law") applied to state criminal proceedings.

Do unreasonable searches and seizures violate the due process clause of the Fourteenth Amendment? It wasn't until 1949 that the Court took up the question in *Wolf v. Colorado* (1949). In fact, the Court was faced with two questions:

1. Does the Fourteenth Amendment due process clause apply the right against unreasonable searches and seizures to the states at all?

2. If it does, is the exclusionary rule part of the right?

The Court answered "Yes" to the first question and "No" to the second. In other words, states have to enforce the ban on unreasonable searches and seizures, but the Fourth Amendment leaves it up to the states how to enforce it.

Twelve years later, in *Mapp v. Ohio* (1961), the Court changed its answer to the second question in *Wolf* to yes. The circumstances surrounding the decision to reverse itself were unusual, to put it mildly. The case started out and reached the Court as a free speech case. Dollree Mapp was convicted of possession of pornography in Ohio. The question the Supreme Court was asked to review—and which both the briefs and the oral argument were almost entirely devoted to—was whether Ohio's pornography statute violated Mapp's right to free speech.

Until the first draft of the opinion circulated among the justices, the only mention of *Wolf* was in three sentences in an **amicus curiae brief** (an argument the Court allows to be submitted by someone—or more likely some interest group—who isn't a party but who has an interest in the case) of the American Civil Liberties Union. In fact, when asked about *Wolf v. Colorado* during oral arguments, Mapp's attorney admitted he'd never heard of the case.

Justice Stewart (1983) later recalled:

> I was shocked when Justice [Tom C.] Clark's proposed Court opinion reached my desk. I immediately wrote him a note expressing my surprise and questioning the wisdom of overruling an important doctrine in a case in which the issue was not briefed, argued, or discussed by the state courts, by the parties' counsel, or at our conferences following the oral argument. After my shock subsided, I wrote a brief memorandum concurring in the judgment and agreeing with Justice Harlan's dissent that the issue was not properly before the Court. The *Mapp* majority, however, stood its ground. The case provides significant insight into the judicial process and the evolution of law—a first amendment controversy was transformed into perhaps the most important search-and-seizure case in history. (1367)

In Mapp v. Ohio (1961), our next case excerpt, the U.S. Supreme Court extended the exclusionary rule to the states when it ruled that evidence seized illegally from Dollree Mapp's home couldn't be used against her in a state prosecution.

 **CASE** Should the Court Exclude the Evidence?

Mapp v. Ohio
367 U.S. 643 (1961)

HISTORY

Dollree Mapp was tried and convicted of illegal possession of pornography. Over her objection, the trial court admitted the pornography in evidence against her. On appeal, the Ohio Supreme Court affirmed. The U.S. Supreme Court reversed.

CLARK, J.

FACTS

On May 23, 1957, three Cleveland police officers arrived at Dollree Mapp's house pursuant to information that "a person was hiding out in the home, who was wanted for questioning in connection with a recent bombing, and that there was a large amount of policy paraphernalia being hidden in the home." Miss Mapp and her daughter by a former marriage lived on the top floor of the two-family dwelling. Upon their arrival at that house, the officers knocked on the door and demanded entrance but Mapp, after telephoning her attorney, refused to admit them without a search warrant. They advised their headquarters of the situation and undertook a surveillance of the house.

The officers again sought entrance some three hours later when four or more additional officers arrived on the scene. When Miss Mapp did not come to the door immediately, at least one of the several doors to the house was forcibly opened and the policemen gained admittance. Officer Carl DeLau testified that "we did pry the screen door to gain entrance"; the attorney on the scene testified that a policeman "tried . . . to kick the door" and then "broke the glass in the door and somebody reached in and opened the door and let them in"; Mapp testified that "The back door was broken."

Meanwhile Miss Mapp's attorney arrived, but the officers, having secured their own entry, and continuing in their defiance of the law, would permit him neither to see Miss Mapp nor to enter the house. It happens that Miss Mapp was halfway down the stairs from the upper floor to the front door when the officers, in this high-handed manner, broke into the hall. She demanded to see the search warrant. A paper, claimed to be a warrant, was held up by one of the officers. She grabbed the "warrant" and placed it in her bosom. A struggle ensued in which the officers recovered the piece of paper as a result of which they handcuffed Mapp because she had been "belligerent" in resisting their official rescue of the "warrant" from her person.

Running roughshod over Mapp, a policeman "grabbed" her, "twisted her hand," and she "yelled and pleaded with him" because "it was hurting." Mapp, in handcuffs, was then forcibly taken upstairs to her bedroom where the officers searched the dresser, a chest of drawers, a closet and some suitcases. They also looked in a photo album and through personal papers belonging to Mapp. The search spread to the rest of the second floor including the child's bedroom, the living room, the kitchen, and a dinette. The basement of the building and a trunk found therein were also searched. The obscene materials for possession of which she was ultimately convicted were discovered in the course of that widespread search.

At the trial no search warrant was produced by the prosecution, nor was the failure to produce one explained or accounted for. At best, "There is, in the record, considerable doubt as to whether there ever was any warrant for the search of defendant's home." The Ohio Supreme Court affirmed.

OPINION

In 1949, 35 years after *Weeks v. U.S.* (1914) was announced, this Court, in *Wolf v. Colorado*, for the first time, discussed the effect of the Fourth Amendment upon the States through the operation of the Due Process Clause of the Fourteenth Amendment. The Court decided that the *Weeks* exclusionary rule would not then be imposed upon the States as "an essential ingredient of the right."

The Court in *Wolf* stated that "the contrariety of views of the States" on the adoption of the exclusionary rule was "particularly impressive"; and it could not "brush aside the experience of the States which deem the incidence of such conduct by the police too slight to call for a deterrent remedy by overriding the States' relevant rules of evidence." While in 1949, prior to the *Wolf* case, almost two-thirds of the States were opposed to the use of the exclusionary rule, now more than half have wholly or partly adopted or adhered to the *Weeks* rule.

Significantly, among those now following the rule is California which, according to its highest court, was "compelled to reach that conclusion because other remedies have completely failed to secure compliance with the constitutional provisions." The second basis elaborated in *Wolf* in support of its failure to enforce the exclusionary doctrine against the States was that other means of protection have been afforded "the right of privacy." The experience of California that such other remedies have been worthless and futile is buttressed by the experience of other States. The obvious futility of relegating the Fourth Amendment to the protection of other remedies has, moreover, been recognized by this Court since *Wolf*.

Since the Fourth Amendment's right of privacy has been declared enforceable against the States through the Due Process Clause of the Fourteenth, it is enforceable against them by the same sanction of exclusion as is used against the Federal Government. Were it otherwise, then the assurance against unreasonable federal searches and seizures would be a form of words, valueless and undeserving of mention in a perpetual charter of inestimable human liberties, so too, without that rule the freedom from state invasions of privacy would be so ephemeral and so neatly severed from its conceptual nexus with the freedom from all brutish means of coercing evidence as not to merit this Court's high regard as a freedom "implicit in the concept of ordered liberty."

There are those who say, as did Justice Cardozo, that under our constitutional exclusionary doctrine "the criminal is to go free because the constable has blundered." In some cases this will undoubtedly be the result. But, there is another consideration—the imperative of judicial integrity. The criminal goes free, if he must, but it is the law that sets him free. Nothing can destroy a government more quickly than its failure to observe its own laws, or worse, its disregard of the charter of its own existence. [*As Justice Brandeis, dissenting in* Olmstead v. U.S. *(1928), wrote:*]

> Our Government is the potent, the omnipresent teacher. For good or for ill, it teaches the whole people by its example. If the Government becomes a lawbreaker, it breeds contempt for law; it invites every man to become a law unto himself; it invites anarchy.

Nor can it lightly be assumed that, as a practical matter, adoption of the exclusionary rule fetters law enforcement. Only last year this Court expressly considered that contention and found that "pragmatic evidence of a sort" to the contrary was not wanting. The Court noted that the federal courts themselves have operated under the exclusionary rule for almost half a century; yet it has not been suggested either that the Federal Bureau of Investigation has thereby been rendered ineffective, or that the administration of criminal justice in the federal courts has thereby been disrupted. Moreover, the experience of the states is impressive. The movement towards the rule of exclusion has been halting but seemingly inexorable.

Our decision, founded on reason and truth, gives to the individual no more than that which the Constitution guarantees him, to the police officer no less than that to which honest law enforcement is entitled, and, to the courts, that judicial integrity so necessary in the true administration of justice.

REVERSED and REMANDED.

DISSENT

HARLAN, J., joined by FRANKFURTER and WHITTAKER, JJ.

At the heart of the majority's opinion in this case is the following syllogism: the rule excluding in federal criminal trials evidence which is the product of an illegal search and seizure is "part and parcel" of the Fourth Amendment; *Wolf* held that the "privacy" assured against federal action by the Fourth Amendment is also protected against state action by the Fourteenth Amendment; and it is therefore "logically and constitutionally necessary" that the *Weeks* exclusionary rule should also be enforced against the States.

This reasoning ultimately rests on the unsound premise that because *Wolf* carried into the States, as part of "the concept of ordered liberty" embodied in the Fourteenth Amendment, the principle of "privacy" underlying the Fourth Amendment, it must follow that whatever configurations of the Fourth Amendment have been developed in the federal precedents are likewise to be deemed a part of "ordered liberty," and as such are enforceable against the States. For me, this does not follow at all.

Since there is not the slightest suggestion that Ohio's policy is "affirmatively to sanction police incursion into privacy" what the Court is now doing is to impose upon the States not only federal substantive standards of "search and seizure" but also the basic federal remedy for violation of those standards. For I think it entirely clear that the *Weeks* exclusionary rule is but a remedy which, by penalizing past official misconduct, is aimed at deterring such conduct in the future.

I would not impose upon the States this federal exclusionary remedy.

QUESTIONS

1. List the reasons the Court gave for overruling *Wolf v. Colorado*. Do you agree?
2. Are Justice Stewart's recollections of any importance? Explain.
3. According to the Court majority, why should Dollree Mapp go free? Because the Cleveland police blundered?
4. What remedies are available to Dollree Mapp besides the exclusion of the evidence? Which would you recommend?

Justifications for the Exclusionary Rule

LO 3, LO 4

To put it mildly, the exclusionary rule is controversial. Critics say it sets criminals free on "technicalities." Supporters reply that these "technicalities" are rights for which our ancestors fought and died. Why do we throw good evidence out of court? The U.S. Supreme Court has relied on three justifications:

1. *Constitutional right.* It's part of the constitutional rights against unreasonable seizure and coerced confessions and the rights to a lawyer and due process of law.
2. *Judicial integrity.* It preserves the honor and honesty of the courts.
3. *Deterrence.* It prevents officers from breaking the law.

The **constitutional right justification** stems from an ancient legal saying, "There's no right without a remedy" (Stewart 1983, 1380–83). One commentator summed it up with this great image: "It's like one hand clapping" (Uviller 1988).

In *Weeks v. U.S.* (1914), the case that created the exclusionary rule for the federal system, U.S. Supreme Court Justice William Rufus Day put it this way:

If letters and private documents can be seized and held illegally, and used in evidence against a citizen accused of an offense, the protection of the Fourth Amendment declaring his right to be secure against such searches and seizures is of no value, and may as well be stricken from the Constitution. (393)

The **judicial integrity justification** maintains that the honor and honesty of courts forbid them from participating in unconstitutional conduct. Dissenting in *Olmstead v. U.S.* (1928), a famous case upholding the constitutionality of wiretapping (Chapter 3), Justice Oliver Wendell Holmes spoke to the dilemma of throwing out good evidence because it was obtained by bad official behavior:

> We must consider two objects of desire, both of which we cannot have, and make up our minds which to choose. It is desirable that criminals should be detected, and to that end that all available evidence should be used. It also is desirable that the Government should not itself foster and pay for other crimes, when they are the means by which the evidence is to be obtained. For my part, I think it is less evil that some criminals should escape than that the Government should play an ignoble part. (470)

The **deterrence justification** says throwing out good evidence because it was obtained illegally sends a strong message to law enforcement. Here's how the distinguished Justice Potter Stewart (who probably knew more about the Fourth Amendment than any other U.S. Supreme Court justice in our history) summed up the deterrence justification:

> The rule is calculated to prevent, not to repair. Its purpose is to deter—to compel respect for the constitutional guaranty in the only effective available way—by removing the incentive to disregard it. (*Elkins v. U.S.* 1960, 217)

Since the 1980s, the Court has relied on deterrence as the only justification for excluding valid evidence. The Court has adopted another form of its old friend, the balancing test, in applying the deterrence justification. This form of the test weighs the social cost of excluding "good" evidence—namely, setting criminals free—against the deterrent effect that excluding good evidence might have on the illegal conduct of law enforcement officers. If the social costs outweigh the deterrent effect, then the evidence comes in.

The constitutional significance of letting evidence seized illegally into court because the social cost of keeping it out is too high is that the exclusionary rule isn't a constitutional right. (See "Social Costs and Deterrence" later for more discussion.) According to the U.S. Supreme Court in *U.S. v. Leon* (1984), excluding evidence isn't a constitutional right; it's a **prophylactic rule**—a protective procedure against violations of constitutional rights (Schroeder 1981, 1378–86).

The exclusionary rule brings into bold relief the tension between ends and means—namely, between result and process in the law of criminal procedure (Chapter 1). By throwing out good evidence because of bad practices, the rule puts the search for truth second to fair procedures. No one put the case for the exclusionary rule better than Associate Justice Louis D. Brandeis in his famous dissent in *Olmstead v. U.S.* (1928):

> Our government is the potent, the omnipresent teacher. For good or for ill, it teaches the whole people by its example. Crime is contagious. If the government becomes a lawbreaker, it breeds contempt for law; it invites every man to become a law unto himself; it invites anarchy.
>
> To declare that in the administration of the criminal law the end justifies the means—to declare that the government may commit crimes in order to secure the conviction of a private criminal—would bring terrible retribution. Against that pernicious doctrine this court should resolutely set its face. (468)

Exceptions to the Exclusionary Rule

The **social cost of the rule**—freeing guilty people and undermining the prosecution's case by keeping good evidence out of court—led the U.S. Supreme Court to limit it to cases it believes are most likely to deter police misconduct. The Court has decided that proceedings outside the trial don't deter police misconduct and that even major parts of the trial have no deterrent effect on police misconduct. The Court has created numerous exceptions to the exclusionary rule to cover cases that it believes don't deter police misconduct.

We'll discuss six of the major exceptions:

1. Collateral use
2. Cross-examination
3. Attenuation of the taint of unconstitutional official conduct
4. Independent source
5. Inevitable discovery
6. The "Good Faith Exception"

Collateral Use

LO 5

The **collateral-use exception** allows the use of illegally obtained evidence in **nontrial proceedings** (*U.S. v. Calandra* 1974). What proceedings does this include? The general answer is proceedings *related* to the case but not the trial of the case. (The term **collateral proceedings** means proceedings "off to the side" of the main case.) Specifically, these include bail hearings (Chapter 12); preliminary hearings (Chapter 12); grand jury proceedings (Chapter 12); and some kinds of habeas corpus proceedings (Chapter 14). So prosecutors can present illegally obtained evidence to deny defendants bail; get grand juries to indict defendants; and get judges in preliminary hearings to send cases on for trial.

Cross-Examination

LO 5

The exclusionary rule applies only to one part of one criminal proceeding: the government's case-in-chief in the criminal trial. **Case-in-chief** means the part of the trial where the government presents its evidence to prove the defendant's guilt. The case-in-chief doesn't include cross-examination of defense witnesses.

In *Walder v. U.S.* (1954), Walder was tried for purchasing and possessing heroin. During direct examination, Walder denied he'd ever bought or possessed heroin. The government then introduced heroin capsules seized during an illegal search to destroy his credibility by proving to the jury that he was a liar. The trial court admitted the capsules but cautioned the jury not to use the heroin capsules to prove Walder's guilt, only to **impeach** (undermine the believability of) his testimony. The U.S. Supreme Court ruled that the exclusionary rule didn't apply. According to the Court, Walder couldn't use the government's "illegal method" to obtain evidence as a shield against exposing his own lies. "Such an extension of the *Weeks* doctrine would be a perversion of the Fourth Amendment" (65).

Attenuation, Independent Source, and Inevitable Discovery

LO 5

These three exceptions apply to the *fruit-of-the-poisonous-tree doctrine*. The basic idea of the doctrine is that the government shouldn't be in a *better* position after it breaks the law. But what if the government's position is *worse*? That's where three complicated exceptions—attenuation, independent source, and inevitable discovery—come in. As you read and try to understand these exceptions, keep in mind that they're *exceptions* to the poisonous-tree doctrine. So their effect is to allow more evidence into court. (Remember that the purpose of the fruit-of-the-poisonous-tree doctrine is to keep evidence out of court.) Maybe it'll help you to think of the exceptions as antidotes to the poison of illegal governmental actions. As the U.S. Supreme Court said, not all evidence is "'fruit of the poisonous tree' simply because it would not have come to light but for the illegal actions of the police" (*Wong Sun v. U.S.* 1963, 488).

The noun *attenuation* (according to the dictionary) means "thinning, weakening, or emaciation." The **attenuation exception** says the illegally obtained evidence can come in if the poisonous connection between illegal police actions and the evidence they got illegally from their actions weakens (attenuates) enough.

The U.S. Supreme Court hasn't written a bright-line attenuation rule. Instead, courts have to decide each case according to the totality of circumstances. One circumstance is the closeness in time between the poisonous tree (illegal government act) and getting its fruit (evidence). For example, in *Wong Sun v. U.S.* (1963, 491), federal narcotics officers in San Francisco illegally broke into James Wah Toy's home and chased him down the hall into his bedroom. Agent Wong pulled his gun, illegally arrested Toy, and handcuffed him. Toy then told the officers Johnny Yee had sold him heroin. The officers immediately went to Yee's home. Yee admitted he had heroin and gave it to the officers. The Court ruled that the time between the illegal arrest and getting the heroin from Yee was too close to dissipate the poison of the arrest.

In the same case, the same narcotics officers arrested another man, Wong Sun, illegally. A few days later, after Wong Sun was charged and released on bail, he went back voluntarily to the Narcotics Bureau, where he told detectives he'd delivered heroin to Johnny Yee and smoked it with him. In his case, the U.S. Supreme Court decided "the connection between the arrest and the statement had become so attenuated as to dissipate the taint."

Another circumstance that might attenuate the poison enough to let the evidence in is an "intervening independent act of free will" after the illegal act. Let's go back to James Wah Toy in his bedroom after the illegal arrest. The government argued that when Toy told the officers that Yee had sold him heroin, he did it of his own free will. But the Court rejected the argument, not because an independent act of free will can't attenuate the poison but because it didn't fit the facts of this case.

According to the Court:

> Six or seven officers had broken the door and followed on Toy's heels into the bedroom where his wife and child were sleeping. He had been almost immediately handcuffed and arrested. Under such circumstances it is unreasonable to infer that Toy's response was sufficiently an act of free will to purge the primary taint of the unlawful invasion. (*Wong Sun v. U.S.* 1963, 416–17)

What if police officers violate the Constitution looking for evidence and, then, in a totally separate action, get the same evidence lawfully? It's admissible under the **independent source exception**. For example, in *U.S. v. Moscatiello* (1985), federal agents entered a South Boston warehouse illegally where they saw marijuana in plain view. They left without touching the marijuana and kept the warehouse under surveillance while they went to get a search warrant. In applying for the warrant, the officers didn't build their probable cause on anything they'd learned during the unlawful entry of the warehouse.

The U.S. Court of Appeals concluded that it was "absolutely certain" that the entry without a warrant entry didn't contribute "in the slightest" to discovering the marijuana in plain view during the later search backed up by a warrant. "The discovery of the contraband in plain view was totally irrelevant to the later securing of a warrant and the successful search that ensued" (603).

The U.S. Supreme Court upheld the Court of Appeals. According to the Court:

> [W]hile the government should not profit from its illegal activity, neither should it be placed in a worse position than it would otherwise have occupied. So long as a later, lawful seizure is genuinely independent of an earlier, tainted one … there is no reason why the independent source doctrine should not apply. (*Murray v. U.S.* 1988, 542–43)

So, in a nutshell, the independent source exception says, even if officers break the law, unless their lawbreaking causes the seizure of evidence, the evidence is admissible in court. But what if official lawbreaking is the cause of getting the evidence? Is the evidence banned from use? Not if officers, acting within the Constitution, would eventually find it anyway. And this is the nub of the **inevitable discovery exception**.

The inevitable discovery exception was the issue in *Nix v. Williams* (1984), an appeal from the retrial of Robert Williams, whom you met in Chapter 8 (excerpted on p. 279–280). Recall that Williams was suspected of brutally murdering 10-year-old Pamela Powers. During an illegal police interrogation, Williams led police officers to the place where he had hidden the body. At the same time, a separate search party was combing the same area near where some of Pamela's clothing had been found. The search party took a break from the search only 2½ miles from where Williams led the officers to the body; the location was within the area they planned to search.

So two searches were converging on the dead body. One search was being lawfully conducted by a search party. The other was the fruit of the poisonous illegal interrogation. The fruit-of-the-poisonous-tree search was the discovery of the body during the legal search party's break. Should the evidence be admitted? Yes, said the U.S. Supreme Court. Why? Because the body would have been discovered anyway by the legal search party.

Emphasizing the purpose of the fruit-of-the-poisonous-tree doctrine, and why the inevitable discovery exception was consistent with that purpose, the Court wrote:

> Exclusion of evidence that would inevitably have been discovered would put the government in a worse position, because the police would have obtained that evidence if no misconduct had taken place. This rationale justifies our adoption of the inevitable discovery exception to the exclusionary rule. (444)

The Good-Faith Exception

LO 5

Perhaps nothing more clearly demonstrates the U.S. Supreme Court's commitment to the balancing test than the **good-faith exception** to the exclusionary rule. The exception allows the government to use evidence obtained from searches based on unlawful search warrants if officers honestly and reasonably believed they were lawful. Good faith implies a subjective standard, which it's not. Chief Justice Roberts acknowledged this: "We (perhaps confusingly) called this objectively reasonable reliance "good faith" (*Herring v. U.S.*, 2009, 701).

Basically, this means that the exclusionary rule shouldn't apply when law enforcement officers are "reasonably" unaware that they're violating the Fourth Amendment because, in the Court's judgment, the rule can't deter police illegal behavior. According to the chief justice, in view of the "enormous social cost" of letting guilty criminals go free, the rule simply can't "pay its way" (704). The good-faith exception last reached the Supreme Court in our next case excerpt, *Herring v. U.S.* (2009).

In this case, the U.S. Supreme Court held that if an officer reasonably believes there's an outstanding arrest warrant against a suspect, but that belief turns out to be wrong because of a negligent bookkeeping error by another police employee, the arrest violates the Fourth Amendment. Nevertheless, the evidence obtained during a search incident to the unlawful arrest is admissible in a later criminal prosecution.

In Herring v. U.S. (2009), the U.S. Supreme Court held that if an officer makes an arrest, reasonably (but wrongly) believing there's an outstanding arrest warrant against the suspect, the arrest violates the Fourth Amendment but evidence obtained during a search incident to the unlawful arrest is admissible in court.

CASE Was the Illegally Seized Evidence Admissible?

Herring v. U.S.
129 S.Ct. 695 (2009)

HISTORY

Bennie Dean Herring (Defendant) was charged with being a convicted felon in possession of firearm and knowingly possessing methamphetamine. The United States District Court for the Middle District of Alabama, Myron H. Thompson, J., denied defendant's motion to suppress evidence recovered in search incident to his arrest. Defendant was subsequently convicted on both counts and he appealed. The United States Court of Appeals for the Eleventh Circuit, Carnes, Circuit Judge, 492 F.3d 1212, affirmed. Certiorari was granted. Affirmed.

ROBERTS, C.J., delivered the opinion of the Court, in which SCALIA, KENNEDY, THOMAS, and ALITO, JJ., joined.

The Fourth Amendment forbids "unreasonable searches and seizures," and this usually requires the police to have probable cause or a warrant before making an arrest. What if an officer reasonably believes there is an outstanding arrest warrant, but that belief turns out to be wrong because of a negligent bookkeeping error by another police employee? The parties here agree that the ensuing arrest is

still a violation of the Fourth Amendment, but dispute whether contraband found during a search incident to that arrest must be excluded in a later prosecution.

Our cases establish that such suppression is not an automatic consequence of a Fourth Amendment violation. Instead, the question turns on the culpability of the police and the potential of exclusion to deter wrongful police conduct. Here the error was the result of isolated negligence attenuated from the arrest. We hold that in these circumstances the jury should not be barred from considering all the evidence.

FACTS

On July 7, 2004, Investigator Mark Anderson learned that Bennie Dean Herring had driven to the Coffee County Sheriff's Department to retrieve something from his impounded truck. Herring was no stranger to law enforcement, and Anderson asked the county's warrant clerk, Sandy Pope, to check for any outstanding warrants for Herring's arrest. When she found none, Anderson asked Pope to check with Sharon Morgan, her counterpart in neighboring Dale County. After checking Dale County's computer database, Morgan replied that there was an active arrest warrant for Herring's failure to appear on a felony charge. Pope relayed the information to Anderson and asked Morgan to fax over a copy of the warrant as confirmation. Anderson and a deputy followed Herring as he left the impound lot, pulled him over, and arrested him. A search incident to the arrest revealed methamphetamine in Herring's pocket, and a pistol (which as a felon he could not possess) in his vehicle.

There had, however, been a mistake about the warrant. The Dale County sheriff's computer records are supposed to correspond to actual arrest warrants, which the office also maintains. But when Morgan went to the files to retrieve the actual warrant to fax to Pope, Morgan was unable to find it. She called a court clerk and learned that the warrant had been recalled five months earlier. Normally when a warrant is recalled the court clerk's office or a judge's chambers calls Morgan, who enters the information in the sheriff's computer database and disposes of the physical copy. For whatever reason, the information about the recall of the warrant for Herring did not appear in the database. Morgan immediately called Pope to alert her to the mixup, and Pope contacted Anderson over a secure radio. This all unfolded in 10 to 15 minutes, but Herring had already been arrested and found with the gun and drugs, just a few hundred yards from the sheriff's office.

Herring was indicted in the District Court for the Middle District of Alabama for illegally possessing the gun and drugs, violations of 18 U.S.C. § 922(g)(1) and 21 U.S.C. § 844(a). He moved to suppress the evidence on the ground that his initial arrest had been illegal because the warrant had been rescinded. The Magistrate Judge recommended denying the motion because the arresting officers had acted in a good-faith belief that the warrant was still outstanding. Thus, even if there were a Fourth Amendment violation, there was "no reason to believe that application of the exclusionary rule here would deter the occurrence of any future mistakes."

The Eleventh Circuit found that the arresting officers in Coffee County "were entirely innocent of any wrongdoing or carelessness." The court assumed that whoever failed to update the Dale County sheriff's records was also a law enforcement official, but noted that "the conduct in question was a negligent failure to act, not a deliberate or tactical choice to act." Because the error was merely negligent and attenuated from the arrest, the Eleventh Circuit concluded that the benefit of suppressing the evidence "would be marginal or nonexistent," and the evidence was therefore admissible under the good-faith rule of *United States v. Leon* (1984).

Other courts have required exclusion of evidence obtained through similar police errors, *e.g.*, *Hoay v. State*, 348 Ark. 80, 86–87, 71 S.W.3d 573, 577 (2002), so we granted Herring's petition for certiorari to resolve the conflict, 552 U.S. ——, 128 S.Ct. 1221, 170 L.Ed.2d 57 (2008). We now affirm the Eleventh Circuit's judgment.

OPINION

The Fourth Amendment protects "the right of the people to be secure in their persons, houses, papers, and effects,

against unreasonable searches and seizures," but "contains no provision expressly precluding the use of evidence obtained in violation of its commands," *Arizona v. Evans* (1995). Nonetheless, our decisions establish an exclusionary rule that, when applicable, forbids the use of improperly obtained evidence at trial. We have stated that this judicially created rule is "designed to safeguard Fourth Amendment rights generally through its deterrent effect." *United States v. Calandra* (1974).

In analyzing the applicability of the rule, *Leon* admonished that we must consider the actions of all the police officers involved. The Coffee County officers did nothing improper. Indeed, the error was noticed so quickly because Coffee County requested a faxed confirmation of the warrant. The Eleventh Circuit concluded, however, that somebody in Dale County should have updated the computer database to reflect the recall of the arrest warrant. The court also concluded that this error was negligent, but did not find it to be reckless or deliberate. That fact is crucial to our holding that this error is not enough by itself to require the extreme sanction of exclusion.

The fact that a Fourth Amendment violation occurred—*i.e.*, that a search or arrest was unreasonable— does not necessarily mean that the exclusionary rule applies. Indeed, exclusion "has always been our last resort, not our first impulse," *Hudson v. Michigan* (2006), and our precedents establish important principles that constrain application of the exclusionary rule.

First, the exclusionary rule is not an individual right and applies only where it results in appreciable deterrence. We have repeatedly rejected the argument that exclusion is a necessary consequence of a Fourth Amendment violation. Instead we have focused on the efficacy of the rule in deterring Fourth Amendment violations in the future.

In addition, the benefits of deterrence must outweigh the costs. We have never suggested that the exclusionary rule must apply in every circumstance in which it might provide marginal deterrence. The principal cost of applying the rule is, of course, letting guilty and possibly dangerous defendants go free—something that offends basic concepts of the criminal justice system. When police act under a warrant that is invalid for lack of probable cause, the exclusionary rule does not apply if the police acted in objectively reasonable reliance on the subsequently invalidated search warrant. We (perhaps confusingly) called this objectively reasonable reliance "good faith." We have also held that the exclusionary rule did not apply when a warrant was invalid because a judge forgot to make "clerical corrections" to it; to warrantless administrative searches performed in good-faith reliance on a statute later declared unconstitutional.

Finally, in *Evans* (1995), we applied this good-faith rule to police who reasonably relied on mistaken information in a court's database that an arrest warrant was outstanding. We held that a mistake made by a judicial employee could not give rise to exclusion for three reasons: (1) The exclusionary rule was crafted to curb police rather than judicial misconduct; (2) court employees were unlikely to try to subvert the Fourth Amendment; and (3) most important, there was no basis for believing that application of the exclusionary rule in those circumstances would have any significant effect in deterring the errors. *Evans* left unresolved whether the evidence should be suppressed if *police personnel* were responsible for the error.

The extent to which the exclusionary rule is justified by these deterrence principles varies with the culpability of the law enforcement conduct. An assessment of the flagrancy of the police misconduct constitutes an important step in the calculus of applying the exclusionary rule. Similarly, evidence should be suppressed only if it can be said that the law enforcement officer had knowledge, or may properly be charged with knowledge, that the search was unconstitutional under the Fourth Amendment.

Indeed, the abuses that gave rise to the exclusionary rule featured intentional conduct that was patently unconstitutional. In *Weeks* (1914), a foundational exclusionary rule case, the officers had broken into the defendant's home (using a key shown to them by a neighbor), confiscated incriminating papers, then returned again with a U.S. Marshal to confiscate even more. Not only did they have no search warrant, which the Court held was required, but they could not have gotten one had they tried. They were so lacking in sworn and particularized information that not even an order of court would have justified such procedure. *Silverthorne Lumber Co. v. United States*, (1920), was similar; federal officials "without a shadow of authority" went to the defendants' office and "made a clean sweep" of every paper they could find. Even the Government seemed to acknowledge that the "seizure was an outrage."

Equally flagrant conduct was at issue in *Mapp v. Ohio* (1961). Officers forced open a door to Ms. Mapp's house, kept her lawyer from entering, brandished what the court concluded was a false warrant, then forced her into handcuffs and canvassed the house for obscenity. An error that arises from nonrecurring and attenuated negligence is thus far removed from the core concerns that led us to adopt the rule in the first place. And in fact since *Leon*, we have never applied the rule to exclude evidence obtained in violation of the Fourth Amendment, where the police conduct was no more intentional or culpable than this.

To trigger the exclusionary rule, police conduct must be sufficiently deliberate that exclusion can meaningfully deter it, and sufficiently culpable that such deterrence is worth the price paid by the justice system. As laid out in our cases, the exclusionary rule serves to deter deliberate, reckless, or grossly negligent conduct, or in some circumstances recurring or systemic negligence. The error in this case does not rise to that level. The pertinent analysis of deterrence and culpability is objective, not an inquiry into the subjective awareness of arresting officers. Our good-faith inquiry is confined to the objectively ascertainable question whether a reasonably well trained officer would have known that the search was illegal in light of all of the circumstances. These circumstances frequently include a particular officer's knowledge and experience, but that does not make the test any more subjective than the one for probable cause, which looks to an officer's knowledge and experience.

We do not suggest that all recordkeeping errors by the police are immune from the exclusionary rule. In this case, however, the conduct at issue was not so objectively culpable as to require exclusion. The marginal or nonexistent benefits produced by suppressing evidence obtained in objectively reasonable reliance on a subsequently invalidated search warrant cannot justify the substantial costs of exclusion. The same is true when evidence is obtained in objectively reasonable reliance on a subsequently recalled warrant.

If the police have been shown to be reckless in maintaining a warrant system, or to have knowingly made false entries to lay the groundwork for future false arrests, exclusion would certainly be justified under our cases should such misconduct cause a Fourth Amendment violation. An officer could not obtain a warrant on the basis of a "bare bones" affidavit, and then rely on colleagues who are ignorant of the circumstances under which the warrant was obtained to conduct the search. Petitioner's fears that our decision will cause police departments to deliberately keep their officers ignorant, are thus unfounded.

The dissent also adverts to the possible unreliability of a number of databases not relevant to this case. In a case where systemic errors were demonstrated, it might be reckless for officers to rely on an unreliable warrant system. But there is no evidence that errors in Dale County's system are routine or widespread. Officer Anderson testified that he had never had reason to question information about a Dale County warrant, and both Sandy Pope and Sharon Morgan testified that they could remember no similar miscommunication ever happening on their watch. That is even less error than in the database at issue in *Evans*, where we also found reliance on the database to be objectively reasonable (similar error "every three or four years"). Because no such showings were made here, the Eleventh Circuit was correct to affirm the denial of the motion to suppress.

Petitioner's claim that police negligence automatically triggers suppression cannot be squared with the principles underlying the exclusionary rule. In light of our repeated holdings that the deterrent effect of suppression must be substantial and outweigh any harm to the justice system, we conclude that when police mistakes are the result of negligence such as that described here, rather than systemic error or reckless disregard of constitutional requirements, any marginal deterrence does not pay its way. In such a case, the criminal should not "go free because the constable has blundered."

The judgment of the Court of Appeals for the Eleventh Circuit is AFFIRMED.

It is so ordered.

DISSENT

GINSBURG, J., joined by STEVENS, SOUTER, and BREYER, JJ.

Bennie Dean Herring was arrested, and subjected to a search incident to his arrest, although no warrant was outstanding against him, and the police lacked probable cause to believe he was engaged in criminal activity. The arrest and ensuing search therefore violated Herring's Fourth Amendment right "to be secure . . . against unreasonable searches and seizures." The Court of Appeals so determined, and the Government does not contend otherwise. The exclusionary rule provides redress for Fourth Amendment violations by placing the government in the position it would have been in had there been no unconstitutional arrest and search. The rule thus strongly encourages police compliance with the Fourth Amendment in the future. The Court, however, holds the rule inapplicable because careless recordkeeping by the police—not flagrant or deliberate misconduct—accounts for Herring's arrest.

I would not so constrict the domain of the exclusionary rule and would hold the rule dispositive of this case: If courts are to have any power to discourage police error of the kind here at issue, it must be through the application of the exclusionary rule. The unlawful search in this case was contested in court because the police found methamphetamine in Herring's pocket and a pistol in his truck. But the "most serious impact" of the Court's holding will be on innocent persons "wrongfully arrested based on erroneous information [carelessly maintained] in a computer data base."

A warrant for Herring's arrest was recalled in February 2004, apparently because it had been issued in error. The warrant database for the Dale County Sheriff's Department, however, does not automatically update to reflect such changes. A member of the Dale County Sheriff's Department—whom the parties have not identified—returned the hard copy of the warrant to the County Circuit Clerk's office, but did not correct the Department's database to show that the warrant had been recalled. The erroneous entry for the warrant remained in the database, undetected, for five months.

On a July afternoon in 2004, Herring came to the Coffee County Sheriff's Department to retrieve his belongings from a vehicle impounded in the Department's lot. Investigator Mark Anderson, who was at the Department that day, knew Herring from prior interactions: Herring had told the district attorney, among others, of his suspicion that Anderson had been involved in the killing of a local teenager, and Anderson had pursued Herring to get him to drop the accusations. Informed that Herring was in the impoundment lot, Anderson asked the Coffee County warrant clerk whether there was an outstanding warrant for Herring's arrest. The clerk, Sandy Pope, found no warrant.

Anderson then asked Pope to call the neighboring Dale County Sheriff's Department to inquire whether a warrant to arrest Herring was outstanding there. Upon receiving Pope's phone call, Sharon Morgan, the warrant clerk for the Dale County Department, checked her computer database. As just recounted, that Department's database preserved an error. Morgan's check therefore showed—incorrectly—an active warrant for Herring's arrest. Morgan gave the misinformation to Pope, who relayed it to Investigator Anderson. Armed with the report that a warrant existed, Anderson promptly arrested Herring and performed an incident search minutes before detection of the error.

The Court of Appeals concluded, and the Government does not contest, "that the failure to bring the Dale County Sheriff's Department records up to date was 'at the very least negligent.'" And it is uncontested here that Herring's arrest violated his Fourth Amendment rights. The sole question presented, therefore, is whether evidence the police obtained through the unlawful search should have been suppressed. The Court holds that suppression was unwarranted because the exclusionary rule's "core concerns" are not raised by an isolated, negligent recordkeeping error attenuated from the arrest. In my view, the Court's opinion underestimates the need for a forceful exclusionary rule and the gravity of recordkeeping errors in law enforcement.

The Court states that the exclusionary rule is not a defendant's right; rather, it is simply a remedy applicable only when suppression would result in appreciable deterrence that outweighs the cost to the justice system. Also, the exclusionary rule serves to deter deliberate, reckless, or grossly negligent conduct, or in some circumstances recurring or systemic negligence. Others have described a more majestic conception of the Fourth Amendment and its adjunct, the exclusionary rule. Protective of the fundamental "right of the people to be secure in their persons, houses, papers, and effects," the Amendment is a constraint on the power of the sovereign, not merely on some of its agents. The exclusionary rule is a remedy necessary to ensure that the Fourth Amendment's prohibitions are observed in fact. The rule's service as an essential auxiliary to the Amendment earlier inclined the Court to hold the two inseparable.

Beyond doubt, a main objective of the rule is to deter—to compel respect for the constitutional guaranty in the only effectively available way—by removing the incentive to disregard it. But the rule also serves other important purposes: It enables the judiciary to avoid the taint of partnership in official lawlessness, and it assures the people—all potential victims of unlawful government conduct—that the government would not profit from its lawless behavior, thus minimizing the risk of seriously undermining popular trust in government.

The exclusionary rule, it bears emphasis, is often the only remedy effective to redress a Fourth Amendment violation. Civil liability will not lie for the vast majority of Fourth Amendment violations—the frequent infringements motivated by commendable zeal, not condemnable malice. Criminal prosecutions or administrative sanctions against the offending officers and injunctive relief against widespread violations are an even farther cry.

The Court maintains that Herring's case is one in which the exclusionary rule could have scant deterrent effect and therefore would not "pay its way." I disagree. The exclusionary rule, the Court suggests, is capable of only marginal deterrence when the misconduct at issue is merely careless, not intentional or reckless. The suggestion runs counter to a foundational premise of tort law—that liability for negligence, *i.e.*, lack of due care, creates an incentive to act with greater care. The Government so acknowledges.

That the mistake here involved the failure to make a computer entry hardly means that application of the exclusionary rule would have minimal value. Just as the risk of *respondeat superior* liability encourages employers to supervise their employees' conduct more carefully, so the risk of exclusion of evidence encourages policymakers and systems managers to monitor the performance of the systems they install and the personnel employed to operate those systems.

Consider the potential impact of a decision applying the exclusionary rule in this case. As earlier observed, the record indicates that there is no electronic connection between the warrant database of the Dale County Sheriff's Department and that of the County Circuit Clerk's office, which is located in the basement of the same building. When a warrant is recalled, one of the many different people that have access to the warrants must find the hard copy of the warrant in the two or three different places where the department houses warrants, return it to the Clerk's office, and manually update the Department's database. The record reflects no routine practice of checking the database for accuracy, and the failure to remove the entry for Herring's warrant was not discovered until Investigator Anderson sought to pursue Herring five months later. Is it not altogether obvious that the Department could take further precautions to ensure the integrity of its database? The Sheriff's Department is in a position to remedy the situation and might well do so if the exclusionary rule is there to remove the incentive to do otherwise.

Is the potential deterrence here worth the costs it imposes? In light of the paramount importance of accurate recordkeeping in law enforcement, I would answer yes, and next explain why, as I see it, Herring's motion presents a particularly strong case for suppression.

Electronic databases form the nervous system of contemporary criminal justice operations. In recent years, their breadth and influence have dramatically expanded. Police today can access databases that include not only the updated National Crime Information Center (NCIC), but also terrorist watchlists, the Federal Government's employee eligibility system, and various commercial databases. Moreover, States are actively expanding information sharing between jurisdictions. As a result, law enforcement has an increasing supply of information within its easy electronic reach.

The risk of error stemming from these databases is not slim. Law enforcement databases are insufficiently monitored and often out of date. Government reports describe, for example, flaws in NCIC databases, terrorist watchlist

databases, and databases associated with the Federal Government's employment eligibility verification system. Inaccuracies in expansive, interconnected collections of electronic information raise grave concerns for individual liberty. The offense to the dignity of the citizen who is arrested, handcuffed, and searched on a public street simply because some bureaucrat has failed to maintain an accurate computer data base is evocative of the use of general warrants that so outraged the authors of our Bill of Rights.

The Court assures that "exclusion would certainly be justified" if "the police have been shown to be reckless in maintaining a warrant system, or to have knowingly made false entries to lay the groundwork for future false arrests." This concession provides little comfort.

First, by restricting suppression to bookkeeping errors that are deliberate or reckless, the majority leaves Herring, and others like him, with no remedy for violations of their constitutional rights. There can be no serious assertion that relief is available under 42 U.S.C. § 1983. The arresting officer would be sheltered by qualified immunity, and the police department itself is not liable for the negligent acts of its employees. Moreover, identifying the department employee who committed the error may be impossible.

Second, I doubt that police forces already possess sufficient incentives to maintain up-to-date records. The Government argues that police have no desire to send officers out on arrests unnecessarily, because arrests consume resources and place officers in danger. The facts of this case do not fit that description of police motivation. Here the officer wanted to arrest Herring and consulted the Department's records to legitimate his predisposition. It has been asserted that police departments have become sufficiently "professional" that they do not need external deterrence to avoid Fourth Amendment violations. But professionalism is a sign of the exclusionary rule's efficacy—not of its superfluity.

Third, even when deliberate or reckless conduct is afoot, the Court's assurance will often be an empty promise: How is an impecunious defendant to make the required showing? If the answer is that a defendant is entitled to discovery (and if necessary, an audit of police databases), then the Court has imposed a considerable administrative burden on courts and law enforcement.

Negligent recordkeeping errors by law enforcement threaten individual liberty, are susceptible to deterrence by the exclusionary rule, and cannot be remedied effectively through other means. Such errors present no occasion to further erode the exclusionary rule. The rule is needed to make the Fourth Amendment something real; a guarantee that does not carry with it the exclusion of evidence obtained by its violation is a chimera. In keeping with the rule's "core concerns," suppression should have attended the unconstitutional search in this case.

For the reasons stated, I would reverse the judgment of the Eleventh Circuit.

QUESTIONS

1. State the Court's reasons for limiting the deterrence justification to law enforcement officers.
2. Identify the dissenting justices' reasons for arguing that the deterrence justification for the good-faith exception should be applied to all government officials.
3. Which of the opinions do you agree with? Support your answer.

Social Costs and Deterrence: The Empirical Findings

In 1960, in *Mapp v. Ohio*, the U.S. Supreme Court, headed by Chief Justice Earl Warren, applied the exclusionary rule to the states because the Court *assumed* that the rule would deter illegal searches and seizures. But there's a social cost for deterring law enforcement officers from violating individuals' rights: Keeping good evidence from juries may set some criminals free. Since the 1970s, in case after case, the majorities of the Burger and the Rehnquist Courts have *assumed* that the social cost is too high a price to pay; deterrence simply can't "pay its way." Which Court's assumption is right?

Ever since the Court decided *Mapp*, a growing stack of empirical studies has tested the correctness of the two assumptions. What's the answer? According to Professor Christopher Slobogin (1999, 368–69), "No one is going to win the empirical debate over whether the exclusionary rule deters the police from committing a significant number of illegal searches and seizures." It's true, say most of the studies, that police officers pay more attention to the Fourth Amendment than they did in 1960. But many officers don't take the rule into account when they're deciding whether to make a search or a seizure. "In short, we do not know how much the rule deters" either individual officers whose evidence courts throw out (special deterrence) or other officers who might be thinking of illegally searching or seizing (general deterrence) (369).

"We probably never will" (369). Why? Because it's hard to conduct empirical research; we have to rely on speculation (370). And what's the speculation? Both supporters and opponents of the rule make plausible claims for their positions. It's reasonable for supporters to claim "officers who know illegally seized evidence will be excluded cannot help but try to avoid illegal searches because they will have nothing to gain from them."

Equally reasonable, the rule's opponents can point out that its most direct consequence is imposed on the prosecutor rather than on law enforcement officers; that police know and count on the fact that the rule is rarely applied (for both legal and not-so-legal reasons); and that the rule can't affect searches and seizures the police believe won't result in prosecution (372).

Despite these limits to the empirical research, some of it provides us with valuable insights. The social costs of letting guilty criminals go free by excluding credible evidence that would convict them might not be as high as we commonly believe. According to Thomas Y. Davies (1983), who studied the exclusionary rule in California and whose research the Court cited in *U.S. v. Leon*, prosecutors almost never reject cases involving violent crimes because of the exclusionary rule.

In California, evidence seized illegally led to dismissals in a mere 0.8 percent of all criminal cases and only 4.8 percent of felonies. Davies found that prosecutors rejected only 0.06 percent of homicides, 0.09 percent of forcible rapes, and 0.13 percent of assault cases because of illegal searches and seizures. They rejected less than 0.50 percent of theft cases and only 0.19 percent of burglary cases. The largest number of cases rejected for prosecution because of illegal searches and seizures involved the possession of small amounts of drugs (644).

Other studies reached similar conclusions—namely, that the exclusionary rule affects only a small portion of cases, and most of those aren't crimes against persons (cited in

Davies 1983). Less than one-tenth of 1 percent of all criminal cases will be dismissed because the police seized evidence illegally. The rule leaves violent crimes and serious property offenses virtually unaffected. Furthermore, not all cases involving illegally obtained evidence that are rejected or lost fail because of the exclusionary rule. Peter F. Nardulli (1987) found, for example, that in some cases of drug possession, the police weren't interested in successful prosecution but rather in getting contraband off the street.

Most criminal justice professionals seem to agree that the exclusionary rule is worth the price. The American Bar Association (1988) gathered information from police officers, prosecutors, defense attorneys, and judges in representative urban and geographically distributed locations on the problems they face in their work. They also conducted a telephone survey of 800 police administrators, prosecutors, judges, and defense attorneys based on a stratified random selection technique to obtain a representative group of small-to-large cities and counties.

The results showed the following:

1. Although the prosecutors and police interviewed believe that a few Fourth Amendment restrictions are ambiguous or complex and, thus, present training and field application problems, they don't believe that Fourth Amendment rights or their protection via the exclusionary rule are a significant impediment to crime control.

2. A number of police officials also report that the demands of the exclusionary rule and resulting police training on Fourth Amendment requirements have promoted professionalism in police departments across the country.

3. Thus, the exclusionary rule appears to be providing a significant safeguard of Fourth Amendment protections for individuals at a modest cost in terms of either crime control or effective prosecution.

4. This "cost," for the most part, reflects the values expressed in the Fourth Amendment itself. It manifests a preference for privacy and freedom over the level of law enforcement efficiency that could be achieved if police were permitted to arrest and search without probable cause or judicial authorization. (11)

In view of its limited application, restrictions on the exclusionary rule hardly seem adequate cause for either critics of the rule to rejoice that these restrictions will make society safer or for supporters to bemoan that they'll throttle individual liberties.

Probably the strongest argument for the exclusionary rule is that it helps to ensure judicial integrity. Courts, by excluding illegally obtained evidence, announce publicly and in writing their refusal to participate in or condone illegal police practices. At the end of the day, what the exclusionary rule does is exact the price of setting a few criminals free to maintain the rule of law for everybody; it sacrifices the correct result in an individual case for the general interest in the essential fairness of constitutional government for all people.

One final point about the exclusionary rule: Every year, there are approximately 175,000 motions to exclude evidence obtained by illegal searches and seizures. In contrast, there are only a few thousand lawsuits against police and a few dozen criminal charges based on illegal searches and seizures (Allen and others 2005, 336). This lopsided distribution may have a large effect on the substance of Fourth Amendment law. The exclusionary rule shapes the kinds of Fourth Amendment cases judges see. All exclusionary claims seek to suppress incriminating evidence; if no incriminating evidence is found, there is nothing for the defendant to exclude. *Thus, judges see the cases where the police find cocaine in the car, not the cases where they find nothing* [emphasis added]. Perhaps that affects the way judges think about car searches. (336)

ETHICAL ISSUES

Social Costs and the Exclusionary Rule

Is it ethical public policy to let criminals go free because police officers violated the Fourth Amendment to obtain evidence? During oral arguments before the U.S. Supreme Court in *Herring v. U.S.* (2009), justices offered these two opposing views:

Chief Justice Roberts: We know what the cost was here, right? I mean, not just a drug peddler, but somebody with an illegal weapon found in his car, a weapon that presumably he would use on an occasion in which it was in his view appropriate to do so.

Justice Stevens: Of course, if you did the cost-benefit analysis, the cost is always zero to the State because they would not have had the evidence if they had obeyed the law.

INSTRUCTIONS

1. Visit the Companion Website and listen to the oral argument in *Herring v. U.S.* (2009). (You can follow along with the transcript of the argument.) See the link under the Chapter 10 Ethical Issues section—login at www.cengagebrain.com.

2. List and summarize the arguments regarding the social cost of the exclusionary rule.

3. Write an essay, answering the question: "Is it ethical public policy to let criminals go free because police officers violated the Fourth Amendment to obtain evidence?"

The Defense of Entrapment

LO 6, LO 7

What if law enforcement agents (usually undercover cops) get people to commit crimes they wouldn't have committed if the government hadn't encouraged them? Sometimes, defendants in such cases are entitled to the *defense of entrapment,* meaning courts will dismiss the criminal charges.

For most of our history, U.S. courts didn't recognize entrapment as a defense. In 1864, a New York court explained why:

> Even if inducements to commit crime could be assumed to exist in this case, the allegation of the defendant would be but the repetition of the pleas as ancient as the world, and first interposed in Paradise: "The serpent beguiled me and I did eat." That defense was overruled by the great Lawgiver, and whatever estimate we may form, or whatever judgment pass upon the character or conduct of the tempter, this plea has never since availed to shield crime or give indemnity to the culprit, and it is safe to say that under any code of civilized, not say Christian ethics, it never will. (*Board of Commissioners v. Backus* 1864, 42)

Another court, in 1904, summed up this attitude toward entrapment:

> We are asked to protect the defendant, not because he is innocent, but because a zealous public officer exceeded his powers and held out a bait. The courts do not look to see who held out the bait, but to see who took it. (*People v. Mills* 1904, 791)

These attitudes stemmed from indifference to government enticements to commit crimes. After all, "once the crime is committed, why should it matter what particular incentives were involved and who offered them?" However, attitudes have shifted from indifference to "limited sympathy" toward entrapped defendants and a growing intolerance of government inducements to entrap individuals who are basically law-abiding people (Marcus 1986).

The present law of entrapment attempts to balance criminal predisposition and law enforcement practices; that is, it casts a net for habitual criminals, while trying not to capture law-abiding people in the net. The practice of entrapment wasn't a response to violent crime or other crimes with complaining victims. Rather, the practice arose because of the difficulty in detecting consensual crimes—namely, illegal drug offenses, gambling, pornography, and prostitution—because "victims" don't want to report the crimes to the police.

The use of government encouragement as a law enforcement tool is neither new nor limited to the United States. The practice has been associated with some highly unsavory characters throughout world history. Ancient tyrants and modern dictators alike have relied on government agents to get innocent people to commit crimes (the infamous agents provocateurs), so that these autocrats could silence and destroy their political opponents. From the days of Henry VIII to the era of Hitler, Mussolini, Franco, and Stalin to Manuel Noriega, Slobodan Milosevic, and Saddam Hussein (and too many others to list) in our own time, police states have used government informers to get dissidents to admit their disloyalty.

Unfortunately, inducement is not just a tool used by dictators to oppress their opponents. In all societies and political systems, it's used in ordinary law enforcement, too, creating the risk that law-abiding people will commit crimes they wouldn't have committed if they hadn't been encouraged. Enticement to commit crimes flies in the face of good government. The great Victorian British Prime Minister William Gladstone admonished government to make it easy to do right and hard to do wrong. And consider the plea in the Christian Lord's Prayer's to "lead us not into temptation, but deliver us from evil" (Carlson 1987).

Encouragement is likely to occur whenever law enforcement officers do any of the following:

1. Pretend they're victims

2. Intend to entice suspects to commit crimes

3. Communicate the enticement to suspects

4. Influence the decision to commit crimes

Here's how encouragement works in typical cases: One officer provides an opportunity for "targets" to commit a crime while other officers witness the event; that way, they have proof of the target's guilt. But it's usually not enough for officers just to present targets an opportunity or even to "ask" them to commit a crime. In most cases, officers actively have to encourage their targets because, like most of us, targets are wary of strangers. Active encouragement usually requires using tactics, such as

• Asking targets over and over to commit a crime

• Developing personal relationships with targets

• Appealing personally to targets

• Supplying or helping targets get contraband (LaFave and Israel 1984, 1:412–13)

The defense of entrapment is not a constitutional right; it's a defense to criminal liability created and defined by statutes and courts. It's what we call an **affirmative**

defense. That means defendants have the burden of introducing some evidence that they were entrapped. If they meet this burden, then the burden shifts to the government to prove defendants were *not* entrapped. The jury—or the judge in trials without juries—decides whether officers, in fact, entrapped defendants. The courts have adopted two types of tests for entrapment: one is subjective, and the other is objective.

The Subjective Test

LO 8

Encouragement is entrapment only if it crosses the line from acceptable to unacceptable encouragement. How do we know when officers have crossed that line? Most states and the federal government have adopted a **subjective test of entrapment**, which focuses on whether defendants had the predisposition to commit the crimes.

According to the subjective test, defendants are entitled to the defense of entrapment if they can show some evidence of two elements:

1.   They had no desire to commit the crime before the government's encouragement.

2.   The government's encouragement caused them to commit the crime.

The crucial question in the subjective test is, "Where did criminal intent originate?" If it originated with the defendant, then the government didn't entrap the defendant. If it originated with the government, then the government did entrap the defendant. Put another way, if the defendant was predisposed to commit the crime and the government only provided her with the opportunity to commit it, then she wasn't entrapped.

According to the Minnesota Court of Appeals, government encouragement has to "go beyond mere solicitation; it requires something in the nature of persuasion, badgering or pressure by the state" (*State v. Fitiwi* 2003). The legal encyclopedia *Corpus Juris Secundum* (2003, § 61) says the government has to use "trickery, persuasion, or fraud."

In a leading U.S. Supreme Court case, *Sherman v. U.S.* (1958), government informant and undercover agent Kalchinian and drug addict Joe Sherman met in a treatment center. Kalchinian struck up a friendship with Sherman and eventually asked Sherman to get him some heroin. At first, Sherman refused. However, after Kalchinian begged and pleaded for several weeks, Sherman finally gave in and got Kalchinian the heroin. The police promptly arrested Sherman. The Court understandably found that the intent originated with the government. According to the Court, given that Sherman was in treatment for his addiction he was hardly predisposed to commit a drug offense.

Once defendants have produced some evidence that the government agent persuaded the defendant to commit the crime, the government then has to prove the defendant was predisposed to commit it. The circumstances the government can use vary somewhat from state to state, but they usually boil down to either the defendants' character or their behavior. Minnesota's list is typical:

1.   Active solicitation of the crime

2.   Prior criminal convictions

3.   Prior criminal activity not resulting in conviction

4.   Defendant's criminal reputation

5.   By any other adequate means (*State v. Wright* 2001)

In *Jacobson v. U.S.* (1992), our next case excerpt, the U.S. Supreme Court held that, according to the subjective test, Keith Jacobson wasn't predisposed to possess child pornography.

In Jacobson v. U.S. (1992), our next case excerpt, the U.S. Supreme Court held that, according to the subjective test of entrapment, Keith Jacobson wasn't predisposed to possess child pornography.

CASE Did the Government Entrap Jacobson?

Jacobson v. U.S.

503 U.S. 540 (1992)

HISTORY

Keith Jacobson was convicted in the U.S. District Court for the District of Nebraska of receiving child pornography through the mail. A panel (3 members) of the Court of Appeals for the Eighth Circuit reversed. On rehearing en banc (the full court) affirmed. The U.S. Supreme Court reversed.

WHITE, J., joined by BLACKMUN, STEVENS, SOUTER, and THOMAS, JJ.

FACTS

In February 1984, Keith Jacobson, a 56-year-old Korean War veteran-turned-farmer who supported his elderly father in Nebraska, ordered two magazines and a brochure from a California adult bookstore. The magazines, entitled *Bare Boys I* and *Bare Boys II*, contained photographs of nude pre-teen and teenage boys. The contents of the magazines startled petitioner, who testified that he had expected to receive photographs of "young men 18 years or older." On cross-examination, he explained his response to the magazines:

> *Prosecutor:* You were shocked and surprised that there were pictures of very young boys without clothes on, is that correct?
>
> *Jacobson:* Yes, I was.
>
> *Prosecutor:* Were you offended?
>
> *Jacobson:* I was not offended because I thought these were a nudist type publication. Many of the pictures were out in a rural or outdoor setting. There was—I didn't draw any sexual connotation or connection with that.

The young men depicted in the magazines were not engaged in sexual activity, and Jacobson's receipt of the magazines was legal under both federal and Nebraska law.

Within three months, the law with respect to child pornography changed; Congress passed the Act illegalizing the receipt through the mails of sexually explicit depictions of children. In the very month the new provision became law, postal inspectors found Jacobson's name on the mailing list of the California bookstore that had mailed him *Bare Boys I* and *II*. There followed over the next 2½ years repeated efforts by two Government agencies, through five fictitious organizations and a bogus pen pal, to explore Jacobson's willingness to break the new law by ordering sexually explicit photographs of children through the mail.

The Government began its efforts in January 1985 when a postal inspector sent Jacobson a letter supposedly from the American Hedonist Society, which in fact was a fictitious organization. The letter included a membership application and stated the Society's doctrine: that members had the "right to read what we desire, the right to discuss similar interests with those who share our philosophy, and finally that we have the right to seek pleasure without restrictions being placed on us by outdated puritan morality." Jacobson enrolled in the organization and returned a sexual attitude questionnaire that asked him to rank on a scale of one to four his enjoyment of various sexual materials, with one being "really enjoy," two being "enjoy," three being "somewhat enjoy," and four being "do not enjoy." Jacobson ranked the entry "pre-teen sex" as a two, but indicated that he was opposed to pedophilia.

For a time, the Government left Jacobson alone. But then a new "prohibited mailing specialist" in the Postal Service found Jacobson's name in a file, and in May 1986, Jacobson received a solicitation from a second fictitious consumer research company, "Midlands Data Research," seeking a response from those who "believe in the joys of sex and the complete awareness of those lusty and youthful lads and lasses of the neophite [*sic*] age."

The letter never explained whether "neophite" referred to minors or young adults. Jacobson responded: "Please feel free to send me more information, I am interested in teenage sexuality. Please keep my name confidential." Jacobson then heard from yet another Government creation, "Heartland Institute for a New Tomorrow" (HINT), which proclaimed it was an organization founded to protect and promote sexual freedom and freedom of choice. We believe that arbitrarily imposed legislative sanctions restricting your sexual freedom should be rescinded through the legislative process.

The letter also enclosed a second survey. Jacobson indicated that his interest in "preteen sex–homosexual" material was above average, but not high. In response to another question, Jacobson wrote:

> Not only sexual expression but freedom of the press is under attack. We must be ever vigilant to counter attack right wing fundamentalists who are determined to curtail our freedoms.

HINT replied, portraying itself as a lobbying organization seeking to repeal "all statutes which regulate sexual activities, except those laws which deal with violent behavior, such as rape. HINT is also lobbying to eliminate any legal definition of 'the age of consent.'" These lobbying efforts were to be funded by sales from a catalog to be published in the future "offering the sale of various items which we believe you will find to be both interesting and stimulating." HINT also provided computer matching of group members with similar survey responses; and, although petitioner was supplied with a list of potential "pen pals," he did not initiate any correspondence.

Nevertheless, the Government's "prohibited mailing specialist" began writing to Jacobson, using the pseudonym "Carl Long." The letters employed a tactic known as "mirroring," which the inspector described as "reflecting whatever the interests are of the person we are writing to." Jacobson responded at first, indicating that his interest was primarily in "male-male items." Inspector "Long" wrote back:

> My interests too are primarily male-male items. Are you satisfied with the type of VCR tapes available? Personally, I like the amateur stuff better if it's well produced as it can get more kinky and also seems more real. I think the actors enjoy it more.

Jacobson responded:

> As far as my likes are concerned, I like good looking young guys (in their late teens and early 20's) doing their thing together.

Jacobson's letters to "Long" made no reference to child pornography. After writing two letters, petitioner discontinued the correspondence.

By March 1987, 34 months had passed since the Government obtained Jacobson's name from the mailing list of the California bookstore, and 26 months had passed since the Postal Service had commenced its mailings to petitioner. Although Jacobson had responded to surveys and letters, the Government had no evidence that petitioner had ever intentionally possessed or been exposed to child pornography. The Postal Service had not checked Jacobson's mail to determine whether he was receiving questionable mailings from persons—other than the Government—involved in the child pornography industry.

At this point, a second Government agency, the Customs Service, included Jacobson in its own child pornography sting, "Operation Borderline," after receiving his name on lists submitted by the Postal Service. Using the name of a fictitious Canadian company called "Produit Outaouais," the Customs Service mailed petitioner a brochure advertising photographs of young boys engaging in sex. Jacobson placed an order that was never filled.

The Postal Service also continued its efforts in the Jacobson case, writing to petitioner as the "Far Eastern Trading Company Ltd." The letter began:

> As many of you know, much hysterical nonsense has appeared in the American media concerning "pornography" and what must be done to stop it from coming across your borders. This brief letter does not allow us to give much comments; however, why is your government spending millions of dollars to exercise international censorship while tons of drugs, which makes yours the world's most crime ridden country are passed through easily.

The letter went on to say:

> We have devised a method of getting these to you without prying eyes of U.S. Customs seizing your mail. . . . After consultations with American solicitors, we have been advised that once we have posted our material through your system, it cannot be opened for any inspection without authorization of a judge.

The letter invited Jacobson to send for more information. It also asked Jacobson to sign an affirmation that he was "not a law enforcement officer or agent of the U.S. Government acting in an undercover capacity for the purpose of entrapping Far Eastern Trading Company, its agents or customers." Jacobson responded. A catalog was sent, and Jacobson ordered *Boys Who Love Boys*, a pornographic magazine depicting young boys engaged in various sexual activities. Jacobson was arrested after a controlled delivery of a photocopy of the magazine.

When Jacobson was asked at trial why he placed such an order, he explained the Government had succeeded in piquing his curiosity: "Well, the statement was made of all the trouble and the hysteria over pornography and I wanted to see what the material was. It didn't describe the—I didn't know for sure what kind of sexual action they were referring to in the Canadian letter."

In Jacobson's home, the Government found the *Bare Boys* magazines and materials that the Government had sent to him in the course of its protracted investigation, but no other materials that would indicate Jacobson collected, or was actively interested in, child pornography.

Jacobson was indicted for violating 18 U.S.C. § 2252(a)(2)(A). The trial court instructed the jury on Jacobson's entrapment defense. The jury was instructed: As mentioned, one of the issues in this case is whether the defendant was entrapped. If the defendant was entrapped he must be found not guilty. The government has the burden of proving beyond a reasonable doubt that the defendant was not entrapped.

Jacobson was convicted, and a divided Court of Appeals for the Eighth Circuit, sitting en banc, affirmed, concluding "Jacobson was not entrapped as a matter of law." We granted certiorari.

OPINION

There can be no dispute about the evils of child pornography or the difficulties that laws and law enforcement have encountered in eliminating it. Likewise, there can be no dispute that the Government may use undercover agents to enforce the law. In their zeal to enforce the law, however, Government agents may not originate a criminal design, implant in an innocent person's mind the disposition to commit a criminal act, and then induce commission of the crime so that the Government may prosecute. Where the Government has induced an individual to break the law and the defense of entrapment is at issue, as it was in this case, the prosecution must prove beyond reasonable doubt that the defendant was disposed to commit the criminal act prior to first being approached by Government agents.

Inducement is not at issue in this case. The Government does not dispute that it induced Jacobson to commit the crime. The sole issue is whether the Government carried its burden of proving that Jacobson was predisposed to violate the law before the Government intervened. The Government's internal guidelines for undercover operations provide that an inducement to commit a crime should not be offered unless:

1. There is a reasonable indication, based on information developed through informants or other means, that the subject is engaging, has engaged, or is likely to engage in illegal activity of a similar type; or

2. The opportunity for illegal activity has been structured so that there is reason for believing that persons drawn to the opportunity, or brought to it, are predisposed to engage in the contemplated illegal activity.

Thus, an agent deployed to stop the traffic in illegal drugs may offer the opportunity to buy or sell drugs and, if the offer is accepted, make an arrest on the spot or later. In such a typical case, or in a more elaborate "sting" operation involving government-sponsored fencing where the defendant is simply provided with the opportunity to commit a crime, the entrapment defense is of little use because the ready commission of the criminal act amply demonstrates the defendant's predisposition. Had the agents simply offered Jacobson the opportunity to order child pornography through the mails, and Jacobson had promptly availed himself of this criminal opportunity, it is unlikely his entrapment defense would have warranted a jury instruction.

But that is not what happened here. By the time Jacobson finally placed his order, he had already been the target of 26 months of repeated mailings and communications from Government agents and fictitious organizations. Therefore, although he had become predisposed to break the law by May 1987, it is our view that the Government did not prove this predisposition was independent and not the product of the attention the Government had directed at Jacobson since January 1985.

The prosecution's evidence of predisposition falls into two categories: evidence developed prior to the Postal Service's mail campaign, and that developed during the course of the investigation. The sole piece of preinvestigation evidence is Jacobson's 1984 order and receipt of the *Bare Boys* magazines. But this is scant if any proof of Jacobson's predisposition to commit an illegal act. It may indicate a predisposition to view sexually oriented photographs that are responsive to his sexual tastes; but evidence that merely indicates a generic inclination to act within a broad range, not all of which is criminal, is of little probative value in establishing predisposition.

Furthermore, Jacobson was acting within the law at the time he received these magazines. Receipt through the mails of sexually explicit depictions of children for noncommercial use did not become illegal under federal law until May 1984, and Nebraska had no law that forbade his possession of such material until 1988. Evidence of predisposition to do what once was lawful is not, by itself, sufficient to show predisposition to do what is now illegal, for there is a common understanding that most people obey the law even when they disapprove of it. Hence, the fact that Jacobson legally ordered and received the *Bare Boys* magazines does little to further the Government's burden of proving he was predisposed to commit a criminal act. This is particularly true given Jacobson's unchallenged testimony that he did not know until they arrived that the magazines would depict minors.

The prosecution's evidence gathered during the investigation also fails to carry the Government's burden. Jacobson's responses to the many communications prior to the ultimate criminal act were at most indicative of certain personal inclinations, including a predisposition to view photographs of preteen sex and a willingness to promote a given agenda by supporting lobbying organizations. Even so, his responses hardly support an inference that he would commit the crime of receiving child pornography through the mails. Furthermore, a person's inclinations and "fantasies are his own and beyond the reach of government."

On the other hand, the strong arguable inference is that, by waving the banner of individual rights and disparaging the legitimacy and constitutionality of efforts to restrict the availability of sexually explicit materials, the Government not only excited Jacobson's interest in sexually explicit materials banned by law but also exerted substantial pressure on Jacobson to obtain and read such material as part of a fight against censorship and the infringement of individual rights.

For instance, HINT described itself as "an organization founded to protect and promote sexual freedom and freedom of choice" and stated that "the most appropriate means to accomplish its objectives is to promote honest dialogue among concerned individuals and to continue its lobbying efforts with State Legislators." These lobbying efforts were to be financed through catalog sales. . . . Mailings from the equally fictitious American Hedonist Society, and the correspondence from the nonexistent Carl Long, endorsed these themes.

Similarly, the two solicitations in the spring of 1987 raised the specter of censorship while suggesting Jacobson ought to be allowed to do what he had been solicited to do. The mailing from the Customs Service referred to "the worldwide ban and intense enforcement on this type of material," observed that "what was legal and commonplace is now an 'underground' and secretive service," and emphasized that "this environment forces us to take extreme measures" to ensure delivery. The Postal Service solicitation described the concern about child pornography as "hysterical nonsense," decried "international censorship," and assured petitioner, based on consultation with "American solicitors," that an order that had been posted could not be opened for inspection without authorization of a judge. It further asked petitioner to affirm he was not a Government agent attempting to entrap the mail order company or its customers. In these particulars, both Government solicitations suggested receiving this material was something Jacobson ought to be allowed to do.

Jacobson's ready response to these solicitations cannot be enough to establish beyond reasonable doubt he was predisposed, prior to the Government acts intended to create predisposition, to commit the crime of receiving child pornography through the mails. The evidence that he was ready and willing to commit the offense came only after the Government had devoted 2½ years to convincing him he had or should have the right to engage in the very behavior proscribed by law.

Rational jurors could not say beyond a reasonable doubt that Jacobson possessed the requisite predisposition prior to the Government's investigation and that it existed independent of the Government's many and varied approaches to him. The Government may not play on the weaknesses of an innocent party and beguile him into committing crimes which he otherwise would not have attempted. Law enforcement officials go too far when they implant in the mind of an innocent person the disposition to commit the alleged offense and induce its commission in order that they may prosecute.

When the Government's quest for convictions leads to the apprehension of an otherwise law-abiding citizen who, if left to his own devices, likely would have never run afoul of the law, the courts should intervene. Because we conclude this is such a case and the prosecution failed to adduce evidence to support the jury verdict Jacobson was predisposed, independent of the Government's acts and beyond a reasonable doubt, to violate the law by receiving child pornography through the mails, we REVERSE the Court of Appeals' judgment affirming the conviction of Keith Jacobson.

DISSENT

O'CONNOR, J., joins with REHNQUIST, C.J.,
and KENNEDY and SCALIA, JJ.

Keith Jacobson was offered only two opportunities to buy child pornography through the mail. Both times, he ordered. Both times, he asked for opportunities to buy more. He needed no Government agent to coax, threaten, or persuade him; no one played on his sympathies, friendship, or suggested that his committing the crime would further a greater good. In fact, no Government agent even contacted him face to face. The Government contends that from the enthusiasm with which Mr. Jacobson responded to the chance to commit a crime, a reasonable jury could permissibly infer beyond a reasonable doubt that he was predisposed to commit the crime. I agree.

Today, the Court holds that Government conduct may be considered to create a predisposition to commit a crime, even before any Government action to induce the commission of the crime. In my view, this holding changes entrapment doctrine. Generally, the inquiry is whether a suspect is predisposed before the Government induces the commission of the crime, not before the Government makes initial contact with him. There is no dispute here that the Government's questionnaires and letters were not sufficient to establish inducement; they did not even suggest that Mr. Jacobson should engage in any illegal activity. Yet, the Court holds that the Government must prove not only that a suspect was predisposed to commit the crime before the opportunity to commit it arose, but also before the Government came on the scene.

While the Court states that the Government "exerted substantial pressure on petitioner to obtain and read such material as part of a fight against censorship and the infringement of individual rights," one looks at the record in vain for evidence of such "substantial pressure." The most one finds is letters advocating legislative action to liberalize obscenity laws, letters which could easily be ignored or thrown away. Much later, the Government sent separate mailings of catalogs of illegal materials. Nowhere did the Government suggest that the proceeds of the sale of the illegal materials would be used to support legislative reforms.

In sum, it was surely reasonable for the jury to infer that Mr. Jacobson was predisposed beyond a reasonable doubt, even if other inferences from the evidence were also possible. Because I believe there was sufficient evidence to uphold the jury's verdict, I respectfully dissent.

QUESTIONS

1. **What specific facts demonstrate that the government induced Keith Jacobson to order the child pornography?**
2. **What evidence demonstrates that Keith Jacobson was predisposed to commit the crime?**
3. **Why did the Court reverse the conviction even though the jury convicted him?**
4. **What does the dissent mean when it says that the majority has changed the law of entrapment?**
5. **Commentary following the Court's decision claimed the decision "ties the hands of law enforcement officers." Do you agree? Defend your answer.**

The Objective Test

LO 8

A growing minority of courts has adopted an **objective test of entrapment**, also called the "hypothetical person" test (*State v. Wilkins* 1983). The objective test of entrapment doesn't focus on the predisposition of the specific defendant in the case. Instead, it focuses on whether the actions of government officers would get a hypothetical "reasonable person" to commit a crime. According to the objective test, if the actions of the officer would induce an "ordinarily law-abiding" person to commit the crime, the court should dismiss the case. This test is a prophylactic rule aimed to deter "unsavory police methods." Courts (not juries) decide whether police methods would cause a hypothetical reasonable person to commit a crime they wouldn't commit otherwise.

U.S. Supreme Court Justice Felix Frankfurter, concurring in *Sherman v. U.S.* (1958, discussed earlier) about the core idea behind the objective test, wrote:

> No matter what the defendant's past record and present inclinations to criminality, or the depths to which he has sunk in the estimation of society, certain police conduct to ensnare him into further crime is not to be tolerated by an advanced society. (382–83)

Summary

LO 1
- Citizens have no constitutional right to either the exclusionary rule or the entrapment defense. The exclusionary rule is a device created by the U.S. Supreme Court to enforce constitutional rights, not a right in its own.

LO 2
- Bad methods refer to police actions and procedures that violate Fourth, Fifth, Sixth, and Fourteenth Amendment rights. Use of the term "good evidence" isn't meant to imply that the evidence was collected using good methods.

LO 3
- The fruit-of-the-poisonous-tree doctrine excludes evidence indirectly associated with an illegal government action. The premise is that courts should ensure the government is never better off after violating the Constitution than it was before it did so.

LO 4
- The Supreme Court established that unreasonable search and seizure violates the due process clause of the Fourteenth Amendment in 1949 and endorsed exclusion of evidence based on that right in 1961.

LO 4
- Justification of the exclusionary rule is based on constitutional rights, the preservation of judicial integrity, and deterring officers from breaking laws.

LO 5
- The exclusionary rule has real social costs and courts seek to mitigate them by defining exceptions. Otherwise inadmissible evidence can be used in hearings outside the trial, such as bail, and in cross-examination to discredit the defendant's testimony.

LO 5
- Evidence that would normally be excluded is admissible if the same evidence was also acquired from a legal source or if discovery of it was inevitable.

LO 4, LO 5
- It's difficult to measure what deterrent effect, if any, the exclusionary rule has had on law officers breaking the law to obtain evidence. It's easier to quantify the social impact on successful prosecution. Many professionals agree the exclusionary rule is used rarely and, when it is, doesn't often involve crimes against persons.

LO 6 • Entrapment occurs when agents get people to commit crimes they wouldn't otherwise commit. The entrapment defense seeks to regulate enforcement tactics by taking criminal disposition into account when assessing guilt.

LO 6 • Encouragement is likely to result when law enforcement officers pretend they're victims, intentionally entice suspects to commit a crime, communicate the enticement to suspects, or influence the decision to commit crimes. Not all encouragement is entrapment.

LO 7 • The entrapment defense isn't provided by constitutional right. It's an affirmative defense, created and defined by statutes and courts.

LO 8 • The subjective test prevents conviction in cases where a defendant had no prior desire to commit the crime and government encouragement caused the defendant to commit it.

LO 8 • The objective test (adopted by a growing minority of courts) doesn't focus on the predisposition of an individual but on whether the government actions would have caused a hypothetical "reasonable person" to commit the crime.

Review Questions

1. Identify two types of remedies against government wrongdoing and the differences between them, and give examples of each.

2. Is there a constitutional right to the exclusionary rule and the defense of entrapment? Explain your answer.

3. Briefly trace the history of the exclusionary rule through the leading U.S. Supreme Court cases that created and expanded it.

4. Identify and explain the rationales behind the three justifications for the exclusionary rule. Which justification does the U.S. Supreme Court use today?

5. Explain the balancing test the U.S. Supreme Court adopted to apply the deterrence justification.

6. Summarize U.S. Supreme Court Justice Louis Brandeis's arguments in favor of the exclusionary rule.

7. List and explain five exceptions to the exclusionary rule.

8. Identify the rationale for the attenuation, independent source, and inevitable discovery exceptions to the exclusionary rule.

9. State the narrow scope of the reasonable good-faith exception to the exclusionary rule.

10. Identify the assumptions of the Warren and Rehnquist Courts regarding the exclusionary rule.

11. According to Professor Christopher Slobogin, why is no one likely to win the empirical debate over the accuracy of the assumptions you identified in question 11?

12. Describe and explain the U.S. Supreme Court's attitude toward the defense of entrapment throughout most of our history.

13. Identify four examples of active law enforcement encouragement.

14. Identify the difference between the subjective and the objective tests of entrapment.

15. Identify two elements in the subjective test of entrapment.

16. What's the crucial question in the subjective test of entrapment?

17. Describe how the U.S. Supreme Court applied the subjective case to the facts of *Sherman v. U.S.*

18. Identify the two kinds of circumstances the government can use to prove defendants' predisposition to commit crimes. Give an example of each.

19. According to U.S. Supreme Court Justice Felix Frankfurter, what's the core idea behind the objective test of entrapment?

Key Terms

exclusionary rule, p. 336
defense of entrapment, p. 336
encouragement, p. 336
"good evidence," p. 336
probative evidence, p. 336
"bad methods," p. 336
fruit-of-the-poisonous-tree
  doctrine, p. 338
amicus curiae brief, p. 339
constitutional right justification, p. 341
judicial integrity justification, p. 342
deterrence justification, p. 342
prophylactic rule, p. 342

social cost of the rule, p. 343
collateral-use exception, p. 343
nontrial proceedings, p. 343
collateral proceedings, p. 343
case-in-chief, p. 343
impeach, p. 343
attenuation exception, p. 344
independent source exception, p. 344
inevitable discovery exception, p. 345
good-faith exception, p. 345
subjective test of entrapment, p. 355
objective test of entrapment, p. 360

11

LEARNING OBJECTIVES

1 Understand the role of criminal intent in cases against officers.

2 Know that civil actions against (a) the federal government and its officers; (b) local, county, and state officers, law enforcement agencies, and government units; and (c) other government employees are controlled by different statutes, court decisions, and government units.

3 Understand constitutional tort actions (*Bivens* actions) against officers and Federal Tort Claims Act actions against public institutions.

4 Recognize and appreciate the role of the courts in maintaining the balance between the right of individuals to recover damages for injuries and the need of well-meaning law enforcement officers to do their job effectively.

5 Know the role of Civil Rights Act actions in holding law enforcement officials responsible for violating the constitutional rights of individuals.

6 Understand the limitations of lawsuits brought against states and their officers.

7 Realize that the Constitution places no duty on officers to protect individuals from each other, and that it doesn't create a right of private parties to sue officers for failing to prevent crime.

8 Know that judges enjoy absolute immunity, and prosecutors have functional immunity.

9 Know of the "special relationship" between the government and persons in custody and the impact that special relationship has on lawsuits brought by prisoners against law enforcement officers.

10 Understand the role of administrative action in remedying misconduct.

Constitutional Violations II: Other Remedies against Official Misconduct

CHAPTER OUTLINE

On the evening of March 10, 1989, Officer Donald Johnson responded to a call reporting a domestic disturbance at the home of Carol Pinder. When he arrived at the scene, Johnson discovered that Pinder's former boyfriend, Don Pittman, had broken into her home. Pinder told Officer Johnson that when Pittman broke in, he was abusive and violent. He pushed her, punched her, and threw various objects at her. Pittman was also screaming and threatening both Pinder and her children, saying he would murder them all. A neighbor, Darnell Taylor, managed to subdue Pittman and restrain him until the police arrived. Johnson arrested Pittman, but later that evening Pittman was released, returned to Pinder's house and set fire to it. Pinder was still at work, but her three children were home asleep and died of smoke inhalation. *Pinder v. Johnson* (1995)

We talked about remedies that affect the determination of guilt (trial stage) in criminal cases against defendants (the exclusionary rule and the defense of entrapment) in Chapter 10. In this chapter, you'll learn about remedies against officers that aren't available in the criminal trial case against defendants. They result from three separate actions:

1. ***Criminal law***. Prosecuting the officer
2. ***Civil law***. Suing the officer, the police department, or the government
3. ***Internal and external departmental review***. Disciplining the officer outside the judicial system

Let's look at these three types of actions and the remedies that flow from them.

Criminal Actions

LO 1

Most police misconduct can be a crime. So a police officer who illegally shoots and kills a person might have committed criminal homicide. Illegal arrests can be false imprisonment. Illegal searches can be trespassing—and maybe breaking and entering, too. But, how likely is it that police officers will be charged with crimes, convicted, and punished when they break the law? Not very. Why? Judges and juries don't see police misconduct as a crime. And with good reason. In our criminal justice system, the government has to prove criminal intent beyond a reasonable doubt. If police officers honestly believe they were enforcing the law, and not committing a crime (which in most cases is either true or difficult to prove otherwise beyond a reasonable doubt), then they're not *criminally* guilty. And this is the way it should be. The standard of proof has to be the same for officers as for everybody else.

There's a second reason. Even if officers are guilty of criminal misconduct, prosecutors hesitate to prosecute, and juries are unwilling to convict, police officers who are "only trying to do their job." This is true especially when the "victims" might be "real" criminals (or at least people who associate with criminals).

Civil Actions

LO 2

Most individuals seeking a remedy for official lawbreaking (**plaintiffs**) want compensation (the law calls them **damages**) for the injuries caused by police misconduct. How do they get damages? The only way is by becoming plaintiffs in a **civil action** (meaning it's not a criminal case).

Who can plaintiffs sue for money damages? Any—or all—of the following:

1. Individual law enforcement officers
2. Officers' superiors (such as police chiefs and sheriffs)
3. Law enforcement agencies
4. Government units in charge of officers and departments (towns, cities, counties, states, and the U.S. government)

Where do they sue? In state and federal courts. We'll look separately at civil actions for damages against (1) federal officers; (2) the U.S. government; (3) local, county, and state officers; (4) local, county, and state law enforcement agencies; (5) local, county, and state government units; and (6) other government employees, because they're controlled by different statutes, court decisions, and government units. We'll also examine what happens when law enforcement officers fail to protect individuals and some of the hurdles to suing the government.

Lawsuits against U.S. Officers and the U.S. Government

LO 3

Lawsuits against individual federal law enforcement officers are called **constitutional tort (*Bivens*) actions**. Lawsuits against the federal government for their officers' constitutional torts are called **Federal Tort Claims Act (FTCA) actions**. Let's look at each.

Lawsuits against U.S. Officers

LO 1, LO 2, LO 3, LO 4

Until 1971, individuals were banned from suing federal officers for violations of their constitutional rights. All that changed after the U.S. Supreme Court decided *Bivens v. Six Unnamed FBI Agents* (1971). In that case, six FBI agents entered Webster Bivens's apartment without a search or arrest warrant. After they searched his apartment "from stem to stern," the agents arrested Bivens for violating federal drug laws and hand-cuffed him in the presence of his wife and children.

The agents took Bivens first to the Brooklyn Federal Courthouse and then to the Federal Bureau of Narcotics, "where he was interrogated, fingerprinted, photographed, subjected to search of his person, and booked." Bivens claimed these events caused him "great humiliation, embarrassment, and mental suffering" and would "continue to do so." He sought damages of $15,000 from each of the six officers (390).

In *Bivens*, the Court created a **constitutional tort**, a private right to sue federal officers for violations of plaintiffs' constitutional rights. In these "*Bivens* actions," plaintiffs have to prove two elements:

1. Officers were acting "under color of authority" or the appearance of power. (Garner 1987, 123–24)

2. Officers' actions deprived the plaintiff of a constitutional right.

Even if plaintiffs prove these two elements, they don't automatically "win" their case. Law enforcement officers have a defense called **qualified immunity** (also called the **"good faith" defense**). According to this complex defense, individual officers can't be held personally liable for official action if

1. Their action meets the test of "objective legal reasonableness."

2. Reasonableness is measured by legal rules "clearly established" at the time the officers acted.

The reason for creating this test was to protect officers' broad discretion to do their job and keep them (and the courts) from being bombarded with frivolous lawsuits.

The U.S. Supreme Court created and explained why it created the qualified immunity defense against constitutional torts in *Anderson v. Creighton* (1987).

In Anderson v. Creighton (1987), our next case excerpt, the U.S. Supreme Court created the qualified immunity defense and held that it applied to an FBI officer who invaded the Creighton home, because his mistaken entry was "objectively reasonable."

CASE Were the FBI Agent's Actions "Objectively Reasonable"?

Anderson v. Creighton

483 U.S. 635 (1987)

HISTORY

Robert E. Creighton Jr., his wife, and others sued FBI Agent Russell Anderson in the U.S. District Court for the District of Minnesota. The U.S. District Court granted **summary judgment** [a motion that the court enter a judgment without a trial because there's not enough evidence to support the plaintiff's claim] in favor of the agent. The Court of Appeals for the Eighth Circuit reversed and remanded. The U.S. Supreme Court granted certiorari, vacated the Circuit Court's judgment and remanded the case.

SCALIA, J., joined by REHNQUIST, C.J., and WHITE, BLACKMUN, POWELL, and O'CONNOR JJ.

FACTS

Russell Anderson is an agent of the Federal Bureau of Investigation. On November 11, 1983, Anderson and other state and federal law enforcement officers conducted a warrantless search of the Creighton family's home. The search was conducted because Anderson believed that Vadaain Dixon, a man suspected of a bank robbery committed earlier that day, might be found there. He was not.

On the night of November 11, 1983, Sarisse and Robert Creighton and their three young daughters were spending a quiet evening at their home when a spotlight suddenly flashed through their front window. Mr. Creighton opened the door and was confronted by several uniformed and plainclothes officers, many of them brandishing shotguns. All of the officers were white; the Creightons are black. Mr. Creighton claims that none of the officers responded when he asked what they wanted.

Instead, by his account (as verified by a St. Paul police report), one of the officers told him to "keep his hands in sight" while the other officers rushed through the door. When Mr. Creighton asked if they had a search warrant, one of the officers told him, "We don't have a search warrant and don't need one; you watch too much TV." Mr. Creighton asked the officers to put their guns away because his children were frightened, but the officers refused.

Mrs. Creighton awoke to the shrieking of her children, and was confronted by an officer who pointed a shotgun at her. She allegedly observed the officers yelling at her three daughters to "sit their damn asses down and stop screaming." She asked the officer, "What the hell is going on?" The officer allegedly did not explain the situation and simply said to her, "Why don't you make your damn kids sit on the couch and make them shut up."

One of the officers asked Mr. Creighton if he had a red and silver car. As Mr. Creighton led the officers downstairs to his garage, where his maroon Oldsmobile was parked, one of the officers punched him in the face, knocking him to the ground, and causing him to bleed from the mouth and the forehead. Mr. Creighton alleges that he was attempting to move past the officer to open the garage door when the officer panicked and hit him. The officer claims that Mr. Creighton attempted to grab his shotgun, even though Mr. Creighton was not a suspect in any crime and had no contraband in his home or on his person. Shaunda, the Creighton's ten-year-old daughter, witnessed the assault and screamed for her mother to come help. She claims that one of the officers then hit her.

Mrs. Creighton phoned her mother, but an officer allegedly kicked and grabbed the phone and told her to "hang up that damn phone." She told her children to run to their neighbor's house for safety. The children ran out and a plainclothes officer chased them. The Creightons' neighbor allegedly told Mrs. Creighton that the officer ran into her house and grabbed Shaunda by the shoulders and shook her. The neighbor allegedly told the officer, "Can't you see she's in shock; leave her alone and get out of my house." Mrs. Creighton's mother later brought Shaunda to the emergency room at Children's Hospital for an arm injury caused by the officer's rough handling.

During the melee, family members and friends began arriving at the Creightons' home. Mrs. Creighton claims that she was embarrassed in front of her family and friends by the invasion of their home and their rough treatment as if they were suspects in a major crime. At this time, she again asked Anderson for a search warrant. He allegedly replied, "I don't need a damn search warrant when I'm looking for a fugitive." The officers did not discover the allegedly unspecified "fugitive" at the Creightons' home or any evidence whatsoever that he had been there or that the Creightons were involved in any type of criminal activity.

Nonetheless, the officers then arrested and handcuffed Mr. Creighton for obstruction of justice and brought him to the police station where he was jailed overnight, then released without being charged.

OPINION

When government officials abuse their offices, actions for damages may offer the only realistic avenue for vindication of constitutional guarantees. On the other hand, permitting damages suits against government officials can entail substantial social costs, including the risk that fear of personal monetary liability and harassing litigation will unduly inhibit officials in the discharge of their duties. Our cases have accommodated these conflicting concerns by generally providing government officials performing discretionary functions with a qualified immunity, shielding them from civil damages liability as long as their actions could reasonably have been thought consistent with the rights they are alleged to have violated.

Somewhat more concretely, whether an official protected by qualified immunity may be held personally liable for an allegedly unlawful official action generally turns on the "objective legal reasonableness" of the action, assessed in light of the legal rules that were "clearly established" at the time it was taken. The contours of the right must be sufficiently clear that a reasonable official would understand that what he is doing violates that right. This is not to say that an official action is protected by qualified immunity unless the very action in question has previously been held unlawful, but it is to say that in the light of pre-existing law the unlawfulness must be apparent.

We vacate the judgment of the Court of Appeals and REMAND the case for further proceedings consistent with this opinion.

DISSENT

STEVENS, J., joined by BRENNAN and MARSHALL, JJ.

The Court announces a new rule of law that protects federal agents who make forcible nighttime entries into the homes of innocent citizens without probable cause, without a warrant, and without any valid emergency justification for their warrantless search. The Court of Appeals understood the principle of qualified immunity to shield government officials performing discretionary functions from exposure to damages liability unless their conduct violated clearly established statutory or constitutional rights of which a reasonable person would have known.

Anderson has not argued that any relevant rule of law—whether the probable-cause requirement or the exigent-circumstances exception to the warrant requirement—was not "clearly established" in November 1983. Rather, he argues that a competent officer might have concluded that the particular set of facts he faced did constitute "probable cause" and "exigent circumstances," and that his own reasonable belief that the conduct engaged in was within the law suffices to establish immunity. Of course, the probable-cause requirement for an officer who faces the situation Anderson did was clearly established.

Although the question does not appear to have been argued in, or decided by, the Court of Appeals, this Court has decided to apply a double standard of reasonableness in damages actions against federal agents who are alleged to have violated an innocent citizen's Fourth Amendment rights. By double standard I mean a standard that affords a law enforcement official two layers of insulation from liability or other adverse consequence, such as suppression of evidence.

Having already adopted such a double standard in applying the exclusionary rule to searches authorized by an invalid warrant, *U.S. v. Leon*, (1984) [discussed in Chapter 10], the Court seems prepared and even anxious in this case to remove any requirement that the officer must obey the Fourth Amendment when entering a private home. I remain convinced that in a suit for damages as well as in a hearing on a motion to suppress evidence, an official search and seizure cannot be both unreasonable and reasonable at the same time. A federal official may not with impunity ignore the limitations which the controlling law has placed on his powers.

The effect of the Court's (literally unwarranted) extension of qualified immunity, I fear, is that it allows federal agents to ignore the limitations of the probable-cause and warrant requirements with impunity. The Court does so in the name of avoiding interference with legitimate law enforcement activities even though the probable-cause requirement, which limits the police's exercise of coercive authority, is itself a form of immunity that frees them to exercise that power without fear of strict liability.

The argument that police officers need special immunity to encourage them to take vigorous enforcement action when they are uncertain about their right to make a forcible entry into a private home has already been accepted in our jurisprudence. We have held that the police act reasonably in entering a house when they have probable cause to believe a fugitive is in the house and exigent circumstances make it impracticable to obtain a warrant. This interpretation of the Fourth Amendment allows room for police intrusion, without a warrant, on the privacy of even innocent citizens.

In *Pierson v. Ray*, we held that police officers would not be liable in an action brought under 42 U.S.C. § 1983 "if they acted in good faith and with probable cause." We explained:

Under the prevailing view in this country a peace officer who arrests someone with probable cause is not liable for false arrest simply because the innocence of the suspect is later proved. A policeman's lot is not so unhappy that he must choose between being charged with dereliction of duty if he does not arrest when he has probable cause, and being mulcted in damages if he does.

Thus, until now the Court has not found intolerable the use of a probable-cause standard to protect the police officer from exposure to liability simply because his reasonable conduct is subsequently shown to have been mistaken. Today, however, the Court counts the law enforcement interest twice and the individual's privacy interest only once. The Court's double-counting approach reflects understandable sympathy for the plight of the officer and an overriding interest in unfettered law enforcement. It ascribes a far lesser importance to the privacy interest of innocent citizens than did the Framers of the Fourth Amendment.

The importance of that interest and the possible magnitude of its invasion are both illustrated by the facts of this case. The home of an innocent family was invaded by several officers without a warrant, without the owner's consent, with a substantial show of force, and with blunt expressions of disrespect for the law and for the rights of the family members. I see no reason why the family's interest in the security of its own home should be accorded a lesser weight than the Government's interest in carrying out an invasion that was unlawful.

Arguably, if the Government considers it important not to discourage such conduct, it should provide indemnity to its officers. Preferably, however, it should furnish the kind of training for its law enforcement agents that would entirely eliminate the necessity for the Court to distinguish between the conduct that a competent officer considers reasonable and the conduct that the Constitution deems reasonable. On the other hand, surely an innocent family should not bear the entire risk that a trial court, with the benefit of hindsight, will find that a federal agent reasonably believed that he could break into their home equipped with force and arms but without probable cause or a warrant.

I respectfully dissent.

QUESTIONS

1. State the test for qualified immunity adopted by the majority.
2. List the reasons the Court gives for defining "qualified immunity" the way it does.
3. Summarize the dissent's objections to the majority's definition of "qualified immunity."
4. Which of the opinions do you agree with?
5. Explain what Justice Stevens means by "the Court counts the law enforcement interest twice and the individual's privacy interest only once."
6. Do you believe Robert and Sarisse Creighton and their children should have received damages for what happened? Defend your answer, relying on the facts and the arguments of the majority and the dissent.

Lawsuits against the U.S. Government

LO 3

Bivens didn't decide whether Webster Bivens could also sue the U.S. government for the six FBI officers' constitutional torts. According to the **doctrine of sovereign immunity** (a holdover from the days when kings didn't have to appear in court), governments can't be sued without their consent. The U.S. and most state governments have laws waiving their sovereign immunity (at least to some degree). That's what Congress did in the Federal Tort Claims Act (FTCA).

After *Bivens,* Congress permitted FTCA suits against the U.S. government for the constitutional torts of federal law enforcement agents "empowered by law to execute searches, to seize evidence, or to make arrests for violations of Federal law." The U.S. government's "deep pockets" make FTCA actions attractive to plaintiffs—probably more attractive than *Bivens* actions against individual officers. But both remedies are available to plaintiffs.

According to Professors Whitebread and Slobogin (2000):

> The plaintiff whose constitutional rights have been violated by a federal police officer in bad faith can be assured of monetary compensation [in an FTCA action] at the same time he can expect direct "revenge" in a *Bivens* action against the official to the extent the official can afford it. (51–52)

LO 1, LO 2,
LO 3, LO 4,
LO5, LO 6

LO 4

Suing State Officers

Plaintiffs can sue individual state officers in two kinds of actions: state tort lawsuits and federal U.S. Civil Rights Act lawsuits. Let's look at each.

State Tort Actions

Most illegal acts by state police, county sheriffs' and their deputies, and local police officers and their chiefs are also **torts**, meaning plaintiffs can sue individual officers for damages for acts such as assault, false arrest or false imprisonment, and trespassing or breaking and entering. But the right to recover damages for injuries caused by officials' torts has to be balanced against law enforcement's job of protecting the public. So, although individual officers are liable for their own torts, there's a huge difference between suing an ordinary person and a police officer.

The **defense of official immunity** limits officers' liability for their torts. This defense says that "a public official charged by law with duties which call for the exercise of his judgment or discretion is not personally liable to an individual unless he is guilty of a willful or malicious wrong." Why? Because "to encourage responsible law enforcement police are afforded a wide degree of discretion precisely because a more stringent standard could inhibit action."

In *Pletan v. Gaines et al.* (1992), the Minnesota Supreme Court balanced the rights of injured individuals and the needs of law enforcement when the court decided a police officer wasn't liable for the death of a small boy he killed during a high-speed chase to catch a fleeing shoplifter. If the officer were held liable, the court said, officers in the future might shy away from vigorously enforcing the law.

U.S. Civil Rights Act (§ 1983) Actions

LO 1, LO 2,
LO 5

Civil Rights Act actions (called **§ 1983 actions** because they're brought under Title 42, Section 1983, of the Civil Rights Act of 1871, passed just after the Civil War) allow plaintiffs to go into federal courts to sue state police officers and their agency heads; county sheriffs and their deputies; and municipal police officers and their chiefs for violating plaintiffs' federal constitutional rights.

Section 1983 provides:

> Every person who, under color of any statute, ordinance, regulation, custom, or usage, of any State or Territory, subjects, or causes to be subjected, any citizen of the United States or other person within the jurisdiction thereof to the deprivation of any rights, privileges, or immunities secured by the Constitution and laws, shall be liable to the party injured. (U.S. Code 2002, Title 42, § 1983)

As interpreted by the U.S. Supreme Court, plaintiffs have to prove two elements similar to those in *Bivens* constitutional tort actions:

1. Officers acted "under color of state law," which includes all acts done within the scope of their employment.

2. Officers' actions caused a deprivation of plaintiffs' rights guaranteed by the U.S. Constitution.

Section 1983 doesn't mean that officers are liable every time they violate individuals' constitutional rights. Far from it. The U.S. Supreme Court has read several limits into the statutory protection. First, plaintiffs can't recover for accidental or even negligent violations; violations have to be deliberate. Second, state and local officers are protected by the same qualified immunity under § 1983 that federal officers have under *Bivens* and the Federal Tort Claims Act.

Suing State and Local Governments

LO 2, LO 6

Plaintiffs have two options in deciding to sue state and local governments instead of (or in addition to) suing individual officers. They can sue governments in state courts for the torts of their officers, or they can sue them under the U.S. Civil Rights Act (see "Suing State Officers"). Let's look at each of these complicated routes to recovering damages from governments instead of individuals.

State Tort Actions

LO 6

What if the boy's parents in the *Pletan v. Gaines et al.* (1992) case (discussed earlier) had sued the local Minnesota police department or the city instead of the individual officer? Under the **doctrine of *respondeat superior***, state and local governments and their agencies are liable for the torts of their employees but only if the employees committed the torts during the course of their employment.

There's another catch; not all states have adopted the doctrine. In these states, government units enjoy the **defense of vicarious official immunity**, which means police departments and local governments can claim the official immunity of its employees. To determine whether government units are entitled to the defense of vicarious official immunity, courts apply a balancing test of local government liability. This test balances two elements:

1. The need for effective law enforcement
2. The need to avoid putting the public at risk

In the Minnesota Supreme Court's application of the balancing test in *Pletan v. Gaines et al.* (1992), the high-speed chase case, the court found the need to enforce the criminal law outweighed the risk to the public created by the high-speed chase. So, the court held, the municipality wasn't liable for the boy's death (42–43).

U.S. Civil Rights Act (§ 1983) Actions

LO 2, LO 6

As you learned from *Anderson v. Creighton* (excerpted p. 368), suing individual officers for violating constitutional rights is a complicated business. Suing a department or a city under § 1983 is even more complicated. In fact, until the Court decided to undertake "a fresh analysis of debate on the Civil Rights Act of 1871" in *Monell v. New York City Department of Social Services* (1978), the Court had interpreted § 1983 to mean Congress didn't intend to allow individuals to sue municipalities and counties at all. But in *Monell*, the Court changed its mind, deciding the legislative history of the act "compels the conclusion that Congress did intend municipalities and other local government units to be included among those persons to whom § 1983 applies."

According to the *Monell* Court, individuals could sue local government units if they could prove two elements:

1. Officers either acted according to written policies, statements, ordinances, regulations, or decisions approved by authorized official bodies or to unwritten custom. The condition was met even if the custom wasn't formally approved through official decision-making channels.

2. The action caused the violation of the plaintiff's constitutional right(s).

So according to the Supreme Court in the *Monell* case:

A local government cannot be sued for an injury inflicted solely by its employees or agents. Instead, it is when execution of a government's policy or custom, whether made by its lawmakers or by those whose edicts or acts may fairly be said to represent official policy, inflicts the injury that the government as an entity is responsible for it under § 1983. (695)

Law Enforcement Failure to Protect

LO 7

Until now, we've talked only about remedies that protect individuals from government violations of their rights, but what about failure by the government to protect people from each other? Most police departments conceive their mission broadly: "To protect and serve." But is their mission "to protect" a constitutional command? In other words, do governments and their officers have a constitutional duty to protect individuals from other private individuals who violate their rights? No. (At least, not most of the time.)

According to the U.S. Supreme Court, neither the language of the due process clauses nor the history of the Fifth and Fourteenth Amendments (which contain the due process clauses) imposes an affirmative duty on law enforcement to protect individuals from other private individuals who would deprive them of their right to life, liberty, or property (*DeShaney v. Winnegabo County* 1989). Nor does it bestow an affirmative right on individuals to be protected from those individuals. So, according to what we'll call the Supreme Court's **no-affirmative-duty-to-protect rule**, plaintiffs can't sue individual officers or government units for failing to stop private people from violating their rights by inflicting injuries on them.

LO 9

According to the U.S. Supreme Court, there's an exception to the no-duty-to-protect rule—the **special-relationship exception**. The special relationship is custody. When the government takes it upon itself to put people in jail, prison, or mental institutions against their will and keeps them there, it's cruel and unusual punishment (in violation of the Eighth Amendment to the U.S. Constitution) to fail to protect them when they can't protect themselves (*DeShaney*, 199).

Some of the U.S. Courts of Appeals have created a second exception not yet approved by the Supreme Court, the **state-created-danger exception** (*Robinson v. Township of Redford* 2002, 929). This is a narrow exception, and, to qualify for it and collect damages under § 1983, plaintiffs have to prove three elements:

1. An officer's actions created a special danger of violent harm to the plaintiff (not to the general public).

2. The officer knows or should have known her actions would encourage this plaintiff to rely on her actions.

3. The danger created by the officer's actions either caused harm from the violence itself or increased the plaintiff's vulnerability to harm from violence.

Other U.S. Courts of Appeals have soundly rejected the state-created-danger exception. For example, the Fourth Circuit Court of Appeals has declined to accept the exception. The court explained why in *Pinder v. Johnson* (1995), our next case excerpt.

In Pinder v. Johnson *(1995), our next case excerpt, the Fourth Circuit Court of Appeals rejected the state-created-danger exception when Carol Pinder argued that an officer's negligence led to the deaths of her three children.*

CASE   Did the Police Have a Constitutional Duty to Protect Her and Her Children?

Pinder v. Johnson
54 F.3d 1169 (CA4 1995)

HISTORY

Carol Pinder filed suit individually and as the survivor of her minor children against the municipality of Cambridge, Maryland, and Donald Johnson PFC, a police officer in the municipality of Cambridge. The U.S. District Court for the District of Maryland denied Johnson's motion for summary judgment. A three-judge panel of the Fourth Circuit Court of Appeals affirmed. An **en banc review** [review by the whole circuit] REVERSED.

WILKINSON, J., joined by HALL, WILKINS, NIEMEYER, and WILLIAMS, JJ. WIDENER, MOTZ, HAMILTON, and LUTTIG, JJ. concurred in part, and concurred in the judgment.

FACTS

The facts of this case are genuinely tragic. On the evening of March 10, 1989, Officer Donald Johnson responded to a call reporting a domestic disturbance at the home of Carol Pinder. When he arrived at the scene, Johnson discovered that Pinder's former boyfriend, Don Pittman, had broken into her home. Pinder told Officer Johnson that when Pittman broke in, he was abusive and violent. He pushed her, punched her, and threw various objects at her.

Pittman was also screaming and threatening both Pinder and her children, saying he would murder them all. A neighbor, Darnell Taylor, managed to subdue Pittman and restrain him until the police arrived.

Officer Johnson questioned Pittman, who was hostile and unresponsive. Johnson then placed Pittman under arrest. After confining Pittman in the squad car, Johnson returned to the house to speak with Pinder again. Pinder explained to Officer Johnson that Pittman had threatened her in the past, and that he had just been released from prison after being convicted of attempted arson at Pinder's residence some ten months earlier. She was naturally afraid for herself and her children, and wanted to know whether it would be safe for her to return to work that evening.

Officer Johnson assured her that Pittman would be locked up overnight. He further indicated that Pinder had to wait until the next day to swear out a warrant against Pittman because a county commissioner would not be available to hear the charges before morning. Based on these assurances, Pinder returned to work.

That same evening, Johnson brought Pittman before Dorchester County Commissioner George Ames, Jr. for an initial appearance. Johnson only charged Pittman with trespassing and malicious destruction of property having a value of less than three hundred dollars, both of which are misdemeanor offenses. Consequently, Ames simply released Pittman on his own recognizance and warned him to stay away from Pinder's home.

Pittman did not heed this warning. Upon his release, he returned to Pinder's house and set fire to it. Pinder was still at work, but her three children were home asleep and died of smoke inhalation. Pittman was later arrested and charged with first degree murder. He was convicted and is currently serving three life sentences without possibility of parole.

Pinder brought this action for herself and for the estates of her three children, seeking damages under 42 U.S.C. § 1983, as well as state law theories, against the Commissioners of Cambridge and Officer Johnson. She alleged that defendants had violated their affirmative duty to protect her and her children, thereby depriving them of their constitutional right to due process under the Fourteenth Amendment.

Johnson moved for summary judgment, arguing that he had no constitutionally imposed affirmative duty to protect the Pinders and that he was shielded from liability by the doctrine of qualified immunity. The district court, however, refused to dismiss plaintiff's due process claim, finding that Officer Johnson was not entitled to qualified immunity. Johnson brought an **interlocutory appeal** [an appeal that takes place before the trial court rules on the case]. A divided panel of this court affirmed, finding that Pinder had stated a cognizable substantive due process claim and that Johnson did not have a valid immunity defense. We granted rehearing en banc, and now reverse the judgment of the district court.

OPINION

Qualified immunity under § 1983 shields officials from civil liability unless their actions violated "clearly established statutory or constitutional rights of which a reasonable person would have known." The linchpin of qualified immunity is objective reasonableness. Important to this reasonableness inquiry is whether the rights alleged to have been violated were clearly established at the time of the challenged actions. If the law supporting the allegedly violated rights was not clearly established, then immunity must lie. Where the law is clearly established, and where no reasonable officer could believe he was acting in accordance with it, qualified immunity will not attach.

The purpose of this doctrine is to ensure that police officers and other government actors have notice of the extent of constitutional restrictions on their behavior. Thus, qualified immunity prevents officials from being blindsided by liability derived from newly invented rights or new, unforeseen applications of pre-existing rights. In short, officials cannot be held to have violated rights of which they could not have known.

Here, the question is simply whether the due process right Pinder claims was clearly established at the time of her dealings with Johnson. This inquiry depends upon an assessment of the settled law at the time, not the law as it currently exists. Also, the rights Pinder asserts must have been clearly established in a particularized and relevant sense, not merely as an overarching entitlement to due process.

Pinder can point to no clearly established law supporting her claim at the time of the alleged violation. Pinder's claim is that Officer Johnson deprived her and her children of their due process rights by failing to protect them from the violent actions of Pittman. Eighteen days before the events giving rise to this action, the Supreme Court handed down its decision in *DeShaney v. Winnebago County Department of Social Services* (1989) which squarely rejected liability under 42 U.S.C. § 1983 based on an affirmative duty theory.

The facts in *DeShaney* were as poignant as those in this case. There, the Winnebago County Department of Social Services (DSS) received a number of reports that a young boy, Joshua DeShaney, was being abused by his father. As this abuse went on, several DSS workers personally observed the injuries that had been inflicted on Joshua. They knew firsthand of the threat to the boy's safety, yet they failed to remove him from his father's custody or otherwise protect him from abuse. Ultimately, Joshua's father beat him so violently that the boy suffered serious brain damage. Joshua's mother brought a § 1983 action on his behalf, arguing that the County and its employees had deprived Joshua of his liberty interests without due process by failing to provide adequate protection against his father's violent acts.

Despite natural sympathy for the plaintiff, the Court held that there was no § 1983 liability under these circumstances. It noted that the Due Process Clause of the Fourteenth Amendment does not require governmental actors to affirmatively protect life, liberty, or property against intrusion by private third parties. Instead, the Due Process Clause works only as a negative prohibition on state action. "Its purpose was to protect the people from the State, not to ensure that the State protected them from each other." This view is consistent with our general conception of the Constitution as a document of negative restraints, not positive entitlements.

The *DeShaney* Court concluded that:

> if the Due Process Clause does not require the State to provide its citizens with particular protective services, it follows that the State cannot be held liable under the Clause for injuries that could have been averted had it chosen to provide them. As a general matter, then, we conclude that a State's failure to protect an individual against private violence simply does not constitute a violation of the Due Process Clause.

The affirmative duty of protection that the Supreme Court rejected in *DeShaney* is precisely the duty Pinder relies on in this case. Joshua's mother wanted the state to be held liable for its lack of action, for merely standing by when it could have acted to prevent a tragedy. Likewise, Pinder argues Johnson could have, and thus should have, acted to prevent Pittman's crimes. *DeShaney* makes clear, however, that no affirmative duty was clearly established in these circumstances.

The *DeShaney* Court did indicate that an affirmative duty to protect may arise when the state restrains persons from acting on their own behalf. The Court explained that

> when the State by the affirmative exercise of its power so restrains an individual's liberty that it renders him unable to care for himself, and at the same time fails to provide for his basic human needs . . . it transgresses the substantive limits on state action set by the Eighth Amendment and the Due Process Clause.

The specific source of an affirmative duty to protect, the Court emphasized, is the custodial nature of a "special relationship."

DeShaney reasoned that "the affirmative duty to protect arises not from the State's knowledge of the individual's predicament or from its expressions of intent to help him, but from the limitation which it has imposed on his freedom to act on his own behalf." Some sort of confinement of the injured party—incarceration, institutionalization, or the like—is needed to trigger the affirmative duty. This Court has consistently read *DeShaney* to require a custodial context before any affirmative duty can arise under the Due Process Clause.

There was no custodial relationship with Carol Pinder and her children in this case. Neither Johnson nor any other state official had restrained Pinder's freedom to act on her own behalf. Pinder was never incarcerated, arrested, or otherwise restricted in any way. Without any such limitation imposed on her liberty, *DeShaney* indicates Pinder was due no affirmative constitutional duty of protection from the state, and Johnson would not be charged with liability for the criminal acts of a third party.

Pinder argues, however, that Johnson's explicit promises that Pittman would be incarcerated overnight created the requisite "special relationship." We do not agree. By requiring a custodial context as the condition for an affirmative duty, *DeShaney* rejected the idea that such a duty can arise solely from an official's awareness of a specific risk or from promises of aid. There, as here, plaintiff alleged that the state knew of the special risk of harm at the hands of a third party. There, as here, plaintiff alleged that the state had "specifically proclaimed, by word and by deed, its intention to protect" the victim. Neither allegation was sufficient to support the existence of an affirmative duty in *DeShaney*, and the same holds true in this case.

Promises do not create a special relationship—custody does. Unlike custody, a promise of aid does not actually place a person in a dangerous position and then cut off all outside sources of assistance. Promises from state officials can be ignored if the situation seems dire enough, whereas custody cannot be ignored or changed by the persons it affects. It is for this reason that the Supreme Court made custody the crux of the special relationship rule. Lacking the slightest hint of a true "special relationship," Pinder's claim in this case boils down to an insufficient allegation of a failure to act.

We also cannot accept Pinder's attempt to escape the import of *DeShaney* by characterizing her claim as one of affirmative misconduct by the state in "creating or enhancing" the danger, instead of an omission. She emphasizes the "actions" that Johnson took in making assurances, and in deciding not to charge Pittman with any serious offense. By this measure, every representation by the police and every failure to incarcerate would constitute "affirmative actions," giving rise to civil liability.

No amount of semantics can disguise the fact that the real "affirmative act" here was committed by Pittman, not by Officer Johnson. The most that can be said of the state functionaries is that they stood by and did nothing when suspicious circumstances dictated a more active role for them.

Given the principles laid down by *DeShaney*, it can hardly be said that Johnson was faced with a clearly established duty to protect Pinder or her children in March of 1989. Indeed, it can be argued that *DeShaney* established exactly the opposite, i.e., that no such affirmative duty existed because neither Pinder nor her children were confined by the state.

It is true, as the district court noted, that some cases have found an "affirmative duty" arising outside the traditional custodial context. None of these cases, however, clearly establish the existence of the right Pinder alleges was violated. First, none of these cases found a particularized due process right to affirmative protection based solely on an official's assurances that the danger posed by a third party will be eliminated. All involved some circumstance wherein the state took a much larger and more direct role in "creating" the danger itself.

These cases involve a wholly different paradigm than that presented here. When the state itself creates the dangerous situation that resulted in a victim's injury the state is not merely accused of a failure to act; it becomes much more akin to an actor itself directly causing harm to the injured party. See, e.g., *Cornelius v. Town of Highland Lake* (11th Cir. 1989) (duty when state brought inmates into victim's workplace); *Wells v. Walker* (8th Cir. 1988) (duty when state brought dangerous prisoners to victim's store); *Nishiyama v. Dickson County* (6th Cir. 1987) (duty when state provided unsupervised parolee with squad car). At most, these cases stand for the proposition that state actors may not disclaim liability when they themselves throw others to the lions. They do not, by contrast, entitle persons who rely on promises of aid to some greater degree of protection from lions at large.

The extensive debate provoked by this case should be proof enough that the law in this area was anything but clearly established at the time Officer Johnson gave assurances to Pinder. To impose liability in the absence of a clearly established constitutional duty is to invite litigation over a limitless array of official acts. There are good reasons why the constitutional right to protection sought by Pinder was not clearly established by the courts. As the First Circuit noted in a similar case, "enormous economic consequences could follow from the reading of the Fourteenth Amendment that plaintiff here urges." The consequences, however, are not just economic, and their gravity indicates why the right Pinder asserts was never clearly established.

The recognition of a broad constitutional right to affirmative protection from the state would be the first step down the slippery slope of liability. Such a right potentially would be implicated in nearly every instance where a private actor inflicts injuries that the state could have prevented. Every time a police officer incorrectly decided it was not necessary to intervene in a domestic dispute, the victims of the ensuing violence could bring a § 1983 action. Every time a parolee committed a criminal act, the victims could argue the state had an affirmative duty to keep the prisoner incarcerated. Indeed, victims of virtually every crime could plausibly argue that if the authorities had done their job, they would not have suffered their loss. Broad affirmative duties thus provide a fertile bed for § 1983 litigation, and the resultant governmental liability would wholly defeat the purposes of qualified immunity.

If the right Pinder asserts were ever clearly established, it would entail other significant consequences. A general obligation of the state to protect private citizens makes law enforcement officials constitutional guarantors of the conduct of others. It is no solution to say that such a right to affirmative protection has its inherent limitations. It is no answer to contend that the duty here was created only by Johnson's promise and Pinder's reliance on that promise, and is limited by Johnson's awareness of the risk. Such "limitations" are no barrier to increased lawsuits.

There are endless opportunities for disagreements over the exact nature of an official's promise, the intent behind it, the degree of the reliance, the causal link between the promise and the injury, and so on. Similarly, the extent of the state's affirmative duty to protect and the degree of the state's awareness of the risk are also subjects that would tie up state and local officials in endless federal litigation.

In cases like this, it is always easy to second-guess. Tragic circumstances only sharpen our hindsight, and it is tempting to express our sense of outrage at the failure of Officer Johnson to protect Pinder's children from Pittman's villainy. The Supreme Court in *DeShaney* specifically rejected the "shocks the conscience" test of *Rochin v. California* (1952) [Chapter 2] as a basis for imposing § 1983 liability in the affirmative duty context, however. We cannot simply ignore the lack of any clearly established constitutional duty to protect and the concomitant immunity from civil liability. Hard cases can make bad law, and it is to protect against that possibility that police officers possess the defense of qualified immunity.

For the foregoing reasons, the judgment of the district court denying qualified immunity to Officer Johnson is REVERSED.

DISSENT

RUSSELL, J., joined by ERVIN, C.J., and MURNAGHAN and MICHAEL, JJ.

Because I believe the Court casually disregards the very real ways in which Officer Johnson's conduct placed Pinder and her children in a position of danger, I respectfully dissent. In March 1989, the time of the fire, the law "clearly established" that the state has a duty to protect an individual where the state, by its affirmative action, creates a dangerous situation or renders an individual more vulnerable to danger. As the Seventh Circuit stated in *Bowers v. DeVito* (1982):

> If the state puts a man in a position of danger from private persons and then fails to protect him, it will not be heard to say that its role was merely passive; it is as much an active **tort feasor** [wrong doer] as if it had thrown him into a snake pit.

The Seventh Circuit and other circuits, including our own, have reaffirmed this duty. The Supreme Court's decision in *DeShaney* did not reject the state's clearly established duty to protect an individual where the state, through its affirmative action, has created a dangerous situation or rendered the individual more vulnerable to danger. The Supreme Court held only that the state has no duty to protect an individual from the actions of third parties where the state was aware of the dangers but played no part in their creation. The fact that the state did not create the danger was central to the Court's holding.

In this case, Officer Johnson was not merely aware of the danger; he placed Pinder and her children in a position of danger. Officer Johnson knew Pittman had broken into Pinder's home and had been abusive and violent. Pittman had punched Pinder and thrown objects at her. When the officers arrived at the scene, Pittman was screaming and threatening that he "wasn't going to jail for nothing this time; this time it would be for murder." After the officers restrained Pittman, Pinder explained to Officer Johnson that Pittman had threatened Pinder before, that he had attempted to set fire to her house ten months earlier, and that he had just finished serving his sentence for the attempted arson.

Given Pittman's threats and violent behavior, Pinder was understandably concerned about the safety of herself and her children. She explained to Officer Johnson that she needed to return to work and specifically asked him whether it was safe to do so. Officer Johnson assured Pinder several times that Pittman would remain in police custody until morning. Officer Johnson indicated to Pinder that Pittman could not be released that night because a county commissioner would not be available until the morning.

Instead of remaining home with her children or making other arrangements for their safety, Pinder, relying on Officer Johnson's assurances, returned to work, leaving her children alone at home. At the police station, Officer Johnson charged Pittman only with two minor offenses, trespassing and malicious destruction of property having a value of less than three hundred dollars. Despite his previous representation to Pinder that no county commissioner would be available before the morning, Officer Johnson brought Pittman before a county commissioner that evening.

Because Officer Johnson charged Pittman only with two misdemeanors, the county commissioner released Pittman on his own recognizance. Upon his release, Pittman went directly to Pinder's house and burned it down, killing the three children in the conflagration.

I cannot understand how the majority can recount these same events in its own opinion and not conclude that Officer Johnson placed Pinder and her children in a position of danger. Officer Johnson made assurances to Pinder that Pittman would remain in police custody overnight and falsely represented that no county commissioner would be available until morning. He induced Pinder to return to work and leave her children vulnerable to Pittman's violence. After witnessing Pittman's violent behavior and murderous threats, he charged Pittman with only minor offenses, assuring his release. Officer Johnson had a duty to protect Pinder and her children from Pittman, at least to an extent necessary to dispel the false sense of security that his actions created.

Unlike the majority, I believe that the law at the time of the incident clearly established that Officer Johnson had a duty to protect Pinder and her children upon Pittman's release. The Court finds it significant that no case before March 1989 contained the precise holding that due process creates a duty of affirmative protection based on an official's assurances that the danger posed by a third party will be eliminated. Such a particular holding, however, is not required in order to conclude that a right was clearly established.

In *Anderson v. Creighton* (1987) [excerpted on p. 368], the Supreme Court explained that "the contours of the right must be sufficiently clear that a reasonable official would understand that what he is doing violated that right." On the other hand, the Court also rejected the view that "an official action is protected by qualified immunity unless the very action in question has previously been held unlawful." Requiring such a level of specificity would transform the defense of qualified immunity into a defense of absolute immunity. Instead, the Court held that the preexisting law had to be only specific enough that the unlawfulness of the official's conduct would be apparent to a reasonable person.

I believe that a reasonable officer in Officer Johnson's position would have recognized that, given his assurances to Pinder that Pittman would remain in police custody until morning and his failure to charge Pittman with an offense serious enough to ensure that he remained in custody overnight, he placed Pinder and her children in a dangerous position. He induced Pinder to let her guard down, dissuading her from taking actions to protect herself and her children from Pittman. Certainly, a reasonable officer would have recognized that he had a duty at least to phone Pinder and warn her that Pittman had been released from police custody.

Pinder's children were left alone at home, vulnerable to the rampage of a violent, intemperate man, and deprived of their mother's protection because of the hollow word of an irresponsible, thoughtless police officer. Today the Court holds that this police officer, who took no action to correct a dangerous situation of his own creation, did not violate Pinder's due process rights and is otherwise immune from prosecution because he did not violate a clearly established right. I disagree.

QUESTIONS

1. List the facts relevant to deciding whether Donald Johnson is liable for damages to Carol Pinder.
2. Apply the facts you listed in (1) to the no-affirmative-duty-to-protect rule, the special-relationship exception, and the state-created-danger exception.
3. Summarize the court's majority and dissenting opinions' arguments in favor of or against the rule and exceptions in (3).
4. Which rule do you favor, and why?

Suing Judges and Prosecutors

LO 8

Most plaintiffs in civil actions sue law enforcement officers, who enjoy qualified immunity from being sued for damages. But what about prosecutors and judges? Can individuals sue them? The answer is "no" to suing a judge, and it's "hardly ever" to suing prosecutors Why? Because judges enjoy **absolute immunity** from civil suits, meaning they can't be sued even if they acted maliciously and in bad faith. The only remedy against misbehaving judges is either impeachment or, if they're elected, voting them out of office.

Prosecutors enjoy what's called **functional immunity**. This means their immunity depends on the function they're performing at the time of the misconduct. When they act as advocates, they're absolutely immune from civil liability, even when plaintiffs prove they acted in bad faith and with malice. When they act as administrators or investigators, they're entitled to qualified immunity; that is, they're immune unless their misconduct violated clearly established law that a reasonable prosecutor would have known.

Before we examine the law regarding prosecutors' functional immunity, be aware of this widely documented observation about prosecutors:

> While certainly the vast majority of prosecutors are ethical lawyers engaged in vital public service, the undeniable fact is that many innocent people have been convicted of crimes as a result of prosecutorial misconduct, and the victims of this misconduct are generally denied any civil remedy because of prosecutorial immunities. (Johns 2005, 53, citing and summarizing many empirical studies, pp. 59–64)

Furthermore, prosecutors rarely suffer for their misconduct (Johns 2005, 70). According to the Center for Public Integrity, since 1970 there have been more than two thousand cases of prosecutorial misconduct but only 44 disciplinary actions and two disbarments (70). Another study found only 100 disciplinary proceedings against prosecutors between the years 1886 and 2000 (70).

In theory, prosecutors are criminally liable for their nonadvocacy functions. But since the Civil Rights Act, § 242, in 1866, created criminal liability for public officials who violate constitutional rights, only one prosecutor has ever been convicted (70–71).

The U.S. Supreme Court developed the functional immunity doctrine in four cases. Here's a summary of each:

1. *Imbler v. Pachtman* (1976). Paul Imbler was convicted of felony murder and sentenced to death following a trial in which District Attorney Richard Pachtman knowingly used false evidence and suppressed exculpatory evidence. Imbler was freed after he served nine years in prison. He sued Pachtman for § 1983 money damages. The Supreme Court ruled that Pachtman was absolutely immune from civil damages, because his misconduct occurred while he was performing his advocacy function.

2. *Burns v. Reed* (1991). Speculating that Kathy Burns had multiple personalities, one of which was responsible for shooting her two sons, Indiana police officers Paul Cox and Donald Scroggins decided to interview Burns under hypnosis. They were concerned that hypnosis "might be an unacceptable investigative technique" and sought Chief Deputy Prosecutor Rick Reed's advice. He told them they could question Burns under hypnosis.

While she was hypnotized, she referred to both herself and the shooter as "Katie." Interpreting this as support for their multiple personality theory, the police detained her and consulted Reed again, who told them they "probably had probable cause" to arrest her (482).

At a probable cause hearing the next day, in response to Reed's questioning, an officer testified that Burns confessed, but neither the officer nor Reed informed the judge about the hypnosis or that Burns had otherwise consistently denied guilt. The judge issued the warrant on the basis of this misleading presentation. When this came to light, the trial judge ordered the confession suppressed, and the prosecutor dropped the charges.

Burns sued the prosecutor, Reed, for damages under § 1983. The trial court dismissed the case, ruling that Reed was entitled to absolute immunity. The Supreme Court agreed, partly. The Court ruled that absolute immunity extended to initiation and presentation of the case, which included the probable cause hearing, but it didn't extend to the advice the prosecutor gave to the officers regarding the confession under hypnosis.

3. *Buckley v. Fitzsimmons* (1993). Stephen Buckley had been incarcerated for three years in the DuPage County jail on rape and murder charges, growing out of the highly publicized murder of 11-year-old Jeanine Nicarico. When he was finally released, he sued DuPage County State's Attorney Michael Fitzsimmons for damages under § 1983 for fabricating evidence during the preliminary investigation.

The fabricated evidence related to a boot print on the door of the Nicarico home, apparently left by the killer when he kicked in the door. Three separate studies by experts from the DuPage County Crime Lab, the Illinois Department of Law Enforcement, and the Kansas Bureau of Identification all failed to make a reliable connection between the print and a pair of boots that Buckley had voluntarily supplied. The respondents (including Fitzsimmons and sheriff's deputies) then obtained a "positive identification" from Louise Robbins, an anthropologist in North Carolina. She was allegedly well known for her willingness to fabricate unreliable expert testimony.

They obtained her opinion during the early stages of the investigation, which was being conducted under the joint supervision and direction of the sheriff and Fitzsimmons, whose police officers and assistant prosecutors were performing essentially the same investigatory functions (262–63).

Was Fitzsimmons acting as an advocate or an investigator when Robbins faked the boot print on the victim's door? The Supreme Court ruled that he was acting as an investigator, because the fabrication took place before there was probable cause to arrest; prior to probable cause to arrest, a prosecutor can't be an advocate.

4. *Kalina v. Fletcher* (1997). Lynne Kalina, a deputy prosecutor in King County, Washington, followed standard practice when she filed three documents to begin second-degree burglary proceedings against Rodney Fletcher based on alleged computer theft from a school. One was an information and the second was a motion for an arrest warrant that required "sworn testimony establishing the grounds for issuing the warrant" (121). To satisfy this requirement, Kalina issued a third document that summarized the evidence supporting the charge. In this "Certification for Determination of Probable Cause" (the equivalent of an affidavit), Kalina "personally vouched for the truth of the facts set forth in the certification under penalty of perjury" (121).

There were two false statements in the affidavit. First, it stated that Fletcher had "never been associated with the school in any manner and did not have permission to enter the school." In fact, he worked in the school and was authorized to enter. She also stated that an electronics store employee identified Fletcher in a mug shot lineup as the person who asked for an appraisal of a computer stolen from the school. The employee didn't identify him.

Based on the affidavit, the trial court found probable cause and issued the warrant. Fletcher was arrested and spent a day in jail. A month later, the charges were dropped on Kalina's motion. Fletcher sued under § 1983 seeking damages from Kalina based on her alleged violations of his constitutional rights (122).

The U.S. Supreme Court ruled that the *preparation* of the three documents, including the preparation of the motion for an arrest warrant was covered by the functional immunity doctrine; Kalina was acting as an advocate and therefore absolutely immune from liability (129). But the Court went on to rule that in *executing* the certification on her own, she was acting as the complaining witness, which any nonlawyer was qualified to do, and which police officers routinely do. Therefore, in executing the certification, she wasn't immune from prosecution (131).

ETHICAL ISSUES

Does Ethical Policy Demand That It's Time to End Absolute Immunity for Prosecutors?

While certainly the vast majority of prosecutors are ethical lawyers engaged in vital public service, the undeniable fact is that many innocent people have been wrongly convicted of crimes as a result of prosecutorial misconduct. Prosecutors are rarely disciplined or criminally prosecuted for their misconduct, and the victims of this misconduct are generally denied any civil remedy because of prosecutorial immunities.

The policy reasons supporting absolute prosecutorial immunity are untenable. The U.S. Supreme Court has justified absolute prosecutorial immunity on the grounds that the threat of civil liability would undermine vigorous prosecutorial performance, constrain independent decision making, and divert time and resources to defending frivolous litigation. In short, in the Court's view, exposing prosecutors to civil liability would burden and undermine the functioning of the criminal justice system.

But contrary to this policy argument, absolute immunity is not needed to prevent frivolous litigation or to protect the judicial process. Absolute immunity protects the dishonest prosecutor but is unnecessary to protect the honest prosecutor since the requirements for establishing a cause of action and the defense of qualified immunity will protect all but the most incompetent and willful wrongdoers. In short, in all cases qualified immunity for prosecutors would provide sufficient protection to the criminal justice system, while providing a necessary remedy for prosecutorial misconduct.

INSTRUCTIONS

1. Visit the Companion Website and read "Reconsidering Absolute Prosecutorial Immunity," by Margaret Z. Johns (2005). See the link under the Chapter 11 Ethical Issues section—login at www.cengagebrain.com.

2. List and summarize the policy and ethical arguments for and against absolute immunity for prosecutors.

3. Write an essay answering the question: Does ethical policy demand that it's time to end absolute immunity for prosecutors?

Source: Johns 2005, 53–55.

Hurdles to Suing Officers and Governments

People who sue the government or its officers (even in the most brutal cases) rarely win. Why? According to Allison Patton (1993), there are three major weaknesses to section 1983 suits:

1. They're difficult and expensive to pursue. Most victims of official misconduct are minorities who can't afford to sue, so only a small proportion of police brutality incidents become lawsuits. Victims who can afford to hire a lawyer have to endure a long, tough legal battle, because police departments rarely settle section 1983 suits.

2. The Supreme Court has severely limited plaintiffs' legal capacity to get court orders (injunctions) to stop police techniques, even those that involve frequent use of excessive force.

3. Juries are more likely to believe police officers' version of events than plaintiffs'. Juries don't want to believe that "their police officers are bad people or liars." So plaintiffs rarely win unless they get help from "independent corroborative witnesses or physical evidence." (753–54)

There are other reasons. Anthony Amsterdam (1974), the legendary lawyer for the defense and constitutional law professor, speaking from long personal experience, adds several more:

Where are the lawyers going to come from to handle these cases for the plaintiffs? What on earth would possess a lawyer to file a claim for damages in an ordinary search-and-seizure case? The prospect of a share in the substantial damages to be expected? The chance to earn a reputation as a police-hating lawyer, so that he can no longer count on straight testimony concerning the length of skid marks in his personal injury cases? The gratitude of his client when his filing of the claim causes the prosecutor to refuse a lesser-included offense plea or to charge priors or pile on "cover" charges? The opportunity to represent his client without fee in these resulting criminal matters?

Police cases are an unadulterated investigative and litigate nightmare. Taking on the police in any tribunal involves a commitment to the most frustrating and thankless legal work I know. And the idea that an unrepresented, inarticulate, prosecution-vulnerable citizen can make a case against a team of professional investigators and testifiers in any tribunal begs belief. Even in a tribunal having recognized responsibilities and some resources to conduct independent investigations, a plaintiff without assiduous counsel devoted to developing his side of the case would be utterly outmastered by the police. No, I think we shall have airings of police searches and seizures on suppression motions or not at all. (430)

Furthermore, immunity and the no-affirmative-duty-to-protect rule protect most officials from being sued successfully. Finally, some plaintiffs don't deserve to get damages, because their cases are, in fact, frivolous (Slobogin 1998, 561).

LO 10

Administrative Remedies

Until now, we've dealt with court cases aimed at making police and other public officials accountable for their violations of individuals' constitutional rights, but accountability for official misconduct isn't limited to lawsuits. In fact, the most common accountability procedure for all kinds of police misconduct (not just violations of constitutional rights) is administrative review and discipline outside the courts.

There are two types of administrative review:

1. *Internal affairs units (IAU) review.* Review of police misconduct by special officers inside police departments

2. *External civilian review.* Review of complaints against police officers with participation by individuals who aren't sworn police officers

Internal Review

Most large and mid-sized police departments have special internal affairs units (IAU) that review police misconduct. According to Professor Douglas W. Perez (1994, 88–89), a former deputy sheriff, "most cops do not like internal affairs." They don't trust IAU, and some even think IAU investigators are traitors. Still, most officers believe IAU operations are a necessary evil. For one thing, they're a good defense against external review. As the famed Chicago chief of police O. W. Wilson said, "It is clearly apparent that if the police do not take a vigorous stand on the matter of internal investigation, outside groups—such as review boards consisting of laymen and other persons outside the police service—will step into the void" (Griswold 1994, 215–21).

Internal review consists of four successive stages:

1. Intake

2. Investigation

3. Deliberation

4. Disposition

FIGURE 11.1   Disposition of Excessive Force Complaints

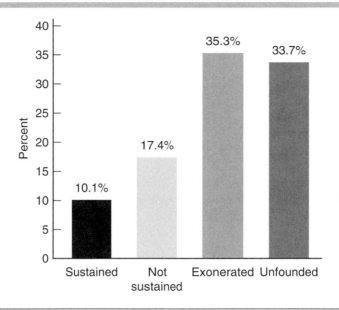

Source: Pate and Fridell 1993, 116.

The Internal Affairs Section of the Oakland, California, Police Department is considered an excellent unit, so we'll use it as an example of how internal review proceeds through these four stages.

The department intake policy is "anyone anywhere should accept a complaint if a citizen wishes it taken." The unit is housed inside the police department building. All complaints alleging excessive force, police corruption, and racial discrimination are followed up (Perez 1994, 92–93).

Then, someone besides the intake officer investigates complaints. The investigator gathers evidence, usually interviewing the officer involved last. If officers refuse to cooperate, they're subject to discipline, such as dismissal for refusing to obey an order of the chief.

Completed investigations go to the IAU supervisor. If the supervisor approves, complaints go to the decision-making, or deliberation, stage. Four possible decisions can be made in the deliberation stage (Figure 11.1):

1. *Unfounded.* The investigation proved that the act didn't take place.

2. *Exonerated.* The acts took place, but the investigation proved that they were justified, lawful, and proper.

3. *Not sustained.* The investigation failed to gather enough evidence to prove clearly the allegations in the complaint.

4. *Sustained.* The investigation disclosed enough evidence to prove clearly the allegations in the complaint. (Perez 1994, 96)

If the decision is "unfounded," "exonerated," or "not sustained," the case is disposed of by closing it. If the decision is "sustained," the supervisor recommends disciplinary action. Recommended disciplinary actions ranked from least to most severe include:

1. Reprimand

2. Written reprimand

FIGURE 11.2 Distribution of Disciplinary Actions

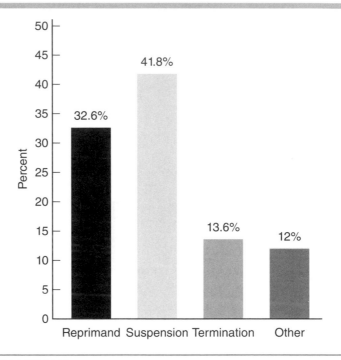

Source: Pate and Fridell 1993, 116.

3. Transfer

4. Retraining

5. Counseling

6. Suspension

7. Demotion

8. Fine

9. Dismissal

After the initial disposition, the case goes up the chain of command inside the department until it finally reaches the chief. In about half the cases, there's a discrepancy between the chief's recommendations and those of the immediate supervisor. These discrepancies are important because the immediate supervisor, usually a sergeant of patrol, works on the street with other patrol officers. The supervisors of sergeants usually go along with the recommendations of sergeants. Chiefs of police, on the other hand, are removed from the day-to-day street operations of patrol officers and their immediate supervisors. They have departmentwide perspectives and are responsible to "local political elites" for their department's performance. So chiefs may find the disciplinary penalty too light and make it heavier. Figure 11.2 shows the distribution of disciplinary measures taken in a national sample of city police departments.

External Review

The basic objection to internal review is that police shouldn't police themselves. To the question, "Who will watch the watchmen?" the answer is, "Not the watchmen!"

So external review has grown. In *external review*, individuals who aren't sworn police officers participate in the review of complaints against the police. Usually called "civilian review," it has sparked controversy for nearly half a century.

Police oppose external review because it interferes with their independence. They have no confidence that outsiders know enough about police work to review it. They also know outside scrutiny could pierce the **blue curtain**, the wall of protection that hides their "real" work from public view.

External review became a popular proposal among some liberal reformers and citizen groups during the 1960s. Strong police unions, chiefs who opposed external review, and the creation of internal review procedures (discussed in the last section) successfully prevented it. However, by the early 1990s, 72 percent of the 50 largest cities had created some form of civilian review procedures (Walker and Bumpus 1992, 1, 3–4). Let's look at the types of external review and how well review by civilians has worked.

The Types of External Review

LO 10

The differences among civilian review procedures all turn on the point in the process when nonofficers participate. The possible entry points are:

1. The initial investigation to collect the facts

2. The review of the investigation reports

3. The recommendation for disposition to the chief

4. The review of decisions made by the chief

Civilian review boards only have the authority to recommend disciplinary action to police chiefs, because under civil service laws only police chiefs can decide disciplinary action against police officers (Walker and Bumpus 1992, 3–4).

The Effectiveness of Civilian Review

LO 10

Does civilian review work? The answer depends on the definition and the measures of effectiveness. "Effectiveness" can mean at least four things, all of which are important in determining the value of civilian review procedures:

1. Maintaining effective control of police misconduct

2. Providing resolutions to complaints that satisfy individual complainants

3. Preserving public confidence in the police

4. Influencing police management by providing "feedback from consumers" (Walker and Bumpus 1992, 8)

It's difficult to measure the effectiveness of civilian review because official data are ambiguous. Take the number of complaints, for example. A large number of complaints might mean a large volume of police misconduct, but it can also indicate confidence in the review procedures. Following the Rodney King incident in Los Angeles, observers noted that San Francisco, a city known for its strong review procedures, received more complaints than the much larger city of Los Angeles.

In Los Angeles, the Independent Commission heard a number of citizen complaints that the LAPD created "significant hurdles" to filing complaints, that they were afraid of the process, and that the complaint process was "unnecessarily difficult or impossible." Further, the ACLU collected evidence suggesting that the LAPD "actively discouraged the filing of complaints." The beating of Rodney King, in fact, would never have come to public attention without the video, according to the Independent

Commission. This is because, according to the commission, the efforts of Rodney King's brother Paul to file a complaint following the beating were "frustrated" by the LAPD (Pate and Fridell 1993, 39).

The numbers and rates of complaints are also difficult to assess because we don't know the numbers of incidents where people don't file complaints. In one national survey, of all the people who said the police mistreated them, only 30 percent said they filed complaints. One thing, however, is clear. Misconduct isn't distributed evenly among individuals and neighborhoods. In one survey, only 40 percent of the addresses in one city had any contact with the police in a year. Most contacts between private individuals and the police occur in poor neighborhoods. In New York City, the rate of complaints ranges from 1 to 5 for every 10,000 people, depending on the neighborhood.

Official data have consistently indicated racial minority males are represented disproportionately among complainants. So the perception of a pattern of police harassment is a major factor in conflict between the police and racial minority communities (Walker and Bumpus 1992, 10).

Whatever the ambiguity of numbers and rates in the official statistics, observers have noted civilian review procedures rarely sustain complaints. Furthermore, the rates of complaints sustained in civilian review are about the same as the rates in internal affairs units (Walker and Bumpus 1992, 16–17).

Summary

LO 1
- For police officers to be charged with crimes, the prosecution must prove criminal intent. Officers who believe they are enforcing the law, generally, are protected.

LO 2
- Civil actions against the federal government and its officers; local, county, and state officers, law enforcement agencies, and government units; and other government employees are controlled by different statutes, court decisions, and government units.

LO 3
- Lawsuits against federal officers were first accepted by the court in 1971 and are called constitutional tort (*Bivens*) actions. Lawsuits against the federal government for their officers' constitutional torts are called Federal Tort Claims Act actions.

LO 4
- The right to recover damages for injuries caused by official torts has to be balanced against law enforcement's job of protecting the public, and official immunity limits liability to malicious wrongdoing.

LO 5
- Civil Rights Act actions are lawsuits against individuals in state and local law enforcement for violating someone's constitutional rights.

LO 6
- Not all states allow citizens to bring suits against them for the constitutional violations of their officers. These states give vicarious diplomatic immunity to officers and other law enforcement officials.

LO 5, LO 6
- A special circumstance exists whereby the government is held responsible for protecting people from state-created dangers.

LO 6
- Other barriers to successfully suing officers and governments include expense, court limitation on injunctions against police techniques, and the preference of juries for police testimony.

LO 7
- Courts impose on officers no constitutional duty to protect and plaintiffs can't sue officers when they fail to prevent other individuals from committing crimes against them or violating their rights.

LO 8
- Judges can't be sued for misconduct because they're protected by a special status of absolute immunity, and prosecutors can hardly ever be sued because they enjoy functional immunity whenever they act as advocates.

LO 9
- A special relationship exists between the government and persons in their custody, and the state has a duty to protect them and prevent other prisoners from injuring them or violating their rights.

LO 10
- Administrative remedies discipline public officials to remedy misconduct. Review of official conduct may be internal to the police department, or it may be conducted externally by civilians.

Review Questions

1. How likely is it that police officers will be charged and convicted of criminal conduct? Why?
2. Summarize the *Bivens v. Six Unnamed FBI Agents* case, and explain its significance.
3. Identify the two elements of the qualified immunity defense, and explain why the test is so easy for officers to pass.
4. What specific remedy does the Federal Tort Claims Act (FTCA) provide plaintiffs, and why is it attractive to plaintiffs?
5. Identify and describe the differences between two kinds of state civil lawsuits against individual state officers.
6. Describe the balance that has to be struck in state cases against state officers.
7. Identify two elements plaintiffs in § 1983 actions against state and local law enforcement officers have to prove.
8. Identify and describe two limits the U.S. Supreme Court placed on § 1983 actions against state and local officers.
9. Describe the extent and limits of state tort actions against state and local governments.
10. Identify the elements in the balancing test used to decide whether to grant the defense of vicarious official immunity.
11. According to the U.S. Supreme Court in *Monell v. New York City Department of Social Services,* what two elements do plaintiffs have to prove to succeed in suing local government units?
12. According to the U.S. Supreme Court, what (if any) constitutional duty do law enforcement officers have to protect private individuals from each other?
13. Identify and explain the three elements in the state-created-danger exception to the no-affirmative-duty-to-protect rule.
14. Can you sue a judge for damages? A prosecutor? Explain.
15. Identify and explain the reasons for the hurdles plaintiffs have to overcome when they sue officers and the governments in charge of them.

16. Identify and briefly describe the two types of administrative remedies against police misconduct.

17. Identify and describe the stages, possible dispositions, and disciplinary actions in internal review procedures.

18. Identify the basic objection to internal review. How is external review supposed to overcome the objection?

19. Identify three reasons why police oppose civilian review.

20. Does civilian review work? Explain.

Key Terms

criminal law, p. 366
civil law, p. 366
internal and external department review, p. 366
plaintiffs, p. 366
damages, p. 366
civil action, p. 366
constitutional tort (*Bivens*) actions, p. 367
Federal Tort Claims Act (FTCA) actions, p. 367
constitutional tort, p. 367
qualified immunity, p. 367
"good faith" defense, p. 367
summary judgment, p. 368
doctrine of sovereign immunity, p. 370
torts, p. 371
defense of official immunity, p. 371

Civil Rights Act actions, p. 371
§ 1983 actions, p. 371
doctrine of *respondeat superior*, p. 372
defense of vicarious official immunity, p. 372
no-affirmative-duty-to-protect rule, p. 373
special-relationship exception, p. 373
state-created-danger exception, p. 373
en banc review, p. 374
interlocutory appeal, p. 374
tort feasor, p. 377
absolute immunity, p. 378
functional immunity, p. 378
internal affairs units (IAU) review, p. 382
external civilian review, p. 382
blue curtain, p. 385

12

CASES COVERED

County of Riverside v. McLaughlin, 500 U.S. 44 (1991)

U.S. v. Salerno, 481 U.S. 739 (1987)

Bell v. Wolfish, 441 U.S. 520 (1979)

Rompilla v. Beard, 545 U.S. 374 (2005)

Renico v. Lett, 2010 WL 1740525 (2010)

LEARNING OBJECTIVES

1 Understand the prosecutor's decision to charge and its role in criminal procedure.

2 Know the difference between criminal complaints, first appearances, and arraignments.

3 Recognize the various forms of pretrial release.

4 Know the constitutional rights that affect bail.

5 Understand the purpose of preventive detention hearings.

6 Know the types of defense counsel; understand the scope and limits of the right to counsel; and appreciate the differences between the rights of those who can afford lawyers and those who can't.

7 Understand preliminary hearings and grand jury reviews and how they differ from trials.

8 Know the meaning of double jeopardy and its effect on criminal procedure.

9 Understand and appreciate the importance of pretrial motions and why counsel devote so much time to preparing them. Pretrial motions may include arguments to prove double jeopardy and requests for a speedy trial, a change of venue, and the suppression of evidence.

Court Proceedings I: Before Trial

The MCC (Metropolitan Correctional Center) differs markedly from the familiar image of a jail; there are no barred cells, dank, colorless corridors, or clanging steel gates. It was intended to include the most advanced and innovative features of modern design of detention facilities. "It represented the architectural embodiment of the best and most progressive penological planning." Jailed defendants sued, challenging the constitutionality of numerous conditions of confinement and practices in the MCC. *Bell v. Wolfish (1979)*

After arrest, interrogation, and identification procedures, the action moves first from the police station to prosecutors' and defense attorneys' offices and then to the courts. In the interval between arrest and the first time defendants appear in court, both the police and the prosecutor have to make critical decisions.

First, the police decide if the case should go forward or be dropped. Police take the strong cases they want prosecuted to the prosecutor's office. Prosecutors then make their own judgments about how to dispose of these cases. If they decide to prosecute, they start formal court proceedings by filing a complaint, information, or indictment.

All three proceedings have a single goal: to test the objective basis for the decision to charge. In these proceedings, either judges or grand juries consider the evidence the government has collected to prove its case. If the government has enough evidence, defendants have to appear and answer the criminal charges against them (called **arraignment**).

The decision to start criminal court proceedings is not just a technicality. According to the U.S. Supreme Court in *Kirby v. Illinois* (1972):

> The initiation of judicial criminal proceedings is far from a mere formalism. It is the starting point of our whole system of adversary criminal justice. For it is only then that the Government has committed itself to prosecute, and only then that the adverse positions of Government and defendant have solidified. It is then that a defendant finds himself faced with the prosecutorial forces of organized society, and immersed in the intricacies of substantive and procedural criminal law. It is this point, therefore, that marks the commencement of the "criminal prosecutions." (689)

In this chapter, we'll look at (1) the decision to charge; (2) the rules regulating probable cause to detain; (3) what happens during defendants' first appearance in court after being charged; (4) bail and pretrial detention; (5) the right to counsel; (6) testing the government's case in grand jury and preliminary hearings; (7) bringing defendants to court to hear and answer the charges against them (arraignment); and (8) pretrial motions: double jeopardy, a speedy trial, a change of venue, and the suppression of illegally obtained evidence.

The Decision to Charge

LO 1

Once the police bring a case to the prosecutor, lawyers take over the management of the criminal process. Although the police fade into the background, they don't disappear. Lawyers need them to clarify, investigate further, and perhaps testify in court. Prosecutors are likely to take at face value the recommendations from officers with a reputation for establishing "good" cases. They're just as likely to discount cases from officers with poor track records.

Prosecutors drop some cases without further action. If they don't think they can prove a case, they drop it and release the suspect outright. Even if they think they can prove their case, prosecutors don't automatically charge suspects. Why? Because of the dual role of prosecutors in our criminal justice system. They represent the public in prosecuting criminal cases, but they're also **officers of the court**. In that capacity, their mission is to "do justice"—and doing justice doesn't always mean charging and prosecuting suspects.

A good example is *People v. Camargo* (1986). Mike Camargo was charged with the criminal sale and possession of cocaine. By the time he was indicted, Camargo was in an advanced stage of AIDS and related complicating illnesses. The virus had invaded his brain and his stomach, and peripheral nerve damage caused him pain and suffering to the extent that doctors ordered him to limit his physical exercise to sitting in a chair for one hour a day. His doctors' prognosis was death within three to four months (1004–5).

The government dropped the case, because "it did not appear that the interest of justice would be substantially served by the defendant's continued prosecution under this indictment." According to the court:

> The uncompromising rampage of the multiple disease processes have condemned this defendant to a painful, imminent death. When the rationale for incarceration becomes unjustifiable because of a deadly disease, it becomes imperative to allow the sufferer to live his last days in the best circumstances possible and with dignity and compassion. (1007)

In the interests of justice, prosecutors also can divert suspects into a program for community service, restitution, substance abuse, or family violence treatment. In **diversion cases**, prosecutors agree to drop the case before formal judicial proceedings begin, on the condition that suspects participate in and complete these programs. The number of cases prosecutors decide not to pursue ranges from a few in some jurisdictions to nearly half of all cases in others (Boland and others 1987).

Several factors determine the **decision to charge**; they're detailed in a complaint, information, or indictment filed in formal court proceedings. Most important is the strength of the case against defendants. For example, if prosecutors don't have enough evidence to prosecute—no witnesses or weak witnesses, poor physical evidence, and no confessions or other admissions by suspects—they won't charge.

Witnesses might be neither reliable nor convincing. Witness problems increase if victims know their assailants in violent crimes. In over half of these cases, witnesses and victims refuse to cooperate because they're either afraid or have a change of heart over prosecuting people they know (and often care about). Sometimes, prosecutors can't use evidence because the police seized it illegally (Chapter 10). But contrary to the popular belief that many guilty criminals go unpunished because of the exclusionary rule, fewer than 2 percent of all cases (and practically no violent crime cases) are dropped because of it (Davies 1983, n. 89; Nardulli 1983).

Selective prosecution also lies behind the decision to charge. Lack of resources makes it impossible to prosecute every case, even when prosecutors have enough evidence and it's in the interests of justice to prosecute. Time and money force prosecutors to set priorities: suspects guilty of petty thefts go to restitution to allow prosecutions for armed robbery; prosecuting violent sex offenses takes precedence over prostitution; and charging a few well-known tax evaders serves as examples to deter tax evasion. According to some critics, selective prosecution cuts into the legislature's power to make the laws. Others argue that selectively prosecuting only some individuals in a category—for example, "fat cats" or notorious tax evaders—undermines impartial law enforcement.

Consider the following scenarios. Which (if any) of the following suspects should a prosecutor selectively charge?

1. A student stole a cassette recorder to record his criminal procedure class because the professor talks too fast. He works part time to pay for school, and although he could've paid for the recorder, it would've been difficult. He has never been in trouble with the law before and says he'll pay for the recorder.

2. A woman who works only occasionally stole a cordless phone for a friend who agreed to pay $35, half the phone's value. The woman has taken compact discs, tape cassettes, and an answering machine from the same store within the past six months.

3. A 50-year-old woman slipped a pair of stereo earphones into her purse. The woman is wealthy and indignantly denied that she intended to steal the earphones. She told the detective she put the device in her bag because she wanted to pick up some film, batteries, and other small items and simply forgot she had put it there.

Review your decisions after completing this chapter.

Despite criticisms of the extent of prosecutorial power, U.S. Supreme Court Justice Robert Jackson's words in 1940 are still true: The prosecutor's power to charge gives her "more control over life, liberty, and reputation than any other person in America" (3). So except for violating due process by vindictively prosecuting individuals or violating equal protection by selectively prosecuting members of groups (Chapter 2)—violations rarely charged and hardly ever successfully when they are—the prosecutor's discretionary power to charge is practically unlimited.

‖‖

Probable Cause to Detain Suspects

LO 1

An urgent situation arises when the following four circumstances combine:

1. Defendants are arrested without warrants.
2. They have no lawyers because they're too poor to hire one.
3. They haven't been charged with any crime.
4. They're locked up in jail.

Both the U.S. Constitution and state laws command that under those conditions, independent magistrates (not police officers whose zeal to root out crime might color their objectivity) have to decide, and decide *soon*, whether there's probable cause to back up this severe deprivation of liberty.

Of course, protecting public safety requires that police have the power to arrest suspects before a judge has decided there was probable cause for the arrest. Otherwise, suspects who turn out to be criminals might escape, commit further crimes, and/or destroy evidence. But once suspects are in jail, these dangers evaporate. Now, the guarantees of due process and protection of innocent people take over.

In *County of Riverside v. McLaughlin* (1991), the U.S. Supreme Court spoke about "reconciling these competing interests" of public safety and individual rights:

> On the one hand, States have a strong interest in protecting public safety by taking into custody those persons who are reasonably suspected of having engaged in criminal activity, even where there has been no opportunity for a prior judicial determination of probable cause. On the other hand, prolonged detention based on incorrect or unfounded suspicion may unjustly "imperil a suspect's job, interrupt his source of income, and impair his family relationships." We sought to balance these competing concerns by holding that States "must provide a fair and reliable determination of probable cause as a condition for any significant pretrial restraint of liberty, and this determination must be made by a judicial officer either before or promptly after arrest." (52)

Before we go on, let's clear up something that might confuse you—there are two kinds of probable cause. **Probable cause to detain a suspect** is decided at a court proceeding called the **first appearance** (sometimes the "probable cause hearing"). **Probable cause to go to trial** is decided in preliminary hearings or grand jury proceedings. Probable cause to detain (Chapter 5) requires fewer facts than probable cause to go to trial.

In *Gerstein v. Pugh* (1975), the U.S. Supreme Court decided that the Fourth Amendment ban on "unreasonable seizure" demands that suspects locked up in jail be taken "promptly" to a magistrate to decide whether there are enough facts to back up the detention. The question is, How prompt is fast enough to satisfy the Fourth Amendment? Lower federal courts and state courts for a long time said that the Fourth Amendment gives the police enough time to complete the "administrative steps incident to arrest." This usually means the police can do all of the following before they take suspects to court (*Sanders v. City of Houston* 1982, 700):

1. Complete paperwork
2. Search the suspect
3. Conduct an inventory search
4. Inventory property found
5. Fingerprint the suspect
6. Photograph the suspect
7. Check for a possible prior criminal record
8. Test laboratory samples
9. Interrogate the suspect
10. Check an alibi
11. Conduct a lineup
12. Compare the crime with similar crimes

Some jurisdictions get more specific; they spell out exactly how much time the police get to finish the administrative steps. Depending on the jurisdiction, times range from 24 to 36 hours (Brandes 1989). The U.S. Supreme Court prescribed a flexible definition of "promptly" in *County of Riverside v. McLaughlin* (1991), our next case excerpt.

In County of Riverside v. McLaughlin *(1991), our next case excerpt, the U.S. Supreme Court provided guidelines for how long jurisdictions can hold suspects before proving they have probable cause to detain them.*

CASE Was Judicial Determination of Probable Cause "Prompt"?

County of Riverside v. McLaughlin
500 U.S. 44 (1991)

HISTORY

Donald Lee McLaughlin and others brought a **class action** [an action in which one person or a small group of people represents the interests of a larger group] under 42 U.S.C. § 1983, challenging how the County of Riverside, California, handles probable cause determinations for individuals arrested without a warrant. The U.S. District court granted a preliminary injunction. The Ninth Circuit U.S. Court of Appeals affirmed. The U.S. Supreme Court granted certiorari, vacated the judgment of the Court of Appeals, and remanded the case.

O'CONNOR, J., joined by REHNQUIST, C.J., and WHITE, KENNEDY, and SOUTER, JJ.

FACTS

In August 1987, Donald Lee McLaughlin filed a complaint in the U.S. District Court for the Central District of California. The complaint alleged that McLaughlin was then currently incarcerated in the Riverside County Jail and had not received a probable cause determination. He requested "an order and judgment requiring that the defendants and the County of Riverside provide in-custody arrestees, arrested without warrants, prompt probable cause, bail and arraignment hearings." A second complaint named three additional plaintiffs—Johnny E. James, Diana Ray Simon, and Michael Scott Hyde. . . . The complaint alleged that each of the named plaintiffs had been arrested without a warrant, had received neither prompt probable cause nor bail hearings, and was still in custody.

In March 1989, plaintiffs asked the District Court to issue a preliminary injunction requiring the County to provide all persons arrested without a warrant a judicial determination of probable cause within 36 hours of arrest. The District Court issued the injunction, holding that the County's existing practice violated this Court's decision in *Gerstein*. Without discussion, the District Court adopted a rule that the County provide probable cause determinations within 36 hours of arrest, except in exigent circumstances.

The court "retained jurisdiction indefinitely" to ensure that the County established new procedures that complied with the injunction. The U.S. Court of Appeals for the Ninth Circuit consolidated this case with another challenging an identical preliminary injunction issued against the County of San Bernardino. On November 8, 1989, the Court of Appeals affirmed the order granting the preliminary injunction against Riverside County.

The Court of Appeals determined that the County's policy of providing probable cause determinations at arraignment within 48 hours was "not in accord with *Gerstein*'s requirement of a determination 'promptly after arrest'" because no more than 36 hours were needed "to complete the administrative steps incident to arrest." The Ninth Circuit thus joined the Fourth and Seventh Circuits in interpreting *Gerstein* as requiring a probable cause determination immediately following completion of the administrative procedures incident to arrest. By contrast, the Second Circuit understands *Gerstein* to "stress the need for flexibility" and to permit States to combine probable cause determinations with other pretrial proceedings. We granted certiorari to resolve this conflict among the Circuits as to what constitutes a "prompt" probable cause determination under *Gerstein*.

OPINION

In *Gerstein v. Pugh* (1975), this Court held unconstitutional Florida procedures under which persons arrested without a warrant could remain in police custody for 30 days or more without a judicial determination of probable cause. In reaching this conclusion we attempted to reconcile important competing interests. On the one hand, States have a strong interest in protecting public safety by taking into custody those persons who are reasonably suspected of having engaged in criminal activity, even where there has been no opportunity for a prior judicial determination of probable cause.

On the other hand, prolonged detention based on incorrect or unfounded suspicion may unjustly "imperil a suspect's job, interrupt his source of income, and impair his family relationships." We sought to balance these competing concerns by holding that States "must provide a fair and reliable determination of probable cause as a condition for any significant pretrial restraint of liberty, and this determination must be made by a judicial officer either before or promptly after arrest." The Court thus established a "practical compromise" between the rights of individuals and the realities of law enforcement. We left it to the individual States to integrate prompt probable cause determinations into their differing systems of pretrial procedures.

Inherent in *Gerstein*'s invitation to the States to experiment and adapt was the recognition that the Fourth Amendment does not compel an immediate determination of probable cause upon completing the administrative steps incident to arrest. Plainly, if a probable cause hearing is constitutionally compelled the moment a suspect is finished being "booked," there is no room whatsoever for "flexibility and experimentation by the States."

Incorporating probable cause determinations "into the procedure for setting bail or fixing other conditions of pretrial release"—which *Gerstein* explicitly contemplated—would be impossible. Waiting even a few hours so that a bail hearing or arraignment could take place at the same time as the probable cause determination would amount to a constitutional violation. Clearly, *Gerstein* is not that inflexible.

But flexibility has its limits; *Gerstein* is not a blank check. A State has no legitimate interest in detaining for extended periods individuals who have been arrested without probable cause. The Court recognized in *Gerstein* that a person arrested without a warrant is entitled to a fair and reliable determination of probable cause and that this determination must be made promptly. Unfortunately, as lower court decisions applying *Gerstein* have demonstrated, it is not enough to say that probable cause determinations must be "prompt." This vague standard simply has not provided sufficient guidance. Instead, it has led to a flurry of systemic challenges to city and county practices, putting federal judges in the role of making legislative judgments and overseeing local jail house operations.

Our task in this case is to articulate more clearly the boundaries of what is permissible under the Fourth Amendment. Although we hesitate to announce that the Constitution compels a specific time limit, it is important to provide some degree of certainty so that States and counties may establish procedures with confidence that they fall within constitutional bounds. Taking into account the competing interests articulated in *Gerstein*, we believe that a jurisdiction that provides judicial determinations of probable cause within 48 hours of arrest will, as a general matter, comply with the promptness requirement of *Gerstein*. For this reason, such jurisdictions will be immune from systemic challenges.

This is not to say that the probable cause determination in a particular case passes constitutional muster simply because it is provided within 48 hours. Such a hearing may nonetheless violate *Gerstein* if the arrested individual can prove that his or her probable cause determination was delayed unreasonably. Examples of unreasonable delay are delays for the purpose of gathering additional evidence to justify the arrest, a delay motivated by ill will against the arrested individual, or delay for delay's sake. In evaluating whether the delay in a particular case is unreasonable, however, courts must allow a substantial degree of flexibility. Courts cannot ignore the often unavoidable delays in transporting arrested persons from one facility to another, handling late-night bookings where no magistrate is readily available, obtaining the presence of an arresting officer who may be busy processing other suspects or securing the premises of an arrest, and other practical realities.

Where an arrested individual does not receive a probable cause determination within 48 hours, the calculus changes. In such a case, the arrested individual does not bear the burden of proving an unreasonable delay. Rather, the burden shifts to the government to demonstrate the existence of a bona fide emergency or other extraordinary circumstance. The fact that in a particular case it may take longer than 48 hours to consolidate pretrial proceedings does not qualify as an extraordinary circumstance. Nor, for that matter, do intervening weekends. A jurisdiction that chooses to offer combined proceedings must do so as soon as is reasonably feasible, but in no event later than 48 hours after arrest.

We conclude that Riverside County is entitled to combine probable cause determinations with arraignments. The record indicates, however, that the County's current policy and practice do not comport fully with the principles we have outlined. The County's current policy is to offer combined proceedings within two days, exclusive of Saturdays, Sundays, or holidays. As a result, persons arrested on Thursdays may have to wait until the following Monday before they receive a probable cause determination. The delay is even longer if there is an intervening holiday. Thus, the County's regular practice exceeds the 48-hour period we deem constitutionally permissible, meaning that the County is not immune from systemic challenges, such as this class action.

As to arrests that occur early in the week, the County's practice is that "arraignments usually take place on the last day" possible. There may well be legitimate reasons for this practice; alternatively, this may constitute delay for delay's sake. We leave it to the Court of Appeals and the District Court, on remand, to make this determination.

The judgment of the Court of Appeals is vacated and the case is REMANDED for further proceedings consistent with this opinion.

DISSENT

SCALIA, J.

"The Fourth Amendment requires a judicial determination of probable cause as a prerequisite to extended restraint of liberty," "either before or promptly after arrest." Determining the outer boundary of reasonableness is an objective and manageable task. The data available are enough to convince me, that certainly no more than 24 hours is needed.

A few weeks before issuance of today's opinion, there appeared in the *Washington Post* the story of protracted litigation arising from the arrest of a student who entered a restaurant in Charlottesville, Virginia, one evening to look for some friends. Failing to find them, he tried to leave—but refused to pay a $5 fee (required by the restaurant's posted rules) for failing to return a red tab he had been issued to keep track of his orders. According to the story, he "was taken by police to the Charlottesville jail" at the restaurant's request. "There, a magistrate refused to issue an arrest warrant," and he was released.

That is how it used to be; but not, according to today's decision, how it must be in the future. If the Fourth Amendment meant then what the Court says it does now, the student could lawfully have been held for as long as it would have taken to arrange for his arraignment, up to a maximum of 48 hours.

Justice Story wrote that the Fourth Amendment "is little more than the affirmance of a great constitutional doctrine of the common law." It should not become less than that. One hears the complaint, nowadays, that the Fourth Amendment has become constitutional law for the guilty; that it benefits the career criminal (through the exclusionary rule) often and directly, but the ordinary citizen remotely if at all.

By failing to protect the innocent arrestee, today's opinion reinforces that view. The common law rule of prompt hearing had as its primary beneficiaries the innocent—not those whose fully justified convictions must be overturned to scold the police; nor those who avoid conviction because the evidence, while convincing, does not establish guilt beyond a reasonable doubt; but those so blameless that there was not even good reason to arrest them. While in recent years we have invented novel applications of the Fourth Amendment to release the unquestionably guilty, we today repudiate one of its core applications so that the presumptively innocent may be left in jail.

Hereafter, a law-abiding citizen wrongfully arrested may be compelled to await the grace of a Dickensian bureaucratic machine, as it churns its cycle for up to two days—never once given the opportunity to show a judge that there is absolutely no reason to hold him, that a mistake has been made. In my view, this is the image of a system of justice that has lost its ancient sense of priority, a system that few Americans would recognize as our own.

QUESTIONS

1. **What reasons does the Court give for deciding that under ordinary circumstances, 48 hours is a reasonable time to satisfy the Fourth Amendment interest in providing a prompt determination of probable cause?**
2. **What interests did the Court balance in making its decision?**
3. **What administrative steps and specific circumstances did the Court consider in balancing these interests?**
4. **What does the history of the common law have to do with a decision made in 1991?**
5. **What rule would you adopt? Why?**

||||||||||||||||||||||||||||||||||||||||||||||||||||||||||||||||||||||||||||||||||||||||||||||||||||||||||||||||||||||

The First Appearance

LO 2

The **criminal complaint** (the document that formally charges defendants with specific crimes) authorizes magistrates to conduct the first appearance. Magistrates complete four tasks at the first appearance:

1. Inform defendants of the charges against them
2. Inform defendants of their constitutional rights
3. Set bail or detain suspects
4. Appoint attorneys for indigent defendants

Felony defendants rarely enter a plea at their first appearance; they wait until their *arraignment* (a proceeding that orders defendants to come to court and plead to the charges against them). Misdemeanor defendants usually plead (almost always guilty) at their first appearance, especially if the penalty is a small fine. When suspects—now called "defendants"—first appear in court, magistrates tell them the charges against them. If defendants don't have a lawyer present, the court gives them copies of the complaint, the police report, and other papers supporting the complaint. The court also informs defendants of their constitutional rights.

Informing defendants of their constitutional rights follows this typical court rule in the Minnesota Rules of Criminal Procedure (2006, Rule 5.01):

> The judge, judicial officer, or other duly authorized personnel shall advise the defendant substantially as follows:
>
> a. That the defendant is not required to say anything or submit to interrogation and that anything the defendant says may be used against the defendant in this or any subsequent proceeding;
> b. That the defendant has a right to counsel in all subsequent proceedings, including police line-ups and interrogations, and if the defendant appears without counsel and is financially unable to afford counsel, that counsel will forthwith be appointed without cost to the defendant charged with an offense punishable upon conviction by incarceration;
> c. That the defendant has a right to communicate with defense counsel and that a continuance will be granted if necessary to enable defendant to obtain or speak to counsel;
> d. That the defendant has a right to a jury trial or a trial to the court;
> e. That if the offense is a misdemeanor, the defendant may either plead guilty or not guilty, or demand a complaint prior to entering a plea;
> f. That if the offense is a designated gross misdemeanor as defined in Rule 1.04(b) and a complaint has not yet been made and filed, a complaint must be issued within 10 days if the defendant is not in custody or within 48 hours if the defendant is in custody.
>
> The judge, judicial officer, or other duly authorized personnel may advise a number of defendants at once of these rights, but each defendant shall be asked individually before arraignment whether the defendant heard and understood these rights as explained earlier.

||||||||||||||||||||||||||||||||||||||||||||||||||||||||||||||||||||||||||||||||||||||||||||||||||||||||||||||||||||||||||||||||||||||||||||||||||||

Bail and Pretrial Detention

LO 3, LO 4, LO 5

Most defendants (in some places more than 90 percent) are released on bail while they wait for trial or the results of a plea bargain (see Chapter 13). Still, locking up even 10 percent of defendants adds to the never-ending problem of crowded jails.

For these defendants detained before trial or guilty plea, their stay in jail can last quite a while (more than 30 days for 33 percent of detainees; more than 90 days for 20 percent). You should be aware of another fact: detention costs money—in most places more than $30 a day for every defendant. About 20 percent of defendants charged with petty offenses are released without even appearing before judges. They receive a **citation release** (like a traffic ticket), or they're released after posting bond according to bail schedules that list amounts for specific offenses (Toborg 1981).

Judges can attach a variety of conditions to release. Sometimes, defendants are **released on recognizance (ROR)**—their promise to appear in court on their court date. Some judges release defendants on the condition that they either report at scheduled times to a pretrial release program or promise not to leave town before their trial.

Sometimes, judges impose supervised release—for example, requiring defendants to report to relatives or their local police department; to participate in a treatment program for illegal drugs, alcohol abuse, or mental illness; or to attend employment programs (Toborg 1981).

Money bonds, in which defendants are released as soon as money is put up, come in several forms. With the unsecured bond, defendants have to pay only if they don't appear for their court date. With the court-administered deposit bond, defendants have to post 10 percent of the amount of the bond; if they appear, the court returns their deposit. Under privately administered bail bonds, bail bondsmen (most are men) or bondswomen charge 10 percent of the amount of the bond they turn over to the courts. Defendants forfeit the 10 percent fee even if they appear (Feeley 1979; also see Chapter 2).

Being locked up before trial is a major loss of freedom, but it's more than that. Temporary loss of wages and even permanent loss of a job, separation from family and friends, restrictions on aiding in their own defense, and loss of reputation are also possible consequences for detained defendants. And—all of these take place before defendants are convicted.

But pretrial release is also a risk to society. Defendants on bail can escape the jurisdiction of the court by fleeing; commit new crimes; and expose the community to anxiety, fear, and outrage over the threats to public safety. Clearly, the decision of whether to release or detain defendants before they're found guilty demands that courts strike the right balance between the right of defendants to be free until they're proved guilty and the need of the community to feel safe from crime and bring criminals to justice.

Striking that balance boils down to two issues:

1. What are the constitutional rights of bailed and detained defendants?
2. What are the legitimate community interests in bailed and detained defendants?

To examine these issues, we'll look at bail and the Constitution; whether preventive detention denies suspects their constitutional rights; and the rights defendants retain during pretrial detention.

Bail and the Constitution

LO 3, LO 4

There's no absolute constitutional right to bail, only a right against *excessive* bail. The Eighth Amendment to the U.S. Constitution provides that "Excessive bail shall not be required," but the word "excessive" is subject to interpretation. So legislatures and courts are left to spell out the precise constitutional limit. In a controversial case from the Cold War era, *Stack v. Boyle* (1951), U.S. Chief Justice Fred M. Vinson wrote for the majority:

> From the passage of the Judiciary Act of 1789, to the present, federal law has unequivocally provided that a person arrested for a non-capital offense shall be admitted to bail.
>
> This traditional right to freedom permits the unhampered preparation of a defense, and serves to prevent the infliction of punishment prior to conviction. Unless this right to bail before trial is preserved, the presumption of innocence, secured only after centuries of struggle, would lose its meaning. (4)

In *Stack v. Boyle*, 12 people were charged with conspiring to violate the Smith Act, which made it a crime to advocate the violent overthrow of the government. The case arose at the height of the Cold War, when anticommunism and fear of radicalism gripped the nation. The trial court fixed bail at $50,000 apiece. The U.S. Supreme Court ruled that amounts that are more than necessary to ensure that petitioners come to court for their trials are "excessive." The Court held that magistrates have to calculate how much money it will take to guarantee that defendants will appear.

Naturally, the amount will vary according to the circumstances of each case, but the main concerns include:

1. The seriousness of the offense
2. The amount of evidence against the defendant
3. The defendant's family ties, employment, financial resources, character, and mental condition
4. The length of the defendant's residence in the community
5. The defendant's criminal history
6. The defendant's prior record for appearing and/or "jumping" bail

Sometimes, no amount of money is enough to guarantee that rich defendants will come to court. In *U.S. v. Abrahams* (1978), Herbert Abrahams had three previous convictions; was an escaped prisoner from another state; had given false information at a prior bail hearing; had failed to appear on a former bail of $100,000; had failed to appear on a previous charge in California from which he was a fugitive; had several aliases; and had recently transferred $1.5 million to Bermuda! The U.S. First Circuit Court of Appeals upheld the U.S. District Court's conclusion that no condition "or any combination will reasonably assure the appearance of defendant for trial if admitted to bail."

At the other extreme (and a lot more common), any amount is too much for poor defendants to pay. Noted bail scholar Professor Caleb Foote (1965) believes our bail system violates the Constitution in three ways when it comes to poor defendants. It denies them:

1. *Due process* of law, because defendants can't help with their own defense if they're locked up
2. *Equal protection* of the law, because they're jailed because they're poor
3. The *right against excessive bail*, because they can't raise any amount required

Pretrial detention is an obstacle to defendants trying to prepare their defense. They can't help investigators find witnesses and physical evidence. Cramped jail quarters and short visiting hours inhibit conferences with their lawyers. Jailing also affects defendants' appearance and demeanor; they can't conceal rumpled clothes and a pale complexion. Free defendants, on the other hand, can help their defense and show the court that they're working and otherwise responsible for themselves and their families.

Preventive Detention

LO 5

Commentators, lawyers, judges, and criminal justice personnel have hotly debated whether the only acceptable purpose for bail and pretrial detention is to make sure defendants come to court. Can courts also deny bail and use pretrial detention to lock up "dangerous" defendants? Yes. **Preventive detention** allows judges to deny bail to defendants who might intimidate, hurt, and terrorize victims and witnesses or who might commit new crimes.

To reduce these dangers, the U.S. Congress enacted the **Bail Reform Act of 1984**, which authorizes federal courts to jail arrested defendants when a judge determines, after a hearing, that no condition of release would "reasonably" guarantee the appearance of the defendant and the safety of the community.

At preventive detention hearings, the Bail Reform Act guarantees defendants' rights:

1. To have an appointed lawyer

2. To testify at the hearing

3. To present evidence

4. To cross-examine witnesses

If the judge decides there's **clear and convincing evidence** (more than probable cause but less than proof beyond a reasonable doubt) that the defendant either won't appear or is a threat to public safety, she can order the defendant to be "preventively detained" (jailed).

Preventive detention gives rise to both empirical and constitutional questions. The major empirical question is, Does probable cause to believe a person has committed a crime predict future dangerous behavior? The question is hard to answer because the word "dangerous" is vague, and because behavior, especially violent behavior, is hard to predict (Moore and others 1984, 1).

The constitutional questions are:

1. Does preventive detention violate the Eighth Amendment ban on "cruel and un-usual punishment"?

2. Does preventive detention violate the Fifth and Fourteenth Amendments and deny defendants liberty without due process of law?

In *U.S. v. Salerno* (1987), our next case excerpt, the U.S. Supreme Court answered "no" to both questions.

*In **U.S. v. Salerno** (1987), our next case excerpt, the U.S. Supreme Court held that preventive detention didn't deny Anthony Salerno and Vincent Cafaro their due process rights.*

CASE Were Their Pretrial Detentions "Punishment"?

U.S. v. Salerno
481 U.S. 739 (1987)

HISTORY

Anthony Salerno and Vincent Cafaro were committed for pretrial detention pursuant to the Bail Reform Act by the U.S. District Court, Southern District of New York. The U.S. Court of Appeals, Second Circuit, vacated the commitment and remanded the case. On writ of certiorari, the U.S. Supreme Court reversed.

REHNQUIST, C.J., joined by WHITE, BLACKMUN, POWELL, O'CONNOR, and SCALIA, JJ.

FACTS

Anthony Salerno and Vincent Cafaro were arrested on March 21, 1986, after being charged in a 29-count indictment alleging various Racketeer Influenced and Corrupt Organizations Act (RICO) violations, mail and wire fraud offenses, extortion, and various criminal gambling violations. The RICO counts alleged 35 acts of racketeering activity, including fraud, extortion, gambling, and conspiracy to commit murder. At their arraignment, the Government moved to have Salerno and Cafaro detained pursuant to § 3142(e) of the Bail Reform Act of 1984 on the ground that no condition of release would assure the safety of the community or any person. The District Court held a hearing at which the Government made a detailed proffer (offer) of evidence.

The Government's case showed that Salerno was the "boss" of the Genovese Crime Family of La Cosa Nostra and that Cafaro was a "captain" in the Genovese Family. According to the Government's proffer, based in large part on conversations intercepted by a court-ordered wiretap, the two respondents had participated in wide-ranging conspiracies to aid their illegitimate enterprises through violent means. The Government also offered the testimony of two of its trial witnesses, who would assert that Salerno personally participated in two murder conspiracies. Salerno opposed the motion for detention, challenging the credibility of the Government's witnesses. He offered the testimony of several character witnesses as well as a letter from his doctor stating that he was suffering from a serious medical condition. Cafaro presented no evidence at the hearing, but instead characterized the wiretap conversations as merely "tough talk."

OPINION

The Bail Reform Act of 1984 allows a federal court to detain an arrestee pending trial if the government demonstrates by clear and convincing evidence after an adversary hearing that no release conditions "will reasonably assure the safety of any other person and the community." The United States Court of Appeals for the Second Circuit struck down this provision of the Act as facially unconstitutional, because, in that court's words, this type of pretrial detention violates "substantive due process." We granted certiorari because of a conflict among the Courts of Appeals regarding the validity of the Act. We hold that . . . the Act fully comports with constitutional requirements. We therefore reverse.

Responding to "the alarming problems of crimes committed by persons on release," Congress formulated the Bail Reform Act of 1984. To this end, § 3141(a) of the Act requires a judicial officer to determine whether an arrestee shall be detained. § 3142(e) provides:

> If, after a hearing pursuant to the provisions of subsection (f), the judicial officer finds that no condition or combination of conditions will reasonably assure the appearance of the person as required and the safety of any other person and the community, he shall order the detention of the person prior to trial.

The judicial officer is not given unbridled discretion in making the detention determination. Congress has specified the consideration relevant to that decision. These factors include

1. the nature and seriousness of the charges,
2. the substantiality of the government's evidence against the arrestee,
3. the arrestee's background and characteristics, and
4. the nature and seriousness of the danger posed by the suspect's release.

Should a judicial officer order detention, the detainee is entitled to expedited appellate review of the detention order.

Respondents present two grounds for invalidating the Bail Reform Act's provisions permitting pretrial detention on the basis of future dangerousness. They rely upon the Court of Appeals' conclusion that the Act exceeds the limitations placed upon the Federal Government by the Due Process Clause of the Fifth Amendment. They contend that the Act contravenes the Eighth Amendment's proscription against excessive bail.

We treat those contentions in turn. Respondents first argue that the Act violates substantive due process because the pretrial detention it authorizes constitutes impermissible punishment before trial. The Government, however, has never argued that pretrial detention could be upheld if it were "punishment."

Pretrial detention under the Bail Reform Act is regulatory, not penal. The government's interest in preventing crime by arrestees is both legitimate and compelling. On the other side of the scale, of course, is the individual's strong interest in liberty. We do not minimize the importance and fundamental nature of this right. But, as our cases hold, this right may, in circumstances where the government's interest is sufficiently weighty, be subordinated to the greater needs of society.

Respondents also contend that the Bail Reform Act violates the Excessive Bail Clause of the Eighth Amendment. We think that the Act survives a challenge founded upon the Eighth Amendment. While we agree that a primary function of bail is to safeguard the courts' role in adjudicating the guilt or innocence of defendants, we reject the proposition that the Eighth Amendment categorically prohibits the government from pursuing other admittedly compelling interests through regulation of pretrial release.

Nothing in the text of the Bail Clause limits permissible government considerations solely to questions of flight. We believe that when Congress has mandated detention on the basis of a compelling interest other than prevention of flight, as it has here, the Eighth Amendment does not require release on bail.

In our society liberty is the norm, and detention prior to trial or without trial is the carefully limited exception. We hold that the provisions for pretrial detention in the Bail Reform Act of 1984 fall within that carefully limited exception. The Act authorizes the detention prior to trial of arrestees charged with serious felonies who are found after an adversary hearing to pose a threat to the safety of individuals or to the community which no condition of release can dispel. We are unwilling to say that this congressional determination, based as it is upon that primary concern of every government—a concern for the safety and indeed the lives of its citizens—on its face violates either the Due Process Clause of the Fifth Amendment or the Excessive Bail Clause of the Eighth Amendment.

The judgment of the Court of Appeals is therefore REVERSED.

DISSENT

MARSHALL, J., joined by BRENNAN, J.

The statute now before us declares that persons who have been indicted may be detained if a judicial officer finds clear and convincing evidence that they pose a danger to individuals or to the community. The conclusion is inescapable that the indictment has been turned into evidence, if not that the defendant is guilty of the crime charged, then that left to his own devices he will soon be guilty of something else. "If it suffices to accuse, what will become of the innocent?"

"It is a fair summary of history to say that the safeguards of liberty have frequently been forged in controversies involving not very nice people." Honoring the presumption of innocence is often difficult; sometimes we must pay substantial social costs as a result of our commitment to the values we espouse. But at the end of the day the presumption of innocence protects the innocent; the shortcuts we take with those whom we believe to be guilty injure only those wrongfully accused and, ultimately, ourselves.

Throughout the world today there are men, women, and children interned indefinitely, awaiting trials which may never come or which may be a mockery of the word, because their governments believe them to be "dangerous." Our Constitution, whose construction began two centuries ago, can shelter us forever from the evils of such unchecked power. Over two hundred years it has slowly, through our efforts, grown more durable, more expansive, and more just. But it cannot protect us if we lack the courage, and the self-restraint, to protect ourselves. Today, a majority of the Court applies itself to an ominous exercise in demolition. Theirs is truly a decision which will go forth without authority, and come back without respect.

QUESTIONS

1. In your opinion, is pretrial detention punishment or a "regulatory device"? What criteria do you use to answer this question?
2. What did Chief Justice John Marshall mean when he asked, "If it suffices to accuse, what will become of the innocent?"
3. Does pretrial detention undermine the presumption of innocence?
4. What, in your opinion, is the proper purpose(s) of bail? Defend your answer.

Conditions of Pretrial Confinement

LO 5

Detention prior to trial, whether to secure defendants' appearance or to protect public safety, is still confinement. Jailed defendants aren't free to leave; they're locked up in cells and subject to jail discipline. They also have to follow rules designed to maintain safety and order. But jailed defendants are legally innocent; they don't forfeit their constitutional rights just because they're in jail. A jail administrator was asked if surveillance in cells through two-way mirrors (prisoners didn't know they were two-way mirrors) violated the prisoners' right to privacy. The administrator replied, "They have no rights." The administrator was wrong. Jailed defendants do have rights, but they're watered down in jail. That's what the U.S. Supreme Court decided in *Bell v. Wolfish* (1979), our next case excerpt.

In Bell v. Wolfish (1979), our next case excerpt, the U.S. Supreme Court held that jailed defendants awaiting trial have constitutional rights but they're severely limited.

CASE Were They "Punished" Before Conviction?

Bell v. Wolfish
441 U.S. 520 (1979)

HISTORY

Jailed defendants sued in U.S. District Court, Southern District of New York, challenging the constitutionality of numerous conditions of confinement and practices in the Metropolitan Correctional Center, a federally operated, short-term custodial facility for pretrial detainees in New York City. The U.S. District Court enjoined various practices in the facility. The U.S. Court of Appeals, Second Circuit, affirmed. On writ of certiorari, the U.S. Supreme Court reversed.

REHNQUIST, J., joined by BURGER, C.J., and STEWART, WHITE, and BLACKMUN, JJ.

FACTS

The MCC (Metropolitan Correctional Center) differs markedly from the familiar image of a jail; there are no barred cells, dank, colorless corridors, or clanging steel gates. It was intended to include the most advanced and innovative features of modern design of detention facilities. "It represented the architectural embodiment of the best and most progressive penological planning." The key design element of the 12-story structure is the "modular" or "unit" concept, whereby each floor designed to house inmates has one or two largely self-contained residential units that replace the traditional cellblock jail construction.

Each unit in turn has several clusters or corridors of private rooms or dormitories radiating from a central 2-story "multipurpose" or common room, to which each inmate has free access approximately 16 hours a day. Because our analysis does not turn on the particulars of the MCC concept design, we need not discuss them further.

When the MCC opened in August 1975, the planned capacity was 449 inmates, an increase of 50% over the former West Street facility. Despite some dormitory accommodations, the MCC was designed primarily to house these inmates in 389 rooms, which originally were intended for single occupancy. While the MCC was under construction, however, the number of persons committed to pretrial detention began to rise at an "unprecedented" rate. The Bureau of Prisons took several steps to accommodate this unexpected flow of persons assigned to the facility, but despite these efforts, the inmate population at the MCC rose above its planned capacity within a short time after its opening.

To provide sleeping space for this increased population, the MCC replaced the single bunks in many of the individual rooms and dormitories with double bunks. Also, each week some newly arrived inmates had to sleep on cots in the common areas until they could be transferred to residential rooms as space became available.

On November 28, 1975, less than four months after the MCC had opened, the named respondents initiated this action by filing in the District Court a petition for writ of habeas corpus. The petition served up a veritable potpourri of complaints that implicated virtually every facet of the institution's conditions and practices. Respondents charged they had been deprived of their statutory and constitutional rights because of overcrowded conditions, undue length of confinement, improper searches, inadequate recreational, educational, and employment opportunities, insufficient staff, and objectionable restrictions on the purchase and receipt of personal items and books.

The District Court intervened broadly into almost every facet of the institution and enjoined no fewer than 20 MCC practices on constitutional and statutory grounds. The Court of Appeals affirmed the District Court's constitutional rulings and in the process held that under the Due Process Clause of the Fifth Amendment, pretrial detainees may be subjected to only those restrictions and privations which inhere in their confinement itself or which are justified by compelling necessities of jail administration. We granted certiorari to consider the important constitutional questions raised by these decisions and to resolve an apparent conflict among the Circuits. We now reverse.

OPINION

Not every disability imposed during pretrial detention amounts to "punishment" in the constitutional sense. Once the Government has exercised its conceded authority to detain a person pending trial, it obviously is entitled to employ devices that are calculated to effectuate this detention. Traditionally, this has meant confinement in a facility which, no matter how modern or antiquated, results in restricting the movement of a detainee in a manner in which he would not be restricted if he simply were free to walk the streets pending trial. Whether it be called a jail, a prison, or a custodial center, the purpose of the facility is to detain.

Loss of freedom of choice and privacy are inherent incidents of confinement in such a facility. And the fact that such detention interferes with the detainee's understandable desire to live as comfortably as possible and with as little restraint as possible during confinement does not convert the conditions or restrictions of detention into "punishment." Judged by this analysis, respondents' claim that "double-bunking" violated their due process rights fails. On this record, we are convinced as a matter of law that "double-bunking" as practiced at the MCC did not amount to punishment and did not, therefore, violate respondents' rights under the Due Process Clause of the Fifth Amendment.

Each of the rooms at the MCC that house pretrial detainees has a total floor space of approximately 75 square feet. Each of them designated for "double-bunking" contains a double bunkbed, certain other items of furniture, a wash basin, and an uncovered toilet. Inmates are generally locked into their rooms from 11 P.M. to 6:30 A.M. and for brief periods during the afternoon and evening head counts. During the rest of the day, they may move about freely between their rooms and the common areas.

We disagree with both the District Court and the Court of Appeals that there is some sort of "one man, one cell" principle lurking in the Due Process Clause of the Fifth Amendment. While confining a given number of people in a given amount of space in such a manner as to cause them to endure genuine privations and hardships over an extended period of time might raise serious questions under the Due Process Clause as to whether those conditions amounted to punishment, nothing even approaching such hardship is shown by this record.

Detainees are required to spend only seven or eight hours each day in their rooms, during most or all of which they presumably are sleeping. During the remainder of the time, the detainees are free to move between their rooms and the common area. While "double-bunking" may have taxed some of the equipment or particular facilities in certain of the common areas, this does not mean that the conditions at the MCC failed to meet the standards required by the Constitution. Our conclusion in this regard is further buttressed by the detainees' length of stay at the MCC. Nearly all of the detainees are released within 60 days. We simply do not believe that requiring a detainee to share toilet facilities and this admittedly small sleeping space with another person for generally a maximum period of 60 days violates the Constitution.

Maintaining institutional security and preserving internal order and discipline are essential goals that may require limitation or retraction of the retained constitutional rights of both convicted prisoners and pretrial detainees. Central to all other corrections goals is the institutional consideration of internal security within the corrections facilities themselves.

Finally, the problems that arise in the day-to-day operations of the corrections facility are not susceptible to easy solutions. Prison administrators therefore should be accorded wide-ranging deference in the adoption and execution of policies and practices that in their judgment are needed to preserve internal order and discipline and to maintain institutional security.

Inmates at all Bureau of Prison facilities, including the MCC, are required to expose their body cavities for visual inspection as part of a strip search conducted after every contact visit with a person from outside the institution. Corrections officials testified that visual cavity searches were necessary not only to discover but also to deter the smuggling of weapons, drugs, and other contraband into the institution. The District Court upheld the strip-search procedure but prohibited the body-cavity searches, absent probable cause to believe that the inmate is concealing contraband.

Because petitioners proved only one instance in the MCC's short history where contraband was found during a body-cavity search, the Court of Appeals affirmed. In its view, the "gross violation of personal privacy inherent in such a search cannot be outweighed by the government's security interest in maintaining a practice of so little actual utility." Admittedly, this practice instinctively gives us the most pause. However, assuming for present purposes that inmates, both convicted prisoners and pretrial detainees, retain some Fourth Amendment rights upon commitment to a corrections facility, we nonetheless conclude that these searches do not violate that Amendment. The Fourth Amendment prohibits only unreasonable searches, and under the circumstances, we do not believe that these searches are unreasonable.

A detention facility is a unique place fraught with serious security dangers. Smuggling of money, drugs, weapons, and other contraband is all too common an occurrence. And inmate attempts to secrete these items into the facility by concealing them in body cavities is documented in this record. That there has been only one instance where an MCC inmate was discovered attempting to smuggle contraband into the institution on his person may be more a testament to the effectiveness of this search technique as a deterrent than to any lack of interest on the part of the inmates to secrete and import such items when the opportunity arises.

There was a time not too long ago when the federal judiciary took a completely "hands-off" approach to the problem of prison administration. In recent years, however, these courts largely have discarded this "hands-off" attitude and have waded into this complex arena. But many of these same courts have, in the name of the Constitution, become increasingly enmeshed in the minutiae of prison operations. Judges, after all, are human. They, no less than others in our society, have a natural tendency to believe that their individual solutions to often intractable problems are better and more workable than those of the persons who are actually charged with and trained in the running of the particular institution under examination.

But under the Constitution, the first question to be answered is not whose plan is best, but in what branch of the Government is lodged the authority to initially devise the plan. The wide range of judgment calls that meet constitutional and statutory requirements are confided to officials outside of the Judicial Branch of Government.

DISSENT

STEVENS, J., joined by BRENNAN, J.

This is not an equal protection case. An empirical judgment that most persons formally accused of criminal conduct are probably guilty would provide a rational basis for a set of rules that treat them like convicts until they establish their innocence. No matter how rational such an approach might be—no matter how acceptable in a community where equality of status is the dominant goal—it is obnoxious to the concept of individual freedom protected by the Due Process Clause. If ever accepted in this country, it would work a fundamental change in the character of our free society.

Nor is this an Eighth Amendment case. That provision of the Constitution protects individuals convicted of crimes from punishment that is cruel and unusual. The pretrial detainees whose rights are at stake in this case, however, are innocent men and women who have been convicted of no crimes. Their claim is not that they have been subjected to cruel and unusual punishment in violation of the Eighth Amendment, but that to subject them to any form of punishment at all is an unconstitutional deprivation of their liberty.

This is a due process case. The most significant—and I venture to suggest the most enduring—part of the Court's opinion today is its recognition of this initial constitutional premise. The Court squarely holds that under the Due Process Clause, a detainee may not be punished prior to an adjudication of guilt in accordance with due process of law. Prior to conviction every individual is entitled to the benefit of a presumption both that he is innocent of prior criminal conduct and that he has no present intention to commit any offense in the immediate future. It is not always easy to determine whether a particular restraint serves the legitimate, regulatory goal of ensuring a detainee's presence at trial and his safety and security in the meantime, or the unlawful end of punishment.

[Double-bunking and searches of mail and cells are omitted from this excerpt.]

The body-cavity search—clearly the greatest personal indignity—may be the least justifiable measure of all. After every contact visit a body-cavity search is mandated by the rule. The District Court's finding that searches have failed in practice to produce any demonstrable improvement in security is hardly surprising. Detainees and their visitors are in full view during all visits, and are fully clad. To insert contraband into one's private body cavities during such a visit would indeed be an imposing challenge to nerves and agility. There is no reason to expect, and the petitioners have established none, that many pretrial detainees would attempt, let alone succeed, in surmounting this challenge absent the challenged rule.

Moreover, as the District Court explicitly found, less severe alternatives are available to ensure that contraband is not transferred during visits. Weapons and other dangerous instruments, the items of greatest legitimate concern, may be discovered by the use of metal detecting devices or other equipment commonly used for airline security. In addition, inmates are required, even apart from the body-cavity searches, to disrobe, to have their clothing inspected, and to present open hands and arms to reveal the absence of any concealed objects. These alternative procedures "amply satisfy" the demands of security. In my judgment, there is no basis in this regard to disagree.

It may well be, as the Court finds, that the rules at issue here were not adopted by administrators eager to punish those detained at MCC. The rules can be explained as the easiest way for administrators to ensure security in the jail. But the easiest course for jail officials is not always one that our Constitution allows them to take. If fundamental rights are withdrawn and severe harms are indiscriminately inflicted on detainees merely to secure minimal savings in time and effort for administrators, the guarantee of due process is violated.

QUESTIONS

1. **Summarize the arguments of the majority and the dissent. Which is better? Defend your answer, relying on the facts and arguments made in the case.**
2. **Distinguish between *detention* and *punishment*.**
3. **One critic said that it was all well and good for Supreme Court justices to say this case involved detention, not punishment, but it probably would be little comfort for the detainees to know that. Do you agree? Explain your answer.**
4. **Does it matter that most pretrial detainees are subject to confinement because they can't afford bail?**
5. **What interests are at stake in this case? How would you balance them?**

|||||||||||||||||||||||||||||||||||||||||||||||||||||||||||||||||||||||||||||||||||||||||||||||||||||||||||||||||||||||||||||||||||||||||||||

The Right to Counsel

LO 6

Lawyers are everywhere in the criminal justice system today, but that wasn't always true. During colonial times and for some time afterward, victims had to find and hire their own private prosecutors. Defendants in felony cases didn't even have the right to a lawyer to defend them during their trials. Until the 1960s due process revolution (Chapter 2), a lawyer's job was to represent people once they got to court, not before they were charged or after they were convicted.

The remaining chapters will show that the right to a lawyer reaches even into prison cells and until the death penalty is carried out. This extension of constitutional protection (and the complex, technical legal rules accompanying it) since the due process revolution has created the need for lawyers not just for suspects, defendants, and convicts but also for police and corrections officers and departments. Police departments and corrections agencies have to hire lawyers, because the Constitution protects people on the street, in police stations, and when they're locked up before trial. Here, we'll concentrate on counsel for suspects, defendants, and appellants.

The Sixth Amendment to the U.S. Constitution provides that "In all criminal prosecutions, the accused shall enjoy the right . . . to have the assistance of counsel for his defense." Courts have always recognized criminal defendants' Sixth Amendment right to **retained counsel** (a lawyer paid for by the client). But they didn't recognize the right to **appointed counsel** (lawyers for people who can't afford to hire lawyers) until well into the 1900s. **Indigent defendants** (defendants too poor to hire their own lawyers) had to rely on **counsel pro bono** (lawyers willing to represent clients at no charge). Even today, many jurisdictions rely on lawyers who donate their services to represent poor defendants.

But most counties with large populations, and the U.S. government, have permanent defenders (called **public defenders**) paid by the public to defend poor clients. As we saw in *Powell v. Alabama* (1932; Chapter 2), the U.S. Supreme Court ruled that "fundamental fairness" requires courts to appoint lawyers for indigent defendants.

In *Johnson v. Zerbst* (1938), the Supreme Court acknowledged that the right to counsel guaranteed in the Sixth Amendment "stands as a constant admonition that, if the constitutional safeguards [the Bill of Rights] provides be lost, justice will not 'still be done.'" The Sixth Amendment recognizes that the "average defendant" doesn't have the legal skills necessary to compete with experienced government lawyers who hold the power to deprive her of life, liberty, and property. "That which is simple, orderly, and necessary to the lawyer—to the untrained layman—may appear intricate, complex, and mysterious" (462).

Nevertheless, *Zerbst* recognized only a narrow right to counsel for the poor: the right to a lawyer at their trial in federal courts. It said nothing about a right to counsel either before trial in federal courts or to any proceedings at all in state courts.

The U.S. Supreme Court confronted the right to counsel in state courts in *Betts v. Brady* (1942). Betts was convicted of robbery and sentenced to prison. At his trial, he asked for a lawyer, claiming that he was too poor to afford one. The judge denied his request because Carroll County, Maryland, the site of the trial, provided counsel only in murder and rape cases. Hearings on Betts's petition for habeas corpus eventually reached the Supreme Court. The Court, adopting the fundamental fairness approach, decided the due process clause didn't incorporate the Sixth Amendment right to counsel.

The Court went further to hold that, except in "special circumstances," denial of counsel doesn't deprive a defendant of a fair trial. In other words, the right to counsel was not "implicit in the concept of ordered liberty" (Chapter 2). The Court reviewed the history of representation by counsel, noting that English courts didn't allow defendants—even if they could afford to hire one—to have a lawyer in felony cases until 1843.

The Court concluded that the Sixth Amendment right to counsel *allowed* defendants to have a lawyer, but it didn't *compel* the government in federal cases to provide one. And, after it reviewed a number of state court decisions, the Court concluded that "in the great majority of the states, it has been the considered judgment of the people, their representatives and their courts that appointment of counsel is not a fundamental right, essential to a fair trial." Therefore, "we are unable to say that the concept of due process incorporated in the Fourteenth Amendment obligates the states, whatever may be their own views, to furnish counsel in every such case" (471).

In *Gideon v. Wainwright* (1963), the Supreme Court agreed to review the Florida Supreme Court's dismissal of Gideon's petition for habeas corpus based on a claim similar to that of Betts. Appearing in court without funds and without a lawyer, Clarence Gideon asked the Florida court to appoint counsel for him, and the following exchange took place:

> *The Court:* Mr. Gideon, I am sorry, but I cannot appoint Counsel to represent you in this case. Under the laws of the State of Florida, the only time the Court can appoint Counsel to represent a Defendant is when that person is charged with a capital offense. I am sorry, but I will have to deny your request to appoint Counsel to defend you in this case.
>
> *The Defendant:* The United States Supreme Court says I am entitled to be represented by Counsel.

The Supreme Court agreed to hear Gideon's appeal and took the occasion to overrule *Betts v. Brady*:

> Upon full consideration we conclude that *Betts v. Brady* should be overruled. In our adversary system of criminal justice, any person haled into court, who is too poor to hire a lawyer, cannot be assured a fair trial unless counsel is provided for him. This seems to us to be an obvious truth.
>
> Governments, both state and federal, quite properly spend vast sums of money to establish machinery to try defendants accused of crime. Lawyers to prosecute are everywhere deemed essential to protect the public's interest in an orderly society. Similarly, there are few defendants charged with crime, few indeed, who fail to hire the best lawyers they can get to prepare and present their defenses. That government hires lawyers to prosecute and defendants who have the money hire lawyers to defend are the strongest indications of the widespread belief that lawyers in criminal courts are necessities, not luxuries.
>
> The right of one charged with crime to counsel may not be deemed fundamental and essential to fair trials in some countries, but it is in ours. From the very beginning, our state and national constitutions and laws have laid great emphasis on procedural and substantive safeguards designed to assure fair trials before impartial tribunals in which every defendant stands equal before the law. This noble ideal cannot be realized if the poor man charged with crime has to face his accusers without a lawyer to assist him.

TABLE 12.1

Critical Stages and the Right to Counsel

Stage of Criminal Process	Right to Counsel?
Investigative stop	No
Frisk for weapons	No
Arrest	No
Search following arrest	No
Custodial interrogation	Yes
Lineup before formal charges	No
Lineup after formal charges	Yes
First appearance	No
Grand jury review/Preliminary hearing	Yes
Arraignment	Yes
Pretrial hearings	Yes
Trial (Chapter 13)	Yes
Appeal/Collateral attack (Chapter 14)	Yes

Let's examine some important questions that the right to the assistance of counsel gives rise to:

1. At what point does the right to counsel kick in?

2. What did the Court mean when it said that the right to counsel applied to "all criminal prosecutions"?

3. How "poor" does a person have to be before the court *has* to appoint defense counsel?

4. Does the right to counsel mean the right to the lawyer of your choice?

5. What does the right to "effective counsel" mean?

Let's look at each of these issues.

When the Right to Counsel Attaches

LO 6

The Sixth Amendment guarantees the right to counsel in all criminal "prosecutions," but what proceedings does prosecution include? Clearly, it includes the trial and appeal, when defendants most need special legal expertise. But what about *before* trial? The U.S. Supreme Court has ruled that the right to counsel attaches to all **critical stages of criminal proceedings**. Table 12.1 shows the stages in the criminal process and indicates the ones the U.S. Supreme Court has declared critical stages. It's clear from the table that defendants have the right to counsel to represent them at all procedures after the first appearance.

But what about at the police station before the first appearance? Specifically, do you have a right to a lawyer during police interrogation and identification procedures (lineups, show-ups, and photo identification; see Chapters 8 and 9)? The U.S. Supreme Court first applied the right to a lawyer in police stations in 1964, in

TABLE 12.2

The Leading Right-to-Counsel Cases

Case	Year	Right Upheld
Powell v. Alabama	1932	Appointed counsel for poor, illiterate, ignorant, isolated defendants in state capital cases
Johnson v. Zerbst	1938	Appointed counsel in federal cases at trial (not before or after)
Betts v. Brady	1942	Appointed counsel in state cases under "special circumstances"
Chandler v. Fretag	1954	Retained (paid for) counsel in all criminal cases
Gideon v. Wainwright	1963	Appointed counsel in state felony cases (overruled *Betts v. Brady*)
Argersinger v. Hamlin	1972	Appointed counsel in any offense punishable by incarceration
Scott v. Illinois	1979	No right to counsel for sentences that don't result in actual jail time

Escobedo v. Illinois (1964). The Court held that the right to counsel attached at the accusatory stage of a criminal case—namely, when a general investigation focused on a specific suspect.

According to the Court, the police reached that point when they decided that Danny Escobedo had committed the murder they were investigating. After they made up their minds that he was the murderer, Chicago police officers tried to get him to confess by interrogating him. During the interrogation, Escobedo asked to see his lawyer, who was in the police station. The officers refused. Eventually, he confessed, and was tried and convicted with the help of the confession. The U.S. Supreme Court said the confession wasn't admissible because it was obtained during the accusatory stage without the help of Escobedo's lawyer.

Just two years later, in *Miranda v. Arizona*, the Court decided that police officers have to tell suspects that they have a right to a lawyer during custodial interrogation (Chapter 8). As for identification procedures, those conducted *after* indictment are a critical stage; those conducted *before* indictment aren't (Chapter 9).

The Meaning of "All Criminal Prosecutions"

LO 6

In 1932, *Powell v. Alabama* (Chapter 2) established the rule that due process commands that appointed counsel represent poor defendants in capital cases. In *Gideon v. Wainwright* (1963), the Court extended the right to counsel to poor defendants prosecuted for felonies against property. In 1972, the Court went further; all poor defendants prosecuted for misdemeanors *punishable by jail terms* have a right to an appointed lawyer.

In *Argersinger v. Hamlin* (1972), Jon Richard Argersinger, a Florida indigent, was convicted of carrying a concealed weapon, a misdemeanor punishable by up to six months' imprisonment, a $1,000 fine, or both. A Florida rule limited assigned counsel to "non-petty offenses punishable by more than six months imprisonment." The Court struck down the rule, holding that states have to provide a lawyer for defendants charged with any offense punishable by incarceration no matter what the state's criminal code calls it (misdemeanor, petty misdemeanor, or felony). Table 12.2 summarizes the leading cases on the right to counsel.

Notice what the Court *didn't* say in *Argersinger*: Poor people have a right to a lawyer paid for by the government in *all* criminal cases. Why? Because the Court was well aware of a practical problem: There isn't enough money to pay for everyone to have a lawyer. Of course, strictly speaking, constitutional rights can't depend on money; but as a practical matter, money definitely affects how many people get their rights in real life. We know many poor people who have a right to a lawyer don't get one because counties and other local governments simply don't have the money to pay for them. Why? Because taxpayers don't want their tax dollars spent on lawyers for "criminals."

This mix of practical reality and constitutional rights surfaced in *Scott v. Illinois* (1979). The Court specifically addressed the question of whether the right to assigned counsel extends to offenses where imprisonment is authorized but not required (**authorized imprisonment standard**) or that don't actually result in prison sentences (**actual imprisonment standard**). Aubrey Scott was convicted of shoplifting merchandise valued at less than $150. An Illinois statute set the maximum penalty at a $500 fine *or* one year in jail, or both. Scott argued that a line of Supreme Court cases, culminating in *Argersinger,* required state-paid counsel whenever imprisonment is an authorized penalty.

The U.S. Supreme Court rejected that argument. Instead, it agreed with the Supreme Court of Illinois, which was "not inclined to extend *Argersinger*" to a case in which the defendant wasn't facing jail time. The statutory offense that Scott was charged with authorized imprisonment upon conviction but courts didn't impose it. The Court held that "the Federal Constitution does not require a state trial court to appoint counsel for a criminal defendant such as [Scott]," who *could've* been, but wasn't actually, sentenced to do jail time (369).

In their dissent, Justices Brennan, Marshall, and Stevens argued that the concern for cost is "both irrelevant and speculative." According to the justices:

1. Constitutional guarantees can't depend on budgetary concerns.

2. Budgetary concerns discriminate against defendants who can't afford to pay.

3. Public defender systems can keep the costs of the authorized imprisonment standard down and won't "clog the courts with inexperienced appointed counsel."

4. The Court's "alarmist prophecies that an authorized imprisonment standard would wreak havoc on the States," are refuted by the reality that "the standard has not produced that result in the substantial number of States that already provide counsel in all cases where imprisonment is authorized—States that include a large majority of the country's population and a great diversity of urban and rural environments. (384–88)

The Standard of Indigence

LO 6

The U.S. Supreme Court has never defined **indigence** (defendants who can't afford to hire a lawyer). However, U.S. Courts of Appeals have established some general guidelines on how to determine whether defendants are poor enough to qualify for a lawyer paid for by the government:

1. Poor defendants don't have to be completely destitute.

2. Earnings and assets count; help from friends and relatives doesn't.

3. Actual, not potential, earnings are the measure.

4. The state can tap defendants' future earnings to get reimbursement for the costs of counsel, transcripts, and fees for expert witnesses and investigators.

According to Rule 5.02 of the Minnesota Rules of Criminal Procedure (2010):

5.02 Appointment of Public Defender
Subd. 3. Standards for Public Defense Eligibility.

A defendant is financially unable to obtain counsel if:

(1) The defendant, or any dependent of the defendant who resides in the same household as the defendant, receives means-tested governmental benefits; or

(2) The defendant, through any combination of liquid assets and current income, would be unable to pay the reasonable costs charged by private counsel in that judicial district for a defense of a case of the nature at issue; or

(3) The defendant can demonstrate that due to insufficient funds or other assets: two members of a defense attorney referral list maintained by the court have refused to defend the case or, if no referral list is maintained, that two private attorneys in that judicial district have refused to defend the case.

The Right to the Counsel of Your Choice

LO 6

All defendants have the right to "effective counsel" to defend them (see "Right to 'Effective' Counsel"). Does this mean that defendants have the right to have the lawyers of their choice? Yes, said the U.S. Supreme Court in *U.S. v. Gonzalez-Lopez* (2006). Cuauhtemoc Gonzalez-Lopez hired Joseph Low to represent him on federal marijuana trafficking charge. Low is an experienced criminal defense lawyer, who has won several national awards for excellence in the courtroom. Low "prides himself on his aggressive approach to criminal defense work and has built his practice around fighting 'oppression by federal and state government'" (Fisher 2006, 2).

Low was just the kind of lawyer Gonzalez-Lopez wanted. He knew that Low recently had gotten another drug defendant a good plea bargain under the same judge as Gonzalez-Lopez's. He insisted he was innocent and wanted an aggressive lawyer to defend him (3). But the trial court judge denied Low's application to represent Gonzalez-Lopez on the ground that Low had violated a professional conduct rule. Then, he blocked Gonzalez-Lopez from meeting or consulting with Low throughout the trial. The jury found Gonzalez-Lopez guilty.

The Supreme Court (6–3) held that the trial court's refusal to allow Low to represent Gonzalez-Lopez deprived him of his constitutional right to counsel and entitled him to a new trial. According to the Court, "[T]he Sixth Amendment guarantees a defendant the right to be represented by an otherwise qualified attorney whom that defendant can afford to hire, or who is willing to represent the defendant even though he is without funds" (*U.S. v. Gonzalez-Lopez* 2006, 144).

Notice that only those who can afford to hire a lawyer can have a lawyer of their choice. That's about 10 percent of all criminal defendants; the remaining 90 percent have the right to effective counsel but not of their choosing.

The Right to "Effective" Counsel

LO 6

In 1932, the U.S. Supreme Court said due process requires not just counsel but *effective counsel*, but the Court didn't say much to clarify what "effective" means. So lower federal courts and state courts stepped in and adopted the **mockery of justice standard**. Under this standard, only lawyers whose behavior is so "shocking" that it turns the trial into a "joke" are constitutionally ineffective. One lawyer called it the "mirror test." (Put a mirror under the lawyer's nose; if it steams up he passes.) What prompted this professional criticism?

In actual cases, appellate courts ruled that lawyers who slept through trials; came to court drunk; couldn't name a single precedent related to the case they were arguing; or were released from jail to represent their clients hadn't turned the proceedings into a joke and met the mockery of justice standard. When one defendant claimed he got ineffective representation because his lawyer slept through the trial, the judge said, "You have a right to a lawyer; that doesn't mean you have a right to one who's awake." That decision was affirmed by the reviewing court.

Courts and commentators have criticized the mockery of justice standard for being too subjective, vague, and narrow. The standard's focus on the trial excludes many serious errors that lawyers make in preparing for trial. Furthermore, in the overwhelming majority of cases disposed of by guilty pleas, the standard is totally irrelevant.

Judge David Bazelon (1973), an experienced and respected federal judge, said the test requires "such a minimal level of performance from counsel that it is itself a mockery of the Sixth Amendment" (28). "I have often been told that if my court were to reverse in every case in which there was inadequate counsel, we would have to send back half the convictions in my jurisdiction" (22–23).

Courts resist getting involved in the touchy question of judging the performance of defense attorneys. Why? For one thing, too much interference can damage not only professional relationships but also the professional independence of defense lawyers and even the adversary system itself. Furthermore, judges who criticize defense lawyers are criticizing fellow professionals, lawyers who appear in their courts regularly.

Most jurisdictions have abandoned the mockery of justice standard, replacing it with the **reasonably competent attorney standard**. According to this standard, judges measure lawyers' performance against the "customary skills and diligence that a reasonably competent attorney would perform under similar circumstances." Attorneys have to be more diligent under the reasonably competent attorney standard than under the mockery of justice standard. Nevertheless, both the mockery of justice and the reasonably competent attorney standards are "vague to some appreciable degree and susceptible to greatly varying subjective impressions" (LaFave and Israel 1984, 2:99–102).

The U.S. Supreme Court tried to increase the clarity of the reasonably competent attorney test by announcing a **two-pronged effective counsel test** to evaluate the effectiveness of counsel. The test was announced in *Strickland v. Washington* (1984). In 1976, David Leroy Washington went on a 10-day crime spree that ended in three murders. After his lawyer, William Tunkey, was appointed, Washington confessed; he also pleaded guilty at his trial. Washington waived his right to an advisory jury to decide whether he should get the death penalty.

During the sentencing phase of the proceedings, Tunkey didn't present any character evidence, didn't present any medical or psychiatric evidence, and only cross-examined some of the state's witnesses. The judge sentenced Washington to death. Washington went through the state and then the federal courts claiming ineffectiveness of counsel. The U.S. Court of Appeals for the Eleventh Circuit ruled in his favor and the state appealed.

The U.S. Supreme Court reversed, applying its new two-pronged test of ineffective counsel. Under the first prong, called the **reasonableness prong**, defendants have to prove that their lawyer's performance wasn't reasonably competent, meaning that the lawyer was so deficient that she "was not functioning as the 'counsel' guaranteed the defendant by the Sixth Amendment."

Under the reasonableness prong, reviewing courts have to look at the totality of the facts and circumstances to decide whether the defense lawyer's performance was reasonably competent. Reviewing courts have to start with a presumption in favor of the defense lawyer's competence, meaning they have lots of leeway to make tactical and strategic decisions that fall within the wide range of available professional judgment. So as long as defense counsel's choices fall within that wide range, representation is presumed reasonable.

If the defendant proves his lawyer's performance was unreasonable, he still has to prove the second-prong of the test, called the **prejudice prong** of the reasonable competence test. Under the prejudice prong, defendants have to prove that their lawyer's incompetence was probably responsible for their conviction. In our next case, *Rompilla v. Beard* (2005), the U.S. Supreme Court (5–4), over a heated dissent, held that Ronald Rompilla's lawyers failed both prongs of the *Strickland* test and reversed his death sentence.

In Rompilla v. Beard *(2005), our next case excerpt, the U.S. Supreme Court held that Ronald Rompilla's right to effective counsel had been violated because his attorneys didn't meet the two-pronged effective counsel test.*

 **CASE** Was He Denied His Right to "Effective" Counsel?

Rompilla v. Beard
545 U.S. 374 (2005)

HISTORY

After his conviction for murder in the first degree, and imposition of the death penalty, and affirmance of a denial of petition for postconviction relief, Ronald Rompilla (defendant) filed a petition for a writ of habeas corpus. The District Court granted the petition; Jeffrey Beard, Pennsylvania Department of Corrections, appealed. The Court of Appeals for the Third Circuit reversed. The U.S. Supreme Court reversed.

SOUTER, J., joined by STEVENS, O'CONNOR, GINSBURG, and BREYER, JJ.

FACTS

On the morning of January 14, 1988, James Scanlon was discovered dead in a bar he ran in Allentown, Pennsylvania, his body having been stabbed repeatedly and set on fire. Ronald Rompilla was indicted for the murder and related offenses, and the Commonwealth gave notice of intent to ask for the death penalty. Two public defenders were assigned to the case.

The jury at the guilt phase of trial found Rompilla guilty on all counts, and during the ensuing penalty phase, the prosecutor sought to prove three aggravating factors to justify a death sentence: that the murder was committed in the course of another felony; that the murder was committed by torture; and that Rompilla had a significant history of felony convictions indicating the use or threat of violence. The Commonwealth presented evidence on all three aggravators, and the jury found all proven. Rompilla's evidence in mitigation consisted of relatively brief testimony: five of his family members argued in effect for residual doubt, and beseeched the jury for mercy, saying that they believed Rompilla was innocent and a good man. Rompilla's 14-year-old son testified that he loved his father and would visit him in prison. The jury acknowledged this evidence to the point of finding, as two factors in mitigation, that Rompilla's son had testified on his behalf and that rehabilitation was possible. But the jurors assigned the greater weight to the aggravating factors, and sentenced Rompilla to death. The

Supreme Court of Pennsylvania affirmed both conviction and sentence.

In December 1995, with new lawyers, Rompilla filed claims under the Pennsylvania Post Conviction Relief Act, including ineffective assistance by trial counsel in failing to present significant mitigating evidence about Rompilla's childhood, mental capacity and health, and alcoholism. The postconviction court found that trial counsel had done enough to investigate the possibilities of a mitigation case, and the Supreme Court of Pennsylvania affirmed the denial of relief.

Rompilla then petitioned for a writ of habeas corpus in Federal District Court, raising claims that included inadequate representation. The District Court found that the State Supreme Court had unreasonably applied *Strickland v. Washington* (1984), as to the penalty phase of the trial, and granted relief for ineffective assistance of counsel. The court found that in preparing the mitigation case the defense lawyers had failed to investigate "pretty obvious signs" that Rompilla had a troubled childhood and suffered from mental illness and alcoholism, and instead had relied unjustifiably on Rompilla's own description of an unexceptional background. A divided Third Circuit panel reversed. The Third Circuit denied rehearing en banc by a vote of 6 to 5. We granted certiorari, and now reverse.

OPINION

This is not a case in which defense counsel simply ignored their obligation to find mitigating evidence, and their workload as busy public defenders did not keep them from making a number of efforts, including interviews with Rompilla and some members of his family, and examinations of reports by three mental health experts who gave opinions at the guilt phase. None of the sources proved particularly helpful. Rompilla's own contributions to any mitigation case were minimal. Counsel found him uninterested in helping, as on their visit to his prison to go over a proposed mitigation strategy, when Rompilla told them he was "bored being here listening" and returned to his cell. To questions about childhood and schooling, his answers indicated they had been normal, save for quitting school in the ninth grade. There were times when Rompilla was even actively obstructive by sending counsel off on false leads.

The lawyers also spoke with five members of Rompilla's family (his former wife, two brothers, a sister-in-law, and his son), and counsel testified that they developed a good relationship with the family in the course of their representation. The state postconviction court found that counsel spoke to the relatives in a "detailed manner," attempting to unearth mitigating information, although the weight of this finding is qualified by the lawyers' concession that "the overwhelming response from the family was that they didn't really feel as though they knew him all that well since he had spent the majority of his adult years and some of his childhood years in custody."

Defense counsel also said that because the family was "coming from the position that [Rompilla] was innocent, they weren't looking for reasons for why he might have done this."

The third and final source tapped for mitigating material was the cadre of three mental health witnesses who were asked to look into Rompilla's mental state as of the time of the offense and his competency to stand trial. But their reports revealed "nothing useful" to Rompilla's case, and the lawyers consequently did not go to any other historical source that might have cast light on Rompilla's mental condition.

When new counsel entered the case to raise Rompilla's postconviction claims, however, they identified a number of likely avenues the trial lawyers could fruitfully have followed in building a mitigation case. School records are one example, which trial counsel never examined in spite of the professed unfamiliarity of the several family members with Rompilla's childhood, and despite counsel's knowledge that Rompilla left school after the ninth grade. Other examples are records of Rompilla's juvenile and adult incarcerations, which counsel did not consult, although they were aware of their client's criminal record. And while counsel knew from police reports provided in pretrial discovery that Rompilla had been drinking heavily at the time of his offense, and although one of the mental health experts reported that Rompilla's troubles with alcohol merited further investigation, counsel did not look for evidence of a history of dependence on alcohol that might have extenuating significance.

Trial counsel and the Commonwealth respond to these unexplored possibilities by emphasizing this Court's recognition that the duty to investigate does not force defense lawyers to scour the globe on the off chance something will turn up; reasonably diligent counsel may draw a line when they have good reason to think further investigation would be a waste. The Commonwealth argues that the information trial counsel gathered from Rompilla and the other sources gave them sound reason to think it would have been pointless to spend time and money on the additional investigation espoused by postconviction counsel, and we can say that there is room for debate about trial counsel's obligation to follow at least some of those potential lines of enquiry. There is no need to say more, however, for a further point is clear and dispositive: the lawyers were deficient in failing to examine the court file on Rompilla's prior conviction.

There is an obvious reason that the failure to examine Rompilla's prior conviction file fell below the level of reasonable performance. Counsel knew that the Commonwealth intended to seek the death penalty by proving Rompilla had a significant history of felony convictions indicating the use or threat of violence, an aggravator under state law. Counsel further knew that the Commonwealth would attempt to establish this history by proving Rompilla's prior conviction for rape and assault, and would emphasize his violent character by introducing a transcript of the rape victim's testimony given in that earlier trial. There is no question that defense counsel were on notice, since they acknowledge that a "plea letter," written by one of them four days prior to trial, mentioned the prosecutor's plans. It is also undisputed that the prior conviction file was a public document, readily available for the asking at the very courthouse where Rompilla was to be tried.

It is clear, however, that defense counsel did not look at any part of that file, including the transcript, until warned by the prosecution a second time. In a colloquy the day before the evidentiary sentencing phase began, the prosecutor again said he would present the transcript of the victim's testimony to establish the prior conviction.

At the postconviction evidentiary hearing, Rompilla's lawyer confirmed that she had not seen the transcript before the hearing in which this exchange took place, and crucially, even after obtaining the transcript of the victim's testimony on the eve of the sentencing hearing, counsel apparently examined none of the other material in the file.

With every effort to view the facts as a defense lawyer would have done at the time, it is difficult to see how counsel could have failed to realize that without examining the readily available file they were seriously compromising their opportunity to respond to a case for aggravation. The prosecution was going to use the dramatic facts of a similar prior offense, and Rompilla's counsel had a duty to make all reasonable efforts to learn what they could about the offense. Reasonable efforts certainly included obtaining the Commonwealth's own readily available file on the prior conviction to learn what the Commonwealth knew about the crime, to discover any mitigating evidence the Commonwealth would downplay, and to anticipate the details of the aggravating evidence the Commonwealth would emphasize.

Without making reasonable efforts to review the file, defense counsel could have had no hope of knowing whether the prosecution was quoting selectively from the transcript, or whether there were circumstances extenuating the behavior described by the victim. The obligation to get the file was particularly pressing here owing to the similarity of the violent prior offense to the crime charged and Rompilla's sentencing strategy stressing residual doubt. Without making efforts to learn the details and rebut the relevance of the earlier crime, a convincing argument for residual doubt was certainly beyond any hope.

The notion that defense counsel must obtain information that the State has and will use against the defendant is not simply a matter of common sense. The American Bar Association Guidelines relating to death penalty defense are explicit:

> Counsel must investigate prior convictions . . . that could be used as aggravating circumstances or otherwise come into evidence. If a prior conviction is

legally flawed, counsel should seek to have it set aside. Counsel may also find extenuating circumstances that can be offered to lessen the weight of a conviction." ABA Guidelines for the Appointment and Performance of Defense Counsel in Death Penalty Cases 10.7, comment.

It flouts prudence to deny that a defense lawyer should try to look at a file he knows the prosecution will cull for aggravating evidence, let alone when the file is sitting in the trial courthouse, open for the asking. No reasonable lawyer would forgo examination of the file thinking he could do as well by asking the defendant or family relations whether they recalled anything helpful or damaging in the prior victim's testimony. Nor would a reasonable lawyer compare possible searches for school reports, juvenile records, and evidence of drinking habits to the opportunity to take a look at a file disclosing what the prosecutor knows and even plans to read from in his case. Questioning a few more family members and searching for old records can promise less than looking for a needle in a haystack, when a lawyer truly has reason to doubt there is any needle there. But looking at a file the prosecution says it will use is a sure bet: whatever may be in that file is going to tell defense counsel something about what the prosecution can produce.

Since counsel's failure to look at the file fell below the line of reasonable practice, there is a further question about prejudice, that is, whether there is a reasonable probability that, but for counsel's unprofessional errors, the result of the proceeding would have been different. Because the state courts found the representation adequate, they never reached the issue of prejudice, and so we examine this element of the *Strickland* claim. We think Rompilla has shown beyond any doubt that counsel's lapse was prejudicial.

If the defense lawyers had looked in the file on Rompilla's prior conviction, it is uncontested they would have found a range of mitigation leads that no other source had opened up. In the same file with the transcript of the prior trial were the records of Rompilla's imprisonment on the earlier conviction, which defense counsel testified she had never seen. The prison files pictured Rompilla's childhood and mental health very differently from anything defense counsel had seen or heard. An evaluation by a corrections counselor states that Rompilla was "reared in the slum environment of Allentown, Pa. vicinity. He early came to the attention of juvenile authorities, quit school at 16, and started a series of incarcerations in and out Penna. often of assaultive nature and commonly related to overindulgence in alcoholic beverages. The same file discloses test results that the defense's mental health experts would have viewed as pointing to schizophrenia and other disorders, and test scores showing a third grade level of cognition after nine years of schooling.

The accumulated entries would have destroyed the benign conception of Rompilla's upbringing and mental capacity defense counsel had formed from talking with Rompilla himself and some of his family members, and from the reports of the mental health experts. With this information, counsel would have become skeptical of the impression given by the five family members and would unquestionably have gone further to build a mitigation case. Further effort would presumably have unearthed much of the material postconviction counsel found, including testimony from several members of Rompilla's family, whom trial counsel did not interview. Judge Sloviter summarized this evidence:

> Rompilla's parents were both severe alcoholics who drank constantly. His mother drank during her pregnancy with Rompilla, and he and his brothers eventually developed serious drinking problems. His father, who had a vicious temper, frequently beat Rompilla's mother, leaving her bruised and black-eyed, and bragged about his cheating on her. His parents fought violently, and on at least one occasion his mother stabbed his father. He was abused by his father who beat him when he was young with his hands, fists, leather straps, belts and sticks. All of the children lived in terror. There were no expressions of parental love, affection or approval. Instead, he was subjected to yelling and verbal abuse. His father locked Rompilla and his brother Richard in a small wire mesh dog pen that was filthy and excrement filled. He had an isolated background, and was not allowed to visit other children or to speak to anyone on the phone. They had no indoor plumbing in the house, he slept in the attic with no heat, and the children were not given clothes and attended school in rags.

The jury never heard any of this and neither did the mental health experts who examined Rompilla before trial. While they found "nothing helpful to Rompilla's case," their postconviction counterparts, alerted by information from school, medical, and prison records that trial counsel never saw, found plenty of "red flags" pointing up a need to test further. When they tested, they found that Rompilla "suffers from organic brain damage, an extreme mental disturbance significantly impairing several of his cognitive functions." They also said that "Rompilla's problems relate back to his childhood, and were likely caused by fetal alcohol syndrome and that Rompilla's capacity to appreciate the criminality of his conduct or to conform his conduct to the law was substantially impaired at the time of the offense."

These findings in turn would probably have prompted a look at school and juvenile records, all of them easy to get, showing, for example, that when Rompilla was 16 his mother "was missing from home frequently for a period of one or several weeks at a time." The same report noted that his mother "has been reported frequently under the influence of alcoholic beverages, with the result that the

children have always been poorly kept and on the filthy side which was also the condition of the home at all times." School records showed Rompilla's IQ was in the mentally retarded range.

This evidence adds up to a mitigation case that bears no relation to the few naked pleas for mercy actually put before the jury, and although we suppose it is possible that a jury could have heard it all and still have decided on the death penalty, that is not the test. It goes without saying that the undiscovered mitigating evidence, taken as a whole, might well have influenced the jury's appraisal of Rompilla's culpability, and the likelihood of a different result if the evidence had gone in is sufficient to undermine confidence in the outcome actually reached at sentencing (*Strickland* 694).

The judgment of the Third Circuit is REVERSED, and Pennsylvania must either retry the case on penalty or stipulate to a life sentence.

It is so ordered.

DISSENT

KENNEDY, J., joined by REHNQUIST, C.J., and SCALIA and THOMAS, JJ.

Today the Court brands two committed criminal defense attorneys as ineffective—"outside the wide range of professionally competent assistance," *Strickland v. Washington* (1984)—because they did not look in an old case file and stumble upon something they had not set out to find. To reach this result, the majority imposes on defense counsel a rigid requirement to review all documents in what it calls the "case file" of any prior conviction that the prosecution might rely on at trial. In order to grant Rompilla habeas relief the Court must say, and indeed does say, that the Pennsylvania Supreme Court was objectively unreasonable in failing to anticipate today's new case file rule.

In my respectful submission it is this Court, not the state court, which is unreasonable. The majority's holding has no place in our Sixth Amendment jurisprudence and, if followed, often will result in less effective counsel by diverting limited defense resources from other important tasks in order to satisfy the Court's new *per se* rule. Under any standard of review the investigation performed by Rompilla's counsel in preparation for sentencing was not only adequate but also conscientious. Rompilla's attorneys recognized from the outset that building an effective mitigation case was crucial to helping their client avoid the death penalty. Rompilla stood accused of a brutal crime. In January 1988, James Scanlon was murdered while he was closing the Cozy Corner Cafe, a bar he owned in Allentown, Pennsylvania. Scanlon's body was discovered later the next morning, lying in a pool of blood. Scanlon had been stabbed multiple times, including 16 wounds around the neck and head. Scanlon also had been beaten with a blunt object, and his face had been gashed, possibly with shards from broken liquor and beer bottles found at the scene of the crime. After Scanlon was stabbed to death his body had been set on fire.

A *per se* rule requiring counsel in every case to review the records of prior convictions used by the State as aggravation evidence is a radical departure from *Strickland*. We have warned against the creation of specific guidelines or checklists for judicial evaluation of attorney performance. No particular set of detailed rules for counsel's conduct can satisfactorily take account of the variety of circumstances faced by defense counsel or the range of legitimate decisions regarding how best to represent a criminal defendant. Any such set of rules would interfere with the constitutionally protected independence of counsel and restrict the wide latitude counsel must have in making tactical decisions. Indeed, the existence of detailed guidelines for representation could distract counsel from the overriding mission of vigorous advocacy of the defendant's cause.

The majority disregards the sound strategic calculation supporting the decisions made by Rompilla's attorneys. Charles and Dantos were aware of [Rompilla's] priors and aware of the circumstances surrounding these convictions. At the postconviction hearing, Dantos also indicated that she had reviewed documents relating to the prior conviction. Based on this information, as well as their numerous conversations with Rompilla and his family, Charles and Dantos reasonably could conclude that reviewing the full prior conviction case file was not the best allocation of resources.

Perhaps the circumstances to which the majority refers are the details of Rompilla's 1974 crimes. Rompilla had been convicted of breaking into the residence of Josephine Macrenna, who lived in an apartment above the bar she owned. After Macrenna gave him the bar's receipts for the night, Rompilla demanded that she disrobe. When she initially resisted, Rompilla slashed her left breast with a knife. Rompilla then held Macrenna at knifepoint while he raped her for over an hour. Charles and Dantos were aware of these circumstances of the prior conviction and the brutality of the crime. It did not take a review of the case file to know that quibbling with the Commonwealth's version of events was a dubious trial strategy. Rompilla was unlikely to endear himself to the jury by arguing that his prior conviction for burglary, theft, and rape really was not as bad as the Commonwealth was making it out to be. Recognizing this, Rompilla's attorneys instead devoted their limited time and resources to developing a mitigation case. That those efforts turned up little useful evidence does not make the ex ante strategic calculation of Rompilla's attorneys constitutionally deficient.

Today's decision will not increase the resources committed to capital defense. (At the time of Rompilla's trial, the Lehigh County Public Defender's Office had two investigators for 2,000 cases.) If defense attorneys dutifully comply with the Court's new rule, they will have to divert resources from other tasks. The net effect of today's holding in many cases—instances where trial counsel reasonably can conclude that reviewing old case files is not an effective use of time—will be to diminish the quality of representation. We have consistently declined to impose mechanical rules on counsel—even when those rules might lead to better representation; I see no occasion to depart from this approach in order to impose a requirement that might well lead to worse representation.

It is quite possible defense attorneys, recognizing the absurdity of a one-size-fits-all approach to effective advocacy, will simply ignore the Court's new requirement and continue to exercise their best judgment about how to allocate time and resources in preparation for trial. While this decision would be understandable—and might even be required by state ethical rules—it leaves open the possibility that a defendant will seek to overturn his conviction based on something in a prior conviction case file that went unreviewed. This elevation of needle-in-a-haystack claims to the status of constitutional violations will benefit undeserving defendants and saddle States with the considerable costs of retrial and/or resentencing.

QUESTIONS

1. Identify and state the two prongs of the *Strickland* "effective assistance of counsel" standard.
2. List the relevant actions defense counsel took, or failed to take, to defend Rompilla at the conviction and sentencing phases of his trial.
3. Summarize the majority's arguments supporting its decision that Pennsylvania deprived Rompilla of the right to the effective assistance of counsel.
4. Summarize the dissent's arguments supporting its conclusion that Rompilla's lawyers passed both prongs of the *Strickland* test.
5. Can you explain why the majority omitted, and the dissent reported, the gory details of the murder and the rape Rompilla was convicted of?
6. Do you agree more with the majority or the dissent? Back up your answer with details from the facts and opinions in the case.
7. Just as the jury was about to be selected in Rompilla's retrial, on August 13, 2007, the Lehigh County, Pennsylvania, County Attorney announced a plea agreement: Rompilla pleaded guilty in exchange for life in prison without the chance of parole. They spent "millions" on Rompilla's case (Associated Press 2007.) Is this a "fair" conclusion to the case?

ETHICAL ISSUES

Is It Ethical to Allow Prosecutors to Appoint Their Opposing Defense Lawyers?

When the state of Georgia ran out of money to pay the lawyers for a man facing the death penalty, the prosecutor, of all people, had an idea. He asked the judge to appoint two over-worked public defenders instead, identifying them by name.

The judge went along. The Georgia Supreme Court, by a 4-to-3 vote, *endorsed* the arrangement in March, saying the defendant, Jamie R. Weis, should have accepted the new lawyers to help solve the state's budget impasse.

The adversary system does not ordinarily let prosecutors pick their opponents. Indeed, most states do not allow established relationships between lawyers and their clients to be interrupted for any but the most exceptional reasons.

Two states, Georgia and Louisiana, take a less sporting attitude, saying poor defendants may be forced to switch lawyers long after the case is under way and must take whomever the state can afford at the time.

The Georgia case is now before the Supreme Court, which will soon decide whether to hear it. . . .

INSTRUCTIONS

1. Visit the Companion Website and read Adam Liptak's "Defendants Squeezed by Georgia's Tight Budget." See the link under the Chapter 12 Ethical Issues section—login at www.cengagebrain.com.

2. Watch Stephen Bright argue Jamie Weis's case (*Weis v. State*) to the Georgia Supreme Court.

3. Write a report that includes:

   a. A list of Liptak's main points

   b. Stephen Bright's arguments to the court

   c. The justices' points made during Bright's argument

   d. Your conclusions about the ethics involved, even if the budget-saving policy is legal

Source: Adam Liptak 2010.

Testing the Government's Case

After the decision to charge, the action moves from the prosecutor's office into court. At this point, decisions inside the courtroom are based more on formal rules than informal discretion. These rules govern the pretrial proceedings to test the government's case and hear motions. Testing the government's case means deciding whether there's enough evidence to go to trial. Still more complex rules control the centerpiece of formal criminal justice, the criminal trial.

But don't be deceived by these public formal proceedings. Discretionary decision making hasn't disappeared; it has just moved out of the courtroom and into the

TABLE 12.3

Contrasts between the Preliminary Hearing and Grand Jury Review

Preliminary Hearing	Grand Jury Review
Held in public	Secret proceeding
Adversarial hearing	Only the government's case is presented
Judge presides	Prosecutor presides
Judge determines the facts	Grand jurors decide the facts
Defendants and their lawyers may attend	Neither defendants nor their lawyers may attend

corridors in and around the courthouse. Here's where plea bargaining takes place—or, where defendants decide they just want to plead guilty without bargaining, hoping to get a lighter sentence by admitting their guilt and saving the court and lawyers time (Chapter 13). In these cases (the vast majority by all counts), courtroom proceedings only ratify what was worked out by informal negotiations.

We saw earlier that the decision to charge (p. 392) demonstrates the government's commitment to criminal prosecution and that the first appearance (p. 398) prepares defendants for the consequences of this decision. But the government's commitment and the first appearance aren't enough by themselves to start a criminal trial.

First, one of two procedures has to test the strength of the government's case against the defendant. There are good reasons for this test. According to the Seventh Circuit U.S. Court of Appeals in *U.S. v. Udziela* (1982):

> While in theory a trial provides a defendant with a full opportunity to contest and disprove charges against him, in practice, the handing up of an indictment will often have a devastating personal and professional impact that a later dismissal or acquittal can never undo. (1001)

Two procedures test the government's case against defendants: (1) **preliminary hearings** and (2) **grand jury review**. A preliminary hearing is an adversarial proceeding that tests the government's case; a grand jury review is a secret proceeding to test the government's case.

When prosecutors draw up a **criminal information** (a written formal charge made by prosecutors without a grand jury indictment), they test their case at a preliminary hearing before a judge. When they seek an **indictment**, they test the government's case by presenting it to a grand jury for grand jury review. If the government passes the test of the grand jury review, the grand jury returns the indictment as a **true bill**, which records the number of **grand jurors** (citizens selected to serve a term) voting for indictment. If the government passes the test in the preliminary hearing, the judge **binds over** the defendant; that is, he sends the case on for trial.

Both preliminary hearings and grand jury review test the government's case, but they differ in several important respects (see Table 12.3). Preliminary hearings are public; grand jury proceedings are secret. Preliminary hearings are adversarial proceedings, in which the defense can challenge the prosecution's case; grand juries hear only the prosecution's case without the defense's participation. Judges preside over preliminary hearings; prosecutors manage grand jury proceedings without judicial participation. In preliminary hearings, magistrates determine whether there's enough evidence to go to trial; grand jury review relies on grand jurors selected to decide whether there's enough evidence. Finally, defendants and their lawyers attend preliminary hearings; defendants and their lawyers are banned from grand jury review (ex parte proceedings).

The differences between preliminary hearings and grand jury proceedings reflect different values in the criminal process. The preliminary hearing stresses adversarial, open, accusatory values and control by experts. Grand jury review, on the other hand, underscores the value of the democratic dimension of the criminal process: lay participation in criminal proceedings. But their goal is the same: deciding whether there's enough evidence to bring defendants to trial.

The Preliminary Hearing

LO 7

Preliminary hearings are held after the first appearance. In most states, all judges are authorized to conduct preliminary hearings, but, in practice, they're conducted by magistrates, justices of the peace, municipal court judges, or other members of the lower court judiciary. There's no constitutional right to a preliminary hearing. But if states do provide for preliminary hearings, the Sixth Amendment guarantees defendants the right to have a lawyer represent them at the hearing (*Gerstein v. Pugh* 1975).

Preliminary hearings are adversarial proceedings. The prosecution presents evidence, and then the defense can challenge it and even present its own evidence. Preliminary hearings are also public. This may sound like a trial, but it's not.

First, the rigid rules of evidence followed during trials are relaxed during preliminary hearings. In some states, preliminary hearing judges even admit illegally seized evidence and hearsay (LaFave and Israel 1984, 2:263–64). Prosecutors reveal only enough of the state's evidence (for example, a witness or two and minimal physical evidence) to satisfy the **bind-over standard** (there's enough evidence for the judge to decide to go to trial). Why? Because it takes time and, probably more important, prosecutors don't want to give away any more of their case than they have to. The defense typically introduces no evidence, because they don't want to give away their case either; instead, defense attorneys limit their participation to cross-examining the state's witnesses.

The objective basis for going to trial is probable cause, but don't confuse this with probable cause to arrest (Chapter 5). Most courts hold that it takes more **probable cause to bind over** someone for trial than it does to arrest the person. Why? Because the consequences of going to trial are graver. Defendants are detained longer, and the ordeals of criminal prosecution, conviction, and punishment are greater. Even if they aren't convicted, defendants have to pay their lawyers; suffer the stigma of prosecution; and subject their families to hardships. As one prominent exonerated defendant asked, "How do I get my reputation back?" The consequences fall not only on defendants but also on the government. The state has to spend scarce resources to prove guilt, and that takes away resources for other services, such as education and road repairs.

The *bind-over standard* reflects the idea that the greater the invasions and deprivations against individuals, the more facts that are needed to back them up. Just how many facts does it take to move a case to trial? Some courts have adopted a **prima facie case rule**. According to this standard, the judge can bind over a defendant if the prosecution presents evidence that could convict if the defense doesn't rebut it at trial. Others have adopted a **directed verdict rule**. According to this rule, preliminary hearing judges should look at the case as if it's a trial and they're deciding whether there's enough believable evidence to send the case to the jury. If there isn't enough, then the judge should dismiss the case. The minimum amount of evidence required to bind over under the directed verdict rule is more than enough to add up to probable cause to arrest but less than enough to "prove the defendant's guilt beyond a reasonable doubt" (*Myers v. Commonwealth* 1973, 824).

Grand Jury Review

LO 7

Grand jury review is ancient. Originating in medieval England as a council of local residents that helped the king look into matters of royal concern (crime, revenues, and official misconduct), the grand jury was an investigating body. However, by the time of the American Revolution, the grand jury had another duty: it screened criminal cases to protect individuals from malicious and unfounded prosecution. So the grand jury had two functions: to act as a sword to root out crime and corruption and as a shield to protect innocent people from unwarranted state intrusion.

Colonists warmly approved of the grand jury shield function, because it "shielded" them from prosecution for their antiroyalist sentiments. For that reason, the Fifth Amendment to the U.S. Constitution provides that "no person shall be held to answer for a capital, or otherwise infamous crime, unless on a presentment or indictment by a Grand Jury." But grand jury indictment is one of the very few provisions in the Bill of Rights that doesn't apply to state court proceedings under the incorporation doctrine (Chapter 2).

THE OTHER CRIMINAL PROCEDURE # White Collar Crime

The Grand Jury and White Collar Crime

Most criminal investigations are conducted without any resort to subpoenaed witnesses or evidence. In most jurisdictions, police investigations are conducted without the benefit of the subpoena power, and in many kinds of cases, the absence of that authority does not significantly impair the effectiveness of the investigation. Ordinarily, investigations of so-called "street crimes" such as murder, rape, robbery, and assault can be conducted effectively without resort to the subpoena power. The victims in such cases are often eager to help the investigators, witnesses are generally willing to volunteer their statements, and physical evidence can be obtained on the scene of the crime or in the course of the subsequent police investigation.

The situation is otherwise with more complex offenses, particularly so-called "white collar" crimes. In many of these cases, such as bribery or financial fraud, there is either no identifiable "victim," or the "victims" are unable to give much useful information about the offense. The "witnesses" to the offense are often participants in the crime and will not willingly come forward to tell what they know. Instead, the only way to obtain the cooperation of those witnesses may be by compelling them to testify by the issuance of a subpoena and perhaps a grant of immunity from prosecution. In addition, the physical evidence that is needed for the prosecution, such as documents revealing the details of the unlawful transactions, is often in the possession of the suspects themselves. The prosecution may not be able to obtain a warrant to search for and seize that evidence because of a lack of probable cause or an inability to describe the evidence with sufficient specificity. In that event, the only way to obtain the needed evidence may be by compelling its production through a **subpoena** *duces tecum* (an order to produce documents).

Source: S. S. Beale, W. C. Bryson, E. Felman, and M. J. Elston. 2004. *Grand Jury Law and Practice.* Eagen, MN: West, 6-3–6-4.

WHAT DO *YOU* THINK?

1. Are the authors correct about police investigations? Are victims and witnesses so willing and eager to help the police?

2. If not, then is the grand jury really more important in white collar crime than in "street crime"?

Grand juries vary from state to state both in their membership and in the procedures they follow. Let's look at grand jury membership, grand jury proceedings, and the debate over grand juries.

The Members of the Grand Jury

We'll use as an example of choosing grand jury members the operation of the federal grand jury in the Southern District of New York, a jurisdiction that includes Manhattan, the Bronx, and several New York counties as far north as Albany (Frankel and Naftalis 1977, Chapter 4).

Federal grand juries consist of 16 to 23 jurors. To qualify, prospective grand jurors have to

1. Be U.S. citizens

2. Be 18 or over

3. Reside in the jurisdiction

4. Have no felony convictions

5. Speak, write, and read English

6. Suffer from no physical impairments that might hamper their participation, such as impaired hearing or vision

The jurisdiction sometimes summons nearly two hundred citizens for jury service—many more than are needed. The process of narrowing down the number of potential jurors and selecting the final 16 to 23 is called "purging" the grand jury. The process does eliminate prospective grand jurors with compelling reasons not to serve—business, family, and health obligations—but it often hinders the selection of a representative grand jury. The resulting composition of federal grand juries overrepresents retired persons and those not burdened with other responsibilities.

Grand Jury Proceedings

After swearing in the grand jurors, judges **charge the grand jury**. Some charges are calls to action against specific dangers. Others resemble stump speeches for law and order or constitutional rights. Almost all include a history and outline of grand jury duties and responsibilities, warnings about the secrecy of grand jury proceedings, and admonitions to protect the innocent and condemn the guilty. Following the charge, judges turn grand jurors over to prosecutors to conduct grand jury proceedings. Unlike preliminary hearings, grand jury proceedings don't require a judge's participation.

Grand jury secrecy severely restricts who's allowed to attend proceedings. In addition to the grand jurors themselves, only the prosecutor, witnesses called to testify, and stenographers appear in the grand jury room. Defendants are banned. So are witnesses' attorneys, even though these witnesses are often themselves grand jury *targets* (individuals who themselves are under suspicion and investigation). But witnesses may (and often do) bring their lawyers to the courthouse for consultation outside the grand jury room.

After all witnesses have testified and prosecutors have introduced any other evidence, prosecutors draw up an indictment and present it to the grand jury for consideration. Prosecutors then sum up the reasons the evidence amounts to a crime and leave during grand jury deliberations, which ordinarily take only a few minutes. Grand juries rarely disagree with prosecutors' recommendations. Forepersons sign both the indictment and the true bill, which records the number of jurors who voted to indict. Federal grand jury proceedings require 12 jurors' concurrence to indict.

The entire grand jury, accompanied by the prosecutor, then proceeds to a designated courtroom to hand up the indictment, an action that amounts to the formal filing of charges, requiring defendants to answer in court. After judges check to ensure all documents are in order, they accept the indictment, which becomes a matter of public record. They also accept the true bill, but it doesn't become a public record. The judges' acceptance initiates the criminal prosecution by indictment.

The Debate over the Grand Jury

Since the 16th century, observers have found a lot to criticize about the grand jury. The Elizabethan justice of the peace William Lambarde's charges to the Kent grand juries have preserved these early criticisms (Read 1962). Justice Lambarde praised the grand juries' capacity to aid in law enforcement but scorned their conduct in carrying out their responsibilities. Mainly, Lambarde attacked their sword function, berating them for being too timid in rooting out crimes. But he also criticized their shield function, too, attacking their weakness in screening cases.

In modern times, the debate has focused almost entirely on the grand jury's screening function. From the early 1900s, confidence in science and experts led many reformers to call for banning nonexperts from participating in criminal justice decision making. Those at the extreme wanted to abolish grand and trial juries and replace them with panels of "trained experts" to weigh evidence. However, two prestigious presidential commissions, the Wickersham Commission, appointed by President Herbert Hoover, and the National Advisory Commission, appointed by President Richard Nixon, were more in the mainstream. Both urged the abolition only of mandatory grand jury review.

Since the early 1980s, most legal commentators have condemned the grand jury. Critics make several arguments against grand jury screening. One line of attack is that grand juries are prosecutors' rubber stamps. According to one former prosecutor, a prosecutor "can indict anybody, at any time, for almost anything before a grand jury." Statistics bear out this claim. Grand juries issue *no-bills* (refusals to indict) in only a tiny percentage of cases. Even the no-bills don't necessarily show grand jury independence.

In sensitive or controversial cases, prosecutors choose grand jury review over preliminary hearings to put the burden for deciding whether or not to charge on the grand jury (LaFave and Israel 1984, 2:282–83). Critics also condemn the nonadversarial nature of grand jury review, charging it prevents either screening cases effectively or protecting citizens adequately against unwarranted prosecutions. Also, the secrecy of grand jury proceedings creates doubts and suspicion. That defendants and their lawyers can't attend grand jury sessions provides further ammunition for critics' charges that this exclusion is both unfair and results in inadequate screening. Critics also argue grand jury review is inefficient, expensive, and time-consuming.

Impaneling and servicing a grand jury is costly in terms of space, human resources, and money. The members have to be selected, notified, sworn, housed, fed, and provided other services. Finally, grand jury screening takes more time than preliminary hearings. The law surrounding grand jury proceedings is complex and technical, creating delays in the proceedings themselves and, later, in successful challenges to grand jury proceedings. In several jurisdictions, the intricacies and complexities of impaneling a grand jury guarantee attack by a skilled defense attorney and frequently result in dismissal of charges for minor discrepancies in the impaneling procedure.

On the other side, supporters of grand jury review have their arguments, too. First, they maintain grand juries cost no more than preliminary hearings. Preliminary hearings, they charge, have turned into needless "minitrials," elaborate affairs to which lawyers, judges, other court personnel, and witnesses devote a great deal of court time. Furthermore, the number of requests that defense attorneys make for continuances leads to a greater delay in, and a better chance of successful challenges to, preliminary hearings than grand jury proceedings.

Grand jury supporters also reject the contention that the grand jury doesn't effectively screen cases. They cite prosecutors who believe that grand juries are valuable sounding boards and argue that grand jurors definitely have minds of their own. The high percentage of indictments grand juries return isn't the important figure, according to supporters. Rather, the percentage of convictions—as high as 98 percent—based on indictments demonstrates that grand juries effectively screen out cases that shouldn't go to trial (Younger 1963).

Finally, grand jury review shows democracy at work. Supporters maintain that what grand jury review loses in secret and nonadversarial proceedings it more than recaptures in community participation in screening criminal cases. Citizen participation enhances public confidence in the criminal justice system. In a system where most cases don't go to trial, grand jury proceedings provide private citizens with their only opportunity to participate actively on the "front lines" of the criminal process. But, in fact, grand jurors aren't as representative of the community as trial jurors—who aren't all that representative either. Grand jury duty spans a long period of time, usually a year, and requires service at least two or three days a week. Only citizens with a lot of free time can devote such extended service in the criminal process (Graham and Letwin 1971, 681).

||||||||||||||||||||||||||||||||||||||||||||||||||||||||||||||||||||||||||||||||||||||||||||||||||||||||||||||||||||||

Arraignment

LO 2

If defendants are indicted or bound over, the next step in the criminal process is arraignment. *Arraignment* means to bring defendants to court to hear and to answer (plead to) the charges against them. Don't confuse arraignment with the first appearance. The first appearance takes place within days of the arrest, and defendants don't have to answer the charges; arraignment happens sometimes months after the arrest, and defendants have to answer something.

There are four possible pleas (answers) to the charges:

1. Not guilty
2. Not guilty by reason of insanity
3. Nolo contendere
4. Guilty (Chapter 13)

Nolo contendere is Latin for defendants who plead "no contest," meaning they don't contest the issue of guilt or innocence. There's no right to plead nolo contendere; the court has to consent to it. Why do defendants plead nolo contendere? Because it might help them in civil lawsuits, a complicated matter we don't need to explore in a criminal procedure course. Also, if a defendant pleads guilty, the court has to decide whether the plea is knowing and voluntary.

||||||||||||||||||||||||||||||||||||||||||||||||||||||||||||||||||||||||||||||||||||||||||||||||||||||||||||||||||||||||||||||||||||||

Pretrial Motions

LO 8, LO 9

Pretrial motions are written or oral requests asking the court to decide questions that don't require a trial to be ruled on. They're an important part of both prosecutors' and defense counsel's work. They definitely spend a lot more time on "motion practice" than they spend trying cases—and probably more time than they do on plea bargaining.

Let's look briefly at the main pretrial motions:

1. Double jeopardy
2. Speedy trial
3. Change of venue
4. Suppression of evidence

Double Jeopardy

LO 8

The Fifth Amendment to the U.S. Constitution guarantees that, "No person . . . shall . . . be subject for the same offence to be twice put in jeopardy of life or limb; . . ." Although the words "life or limb" suggest only death and corporal punishment, this guarantee against double jeopardy applies to all crimes, including decisions in juvenile proceedings.

The ban on **double jeopardy** protects several interests both of the state and defendants (Table 12.4). It's supposed to allow the government "one fair shot" at convicting criminals. At the same time, it bans the government's use of its greater share of power and resources to subject less-powerful citizens accused of crimes to repeated attempts to convict them. Furthermore, it protects individuals from the embarrassment, expense, and ordeal—and the anxiety and insecurity—that repeated prosecutions generate.

Defendants also have an interest in completing their trials under one tribunal and jury. In addition, both the state and defendants have an interest in the finality and integrity of judgments that aren't susceptible to repeated reconsideration. Finally, the prohibition against double jeopardy reduces costs both to defendants and to the state. Retrials consume time and impede the efficient and economical disposition of other cases on crowded criminal court calendars.

The Fifth Amendment prohibition against double jeopardy kicks in as soon as the state "puts defendants to trial." In jury trials, this happens when the jury is impaneled

TABLE 12.4

Interests Protected by a Ban on Double Jeopardy

Interest	State	Defendant
Allows one fair shot at convicting defendants	Yes	
Limits the government's advantage of greater resources		Yes
Reduces prolonged stress that multiple trials would lead to		Yes
Promotes finality (closure) in criminal cases	Yes	Yes
Reduces the costs that multiple trials would lead to	Yes	Yes

and sworn in. The U.S. Supreme Court referred to the history of this definition of jury trials in *Crist v. Bretz* (1978), when it struck down Montana's rule that, despite swearing in the jury, jeopardy didn't attach until the first witness started testifying. The reason that jeopardy attaches when the jury is impaneled and sworn in is to

> protect the interest of an accused in retaining a chosen jury, an interest with roots deep in the historic development of trial by jury in the Anglo-American system of criminal justice. Throughout that history there ran a strong tradition that once banded together a jury should not be discharged until it had completed its solemn task of announcing a verdict. (36)

In **bench trials**—trials without juries, in which judges find the facts—jeopardy kicks in when the court begins to hear evidence. Why? Because until the court begins to hear evidence, the trial hasn't started. The point when jeopardy kicks in, or attaches, has been called the "linchpin" of the double jeopardy inquiry, but the Fifth Amendment prohibits only double jeopardy. So the attachment of jeopardy is necessary but not enough to kick in double jeopardy; it's only enough when defendants are exposed to double jeopardy.

What actions are protected by the ban on double jeopardy? According to the U.S. Supreme Court, the double jeopardy prohibition bans these three actions:

1. A second prosecution for the same offense after conviction
2. A second prosecution for the same offense after acquittal
3. Multiple punishments for the same offense

In cases in which jeopardy has kicked in but the proceedings end before conviction or acquittal, the double jeopardy clause doesn't prevent a second prosecution for the same offense. This can happen in two types of cases. First, if the defendant moves to dismiss the case (or asks for or accepts a mistrial), and the judge rules in the defendant's favor, the prosecution can reprosecute. Second, the government can reprosecute for the same offense if the judge dismissed the case or ordered a mistrial because dismissal "serves the ends of justice" (**manifest necessity doctrine**).

The classic example of manifest necessity is the **hung jury**—a jury unable to reach a verdict. Why? According to the U.S. Supreme Court (*U.S. v. Perez* 1824):

> We think that in cases of this nature, the law has invested Courts of justice with the authority to discharge a jury from giving any verdict, whenever, in their opinion, taking all the circumstances into consideration, there is a manifest necessity for the act, or the ends of public justice would otherwise be defeated. They are to exercise a sound discretion on the subject; and it is impossible to define all the

circumstances, which would render it proper to interfere. To be sure, the power ought to be used with the greatest of caution, under urgent circumstances. (580)

The U.S. Supreme Court revisited the hung jury question in *Renico v. Lett* (2010), our next case excerpt. After a jury trial that lasted nine hours from jury selection to jury instructions plus four hours of deliberation, the jury foreperson told the judge that the jury wasn't able to reach a verdict. The judge immediately declared a mistrial, dismissed the jury, and scheduled a new trial. At the second trial, the jury reached a verdict after three hours. On appeal, Lett argued that the second trial violated his right against double jeopardy because the trial judge had declared a mistrial without manifest necessity. The U.S. Supreme Court decided that the judge had not abused her "sound discretion" when she concluded that the jury was deadlocked.

In **Renico v. Lett** *(2010), our next excerpt, the U.S. Supreme Court held that Reginald Lett's conviction in a retrial, following the dismissal of his first trial after a hung jury, didn't violate his right against double jeopardy.*

CASE   Did the Retrial Place Him in Jeopardy Twice?

Renico v. Lett

2010 WL 1740525 (2010)

HISTORY

Following reversal by intermediate state appellate court of Reginald Lett's (Petitioner's) conviction for second-degree murder and possession of a firearm during the commission of a felony, the Supreme Court of Michigan, reversed and remanded, and the intermediate appellate court affirmed on remand. Lett then sought federal habeas relief. The United States District Court for the Eastern District of Michigan, granted relief, and the government appealed. The United States Court Of Appeals for the Sixth Circuit, Cole, Circuit Judge, affirmed. Certiorari was granted. The U.S. Supreme Court REVERSED and REMANDED.

ROBERTS, C.J., joined by SCALIA, KENNEDY, THOMAS, GINSBURG, and ALITO, JJ.

FACTS

On August 29, 1996, an argument broke out in a Detroit liquor store. The antagonists included Adesoji Latona, a taxi driver; Charles Jones, a passenger who claimed he had been wrongfully ejected from Latona's cab; and Reginald

Lett, a friend of Jones's. After the argument began, Lett left the liquor store, retrieved a handgun from another friend outside in the parking lot, and returned to the store. He shot Latona twice, once in the head and once in the chest. Latona died from his wounds shortly thereafter. Michigan prosecutors charged Lett with first-degree murder and possession of a firearm during the commission of a felony. His trial took place in June 1997. From jury selection to jury instructions the trial took less than nine hours, spread over six different days.

The jury's deliberations began on June 12, 1997, at 3:24 P.M., and ran that day until 4 P.M. After resuming its work the next morning, the jury sent the trial court a note—one of seven it sent out in its two days of deliberations—stating that the jurors had "a concern about our voice levels disturbing any other proceedings that might be going on." Later, the jury sent out another note, asking "What if we can't agree? Mistrial? Retrial? What?"

At 12:45 P.M. the judge called the jury back into the courtroom, along with the prosecutor and defense counsel. Once the jury was seated, the following exchange took place:

> *The Court:* I received your note asking me what if you can't agree? And I have to conclude from that that that is your situation at this time. So, I'd like to ask the foreperson to identify themselves, please?

The Foreperson: [Identified herself.]

The Court: Okay, thank you. All right. I need to ask you if the jury is deadlocked; in other words, is there a disagreement as to the verdict?

The Foreperson: Yes, there is.

The Court: All right. Do you believe that it is hopelessly deadlocked?

The Foreperson: The majority of us don't believe that–

The Court: (Interposing) Don't say what you're going to say, okay?

The Foreperson: Oh, I'm sorry.

The Court: I don't want to know what your verdict might be, or how the split is, or any of that. Thank you. Okay? Are you going to reach a unanimous verdict, or not?

The Foreperson: (No response)

The Court: Yes or no?

The Foreperson: No, Judge."

The judge then declared a mistrial, dismissed the jury, and scheduled a new trial for later that year. Neither the prosecutor nor Lett's attorney made any objection.

Lett's second trial was held before a different judge and jury in November 1997. This time, the jury was able to reach a unanimous verdict—that Lett was guilty of second-degree murder—after deliberating for only 3 hours and 15 minutes.

Lett appealed his conviction to the Michigan Court of Appeals. The Michigan Court of Appeals reversed his conviction. The State appealed to the Michigan Supreme Court, which reversed the Court of Appeals. The court explained that under our decision in *United States v. Perez* (1824), a defendant may be retried following the discharge of a deadlocked jury, even if the discharge occurs without the defendant's consent. There is no Double Jeopardy Clause violation in such circumstances, it noted, so long as the trial court exercised its "sound discretion" in concluding that the jury was deadlocked and thus that there was a "manifest necessity" for a mistrial. The court further observed that, under our decision in *Arizona v. Washington* (1978), an appellate court must generally defer to a trial judge's determination that a deadlock has been reached.

After setting forth the applicable law, the Michigan Supreme Court determined that the judge at Lett's first trial had not abused her discretion in declaring the mistrial. The court cited the facts that the jury "had deliberated for at least four hours following a relatively short, and far from complex, trial," that the jury had sent out several notes, including one that appears to indicate that its discussions may have been "particularly heated," and—"most important"—that the jury foreperson expressly stated that the jury was not going to reach a verdict.

Lett petitioned for a federal writ of habeas corpus. Again he argued that the trial court's declaration of a mistrial constituted an abuse of discretion because there was

no manifest necessity to cut short the jury's deliberations. He further contended that the Michigan Supreme Court's rejection of his double jeopardy claim amounted to "an unreasonable application of . . . clearly established Federal law, as determined by the Supreme Court of the United States," and thus that he was not barred by AEDPA (Anti-Terrorism and Effective Death Penalty Act), 28 U.S.C. § 2254(d)(1), from obtaining federal habeas relief. The District Court agreed and granted the writ. On appeal, a divided panel of the U.S. Court of Appeals for the Sixth Circuit affirmed. The State petitioned for review in our Court, and we granted certiorari.

OPINION

It is important at the outset to define the question before us. That question is not whether the trial judge should have declared a mistrial. It is not even whether it was an abuse of discretion for her to have done so—the applicable standard on direct review. The question under AEDPA is instead whether the determination of the Michigan Supreme Court that there was no abuse of discretion was "an unreasonable application of . . . clearly established Federal law." § 2254(d)(1).

We have explained that "an *unreasonable* application of federal law is different from an *incorrect* application of federal law." This distinction creates "a substantially higher threshold" for obtaining relief than *de novo* review. AEDPA thus imposes a "highly deferential standard for evaluating state-court rulings," and "demands that state-court decisions be given the benefit of the doubt." The "manifest necessity" standard "cannot be interpreted literally," and that a mistrial is appropriate when there is a "high degree" of necessity. The decision whether to grant a mistrial is reserved to the "broad discretion" of the trial judge, a point that "has been consistently reiterated in decisions of this Court."

The reasons for "allowing the trial judge to exercise broad discretion" are "especially compelling" in cases involving a potentially deadlocked jury. There, the justification for deference is that "the trial court is in the best position to assess all the factors which must be considered in making a necessarily discretionary determination whether the jury will be able to reach a just verdict if it continues to deliberate." In the absence of such deference, trial judges might otherwise "employ coercive means to break the apparent deadlock," thereby creating a "significant risk that a verdict may result from pressures inherent in the situation rather than the considered judgment of all the jurors."

This is not to say that we grant *absolute* deference to trial judges in this context. The judge's exercise of discretion must be "sound," and we have made clear that "if the record reveals that the trial judge has failed to exercise the 'sound discretion' entrusted to him, the reason for such deference by an appellate court disappears." In light of all the foregoing, the Michigan Supreme Court's decision in this case was not unreasonable under AEDPA, and the decision of the Court of Appeals to grant Lett a writ of habeas corpus must be reversed.

AEDPA prevents defendants—and federal courts—from using federal habeas corpus review as a vehicle to second-guess the reasonable decisions of state courts. Whether or not the Michigan Supreme Court's opinion reinstating Lett's conviction in this case was *correct,* it was clearly *not unreasonable.*

The judgment of the Court of Appeals is REVERSED, and the case is REMANDED for further proceedings consistent with this opinion.

It is so ordered.

DISSENT

STEVENS, J., joined by SOTOMAYOR and BREYER, JJ.

At common law, courts went to great lengths to ensure the jury reached a verdict. Fourteenth-century English judges reportedly loaded hung juries into oxcarts and carried them from town to town until a judgment "bounced out." Less enterprising colleagues kept jurors as *de facto* "prisoners" until they achieved unanimity. The notion of a mistrial based on jury deadlock did not appear in Blackstone's Commentaries; it is no surprise, then, that colonial juries virtually always returned a verdict. Well into the 19th and even the 20th century, some American judges continued to coax unresolved juries toward consensus by threatening to deprive them of heat, sleep, or sustenance or to lock them in a room for a prolonged period of time.

Mercifully, our legal system has evolved, and such harsh measures are no longer tolerated. Yet what this history demonstrates—and what has not changed—is the respect owed "a defendant's valued right to have his trial completed by a particular tribunal." Our longstanding doctrine applying the Double Jeopardy Clause attests to the durability and fundamentality of this interest.

The underlying idea is that the State with all its resources and power should not be allowed to make repeated attempts to convict an individual for an alleged offense, thereby subjecting him to embarrassment, expense and ordeal and compelling him to live in a continuing state of anxiety and insecurity, as well as enhancing the possibility that even though innocent he may be found guilty.

We have come over the years to recognize that jury coercion poses a serious threat to jurors and defendants alike, and that the accused's interest in a single proceeding must sometimes yield to the public's interest in fair trials designed to end in just judgments; and we have therefore carved out exceptions to the common-law rule. But the exceptions are narrow. For a mistrial to be granted at the prosecutor's request, the prosecutor must shoulder the burden of justifying the mistrial if he is to avoid the double jeopardy bar. His burden is a heavy one. A judge who acts *sua sponte* in declaring a mistrial must similarly make sure, and must enable a reviewing court to confirm, that there is a "manifest necessity" to deprive the defendant of his valued right.

In this case, the trial judge did not meet that burden. The record suggests that she discharged the jury without considering any less extreme courses of action, and the record makes quite clear that she did not fully appreciate the scope or significance of the ancient right at stake. The Michigan Supreme Court's decision rejecting Reginald Lett's double jeopardy claim was just as clearly in error.

No one disputes that a "genuinely deadlocked jury" is "the classic basis" for declaring a mistrial or that such declaration, under our doctrine, does not preclude reprosecution; what is disputed in this case is whether the trial judge took adequate care to ensure the jury was genuinely deadlocked. A long line of precedents from this Court establishes the "governing legal principles," for resolving this question. Although the Court acknowledges these precedents, it minimizes the heavy burden we have placed on trial courts.

We have repeatedly reaffirmed that the power to discharge the jury prior to verdict should be reserved for "extraordinary and striking circumstances," unless and until he has "scrupulously" assessed the situation and "taken care to assure himself that it warrants action on his part foreclosing the defendant from a potentially favorable judgment by the tribunal," that, to exercise sound discretion, the judge may not act "irrationally," "irresponsibly," or "precipitately" but must instead act "deliberately" and "carefully," and that, in view of "the elusive nature of the problem," mechanical rules are no substitute in the double jeopardy mistrial context for the sensitive application of general standards.

The Court accurately describes the events leading up to this trial judge's declaration of mistrial, but it glides too quickly over a number of details that, taken together, show her decision-making was neither careful nor well considered. If the "manifest necessity" and "sound discretion" standards are to have any force, we must demand more from our trial courts.

I fail to see how the trial judge exercised anything resembling "sound discretion" in declaring a mistrial, as we have defined that term. Indeed, I fail to see how a record could disclose much less evidence of sound decision-making. Within the realm of realistic, nonpretextual possibilities, this mistrial declaration was about as precipitate as one is liable to find. Four hours is not a long time for jury deliberations, particularly in a first-degree murder case. Indeed, it would have been remarkable if the jurors could review the testimony of all the witnesses in the time they were given, let alone conclude that they were deadlocked.

The jury's note pertaining to its volume level does not necessarily indicate anything about the heatedness of its discussion. "There is no other suggestion in the record that such was the case, and the trial judge did not draw that conclusion." Although it would have been preferable if Lett had tried to lodge an objection, defense counsel was given no meaningful opportunity to do so—the judge discharged the jury simultaneously with her mistrial order, counsel received no advance notice of either action, and he may not even have been informed of the content of the jury's notes. "At no point before the actual declaration of the mistrial was it even mentioned on the record as a potential course of action by the court. The summary nature of the trial court's actions . . . rendered an objection both unlikely and meaningless. Counsel's failure to object is therefore legally irrelevant. And, as detailed above, the foreperson's remarks were far more equivocal and ambiguous, in context, than the Michigan Supreme Court allowed.

In this case, Reginald Lett's constitutional rights were violated when the trial court terminated his first trial without adequate justification and he was subsequently prosecuted for the same offense. The majority does not appear to dispute this point, but it nevertheless denies Lett relief by applying a level of deference to the state court's ruling that effectively effaces the role of the federal courts. Nothing one will find in the United States Code or the United States Reports requires us to turn a blind eye to this manifestly unlawful conviction.

QUESTIONS

1. List all the relevant details surrounding the jury deliberations in Reginald Lett's first trial.
2. Summarize Chief Justice Roberts's argument for the Court's holding that the trial judge didn't abuse her discretion when she declared a mistrial due to a hung jury.
3. Summarize Justice Stevens's argument that the trial judge didn't meet her burden to make sure there was a "manifest necessity" to declare a mistrial because the jury was "hung."
4. Who has the more convincing arguments? Defend your answer with specifics from the arguments and relevant facts.

The double jeopardy clause bans both multiple *punishments* and multiple *prosecutions*. Nevertheless, it's not double jeopardy to prosecute and punish a defendant for the same acts in separate jurisdictions. The main purpose of the double jeopardy clause is to restrain prosecutors and judges. According to the **dual sovereignty doctrine**, a crime arising out of the same facts in one state is not the same crime in another state. This also holds when the same conduct is a crime under both state and federal law.

In *Heath v. Alabama* (1985), Larry Heath hired Charles Owens and Gregory Lumpkin for $2,000 to kill his wife, who was then nine months' pregnant. The killers fulfilled their part of the deal. Heath was sentenced to life imprisonment in a Georgia court after he pleaded guilty. However, part of the crime was committed in Alabama, so Alabama prosecuted Heath, too. He was convicted in Alabama of murder committed during a kidnapping and sentenced to death. He appealed the conviction on the grounds of double jeopardy. The U.S. Supreme Court affirmed the conviction, holding that successive prosecutions for the same crime in two different states didn't put him in jeopardy twice.

According to Justice O'Connor, writing for the majority of the Court:

> To deny a State its power to enforce its criminal laws because another State has won the race to the courthouse "would be a shocking and untoward deprivation of the historic right and obligation of the States to maintain peace and order within their confines." Such a deprivation of a State's sovereign powers cannot be justified by the assertion that under "interest analysis" the State's legitimate penal interests will be satisfied through a prosecution conducted by another State. A State's interest in vindicating its sovereign authority through enforcement of its laws by definition can never be satisfied by another State's enforcement of its own laws. The Court has always understood the words of the Double Jeopardy Clause to reflect this fundamental principle, and we see no reason why we should reconsider that understanding today. (93)

Also, it doesn't put defendants in double jeopardy to prosecute them in multiple trials for separate offenses arising out of the same incident. The U.S. Supreme Court decided this in the horrible multiple-murder case, *Ciucci v. Illinois* (1958). Vincent Ciucci was married and had three children. When he fell in love with a 21-year-old woman he wanted to marry, his wife wouldn't give him a divorce. So he shot her and all three of his children in the head one by one while they slept. Illinois used the same evidence to convict Ciucci in three separate murder trials. The Court decided that the multiple trials, even if they stemmed from the same incident, didn't put Ciucci in jeopardy more than once.

A Speedy Trial

LO 9

According to the Sixth Amendment, "In all criminal trials, the accused shall enjoy the right to a speedy . . . trial." The idea of speedy justice is more than 900 years older than the Bill of Rights. In 1187, King Henry II provided for "speedy justice" in the Assizes of Clarendon. King John promised in the Magna Carta in 1215 that "every subject of this realm . . . may . . . have justice . . . speedily without delay." In his *Institutes*—called by Thomas Jefferson, "the universal elementary book of law students" (*Klopfer v. North Carolina* 1967, 225)—Sir Edward Coke (1797) wrote that the English itinerant justices in 1600 "have not suffered the prisoner to be long detained, but, at their next coming, have given the prisoner full and speedy justice, . . . without detaining him long in prison" (*Klopfer v. North Carolina* 1967, 224). The Virginia Declaration of Rights in 1776 (the state's "bills of rights") and the speedy trial clause of the Sixth Amendment reflect this history. And even though the state constitutions guarantee a speedy trial, the U.S. Supreme Court has extended the federal speedy trial protection of the Sixth Amendment to the states (225).

The speedy trial clause promotes and balances several interests. For the accused, it prevents prolonged detention before trial; reduces the anxiety and uncertainty surrounding criminal prosecution; and guards against weakening the defense's case through loss of alibi witnesses and other evidence. And because most detained defendants are poor, both the process interest in ensuring equal protection of the laws and the societal interest in protecting the poor and less powerful are at stake in speedy trial decisions (*Report to the Nation on Crime and Justice* 1988, 123).

The speedy trial provision also promotes the interest in obtaining the correct result. Delay means lost evidence and lost witnesses—or at least the loss of their memory—not only for the defense but also for the prosecution. The clause also promotes process goals, particularly that decisions should be made in a timely fashion. Organizational interests are at stake as well. Failure to provide prompt trials contributes to large case backlogs, particularly in urban areas. Furthermore, long pretrial detention is costly to taxpayers. In addition to feeding and housing detained defendants, lost wages and greater welfare burdens result from incarceration.

According to the U.S. Supreme Court, the Sixth Amendment "speedy trial clock" doesn't start ticking until suspects are charged formally with crimes. Before they're charged, defendants have to depend on either statutes spelling out the length of time allowed between the commission of crimes and the filing of charges (statutes of limitations) or the due process clauses. So in rejecting a speedy trial violation in a delay of three years between the commission of the crime and an indictment, the Court said:

> The due process clause of the Fifth Amendment would require dismissal of the indictment if it were shown at trial that the pre-indictment delay . . . caused substantial prejudice to appellants' rights to a fair trial and that the delay was an intentional device to gain tactical advantage over the accused. (*U.S. v. Marion* 1971, 324)

The speedy trial clause bans only *undue* delays. According to the U.S. Supreme Court, flexibility governs whether delays are undue enough to violate the speedy trial clause. The Court has adopted another one of its balancing tests to decide whether delays hurt ("prejudice," if you want the technical term) defendants' cases. Four elements make up the balance:

1. The length of the delay

2. The reason for the delay

3. The defendant's assertion of his or her right to a speedy trial

4. The prejudice (harm) the delay causes to the defendant's case

What are the consequences of violating the speedy trial guarantee? According to the Court, there are only two remedies for the violation of the speedy trial clause:

1. **Dismissal without prejudice.** Allows a new prosecution for the same offense

2. **Dismissal with prejudice.** Terminates the case with the provision that it can't be prosecuted again

According to a unanimous U.S. Supreme Court, even though there's enough evidence for conviction, undue delay subjects defendants to "emotional stress" that requires dismissal as "the only possible remedy." The Court's ruling has raised the strong objection that the high price of dismissal will make courts "extremely hesitant" to find speedy trial violations because judges don't want to be responsible for freeing criminals (*Strunk v. U.S.* 1973).

Although the Sixth Amendment doesn't require it, several states have enacted statutes or court rules that set time limits for bringing cases to trial. These limits vary widely among the states. The Federal Speedy Trial Act provides definite time periods for bringing defendants to trial. The government has to start prosecution within 30 days after arrest (60 days if there's no grand jury in session); arraign defendants within 10 days after filing indictments or informations; and bring defendants to trial within 60 days following arraignment.

According to the act, the following delays don't count in computing days:

- Delays needed to determine the defendant's competency to stand trial

- Delays due to other trials of the defendant

- Delays due to hearings on pretrial motions

- Delays because of *interlocutory appeals*—provisional appeals that interrupt the proceedings, such as an appeal from a ruling on a pretrial motion

A Change of Venue

LO 9

The Sixth Amendment provides that "in all criminal prosecutions, the accused shall enjoy the right to a . . . public trial, by an impartial jury of the State and district wherein the crime shall have been committed." A defendant's pretrial motion to change the venue (the place where the trial is held) waives the Sixth Amendment right to have a trial in the state and district where the crime was committed. Only defendants, not the prosecution, may move to change the venue, and changes of venue aren't automatic.

According to Rule 21(a) of the *Federal Rules of Criminal Procedure* (2002):

The court upon motion of the defendant shall transfer the proceeding as to that defendant to another district . . . if the court is satisfied that there exists in the district where the prosecution is pending so great a prejudice against the defendant that the defendant cannot obtain a fair and impartial trial at any place fixed for holding court in that district.

Why do defendants give up their right to a trial in the place where the crime was committed? Because they believe they can't get an impartial public trial in that location. When courts rule on the motion, they balance the right to a public trial in the place where the crime was committed against the right to an impartial trial. In that respect, changing venue reflects the interest in obtaining a proper result in the individual case—prejudiced jurors can't find the truth. Process values are also at stake: the integrity of the judicial process requires a calm, dignified, reflective atmosphere; due process demands unbiased fact-finding; the equal protection clause prohibits trying defendants who are the object of public outrage differently from other defendants.

In *Sheppard v. Maxwell* (1966), the U.S. Supreme Court held that "where there is a reasonable likelihood that the prejudicial news prior to trial will prevent a fair trial, the judge should continue the case until the threat abates, or transfer it to another county not so permeated with publicity" (363).

In this case, Ohio tried Dr. Sam Sheppard for the bludgeoning murder of his pregnant wife, Marilyn, a Cleveland socialite. The case dominated the news and gripped the public's attention before, during, and after the trial. Lurid headlines and long stories appeared regularly, detailing the brutality of the murder and Sheppard's failure to cooperate with authorities. The editorials accused Sheppard of the murder. One charged on the front page that "somebody is getting away with murder," alleging that Sheppard's wealth and prominent social position protected him from a full-fledged investigation by police. Finally, the papers printed detailed analyses of evidence that came to light during the investigation, editorializing about its credibility, relevance, and materiality to the case.

As for the trial itself, the press, the public, and other observers packed the courtroom every day. One local radio station set up broadcasting facilities on the third floor of the courthouse. Television and newsreel cameras waiting outside on the courthouse steps filmed jurors, lawyers, witnesses, and other participants in the trial. All the jurors were exposed to the heavy publicity prior to the trial. The public was so fascinated by the case that television later based the popular 1960s drama *The Fugitive* (and the 1993 movie) on it. (The fascination continued for television viewers who watched a short-lived 2001 version of *The Fugitive*.)

Sheppard was convicted, and his appeals made it to the U.S. Supreme Court. In granting Sheppard a new trial, the Court ruled that the proceedings should have been postponed or the trial venue moved because of a reasonable likelihood of prejudice.

The **reasonable-likelihood-of-prejudice test** requires courts to balance four elements in each change-of-venue case:

1. The kind and amount of community bias that endangers a fair trial
2. The size of the community where jury panels are selected
3. The details and seriousness of the offense
4. The status of the victim and the accused

These elements may vary in intensity, and they don't all have to be present in each case; they're guidelines for judges when they measure the likelihood the defendant will receive a fair trial.

Most courts don't grant changes of venue even if defendants show there's a reasonable likelihood of prejudice. Instead, they adopt an **actual prejudice test** to determine whether to change the venue or take less drastic measures. Under the actual prejudice test, courts have to decide whether jurors were, in fact, prejudiced by harmful publicity.

TABLE 12.5
Factors Considered in Change-of-Venue Motions

- Trials at distant locations burden witnesses.
- Communities have a substantial interest in the trial taking place where the crime was committed.
- Changing prosecutors disrupts the state's case.
- Courts can't decide the partiality question until the jury has been impaneled.
- Courts don't want to transfer a case after all the time spent in picking a jury.

Referring to the "carnival atmosphere" at Sheppard's trial, the U.S. Supreme Court concluded that he was entitled to a new trial without showing actual prejudice—a reasonable likelihood of prejudice was sufficient.

In another case, *Swindler v. State* (1979), John Edward Swindler proved that three jurors had read and heard about the case and that over 80 percent of prospective jurors were excused for cause. But this didn't stop the Arkansas Supreme Court from rejecting Swindler's claim that the trial court's refusal to grant his motion for change of venue denied him a fair trial and upholding Swindler's death sentence. The Supreme Court didn't find proof of actual prejudice during the trial. Swindler's experience is an example of how rare change of venue is.

In deciding whether the venue should be changed, courts consider a number of issues (Table 12.5). Moving proceedings to jurisdictions farther away, providing for witnesses to appear, and working in unfamiliar court surroundings hinder smooth, efficient, economical resolution of criminal cases. Furthermore, society has a strong interest in maintaining public confidence in the criminal justice system and providing an outlet for community reaction to crime. Citizens resent moving trials both because they want to follow the proceedings, and they feel insulted by a ruling that their own jurisdiction can't guarantee a fair trial.

The Suppression of Evidence

LO 9

As you've already learned, almost every case excerpt dealing with police work is about a struggle between defendants who want to keep evidence out of court and prosecutors who want to get it in. The reason for this struggle is the exclusionary rule (Chapter 11). Whether the exclusionary rule applies is decided in a pretrial hearing triggered by a defense motion to suppress evidence that law enforcement officers obtained by searches, seizures, confessions, or identification procedures (Chapters 4–9). The decision whether to let evidence in or keep it out is a legal question, meaning judges, not juries, decide whether to exclude evidence.

Summary

LO 1

- Prosecutors drop cases if they don't think they can prove them, or if, as "officers of the court," they feel prosecution wouldn't serve justice.

LO 1

- Selective prosecution is a necessity based on limited resources.

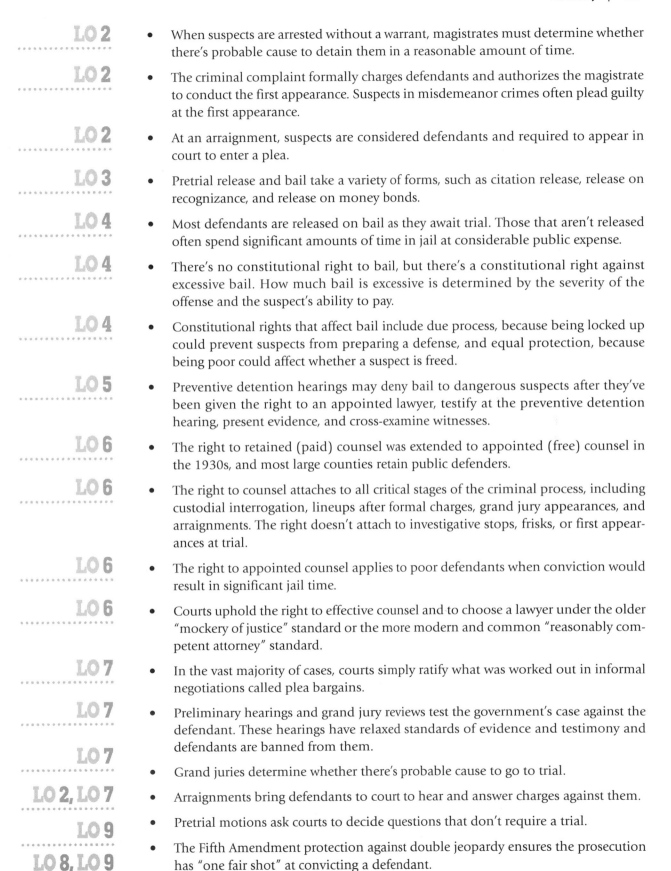

LO 2 • When suspects are arrested without a warrant, magistrates must determine whether there's probable cause to detain them in a reasonable amount of time.

LO 2 • The criminal complaint formally charges defendants and authorizes the magistrate to conduct the first appearance. Suspects in misdemeanor crimes often plead guilty at the first appearance.

LO 2 • At an arraignment, suspects are considered defendants and required to appear in court to enter a plea.

LO 3 • Pretrial release and bail take a variety of forms, such as citation release, release on recognizance, and release on money bonds.

LO 4 • Most defendants are released on bail as they await trial. Those that aren't released often spend significant amounts of time in jail at considerable public expense.

LO 4 • There's no constitutional right to bail, but there's a constitutional right against excessive bail. How much bail is excessive is determined by the severity of the offense and the suspect's ability to pay.

LO 4 • Constitutional rights that affect bail include due process, because being locked up could prevent suspects from preparing a defense, and equal protection, because being poor could affect whether a suspect is freed.

LO 5 • Preventive detention hearings may deny bail to dangerous suspects after they've been given the right to an appointed lawyer, testify at the preventive detention hearing, present evidence, and cross-examine witnesses.

LO 6 • The right to retained (paid) counsel was extended to appointed (free) counsel in the 1930s, and most large counties retain public defenders.

LO 6 • The right to counsel attaches to all critical stages of the criminal process, including custodial interrogation, lineups after formal charges, grand jury appearances, and arraignments. The right doesn't attach to investigative stops, frisks, or first appearances at trial.

LO 6 • The right to appointed counsel applies to poor defendants when conviction would result in significant jail time.

LO 6 • Courts uphold the right to effective counsel and to choose a lawyer under the older "mockery of justice" standard or the more modern and common "reasonably competent attorney" standard.

LO 7 • In the vast majority of cases, courts simply ratify what was worked out in informal negotiations called plea bargains.

LO 7 • Preliminary hearings and grand jury reviews test the government's case against the defendant. These hearings have relaxed standards of evidence and testimony and defendants are banned from them.

LO 7 • Grand juries determine whether there's probable cause to go to trial.

LO 2, LO 7 • Arraignments bring defendants to court to hear and answer charges against them.

LO 9 • Pretrial motions ask courts to decide questions that don't require a trial.

LO 8, LO 9 • The Fifth Amendment protection against double jeopardy ensures the prosecution has "one fair shot" at convicting a defendant.

LO 9
- The constitution guarantees a speedy trial, so prosecution must begin promptly.

LO 9
- The constitution ensures that changes of venue occur only at the defendant's request and only where great prejudice would otherwise exist.

Review Questions

1. Describe what occurs following arrest, interrogation, and identification procedures.

2. List the reasons that affect whether police drop cases or take them to prosecutors.

3. Identify the two roles of prosecutors and how the roles affect their decisions.

4. According to the U.S. Supreme Court, why is the initiation of judicial proceedings not just a "mere formalism"?

5. List and explain the importance of the reasons behind the decision of prosecutors to charge, divert, or drop criminal cases.

6. Why and when do police officers have to take arrested suspects to a magistrate?

7. Explain the difference between probable cause to detain a suspect and probable cause to go to trial.

8. What's the significance of the U.S. Supreme Court case *Gerstein v. Pugh*?

9. List the "administrative steps" police officers can complete before they take detained suspects to magistrates.

10. Identify and describe the consequences of detention before trial.

11. Describe the balance struck in the decision to bail or detain defendants.

12. Exactly what does the constitutional right to bail consist of?

13. Identify three constitutional rights our bail system denies to poor defendants, and explain how each is denied.

14. Describe the obstacles pretrial detention creates for defendants trying to prepare their defense.

15. According to the 1984 Bail Reform Act, when can judges preventively detain defendants?

16. What constitutional rights do pretrial detainees have regarding the conditions of their confinement?

17. List the "critical stages" of criminal prosecutions.

18. Summarize the facts of the U.S. Supreme Court decision in *Argersinger v. Hamlin*.

19. List four guidelines for defining indigence developed by the U.S. Courts of Appeals, and summarize the detailed definition of indigence adopted in Minnesota.

20. Identify, define, and explain the two-prongs of the U.S. Supreme Court's test of "effective" counsel adopted in *Strickland v. Washington*.

21. List and describe the differences between testing the government's case by grand jury review and by preliminary hearing.

22. Identify the four possible pleas defendants can enter at their arraignment.

23. Describe and explain the significance of the U.S. Supreme Court decisions in *Heath v. Alabama* and *Ciucci v. Illinois*.

24. According to the Federal Speedy Trial Act, when does the government have to begin prosecution? Arraign defendants? Bring defendants to trial?

25. Summarize the arguments against changes of venue.

26. Describe and summarize the significance of the U.S. Supreme Court decision in *Sheppard v. Maxwell.*

27. What kind of question is answered by the motion to suppress evidence?

Key Terms

13

CASES COVERED

Snyder v. Louisiana, 452 U.S. 472 (2008)

North Carolina v. Alford, 400 U.S. 25 (1970)

LEARNING OBJECTIVES

1 Understand that jury trials promote fact-finding and check government power, while plea negotiation promotes efficiency.

2 Know the constitutional rights that the jury selection process must protect.

3 Understand the right to a public trial by jury, and know the stages of a jury trial.

4 Know the process of jury selection, the types of verdicts juries can give, and the purpose of the unanimous verdict requirement.

5 Understand the difference between straight guilty pleas, negotiated guilty pleas, charge bargaining, and sentence bargaining.

6 Know the historical developments that contributed to the prevalence of plea bargaining.

7 Know the circumstances under which guilty pleas and plea bargaining are constitutional.

8 Understand the rights that defendants waive when they enter a guilty plea.

9 Know, understand, and appreciate the empirical research regarding plea bargains in and outside "the shadow of trial."

Court Proceedings II: Trial and Conviction

After Allen Snyder and his wife, Mary, had separated, they discussed the possibility of reconciliation, and Mary agreed to meet with Allen the next day. That night, Mary went on a date with Howard Wilson. At approximately 1:30 A.M., Wilson drove up to the home of Mary's mother to drop Mary off. Allen was waiting at the scene armed with a knife. He opened the driver's side door of Wilson's car and repeatedly stabbed the occupants, killing Wilson and wounding Mary. Snyder was convicted of first-degree murder. Snyder asked the U.S. Supreme Court to review his claim that the prosecution exercised some of its peremptory jury challenges based on race. *Snyder v. Louisiana* (2008)

Court proceedings are sharply divided into adversarial proceedings inside the courtroom and informal negotiations outside the courtroom. Three constitutional commands lie behind the trial and conviction of defendants in criminal cases:

1. *Article III, § 2.* The Trial of all Crimes, except in Cases of Impeachment, shall be by Jury; and such Trial shall be held in the State where the Crimes shall have been committed.

2. *The Fifth Amendment.* No person shall be . . . compelled in any criminal case to be a witness against himself.

3. *The Sixth Amendment.* In all criminal prosecutions, the accused shall enjoy the right to a speedy and public trial, by an impartial jury of the State and District wherein the crime shall have been committed . . . to be confronted with the witnesses against him, . . . and to have the assistance of Counsel for his defense.

These constitutional commands set high standards because conviction for a crime can result in the greatest deprivations (loss of property, liberty, privacy, and perhaps even life itself) in the criminal process. These commands are directed almost exclusively at criminal trials.

Although trials receive most of the attention in the news, and of course in movies and television, they account for only about 5 out of every 100 convictions (Table 13.1). The other 90 result from guilty pleas. Some of these guilty pleas result from plea bargaining, but many are *straight guilty pleas* (pleas of guilty without negotiation).

Trials and guilty pleas promote different interests. The trial promotes fact-finding by the adversarial process, procedural regularity, and public participation in criminal proceedings. The guilty plea promotes efficiency, economy, harmony, and speed. Plea negotiations also promote fact-finding by informal discussion and the give-and-take that occur in reaching an agreement over the plea.

In this chapter, we'll examine the constitutionally mandated trial by jury, the stages and rules of jury trials, and conviction by guilty pleas.

TABLE 13.1
Types of Felony Convictions in State Courts

Most Serious Conviction Offense	Percent of Felons Convicted By—				
		Trial			
	Total %	Total* %	Jury %	Bench %	Guilty Plea %
All offenses	100%	6	4	2	94
Violent offenses	100%	10	8	2	90
Murder/ Nonnegligent manslaughter	100	39	36	2	61
Sexual assault	100	12	10	2	88
Rape	100	16	13	3	84
Other sexual assault	100	9	8	2	91
Robbery	100	11	9	2	89
Aggravated assault	100	8	5	3	92
Other violent	100	7	5	2	93
Property offenses	100	5	3	2	95
Burglary	100	6	4	2	94
Larceny	100	5	3	2	95
Motor vehicle theft	100	4	4	—	96
Fraud/Forgery	100	5	3	2	95

TABLE 13.1 (continued)

| Most Serious Conviction Offense | Percent of Felons Convicted By— | | | | |
| | | | Trial | | |
	Total %	Total* %	Jury %	Bench %	Guilty Plea %
Drug offenses	100	4	3	2	96
Possession	100	2	1	1	98
Trafficking	100	6	3	2	94
Weapon offenses	100	7	5	2	93
Other specified offenses	100	3	3	1	97

Source: Bureau of Justice Statistics. *Felony Sentences in State Courts, 2006—Statistical Tables.* December 2009, NCJ 226846.

*Note: Data may not sum to the total because of rounding.

Trial by Jury

LO 1, LO 2

Trial by jury is ancient, with roots in the societies of the Teutonic tribes in Germany and the Normans before their conquest of England. The Assizes of Clarendon in 1187 and the Magna Carta in 1215 also contain traces of its origins. The jury trial was provided for specifically in the English Bill of Rights in 1689, and it then became common practice in the British American colonies.

From the start, the colonists resented royal interference with the right to a jury trial. Complaints regarding that interference appear in the Stamp Act, the First Continental Congress's resolves, and the Declaration of Independence. Article III, § 2, in the body of the U.S. Constitution, and the Sixth Amendment reflect the new nation's commitment to jury trial. Every state constitution guarantees it, and the U.S. Supreme Court has interpreted the due process clause of the Fourteenth Amendment to require states to provide it (*Duncan v. Louisiana* 1968).

Trial by jury promotes several interests. It checks and balances government power by putting an independent community-dominated body between the state, with all its resources, and a single individual. Jury trial also balances official power with citizen participation in criminal law enforcement. In addition, it guarantees that accused citizens who prefer that other citizens decide their innocence or guilt will have that preference honored.

In extending the Sixth Amendment's jury trial right to the states, Justice Byron R. White wrote the following:

The guarantees of jury trial reflect a profound judgment about the way in which law should be enforced and justice administered. Providing an accused with the right to be tried by a jury of his peers gave him an inestimable safeguard against the corrupt or overzealous prosecutor and against the compliant, biased, or eccentric judge. Beyond this, the jury trial reflects a reluctance to entrust plenary powers over the life and liberty of the citizen to one judge or to a group of judges. Fear of unchecked power, so typical of our State and Federal Governments in other respects, found expression in the criminal law in this insistence upon community participation in the determination of guilt or innocence. (*Duncan v. Louisiana* 1968, 156)

Let's explore more fully the meaning of the right to a trial by jury by examining how this right is affected by the moral seriousness standard, the issue of how many citizens are required to sit on a jury, the jury selection process, and the right to a public trial.

The Moral Seriousness Standard

LO 1, LO 2

According to the U.S. Supreme Court, there's one major exception to the right to a jury trial for "all crimes," in Article III, § 2, and "all criminal prosecutions," in the Sixth Amendment. That exception is for "petty offenses" (*Duncan v. Louisiana* 1968, 160). But in setting the **moral seriousness standard**, the Court extended the Sixth Amendment right to a jury trial to morally serious misdemeanors that can lead to jail time. In jurisdictions where there's no specific law drawing a line between petty and other offenses, the Court has used six months' imprisonment as the dividing line (*Baldwin v. New York* 1970).

By taking the "moral quality" of offenses into account, courts have declared some offenses serious even if the penalty is less than six months' imprisonment. So, under this *moral seriousness standard*, courts have decided defendants had a right to a jury trial when charged with conspiring to deceive immigration officials (*U.S. v. Sanchez-Meza* 1976), driving while intoxicated (*U.S. v. Craner* 1981), and shoplifting (*State v. Superior Court* 1978), even though the penalty for these offenses was less than six months in jail.

The 12-Member Jury Requirement

LO 1, LO 2

The 12-member jury at one time was regarded by the U.S. Supreme Court as essential to the right to a jury trial (*Thompson v. Utah* 1898). The Court has since retreated from that position. Justice Byron R. White spelled out the reasons in *Williams v. Florida* (1970):

1. We can't "pretend" to know the Framers' intent.
2. The number 12 is based on superstition about the number (12 apostles, 12 tribes).
3. History doesn't give good enough reasons to stick to 12 members in today's world.

So, according to the Court in *Williams v. Florida* (1970), the Sixth Amendment only demands enough jurors to achieve the goals of a jury trial: to find the truth and allow for community participation in criminal justice decision making. And that number isn't necessarily 12:

> That the jury at common law was composed of precisely 12 is a historical accident, unnecessary to effect the purposes of the jury system and wholly without significance "except to mystics." To read the Sixth Amendment as forever codifying a feature so incidental to the real purpose of the Amendment is to ascribe a blind formalism to the Framers which would require considerably more evidence than we have been able to discover in the history and language of the Constitution or in the reasoning of our past decisions. (102)

The 12-member jury has strong supporters, despite the Court's dismissal of it as superstitious. Justice John Marshall Harlan called the accident of superstition argument "much too thin." If the number 12 was merely an accident, it was one that "has recurred without interruption since the 14th century." Also, according to Justice Harlan:

> If 12 jurors are not essential, why are six? Can it be doubted that a unanimous jury of 12 provides a greater safeguard than a majority vote of six? The uncertainty that will henceforth plague the meaning of trial by jury is itself a further reason for not hoisting the anchor of history. . . . The [Court's] circumvention of history is compounded by the cavalier disregard of numerous pronouncements of this Court that reflect the understanding of the jury as one of twelve members and have fixed expectations accordingly. (*Baldwin v. New York* 1970, 126)

Judges aren't the only ones who support the 12-member jury. Social scientists have found that juries with 12 members are right more often, and they represent the community better than juries with fewer than 12 members. Hans Zeisel, a major authority on the jury, had this to say about the 12-member jury:

> Suppose that in a given community, 90 percent of the people share one viewpoint and the remaining 10 percent have a different viewpoint. Suppose further that we draw 100 twelve-member and 100 six-member juries. Using standard statistical methods, it can be predicted that approximately 72 of the twelve-member juries will contain a representative of the 10 percent minority, as compared to only 47 juries composed of six persons. This difference is by no means negligible. (LaFave and Israel 1984, 2:696, n. 57)

Six-member juries are enough to satisfy the Sixth Amendment but what about five? The Supreme Court answered "no" in *Ballew v. Georgia* (1978).

Jury Selection

According to the U.S. Supreme Court, the Sixth Amendment right to an "impartial jury" requires that juries represent a "fair cross section" of the community. Furthermore, the equal protection clause of the Fourteenth Amendment bars the systematic exclusion of members of defendants' racial, gender, ethnic, or religious group. The **Federal Jury Selection and Service Act** meets these constitutional requirements by requiring that juries be "selected at random from a fair cross section of the community in the district or division wherein the court convenes," and "No citizen shall be excluded from service as a grand or petit juror in the district courts of the United States on account of race, color, religion, sex, national origin, or economic status."

Most states have similar provisions. To implement them, jurisdictions select jurors at random from the following sources:

- Local census reports
- Tax rolls
- City directories
- Telephone books
- Driver's license lists

Some states, mainly in New England and the South, use the **key-man system**, in which civic and political leaders recommend people from these lists that they know personally or by reputation. Understandably, the key-man system faces repeated challenges

TABLE 13.2

Common Excuses for Exemption from Jury Service

- Economic hardship
- Need to care for small children
- Advanced age
- Distance between home and the courthouse is too far
- Illness

that it doesn't represent a fair cross section of the community and that it discriminates against various segments in the community (LaFave and Israel 1984, 2:708).

Jury service isn't popular; most prospective jurors ask to be excused (Table 13.2). Courts rarely refuse their requests because it's "easier, administratively and financially, to excuse unwilling people" (LaFave and Israel 1984, 2:708). Some groups are ordinarily exempt from jury service, including:

- Persons below voting age
- Convicted felons
- Persons who can't write and read English

Some occupations are also exempt in some states:

- Doctors
- Pharmacists
- Teachers
- Clergy
- Lawyers
- Judges
- Criminal justice professionals
- Some other public employees (LaFave and Israel 1984, 2:708–9)

From the **jury panel** (the potential jurors drawn from the list of eligible citizens not excused), the attorneys for the government and the defendant pick the jurors who will actually serve. The process of picking the actual jurors from the pool of potential jurors by questioning them is called the *voir dire*—literally, "to speak the truth." Both prosecutors and defense attorneys can remove jurors during the *voir dire*. There are two ways of removing (usually called "striking") potential jurors, **peremptory challenges** (striking without having to give a reason) and **challenges for cause** (striking by showing the juror is biased). Lawyers almost always use their peremptory challenges to strike potential jurors who it appears will sympathize with the other side. Attorneys use challenges for cause only when they can convince judges of juror bias.

The number of peremptory challenges depends on the jurisdiction; the number of challenges for cause is unlimited. In the federal courts, both the prosecution and the defense have 20 peremptories in capital offenses and 3 in misdemeanors. In felony cases, defendants have 10, and the government has 6. Both sides rarely exercise their right to challenges for cause—usually one to three times to assemble a jury of 12 (Van Dyke 1977, 14).

Inquiring into racial prejudice during *voir dire* is sensitive. We know that prejudice can sway some jurors' judgment (*Strauder v. West Virginia* 1880). Prejudice can cause specific defendants harm when discrimination infects jury selection. But it can also harm certain groups generally. For example, by drawing racial, gender, sexual orientation, and other group lines in picking juries, prosecutors "establish state-sponsored group stereotypes rooted in, and reflective of, historical prejudice" (*Miller-El v. Dretke* 2005, 237–38). The harm doesn't stop with minorities.

> When the government's choice of jurors is tainted with racial bias, that overt wrong casts doubt over the obligation of the parties, the jury, and indeed the court to adhere to the law throughout the trial. That is, the very integrity of the courts is jeopardized when a prosecutor's discrimination invites cynicism respecting the jury's neutrality, and undermines public confidence in adjudication. (238)

As a result, since 1880, the U.S. Supreme Court has "consistently and repeatedly reaffirmed that racial discrimination by the State in jury selection offends the equal protection clause." It's clear, therefore, that the Court recognizes the problem of discrimination. "The rub has been the practical difficulty of ferreting out discrimination in selections discretionary by nature, and choices subject to myriad legitimate influences, whatever the race of the individuals on the panel from which jurors are selected" (238).

In *Swain v. Alabama* (1965), the Court addressed the problem of the amount of proof to show intentional discrimination without disturbing both the prosecution's and defense's "historical prerogative to make a peremptory strike or challenge, the very nature of which is traditionally without a reason stated" (238). The Court presumed that the prosecution's strikes were legitimate, "except in the face of a longstanding pattern of discrimination." Specifically, "when 'in case after case, whatever the circumstances,' no blacks served on juries, then 'giving the widest leeway to the operation of irrational but trial-related suspicions and antagonisms, it would appear that the purposes of the peremptory challenge were being perverted'" (238–39).

The rule in *Swain* didn't work. The requirement to show an extended pattern of discrimination imposed a "crippling burden of proof that left prosecutors' use of peremptories largely immune from constitutional scrutiny. So, in *Batson v. Kentucky* (1986), the Court tried again to solve the tough problem of ferreting out discrimination without strangling the "right" of striking potential jurors without cause. The Court held that a defendant could make a **prima facie case** (enough facts to prove discriminatory jury selection unless rebutted by the prosecution) by the "totality of the relevant facts" about a prosecutor's conduct during the defendant's own trial (*Batson*, 94, 96). "Once the defendant makes a prima facie showing, the burden shifts to the State to come forward with a neutral explanation for challenging jurors within an arguably targeted class" (97). The trial court then has the duty to decide if the defendant has proved intentional discrimination (98). Unfortunately, *Batson* came with its own weakness: if *any* explanation on its face is enough to rebut the defendant's prima facie case, then *Batson* didn't do much more than *Swain*.

Defendants now have another hurdle if a trial court finds that the prosecutor's explanations are race-neutral: the Antiterrorism and Effective Death Penalty Act of 1996 (AEDPA) (28 U.S.C. § 2254(d)(2). Under the act, defendants can only obtain equal protection relief by proving that the trial court's finding is "an unreasonable determination of the facts in light of the evidence presented in the state court proceeding" (*Miller-El v. Dretke* 2005, 239–40).

In *Snyder v. Louisiana* (2008), our next case excerpt, the Supreme Court applied the *Miller-El v. Dretke* "unreasonable determination of the facts" test and held that the "trial court committed clear error" when it rejected Allen Snyder's claim that some of the prosecution's peremptory challenges were race-based in violation of *Batson v. Kentucky*.

In Snyder v. Louisiana *(2008), our next case excerpt, the Supreme Court held that the trial court had violated Allen Snyder's right to a jury free of race-based exclusions in violation of* Batson v. Kentucky.

CASE Were the Peremptory Challenges Based on Race?

Snyder v. Louisiana
452 U.S. 472 (2008)

HISTORY

Allen Snyder (Petitioner/Defendant) was convicted in the Twenty-Fourth Judicial District Court, Parish of Jefferson, Kernan A. Hand, J., of first-degree murder and was sentenced to death. Defendant appealed. The Supreme Court of Louisiana, affirmed. Granting defendant's petition for a writ of certiorari, the Supreme Court vacated the judgment and remanded for further consideration. On remand, the Supreme Court of Louisiana affirmed. Certiorari was granted. The Supreme Court, Justice Alito, held that prosecutor's proffered reasons for striking black prospective jurors were pretext for racial discrimination. Reversed and remanded.

ALITO, J., joined by ROBERTS, C.J., and STEVENS, KENNEDY, SOUTER, GINSBURG, and BREYER, JJ.

Petitioner Allen Snyder was convicted of first-degree murder in a Louisiana court and was sentenced to death. He asks us to review a decision of the Louisiana Supreme Court rejecting his claim that the prosecution exercised some of its peremptory jury challenges based on race, in violation of *Batson v. Kentucky*. We hold that the trial court committed clear error in its ruling on a *Batson* objection, and we therefore reverse.

FACTS

The crime for which petitioner was convicted occurred in August 1995. At that time, petitioner and his wife, Mary, had separated. On August 15, they discussed the possibility of reconciliation, and Mary agreed to meet with petitioner the next day. That night, Mary went on a date with petitioner the next day. That night, Mary went on a date with

Howard Wilson. During the evening, petitioner repeatedly attempted to page Mary, but she did not respond. At approximately 1:30 A.M. on August 16, Wilson drove up to the home of Mary's mother to drop Mary off. Petitioner was waiting at the scene armed with a knife. He opened the driver's side door of Wilson's car and repeatedly stabbed the occupants, killing Wilson and wounding Mary.

The State charged petitioner with first-degree murder and sought the death penalty based on the aggravating circumstance that petitioner had knowingly created a risk of death or great bodily harm to more than one person.

Voir dire began on Tuesday, August 27, 1996, and proceeded as follows. During the first phase, the trial court screened the panel to identify jurors who did not meet Louisiana's requirements for jury service or claimed that service on the jury or sequestration for the duration of the trial would result in extreme hardship. More than 50 prospective jurors reported that they had work, family, or other commitments that would interfere with jury service. In each of those instances, the nature of the conflicting commitments was explored, and some of these jurors were dismissed. App. 58–164.

In the next phase, the court randomly selected panels of 13 potential jurors for further questioning. The defense and prosecution addressed each panel and questioned the jurors both as a group and individually. At the conclusion of this questioning, the court ruled on challenges for cause. Then, the prosecution and the defense were given the opportunity to use peremptory challenges (each side had 12) to remove remaining jurors. The court continued this process of calling 13-person panels until the jury was filled. In accordance with Louisiana law, the parties were permitted to exercise "backstrikes." That is, they were allowed to use their peremptories up until the time when the final jury was sworn and thus were permitted to strike jurors whom they had initially accepted when the jurors' panels were called.

Eighty-five prospective jurors were questioned as members of a panel. Thirty-six of these survived challenges for cause; 5 of the 36 were black; and all 5 of the prospective black jurors were eliminated by the prosecution through the use of peremptory strikes. The jury found petitioner guilty of first-degree murder and determined that he should receive the death penalty.

On direct appeal, the Louisiana Supreme Court conditionally affirmed petitioner's conviction. The court rejected petitioner's *Batson* claim but remanded the case for a retroactive determination of petitioner's competency to stand trial. Two justices dissented and would have found a *Batson* violation.

On remand, the trial court found that petitioner had been competent to stand trial, and the Louisiana Supreme Court affirmed that determination. Petitioner petitioned this Court for a writ of certiorari, and while his petition was pending, this Court decided *Miller-El v. Dretke* (2005). We then granted the petition, vacated the judgment, and remanded the case to the Louisiana Supreme Court for further consideration in light of *Miller-El*. On remand, the Louisiana Supreme Court again rejected Snyder's *Batson* claim, this time by a vote of 4 to 3. We again granted certiorari, and now reverse.

OPINION

Batson provides a three-step process for a trial court to use in adjudicating a claim that a peremptory challenge was based on race:

> First, a defendant must make a prima facie showing that a peremptory challenge has been exercised on the basis of race;
>
> Second, if that showing has been made, the prosecution must offer a race-neutral basis for striking the juror in question; and
>
> Third, in light of the parties' submissions, the trial court must determine whether the defendant has shown purposeful discrimination.

On appeal, a trial court's ruling on the issue of discriminatory intent must be sustained unless it is clearly erroneous. The trial court has a pivotal role in evaluating *Batson* claims. Step three of the *Batson* inquiry involves an evaluation of the prosecutor's credibility, and "the best evidence of discriminatory intent often will be the demeanor of the attorney who exercises the challenge. In addition, race-neutral reasons for peremptory challenges often invoke a juror's demeanor (*e.g.*, nervousness, inattention), making the trial court's first-hand observations of even greater importance.

In this situation, the trial court must evaluate not only whether the prosecutor's demeanor belies a discriminatory intent, but also whether the juror's demeanor can credibly be said to have exhibited the basis for the strike attributed to the juror by the prosecutor. We have recognized that these determinations of credibility and demeanor lie peculiarly within a trial judge's province, and we have stated that in the absence of exceptional circumstances, we would defer to the trial court.

Petitioner centers his *Batson* claim on the prosecution's strikes of two black jurors, Jeffrey Brooks and Elaine Scott. Because we find that the trial court committed clear error in overruling petitioner's *Batson* objection with respect to Mr. Brooks, we have no need to consider petitioner's claim regarding Ms. Scott.

When defense counsel made a *Batson* objection concerning the strike of Mr. Brooks, a college senior who was attempting to fulfill his student-teaching obligation, the prosecution offered two race-neutral reasons for the strike. The prosecutor explained:

> I thought about it last night. Number 1, the main reason is that he looked very nervous to me throughout the questioning. Number 2, he's one of the fellows that came up at the beginning of *voir dire* and said he was going to miss class. He's a student teacher. My main concern is for that reason, that being that he might, to go home quickly, come back with guilty of a lesser verdict so there wouldn't be a penalty phase. Those are my two reasons.

Defense counsel disputed both explanations, and the trial judge ruled as follows: "All right. I'm going to allow the challenge. I'm going to allow the challenge."

We discuss the prosecution's two proffered grounds for striking Mr. Brooks in turn. With respect to the first reason, the Louisiana Supreme Court was correct that "nervousness cannot be shown from a cold transcript, which is why the trial judge's evaluation must be given much deference." As noted above, deference is especially appropriate where a trial judge has made a finding that an attorney credibly relied on demeanor in exercising a strike. Here, however, the record does not show that the trial judge actually made a determination concerning Mr. Brooks' demeanor. The trial judge was given two explanations for the strike. Rather than making a specific finding on the record concerning Mr. Brooks' demeanor, the trial judge simply allowed the challenge without explanation. It is possible that the judge did not have any impression one way or the other concerning Mr. Brooks' demeanor. Mr. Brooks was not challenged until the day after he was questioned, and by that time dozens of other jurors had been questioned. Thus, the trial judge may not have recalled Mr. Brooks' demeanor. Or, the trial judge may have found it unnecessary to consider Mr. Brooks' demeanor, instead basing his ruling completely on the second proffered justification for the strike. For these reasons, we cannot presume that the trial judge credited the prosecutor's assertion that Mr. Brooks was nervous.

The second reason proffered for the strike of Mr. Brooks—his student-teaching obligation—fails even under the highly deferential standard of review that is applicable here. At the beginning of *voir dire*, when the trial court asked the members of the venire whether jury service or sequestration would pose an extreme hardship, Mr. Brooks was 1 of more than 50 members of the venire who expressed concern that jury service or sequestration would interfere with work, school, family, or other obligations.

When Mr. Brooks came forward, the following exchange took place:

Mr. Jeffrey Brooks: . . . I'm a student at Southern University, New Orleans. This is my last semester. My major requires me to student teach, and today I've already missed a half a day. That is part of my—it's required for me to graduate this semester.

[Defense Counsel]: Mr. Brooks, if you—how many days would you miss if you were sequestered on this jury? Do you teach every day?

Mr. Jeffrey Brooks: Five days a week.

[Defense Counsel]: Five days a week.

Mr. Jeffrey Brooks: And it's 8:30 through 3:00.

[Defense Counsel]: If you missed this week, is there any way that you could make it up this semester?

Mr. Jeffrey Brooks: Well, the first two weeks I observe, the remaining I begin teaching, so there is something I'm missing right now that will better me towards my teaching career.

[Defense Counsel]: Is there any way that you could make up the observed observation [*sic*] that you're missing today, at another time?

Mr. Jeffrey Brooks: It may be possible, I'm not sure.

[Defense Counsel]: Okay. So that—

The Court: Is there anyone we could call, like a Dean or anything, that we could speak to?

Mr. Jeffrey Brooks: Actually, I spoke to my Dean, Doctor Tillman, who's at the university probably right now.

The Court: All right.

Mr. Jeffrey Brooks: Would you like to speak to him?

The Court: Yeah.

Mr. Jeffrey Brooks: I don't have his card on me.

The Court: Why don't you give [a law clerk] his number, give [a law clerk] his name and we'll call him and we'll see what we can do.

(Mr. Jeffrey Brooks left the bench.) App. 102–104.

Shortly thereafter, the court again spoke with Mr. Brooks:

The Law Clerk: Jeffrey Brooks, the requirement for his teaching is a three hundred clock hour observation. Doctor Tillman at Southern University said that as long as it's just this week, he doesn't see that it would cause a problem with Mr. Brooks completing his observation time within this semester.

(Mr. Brooks approached the bench.)

The Court: We talked to Doctor Tillman and he says he doesn't see a problem as long as it's just this week, you know, he'll work with you on it. Okay?

Mr. Jeffrey Brooks: Okay.

(Mr. Jeffrey Brooks left the bench.)

Once Mr. Brooks heard the law clerk's report about the conversation with Doctor Tillman, Mr. Brooks did not express any further concern about serving on the jury, and the prosecution did not choose to question him more deeply about this matter. The colloquy with Mr. Brooks and the law clerk's report took place on Tuesday, August 27; the prosecution struck Mr. Brooks the following day, Wednesday, August 28; the guilt phase of petitioner's trial ended the next day, Thursday, August 29; and the penalty phase was completed by the end of the week, on Friday, August 30.

The prosecutor's second proffered reason for striking Mr. Brooks must be evaluated in light of these circumstances. The prosecutor claimed to be apprehensive that Mr. Brooks, in order to minimize the student-teaching hours missed during jury service, might have been motivated to find petitioner guilty, not of first-degree murder, but of a lesser included offense because this would obviate the need for a penalty phase proceeding. But this scenario was highly speculative. Even if Mr. Brooks had favored a quick resolution, that would not have necessarily led him to reject a finding of first-degree murder. If the majority of jurors had initially favored a finding of first-degree murder, Mr. Brooks' purported inclination might have led him to agree in order to speed the deliberations. Only if all or most of the other jurors had favored the lesser verdict would Mr. Brooks have been in a position to shorten the trial by favoring such a verdict.

Perhaps most telling, the brevity of petitioner's trial—something that the prosecutor anticipated on the record during *voir dire*—meant that serving on the jury would not have seriously interfered with Mr. Brooks' ability to complete his required student teaching. As noted, petitioner's trial was completed by Friday, August 30. If Mr. Brooks, who reported to court and was peremptorily challenged on Wednesday, August 28, had been permitted to serve, he would have missed only two additional days of student teaching, Thursday, August 29, and Friday, August 30. Mr. Brooks' dean promised to "work with" Mr. Brooks to see that he was able to make up any student-teaching time that he missed due to jury service; the dean stated that he did not think that this would be a problem; and the record contains no suggestion that Mr. Brooks remained troubled after hearing the report of the dean's remarks. In addition, although the record does not include the academic calendar of Mr. Brooks' university, it is apparent that the trial occurred relatively early in the fall semester. With many weeks remaining in the term, Mr. Brooks would have needed to make up no more than an hour or two per week in order to compensate for the time that he would have lost due to jury service. When all of these considerations are taken into account, the prosecutor's second proffered justification for striking Mr. Brooks is suspicious.

The implausibility of this explanation is reinforced by the prosecutor's acceptance of white jurors who disclosed conflicting obligations that appear to have been at least as serious as Mr. Brooks'. We recognize that a retrospective comparison of jurors based on a cold appellate record may be very misleading when alleged similarities were not raised at trial. In that situation, an appellate court must be mindful that an exploration of the alleged similarities at the time of trial might have shown that the jurors in question were not really comparable. In this case, however, the shared characteristic, *i.e.*, concern about serving on the jury due to conflicting obligations, was thoroughly explored by the trial court when the relevant jurors asked to be excused for cause.

A comparison between Mr. Brooks and Roland Laws, a white juror, is particularly striking. During the initial stage of *voir dire*, Mr. Laws approached the court and offered strong reasons why serving on the sequestered jury would cause him hardship. Mr. Laws stated that he was "a self-employed general contractor," with "two houses that are nearing completion, one with the occupants moving in this weekend. He explained that, if he served on the jury, "the people won't be able to move in." Mr. Laws also had demanding family obligations:

> My wife just had a hysterectomy, so I'm running the kids back and forth to school, and we're not originally from here, so I have no family in the area, so between the two things, it's kind of bad timing for me.

Although these obligations seem substantially more pressing than Mr. Brooks', the prosecution questioned Mr. Laws and attempted to elicit assurances that he would be able to serve despite his work and family obligations. (prosecutor [*sic*] asking Mr. Laws "if you got stuck on jury duty anyway would you try to make other arrangements as best you could?"). And the prosecution declined the opportunity to use a peremptory strike on Mr. Laws. If the prosecution had been sincerely concerned that Mr. Brooks would favor a lesser verdict than first-degree murder in order to shorten the trial, it is hard to see why the prosecution would not have had at least as much concern regarding Mr. Laws.

The situation regarding another white juror, John Donnes, although less fully developed, is also significant. At the end of the first day of *voir dire*, Mr. Donnes approached the court and raised the possibility that he would have an important work commitment later that week. Because Mr. Donnes stated that he would know the next morning whether he would actually have a problem, the court suggested that Mr. Donnes raise the matter again at that time. The next day, Mr. Donnes again expressed concern about serving, stating that, in order to serve, "I'd have to cancel too many things," including an urgent appointment at which his presence was essential. Despite Mr. Donnes' concern, the prosecution did not strike him.

As previously noted, the question presented at the third stage of the *Batson* inquiry is whether the defendant has shown purposeful discrimination. The prosecution's proffer of this pretextual explanation naturally gives rise to an inference of discriminatory intent. In other circumstances, we have held that, once it is shown that a discriminatory intent was a substantial or motivating factor in an action taken by a state actor, the burden shifts to the party defending the action to show that this factor was not determinative.

We have not previously applied this rule in a *Batson* case, and we need not decide here whether that standard governs in this context. For present purposes, it is enough to recognize that a peremptory strike shown to have been motivated in substantial part by discriminatory intent could not be sustained based on any lesser showing by the prosecution. And in light of the circumstances here— including absence of anything in the record showing that the trial judge credited the claim that Mr. Brooks was nervous, the prosecution's description of both of its proffered explanations as "main concerns," and the adverse inference noted above—the record does not show that the prosecution would have pre-emptively challenged Mr. Brooks based on his nervousness alone. Nor is there any realistic possibility that this subtle question of causation could be profitably explored further on remand at this late date, more than a decade after petitioner's trial.

We therefore REVERSE the judgment of the Louisiana Supreme Court and REMAND the case for further proceedings not inconsistent with this opinion.

It is so ordered.

DISSENT

Justice THOMAS, with whom Justice SCALIA joins, dissenting.

Petitioner essentially asks this Court to second-guess the fact-based determinations of the Louisiana courts as to the reasons for a prosecutor's decision to strike two jurors. The evaluation of a prosecutor's motives for striking a juror is at bottom a credibility judgment, which lies peculiarly within a trial judge's province. None of the evidence in the record as to jurors Jeffrey Brooks and Elaine Scott demonstrates that the trial court clearly erred in finding they were not stricken on the basis of race. Because the trial court's determination was a permissible view of the evidence, I would affirm the judgment of the Louisiana Supreme Court.

The Court's conclusion reveals that it is only paying lip service to the pivotal role of the trial court. The Court second-guesses the trial court's determinations in this case merely because the judge did not clarify which of the prosecutor's neutral bases for striking Mr. Brooks was dispositive. But we have never suggested that a reviewing court should defer to a trial court's resolution of a *Batson* challenge only if the trial court made specific findings with respect to each of the prosecutor's proffered race-neutral reasons. To the contrary, when the grounds for a trial court's decision are ambiguous, an appellate court should not presume that the lower court based its decision on an improper ground, particularly when applying a deferential standard of review.

QUESTIONS

1. **State the test the Court used to determine whether the prosecutor's peremptory challenges were race-based.**
2. **Summarize the majority's arguments supporting its remand for further consideration.**
3. **Summarize the dissent's arguments opposing the remand.**
4. **Which opinion do you support? Back up your answer with details from the facts and opinions.**

Should It Be Ethical to Take Race, Ethnicity, and Gender into Account When Selecting Jurors?

Although a long line of U.S. Supreme Court decisions forbids packing juries based on race or gender, lawyers admit they do it frequently. Asians are conservative. African-Americans distrust cops. Latins are emotional. Jews are sentimental. Women are hard on women—or so goes some of the lore that litigators have all heard. Clatsop County, Ore., District Attorney Joshua Marquis, who is the co-chairman of the National District Attorneys Association's death-penalty committee, said that he would not have let his own father sit on a jury in a capital case. "It would be a little disingenuous for me to say that I would have allowed my father—a refugee from Nazi Germany—to sit in a capital case," he said.

The issue of packing juries along racial and gender lines garnered national attention recently when former Alameda County, Calif., prosecutor John Quatman claimed that it was standard practice to exclude Jews and black women from juries in capital cases because they would never vote for death. Yet every litigator interviewed for this article considers race and gender when picking a jury. At the conclusion of a recent evidentiary hearing ordered by the California Supreme Court to determine the truth of some of the allegations that Quatman made in a declaration in a capital habeas case (*In re Freeman,* No. S122590), a judge found Quatman not credible. But the lower court was not asked to determine whether Quatman's alleged standard practices exist.

INSTRUCTIONS

1. Visit the Companion Website and read Leonard Post's, "A Loaded Box of Stereotypes: Discrimination in Jury Selection." See the link under the Chapter 13 Ethical Issues section—login at www.cengagebrain.com.

2. List all the reasons prosecutors try to—and usually succeed—pack juries based on race, ethnicity, gender, and other "unconstitutional" categories.

3. List all the reasons prosecutors shouldn't try to "pack" juries by using "unconstitutional" categories.

4. Write an essay answering, "Should it be ethical to take race, ethnicity, and gender into account when selecting jurors?"

Source: Post 2005.

The Right to a Public Trial

LO 3

Three constitutional amendments guarantee defendants the right to a public trial:

1. The Sixth Amendment right to confront witnesses
2. The Fifth Amendment due process right
3. The Fourteenth Amendment due process right

Public trials protect two distinct rights:

1. *Public access.* The right of the public to attend the proceedings
2. *Defendants' rights.* The right of defendants to attend their own trials

The right to a public trial extends to "every stage of the trial," including jury selection, communications between the judge and the jury, **jury instructions** (judges' explanations of the law to the jury), and in-chamber conversations between the judge and jurors. It doesn't include brief conferences at the bench outside the defendant's hearing or other brief conferences involving only questions of law.

Public trials support defendants' interests in avoiding persecution through secret proceedings, enhance community participation in law enforcement, and aid in the search for truth by encouraging witnesses to come forward who otherwise might not.

These interests aren't absolute. Courtroom size limits public access. Furthermore, the need to protect threatened witnesses even justifies closing the courtroom. Protecting undercover agents also authorizes exclusion of the public during their testimony. Moreover, public trials may discourage shy and introverted witnesses from coming forward. Finally, judges can limit public access during sensitive proceedings. For example, it's justifiable to exclude spectators while alleged rape victims are testifying about the "lurid details" of the crime (*U.S. ex rel. Latimore v. Sielaff* 1977).

Defendants don't have an absolute right to attend their own trials; they can forfeit that right by their disruptive behavior. For example, in *Illinois v. Allen* (1970), William Allen, while being tried for armed robbery, repeatedly interrupted the judge in a "most abusive and disrespectful manner." He also threatened him, "When I go out for lunchtime, you're going to be a corpse here." When the judge warned Allen that he could attend only as long as he behaved himself, Allen answered, "There is going to be no proceeding. I'm going to start talking all through the trial. There's not going to be no trial like this."

According to the U.S. Supreme Court, the judge properly removed Allen from the courtroom:

> It is essential to the proper administration of criminal justice that dignity, order, and decorum be the hallmarks of all court proceedings in our country. The flagrant disregard in the courtroom of elementary standards of proper conduct should not and cannot be tolerated. We believe that trial judges confronted with disruptive, contumacious, stubbornly defiant defendants must be given sufficient discretion to meet the circumstances of each case. We think there are at least three constitutionally permissible ways for a trial judge to handle an obstreperous defendant like Allen: (1) bind and gag him, thereby keeping him present; (2) cite him for contempt; (3) take him out of the courtroom until he promises to conduct himself properly. (343)

Judges can also exclude defendants during the questioning of child witnesses in sexual abuse cases. For example, in *Kentucky v. Stincer* (1987), Sergio Stincer was on trial for sodomizing two children, ages 7 and 8. The trial court conducted an in-chambers hearing to determine whether the children could remember certain details and whether they understood the significance of telling the truth in court. The judge permitted his lawyer to attend but refused Stincer's request to do so. The U.S. Supreme Court upheld the judge's ruling because Stincer had an adequate opportunity to "confront" the children during the trial.

Courts can also require dangerous defendants to appear under guard to protect the public, witnesses, and court officials from harm and to prevent defendants from escaping. However, defendants ordinarily have the right not just to be at their trial but also to be presented in a way that doesn't prejudice their case. For example, the government can't bring defendants to court in jail dress (*Estelle v. Williams* 1976) or make defense witnesses testify in shackles, because their dress prejudices the jury, furthers no state policy, and mainly hurts poor defendants (*Holbrook v. Flynn* 1986).

||||||||||||||||||||||||||||||||||||||||||||||||||||||||||||||||||||||||||||||||||||||||||||||||||||||||||||||||||||||

The Stages and Rules of Jury Trials

LO 3

The adversarial process reaches its high point in the jury trial. Strict, technical rules control trials. The main stages in the criminal trial include:

1. Opening statements, with the prosecution first, followed by the defense

2. Presenting the evidence—the state's and the defendants' cases

3. Closing arguments

4. Instructions to the jury

5. Jury deliberations

Let's look at each of these stages. Then, we'll examine the issues of whether the law requires unanimous verdicts and jury nullification.

Opening Statements

LO 3

Prosecutors and defense counsel can make **opening statements**—that is, address the jury before they present their evidence. Prosecutors make their opening statements first; defense counsel address the jury either immediately after the prosecutor's opening statement or, in a few jurisdictions, following the presentation of the state's case. The opening statements have a narrow scope: to outline the case that the two sides hope to prove, not to prove the case. Proving the case takes place during the presentation-of-evidence phase of the criminal trial. In fact, it's unprofessional for either side to refer to any evidence they don't honestly believe will be admissible in court. Although it's rare for them to do so, appeals courts sometimes reverse cases in which prosecutors have referred to points they intend to prove with evidence they know is inadmissible, incompetent, or both (LaFave and Israel 1984, 3:12).

Presenting Evidence

LO 3

The prosecution presents its case first because of its burden to prove defendants' guilt. In presenting its case, the rules of evidence restrict what evidence the state may use, mainly excluding illegally obtained testimony and physical evidence and most hearsay. The prosecution has to prove every element in the case, but the defense frequently **"stipulates"** (agrees not to contest) some facts, particularly those that might prejudice the defendant's case—detailed photographs and descriptions of a brutally murdered victim, for example. The prosecution can decline a stipulation. Most courts don't compel the prosecution to accept stipulations, because it might weaken the state's case (*People v. McClellan* 1969).

The state ordinarily presents all the available eyewitnesses to the crime. In some instances, if the prosecution doesn't call a material witness, particularly a victim, the defense can ask for a **"missing witness instruction"**—an instruction that jurors can infer that the witness's testimony would have been unfavorable to the prosecution. The prosecution can ask the court to inform the jury that a key witness is unavailable and not to draw negative inferences from his failure to testify. Prosecutors also may decide not to call witnesses—such as spouses, priests, and doctors—that they know will claim a valid privilege; doing so might result in reversible error (*Bowles v. U.S.* 1970).

Issues that affect the presenting of evidence include cross-examination, the admission of hearsay evidence, compelling witnesses to testify, the prosecutor's burden to prove all elements of a crime, and proof beyond a reasonable doubt. Let's look at each.

Cross-Examination

The **Sixth Amendment confrontation clause** includes the right to cross-examine the prosecution's witnesses. In *Smith v. Illinois* (1968), when the prosecution's key witness, an informant, testified that he bought heroin from Smith, the trial court allowed him to use an alias, concealing his real name and address. The U.S. Supreme Court ruled that this violated Smith's right to confrontation:

> When the credibility of a witness is at issue, the very starting point in "exposing falsehood and bringing out the truth" through cross-examination must necessarily be to ask the witness who he is and where he lives. The witness's name and address open countless avenues of in-court examination and out-of-doors investigation. It is of the essence of a fair trial that reasonable latitude be given to the cross-examiner, even though he is unable to state to the court what facts a reasonable cross-examination might develop. (132)

Hearsay Evidence

The confrontation clause also restricts the prosecution's use of **hearsay testimony**— out-of-court statements offered to prove the truth of the statements. Hearsay violates the confrontation clause because defendants can't ferret the truth through the adversarial process unless the defense can cross-examine the witnesses against them. Therefore, the jury can't have an adequate basis for fact-finding.

The confrontation clause doesn't bar hearsay testimony totally. The prosecution can introduce hearsay if the government meets two tests:

1. It demonstrates the witness's unavailability and, hence, the necessity to use out-of-court statements.
2. It shows that the state obtained the evidence under circumstances that clearly establish its reliability.

In *Ohio v. Roberts* (1980), the majority of the Supreme Court found that the state satisfied the tests under these circumstances:

1. The witness's mother said the witness, her daughter, had left home, saying she was going to Tucson, two years earlier.
2. Shortly thereafter, a San Francisco social worker contacted the mother concerning a welfare claim her daughter had filed there.
3. The mother was able to reach her daughter only once, by phone.
4. When the daughter called a few months prior to the trial, she told her mother she was traveling but didn't reveal her whereabouts.

The dissent argued that relying solely on the parents wasn't sufficient; the prosecution had the burden to go out and find the witness. The Court disagreed.

Compulsory Process

The Sixth Amendment guarantees the defendant's right "to have **compulsory process for obtaining witnesses** in [his or her] . . . favor." This means defendants can compel witnesses to come to court to testify for them. Most states pay for poor defendants' process, but they don't pay for process to get evidence that only corroborates (adds to) evidence already available. And most states make defendants spell out exactly why they need the evidence.

The Burden of Proof

The Fifth Amendment provides that "no person . . . shall be compelled in any criminal case to be a witness against himself." This means the state can't call defendants to the witness stand in criminal trials. It also bars the prosecution from commenting on defendants' refusal to testify; it even entitles defendants to ask judges to instruct juries not to infer guilt from their silence. However, if defendants decide to take the stand to tell their side of the story, the prosecution can cross-examine them as they would any other witness.

The defense doesn't have to present a case; cross-examining the prosecution's witnesses by itself can raise a reasonable doubt about the proof against the defendant. Or defendants may call their own witnesses for the sole purpose of rebutting the prosecution's witnesses. Of course, they may also call witnesses to create a reasonable doubt about their guilt—to establish alibis, for example.

Defendants may also have affirmative defenses that justify or excuse what would otherwise be criminal conduct (self-defense, insanity, duress, and entrapment). Or maybe they have evidence that reduces the grade of the offense, such as provocation to reduce murder to manslaughter or diminished capacity to reduce first-degree murder to second-degree murder. The prosecution, of course, has the right to cross-examine defense witnesses.

Proof beyond a Reasonable Doubt

Defendants don't have to prove their innocence or help the government prove their guilt. The right against self-incrimination gives defendants an absolute right to say nothing at all and not have it count against them. So trials can proceed, and some do, where neither defendants nor their lawyers present a case. Sometimes, no defense is the best defense. The **reasonable doubt standard** requires the government to carry the whole burden of proving defendants are guilty beyond a reasonable doubt.

The U.S. Supreme Court ruled in *In re Winship* (1970) that due process requires both federal and state prosecutors to prove every element of a crime beyond a reasonable doubt. According to the Court, "The reasonable doubt standard is bottomed on a fundamental value determination of our society that it is far worse to convict an innocent man than to let a guilty man go free" (373).

Despite the constitutional requirement of proof beyond a reasonable doubt, the U.S. Supreme Court hasn't decided that due process requires judges to define proof beyond a reasonable doubt. Nevertheless, courts struggle to tell jurors what reasonable doubt means. Table 13.3 provides some examples of courts' definitions.

Closing Arguments

After they've presented their evidence, both the state and the defense make their closing arguments. Prosecutors close first, the defense follows, and then the prosecution rebuts. Prosecutors can't waive their right to make a closing argument and save their remarks for rebuttal. If they waive their right to make a closing argument, they're barred automatically from making a rebuttal. Prosecutors can't raise "new" matters in rebuttal

TABLE 13.3

Sample of Trial Court Definitions of Proof beyond a Reasonable Doubt

- A doubt that would cause prudent people to hesitate before acting in a matter of importance to themselves
- A doubt based on reason and common sense
- A doubt that's neither frivolous nor fanciful and that can't be explained away easily
- Substantial doubt
- Persuasion to a reasonable or moral certainty
- Doubt beyond that which is reasonable; about "7½ on a scale of 10" (rejected by the appellate court)
- When the "scales of justice are substantially out of equipoise" (rejected by the appellate court)

either; they can only rebut what either they or the defense counsel brought up during closing arguments. Why? It's only fair that the defense should hear all the arguments in favor of conviction before responding to them.

Formally, prosecutors have the duty not only to convict criminals but also to seek justice. The American Bar Association's *Standards for Criminal Justice* (1980, § 3.5) includes the following guidelines for prosecutors. It's improper to

- Misstate intentionally the evidence or mislead the jury
- Refer to evidence excluded or not introduced at trial
- Express personal beliefs or opinions about the truth or falsity of the evidence or the defendant's guilt
- Engage in arguments that divert jurors' attention by injecting issues beyond the case or predicting consequences of the jury's verdict
- Make arguments calculated to inflame jurors' passions and prejudices

Violating these standards rarely results in reversal. According to the Supreme Court:

> If every remark made by counsel outside of the testimony were grounds for a reversal, comparatively few verdicts would stand, since in the ardor of advocacy, and in the excitement of the trial, even the most experienced counsel are occasionally carried away by this temptation. (*Dunlop v. U.S.* 1897)

When determining whether to reverse convictions based on improper closing arguments, appellate courts consider whether:

- Defense counsel invited or provoked the remarks.
- Defense counsel made timely objection to the remarks.
- The trial judge took corrective action, such as instructing the jury to disregard the remarks.
- The comments were brief and isolated in an otherwise proper argument.
- Other errors occurred during the trial.
- The evidence of guilt was overwhelming. (LaFave and Israel 1984, 3:15)

Although appellate courts rarely reverse convictions for these abuses, they frequently express their displeasure with prosecutors' improper remarks made during closing arguments. In *Bowen v. Kemp* (1985), Charlie Bowen was convicted of raping and murdering a 12-year-old girl. The prosecutor, in the course of the closing statement, made several comments focusing on the accused:

> And now we come up here with this idea that a man is subject to be rehabilitated and released back into society. Yeah, I guess he can be rehabilitated. Hitler could have been. I believe in about six or eight months if I'd had him chained to a wall and talked to him and beat him on one side of the head for a while with a stick telling him you believe this don't you then beat him on the other side with a stick telling him you believe that don't you I believe I could have rehabilitated Hitler. (678)

The prosecutor went on to call Bowen "a product of the devil" and a "liar" who was "no better than a beast":

> And, you know for a criminal to go without proper punishment is a disgrace to the society we live in and it's shown to us every day by the fruits that we reap from day to day in our society when we have the bloody deeds such as this occur. (680)

Bowen appealed his conviction on the basis that the prosecutor's remarks affected the jury's verdict. While conceding that the remarks were improper, the circuit court of appeals affirmed the conviction. It found "no reasonable probability that, absent the improper statements of opinion, Bowen would not have been sentenced to death" (682).

Jury Instructions

LO 3

Before jurors begin their deliberations, judges "instruct" them on what the law is and how they should apply it. Jury instructions usually inform the jury about the following subjects:

- The respective roles of the judge to decide the law and the jury to decide the facts
- The principle that defendants are presumed innocent until proven guilty
- The principle that the state bears the burden of proving guilt beyond a reasonable doubt
- The definition of all the elements of the crime with which the defendant is charged

Both the prosecution and the defense can ask the judge to provide the jury with specific instructions. And they can object if the judge refuses to give the requested instruction and frequently do base appeals on such refusals.

A number of jurisdictions use *pattern instructions*—published boilerplate instructions that fit most cases. Supporters praise the clarity, accuracy, impartiality, and efficiency of pattern instructions; critics say they're too general to help jurors. However, most empirical evaluations show that jurors understand only about half of judges' instructions, whether patterned or individually crafted (LaFave and Israel 1984, 3:39–40).

Jury Deliberations

LO 3

After the judge instructs the jury, she orders them to retire to a separate room under supervision and without interruption to deliberate until they reach a verdict. The jurors

TABLE 13.4

Arguments for Unanimous Verdicts

- They instill confidence in the criminal justice process.
- They guarantee that the jury carefully reviews the evidence.
- They ensure the hearing and consideration of minority viewpoints.
- They prevent government oppression.
- They support the principle that convicting innocent defendants is worse than freeing guilty ones.
- They fulfill the proof-beyond-a-reasonable-doubt requirement.

Source: LaFave and Israel 1984, 698.

take the instructions, any exhibits received in evidence, and a list of the charges against the defendant with them into the jury room. During the course of their deliberations, they may ask the court for further instruction or information concerning the evidence or any other matter. The court can discharge *hung juries*—juries unable to reach a verdict after protracted deliberations (Chapter 12).

Jury Verdicts

LO 4

Juries can return one of three verdicts:

1. Guilty

2. Not guilty

3. Special, mainly related to insanity or capital punishment

If the jury acquits, or issues the not guilty verdict, the defendants' ordeal with the criminal process stops immediately; they're free to go. If the jury convicts, the case continues to **judgment**—the court's final decision on the legal outcome of the case. Juries can't pass legal judgment; their word is final only as to the facts. Following the court's judgment of guilt or acquittal, the criminal trial ends.

Let's look more closely at the issue of whether juries' verdicts must be unanimous—and what happens when they aren't—and why juries sometimes choose to nullify the evidence with their verdicts.

The "Unanimous Verdict" Requirement

LO 4

Like 12-member juries (discussed earlier), unanimous verdicts are an ancient requirement and still enjoy strong support (Table 13.4). In 1900, the U.S. Supreme Court held that the Sixth Amendment demanded conviction by unanimous jury verdicts. But the Court changed its mind in 1972 when it ruled, in *Apodaca v. Oregon*, that verdicts of 11–1 and 10–2 didn't violate two convicted felons' right to a jury trial:

> A requirement of unanimity . . . does not materially contribute to . . . [the jury's] common-sense judgment. . . . A jury will come to such a verdict as long as it consists of a group of laymen representative of a cross section of the community who have the duty and the opportunity to deliberate, free from outside attempts at intimidation, on the question of a defendant's guilt. In terms of this function we perceive no difference between juries required to act unanimously and those

permitted to convict or acquit by votes of 10 to two or 11 to one. Requiring unanimity would obviously produce hung juries in some situations where nonunanimous juries will convict or acquit. But in either case, the interest of the defendant in having the judgment of his peers interposed between himself and the officers of the state who prosecute and judge him is equally well served. (411)

In *Johnson v. Louisiana* (1972), in upholding a robbery conviction based on a 9–3 verdict, Justice Byron R. White wrote:

> Nine jurors—a substantial majority of the jury—were convinced by the evidence. Disagreement of the three jurors does not alone establish reasonable doubt, particularly when such a heavy majority of the jury, after having considered the dissenters' views, remains convinced of guilt. (362)

Still, the Supreme Court hasn't answered the question of how many votes short of unanimity are required to satisfy the Sixth Amendment. What about less than unanimous verdicts by fewer than 12-member juries? A unanimous U.S. Supreme Court in *Burch v. Louisiana* (1979) struck down a Louisiana statute providing that misdemeanors punishable by more than six months "shall be tried before a jury of six persons, five of whom must concur to render a verdict." According to the Court, to preserve the right to jury trial, it had to draw a line at nonunanimous verdicts of six-member juries—a line supported by the "near-uniform judgment of the nation" (only two other states had permitted these verdicts).

Jury Nullification

The jury's function is to decide the facts in a case and apply them to the law as the judge has defined the law. Nevertheless, juries have the power to acquit even when the facts clearly fit the law. Jury acquittals are final, meaning the prosecution can't appeal them. The practice of acquitting in the face of proof beyond a reasonable doubt is called **jury nullification.** Why do juries nullify? Usually, it's because either they sympathize with particular defendants (for example, in a mercy killing) or because the state has prosecuted defendants for breaking unpopular laws (for example, possession of small amounts of marijuana for personal use).

Jury nullification has an ancient lineage. The "pages of history shine on instances of the jury's exercise of its prerogative to disregard uncontradicted evidence and instructions of the judge." In the famous John Peter Zenger case (*New York v. Zenger* 1735), the jury ignored the facts and the judge's instructions and acquitted Zenger of the charge of sedition (LaFave and Israel 1984, 3:700).

The U.S. Supreme Court has indirectly approved jury nullification. Although the Court obviously didn't like the jury's power, it conceded in *Sparf and Hansen v. U.S.* (1895):

> If a jury may rightfully disregard the direction of the court in matters of law and determine for themselves what the law is in the particular case before them, it is difficult to perceive any legal ground upon which a verdict of conviction can be set aside by the court as being against law. (101)

Probably more than any other doctrine in criminal procedure we've studied, nullification promotes community participation in criminal law enforcement. As community representatives, juries act as safety valves in exceptional cases by allowing "informal communication from the total culture" to override the strict legal bonds of their instructions from the judge (*U.S. v. Dougherty* 1972).

|||||||||||||||||||||||||||||||||||||||||||||||||||||||||||||||||||||||||||||||||||||||||||||||||||||||||||||||||||||||||||||||||||||

Conviction by Guilty Plea

There are two types of guilty plea: (1) straight pleas and (2) negotiated pleas. **Straight guilty pleas** (pleading guilty without negotiation) are ordinarily made in what are called "dead bang" cases, meaning proof of guilt is overwhelming. **Negotiated guilty pleas** (pleading guilty in exchange for concessions by the state) appear mainly in large urban courts. The concessions consist of three types: **Charge bargaining** refers to bargaining for a reduction in either the number or severity of criminal charges. **Sentence bargaining** refers to a favorable sentence *recommendation* by the prosecutor to the judge, or bargaining directly with the judge for a favorable sentence. In **fact bargaining**, the prosecutor agrees not to challenge the defendant's version of the facts or not to reveal aggravating facts to the judge.

Several historical developments have contributed to the growth and prevalence of plea bargaining. They include:

1. Increasing complexity of the criminal trial process

2. Expansion of the criminal law

3. Increasing crime rates

4. Larger caseloads

5. Political corruption in urban courts

6. Increase in the number of criminal justice professionals (police, public prosecutors, and defense lawyers)

7. Increasing statutory powers of prosecutors (Alschuler 2002, 756)

The plea-bargaining system is highly complex in operation. Consequently, participants offer multiple and conflicting descriptions of how and why it works as it does. Professor Albert Alschuler (2002), a plea-bargaining scholar, describes some of these conflicting views, based on what he hears from scholars and practitioners at plea-bargaining conferences:

- "When experienced lawyers can predict the outcome of a trial, there's no need to have a trial."

- "No one can predict how a trial will turn out; all we know is that one side will win big and the other side will lose big. The goal of bargaining *isn't* to get the same result as a trial but to steer the risks of trial into a sensible middle ground where each side gets, and gives up, something."

- "The goal is to 'escape altogether the irrationalities of an overly legalized trial system and achieve "substantive justice" without regard to technicalities.'"

- "The lawyer's goal in plea bargaining is 'to take as much as possible from the other side by threat, bluster, charm, bluff, campaign contributions, personal appeals, friendship, or whatever else works.'"

- "Sometimes the dominant motive for lazy lawyers and judges is to take the money and go home early." (756–57)

Professor Alschuler concludes that:

Of course, to some extent, all of these things are going on at the same time. . . . [I]n view of the different forms that plea bargaining may take and the many considerations that may influence it, mathematical models of plea negotiation of the sort developed by economists generally seem artificial to practicing lawyers. (757)

The Constitution and Guilty Pleas

LO 7, LO 8

Although widely used for more than a century, courts didn't recognize negotiated pleas formally until 1970. In that year, in *Brady v. U.S.*, the U.S. Supreme Court ruled that bargained pleas are constitutional. According to the Court, "the chief virtues of the plea system are speed, economy, and finality." Whatever might be the situation in an ideal world, plea bargaining and guilty pleas are important (and can be beneficial) parts of our criminal justice system" (*Blackledge v. Allison* 1977, 71).

When they plead guilty, defendants *waive* (give up) three constitutional rights:

1. The Fifth Amendment right to remain silent
2. The Sixth Amendment right to a trial by jury
3. The Sixth Amendment right to confront the witnesses against them

The Court has ruled that, to give up these constitutional rights, defendants have to do so knowingly (also called "intelligently") and voluntarily (*Brady v. U.S.* 1970, 748).

It's up to trial judges to make sure defendants' pleas are voluntary and knowing in view of the totality of the circumstances surrounding the plea. The Court has established the following standard for trial judges' inquiries:

> A plea of guilty entered by one fully aware of the direct consequences, including the actual value of any commitments made to him by the court, prosecutor, or his own counsel, must stand unless induced by threats (or promises to discontinue improper harassment), misrepresentation (including unfulfilled or unfulfillable promises), or perhaps by promises that are by their nature improper as having no prior relationship to the prosecutor's business (e.g., bribes). (*Brady v. U.S.* 1970, 756)

The Supreme Court has held that a trial judge's failure to ask defendants questions concerning their plea in open court is **reversible error**—grounds to reverse the trial court's judgment of guilt. Why? Because the trial court accepted the plea "without an affirmative showing that it was intelligent and voluntary" (*Boykin v. Alabama* 1969). A court can't presume "from a silent record" that by pleading guilty defendants give up fundamental rights. Judges have to make clear to defendants when they plead guilty that they're giving up their rights to trial (Sixth Amendment), to confrontation (Sixth Amendment), and not to incriminate themselves (Fifth Amendment).

According to the Court, defendants have to know "the true nature of the charges" against them. For example, in one case, the defendant pleaded guilty to second-degree murder without knowing the elements of the crime. Neither his lawyer nor the trial judge had explained to him that second-degree murder required an intent to kill and that his version of what he did negated intent. The U.S. Supreme Court ruled that the record didn't establish a knowing plea.

Most jurisdictions now require that judges determine that there's a **factual basis for guilty pleas**. To determine the factual basis, for example, judges might ask defendants to describe the conduct that led to the charges, ask the prosecutor and defense attorney similar questions, and consult presentence reports. But in *North Carolina v. Alford* (1970), the U.S. Supreme Court held that there are no constitutional barriers to prevent a judge from accepting a guilty plea from a defendant who wants to plead guilty while still protesting his innocence. (It's called an *Alford* plea.)

So are defendants who believe they're **factually innocent** (they didn't commit the crime) but **legally guilty** (the government has enough evidence to convict them), and who plead guilty because they don't want to risk going to trial and receiving a harsher sentence if convicted, knowingly and voluntarily pleading guilty? "Yes," the U.S. Supreme Court answered in *North Carolina v. Alford* (1970), our next case excerpt.

In **North Carolina v. Alford (1970),** *our next case excerpt, the U.S. Supreme Court found Henry Alford's guilty plea was knowing and voluntary despite his denial of factual guilt in the murder.*

CASE   Was His Guilty Plea Voluntary?

North Carolina v. Alford
400 U.S. 25 (1970)

HISTORY

Henry Alford was indicted for the capital offense of first-degree murder. North Carolina law provided for three possible punishments for murder: (1) life imprisonment when a plea of guilty was accepted for first-degree murder; (2) death following a jury verdict of guilty of first-degree murder unless the jury recommended life imprisonment; (3) two to thirty years' imprisonment for second-degree murder. Alford's attorney recommended that Alford plead guilty to second-degree murder, which the prosecutor accepted. Alford pleaded guilty and was sentenced to 30 years in prison. On writ of habeas corpus, the U.S. Court of Appeals found Alford's plea involuntary. On writ of certiorari, the U.S. Supreme Court reversed.

WHITE, J., joined by BURGER, C.J., and HARLAN, STEWART, and BLACKMUN, JJ.

FACTS

On December 2, 1963, Alford was indicted for first-degree murder, a capital offense under North Carolina law. The court appointed an attorney to represent him, and this attorney questioned all but one of the various witnesses who appellee said would substantiate his claim of innocence. The witnesses, however, did not support Alford's story but gave statements that strongly indicated his guilt. Faced with strong evidence of guilt and no substantial evidentiary support for the claim of innocence, Alford's attorney recommended that he plead guilty, but left the ultimate decision to Alford himself. The prosecutor agreed to accept a plea of guilty to a charge of second-degree murder, and on December 10, 1963, Alford pleaded guilty to the reduced charge.

Before the plea was finally accepted by the trial court, the court heard the sworn testimony of a police officer who summarized the State's case. Two other witnesses besides Alford were also heard. Although there was no eyewitness to the crime, the testimony indicated that shortly before the killing Alford took his gun from his house, stated his intention to kill the victim and returned home with the declaration that he had carried out the killing.

After the summary presentation of the State's case, Alford took the stand and testified that he had not committed the murder but that he was pleading guilty because he faced the threat of the death penalty if he did not do so. In response to the questions of his counsel, he acknowledged that his counsel had informed him of the difference between second- and first-degree murder and of his rights in case he chose to go to trial.

The trial court then asked Alford if, in light of his denial of guilt, he still desired to plead guilty to second-degree murder and appellee answered, "Yes, sir. I plead guilty on—from the circumstances that he [Alford's attorney] told me." After eliciting information about Alford's prior criminal record, which was a long one, the trial court sentenced him to 30 years' imprisonment, the maximum penalty for second-degree murder.

After giving his version of the events of the night of the murder, Alford stated: "I pleaded guilty on second degree murder because they said there is too much evidence, but I ain't shot no man, but I take the fault for the other man. We never had an argument in our life and I just pleaded guilty because they said if I didn't they would gas me for it, and that is all." In response to questions from his attorney, Alford affirmed that he had consulted several times with his attorney and with members of his family and had been informed of his rights if he chose to plead not guilty. Alford then reaffirmed his decision to plead guilty to second-degree murder:

Q: [by Alford's attorney] And you authorized me to tender a plea of guilty to second degree murder before the court?

A: Yes, sir.

Q: And in doing that, you have again affirmed your decision on that point?

A: Well, I'm still pleading that you all got me to plead guilty. I plead the other way, circumstantial evidence; that the jury will prosecute me on—on the second. You told me to plead guilty, right. I don't—I'm not guilty but I plead guilty.

On appeal, a divided panel of the Court of Appeals for the Fourth Circuit reversed on the ground that Alford's guilty plea was made involuntarily.

OPINION

The standard [for determining the validity of a quality plea is] whether the plea represents a voluntary and intelligent choice among the alternative courses of action open to the defendant. Ordinarily, a judgment of conviction resting on a plea of guilty is justified by the defendant's admission that he committed the crime charged against him and his consent that judgment be entered without a trial of any kind. The plea usually subsumes both elements, and justifiably so, even though there is no separate, express admission by the defendant that he committed the particular acts claimed to constitute the crime charged in the indictment.

Here Alford entered his plea but accompanied it with the statement that he had not shot the victim. While most pleas of guilty consist of both a waiver of trial and an express admission of guilt, the latter element is not a constitutional requisite to the imposition of criminal penalty. An individual accused of crime may voluntarily, knowingly, and understandably consent to the imposition of a prison sentence even if he is unwilling or unable to admit his participation in the acts constituting the crime.

Nor can we perceive any material difference between a plea that refuses to admit commission of the criminal act and a plea containing a protestation of innocence when, as in the instant case, a defendant intelligently concludes that his interests require entry of a guilty plea and the record before the judge contains strong evidence of actual guilt.

Here the State had a strong case of first-degree murder against Alford. Whether he realized or disbelieved his guilt, he insisted on his plea because in his view he had absolutely nothing to gain by a trial and much to gain by pleading. Because of the overwhelming evidence against him, a trial was precisely what neither Alford nor his attorney desired.

Confronted with the choice between a trial for first-degree murder, on the one hand, and a plea of guilty to second-degree murder, on the other, Alford quite reasonably chose the latter and thereby limited the maximum penalty to a 30-year term. When his plea is viewed in light of the evidence against him, which substantially negated his claim of innocence and which further provided a means by which the judge could test whether the plea was being intelligently entered, its validity cannot be seriously questioned. In view of the strong factual basis for the plea demonstrated by the State and Alford's clearly expressed desire to enter it despite his professed belief in his innocence, we hold that the trial judge did not commit constitutional error in accepting it.

Alford now argues in effect that the State should not have allowed him this choice but should have insisted on proving him guilty of murder in the first degree. The States in their wisdom may take this course by statute or otherwise and may prohibit the practice of accepting pleas to lesser included offenses under any circumstances. But this is not the mandate of the Fourteenth Amendment and the Bill of Rights. The prohibitions against involuntary or unintelligent pleas should not be relaxed, but neither should an exercise in arid logic render those constitutional guarantees counterproductive and put in jeopardy the very human values they were meant to preserve.

The Court of Appeals judgment directing the issuance of the writ of habeas corpus is vacated and the case is REMANDED to the Court of Appeals for further proceedings consistent with this opinion. It is so ordered.

DISSENT

BRENNAN, J., joined by DOUGLAS and MARSHALL, JJ.

Last Term, this Court held, over my dissent, that a plea of guilty may validly be induced by an unconstitutional threat to subject the defendant to the risk to death, so long as the plea is entered in open court and the defendant is represented by competent counsel who is aware of the threat, albeit not of its unconstitutionality. *Brady v. U.S.* (1970). Today the Court makes clear that its previous holding was intended to apply even when the record demonstrates that the actual effect of the unconstitutional threat was to induce a guilty plea from a defendant who was unwilling to admit his guilt.

I adhere to the view that, in any given case, the influence of such an unconstitutional threat must necessarily be given weight in determining the voluntariness of a plea. I believe that at the very least such a denial of guilt is a relevant factor in determining whether the plea was voluntarily and intelligently made. With these factors in mind, it is sufficient in my view to state that the facts set out in the majority opinion demonstrate that Alford was "so gripped by fear of the death penalty" that his decision to plead guilty was not voluntary but was "the product of duress as much so as choice reflecting physical constraint."

QUESTIONS

1. **Did Henry Alford knowingly and voluntarily plead guilty?**
2. **Consider the dissent's comment that Henry Alford was "so gripped by fear of the death penalty" that his decision was "the product of duress." Should defendants ever be allowed to plead guilty if they believe they're innocent? Why? or Why not? Back up your answer with arguments from the majority and dissenting opinions.**

The Debate over Conviction by Guilty Plea

**LO 7, LO 8,
LO 9**

The arguments for and against conviction by guilty plea are heated, complex, and by no means empirically resolved:

- Some say negotiation better serves the search for truth; others argue that the adversarial process best serves the ends of justice.

- Some maintain guilty pleas save time; others contend plea negotiations more than make up for the time it takes to go to trial.

- Some insist the criminal justice system would collapse under its own weight if only a few of the now vast majority of defendants who plead guilty asserted their right to trial; others contend banning plea bargaining would make little difference in how many defendants plead guilty.

- Some maintain the guilty plea intimidates the innocent and emboldens the guilty; others say outcomes between jury trials and guilty pleas don't differ much at all.

The public and police officers usually oppose plea bargaining, because they believe it "lets criminals off"; the courts and lawyers, who are responsible for it, mostly support it. Finally, recent empirical research in the behavioral law and economics field casts doubt on the underlying assumption that the parties to plea bargaining, and the process, are involved in a totally rational process.

Legal academic research and empirical law and behavioral science research are in conflict on this issue. In this section, we'll look at two models of plea bargaining: one that reflects the legal scholarship and the other that reflects behavioral science empirical research.

Most academic legal research by lawyers assumes that prosecutors and defense attorneys act rationally to settle disputes according to the "strength of the evidence and the expected punishment after trial" (Bibas 2003–4, 2467). In the **plea bargaining in the "shadow of trial" model**, prosecutors, judges, and defense attorneys act rationally to forecast the outcome of a trial. They make bargains that leave both sides better off by splitting the costs they save by not going to trial. Of course, plea bargains aren't perfect, but trials aren't perfect either. These scholars contend that plea bargains still produce results "roughly as fair" as trials (Bibas 2003–4, 2464–5).

But a growing body of law and behavioral science research finds this model "far too simplistic" (2466) and rejects its assumption of rationality. In the real world of plea bargaining, which they call **plea bargaining outside the "shadow of trial,"** legally irrelevant factors sometimes skew the fair allocation of punishment. As a result, some defendants strike skewed bargains. Other defendants plead when they would otherwise go to trial, or go to trial (and usually receive heavier sentences) when they would otherwise plead (2467–8).

In the view of these researchers, "structural forces and psychological biases" can "inefficiently prevent mutually beneficial bargains or induce harmful ones" (2467). In other words, prosecutors and defense lawyers aren't "perfectly selfless, perfect agents of the public interest" (2470). The strength of the evidence may be the most important influence on plea bargaining, but there are others. Self-interest pushes prosecutors, defense lawyers, and judges to settle cases for several personal reasons. For example, they all want to spend more time with their families. Also, winning "boosts their egos, their esteem, their praise by colleagues, and their prospects for promotion, and career advancement" (2471). Losing, on the other hand, is painful. Prosecutors tend to be loss averse. They may strike some plea bargains, Stephanos Bibas argues, because they "hate losing more than they like winning" (2472, n. 26).

There's another problem with the "shadow of trial" model, demonstrated by cognitive psychologists: **bounded rationality**. Bounded rationality refers to the strongly documented finding that people don't "attempt to ruthlessly maximize utility." Instead, once they identify an option that's "good enough," they stop looking and choose it. Bounded rationality creates a problem as a model for the rational view of plea bargaining, which requires the calculation of the value of pleas based on many "difficult-to-predict inputs" (Covey 2007–8, 216).

According to Russell Covey (2007–8),

> To make the correct decision, the parties must at a minimum estimate the probability that the defendant will be convicted at trial; predict what punishment will be imposed if the defendant is convicted; estimate the costs involved in the litigation, including attorneys fees, time lost waiting in court, and the psychological stress of nonresolution; and then calculate the forecasted trial sentence by multiplying the expected trial sentence by the probability of conviction, discounted by estimated process costs. They then must predict what punishment will be imposed if they enter a guilty plea and compare those two values in order to decide which course of action to take. (217)

Add to these complex tasks the "information deficits" during bargaining. Defendants may not know what evidence the prosecution has or how it will affect jurors. They don't know if witnesses will show up, what they'll say if they do, or whether it'll persuade the jury. They don't know who will be on the jury. There's more, but this should make clear to you what to defendants is only a "fuzzy notion" of the consequences of their guilty plea (217).

As if these difficulties aren't enough to cast doubt on the chances for rational plea bargaining, decades of empirical and experimental cognitive psychology research have shown that human reasoning diverges from the rational choice model in several ways. One is especially relevant here: People "aren't very good at assessing probabilities, particularly when the outcome in question is a rare event, or where there is limited information available from which to make a prediction" (213).

THE OTHER CRIMINAL PROCEDURE ## White Collar Crime

Refusing to Plea Bargain Extracts a Heavy Price

"Olis Testified He Couldn't 'Ruin Those People's Lives'"

Jamie Olis repeatedly turned down offers to cooperate with prosecutors, even after the former Dynegy worker was sentenced to 24 years in prison. "I just couldn't do it," he testified in a civil trial this month. Olis spoke by phone from federal prison in Bastrop during the trial, where his former attorney won legal fees from Dynegy that he claimed the company held back under pressure from prosecutors. A recording of the testimony was obtained by the *Houston Chronicle*. Olis testified that in May 2003, shortly before he and two co-workers were indicted for their roles in Project Alpha, the government pressured him to make a deal. Olis said an assistant U.S. attorney took him aside after a hearing and said: "Hey, we know you're the small guy on this stuff, plead guilty and you don't owe anybody anything."

Olis declined, and he and his boss, Gene Foster, and co-worker Helen Sharkey were indicted on June 12. In August 2003, after Foster and Sharkey entered plea agreements, Olis said he was offered a similar deal but he didn't take it. Even after he was found guilty in November 2003 and later sentenced to 24 years in prison, he said prosecutors tried to get him to enter into a deal that would reduce his sentence. Lloyd Kelley, an attorney, asked if he was tempted to take it. "I did think about it, but there was no way I could have done it," Olis said. "Why?" Kelley asked. "Because it wasn't a matter of just pleading guilty," Olis said, his voice trembling with emotion. "What they wanted was for me to tell the story that I and everyone else engaged in a conspiracy."

The "everyone else" was a list of more than a half-dozen Dynegy workers that Foster said in the criminal trial had conspired to withhold information about Alpha from outside accountants. No one beside Olis, Foster and Sharkey has been charged. "And I couldn't ruin those people's lives," Olis continued in a halting voice. "I'm Catholic. And I can't do that." Olis claimed Foster's testimony about a conspiracy wasn't truthful. "We were all consistent in our SEC depositions, and we never talked to each other," he said, referring to statements the three gave to the Securities and Exchange Commission. "Then at the trial Mr. Foster comes on after pleading guilty and does a 180, and starts to say we had a conversation."

Foster's attorney declined to comment.

Source: Tom Fowler. 2007. "Olis Testified He Couldn't 'Ruin Those People's Lives.'" *Houston Chronicle* (May 27): Business p. 5.

White-Collar Plea Bargaining

Section 2B1.1 of the U.S. Sentencing Guidelines keys the base offense level to the statutory maximum sentence of the crime charged. If the prosecutor chooses to file a mail or wire fraud charge, the base offense level is seven, but if the prosecutor chooses instead to charge it as simple embezzlement or false statements to the government, the base offense level is six. This one-level difference frequently means the difference between brief imprisonment and probation and gives prosecutors leverage to extract pleas. Moreover, prosecutors can choose to decline or divert charges for civil resolution or restitution, enter into non-prosecution agreements, or sign cooperation agreements. All of these avenues leave prosecutors the keys to the prison.

Alternatively, if prosecutors want to imprison someone for only a short time, they can charge bargain down to misdemeanors or other offenses with low statutory maxima. For example, Jamie Olis's two codefendants in the Dynegy scandal accepted charge bargains that capped their sentences at five years, but Olis insisted on going to trial and lost. His penalty for exercising his constitutional right to trial was steep: the Sentencing Guidelines demanded a sentence of at least 292 months, more than 24 years.

Moreover, prosecutors have substantial room to bargain over the facts. Fraud sentences depend on the dollar amount of losses. If prosecutors pull out all the stops to dig up every last victim and dollar lost, they can raise sentences substantially. Conversely, prosecutors can lower sentences if they agree not to press arguable but speculative losses and if they terminate investigations after the defendant quickly agrees to plead guilty. Prosecutors can also manipulate other vaguely worded enhancements, such as whether a crime involved sophisticated means, substantially endangered a company's solvency, or abused the company's trust.

Why did prosecutors push for these guideline enhancements? In part, they were understandably frustrated with lenient judges. A minority of judges do not view white-collar crime as serious and refuse to impose jail sentences unless forced to do so. Part of the prosecutors' motivation was to create more specific deterrence and retribution. But prosecutors themselves show enough mercy and carve out enough exceptions through charge- and fact-bargaining that toughness is not the sole explanation.

Rather, these huge penalties give prosecutors, and not judges, control over the key decision: will a defendant be imprisoned? Prosecutors trust their own gatekeeping abilities and sense of justice. Their ability to create huge disparities between post-plea and post-trial sentences allows them to make credible threats and promise huge rewards to induce pleas. White-collar defendants, who might otherwise roll the dice in all-or-nothing gambles to clear their names, undoubtedly become more pliable when faced with enormous sentencing differentials.

This plea-bargaining leverage is particularly important in cracking large, multi-defendant frauds and conspiracies. Prosecutors have to start with the small fry and flip them to use their testimony in going after the big fish. Lower-level employees may feel loyalty to their bosses, and the code of silence may inhibit them from revealing their crimes. The threat of substantial prison terms makes these employees more willing to cooperate with the government, as section 5K1.1 (U.S. Sentencing Guidelines) cooperation letters are often the only way around otherwise mandatory sentencing guidelines. This need for leverage to flip lower-level employees was one of the Department of Justice's justifications for seeking to raise sentences for lower-loss frauds.

Source: Stephanos Bibas. 2005 (December). "White-Collar Plea Bargaining and Sentencing after *Booker*." *William and Mary Law Review* 47:721.

WHAT DO *YOU* THINK?

1. Was it fair to sentence Olis to 24 years when his colleagues received 5 years because they co-operated?

2. What do you think the sentence differential should be?

Summary

LO 1	• Prosecutors drop cases if they don't think they can prove them, or if, as "officers of the court," they feel prosecution wouldn't serve justice.
LO 1, LO 3	• The right to a jury trial is extended to all crimes of "moral seriousness." This generally excludes petty offenses but could include crimes where the "moral quality" of the offense is serious, even when long prison terms aren't at stake.
LO 1, LO 2	• The 12-member jury has strong traditional support from legal experts and social scientists, but it isn't an exclusive rule. The Sixth Amendment is satisfied by a jury of fewer members.
LO 2	• The Fourteenth Amendment ensures that juries are selected from a random cross section of the public using local census reports, tax rolls, city directories, and more.
LO 3	• Stages of a jury trial include opening statements (starting with the prosecution), presenting evidence, closing arguments, instructions to the jury, and jury deliberations.

LO 3 • The right to a public trial is based on the Sixth Amendment right to confront witnesses, the Fifth Amendment due process right, and the Fourteenth Amendment due process right. Public trials also protect the right of the public to attend proceedings and the right of defendants to attend their own trials.

LO 3 • Defendants don't have to prove their innocence. Instead, prosecutors must prove their guilt "beyond a reasonable doubt."

LO 3 • Prosecutors have a formal duty not only to convict criminals but also to do justice, prohibiting such behavior as intentionally misstating evidence, misleading juries, or inflaming jurors' passions or prejudices.

LO 4 • Juries can return "guilty," "not guilty," or "special" verdicts. Special verdicts, generally, are related to insanity or capital punishment. The requirement for a unanimous verdict instills confidence in the criminal justice process, guarantees careful review of evidence, ensures the hearing of minority viewpoints, and more. The U.S. Supreme Court has held that nonunanimous guilty verdicts are constitutional.

LO 5 • Guilty pleas include straight pleas and negotiated pleas (bargaining on the severity of charges or severity of punishment).

LO 7 • Guilty pleas are constitutional when defendants waive rights knowingly and voluntarily. According to the U.S. Supreme Court, the guilty plea must have a factual basis, meaning that defendants' pleas reflect an understanding of the "true nature" of the charges against them. When a judge fails to question defendants about their plea and establish it as knowing and voluntary, the conviction may be reversed.

LO 7 • Courts hold that a guilty plea may be "knowing and voluntary" even if the defendant didn't commit the crime. For example, pleas are accepted where innocent defendants want to avoid the risk of a long sentence at trial.

LO 8 • Defendants who plead guilty waive their Fifth Amendment right to remain silent, and the Sixth Amendment rights to trial by jury and to confront witnesses.

LO 9 • Under the "shadow of trial" model, prosecutors and defense attorneys rationally forecast the outcome of a trial and make bargains that often leave both sides better off.

LO 9 • Legal and behavioral research demonstrates that parties involved in a plea bargain negotiate based on legally irrelevant factors. For example, prosecutors and defense lawyers might have their own motivations to settle that aren't shared by the people they represent.

LO 9 • Cognitive research into "bounded rationality" creates problems for the "shadow of trial" model, because it shows people stop looking for solutions when they've found one that's "good enough." Faced with many "difficult-to-predict inputs," people are likely to accept the first plea they think they can live with.

LO 9 • Prosecutors of white-collar crimes pushed for guideline enhancements, because they were frustrated with lenient judges who didn't view fraud offenses as serious enough to justify jail sentences.

1. Contrast conviction by trial with conviction by guilty plea.

2. Identify five sources most jurisdictions use to draw up jury lists, and list six reasons jurors give to be excused from jury service. Why do most courts accept their excuses?

3. Explain the difference between peremptory challenges and challenges for cause.

4. List and briefly summarize the stages in the criminal trial.

5. Describe and explain the significance of the U.S. Supreme Court case of *In re Winship*.

6. What's the difference between the jury's verdict and the judgment of the court?

7. Describe and explain the significance of the U.S. Supreme Court decisions in *Apodaca v. Oregon* and *Johnson v. Louisiana*.

8. Explain the difference between straight and negotiated guilty pleas.

9. Summarize the arguments for and against plea bargaining.

10. List three constitutional rights defendants waive when they plead guilty.

11. Explain how a defendant can be factually innocent but legally guilty.

12. Describe and explain the significance of the U.S. Supreme Court decision in *Brady v. U.S.*

13. List reasons why a plea bargain might not be a rational attempt to settle a dispute according to the "strength of the evidence and the expected punishment after trial."

14. Explain why plea bargains have special importance to prosecutors of white-collar crimes.

Key Terms

14

CASES COVERED

Lockyer, Attorney General of California v. Andrade, 538 U.S. 63 (2003)

Gall v. U.S., 552 U.S. 38 (2007)

LEARNING OBJECTIVES

1 Understand how the rights of a defendant differ from those of a convicted offender.

2 Understand how public demands for uniformity and certainty can affect how much discretion judges are given when it comes to sentencing.

3 Know the role of sentencing guidelines and how departures from them depend on a crime's seriousness and an offender's criminal history.

4 Know what mandatory minimum sentencing laws are and how they impact a judge's sentence.

5 Understand the proportionality principle, and know how it defines cruel and unusual punishment under the Eighth Amendment.

6 Know the forces that led courts to start imposing harsher penalties on white-collar criminals.

7 Understand the *Apprendi* bright-line rule and its impact on sentences that are harsher than the relevant guideline.

8 Know that there's no constitutional right to appeal, but every jurisdiction has created a statutory right to appeal.

9 Understand why habeas corpus is a "collateral attack" and how civil trials are used to determine whether convicts have been unlawfully detained.

10 Know the relative roles of state and federal review and the circumstances under which they apply.

After Conviction

In February or March 2000, Brian Gall, a second-year college student at the University of Iowa, was invited by Luke Rinderknecht to join an ongoing enterprise distributing a controlled substance popularly known as "ecstasy." Gall—who was then a user of ecstasy, cocaine, and marijuana—accepted the invitation. During the ensuing seven months, Gall delivered ecstasy pills, which he received from Rinderknecht, to other conspirators, who then sold them to consumers. He netted over $30,000.

A month or two after joining the conspiracy, Gall stopped using ecstasy. A few months after that, in September 2000, he advised Rinderknecht and other co-conspirators that he was withdrawing from the conspiracy. He has not sold illegal drugs of any kind since. He has, in the words of the District Court, "self-rehabilitated." He graduated from the University of Iowa in 2002, and moved first to Arizona, where he obtained a job in the construction industry, and later to Colorado, where he earned $18 per hour as a master carpenter. He has not used any illegal drugs since graduating from college. *Gall v. U.S.* 2007

LO 1

After conviction defendants become "offenders." Don't mistake this for a mere change of words. It's a dramatic shift in status with grave consequences. In court before conviction, the shield of constitutional rights protects "defendants" by the presumption of innocence and all that goes with it (Chapters 12 and 13). But in the three main procedures following conviction—sentencing, appeal, and habeas corpus—a tough-to-overcome **presumption of guilt** rules the day. The significance of this presumption is the reduction or even absence of rights for convicted offenders during sentencing and appeal. They also face growing restrictions on the **right of habeas corpus**, a civil action to determine if the offender is being lawfully detained.

There's a powerful assumption (not necessarily backed up by empirical evidence) that by the time defendants are convicted, the state and defendants have had one fair shot at justice, and that's enough. Lots of time, energy, and money are devoted to deciding guilt. For their part, prosecutors have enormous resources at their command—the whole law enforcement machinery—to help them make their case. To offset the state's advantage, defendants are shielded by an array of constitutional rights. (We've examined them in previous chapters.)

After that fair shot, there's a strong consensus that we're wasting time, money, and energy to allow defendants to climb up, first, the ladder of appeals and then up a second ladder of **collateral attack** (habeas corpus review of convictions by offenders in a separate civil action) to decide if they're being lawfully detained. As in all things (even the pursuit of justice), there comes a time to call it quits and move on—for the state to fight other crimes and for offenders to pay for their crimes, put their lives together, and get back into society as productive members of their community.

Before 2000, the answer to the question "Which constitutional rights apply to convicted defendants during sentencing?" would have been simple. Hardly any. Since then, a series of U.S. Supreme Court decisions has applied the constitutional rights of trial by jury and proof beyond a reasonable doubt to sentencing.

We'll devote most of the chapter to sentencing, because it's where most activity after conviction occurs. Then, we'll study the extent to which the constitutional rights that protect defendants before conviction apply to convicted defendants during sentencing. Finally, we'll look at the appeals process and habeas corpus proceedings.

III

Sentencing

LO 2

For more than a thousand years, policy makers have debated whether to fit sentences to the crime or to tailor sentences to suit the criminal. As early as A.D. 700, the Roman Catholic Church's penitential books revealed a tension between prescribing penance strictly according to the sin and tailoring it to suit individual sinners (Samaha 1978). **Determinate, or fixed, sentencing** (fitting punishment to the crime) puts sentencing authority in the hands of legislators. **Indeterminate sentencing** (tailoring punishment to suit the criminal) puts the power to sentence in the hands of judges and parole boards.

Like the ancient tension between fixed and indeterminate sentencing, there's an ancient debate about judicial discretion in sentencing. Arguments over who should impose sentences indelibly mark the history of sentencing (Samaha 1989). There's also an ancient debate over what sentences to impose—about capital and corporal punishment, the length of imprisonment, what kinds of prisons to put prisoners in, and how to treat them while they're there. The early arguments regarding sinners and penance, judges and punishment, and the aims and kinds of punishment all sound a lot like current debates over the proper authority, aims, kinds, and amounts of punishment sentences ought to reflect.

In this section, we'll concentrate on fixed and indeterminate sentencing. We'll begin by looking at the history of sentencing, examine more closely the division of sentencing authority, and then look at sentencing guidelines.

The History of Sentencing

LO 2

Fixed sentencing, tailored to fit the crime, prevailed in the United States from the 1600s to the late 1800s. Then, a shift toward *indeterminate sentencing,* tailored to fit individual criminals, began. However, neither fixed nor indeterminate sentences have ever totally dominated criminal sentencing. The tension between the need for both certainty *and* flexibility in sentencing decisions has always required both a measure of predictability (fixed sentences) and a degree of flexibility (indeterminate sentences). Shifting ideological commitments and other informed influences on sentencing ensure that neither fixed nor indeterminate sentences will ever exclusively prevail in sentencing policies and practices.

Following the American Revolution, fixed but relatively moderate penalties became the rule. States abolished the death penalty for many offenses. The rarity of the use of **corporal punishment** (whipping), mutilation (cutting off ears and slitting tongues), and shaming (the ducking stool) led to their extinction. By 1850, imprisonment—which up to that time had been used mainly to detain accused people while they waited for their trial—had become the dominant form of criminal punishment after conviction.

Statutes fixed prison terms for most felonies. In practice, liberal use of pardons, early release for "good time," and other devices permitted judges to use informal discretionary judgment in altering formally fixed sentences (Rothman 1971).

The modern history of sentencing began around 1870. Demands for reform grew out of deep dissatisfaction with legislatively fixed *harsh* prison sentences. Reformers complained that prisons were nothing more than warehouses for the poor and the undesirable, and that harsh prison punishment didn't work. Proof of that, the reformers maintained, were the crime rates that continued to grow at unacceptable rates despite harsh, fixed prison sentences. Furthermore, the reformers documented that the prisons were full of recent immigrants and others on the lower rungs of society. Many public officials and concerned citizens agreed. Particularly instrumental in demanding reform were prison administrators and other criminal justice officials. By 1922, all but four states had adopted some form of indeterminate sentencing law.

When the indeterminate sentence became the prevailing practice, administrative sentencing by parole boards and prison officials took precedence over legislative and judicial sentence fixing. At its extreme, judges set no time on sentencing, leaving it wholly to parole boards and correctional officers to determine informally the length of a prisoner's incarceration. More commonly, judges were free to grant probation, suspend sentences in favor of alternatives to incarceration such as community service, or pick confinement times within minimums and maximums prescribed by statutes. Then, parole boards and corrections officers determined the exact release date.

Indeterminate sentencing remained dominant until the 1970s, when several forces coalesced to oppose it. Prison uprisings, especially at Attica and the Tombs in New York in the late 1960s, dramatically portrayed rehabilitation as little more than rhetoric and prisoners as deeply and dangerously discontented. Advocates for individuals' rights challenged the widespread and unreviewable informal discretionary powers exercised by criminal justice officials in general and judges in particular. Demands for increased formal accountability spread throughout the criminal justice system. Courts required public officials to justify their decisions in writing and empowered defendants to dispute allegations against them at sentencing. The courts required even prisons to publish their rules and to grant prisoners the right to challenge the rules they were accused of breaking.

At the same time, statistical and experimental studies showed a pernicious discrimination in sentencing. In particular, some research strongly suggested that poor people and Blacks were sentenced more harshly than middle- and upper-class Americans and Whites. Finally, official reports showed steeply rising street crime rates. The National Research Council created a distinguished panel to review sentencing. It concluded that by the early 1970s, a "remarkable consensus emerged along left and right, law enforcement officials and prisoners groups, reformers and bureaucrats that the indeterminate sentencing era was at its end" (Blumstein et al. 1983, 48–52).

By the late 1970s, the emphasis in crime policy had shifted from fairness to crime prevention. Crime prevention was based on incarceration, general deterrence, and retribution; prevention by rehabilitation was definitely losing ground. Civil libertarians and "law and order" supporters alike called for sentencing practices that would advance swift and certain punishment. They differed on only one fundamental element of sentences—their length. To civil libertarians, determinate sentencing meant short, fixed sentences; to conservatives, it meant long, fixed sentences.

Three ideas came to dominate thinking about sentencing:

1. All crimes deserve some punishment to retain the deterrent potency of the criminal law.

2. Many offenders deserve severe punishment, because they've committed serious crimes.

3. Repeat career offenders require severe punishment to incapacitate them.

According to the National Council on Crime and Delinquency (1992):

By 1990, the shift in goals of sentencing reform was complete. Virtually all new sentencing law was designed to increase the certainty and length of prison sentences to incapacitate the active criminal and deter the rest. (6)

Harsher penalties accompanied the shift in the philosophy of punishment. Public support for the death penalty grew; the U.S. Supreme Court ruled that the death penalty was not cruel and unusual punishment; courts sentenced more people to death; and the states began to execute criminals. Judges sentenced more people to prison and to longer prison terms. By 2009, the United States was sentencing more people to prison per 100,000 people than any other country in the world (*World Prison Population List* 2009).

The Division of Sentencing Authority

LO 2

Throughout U.S. history, three institutions—legislatures, courts, and administrative agencies—have exercised sentencing power. In the **legislative sentencing model**, legislatures prescribe specific penalties for crimes without regard to the persons who committed them. The punishment fits the crime, not the criminal, and judges and parole boards can't alter these penalties. Removing discretion from judges and parole boards doesn't eliminate evils arising from prejudicial laws that criminalize conduct peculiar to certain groups in society, but it does limit the making of criminal law to legislatures.

In the **judicial sentencing model**, judges prescribe sentences within broad formal contours set by legislative acts. Typically, a statute prescribes a range, such as 1 to 10 years, 0 to 5 years, or 20 years to life. Judges then fix the exact time that convicted criminals serve.

In the **administrative sentencing model**, both the legislature and the judge prescribe a wide range of allowable prison times for particular crimes. Administrative agencies, typically parole boards and prison administrators, determine the exact release date. Under this model, administrative agencies have broad discretion to determine how long prisoners serve and under what conditions they can be released.

As models, these sentencing schemes never operate in pure form. At all times in U.S. history, all three sentencing institutions have overlapped considerably; all have included the exercise of wide discretion. For example, plea bargaining (Chapter 13) has prevented fixing sentencing authority in any of these three. Charge bargaining gets around legislatively fixed sentences, sentence bargaining avoids judicially fixed sentencing, and both alter administratively fixed sentences.

But until sentencing reforms in the 1970s began to change policy and practice, legislatures set the general range of penalties, judges picked a specific penalty within that range, and parole boards released offenders after some time spent in prison. Under this practice, judges, parole boards, and prison authorities had considerable discretion in sentencing criminal defendants.

Sentencing Guidelines and Mandatory Minimum Sentences

LO 3

Throughout these sections on guidelines and mandatory minimum sentence regimes, remember this important fact: The indeterminate sentence, parole boards, and good time still remain a part of the sentencing structure of many states. But the adoption of fixed sentencing regimes is growing. Fixed sentencing has taken two primary forms—sentencing guidelines and mandatory minimum prison sentences. The federal government and most states have adopted both forms. Both are based, at least in theory, on limiting—or even eliminating—discretion in sentencing. Both respond to three demands of experts and the public:

1. *Uniformity.* Similar offenses should receive similar punishment.

2. *Certainty and truth in sentencing.* Convicted offenders, victims, and the public should know that the sentence imposed is similar to the sentence actually served. ("Do the crime; do the time.")

3. *Retribution, deterrence, and incapacitation.* The rehabilitation of individual offenders isn't the primary aim of punishment.

Let's look more closely at sentencing guidelines and mandatory minimum prison sentences.

Sentencing Guidelines

In **sentencing guidelines** regimes, a commission establishes a relatively narrow range of penalties, and judges are supposed to choose a specific sentence within that range. The guideline ties sentences to two criteria:

1. The seriousness of the crime

2. The offender's criminal history (Figure 14.1)

Sentences are either presumptively incarceration or presumptively nonprison penalties. Judges can depart from the range set in the guidelines, but they have to give written reasons for their **departure.** The guidelines specify what reasons the judges can choose. For example, vulnerable victims are a reason for upward departures; being only a minor participant in a crime is a reason for downward departure. The government can appeal *downward* departures; the defendant can appeal *upward* departures.

Sentencing guideline grids, like Minnesota's in Figure 14.1, commonly depict these elements of guidelines sentencing. The rows along the left list the crimes and their seriousness; the columns show the offenders' criminal history. For example, the recommended sentence for residential burglary is 33 months; the judge has the discretion to go down to 29 months or up to 39 months. The shaded area depicts the discretionary dispositional sentences.

Letting judges choose within a range without departing from the guidelines builds a flexibility into the system. This allows for differences in individual cases without undermining the basic goals of uniformity and equity. Uniformity and equity are the *goals* of guidelines' regimes. But what about the reality? Empirical research has some answers. That research demonstrates that context affects most courtroom decision making, including sentencing. Judges don't impose sentences in a social vacuum; the social, political, and organizational environment influences the sentences they impose, even in guidelines regimes. So sentences are likely to vary from one region, state, district, and even courtrooms in the same district, to another.

According to available research, they *do* vary (Johnson 2005). Elements of the courtroom social context that "matter" include:

• Urbanization

• Bureaucratization

• Court size

FIGURE 14.1 Minnesota Sentencing Guidelines Grid

IV. Sentencing Guidelines Grid
Presumptive sentence lengths in months

Italicized numbers within the grid denote the range within which a judge may sentence without the sentence being deemed a departure. Offenders with non-imprisonment felony sentences are subject to jail time according to law.

Criminal History Score

Severity Level of Conviction Offense (common offenses listed in italics)		0	1	2	3	4	5	6 or more
Murder, 2nd degree (intentional murder; drive-by-shootings)	XI	306 261–367	326 278–391	346 295–415	366 312–439	386 329–463	406 346–480[2]	426 363–480[2]
Murder, 3rd degree Murder, 2nd degree (unintentional murder)	X	150 128–180	165 141–198	180 153–216	195 166–234	210 179–252	225 192–270	240 204–288
Assault, 1st degree Controlled substance crime, 1st degree	IX	86 74–103	98 84–117	110 94–132	122 104–146	134 114–160	146 125–175	158 135–189
Aggravated robbery, 1st degree Controlled substance crime, 2nd degree	VIII	48 41–57	58 50–69	68 58–81	78 67–93	88 75–105	98 84–117	108 92–129
Felony DWI	VII	36	42	48	54 46–64	60 51–72	66 57–79	72 62–84[2]
Controlled substance crime, 3rd degree	VI	21	27	33	39 34–46	45 39–54	51 44–61	57 49–68
Residential burglary Simple robbery	V	18	23	28	33 29–39	38 33–45	43 37–51	48 41–57
Nonresidential burglary	IV	12[1]	15	18	21	24 21–28	27 23–32	30 26–36
Theft crimes (Over $5,000)	III	12[1]	13	15	17	19 17–22	21 18–25	23 20–27
Theft crimes ($5,000 or less) Check forgery ($251–$2,500)	II	12[1]	12[1]	13	15	17	19	21 18–25
Sale of simulated controlled substance	I	12[1]	12[1]	12[1]	13	15	17	19 17–22

☐ Presumptive commitment to state imprisonment. First-degree murder has a mandatory life sentence and is excluded from the guidelines by law. See guidelines section II.E., Mandatory sentences, for policy regarding those sentences controlled by law.

▨ Presumptive stayed sentence; at the discretion of the judge, up to a year in jail and/or other non-jail sanctions can be imposed as conditions of probation. However, certain offenses in this section of the grid always carry a presumptive commitment to state prison. See, guidelines sections II.C. Presumptive sentence and II.E. Mandatory sentences.

[1]One year and one day

[2]M.S. § 244.09 requires the sentencing guidelines to provide a range for sentences which are presumptive commitment to state imprisonment of 15% lower and 20% higher than the fixed duration displayed, provided that the minimum sentence is not less than one year and one day and the maximum sentence is not more than the statutory maximum. See, guidelines sections II.H. Presumptive sentence durations that exceed the statutory maximum sentence and II.I. Sentence ranges for presumptive commitment offenses in shaded areas of grids.

Effective August 1, 2009

Source: Minnesota Sentencing Commission. 2009. http://www.msgc.state.mn.us/msgc5/guidelines.htm.

TABLE 14.1

Odds of Receiving Departures by Race, Ethnicity, Sex, and Age

1. The odds of receiving *downward* departures is

    a. 56% less for Hispanics than Whites
    b. 25% less for Blacks than Whites
    c. 63% greater for a female than a male
    d. 71% greater for a 65-year-old than a 20-year-old (464–66)

2. The odds of receiving *upward* departures are

    a. 39% higher for Hispanics than Whites
    b. 21% higher for Blacks than Whites
    c. 31% higher for males than females
    d. Significantly higher for younger than older people (468)

Source: Johnson 2003, 464–66; 468.

- Unemployment

- Race

- Crime rates

- Court resources (Johnson 2005, 763)

Let's look closer at one aspect of this research, the focus on the extralegal categories of race, ethnicity, gender, and age on judicial discretion to impose unwarranted departures from recommended sentences. Most of this research has found varying degrees of disparities based on these extralegal categories. Brian D. Johnson (2003) found that

- Black and Hispanic defendants are *less* likely to receive *downward* departures and *more* likely to receive *upward* departures than Whites.

- Men are *less* likely to receive *decreased* departures and *more* likely to receive *upward* departures than women.

- Younger defendants are *more* likely to receive *upward* departures and *less* likely to receive *downward* departures than older defendants. (464–66; 468; Table 14.1)

Like all good researchers, Johnson ends on a cautionary note. Sentencing decision making is inherently complex, and circumstances change. Future research, therefore, should replicate his findings in other places and times (482–83).

Johnson's empirical work and other studies have focused on characteristics of *defendants* to demonstrate unwarranted disparities in departures from recommended guidelines sentences. But what about the characteristics of *judges*? "Most scholars and observers agree that political-ideological preferences are at play when judges sentence criminals" (Schanzenbach and Tiller 2008, 725).

One empirical study tested whether political affiliation is a source of unwarranted departures under the U.S. Sentencing Guidelines regime. Schanzenbach and Tiller examined the relationship between U.S. District judges' sentencing decisions and reviews by their supervising U.S. Circuit judges under the U.S. Sentencing Guidelines regime following *Booker*. They assessed whether District Court judges use the tools of offense-level adjustments and departures as strategies "to attain sentencing outcomes closer to their personal preferences" instead of the primary goals of the U.S. Sentencing Guidelines—namely, certainty and fairness.

Here's what Schanzenbach and Tiller found:

1. "Policy preferences matter in sentencing. Liberal (Democratic-appointed) judges give different (generally lower) sentences than conservative (Republican-appointed) judges for certain categories of crime."

2. The length of the sentence given by U.S. District Court sentencing judges depends on the amount of political alignment between the sentencing judge and the U.S. Circuit judges who "supervise" their decisions.

3. "Sentencing judges selectively use adjustments and departures to enhance or reduce sentences, and the use of departures is influenced by the degree of political alignment between the sentencing judge and the overseeing circuit court, while the use of adjustment is not so limited." (727)

Mandatory Minimum Sentences

LO 4

The other type of fixed sentence, **mandatory minimum sentences**, requires judges to impose a nondiscretionary minimum amount of prison time that all offenders convicted of the offense have to serve. Judges can sentence offenders to *more* than the minimum but not *less*. Mandatory minimum sentence laws promise that "If you do the crime, you *will* do the time."

Mandatory penalties are very old. The "eye for an eye" and "tooth for a tooth" in the Old Testament were mandatory penalties. The Anglo-Saxon king Alfred prescribed a detailed mandatory penal code, including such provisions as "If one knocks out another's eye, he shall pay 66 shillings, $6^1/3$ pence. If the eye is still in the head, but the injured man can see nothing with it, one-third of the payment shall be withheld" (Lee n.d.).

As early as 1790 in the United States, most states had established mandatory penalties for capital crimes. Throughout the 19th century, Congress enacted mandatory penalties—usually short prison sentences—for a long list of crimes, including refusal to testify before Congress, failure to report seaboard saloon purchases, or causing a ship to run aground by use of a false light (Wallace 1993, 9).

From 1900 to the 1950s, the use of mandatory minimum penalties fell into disuse. The Boggs Act (1951), named after its sponsor, Alabama Representative Hale Boggs, signaled a shift to mandatory minimum sentences. It set minimum sentences for those convicted of importing drugs or distributing marijuana. In the 1950s, fear that crime and drug problems were caused by a Communist plot to get Americans "hooked" on especially potent "pure Communist heroin" from China led Congress to enact the Narcotic Control Act of 1956 (U.S. Congress 1954, 7). It further increased the penalties set in the Boggs Act.

In 1956, the Senate Judiciary explained why Congress needed a mandatory minimum sentence drug law:

> There is a need for the continuation of the policy of punishment of a severe character as a deterrent to narcotic law violations. [The Committee] therefore recommends an increase in maximum sentences for first as well as subsequent offenses. With respect to the mandatory minimum features of such penalties, and prohibition of suspended sentences or probation, the Committee recognizes objections in principle. It feels, however, that, in order to define the gravity of this class of crime and the assured penalty to follow, these features of the law must be regarded as essential elements of the desired deterrents, although some differences of opinion still exist regarding their application to first offenses of certain types. (U.S. Sentencing Commission 1991, 5–7)

The 1956 statute imposed stiff mandatory minimum sentences for narcotics offenses, requiring judges to pick within a range of penalties. Judges couldn't suspend sentences or put convicted offenders on probation. In addition, offenders weren't eligible for parole if they were convicted under the act. For example, the act punished the first conviction for selling heroin by a term of from 5 to 10 years of imprisonment. Judges had to sentence offenders to at least 5 years in prison, judges couldn't suspend the sentence or put offenders on probation, and offenders weren't eligible for parole for at least the minimum period of the sentence. For second offenders, the mandatory minimum was raised to 10 years. The penalty for the sale of narcotics to persons under 18 ranged from a mandatory minimum of 10 years to a maximum of life imprisonment or death (U.S. Sentencing Commission 1991, 6).

In 1970, Congress retreated from the mandatory minimum sentence approach. In the Comprehensive Drug Abuse Prevention and Control Act of 1970, Congress repealed virtually all of the mandatory minimum provisions adopted in the 1956 act, because the increased sentence lengths "had not shown the expected overall reduction in drug law violations." Among the reasons for the repeal of mandatory minimum penalties for drug law offenses were that they

1. Alienated youths from the general society

2. Hampered the rehabilitation of drug offenders

3. Infringed on judicial authority by drastically reducing discretion in sentencing

4. Reduced the deterrent effect of drug laws because even prosecutors thought the laws were too severe

According to the House committee that considered the repeal of the bill:

> The severity of existing penalties, involving in many instances minimum sentences, have [sic] led in many instances to reluctance on the part of prosecutors to prosecute some violations, where the penalties seem to be out of line with the seriousness of the offenses. In addition, severe penalties, which do not take into account individual circumstances, and which treat casual violators as severely as they treat hardened criminals, tend to make conviction more difficult to obtain. (U.S. Congress 1970, 11)

The retreat from mandatory minimum sentences was short-lived, because public concern about violence and drugs again rose to the top of the national agenda. The public and legislatures blamed rising crime rates on the uncertainty and "leniency" of indeterminate sentences. Beginning in the early 1970s, the states and the federal government enacted more and longer mandatory minimum prison sentences. By 1991, 46 states and the federal government had enacted mandatory minimum sentencing laws. Although the list of mandatory minimum laws is long (the U.S. Criminal Code contains at least one hundred), the main targets of mandatory minimum sentences are drug offenses, violent crimes, and crimes committed with a weapon (Wallace 1993, 11).

Mandatory minimum sentences are supposed to satisfy three basic aims of criminal punishment: retribution, incapacitation, and deterrence. According to supporters, mandatory minimum sentence laws mean those committing serious crimes will receive severe punishment. Furthermore, violent criminals, criminals who use weapons, and drug offenders can't harm the public if they're in prison. And the knowledge that committing mandatory minimum crimes will bring certain, swift, and severe punishment should deter these types of crimes.

Several evaluations, however, suggest that, in practice, mandatory minimum penalties don't always achieve the goals their supporters hoped they would. In 1990,

Congress ordered the U.S. Sentencing Commission to evaluate the rapidly increasing number of mandatory minimum sentencing provisions in the federal system. The results of the commission's study provided little empirical support for the success of mandatory sentencing laws, as these findings demonstrate:

1. Only a few of the mandatory minimum sentencing provisions are ever used. Nearly all those used relate to drug and weapons offenses.

2. Only 41 percent of defendants whose characteristics and behavior qualify them for mandatory minimum sentences actually receive them.

3. Mandatory minimum sentences actually introduce disparity in sentencing. For example, the commission found that race influences disparity in a number of ways. Whites are less likely than Blacks and Hispanics to be indicted or convicted at the mandatory minimum. Whites are also more likely than Blacks and Hispanics to receive reductions for "substantial assistance" in aiding in the prosecution of other offenders. The mandatory minimum sentence laws allow an exception for offenders who provide "substantial assistance" in investigating other offenders. But judges can reduce the minimum for substantial assistance only on the motion of the prosecutors.

4. Substantial assistance also leads to disparities quite apart from race. It tends to favor the very people the law was intended to reach—those higher up in the chain of drug dealing, because underlings have less to offer the government. In one case, for example, Stanley Marshall, who sold less than one gram of LSD, got a 20-year mandatory prison sentence. Jose Cabrera, on the other hand, who the government estimated made more than $40 million from importing cocaine and who would have qualified for life plus 200 years, received a prison term of 8 years for providing "substantial assistance" in the case of Manuel Noriega. According to Judge Terry J. Hatter, Jr., "The people at the very bottom who can't provide substantial assistance end up getting [punished] more severely than those at the top." (*Criminal Justice Newsletter* 1993, 5; Wallace 1993, 11)

5. Mandatory minimum sentences don't eliminate discretion; they just shift it from judges to prosecutors. Prosecutors can use their discretion in a number of ways, including manipulating the "substantial assistance" exception and deciding not to charge defendants with crimes carrying mandatory minimum sentences or to charge them with mandatory minimum crimes of lesser degree.

The U.S. Sentencing Commission recommended further study before making any final conclusions about the effectiveness of mandatory penalties. But their findings, along with other research on federal and state mandatory minimum sentences, suggest that mandatory minimum penalties aren't the easy answer to the crime problem that politicians promise and the public hopes for (Campaign for an Effective Crime Policy 1993; Schulhofer 1993, 199).

ETHICAL ISSUES

Juveniles: A Life Sentence without the Chance of Parole?

WASHINGTON—Terrance Jamar Graham was 16 in 2003, when he and two accomplices broke into a Jacksonville restaurant and tried to rob the place. He pleaded guilty and got three years' probation on the condition he stay out of trouble. A year later, Graham and another pair of accomplices forced their way into an apartment and robbed two men. That landed him in prison for life, without parole.

INSTRUCTIONS

1. Visit the Companion Website and read Joan Biskupic's, "High Court Justices to Ponder Life Imprisonment for Juveniles," and Joan Biskupic and Martha T. Moore's, "Court Limits Harsh Terms for Youths." See the links under the Chapter 14 Ethical Issues section—login at www.cengagebrain.com.

2. Based on the information in the articles, write an essay answering the question: "Even though the U.S. Supreme Court ruled that it's *always* cruel and unusual punishment to sentence a juvenile to life without parole, do you believe it should be ethical to sentence Terrance Jamar Graham to life without parole?"

The Constitution and Sentencing

LO 5

There are two kinds of constitutional questions regarding sentencing. One has to do with the sentence itself—namely, whether it's banned by the Eighth Amendment "cruel and unusual punishment" clause. Whether it's cruel and unusual depends on the answer to another question, "Does the Eighth Amendment embody a proportionality requirement?" The **proportionality principle** states that a punishment is cruel and unusual if its harshness is "grossly disproportionate" to the "gravity of the offense" (*Harmelin v. Michigan* 1991, 997).

The other constitutional question has to do with the procedures used to determine the sentence. That question is, "What, if any, rights that defendants enjoyed *before* conviction during trial and plea bargaining do they enjoy *after* conviction during sentencing?" Let's look at each of these questions.

The Proportionality Principle and the Sentence of Death

LO 5

A majority of the U.S. Supreme Court has made it clear that the proportionality principle applies to death sentences because "death is different." A minority have concluded that the Eighth Amendment includes no proportionality requirement. Or, if it does, it's legislatures elected by the people, not the unelected "undemocratic" judges appointed for life, who should decide what's a disproportionate, or cruel and unusual, sentence.

As of 2010, the Court has ruled that the sentence of death fits only the crime of murder (*Gregg v. Georgia* 1976), with several categorical exceptions: mentally retarded persons who kill (*Atkins v. Virginia* 2002); juveniles under the age of 18 (*Roper v. Simmons* 2005); and felony murderers who didn't do the actual killing and lacked the intent to kill (*Enmund v. Florida* 1982).

We also know that a death sentence for raping an adult woman is "grossly disproportionate" (*Coker v. Georgia* 1977, 592). The same applies to raping a child, as in the disturbing case of an 8-year-old girl whose stepfather raped her in Harvey, Louisiana, across the river from New Orleans. The little girl was awakened early in the morning to find Patrick Kennedy (her 300-pound stepfather) on top of her, undressing her, with his hand over her mouth to keep her quiet before forcing himself inside her, causing internal injuries and heavy bleeding.

The U.S. Supreme Court overturned his death sentence because even in this awful crime, death was "grossly disproportionate" (*Kennedy v. Louisiana* 2008). According to the Court:

Consistent with evolving standards of decency and the teachings of our precedents we conclude that, in determining whether the death penalty is excessive, there is a distinction between intentional first-degree murder on the one hand, and non-homicide crimes against individual persons, even including child rape, on the other. The latter crimes may be devastating in their harm, as here, but in terms of moral depravity and of the injury to the person and to the public, they cannot be compared to murder in their severity and irrevocability. (27)

The Proportionality Principle and Sentences of Imprisonment

LO 5

When it comes to sentences of imprisonment, the Court is deeply divided. Some justices have concluded that proportionality never applies to sentences of imprisonment. A narrow and shifting majority has concluded that there's a "narrow proportionality principle" regarding prison sentences (*Harmelin v. Michigan* 1991, 997). For example, it would be cruel and unusual punishment to sentence someone to life in prison for failing to pay a parking ticket (*Rummell v. Estelle* 1980, 274, n. 11).

By a slim majority and over strong dissents, the Supreme Court held that it was not cruel and unusual punishment to sentence first-time offender Ronald Allen Harmelin to life in prison with no chance of parole for possessing 672 grams of cocaine (*Harmelin v. Michigan* 1991). The majority, however, couldn't agree as to why. Justice Scalia and Chief Justice Rehnquist's reason was because there's no proportionality requirement in the Eighth Amendment. Justices O'Connor, Kennedy, and Souter concluded that the sentence wasn't grossly disproportionate to the crime. Four justices dissented, arguing that the sentence was grossly disproportionate to the crime. (See the White Collar Crime box for more on proportionality in sentencing.)

THE OTHER CRIMINAL PROCEDURE **White Collar Crime**

Sentencing White Collar Offenders after *U.S. v. Booker* (2005)

LO 6

Until 2004, white-collar sentencing appeared to exemplify the ratchet effect. As the media exposed ever more corporate corruption and shady dealing, lawmakers competed to prove their toughness on crime by raising sentences. This irresistible force, however, met a seemingly immovable object: The Supreme Court's new Sixth Amendment limits on judicial sentencing (*Apprendi v. New Jersey*, *Blakely v. Washington*, and *United States v. Booker*) have upended sentencing law by requiring juries, not judges, to find beyond a reasonable doubt facts that raise maximum sentences. *Booker*'s remedy was to invalidate the binding force of the U.S. Sentencing Guidelines. *Apprendi* and *Blakely* have had large and obvious effects on violent and drug crime prosecutions. These cases, however, also portend a revolution in white-collar plea bargaining and sentencing.

Traditionally, penalties for white-collar crimes such as fraud, embezzlement, and insider trading were significantly lower than penalties for violent, drug, or even physical property crimes. White-collar offenders were much more likely to receive probation than thieves who stole equivalent amounts, and when white-collar offenders did go to prison their sentences were substantially shorter. For example, before the Sentencing Guidelines, an average of 59% of fraud defendants received straight probation sentences, and the average prison time served was seven months. For tax defendants, the figures were comparable: 57% received straight probation, and the average prison time served was five and a half months. Generally, these white-collar defendants came from well-off backgrounds, had no criminal histories, and seemed unlikely to recidivate, let alone endanger anyone. So there was little need for specific deterrence, and few people thought retribution required imprisonment. Thus, white-collar criminals usually got probation, community service, restitution, or similar soft punishments (721).

Our thinking about white-collar crime has undergone a sea change in the last two decades. White-collar crime came to epitomize greed, which increasingly seemed morally wrong and more deserving of retribution. Moreover, the sentencing-reform movement focused on meting out equal sentences for equally bad crimes. If we imprison the black teenager who steals a $25,000 car, equal treatment demands that we also imprison the middle-aged white guy who steals $25,000. Otherwise, sentencing judges may be indulging unconscious racial and class stereotypes by going easy on defendants who remind judges of themselves or with whom judges can identify (723).

In addition, white-collar crime is more rational, cool, and calculated than sudden crimes of passion or opportunity, so it should be a prime candidate for general deterrence. An economist would argue that if one increased the expected cost of white-collar crime by raising the expected penalty, white-collar crime would be unprofitable and would thus cease (724).

Nevertheless, many judges lean toward home confinement or probation. Although economists may focus on ex ante deterrence, judges may prefer to look ex post at the sympathetic, white, educated offender who reminds judges of themselves and seems to pose no danger. Allowing these offenders to escape imprisonment, however, is inequitable and undercuts the law's deterrent and moral message condemning white-collar crime (724).

Among other recommendations for reform, Professor Bibas proposes this one:

The Sentencing Commission should calibrate white-collar sentences to their core purpose. The prospect of routine probation for white-collar offenders in the old days rightly troubled many people. Fines seemed like a mere tax on business that allowed wealthy criminals to buy their way out of real punishment. Short but certain terms of imprisonment would go a long way toward satisfying the demand for unequivocal condemnation. Few white-collar defendants deserve decades in prison, as if they were three times worse than rapists. Rather, one could add bite to short white-collar prison terms by coupling them with shaming penalties. As Professors Dan Kahan and Eric Posner have argued, white-collar offenders have a great deal of reputational capital and are particularly sensitive to shaming. A mere sentence of community service or charitable works would not effectively communicate condemnation of the crime. Felons ought to spend a few years in prison, not home detention or halfway houses. But they should also have to apologize and make restitution to victims and communities, and in appropriate cases they should endure some stigmatizing publicity as well. This combination of punishments might foster deterrence, inflict retribution, express condemnation, and heal victims at a fraction of the cost. It would condemn and deter crime ex ante without sacrificing ex post individualized justice.

WHAT DO *YOU* THINK?

1. Which of Professor Bibas's recommendations are fair?

2. Which are practical?

3. How would or could they be enforced?

Source: Stephanos Bibas. 2005. "White-Collar Sentencing and Plea Bargaining after *Booker. William and Mary Law Review* 47:721–41.

In *Lockyer v. Andrade* (2003), our next case excerpt, the U.S. Supreme Court held narrowly that it wasn't cruel and unusual punishment to sentence Leandro Andrade to 50 years for shoplifting $150 worth of videos under California's "three strikes" law.

In Lockyer v. Andrade (2003), our next case excerpt, the U.S. Supreme Court held that it wasn't cruel and unusual punishment to sentence Leandro Andrade to 50 years for shoplifting $150 worth of videos under California's "three strikes" law.

CASE Was 50 Years in Prison for Shoplifting $150 Worth of Videos "Cruel and Unusual Punishment"?

Lockyer, Attorney General of California v. Andrade

538 U.S. 63 (2003)

HISTORY

Leandro Andrade (State prisoner/petitioner) who was convicted on two counts of petty theft and sentenced to life in prison under California's Career Criminal Punishment Act, also known as the Three Strikes law, petitioned for a writ of habeas corpus. The United States District Court for the Central District of California, Christina A. Snyder, J., denied his petition, and the prisoner appealed. The United States Court of Appeals for the Ninth Circuit, Paez, Circuit Judge, reversed and remanded. Certiorari was granted. The Supreme Court held that California Court of Appeal's decision affirming petitioner's two consecutive terms of 25 years to life in prison for a "third strike" conviction was not "contrary to" or an "unreasonable application" of the "clearly established" gross disproportionality principle set forth by *Rummel*, *Solem* and *Harmelin* decisions of United States Supreme Court and thus did not warrant federal habeas relief. The Supreme Court reversed.

O'CONNOR, J., joined by REHNQUIST, C.J., and SCALIA, KENNEDY, and THOMAS, JJ.

This case raises the issue whether the United States Court of Appeals for the Ninth Circuit erred in ruling that the California Court of Appeal's decision affirming Leandro Andrade's two consecutive terms of 25 years to life in prison for a "third strike" conviction is contrary to, or an unreasonable application of, clearly established federal law as determined by this Court within the meaning of 28 U.S.C. § 2254(d)(1).

FACTS

On November 4, 1995, Leandro Andrade stole five video-tapes worth $84.70 from a Kmart store in Ontario, California. Security personnel detained Andrade as he was leaving the store. On November 18, 1995, Andrade entered a different Kmart store in Montclair, California, and placed four videotapes worth $68.84 in the rear waistband of his pants. Again, security guards apprehended Andrade as he was exiting the premises. Police subsequently arrested Andrade for these crimes.

These two incidents were not Andrade's first or only encounters with law enforcement. According to the state probation officer's presentence report, Andrade has been in and out of state and federal prison since 1982. In January 1982, he was convicted of a misdemeanor theft offense and was sentenced to 6 days in jail with 12 months' probation. Andrade was arrested again in November 1982 for multiple counts of first-degree residential burglary. He pleaded guilty to at least three of those counts, and in April of the following year he was sentenced to 120 months in prison. In 1988, Andrade was convicted in federal court of "transportation of marijuana," and was sentenced to eight years in federal prison. In 1990, he was convicted in state court for a misdemeanor petty theft offense and was ordered to serve 180 days in jail. In September 1990, Andrade was convicted again in federal court for the same felony of "transportation of marijuana," and was sentenced to 2,191 days in federal prison. And in 1991, Andrade was arrested for a state parole violation-escape from federal prison. He was paroled from the state penitentiary system in 1993.

A state probation officer interviewed Andrade after his arrest in this case. The presentence report notes:

The defendant admitted committing the offense. The defendant further stated he went into the K-Mart Store to steal videos. He took four of them to sell so he could buy heroin. He has been a heroin addict since 1977. He says when he gets out of jail or prison he always does something stupid. He admits his addiction controls his life and he steals for his habit.

Because of his 1990 misdemeanor conviction, the State charged Andrade in this case with two counts of petty theft with a prior conviction, in violation of Cal. Penal Code Ann. § 666 (West Supp.2002). Under California law, petty theft with a prior conviction is a so-called "wobbler" offense because it is punishable either as a misdemeanor or as a felony. The decision to prosecute petty theft with a prior conviction as a misdemeanor or as a felony is in the discretion of the prosecutor. The trial court also has discretion to reduce the charge to a misdemeanor at the time of sentencing.

Under California's three strikes law, any felony can constitute the third strike, and thus can subject a defendant to a term of 25 years to life in prison. See Cal.Penal Code Ann. § 667(e)(2)(A) (West 1999). In this case, the prosecutor decided to charge the two counts of theft as felonies rather than misdemeanors. The trial court denied Andrade's motion to reduce the offenses to misdemeanors, both before the jury verdict and again in state habeas proceedings.

A jury found Andrade guilty of two counts of petty theft with a prior conviction. According to California law, a jury must also find that a defendant has been convicted of at least two serious or violent felonies that serve as qualifying offenses under the three strikes regime. In this case, the jury made a special finding that Andrade was convicted of three counts of first-degree residential burglary. A conviction for first-degree residential burglary qualifies as a serious or violent felony for the purposes of the three strikes law. As a consequence, each of Andrade's convictions for theft under Cal.Penal Code Ann. § 666 (West Supp.2002) triggered a separate application of the three strikes law. Pursuant to California law, the judge sentenced Andrade to two consecutive terms of 25 years to life in prison. See §§ 667(c)(6), 667(e)(2)(B).

On direct appeal in 1997, the California Court of Appeal affirmed Andrade's sentence of two consecutive terms of 25 years to life in prison. After the Supreme Court of California denied discretionary review, Andrade filed a petition for a writ of habeas corpus in Federal District Court. The District Court denied his petition. The Ninth Circuit granted Andrade a certificate of appealability, and subsequently reversed the judgment of the District Court.

OPINION

Andrade's argument in this Court is that two consecutive terms of 25 years to life for stealing approximately $150 in videotapes is grossly disproportionate in violation of the Eighth Amendment. Andrade similarly maintains that the state court decision affirming his sentence is "contrary to, or involved an unreasonable application of, clearly established Federal law, as determined by the Supreme Court of the United States." 28 U.S.C. § 2254(d)(1). AEDPA (Antiterrorism and Effective Death Penalty Act) circumscribes a federal habeas court's review of a state court decision. Section 2254 provides:

(d) An application for a writ of habeas corpus on behalf of a person in custody pursuant to the judgment of a State court shall not be granted with respect to any claim that was adjudicated on the merits in State court proceedings unless the adjudication of the claim—

(1) resulted in a decision that was contrary to, or involved an unreasonable application of, clearly established Federal law, as determined by the Supreme Court of the United States.

One governing legal principle emerges as "clearly established" under § 2254(d)(1): A gross disproportionality principle is applicable to sentences for terms of years. Our cases exhibit a lack of clarity regarding what factors may indicate gross disproportionality. In *Solem* (the case upon which Andrade relies most heavily), we stated: "It is clear that a 25-year sentence generally is more severe than a 15-year sentence, but in most cases it would be difficult to decide that the former violates the Eighth Amendment while the latter does not." Thus, in this case, the only relevant clearly established law amenable to the "contrary to" or "unreasonable application of" framework is the gross disproportionality principle, the precise contours of which are unclear, applicable only in the "exceedingly rare" and "extreme" case. The final question is whether the California Court of Appeal's decision affirming Andrade's sentence is "contrary to, or involved an unreasonable application of," this clearly established gross disproportionality principle.

First, a state court decision is contrary to our clearly established precedent if the state court applies a rule that contradicts the governing law set forth in our cases or if the state court confronts a set of facts that are materially indistinguishable from a decision of this Court and nevertheless arrives at a result different from our precedent. In terms of length of sentence and availability of parole, severity of the underlying offense, and the impact of recidivism, Andrade's sentence implicates factors relevant in both *Rummel* and *Solem*. It was not contrary to our clearly established law for the California Court of Appeal to turn to *Rummel* in deciding whether a sentence is grossly disproportionate. *Harmelin*. Indeed, *Harmelin* allows a state court to reasonably rely on *Rummel* in determining whether a sentence is grossly disproportionate. The California Court of Appeal's decision was therefore not "contrary to" the governing legal principles set forth in our cases.

Andrade's sentence also was not materially indistinguishable from the facts in *Solem*. The facts here fall in between the facts in *Rummel* and the facts in *Solem*. *Solem* involved a sentence of life in prison without the possibility of parole. The defendant in *Rummel* was sentenced to life in prison with the possibility of parole. Here, Andrade retains the possibility of parole. *Solem* acknowledged that *Rummel* would apply in a "similar factual situation." And while this case resembles to some degree both *Rummel* and *Solem*, it is not materially indistinguishable from either. Consequently, the state court did not confront a set of facts that are materially indistinguishable from a decision of this Court and nevertheless arrive at a result different from our precedent.

Second, under the "unreasonable application" clause, a federal habeas court may grant the writ if the state court identifies the correct governing legal principle from this Court's decisions but unreasonably applies that principle to the facts of the prisoner's case. The "unreasonable application" clause requires the state court decision to be more than incorrect or erroneous. The state court's application of clearly established law must be objectively unreasonable.

It is not enough that a federal habeas court, in its independent review of the legal question, is left with a firm conviction that the state court was erroneous. We have held precisely the opposite: "Under § 2254(d)(1)'s 'unreasonable application' clause, then, a federal habeas court may not issue the writ simply because that court concludes in its independent judgment that the relevant state-court decision applied clearly established federal law erroneously or incorrectly." Rather, that application must be objectively unreasonable.

Section 2254(d)(1) permits a federal court to grant habeas relief based on the application of a governing legal principle to a set of facts different from those of the case in which the principle was announced. Here, however, the governing legal principle gives legislatures broad discretion to fashion a sentence that fits within the scope of the proportionality principle—the "precise contours" of which "are unclear." And it was not objectively unreasonable for the California Court of Appeal to conclude that these "contours" permitted an affirmance of Andrade's sentence.

The gross disproportionality principle reserves a constitutional violation for only the extraordinary case. In applying this principle for § 2254(d)(1) purposes, it was not an unreasonable application of our clearly established law for the California Court of Appeal to affirm Andrade's sentence of two consecutive terms of 25 years to life in prison.

The judgment of the United States Court of Appeals for the Ninth Circuit, accordingly, is REVERSED.

It is so ordered.

DISSENT

SOUTER, J., joined by STEVENS, GINSBURG, and BREYER, JJ.

Andrade's sentence cannot survive Eighth Amendment review. His criminal history is less grave than Ewing's [*Ewing v. California* 2003], and yet he received a prison term twice as long for a less serious triggering offense. To be sure, this is a habeas case and a prohibition couched in terms as general as gross disproportion necessarily leaves state courts with much leeway under the statutory criterion that conditions federal relief upon finding that a state court unreasonably applied clear law, see 28 U.S.C. § 2254(d). This case nonetheless presents two independent reasons for holding that the disproportionality review by the state court was not only erroneous but unreasonable, entitling Andrade to relief. I respectfully dissent accordingly.

The first reason is the holding in *Solem*, which happens to be our most recent effort at proportionality review of recidivist sentencing. *Solem* is controlling here because it established a benchmark in applying the general principle. We specifically held that a sentence of life imprisonment without parole for uttering a $100 "no account" check was disproportionate to the crime, even though the defendant had committed six prior nonviolent felonies. In explaining our proportionality review, we contrasted the result with *Rummel's* on the ground that the life sentence there had included parole eligibility after 12 years.

The facts here are on all fours with those of *Solem* and point to the same result. Andrade, like the defendant in *Solem*, was a repeat offender who committed theft of fairly trifling value, some $150, and their criminal records are comparable, including burglary (though Andrade's were residential), with no violent crimes or crimes against the person. The respective sentences, too, are strikingly alike. Although Andrade's petty thefts occurred on two separate occasions, his sentence can only be understood as punishment for the total amount he stole. The two thefts were separated by only two weeks; they involved the same victim; they apparently constituted parts of a single, continuing effort to finance drug sales; their seriousness is measured by the dollar value of the things taken; and the government charged both thefts in a single indictment. The results under the Eighth Amendment should therefore be the same in each case. The only ways to reach a different conclusion are to reject the practical equivalence of a life sentence without parole and one with parole eligibility at 87. The former is unrealistic; an 87-year-old man released after 50 years behind bars will have no real life left, if he survives to be released at all. And the latter, disparaging *Solem* as a point of reference on Eighth Amendment analysis, is wrong as a matter of law.

The second reason that relief is required even under the § 2254(d) unreasonable application standard rests on the alternative way of looking at Andrade's 50-year sentence as two separate 25-year applications of the three-strikes law, and construing the challenge here as going to the second, consecutive 25-year minimum term triggered by a petty theft. To understand why it is revealing to look at the sentence this way, it helps to recall the basic difficulty inherent in proportionality review. We require the comparison of offense and penalty to disclose a truly gross disproportionality before the constitutional limit is passed, in large part because we believe that legislatures are institutionally equipped with better judgment than courts in deciding what penalty is merited by particular behavior. In this case, however, a court is substantially aided in its reviewing function by two determinations made by the State itself.

The first is the State's adoption of a particular penalogical [*sic*] theory as its principal reason for shutting a three-strikes defendant away for at least 25 years. Although the State alludes in passing to retribution or deterrence, its only serious justification for the 25-year minimum treats the sentence as a way to incapacitate a given defendant from further crime; the underlying theory is the need to protect the public from a danger demonstrated by the prior record of violent and serious crime. The State, in other words, has not chosen 25 to life because of the inherent moral or social reprehensibility of the triggering offense in isolation; the triggering offense is treated so seriously, rather, because of its confirmation of the defendant's danger to society and the need to counter his threat with incapacitation. As to the length of incapacitation, the State has made a second helpful determination, that the public risk or danger posed by someone with the specified predicate record is generally addressed by incapacitation for 25 years before parole eligibility. The three-strikes law, in sum, responds to a condition of the defendant shown by his prior felony record, his danger to society, and it reflects a judgment that 25 years of incapacitation prior to parole eligibility is appropriate when a defendant exhibiting such a condition commits another felony.

That said, I do not question the legitimacy of repeatedly sentencing a defendant in light of his criminal record: the Federal Sentencing Guidelines provide a prime example of how a sentencing scheme may take into account a defendant's criminal history without resentencing a defendant for past convictions. The point is merely that the triggering offense must reasonably support the weight of even the harshest possible sentences.

Whether or not one accepts the State's choice of penalogical [sic] policy as constitutionally sound, that policy cannot reasonably justify the imposition of a consecutive 25-year minimum for a second minor felony committed soon after the first triggering offense. Andrade did not somehow become twice as dangerous to society when he stole the second handful of videotapes; his dangerousness may justify treating one minor felony as serious and warranting long incapacitation, but a second such felony does not disclose greater danger warranting substantially longer incapacitation. Since the defendant's condition has not changed between the two closely related thefts, the incapacitation penalty is not open to the simple arithmetic of multiplying the punishment by two, without resulting in gross disproportion even under the State's chosen benchmark. Far from attempting a novel penal theory to justify doubling the sentence, the California Court of Appeal offered no comment at all as to the particular penal theory supporting such a

punishment. Perhaps even more tellingly, no one could seriously argue that the second theft of videotapes provided any basis to think that Andrade would be so dangerous after 25 years, the date on which the consecutive sentence would begin to run, as to require at least 25 years more. I know of no jurisdiction that would add 25 years of imprisonment simply to reflect the fact that the two temporally related thefts took place on two separate occasions, and I am not surprised that California has found no such case, not even under its three-strikes law. In sum, the argument that repeating a trivial crime justifies doubling a 25-year minimum incapacitation sentence based on a threat to the public does not raise a seriously debatable point on which judgments might reasonably differ. The argument is irrational, and the state court's acceptance of it in response to a facially gross disproportion between triggering offense and penalty was unreasonable within the meaning of § 2254(d).

This is the rare sentence of demonstrable gross disproportionality, as the California Legislature may well have recognized when it specifically provided that a prosecutor may move to dismiss or strike a prior felony conviction "in the furtherance of justice." Cal.Penal Code Ann. § 667(f)(2) (West 1999). In this case, the statutory safeguard failed, and the state court was left to ensure that the Eighth Amendment prohibition on grossly disproportionate sentences was met. If Andrade's sentence is not grossly disproportionate, the principle has no meaning. The California court's holding was an unreasonable application of clearly established precedent.

QUESTIONS

1. How does the majority *know* that the three-strikes law isn't cruel and unusual?
2. How does the dissent know that it *is* cruel and unusual?
3. Are their opinions purely subjective, or are they based on some standards? If so, what are the standards?
4. Should the California legislature or the U.S. Supreme Court decide whether punishments are cruel and unusual? Explain your answer.
5. Do you believe 25 years to life is "grossly disproportionate" to Leandro Andrade's crime? How do *you* know whether it is or isn't?

Trial Rights at Sentencing

LO 5

Until the present era of sentencing guidelines and mandatory minimum sentencing, the U.S. Supreme Court adopted a **hands-off approach to sentencing procedures**, leaving sentencing decisions to trial judges' discretionary judgment. Put another way, the Constitution places few, if any, limits on judicial discretionary decision making. The hands-off approach was a hallmark of the indeterminate sentencing era (1870–1970), when the rehabilitative ideal and judicial discretion as a means to achieve it dominated "advanced" penological thinking.

In the leading case applying the hands-off approach, *Williams v. New York* (1949), Samuel Titto Williams was sentenced to death by the trial judge even though the jury recommended life imprisonment. In open court, the trial judge pointed out that he had considered the evidence that the jury heard "in light of additional information obtained through the court's Probation Department, and through other sources." The additional information "revealed many material facts concerning appellant's background which though relevant to the question of punishment could not properly have been brought to the attention of the jury in its consideration of the question of guilt" (242–44).

Williams contended that sentencing him to death based on the additional information would deny him life without due process of law. The court rejected his contention:

> Tribunals passing on the guilt of a defendant always have been hedged in by strict evidentiary procedural limitations. But both before and since the American colonies became a nation, courts in this country and in England practiced a policy under which a sentencing judge could exercise a wide discretion in the sources and types of evidence used to assist him in determining the kind and extent of punishment to be imposed within limits fixed by law. Out-of-court affidavits have been used frequently, and of course in the smaller communities sentencing judges naturally have in mind their knowledge of the personalities and backgrounds of convicted offenders. (246)

In addition to history, the Court continued, there are "sound practical reasons" for different rules governing trials and sentencing procedures. "Rules of evidence have been fashioned for criminal trials which narrowly confine the trial contest to evidence that is strictly relevant to the particular offense charged." But, at sentencing, a judge isn't "confined to the narrow issue of guilt. His task is to determine the type and extent of punishment after the issue of guilt has been determined."

> And modern concepts individualizing punishment have made it all the more necessary that a sentencing judge not be denied an opportunity to obtain pertinent information by a requirement of rigid adherence to restrictive rules of evidence properly applicable to the trial. (246–47)

LO 7

That was 1949, when the rehabilitative ideal and judicial discretion was in full favor. Then came the history that saw the adoption of sentencing guidelines and mandatory minimum sentencing laws based on retribution, deterrence, and incapacitation and the accompanying curbs on judicial discretion. All this history came to a head in 2000 when the U.S. Supreme Court, to the surprise of many, dropped the hands-off approach and brought the Constitution into sentencing proceedings in *Apprendi v. New Jersey*.

Charles Apprendi, Jr., was convicted of possessing a firearm with an unlawful purpose, a felony in New Jersey normally punishable by 5 to 10 years in prison. New Jersey also had a hate crime statute providing for an extended punishment of 10 to 20 years if the judge found by a preponderance of the evidence that the defendant committed the crime with a "purpose to intimidate an individual or group of individuals because of race, color, gender, handicap, religion, sexual orientation or ethnicity" (469).

Apprendi argued that "racial purpose" was an element of the crime that required proof beyond a reasonable doubt. New Jersey argued that the choice of elements of offenses is for legislatures to make and that New Jersey's legislature chose to make "racial purpose" a "sentencing factor." The 5-member majority agreed with Apprendi and adopted the *Apprendi* **bright-line rule**:

> Other than the fact of prior conviction, any fact that increases the penalty for a crime beyond the prescribed statutory maximum must be submitted to a jury, and proved beyond a reasonable doubt. (490)

TABLE 14.2
Major U.S. Supreme Court Sentencing Rights Cases

Case	Sentencing Rights Affected
1. *Apprendi v. New Jersey,* 530 U.S. 466 (2000), 5–4	Struck down a New Jersey statute empowering judges to impose maximum sentences based on facts they found to be true by a preponderance of evidence but not found by juries beyond a reasonable doubt or confessed to by defendants
2. *Apprendi v. New Jersey,* 530 U.S. 466 (2000), 5–4	Affirmed judges' power to increase maximum sentence based on prior convictions without juries finding there were prior convictions or defendants confessing to them
3. *Harris v. U.S.,* 536 U.S. 545 (2002), 4-member plurality	Upheld a statute permitting judges to raise mandatory minimum sentences based on facts found by judges, not juries, as long as the increase doesn't exceed the statutory maximum
4. *Blakely v. Washington,* 542 U.S. 296 (2004), 5–4	Struck down a Washington State statute that empowered judges to *increase* the length of prison time beyond the "standard range" prescribed by Washington's sentencing guidelines based on facts not found by juries beyond a reasonable doubt
5. *U.S. v. Booker,* 543 U.S. 220 (2005), 5–4	• Struck down provisions in the U.S. Sentencing Guidelines that allowed judges to *increase* individual sentences beyond the standard range based on facts not found by juries beyond a reasonable doubt • Ruled that the U.S. Sentencing Guidelines are *advisory,* but they enjoy the presumption of reasonableness
6. *Rita v. U.S.,* 551 U.S. 338 (2007), 9–1	Ruled that when the District Court judge's discretionary sentencing decision falls *within* recommended ranges in the U.S. Sentencing Guidelines, the Courts of Appeals *may* presume that the sentence is reasonable
7. *Gall v. U.S.,* 552 U.S. 38 (2007), 7–2	Under post-*Booker* advisory Sentencing Guidelines regime: • District judge must consider the extent of any departure from guidelines and explain appropriateness of an unusually lenient or harsh sentence with sufficient justifications • Appellate review of sentencing decisions is limited to determining whether they're "reasonable" • Courts of appeals must review all sentences (whether inside, just outside, or significantly outside guidelines range) under deferential abuse-of-discretion standard (see case excerpt, p. 493)

Four justices dissented. According to Justice O'Connor:

The Court has long recognized that not every fact that bears on a defendant's punishment need be charged in an indictment, submitted to a jury, and proved by the government beyond a reasonable doubt. We have declined to establish any bright-line rule for making such judgments and have instead approached each case individually, sifting through the considerations most relevant to determining whether the legislature has acted properly within its broad power to define crimes and their punishments or has sought to evade the constitutional requirements associated with the characterization of a fact as an offense element. (524–25)

Apprendi was supposed to be a "ringing endorsement of the right to trial by jury" (Allen and others 2005, 1718). Sentencing guidelines and mandatory minimum sentencing laws allowed trial judges to decide facts related to defendants' punishment. This threatened the democratic right to have our peers decide those critical facts. *Apprendi* was supposed to eliminate that threat. But did it? The answer is by no means clear in the summer of 2010 as I write this edition of your book. The Court followed *Apprendi* with four other decisions, made up of shifting 5–4 majorities (Table 14.2) and several concurring opinions—overall displaying a badly splintered Court.

After *U.S. v. Booker* (2005), the touchstone for trial courts' use of facts to impose specific punishments—and for appellate courts in reviewing trial courts' sentences—is "reasonableness." The bright-line rule that juries have to decide all facts relied on to impose a specific sentence (except for the fact of prior convictions) is no longer the standard. But what does "reasonableness" mean? The Court grappled with the answer in *Gall v. U.S.* (2007), our next case excerpt.

In Gall v. U.S. (2007), *our next case excerpt, the U.S. Supreme Court found that the trial judge's explanation for sentencing Brian Gall to less than the terms of the sentencing guidelines was reasonable.*

CASE   Was the Trial Judge's Sentence "Reasonable"?

Gall v. U.S.
552 U.S. 38 (2007)

HISTORY

Brian Michael Gall (Defendant/petitioner) was convicted, on his guilty plea, in the United States District Court for the Southern District of Iowa, Robert W. Pratt, J., of conspiracy to distribute ecstasy, and was sentenced to 36 months of probation. The government appealed, challenging the sentence. The Eighth Circuit Court of Appeals, Smith, Circuit Judge, remanded for resentencing. The U.S. Supreme Court granted certiorari, and reversed.

STEVENS, J., joined by ROBERTS, C.J., and SCALIA, KENNEDY, SOUTER, GINSBURG, and BREYER, JJ.

FACTS

In February or March 2000, petitioner Brian Gall, a second-year college student at the University of Iowa, was invited by Luke Rinderknecht to join an ongoing enterprise distributing a controlled substance popularly known as "ecstasy." Gall—who was then a user of ecstasy, cocaine, and marijuana—accepted the invitation. During the ensuing seven months, Gall delivered ecstasy pills, which he received from Rinderknecht, to other conspirators, who then sold them to consumers. He netted over $30,000.

A month or two after joining the conspiracy, Gall stopped using ecstasy. A few months after that, in September 2000, he advised Rinderknecht and other co-conspirators that he was withdrawing from the conspiracy.

He has not sold illegal drugs of any kind since. He has, in the words of the District Court, "self-rehabilitated." He graduated from the University of Iowa in 2002, and moved first to Arizona, where he obtained a job in the construction industry, and later to Colorado, where he earned $18 per hour as a master carpenter. He has not used any illegal drugs since graduating from college.

After Gall moved to Arizona, he was approached by federal law enforcement agents who questioned him about his involvement in the ecstasy distribution conspiracy. Gall admitted his limited participation in the distribution of ecstasy, and the agents took no further action at that time. On April 28, 2004—approximately a year and a half after this initial interview, and three and a half years after Gall withdrew from the conspiracy—an indictment was returned in the Southern District of Iowa charging him and seven other defendants with participating in a conspiracy to distribute ecstasy, cocaine, and marijuana, that began in or about May 1996 and continued through October 30, 2002. The Government has never questioned the truthfulness of any of Gall's earlier statements or contended that he played any role in, or had any knowledge of, other aspects of the conspiracy described in the indictment. When he received notice of the indictment, Gall moved back to Iowa and surrendered to the authorities. While free on his own recognizance, Gall started his own business in the construction industry, primarily engaged in subcontracting for the installation of windows and doors. In his first year, his profits were over $2,000 per month.

Gall entered into a plea agreement with the Government, stipulating that he was "responsible for, but did not necessarily distribute himself, at least 2,500 grams of ecstasy, or the equivalent of at least 87.5 kilograms of marijuana." In the agreement, the Government acknowledged that by "on or about September of 2000," Gall had communicated his intent to stop distributing ecstasy to Rinderknecht and other members of the conspiracy. The agreement further provided that recent changes in the Guidelines that enhanced the recommended punishment for distributing ecstasy were not applicable to Gall because he had withdrawn from the conspiracy prior to the effective date of those changes.

In her presentence report, the probation officer concluded that Gall had no significant criminal history; that he was not an organizer, leader, or manager; and that his offense did not involve the use of any weapons. The report stated that Gall had truthfully provided the Government with all of the evidence he had concerning the alleged offenses, but that his evidence was not useful because he provided no new information to the agents. The report also described Gall's substantial use of drugs prior to his offense and the absence of any such use in recent years. The report recommended a sentencing range of 30 to 37 months of imprisonment.

The record of the sentencing hearing held on May 27, 2005, includes a "small flood" of letters from Gall's parents and other relatives, his fiancée, neighbors, and representatives of firms doing business with him, uniformly praising his character and work ethic. The transcript includes the testimony of several witnesses and the District Judge's colloquy with the Assistant United States Attorney (AUSA) and with Gall. The AUSA did not contest any of the evidence concerning Gall's law-abiding life during the preceding five years, but urged that "the Guidelines are appropriate and should be followed," and requested that the court impose a prison sentence within the Guidelines range. He mentioned that two of Gall's co-conspirators had been sentenced to 30 and 35 months, respectively, but upon further questioning by the District Court, he acknowledged that neither of them had voluntarily withdrawn from the conspiracy.

The District Judge sentenced Gall to probation for a term of 36 months. In addition to making a lengthy statement on the record, the judge filed a detailed sentencing memorandum explaining his decision, and provided the following statement of reasons in his written judgment:

> The Court determined that, considering all the factors under 18 U.S.C. 3553(a), (Figure 14.2) the Defendant's explicit withdrawal from the conspiracy almost four years before the filing of the Indictment, the Defendant's post-offense conduct, especially obtaining a college degree and the start of his own successful business, the support of family and friends, lack of criminal history, and his age at the time of the offense conduct, all warrant the sentence imposed, which was sufficient, but not greater than necessary to serve the purposes of sentencing.

At the end of both the sentencing hearing and the sentencing memorandum, the District Judge reminded Gall that probation, rather than "an act of leniency," is a "substantial restriction of freedom." In the memorandum, he emphasized:

> Gall will have to comply with strict reporting conditions along with a three-year regime of alcohol and drug testing. He will not be able to change or make decisions about significant circumstances in his life, such as where to live or work, which are prized liberty interests, without first seeking authorization from his Probation Officer or, perhaps, even the Court. Of course, the Defendant always faces the harsh consequences that await if he violates the conditions of his probationary term.

Finally, the District Judge explained why he had concluded that the sentence of probation reflected the seriousness of Gall's offense and that no term of imprisonment was necessary:

> Any term of imprisonment in this case would be counter effective by depriving society of the contributions of the Defendant who, the Court has found, understands the consequences of his criminal conduct and is doing everything in his power to forge a new life. The Defendant's post-offense conduct indicates neither that he will return to criminal behavior nor that the Defendant is a danger to society. In fact, the Defendant's post-offense conduct was not motivated by a desire to please the Court or any other governmental agency, but was the pre-Indictment product of the Defendant's own desire to lead a better life.

The Court of Appeals reversed and remanded for resentencing. Relying on its earlier opinion in *United States v. Claiborne* (C.A.8 2006), it held that a sentence outside of the Guidelines range must be supported by a justification that "is proportional to the extent of the difference between the advisory range and the sentence imposed." Characterizing the difference between a sentence of probation and the bottom of Gall's advisory Guidelines range of 30 months as "extraordinary" because it amounted to "a 100% downward variance," the Court of Appeals held that such a variance must be—and here was not—supported by extraordinary circumstances.

Rather than making an attempt to quantify the value of the justifications provided by the District Judge, the Court of Appeals identified what it regarded as five separate errors in the District Judge's reasoning:

1. He gave "too much weight to Gall's withdrawal from the conspiracy";

2. given that Gall was 21 at the time of his offense, the District Judge erroneously gave "significant weight" to studies showing impetuous behavior by persons under the age of 18;

3. he did not "properly weigh" the seriousness of Gall's offense;

4. he failed to consider whether a sentence of probation would result in "unwarranted" disparities; and

5. he placed "too much emphasis on Gall's post-offense rehabilitation."

FIGURE 14.2 U.S. Sentencing Guidelines, 18 U.S.C. § 3553

Imposition of a Sentence

§ 3553 (a). Factors To Be Considered in Imposing a Sentence. The court shall impose a sentence sufficient, but not greater than necessary, to comply with the purposes set forth in paragraph (2) of this subsection. The court, in determining the particular sentence to be imposed, shall consider—

(1) the nature and circumstances of the offense and the history and characteristics of the defendant;

(2) the need for the sentence imposed—

    (A) to reflect the seriousness of the offense, to promote respect for the law, and to provide just punishment for the offense;

    (B) to afford adequate deterrence to criminal conduct;

    (C) to protect the public from further crimes of the defendant; and

    (D) to provide the defendant with needed educational or vocational training, medical care, or other correctional treatment in the most effective manner;

(3) the kinds of sentences available;

(4) the kinds of sentence and the sentencing range established for—

    (A) the applicable category of offense committed by the applicable category of defendant as set forth in the guidelines—

        (i) issued by the Sentencing Commission pursuant to section 994 (a)(1) of title 28, United States Code, subject to any amendments made to such guidelines by act of Congress (regardless of whether such amendments have yet to be incorporated by the Sentencing Commission into amendments issued under section 994 (p) of title 28); and

        (ii) that, except as provided in section 3742 (g), are in effect on the date the defendant is sentenced; or

    (B) in the case of a violation of probation or supervised release, the applicable guidelines or policy statements issued by the Sentencing Commission pursuant to section 994 (a)(3) of title 28, United States Code, taking into account any amendments made to such guidelines or policy statements by act of Congress (regardless of whether such amendments have yet to be incorporated by the Sentencing Commission into amendments issued under section 994 (p) of title 28);

(5) any pertinent policy statement—

    (A) issued by the Sentencing Commission pursuant to section 994 (a)(2) of title 28, United States Code, subject to any amendments made to such policy statement by act of Congress (regardless of whether such amendments have yet to be incorporated by the Sentencing Commission into amendments issued under section 994 (p) of title 28); and

    (B) that, except as provided in section 3742 (g), is in effect on the date the defendant is sentenced.

(6) the need to avoid unwarranted sentence disparities among defendants with similar records who have been found guilty of similar conduct; and

(7) the need to provide restitution to any victims of the offense.

We are not persuaded that these factors are sufficient to support the conclusion that the District Judge abused his discretion.

OPINION

In *Booker* we invalidated both the statutory provision, 18 U.S.C. § 3553(b)(1) (2000 ed., Supp. IV), which made the Sentencing Guidelines mandatory, and § 3742(e) (2000 ed. and Supp. IV), which directed appellate courts to apply a *de novo* standard of review to departures from the Guidelines. As a result of our decision, the Guidelines are now advisory, and appellate review of sentencing decisions is limited to determining whether they are "reasonable." Our explanation of "reasonableness" review in the *Booker* opinion made it pellucidly clear that the familiar abuse-of-discretion standard of review now applies to appellate review of sentencing decisions. [*Abuse of discretion is an appellate court's standard for reviewing a trial court's decision that is asserted to be grossly unsound, unreasonable, illegal, or unsupported by the evidence.*]

It is also clear that a district judge must give serious consideration to the extent of any departure from the Guidelines and must explain his conclusion that an unusually lenient or an unusually harsh sentence is appropriate in a particular case with sufficient justifications. For even though the Guidelines are advisory rather than mandatory, they are the product of careful study based on extensive empirical evidence derived from the review of thousands of individual sentencing decisions.

In reviewing the reasonableness of a sentence outside the Guidelines range, appellate courts may therefore take the degree of variance into account and consider the extent of a deviation from the Guidelines. We reject, however, an appellate rule that requires "extraordinary" circumstances to justify a sentence outside the Guidelines range. We also reject the use of a rigid mathematical formula that uses the percentage of a departure as the standard for determining the strength of the justifications required for a specific sentence. The approaches we reject come too close to creating an impermissible presumption of unreasonableness for sentences outside the Guidelines range. The fact that we permit courts of appeals to adopt a presumption of reasonableness does not mean that courts may adopt a presumption of unreasonableness. Even the Government has acknowledged that such a presumption would not be consistent with *Booker*.

It has been uniform and constant in the federal judicial tradition for the sentencing judge to consider every convicted person as an individual, and every case as a unique study in the human failings that sometimes mitigate, sometimes magnify, the crime and the punishment to ensue. The uniqueness of the individual case, however, does not change the deferential abuse-of-discretion standard of review that applies to all sentencing decisions.

The opinion of the Court of Appeals in this case does not reflect the requisite deference and does not support the conclusion that the District Court abused its discretion.

The District Judge committed no significant procedural error. He correctly calculated the applicable Guidelines range, allowed both parties to present arguments as to what they believed the appropriate sentence should be, considered all of the § 3553(a) factors, and thoroughly documented his reasoning.

The Court of Appeals gave virtually no deference to the District Court's decision that the § 3553(a) factors justified a significant variance in this case. Although the Court of Appeals correctly stated that the appropriate standard of review was abuse of discretion, it engaged in an analysis that more closely resembled *de novo* review of the facts presented and determined that, in its view, the degree of variance was not warranted.

The Court of Appeals thought that the District Court "gave too much weight to Gall's withdrawal from the conspiracy because the court failed to acknowledge the significant benefit Gall received from being subject to the 1999 Guidelines." This criticism is flawed in that it ignores the critical relevance of Gall's voluntary withdrawal, a circumstance that distinguished his conduct not only from that of all his codefendants, but from the vast majority of defendants convicted of conspiracy in federal court. The District Court quite reasonably attached great weight to the fact that Gall voluntarily withdrew from the conspiracy after deciding, on his own initiative, to change his life. This lends strong support to the District Court's conclusion that Gall is not going to return to criminal behavior and is not a danger to society. Compared to a case where the offender's rehabilitation occurred after he was charged with a crime, the District Court here had greater justification for believing Gall's turnaround was genuine, as distinct from a transparent attempt to build a mitigation case.

Finally, the Court of Appeals thought that, even if Gall's rehabilitation was dramatic and permanent, a sentence of probation for participation as a middleman in a conspiracy distributing 10,000 pills of ecstasy "lies outside the range of choice dictated by the facts of the case." If the Guidelines were still mandatory, and assuming the facts did not justify a Guidelines-based downward departure, this would provide a sufficient basis for setting aside Gall's sentence because the Guidelines state that probation alone is not an appropriate sentence for comparable offenses.

But the Guidelines are not mandatory, and thus the "range of choice dictated by the facts of the case" is significantly broadened. Moreover, the Guidelines are only one of the factors to consider when imposing sentence, and § 3553(a)(3) directs the judge to consider sentences other than imprisonment. The District Court quite reasonably attached great weight to Gall's self-motivated rehabilitation, which was undertaken not at the direction of, or under supervision by, any court, but on his own initiative. This also lends strong support to the conclusion that imprisonment was not necessary to deter Gall from engaging in future criminal conduct or to protect the public from his future criminal acts.

The Court of Appeals clearly disagreed with the District Judge's conclusion that consideration of the § 3553(a) factors justified a sentence of probation; it believed that the circumstances presented here were insufficient to sustain such a marked deviation from the Guidelines range. But it is not for the Court of Appeals to decide *de novo* whether the justification for a variance is sufficient or the sentence reasonable. On abuse-of-discretion review, the Court of Appeals should have given due deference to the District Court's reasoned and reasonable decision that the § 3553(a) factors, on the whole, justified the sentence. Accordingly, the judgment of the Court of Appeals is REVERSED.

It is so ordered.

DISSENT

ALITO, J.

Booker did not explain exactly what it meant by a system of "advisory" guidelines or by "reasonableness" review, and the opinion is open to different interpretations. It is possible to read the opinion to mean that district judges, after giving the Guidelines a polite nod, may then proceed essentially as if the Sentencing Reform Act had never been enacted. While this is a possible understanding of the opinion, a better reading is that sentencing judges must still give the Guidelines' policy decisions some significant weight and that the courts of appeals must still police compliance. [Under this reading] district courts are still required to give some deference to the policy decisions embodied in the Guidelines and that appellate review must monitor compliance.

Moreover, the Court expressed confidence that appellate review for reasonableness would help to avoid excessive sentencing disparities and would tend to iron out sentencing differences. Indeed, a major theme was that the post-*Booker* sentencing regime would still promote the Sentencing Reform Act's goal of reducing sentencing disparities. It is unrealistic to think this goal can be achieved over the long term if sentencing judges need only give lip service to the Guidelines. On the contrary, sentencing disparities will gradually increase. Appellate decisions affirming sentences that diverge from the Guidelines (such as the Court's decision today) will be influential, and the sentencing habits developed during the pre-*Booker* era will fade.

Finally, we should not forget the decision's constitutional underpinnings. *Booker* and its antecedents are based on the Sixth Amendment right to trial by jury. The Court has held that (at least under a mandatory guidelines system) a defendant has the right to have a jury, not a judge, find facts that increase the defendant's authorized sentence. It is telling that the rules set out in the Court's opinion in the present case have nothing to do with juries or factfinding and, indeed, that not one of the facts that bears on petitioner's sentence is disputed. What is at issue, instead, is the allocation of the authority to decide issues of substantive sentencing policy, an issue on which the Sixth Amendment says absolutely nothing. The yawning gap between the Sixth Amendment and the Court's opinion should be enough to show that the *Blakely-Booker* line of cases has gone astray.

QUESTIONS

1. State the majority opinion's definition of "reasonableness" as it applies to (a) the trial court's sentencing discretionary decision making and (b) the appellate court's review of the trial court's decision. Do these definitions help you understand what "reasonableness" *really* means?

2. List the facts, and summarize the trial court's arguments, that led the judge to depart from the guidelines and sentence Brian Michael Gall to probation instead of prison.

3. List the facts that led the state to argue that the trial court abused its discretion when it departed from the guidelines and sentenced Brian Michael Gall to probation instead of prison.

4. Do you believe the trial court abused its discretion? Back up your answer with facts and arguments in questions 1–3.

5. If you were the trial judge, what sentence would you have imposed? Back up your answer with facts and arguments in questions 1–3.

Death Sentence Procedure Rights

LO 7

As you learned earlier ("The Proportionality Principle and the Death Sentence"), capital punishment is different from all other punishments, which means death *sentences* are different, too. The Court has held that capital punishment for murder isn't cruel and unusual, only if:

1. The sentencing process allows the judge or jury to consider mitigating and aggravating circumstances and offers adequate guidance in weighing them (see Table 14.3).

2. The law provides for a review procedure to ensure against discriminatory application of the death penalty (*Lockett v. Ohio* 1978).

TABLE 14.3

Aggravating and Mitigating Circumstances in Death Penalty Cases

Aggravating Circumstances	Mitigating Circumstances
Prior record of violent felony	No significant prior criminal record
Felony murder	Extreme mental or emotional disturbance
Murder of more than one person	Minor participant in the murder
Murder of police officer or other public official	Youth at the time of the murder
Torture or other heinous killing	
Killing to avoid arrest	
Killing during escape from lawful custody	

According to the Court, the rationale for this process is that "it is of vital importance to the defendant, and to the community, that any decision to impose the death sentence be, and appear to be, based on reason rather than caprice or emotion" (*Gardner v. Florida* 1977).

Statistics indicate that there's a pronounced racial disparity in death sentences (Figure 14.3). Blacks and Whites who kill Whites are more likely to receive the death sentence than either Blacks who kill Blacks or Whites who kill Blacks (Baldus and Woodworth 1998, 399–400).

The U.S. Supreme Court has conceded that these numbers may well prove that race infects death sentencing decisions, in *general*, but that they're not enough to prove cruel and unusual punishment in *individual cases*. To overturn a death sentence, individual defendants have to prove that the death sentencing decision in their case was infected by racial views. Specifically, they have to prove that the prosecutor, the jury, or their lawyer's decisions were motivated by race (*McCleskey v. Kemp* 1987).

IIIIIIIIIIIIIIIIIIIIIIIIIIIIIIIIIIIIIIIIIIIIIIIIIIIIIIIIIIIIIIIIIIIIIIIIIIIIIIIIIIIIIIIIIIIIIIIIIIIIIIIIIIIIIIIIIII

Appeals

LO 8

It may surprise you to learn (as it surprises most of my students) that convicted offenders don't have a constitutional right to appeal their convictions. According to the U.S. Supreme Court in *Ross v. Moffitt* (1974), "It is clear that the State need not provide any appeal at all." Based on that principle, the Court upheld a state court decision that denied a poor defendant a right to a lawyer for his appeal to the state supreme court. According to the Court:

> There are significant differences between the trial and appellate stages of a criminal proceeding. The purpose of the trial stage from the State's point of view is to convert a criminal defendant from a person presumed innocent to one found guilty beyond a reasonable doubt. To accomplish this purpose, the State employs a prosecuting attorney who presents evidence to the court, challenges any witnesses offered by the defendant, argues rulings of the court, and makes direct arguments to the court and jury seeking to persuade them of the defendant's guilt. Under these circumstances reason and reflection require us to recognize that in our adversary system of criminal justice, any person haled into court,

FIGURE 14.3 Death Penalty: The Numbers

Race of Death Row Inmates

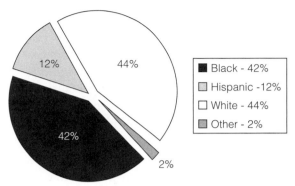

- ■ Black - 42%
- ▨ Hispanic - 12%
- □ White - 44%
- ▨ Other - 2%

Race of Defendants Executed

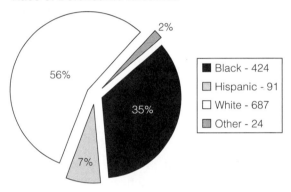

- ■ Black - 424
- ▨ Hispanic - 91
- □ White - 687
- ▨ Other - 24

Race of Victim in Death Penalty Cases

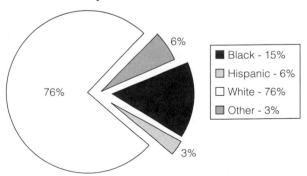

- ■ Black - 15%
- ▨ Hispanic - 6%
- □ White - 76%
- ▨ Other - 3%

Source: Death Penalty Information Center. 2010. "Death Penalty Fact Sheet," http://www.deathpenaltyinfo.org.

who is too poor to hire a lawyer, cannot be assured a fair trial unless counsel is provided for him.

By contrast, it is ordinarily the defendant, rather than the state, who initiates the appellate process, seeking not to fend off the efforts of the state's prosecutor but rather to overturn a finding of guilty made by a judge or a jury below. The defendant needs an attorney on appeal not as a shield to protect him against being "haled into court" by the state and stripped of his presumption of innocence, but rather as a sword to upset the prior determination of guilt. This difference is significant for, while no one would agree that the state may simply dispense with the trial stage of proceedings without a criminal defendant's consent, it is clear that the state need not provide any appeal at all. (609)

Even though there's no *constitutional* right to appeal, every jurisdiction has created a **statutory right to appeal**. To understand this statutory right, refer to Figure 1.2 in Chapter 1, which depicts our three-tiered judicial system: trial courts, intermediate appeals courts, and supreme courts of appeal. The statutory right to appeal applies only to the *intermediate* appellate courts (and in capital cases, to the supreme courts).

Appeals to *supreme* courts of the states and to the U.S. Supreme Court, on the other hand, are discretionary. Most of the cases in this book, for example, appeals to the U.S. Supreme Court, are **discretionary appeal** cases. The *writ of* certiorari is a discretionary writ, allowing appeals only in cases that the U.S. Supreme Court or the state supreme courts decide are of significance beyond the interests of the particular defendants appealing them (Chapter 1, "Appellate Court Cases").

Since the late 1980s, the U.S. Supreme Court has sharply reduced the number of cases it accepts by means of certiorari. By this reduction, the Court has reaffirmed the principle that final appeal isn't a right; it's a matter of discretionary judgment.

Three principal doctrines define the scope of appellate review of criminal cases in state courts:

1. Mootness

2. Raise or waive

3. Plain error

Traditionally, the **mootness doctrine** banned appeals by offenders who had finished their prison sentences or who had paid their fines. Some jurisdictions have retained this traditional definition of mootness. Several others have gone to the other extreme, holding that criminal cases are *never* moot, because defendants always have an interest in removing the "stigma of guilt." Most jurisdictions have taken a middle ground, retaining the mootness doctrine but carving out exceptions to it.

The **collateral consequences exception** says that if defendants might suffer legal consequences from a criminal conviction, then even if they have fully served their sentence the case isn't moot. These consequences include the possibility of the loss of a professional license, rejection for admission to a professional school, or loss of employment.

The **raise-or-waive doctrine** says defendants have to raise their objections at trial; if they don't, they give up their right to appeal. Why? The **doctrine of judicial economy** says we shouldn't spend time and money on appeals that defendants could have avoided by objecting during the trial. However, defendants don't always waive their right to appeal when they fail to object at trial. When procedural requirements don't provide adequate time for a defendant to object to a trial court error, the defendant doesn't waive the right to appeal the error. Also, circumstances can make it impossible for a defendant to comply with the raise-or-waive rule. And obviously, incompetent lawyers don't object to their own ineffectiveness (LaFave and Israel 1984, 3:252–54).

A major exception to the raise-or-waive rule is the **plain-error rule**, which applies even if defendants don't object to the errors at trial. It applies when "plain errors affecting substantial rights" cause "manifest injustice or miscarriage of justice." Most courts apply the rule "sparingly." Plain error doesn't require or justify a review "of every alleged trial error that has not been properly preserved for appellate review."

Furthermore, in most jurisdictions, the defendant bears the burden of proving that an alleged error is of such magnitude that it constitutes plain error.

||||||||||||||||||||||||||||||||||||||||||||||||||||||||||||||||||||||||||||||||||||||||||||||||||||||||||||||||||||||||||||||||||||||||||||||

Habeas Corpus (Collateral Attack)

LO 9, LO 10

A defendant's criminal conviction becomes final when it's either affirmed on appeal to the jurisdiction's highest court or the highest court denies his or her petition for review. Appeals are called **direct attacks**, because they attack the decisions made by the trial court and/or the jury's guilty verdict in the specific defendant's criminal trial.

But the story doesn't necessarily end there. In every state, and in the federal system, convicted defendants get one more chance for review. This review is called a **habeas corpus proceeding**, or a "**collateral attack**." They're called collateral because they indirectly attack the judgment in a new and separate noncriminal (civil) lawsuit. In that new case, the defendant in the criminal case (now the petitioner or plaintiff in the civil case) asks (**petitions the court**) for review on various grounds.

There are three kinds of collateral attack:

1. State court collateral review for defendants who were convicted in a state court

2. Federal court collateral review for defendants convicted in federal courts

3. Federal court habeas corpus review for defendants convicted in state courts (Allen and others 2005, 1574)

State review varies too much to generalize about it, and procedures for review of federal criminal defendants are similar to federal review of state criminal defendants. So we'll concentrate on federal habeas corpus review of state criminal defendants' convictions.

If the court issues the writ, the writ orders the person (usually a prison warden) who's detaining the plaintiff to bring him or her before the judge and "show cause" for the detention. The object is to find out if the court in the criminal case had the authority (*jurisdiction*) to enter the judgment that put the plaintiff in prison and, if so, whether the judgment was reached properly. Depending on the evidence produced, the plaintiff is either set free, bailed, tried, or sent back to prison (Fisher 1888, 454).

Habeas corpus has a long and distinguished history. It's called the "**great writ of liberty**," because it originated as a bulwark against tyrannical English kings. The U.S. Constitution's founders placed enormous confidence in the "Great Writ." Alexander Hamilton called it a bulwark against the "practice of arbitrary imprisonments in all ages, among the favorite and most formidable instruments of tyranny" (Hamilton 1788).

According to the 19th-century historian of habeas corpus, Sydney George Fisher (1888):

> These rulers of men often want to rid themselves quickly of their personal enemies or of those whom they choose to consider enemies of their country, and of the easiest methods is to arrest on any sort of charge or suspicion, and keep the victim in confinement simply by not allowing him to be brought to trial. And it has often been said,—and the Bastille and the Tower of London will warrant the assertion— that the power to secretly hurry a man to jail, where his sufferings will be unknown or soon forgotten, is more dangerous than all the engines of tyranny. (454)

Fisher contrasted this abuse of the English kings' power with President Lincoln's suspension of the writ of habeas corpus during the Civil War. Fisher vigorously defended Lincoln and scoffed at Lincoln's critics who called him a dictator because, Fisher argued, it was right to take extreme measures to save the Union.

Of course, we're a long way from tyrannical kings, and even from Lincoln's use of the writ. Today, most habeas corpus proceedings begin only after criminal cases have run through their full course of direct attack in state trial and appellate courts. After this long and involved process, habeas corpus proceedings start in U.S. District Court, proceed through the U.S. Court of Appeals, and can eventually reach the U.S. Supreme Court for final review.

According to the U.S. Constitution Article I: "The privilege of the Writ of Habeas Corpus shall not be suspended, unless when in Cases of Rebellion or Invasion the public Safety may require it." Two U.S. statutes elaborated on Article I by granting power to U.S. courts to hear petitions of habeas corpus and issue writs of habeas corpus.

The U.S. Judiciary Act of 1789 authorized U.S. courts to deal with the petitions of federal prisoners. The Habeas Corpus Act of 1867 (LaFave and Israel 1984, 292) extended the power of U.S. Courts to deal with habeas corpus petitions of state prisoners. According to the 1867 act:

> The several courts of the United States within their respective jurisdictions, in addition to the authority already conferred by law, shall have power to grant writs of habeas corpus in all cases where any person may be restrained of his or her liberty in violation of the Constitution, or of any treaty or law of the United States. (292)

The original purpose of the Act was to protect newly freed slaves and Federal Reconstruction officials who were wrongly convicted of crimes in Southern state courts in violation of their federal constitutional rights (Allen and others 2005, 1576). For almost a century, courts interpreted habeas review narrowly. According to the **narrow interpretation**, the act authorizes the courts only to review the jurisdiction of the court—that is, its authority over the person and the subject matter of the case. The review asks only whether the court has the power to hear criminal cases and whether it can decide criminal cases involving the prisoner. According to the **broad interpretation**, the act empowers the federal courts to review the whole state proceeding to determine possible violations of federal law and constitutional provisions (LaFave and Israel 1984, 3:292–94).

During the years of the Warren Court (Chief Justice Earl Warren, 1953–1969), when federal rights were expanding through the incorporation doctrine (Chapter 2), the Court opted for a broad view of habeas corpus. The leader of the broad view, Associate Justice William Brennan, argued that the broader view fulfilled the historical purpose of habeas corpus, "providing relief against the detention of persons in violation of their fundamental liberties." As to objections that such expansive review of lower court proceedings threatened the interest in finality, he argued that "conventional notions of finality of litigation" should "have no place where life or liberty is at stake and infringement of constitutional rights is alleged."

In addition to preserving fundamental liberties, the broader view, according to its supporters, furthers the interest in correct results. The more chances to review, the greater the accuracy of the final decision. According to one judge: "We would not send two astronauts to the moon without providing them with at least three or four back-up systems. Should we send literally thousands of men to prison with even less reserves? With knowledge of our fallibility and a realization of past errors, we can hardly insure our confidence by creating an irrevocable end to the guilt determining process" (LaFave and Israel 1984, 3:298–99).

Justice Brennan's and the Warren Court majority's view have received harsh criticism from judges and commentators. Most of the criticism focuses on the threat to finality and the costs of "endless" reviews of legal issues, which sometimes go on for years. No one has put the argument for finality better than the great advocate John W. Davis in his last argument before the U.S. Supreme Court: "Somewhere, sometime to every principle comes a moment of repose when it has been so often announced, so confidently relied upon, so long continued, that it passes the limits of judicial discretion and disturbance" (*Brown v. Board of Education* 1954).

Others doubt that the broad view really protects prisoners' fundamental rights. Associate Supreme Court Justice Robert H. Jackson, in *Brown v. Allen* (1953), argued that we have no reason to expect more accuracy in a second review than in the initial decision:

> Reversal by a higher court is not proof that justice is thereby better done. There is no doubt that if there were a super–Supreme Court, a substantial proportion of our reversals of state courts would also be reversed. We are not final because we are infallible, but we are infallible only because we are final. (540)

Justice Jackson attributed the controversy over habeas corpus to three causes:

1. The Supreme Court's use of the due process clause of the Fourteenth Amendment to "subject state courts to increasing federal control"

2. The determination of what due process means by "personal notions of justice instead of by known rules of law"

3. The "breakdown of procedural safeguards against abuse of the writ"

The Burger (Chief Justice Warren Burger, 1969–1986) and Rehnquist (Chief Justice William Rehnquist, 1986–2005) Courts adopted the *narrow view of habeas corpus*—the power to review only the jurisdiction of the court over the person and the subject matter of the case. The Rehnquist Court emphasized the balance of interests that habeas corpus proceedings require. On one side of the balance are the constitutional rights of individuals and the need to control government misconduct. On the other side are the following interests:

1. The finality of decisions

2. Reliability, or obtaining the correct result

3. Certainty in decisions, or promoting reliance on decisions

4. The stability of decisions, or promoting the permanence of decisions

5. Federalism, or respect for state criminal court decisions

6. The burden on federal judicial resources in hearing repeated challenges

7. Contempt for the system from repeated and long-drawn-out proceedings

8. The impediment that many frivolous claims are to the success of meritorious claims

To the Rehnquist Court, the main problem in habeas corpus was an "endless succession of writs." Historically, an English subject could take a petition to every judge in England. The rule of *res judicata*—that once a matter is decided it cannot be reopened—didn't apply to habeas corpus. Remnants of res judicata linger in the rule that denial of a first petition for habeas corpus doesn't prohibit filing a second petition.

But, according to the Rehnquist Court in *McCleskey v. Zant* (1991), just because the rule of res judicata doesn't apply doesn't mean that prisoners can file an unlimited number of petitions. Courts have the discretion to deny successive petitions, especially if petitioners try to raise issues they failed to raise in their first petition.

In the wake of the bombing of the Federal Building in Oklahoma City in 1995, and a wave of anticrime sentiment in 1996, Congress enacted the **Antiterrorism and Effective Death Penalty Act (AEDPA)** (U.S.C.A. §§ 2241–66). AEDPA substantially amends federal habeas corpus law as it applies to both state and federal prisoners, whether they're on death row or imprisoned for any length of time. Federal habeas corpus is the statutory procedure (28 U.S.C. 2241–and following) that enables state and federal prisoners to petition the federal courts to review their convictions and sentences to determine whether they're being held contrary to the laws or the Constitution of the United States. AEDPA greatly narrows these prisoners' habeas statutory right to petition.

Here are some highlights of AEDPA's habeas amendments:

1. An almost total ban on federal habeas reconsideration of legal and factual issues ruled upon by state courts

2. The creation of a general one-year statute of limitations on filing habeas petitions for prisoners serving life sentences or less. The time begins at the date of the completion of direct appeal in the prisoner's criminal case. The limit in death penalty cases is 6 months.

3. An encouragement for states to appoint counsel for indigent state death row inmates during state habeas or other appellate proceedings

4. A requirement that the appellate court approve repetitious habeas petitions before they proceed

Summary

LO 1
- After conviction, defendants become "offenders" and lose constitutional protections they received as defendants. Few rights are recognized at sentencing and appeal. People assume that by the time defendants are convicted, they've had one fair shot at justice. This makes them less supportive of devoting public resources to determine if a convict was unlawfully detained.

LO 2
- Supporters of fixed sentencing argue that the punishment should fit the crime, while advocates of indeterminate sentencing think the punishment should be tailored to individual circumstances. Historically, both fixed and indeterminate sentencing played important roles, but indeterminate sentencing largely has given way to fixed sentences in the last few decades as rehabilitation lost favor to retribution.

LO 2, LO 3
- Throughout history, legislatures, courts, and administrative agencies have exercised sentencing authority. In judicial sentencing, judges prescribe sentences. In administrative sentencing, the legislature and judges prescribe a range of prison times for a particular crime, and administrative agencies such as parole boards determine

the exact release date. Limiting discretion in sentencing responds to demands for uniformity and certainty of punishment. It also responds to demands for retribution, deterrence, and incapacitation. Scholars and observers agree that the social context of the courtroom and the political-ideological preferences of the judge play significant roles in sentencing.

LO 3, LO 4

- Sentencing guidelines establish a relatively narrow range of penalties and give judges room to depart from the specified ranges where justified by the seriousness of the crime and the offender's criminal history. Mandatory minimum sentencing laws seek to ensure judges depart from guidelines only to issue harsher penalties.

LO 5

- The proportionality principle deems sentences cruel and unusual if they're "grossly disproportionate" to the "gravity of the offense." A minority of judges believe the Eighth Amendment contains no proportionality principle, or, if it does, that it's up to the legislature to decide what sentences are disproportionate. The U.S. Supreme Court has held that the death penalty is proportionate punishment only when a mentally fit adult kills and is convicted of murder.

LO 6

- Long prison terms for white-collar criminals are modern attempts to match the harsh penalties often given to their non-white-collar counterparts and to deter the more rational, calculated crimes they're likely to commit.

LO 7

- The Constitution places few limits on judicial sentencing, and until the present era of mandatory minimum sentencing, the U.S. Supreme Court adopted a "hands-off" approach. Sentencing procedures (not just sentences themselves) vary widely based on what the Supreme Court deems "sound practical reasons" for variation.

LO 7

- In the *Apprendi* bright-line rule, any departure from sentencing guidelines that increases the penalty for a crime must be submitted to a jury.

LO 7

- The Supreme Court has held that the sentencing procedure in capital punishment cases must allow adequate room for the jury to consider mitigating circumstances and must include a formal review procedure.

LO 8

- Convicted criminals don't base their appeals on any constitutional right but on a statutory right to appeal noncapital convictions in intermediate appellate courts and capital convictions to any court. Appellate review of criminal cases is affected by principles of mootness (the punishment is complete), raise or waive (the defendant didn't object to the error at trial), and plain error (substantial rights were affected and injustice resulted). A conviction becomes final when it's affirmed on appeal to the highest court of the land or when the highest court declines to review it.

LO 9, LO 10

- Habeas corpus is a "collateral attack" where convicted criminals seek to prove they've been unlawfully detained in a civil lawsuit against the government. State courts provide collateral review for defendants convicted in state court. Federal courts review cases brought by defendants convicted in both federal courts and state courts. The broad view of habeas corpus holds that the more judicial review a conviction receives, the more accurate it will be. Opponents argue that excessive review is costly, jeopardizes a sense of finality, and harms offenders if subsequent trial results are worse than the first.

Review Questions

1. Why is the change of status from defendant to offender more than "just a change of words"?

2. Describe the reasons for the assumption that one shot of justice is enough.

3. In the debate over sentencing, identify the two sides that have characterized its history for more than a thousand years.

4. Trace the history of sentencing from A.D. 700 to the present.

5. List three ideas that came to dominate thinking about sentencing in the 1970s.

6. Identify and describe the three divisions of sentencing authority.

7. Identify three aims of both sentencing guidelines and mandatory minimum sentences.

8. Compare and contrast sentencing guidelines with mandatory minimum sentences.

9. What two elements are balanced in sentencing guidelines?

10. List the reasons for the revival of mandatory minimum sentences in the 1950s.

11. List the reasons for the abandonment of mandatory minimum sentences in the 1970s.

12. Identify the two main targets of current mandatory minimum sentences.

13. Identify the three aims of criminal punishment that mandatory minimum sentences are supposed to satisfy.

14. List and summarize the five main findings of empirical research on the effectiveness of mandatory minimum sentences.

15. Explain how the proportionality principle affects challenges to the constitutional ban on cruel and unusual punishments.

16. Identify and summarize the procedure rights convicted offenders enjoy during sentencing procedures.

17. Summarize the significance of *Williams v. New York* (1949); *Apprendi v. New Jersey* (2000); *Harris v. U.S.* (2002); *Blakely v. Washington* (2004); *U.S. v. Booker* (2005); *Rita v. U.S.* (2007); and *Gall v. U.S.* (2007).

18. When is the sentence of death not cruel and unusual punishment?

19. Identify the nature and circumstances of the right to appeal a conviction.

20. What's the difference between an *appeal* and a *collateral attack*?

21. Describe appellate review of criminal convictions by direct appeal and collateral attack.

22. Summarize the difference between the broad and narrow views of habeas corpus review.

23. List the three causes of the controversy over habeas corpus identified by U.S. Supreme Court Justice Robert Jackson.

24. Identify eight interests furthered by limits to habeas corpus review.

25. According to the Rehnquist Court, what's the main problem in habeas corpus review?

Key Terms

15

CASES COVERED

Boumediene and others v. Bush and others, 579 F.Supp.2d 191 (2008)

U.S. v. Martinez-Fuerte, 428 U.S. 543 (1976)

Demore v. Kim, 538 U.S. 510 (2003)

LEARNING OBJECTIVES

1 Understand how and why emergency times change the balance between government power and individual liberty.

2 Realize that the way war is waged in modern times affects government use of emergency powers.

3 Recognize Tier 1, Tier 2, and Tier 3 surveillance, and know when each type can be used.

4 Understand how sneak-and-peak searches are used and the restrictions placed upon them.

5 Understand the executive, legislative, and judicial actions that have affected the detainment of unlawful combatants and their access to federal courts.

6 Understand how interrogation techniques used to prevent unlawful combatants from conducting further attacks differ from those used to gain confessions from ordinary suspects.

7 Understand the controversy over *Miranda* warnings for persons detained on suspicion of terrorist acts.

8 Know how the recruitment of "white collar" terrorists raises questions about existing strategies for combating foreign extremists.

9 Know the factors involved in deciding whether to use federal courts or military commissions to try noncitizens for terrorist acts.

10 Understand how courts balance government needs against Fourth Amendment privacy rights when individuals are detained to determine their immigration status.

11 Recognize the controversy raised by Arizona Immigration Law SB 1070, and know the statute's relation to existing federal principles and laws.

Criminal Procedure in Crises Times

The Constitution of the United States is a law for rulers and people, equally in war and in peace, and covers with the shield of its protection all classes of men, at all times, and under all circumstances. *Ex Parte Milligan (1866)*

A strict observance of the written laws is doubtless one of the high duties of a good citizen, but it is not the highest. The laws of necessity, of self-preservation, of saving our country when in danger, are of higher obligation. To lose our country by a scrupulous adherence to written law, would be to lose the law itself, with life, liberty, property and all those who are enjoying them with us; thus absurdly sacrificing the ends to the means. *Thomas Jefferson, September 20, 1810 (1904, I:146)*

As terrible as 9/11 was, it didn't repeal the Constitution.
Judge Rosemary Pooler, November 17, 2003 (Hamblett 2003, 12)

We end our journey through the criminal process the way we began—by looking at the balance between government power and individual liberty and privacy. But this time, we'll examine the balance when it's most stressed—during emergencies. You're probably familiar with governors who declare state emergencies during storms, floods, and fires and call out the state National Guard to enforce government orders to evacuate and stay out of the danger areas. Even local governments can declare emergencies and take extraordinary measures. For example, for those of us who live in Minnesota, the city or town government infringes on our freedom by ordering us not to park on the streets during "snow emergencies."

The simple lesson of these examples is that emergency times call for recalibrating the balance between government power and individual liberty and privacy. The balance tips to expanding government power and limiting individual liberty and privacy. But emergency powers are limited by two conditions:

1. *Necessity.* Government can exercise extraordinary power only when and to the extent that it's absolutely needed to protect the people from the dangers created by the emergency.

2. *Temporary nature.* Government has to give up its extraordinary power as soon as the emergency is over.

In this chapter, we'll examine how two types of emergencies—military conflicts and immigration crises—have affected the balance in criminal procedure. Recalibration of the balance is not new, so we'll place both in some historical perspective before we look at the current "crisis" in each.

Criminal Procedure in Wartime

In fires, floods, and storms, it's easy to apply the conditions that limit emergency powers, because the emergencies are easy to define: Our senses clearly tell us the fires, floods, and snowstorms are here; the responses to them are widely known and followed (build firewalls and levies; plow the snow); and it's easy to tell when they're over (we can see the fires and floods have stopped and the snow's gone, or at least they're under control).

All these things used to be true of wartime emergencies. Wars began when governments of one country declared war on another country. They were fought according to long-standing **laws of war**—rules written, understood, and agreed to by almost all the countries fighting the wars (Avalon Project 2003). And they ended when the countries signed peace treaties.

Not all nations always followed the laws of war, and, even if they did, there was plenty of "play in the joints" for interpreting many of the rules. Also, some argue that the "new" wars—the "world" wars—differed from the earlier wars for which the rules were made. The difference was that "World" Wars I and II were **"total wars,"** meaning the whole people, the governments, and the countries' resources were mobilized for fighting and winning the war. The rules had to change to meet the challenges brought about by total war. But even in total wars, most of the basics were the same as they'd always been. The enemies were identifiable foreign nations. Wars began with declarations of war (even if the declaration was by a "sneak attack" like the Japanese attack on Pearl Harbor). Wars ended when treaties were signed between the warring nations.

Then came the Cold War. International communism crossed national boundaries. Communist spies came to the United States. They looked and acted like non-Communists. They got jobs in strategic industries and government for the purpose of "boring from within" to learn secrets and pass them on to Communist governments. They became the feared "invisible enemy within." Waging the Cold War required great emphasis on an old feature of war—**enemy intelligence** (information about the enemy).

The U.S. and many state governments took strong measures to respond to the Communist "hidden enemy within." These measures were of two types. First, the government sought to get evidence either to prosecute and convict the foreign enemies of crimes or to find and deport them. Second, but far more important, law enforcement focused on gathering intelligence to prevent further Communist infiltration and activity in the United States. The emphasis on intelligence gathering for the purpose of prevention differed fundamentally from what we've studied throughout this book—balancing the need for getting evidence for criminal prosecution against the rights of individuals to fair proceedings.

This shift in emphasis from *prosecuting* terrorists for crimes to *preventing* them continues in most of today's measures used (with some modifications) to respond to domestic and international terrorism. We'll discuss both the terrorism prevention and the criminal prosecution elements of antiterrorism laws, court decisions, and procedures *before* September 11, 2001. We'll also look at modifications made *after* September 11 by the 2001 USA Patriot Act (short for Uniting and Strengthening America by Providing Appropriate Tools Required to Intercept and Obstruct Terrorism); the Detainee Treatment Act of 2005 (DTA); and the Military Commissions Act of 2006. Then, we'll see how these laws have fared in the courts, especially in the major U.S. Supreme Court cases since 2001.

Former U.S. Attorney General John Ashcroft (2002) stated clearly the shift in the FBI's role brought about by the September 11 attacks, a shift that remains the same in 2010:

> The FBI plays a central role in the enforcement of federal laws and in the proper administration of justice in the United States. In discharging this function, the highest priority is to protect the security of the nation and the safety of the American people against terrorists and foreign aggressors. Investigations by the FBI are premised on the fundamental duty of government to protect the public against those who would threaten the fabric of society through terrorism or mass destruction. (2)

In studying the balance between government power and individual autonomy since 9/11, we're faced with a significant restriction—the need for government secrecy. The government can't tell us things that might tip off terrorists—things that might help us learn more about the laws but would at the same time help terrorists plan future attacks. With this limit in mind, let's look at what the antiterrorism laws say and (as much as possible) how they're operating regarding four issues you've learned about outside the area of national security:

1. Surveillance (Chapter 3)

2. Search and seizure (Chapters 4–7)

3. Detention (Chapters 4–6, 12)

4. Trial rights (Chapters 13–14)

As you read about these four issues, remember that just as in ordinary criminal procedure, federal antiterrorism procedures are based on the requirement in a constitutional democracy to balance the need for enough government power to prevent and prosecute terrorist acts against the rights of individuals guaranteed by the U.S. Constitution. Comments from Charles Doyle (2002), senior specialist at the Congressional Research Center, on the intelligence gathering provisions of the Patriot Act underscore this emphasis: It "was erected for the dual purpose of protecting the confidentiality of private telephone, face-to-face, and computer communications while enabling authorities to identify and intercept criminal communications" (2).

One last point before we begin our journey through national security law and its application to antiterrorism. There's a lot of chatter about the dramatic changes in the balance between power and liberty brought about by three statutes: the USA Patriot Act, the Detainee Treatment Act (DTA), and the Military Commissions Act (MCA). These are actions taken by the executive branch of the U.S. government and its intelligence and law enforcement agencies. On one side, we're warned that under this "new" regime, we'll lose our liberty and privacy to our own government. On the other side, we're warned that without the expanded government powers, we'll lose our liberty and privacy to foreign terrorist organizations. You'll have to decide for yourself whether these extreme positions on the antiterrorism laws are correct or the changes are less extreme adjustments to existing laws.

Surveillance

LO 3

You're already familiar with law enforcement's use of surveillance to gather evidence in criminal cases, especially in illegal drug cases. You learned in Chapter 3 that, according to the U.S. Supreme Court, the Fourth Amendment ban on unreasonable searches and seizures doesn't protect any of the following highly personal information from law enforcement officers who intercept communications and capture it without warrants or probable cause:

1. Conversations of private individuals secretly listened to after wiring informants for sound (*U.S. v. White* [1971], case excerpt Chapter 3)

2. Telephone company lists of the phone numbers of outgoing calls (**pen registers**) (*Smith v. Maryland* [1979], Chapter 3) and incoming calls (**trap and trace**) to a specific telephone

3. Bank records of individuals' financial dealings (*U.S. v. Miller* [1976], Chapter 3)

Recall the rationale for the Court's decisions in these cases: The Fourth Amendment bans "unreasonable searches and seizures" by the government, but not all government actions are searches and seizures. If a government action isn't a search or seizure, the ban doesn't apply at all. In other words, it's left to government discretionary judgment whether to act. Here's another "but": Legislatures can control this discretion. And Congress has decided to control government's discretion not just in ordinary criminal cases but in antiterrorism cases, too. Congress passed legislation balancing government power to use electronic surveillance and individual privacy. The USA Patriot Act modified this general legislation.

Federal law has established a three-tiered system to balance government power and individual privacy in government surveillance (see Table 15.1). Tier 1 restricts government power and protects privacy most. Tier 2 authorizes more government power

TABLE 15.1

Three Tiers of Federal Law Balancing Government Power and Individual Privacy

Tier 1 Least government power/Most privacy protection	Tier 2 More government power/Less privacy protection	Tier 3 Most government power/Least privacy protection
1. General ban on electronic surveillance, interception, and capture	1. Stored communications and transactions subject to surveillance, interception, and capture of information	1. Pen registers and trap-and-trace devices allowed for surveillance, interception, and capture of information
2. Exception: serious crime	2. Applies to all crimes, not just "serious" crimes	2. Applies to all crimes, not just "serious" crimes
3. Safeguards: detailed and approved by courts	3. Safeguards: court order, warrant, or subpoena required	3. Safeguard: certification by law enforcement agency supervisory officer without the need for approval by court order

and provides less protection for individual privacy. Tier 3 authorizes the most government power and provides the least protection for individual privacy. The tiers are nothing new; they've been around since the 1960s. We'll look at how terrorism has affected surveillance procedures for each of the three tiers. Then, we'll look at a controversial tool codified in the Patriot Act, sneak-and-peek searches.

Tier 1: "Real Time" Electronic Surveillance

The first tier, "Real Time" electronic surveillance, was created in the **Crime Control and Safe Streets Act of 1968** (U.S. Code 2003, Title 18, Chapter 119, §§ 2510–22). This act provides the most protection for individual privacy by banning government interception of "wire, oral, or electronic communications" while they're taking place (§ 2511). However, the ban contains a **serious crime exception**. Serious crimes are defined as crimes punishable by death or more than one year in prison (§ 2516). The exception contains specific conditions aimed at protecting individual privacy. They include the following:

1. The U.S. attorney general or other senior Department of Justice officials have to approve a law enforcement officer's application for a court order from a federal judge to allow the officer to secretly intercept and capture conversations.

2. The judge may issue the order if the interception "may provide or has provided evidence of any offense punishable by death or imprisonment for more than one year."

3. The application includes

    a. A "full and complete statement of the facts and circumstances relied upon by the applicant, to justify the belief that an order should be issued"

    b. "A full and complete statement as to whether other investigative procedures have been tried and failed or why they reasonably appear to be unlikely to succeed if tried or to be too dangerous"

    c. A statement of how long the interception is going to last

The Patriot Act also adds several terrorist crimes to the list of serious crimes excepted from the ban on electronic surveillance (Table 15.2).

TABLE 15.2

Terrorist Crimes Not Subject to a Ban on Electronic Surveillance

- Chemical weapons offenses (18 U.S.C. § 229) [same as U.S. Code, Title 18, Section 229]
- Terrorist acts of violence against Americans overseas (§ 2332)
- Use of weapons of mass destruction (§ 2332a)
- Financial transactions with countries that support terrorists (§ 2332d)
- Providing material support for terrorists (§ 2339A)
- Providing material support for terrorist organizations (§ 2339B)

Source: U.S. Code. 2010. Title 18, Part 1. Chapters 11B and 113B. http://www.law.cornell.edu/uscode/html/uscode18/usc_sup_01_18_10_I.html.

Tier 2: Surveilling Stored Electronic Communications

Tier 2 legislation (the **USA Patriot Act** 2001) tips the balance *somewhat* in favor of government power and guarantees *somewhat* less protection for individual privacy. The Patriot Act has significantly expanded government surveillance power beyond the Crime Control and Safe Streets Act of 1968. First, it allows the government to access stored "wire and electronic communications," such as voice mail and e-mail. Second, the power applies to "any criminal investigation," not just to the serious crimes in Tier 1.

The Patriot Act includes *significant* limits to the government's Tier 2 power. The decision to intercept and capture stored information isn't left to law enforcement's discretionary judgment. If the e-mail and voice mail messages have been stored less than six months, officers have to get a warrant based on probable cause (U.S. Code 2003, Title 18, § 2703; see Chapter 6, "Search," on search warrants).

For communications stored for more than six months, the government still needs a warrant to access the information. But they don't have to tell subscribers about the warrant for 90 days "if the court determines" there's "reason to believe" this "may have an adverse result" on the investigation (§ 2705(a)(1)(A)). "Adverse results" include endangering life, flight from prosecution, destruction of evidence, intimidating potential witnesses, or "otherwise seriously jeopardizing an investigation or unduly delaying a trial" (§ 2705(a)(2)).

Tier 3: Secret "Caller ID"

Government power in Tier 3 legislation is broader than in Tiers 1 and 2 but doesn't invade individual privacy as deeply as they do. Tier 3 grants the power to capture a record of all telephone numbers (not conversations) from a subscriber's phone, using pen registers and trap-and-trace devices (U.S. Code 2003, Title 18, §§ 3121–27). This **secret "caller ID"** is available to investigate "any crime," without court approval and without officers' ever notifying subscribers they have it or what they learned from it. Officers are limited in getting and using the secret caller IDs only by having to get the approval of a department senior official.

The Patriot Act expands pen register and trap and trace in two ways (§§ 3121, 3123). First, it allows the use of pen registers and trap-and-trace devices to capture e-mail headers (not messages). Before the act, pen registers and trap and trace were authorized only to capture telephone numbers. Second, it expands the geographical area the pen register and trap-and-trace order covers. Before the act, the court's power was limited to issuing orders only within its own district; the act empowers the court to issue orders to "anywhere in the United States" (§ 3123(b)(1)(C)).

To address objections that e-mail headers reveal more information than telephone numbers, the act (§ 3123(a)(3)) requires any agency getting the court order to submit a detailed report to the court showing:

1. The name of the officer who installed and/or accessed the device
2. The date and time the device was installed, accessed, and uninstalled
3. The configuration of the device when it was installed and any modifications made after installation
4. Information captured by the device

"Sneak and Peek" Searches

You've already learned that searches of private places are "unreasonable searches." They're banned by the Fourth Amendment unless officers are backed up by warrants based on probable cause, and they "knock and announce" their presence before they enter and search (Chapter 6). But you also learned that there's a "no knock" emergency exception to the knock-and-announce rule. **"Sneak and peek" searches** are a variation of no-knock entries. **Sneak-and-peek search warrants** allow officers to enter private places without the owner or (occupant) consenting or even knowing about it.

Sneak and peek is not exactly a new practice. During the 1980s, the FBI and DEA (Drug Enforcement Agency) asked for, and judges issued, at least thirty-five sneak-and-peek warrants ("Sneak and Peek Warrants," 2002, 1). Here's a description of these warrants from the 1980s:

> Under those warrants the search occurred only when the occupants were absent from the premises. The entry and the search were conducted in such a way as to keep them secret. The warrants prohibited seizures of anything except intangible evidence, i.e., information concerning what had been going on, or now was located, inside the premises. No tangible evidence was seized. The searching officers usually took photographs inside the premises searched. No copy of the warrant or receipt was left on the premises. The time for giving notice of the covert entry might be postponed by the court one or more times. The same premises might be subjected to repeated covert entries under successive warrants. At the end of the criminal investigation the premises previously searched under a sneak and peek warrant were usually searched under a conventional search warrant and tangible evidence was then seized. Generally, it was not until after the police made an arrest or returned with a conventional search warrant that the existence of any covert entries was disclosed. Sometimes this was weeks or even months after the surreptitious search or searches. (1)

Both the Second and Ninth Circuit U.S. Courts of Appeals have upheld the admission of evidence obtained during sneak-and-peek searches. In *U.S. v. Villegas* (1990), the Second Circuit said they were reasonable searches (see Chapter 6). And, in *U.S. v. Freitas* (1988), the Ninth Circuit said the evidence was admissible under the "good faith" exception to the exclusionary rule (see Chapter 10).

The Patriot Act was the first time that sneak-and-peek warrants became part of a statute (§ 213). Section 213 of the Patriot Act authorizes judges to issue sneak-and-peek warrants if:

1. The court finds reasonable cause to believe that providing immediate notification of the execution of the warrant may have an adverse effect ["adverse effect" includes: "endangering life; flight from prosecution; destruction of evidence; intimidating potential witnesses; or otherwise seriously jeopardizing an investigation or unduly delaying a trial"].

2. The warrant prohibits the seizure of any tangible [personal] property . . . except where the court finds reasonable necessity for the seizure.

3. The warrant provides for the giving of such notice within a reasonable period of its execution, which period may thereafter be extended by the court for good cause shown.

Section 213 set off a storm of protest. According to *The Georgia Defender* ("Sneak and Peek Warrants" 2002), the publication of the Georgia defense bar:

It is obvious that these restrictions [reasonable cause, property seizure, and notice] on issuing sneak and peek search warrants border on the meaningless, especially in light of the somber reality that search warrants are issued secretly and *ex parte* [in the defendant's absence from the proceeding], that they are typically issued on the basis of recurring, generalized, boilerplate allegations, and that the judicial officials who issue them tend to be rubber stamps for law enforcement. (1)

On the other side, Massachusetts U.S. Attorney Michael Sullivan told the Boston Anti-Terrorism Task Force that sneak and peek is part of the Patriot Act's "series of necessary, measured, and limited tools without which we would be greatly hampered in the struggle against terrorism" (Murphy 2003).

We can't settle this debate here, but keep in mind that most of what Section 213 did was write into a statute combating terrorism what law enforcement had been doing in enforcing drug laws for at least twenty years (and off the record probably a lot longer). Further, courts also previously had admitted evidence obtained from these searches either because they were "reasonable" Fourth Amendment "searches" or qualified as a "good faith" exception to the exclusionary rule.

Detention

LO 5

In Chapter 4, you learned that in ordinary times, under ordinary circumstances, detaining someone on the street for just a few minutes is an "unreasonable" Fourth Amendment seizure (a stop), unless it's backed up by reasonable suspicion. You know from Chapter 5 that arresting and detaining someone for hours (and maybe a few days) at a police station is an "unreasonable seizure" if it's not backed up by probable cause. And, in Chapter 12, you learned that both the Fourth Amendment and the Sixth Amendment "speedy trial" clause require officers to take detained suspects before a judge promptly (usually within 48 hours). The judge can (1) decide whether there's probable cause to detain them; (2) inform them of their rights; (3) set or deny them bail; and (4) provide them with a lawyer if they can't afford one (see Figure 15.1).

But we're not living in ordinary times under ordinary circumstances. September 11 changed that. Of course, during all armed conflicts, combatants capture enemy combatants. So there's always the question of what to do with the captives. But

FIGURE 15.1 Foreign Terrorism Case Defendants Awaiting Trial by U.S. Federal Courts

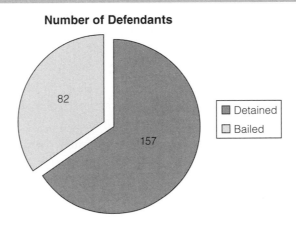

Number of Defendants

82 — Detained
157 — Bailed

Source: Richard Zabel and James Benjamin, Jr., 2009 (July), *In Pursuit of Justice: Prosecuting Terrorism Cases in the Federal Courts*, Fig. 13 (Washington, D.C.: Human Rights First). http://www.humanrightsfirst.org.

detainees captured since September 11, 2001, have given rise to especially tangled and contentious detention issues. Let's look at the development of the detention regime established after 9/11.

One note here: Although much of what follows refers to the regime established under President George W. Bush's administration, as of July 2010, it has continued with only a few minor alterations under President Obama's administration.

On September 14, 2001, President George W. Bush declared a "national emergency by reason of certain terrorist attacks" in **Presidential Proclamation 7463** (Presidential Documents 2001 [Sept. 18], 48199). On that same day, Congress threw its weight behind the president's war power in a Joint Resolution, **Authorization for Use of Military Force (AUMF)**. Section 2 of the AUMF provides:

> That the President is authorized to use all necessary and appropriate force against those nations, organizations, or persons he determines planned, authorized, committed, or aided the terrorist attacks that occurred on September 11, 2001, or harbored such organizations or persons, in order to prevent any future acts of international terrorism against the United States by such nations, organizations or persons. (U.S. Senate 2001)

Then, President Bush issued the **Military Order of November 13, 2001**, "Detention, Treatment, and Trial of Certain Non-Citizens in the War against Terrorism" (Presidential Documents 2001 [Nov. 16], 57831–36). According to the order, "certain non-citizens" included "any individual who is not a U.S. citizen that there is reason to believe:

1. Is or was a member of al Qaida

2. Has engaged in, aided or abetted, or conspired to commit, acts of international terrorism, or acts in preparation therefore, that have caused, threaten to cause, or have as their aim to cause, injury to or adverse effects on the U.S., its citizens, national security, foreign policy, or economy, or

3. Has knowingly harbored one or more individuals described in 1 or 2 . . . shall be detained by the secretary of defense."

Under this detention regime, the Bush administration (and the Obama administration with some minor alterations) declared that most of the detainees captured in the war in Afghanistan were **unlawful enemy combatants**. An unlawful enemy combatant is "a person who has engaged in hostilities or who has purposefully and materially supported hostilities against the United States or its co-belligerents who is not a lawful enemy combatant (including a person who is part of the Taliban, al-Qaida, or associated forces)" (Military Commissions Act 2006, 948a). A **lawful enemy combatant** means a person who is

(A) a member of the regular forces of a State party engaged in hostilities against the United States;

(B) a member of a militia, volunteer corps, or organized resistance movement belonging to a State party engaged in such hostilities, which are under responsible command, wear a fixed distinctive sign recognizable at a distance, carry their arms openly, and abide by the law of war; or

(C) a member of a regular armed force who professes allegiance to a government engaged in such hostilities, but not recognized by the United States. (Military Commissions Act 2006, 948a)

Let's look at how the courts have handled challenges from detainees held at Guantanamo Bay; the case of *Boumediene v. Bush*, which defined who would be considered an enemy combatant and thus ineligible for habeas corpus review before the court; and habeas corpus after *Boumediene*.

Challenging Detention at Guantanamo Bay

After the decision to detain the captives at Guantanamo Bay as enemy combatants, some detainees wasted no time challenging their detentions. Before we get to some of their stories, and others the U.S. Supreme Court has dealt with since 9/11, let's go back to 1950, when the Court decided ***Johnson v. Eisentrager* (1950)**, the case that the Court relied on in all of the leading detention cases. Luther Eisentrager and 21 other German nationals were captured and detained in China by the U.S. Army in 1945. They were tried by a U.S. military commission in China. After the commission convicted them of war crimes—namely, helping the Japanese in the time between the German surrender early in May 1945 and the Japanese capitulation in August 1945—they were returned to Germany and incarcerated in Landsberg Prison. The prison was under the control of the U.S. Army. From their prison in Germany, they filed a habeas corpus petition in the U.S. District Court for the District of Columbia, alleging that they were being detained unlawfully.

In a unanimous opinion written by Justice Robert Jackson, the U.S. Supreme Court denied these Germans access to American Courts. Justice Jackson listed seven facts that taken together banned the prisoners from suing for a writ of habeas corpus in U.S. courts:

1. They were enemy aliens.

2. They had never been, or resided, in the United States.

3. They were captured outside U.S. territory.

4. They were being held in military custody as prisoners of war.

5. They were tried and convicted by a military commission sitting outside the United States.

FIGURE 15.2 *Johnson v. Eisentrager (1950)*

Key Points

1. American law has come a long way since the time when outbreak of war made every enemy national an outlaw, subject to both public and private slaughter, cruelty and plunder. But even by the most magnanimous view, our law does not abolish inherent distinctions recognized throughout the civilized world between citizens and aliens, nor between aliens of friendly and of enemy allegiance, nor between resident enemy aliens who have submitted themselves to our laws and nonresident enemy aliens who at all times have remained with, and adhered to, enemy governments.

2. The alien, to whom the United States has been traditionally hospitable, has been accorded a generous and ascending scale of rights as he increases his identity with our society. Mere lawful presence in the country creates an implied assurance of safe conduct and gives him certain rights; they become more extensive and secure when he makes preliminary declaration of intention to become a citizen, and they expand to those of full citizenship upon naturalization.

3. But, in extending constitutional protections beyond the citizenry, the Court has been at pains to point out that it was the alien's presence within its territorial jurisdiction that gave the Judiciary power to act. Since most cases involving aliens afford this ground of jurisdiction, and the civil and property rights of immigrants or transients of foreign nationality so nearly approach equivalence to those of citizens, courts in peace time have little occasion to inquire whether litigants before them are alien or citizen.

4. It is war that exposes the relative vulnerability of the alien's status. The security and protection enjoyed while the nation of his allegiance remains in amity with the United States are greatly impaired when his nation takes up arms against us. While his lot is far more humane and endurable than the experience of our citizens in some enemy lands, it is still not a happy one. But disabilities this country lays upon the alien who becomes also an enemy are imposed temporarily as an incident of war and not as an incident of alienage. (768–72).

Source: Johnson v. Eisentrager 1950. 339 U.S. 763, 768–72.

6. They were convicted of offenses against laws of war committed outside the United States.

7. They had been at all times imprisoned outside the United States.

Justice Jackson's opinion contained several important points about citizenship and detention. Some are included in Figure 15.2.

Now, let's turn to the Court's detention decisions, beginning with *Rasul v. Bush* (2004). Shafiq Rasul, a British national, and several other non–U.S. detainees, arrived in Guantanamo in January 2002, where the "Bush Administration planned to hold them with no legal process and no access to court or counsel" (Report from Former Judges 2010, 6).

On February 19, 2002, they filed a petition for habeas corpus in the U.S. District Court for the District of Columbia. Relying on *Johnson v. Eisentrager*, the U.S. government moved to dismiss the petitions, arguing that the "detainees were beyond the jurisdiction of the federal courts." The District Court agreed, and the U.S. Court of Appeals for the D.C. Circuit affirmed. The U.S. Supreme Court granted certiorari in November 2003, to decide the "narrow but important question of whether the U.S. courts lack jurisdiction to consider challenges to the legality of the detention of *foreign* nationals captured abroad in connection with hostilities and incarcerated in Guantanamo Bay Naval Base" (Report from Former Judges 2010, 6).

The Supreme Court reversed, holding that the U.S. Habeas Corpus Statute (28 U.S.C. § 2241–and following) empowered the federal courts to hear and decide the petition. Justice Stevens, writing for the majority of six justices, pointed out that, unlike the *Eisentrager* petitioners, the petitioners in this case

1. Weren't nationals of countries at war with the United States

2. Had "never been afforded access to any tribunal, much less charged with and convicted of wrongdoing"

3. Had "been imprisoned in territory over which the U.S. exercises exclusive jurisdiction and control" (476)

Congress responded by passing the **Detainee Treatment Act of 2005 (DTA)**. DTA amended the Habeas Corpus Act to strip federal courts of jurisdiction over habeas petitions filed by Guantanamo Bay detainees (DTA § (e) 1005). But the Supreme Court in *Hamdan v. Rumsfeld* (2006) held that DTA didn't apply to petitions filed prior to its enactment. Then, Congress, in response to *Hamdan*, enacted the **Military Commissions Act of 2006**, which stripped all federal courts of jurisdiction over *all* habeas petitions filed by Guantanamo Bay detainees regardless of when it was filed. It also limited detainees to the review process set up in DTA (see "Military Commissions").

Boumediene v. Bush

LO 5

These cases set up "the historic questions" decided in the U.S. Supreme Court case of *Boumediene v. Bush* (2008):

1. Are Guantanamo Bay detainees guaranteed the *constitutional* (not just the statutory) right to habeas corpus unless Congress suspends the writ under the **suspension clause**? (Article I, Section 9 of the U.S. Constitution provides "The privilege of the writ of habeas corpus shall not be suspended, unless when in cases of rebellion or invasion the public safety may require it.")

2. If so, is the DTA review process an adequate substitute for habeas corpus review in the regular courts?

In *Boumediene*, Lakhdar Boumediene and six other natives of Algeria emigrated to Bosnia and Herzegovina during the 1990s. Five acquired Bosnian citizenship, while the sixth acquired permanent residency. At the time of the brutal attacks of September 11, 2001, each was living peacefully with his family in Bosnia. None traveled to Afghanistan during the U.S. engagement in hostilities there. None had waged war or committed belligerent acts against the United States or its allies. All six were arrested by Bosnian police in October 2001, on suspicion of plotting to attack the U.S. embassy in Sarajevo. The Bosnian authorities had no evidence for this charge. Rather, they acted under pressure from U.S. officials, who threatened to cease diplomatic relations with Bosnia if the six weren't arrested.

On January 17, 2002, the Supreme Court of the Federation of Bosnia and Herzegovina, acting with the concurrence of the Bosnian prosecutor, ordered all six released after a three-month international investigation (with collaboration from the U.S. embassy and Interpol) failed to support the charges. On the same day, the Human Rights Chamber for Bosnia and Herzegovina—a tribunal established under

the U.S.-brokered Dayton Peace Agreement and staffed by judges from several European countries—issued an order forbidding their removal from Bosnian territory.

Late that day, as they were being released from the Central Prison in Sarajevo, Bosnian police—acting again under pressure from U.S. officials and in defiance of the Human Rights Chamber's order—again seized and delivered them to U.S. military personnel stationed in Bosnia. The U.S. military transported them to Guantanamo Bay, where they continued to be held. They had no direct contact with their families, and the government closely limited the frequency and length of counsel visits (*Boumediene and others v. Bush.* Brief for Petitioners 2007, 1–2).

In 2008, the U.S. Supreme Court (5–4) held that Boumediene and his fellow Algerians had a constitutional right to go to the U.S. federal courts to challenge their detention by a petition for habeas corpus. The Court declared unconstitutional a provision in the Military Commissions Act of 2006 that stripped the federal courts of their power to hear habeas corpus petitions from detainees seeking to challenge their designation as enemy combatants. According to the majority, the Detainee Treatment Act of 2005 "falls short of being a constitutionally adequate substitute" (2272) because it didn't offer "the fundamental procedural protections of habeas corpus." Justice Anthony Kennedy wrote, "The laws and Constitution are designed to survive, and remain in force, in extraordinary times" (2227).

In his dissenting opinion, Justice Scalia wrote that the Court's "decision is devastating":

> At least 30 of those prisoners hitherto released from Guantanamo Bay have returned to the battlefield. Some have been captured or killed. But others have succeeded in carrying on their atrocities against innocent civilians. In one case, a detainee released from Guantanamo Bay masterminded the kidnapping of two Chinese dam workers, one of whom was later shot to death when used as a human shield against Pakistani commandoes. Another former detainee promptly resumed his post as a senior Taliban commander and murdered a United Nations engineer and three Afghan soldiers. Still another murdered an Afghan judge. It was reported only last month that a released detainee carried out a suicide bombing against Iraqi soldiers in Mosul, Iraq. (2294–95)

The government can detain noncitizen *and* U.S. citizen terrorist suspects. Let's look at what the government can do with suspects while they're detained. According to the Military Order of November 13, 2001, detainees "*shall* be:

1. Treated humanely, without any adverse distinction based on race, color, religion, gender, birth, wealth, or any similar criteria;

2. Afforded adequate food, drinking water, shelter, clothing, and medical treatment;

3. Allowed the free exercise of religion consistent with the requirements of such detention; and

4. Detained in accordance with such other conditions as the secretary of defense shall prescribe." (Presidential Document 2001 [Nov. 16], 57834)

Habeas Corpus after Boumediene

LO 5

Prior to *Boumediene*, in *Hamdi v. Rumsfeld* (2004), the U.S. military detained Yaser Hamdi, a U.S. citizen, at Guantanamo Bay, because he "was carrying a weapon against American troops on a foreign battlefield"; hence, he was an enemy combatant. The U.S. Supreme Court held that "a citizen-detainee seeking to challenge his classification

as an enemy combatant must receive notice of the factual basis for his classification, and a fair opportunity to rebut the Government's factual assertions before a neutral decision maker" (533). More important for us here, the Court, conceding that "the legal category of enemy combatant has not been elaborated upon in great detail," held that "the permissible bounds of the category will be defined by the lower courts as subsequent cases are presented to them" (521).

When the Court in *Boumediene v. Bush* (2008) held that Boumediene and the other Algerians could pursue their habeas petitions in U.S. District Courts, it also reaffirmed its confidence in the lower courts to work out the standards for detention. Let's look at what happened to Boumediene and the other detainees when their cases were remanded to the U.S. District Court for the District of Columbia to hear their petitions for habeas corpus.

The District Court's decision, *Boumediene v. Bush* (2008a), gives us the opportunity to see how one "lower court" adopted and applied its standard. Judge Richard J. Leon, appointed by President George W. Bush, held two hearings in the case. First, the Court held a hearing to determine the appropriate definition of "enemy combatant." The government argued for a broad definition; the defense argued for a narrow definition, "requiring that 'civilians,' like the detainees here, directly participate in hostilities as part of an organized armed force in an armed conflict against the U.S." (*Boumediene v. Bush* 2008b, 134).

Judge Leon explained the definition he would apply:

> I indicated at the close of the hearing on October 23, 2008 that my initial sense was that both sides were going too far, and that I was likely to end up somewhere in the middle. After a weekend of reading and reviewing the voluminous materials and pleadings in this case, my initial impression has not changed. Indeed, I would say it has solidified even further. (134)
>
> Fortunately, there is a definition that was crafted by the Executive, not the courts, and blessed by Congress, which in my judgment passes muster under both the AUMF and Article II. That definition, ironically, is the very first one crafted by the Department of Defense in 2004 for the type of Combatant Status Review Tribunal ("CSRT") proceedings that these six detainees were given. And that definition was later, in effect, blessed by Congress when, in response to the Supreme Court's *Hamdan v. Rumsfeld* (2006) decision, it drafted and passed the Military Commissions Act of 2006. On that occasion, Congress, in defining the term "unlawful enemy combatant," specifically provided that it included persons who had been "determined to be an unlawful enemy combatant by a Combatant Status Review Tribunal or another competent tribunal established under the authority of the President or the Secretary of Defense." (134)
>
> Accordingly, for the reasons set forth above and on the record at the October 27, 2008 hearing, the Court adopts the following definition of "enemy combatant" to govern the proceedings in this case:
>
>> An "enemy combatant" is an individual who was part of or supporting Taliban or al Qaeda forces, or associated forces that are engaged in hostilities against the United States or its coalition partners. This includes any person who has committed a belligerent act or has directly supported hostilities in aid of enemy armed forces. (135)

In the second stage, the Court applied the definition, granting the petition, ordering the release of five of the petitioners, and denying the petition of the sixth.

In **Boumediene v. Bush** *(2008), our next case excerpt, the U.S. District Court for the District of Columbia granted petitions of habeas corpus of five Guantanamo Bay detainees and ordered their release, while denying a habeas petition of the sixth.*

CASE Do Guantanamo Detainees Have a Constitutional Right to Habeas Corpus?

Boumediene and others v. Bush and others

579 F.Supp.2d 191 (2008)

HISTORY

Lakhdar Boumediene, Belkacem Bensayah, Mohamed Nechla, Hadj Boudella, Mustafa Ait Idir, and Saber Lahmar, Algerian aliens detained as enemy combatants at United States Naval Station at Guantanamo Bay, Cuba, petitioned for a writ of habeas corpus. Judge Leon granted the petition of Boumediene, Nechla, Boudella, Idir, and Lahmar. Judge Leon denied the petition of Bensayah. Judge Leon directed the Respondents, President George W. Bush, Secretary of Defense Robert M. Gates, Army Brigade General Jay Hood, and Army Colonel Nelson J. Cannon (the "Government") to take all necessary and appropriate diplomatic steps to facilitate the release of Petitioners Lakhdar Boumediene, Mohamed Nechla, Hadj Boudella, Mustafa Ait Idir, and Saber Lahmar forthwith.

LEON, District Judge.

Petitioners are six prisoners at the U.S. Naval Base at Guantanamo Bay, Cuba and allege that they are being unlawfully detained by the Government. On November 6, 2008, this Court commenced habeas corpus hearings for petitioners Lakhdar Boumediene, Mohamed Nechla, Hadj Boudella, Belkacem Bensayah, Mustafa Ait Idir, and Saber Lahmar (collectively "petitioners" or "detainees"). That morning, counsel for both parties made unclassified opening statements in a public hearing.

In the afternoon of November 6th, this Court convened a closed door session with counsel to begin reviewing certain classified evidence being relied upon by both sides in this case. These closed door sessions continued throughout the remaining six days of hearings. On November 12, 2008, the Government rested its case in chief. Petitioners' counsel thereafter put two of the detainees on the stand via video-teleconference from Guantanamo Bay, Cuba. The detainees, Mr. Ait Idir and

Mr. Boudella, were questioned by their own counsel and cross-examined by Government counsel. Thereafter, the Government exercised its right to put on a rebuttal case. Its rebuttal focused primarily on evidence relating to Mr. Bensayah.

On November 14, 2008, counsel for petitioners and the Government presented nearly four and a half hours of closing arguments. Once again, because the information discussed in those arguments was overwhelmingly classified, they had to be held in a closed door session. As a result, neither the public nor the petitioners were able to listen to the arguments. At the end of the final arguments, the Court informed the parties that it would hold a public hearing today to announce its decision. A closed hearing will be held hereafter to discuss in greater detail the Court's reasoning based on the classified evidence relevant to these six detainees.

FACTS

To say the least, this is an unusual case. At the time of their arrest, all six petitioners, who are native Algerians, were residing in Bosnia and Herzegovina (hereinafter "Bosnia"), over a thousand miles away from the battlefield in Afghanistan. Petitioners held Bosnian citizenship or lawful permanent residence, as well as their native Algerian citizenship. All six men were arrested by Bosnian authorities in October 2001 for their alleged involvement in a plot to bomb the U.S. Embassy in Sarajevo. (Between October 18 and 21, 2001, Bosnian police took Nechla, Boumediene, Ait Idir, Boudella, and Lahmar into custody. At this time, Bensayah was already in custody for alleged immigration charges.) Respondents have since withdrawn that allegation as a basis for the petitioners' detention.

On January 17, 2002, upon their release from prison in Sarajevo, petitioners were detained by Bosnian authorities and U.S. personnel. Petitioners were transported to the U.S. Naval Station at Guantanamo Bay and have remained there since their arrival on January 20, 2002. In July 2004, after the Supreme Court's decision in *Rasul v.*

Bush, (2004) holding that 28 U.S.C. § 2241 extended statutory habeas corpus jurisdiction to Guantanamo, detainees filed, on their own behalf and through certain relatives as their "next friend," a petition for writs of habeas corpus, alleging, among other things, that the U.S. Government holds them in violation of the Constitution and various U.S. and international laws. The Government moved to dismiss this action in October 2004.

In January 2005, this Court granted the Government's motion to dismiss, holding that Guantanamo Bay detainees had no rights that could be vindicated in a habeas corpus proceeding. After intervening Supreme Court precedent and legislation changed the legal landscape in which these petitions were brought (*See, e.g.,* Detainee Treatment Act of 2005 ("DTA"), *Hamdan v. Rumsfeld* (2006); Military Commissions Act of 2006) the Supreme Court, on June 12, 2008, reversed this Court and held in *Boumediene v. Bush,* that Guantanamo detainees are "entitled to the privilege of habeas corpus to challenge the legality of their detention."

Although the Supreme Court made it clear that the privilege of habeas corpus "entitles the prisoner to a meaningful opportunity to demonstrate that he is being held pursuant to 'the erroneous application or interpretation' of relevant law," it left largely to the habeas court's discretion to craft, in the first instance, the framework in which these unique habeas cases would proceed. (Accommodating the Government's "legitimate interest in protecting sources and methods of intelligence gathering" and "other remaining questions are within the expertise and competence of the District Court to address in the first instance.")

Indeed, the Supreme Court even delegated the decision as to which definition of "enemy combatant" should govern these proceedings. Above all, the Supreme Court made it very clear that the detainees were "entitled to a prompt habeas corpus hearing" noting that "while some delay in fashioning new procedures is unavoidable, the costs of delay can no longer be borne by those who are held in custody."

With *Boumediene*'s instruction that habeas be "an adaptable remedy," and the admonition in *Hamdi v. Rumsfeld,* that the district courts should proceed in a "prudent" and "incremental" fashion in wartime habeas proceedings, this Court held its first status conference with Government and petitioners' counsel on July 24, 2008. During that session, it received invaluable insight into the unique nature of this case and the array of logistical and legal questions that it would need to resolve.

Several weeks later, the Court received consolidated briefing on the procedural issues common to all of its Guantanamo habeas cases. On August 21, 2008, the Court held oral argument on those issues. The following day, the Government, pursuant to an earlier order, filed its Amended Factual Return. The Government's Return contained approximately 650 pages of exhibits and a 53-page narrative, setting forth the Government's alleged legal and factual basis for holding the six petitioners as "enemy combatants."

On August 27, 2008, the Court issued its Case Management Order ("CMO"), setting forth the procedural framework for the litigation of these six detainees' habeas petitions. Petitioners' counsel, pursuant to the CMO, submitted ten motions seeking discovery from the Government, totaling well over 80 individual requests for documents and/or information. The Court held over 50 hours of hearings to address and resolve the various discovery requests. Petitioners' counsel was successful in a number of instances, and the Court ordered the Government to produce additional non-exculpatory information in response to petitioners' requests. As a result of the breadth and complexity of the legal issues presented in this case, the Court had to twice reschedule both the deadline for the petitioners' Traverse and the start date of the habeas corpus hearings.

On October 17, 2008, petitioners' counsel filed the factual portion of their Traverse, setting forth their factual bases for opposing the Government's Return. Petitioners' Traverse included approximately 1,650 pages of exhibits and over 200 pages of narrative, discussing the alleged deficiencies in the Government's case. Three days later, petitioners' counsel submitted the legal portion of their Traverse, setting forth their legal arguments in opposition to the Government's Return.

On October 23, 2008, the Court heard oral arguments from the parties regarding the appropriate definition of "enemy combatant" to be employed in these hearings. Four days later, the Court issued a Memorandum Order, adopting the definition, which had been drafted by the Department of Defense in 2004 for the type of Combatant Status Review Tribunal ("CSRT") proceedings that these detainees were given.

Finally, in the weeks leading up to these hearings, the Court met on a number of occasions with counsel for both parties in an effort to narrow the focus of these hearings to the material issues of fact in dispute between the parties. Based on a careful review of the Amended Factual Return and Traverse, and after hearing arguments over the seven days of habeas hearings on the factual issues in dispute, the following is the Court's ruling on the six detainees' petitions.

OPINION

Legal Standard

Under the CMO, the Government bears the burden of proving "by a preponderance of the evidence, the lawfulness of the petitioner's detention." The following definition of "enemy combatant" governs the proceedings in this case:

> An "enemy combatant" is an individual who was part of or supporting Taliban or al Qaeda forces, or associated forces that are engaged in hostilities against the United States or its coalition partners. This includes any person who has committed a belligerent act or has directly supported hostilities in aid of enemy armed forces.

Accordingly, the question before this Court is whether the Government has shown by a preponderance of the evidence that each petitioner is being lawfully detained—*i.e.,* that each is an "enemy combatant" under the definition adopted by this Court.

Analysis

The Government sets forth two theories as to why these men should be lawfully detained as enemy combatants. First, as to all six petitioners, the Government contends that they planned to travel to Afghanistan in late 2001 and take up arms against U.S. and allied forces. Additionally, as to Belkacem Bensayah alone, the Government contends that he is an al-Qaida member and facilitator. (In its Amended Factual Return, the Government initially alleged that Bensayah is an al-Qaida member, facilitator, *and financier.* However, during the habeas hearings, the Government did not advance the theory that Bensayah was an al-Qaida *financier.* Instead, respondents focused primarily on the allegation that Bensayah is an al-Qaida facilitator. Accordingly, the Court will focus its analysis with respect to Bensayah on his role as an al-Qaida facilitator.)

The Court will address each of these theories in turn.

I. The Plan to Travel to Afghanistan to Engage U.S. and Allied Forces The Government alleges that all six petitioners planned to travel to Afghanistan to take up arms against U.S. and allied forces and that such conduct constitutes "support" of al-Qaida under the "enemy combatant" definition adopted by this Court. Petitioners disagree. Petitioners contend that the Government has not shown by a preponderance of the evidence that any of the petitioners planned to travel to Afghanistan to engage U.S. forces, and, even if the Government *had shown* that petitioners had such a plan, a *mere plan,* unaccompanied by any concrete acts, is not—as a matter of law—"supporting" al-Qaida within the meaning of the Court's definition of "enemy combatant." For the following reasons, the Court finds that the Government has failed to show by a preponderance of the evidence that any of the petitioners, other than Mr. Bensayah, either had, or committed to, such a plan.

To support its claim that petitioners had a plan to travel to Afghanistan to engage U.S. and allied forces, the Government relies exclusively on the information contained in a classified document from an unnamed source. This source is the only evidence in the record directly supporting each detainee's alleged knowledge of, or commitment to, this supposed plan. And while the Government has provided some information about the source's credibility and reliability, it has not provided the Court with enough information to adequately evaluate the credibility and reliability of this source's information. For example, the Court has no knowledge as to the circumstances under which the source obtained the information as to each petitioner's alleged knowledge and intentions.

In addition, the Court was not provided with adequate corroborating evidence that these petitioners knew of and were committed to such a plan. Because I cannot, on the record before me, adequately assess the credibility and reliability of the *sole* source information relied upon, for five of the petitioners, to prove an alleged plan by them to travel to Afghanistan to engage U.S. and coalition forces, the Government has failed to carry its burden with respect to these petitioners. Unfortunately, due to the classified nature of the Government's evidence, I cannot be more specific about the deficiencies of the Government's case at this time.

Suffice it to say, however, that while the information in the classified intelligence report, relating to the credibility and reliability of the source, was undoubtedly sufficient for the intelligence purposes for which it was prepared, it is *not* sufficient for the purposes for which a habeas court must now evaluate it. To allow enemy combatancy to rest on so *thin* a reed would be inconsistent with this Court's obligation under the Supreme Court's decision in *Hamdi* to protect petitioners from the risk of erroneous detention.

Having concluded that the Government has not met its burden with respect to the *existence* of a plan to travel to Afghanistan to engage U.S. and coalition forces by these five petitioners, because the Government has failed to establish by a preponderance of the evidence the plan that is the *exclusive* basis for the Government's claim that Messrs. Boumediene, Nechla, Boudella, Ait Idir, and Lahmar are enemy combatants, the Court must, and will, grant their petitions and order their release.

II. Belkacem Bensayah's Role as an Al-Qaida Facilitator As to Mr. Bensayah, however, the Government has met its burden by providing additional evidence that sufficiently corroborates its allegations from this unnamed source that Bensayah is an al-Qaida facilitator. The Government contends that Mr. Bensayah planned to go to Afghanistan to both take up arms against U.S. and allied forces and to facilitate the travel of unnamed others to Afghanistan and elsewhere. In order to establish Bensayah's role as an al-Qaida facilitator, the Government depends on the same intelligence information described above, but also puts forth a series of other intelligence reports based on a variety of sources and evidence, which it contends corroborate the facilitator allegation. I agree.

Although the Court is once again restrained in its ability to discuss and analyze the classified information relied upon by the Government, the Court can describe the information in general terms. The Government provides credible and reliable evidence linking Mr. Bensayah to al-Qaida and, more specifically, to a senior al-Qaida facilitator. The Government additionally provides credible and reliable evidence demonstrating Mr. Bensayah's skills and abilities to travel between and among countries using false passports in multiple names. Finally, the Government creates sufficient doubt as to Bensayah's credibility that his proffered explanations in response to the

Government's allegations should not, in this Court's judgment, be credited.

For all of those reasons and more, the Court concludes that the Government has established by a preponderance of the evidence that it is more likely than not Mr. Bensayah not only planned to take up arms against the United States but also facilitate the travel of unnamed others to do the same. There can be no question that facilitating the travel of others to join the fight against the United States in Afghanistan constitutes direct support to al-Qaida in furtherance of its objectives and that this amounts to "support" within the meaning of the "enemy combatant" definition governing this case. The Court accordingly holds that Belkacem Bensayah is being lawfully detained by the Government as an enemy combatant. As such, the Court must, and will, deny Bensayah's petition for writ of habeas corpus and will *not* order his release.

QUESTIONS

1. **Summarize Judge Leon's reasons for granting the petitions to Lakhdar Boumediene and the four other detainees.**
2. **Summarize Judge Leon's reasons for denying the petition to Belkacem Bensayah.**
3. **Do you agree with the judge's decisions? Explain your answer.**
4. Consider Justice Scalia's dissent (p. 521) in *Boumediene v. Bush* (2008a). **Does it apply to any or all of these petitioners? Explain your answer.**

THE OTHER CRIMINAL PROCEDURE **White Collar Crime**

LO 8

The Christmas Day Bomb Suspect

THE PRIVILEGED STUDENT WHO EMBRACED AL-QA'IDA AND TRIED TO BLOW A TRANSATLANTIC JET OUT OF THE SKY

With his wealth, privilege and education at one of Britain's leading universities, Abdul Farouk Abdulmutallab had the world at his feet—able to choose from a range of futures in which to make his mark on the world. Instead, the son of one of Nigeria's most important figures opted to make his impact in a very different way—by detonating 80g of explosives sewn into his underpants, and trying to destroy a passenger jet as it came in to land at Detroit Airport on Christmas Day. As he was charged by U.S. authorities last night with attempting to blow up an airliner, a surprising picture emerged of the would-be bomber.

Abdulmutallab, 23, had lived a gilded life, and, for the three years he studied in London, he stayed in a £2m flat. He was from a very different background to many of the other al-Qa'ida recruits who opt for martyrdom. The charges were read out to him by U.S. District Judge Paul Borman in a conference room at the medical centre where he is receiving treatment for burns. Agents brought Abdulmutallab, who had a blanket over his lap and was wearing a green hospital robe, into the room in a wheelchair.

Abdulmutallab's father, Umaru, is the former economics minister of Nigeria. He retired earlier this month as the chairman of the First Bank of Nigeria but is still on the boards of several of Nigeria's biggest firms, including Jaiz International, a holding company for the Islamic Bank. The 70-year-old, who was also educated in London, holds the Commander of the Order of the Niger as well as the Italian Order of Merit. Dr Mutallab said he was planning to meet with police in Nigeria last night after realising his son had joined the notorious roster of al-Qa'ida terrorists, and is said to have warned the U.S. authorities about his son's extreme views six months ago.

Police in London were collaborating with the American-led investigation into the would-be bomber. Scotland Yard detectives were searching his flat and two others in the same mansion block in Marylebone, central London. They later cordoned off the street lined with Rolls-Royce, Jaguar and Mercedes cars. Police were also understood to be searching the basement of the building. Abdulmutallab was reportedly on a security watch list, but those who studied with him expressed shock that the person who seemed so quiet and unassuming—a devout Muslim but not radical—apparently came close to perpetrating a Christmas Day massacre.

Fabrizio Cavallo Marincola, 22, who studied mechanical engineering beside Abdulmutallab—nicknamed Biggie—at University College London, said that he graduated in May 2008 and showed no signs of radicalisation or of links to al-Qa'ida. "We worked on projects together," he said. "He always did the bare minimum of work and would just show up to classes. When we were studying, he always would go off to pray. "He was pretty quiet and didn't socialise much or have a girlfriend that I knew of. I didn't get to talk to him much on a personal level. I was really shocked when I saw the reports. You would never imagine him pulling off something like this."

After graduating, Abdulmutallab tried to return to Britain but his visa request was refused. He applied to return for a six-month course, but was barred by the UK Border Agency which judged that the college he applied to was "not genuine." Reports from Nigeria suggested that Abdulmutallab's family had seen a very different person to the one studying at UCL. He apparently cut all contact with his family after university, but is thought to have visited Egypt and then Dubai. "I believe he might have been to Yemen, but we are investigating to determine that," his father said.

Nigerian newspapers reported that Abdulmutallab's father, who lives in Katsina, Nigeria, had informed the U.S. embassy of his son's activities because he had become so concerned about his religious views. A source said Dr. Mutallab was "devastated" at the news but also "surprised" his son had been allowed to travel after he had reported him to the authorities. Abdulmutallab had allegedly become noted for his extreme religious views when he was at the British International School in Togo, where he is said to have preached Islam to his friends.

An official briefing on the attack said the U.S. had known for at least two years that the suspect could have terrorist ties. Abdulmutallab has been on a list that included people with known or suspected contacts or ties to a terrorist or terrorist organisation. The list is maintained by the U.S. National Counterterrorism Center and includes about 550,000 names. The impact of the intended attack will lead airports and governments to again review security measures as terrorists seek more ingenious ways of smuggling explosives through sophisticated security measures.

The failed attempt to blow up flight 253 as it came in to land at Detroit airport is the latest in an ominous pattern of terror attacks that have emerged from, or have been attempted in, the United Kingdom over the past few years. Dr. Sally Leivesley, a leading terror expert who advises governments and businesses, said yesterday there have been several incidents where detonators have failed to ignite devices, with a major terror attack averted through luck or human error.

A significant factor is the report that the bomber was an engineering student at University College London. Dr. Leivesley said that al-Qa'ida was recruiting people with engineering qualifications as well as highly placed scientists, particularly in the nuclear field. "Al-Qa'ida is finding it difficult to recruit young people," she said. "And, interestingly, the election of Barack Obama is a factor in that, because, whatever you think of him as a president, the fact of him shows young people that there is an alternative to killing yourself. Al-Qa'ida is, however, targeting more highly skilled people."

WHAT DO *YOU* THINK?

1. Why did Abdulmutallab try to blow up a plane?

2. What's the significance of his social status?

3. What implications, if any, does his story have for policies designed to combat foreign extremists who try to attack the U.S. homeland?

Source: Andrew Johnson and Emily Dugan. 2009 (December 27). *The Independent World.*

http://www.independent.co.uk/news/world/americas/wealthy-quiet-unassuming-the-christmas-day-bomb-suspect-1851090.html (visited July 1, 2010).

Interrogation

LO 6

The major purpose of detention is to prevent further fighting by captured fighters. But it's not the only purpose. It's also for gathering information (intelligence) to prevent further extremist attacks. Finally, it's for obtaining information (evidence) to prosecute unlawful enemy combatants for war crimes. U.S. government officials have rejected the most extreme tactic for gathering information from detainees—torture. According to Military Commission Instruction No. 10 (2006):

> The President has repeatedly reaffirmed the long-standing policy that the United States will neither commit nor condone torture. The United States has assumed an obligation under Article 15 of the Convention against Torture and Other Cruel, Inhuman, or Degrading Treatment or Punishment to "ensure that any statement which is established to have been made as a result of torture shall not be invoked as evidence in any proceedings, except against a person accused of torture as evidence that the statement was made." (1)

Civil libertarians question whether the interrogators' actions will match their words when it comes to using torture to get information from suspects. They point to the well-publicized examples of abuse at Abu Ghraib and stories by former suspects *and* interrogators and their superiors about abuses they experienced or practiced (Ross and Esposito 2005).

This highly emotional subject raises serious issues—and little or no agreement about any of them—including (1) the definition of "torture"; (2) the number and kinds of abuses (Table 15.3 describes some of the tactics reported by CIA interrogators and their superiors); (3) whether torture "works"; and (4) whether it violates the U.S. Constitution.

In this section, we'll look more closely at what, if any, constitutional protections terrorists suspects are guaranteed during interrogations and how and when *Miranda* is applied to these suspects.

Interrogation, Terrorism Suspects, and the Constitution

LO 6

We can't begin to answer these questions here, but we can at least touch on the *constitutionality* of tactics that exceed what's acceptable in the interrogation of suspects in ordinary criminal cases that you learned about in Chapter 8. Recall that in ordinary interrogation, officers can use pressure and some unsavory tactics without violating the bar on coerced confessions. Recall also that in our first case excerpt in Chapter 2,

TABLE 15.3

CIA Interrogation Tactics

- *The Attention Grab.* The interrogator forcefully grabs the shirt front of the prisoner and shakes him.

- *The Attention Slap.* An open-handed slap aimed at causing pain and triggering fear.

- *The Belly Slap.* A hard open-handed slap to the stomach. The aim is to cause pain but not internal injury. Doctors consulted advised against using a punch, which could cause lasting internal damage.

- *Long Time Standing.* This technique is described as among the most effective. Prisoners are forced to stand, handcuffed and with their feet shackled to an eye bolt in the floor, for more than forty hours. Exhaustion and sleep deprivation are effective in yielding confessions.

- *The Cold Cell.* The prisoner is left to stand naked in a cell kept near 50 degrees. Throughout the time in the cell, the prisoner is doused with cold water.

- *Water Boarding.* The prisoner is bound to an inclined board, feet raised and head slightly below the feet. Cellophane is wrapped over the prisoner's face and water is poured over him. Unavoidably, the gag reflex kicks in and a terrifying fear of drowning leads to almost instant pleas to bring the treatment to a halt.

Source: Ross and Esposito 2005.

Rochin v. California (1952), the Supreme Court ruled that officers' actions to retrieve heroin capsules from Antonin Rochin denied him due process:

> We are compelled to conclude that the proceedings by which this conviction was obtained do more than offend some fastidious squeamishness or private sentimentalism about combating crime too energetically. This is conduct that shocks the conscience. Illegally breaking into the privacy of Rochin, the struggle to open his mouth and remove what was there, the forcible extraction of his stomach's contents—this course of proceeding by agents of government to obtain evidence is bound to offend even hardened sensibilities. They are methods too close to the rack and the screw to permit of constitutional differentiation. (172–73)

Of course, there's a significant difference between *Rochin* and the interrogation of terrorist suspects. The constitutional question in ordinary criminal cases is whether confessions are admissible against suspects to prove their guilt at trial. The interest in getting information from terrorist suspects is not only—or even mainly—to prove their guilt but to prevent another terrorist attack. (Of course, information gained from terrorists may be used for prosecution in military trials, where self-incrimination is clearly relevant and banned; the point here is that it's not the *main* reason.)

When, if ever, do interrogation tactics "shock the conscience"; that is, do they ever violate the Constitution when their object isn't to prosecute but to discover and prevent terrorist attacks? U.S. Seventh Circuit Court of Appeals Judge Richard Posner (2006) poses the constitutional question clearly:

> What process is due a person who refuses to divulge information of utmost importance to the welfare of society? Can the "conscience shocking" effect of a stomach pump be divorced from the circumstances in which the government officers resort to that method of obtaining information, so that the greater the necessity of getting the information the less will forcible methods of getting it shock the conscience? All these are open questions. (81)

Miranda v. Arizona *and Terrorism Suspects*

LO 7

In May 2010, the Obama administration announced that it "would seek a law allowing investigators to interrogate terrorism suspects without informing them of their rights." Attorney General Eric Holder proposed "carving out a broad new exception" to *Miranda v. Arizona* (1966). Before we discuss the Obama administration's proposed "law," recall three important points you learned in Chapter 8. The *Miranda* decision bans prosecutors from using incriminating statements in evidence unless law enforcement officers give suspects the *Miranda* warnings. The "public safety exception" that the U.S. Supreme Court created in *New York v. Quarles* (1984) applies when "the need for answers to questions in a situation posing a threat to public safety outweighs the need for the rule protecting the privilege against self-incrimination" (657). Finally, even when suspects get the warnings, empirical research demonstrates that most of them talk anyway (Chapter 8).

Now, let's turn to two cases that sparked a furious debate over the *Miranda*'s application to terrorism suspects. The first was the attempted bombing of an airplane bound for Detroit on December 25, 2009. The FBI questioned Farouk Abdulmutallab for 50 minutes before they "mirandized" him. The second was the attempt to detonate an SUV packed with explosives in Times Square on May 1, 2010. The FBI questioned Faisal Shahzad for "three or four hours" before they mirandized him.

Critics contend that declaring these suspects enemy combatants would have provided a longer time to interrogate the suspects. Former U.S. attorney and New York City mayor Rudolph Giuliani said, "I would not have given him *Miranda* warnings after just a couple of hours of questioning," Mr. Giuliani said. "I would have instead declared him an enemy combatant, asked the president to do that, and at the same time, that would have given us the opportunity to question him for a much longer period of time" (Savage 2010). The government points out that Shahzad continued to talk after he received the warnings, providing the government with both valuable intelligence and enough evidence to lead to Shahzad's guilty plea (Savage 2010).

Farouk Abulmutallab cooperated without the warnings until he was taken into surgery for burns he suffered during the botched airliner Detroit airliner bombing. Afterward, he got the *Miranda* warnings and at first didn't resume cooperating (Savage 2010). But then he started talking to FBI agents and "has not stopped" two government agents said. The officials declined to say exactly what they learned, only that "it was aiding in the investigation of the attempted terrorist attack." According to FBI Director, Robert S. Mueller III, "Mr. Abdulmutallab had provided valuable intelligence," but he did not elaborate. A law enforcement official said that "they had offered no plea bargain in exchange for Abdulmutallab's cooperation" (Zelaney and Savage 2010).

Trials

LO 9

Suspected terrorists can be tried in two kinds of proceedings: ordinary courts or special military courts. The ordinary courts are called **Article III courts** because their authority comes from Article III of the U.S. Constitution, which created the judiciary. These trials include crimes against the state (such as treason and sedition; "ordinary crimes" (such as murder and rape); and terrorism-related crimes included in the U.S. Criminal Code. Suspected terrorists can also be tried for **war crimes** (such as fighting for al Qaeda or the Taliban) by special military courts called **military commissions**. Military commissions are also sometimes known as **military tribunals**. In the following sections, we'll examine trial by federal Article III courts and trial by military commissions.

FIGURE 15.3 Outcomes in Terrorism Cases in Federal Courts by Disposition Type

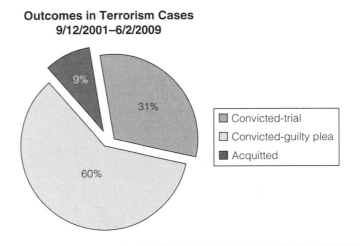

Outcomes in Terrorism Cases
9/12/2001–6/2/2009

- Convicted-trial
- Convicted-guilty plea
- Acquitted

Source: Richard Zabel and James Benjamin, Jr., 2009 (July), *In Pursuit of Justice: Prosecuting Cases in the Federal Courts* (Washington, D.C.: Human Rights First, p. 12). http://www.humanrightsfirst.org.

Trials in Federal Courts

Between September 11, 2001, and June 2, 2009, Article III courts dealt with 289 terrorism defendants; 214 had the charges against them resolved. Of those 214, 195 (91%) were found guilty of at least one offense related to terrorism; 19 (9%) were acquitted. Figure 15.3 shows the outcome of those trials, the rates, and types of conviction (Zabel and Benjamin 2009, 12).

In addition to these defendants, President Obama's Guantanamo Review Task Force has referred 44 of the remaining 240 detainees at Guantanamo for prosecution either in federal court or a military commission (Final Report 2010, ii). The Task Force followed the guidelines for federal prosecutors to determine whether to charge a case. According to the guidelines, "[A] case should be recommended for prosecution if the detainee's conduct constitutes a federal offense and the potentially available admissible evidence will probably be sufficient to obtain and sustain a conviction" (Final Report 7–8).

Key factors in the determination include:

1. The nature and seriousness of the offense

2. The detainee's culpability in the offense

3. The detainee's willingness to cooperate in the investigation or prosecution of others

4. The probable sentence or other consequences if the detainee is convicted (8)

The federal courts have imposed severe sentences on defendants convicted of crimes related to terrorism, whether by trial or guilty plea. This is based on the special provision in the U.S. Sentencing Guidelines (U.S. Sentencing Guidelines Manual 2009, § 3A1.4) for those convicted of the **federal crime of terrorism**. This section automatically triggers a range of 210 to 262 months for defendants convicted of crimes that "involved, or was intended to promote, a federal crime of terrorism." A federal crime of terrorism "means an offense that is calculated to influence or affect the conduct of government by intimidation or coercion, or to retaliate against government conduct" (U.S. Criminal Code 2009, § 2332(g)(5)).

In *U.S. v. Benkala* (2008), for example, the U.S. Fourth Circuit Court of Appeals affirmed Sabri Benkala's sentence of 121 months. According to the court:

> Benkahla was part of a network of people the government was investigating for crimes connected to radical Islamic terrorism and violent jihad. The FBI questioned him and prosecutors twice called him before grand juries. Then he was prosecuted himself for false declarations, false statements, and obstructing justice. (303)

Trial by Military Commission

LO 9

Here, we'll examine the relaxed rules of procedure and proof and the diminished rights for defendants that apply to military commissions. A military commission consists of a panel of military officers acting under military authority to try enemy combatants for war crimes—acts committed during wartime that inflict "needless and disproportionate suffering and damages" in pursuit of a "military objective." (Don't confuse military commissions with military **courts-martial**, which are also made up of military officers, but they try members of U.S. armed forces for violating the Uniform Code of Military Justice) (Elsea 2001, 7, 16).

The Military Order of November 13, 2001 (Presidential Documents 2001 [Nov. 16], 57831–36) spells out the rules governing military commissions to try suspected terrorists. Let's look at the main points in the Military Order that are relevant to military commissions: the source and the jurisdiction of their authority and the trial proceedings before them.

1. *The Sources of Military Commission Authority.* The president bases his authority to establish military commissions on three sources:

   a. The U.S. Constitution, Article II, Section 2, makes the president the "commander in chief" of the armed forces. As commander in chief, he's responsible for trying terrorists.

   b. Article II, Section 2, also imposes responsibility on the president to "take care that the laws shall be faithfully executed." In this case, according to the Military Order, the laws include trying war crimes under the Articles of War and the Authorization for Use of Military Force, passed by a joint resolution of Congress on September 14, 2001.

   c. The joint resolution authorized the president to use "all necessary and appropriate force against those nations, organizations, or persons he determines planned, authorized, committed, or aided" or "harbored" them.

2. *The Jurisdiction of Military Commissions.* The provisions of the order apply only to "certain non-citizens in the war against terrorism" (Presidential Documents 2001 [Nov. 16], 57833). This means the military commission's authority only applies to noncitizens. Here's how Section 2 of the order defines noncitizens and outlines restrictions on their rights, including taking away the power (jurisdiction) of ordinary courts to review military commission decisions regarding them:

> [A]ny individual who is not a United States citizen with respect to whom I determine from time to time in writing that:
>
> 1. there is reason to believe that such individual, at the relevant times,
>
> 2. is or was a member of the organization known as al Qaida;
>
> 3. has engaged in, aided or abetted, or conspired to commit, acts of international terrorism, or acts in preparation therefor, that have caused, threaten to cause, or have as their aim to cause, injury to or adverse effects on the United States, its citizens, national security, foreign policy, or economy; or

4. has knowingly harbored one or more individuals described in subparagraphs (i) or (ii) of subsection 2(a)(1) of this order; and

5. it is in the interest of the United States that such individual be subject to this order. (57834)

As noncitizens, the individuals the order applies to don't "necessarily enjoy the same constitutional rights as citizens" even if they're legally in the country. During wartime, aliens of enemy nations can be detained and deported, and their property can be confiscated. "They may also be denied access to the courts of the United States if they would use the courts to the advantage of the enemy or to impede the U.S. prosecution of a war" (Elsea 2001, 28–29).

3. *Trial Proceedings of Military Commissions.* Military commissions aren't bound by the constitutional requirements that apply to ordinary (Article III) courts.

On April 27, 2010, the Department of Defense released new rules governing the military commission proceedings (U.S. Manual for Military Commissions 2010). Here's a list of key provisions:

1. Provides defendants in capital cases the right to at least one additional lawyer who's an expert on the law relating to death penalty cases (under the old rules, defendants in capital cases had no such right)

2. Permits evidence derived from statements obtained by cruel, inhumane, and degrading treatment if "use of such evidence would otherwise be consistent with the interests of justice" (unlike courts-martial and regular federal courts)

3. Continues to permit defendants to be tried ex-post facto for conduct not considered to constitute a war crime at the time it was committed, such as material support for terrorism

Debate: Military Commissions vs. Trial in U.S. Federal Courts

LO 9

The debate centers around two stark views—terrorism as war and terrorism as crime. The strongest of the terrorism as war view is that getting tough on terrorism calls for trying all foreign suspects by military commissions. At the other end are those who say we should abolish military commissions, treat terrorism as a crime, and try those who commit terrorist acts in U.S. criminal courts. Let's look at the arguments on each side of this debate.

1. *Terrorism as War.* Let's look at the arguments of Andrew C. McCarthy (Weiser 2010), who was the "lead prosecutor in one of the country's biggest terrorism trials." It was the 1995 trial of the blind sheik who led a group of men in a plot to blow up the United Nations, the Lincoln and Holland Tunnels, and other New York City landmarks. At that trial, he asked the jury in the Manhattan federal court, "Are you ready to surrender the rule of law to the men in this courtroom?" On December 5, 2009, he declared, "A war is a war. A war is not a crime, and you don't bring your enemies to the courthouse. Will Americans finally grasp how insane it is to regard counterterrorism as a law-enforcement project rather than a matter of national security?"

Here are a few of McCarthy's main points:

a. A prosecutor's job isn't national security. We indicted Osama bin Laden; three months later, al Qaeda blew up two of our embassies. "I mean we could go into a grand jury and indict him three times a week. But, to do anything about it, you needed the Marines. You didn't need us. In the main, international terrorism is a military problem, not a criminal-justice issue."

b. Terrorists can use criminal trials as an "intelligence gathering tool." He refers to a document provided in the discovery process in the 1995 trial in the sheik's case that contained a long list of witnesses.

c. The country's in a "very bad spot right now," and he's "doing what I'm supposed to be doing. It just seemed to me like since 9/11 we've been drifting away and away from the moment of clarity we had."

2. *Trials in U.S. Criminal Courts.* Former and current national security officials from the Bush and Obama administrations (Savage and Shane 2010) make the following arguments in favor of trials in ordinary courts:

a. Some nations won't extradite terrorism suspects or provide evidence to the United States except for civilian trials.

b. Federal courts offer a greater variety of charges for use in pressuring a defendant to cooperate.

c. Military commission rules don't authorize a judge to accept a guilty plea from a defendant in a capital case.

d. The military system is legally untested, so any guilty verdict is vulnerable to being overturned on appeal.

Juan C. Zarate, who served as deputy national security advisor for combating terrorism to President Bush from 2005 to 2009, argues that the government would hamstring itself by outlawing civilian terrorism trials. "We shouldn't inadvertently handcuff ourselves by taking this tool completely out of our toolkit."

3. *Keep Both Options.* The same experts who support the terrorism as crime view are part of a middle course—keep both options (Savage and Shane 2010):

a. Juan C. Zarate, President Bush's deputy national security advisor for combating terrorism, 2005–9, sees the value of military commissions but wants to keep civilian terrorism trials in the "tool kit."

b. "This rush to military commissions is based on premises that are not true," said John B. Bellinger III, a top legal advisor to the National Security Council and the State Department under President George W. Bush. "I think it is neither appropriate nor necessary to limit terrorism cases to either military commissions alone or federal trials alone."

c. Kenneth L. Wainstein, who was assistant attorney general for national security in the Bush administration, said, "Denying yourself access to one system in favor of the other could be counterproductive. I see the benefit of having both systems available. That's why I applauded the Obama administration when, despite expectations to the contrary, they decided to retain military commissions. It's good to have flexibility."

||||||||||||||||||||||||||||||||||||||||||||||||||||||||||||||||||||||||||||||||||||||||||||||||||||||||||||||

Illegal Immigrants and the Constitution

LO 10

Throughout U.S. history, the flow of immigrants into and out of the country has ebbed and flowed greatly. Official policies have varied from "open borders," until about 1850, to immigrant quotas for many countries of origin until the 1930s, to our present situation, which is in flux. One thing, however, has remained constant from colonial times—widespread opposition to allowing alien known criminals to enter or remain in the country.

Keep in mind that aliens who commit a "new" crime while on U.S. soil and come into the criminal process are entitled to the full protection of all the rights and proceedings you've learned in earlier chapters. We'll concentrate here on the Constitution and the detention of deportable illegal immigrants during deportation proceedings. This is predominantly a Fourth Amendment question.

The Fourth Amendment and "Deportable Aliens"

LO 10

In 1976, the U.S. Supreme Court made it clear that it's a Fourth Amendment seizure to stop a deportable alien for suspected immigration law crimes (*U.S. v. Martinez-Fuerte* [1976], excerpted in the next section). A **deportable alien** is "a person who has been found to be deportable by an immigration judge, or who admits his deportability upon questioning by official agents" (553). But, in the same year, the Court held that according to the *Terry* balancing test (Chapter 4), the strong government interest in investigating illegal immigration outweighed the minimal liberty and privacy intrusion of a brief detention at a permanent immigration checkpoint.

On the government interest side of the balance, the Court noted that, "It has been national policy for many years to limit immigration into the United States." Then, the Court pointed to a finding that there were "as many as 10 or 12 million aliens illegally in the country." The reason, according to the Court, is that there were far more aliens than the then-existing Western Hemisphere quota of 120,000 who wanted to live and work in the United States. Most came from Mexico because "economic opportunities are significantly greater in the United States than they are in Mexico." According to the Court, "Interdicting the flow of illegal entrants from Mexico poses formidable law enforcement problems" (551).

On the other side of the balance—the individual Fourth Amendment privacy and liberty interests—the Court found the invasions "quite limited," lasting only a few minutes. Travelers are asked only to answer a question or two and "possibly [produce] a document evidencing a right to be in the United States. Neither the vehicle nor its occupants are searched, and visual inspection of the vehicle is limited to what can be seen without a search" (558).

The Court then turned to the effectiveness of the permanent border checkpoint near San Clemente, California, the same checkpoint that the Court dealt with in *U.S. v. Martinez-Fuerte*. Here are the details the Court presented:

> Approximately 10 million cars pass the checkpoint location each year, although the checkpoint actually is in operation only about 70% of the time. "Down" periods are caused by personnel shortages, weather conditions, and at San Clemente peak traffic loads. In calendar year 1973, approximately 17,000 illegal aliens were apprehended there. During an eight-day period in 1974 that included the arrests involved in No. 74–1560, roughly 146,000 vehicles passed through the checkpoint during 124 1/6 hours of operation. Of these, 820 vehicles were referred to the secondary inspection area, where Border Patrol agents found 725 deportable aliens in 171 vehicles. In all but two cases, the aliens were discovered without a conventional search of the vehicle. A similar rate of apprehensions throughout the year would have resulted in an annual total of over 33,000, although the Government contends that many illegal aliens pass through the checkpoint undetected. (554)

Six justices had no difficulty holding that the government interest outweighed the individual rights of the deportable illegal immigrant Amado Martinez-Fuerte.

In Martinez-Fuerte (1976), our next case excerpt, the U.S. Supreme Court held that it was reasonable to stop Amado Martinez-Fuerte's vehicle at a checkpoint to question him and other occupants briefly even though police lacked individualized reasonable suspicion.

CASE   Was the Stop without Individualized Suspicion Reasonable?

U.S. v. Martinez-Fuerte

428 U.S. 543 (1976)

HISTORY

Amado Martinez-Fuerte (Respondent) was charged with two counts of illegally transporting aliens in violation of 8 U.S.C. § 1324(a)(2). He moved before trial to suppress all evidence stemming from the stop on the ground that the operation of the checkpoint was in violation of the Fourth Amendment. The motion to suppress was denied, and he was convicted on both counts after a jury trial. Martinez-Fuerte appealed his conviction, and the Government appealed the granting of the motion. The Court of Appeals for the Ninth Circuit held, with one judge dissenting, that these stops violated the Fourth Amendment. It reversed Martinez-Fuerte's conviction, and affirmed the orders to suppress in the other cases. The U.S. Supreme Court reversed and remanded.

POWELL, J., joined by BURGER, C.J., and STEWART, WHITE, BLACKMUN, REHNQUIST, and STEVENS, JJ.

These cases involve criminal prosecutions for offenses relating to the transportation of illegal Mexican aliens. Whether the Fourth Amendment was violated turns primarily on whether a vehicle may be stopped at a fixed checkpoint for brief questioning of its occupants even though there is no reason to believe the particular vehicle contains illegal aliens. We hold today that such stops are consistent with the Fourth Amendment. We also hold that the operation of a fixed checkpoint need not be authorized in advance by a judicial warrant.

FACTS

Approximately one mile south of the permanent immigration checkpoint on Interstate 5 near the San Clemente, California checkpoint is a large black on yellow sign with flashing yellow lights over the highway stating "ALL VEHICLES, STOP AHEAD, 1 MILE." Three-quarters of a mile further north are two black on yellow signs suspended over the highway with flashing lights stating "WATCH FOR BRAKE LIGHTS." At the checkpoint, which is also the location of a State of California weighing station, are two large signs with flashing red lights suspended over the highway. These signs each state "STOP HERE U.S. OFFICERS." Placed on the highway are a number of orange traffic cones funneling traffic into two lanes where a Border Patrol agent in full dress uniform, standing behind a white on red "STOP" sign checks traffic. Blocking traffic in the unused lanes are official U.S. Border Patrol vehicles with flashing red lights. In addition, there is a permanent building which houses the Border Patrol office and temporary detention facilities. There are also floodlights for nighttime operation.

The "point" agent standing between the two lanes of traffic visually screens all northbound vehicles, which the checkpoint brings to a virtual, if not a complete, halt. Most motorists are allowed to resume their progress without any oral inquiry or close visual examination. In a relatively small number of cases the "point" agent will conclude that further inquiry is in order. He directs these cars to a secondary inspection area, where their occupants are asked about their citizenship and immigration status. The Government informs us that at San Clemente the average length of an investigation in the secondary inspection area is three to five minutes. A direction to stop in the secondary inspection area could be based on something suspicious about a particular car passing through the checkpoint, but the Government concedes that none of the three stops at issue in No. 74–1560 was based on any articulable suspicion. [Only Martinez-Fuerte's stop is included in this excerpt.] During the period when these stops were made, the checkpoint was operating under a magistrate's "warrant of inspection," which authorized the Border Patrol to conduct a routine-stop operation at the San Clemente location.

Respondent Amado Martinez-Fuerte approached the checkpoint driving a vehicle containing two female passengers. The women were illegal Mexican aliens who had entered the United States at the San Ysidro port of entry by using false papers and rendezvoused with Martinez-Fuerte in San Diego to be transported northward. At the checkpoint their car was directed to the secondary inspection area. Martinez-Fuerte produced documents showing him to be a lawful resident alien, but his passengers admitted being present in the country unlawfully. He was charged, Inter alia, with two counts of illegally transporting aliens in violation of 8 U.S.C. § 1324(a)(2). He moved before trial to suppress all evidence stemming from the stop on the ground that the operation of the checkpoint was in violation of the Fourth Amendment. The motion to suppress was denied, and he was convicted on both counts after a jury trial.

OPINION

It has been national policy for many years to limit immigration into the United States. Since July 1, 1968, the annual quota for immigrants from all independent countries of the Western Hemisphere, including Mexico, has been 120,000 persons. Act of Oct. 3, 1965, § 21(e), 79 Stat. 921. Many more aliens than can be accommodated under the quota want to live and work in the United States. Consequently, large numbers of aliens seek illegally to enter or to remain in the United States. Estimates of the number of illegal immigrants (already) in the United States vary widely. A conservative estimate in 1972 produced a figure of about one million, but the Immigration and Naturalization Service now suggests there may be as many as 10 or 12 million aliens illegally in the country. It is estimated that 85% of the illegal immigrants are from Mexico, drawn by the fact that economic opportunities are significantly greater in the United States than they are in Mexico.

Interdicting the flow of illegal entrants from Mexico poses formidable law enforcement problems. The principal problem arises from surreptitious entries. The United States shares a border with Mexico that is almost 2,000 miles long, and much of the border area is uninhabited desert or thinly populated arid land. Although the Border Patrol maintains personnel, electronic equipment, and fences along portions of the border, it remains relatively easy for individuals to enter the United States without detection. It also is possible for an alien to enter unlawfully at a port of entry by the use of falsified papers or to enter lawfully but violate restrictions of entry in an effort to remain in the country unlawfully. Once within the country, the aliens seek to travel inland to areas where employment is believed to be available, frequently meeting by prearrangement with friends or professional smugglers who transport them in private vehicles.

The Border Patrol conducts three kinds of inland traffic-checking operations in an effort to minimize illegal immigration. Permanent checkpoints, such as those at San Clemente and Sarita, are maintained at or near intersections of important roads leading away from the border. They operate on a coordinated basis designed to avoid circumvention by smugglers and others who transport the illegal aliens. Temporary checkpoints, which operate like permanent ones, occasionally are established in other strategic locations. Finally, roving patrols are maintained to supplement the checkpoint system. In fiscal 1973, 175,511 deportable aliens (a person who has been found to be deportable by an immigration judge, or who admits his deportability upon questioning by official agents) were apprehended throughout the Nation by "line watch" agents stationed at the border itself.) Traffic-checking operations in the interior apprehended approximately 55,300 more deportable aliens. Most of the traffic-checking apprehensions were at checkpoints, though precise figures are not available.

The record provides a rather complete picture of the effectiveness of the San Clemente checkpoint. Approximately 10 million cars pass the checkpoint location each year, although the checkpoint actually is in operation only about 70% of the time. "Down" periods are caused by personnel shortages, weather conditions, and at San Clemente peak traffic loads.

In calendar year 1973, approximately 17,000 illegal aliens were apprehended there. During an eight-day period in 1974 that included the arrests involved in No. 74–1560, roughly 146,000 vehicles passed through the checkpoint during 124 1/6 hours of operation. Of these, 820 vehicles were referred to the secondary inspection area, where Border Patrol agents found 725 deportable aliens in 171 vehicles. In all but two cases, the aliens were discovered without a conventional search of the vehicle. A similar rate of apprehensions throughout the year would have resulted in an annual total of over 33,000, although the Government contends that many illegal aliens pass through the checkpoint undetected. The record in No. 75–5387 does not provide comparable statistical information regarding the Sarita checkpoint. While it appears that fewer illegal aliens are apprehended there, it may be assumed that fewer pass by undetected, as every motorist is questioned.

The Fourth Amendment imposes limits on search-and-seizure powers in order to prevent arbitrary and oppressive interference by enforcement officials with the privacy and personal security of individuals. In delineating the constitutional safeguards applicable in particular contexts, the Court has weighed the public interest against the Fourth Amendment interest of the individual (*Terry v. Ohio* 1968 [excerpted Chapter 4]), a process evident in our previous cases dealing with Border Patrol traffic-checking operations.

It is agreed that checkpoint stops are "seizures" within the meaning of the Fourth Amendment. Our previous cases have recognized that maintenance of a traffic-checking program in the interior is necessary because the flow of illegal aliens cannot be controlled effectively at the border. We note here the substantiality of the public interest in the practice of routine stops for inquiry at permanent checkpoints, a practice which the Government identifies as the most important of the traffic-checking operations. These checkpoints are located on important highways; in their absence such highways would offer illegal aliens a quick and safe route into the interior. Routine checkpoint inquiries apprehend many smugglers and illegal aliens who succumb to the lure of such highways. And the prospect of such inquiries forces others onto less efficient roads that are less heavily traveled, slowing their movement and making them more vulnerable to detection by roving patrols.

A requirement that stops on major routes inland always be based on reasonable suspicion would be impractical because the flow of traffic tends to be too heavy to allow the particularized study of a given car that would enable it to be identified as a possible carrier of illegal aliens. In particular, such a requirement would largely eliminate any deterrent to the conduct of well-disguised smuggling operations, even though smugglers are known to use these highways regularly.

While the need to make routine checkpoint stops is great, the consequent intrusion on Fourth Amendment interests is quite limited. The stop does intrude to a limited extent on motorists' right to free passage without interruption, and arguably on their right to personal security. But it involves only a brief detention of travelers during which all that is required of the vehicle's occupants is a response to a brief question or two and possibly the production of a document evidencing a right to be in the United States. Neither the vehicle nor its occupants are searched, and visual inspection of the vehicle is limited to what can be seen without a search. This objective intrusion—the stop itself, the questioning, and the visual inspection—also existed in roving-patrol stops. But we view checkpoint stops in a different light because the subjective intrusion—the generating of concern or even fright on the part of lawful travelers—is appreciably less in the case of a checkpoint stop. The circumstances surrounding a checkpoint stop and search are far less intrusive than those attending a roving-patrol stop. Roving patrols often operate at night on seldom-traveled roads, and their approach may frighten motorists. At traffic checkpoints the motorist can see that other vehicles are being stopped, he can see visible signs of the officers' authority, and he is much less likely to be frightened or annoyed by the intrusion.

Routine checkpoint stops do not intrude on the motoring public. First, the potential interference with legitimate traffic is minimal. Motorists using these highways are not taken by surprise as they know, or may obtain knowledge of, the location of the checkpoints and will not be stopped elsewhere. Second, checkpoint operations both appear to and actually involve less discretionary enforcement activity. The regularized manner in which established checkpoints are operated is visible evidence, reassuring to law-abiding motorists, that the stops are duly authorized and believed to serve the public interest. The location of a fixed checkpoint is not chosen by officers in the field, but by officials responsible for making overall decisions as to the most effective allocation of limited enforcement resources. We may assume that such officials will be unlikely to locate a checkpoint where it bears arbitrarily or oppressively on motorists as a class. And since field officers may stop only those cars passing the checkpoint, there is less room for abusive or harassing stops of individuals than there was in the case of roving-patrol stops.

The defendants arrested at the San Clemente checkpoint suggest that its operation involves a significant extra element of intrusiveness in that only a small percentage of cars are referred to the secondary inspection area, thereby "stigmatizing" those diverted and reducing the assurances provided by equal treatment of all motorists. We think defendants overstate the consequences. Referrals are made for the sole purpose of conducting a routine and limited inquiry into residence status that cannot feasibly be made of every motorist where the traffic is heavy. The objective intrusion of the stop and inquiry thus remains minimal. Selective referral may involve some annoyance, but it remains true that the stops should not be frightening or offensive because of their public and relatively routine nature. Moreover, selective referrals rather than questioning the occupants of every car tend to advance some Fourth Amendment interests by minimizing the intrusion on the general motoring public.

The defendants note correctly that to accommodate public and private interests some quantum of individualized suspicion is usually a prerequisite to a constitutional search or seizure. But the Fourth Amendment imposes no irreducible requirement of such suspicion. One's expectation of privacy in an automobile and of freedom in its operation are significantly different from the traditional expectation of privacy and freedom in one's residence. And the reasonableness of the procedures followed in making these checkpoint stops makes the resulting intrusion on the interests of motorists minimal. On the other hand, the purpose of the stops is legitimate and in the public interest, and the need for this enforcement technique is demonstrated by the records in the cases before us. Accordingly, we hold that the stops and questioning at issue may be made in the absence of any individualized suspicion at reasonably located checkpoints.

In summary, we hold that stops for brief questioning routinely conducted at permanent checkpoints are consistent with the Fourth Amendment and need not be authorized by warrant. We REVERSE the judgment of the Court of Appeals for the Ninth Circuit and REMAND the case with directions to affirm the conviction of Martinez-Fuerte and to REMAND the other cases to the District Court for further proceedings.

It is so ordered.

DISSENT

BRENNAN, joined by MARSHALL, J.

Today's decision continues the evisceration of Fourth Amendment protections against unreasonable searches and seizures. Consistent with this purpose to debilitate Fourth Amendment protections, the Court's decision today virtually empties the Amendment of its reasonableness requirement by holding that law enforcement officials manning fixed checkpoint stations who make standardless seizures of persons do not violate the Amendment. While the requisite justification for permitting a search or seizure may vary in certain contexts, even in the exceptional situations permitting intrusions on less than probable cause, it has long been settled that justification must be measured by objective standards. *Terry v. Ohio* made clear what common sense teaches: Conduct, to be reasonable, must pass muster under objective standards applied to specific facts.

We are told today, however, that motorists without number may be individually stopped, questioned, visually inspected, and then further detained upon nothing more substantial than inarticulate hunches. This defacement of Fourth Amendment protections is arrived at by a balancing process that overwhelms the individual's protection against unwarranted official intrusion by a governmental interest said to justify the search and seizure. But that method is only a convenient cover for condoning arbitrary official conduct.

In any event, the subjective aspects of checkpoint stops require some principled restraint on law enforcement conduct. The motorist whose conduct has been nothing but innocent and this is overwhelmingly the case surely resents his own detention and inspection. And checkpoints, unlike roving stops, detain thousands of motorists, a dragnet-like procedure offensive to the sensibilities of free citizens. Also, the delay occasioned by stopping hundreds of vehicles on a busy highway is particularly irritating.

In addition to overlooking these dimensions of subjective intrusion, checkpoint officials, uninhibited by any objective standards and therefore free to stop any or all motorists without explanation or excuse, wholly on whim, will perforce target motorists of Mexican appearance. The process will then inescapably discriminate against citizens of Mexican ancestry and Mexican aliens lawfully in this country for no other reason than that they unavoidably possess the same "suspicious" physical and grooming characteristics of illegal Mexican aliens.

Every American citizen of Mexican ancestry and every Mexican alien lawfully in this country must know after today's decision that he travels the fixed checkpoint highways at the risk of being subjected not only to a stop, but also to detention and interrogation, both prolonged and to an extent far more than for non-Mexican appearing motorists. To be singled out for referral and to be detained and interrogated must be upsetting to any motorist. One wonders what actual experience supports my Brethren's conclusion that referrals "should not be frightening or offensive because of their public and relatively routine nature." In point of fact, referrals, viewed in context, are not relatively routine; thousands are otherwise permitted to pass. But for the arbitrarily selected motorists who must suffer the delay and humiliation of detention and interrogation, the experience can obviously be upsetting. And that experience is particularly vexing for the motorist of Mexican ancestry who is selectively referred, knowing that the officers' target is the Mexican alien. That deep resentment will be stirred by a sense of unfair discrimination is not difficult to foresee.

The cornerstone of this society, indeed of any free society, is orderly procedure. The Constitution, as originally adopted, was therefore, in great measure, a procedural document. For the same reasons the drafters of the Bill of Rights largely placed their faith in procedural limitations on government action. The Fourth Amendment's requirement that searches and seizures be reasonable enforces this fundamental understanding in erecting its buffer against the arbitrary treatment of citizens by government. But to permit, as the Court does today, police discretion to supplant the objectivity of reason and, thereby, expediency to reign in the place of order, is to undermine Fourth Amendment safeguards and threaten erosion of the cornerstone of our system of a government, for, as Mr. Justice Frankfurter reminded us, "the history of American freedom is, in no small measure, the history of procedure."

QUESTIONS

1. Describe the government interest in detail.
2. Describe the individual interest in detail.
3. Identify the objective basis the Court established, and list the relevant facts that supported the reasonableness of the seizure.
4. Do the facts of the case support the dissent's claim that:

    Every American citizen of Mexican ancestry and every Mexican alien lawfully in this country must know after today's decision that he travels the fixed checkpoint highways at the risk of being subjected not only to a stop, but also to detention and interrogation, both prolonged and to an extent far more than for non-Mexican appearing motorists?

LO 11

ETHICAL ISSUES

Is It Ethical to Refuse to Enforce Arizona's Immigration Law?

On April 23, 2010, Gov. Jan Brewer of Arizona signed a law—SB 1070—that prohibits the harboring of illegal aliens and makes it a state crime for an alien to commit certain federal immigration crimes. It also requires police officers who, in the course of a traffic stop or other law-enforcement action, come to a "reasonable suspicion" that a person is an illegal alien verify the person's immigration status with the federal government.

Professor Kris Kobach
University of Missouri at Kansas City
Attorney General John Ashcroft's chief advisor on immigration law and border security from 2001 to 2003
Presently advisor to Arizona Governor
New York Times

May 27, 2010. An Arizona sheriff said that he has "no intention of complying" with the state's controversial new immigration law, calling it "abominable" and a "national embarrassment." The defiance by Pima County Sheriff Clarence Dupnik was perhaps the sharpest rebuke to Arizona Gov. Jan Brewer for signing into law last Friday a bill that empowers police in the state to stop people they suspect may be illegal immigrants and demand identification. Critics rallied around the country today, claiming the law fosters racism and was a bad policing measure.

ABC News and the Associated Press

INSTRUCTIONS

1. Visit the Companion Website and read the two selections discussed below. See the links under the Chapter 15 Ethical Issues section of the Companion Website—login at www .cengagebrain.com.

2. Read Professor Kobach's full article.

3. Read the full report of Pima County Sheriff Clarence Dupnik's remarks.

4. Write an essay that includes the following:

    a. A summary of Kobach's article supporting the Arizona law.

    b. A summary of Sheriff Dupnik's reasons for saying he won't comply with the law.

    c. Your position on whether Sheriff Dupnik's refusal to comply with the law would be ethical. Back up your answer with your summaries from 4a and 4b.

Noncitizen Detention and the Fourth Amendment

LO 10

Detention during **noncriminal (civil) deportation proceedings** is a subject of much debate. Recall that the Fourth Amendment protects against "unreasonable searches and seizures" (Chapters 3–7). Detention is clearly a seizure. And "detention is clearly an important element in an effective immigration enforcement system" (*Demore v. Kim* "Amicus Brief for T. Alexander Aleinikoff and others" 2002, 3). Most agree with this statement by several former high-ranking officials in the Immigration and Naturalization Services (INS). Most also agree that two criteria should determine the reasonableness of detaining noncitizens or allowing them to remain free during deportation and removal proceedings:

1. The risk that the noncitizen will flee

2. The danger that the noncitizen poses to the community

There the agreement stops. There's heated debate over several issues, especially over how to decide whom to detain. Some courts and commentators have called for "an individualized determination of flight risk and dangerousness before subjecting lawful permanent residents to sustained detention" (*Demore v. Kim* 2002, Amicus Brief, 3). Other courts and commentators call for mandatory detention of all "criminal" aliens while the question of deportation is being decided. But we're not talking about detaining noncitizens during *criminal* investigations and prosecutions for crimes committed in the United States (Chapters 3–6, on search and seizure; Chapter 12, on bail and detention). This debate is over those involved in noncriminal, or civil, deportation proceedings.

The U.S. Supreme Court resolved the conflict—at least in the courts—in *Demore v. Kim* (2003), our next case excerpt. The Court held (6–3) that "Congress, justifiably concerned that deportable criminal aliens who are not detained continue to engage in crime and fail to appear for their removal hearings in large numbers, may require that persons such as respondent be detained for the brief period necessary for their removal proceedings" (513).

The Court readily conceded that the Constitution "entitles aliens to due process of law in deportation proceedings." But the Court also "recognized detention during deportation proceedings as a constitutionally valid aspect of the deportation process. As we said more than a century ago, deportation proceedings 'would be vain if those accused could not be held in custody pending the inquiry into their true character'" (523).

Before we go to the excerpt, let's look at the nature of the detention and removal process so you can get a better perspective on the situation that led to the mandatory detention laws enacted during the 1990s, which are still the law today. Traditionally, the **Immigration and Nationality Act (INA)** has authorized the U.S. attorney general, in his or her *discretion*, to detain *suspected* deportable aliens found in the United States to make sure they're available for deportation proceedings and to reduce the danger to the community (INA, 8 U.S.C. § 1226a). The decision to arrest, detain, or release aliens subject to deportation proceedings on bond or other conditions was made on a case-by-case basis, typically within a day of arrest (8 C.F.R. § 236.1(d)(1)).

Aliens, except for arriving aliens, can appeal the detention decision to an immigration judge, who follows a "streamlined bond redetermination" procedure, conducted informally either in person or by telephone (8 C.F.R. § 3.19(b)). The judge can consider any information provided by the Immigration and Naturalization Service (INS) or the alien. Information that's made available independently to the judge may also be considered. The judge can approve the release conditions, modify them, or release on recognizance (8 C.F.R § 236.1(d)(1)). The alien or the INS also can appeal the judge's decision to the Board of Immigration Appeals (BIA) in expedited informal proceedings (8 C.F.R § 236.1(d)(3)).

This procedure is still the law for *non*criminal aliens. But the **Illegal Immigration Reform and Immigrant Responsibility Act (IIRIRA) of 1996** amended the INA. It now provides that "the Attorney General *shall* take into custody any alien who" has committed a fairly long list of crimes (8 U.S.C. § 1226 (c)). (Figure 15.4 details the conditions that qualify aliens for deportation.)

The statute further orders the attorney general to develop a coordinated system to identify and transfer these aliens from federal, state, and local law enforcement to INS custody (Figure 15.5).

Now, let's turn to our next case excerpt, *Demore v. Kim* (2003). The issue in this case was whether the Immigration and Nationality Act violated the rights of lawful permanent resident aliens by requiring no bail for their civil detention while awaiting

FIGURE 15.4   Offenses that qualify aliens for mandatory detention during deportation proceedings

---

Section 1227. Deportable Aliens

(a) Classes of deportable aliens

Any alien (including an alien crewman) in and admitted to the United States shall, upon the order of the Attorney General, be removed if the alien is within one or more of the following classes of deportable aliens:

   (2) Criminal offenses

   (A) General crimes

   (i) Crimes of moral turpitude

   Any alien who—

   (I) is convicted of a crime involving moral turpitude committed within five years (or 10 years in the case of an alien provided lawful permanent resident status ...) and ...

   (II) is convicted of a crime for which a sentence of one year or longer may be imposed, is deportable.

   (ii) Multiple criminal convictions

   Any alien who at any time after admission is convicted of two or more crimes involving moral turpitude, not arising out of a single scheme of criminal misconduct, regardless of whether confined therefor and regardless of whether the convictions were in a single trial, is deportable.

   (iii) Aggravated felony ...

   (iv) High speed flight ...

   (v) Failure to register as a sex offender ...

   (B) Controlled substances

   (i) Conviction

   Any alien who at any time after admission has been convicted of a violation of (or a conspiracy or attempt to violate) any law or regulation of a State, the United States, or a foreign country relating to a controlled substance, other than a single offense involving possession for one's own use of 30 grams or less of marijuana, is deportable.

   (ii) Drug abusers and addicts

   Any alien who is, or at any time after admission has been, a drug abuser or addict is deportable.

   (C) Certain firearm offenses

   Any alien who at any time after admission is convicted under any law of purchasing, selling, offering for sale, exchanging, using, owning, possessing, or carrying, or of attempting or conspiring to purchase, sell, offer for sale, exchange, use, own, possess, or carry, any weapon, part, or accessory which is a firearm or destructive device (as defined in section 921 (a) of title 18) in violation of any law is deportable.

   (D) Miscellaneous crimes

   Any alien who at any time has been convicted of, or has been so convicted of a conspiracy or attempt to violate—

   (i) ... espionage, sabotage, or treason and sedition ... for which a term of imprisonment of five or more years may be imposed;...

   (iii) a violation of any provision of the Military Selective Service Act ... is deportable.

FIGURE 15.4 *Continued*

(E) Crimes of domestic violence, stalking, or violation of protection order, crimes against children and

   (i) Domestic violence, stalking, and child abuse

     Any alien who at any time after admission is convicted of a crime of domestic violence, a crime of stalking, or a crime of child abuse, child neglect, or child abandonment is deportable. ...

   (ii) Violators of protection orders

     Any alien who at any time after admission is enjoined under a protection order issued by a court and whom the court determines has engaged in conduct that violates the portion of a protection order that involves protection against credible threats of violence, repeated harassment, or bodily injury to the person or persons for whom the protection order was issued is deportable. ...

(3) Failure to register and falsification of documents

  (D) Falsely claiming citizenship

    (i) In general

      Any alien who falsely represents, or has falsely represented, himself to be a citizen of the United States for any purpose or benefit under this chapter ... or any Federal or State law is deportable.

Source: U.S. Code. 2010. 8 U.S.C. § 1227(a).

FIGURE 15.5 **Illegal Immigration Reform and Immigrant Responsibility Act (IIRIRA) of 1996**

---

§ 1226. Apprehension and Detention of Aliens

(d) Identification of criminal aliens

  (1) The Attorney General shall devise and implement a system—

    (A) to make available, daily (on a 24-hour basis), to Federal, State, and local authorities the investigative resources of the Service to determine whether individuals arrested by such authorities for aggravated felonies are aliens;

    (B) to designate and train officers and employees of the Service to serve as a liaison to Federal, State, and local law enforcement and correctional agencies and courts with respect to the arrest, conviction, and release of any alien charged with an aggravated felony; and

    (C) which uses computer resources to maintain a current record of aliens who have been convicted of an aggravated felony, and indicates those who have been removed.

  (2) The record under paragraph (1)(C) shall be made available—

    (A) to inspectors at ports of entry and to border patrol agents at sector headquarters for purposes of immediate identification of any alien who was previously ordered removed and is seeking to reenter the United States, and

    (B) to officials of the Department of State for use in its automated visa lookout system.

  (3) Upon the request of the governor or chief executive officer of any State, the Service shall provide assistance to State courts in the identification of aliens unlawfully present in the United States pending criminal prosecution.

Source: U.S. Code. 2010. 8 U.S.C. § 1226(d).

deportation proceedings. Hyung Joon Kim wasn't protesting his classification as a deportable alien following his criminal conviction for crimes defined under INA. Rather, he argued that making him ineligible for bail without an individualized hearing violated his due process rights.

In Demore v. Kim (2003), our next case excerpt, the U.S. Supreme Court ruled that the no-bail, civil detention requirement of the Immigration Nationality Act didn't violate the due process rights of Hyung Joon Kim, a lawful permanent resident alien.

CASE   Did His Detention Deprive Him of Liberty without "Due Process of Law"?

Demore v. Kim

538 U.S. 510 (2003)

HISTORY

Hyung Joon Kim (Respondent), a lawful permanent resident alien (LPR) filed a habeas petition challenging the no-bail provision of the Immigration and Nationality Act (INA), pursuant to which he had been held for six months during pendency of removal proceedings against him. The United States District Court for the Northern District of California, Susan Y. Illston, J., entered an order, holding the statute unconstitutional on its face and directing the Immigration and Naturalization Service (INS) to hold a bail hearing. The Government appealed. The United States Court of Appeals for the Ninth Circuit, affirmed. Certiorari was granted. The Supreme Court reversed.

REHNQUIST, C.J., joined by KENNEDY, STEVENS, SOUTER, GINSBURG, BREYER, O'CONNOR, SCALIA, and THOMAS, JJ.

Section 236(c) of the Immigration and Nationality Act, as amended, 8 U.S.C. § 1226(c), provides that "the Attorney General *shall* take into custody any alien who is removable from this country because he has been convicted of one of a specified set of crimes." [emphasis added]

FACTS

Hyung Joon Kim (Respondent) is a citizen of the Republic of South Korea. He entered the United States in 1984, at the age of six, and became a lawful permanent resident of the United States two years later. In July 1996, he was

convicted of first-degree burglary in state court in California and, in April 1997, he was convicted of a second crime, "petty theft with priors." The Immigration and Naturalization Service (INS) charged respondent with being deportable from the United States in light of these convictions, and detained him pending his removal hearing. We hold that Congress, justifiably concerned that deportable criminal aliens who are not detained continue to engage in crime and fail to appear for their removal hearings in large numbers, may require that persons such as respondent be detained for the brief period necessary for their removal proceedings.

Respondent does not dispute the validity of his prior convictions, which were obtained following the full procedural protections our criminal justice system offers. Respondent also did not dispute the INS's conclusion that he is subject to mandatory detention under § 1226(c). As respondent explained: "The statute requires the [INS] to take into custody any alien who 'is deportable' from the United States based on having been convicted of any of a wide range of crimes. . . . [Respondent] does not challenge INS's authority to take him into custody after he finished serving his criminal sentence. His challenge is solely to Section 1226(c)'s absolute prohibition on his release from detention, even where, as here, the INS never asserted that he posed a danger or significant flight risk."

In conceding that he was deportable, respondent forwent a hearing at which he would have been entitled to raise any nonfrivolous argument available to demonstrate that he was not properly included in a mandatory detention category. Respondent instead filed a habeas corpus action pursuant to 28 U.S.C. § 2241 in the United States

District Court for the Northern District of California challenging the constitutionality of § 1226(c) itself.

The District Court agreed with respondent that § 1226(c)'s requirement of mandatory detention for certain criminal aliens was unconstitutional. The District Court therefore granted respondent's petition subject to the INS's prompt undertaking of an individualized bond hearing to determine whether respondent posed either a flight risk or a danger to the community. Following that decision, the District Director of the INS released respondent on $5,000 bond. The Court of Appeals for the Ninth Circuit affirmed. We granted certiorari to resolve this conflict, and now reverse.

OPINION

Section 1226(c) of the Immigration and Nationality Act (INA) mandates detention during removal proceedings for a limited class of deportable aliens—including those convicted of an aggravated felony. Congress adopted this provision against a backdrop of wholesale failure by the INS to deal with increasing rates of criminal activity by aliens. Criminal aliens were the fastest growing segment of the federal prison population, already constituting roughly 25% of all federal prisoners, and they formed a rapidly rising share of state prison populations as well.

Congress's investigations showed, however, that the INS could not even *identify* most deportable aliens, much less locate them and remove them from the country. One study showed that, at the then-current rate of deportation, it would take 23 years to remove every criminal alien already subject to deportation. Making matters worse, criminal aliens who were deported swiftly reentered the country illegally in great numbers.

The INS's near-total inability to remove deportable criminal aliens imposed more than a monetary cost on the Nation. Deportable criminal aliens who remained in the United States often committed more crimes before being removed. One 1986 study showed that, after criminal aliens were identified as deportable, 77% were arrested at least once more and 45%—nearly half—were arrested multiple times before their deportation proceedings even began.

Congress also had before it evidence that one of the major causes of the INS's failure to remove deportable criminal aliens was the agency's failure to detain those aliens during their deportation proceedings. The Attorney General at the time had broad discretion to conduct individualized bond hearings and to release criminal aliens from custody during their removal proceedings when those aliens were determined not to present an excessive flight risk or threat to society. Despite this discretion to conduct bond hearings, however, in practice the INS faced severe limitations on funding and detention space, which considerations affected its release determinations. Once released, more than 20% of deportable criminal aliens failed to appear for their removal hearings.

Congress amended the immigration laws several times toward the end of the 1980's. In 1988, Congress limited the Attorney General's discretion over custody determinations with respect to deportable aliens who had been convicted of aggravated felonies. Then, in 1990, Congress broadened the definition of "aggravated felony," subjecting more criminal aliens to mandatory detention. At the same time, however, Congress added a new provision, authorizing the Attorney General to release permanent resident aliens during their deportation proceedings where such aliens were found not to constitute a flight risk or threat to the community.

During the same period in which Congress was making incremental changes to the immigration laws, it was also considering wholesale reform of those laws. Some studies presented to Congress suggested that detention of criminal aliens during their removal proceedings might be the best way to ensure their successful removal from this country. It was following those Reports that Congress enacted 8 U.S.C. § 1226, requiring the Attorney General to detain a subset of deportable criminal aliens pending a determination of their removability.

In the exercise of its broad power over naturalization and immigration, Congress regularly makes rules that would be unacceptable if applied to citizens. This Court has firmly and repeatedly endorsed the proposition that Congress may make rules as to aliens that would be unacceptable if applied to citizens. In his habeas corpus challenge, respondent did not contest Congress's general authority to remove criminal aliens from the United States. Nor did he argue that he himself was not "deportable" within the meaning of § 1226(c). Rather, respondent argued that the Government may not, consistent with the Due Process Clause of the Fifth Amendment, detain him for the brief period necessary for his removal proceedings.

It is well established that the Fifth Amendment entitles aliens to due process of law in deportation proceedings. At the same time, however, this Court has recognized detention during deportation proceedings as a constitutionally valid aspect of the deportation process. As we said more than a century ago, deportation proceedings "would be vain if those accused could not be held in custody pending the inquiry into their true character." Despite this Court's longstanding view that the Government may constitutionally detain deportable aliens during the limited period necessary for their removal proceedings, respondent argues that the narrow detention policy reflected in 8 U.S.C. § 1226(c) violates due process.

In the present case, the statutory provision at issue governs detention of deportable criminal aliens *pending their removal proceedings.* Such detention necessarily serves the purpose of preventing deportable criminal aliens from fleeing prior to or during their removal proceedings, thus increasing the chance that, if ordered removed, the aliens will be successfully removed. Respondent disagrees, arguing that there is no evidence that mandatory detention is necessary because the Government has never shown that individualized bond hearings would be ineffective. But, in adopting § 1226(c), Congress had before it evidence suggesting that permitting discretionary release of aliens pending their removal hearings would lead to large numbers of deportable criminal aliens skipping their hearings and remaining at large in the United States unlawfully.

Respondent argues that these statistics are irrelevant and do not demonstrate that individualized bond hearings "are ineffective or burdensome." It is of course true that when Congress enacted § 1226, individualized bail determinations had not been tested under optimal conditions, or tested in all their possible permutations. But when the Government deals with deportable aliens, the Due Process Clause does not require it to employ the least burdensome means to accomplish its goal. The evidence Congress had before it certainly supports the approach it selected even if other, hypothetical studies might have suggested different courses of action.

The Executive Office for Immigration Review has calculated that, in 85% of the cases in which aliens are detained pursuant to § 1226(c), removal proceedings are completed in an average time of 47 days and a median of 30 days. In the remaining 15% of cases, in which the alien appeals the decision of the Immigration Judge to the Board of Immigration Appeals, appeal takes an average of four months, with a median time that is slightly shorter.

These statistics do not include the many cases in which removal proceedings are completed while the alien is still serving time for the underlying conviction. In those cases, the aliens involved are never subjected to mandatory detention at all. In sum, the detention at stake under § 1226(c) lasts roughly a month and a half in the vast majority of cases in which it is invoked, and about five months in the minority of cases in which the alien chooses to appeal. Respondent was detained for somewhat longer than the average—spending six months in INS custody prior to the District Court's order granting habeas relief, but respondent himself had requested a continuance of his removal hearing.

For the reasons set forth above, respondent's claim must fail. Detention during removal proceedings is a constitutionally permissible part of that process. The INS detention of respondent, a criminal alien who has conceded that he is deportable, for the limited period of his removal proceedings, is governed by these cases. The judgment of the Court of Appeals is

REVERSED.

CONCURRING and DISSENTING SOUTER, J., joined by STEVENS and GINSBURG, JJ.

It has been settled for over a century that all aliens within our territory are "persons" entitled to the protection of the Due Process Clause. The constitutional protection of an alien's person and property is particularly strong in the case of aliens lawfully admitted to permanent residence (LPRs). The immigration laws give LPRs the opportunity to establish a life permanently in this country by developing economic, familial, and social ties indistinguishable from those of a citizen. In fact, the law of the United States goes out of its way to encourage just such attachments by creating immigration preferences for those with a citizen as a close relation, and those with valuable professional skills or other assets promising benefits to the United States.

Resident aliens, like citizens, pay taxes, support the economy, serve in the Armed Forces, and contribute in myriad other ways to our society. And if they choose, they may apply for full membership in the national polity through naturalization. The attachments fostered through these legal mechanisms are all the more intense for LPRs brought to the United States as children. They grow up here as members of the society around them, probably without much touch with their country of citizenship, probably considering the United States as home just as much as a native-born, younger brother or sister entitled to United States citizenship. Many resident aliens have lived in this country longer and established stronger family, social, and economic ties here than some who have become naturalized citizens.

Kim is an example. He moved to the United States at the age of six and was lawfully admitted to permanent residence when he was eight. His mother is a citizen, and his father and brother are LPRs. LPRs in Kim's situation have little or no reason to feel or to establish firm ties with any place besides the United States.

Kim's claim is a limited one: not that the Government may not detain LPRs to ensure their appearance at removal hearings, but that due process under the Fifth Amendment conditions a potentially lengthy detention on a hearing and an impartial decision maker's finding that detention is necessary to a governmental purpose. He thus invokes our repeated decisions that the claim of liberty protected by the Fifth Amendment procedural due process is at its strongest when government seeks to detain an individual. Due process calls for an individual determination before someone is locked away.

In none of our prior cases cited [omitted here], did we ever suggest that the government could avoid the Due Process Clause by doing what § 1226(c) does, by selecting a class of people for confinement on a categorical basis and denying members of that class any chance to dispute the necessity of putting them away.

Due process requires a special justification for physical detention that outweighs the individual's constitutionally protected interest in avoiding physical restraint as well as adequate procedural protections. Finally, procedural due process requires, at a minimum, that a detainee have the benefit of an impartial decisionmaker able to consider particular circumstances on the issue of necessity.

I would affirm the judgment of the Court of Appeals requiring the INS to hold a bail hearing to see whether detention is needed to avoid a risk of flight or a danger to the community. This is surely little enough, given the fact that 8 U.S.C. § 1536 gives an LPR charged with being a foreign terrorist the right to a release hearing pending a determination that he be removed. Although Kim is a convicted criminal, we are not concerned here with a State's interest in punishing those who violate its criminal laws. Kim completed the criminal sentence imposed by the California courts on February 1, 1999, and California no longer has any interest in incarcerating him.

The Court says that § 1226(c) "serves the purpose of preventing deportable criminal aliens from fleeing prior to or during their removal proceedings." Yes it does, and the statute served the purpose of preventing aliens ordered to be deported from fleeing prior to actual deportation. But, the fact that a statute serves its purpose in general fails to justify the detention of an individual in particular. Some individual aliens covered by § 1226(c) have meritorious challenges to removability or claims for relief from removal.

The Court appears to respond that Congress may require detention of removable aliens based on a general conclusion that detention is needed for effective removal of criminal aliens on a class-wide basis. The Court's closest approach to a reason justifying class-wide detention without exception here is a Senate Report stating that over 20% of nondetained criminal aliens failed to appear for removal hearings. To begin with, the Senate Report's statistic treats all criminal aliens alike and does not distinguish between LPRs like Kim, who are likely to have developed strong ties within the United States, and temporary visitors or illegal entrants. Even more importantly, the statistic tells us nothing about flight risk at all because, as both the Court and the Senate Report recognize, the INS was making its custody determinations not on the ground of likelihood of flight or dangerousness, but in large part, according to the number of beds available in a particular region. This meant that the INS often could not detain even the aliens who posed serious flight risks. The INS had only 3,500 detention beds for criminal aliens in the entire country and the INS district comprising Pennsylvania, Delaware, and West Virginia had only 15.

The desperate lack of detention space likewise had led the INS to set bonds too low, because "if the alien is not able to pay, the alien cannot be released, and a needed bed space is lost." The Senate Report also recognized that, even when the INS identifies a criminal alien, the INS "often refuses to take action because of insufficient agents to transport prisoners, or because of limited detention space." Four former high-ranking INS officials explained the Court's statistics as follows: "Flight rates were so high in the early 1990s not as a result of chronic discretionary judgment failures by the INS in assessing which aliens might pose a flight risk. Rather, the rates were alarmingly high because decisions to release aliens in proceedings were driven overwhelmingly by a lack of detention facilities."

Relevant to this case, and largely ignored by the Court, is a recent study conducted at the INS's request concluding that 92% of criminal aliens (most of whom were LPRs) who were released under supervisory conditions attended all of their hearings. Even without supervision, 82% of criminal aliens released on recognizance showed up, as did 77% of those released on bond, leading the reporters to conclude that "supervision was especially effective for criminal aliens" and that "mandatory detention of virtually all criminal aliens is not necessary." In sum, the Court's inapposite statistics do not show that detention of criminal LPRs pending removal proceedings, even on a general level, is necessary to ensure attendance at removal hearings, and the study reinforces the point by establishing the effectiveness of release under supervisory conditions.

The Court's second effort is its claim that mandatory detention under § 1226(c) is generally of a "much shorter duration" than the incarceration at issue in *Zadvydas* [omitted in this excerpt]. While it is true that removal proceedings are unlikely to prove "indefinite and potentially permanent," they are not formally limited to any period, and often extend beyond the time suggested by the Court, that is, "an average time of 47 days" or, for aliens who exercise their right of appeal, "an average of four months." Revealing is an explanation of the raw numbers that are averaged out. As the Solicitor General conceded, the length of the average detention period in great part reflects the fact that the vast majority of cases involve aliens who raise no challenge to removability at all. LPRs like Kim, however, will hardly fit that pattern. Unlike many illegal entrants and temporary nonimmigrants, LPRs are the aliens most likely to press substantial challenges to removability requiring lengthy proceedings. Successful challenges often require several months of proceedings; detention for an open-ended period like this falls far short of the "stringent time limitations" held to be significant in *Salerno* [Chapter 12, pp. 402]. The potential for several months of confinement requires an individualized finding of necessity.

This case is not about the National Government's undisputed power to detain aliens in order to avoid flight or prevent danger to the community. The issue is whether that power may be exercised by detaining a still lawful permanent resident alien when there is no reason for it and no way to challenge it. The Court's holding that the Due Process Clause allows this under a blanket rule is devoid of even ostensible justification in fact and at odds with the settled standard of liberty. I respectfully dissent.

QUESTIONS

1. **Summarize Section 1226(c) of the Immigration and Nationality Act (INA).**
2. **Describe how Section 1226(c) changed prior law.**
3. **According to the majority opinion, why did Congress enact the law?**
4. **Summarize the majority's arguments supporting Kim's detention.**
5. **Summarize the dissent's arguments opposing Kim's detention.**
6. **Which side do you agree with? Support your answer with specific details from the case excerpt and your text.**

Summary

LO 1
- Periods of emergency change the balance between government power and individual liberty to protect people from danger, but the government must give up its extraordinary powers when the emergency is over.

LO 2
- Wars are waged differently in modern times, and the government's use of emergency powers has changed, too, as it monitors citizens to prevent espionage and terrorism.

LO 3
- The Crime Control and Safe Streets Act of 1968 allowed real-time surveillance (Tier 1) during investigations of serious crimes. The Patriot Act allows warrants to be obtained for e-mail and voice message surveillance (Tier 2) and caller ID surveillance (Tier 3) in any criminal investigation without a warrant.

LO 4
- Although sneak-and-peak searches aren't new, their first appearance in statute occurred in the Patriot Act, Section 213. It authorized their use when tangible evidence won't be seized and notifying the resident might affect an investigation.

LO 5
- The Supreme Court denied enemy combatants access to U.S. federal courts in *Johnson v. Eisentrager* (1950). In *Rasul v. Bush* (2004), the Supreme Court held that federal courts may hear petitions from noncitizens detained as enemy combatants at Guantanamo Bay. Congress prevented courts from taking petitions from detainees with the Detainee Treatment Act of 2005 and the Military Commission Act of 2006. But, in *Boumediene v. Bush,* the Supreme Court decided that detainees have a constitutional right to challenge their detainment in federal courts.

LO 5, LO 6
- The Military Order of November 13, 2001, requires that detainees be treated humanely and allowed to exercise their religion. The power to decide whether a citizen or a noncitizen is an unlawful enemy combatant was given to the Combatant Status Review Tribunal (CSRT) by the Executive and Congress, and its role has been upheld by the courts.

LO 6, LO 7
- The interrogation techniques used to gain confessions from ordinary suspects are expanded to include very severe techniques when unlawful combatants are interrogated to prevent further attacks. When and whether to give *Miranda* warnings to persons detained on suspicion of terrorist acts is a hotly debated issue, in part because some may be held as unlawful combatants.

LO 8
- As wealthy, white-collar engineers are recruited successfully and commit terrorist acts, questions arise about the effectiveness of existing strategies for combating foreign extremists.

LO 9
- Persons detained as unlawful combatants face federal court trials according to the nature and seriousness of the offense, the defendant's culpability, and their willingness to cooperate. Federal courts have high conviction rates and traditionally give long sentences in terrorism trials.

LO 9
- Military commissions are established by the president as commander in chief, replace the authority of federal courts in trying noncitizens for terrorist acts, and aren't bound by constitutional requirements.

LO 9
- The "terrorism as war" position emphasizes trial by military commissions, a focus on national security, and secret proceedings that prevent enemies from gaining

intelligence. The "terrorism as crime" position criticizes the untested nature of the military court system and relies on federal courts to gain extradition and access a wider variety of charges and pleas.

LO 10
- The Supreme Court has held that stopping a deportable alien for suspected immigration crimes at a checkpoint is a Fourth Amendment seizure but that the national interest in controlling immigration outweighs the intrusion of a brief detention.

LO 10
- The reasonableness of detaining noncitizens during deportation proceedings depends on the risk of flight and the danger he or she may pose to the community. The Illegal Immigration Reform and Immigration Responsibility Act (IIRIRA) of 1996 requires that the attorney general take into custody any alien who has committed a long list of crimes and deport any alien convicted of serious offenses in their home country.

LO 11
- Proponents of Arizona Immigration Law SB 1070 argue that it's based on existing federal laws and expressly prohibits racial profiling when officers make stops or determine immigration status. Opponents of SB 1070 argue that enforcing it would require racial profiling, open law enforcement to civil lawsuits, and be unfair to legal immigrants pressed for documentation when stopped for other offenses.

Review Questions

1. Identify and describe two limits on government's emergency powers.
2. Summarize the history of criminal procedure in wartime.
3. Identify the difference between the responses to ordinary crime we've studied in previous chapters and the responses to domestic and international terrorism.
4. Describe how our study of antiterrorism laws is limited, and give two reasons for this limitation.
5. What requirement of a constitutional democracy are all federal antiterrorism procedure laws based on?
6. Describe both sides of the argument about the changes in the balance between power and liberty brought about by the September 11, 2001, attacks.
7. Identify three types of personal information not protected from electronic surveillance by the Fourth Amendment.
8. According to the U.S. Supreme Court, why aren't they protected?
9. Identify and describe the three tiers of the surveillance system designed to balance government power and individual privacy. Include in your description both government powers and the limits on that power in each tier.
10. How, if at all, has the Patriot Act modified this balance?
11. What were "sneak and peek" searches originally used for, and how has their legal status and definition changed since 9/11?
12. List and describe the three conditions under which the Patriot Act authorizes judges to issue sneak-and-peek warrants.
13. Summarize the two sides of the argument over sneak-and-peek warrants that followed passage of the Patriot Act.

14. How are lawful enemy combatants distinguished from unlawful enemy combatants?

15. What reasons did the U.S. Supreme Court give for denying German combatants in Japan access to U.S. federal courts after World War II?

16. Describe how the court's opinion on habeas corpus rights for detainees changed under *Rasul v. Bush,* and summarize the reasons they gave for that change.

17. Explain how Congress has responded to the Supreme Court expanding habeas corpus rights to Guantanamo Bay detainees.

18. Describe how habeas corpus rights changed after *Boumediene v. Bush.*

19. Describe how Abdul Farouk Abdulmutallab's Christmas attack differs from past incidents and how views of "terrorism as war" and "terrorism as crime" are affected by his case.

20. Identify and describe the two kinds of proceedings for the trial of suspected terrorists.

21. Identify the sources of authority for the Military Order of November 13, 2001, and describe the jurisdiction of military commissions created by the order.

22. How do the constitutional requirements that apply to Article III (ordinary) criminal courts differ from those of military commissions?

23. List and summarize the major provisions in the Military Commissions Act of 2006. Sort them according to the power of the government and the rights of the accused.

24. List some factors the court considered when judging whether one immigration checkpoint met constitutional requirements to balance personal privacy with government need.

25. Distinguish between the rights we give an illegal immigrant detained on suspicion of crimes in the United States and the rights of an immigrant detained on suspicion of having a criminal record overseas.

26. Identify two major considerations in deciding whether to detain noncitizens during noncriminal deportation proceedings.

27. How did the Immigration and Nationality Act affect detainment during deportation proceedings?

28. How did the Illegal Immigration Reform and Immigration Responsibility Act affect detention during criminal deportation proceedings?

29. Explain the connection between Arizona's Immigration Law SB 1070 and existing federal laws.

30. What concerns have law enforcement officers expressed about enforcing Arizona's Immigration Law SB 1070 effectively and fairly?

Key Terms

Selected Amendments of the Constitution of the United States

Amendment IV

The right of the people to be secure in their persons, houses, papers, and effects, against unreasonable searches and seizures, shall not be violated, and no Warrants shall issue, but upon probable cause, supported by Oath or affirmation, and particularly describing the place to be searched, and the persons or things to be seized.

Amendment V

No person shall be held to answer for a capital, or otherwise infamous crime, unless on a presentment or indictment of a Grand Jury, except in cases arising in the land or naval forces, or in the Militia, when in actual service in time of War or public danger; nor shall any person be subject for the same offence to be twice put in jeopardy of life or limb; nor shall be compelled in any criminal case to be a witness against himself, nor be deprived of life, liberty, or property, without due process of law; nor shall private property be taken for public use, without just compensation.

Amendment VI

In all criminal prosecutions, the accused shall enjoy the right to a speedy and public trial, by an impartial jury of the State and district wherein the crime shall have been committed, which district shall have been previously ascertained by law, and to be informed of the nature and cause of the accusation; to be confronted with the witnesses against him; to have compulsory process for obtaining witnesses in his favor, and to have the Assistance of Counsel for his defence.

Amendment VIII

Excessive bail shall not be required, nor excessive fines imposed, nor cruel and unusual punishments inflicted.

Amendment XIV

Passed by Congress June 13, 1866. Ratified July 9, 1868.

Section 1 All persons born or naturalized in the United States, and subject to the jurisdiction thereof, are citizens of the United States and of the State wherein they reside. No State shall make or enforce any law which shall abridge the privileges or immunities of citizens of the United States; nor shall any State deprive any person of life, liberty, or property, without due process of law; nor deny to any person within its jurisdiction the equal protection of the laws.

absolute immunity the absence of liability for actions within the scope of duties; judges have it.

accusatory stage of the criminal process the point at which the criminal process focuses on a specific suspect.

accusatory system rationale a system in which the government bears the burden of proof.

acquisition of memory information the brain takes in at the time of the crime.

actual authority (subjective) third-party consent third-party consent searches aren't valid unless the person consenting had actual authority to consent for another person.

actual imprisonment standard offenses that don't actually result in prison sentences.

actual prejudice test courts have to decide whether jurors were in fact prejudiced by harmful publicity.

actual seizures when officers physically grab individuals with the intent to keep them from leaving.

administrative sentencing model a sentencing structure in which parole boards and prison administrators determine the exact release date within sentences prescribed by legislatures and judges.

affidavit a sworn statement under oath to the facts and circumstances amounting to probable cause.

affirmative defense a defense, such as self-defense or insanity, that requires defendants to present facts that support their innocence in addition to denying the charge.

affirmed an appellate court decision upholding the decision of a lower court.

agency source of third-party consent authority consent by someone authorized to consent for someone else.

amicus curiae brief brief filed in court by someone interested in, but not a party to, the case.

Antiterrorism and Effective Death Penalty Act (AEDPA) limits the use of federal habeas corpus law by both state and federal prisoners, whether they're on death row or imprisoned for any length of time.

apparent authority (objective) third-party consent individuals who it's reasonable to believe (but in fact don't) have authority to consent to a search.

appellant the party appealing in an appellate court case.

appellate court case case in which a lower court has already taken some action and one of the parties has asked a higher court to review the lower court's action.

appellee the party appealed against in an appellate court case.

appointed counsel lawyers for people who can't afford to hire lawyers.

Apprendi **bright-line rule** other than a prior conviction, any fact that increases the penalty for a crime beyond the prescribed statutory maximum must be submitted to a jury and proved beyond a reasonable doubt.

archival research consists of analyzing real procedures used in actual criminal cases.

arraignment to bring defendants to court to answer the criminal charges against them.

arrest officers take suspects to the police station and keep them there against their will.

Article III courts regular federal courts whose authority comes from Article III of the U.S. Constitution, which created the judiciary.

articulable facts facts officers can name to back up their stops of citizens.

assumption of risk source of third-party consent authority consenting party takes the chance that someone else might consent for her.

555

attenuation exception illegally seized evidence is admissible in court if the poisonous connection between illegal police actions and the evidence they illegally got from their actions weakens enough.

Authorization for Use of Military Force (AUMF) joint resolution of Congress passed following the September 11 attacks, supporting the president's war power to use "all necessary and appropriate force."

authorized imprisonment standard offenses where imprisonment is authorized but not required.

"bad methods" using unconstitutional means to obtain evidence.

Bail Reform Act of 1984 authorizes federal courts to jail arrested defendants when a judge determines, after a hearing, that no condition of release would "reasonably" guarantee the appearance of the defendant and the safety of the community.

balancing element the need to search and/or seize outweighs the invasion of individual liberty and/or privacy.

bench trials trials without juries, in which judges find the facts.

bind over to decide to send a case to trial.

bind-over standard enough evidence exists for the judge in a preliminary hearing to decide to send the case to trial.

bite-and-hold technique technique in which a police dog given a "find" command will find, "bite," and "hold" a suspect until commanded to release.

blind administrator a person conducting a lineup who doesn't know which person in the lineup is the suspect.

blue curtain wall of protection that hides "real" police work from public view.

border search exception searches at international borders are reasonable without probable cause or warrants, because the government interest in what and who enters the country outweighs the invasion of privacy of persons entering.

bounded rationality strongly documented finding that people don't "attempt to ruthlessly maximize utility"; instead, once they identify an option that's "good enough," they stop looking and choose it.

briefing a case putting a case summary into a format that will help you in class, for review, and to compare and contrast it with other cases.

"bright-line" rules rules that spell out officers' power and apply to all cases rather than assessing the totality of circumstances on a case-by-case basis.

broad interpretation (of habeas corpus) view that courts should review all claims that persons are being detained in violation of their fundamental liberties.

case-by-case basis deciding whether constitutional requirements were satisfied in each case.

case citation tells where you can find the published report of a case.

case-in-chief the part of the trial where the government presents its evidence to prove the defendants' guilt.

categorical suspicion refers to suspicion that falls on suspects because they fit into a broad category of people, such as being in a particular location, being members of a particular race or ethnicity, or fitting a profile.

cautionary instruction instruction in which judges explain the weaknesses of eyewitness identification evidence to juries.

certiorari Latin for "to be certified," it's a discretionary order of the Supreme Court to review a lower court decision.

challenges for cause removal of prospective jurors upon showing their partiality.

charge bargaining bargaining for a reduction in either the number or severity of criminal charges.

charge the grand jury the address of the judge to the grand jury.

charging by information prosecutors charge defendants directly rather than having grand juries indict them.

citation an order to appear before a judge on a certain date to defend against a charge, often a traffic violation.

citation release defendants charged with petty offenses can receive this type of ticket and be released without even appearing before a judge.

civil action a noncriminal case.

civil law remedy against constitutional violations that involves suing the officer, the police department, or the government.

Civil Rights Act actions lawsuits initiated by private individuals in federal court against state officers for violating the individuals' constitutional rights; also called § 1983 actions.

class action an action in which one person or a small group of people represent the interests of a larger group.

clear and convincing evidence more than probable cause but less than proof beyond a reasonable doubt.

collateral attack a proceeding to review the constitutionality of detention or imprisonment.

collateral consequences exception the principle that cases aren't moot if conviction can still cause legal consequences despite completion of the sentence.

collateral proceedings proceedings "off to the side" of the main case (for example, grand jury proceedings and bail hearings).

collateral-use exception allows the use of illegally obtained evidence in nontrial proceedings.

compliant confessions mere acts of public compliance by a suspect who comes to believe that the short-term benefits of confession outweigh the long-term costs.

compulsory process for obtaining witnesses Sixth Amendment guarantee of defendants' right to compel the appearance of witnesses in their favor.

concurring opinion statements in which justices agree with the decision but not the reasoning of a court's opinion.

confession suspect's written or oral acknowledgement of guilt, often including details about the crime.

consent searches searches the government can prove by the totality of the circumstances suspects consented to don't require probable cause or warrants.

constitutional democracy the balance between the power of government and the rights of individuals.

constitutionalism refers to the idea that constitutions adopted by the whole people are a higher form of law than ordinary laws passed by legislatures.

constitutional question court's action that decides what happens to the defendant and to the government.

constitutional right justification the idea that the exclusionary rule is an essential part of constitutional rights.

constitutional tort a private right to sue federal officers for violations of plaintiffs' constitutional rights.

constitutional tort (*Bivens*) actions lawsuits against individual federal law enforcement officers.

contemporaneous with arrest also called "incident to arrest," it includes the time before, during, and after arrest.

conventional Fourth Amendment approach the warrant and reasonableness clauses are firmly connected, according to the U.S. Supreme Court, when ruling on stop-and-frisk law cases.

corporal punishment physical punishment, such as whipping.

counsel pro bono lawyers willing to represent clients at no charge.

court opinions written explanation for a court's decision.

courts-martial military courts made up of military officers to try members of the U.S. armed forces for violating the Uniform Code of Military Justice.

Crime Control and Safe Streets Act of 1968 provides for a general ban on the interception of "wire, oral, or electronic communications" while they're taking place.

criminal complaint the formal charging document.

criminal information a written formal charge made by prosecutors without a grand jury indictment.

criminal law remedy against official misconduct that involves suing the officer.

critical stages in criminal prosecutions includes all those stages that occur after the government files formal charges; the view that custodial interrogation is so important in criminal prosecutions that during it suspects have a right to a lawyer.

critical stages of criminal proceedings see *critical stages in criminal prosecutions*.

curtilage the area immediately surrounding a house, such as garages, patios, and pools, aren't part of the open fields doctrine.

custodial arrest an official taking a person into custody and holding her to answer criminal charges.

custodial interrogation the questioning that occurs after the police have taken suspects into custody.

custody depriving people of their "freedom of action in any significant way."

damages a remedy in private lawsuits in the form of money for injuries.

deadly force constraint capable of producing death.

decision to charge the prosecutor's decision to begin formal proceedings against a suspect.

defense of entrapment defense to criminal liability based on proof that the government induced the defendant to commit a crime she wouldn't have committed otherwise.

defense of official immunity a public official charged by law with duties calling for discretionary decision making isn't personally liable to an individual except for willful or malicious wrongdoing.

defense of vicarious official immunity police departments and local governments can claim the official immunity of their employees.

"deliberately eliciting a response" test the test for interrogation focuses on police intent.

departure judge imposes a sentence outside of sentencing guidelines.

deportable alien a person who has been found deportable by an immigration judge or who admits his deportability upon questioning by official agents.

Detainee Treatment Act of 2005 (DTA) amended the Habeas Corpus Act to strip federal courts of jurisdiction over habeas petitions filed by Guantanamo Bay detainees.

determinate sentencing see *fixed sentencing*.

deterrence justification the justification that excluding evidence obtained in violation of the Constitution prevents illegal law enforcement.

direct attack appeal attacking directly decisions made by trial courts.

directed verdict rule enough evidence exists to decide a case without submitting it to the jury.

direct information information that officers know firsthand, acquired directly through their physical senses.

direct information in probable cause to arrest firsthand information known to arresting officers through what they see, hear, feel, taste, and smell.

discovery a legal action asking a court order to compel one side in a case to turn over information that might help the other side.

discretionary appeal allowing appeals only in cases the U.S. Supreme Court or the state supreme courts decide are of significance beyond the interests of the particular defendants appealing them.

discretionary decision making informal decision making by professionals based on their training and experience and unwritten rules.

discriminatory effect proving that race or some other illegal group characteristic (not a legitimate criterion, such as seriousness of the offense or criminal record) accounts for the official decision.

discriminatory purpose a named official in the case at hand intended to discriminate against a named individual because of race or other illegal criteria.

dismissal without prejudice the termination of a case with the provision that it can be prosecuted again.

dismissal with prejudice the termination of a case with the provision that it can't be prosecuted again.

dissenting opinion part of an appellate court case in which justices write opinions disagreeing with the decision and reasoning of a court.

distinguishing cases a court decides that a prior decision doesn't apply to the current case because the facts are different.

diversion cases prosecutors agree to drop a case before formal judicial proceedings begin if suspects participate in specified programs (for example, community service, restitution, substance abuse, or family violence treatment).

DNA profiling a special type of DNA pattern that distinguishes one individual from all others.

doctrine of judicial economy rule that says that time and money shouldn't be spent on appeals defendants could've avoided by objecting during the trial.

doctrine of *respondeat superior* employers are legally liable for their employees' illegal acts.

doctrine of sovereign immunity governments can't be sued by individuals without the consent of the government.

double jeopardy constitutional protection against being subject to liability for the same offense more than once.

drug courier profile lists of characteristics that drug traffickers are supposed to possess.

dual sovereignty doctrine the principle that holds that a crime arising out of the same facts in one state isn't the same crime in another state.

due process a broad and vague guarantee of fair procedures in deciding cases; the Fifth and Fourteenth Amendment provisions prohibiting the federal government and the states, respectively, from depriving citizens of life, liberty, or property without due process of law.

due process approach to confessions confessions must be voluntary; involuntary confessions violate due process, not because they're compelled but because they might not be true.

due process revolution U.S. Supreme Court application of the Bill of Rights to state criminal proceedings.

emergency searches also called *"exigent circumstance searches"*; are based on the idea that it's sometimes impractical (even dangerous) to require officers to obtain warrants before they search.

en banc see *en banc review*.

en banc review a hearing by all the judges on the Court.

encouragement a widely used undercover police tactic directed mainly at consensual crimes, such as official corruption, and crimes without complaining victims, such as illegal drugs, pornography, and prostitution.

enemy intelligence gathering all kinds of information (not just criminal evidence) about enemies.

equal protection state officials can't investigate, apprehend, convict, and punish people for unacceptable reasons.

errors of commission a *retrieval of memory* error, such as picking an innocent person in a photo array.

errors of omission a *retrieval of memory* error, such as failure to recall some detail or to recognize a perpetrator.

exclusionary rule the rule that illegally seized evidence can't be admitted in criminal trials.

exigent circumstances circumstances requiring prompt action, eliminating the warrant requirement for a search.

experimental research researchers *create* crimes (live staged or videotaped) that unsuspecting people witness, then question them about what they witnessed and show them a lineup.

express waiver test the suspect specifically says or writes that she knows her rights, knows she's giving them up, and knows the consequences of giving them up.

external review review of complaints against police officers with participation by individuals who aren't sworn police officers.

eyewitness recall information retrieved from memory at the time of the lineup, show-up, or picture identification; eyewitnesses are given hints, such as a time frame, and then asked to report what they observed.

eyewitness recognition information retrieved from memory at the time of the lineup, show-up, or picture identification; eyewitnesses are shown persons or objects and then asked to indicate whether they were involved in the crime.

eyewitness retrospective self-reports witnesses' in-court recollections.

fact bargaining the prosecutor agrees not to challenge the defendant's version of the facts or not to reveal aggravating facts to the judge.

factual basis for guilty pleas judges might ask defendants to describe the conduct that led to the charges, ask the prosecutor and defense attorney similar questions, and consult presentence reports to determine whether the facts support a guilty plea.

factually innocent the defendant didn't commit the crime.

federal crime of terrorism an offense calculated to influence or affect the conduct of government by intimidation or coercion or to retaliate against government conduct.

Federal Jury Selection and Service Act requires that juries be "selected at random from a fair cross section of the community in the district or division wherein the court convenes" and forbids exclusion based on race, color, religion, sex, national origin, or economic status.

federal rights floor minimum standards set by the U.S. Constitution.

Federal Tort Claims Act (FTCA) actions lawsuits against the federal government for their officers' constitutional torts.

fillers persons known to be innocent who participate in a line-up.

find-and-bark technique technique in which dogs are trained to find suspects and then bark until officers can get control of the suspect.

first appearance the appearance of a defendant in court for determination of probable cause, determination of bail, assignment of an attorney, and notification of rights; also called a "probable cause hearing."

fixed (determinate) sentencing sentences that fit the punishment to the crime.

formal decision making consists of decisions made according to the law of criminal procedure—namely, the rules spelled out in the Constitution, judicial opinions, laws, other written sources, and cases.

Fourth Amendment frisks once-over-lightly pat downs of outer clothing by officers to protect themselves by taking away suspects' weapons.

Fourth Amendment stops brief, on-the-spot detentions that freeze suspicious situations so that law enforcement officers can determine whether to arrest, investigate further, or terminate further action.

free will rationale involuntary confessions aren't just unreliable and contrary to the accusatory system of justice; they're also coerced if they're not "the product of a rational intellect and a free will."

fruit-of-the-poisonous-tree doctrine the principle that evidence derived from illegally obtained sources isn't admissible.

"functional equivalent of a question" test interrogation refers not only to express questioning but also to any words or actions that the police should know are reasonably likely to elicit an incriminating response from the suspect.

functional immunity whether prosecutors have immunity depends on the function they're performing at the time of their misconduct.

fundamental attribution error tendency of juries to overestimate the role of defendants' "nature" (disposition) in evaluating their actions, while they underestimate the role of the interrogation situation.

fundamental fairness doctrine due process is a command to the states to provide two basics of a fair trial: notice and a hearing.

general warrant empowered royal agents of the English Crown to search anyone, anywhere, anytime.

"good" evidence probative evidence, or proof of guilt.

"good faith" defense officers can't be held personally liable for their actions if they acted according to rules clearly established at the time of their actions; also called "qualified immunity."

good-faith exception searches conducted by officers with warrants they honestly and reasonably believe satisfy the Fourth Amendment requirements.

grabbable area searchable area that includes the arrestee's person and area within his reach.

graduated objective basis requirement the greater the government invasion, the more facts required to back it up.

grand jurors members of the grand jury.

grand jury review a secret proceeding to test a government case.

"great writ of liberty" refers to the use of habeas corpus during the 19th century.

habeas corpus Latin for "you have the body," it's an action that asks those who hold defendants to justify their detention.

habeas corpus proceedings civil action, also called "collateral attack," brought by defendants attacking the lawfulness of their detention.

hands-off approach to sentencing procedures U.S. Supreme Court policy of leaving decisions about the way sentences were determined to trial judges.

hearsay information facts and circumstances officers learn secondhand from victims, witnesses, other police officers, and anonymous, professional, or paid informants.

hearsay rule in arrests courts don't admit secondhand evidence to prove guilt, but, if it's reliable and truthful, they'll accept it to show probable cause to arrest.

hearsay testimony evidence from witnesses that they don't know firsthand.

holding of the court the holding refers to the legal rule the court applied to the facts of the cases.

hung jury a jury that's unable to reach a verdict after protracted deliberations.

Illegal Immigration Reform and Immigrant Responsibility Act (IIRIRA) of 1996 amended the *INA* to provide that "the Attorney General *shall* take into custody any alien who" has committed crimes specified within the act.

Immigration and Nationality Act (INA) authorized the U.S. attorney general, in his or her discretion, to detain suspected deportable aliens to make sure they're available for deportation proceedings and to reduce the danger to the community.

impeach to show that a witness's credibility is suspect.

implied waiver test the totality of circumstances in each case adds up to proof that before suspects talked they knew they had the right to remain silent and knew they were giving up the right.

incident to arrest sometimes called "contemporaneous with arrest," it includes the time before, during, and after arrest.

incorporation doctrine the principle that the Fourteenth Amendment due process clause incorporates the provisions of the Bill of Rights and applies them to state criminal procedure.

incriminating statements statements that fall short of full confessions.

independent source exception evidence is admissible even if police officers violate the Constitution to obtain it if in a totally separate action, they obtain the same evidence lawfully.

indeterminate sentencing tailoring punishment to suit the criminal; sentencing that relies heavily on the discretion of judges and parole boards in exercising sentencing authority.

indictment a formal criminal charge issued by a grand jury.

indigence financial hardship in which defendants can't afford an attorney.

indigent defendants defendants too poor to hire their own lawyers.

individualized suspicion suspicion that points to specific individuals and consists of "facts that would tell both the officer on the street and a court ruling on a suppression motion whether or not there was reasonable suspicion."

inevitable discovery exception evidence obtained illegally is admissible if officers would've legally discovered it eventually.

inherently coercive custodial interrogation is coercive because police hold suspects in strange surroundings while trying to crack their will, and suspects don't have anyone there to support them.

in loco parentis the principle by which the government stands in place of parents; school administrators are substitute parents while students are in school and have the legal authority to search students and their stuff during school hours and activities.

interlocutory appeal an appeal that takes place before the trial court rules on the case.

internal affairs units (IAU) review review of police misconduct by special officers inside police departments.

internal and external departmental review remedy against official misconduct that involves disciplining the officer outside the judicial system.

internalized false confessions innocent, but vulnerable, suspects under "highly suggestive interrogation tactics," come not just to give in to get the situation over with but to believe that they actually committed the crime.

interrogation police questioning suspects while holding them against their will, usually in a police station but sometimes in other places; has constitutional significance in the Fourth, Fifth, and Fourteenth Amendments; in each eliciting a response from a suspect can invoke rights under the amendment.

inventory searches searches conducted without probable cause or warrants to protect property and the safety of police and to prevent claims against police.

Johnson v. Eisentrager **(1950)** the case that the U.S. Supreme Court relied on in all of the leading detention cases.

judgment the final outcome of a case.

judgment (disposition) of the case see *judgment*.

judicial integrity justification the idea that the honor and honesty of the courts justify the exclusionary rule.

judicial review courts, and ultimately the U.S. Supreme Court, *not* the Congress and *not* the president, have the final word on what the Constitution means.

judicial sentencing model a structure in which judges prescribe sentences within broad contours set by legislative acts.

jurisdiction the power to hear and decide cases in a specific geographical area (such as a county, a state, or a federal district) or the subject matter (for example, criminal appeals) the court controls.

jury instructions instructions from the judge to the jury on what the law is and how they should apply it.

jury nullification the jury's authority to reach a not guilty verdict despite proof of guilt.

jury panel potential jurors drawn from the list of eligible citizens not excused.

key-man system jury lists are made up by civic and political leaders selected from individuals they know personally or by reputation.

knock-and-announce rule the practice of law enforcement officers knocking and announcing their presence before entering a home to search it.

lawful enemy combatant a member of the regular forces, militia, volunteer corps, or organized resistance movement of a state party engaged in hostilities against the United States that wears a fixed distinctive sign recognizable at a distance, carries their arms openly, and abides by the *laws of war.*

law of criminal procedure the rules that government has to follow to detect and investigate crimes, apprehend suspects, prosecute and convict defendants, and punish criminals.

laws of war rules written, understood, and agreed to by almost all the countries fighting the wars.

legally guilty cases in which the government has proved beyond a reasonable doubt the guilt of defendants.

legislative sentencing model a structure in which legislatures exercise sentencing authority.

liberty the right of citizens to come and go as they please (locomotion) without government interference.

lineup an identification procedure in which the suspect stands in a line with other individuals.

majority opinion a decision rendered by five or more Supreme Court justices, which becomes the law.

mandatory minimum sentences the legislatively prescribed, nondiscretionary amount of prison time that all offenders convicted of the offense must serve.

manifest necessity doctrine the government can reprosecute a defendant for the same offense if the judge dismissed the case or ordered a mistrial because dismissal "served the ends of justice."

memory experts scientists whose profession is providing empirical demonstrations of how memory actually functions.

might-or-might-not-be-present instruction one of the ways to improve the reliability of eyewitness identification of strangers is to tell witnesses the suspect might or might not be among the photos or members of a lineup.

military commissions non–Article III courts, consisting of a panel of military officers acting under military authority to try enemy combatants for war crimes.

Military Commissions Act of 2006 stripped all federal courts of jurisdiction over all habeas petitions filed by Guantanamo Bay detainees regardless of when it was filed, limiting detainees to the review process set up in the *Detainees Treatment Act (DTA).*

Military Order of November 13, 2001 president's order defining who could be detained following September 11, 2001, and prescribing the conditions of their detention.

military tribunals see *military commissions.*

missing witness instruction instruction that jurors can infer that the witness's testimony would have been unfavorable to the prosecution.

mockery of justice standard the standard under which counsel is deemed ineffective only if circumstances reduced the trial to a farce.

Model Code of Pre-Arraignment Procedure American Law Institute's (group of distinguished judges, lawyers, criminal justice professionals, law enforcement professionals, and scholars) model of criminal procedure law for law enforcement and courts.

money bonds can be unsecured, a court-administered deposit, or privately administered, and defendants are released as soon as money is put up.

mootness doctrine ban on appeals by offenders who have finished their prison sentences or paid their fines.

moral seriousness standard the principle that the Sixth Amendment right to a jury trial extends to morally serious misdemeanors.

narrow interpretation (of habeas corpus) power to review only the jurisdiction of the court over the person and the subject matter of the case.

natural law a body of unchanging moral principles regarded as a basis for all human conduct.

negotiated guilty plea a plea of guilty in exchange for a concession to the defendant by the government.

neutral magistrate a disinterested judge who decides whether there's probable cause before officers arrest suspects.

no-affirmative-duty-to-protect rule plaintiffs can't sue individual officers or government units for failing to stop private people from violating their rights.

nolo contendere Latin for defendants who plead "no contest," meaning they don't contest the issue of guilt or innocence.

noncriminal (civil) deportation proceedings hearings to decide whether an alien is deportable.

nonsearch-related plain view refers to plain view that doesn't involve a Fourth Amendment intrusion at all.

nontrial proceedings proceedings related to the case but not the trial of the case, including bail hearings, preliminary hearings, grand jury proceedings, and some kinds of habeas corpus proceedings.

objective basis the factual justification for government invasions of individual privacy, liberty, and property.

objective basis requirement facts, not hunches, have to back up government invasions of individual liberty and privacy.

objective privacy whether the subjective expectation of privacy is "one that society is prepared to recognize as 'reasonable.'"

objective standard of reasonable force the Fourth Amendment permits officers to use the amount of force necessary to apprehend and bring suspects under control.

objective test of entrapment focuses on whether the actions of government agents would induce a hypothetical reasonable person to commit crimes.

officers of the court part of the dual role of prosecutors in our criminal justice system, in which their mission is to do justice.

open fields doctrine the rule that the Fourth Amendment doesn't prevent government officials from gathering and using information they see, hear, smell, or touch in open fields.

opening statements addresses to the jury by the prosecution and defense counsel before they present their evidence.

parallel rights state-granted rights similar to those in the U.S. Constitution and Bill of Rights.

particularity requirement the requirement that a warrant must identify the person or place to be searched and the items or persons to be seized.

pen register telephone company lists of the phone numbers of outgoing calls from a particular telephone number.

peremptory challenges removal of jurors without showing cause.

per se approach looking at the totality of circumstances to determine whether an identification should be admitted into evidence.

per se rule often called a *"bright-line rule."*

petitioner a defendant in a noncriminal case who asks a higher court to review a decision made either by a lower court or some other official.

petitions the court asks the court for a review of facts.

photo array witnesses try to pick the suspect from one (photo show-up) or several (photo lineup) mug shots.

plain-error rule review of convictions should take place only when "plain errors affecting substantial rights" cause "manifest injustice or miscarriage of justice."

plaintiff the party who brings a civil action.

plain view doctrine doctrine that it's not a "search" to discover evidence inadvertently obtained through ordinary senses if the officers are where they have a right to be and are doing what they have a right to do.

plea bargaining in the "shadow of trial" model prosecutors, judges, and defense attorneys act rationally to forecast the outcome of a trial, then make bargains that leave both sides better off by splitting the costs they save by not going to trial.

plea bargaining outside the "shadow of trial" model the real world of plea bargaining, in which legally irrelevant factors sometimes skew the fair allocation of punishment and some defendants strike skewed bargains.

plurality opinion a statement in which the greatest number, but not a majority, of the justices favor a court's decision.

precedent a prior decision that's binding on a similar present case.

prejudice prong the second of a two-prong test of reasonable competence, in which defendants have to show that bad "lawyering" deprived them of a fair trial with a reliable result.

preliminary hearing the adversary proceeding that tests the government's case.

preponderance of the evidence more evidence than not supports a conclusion.

Presidential Proclamation 7463 proclamation declaring a national emergency by reason of the terrorist attacks of September 11, 2001.

presumption of guilt the reduction of rights of convicted offenders during sentencing, appeal, and habeas corpus processes.

presumption of regularity presumes government actions are lawful in the absence of "clear evidence to the contrary."

pretext arrests arrests for one offense where probable cause exists motivated by officers' desire to search for evidence of another unrelated offense where probable cause doesn't exist.

pretrial motions written or oral requests asking the court to decide questions that don't require a trial to be ruled on.

preventive detention confining defendants to jail before conviction because they're a threat to public safety.

prima facie case see *prima facie case rule.*

prima facie case rule enough evidence exists to make a decision unless the evidence is contradicted.

privacy the value that's sometimes referred to as "the right to be let alone from government invasions."

privacy doctrine the doctrine that holds that the Fourth Amendment protects persons, not places, when persons have an expectation of privacy that society is prepared to recognize.

probable cause to arrest requires that an officer, in the light of her training and experience, knows enough facts and circumstances to reasonably believe that a crime has been, is being, or is about to be committed and the person arrested has committed, is committing, or is about to commit the crime.

probable cause to bind over higher than the standard for probable cause to arrest, the objective basis for requiring a suspect to stand trial.

probable cause to detain a suspect the objective basis for detaining a suspect following arrest.

probable cause to go to trial requires a higher objective basis than probable cause to detain and is tested by a preliminary hearing or grand jury review.

probative evidence evidence that proves (or at least helps to prove) defendants committed the crimes they're charged with.

procedural due process guarantee of fair procedures for deciding cases.

procedural history of a case a brief description of the procedural steps and judgments (decisions) made by each court that has heard the case.

profiles popular law enforcement tool that consist of lists of circumstances that might, or might not, be linked to particular kinds of behavior.

property source of third-party consent authority consent based on the property interest of the consenting party.

prophylactic rule mechanisms that aren't themselves constitutional rights but are used to guarantee those rights.

proportionality principle a punishment is cruel and unusual if its harshness is "grossly disproportionate" to the "gravity of the offense."

public defender permanently employed defense lawyers paid for at public expense.

public safety exception the rule that *Miranda* warnings need not be administered if doing so would endanger the public.

qualified immunity grants immunity from tort actions if the party was acting reasonably within the scope of his or her duties; also called the *"good faith" defense.*

quantum of proof the amount of evidence backing up a government invasion.

raise-or-waive doctrine the rule that defendants must raise and preserve objections to errors at trial or waive their right to appeal the errors.

reasonable doubt standard due process requires both federal and state prosecutors to prove every element of a crime beyond a reasonable doubt.

reasonable expectation of privacy the kind of expectation any citizen might have with respect to any other citizen applies to law enforcement as well.

reasonable-likelihood-of-prejudice test the determination that circumstances may prevent a fair trial.

reasonable manner of arrest requirement to satisfy the Fourth Amendment, arrests have to be executed in a way that's reasonable.

reasonableness clause the clause in the Fourth Amendment that bans "unreasonable searches and seizures" as opposed to the "warrant clause," which outlines the requirements for obtaining arrest and search warrants.

reasonableness Fourth Amendment approach the warrant and the reasonableness parts of the Fourth Amendment are separate elements that address separate problems.

reasonableness prong defendants have to prove that their lawyer's performance wasn't reasonably competent, meaning that the lawyer was so deficient that she "was not functioning as the 'counsel' guaranteed the defendant by the Sixth Amendment."

reasonableness test the reasonableness of searches and seizures depends on balancing government and individual interests and the objective basis of the searches and seizures.

"reasonable person would not feel free to leave" definition of seizure standard used by most courts to determine whether a person was "seized" by law enforcement.

reasonable suspicion the totality of articulable facts and circumstances that would lead an officer, in the light of her training and experience, to suspect that a crime might be afoot.

reasonably competent attorney standard performance measured by customary skills and diligence.

reasoning of the court the reasoning refers to the reasons and arguments the court gives to support its holding.

relative judgment witnesses select the person in the lineup who looks most like the culprit.

release on recognizance (ROR) release from custody on a mere promise to appear.

reliability rationale for due process the justification for reviewing state confessions based on their untrustworthiness.

reliability test of eyewitness evidence allows the admission of identification evidence based on "unnecessarily suggestive" identification procedures *unless* defendants can prove that the suggestive procedure creates a "very substantial likelihood of misidentification."

remanded the appellate court sent the case back to the lower court for further action.

res judicata once a matter is decided it cannot be reopened.

retained counsel a lawyer paid for by the client.

retention of memory information the brain stores between the time of the crime and the lineup, show-up, or picture identification.

retrieval of memory information retrieved from memory at the time of the lineup, show-up, or picture identification.

reversed the appellate court set aside, or nullified, the lower court's judgment.

reversible error an error that requires an appellate court to reverse the trial court's judgment in the case.

right of habeas corpus the right to a civil action to determine if the offender is being lawfully detained.

right of locomotion the freedom to come and go as we please.

right-to-counsel approach relies on the clause in the Sixth Amendment that guarantees the right to a lawyer in "all criminal prosecutions."

roadblocks stopping everyone who passes a point on a road during a specific time period.

Robinson **rule** *bright-line rule* that officers can always search anyone they're authorized to take into custody.

routine-procedure limit inventory searches are reasonable if officers follow department guidelines in conducting them.

rule of four the requirement that four Supreme Court justices must vote to review a case for its appeal to be heard by the Supreme Court.

searches incident to arrest a search made of a lawfully arrested suspect without probable cause or warrant.

search-related plain view refers to items in plain view that officers discover while they're searching for items for which they're specifically authorized to search.

secret "caller ID" the power of government to capture a record of all telephone numbers (not conversations) from a subscriber's phone in the investigation of "any crime."

§ 1983 actions lawsuits brought by private individuals against law enforcement officers under § 1983 of the U.S. Civil Rights Act.

selective incorporation doctrine some of the Bill of Rights is incorporated in due process, and states must follow these procedures as defined by the U.S. Supreme Court.

selective prosecution lack of resources leads prosecutors to base decisions to charge on priorities.

sentence bargaining a favorable sentence recommendation by the prosecutor to the judge, or bargaining directly with the judge for a favorable sentence.

sentencing guidelines a narrow range of penalties established by a commission within which judges are supposed to choose a specific sentence.

sequential presentation present members of a lineup one at a time and require witnesses to answer "yes" or "no" as they're presented.

serious crime exception provides for an exception for serious crimes to the Crime Control and Safe Streets Act's general ban on the interception of "wire, oral, or electronic communications" in real time, or while they're taking place.

show-of-authority seizures take place when officers display their authority by ordering suspects to stop, drawing their weapons, or otherwise acting such that a reasonable person wouldn't feel free to leave.

show-up a procedure in which the witness identifies the suspect without other possible suspects present.

simultaneous presentation a traditional lineup, in which members are standing together at the same time, giving witnesses the opportunity to treat the procedure like a multiple-choice test with a "best," but maybe not "right," answer.

Sixth Amendment confrontation clause the right to cross-examine the prosecution's witnesses.

sneak-and-peek searches a variation of no-knock entries in which officers enter private places without the owner or (occupant) consenting or even knowing about it.

sneak-and-peek search warrants warrants that allow officers to enter private places without the owner or (occupant) consenting or knowing about it.

social cost of the rule the exclusionary rule might free guilty people and undermine the prosecution's case by keeping good evidence out of court.

special-needs searches government inspections and other regulatory measures not conducted to gather criminal evidence.

special-relationship exception exception to the *no-affirmative-duty-to-protect rule,* which says that governments have a duty to protect individuals they hold in custody.

stare decisis the doctrine in which a prior decision binds a present case with similar facts.

state-created-danger exception exception to the *no-affirmative-duty-to-protect rule,* which tests government liability by examining whether (1) the officer's actions created a special danger of violent harm to the plaintiff in the lawsuit; (2) the officer knew or should have known her actions would encourage this plaintiff to rely on her actions; and (3) the danger created by the officer's actions caused either harm or vulnerability to harm.

statutory right to appeal nonconstitutional right to appeal a criminal conviction.

stipulates defense counsel agrees not to contest some evidence prevented by the prosecution.

"stop and identify" statutes statutes in 21 states that allow officers to ask for suspects' names and identification.

stops see *Fourth Amendment stop.*

straight guilty pleas plea of guilty not based on negotiation, usually when the proof of guilt is overwhelming.

subjective privacy whether a person exhibited an actual personal expectation of privacy.

subjective test of entrapment the test of entrapment that focuses on whether defendants had the predisposition to commit the crimes.

subpoena *duces tecum* an order to produce documents.

suggestion eyewitness's interpretation of events is shaped by other people's suggestions.

summary judgment a motion that the court enter a judgment without a trial because there's not enough evidence to support the plaintiff's claim.

supervisory power the power of the U.S. Supreme Court to make rules to manage how lower federal courts conduct their business.

suppression hearing a proceeding in an appellate case to determine whether evidence obtained by law enforcement officers during searches and seizures, interrogation, and identification procedures, such as lineups, should be thrown out.

supremacy clause U.S. Constitution, Article VI, which says that the U.S. Constitution is the last word in criminal procedure.

testimony the content of what you say and write against yourself.

thermal imagers devices that detect, measure, and record infrared radiation not visible to the naked eye.

third-party consent searches one person can consent for another person to a search.

title of the case the name of the case as it appears in the formal legal documents and in secondary sources.

tort feasor the accused wrongdoer in a tort case.

torts civil lawsuits for damages over private wrongs.

total incorporation doctrine that says the states have to apply the provisions outlined in the Bill of Rights and that all the provisions were incorporated under the due process clause.

totality-of-circumstances approach weighing all the facts surrounding the government's establishing identification of the suspect to determine if it's reliable enough to be admitted; also called the *"per se approach."*

totality-of-circumstances test the conditions used to determine abandonment and the voluntariness of a waiver of rights and of incriminating statements.

totality-of-facts-and-circumstances test usually called the *"totality-of-circumstances test,"* it's a favorite standard the Court applies to decide whether official actions are constitutional.

total wars the whole people, the governments, and the countries' resources are mobilized for fighting and winning a war.

trap and trace telephone company lists of the phone numbers of incoming calls to a particular phone number.

trespass doctrine the Fourth Amendment doctrine that requires physical intrusions into a "constitutionally protected area" to qualify as a search.

true bill the record of the number of grand jurors voting for indictment.

two-pronged effective counsel test U.S. Supreme Court test of "effectiveness of counsel," which requires the defense to prove a lawyer's performance wasn't reasonably competent and that the incompetence affected the outcome of the case in favor of conviction.

unequivocal acts or statements withdrawal of consent rule people can withdraw their consent, but it must be with actions or statements that are unambiguously clear.

unlawful enemy combatants a person who has engaged in hostilities or purposefully and materially supported hostilities against the United States or its co-belligerents who is not a *lawful enemy combatant* (including a person who is part of the Taliban, al-Qaida, or associated forces).

unnecessarily and impermissibly suggestive one of the requirements a defendant must prove to have a lineup, show-up, or photo array identification thrown out on due process grounds.

USA Patriot Act short for <u>U</u>niting and <u>S</u>trengthening <u>A</u>merica by <u>P</u>roviding <u>A</u>ppropriate <u>T</u>ools <u>R</u>equired to <u>I</u>ntercept and <u>O</u>bstruct <u>T</u>errorism, the bill was passed after 9/11 to give the government more powers.

vehicle exception exception to the Fourth Amendment that says that if officers have probable cause to believe that a vehicle contains that which by law is subject to seizure, then search and seizure are valid.

very substantial likelihood of misidentification one of two requirements to have identification evidence thrown out based on due process grounds; the totality of circumstances must prove that "unnecessarily and impermissibly suggestive" procedures probably led to a misidentification.

violent crime–automatic-frisk exception facts that back up a stop don't automatically also back up a frisk, except when suspects are stopped for crimes of violence

voir dire the process of picking jurors from the pool of potential jurors by questioning them.

voluntariness test of consent searches a test in which the totality of circumstances is used to determine whether a consent to search was obtained without coercion, deception, or promises.

voluntary false confessions innocent people confess without police prompting or pressure.

war crimes crimes committed during wartime that inflict "needless and disproportionate suffering and damages" in pursuit of a "military objective."

warrant clause the part of the Fourth Amendment that outlines the requirements for obtaining arrest and search warrants.

whole picture test looking at all the facts and circumstances in each case to determine the constitutionality of government actions.

writ of certiorari an order to the court that decided the case to send up the record of its proceedings to the U.S. Supreme Court for review.

writs of assistance issued by the English Crown for the life of the monarch, they empowered royal agents to search anyone, anywhere, anytime and to order anyone who happened to be nearby to help execute the warrant.

Abel v. U.S. 1960. 362 U.S. 217.

Adamson v. California. 1947. 332 U.S. 46.

Adams v. Williams. 1972. 407 U.S. 143.

Agnello v. U.S. 1925. 269 U.S. 20.

Alabama v. White. 1990. 496 U.S. 325.

Allen, Francis A. 1978. "The Law as a Path to the World." *Michigan Law Review* 77.

Allen, Ronald J., Joseph L. Hoffman, Debra A. Livingston, and William J. Stuntz. 2005. *Comprehensive Criminal Procedure.* New York: Aspen Publishers.

Allison v. State. 1974. 214 N.W.2d 437 (Wisc.).

Alschuler, Albert. 2002. "Guilty Plea: Plea Bargaining." In *Encyclopedia of Crime & Justice*, 2d ed., edited by Joshua Dressler. New York: Macmillan Reference USA, 754–62.

Amacost, Barbara E. 2010. "*Arizona v. Gant:* Does It Matter?" *Supreme Court Review 2009.* Chicago: University of Chicago Press.

American Bar Association. 1980. *Standards for Criminal Justice.* 2d ed. Chicago: ABA.

_____. 1988. *Criminal Justice in Crisis.* Chicago: ABA.

American Law Institute. 1975. *Model Code of Pre-Arraignment Procedure.* Philadelphia: ALI.

Amsterdam, Anthony. 1970. "The Supreme Court and the Rights of Suspects in Criminal Cases." *New York University Law Review* 45:785.

_____. 1974. "Perspectives on the Fourth Amendment." *Minnesota Law Review* 58:430.

Anderson v. Creighton. 1987. 483 U.S. 635.

Annals of Congress. 1789. House of Representatives, 1st Cong., 1st sess. Accessed August 31, 2010. http://lcweb2.loc.gov/cgi-bin/ampage?collId=llac&fileName=001/llac001.db&recNum=51.

Apodaca v. Oregon. 1972. 406 U.S. 404.

Apprendi v. New Jersey. 2000. 530 U.S. 466.

Archibold, Randal. 2010. "Arizona Enacts Stringent Law on Immigration." *New York Times*, April 23. Accessed July 4, 2010. http://www.nytimes.com/2010/04/24/us/politics/24immig.html?_r=1.

Argersinger v. Hamlin. 1972. 407 U.S. 25.

Arizona v. Evans. 1995. 514 U.S. 1.

Arizona v. Gant. 2008. "Amicus Brief of State Officials Supporting Arizona." 2008 WL 2151707.

_____. 2009. 129 S.Ct. 1710.

Arizona v. Johnson. 2009. 129 S.Ct. 781. SCOTUS Wiki. Accessed February 20, 2010. http://www.scotuswiki.com/index.php?title=Arizona_v._Johnson.

Ashcroft, John. 2002. *Attorney General's Guidelines on General Crimes, Racketeering Enterprise and Terrorism Enterprise Investigations.* Washington, D.C.: U.S. Department of Justice, May 30.

Associated Press. 2007. "Death Row Inmate Gets New Life Term," *USA Today.* Accessed August 31, 2010. http://www.usatoday.com/news/topstories/2007-08-13-477084247_x.htm.

Atkins v. Virginia. 2002. 536 U.S. 304.

Atwater v. City of Lago Vista. 2001. 532 U.S. 318.

Avalon Project at the Yale Law School. 2003. *The Laws of War.* Accessed September 2, 2010. http://avalon.law.yale.edu/subject_menus/lawwar.asp.

Baldus, David C., and George Woodworth. 1998. "Race Discrimination and the Death Penalty: An Empirical and Legal Overview." In *America's Experiment with Capital Punishment*, edited by James R. Acker, Robert S. Bohm, and Charles S. Lanier. Durham, N.C.: Carolina Academic Press.

Baldwin v. New York. 1970. 399 U.S. 66.

Ballew v. Georgia. 1978. 435 U.S. 223.

Barnes v. State. 1975. 520 S.W.2d 401 (Tex.Crim.App.).

Barron v. Baltimore. 1833. 32 U.S. (7 Pet.) 243.

Batson v. Kentucky. 1986. 476 U.S. 79.

Bazelon, David. 1973. "Defective Assistance of Counsel." *University of Cincinnati Law Review* 42:1.

Beale, Sara S., William C. Bryson, James E. Felman, and Michael J. Elston. 2004. *Grand Jury Law and Practice.* Eagan, Minn.: West, 6-3-6-4.

Behrman, Bruce W., and Richards, Regina E. 2005. "Suspect/Foil Identification in Actual Crimes and in the Laboratory: A Reality Monitoring Analysis." *Law and Human Behavior* 29:279–301.

Bell v. Irwin. 2003. 321 F.3d 637 (CA7 Ill.).

Bell v. Wolfish. 1979. 441 U.S. 520.

Berghuis v. Thompkins. 2010. 130 S.Ct. 2250.

Berkemer v. McCarty. 1984. 468 U.S. 420.

Betts v. Brady. 1942. 316 U.S. 455.

Bibas, Stephanos. 2003–2004. "Plea Bargaining Outside the Shadow of Trial." *Harvard Law Review.* 117:2464.

Bibas, Stephanos. 2005. "White-Collar Plea Bargaining and Sentencing after *Booker.*" *William and Mary Law Review* 47(December):721.

Bivens v. Six Unnamed FBI Agents. 1971. 403 U.S. 388.

Blackledge v. Allison. 1977. 431 U.S. 63.

Blakely v. Washington. 2004. 542 U.S. 296.

Blumstein, Alfred, Jacqueline Cohen, Susan E. Martin, and Michael H. Tonry, eds. 1983. *Research on Sentencing: The Search for Reform.* Washington, D.C.: National Academy Press.

Board of Commissioners v. Backus. 1864. 29 How. Pr. 33.

Board of Education of Independent School District No. 92 of Pottawatomie County v. Earls. 2002. 535 U.S. 822.

Boggs Act. 1951. U.S. Code. Act of November 2, 1951, 65 Stat. 767.

Boland, Barbara, Wayne Logan, Ronald Sones, and William Martin. 1987. *The Prosecution of Felony Arrests, 1982.* Washington, D.C.: U.S. Department of Justice, BJS, May.

Borchard, Edwin. 1932. *Convicting the Innocent.* Garden City, N.J.: Garden City Publishing.

Boumediene and others v. Bush and others. 2007. "Brief for Petitioners." 2007 WL 2441590.

———. 2008. 579 F.Supp.2d 191.

———. 2008a. 553 U.S. 723.

———. 2008b. 583 F.Supp.2d 133.

Bowen v. Kemp. 1985. 769 F.2d 672 (CA11 Ga.).

Bowles v. U.S. 1970. 439 F.2d 536 (CADC).

Boykin v. Alabama. 1969. 395 U.S. 238.

Bradfield, Amy. L., Gary L. Wells, and Elizabeth. A. Olson. 2002. "The Damaging Effect of Confirming Feedback on the Relation between Eyewitness Certainty and Identification Accuracy." *Journal of Applied Psychology* 87:112–20.

Bradley, Craig M. 1985. "Two Models of the Fourth Amendment." *Michigan Law Review* 83:1471.

Brady v. U.S. 1970. 397 U.S. 742.

Brandes, Wendy. 1989. "Post-Arrest Detention and the Fourth Amendment: Refining the Standard of *Gerstein v. Pugh.*" *Columbia Journal of Law and Contemporary Problems* 22:445–88.

Brazil, Jeff, and Steve Berry. 1992. "Color of Driver Is Key to Stops in I-95 Videos." *Orlando Sentinel,* August 23.

Brennan, William J. 1977. "State Constitutions and the Protection of Individual Rights." *Harvard Law Review* 90:489–504.

Brewer v. Williams. 1977. 430 U.S. 387.

Brigham City Utah v. Charles Stuart, Shayne Taylor, and Sandra Taylor. 2006. 547 U.S. 398.

Brinegar v. United States. 1949. 338 U.S. 160.

Brown v. Allen. 1953. 344 U.S. 443.

Brown v. Board of Education. 1954. 347 U.S. 483. Oral Argument.

Brown v. Mississippi. 1936. 297 U.S. 278.

Brown v. Texas. 1979. 443 U.S. 47.

Buckhout, Robert. 1975. "Eyewitness Testimony." *Jurimetrics Journal* 171 (Spring):171–87.

Buckley v. Fitzsimmons. 1993. 509 U.S. 259.

Bull v. City and County of San Francisco. 2010. 595 F.3d 964 (CA9 Calif.).

Bumper v. North Carolina. 1968. 391 U.S. 543.

Burch v. Louisiana. 1979. 441 U.S. 130.

Bureau of Justice Statistics. 2009. *Felony Sentences in State Courts, 2006—Statistical Tables.* Washington, D.C.: NCJ 226846, December.

Burns v. Reed. 1991. 500 U.S. 478.

Bynum v. State. 2005. 929 So.2d 324 (Miss.App.).

California v. Acevedo. 1991. 500 U.S. 565.

California v. Beheler. 1983. 463 U.S. 1121.

California v. Ciraolo. 1986. 476 U.S. 207.

California v. Gilbert. 1967. 388 U.S. 263.

California v. Greenwood. 1988. 486 U.S. 35.

California v. Hodari D. 1991. 499 U.S. 621.

Campaign for an Effective Crime Policy. 1993. "Evaluating Mandatory Minimum Sentences." Washington, D.C.: Campaign for an Effective Crime Policy, October. Unpublished manuscript.

Cardozo, Benjamin. 1921. *The Nature of the Judicial Process.* New Haven, Conn.: Yale University Press.

Carlson, Jonathan. 1987. "The Act Requirement and the Foundations of the Entrapment Defense." *Virginia Law Review* 73:1011.

Carroll v. U.S. 1925. 267 U.S. 132.

Center for Constitutional Rights. 2009. "Racial Disparity in NYPD Stops-and-Frisks." New York: Center for Constitutional Rights. Accessed July 8, 2010. http://ccrjustice.org/stopandfrisk.

Chandler v. Florida. 1981. 499 U.S. 560.

Chandler v. Fretag. 1954. 348 U.S. 3.

Chimel v. California. 1969. 395 U.S. 752.

Ciucci v. Illinois. 1958. 356 U.S. 571.

Clarke v. Caspari. 2002. 274 F.3d 507 (CA8).

Cloud, Morgan. 1985. "Search and Seizure by the Numbers: The Drug Courier Profile and Judicial Review of Investigative Formulas." *Boston University Law Review* 65:843.

Coke, Edward. 1797. *The Second Part of the Institutes of the Laws of England.* 5th ed. London: Brooke.

Coker v. Georgia. 1977. 433 U.S. 584.

Cole, David. 1999. *No Equal Justice.* New York: New Press.

Coleman, Howard, and Eric Swenson. 1994. *DNA in the Courtroom: A Trial Watcher's Guide.* Seattle: Genelex Corp.

Colorado v. Bertine. 1987. 479 U.S. 367.

Colorado v. Connelly. 1986. 479 U.S. 157.

Colorado v. Mendez. 1999. 986 P.2d 285 (Colo.).

Connecticut v. Barrett. 1987. 479 U.S. 523.

Cooper v. State. 1985. 480 So.2d 8 (Ala.Crim.App.).

Copacino, John M. 1994. "Suspicionless Criminal Seizures after *Michigan Department of State Police v. Sitz.*" *American Criminal Law Review* 31:215.

Corpus Juris Secundum. 2003. St Paul, Minn.: West, § 61.

Cortner, Richard C. 1981. *The Supreme Court and the Second Bill of Rights.* Madison: University of Wisconsin Press.

County of Riverside v. McLaughlin. 1991. 500 U.S. 44.

Covey, Russell. 2007–2008. "Reconsidering the Relationship between Cognitive Psychology and Plea Bargaining." *Marquette Law Review* 91:213–47.

Criminal Justice Newsletter. 1993. Washington, D.C.: Pace Publications, November 15.

Crist v. Bretz. 1978. 437 U.S. 28.

Cronin, Thomas E., Tania Cronin, and Michael Milakovich. 1981. *U.S. v. Crime in the Streets*. Bloomington: Indiana University Press.

Crooker v. California. 1958. 357 U.S. 433.

Cruz v. City of Laramie. 2001. 239 F.3d 1183 (CA10 Wyo.).

Culombe v. Connecticut. 1961. 367 U.S. 568.

Cupp v. Murphy. 1973. 412 U.S. 291.

Davenport, Jennifer L., and Steven Penrod. 1997. "Eyewitness Identification Evidence: Evaluating Commonsense Evaluations." *Psychology, Public Policy, and Law* 3:338–61.

Davies, Thomas Y. 1983. "A Hard Look at What We Know (and Still Need to Learn) about the 'Social Costs' of the Exclusionary Rule: The NIJ Study and Other Studies of 'Lost' Arrests." *American Bar Foundation Research Journal* 640.

———. 1999. "Recovering the Original Fourth Amendment." *Michigan Law Review* 98:547.

Death Penalty Information Center. 2010. "Death Penalty Fact Sheet." Accessed August 31, 2010. http://www.deathpenaltyinfo.org.

Demore v. Kim. 2002. "Amicus Brief for T. Alexander Aleinikoff and Others." 2002 WL 31455523.

Demore v. Kim. 2003. 538 U.S. 510.

Deorle v. Rutherford. 2001. 272 F.3d 1272 (CA9 Calif.).

DeShaney v. Winnebago County. 1989. 489 U.S. 189.

Detainee Treatment Act (DTA). 2005. Accessed August 27, 2010. http://jurist.law.pitt.edu/gazette/2005/12/detainee-treatment-act-of-2005-white.php.

Dickerson v. U.S. 2000. 530 U.S. 428.

District Attorney's Office for the Third Judicial District and others v. William G. Osborne. 2009. 129 S.Ct. 2308.

Dix, George E. 1985. "Nonarrest Investigatory Detentions in Search and Seizure Law." *Duke Law Journal* 849.

Douglass, Amy B., and Dawn McQuiston-Surrett. 2006. "Post-Identification Feedback: Exploring the Effects of Sequential Photospreads and Eyewitnesses' Awareness of the Identification Task." *Applied Cognitive Psychology* 20:991–1007.

Dow Chemical Co. v. U.S. 1986. 476 U.S. 227.

Doyle, Charles. 2002. *The USA Patriot Act: A Legal Analysis*. Washington, D.C.: Congressional Research Service.

Draper v. Reynolds. 2004. 369 F.3d 1270 (CA11 Ga.).

Draper v. U.S. 1959. 358 U.S. 307.

Drizin, Steven A., and Richard A. Leo. 2003–2004. "The Problem of False Confessions in the Post-DNA World." *North Carolina Law Review* 82:891.

Drizin, Steven A., and Marissa J. Reich. 2004. "Heeding the Lessons of History: The Need for Mandatory Recording of Police Interrogations to Accurately Assess the Reliability and Voluntariness of Confessions." *Drake Law Review* 52:619.

Duarte v. Commonwealth. 1991. 407 S.E.2d 41.

Duncan v. Louisiana. 1968. 391 U.S. 145.

Dunlop v. U.S. 1897. 165 U.S. 486.

Elkins v. U.S. 1960. 364 U.S. 206.

Elsea, Jennifer. 2001. *Terrorism and the Law of War: Trying Terrorists as War Criminals before Military Commissions*. Washington, D.C.: Congressional Research Service.

Enmund v. Florida. 1982. 458 U.S. 782.

Ervin, Sam J., Jr. 1983. "The Exclusionary Rule: An Essential Ingredient of the Fourth Amendment." *Supreme Court Review*. Chicago: University of Chicago Press.

Escobedo v. Illinois. 1964. 378 U.S. 478.

Estelle v. Williams. 1976. 425 U.S. 501.

Ewing v. California. 2003. 538 U.S. 11.

Ex Parte Milligan. 1866. 71 U.S. 2.

Federal Rules of Criminal Procedure. 2002. 41(d)(3). Accessed September 2, 2010. http://www.law.cornell.edu/rules/frcrmp/Rule4.htm.

Feeley, Malcolm M. 1979. *The Process Is the Punishment: Handling Cases in a Lower Criminal Court*. New York: Russell Sage Foundation.

Ferguson, Andrew Guthrie, and Damien Bernache. 2008. "The 'High-Crime Area' Question: Requiring Verifiable and Quantifiable Evidence for Fourth Amendment Reasonable Suspicion Analysis." *American University Law Review* 57:1587–644.

Ferguson v. City of Charleston. 2001. 532 U.S. 67.

Final Report. 2010. Guantanamo Review Task Force. Washington, D.C.: Department of Justice, Department of Defense, Department of State, Department of Homeland Security, Office of the Director of National Intelligence, Joint Chiefs of Staff.

Fisher, Jeffrey. 2006. "Respondent's Brief." *U.S. v. Gonzalez-Lopez*. 2006 WL 838892.

———. 2008. "Brief for Amicus Curiae National Association of Criminal Defense Lawyers in Support of Respondent." *Gant v. U.S.* 2008 WL 39111137.

Fisher, Sydney George F. 1888. "The Suspension of Habeas Corpus during the War of Rebellion." *Political Science Quarterly* 3.

Florida v. Bostick. 1991. 501 U.S. 429.

Florida v. Jimeno. 1991. 500 U.S. 248.

Florida v. J. L. 2000. 529 U.S. 266.

Florida v. Royer. 1983. 460 U.S. 491.

Foote, Caleb. 1965. "The Coming Constitutional Crisis in Bail." *University of Pennsylvania Law Review* 113:959–1185.

Fowler, Tom. 2007. "Olis Testified He Couldn't 'Ruin Those People's Lives.'" *Houston Chronicle*, May 27, Business, 5.

Fraizer v. Roberts. 1971. 441 F.2d 1224 (CA8 Ark.).

Frankel, Marvin E., and Gary F. Naftalis. 1977. *The Grand Jury: An Institution on Trial*. New York: Hill and Wang.

Frazier v. Cupp. 1969. 394 U.S. 731.

Friendly, Henry J. 1965. "The Bill of Rights as a Code of Criminal Procedure." *California Law Review* 53:929.

Friendly, Henry J. 1968. "The Fifth Amendment Tomorrow: The Case for Constitutional Change." *University of Cincinnati Law Review* 37:671.

Frontline. 1999. "Snitch" Transcript. Accessed September 3, 2010. http://www.pbs.org/wgbh/pages/frontline/shows/snitch/etc/script.html.

Gall v. U.S. 2007. 552 U.S. 38.

Gardner, James A. 1991. "The Failed Discourse of State Constitutionalism." *Michigan Law Review* 90:761.

Gardner v. Florida. 1977. 430 U.S. 349.

Garner, Bryan A. 1987. *Dictionary of Modern Legal Usage.* New York: Oxford University Press.

Gayarré, Charles. 1903. *History of Louisiana, Vol. IV.* New Orleans: F. F. Hansell & Bro.

Georgia v. Randolph. 2006. 126 S.Ct. 1515.

Gerstein v. Pugh. 1975. 420 U.S. 103.

Gideon v. Wainwright. 1963. 372 U.S. 335.

Gilbert v. California. 1967. 388 U.S. 263.

Goldstein, Abraham S. 1987. "The Search Warrant, the Magistrate, and Judicial Review." *New York University Law Review* 62:1173.

Goldstein, Joseph. 1960. "The State and the Accused: Balance and Advantage in Criminal Procedure." *Yale Law Journal* 69.

Graham, Fred. 1970. *The Self-Inflicted Wound.* New York: Macmillan.

Graham, Kenneth, and Leon Letwin. 1971. "The Preliminary Hearing in Los Angeles: Some Field Findings and Legal-Policy Questions." *UCLA Law Review* 18:636.

Graham v. Connor. 1989. 490 U.S. 386.

Gregg v. Georgia. 1976. 428 U.S. 153.

Griffin v. Wisconsin. 1987. 483 U.S. 868.

Griswold, David B. 1994. "Complaints against the Police: Predicting Dispositions." *Journal of Criminal Justice* 22.

Gross, Samuel R. 1987. "Loss of Innocence: Eyewitness Identification and Proof of Guilt." *Journal of Legal Studies* 16.

Haber, Ralph Norman, and Lyn Haber. 2000. "Experiencing, Remembering, and Reporting Events." *Psychology, Public Policy, and Law* 6(4):1057–97.

Haddad, James B. 1977. "Well-Delineated Exceptions, Claims of Sham, and Fourfold Probable Cause." *Journal of Criminal Law and Criminology* 68:198–225.

Hall, Jerome. 1942. "Objectives of Federal Criminal Rules Revision." *Yale Law Journal* 725.

Hall, John Wesley, Jr. 1993. *Search and Seizure.* 2d ed. New York: Clark, Boardman, Callaghan.

———. 2009. "A Great Awakening." *Champion Magazine,* June.

Hamblett, Mark. 2003. "Tough Questions for U.S. on Detention." *Legal Times,* November 24.

Hamdan v. Rumsfeld. 2006. 126 S.Ct. 2749.

Hamdi v. Rumsfeld. 2004. 542 U.S. 507.

Hamilton, Alexander. 1788. "The Federalist No. 78: The Judiciary Department." Accessed June 7, 2010. http:// press-pubs.uchicago.edu/founders/documents/bill_of_rightss7.html.

Hancock, Catherine. 1982. "State Court Activism and Searches Incident to Arrest." *Virginia Law Review* 68:1085.

Hand, Learned. 1922. *U.S. v. Garsson.* 291 Fed. 646 (S.D.N.Y.).

Harmelin v. Michigan. 1991. 501 U.S. 957.

Harris, David A. 1998. "Particularized Suspicion, Categorical Judgments: Supreme Court Rhetoric versus Lower Court Reality under *Terry v. Ohio.*" *St. John's Law Review* 72:975.

Harris v. U.S. 1947. 331 U.S. 145.

Harris v. U.S. 2002. 536 U.S. 545.

Harvey v. Horan. 2002. 285 F.3d 298 (CA4).

Heath v. Alabama. 1985. 474 U.S. 82.

Hedgepeth v. Washington Metro Area Transit and others. 2003. 284 F.Supp.2d 145 (D.D.C.).

Heffernan, William C. 2001–2002. "Fourth Amendment Privacy Interests." *Journal of Criminal Law & Criminology* 92:1–126.

Henderson v. Florida. 1985. 473 U.S. 916.

Henderson v. U.S. 1967. 390 F.2d 805 (CA9 Calif.).

Herring v. U.S. 2009.129 S.Ct. 695.

Hester v. U.S. 1924. 265 U.S. 57.

Hickey, Thomas, and Michael Axline. 1992. "Drunk-Driving Roadblocks under State Constitutions: A Reasonable Alternative to *Michigan v. Sitz.*" *Criminal Law Bulletin* 28.

Hiibel v. Sixth Judicial District Court of Nevada, Humboldt County et al. 2004. 542 U.S. 177.

Hockett, Jeffrey D. 1991. "Justice Robert H. Jackson, the Supreme Court, and the Nuremberg Trial." *Supreme Court Review.* Chicago: University of Chicago Press.

Hoffa v. U.S. 1966. 385 U.S. 293.

Holbrook v. Flynn. 1986. 475 U.S. 560.

Holy Bible, Authorized (King James) Version. 1990. Nashville: Thomas Nelson.

Horton v. California. 1990. 496 U.S. 128.

Howard v. Bouchard. 2008. 405 F.3d 459 (CA6).

Hudson v. Palmer. 1984. 468 U.S. 523.

Hurtado v. California. 1884. 110 U.S. 516.

Hutson, H. Range, Deirdre Anglin, Gilbert Pineda, Christopher Flynn, and James McKeith. 1997. "Law Enforcement and K-9 Dog Bites: Injuries, Complications, and Trends." *Annals of American Emergency Medicine* 25(5): 637–42.

Illinois v. Allen. 1970. 397 U.S. 337.

Illinois v. Caballes. 2005. 543 U.S. 405.

Illinois v. Rodriquez. 1990. 497 U.S. 177.

Illinois v. Wardlow. 1999. "U.S. Supreme Court Amicus Brief." 1999 WL 451226.

Illinois v. Wardlow. 2000. 528 U.S. 119.

Imbler v. Pachtman. 1976. 424 U.S. 409.

Immigration and Nationality Act. 2004. 8 U.S.C. § 1226a. Accessed August 27, 2010. http://vlex.com/vid/suspected-terrorists-habeas-corpus-19271949.

In re Winship. 1970. 397 U.S. 358.

Inbau, Fred E. 1961. "Police Interrogation and Limitations." *Journal of Criminal Law, Criminology, and Police Science* 52:19.

Inbau, Fred E., James R. Thompson, James B. Zagel, and James P. Manak. 1984. *Criminal Law and Its Administration.* 4th ed. Mineola, N.Y.: Foundation Press.

Innocence Project. 2010. "Eyewitness Misidentification." Accessed April 23, 2010. http://www.innocenceproject.org/understand/Eyewitness-Misidentification.php.

Innocence Project. 2010. "False Confessions and Mandatory Recording of Interrogations." Fix the System. Accessed May 22, 2010. http://www.innocenceproject.org/fix/False-Confessions.php.

INS v. Delgado. 1984. 466 U.S. 210.

Isom v. Town of Warren. 2004. 360 F.3d 7 (CA1 R.I.).

Israel, Jerold H. 1982. "Selective Incorporation: Revisited." *Georgetown Law Journal* 71:274.

Jackson, Robert. 1940. "The Federal Prosecutor." *Journal of Criminal Law and Criminology* 31:3.

Jacobson v. U.S. 1992. 503 U.S. 540.

Jefferson, Thomas. 1904. *Works.* London: Putnam and Sons.

Johns, Margaret Z. 2005. "Reconsidering Absolute Prosecutorial Immunity." *Brigham University Law Review* 53.

Johnson, Andrew, and Emily Dugan. 2009. *Independent World,* December 27. Accessed July 1, 2010. http://www.independent.co.uk/news/world/americas/wealthy-quiet-unassuming-the-christmas-day-bomb-suspect-1851090.html.

Johnson, Brian D. 2003. "Racial and Ethnic Disparities in Sentencing Departures across Modes of Conviction." *Criminology* 41(2):449–90.

———. 2005. "Contextual Disparities in Guidelines Departures: Courtroom Social Contexts, Guidelines Compliance, and Extralegal Disparities in Criminal Sentencing." *Criminology* 43(3):761–96.

Johnson v. Eisentrager. 1950. 339 U.S. 763.

Johnson v. Louisiana. 1972. 406 U.S. 356.

Johnson v. Zerbst. 1938. 304 U.S. 458.

Jonas, Daniel S. 1989. "Comment, Pretextual Searches, and the Fourth Amendment: Unconstitutional Abuses of Power." *University of Pennsylvania Law Review* 137:1791.

Jones, Elizabeth O. 2007. "The Fourth Amendment and Dormitory Searches." *Journal of College and University Law* 33:597.

Jones v. U.S. 1959. 266 F.2d 924 (CADC).

Juvelir, Hon. Michael R. 1998. "A Prosecutor's Perspective." *St. John's Law Review* 72:741.

Kalina v. Fletcher. 1997. 522 U.S. 118.

Kassin, Saul M., and Gisli Gudjonsson. 2004. *Psychological Science in the Public Interest* 5(2):33.

Kassin, Saul M., Christian A. Meissner, and Rebecca J. Norwick. 2005. "I'd Know a False Confession If I Saw One: A Comparative Study of College Students and Police Investigators." *Law and Human Behavior* 29(2):211–27.

Katz, Lewis. 2004. "*Terry v. Ohio* at Thirty-Five: A Revisionist View." *Mississippi Law Journal* 74:423.

Katz v. U.S. 1967. 389 U.S. 347, 88 S.Ct. 507, 19 L.Ed.2d 576.

Kennedy, Randall. 1997. *Race, Crime, and the Law.* New York: Random House.

Kennedy v. Louisiana. 2008. 554 U.S. ___ (Slip opinion).

Kentucky v. Stincer. 1987. 107 S.Ct. 2658.

Ker v. California. 1963. 374 U.S. 23.

Keys, Karl. 2007. "Ronald Rompilla Pleads to Life." *Capital Defense Weekly,* August 13. Accessed May 30, 2010. http://www.capitaldefenseweekly.com/blog/?p=2251.

Kirby v. Illinois. 1972. 406 U.S. 682.

Kirk v. Louisiana. 2002. 536 U.S. 635.

Klobuchar, Amy, Nancy Steblay, and Hilary Caligiuri. 2006. "Improving Eyewitness Identifications: Hennepin County's Blind Sequential Lineup Pilot Project." *Cardozo Public Law, Policy and Ethics Journal* (April).

Klockars, Carl B. 1980. "The Dirty Harry Problem." *Annals of the American Academy of Political and Social Science* 452:3.

Klopfer v. North Carolina. 1967. 386 U.S. 213.

Knowles v. Iowa. 1998. 525 U.S. 113.

Kobach, Kris. 2010. "Why Arizona Drew a Line." *New York Times,* April 29. Accessed July 4, 2010. http://www.nytimes.com/2010/04/29/opinion/29kobach.html?th&emc=th.

Kopec v. Tate. 2004. 361 F.3d 772 (CA3 Penn.).

Kuha v. City of Minnetonka. 2003. 365 F.3d 590 (CA8 Minn.).

Kurland, Philip B., and Gerhard Casper, eds. 1975. "Brief for the NAACP Legal Defense and Educational Fund, Inc., as Amicus Curiae." *Terry v. Ohio. Landmark Briefs and Arguments of the Supreme Court of the United States.* Washington, D.C.: University Publications of America.

Kyllo v. U.S. 2001. 533 U.S. 27.

LaFave, Wayne R. 1993. "Police Rule Making and the Fourth Amendment." In *Discretion in Criminal Justice,* edited by Lloyd Ohlin and Frank Remington. Albany, N.Y.: State University of New York Press.

———. 2004. *Search and Seizure.* 4th ed. St. Paul, Minn.: Thomson West.

LaFave, Wayne R., and Jerold H. Israel. 1984. *Criminal Procedure.* St. Paul, Minn.: West.

LaFave, Wayne, Jerold H. Israel, Nancy King, and Orin Kerr. 2009. *Criminal Procedure.* 5th ed. St. Paul: West.

Lanza v. New York. 1962. 370 U.S. 139.

Latzer, Barry. 1991. *State Constitutions and Criminal Justice.* Westport, Conn.: Greenwood.

Lee, F. N. n.d. *King Alfred the Great and Our Common Law.* http://www.dr-fnlee.org/docs6/alfred/alfred.pdf.

Leo, Richard A. 1996. "The Impact of *Miranda* Revisited." *Journal of Criminal Law and Criminology* 86:621.

———. 1998. "From Coercion to Deception: The Changing Nature of Police Interrogation in America."

In *The Miranda Debate: Law, Justice and Policing*, edited by Richard Leo and George C. Thomas III. Boston: Northeastern University, 2002.

Levy, Leonard. 1968. *The Origins of the Fifth Amendment*. New York: Oxford University Press.

Lewis, Anthony. 1994. "The Blackmun Legacy." *New York Times*, April 8.

Lewis v. U.S. 1966. 385 U.S. 206.

Lichtenberg, Illya. 2001. "*Miranda* in Ohio: The Effects of 'Voluntary' Waiver of Fourth Amendment Rights." *Howard Law Journal* 44:349.

Lichtenberg, Illya, and Alisa Smith. 2001. "How Dangerous Are Routine Police-Citizen Traffic Stops?" *Journal of Criminal Justice* 29:419–28.

Liptak, Adam. 2010. "Defendants Squeezed by Georgia's Tight Budget." *New York Times*, July 5. Accessed July 6, 2010. http://www.nytimes.com/2010/07/06/us/06bar.html?th&emc=th.

Lisenba v. California. 1941. 314 U.S. 219.

Llaguno v. Mingey. 1985. 763 F.2d 1560 (CA7 Ill.).

Lockett v. Ohio. 1978. 438 U.S. 586.

Lockyer v. Andrade. 2003. 538 U.S. 63.

Loftus, Elizabeth F. 1996. *Eyewitness Identification.* Rev. ed. Cambridge: Harvard University Press.

_____. 2004. "The Devil in Confessions." *Psychological Science in the Public Interest* 5(2):i.

Loftus, Geoffrey, and Erin M. Harley. 2005. "Why Is It Easier to Identify Someone Close Than Far Away?" *Psychonomic Bulletin & Review* 12(1):43–65.

Madison, James. 1787. "The Federalist No. 51." In *The Federalist*, edited by Jacob E. Cooke. Middletown, Conn.: Wesleyan University Press, 1961, 349.

Magid, Laurie. 2001. "Deceptive Police Interrogation Practices: How Far Is Too Far?" *Michigan Law Review* 99(5): 1168.

Malloy v. Hogan. 1964. 378 U.S. 1.

Manson v. Brathwaite. 1977. 432 U.S. 98.

Mapp v. Ohio. 1961. 367 U.S. 643.

Marbury v. Madison. 1803. 5 U.S. 137.

Marcus, Paul. 1986. "The Development of Entrapment Law." *Wayne Law Review* 336:5.

Mary Beth G. and Sharon N. v. City of Chicago. 1983. 723 F.2d 1262, 1263 (CA7 Ill.).

Maryland v. Wilson. 1997. 519 U.S. 408.

Massiah v. U.S. 1964. 377 U.S. 201.

McCleskey v. Kemp. 1987. 481 U.S. 279.

McCleskey v. Zant. 1991. 499 U.S. 467.

McCormick v. City of Fort Lauderdale. 2003. 333 F.3d 1234 (CA11 Fla.).

McCulloch v. Maryland. 1819. 17 U.S. 316.

McFadden v. Cabana. 1988. 851 F.2d 784 (CA5 Miss.).

Meares, Tracey L., and Bernard Harcourt. 2000. "Foreword: Transparent Adjudication and Social Science Research in Criminal Procedure." *Journal of Criminal Law & Criminology* 90(3):733.

Michigan v. Clifford. 1984. 464 U.S. 287.

Michigan v. Sitz. 1990. 496 U.S. 444.

Michigan v. Summers. 1981. 452 U.S. 692.

Military Commissions Act of 2006. 2006. 10 U.S.C. 948a, Section 1, Subchapter I.

Military Instruction No. 10. 2006. "Certain Evidentiary Determinations." U.S. Department of Defense. http://www.defense.gov/news/Mar2006/d20060327MCI10.pdf.

Miller-El v. Dretke. 2005. 545 U.S. 231.

Miller v. Clark County. 2003. 340 F. 3d 959 (CA9 Wash.).

Minnesota Rules of Criminal Procedure. 2006. Accessed September 2, 2010. http://www.courts.state.mn.us/rules/criminal/RCRP.htm#cr501.

Minnesota Rules of Criminal Procedure. 2010. Accessed August 21, 2010. http://www.lawlibrary.state.mn.us/archive/supct/9808/finamd.htm.

Minnesota Sentencing Commission. 2009. Accessed September 2, 2010. http://www.msgc.state.mn.us/msgc5/guidelines.htm.

Minnesota v. Dickerson. 1993. 508 U.S. 366.

Minnesota v. Murphy. 1984. 465 U.S. 420.

Miranda v. Arizona. 1966. 384 U.S. 436, 86 S.Ct. 1602.

Missouri v. Seibert. 2004. 542 U.S. 600.

Monell v. New York City Department of Social Services. 1978. 436 U.S. 658.

Moore, Mark H., Susan R. Estrich, Daniel McGillis, and William Spelman. 1984. *Dangerous Offenders: The Elusive Target of Justice.* Cambridge, Mass.: Harvard University Press.

Moore v. Student Affairs Committee of Troy State University. 1968. 284 F. Supp. 725.

Moskovitz, Myron. 2002. "A Rule in Search of a Reason: An Empirical Reexamination of *Chimel* and *Belton*." *Michigan Law Review* 2002:657–97.

Moylan, Charles E., Jr. 1977. "The Fourth Amendment Inapplicable vs. the Fourth Amendment Satisfied: The Neglected Threshold of 'So What.'" *Southern Illinois University Law Journal* 75.

Murphy, Shelley. 2003. "Prosecutors Defend 'Sneak and Peek' Warrant." *Boston Globe*, October 20.

Murray v. U.S. 1988. 487 U.S. 533.

Myers v. Commonwealth. 1973. 298 N.E.2d 819 (Mass.).

Nadler, Janice. 2002. "No Need to Shout: Bus Sweeps and the Psychology of Coercion." *Supreme Court Review*. Chicago: University of Chicago Press.

Nardulli, Peter F. 1983. "The Societal Cost of the Exclusionary Rule: An Empirical Assessment." *American Bar Foundation Research Journal* (Summer):585–609.

_____. 1987. "The Societal Cost of the Exclusionary Rule: Revisited." *University of Illinois Law Review* 223–239.

Nartarajan, Radha. 2003. "Racialized Memory and Reliability: Due Process Applied to Cross-Racial Eyewitness Identifications." *New York University Law Review* 78:1821–58.

National Council on Crime and Delinquency. 1992. *Criminal Justice Sentencing Policy Statement*. San Francisco: NCCD.

National Treasury Employees Union v. Von Raab. 1989. 489 U.S. 656.

Nelson, William E. 1988. *The Fourteenth Amendment: From Political Principle to Judicial Doctrine.* Cambridge, Mass.: Harvard University Press.

New Jersey v. T. L. O. 1985. 469 U.S. 325.

New York Civil Liberties Union. 2009. "Record Number of Innocent New Yorkers Stopped, Interrogated by NYPD." New York Civil Liberties Union. Accessed September 2, 2010. http://www.nyclu.org/node/2389.

New York Office of the Attorney General. 1999. *New York City Police Department's "Stop and Frisk" Practices: A Report to the People of the State of New York from the Office of the Attorney General.* New York: Attorney General's Office.

New York v. Belton. 1981. 453 U.S. 454.

New York v. Quarles. 1984. 467 U.S. 649.

New York v. Zenger. 1735. 17 Howell's St. Tr. 675, 721–22.

Nix v. Williams. 1984. 467 U.S. 431.

North Carolina v. Alford. 1970. 400 U.S. 25.

North Carolina v. Butler. 1979. 441 U.S. 369.

Ohio v. Roberts. 1980. 448 U.S. 56.

Ohio v. Robinette. 1996. 117 S.Ct. 417.

Okie, Susan. 2009. "The Epidemic That Wasn't." *New York Times,* January 27. Accessed August 31, 2010. http://www.nytimes.com/2009/01/27/health/27coca.html?_r=2.

Oliver v. U.S. 1984. 466 U.S. 170.

Olmstead v. U.S. 1928. 277 U.S. 438.

Oregon v. Mathiason. 1977. 429 U.S. 492.

Orozco v. Texas. 1969. 394 U.S. 324.

Orr v. State. 1980. 382 So.2d 860 (Fla.App.).

Padgett v. Donald. 2005. 401 F.3d 1273 (CA11 Ga.).

Palko v. Connecticut. 1937. 302 U.S. 319.

Pate, Anthony M., and Lorie A Fridell. 1993. Police Use of Force: Official Reports, Citizen Complaints, and Legal Consequences. Washington, D.C.: Police Foundation.

Patton, Allison. 1993. "The Endless Cycle of Abuse: Why 42 U.S.C. § 1983 Is Ineffective in Deterring Police Brutality." *Hastings Law Journal* 44:753.

Payne v. Pauley. 2003. 337 F.3d 767 (CA7 Ill.).

Payton v. New York. 1980. 445 U.S. 573.

Pearce v. Pearce. 1846. 63 E.R. 950.

Pennsylvania v. Mimms. 1977. 434 U.S. 106.

Penrod, Steven. 2003. "Eyewitness Identification Evidence." American Bar Association. Accessed September 2, 2010. http://www.abanet.org/crimjust/spring2003/eyewitness.html.

People v. Brooks. 1989. 257 Cal.Rptr. 840 (Cal.App.).

People v. Brown. 1969. 248 N.E.2d 867 (N.Y.).

People v. Camargo. 1986. 516 N.Y.S.2d 1004 (N.Y.).

People v. Defore. 1926. 242 N.Y. 13.

People v. Kelly. 1961. 195 Cal.App.2d 669.

People v. McClellan. 1969. 457 P.2d 871 (Calif.).

People v. Mills. 1904. 70 N.E. 786 (N.Y.).

People v. Superior Court of Santa Clara County. 2006. 49 Cal.Rptr.3d 831 (Cal.App.).

People v. Washington. 1987. 236 Cal.Rptr. 840 (Cal.App.).

Perez, Douglas W. 1994. *Common Sense about Police Review.* Philadelphia: Temple University Press.

Pinder v. Johnson. 1995. 54 F.3d 1169 (CA4 Md.).

Pletan v. Gaines et al. 1992. 494 N.W.2d 38 (Minn.).

Pointer v. Texas. 1965. 380 U.S. 400.

Posner, Richard. 2006. *Not a Suicide Pact: The Constitution in a Time of National Emergency.* New York: Oxford University Press.

Post, Leonard. 2005. "A Loaded Box of Stereotypes: Discrimination in Jury Selection." *National Law Journal* (April 25).

Pound, Roscoe. 1921. "The Future of the Criminal Law." *Columbia Law Review* 21.

Powell v. Alabama. 1932. 287 U.S. 45.

Presidential Documents. 2001 (September 18). "Declaration of National Emergency by Reason of Certain Terrorist Attacks, Proclamation 7463 of September 14, 2001." *Federal Register* 66(181):48199. Accessed September 2, 2010. http://frwebgate.access.gpo.gov/cgi-bin/getdoc.cgi?dbname=2001_register&docid=01–23358-filed.

_____. 2001 (November 16). "Military Tribunals for Non-Citizens Involved in Terrorism Activities; Authorization (Military Order of November 13, 2001), Administrative Orders." *Federal Register* 66(222):57831–36 [01–28904]. Accessed September 2, 2010. http://frwebgate.access.gpo.gov/cgi-bin/getdoc.cgi?dbname=2001_register&docid=01–28904-filed.

Priar, L. L., and T. F. Martin. 1954 (November–December). "Searching and Disarming Criminals." *Journal of Criminal Law, Criminology, and Police Science* 45(4):481.

RAND Corporation. 2008. "Do NYPD's Pedestrian Stop Data Indicate Racial Bias?" Research Brief. Santa Monica: RAND. Accessed July 8, 2010. http://www.rand.org/pubs/research_briefs/RB9325/index1.html.

Rasul v. Bush. 2004. 542 U.S. 466.

Raymond, Margaret. 1999. "Down on the Corner, Out on the Street: Considering the Character of the Neighborhood in Evaluating Reasonable Suspicion." *Ohio State Law Journal* 90:99.

Read, Conyers, ed. 1962. *William Lambarde and Local Government.* Ithaca, N.Y.: Cornell University Press.

Rehnquist, William H. 1974. "Is an Expanded Right of Privacy Consistent with Fair and Effective Law Enforcement? Or: Privacy, You've Come a Long Way Baby." *Kansas Law Review* 23.

_____. 2000. *Dickerson v. U.S.* 530 U.S. 428. Accessed August 31, 2010. http://www.oyez.org/cases/1990–1999/1999/1999_99_5525/opinion.

Reid v. Georgia. 1980. 448 U.S. 438.

Remington, Frank. 1960. "The Law Relating to 'On the Street' Detention, Questioning, and Frisking of

Suspected Persons and Police Arrest Privileges in General." *Journal of Criminal Law, Criminology, and Police Science* 50.

Renico v. Lett. 2010. 2010 WL 1740525.

Report from Former Judges. 2010. *Habeas Works: Federal Courts' Proven Capacity to Handle Guantanamo Cases.* Washington, D.C.: Human Rights First.

Report to the Nation on Crime and Justice. 1988. 2d ed. Washington, D.C.: Bureau of Justice Statistics.

Rhode Island v. Innis. 1980. 446 U.S. 291.

Richards v. Wisconsin. 1997. 520 U.S. 385.

Rimer, Sara. 2002. "Convict's DNA Sways Labs, Not a Determined Prosecutor." *New York Times*, February 26. Accessed May 22, 2010. http://www.nytimes .com/2002/02/06/us/convict-s-dna-sways-labs-not-a-determined-prosecutor.html?scp=1&sq=convict%27s+dna+sways+labs&st=nyt.

Rita v. U.S. 2007. 551 U.S. 338.

Rivera v. Murphy. 1992. 979 F.2d 259 (CA1 Mass.).

Robinson v. California. 1962. 370 U.S. 660.

Robinson v. Township of Redford. 2002. 48 Fed. Appx. 925 (CA6 Mich.). Unpublished.

Rochin v. California. 1952. 342 U.S. 165.

Rogers v. Richmond. 1961. 365 U.S. 534.

Rompilla v. Beard. 2005. 545 U.S. 374.

"Ronald Rompilla Pleads Guilty to Life." 2007. *Capital Defense Weekly*, August 13. Accessed May 30, 2010. http://www.capitaldefenseweekly.com/blog/?p=2251.

Roper v. Simmons. 2005. 543 U.S. 551.

Ross v. Moffitt. 1974. 417 U.S. 600.

Ross, Brian, and Richard Esposito. 2005. "CIA's Harsh Interrogation Techniques Lead to Questionable Confessions, Sometimes to Death." *ABC News*, November 18. Accessed August 31, 2010. http://abcnews.go.com/WNT/Investigation/story?id=1322866.

Rossiter, Clinton. 1948. *Constitutional Dictatorship.* Princeton, N.J.: Princeton University Press.

Rothman, David. 1971. *The Discovery of the Asylum.* Boston: Little, Brown.

Ruffin v. Commonwealth. 1871. 62 Va. 1025.

Rummell v. Estelle. 1980. 445 U.S. 263.

Samaha, Joel. 1978. "Discretion and Law in the Early Penitential Books." In *Social Psychology and Discretionary Law*, edited by Richard Abt. New York: Norton.

———. 1989. "Fixed Sentences and Judicial Discretion in Historical Perspective." *William Mitchell Law Review* 15:217.

Samson v. California. 2006. 126 S.Ct. 2193.

Sanders v. City of Houston. 1982. 543 F.Supp. 694 (S.D. Texas).

Savage, Charlie. 2010. "Holder Backs a *Miranda* Limit for Terrorist Suspects." *New York Times*, May 9. Accessed June 24, 2010. http://www.nytimes.com/2010/05/10/us/politics/10holder.html.

Savage, Charlie, and Scott Shane. 2010. "Experts Urge Keeping Two Options for Terror Trials." *New York Times*, March 8. Accessed June 25, 2010. http://

www.nytimes.com/2010/03/09/us/politics/09terror .html?th&emc=th.

Schantzenbach, Max M., and Emerson H. Tiller. 2008. "Reviewing the Sentencing Guidelines; Judicial Politics, Empirical Evidence, and Reform." *University of Chicago Law Review* 75:715.

Schauer, Frederick. 1987. "Precedent." *Stanford Law Review* 39.

Scheck, Barry. 1997. "Frontline: What Jennifer Saw." Washington, D.C.: Public Broadcasting Corporation. Accessed April 23, 2010. http://www.pbs.org/wgbh/pages/frontline/shows/dna/etc/script.html.

Schmerber v. California. 1966. 384 U.S. 757.

Schneckloth v. Bustamonte. 1973. 412 U.S. 218.

Schroeder, William A. 1981. "Deterring Fourth Amendment Violations." *Georgetown Law Journal* 69:1361.

Schulhofer, Stephen J. 1993. "Rethinking Mandatory Minimums." *Wake Forest Law Review* 28.

Scott v. Illinois. 1979. 440 U.S. 367.

Seidman, Louis. 2002. "Confessions." In *Encyclopedia of Crime and Justice*, 2d ed., edited by Joshua Dressler. New York: Macmillan Reference USA.

Shay, Giovanna, and Timothy P. O'Toole. 2006. "*Manson v. Brathwaite* Revisited: Towards a New Rule of Decision for Due Process Challenges to Eyewitness Identification Procedures." *Valparaiso University Law Review* 41: 109.

Sheppard v Maxwell. 1966. 384 U.S. 333.

Sherman v. U.S. 1958. 356 U.S. 369.

Sibron v. New York. 1968. 392 U.S. 40.

Silverthorne Lumber Company v. U.S. 1920. 251 U.S. 385.

Skinner v. Railway Labor Executive Association. 1989. 489 U.S. 602.

Slobogin, Christopher. 1998. *Criminal Procedure: Regulation of Police Investigation.* Charlottesville, Va.: LEXIS.

———. 1999. "Why Liberals Should Chuck the Exclusionary Rule." *University of Illinois Law Review* 363.

———. 2003. "Toward Taping." *Ohio State Journal of Criminal Law* 1:309.

Smith, Page. 1962. *John Adams.* New York: Doubleday.

Smith v. Illinois. 1968. 390 U.S. 129.

Smith v. Maryland. 1979. 442 U.S. 745.

"Sneak and Peek Warrants and the USA Patriot Act." 2002. *Georgia Defender*, September. Accessed September 2, 2010. http://www.law.uga.edu/academics/profiles/dwilkes_more/37patriot.html.

Snyder v. Louisiana. 2008. 452 U.S. 472.

South Dakota v. Opperman. 1976. 428 U.S. 364.

Sparf and Hansen v. U.S. 1895. 156 U.S. 51.

Spitzer, Eliot. 1999. *The New York City Police Department's "Stop & Frisk" Practices: A Report to the People of the State of New York from the Attorney General.* New York: Civil Rights Bureau.

Stack v. Boyle. 1951. 342 U.S. 1.

State v. Bowe. 1994. 881 P.2d 538.

State v. Bumpus. 1990. 459 N.W.2d 619 (Iowa).

State v. Carty. 2002. 790 A.2d 903 (N.J.).

State v. Clopten. 2009. 223 P.3d 1103 (Utah).

State v. Cook. 2004. 847 A.2d 530 (N.J.).

State v. Ellis. 2006. WL 82736 (OhioApp.).

State v. Fitiwi. 2003. Minnesota Court of Appeals. Not reported.

State v. Holeman. 1985. 693 P.2d 89 (Wash.).

State v. Hunter. 1992. 831 P.2d 1033 (UtahApp.).

State v. Johnson. 2005. 836 N.E. 2d 1243 (OhioApp.).

State v. Long. 1986. 721 P.2d 483 (Utah).

State v. Raines. 2004. 857 A.2d 19 (Md.).

State v. Richards. 1996. 549 N.W.2d 218 (Wisc.).

State v. Superior Court. 1978. 589 P.2d 48 (Ariz.App.).

State v. Thompson. 2004. 839 A.2d 622 (Conn.App.).

State v. Wilkins. 1983. 473 A.2d 295 (Vt.).

State v. Wright. 2001. WL 96203 (Minn.App.).

Stein v. New York. 1953. 346 U.S. 156.

Stern, Loren G. 1967. "Stop and Frisk: An Historical Answer to a Modern Problem." *Journal of Criminal Law, Criminology, and Police Science* 58.

Stewart, Potter. 1983. "The Road to *Mapp v. Ohio* and Beyond: The Origins, Development, and Future of the Exclusionary Rule in Search-and-Seizure Cases." *Columbia Law Review* 83.

Stoner v. California. 1964. 376 U.S. 483.

Stovall v. Denno. 1967. 388 U.S. 293.

Strauder v. West Virginia. 1879. 100 U.S. 303.

Strickland v. Washington. 1984. 104 S.Ct. 2052.

Strunk v. U.S. 1973. 412 U.S. 434.

Stuntz, William. 2002. "Search and Seizure." In *Encyclopedia of Crime & Justice,* 2d ed., edited by Joshua Dressler. New York: Macmillan Reference USA.

Sussman, Jake. 2001–2002. "Suspect Choices: Lineup Procedures and the Abdication of Judicial Authority." *New York University Review of Law & Social Change* 27:507.

Sutherland, Brian. 2006. "Whether Consent to Search Was Given Voluntarily: A Statistical Analysis of Factors That Predict the Suppression of Rulings of Federal District Courts." *New York University Law Review* 81:2192–227.

Sutton, Paul. 1986. "The Fourth Amendment in Action: An Empirical View of the Search Warrant Process." *Criminal Law Bulletin* 22:405.

Swain v. Alabama. 1965. 380 U.S. 202.

Swindler v. State. 1979. 592 S.W.2d 91 (Ark.).

Taylor, Telford. 1969. *Two Studies in Constitutional Interpretation.* Columbus: Ohio State University Press.

Tennessee v. Garner. 1985. 471 U.S. 1.

Terry v. Ohio. 1968. 392 U.S. 1.

Thompson v. Utah. 1898. 170 U.S. 343.

Thornton v. U.S. 2004. 541 U.S. 615.

Tiffany, Lawrence P., Donald M. McIntyre, Jr., and Daniel L. Rotenberg. 1967. *Detection of Crime: Stopping and Questioning, Search and Seizure, Encouragement, and Entrapment.* Boston: Little, Brown.

Toborg, Mary A. 1981. *Pretrial Release: A National Evaluation of Practices and Outcomes.* Washington, D.C.: National Institute of Justice.

Townsend v. Sain. 1963. 372 U.S. 293.

Twenty-Sixth Annual Review of Criminal Procedure. 1997. *Georgetown Law Journal* 85.

U.S. Code. 2002. Title 42. Accessed September 3, 2010. http://www.law.cornell.edu/uscode/42/usc_sup_01_42.html.

———. 2003. Title 18. Parts I and II. Chapters 119, "Wire and Electronic Communications Interceptions and Interceptions of Oral Communications"; 121; and 206. Accessed September 3, 2010. http://www.law.cornell.edu/uscode/html/uscode18/usc_sup_01_18.html. http://www4.law.cornell.edu/uscode/18/pIch119.html.

———. 2007. § 1861. Title 50, Chapter 36, Subchapter IV, § 1861. "Access to Certain Business Records for Foreign Intelligence and International Terrorism Investigations." Accessed September 3, 2010. http://www.law.cornell.edu/uscode/search/display.html?terms=1861(a)(1)&url=/uscode/html/uscode50/usc_sec_50_00001861——000-.html.

———. 2010. Title 18, Part 1. Chapters 11B and 113B. Accessed September 3, 2010. http://www.law.cornell.edu/uscode/html/uscode18/usc_sup_01_18_10_I.html.

U.S. Congress. 1954. Senate, Committee on the Judiciary, Hearing before the Subcommittee to Investigate Juvenile Delinquency, Miami, Florida, 83d Cong., 2d sess. Washington, D.C.: Government Printing Office.

———. 1970. H. Rep. No. 1444, 91st Cong., 2d sess. Washington, D.C.: Government Printing Office.

U.S. Criminal Code, Title 18. 2009. Accessed September 3, 2010. http://www.law.cornell.edu/uscode/718/usc_sup_01_18_10_I.html.

U.S. ex rel. Latimore v. Sielaff. 1977. 561 F.2d 691 (CA7 Ill.).

U.S. Food and Drug Administration. Accessed July 5, 2010. http://www.fda.gov/ForConsumers/ConsumerUpdates/ucm048377.htm.

U.S. Manual for Military Commissions. 2010. Washington, D.C.: U.S. Department of Defense. Accessed July 6, 2010. http://www.defense.gov/news/commissionsmanual.html.

U.S. Senate. 2001 (September 14). Authorization for the Use of Military Force. S.J. Res. 23. 107th Cong., 1st sess. Accessed September 3, 2010. http://news.findlaw.com/hdocs/docs/terrorism/sjres23.enr.html.

U.S. Sentencing Commission. 1991. *Mandatory Minimum Penalties in the Federal Criminal Justice System.* Washington, D.C.: U.S. Sentencing Commission.

U.S. Sentencing Guidelines Manual. 2009. Accessed July 4, 2010. http://www.ussc.gov/2009guid/TABCON09.htm.

U.S. v. Abrahams. 1978. 575 F.2d 3 (CA1 Mass.).

U.S. v. Armstrong. 1996. 517 U.S. 456.

U.S. v. Banks. 1995. 78 F.3d 1190 (CA7 Ill.).

U.S. v. Banks. 2003. 540 U.S. 31.

U.S. v. Barahona. 1993. 990 F.2d 412 (CA8 Mo.).

U.S. v. Benkala. 2008. 530 F.3d 300 (CA4 Va.).

U.S. v. Bily. 1975. 406 F.Supp. 726 (E.D.Pa.).

U.S. v. Blake. 1988. 718 F.Supp. (S.D.Fla.).

⸻. 1989. 888 F.2d 795 (CA11 Fla.).

U.S. v. Booker. 2005. 543 U.S. 220.

U.S. v. Caicedo. 1996. 85 F.3d 1184 (CA6 Ohio).

U.S. v. Calandra. 1974. 414 U.S. 338.

U.S. v. Ceballos. 1987. 812 F.2d 42 (CA2 N.Y.).

U.S. v. Cortez. 1981. 449 U.S. 411.

U.S. v. Craner. 1981. 652 F.2d 23 (CA9 Calif.).

U.S. v. Dichiarinte. 1971. 445 F.2d 126 (CA7 Ill.).

U.S. v. Doe. 1985. 819 F.2d 206 (CA9 Ariz.).

U.S. v. Dougherty. 1972. 473 F.2d 1113 (CADC).

U.S. v. Drayton. 2002. 536 U.S. 194.

U.S. v. Dunn. 1987. 480 U.S. 294.

U.S. v. Edwards. 1974. 415 U.S. 800.

U.S. v. Elmore. 1979. 595 F.2d 1036 (CA5 Ga.).

U.S. v. Freitas. 1988. 800 F.2d 1451 (CA9 Calif.).

U.S. v. Garcia-Camacho. 1995. 53 F.3d 244 (CA9 Calif.).

U.S. v. Gonzalez-Lopez. 2006. 548 U.S. 140.

U.S. v. Gray. 2004. 369 F.3d 1024 (CA8 Ark.).

U.S. v. Halls. 1995. 40 F.3d 275 (CA8 Iowa).

U.S. v. Ibarra. 1990. 731 F.Supp. 1037 (D.Wyo.).

U.S. v. Jacobsen. 1984. 466 U.S. 109.

U.S. v. Jaramillo. 1994. 25 F.3d 1146 (CA2 N.Y.).

U.S. v. Kelly. 2002. 302 F.3d 291 (CA5 Texas).

U.S. v. Kim. 1976. 415 F.Supp. 1252 (D.Hawaii).

U.S. v. Knights. 2001. 524 U.S. 112.

U.S. v. Lambert. 1995. 46 F.3d 1064 (CA10 Kans.).

U.S. v. Leon. 1984. 468 U.S. 897.

U.S. v. Lindsey. 1989. 877 F.2d 777 (CA9 Calif.).

U.S. v. Marion. 1971. 404 U.S. 307.

U.S. v. Martinez-Fuerte. 1976. 428 U.S. 543.

U.S. v. Matlock. 1974. 415 U.S. 164.

U.S. v. Mendenhall. 1980. 446 U.S. 544, 100 S.Ct. 1870, 64 L.Ed.2d 497.

U.S. v. Miller. 1976. 425 U.S. 435.

U.S. v. Miner. 1973. 484 F.2d 1075 (CA9 Calif.).

U.S. v. Mitchell. 1959. 179 F.Supp. 636 (CADC).

U.S. v. Montero-Camargo. 2000. 208 F.3d 1122 (CA9 Calif.).

U.S. v. Montoya de Hernandez. 1985. 473 U.S. 531.

U.S. v. Moscatiello. 1985. 771 F.2d 589 (CA1 Mass.).

U.S. v. Perea. 2006. 978 [179 Fed.Appx.] 474 (CA10 N.M.).

U.S. v. Perez. 1824. 22 U.S. (9 Wheat.) 579.

U.S. v. Ramsey. 1977. 431 U.S. 606.

U.S. v. Robinson. 1973. 414 U.S. 218.

U.S. v. Rodney. 1992. 956 F.2d 295 (CADC).

U.S. v. Salerno. 1987. 481 U.S. 739.

U.S. v. Sanchez-Meza. 1976. 547 F.2d 461 (CA9 Calif.).

U.S. v. Sanders. 2005. 424 F.3d 768 (CA8 Iowa).

U.S. v. Santana. 1976. 427 U.S. 38.

U.S. v. Sharpe and Savage. 1985. 470 U.S. 675.

U.S. v. Smith. 1986. 799 F.2d 704 (CA11 Fla.).

U.S. v. Sokolow. 1989. 490 U.S. 1.

U.S. v. Spikes. 1998. 158 F.3d 913 (CA6 Ohio).

U.S. v. Tapia. 1990. 912 F.2d 1367 (CA11 Ala.).

U.S. v. Udziela. 1982. 671 F.2d 995 (CA7 Ill.).

U.S. v. U.S. District Court. 1972. 407 U.S. 297.

U.S. v. Vaneaton. 1995. 49 F.3d 1423 (CA9 Ore.).

U.S. v. Villegas. 1990. 899 F.2d 1324 (CA2 N.Y.).

U.S. v. Wade. 1967. 388 U.S. 218.

U.S. v. Warner. 1988. 843 F.2d 401 (CA9 Calif.).

U.S. v. Weaver. 1992. 966 F.2d 391 (CA8 Mo.).

U.S. v. White. 1971. 401 U.S. 745.

U.S. v. Winsor. 1988. 846 F.2d 1569 (CA9 Calif.).

U.S. v. Wong. 1994. 40 F.3d 1347 (CA2).

USA Patriot Act. 2001. P.L. 107–156, 115 Stat. 272.

Uviller, H. Richard. 1986. "Seizure by Gunshot: The Riddle of the Fleeing Felon." *New York University Review of Law of Social Change* 14:705.

⸻. 1988. *Tempered Zeal*. Chicago/New York: Contemporary Books.

Van Dyke, Jon. 1977. *Jury Selection Procedures*. Cambridge, Mass.: Ballinger.

Vernonia School District v. Acton. 1995. 515 U.S. 646.

Vinyard v. Wilson. 2002. 311 F.3d 1340 (CA11 Ga.).

Walder v. U.S. 1954. 347 U.S. 62.

Walker, Samuel, and Vic W. Bumpus. 1992. "The Effectiveness of Civilian Review." *American Journal of Police* 11.

Wallace, Henry Scott. 1993. "Mandatory Minimums and the Betrayal of Sentencing Reform: A Legislative Dr. Jekyll and Mr. Hyde." *Federal Probation*, September.

Warden v. Hayden. 1967. 387 U.S. 294.

Washington v. Texas. 1967. 388 U.S. 14.

Watkins v. Virginia. 1986. 475 U.S. 1099.

Watts v. Indiana. 1949. 338 U.S. 49.

Weeks v. U.S. 1914. 232 U.S. 383.

Weiner, William P., and Larry S. Royster. 1991. "Sobriety Checkpoints in Michigan: The *Sitz* Case and Its Aftermath." *T. M. Cooley Law Review* 8:243.

Weiser, Benjamin. 2010. "Top Terror Prosecutor Is a Critic of Civilian Trials." *New York Times*, February 19. Accessed June 26, 2010. http://www.nytimes.com/2010/02/20/nyregion/20prosecutor.html?ref=military_commissions.

Weis v. State. 2009. Argument. Accessed September 5, 2010. http://multimedia.dailyreportonline.com/2009/11/video-robert-smith-in-weis-v-state/.

Wellentine, Ken. 2009. "PoliceOne Analysis: *Arizona v. Gant*." Comment posted by rebelranger79 on Thursday, April 23, 2009, 10:29 a.m. pdt. Accessed July 13, 2010. http://www.policeone.com/legal/articles/1813475.

Wells, Gary L. 2002. "Eyewitness Identification: Psychological Aspects." In *Encyclopedia of Crime & Justice*, 2d ed., edited by Joshua Dressler. New York: Macmillan Reference USA.

Wells, Gary L., and M. Leippe. 1981. "How Triers of Fact Infer the Accuracy of Eyewitness Identification." *Journal of Applied Psychology* 66:682.

Wells, Gary L., Amina Memon, and Steven D. Penrod. 2006. "Eyewitness Evidence: Improving Its

Probative Value." *Psychological Science in the Public Interest* 7(2):45–75.

Wells, Gary L., and Elizabeth A. Olson. 2003. "Eyewitness Testimony." *Annual Review of Psychology* 54:277–95.

Wells, Gary L., and Deah S. Quinlivan. 2009. "Suggestive Eyewitness Identification Procedures and the Supreme Court's Reliability Test in Light of Eyewitness Science: 30 Years Later." *Law and Human Behavior* 33:1–24.

Whitebread, Charles H., and Christopher Slobogin. 2000. *Criminal Procedure*. New York: Foundation Press.

Whren v. U.S. 1996. 517 U.S. 806.

_____. 1996a. "Petitioners' Brief." http://www.soc.umn .edu/~samaha/cases/whren_v_us_petitioner.htm.

Williams v. Florida. 1970. 399 U.S. 78.

Williams v. New York. 1949. 337 U.S. 241.

Wilson v. Arkansas. 1995. 514 U.S. 927.

Wilson, James Q. "Take Away Their Guns." Accessed July 8, 2010. http://www.nytimes.com/1994/03/20/ magazine/just-take-away-their-guns.html.

Wisconsin Attorney General. 2010. *Model Policy and Procedure for Eyewitness Identification*. State of Wisconsin, Wisconsin Department of Justice, Bureau of Training and Standards for Criminal Justice. Accessed May 7,

2010. http://www.thejusticeproject.org/reports/ model-policy-and-procedure/.

Wolf v. Colorado. 1949. 338 U.S. 25.

Wong Sun v. U.S. 1963. 371 U.S. 471.

World Prison Population List. 2009. Kings College London. Accessed June 7, 2010. http://www.kcl.ac.uk/depsta/ law/research/icps/news.php?id=203.

Wyoming v. Houghton. 1999. 526 U.S. 295.

Yant, Martin. 1991. *Presumed Guilty: When Innocent People Are Wrongly Convicted*. Buffalo: Prometheus Books.

Ybarra v. Illinois. 1979. 444 U.S. 85.

Younger, Richard D. 1963. *The People's Panel*. Providence, R.I.: Brown University Press.

Zabel, Richard, and James Benjamin, Jr. 2009. *In Pursuit of Justice: Prosecuting Terrorism Cases in the Federal Courts*. Washington, D.C.: Human Rights First, July, Figure 13. http://www.humanrightsfirst.org/ pdf/090723-LS-in-pursuit-justice-09-update.pdf.

Zelaney, Jeff, and Charlie Savage. 2010. "Officials Say Terrorism Suspect Is Cooperating." *New York Times*, February 3. Accessed July 1, 2010. http:// www.nytimes.com/2010/02/03/us/03terror .html?ref=umar_farouk_abdulmutallab.

Page numbers in **boldface** denote glossary terms.